COMPUTER
FUNDAMENTALS
& APPLICATIONS

FOR BUSINESS

COMPUTER
FUNDAMENTALS
& APPLICATIONS
FOR BUSINESS

DOS
WordPerfect® 5.1
Lotus® 1-2-3® Release 2.3/2.4
dBASE IV® Version 1.5/2.0

■   ■   ■

Roy Ageloff University of Rhode Island
Scott Zimmerman Brigham Young University
Beverly Zimmerman Brigham Young University
Dennis A. Adams University of Houston

Course Technology, Inc. One Main Street, Cambridge, MA 02142

Computer Fundamentals & Applications for Business: DOS, WordPerfect 5.1, Lotus 1-2-3 Release 2.3/2.4, dBASE IV Version 1.5/2.0 is published by Course Technology, Inc.

Editorial Director	Joseph B. Dougherty
Product Managers	Susan Solomon Communications
	Katherine T. Pinard
	Pete Alcorn
Production Managers	Josh Bernoff
	Thomas E. Dorsaneo
Production Editor	Robin M. Geller
Editorial Assistant	Erin Bridgeford
Desktop Publishers	Debbie Masi Kim Munsell Rosalie Blazej
Artists	Stacey Alickman Mark Valentine
	Darrell Judd Winston Sin
Copyeditors	Nancy Wirtes
	Janet Reed
Proofreader	Darlene Bordwell
Quality Assurance Supervisor	Rob Spadoni
Quality Assurance Group	Peter Came Betsy Paquelet Jeff Goding
	David Crocco Jeremy Parker John Mihnos
	John Harvie Nicole Jones Steve Bayle
	Mark Valentine Marjorie Osterhout
	Mark Vodnik M. David Smith
Manufacturing and Package Designer	Mark Dec
Cover Designer	Darci Mehall

Computer Fundamentals & Applications for Business: DOS, WordPerfect 5.1, Lotus 1-2-3 Release 2.3/2.4, dBASE IV Version 1.5/2.0 © 1993 Course Technology, Inc.

Trademarks

Course Technology and the open book logo are registered trademarks of Course Technology, Inc.
dBASE and dBASE IV are registered trademarks of Borland International, Inc.
Lotus and 1-2-3 are registered trademarks of Lotus Development Corporation.
WordPerfect is a registered trademark of WordPerfect Corporation.
Some of the product names used in this book have been used for identification purposes only and may be trademarks or registered trademarks of their respective manufacturers and sellers.

Disclaimer

Course Technology, Inc., reserves the right to revise this publication and from time to time make changes in its content without notice.

ISBN 1-56527-072-X (text and 3½-inch Data Disk)
ISBN 1-56527-074-6 (text and 3½-inch Data Disk, Lotus 1-2-3 Release 2.4, and dBASE IV Version 1.5)
ISBN 1-56527-073-8 (text and 3½-inch Data Disk and Lotus 1-2-3 Release 2.4)
ISBN 1-56527-092-4 (text and 3½-inch Data Disk and dBASE IV Version 1.5)

Printed in the United States of America.
10 9 8 7 6 5 4 3

Preface

Computer Fundamentals & Applications for Business represents a new approach to computer education by combining a carefully developed text with fully functional software. It is designed for any first course on how word processing, spreadsheets, and database management are used in business.

The Textbook

This textbook presents a unique approach to teaching fundamental computer concepts along with comprehensive sections on how to use DOS, WordPerfect, Lotus 1-2-3, and dBASE IV. Students learn to plan before they press keys. They learn to analyze the business problem and design their solution — whether it be a memo or letter, a worksheet or graphic, a query or a report. Then they solve the problem by following a distinctive step-by-step methodology, frequently referring back to their original plan. From this process students learn that word processing, spreadsheets, and database management are valuable tools to help make informed business decisions.

Organization

The textbook consists of five parts:

Part I   *Computer Fundamentals*
Part II   *DOS Tutorials*
Part III   *WordPerfect 5.1 Tutorials*
Part IV   *Lotus 1-2-3 Release 2.3/2.4 Tutorials*
Part V   *dBASE IV Version 1.5/2.0 Tutorials*

Part I, *Computer Fundamentals*, provides students with a thorough foundation to computer software, hardware and systems. These topics are introduced using a continuous case study, the Buena Vista Office Supply Company (BVOS). Students are also encouraged to apply what they learn within a unique problem solving framework that is reinforced throughout the entire text.

The two DOS tutorials give students step-by-step instructions on how to use DOS for file management in both diskette and hard-disk environments. Both the concepts chapters and the DOS tutorials are unique in their approach. They motivate all of the concepts and skills they teach by explaining *why* students need to learn them.

Parts III, IV, and V contain hands-on tutorials with step-by-step instructions on how to use today's most popular microcomputer applications.

Approach

The tutorials in *Computer Fundamentals & Applications for Business* textbook employ a problem-solving approach to teach students how to use WordPerfect 5.1, Lotus 1-2-3 Release 2.3/2.4, and dBASE IV Version 1.5/2.0. This approach is achieved by including the following features in each tutorial:

Objectives   A list of objectives orients students to the goals of each tutorial.

Tutorial Case   This case presents the business problem that students will solve in the tutorial and that they could reasonably encounter in an entry-level job. Moreover, each business problem is geared to what the typical student taking this course is likely to know about business. Thus, the process of solving the problem using the microcomputer tool will be meaningful to the student. All of the key business areas — accounting, finance, marketing, production, and management — are represented.

Planning Section   Each tutorial's case also includes discussion about planning the document, the worksheet, or the database management activity. Students learn to analyze the business problem and then set clear goals for the solution before they press keys. Outlines, planning sheets, worksheet sketches, and record layout sheets are introduced as basic tools.

Step-by-Step Methodology   The unique CTI methodology integrates concepts and keystrokes. Students are asked to press keys always within the context of solving the problem. The text constantly guides students, letting them know where they are in the problem-solving process and referring them back to their original plan.

Page Design   Each page is designed to help students easily differentiate between what they are to *do* and what they are to *read*. In addition, the numerous screen shots include labels that direct students' attention to what they should look at on the screen.

Exercises   Each tutorial concludes with meaningful, conceptual questions that test students' understanding of what they learned in the tutorial.

Tutorial Assignments   These assignments provide students with additional practice on the particular skills that they learned in the tutorial. Students practice these skills by modifying the business problem that they solved in the tutorial.

Case Problems   Each tutorial concludes with several additional business problems that have approximately the same scope as the Tutorial Case. Students are asked to use the skills they learned in the tutorial to solve these case problems.

The Software — Lotus 1-2-3 Release 2.4 and dBASE IV Version 1.5/2.0

Computer Fundamentals & Applications for Business is available with either Lotus 1-2-3 or dBASE IV, or both.

Lotus 1-2-3 Release 2.4 is a full-sized (256 columns by 8,192 rows) and full-capacity version of the Lotus 1-2-3 spreadsheet software that includes the WYSIWYG and SmartIcons add-ins. All 1-2-3 features are included with the exception of the Translator, Access, Viewer, Backsolver, and Auditor add-ins.

The student version of dBASE IV Version 1.5 is limited to 120 records (or 120 rows in an SQL table). The dBASE IV tutorials can also be used with dBASE IV Version 2.0.

Both Lotus 1-2-3 and dBASE IV are available in 3½-inch format. (If you need 5¼-inch diskettes, see your instructor.)

Coupon   Students who buy this textbook packaged without Lotus 1-2-3 software can purchase their own copy of the software for a nominal price. Look for the valuable upgrade coupon included with this textbook.

CTI Quick Reference   These invaluable references are included in every book and provide lists of functions, menu trees, and summaries of commonly used commands for all of the software covered in the text.

CTI Keyboard Template   This useful aid is a laminated strip with WordPerfect 5.1 keyboard commands on one side and Lotus 1-2-3 function keys and commands on the other.

The Supplements

Data Disk

The Data Disk includes all of the documents, worksheets, and database files needed to complete all of the Tutorial Cases, Tutorial Assignments, and Case Problems. It is available in 3½-inch format. (If you need 5¼-inch diskettes, see your instructor.)

Instructor's Manual

The Instructor's Manual is written by the authors and is quality assured. It includes:

- Answers and solutions to the all of the text's end of chapter material.
- A 3½-inch diskette containing solutions to all of the text's Tutorial Assignments, and Case Problems
- Transparency Masters of key illustrations in the text

Test Bank

This supplement contains approximately 50 questions per tutorial or chapter in true/false, multiple choice, matching, and short answer formats. Each question has been quality-assurance tested by students for accuracy and clarity.

Electronic Test Bank

This Electronic Test Bank allows professors to edit individual test questions, select questions individually or at random, and print out scrambled versions of the same test to any supported printer.

Acknowledgments

As the Course Technology, Inc. *Microcomputer Applications for Business Series* has grown, so too has the list of adopters, editors, reviewers, production and manufacturing professionals, technical reviewers, helpful colleagues, supportive spouses and family members, and sales and marketing representatives that all require our thanks. So, let us simply say thank you because without all of you the product you see here would not be possible.

Roy Ageloff
Scott Zimmerman
Beverly Zimmerman
Dennis A. Adams

■   ■   ■

Brief Contents

Part Four   Lotus 1-2-3 Tutorials and Modules

Part Five   dBASE IV v1.5/2.0 Tutorials

Contents

Part Three
WordPerfect 5.1 Tutorials

Part Four
Lotus 1-2-3 Tutorials

Part Five
dBASE IV v1.5/2.0 Tutorials

Photography Credits for *Computer Fundamentals*

Chapter 1. Figures 1-2, 1-5, 1-6, 1-8, 1-9, 1-11a, 1-11b courtesy of International Business Machines Corporation. Figure 1-3 © John William Lund. Figure 1-7 courtesy of Cray. Figure 1-10 reprinted from *POPULAR ELECTRONICS*, January 1975, copyright ©1975, Ziff-Davis Publishing Company. Figure 1-11c photo courtesy of Hewlett-Packard Company.

Chapter 2. Figures 2-1, 2-2, 2-3 courtesy of International Business Machines Corporation. Figures 2-4, 2-5a, 2-5c courtesy of Apple Computer, Inc. Figures 2-5b, 2-5d, 2-7 © John William Lund. Figures 2-6, 2-8 courtesy of Microsoft Corporation. Figure 2-9 courtesy of Hewlett-Packard Company.

Chapter 3. Figures 3-5, 3-7, 3-14 courtesy of International Business Machines Corporation. Figure 3-12 © John William Lund.

Chapter 4. Figures 4-4, 4-7, 4-15, 4-19, 4-21a, 4-21b, 4-22a, 4-23 © John William Lund. Figure 4-10 courtesy of Hewlett-Packard Company. Figure 4-17 courtesy Central Point Software, Inc. Figures 4-20, 4-21c, 4-22c, 4-24 courtesy International Business Machines Corporation.

Chapter 5. Figure 5-10 UPI/Bettmann Newsphoto. Figure 5-16a Bettmann/Hulton. Figure 5-16b, The Bettmann Archives. Figure 5-25b © John William Lund.

Chapter 6. Figures 6-2, 6-3, 6-5, 6-6, 6-7, 6-9, 6-10, 6-14, 6-15, 6-16, 6-17, 6-18, 6-19, 6-20, 6-21, 6-22, 6-23a, 6-23b, 6-24 © John William Lund. Figure 6-8 UPI/Bettmann. Figure 6-9 courtesy Intel Corporation. Figure 6-25 (left) courtesy of International Business Machines Corporation. Figure 6-25 (right) courtesy of Hewlett-Packard Company.

Chapter 7. Figures 7-8, 7-10, 7-11, 7-27, 7-28 © John William Lund. Figures 7-12, 7-14, 7-16, 7-21a, 7-21b courtesy of International Business Machines Corporation. Figure 7-13 courtesy of Summagraphics Corporation. Figures 7-22a, 7-22b, 7-22c, 7-22d courtesy of Apple Computer, Inc. Figure 7-15 courtesy of Hewlett-Packard Company.

Chapter 8. Figures 8-6, 8-7, 8-13, 8-14, 8-15, 8-16, 8-17 © John William Lund.

Chapter 9. Figure 9-3a, 9-3b, 9-6 © John William Lund. Figure 9-11 courtesy of International Business Machines Corporation.

Chapter 10. Figure 10-8 courtesy Microsoft Corporation. Figure 10-16 courtesy Unix Systems Laboratories.

Chapter 12. Figures 12-2, 12-3 courtesy of International Business Machines Corporation.

Chapter 13. Figure 13-9 courtesy Popkin Software & Systems Incorporated. Figure 13-10 courtesy of International Business Machines Corporation.

Creating Your Data Diskettes for the Tutorials

Before you do the tutorials in Computer Fundamentals & Applications for Business, you must create data diskettes for each of the applications discussed. The Disk Maker Program Disk included with this textbook contains the data files you will need. You cannot use the Disk Maker Program Disk to work through the steps in the Tutorials.

Before you begin, make sure you have the following items:

- Four blank, formatted 5¼-inch or 3½-inch diskettes. The size of the disks should match the size of the Disk Maker Program Disk that came with this book. If you don't know how to format a diskette, see your instructor or technical support person, or follow the instructions on pages DOS 21 through DOS 23.
- Four blank diskette labels and a felt-tip pen.
- The Disk Maker Program Disk that came with this book.

After you collect these items, you are ready to create your data diskettes.

Carefully follow these steps to create your data diskettes:

❶ Using a felt-tip pen, write the words "DOS data diskette" on the label of the first blank formatted diskette; write "WordPerfect 5.1 data diskette" on the second blank, formatted diskette; write "Lotus 1-2-3 Release 2.3/2.4 data diskette" on the third blank, formatted diskette; and write "dBASE IV data diskette" on the fourth blank, formatted diskette.

❷ Start your computer. If you need help see your technical support person or follow the instructions on pages DOS 5 and DOS 6.

❸ If there is a diskette in drive A remove it. Then insert the Disk Maker Program Disk in drive A.

If your Disk Maker Program Disk doesn't match drive A but does match drive B, insert it in drive B instead. Then use drive B instead of drive A in the following instructions.

If you don't know how to determine which diskette drive is drive A and which is drive B, or if you don't know how to insert a disk into a diskette drive, see page DOS 4.

❹ Type **a:** and press **[Enter]**. (If you inserted the Disk Maker Program Disk in drive B, type **b:** and press **[Enter]**.)

❺ Type **diskmake** and press **[Enter]**. The screen shown in Figure 1 appears.

This is the Disk Maker Main Menu screen. The highlight (a solid rectangle) is currently on the words "Exit to DOS."

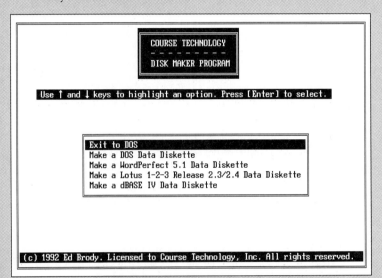

Figure 1
Disk Maker
Program Main
Menu

❻ Press **[↓]** (down-arrow key) until you have moved the highlight to the type of data diskette you are creating. For example, to create your DOS data diskette, move the highlight to the words "Make a DOS Data Diskette." If you cannot find the down-arrow key, or if pressing it does not move the highlighted bar, try pressing the [Num Lock] key. If this fails, ask your instructor or technical support person for help.

❼ Make sure the highlight bar is on the correct option. For example, if you are creating your DOS data diskette, make sure the highlight bar is on "Make a DOS Data Diskette." Press **[Enter]**. Messages appear and then the screen shown in Figure 2 appears.

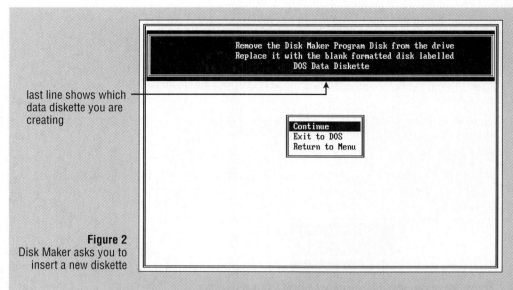

last line shows which
data diskette you are
creating

Figure 2
Disk Maker asks you to
insert a new diskette

⑧ Remove the Disk Maker Program Disk. Replace it with the data diskette you are creating (one of the blank, formatted diskettes you labeled in Step 1). For example, if
you are creating your DOS data diskette, replace the Disk Maker Program Disk
with your DOS data diskette.

⑨ Be sure the highlight bar is on the word "Continue," then press **[Enter]**.

⑩ Messages appear on your screen. Eventually, you will see the message telling you
that your data diskette has been created. For example, if you are creating your
DOS data diskette, you will see the message "DOS data diskette created." Remove
your data diskette from the disk drive.

After you have created the first data diskette, repeat steps 3 through 10 to create each of
your data diskettes. After you have created all four of your data diskettes, put your Disk Maker
Program Disk in a safe place. If any of your data diskettes becomes damaged, you can create
a replacement using the Disk Maker Program Disk.

Now that you have created your data diskettes, you are ready to begin learning about
DOS.

Computer Fundamentals

■   ■   ■

- Unit I · The World of Computing
- Unit II · Solving Problems with Software
- Unit III · Hardware and Operating Systems
- Unit IV · Organizational Solutions

The World of Computing

Unit I

Opening a New BVOS Franchise

INTRODUCTION

CHAPTER 1
An Overview of Computers
and Computer Users

CHAPTER 2
The Computer Industry

In reading this unit, you will get the "big picture." We will discuss computers in the broadest sense: what they are, how they are used, who makes them, and who uses them.

In terms of the problem-solving model, which we will establish in the Introduction that follows, we will principally address step 2: understanding the problem, as shown in Figure I-1. Your problem at BVOS is to research, purchase, and install a computer system that will make your business as efficient as possible. There are two key points here. First, you need more than a computer; you need a computer *system*. Chapter 1 addresses this point in detail. By the end of the first chapter, you will know the various parts of the computer itself, and you will know the parts of the system.

Second, in Chapter 2 you will learn how some well-known companies have used computer systems to become more efficient and more effective. And you will gain some background on a few of the companies that provide the computer products that can help you in your efforts.

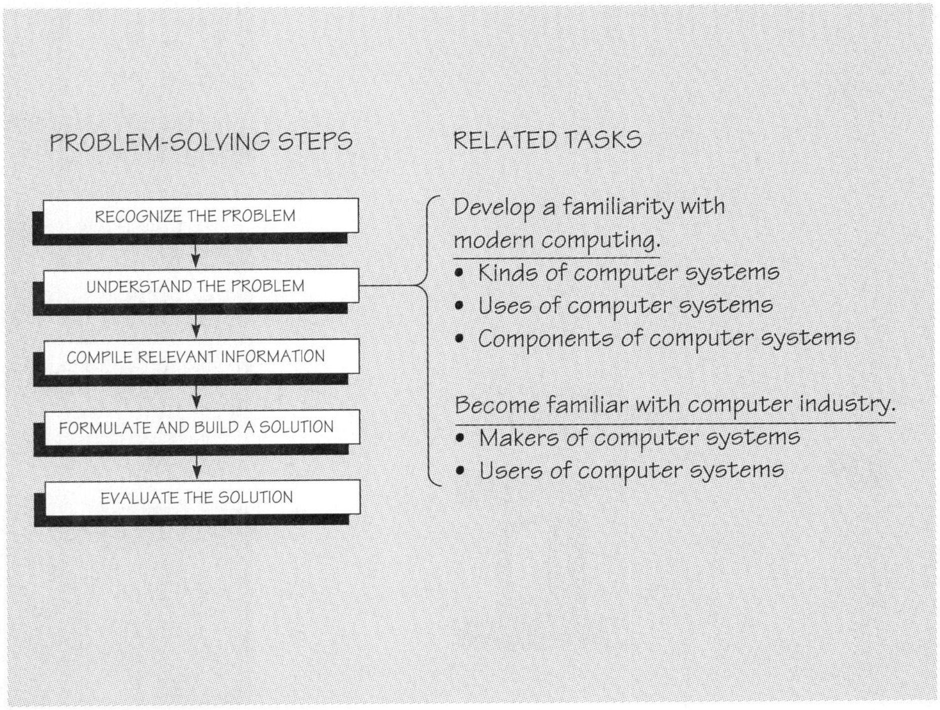

PROBLEM-SOLVING STEPS

RELATED TASKS

RECOGNIZE THE PROBLEM

UNDERSTAND THE PROBLEM

COMPILE RELEVANT INFORMATION

FORMULATE AND BUILD A SOLUTION

EVALUATE THE SOLUTION

Develop a familiarity with
modern computing.
- Kinds of computer systems
- Uses of computer systems
- Components of computer systems

Become familiar with computer industry.
- Makers of computer systems
- Users of computer systems

Figure I-1   In this unit, we will focus on step 2 of the problem-solving process.

Introduction

The Buena Vista Scenario: Following a Problem-Solving Approach

In order to show how all of the computer topics presented here are integrated, we have used a single running example throughout the book. The example involves a fictitious business: Buena Vista Office Supply, or BVOS. You, the reader, play the part of an entrepreneur who is opening a branch of Buena Vista in your own community (Figure I-2).

As the owner of the new BVOS branch, you will be faced with a number of problems. Like any good entrepreneur, you want to turn those problems into opportunities, and maybe

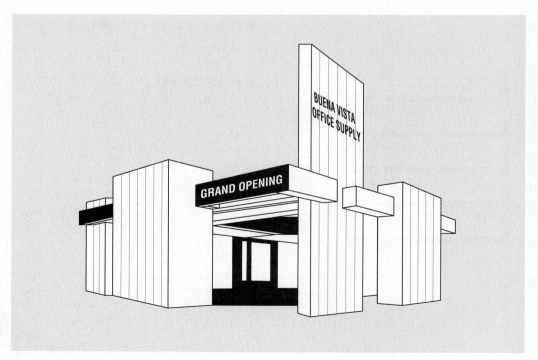

Figure I-2
In this book, you will be making decisions related to a business you are opening, a local branch of Buena Vista Office Supply.

even advantages! You ask the question, "How can I use computers to make my business run efficiently?" To solve this central problem, you will follow a standard problem-solving technique, which consists of five steps:

1. Recognizing the problem
2. Understanding the problem
3. Compiling relevant information
4. Designing and building the solution
5. Evaluating the solution

Each step, in turn, requires particular actions and decisions, depending on the problem at hand. Throughout this book, we will provide diagrams similar to Figure I-3 to help you see what is required to accomplish each step.

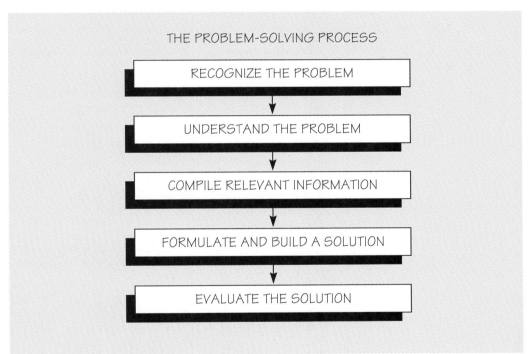

THE PROBLEM-SOLVING PROCESS

RECOGNIZE THE PROBLEM

UNDERSTAND THE PROBLEM

COMPILE RELEVANT INFORMATION

FORMULATE AND BUILD A SOLUTION

EVALUATE THE SOLUTION

Figure I-3
The problem-solving process. You will find figures similar to this one at key points throughout this book.

Step 1: Recognizing The Problem

Because we have created this scenario for you, the first step is already done. We begin at a stage in which you have researched the office supply market in your area and found that there is a need for an office supply store to service local businesses. You showed your findings to the headquarters of Buena Vista Office Supply in Toronto, Canada, and they agreed that you should open a branch of BVOS in your town.

In your discussions with BVOS headquarters personnel, they outlined to you how most local branches operate. Your customers are local businesses that need office supplies, such as copy paper, office furniture, writing materials, staplers, file folders, and so on. The staff of your branch takes orders from local businesses over the phone or by fax. The staff then fills the orders with the supplies obtained from the regional distributor and delivers the supplies using your delivery vans. A graphic of your merchandise is shown in Figure I-4.

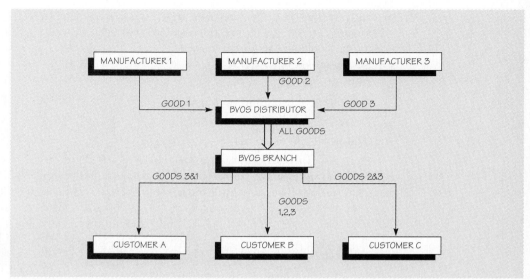

Figure I-4
A flowchart illustrating your role in bringing office supplies to your customers.

To start your new branch, you have estimated that you will need 12 employees:

- Three salespeople will take orders from local businesses.
- Three stockroom workers will fill the orders, box them, and load them onto the delivery vans.
- Five drivers will deliver the supplies to local businesses.
- One inventory manager will monitor your stock of office supplies and, when necessary, order new supplies from the regional distributor. The inventory manager will also be your accountant — billing customers, paying the regional distributor, and paying your employees.

Figure I-5 diagrams your staff members and their functions in your branch office.

To give you a better idea of how valuable computer technology is, executives at BVOS

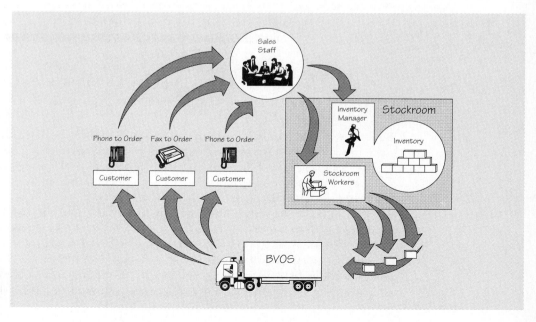

Figure I-5
Your employees and their functions at BVOS.

headquarters showed you profit reports, accounting records, and inventory lists from various BVOS branches before and after computerization. It was obvious that the branches made considerably more money once they implemented computer systems and that their business practices were much more efficient.

Once you saw those financial reports, you saw clearly the task ahead of you. You needed to buy a computer system to make your new business as efficient as possible.

Step 2: Understanding the Problem

Now that you recognize you have a problem worth solving, the next step is to gain a better understanding of that problem. Unfortunately, you don't know much about computers. You have heard a great deal, and you've seen them in many other businesses. But now you will be faced with a lot of purchasing decisions, and you don't have any idea of what you ought to buy.

Fortunately, that's just what you're going to learn about in this book. Each new topic you encounter here begins by covering the basic concepts. You need to master these basic concepts in order to understand what products your new business needs. First, in Unit I, you will get an overview of computers and gain a perspective on the entire computer industry. In Unit II, you will build your understanding of computer software, the most important problem-solving tool of the computer user. In Unit III, you will study the fundamentals of computer hardware — the parts of the computer that you can see and touch. Finally, in Unit IV, you will begin to understand how computers are used to solve business problems.

Step 3: Compiling Relevant Information

After gaining an understanding of each new computer topic, move on to step 3 of the problem-solving process: compiling relevant information. We will provide you with some of the information you need. However, any product data we give you will be out of date by the time you read this book. In order to make an informed decision about what to buy for your new business, you will need to do some current research to find out what computer products are available, the advantages and disadvantages of each product, and how much each costs.

Part of compiling relevant information is knowing where the relevant information is and how to find it. Throughout this book, you will be asked to search magazines, newspapers, and trade catalogs to discover what's available. By the time you get through the book, you will have an excellent sense of the kind of information you will need and where to find it.

Step 4: Designing and Building a Solution

Once you have fully researched the products that are available to you in the computer market, you are ready to enter the fourth step of the problem-solving process: designing and building the solution. As its name implies, this step is divided into two phases. In the first phase, you design your solution; in the second phase, you actually build it.

In the exercises associated with Units II and III of this book, you will become deeply involved in choosing hardware and software for your branch of BVOS. And, in Unit IV, you will examine how the hardware and software work together to solve many of your business problems. In other words, you will design your own solution. This book will provide advice and guidelines, but in the end, the decision about what to purchase will be up to you.

Step 5: Evaluating the Solution

An essential step in any solution is your evaluation. In order to learn from your successes as well as your mistakes, you must always look back at what you have done and make judgments about the job you did.

Summary

Now you understand your challenge as the owner of a new business. Computers will clearly play a large part in setting up the new venture. You have many decisions to make, so don't forget the problem-solving techniques illustrated here. Let's get started with Unit I, "The World of Computing."

An Overview of Computers and Computer Users

Key Terms

automated teller machine (ATM)
communication device
computer
computer system
data
general purpose computer
hardware
input device
laptop
load
mainframe
microcomputer
minicomputer
notebook computer
output device
palmtop computer
point of sale (POS) computer
portable computer
processing device
program
robot
software
special purpose computer
storage device
supercomputer
user
workstation

Objectives

In this chapter, you will learn to:

- Understand what a computer is and name its three essential functions
- Explain the differences between special purpose computers and general purpose computers
- Compare the uses of supercomputers, mainframes, minicomputers, and microcomputers
- Name and describe the four parts of a computer system
- Identify the five types of computer hardware

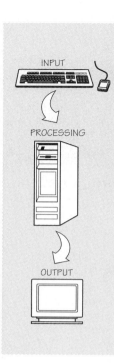

Figure 1-1
The essence of the computing process is input, processing, and output.

What Is a Computer?

A **computer** is an electronic device for processing data. Its purpose is to accept available data and turn it into useful information.

At the very minimum, a computer must have three parts, as shown in Figure 1-1. At the heart of the computer are **processing devices**, which consist of sets of electronic circuits. Their purpose is to manipulate data using a written set of instructions. Attached to the processing device, there must be at least one input device and one output device. The **input device** accepts data from the person or machine using the computer and transmits it to the processing devices. The **output device** accepts processed data from the processing devices and returns it as information to the person or machine using the computer.

Special Purpose Computers

Computers are everywhere. There are computers on our desks at work, in our televisions at home, in our cars, at the supermarket, at the bank — even in the kitchen (such as those controlling microwave ovens and refrigerators). It is important to realize, however, that the computers that sit on our desktops at work and at home — the machines that we usually think of as computers — are very different from the other examples we just mentioned. The difference between them is that desktop computers are general purpose computers, and most of the others are special purpose computers.

Most of this book is devoted to general purpose computers such as the one in Figure 1-2, and how they are used to solve business problems. Before we turn our attention to the main topic, though, let's take a quick look at some of the other kinds of computers we find in our everyday lives. These computers are referred to as **special purpose computers** because each one is designed to address just one kind of problem.

Figure 1-2   A general purpose computer.

Figure 1-3   An automated teller machine, or ATM.

ATMs

Perhaps the most common type of special purpose computer that we interact with directly in our day-to-day lives is the bank's **automated teller machine,** or **ATM** (Figure 1-3). For many years, banking customers had to coordinate their banking around the hours that banks were open. The term "banker's hours," in fact, was used disparagingly in describing the schedule of someone who worked only a few hours a day. Advancements in computer technology and competition among banks led to the development of the ATM. Today, ATMs are so prevalent that a bank has difficulty attracting customers if it doesn't offer an ATM card with each type of account.

An ATM has a small keypad, a video monitor, a card reader, a small printer, and a transaction drawer (Figure 1-4). The keypad and card reader are input devices. The video monitor, printer, and cash tray are output devices. Because the ATM is a computer, we know that there is also a processing device behind the facade that we see.

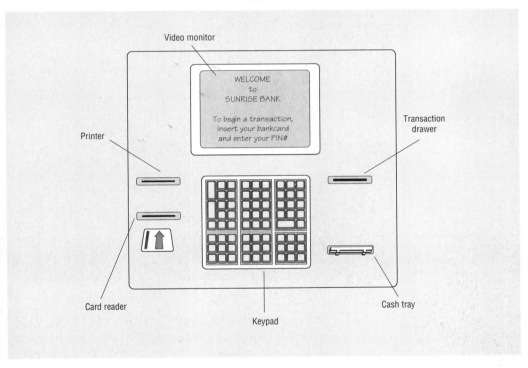

Figure 1-4
An ATM and its input and output devices.

To use an ATM, the bank customer inserts his or her bank card into the card reader and enters a code on the keypad. The ATM's processor checks to see if this code matches the code recorded on the card's magnetic strip. If it does, the processor uses the video monitor to prompt the customer to choose among the options listed. The customer uses the keypad to enter a request for some type of banking transaction.

At this point, the ATM uses a device called a *modem* to call a central computer that keeps track of the customer's account. The central computer checks to see that the requested transaction is acceptable and returns a response to the ATM through its modem. The ATM then prints the results of the transaction using its printer. If the customer is withdrawing cash, the transaction drawer or cash tray gives out cash. If the customer is depositing cash or checks, the transaction drawer accepts them.

Point of Sale Computers

Another common type of special purpose computer is the **point of sale**, or **POS, computer**. They were developed to make it easier for large stores to keep track of inventory. POS computers are usually housed in cash registers attached to scanning devices, such as bar-code readers (Figure 1-5). The bar-code reader and the register keys are the computer's input devices. Like the ATM, the POS terminal's output devices include a printer, a small video monitor, and a cash drawer. In this case, however, the POS computer does not directly control the flow of cash, but simply opens the cash drawer at the appropriate time.

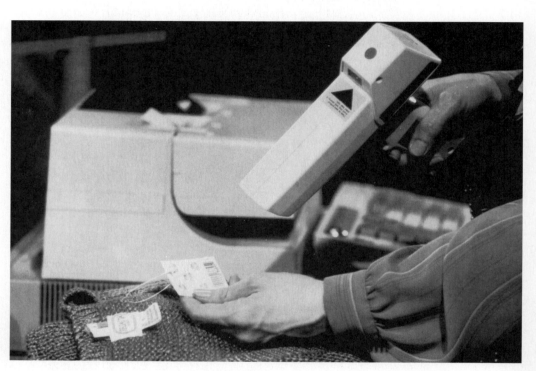

Figure 1-5
POS computers are now found in many retail environments.

Each POS computer is connected to another, more powerful computer somewhere in the store. This central computer acts in much the same way as the computer accessed by the ATM. The central store computer keeps inventories and prices in a computerized file. When the bar code on the item is scanned, the inventory account for that item is decreased by one and the item's price is passed to the cash register.

POS computers have allowed retailers to trim inventories and serve customers better. The scanners get customers through the lines faster, and the charges are more accurate. With ATM systems attached to the POS system, customers can pay for items without ever handling money or a check, thus speeding up the transaction process.

Computers in Manufacturing

From Nike shoes to Chrysler cars, computers are incorporated into the design and manufacture of consumer products. In fact, at companies like IBM and Compaq, computers are used to make computers.

Figure 1-6
Robots like this one have become commonplace in manufacturing.

Employing technologies such as robotics, manufacturers are using computers to decrease production costs and increase the quality of the products they create. A **robot** is a computer that accepts electronic input and performs mechanical output (Figure 1-6). Robots are able to perform hazardous activities, work accurately and consistently, and perform 24 hours a day. The types of activities that are possible with robotics are almost limitless. For example, in the automotive industry, robots are used to paint cars, do spot welding, and put lights in dashboards.

But including computers in manufacturing means much more than robotics. Computers — usually general purpose computers — are also used as high-powered accounting tools to calculate exactly how much raw material is needed to produce a given number of products. They can then be used to manage the whole production process, including ordering materials when necessary.

Comprehension Questions

1. Is the physical movement of a robot's arm considered input, processing, output, or none of the three?

2. A mechanical cash register simply adds numbers that are punched in. Why isn't a mechanical cash register considered a computer?

3. Although a mechanical cash register is not a computer, a pocket calculator is. Explain why a pocket calculator fits the definition of a computer.

Using What You Know

1. Name at least two special purpose computers that were not mentioned in the last section. Identify their input and output devices.

2. Describe a special purpose computer that could be useful to you in your everyday life. Explain what type of data it would accept as input and in what form it would present the output.

3. Which of the special purpose computers mentioned in the last section could be used at BVOS? Explain how and why the computer would be used.

General Purpose Computers

All of the computers mentioned in the previous section are created to perform a specific task. The computers that are used in the office or at home, however, must be able to solve a variety of problems, so they are referred to as **general purpose computers**. These computers can help create everything from documents to art. They can perform mathematical calculations and manage massive collections of data, called *databases*.

Despite the name, different types of general purpose computers are best suited to perform different kinds of tasks. They are therefore categorized by the size of the problems they are designed to address. In general, there are four types: supercomputers, mainframes, minicomputers, and microcomputers. However, you will find that these terms are gradually losing their meaning. You may see references to "mini-mainframes," "super minis," and "super micros," which represent categories that don't fall neatly into the four historical groups.

Supercomputers

Supercomputers like the one shown in Figure 1-7 are designed to solve large, complex mathematical problems. Oil companies use supercomputers to analyze seismic data in their search for oil. The National Oceanographic and Aeronautic Agency uses them to help predict the weather. Researchers in medicine and biochemistry use them to investigate combinatorial DNA in attempting to detect, predict, and cure diseases genetically. Each of these tasks requires a computer that can accept and process huge amounts of numerical data. Super-computers are not used for common office work, such as creating documents or keeping track of clients, because even though they can perform those functions, it would not be cost effective to do so.

Some of today's supercomputers have thousands of small computers inside them, each of which is more powerful than the typical desktop computer found at home or in the office. They are sometimes called *multiprocessors* or *parallel processors* because of this design.

To protect them from smoke, dust, and other small particles or environmental hazards, supercomputers are often housed in special rooms. The temperature and humidity in these rooms is strictly controlled, and the power supply is filtered to make sure that power surges and dips are smoothed out. Today's supercomputers are smaller than their predecessors, and many no longer need special environments.

The manufacturers of supercomputers include Cray, NEC, Intel, Thinking Machines, and Hypercube.

Figure 1-7 A Cray supercomputer.

Figure 1-8 A mainframe computer, the IBM 370.

Mainframes

Until the mid-1970s, the most common type of computer was the **mainframe** (Figure 1-8). Mainframes are used by large companies and organizations in which many people need access to the company's or organization's files. Mainframes are not as specialized as supercomputers because they must be able to perform many types of business-related tasks. The size of the mainframe is determined by the amount of data it can hold and by the number of people that need access to it at the same time. A small mainframe might be used by only a handful of people, while a large one might be used by thousands.

Like some supercomputers, the processing devices of a mainframe are often housed in a special environment that protects the computer. The biggest manufacturer of mainframes, by far, is IBM. Other companies that make mainframes include Amdahl, DEC, and Groupe Bull.

Minicomputers

The expense of purchasing a mainframe led Digital Equipment Corporation to develop the **minicomputer**, the first of which was released in 1959. These machines were much smaller and easier to use than the mainframes of the time, and they did not require the same sophisticated operating environments. The types of tasks they were used to perform, however, are very similar to that of mainframes. Though they are still known by their original name, they are also sometimes called *departmental computers* because they are inexpensive enough to be purchased by individual departments of large companies. Minicomputers became commonplace in small companies for the same reason. Some minis are designed to be used by a single person; others can be accessed by hundreds of people simultaneously. Figure 1-9 shows a typical minicomputer.

Microcomputers

First appearing on the market in the mid-1970s (Figure 1-10), **microcomputers**, which fit on a desktop, were also known as personal computers because they were intended to be used by individuals, rather than by whole companies or organizations. As these computers became more powerful, they began to enter the business world, taking over at least part of the role that had been played by minis and mainframes. Microcomputers have not completely replaced mainframes in large organizations, however, because micros cannot handle the same volume of data. Because most microcomputers are designed to service the needs of a

Figure 1-9   A minicomputer. The processing components are in the cabinet on the left.

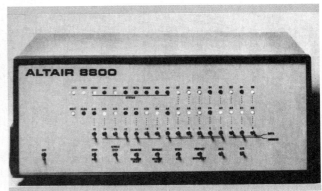

Figure 1-10   The first commercially successful microcomputer, the Altair.

single person, they tend to be less expensive, easier to use, and more flexible than either minis or mainframes. Some of today's micros, however, can be used by more than one person at a time. These new high-powered personal computers have created a new and important category called **workstations**. Workstations that can easily fit on a desktop rival the speed and power of popular minicomputers of the 1960s and 1970s. Engineers are the most common users of workstations.

Today, microcomputers are themselves categorized by size. The original microcomputers, and still the most common size used, are known as *desktop computers* (Figure 1-11a) because they fit on a desk. This term has become a bit of a misnomer, because many full-size microcomputers are now designed to sit on the floor beneath a desk. The first portable microcomputers were released by a company called Osborne. Throughout the 1980s, **portables**, which folded up to the size of a briefcase, remained popular. Today, however, portables have largely been replaced by smaller computers called **laptops** (Figure 1-11b). Laptops weigh less than 10 pounds and fold down to the size of a two-inch-thick pad of paper, though sizes continue to decrease. Small laptops are often called **notebooks**.

As computers become smaller, people are more and more likely to carry them with them all of the time. Today, very small, limited-purpose computers, known as **palmtops** or **personal digital assistants** (**PDAs**) (Figure 1-11c), can perform a number of applications, such as keeping schedules, storing telephone numbers, taking notes, and so on. Some of these systems will even dial a telephone for you. These computers have several batteries and enough RAM to support whatever applications are built into the system, but they cannot run large programs like Windows or WordPerfect. Many PDAs are still a bit clumsy to use because the keypads are very small, and the LCD screens can be difficult to read. In the future, however, voice and written interaction will provide a more natural interface.

(a)   (b)   (c)

Figure 1-11   (a) A desktop computer; (b) a laptop; (c) a palmtop.

Parts of a Computer System

General purpose computers do not operate on their own like some special purpose computers, such as those found in a car. General purpose computers are interactive devices that must be part of a computer system in order to be useful. As shown in Figure 1-12 (on the next page), **computer systems** include four essential elements: hardware, software, data, and people. So far in this chapter, we have focused on computer hardware, but we must consider the entire system to understand how a computer can be used to perform useful work.

Hardware

The center of any computer system is, of course, the hardware. **Hardware** is the machinery of the computer system. It is what most people think of when they talk about computers. Therefore, when we use the term *computer* in this book, we mean hardware.

Early in this chapter, we defined a computer as "a device for processing data." Because the term *computer*, used alone, means "hardware," hardware is the set of devices that are used to process data. You can think of hardware as the part of the computer you can touch. We also said that a computer must have at least three parts: a processing device, an input device, and an output device.

The "guts" of a computer include the central processing unit (CPU) and memory. In a microcomputer, the CPU is called a *microprocessor*, because it consists of millions of microscopic circuits etched on a silicon chip. The most common input device for a computer is the keyboard. Other input devices can include a mouse, a trackball, a scanner, and a stylus and digitizer tablet. The most common output devices for general purpose computers are the monitor and the printer.

In addition to input, processing, and output devices, most computers contain one or two other important parts. **Storage devices** hold data much the way your brain stores memories. The most common storage devices are hard disk drives and diskette drives. Other storage devices include magnetic tape drives and CD-ROM drives. **Communication devices** enable computer systems to share data. When computer systems need to share data over distances, they do so using telephone lines with the help of a modem. Computers can also share data by connecting them to form a network. Figure 1-13 summarizes the most common micro-computer devices.

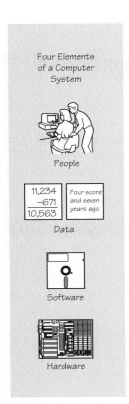

Four Elements of a Computer System

People

Data

Software

Hardware

Figure 1-12
Every computer system must include hardware, software, data, and people.

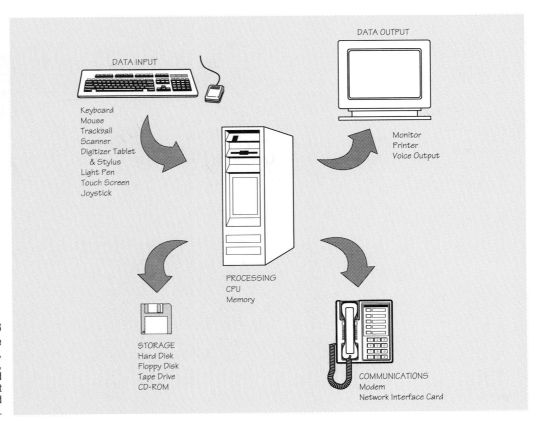

DATA OUTPUT

DATA INPUT

Keyboard
Mouse
Trackball
Scanner
Digitizer Tablet
  & Stylus
Light Pen
Touch Screen
Joystick

Monitor
Printer
Voice Output

PROCESSING
CPU
Memory

STORAGE
Hard Disk
Floppy Disk
Tape Drive
CD-ROM

COMMUNICATIONS
Modem
Network Interface Card

Figure 1-13
Microcomputers include devices for input, processing, output, storage, and communication. The most common devices are listed here under their function.

Software

To be useful for processing data, a general purpose computer needs sets of instructions, which are called **programs**. A collection of programs is called **software**. The two terms are often used interchangeably.

In some special purpose computers, software is not required, because electronic instructions have been built into the circuitry of the hardware. In general purpose computers, however, software is always required. Another way to say this is that general purpose computers are programmable machines. The hardware is built to perform many different types of processing; the software tailors the hardware to perform the type that is needed.

Two main types of software are used in general purpose computers: operating systems and application software. The operating system contains the basic instructions that manage the various hardware devices. The operating system must be loaded before any application software can. To **load** a piece of software is to move it from a storage device into the computer's memory, which is a processing device. Application software is what you use to perform a certain type of task. For example, word processing software is used to create text documents on a computer. Database management software is used to access, manipulate, and organize large amounts of data. Figure 1-14 lists some of the most popular application programs and operating systems.

Data

The third essential element of the computer system is data. For most general purpose computers, **data** consists of numbers, letters, images, and sounds. The type of data that is processed by the computer is determined by the software being used. For example, word

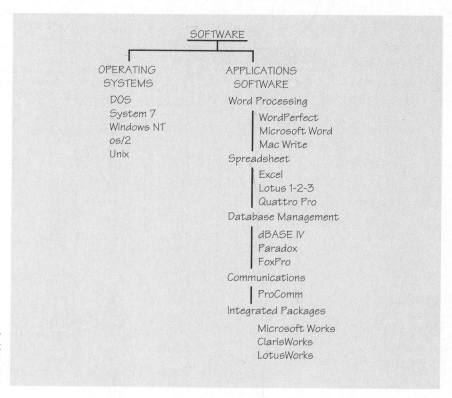

Figure 1-14
Just a few of the most popular application programs and operating systems.

processing software is designed to process text. Spreadsheet software can process text, but it is especially useful in processing numbers. Graphics software is used to process images. Multimedia software can process all three of these types, plus sound and video.

People

Naturally, a computer system isn't going to do much on its own; it generally requires a person to operate it. Because the computer is a tool that is used to accomplish a task, the person operating the computer is often referred to as the **user**.

Comprehension Questions

1. Is a single computer used by 10 people in a small office likely to be a supercomputer, mainframe, a minicomputer, or a microcomputer? Why?
2. Name a type of computer that is appropriate for a businessperson who needs to take a computer along on trips.
3. Is a monitor hardware or software? Is a standard computer monitor a processing device, an input device, or an output device?

Using What You Know

1. General purpose computer systems consist of hardware, software, data, and people, but special purpose computers often do not. Which of the four elements are missing from many special purpose computers? Give three examples.
2. List three reasons why you, as president of BVOS, might want to have a laptop rather than a desktop computer for your personal use.
3. Rather than calling them storage and communication devices, some people refer to disk drives and modems as input/output devices. How can you defend this terminology?

Summary Points

What Is a Computer?

- A computer is an electronic device for processing data.
- At the minimum, a computer must have an input device, a processing device, and an output device.

Special Purpose Computers

- Special purpose computers are designed to address just one kind of problem. Automated teller machines (ATMs) and point of sale (POS) computers are two examples of special purpose computers.

General Purpose Computers

- Business and home computers are general purpose computers because they are used to perform a variety of tasks.

Supercomputers

- Supercomputers are very powerful computers using many processors working in parallel to solve large mathematical problems.
- Supercomputers are often kept in special rooms where they are protected from dust, temperature changes, and electrical surges.

Mainframes

- Mainframes are used by large organizations where many people need access to large company data files.
- A mainframe must be able to accomplish a variety of business-related tasks.
- Many mainframes must also be kept in special rooms.

Minicomputers

- A minicomputer is a small, less expensive version of a mainframe.

Microcomputers

- Microcomputers were originally intended to be used by individuals, though multiuser micros are now available.
- The microcomputer has taken over part of the role of the corporate mainframe.
- Most micros are referred to as desktop computers; the smaller models are called portables, laptops, notebooks, palmtops, or PDAs; larger models are referred to as workstations.

Parts of a Computer System

Hardware

- The term *computer* generally means hardware.
- Hardware devices are categorized into processing, input, output, storage, and communication devices.

Software

- Software is the collection of instructions that tell the hardware what to do.
- The operating system must be loaded before application software because it is in charge of managing the hardware devices.
- Application software turns the computer into a specialized tool capable of performing a specific kind of task.

Data

- For general purpose computers, data consists of numbers, letters, images, and sounds.

People

- An integral part of the computer system, people interact with computers at all levels.

Knowing the Facts

True/False

1. Some microcomputers can be used by more than one person simultaneously.

2. Disk drives are storage devices.

3. The leading manufacturer of supercomputers is DEC.

4. Software determines the type of data that is processed.

5. Supercomputers are designed to handle large mathematical problems.

6. At the minimum, a computer must have five parts: processing, input, output, communication, and storage devices.

7. Supercomputers and mainframes are often kept in special rooms.

8. Application software must be loaded before any other type of software.

9. Some mainframes can be used by thousands of people at once.

10. Until the mid-1970s, the most common type of computer was the minicomputer.

Short Answer

1. The keypad on the bank's ATM is a(n) _____ device.

2. A computer designed to address just one kind of problem is a _____.

3. The biggest manufacturer of mainframes is _____.

4. Computer systems consist of hardware, software, _____, and people.

5. The terms *software* and _____ are used interchangeably.

6. In a computer system, _____ tailors the hardware to perform the task that is needed.

7. A monitor is a(n) _____ device.

8. In which decade were the first microcomputers released?

9. The Digital Equipment Corporation developed the first _____ in 1959.

10. What type of computer does the National Oceanographic and Aeronautic Agency use to help predict the weather?

Answers

True/False

1. T
2. T
3. F
4. T
5. T
6. F
7. T
8. F
9. T
10. F

Short Answer

1. input
2. special purpose computer
3. IBM
4. data
5. programs
6. software
7. output
8. 1970s
9. minicomputer
10. supercomputer

Challenging Your Understanding

1. How are business users like scientific users? How are they different?

2. Summarize the differences among mainframes, minicomputers, and microcomputers. What do you think the differences among these systems will be in the future?

3. Do you think there will be more general purpose or special purpose computers in the future? Why?

4. Some think that the ATM is an example of a stop-gap technology. A stop-gap technology is something that exists to help an organization or society move from one technological infrastructure to another. The ATM provides relatively quick access to cash which can be used for purchases at stores that for some reason do not accept checks or credit cards. The stop-gap service the ATM provides is to supply currency for transactions that are not yet computerized. The fax, or facsimile machine, may also be a stop-gap technology. Do you think the ATM is a stop-gap technology? Why or why not? What about the fax?

The Computer Industry

Key Terms

Apple II
Apple Computer, Inc.
Borland International
Compaq Computer Corporation
compatible (clone)
competitive advantage
competitive necessity
computer information systems
Digital Equipment Corporation (DEC)
Hewlett-Packard Company
IBM Corporation
IBM PC
Lotus Development Corporation
Lotus 1-2-3
Macintosh
Microsoft Corporation
personal computer (PC)
timesharing
user friendly
WordPerfect
WordPerfect Corporation

Objectives

In this chapter, you will learn to:

- Be aware of the three biggest companies in the micro-computer industry today and give background information on each
- Understand the speed at which computer companies evolve
- Identify the difference between competitive advantage and competitive necessity
- Describe at least three cases in which computer information systems helped companies gain competitive advantages
- Describe the various roles that can be played by computer services companies

Hardware and Software Companies

The computer industry is composed of four parts:
- manufacturers of computer hardware and software
- companies that use computers
- companies that provide computer services
- individual computer users

In the 1960s and 1970s, the computer industry was already huge, but it was relatively stable. Computer hardware and software was made by large companies for large companies. Most computers were mainframes or early minicomputers bought by corporations or organizations that could afford them. During this period mainframe companies sold solutions — hardware and software bundled together for one purpose. It was many years before a separate software industry developed. The biggest mainframe producer by far was IBM, although other companies, such as DEC, Sperry, Hewlett-Packard, NCR, and Control Data, were also important.

Since the introduction of the microcomputer in the mid-1970s, the computer industry has exploded. At the same time, the stability of the business has disappeared. There are now thousands of companies making hardware and software, and many seem to appear and disappear overnight. Nevertheless, several companies have evolved and still maintain influence over the industry. In some cases, such as that of Control Data, the older companies have held on to their role in the large-computer market, choosing (for the most part) to avoid the volatile microcomputer industry. In other cases, such as those of Hewlett-Packard and IBM, the companies have diversified to capitalize on technological improvements and consumer demand for smaller computers. In addition, several important new companies have emerged.

A powerful example of the volatility in the computer industry is a company called Compaq, which we will examine more closely later in this chapter. The company, founded in 1982, quickly grew to challenge the giants, IBM and Apple, as a producer of microcomputers. At one point Compaq was the fastest growing company of all time, in any industry. However, as soon as Compaq undercut its chief rival IBM by establishing a reputation for quality and technological innovation, Compaq was itself undercut. A new breed of companies, led by Dell Computers, offered even lower prices and more innovative sales methods. The quick success of these companies spawns new questions. Will Compaq return to its former prominence? Will IBM? How will Dell counter? We really don't know how the race for domination will turn out. What we do know is that we must acknowledge this market volatility and always consider it when making personal or professional computer-related decisions.

To give you a sense for the industry — how it has evolved and who are the biggest names — here are a few of its most famous success stories.

IBM

Herman Hollerith was an employee with the U.S. Census Bureau during the latter part of the nineteenth century. In those days, all census data was tabulated by hand — a huge, expensive, and time-consuming task. In 1890, it was estimated that the process of counting the census data for that year would take more than 10 years. Because the census was (and is) taken every 10 years, this meant the data for one census wouldn't be available until after the next census was taken.

Figure 2-1

Herman Hollerith and his tabulating machine.

Noting this gross inefficiency, Mr. Hollerith invented an electrical tabulating machine that was capable of reading punched cards the size of a one-dollar bill. Using Hollerith's machine (shown in Figure 2-1), the Census Bureau was able to finish tabulating the 1890 census in two and a half years, thus saving five million dollars on the project. With his invention, Hollerith formed the Tabulating Machine Company and sold the machines around the world. Most of Hollerith's machines were used for accounting purposes.

In 1911, Hollerith's company merged with two clock makers and a company that made scales and food slicers to become the Computing-Tabulating-Recording Company (CTR). In 1914, Thomas J. Watson joined the company. Ten years later, he took over and renamed it **International Business Machines Corporation**, or **IBM**.

IBM began manufacturing computers in 1953 with the 701 model. The company's first major success was the IBM 650 in 1954, and its second, the 1401, in 1959. The System/360, introduced in 1964, was the first family of compatible computers and set a standard for all IBM mainframes still in use today. By the 1970s IBM controlled more than 70 percent of the computer market.

In 1981, IBM entered the microcomputer market with the **IBM PC** (Figure 2-2 on the following page). The IBM PC was designed to be easy to use and expandable. The microcomputer had emerged only a few years earlier when the first successful microcomputer kits were sold to computer hobbyists. Throughout the mid- and late 1970s, a number of manufacturers sold microcomputers, but the industry continued to be dominated by hobbyists and home programmers. These early users envisioned the microcomputer progressing to the point of becoming a valuable tool for the home.

To the surprise of the industry, however, the home computer market did not evolve as quickly as many experts predicted. Instead, the first major users of the PC were businesses, and the first programs that were created for the IBM PC were aimed for business users. As it turned out, this turn of events worked well for IBM. Because businesses naturally needed to communicate with one another, there was an urgent need for standards in the tumultuous microcomputer market. Within 18 months, the IBM PC was a clear market leader and the de facto standard.

In addition to its immediate success, another reason the IBM PC became the market standard was that its design was easily copied. In fact, the computer's specifications were made public. As a result, a number of **clones** or **compatibles** were developed to take advantage of the marketing opportunity IBM had opened up. Ten years after the introduction of the PC, clone makers such as Compaq and Dell have undermined the dominance of IBM, whose market share is less than one quarter of what it once was. The term **personal computer**, or **PC** came to refer to both IBMs and compatibles. In this book, we use this common meaning for PC. When we refer to IBM's machine, we call it the IBM PC.

Despite IBM's diminished market share, the company still had revenue of $64.8 billion in 1991. IBM still controls 33 percent of the large-computer market — twice as much as the second largest manufacturer, Fujitsu. In the personal computer market, IBM, which has just been surpassed by Apple, now controls only 15 percent. One of IBM's most successful microcomputer models, the PS/2, is shown in Figure 2-3. IBM's massive market presence is the reason industry experts say, "When IBM sneezes, the computer industry catches cold."

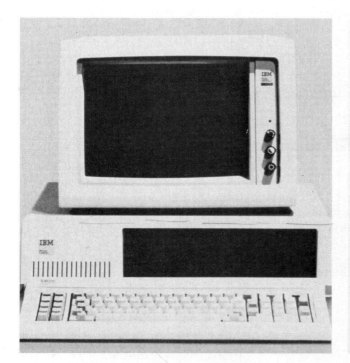

Figure 2-2   The original IBM PC, released in 1981.

Figure 2-3   One of IBM's biggest sellers, the PS/2.

Apple Computer, Inc.

On April 1, 1976, Steve Jobs and Steve Wozniak (Figure 2-4) founded **Apple Computer, Inc.** to manufacture microcomputers. They started in a garage in Palo Alto, California, in what

Figure 2-4
Steve Wozniak and Steve Jobs, founders of Apple Computer. They are shown holding the system board for the Apple I.

later came to be called Silicon Valley. In six years, Apple was on the Fortune 500 list and earned revenue of almost one billion dollars.

Apple's first computer, the Apple I, was introduced in 1976 at the Palo Alto Homebrew Computer Club. The first Apple Is took 60 hours to build, had no keyboard, power supply, or monitor, and had very little memory. They were intended for computer hobbyists who wanted to write programs. In 1977, Apple released the first **Apple II**, the series that brought the company success (Figure 2-5). The Apple II had an open architecture, which meant that

Figure 2-5 The evolution of Apple's computers, left to right starting with the top row: The Apple II, the Mac SE, the Mac II, and the PowerBook.

as the user's needs changed, the computer could be expanded with hardware from Apple and other vendors. The various versions of the Apple II became especially popular in elementary and high schools, primarily because of grant programs that the company provided as an incentive to use computers. Hundreds of educational programs are written for the Apple II.

The infiltration by IBM into the microcomputer industry was hard on Apple. In just a few years, IBM PCs and compatibles virtually controlled the market. In 1983, the former president of PepsiCo, John Sculley, took over Apple, and a series of new computer products were developed. Most notably, Apple released the Lisa, a graphics-oriented computer that was easy to use. Using a pointing device called a *mouse* to move items around on the screen, the user could learn to use the Lisa in far less time than it took to learn the Apple II. Unfortunately, the Lisa was priced too high and was not a commercial success.

Apple Computer's biggest success, however, came with the **Macintosh**, or the Mac, as it came to be known. The Mac was first released in 1984 and quickly became the epitome of the term **user friendly**, meaning it was easy to use. The first Macs, the Macintosh and the Mac Plus, came in a semiportable unit with a small, built-in monitor, a separate keyboard, and a mouse.

The Mac family of computers steadily diversified. In 1987, Apple introduced the Mac II, which had a larger, separate monitor that was available with color. The original Mac did not gain widespread use in the lucrative business market. With the Mac II, however, which looked more like the PC, the Mac's popularity broadened. Today, the Macintosh line is a strong competitor of the PC, and Apple continues its prominence in the areas of user-friendly design and high-quality graphics output.

Microsoft Corporation

The creation of **Microsoft Corporation** is another legendary success story of the microcomputer industry. The story actually begins at a college prep school in Seattle, Washington, where Bill Gates and Paul Allen began learning to program in the school's new computer lab. The young friends' computer skills became so advanced that they obtained free computer time in return for finding flaws in the minicomputer they were using.

In 1975, Gates saw an article for the new Altair 8800, which was being sold by Micro Instrumentation and Telemetry Systems (MITS). Gates and Allen (shown in Figure 2-6) knew that the new computer was not useful to hobbyists without a programming language — preferably BASIC — that would run on it. The two young men created their own version of BASIC to run on the machine and flew to Albuquerque to sell their product to MITS. After initial success, Gates dropped out of Harvard, moved to New Mexico with Allen, and formed Microsoft to continue work on MBASIC, or Microsoft BASIC. Soon they were adapting MBASIC to run on other new microcomputers, and Microsoft became a highly profitable business.

Gates and Allen got their biggest break, however, when IBM came to them in 1980 to create an operating system for its first microcomputer, the IBM PC. For a small company like Microsoft, the undertaking was enormous, and they were given only one year to complete the whole job. Fortunately, Microsoft was able to purchase another company's operating system and adapt it to IBM's needs. Microsoft met its deadline, and the PC was released with a new operating system called DOS. Although the success of the PC essentially spelled success for Microsoft, the software company made even more money by selling DOS to other microcomputer vendors who make clones.

But Microsoft did not stop with DOS and BASIC, as you can see by the products shown in Figure 2-7 on the following page. Gates was quick to diversify and create other pieces of

Figure 2-6
The founders of Microsoft, Paul Allen and Bill Gates.

Figure 2-8
Bill Gates.

software. During the 1980s, Microsoft entered the application software market with Microsoft Works, Word, and Excel. There were two versions of each program: one for the Mac and one for the PC. All three programs were extremely successful. Later, Microsoft introduced Windows, a graphics-based operating environment that runs under DOS and is similar to the Macintosh interface. Two or more applications can be open and running at one time, and users can switch back and forth between them.

With DOS alone, Microsoft could have been the biggest player in the microcomputer software industry. With BASIC and Microsoft's heavy arsenal of application software, there is no contest. Microsoft, still under Gates's direction (Figure 2-8), is now the number one influence on microcomputer software.

Other Important Companies

There are so many makers of computer equipment and developers of computer software that it would be impossible even to list them here. It also would not be appropriate, because we acknowledge the ever-changing landscape of the computer industry as one of the few constants. In the interest of acquainting you with a few more, here is a short list.

DEC. Digital Equipment Corporation, commonly known as Digital or **DEC**, was founded in 1957 by an MIT researcher named Kenneth Olsen. Olsen wanted to build computers that were powerful, yet relatively inexpensive. These computers, which sold for far less than their million-dollar competitors, were controlled with the help of a television monitor and a keyboard. With the success of DEC's PDP series, the minicomputer was born. By the mid-1970s, DEC was a leader in the minicomputer market and posed a significant challenge to IBM's dominance of the computer industry. In 1977, DEC released its first VAX computer. VAX computers come in all sizes, from micro to mainframe, and the same programs can be run on all of them. The VAX achieved widespread popularity during the 1980s. In addition, DEC makes compatibles and printers that compete in the PC market.

Compaq Computer Corporation. Compaq Computer Corporation was founded in 1982 and achieved initial success by making some of the first portable clones. Compaq continues to make both desktop microcomputers and portables. Compaq's success lies in the quality of its systems; the failure rate for Compaq computers is far below the average for clones. Compaq remains one of the largest microcomputer manufacturers. Other major clone manufacturers include Dell, NEC, and Toshiba.

Hewlett-Packard Company. **Hewlett-Packard Company** started making computers in the mid-1960s. Much greater customer recognition came, however, when the company released the HP-35, the first pocket calculator, in 1972 (Figure 2-9a). Today, it is a major presence in the microcomputer industry, largely thanks to the HP LaserJet (Figure 2-9b), a desktop laser printer released in 1984, which made high-quality print and graphics available for microcomputers. Other major producers of printers include Panasonic, Epson, Okidata, and Apple.

(a)

(b)

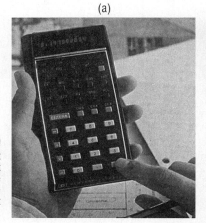 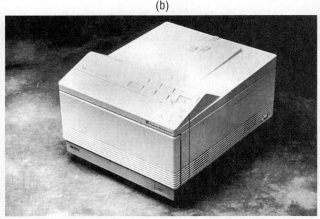

Figure 2-9
(a) Hewlett-Packard's first big success, a pocket calculator called the HP-35; (b) the Hewlett-Packard LaserJet printer.

Lotus Development Corporation. **Lotus Development Corporation** created the industry standard for spreadsheet software with **Lotus 1-2-3** (Figure 2-10). Microsoft Excel and Borland's Quattro Pro now pose a major threat to Lotus' domination of the market, but all other spreadsheets are still compared to 1-2-3.

```
D8: (H) +SALES-(VCOST%*SALES)-FCOSTS                              READY

      A        B       C       D       E       F       G       H
 1  S5TREK3.WK1
 2  Hillary Clarke
 3  2/12/93
 4  Projected Net Income Before Taxes Using a Data Table
 5  *****************************************************************
 6                                          Net Income Before Taxes
 7  Input Area                       Sales  Variable Costs
 8  --------------------------         _       62%     63%     64%     65%
 9  Sales                   50         50    -16.00  -16.50  -17.00  -17.50
10  Variable Costs          64%        75     -6.50   -7.25   -8.00   -8.75
11  Fixed Costs             35        100      3.00    2.00    1.00    0.00
12                                    125     12.50   11.25   10.00    8.75
13                                    150     22.00   20.50   19.00   17.50
14                                    175     31.50   29.75   28.00   26.25
15  Range Names                       200     41.00   39.00   37.00   35.00
16  FCOSTS    C11                     225     50.50   48.25   46.00   43.75
17  SALES     C9                      250     60.00   57.50   55.00   52.50
18  VCOST%    C10                     275     69.50   66.75   64.00   61.25
19                                    300     79.00   76.00   73.00   70.00
20
C10FIG1.WK1
```

Figure 2-10
Lotus 1-2-3, the industry standard in electronic spreadsheets.

WordPerfect Corporation.   During the late 1980s, the equivalent of Lotus in the word processing market was the **WordPerfect Corporation**, with its industry-standard word processor, **WordPerfect** (Figure 2-11). As with 1-2-3, WordPerfect's lead is being challenged, in this case by Microsoft Word.

```
File Edit Search Layout Mark Tools Font Graphics Help        <Press F3 for Help>
                          Shane Miller
                    Total Engineering Concepts
                         42 Scatman Way
                       Cruthers, GA  29987


April 21, 1993


Mark Lakeman
Waste Disposal Inc.
4780 Skypark Drive
Torrance, CA  90505

Dear Mr. Lakeman,

I found last Thursday's meeting to be both productive and
enjoyable.  While investigating your question regarding the
isotopic composition of our nitrogen bath, a number of new issues
have presented themselves.  For example, the need for a catalytic
reagent in Phase III electrolysis may preclude the achievement of
.001M impurity levels in Phase IV separations.  Additionally, the
C:\CORRES\BFD1PERM\3DVISWP.DOC                     Doc 1 Pg 1 Ln 2.5" Pos 3.65"
```

Figure 2-11
WordPerfect.

Borland International.   Since its acquisition of Ashton-Tate, **Borland International** has dominated the market for database management software. Ashton-Tate created dBASE II, the first database program for microcomputers. The latest version, dBASE IV, is the market leader. Borland also acquired another popular database program called Paradox (Figure 2-12). In addition, Borland is the leader in the computer language field.

System File Edit Database Record Program Window Browse					
PERSONAL					
Lastname	Firstname	Mi	Spousename	Address	City	St
Gossnergan	Ed	Y	Turan	321 Strata Ln.	Boulder	CO
Mikelk	Warren		Judy	5 Sign Drive	Los Angeles	CA
English	Jo	G	Richard	12 Davis Plaza	Sausalito	CA
Mostov	Dave	S	Jill	20 Turbofan Drive	Greensboro	NC
Fox	Reid	M	Martha	8681 Absence Freya Estat	Eureka	CA
Byron	Peter		Liz	8 Bogota Road	Havelock	NC
Sine	Marty	N	Nadine	204 Roadside Dr.	New Orleans	LA
Pecukonis	Ronald	C		869 Linus Melcher Plaza	Houston	TX
Barrett	Judy	R	Leo	3 Regent Saloon Avenue	Oak Park	IL
Casey	Jeff	S	Lee	9692 Hebrew Blvd.	Chicago	IL
Barkoe	Barbara		Bert	111 Dash Spurn Street	Madison	WI
Hale	Carol	L	Neal	68 Conspire	Fort Collins	CO
Barkoe	Martha			8819 Viscous Tied Lane	Newburyport	MA
Pierson	Michelle		Glenn	145 Downbeat Drive	W. Palm Beach	FL
Bush	Don	S		Mung Drive 712	Saxtus River	VT
Paretta	Lenny	R	Joan	6 Toward Somber	Hamden	CT
Mikelk	Pat	K		1409 Unknown Trail	Huntington Bc	CA
Colby	Parky	L	Louis	425 Dollop Pk.	METAIRIE	LA
Davis	Edward	L	M.	100 Thulium Squibb Junct	Chico	CA
Rasmussen	Mike	S		6622 Conn Trail	Nashua	NH

Figure 2-12
Paradox, sold by Borland.

Comprehension Questions

1. Could Compaq claim to make a PC if the original PC was made by IBM? Why or why not?
2. Which was more user friendly, the Lisa or the Apple II?
3. What type of computer do you think kept the price of the IBM PC down?

Using What You Know

1. Why do you think IBM made the specifications for the PC public?
2. Why do you think John Sculley was hired by Apple Computer?
3. Why do you think software companies appear and disappear more quickly than hardware companies?

Major Computer Users

Computers can be used to make a process either more efficient or more effective. In the business world, using computers to increase efficiency or effectiveness is most often done to gain a competitive advantage or as a competitive necessity. If a company uses computers in a new way that its competitors have not tried, the company is pursuing a **competitive advantage**. Innovations in using computers are therefore often associated with gaining competitive advantage. Once one company comes up with an innovative computer solution, though, other companies must eventually adopt the same innovation or come up with their own. Adopting a computer solution to keep up with competitors is a **competitive necessity**. For example, most modern companies have computerized accounting systems as a competitive necessity, because doing it any other way would put them at a disadvantage.

One of the current focuses of corporate management is on computer information systems for competitive advantage. A **computer information system** is an organized means of collecting and processing data to make the data useful to a company. Usually, a computer information system includes one or more computers, a collection of data called a database, and the programs for using the database.

Innovative computer solutions that help gain competitive advantage are often expensive and therefore risky. The following cases are well-known examples of how information can be used for competitive advantage. These cases demonstrate that the strategic value of a computer information system arises from the data that can be collected and made accessible, as well as the creativity with which computers are used to process that data.

American Airlines' Sabre System

Sabre has been highly publicized as one of the most successful examples of a computer information system. In brief, Sabre is the system American Airlines developed to help the company determine how many flights it should schedule and how many passengers must be on a flight for it to be profitable. With Sabre (Figure 2-13 on the next page), American Airlines maintains an accurate and up-to-date accounting of airline seats. The system has allowed the company to fine-tune its daily operations to maximize occupancy and compute load factors affecting the planes.

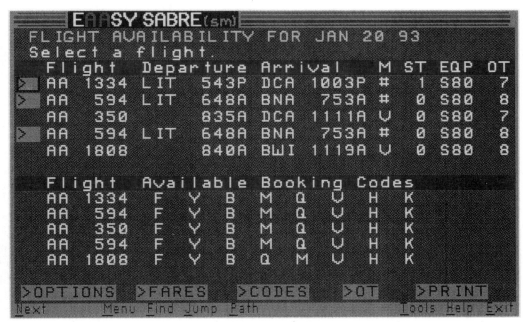

Figure 2-13
American Airlines' Sabre program gave the company a competitive advantage by streamlining its sales operation and maximizing flight occupancy.

One of the major benefits of obtaining this information was discovering that 20 percent of American Airlines' customers were accounting for a far greater percentage of the total seats booked. When the company's marketing personnel saw these statistics, they invented the frequent flyer program. This is an example of changes that were aimed at making a company more efficient, which ended up making it more effective as well.

Sabre's success is measured in more than its 500 percent return on investment. It is also measured by the marketing innovation of the first frequent flyer program and by the information gained about the marketing strategies of competitors.

American Hospital Supply Corporation's ASAP System

Another firm that has been recognized for its innovative use of computer information systems is American Hospital Supply Corporation. Its Analytic Systems Automatic Purchasing (ASAP) system was originally designed to solve its inefficient order-taking and delivery system, which had caused problems with one of the company's major customers.

The ASAP system allowed customers to place their orders directly, using computer terminals located at the hospital. As hospitals realized the ease with which they could order supplies, they tended to switch to American Hospital as their primary supplier. Hospitals saw availability of information and ease of ordering as valuable enhancements in service. Hospital agents were able to scan through up-to-date price lists quickly and conveniently, and then place their orders, which were filled promptly.

The information provided by ASAP to American Hospital Supply's customers, and vice versa, proved to be the competitive edge that ensured the company's success. As a result of ASAP, many of American Hospital's minor competitors suffered significant losses and were forced out of the industry. Other competitors, such as Johnson & Johnson, suffered reductions in their market share.

USAA

USAA is an insurance company that caters to military personnel and their families. In a bold, risky move, USAA decided to use information technology in an effort to reengineer its organizational processes. One notable change USAA made was to adopt what is known as a *document imaging system*.

Insurance companies must manage massive amounts of correspondence — much of it in the form of standardized forms — related to individual clients and cases. Part of USAA's solution to this information management problem was to open all customer correspondence in the mail room and place the letters or forms on a scanning device that looks like a photocopier. The scanner makes an image of the correspondence, which is stored in the company's computer system. The information from the scanned image is then available instantly to anybody using the computer system.

At USAA, insurance agents and claims representatives no longer have to wait while a single copy of an important document makes its way around the office. Now when a customer calls, the telephone system alerts an operator about who is calling, and the customer's information file is automatically presented to the operator before the call is even answered. By having all of the important information immediately available, the operator is able to better serve the customer.

Imaging systems have dramatically changed the ways that companies like USAA operate. In a manual system, information must travel sequentially around an office or from one office to another. Processing of documents must also occur in sequence, and it is difficult to share information. An imaging system allows several employees to use information at the same time, and the whole processing job happens much more quickly. USAA's system made the company far more effective because customers had their claims settled in far less time than it took using the manual system.

American Express

The American Express card operates without a preset credit limit. Instead, American Express (AMEX) uses a computer system to make decisions about credit approval each time a card member makes a purchase. The store salesperson swipes the card through a special card reader that translates information contained on the card's magnetic strip to a central American Express office. Potential card purchases are analyzed to determine whether they are consistent with previous purchases. If they are, then the purchase is automatically approved. If the purchase is large and inconsistent with previous purchases, an AMEX representative will pick up the phone and gather more information.

Before AMEX adopted its new computer information system, all authorizations were made manually by a set of authorizers — a time-consuming and expensive process. The automated authorization process was created to speed authorization and to save AMEX the cost of hiring authorizers. The rules for AMEX authorization were created by interviewing the authorizers. The criteria the authorizers used were programmed into the automatic authorization program. Now most credit approvals are made without human intervention. Other credit card issuers have followed American Express's lead in the credit authorization procedure.

Computer Services Companies

In between the organizations using computers and the companies making hardware or developing software, there is a third group that has emerged: computer services companies.

Timesharing

The meaning of the term *computer services* has changed over the years. During the 1960s and 1970s, most computers were mainframes and minicomputers. Because these large computers allowed many employees to use them simultaneously, companies could often address many of their problems by buying a single computer.

Still, buying a single computer was expensive. Companies with computers looked for any way possible to recoup the cost of the machine. One common method they used was the timesharing system. In general, **timesharing** refers to multiple users sharing a single central processing unit (CPU). As a computer service, timesharing is something that companies with computers offer to companies without computers. Large computer systems are not turned on and off, so there is usually a lot of time when a company is not using its computer. If the company offers timesharing, other companies or individuals can pay the company for the privilege of using the unused computer time. Timesharing in this sense has become less common as microcomputers have gained in popularity and power.

You will also hear the word *timesharing* used as a generic term for the practice of many individuals within a single organization sharing the resources of the mainframe computer. Timesharing is the process of dividing the computer's attention among many users, one user after another. Because a mainframe computer can execute hundreds or even thousands of instructions in the time it takes a human to execute two keystrokes, it seems as if every user is getting the computer's complete attention.

Consulting

Almost every industry uses computers in one way or another. In many cases, the way companies use computers has become quite exotic. In most of the situations described in the last section, the company using the computer solution is not entirely responsible for the development of the solution. In some cases, a computer services company has been responsible for masterminding and setting up the computer information system that fostered the competitive advantage.

Many modern computer services companies are a type of consulting firm that specializes in setting up computer information systems for other companies. Some of the best-known computer services companies are Andersen Consulting, Perot Systems, EDS, Businessland, Systematics, and Computer Sciences Corporation. Some larger companies such as IBM, McDonnell Douglas, and Martin Marietta have computer services branches. One of the more famous firms, Electronic Data Systems, or EDS, was founded by H. Ross Perot, who mounted a much publicized presidential candidacy in 1992.

The employees of computer services companies are often the graduates of MIS (Management Information Systems) departments. In fact, some of the most common employers of MIS graduates are computer services companies.

Software Developers

Some computer services companies are considered software developers rather than consulting firms. Similarly, some software developers are considered computer services companies. Sometimes a company is both. The reason is that developing computer information systems can involve either writing a new program or tailoring an existing program to meet a particular need.

For example, the software that is sold as database management software is normally very open-ended, meaning you can use the software to manage data in a variety of ways. The software is so open-ended, in fact, that using it to manage data just the way you want may take a considerable investment of time. As a result, many programs have emerged that manage databases for specific purposes, such as accounting, project management, and so on.

The companies that develop such software are considered computer services companies. Depending on the way they define the term, some people describe all software developers as computer services companies, simply because they are providing business tools.

Comprehension Questions

1. If you were starting an airline company today, would installing a computer system to track reservations be a competitive advantage or a competitive necessity?

2. Does the creation of a customer service department make a company (primarily) more efficient or more effective?

3. Why aren't innovations in computer information systems associated with competitive necessity?

Using What You Know

1. Explain how a system similar to Sabre might be used at BVOS.

2. If you, as an entrepreneur, are seeking a competitive advantage, why might it be better to find a computer services company that is not also a software developer?

3. How might a system like ASAP be used at BVOS?

Summary Points

Hardware and Software Companies

☐ The introduction of the microcomputer destabilized an industry that had been dominated by a few large companies, especially IBM.

☐ Some of the most important hardware companies in the microcomputer industry today are Apple, Digital Equipment Corporation (DEC), Compaq, and Hewlett-Packard.

☐ The most influential software companies in the microcomputer industry include Microsoft, Lotus, Word-Perfect, and Borland.

Major Computer Users

☐ Companies try to gain a competitive advantage with innovation in computer information systems; they adopt widely used techniques as competitive necessity. Examples of such systems are American Airlines' Sabre system, American Hospital Supply Corporation's ASAP system, the image processing system adopted by USAA, and the automated credit approval system used by American Express.

Computer Services Companies

Timesharing

☐ The original computer service was timesharing, in which companies with computers sell the unused time on their large-computer systems to companies that lack such systems.

☐ Timesharing also refers to the process of dividing a mainframe computer's attention among many users while appearing to serve them all simultaneously.

Consulting

☐ Many modern computer services companies are consultants that help other companies set up computer information systems.

Software Developers

☐ Companies that create computer information systems can very easily become software developers because they often create programs to solve their clients' problems.

☐ Some people consider all software development companies to be computer services companies.

Knowing the Facts

True/False

1. Timesharing as a computer service is an arrangement between a company with a computer and one without.

2. A document imaging system can be part of a computer information system used to gain competitive advantage.

3. At one point, Compaq was the fastest growing company of all time.

4. IBM is the biggest player in the microcomputer hardware industry.

5. Innovations in computer information systems are usually associated with competitive necessity.

6. Hewlett-Packard gained widespread recognition by making the first pocket calculator.

7. DEC initially gained success by manufacturing minicomputers.

8. Compaq initially gained success making portable PCs.

9. Microsoft's first product was DOS, the operating system for the IBM PC and the compatibles.

10. The first computer by Apple had no keyboard and no monitor.

Short Answer

1. The introduction of the _____ in the mid-1970s destabilized the computer industry.

2. _____ created an electronic tabulating machine for the U.S. Census Bureau.

3. Although they do not all do consulting or work for individual clients, some people consider all _____ to be computer services companies, because their products help businesses and organizations.

4. Dividing a computer's attention among many users is known as _____.

5. Some of the most common employers of MIS graduates are _____.

6. The term _____ can include IBM microcomputers and compatibles.

7. When a computer information system is adopted by most of the firms in a given type of business, the system becomes a _____.

8. The product that sealed Microsoft's success was _____.

9. Two of the leading database programs, dBASE IV and Paradox, are both owned by _____ _____.

10. Jobs and Wozniak were the founders of _____ _____.

Answers

True/False

1. T
2. T
3. T
4. F
5. F
6. T
7. T
8. T
9. F
10. T

Short Answer

1. microcomputer
2. Herman Hollerith
3. software developers
4. timesharing
5. computer services companies
6. PC
7. competitive necessity
8. DOS
9. Borland International
10. Apple Computer

Challenging Your Understanding

1. In 1992, Bill Gates, CEO of Microsoft, was the richest American. What are the components of his success? What can Microsoft do in the future to maintain its power in the software market?

2. Is the term "clone" appropriate these days? Why or why not?

3. During the 1960s and 1970s, IBM spent more money on research and development (R&D) than its closest competitors made in revenues. What part does R&D play in the profitability of a computer company?

4. Most computer manufacturers have begun marketing their services as much or more than their products. Why do you think this is happening?

5. Do you think a computer can give a company a sustainable competitive advantage or just a temporary advantage?

Unit I Project

Identifying Market Leaders in the Computer Industry

Yamamoto and Company (Y&C) is a world-renowned business consulting company that monitors, analyzes, and forecasts worldwide issues related to the law, energy, technology, medicine, finance, demography, and culture. Yamamoto boasts the services of Nobel laureates, leading economists, and well-known scholars.

Your broad background, education, and quick intelligence have landed you an attractive junior analyst position in the U.S. office of Y&C. Your first assignment is in technology. When you report to work, you are assigned to Jennifer Andrews, senior technology analyst. Ms. Andrews is preparing an analysis of the computer industry.

Your job is to prepare a report detailing the major companies in the computer industry. Use any resources you feel are necessary to show market share, revenues, and other indicators for mainframe, minicomputer, and microcomputer manufacturers, as well as software developers and computer services companies. Your report should include graphs and tables detailing your findings.

Because you want to impress your boss, you are going one step further than requested. Using the data and your best guesses, forecast the future of the computer industry in the next decade. Be sure to tell Ms. Andrews what you found, how you arrived at your forecast, and what assumptions you made in order to create the forecast.

Solving Problems with Software

Understanding the Needs of BVOS Staff

Recall from the Introduction that the problem-solving process can be broken into five stages:

1. Recognizing the problem
2. Understanding the problem
3. Compiling relevant information
4. Formulating and building the solution
5. Evaluating the solution

In the last unit, we looked at the big picture and tried to understand the problem of purchasing a computer system in general terms by giving an overview of the entire computer industry, both the producers and the users of hardware and

PROBLEM-SOLVING STEPS   **RELATED TASKS**

RECOGNIZE THE PROBLEM

Determine what processes should be computerized.
- Writing memos, reports, correspondence
- Analyzing financial data
- Keeping records of customer transactions
- Communicating within branch and with Toronto

UNDERSTAND THE PROBLEM

Determine software needs.
- Word processing, spreadsheet, database, and communications packages.

COMPILE RELEVANT INFORMATION

Find appropriate sources of information.
- Computer magazines
- Colleagues and friends

Determine what is relevant.
- Decide which software features are necessary to meet your needs.

FORMULATE AND BUILD A SOLUTION

Take action.
- Compare prices and features for popular packages in each of the four application areas needed.

EVALUATE THE SOLUTION

Figure II-1   Steps 2, 3, and 4 of the problem-solving process involve several tasks that relate to software.

software. Now that you have a better idea of how Buena Vista Office Supply (BVOS) relates to other companies using computers, it's time to look more closely at the specific needs of your new company, do some research on the software market, and make some purchasing decisions. In other words, you will be moving through steps 2, 3, and 4 of the problem-solving process, focusing exclusively on software. Figure II-1 on the previous page details the tasks required by each step. We will add to these tasks when we repeat steps 2, 3, and 4 in the next unit, which focuses on hardware.

Dear _____,

    As we agreed in our telephone conversation on Friday, you will be installing a computer system in your new branch office. The figures showing the difference between the revenue achieved by branches with and without computer systems speak for themselves.

    The most important advantage of installing a computer system is the ability to automate the process of keeping track of inventory and taking customer orders. Branch owners who have switched from manual inventory methods to computerized methods will attest to greater efficiency, fewer errors, and even better job satisfaction among employees.

    Automating your record keeping consists mainly of creating a database that contains:

- an itemized listing of your current inventory of office supplies
- a record of the inventory you have on order from the regional distributor
- a record of current orders from customers

    All of this data is accessed automatically by your accounting system, which can keep track of accounts payable (essentially, money due to the regional distributor plus payroll) and accounts receivable (money due from your customers).

    Because most of our branches use dBASE IV, that is the database software you should buy. Using dBASE will make it easier for you to trade information with the other branches. You have more leeway in other software-purchasing decisions, since compatibility with headquarters will not be as critical as with the database software. We will be more than happy, however, to give you advice about which products we like, which we don't, and which products our in-house system experts are familiar with.

    I understand that you probably don't have much experience in setting up a computer system, much less an inventory database. Don't worry. As soon as you have your system running, we'll send down our in-house system experts, Diane Lindstrom and Mary Soriano, to help you set up the database and get you moving in the right direction. Essentially, they'll design the database for you and train your people how to use it. Lisa Yep, your accountant and inventory manager, will need to spend quite a bit of time with Diane and Mary while they are there, since Lisa will naturally become your local expert on the system.

Figure II-2   A letter from Elmer Phillips, the vice president of BVOS in Toronto.

The reason for focusing on software before hardware is that software is the real problem-solving tool of the computer system. You should find the software program that best fits your specific needs in terms of both function and final output format. Whatever gap exists between what your software can do and what you want it to do must be bridged by the most expensive element of the problem-solving process — human labor. Also, your system hardware will limit the kind of software you can choose. Since you don't yet own any hardware and you want the greatest possible freedom when choosing software, you should pick the software first. Once you have chosen the appropriate software to solve your business problems, you can make informed decisions about purchasing the right hardware to run your software.

What Your Computers Are For

Let's look now at the things you need software to do for you at BVOS.

The Inventory Database

When Elmer Phillips, the vice president of BVOS in Toronto, first introduced the idea of purchasing a computer system for your BVOS branch, he mainly talked about the advantages of keeping track of inventory and customer orders. Figure II-2 (on the previous page) is the first part of a letter he sent to you regarding the advantages of computerizing your office. Figure II-3 is a graph that shows the average BVOS revenue at branches with and without computer systems.

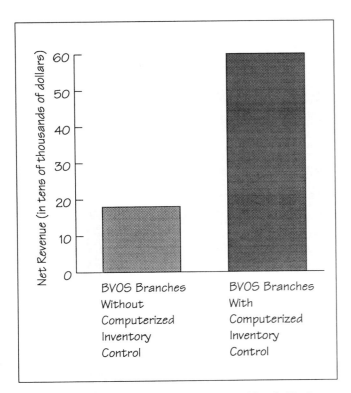

Figure II-3 Average revenue at BVOS branches with and without computer systems

Analyzing Financial Data

As president, your primary concern will be making sure your new enterprise is profitable. Therefore, another important advantage to having a computer system is the ability to keep track of your accounts, analyze financial data and create budgets like the one shown in Figure II-4 (on the next page). You will want to know what products are selling best, which are generating the most revenue, and how much revenue you need to turn a given profit. You can use your computer system to calculate, for example, how many dollars per square foot of floor space per year of profit must be figured and balanced with the needs of customers for low-profit items. There are numerous money-related questions that you will want to answer as your business gets moving.

Sending Correspondence to Clients and Associates

Another basic need you foresee is the ability to send letters to customers, potential customers, and head-quarters. Rather than write letters by hand (which is unprofessional) or on a typewriter (which is cumbersome and slow), you would like to create, edit, and store your correspondence on your computer. Lisa, your manager, also wants to correspond with customers and headquarters using a computer.

Sending and Receiving Data Over the Phone Lines

You will need to obtain a great deal of data from headquarters on a regular basis. BVOS headquarters constantly adjusts prices, and you will need to keep abreast of these changes to keep your books straight. To serve their existing branch offices, headquarters has created a link to the BVOS mainframe in Toronto. The computer systems at your branch will be able to share information with the main computer system hundreds of miles away.

Finding Software Solutions

These four tasks — maintaining inventory and customer orders, analyzing financial data, sending correspondence, and exchanging information — can be accomplished with the aid of software. In order to solve these problems for BVOS, you will need to decide what software products are the right tools for the job. When you reach Chapter 4, you will make several purchasing decisions. Before you do so, however, we will first explain what software is and describe the various types that exist. Next, we will describe the most common software tools that are used in business today and look at a few of the most popular products. Finally, we will explain what programming is and how software is made.

When you are done with this unit, not only will you know what software is, you will understand the process of choosing software for a given type of problem, and you'll know how software is developed.

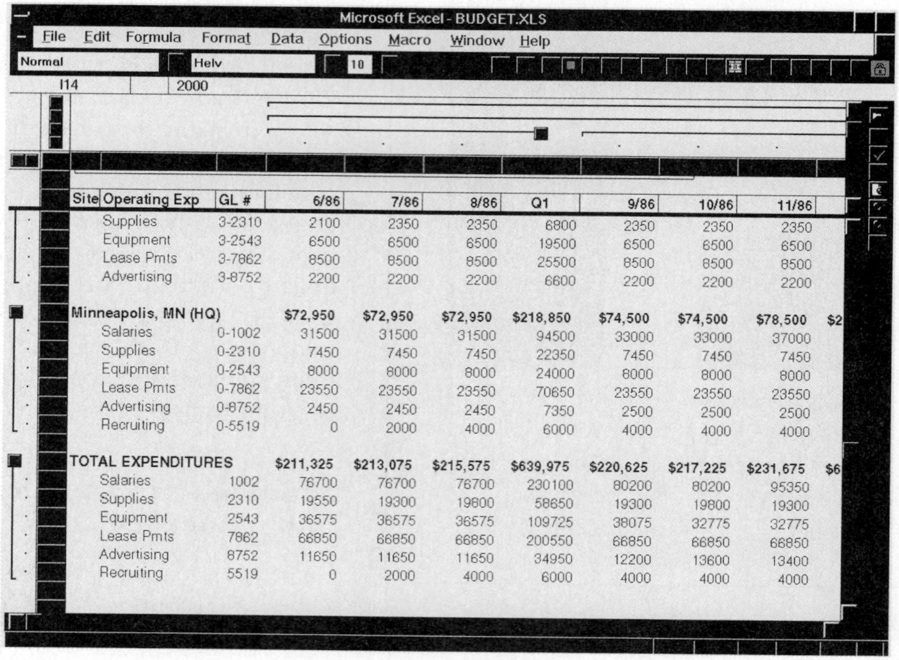

Site	Operating Exp	GL #	6/86	7/86	8/86	Q1	9/86	10/86	11/86	
	Supplies	3-2310	2100	2350	2350	6800	2350	2350	2350	
	Equipment	3-2543	6500	6500	6500	19500	6500	6500	6500	
	Lease Pmts	3-7862	8500	8500	8500	25500	8500	8500	8500	
	Advertising	3-8752	2200	2200	2200	6600	2200	2200	2200	
Minneapolis, MN (HQ)			$72,950	$72,950	$72,950	$218,850	$74,500	$74,500	$78,500	$2
	Salaries	0-1002	31500	31500	31500	94500	33000	33000	37000	
	Supplies	0-2310	7450	7450	7450	22350	7450	7450	7450	
	Equipment	0-2543	8000	8000	8000	24000	8000	8000	8000	
	Lease Pmts	0-7862	23550	23550	23550	70650	23550	23550	23550	
	Advertising	0-8752	2450	2450	2450	7350	2500	2500	2500	
	Recruiting	0-5519	0	2000	4000	6000	4000	4000	4000	
TOTAL EXPENDITURES			$211,325	$213,075	$215,575	$639,975	$220,625	$217,225	$231,675	$6
	Salaries	1002	76700	76700	76700	230100	80200	80200	95350	
	Supplies	2310	19550	19300	19800	58650	19300	19800	19300	
	Equipment	2543	36575	36575	36575	109725	38075	32775	32775	
	Lease Pmts	7862	66850	66850	66850	200550	66850	66850	66850	
	Advertising	8752	11650	11650	11650	34950	12200	13600	13400	
	Recruiting	5519	0	2000	4000	6000	4000	4000	4000	

Figure II-4
Budgets help managers keep their businesses profitable.

C H A P T E R 3

Introduction to Software

Key Terms

application
application package
application software
batch processing
command-line interface
game software
graphical user interface (GUI)
icon
interactive program
menu-driven interface
operating system software
program
real-time processing
simulation software
software
tutorial software
user interface
utilities
overview

Objectives

In this chapter you will learn to:

- Understand in general terms what software is and the decision-making process involved in selecting software
- Compare the three main types of software used in business
- Name and describe at least five other software applications
- Compare the three types of user interface
- Describe the difference between real-time and batch processing

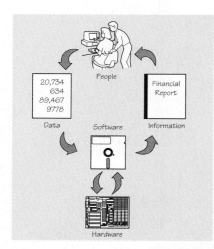

Figure 3-1

Software is the crucial link among people, the data they must process, and the hardware they use to do so.

Software and the Computer System

Software forms the link among people, hardware, data, and information, as shown in Figure 3-1. Specifically, software is what people use to manipulate data on a computer in order to obtain information.

To understand how software makes this interaction possible, this chapter will give you a comprehensive sense of what software is. We will start with a general definition, then fill it out by describing the major types of software that are available. Finally, we will explain briefly how software works.

What Is Software?

Software is the term used to describe the sets of instructions that control the computer. A piece of software — a series of instructions that perform a particular task — is commonly called a **program**. A group of program instructions is shown in Figure 3-2. Because most software products are created for accomplishing specific tasks, we refer to software as the main problem-solving component of the computer system.

In general, no matter what the task, software is designed to accept data and process it so it becomes useful and appears as information. The instructions that comprise the program tell the hardware how to interpret the data, how to manipulate or process it, and how to present it.

Types of Software

There are three main types of software discussed in this book: application software, utility software, and operating system software.

```
 System  File  Edit  Database  Record  Program  Window
                          W-ICITEM.PRG
 close data
 use inmprodt in 1 alias old
 use icitem-w in 2 alias new
 sele old
 go bottom
 m_oldrec=recno()
 sele new
 dele all
 pack
 go bottom
 m_newrec=recno()
 sele new

 if m_oldrec <> m_newrec then
     for i = 1 to (m_oldrec - m_newrec) + 1
         append blank
     endfor
 endif

        |<E:>|           |           |            |Ins  |Num
```

Figure 3-2

Each line in this program is an instruction that tells the computer what to do.

Application Software

Application software refers to any program the user employs to accomplish a specific type of task, as shown in Figure 3-3. The most common **applications** (tasks) that these programs accomplish are creating documents through word processing, creating spreadsheets, managing databases, creating graphic images, and communicating with other computers. There are, however, many other applications for which programs have been written. For a program to be called application software, the tasks it accomplishes must exist independent of the computer. For example, word processing is an application because the need to create documents would still exist even if there were no computers available to help us. Application programs are often characterized by enabling the user to obtain formatted output.

Some application software products you may have heard of are WordPerfect and Microsoft Word (word processing), Lotus 1-2-3 (spreadsheet), dBASE (database management), Harvard Graphics (graphics), and ProComm (communications).

Specific pieces of application software are often referred to as **application packages**, or simply as applications. Thus, the term *application* is sometimes used to mean the task, but it can also mean the software. A piece of application software is referred to as a package because it is capable of performing a number of different functions.

There are actually many other types of application software. Another type of application especially familiar to young people is **game software**, an example of which is shown in Figure 3-4 on the next page. Video game systems for the home, such as Nintendo and Sega, require software to operate. In fact, the software represents a bigger source of income for these companies than the hardware. Game software is also available to run on microcomputers.

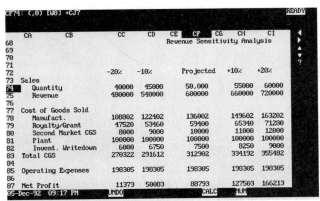

(a)

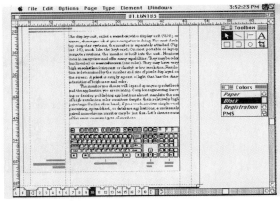

(b)

(c)

Figure 3-3

Three pieces of application software: (a) a spreadsheet program; (b) a desktop publishing program; (c) a program for composing music.

Although the topic is not often discussed in computer textbooks, it isn't uncommon to find game software on computers that people use at work. If you watch your employees at BVOS, you may find that, over time, they will collect a few games to entertain themselves during their free time or when things are slow around the office.

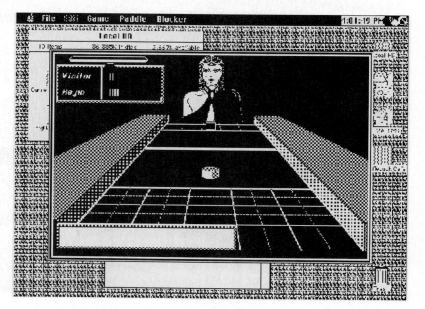

Figure 3-4
The computer game shown here is a type of application software.

The field of education has adopted some of the previously mentioned types of application software and added a few more, as shown in Figure 3-5. **Tutorial software** teaches a subject by directing the student through a series of steps — instructions that appear on-screen. In the more advanced tutorials, the program actually tests the student's comprehension during the program and reteaches material that the student did not properly understand. (Many application programs come with their own tutorials that teach you how to use the software.) At the other end of the scale in terms of complexity, businesses and government have developed simulation software to train employees. **Simulation software** uses the computer to imitate the interaction of real-world objects and activities, such as designing, building, operating, or repairing a car, jet, or forklift. Perhaps the best-known simulation software is the flight simulator. Extremely complex flight simulators are used to train astronauts and pilots, while scaled-down simulators are used as game software on microcomputers and home video game systems.

An exreme outgrowth of computer simulation, known as **virtual reality**, is in its infancy. This new field attempts to replace reality and fool our human senses. In the field of medicine, doctors can put on special headgear and visors with gloves in order to "operate" on the simulation of a real patient. The computer generates a stimulus that allows the doctor to experience the sight and touch of an operation — all without picking up a scalpel.

Utility Software

A second type of software are programs called **utilities**. Utilities accomplish specific tasks that relate to the internal functioning of the computer. Utility programs sort, copy, compare, search, and list files; they also perform diagnostic routines that gauge the condition and performance of the computer system. Operating systems, which we dicuss next, incorporate

Figure 3-5
Tutorial and simulation software are types of application software used in education.

some utility functions. Other utilities are packaged separately. Some utility programs that you may have heard of are the Norton Utilities, Stacker, and FastBack. A screen from the PC Tools utility package is shown in Figure 3-6.

Programmers still use other types of utility programs called compilers and interpreters. These programs translate the material that the programmer writes into instructions the computer can understand. By doing so, these programs save today's software developers countless hours of work that previously had to be done by hand.

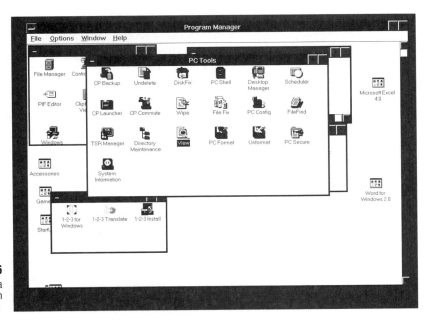

Figure 3-6
The PC Tools packages a set of utility programs in Macintosh or IBM versions

Operating System Software

The third type of software that you will learn about in this book is **operating system software** (usually referred to as simply **operating systems**, but also sometimes called **system software**). Before a microcomputer can load any other piece of software, it needs to load an operating system, or **OS**. The OS of a microcomputer contains basic instructions that help all the hardware components work together and help other software interact with the hardware. Some common operating systems are DOS, the Macintosh's System 7, OS/2, Windows NT, and Unix.

Although we will cover application and utility software in this unit, we will not cover operating systems until Unit III. The reason for this sequence is that understanding operating systems requires understanding the hardware that the OS controls.

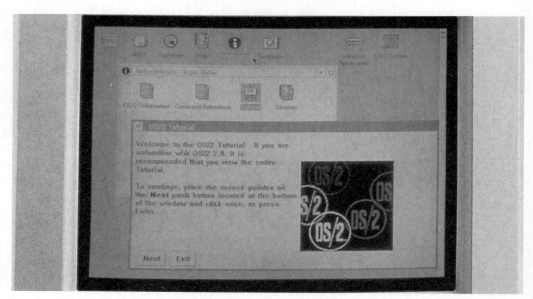

Figure 3-7
OS/2 2.0, an operating
system for IBMs and
compatibles.

Comprehension Questions

1. Autodesk, Inc., makes a software package that helps you design houses. What type of software do you think it is? Why?

2. Microsoft Windows includes a program that displays a clock on the screen. What type of software do you think the program is? Why?

3. Broderbund makes a program for the Macintosh that reviews an entire year of geometry and tests your understanding as you go. What type of software do you think the program is? Why?

Using What You Know

1. See if you can find out what types of software the following are: AfterDark, Quattro Pro, AutoCAD, Mathematica, and Where in the World Is Carmen Sandiego?

2. Can you think of how and why BVOS could use Lotus 1-2-3, Paradox, and WordPerfect?

3. Using a computer magazine, find 10 pieces of software that you haven't heard of. Using the information in the magazine, try to describe what the software does and what type of software it is.

How Software Works

When software is loaded into the computer's memory, it does its job by controlling the central processing unit (CPU) that is the brains of any microcomputer. Once the software is loaded, the sets of instructions that comprise it take over and control the hardware, which reads the instructions and carries them out. In general, software instructions tell the hardware how to do one of two things:

- Some instructions tell the computer how to handle input and output.
- Other instructions tell the computer how to process and store the data it receives.

Input and Output Through User Interfaces

The computer is a machine for processing data in what is called the **processing cycle**. Let's expand on this definition a bit. People, whom we call users, provide data — in one form or another — to computers. This process is called **input**. Computers process the data by carrying out software instructions and the commands issued by the user. Computers then present the processed data back to users. This process is called **output**. The software controls how the computer accepts data and commands as input, and to some degree, controls how it presents data as output through its **user interface**.

In general, there are three basic kinds of user interface: command-line interfaces, menu interfaces, and graphical user interfaces. The most important differences among the three lie in how the user issues processing commands.

Command-Line Interfaces. In a **command-line interface**, the user controls the program by typing commands at the keyboard. The earliest microcomputer programs all used command-line interfaces, primarily because this type of interface is the easiest to create. But many programs that are popular today still use command-line interfaces. The best example is DOS, an operating system created by Microsoft Corporation that is the most widely used piece of software in the world.

An example of the DOS command-line interface is shown in Figure 3-8 on the next page. The "C:\" at the beginning of some lines is the command prompt. The characters that follow the prompt, such as "ver" and "dir," are commands that have been entered by the user. Lines that do not begin with a command prompt are the computer's responses to the commands, that is, output. For example, when you enter "ver," this is input that tells the computer to output the DOS version number on the screen.

Menu-Driven Interfaces. A command-line interface requires the user to know what commands are available and how to use them. **Menu-driven interfaces** relieve some of the burden by providing lists of options from which the user can choose. A given menu option can either invoke a command or bring up another menu that allows the user to further clarify the option selected in the previous menu. Moving from one menu to another is known as "navigating through the menu system."

```
C:\TEMP>ver

MS-DOS Version 5.00


C:\TEMP>dir

 Volume in drive C is JACK STRAW
 Volume Serial Number is 18F6-523A
 Directory of C:\TEMP

.              <DIR>      08-31-92   6:16p
..             <DIR>      08-31-92   6:16p
UNZIP          <DIR>      09-30-92   8:56p
CHKLIST  CPS        108   11-25-92  10:49p
FIG-TEMP ZIP      31518   10-20-92   2:25a
LIBDBF   ZIP     195305   11-26-92   2:23a
PCMAG    ZIP     256610   11-29-92   2:24a
PLAT     ZIP      57240   11-11-92   9:21p
RPMSWAP  TMP     950272   12-05-92   9:10p
WINTN2   ZIP     168364   04-29-92  10:51a
        10 file(s)     1659417 bytes
                      13537280 bytes free

C:\TEMP>
```

Figure 3-8
In DOS command interface, characters following the command prompt, C:\, are commands input by the user.

CompuServe, an information service users can access through telephone lines, uses a menu-driven interface (although users can also type commands at a command prompt). Figure 3-9 shows a WordPerfect 5.1 menu for formatting text.

Graphical User Interfaces.   The Apple Macintosh popularized a third kind of interface, the **graphical user interface**, or **GUI** (pronounced "gooey"). With a graphical user interface, the user usually controls the program by using a pointing device called a **mouse** to select actions, objects, and programs that are represented on the screen. In addition to text and menus, a graphical user interface often includes little pictures, called **icons**, that are used to represent programs, data files, and commands.

```
Format: Line

    1 - Hyphenation                           No

    2 - Hyphenation Zone - Left               10%
                           Right              4%

    3 - Justification                         Full

    4 - Line Height                           Auto

    5 - Line Numbering                        No

    6 - Line Spacing                          1

    7 - Margins - Left                        1"
                  Right                       1"

    8 - Tab Set                               Rel: -1", every 0.5"

    9 - Widow/Orphan Protection               No


Selection: 0
```

Figure 3-9
A menu-driven interface in WordPerfect 5.1.

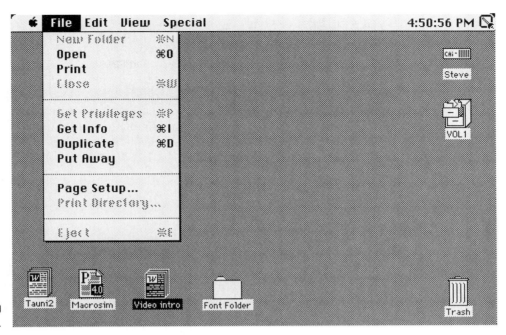

Figure 3-10
The Macintosh's GUI.

Figure 3-10 shows the Macintosh's GUI. The words along the top of the screen are the names of "pull-down menus," which the user accesses with a mouse. In the figure, the File menu is currently open. Below the menus are several icons.

Advantages and Disadvantages of Each Interface. Since the introduction of the original Macintosh in 1984, computer users have been debating the advantages and disadvantages of these interfaces. From a novice's point of view, the advantages of the GUI are obvious: Pointing to parts of the screen and selecting menu options or icons is a far more intuitive process than typing commands at the keyboard. With a GUI, it is often possible to start using a new piece of software without ever touching a software manual. For this reason, GUIs are often referred to as "user friendly." Simple menu-driven interfaces are less intuitive than GUIs but more intuitive than command-line interfaces. Some people choose menu-driven interfaces over GUIs because they prefer working entirely from the keyboard, without using a mouse.

The advantages of a command-line interface may not be as obvious, but they can be equally compelling. One advantage cited by the command-line advocates is that issuing a command from the keyboard — even a complex command — is usually more efficient than navigating through a system of menus. Naturally, this advantage is true only if you are a competent typist and are familiar with the commands. Another advantage of the command line is that the programs that use them tend to be smaller and therefore faster. Finally, command-line allies will tell you that having to learn something about a program from the manual before you sit down at the computer will make you a more informed and more efficient user in the long run.

In evaluating the various user interface options, the focus must always be on understanding the skill and experience of the intended user.

Types of Processing

There are two basic ways that computers process the data they receive: real-time processing and batch processing.

When you use a microcomputer, you generally require real-time processing. **Real-time processing** means that you give the computer a command and it is carried out immediately, as demonstrated in Figure 3-11. The same user is the source of input and the recipient of output. The user gets a response from the computer in a time frame that is relevant for a user sitting at a computer. Real-time processing is often associated with **interactive programs**, which require user input to function.

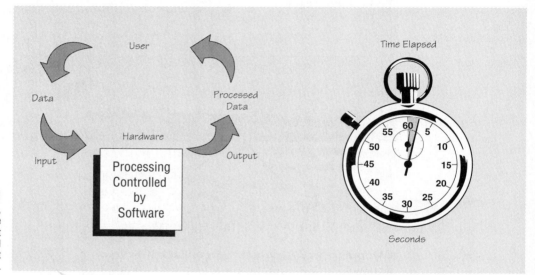

Figure 3-11
In real-time processing, the hardware and software process data as soon as it is input by the user, and generate output immediately.

A bank ATM such as the one shown in Figure 3-12 is an example of an interactive program that uses real-time processing. When you use the machine, you enter your identification number, access your account, and withdraw or deposit money in just a few seconds. Your account information is updated immediately. If it weren't, you could drive from one ATM to another and withdraw the maximum amount of money from each one with no regard for how much money was actually in your account.

The alternative to real-time processing is batch processing. **Batch processing** does not require user input while the program is running. Instead, the program collects data over a period of time and then processes the data all at

Figure 3-12
This bank's ATM uses real-time processing so your account balance can be figured immediately each time you perform a transaction.

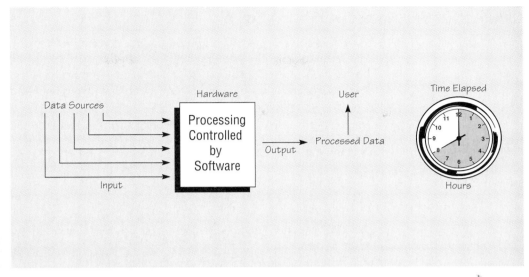

Figure 3-13
In batch processing, data is collected over a period of time, often from a variety of sources; output is generated only periodically.

Figure 3-14
Mainframes like this one are often used to perform batch processing.

once, as demonstrated in Figure 3-13. The user of the processed data is not necessarily the source of input data. Although almost everything done on microcomputers uses real-time processing, it is important to realize that mainframes often use batch processing, as shown in Figure 3-14. Mainframes tend to stay on 24 hours a day. Batch processing is an efficient way to use a mainframe when most of the users are not at work.

Banks use batch processing to enter checks into accounts. When the bank has collected enough checks, it processes them all in sequence and updates the accounts. Batch processing is very efficient because the computer can be used for other activities while the batches of data are being collected.

Comprehension Questions

1. The DOS command A:\DIR gives a directory listing of all files in drive A. The same command in a command-line Unix operating system is A:\LS-A. Which do you think is more intuitive? Why?

2. What types of interfaces are illustrated in Figure 3-5?

3. Imagine that you are not limited by current technology. Describe an advanced user interface that is more intuitive and user friendly than any of the three types mentioned.

Using What You Know

1. Pick which interface your salespeople will use, and justify your choice with three reasons.

2. Of the three most popular interfaces available, which would you pick to win the battle over types of interfaces? Why?

3. Name two examples of batch processing that are not mentioned in this chapter.

Summary Points

What Is Software?

☐ A piece of software, also known as a program, is a set of instructions that controls the computer and makes it useful for accomplishing a specific task.

☐ Software is the primary problem-solving tool of the computer system.

☐ Software instructions tell the computer how to interpret data, how to process it, and how to present the processed result.

Types of Software

Application Software

☐ Application software refers to any program that is used to accomplish a user-defined task that exists independent of the computer.

☐ Common applications are word processing, creating spreadsheets, managing databases, creating graphic images, and communicating with other computers.

☐ Application packages consist of sets of interconnected programs that work together to perform the desired task.

☐ Game software is played on microcomputers or on special video game systems.

☐ The field of education has created tutorial software and simulation software.

☐ Modern programming requires programs called compilers and interpreters.

Utility Software

☐ Utility programs are used to accomplish tasks that relate to the internal functioning of the computer system.

Operating System Software

☐ The operating system is the first program loaded into the computer.

☐ The OS contains basic instructions that allow the hardware to work and that help software interact with the hardware.

How Software Works

☐ Software instructions must be loaded into memory to be carried out.

Input and Output Through User Interfaces

Command-Line Interfaces

☐ With a command-line interface, the user directs the computer by typing commands from the keyboard.

Menu-Driven Interfaces

☐ With a menu-driven interface, the user directs the computer by choosing from a menu of options. If the option is a complete command, the computer carries it out. If the option needs further clarification, the user is shown a different menu.

Graphical User Interfaces
☐ With a GUI, the user directs the computer by using a pointing device to select text, menus, and icons.

Advantages and Disadvantages of Each Interface
☐ Menu-driven interfaces are less intuitive than GUIs but more intuitive than command-line interfaces. They do not require a mouse.
☐ GUIs are more intuitive than command-line interfaces.
☐ Command-line interfaces tend to be more efficient once the user becomes familiar with the commands.
☐ GUIs will win out in the end because they are preferred by new users.

Types of Processing
☐ Interactive programs that use real-time processing require user input and give responses in a time frame that is relevant for the user.
☐ Programs that use batch processing collect data over a period of time and process it all at once without requiring user input.

Knowing the Facts

True/False

1. Application software supports tasks related to the internal functions of the computer.
2. An operating system must be loaded into a computer before any other type of software is loaded.
3. The instructions that comprise any program tell the computer how to accept data, process it, and present it.
4. The most intuitive type of interface is the graphical user interface, or GUI.
5. Game software requires a computer designed for games, such as a Nintendo or an arcade machine.
6. An ATM at a bank uses real-time processing.
7. Application packages are generally smaller than utility programs.
8. Simulation software is usually more complex than tutorial software.
9. The first user interfaces were menu-driven interfaces.
10. DOS includes a command-line interface.

Short Answer

1. Small pictures called _____ are often used in GUIs.
2. Name two types of software used in education.
3. Sets of instructions that control the computer are called _____.
4. The added efficiency of a command-line interface may be lost if the user cannot _____.
5. Mainframe systems use _____ processing to take advantage of times when few users are present.
6. What are the three main types of software?
7. What line of computers popularized the graphical user interface?
8. Which type of software is best described as problem-solving software?
9. Real-time processing is generally associated with _____ programs, while batch processing does not require user input while the program is running.
10. Of the three main types of software, understanding _____ requires the most knowledge of computer hardware.

Answers

True/False		Short Answer	
1. F		1.	icons
2. T		2.	tutorial, simulation
3. T		3.	software or programs
4. T.		4.	type
5. F.		5.	batch
6. T		6.	operating system, software, application software, and utilities
7. F		7.	Macintosh
8. T.		8.	application software
9. F.		9.	interactive
10. T		10.	operating system software

Challenging Your Understanding

1. We described two types of educational software. But the field of education might also use some of the other types we described. How might other kinds of application software and utility programs be used in education?

2. We claimed that "software forms the link among people, hardware, and data." Support this idea by explaining why software, rather than hardware or data, forms the link.

3. See if you can find out what type of software Windows 3.0 or 3.1 is.

4. During the 1980s, the most common type of computer in elementary schools was the Apple II. Much of the educational software written for the Apple II uses menu-driven interfaces. Is a menu-driven interface the best type for elementary school students? Why or why not?

5. Virtual reality involves the use of computers to create artificial worlds that allow humans to explore, create, learn, and work in environments that would normally be hostile or difficult to create. How might virtual reality be used in business applications?

6. What kind of computer interface do you prefer? Why?

Application Software and Utility Software

Key Terms

analytic graphics
antivirus software
artificial intelligence
backing up (archiving)
bitmap
bulletin board service (BBS)
communications software
computer-aided design (CAD)
context-sensitive help
query
copy-protected software
database
database file
database management
    system (DBMS)
data compression
desktop publishing (DTP)
documentation
downloading
draw program
edit
electronic mail (E-mail)
expert system
field
file management
    (hard disk management)
font
font manager
graphics
graphics software
help features

hot links
hypermedia software
installation
integrated application package
knowledge base
knowledge engineer
modem
modules
multimedia
paint program
presentation graphics
public domain software
query
record
screen saver
shareware
site license
software piracy
spreadsheet
telephone support
typeface
upgrade
uploading
utility package
vector graphics
version
virus
what-if capability
word processing
WYSIWYG

Objectives

In this chapter you will learn to:

- Have an understanding of the most popular types of application software and explain the function of each
- Understand the important capabilities of a DBMS
- Briefly explain the difference between paint and draw programs
- Name four activities that communications software can help you perform
- Describe the advantages and disadvantages of integrated software
- Name five types of utility software and explain the function of each
- List at least three periodicals that cover computer products
- Explain the advantages of getting information from friends and business associates
- Name the six criteria you should consider when shopping for a software package
- Describe the three principal types of software support
- Describe the four steps of software installation
- Explain the significance of software piracy and describe the steps software companies are taking to deter it

Applications Software

Recall the four basic problems that you, as president of the new BVOS branch, need to solve:

- Setting up and maintaining your inventory database
- Analyzing financial data
- Sending correspondence
- Communicating via computer with Buena Vista headquarters

Since the term *application software* refers to a program that solves a particular type of task, you will be addressing these four problems with application software. In this chapter, we will cover the various types of application software. Then we will cover some popular types of utility software, which you may also want to purchase for BVOS. Finally, we will look at the issues involved in selecting an application package.

Common Applications

Most users have very similar computing needs. They need to collect and analyze data, and they need to communicate their findings. Software producers have responded to these needs by creating a wealth of certain types of application packages.

Database management systems were created to help users collect and organize data. To analyze data, you might use either a database manager or a spreadsheet package.

Several types of application packages are available for communicating ideas. For text communication, the most common type of software is the word processor. If the text requires complex formatting and integration of graphics, you might use desktop publishing software. If you want to communicate your ideas graphically, there are many graphics packages to choose from. And if you need to communicate your ideas to someone through the phone lines, you will use a communications package. All of these appplications can be performed on the same microcomputer, as demonstrated in Figure 4-1.

Let's look at the most common types of application software in greater detail.

Database Software

A **database** is a collection of data that is stored and ordered to help users answer certain questions. A database can include all kinds of digital data, text, graphics, numbers, full-motion video, and sound. Databases used for business, however, generally include only text and

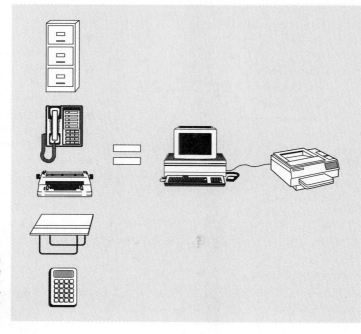

Figure 4-1
With the right application software, a single microcomputer can take the place of many cumbersome pieces of office equipment.

numbers. A text-based database is organized into fields, records, and files. A **field** is a relatively small unit of text. Each field lists a certain type of data. For example, in your position at BVOS, you might want a personal database that includes data on business contacts, such as last name, phone number, and so on. Fields are grouped into records. A **record** contains a set of data about a particular person, place, or event. For example, the fields for the name, department, Social Security number, and address of one of your employees could be listed in a database as a record. A group of related records, such as those pertaining to the the illustrations in this book, can be grouped together in a **database file** such as the one shown in Figure 4-2.

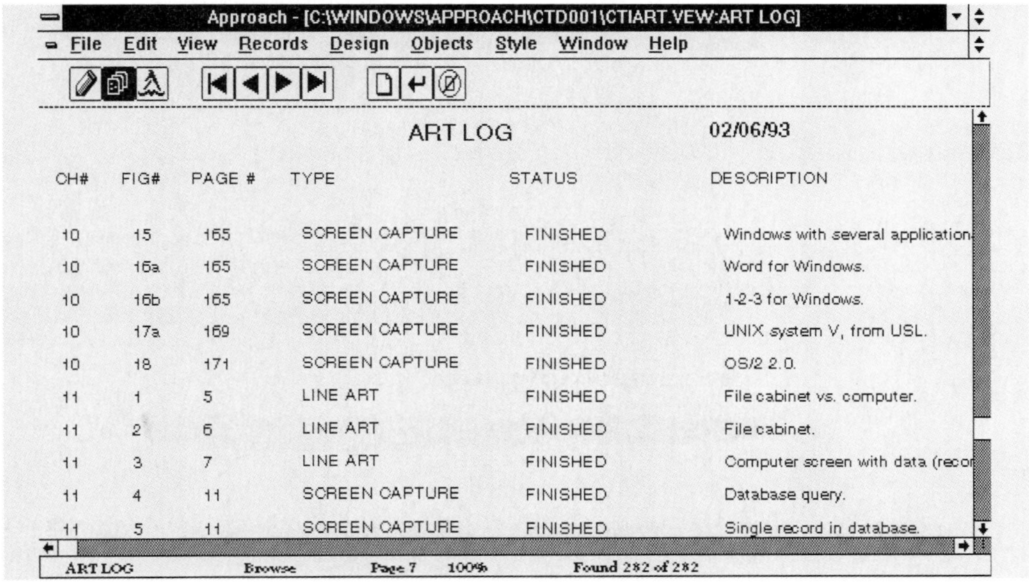

CH#	FIG#	PAGE #	TYPE	STATUS	DESCRIPTION
10	15	165	SCREEN CAPTURE	FINISHED	Windows with several application
10	16a	165	SCREEN CAPTURE	FINISHED	Word for Windows.
10	16b	165	SCREEN CAPTURE	FINISHED	1-2-3 for Windows.
10	17a	169	SCREEN CAPTURE	FINISHED	UNIX system V, from USL.
10	18	171	SCREEN CAPTURE	FINISHED	OS/2 2.0.
11	1	5	LINE ART	FINISHED	File cabinet vs. computer.
11	2	6	LINE ART	FINISHED	File cabinet.
11	3	7	LINE ART	FINISHED	Computer screen with data (reco
11	4	11	SCREEN CAPTURE	FINISHED	Database query.
11	5	11	SCREEN CAPTURE	FINISHED	Single record in database.

Figure 4-2
A small database file: each column of data is a field, and each row is a record.

A database comprises a group of related database files. In order to be related, each file in the database must share at least one field with one other file.

Database software is an informal term for a program that manages a database. The formal term is **database management system**, or **DBMS**. Database management systems on microcomputers began in 1981 when George Tate and Hal Lashlee, owners of a software marketing firm, received orders for a software package written by Wayne Ratliff. The three men formed a company, Ashton-Tate, and began marketing dBASE II, the DBMS that revolutionized the industry. The most popular DBMSs for microcomputers are compatible with dBASE III+, a product written by Ashton-Tate and now sold by Borland International. Another DBMS sold by Borland is Paradox (Figure 4-3 on the next page).

Modern DBMSs have several important capabilities that make them valuable tools. A DBMS should allow you to:

- Sort records according to the contents of fields.
- Ask certain questions, called **queries**, about the data in the database. Queries generally list files that meet certain criteria, count files, or make computations based on numerical data.
- Ensure the security of the data. With a password system, for example, only certain users are allowed to view or change certain fields.

```
System  File  Edit  Database  Record  Program  Window  Browse
                              CLIENTS                                    ≡
   Company                Address                City      State Zip   ▲
  California Beauty Inc.  900 Tenable Court      Woodsboro  TX   78393♦
  Carolina Systems        5 Mention Trail        Washington NC   27889
  Citibank Communication  7930 Rhubarb Towers 6  Bakersfield CA   93309
  City Greeley            6 Zing Rd.             Richardson TX   75080
  Commercial Room         45 Ports Font Drive 93 Golden     CO   80401
  Computer Directions     9603 Befallen Typhoon  Long Beach CA   90805
  Computer Services       378 Phillips Plaza     Morehead City NC 28557
  Computing Consultants   3710 Scramble Blvd.    Los Angeles CA  90048
  Control Services Computin 40 Inside Nicosia Pk. 3 Bryan   TX   77802
  Cox Computer Gaucher    426 Hubert Dr.         Cupertino  CA   95014
  Cubinets & Opera        774 Saracen Circle     Camden     NJ   08103▼
 «◄●                                                              ►.
                                          run cls
                                          set disp to mono
                                          run rpm
                                          run cap
                                          run cls
```

Figure 4-3
Paradox is one of
the latest DBMSs for
microcomputers.

DBMSs are one of the most widely used and yet most difficult to understand of the application types. Because they are both valuable and confusing, we will devote an entire chapter, Chapter 12, to them.

Spreadsheet Software

A **spreadsheet** is a grid divided into rows and columns. Data entered into this grid is used to perform calculations on large sets of numbers. Until the 1980s, most accountants and bookkeepers used manual spreadsheets like the one shown in Figure 4-4, which they kept on large sheets of paper. The concept of the electronic spreadsheet was created by Daniel Bricklin in 1979 while he was a student at the Harvard Business School. He and Robert Frankston developed VisiCalc (the "visible calculator") to solve accounting problems they were assigned in school. More than a means for organizing numerical data, VisiCalc allowed the user to enter a formula into a spreadsheet cell (the intersection of a row and a column) that would compute an error-free result based on the numerical values of other cells. Thus, for instance, totals of columns of numbers could be calculated automatically. The spreadsheet program will recalculate the formulas each time the data changes.

Figure 4-4
Before the electronic
spreadsheet was invented,
accountants kept their
records on manual
spreadsheets.

Electronic spreadsheets have revolutionized modern business with their simplicity, flexibility, and **what-if capability**. *What-if* means that you can ask a hypothetical question and consider alternatives simply by entering new data or changing a formula. For example, say you have constructed a spreadsheet to keep track of expenses, revenues, and net profit. If you wanted to see the impact on net profit of an across-the-board employee salary increase, you could add a column that computes a given percentage increase for each salary and creates a new total for all the salaries. The spreadsheet automatically computes a new total expenses figure that reflects the total salary figure, then computes a new net profit to reflect the new total expenses.

Another valuable characteristic of modern spreadsheet packages is their ability to generate graphs of the spreadsheet data using 3-D effects, color, and multiple typefaces. For instance, given a column of numbers that lists the total revenue for each month, you could select the entire column and automatically generate a pie chart that illustrates each month's total as a part of the year's total. The spreadsheet and line graph shown in Figure 4-5 were created with Microsoft Excel.

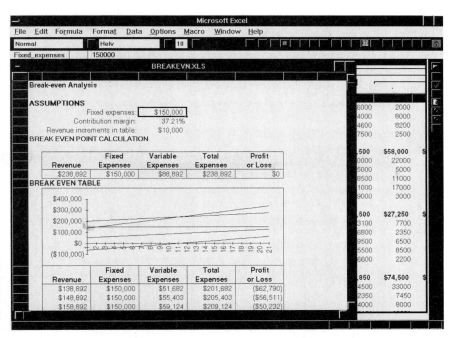

Figure 4-5
Many modern spreadsheet packages, such as Microsoft Excel, allow you to generate graphs and combine them with data.

Word Processing Software

Word processing is the process of creating text documents on a computer. Word processing software, commonly called a word processor (although the same term can also refer to the person using the software), is designed to make it easier to draft and edit text. With a word processor like the one shown in Figure 4-6 on the next page, you can move and delete text, check spelling, create tables and columns, modify margins, draw lines, change the appearance of text, and view how a document will appear before you print it.

The first word processing software was conceived as an improvement on the typewriter. The most striking advantage of creating documents on a computer is that the process of creating the document is separated from printing the document. This makes it possible to **edit**, or make changes to, a document without retyping the entire text. As word processors have become more sophisticated, many features have been added, so that word processing software can hardly be compared to a typewriter any longer.

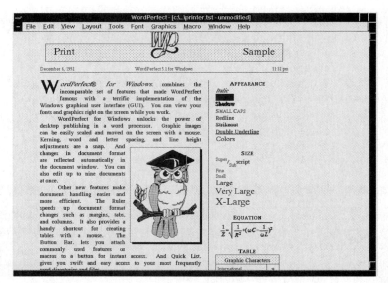

Figure 4-6
This document was created using WordPerfect for Windows.

Desktop Publishing Software

Desktop publishing (also known as **DTP**) is the use of a computer to create high-quality documents that are ready to be sent to a printer. Although desktop publishing software shares many of the same capabilities as modern word processing software, DTP software specializes in the most advanced features, especially the ability to incorporate a wide variety of typefaces and the ability to combine text and graphics. The goal of DTP is to allow the greatest possible flexibility in how the printed page will look, as shown in Figure 4-7.

Figure 4-7
These complex pages were created with DTP software.

Many businesses find DTP to be a cost-efficient way to produce publications, because it requires fewer people, less equipment, and less time than the traditional publishing production process.

Although it is often possible to create graphics and text in a DTP program, it is far more common to import text from a word processing program and graphics from a graphics program to combine them in a DTP file. For example, as Figure 4-8 illustrates, the pages of this book were composed using a DTP package called Ventura Publisher. The text, however, was originally input using Microsoft Word for Windows.

Graphics Software

Graphics software allows you to create **graphics** — illustrations, diagrams, graphs, and charts — on a computer. Research shows that most people can understand and retain more

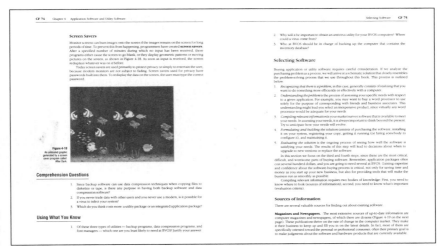

Figure 4-8
A page of this book set up
with DTP software.

information when it is presented in a graphical format. Consequently, most business presentations and many of those made in school are most effective when they include graphics that support the message. The purpose of a graphic is primarily communication.

Analytic graphics are used to display numerical information. They include such formats as pie charts, line graphs, and bar graphs. The graphical capabilities of spreadsheet software, for example, are referred to as analytic graphics. **Presentation graphics** packages are separate pieces of software that provide sophisticated capabilities for creating professional quality analytic graphics using color, multiple typefaces, and 3-D effects. Figure 4-9 is an example of a presentation graphics package.

In addition to analytical software and presentation graphics software, there are many paint and draw programs that allow you to create images from scratch using a mouse or a graphics drawing tablet. **Draw programs** enable you to create pictures by manipulating and combining graphic elements, such as straight lines, circles, and curves. In a vector graphics program — which includes draw programs and **computer-aided design (CAD)** programs — an image is stored as a pattern of lines. CAD programs are similar to draw programs. However, draw programs usually provide effects and capabilities for creating illustrations, while CAD programs are used to create highly specialized designs requiring

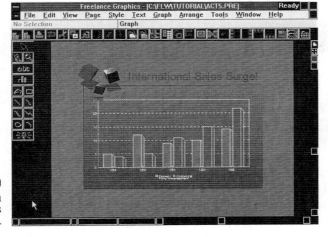

Figure 4-9
A graphic created using a
presentation graphics
program.

Figure 4-10
This microcomputer is equipped with CAD software.

precise, scaled graphic images such as those created by engineers and architects. Figure 4-10 shows a CAD program running on a microcomputer.

Paint programs such as MacPaint, shown in Figure 4-11, allow the user to produce the effect of painting on the screen using a graphics tablet or mouse and a range of colors, known as the palette. A computer displays an image as a set of tiny dots, set close to each other. The simplest types of output equipment uses one bit to control each dot. The image can therefore be stored as a map that shows which bits are supposed to be on and which are off. An image stored in this way is appropriately named a **bitmap**. Paint programs form images using bitmaps.

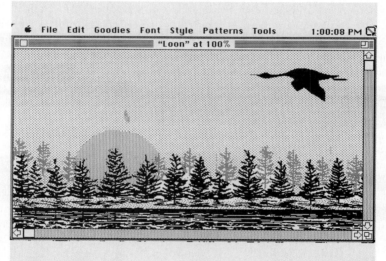

Figure 4-11
An illustration created with MacPaint.

Communications Software

Communications software manages the transmission of data, usually over telephone lines, with the help of a hardware device called a **modem**. Communications software and a modem allow a computer user to:

- Transfer files to and from another computer equipped with communications software and a modem. Sending a file to another computer is called **uploading**. Retrieving a file is called **downloading**.

- Access electronic **bulletin boards services**, or **BBS,** which are an electronic means for information exchange. Users can see and respond to messages from other users. They can also upload or download entire files and, in some cases, entire software programs. There are hundreds of BBS around the country. Some cater to special interests, hobbies, or particular industries; others are more general. Around the world there are literally thousands of BBS. A few examples are Boston Citinet (information

```
copyright 1984 NETI; licensed by Unicon Inc.

          Welcome to The WELLcome Conference!

NEW USERS:  Please read topics 1 and 2 for important information about
this conference.  Type:  s 1 2   and press [Return] at the "OK" prompt.

Gotta question?  Ask away over in topic 55:   type   s 55 nor    then type   r
Introduce yourself in topic 56:               type   s 56 nor    then type   r
For immediate help from a real person:        type   support

3 newresponse topics
First topic 1, last 56

Topic - Number of responses - Header

 51  83 WELL Office Party - Fri, Nov 20 6PM - Presidio Yacht Club - Lissen up, P
ilgrim!
    <topic is frozen>
    <linked topic>
 55  22 Questions and Answers
 56  21 Introduce Yourself here!

Ok (? for help):
Alt-Z FOR HELP| ANSI      | FDX  | 2400 N81 | LOG CLOSED | PRINT OFF | ON-LINE
```

Figure 4-12
An electronic bulletin board.

about Boston), the Federal Job Information Center, OSprey's Nest (discussion of birdwatching), Take 3 (reviews of movies, video, and film), and OCRWM Infolink (information about radioactive waste).The BBS shown in Figure 4-12 is The Well, a general-interest service located in Sausalito, California.

- Access information services. By going on-line with an information service, subscribers can perform a wide range of activities, including shopping, getting news, posting want ads, obtaining up-to-the-minute stock quotes, playing games, and ordering airline tickets. Some information services charge by how many minutes you are on-line; some bill a flat monthly fee. Prodigy and CompuServe are examples of information services.

- Send **electronic mail**, usually called **E-mail**. E-mail systems allow you to send electronic messages to other users who are not necessarily on line when you leave the message. When the other user accesses the E-mail system, the system will automatically tell the user that he or she has a message.

With special communications software and a fax modem, it is possible to send faxes to and receive faxes from a facsimile machine through a microcomputer. Fax modems are less expensive than stand-alone fax machines and, given the right equipment, can deliver higher quality output.

Integrated Application Packages and Their Alternatives

Integrated application packages combine a collection of applications in one package with a common interface. Common applications found in an integrated package include a word processor, a database, a spreadsheet, a graphics system, and a communications system. When included in integrated packages, the individual applications are usually called **modules**. Figure 4-13 on the next page shows the opening screen for Microsoft Works for the Mac. Here you can choose which of the five applications you want to use.

Integrated packages have several advantages. The first is price; integrated packages often cost significantly less than purchasing all the applications separately. Another is the advantage of a single interface, which makes it more comfortable — especially for new users — to switch between applications. Third, these packages allow data to be transferred from one application to another, a process that can be difficult for some operating systems. With such a package, data from a database can be easily graphed in a spreadsheet and then incorporated

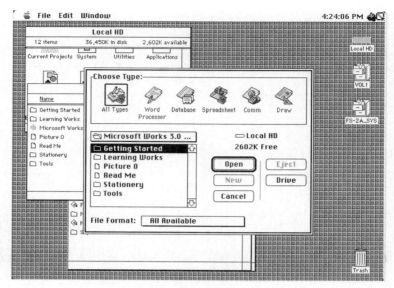

Figure 4-13
In Microsoft Works for the Mac, the user can choose from among five applications.

into a report on the word processor. Some of these packages allow a data change in the database or spreadsheet modules to be reflected in word processing documents or wherever that data may be used. The automatic updates of files between modules are called **hot links**.

The primary disadvantage of integrated software is that a specialized package offers more advanced capabilities. For example, the spreadsheet component of an integrated package may not provide as large a grid as a stand-alone package such as Lotus 1-2-3.

There are alternatives to integrated packages. Some stand-alone programs have the ability to pass data back and forth. For example, in Windows you can create a spreadsheet and a graph in Lotus 1-2-3, import them to a WordPerfect document to add text, and then merge that document with information in Paradox, provided the applications have been designed for use with Windows (Figure 4-14). However, this capability tends to be more cumbersome with stand-alone packages than with the integrated package.

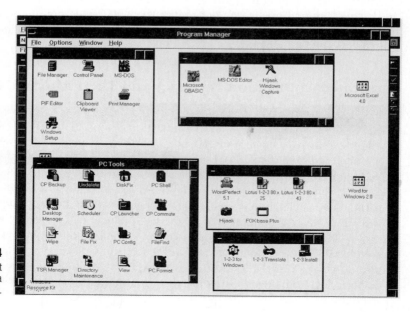

Figure 4-14
All Windows environment applications can trade data easily.

Hypermedia

Hypermedia software such as HyperCard, shown in Figure 4-15, is a subset of the database family that incorporates the advantages of multimedia for conveying information. **Multimedia** refers to the use of several communications media within a single presentation. Multimedia generally includes text, audio, graphics, animation graphics, and full-motion video. Both hypermedia and multimedia are appealing because they encourage nonsequential exploration of the various media.

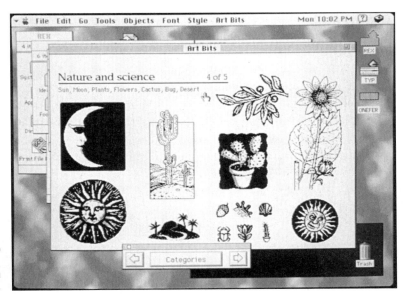

Figure 4-15
A screen from HyperCard, a hypermedia application for the Macintosh.

A hypermedia database of the War of 1812, for example, might contain audio recordings of battle recreations, maps, and text describing the war and important battles. Certain words or phrases could be selected from the text for more information about the subject. While reading about the War of 1812, you could highlight the name Napoleon and read a short biography of the emperor of France. Or while reading about the battle of Waterloo you might highlight the word Waterloo and see a map of where that battle was fought. You might also run across a reference to Tchaikovsky's *1812 Overture* and listen to part of that music. Hypermedia aims to bring life to the text and numbers in a database.

Artificial Intelligence and Expert Systems

Computers have long been used to help humans solve problems. Given precise instructions, a computer can repeatedly and consistently provide a predictable answer. The computer is not thinking; it is simply reproducing the actions that were programmed into it. **Artificial intelligence** is a broad field that attempts to endow computers with the ability to think and reason in ways that are similar to human thought processes. The term *artificial intelligence* was coined in 1956 by John McCarthy, a key figure in the development of the field.

One of the advancements in the field of artificial intelligence has been made in the area of expert systems. An **expert system** is a system that has been created to mimic the human decision-making process in a very narrow problem area. For example, a medical expert system called MYCIN helps physicians diagnose medical problems. MYCIN allows the physician to enter a patient's symptomology and receive suggestions for further testing. If enough information is given, MYCIN suggests a diagnosis and in some cases a series of procedures for treating the problem. The physician using MYCIN can also ask the system how it made its diagnosis. MYCIN will then produce the set of logic it used. From this the physician can learn from the system or choose to interpret the results differently.

MYCIN was created by asking expert diagnosticians how they did their job. By capturing this expertise, the MYCIN programmers, called **knowledge engineers** (a generic term for expert systems programmers), were able to create a program that mimicked the actions of many experts. The coded knowledge or expertise is entered into a **knowledge base**, a database of computer logic and rules based upon human expertise.

Comprehension Questions

1. Why do you think integrated packages usually include word processing, spreadsheet, database, communications, and graphics applications?
2. Is a DBMS a type of hypermedia software, or is it the other way around?
3. The ability to format text is generally associated with word processing software, but it is included in many other packages. What other types of application software might include text-formatting capabilities?

Using What You Know

1. The computers at your school probably have access to certain application packages. Find out what they are.
2. At the beginning of this unit, we outlined four tasks that you will face at BVOS. What four types of application software will you need to purchase to accomplish these tasks?
3. How might you use DTP software at BVOS? How could you use hypermedia software?

Utility Software

Software applications and the computers on which they run are selected to help users solve problems. For many users, this is all that is required. However, at times additional software tools are needed to make the computer easier to use, more efficient, more effective, or safer. Utility software supplies functionality that is not included in the set of applications that run on the computer. For example, software developers have created utility programs to protect display monitors, to facilitate making backup copies of data, and to protect against computer viruses — all functions not commonly performed by a word processing or spreadsheet application package. Most utility software programs are optional and must be purchased separately; however, utility functions are becoming increasingly available as part of operating systems. Utility software can make a substantial difference in how a computer is used and how well hardware, software, and data are preserved.

Utility Packages

Some developers, such as Symantec and Central Point, offer **utility packages**, which include a set of useful programs that either act as conveniences or protect the computer system.

Probably the most famous utility package is the Norton Utilities. This package lets the user perform such tasks as maintaining the hard disk, restoring files that have been deleted or damaged, formatting disks, and searching for files.

Backup Systems

Backing up or **archiving** your data is nothing more than copying data and software from the computer's hard disk (the large storage area built into most microcomputers) and storing the copy in a safe location. It seems that we all understand the importance of backing up: Data is vulnerable to loss or damage from countless causes. But we don't all practice what we preach. Part of the problem is that the process of creating a backup copy is time consuming, especially if we are simply using the operating system to copy data and software to diskettes. Backing up a 100 MB hard disk this way could easily take several hours. Consequently, software companies have written utilities that help create backups quickly and relatively painlessly.

These tools first read a portion of the software or data from the hard disk. Then the files are compressed. **Data compression** is a technique of logical and mathematical methods to minimize the amount of storage space that the software or data occupies. Data compression has been compared to moving furniture using a moving truck. It doesn't make sense to arrange the furniture in the truck the same way it is arranged in your living room. It is much better to eliminate the excess space between the items. Programs that use data compression work in a similar way.

After data compression, the backup software copies the data to a tape or diskette. The process of backing up a hard disk with data compression is illustrated in Figure 4-16. The user then stores the tape or diskette in a safe place. If the data on the hard disk is ever damaged, the backup copy can be used to restore the hard disk.

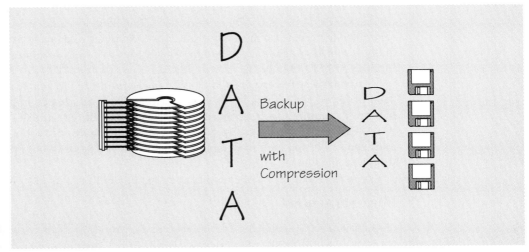

Figure 4-16
The backup process.

Data Compression Software

The amount of room that software takes up on a computer is increasing at an astounding pace. It seems that every new release of a program requires more and more space. Although the size of hard disks is also growing, users often find that their hard disks are full long before they are ready to buy a new one.

One solution — at least a partial solution — is proper file management. **File management**, sometimes called **hard disk management**, means organizing your software and data in a meaningful way on your hard disk, making frequent backups, and eliminating old files. Improper file management can cause a hard disk to fill quickly.

Even with proper file management, however, hard disks can become crowded. To address this issue, many users turn to data compression software that will squeeze as much data and information into a computer as possible, as discussed in the preceding section. Some data compression mechanisms can effectively double the amount of disk space that you have. Unfortunately, data compression software can slow down your computer, because it must first decompress the files before you can use them.

It is now common practice for software companies to ship their software in compressed format. The software is decompressed when it is installed.

Antivirus Software

During the 1980s, some computer users began to notice that their computers were acting strangely. Computers would fail to start one day, or would begin to lose files, or would display odd messages on the screen. These computers had been "infected" by a rogue program, called a **virus**, that attached itself to legitimate programs and automatically copied itself into other programs. This copying process occurs indefinitely, with the virus replicating itself wherever it can. Viruses are also called Trojan horses, logic bombs, or worms.

Although viruses that cause colds in humans occur naturally, computer viruses don't. Every virus must be created by a programmer. Also, a virus doesn't just appear on a computer. It is introduced into a computer when a user inserts an infected disk or when a modem is used to connect to an infected computer via telephone lines.

A virus can cause substantial harm. One virus created by Robert Morris, a student at Cornell University, infected more than 6,000 computers nationwide and reportedly caused millions of dollars's worth of damage. Other viruses are more benign, displaying messages or causing odd effects on the screen. The Michelangelo virus — so named because it was scheduled to activate on the artist's birthday — did minimal damage because people found out about it ahead of time. Some people elected not to use their computers on Michelangelo's birthday. Others changed the date on their computer's internal clock to the day after his birthday.

Antivirus software is used to detect and eradicate viruses. An advertisement for one such program, along with a few of the viruses that it can detect, is shown in Figure 4-17. It can protect computers from infection by inspecting all data and software that are used on the system, or just new files. An important practice is "safe computing" — check all software and data for viruses before you use them. Very few computer environments are totally safe from infection.

Font Managers

If you pick up a typical magazine and look at the ways that characters can appear on a printed page, you will find a wide variety of typefaces. A **typeface** is a complete set of printed characters (all the letters, numbers, punctuation marks, and special characters, such as dollar signs and asterisks) that are created with a single style. Common typefaces are Courier, Helvetica, and Times Roman. A typeface can be any size. One set of characters in a specific typeface, in a specific size, is called a **font**. Fonts are measured in points; one point equals 1/72 of an inch. For example, typewriter characters are usually 10-point or 12-point Courier. Table 4-1 shows several of the most common fonts.

Figure 4-17
Antivirus software detects and eradicates viruses.

Computers use sets of fonts that can be displayed on the screen and printed. Because the resolution of a screen and a printer almost always differ, computers must work with separate screen fonts and printer fonts. The appearance and size (proportionally speaking) of screen fonts and printer fonts must be properly matched in order to achieve *WYSIWYG* (meaning What You See Is What You Get and pronounced *wiz-ee-wig*). **WYSIWYG** refers to the ability to display text and graphics on-screen the same way they will be printed. To control the fonts that are available for use — which ones can be displayed and which can be printed — software developers have created **font managers**, utilities that tell the computer how to display and print each font.

Courier

Garamond

Helvetica

Times

AvantGarde

Palatino

Bookman

Century Schoolbook

Zapf Chancery

Table 4-1
Some common fonts.

Screen Savers

Monitor screens can burn images onto the screen if the images remain on the screen for long periods of time. To prevent this from happening, programmers have created **screen savers**. After a specified number of minutes during which no input has been received, these programs either cause the screen to go blank, or they display geometric patterns or moving pictures on the screen, as shown in Figure 4-18. As soon as input is received, the screen redisplays whatever was on it before.

Today screen savers are used primarily to protect privacy or simply to entertain the user, because modern monitors are not subject to fading. Screen savers used for privacy have passwords built into them. To redisplay the data on the screen, the user must type the correct password.

Figure 4-18
An animated graphic generated by a screen saver program called AfterDark.

Comprehension Questions

1. Since backup software can use data compression techniques when copying files to diskettes or tape, is there any purpose in having both backup software and data compression software?

2. If you never trade data with other users and you never use a modem, is it possible for a virus to infect your system?

3. Which do you think costs more: a utility package or an integrated application package?

Using What You Know

1. Of these three types of utilities — backup programs, data compression programs, and font managers — which one are you least likely to need at BVOS? Justify your answer.

2. Why will it be important to obtain an antivirus utility for your BVOS computers? Where could a virus come from?

3. Who at BVOS should be in charge of backing up the computer that contains the inventory database?

Selecting Software

Buying application or utility software requires careful consideration. If we analyze the purchasing problem as a process, we will arrive at a schematic solution that closely resembles the problem-solving process that we use throughout this book. This process is outlined below.

1. *Recognizing that there is a problem,* in this case, generally consists of realizing that you want to do something more efficiently or effectively with a computer.

2. *Understanding the problem* is the process of assessing your specific needs with respect to a given application. For example, you may want to buy a word processor to use solely for the purpose of corresponding with friends and business associates. This understanding might lead you select an inexpensive product, since virtually any word processor would be adequate for your needs.

3. *Compiling relevant information* is your market survey of software that is available to meet your needs. In assessing your needs, it is always important to think beyond the present. Try to anticipate how your needs will evolve.

4. *Formulating and building the solution* consists of purchasing the software, installing it on your system, registering your copy, getting it running (or hiring somebody to configure it), and maintaining it.

5. *Evaluating the solution* is the ongoing process of seeing how well the software is satisfying your needs. The results of this step will lead to decisions about when to upgrade to new versions or replace the software.

In this section we focus on the third and fourth steps, since these are the most critical, difficult, and worrisome parts of buying software. Remember, application packages often cost several hundred dollars, and you are going to need several at BVOS. Gaining expertise and confidence about the software-buying process is critical, not only for saving time and money as you start up your new business, but also for providing tools that will make the business run as smoothly as possible.

Compiling relevant information requires two bodies of knowledge: First, you need to know where to look (sources of information); second, you need to know what's important (evaluation criteria).

Sources of Information

There are several valuable sources for finding out about existing software.

Magazines and Newspapers. The most extensive sources of up-to-date information are computer magazines and newspapers, of which there are dozens (Figure 4-19 on the next page). These publications thrive on the rate of change in the computer market. They make it their business to keep up and fill you in on the latest details. In fact, most of them are specifically oriented toward the personal or professional consumer; often their primary goal is to make judgments about the software and hardware products that are currently available.

Figure 4-19
Computer industry
periodicals are some of the
best sources of
information about software.

PC Magazine is often the heftiest publication on a magazine rack. It comes out every two weeks and often runs to 600 pages. As the name implies, its focus is on the family of computers and software that are compatible with the IBM PC. Each issue contains numerous evaluations of new products and comparisons of similar hardware or software. As you might imagine, there are a lot of ads in 600 pages of text, but when you're faced with a purchasing decision, the ads can be as valuable as the articles.

PC World is another popular magazine oriented toward new products available for IBM-compatible machines. *PC World* is very similar to its main competitor, *PC Magazine,* although *PC World* costs slightly more. Like *PC Magazine,* information and even software are available through the on-line service the publication offers through CompuServe.

Macworld is published by the same company as *PC World* and is based on a similar format. The difference, of course, is that *Macworld* focuses on hardware and software available for the Apple Macintosh line of computers.

Infoworld and *PC Week,* both of which are tabloid-format newspapers, are good sources for software reviews and are especially popular with larger business organizations.

Other publications that are worth looking at when faced with a purchasing decision are *MacUser,* which competes with *Macworld; Byte,* which addresses the entire microcomputer industry rather than limiting itself to a single type of platform; and another computer newspaper, *Computerworld.*

Friends and Associates.   Another valuable source of information about computers is your friends and business associates who are computer users. Although the people you know may not have as much information as the periodicals mentioned above, there are a few advantages of word-of-mouth advice:

- Usually, it's free.

- It is easier to ask specific questions.

- Your friends are likely to be more candid about their feelings than magazines can be.

- These are the people with whom you will be trading data. If they have good things to say about the products they are using and you buy the same ones, you will have no compatibility problems (discussed in the next section).

Computer User Groups.   A user group is an organization of users who share experiences, ideas, and advice about a particular piece of hardware or software. User groups are excellent sources of information, and they are free. Some groups invite vendors to demonstrate and discuss new products. In fact, user groups can be influential in getting vendors to change or enhance their products (Figure 4-20).

Other Sources of Information.   If you can afford their cost, many firms provide consulting services regarding software, as well as other computer issues. For example, EDS and Andersen Consulting help their clients solve computer-related problems.

Evaluation Criteria

Knowing how to evaluate a given software product is the crucial component of making a wise purchasing decision. Several issues must be considered, no matter what type of software you are looking for.

Compatibility. First, if you own the hardware for your computer system, the field of software choices has already narrowed. This is because most software products will run on only one type of machine. For example, the perfect application package for your needs may exist, but only for a computer you don't have.

Figure 4-20
A vendor demonstrating a new application package to a user group.

Although this sounds like a serious problem, it rarely is, at least from a purchasing standpoint. A wide variety of quality software exists for many different kinds of computers, especially for PCs (and compatibles) and Macs.

Software Features. This evaluation criterion is the most obvious. Every competing software product has a slightly different set of features or capabilities. When deciding which product to buy, you need to consider several scenarios and decide which one best describes your situation. First, can you buy an application off the shelf that is designed to meet your particular needs? There are specialty software programs for all kinds of businesses (Figure 4-21). For example, although you can manage a payroll with a DBMS program, it's cheaper and easier to buy a program, such as QuickPay, that already has payroll functions set up. If you manage an apartment building, you can buy apartment manager software with fields predefined for tracking rents, maintenance costs, tenant histories, and other relevant matters.

Second, if a specific application does not exist, can a software package such as dBASE IV, Lotus 1-2-3, or WordPerfect be configured to solve your problem?

The third scenario is the most problematic. If the appropriate application does not exist, you must write it from scratch, or more realistically, hire someone to do so. To understand

Figure 4-21
Businesses must often choose from among (a) a specific software package such as SBT Accounting Systems, (b) a general application like Lotus 1-2-3, or (c) hiring someone to create a custom-made program.

(a)

(b)

(c)

this process you need to understand computer programming, which we cover in the next chapter.

User Interface. As we discussed in Chapter 3, one important factor affecting all software is the user interface. Programs can be built with a command-line interface, a menu interface, or a graphical user interface (GUI). In some cases, as with the Macintosh and programs written to run under Microsoft Windows, the interface is predetermined. With programs that run under DOS, however, the nature of the user interface may be a deciding factor in your choice.

Reputation. As with any product purchase, the reputation of the manufacturer is an issue. Over time, a software developer establishes a certain reputation. If you ask experienced users or professionals in the computer industry, they will be able to give you their opinions of all the major software companies. You can count on the big ones — Microsoft, Lotus, WordPerfect, Borland, and several others — to put out quality products, because their reputations depend on it. Nevertheless, even among these companies, you will discover nuances of behavior that may affect your purchasing decisions.

Software Support. One of the biggest factors affecting a company's reputation is the support it offers for its software. Software support comes in three basic forms: documentation, help features, and telephone support (Figure 4-22). **Documentation** is the printed material that comes with the software. Sometimes there are several booklets that are packaged with

(a)

Figure 4-22
Software support:
(a) software manuals,
(b) on-line help screen,
and (c) telephone support.

(b)

(c)

the diskettes, but the most important single item is the manual. The quality of the manual can determine how well you are able to learn and use the software.

W. Windows)

Help features are files, built into the software package, that you can access while you are using the software. Normally they can give you information about all of the commands and procedures that you can use. The major factors affecting the quality of the help features are how informative the help screens are and how easy it is to find the relevant help. Some programs have **context-sensitive help** that will automatically display the relevant help screen, depending on the part of the software that the user is working on.

In addition to documentation and help features, many software manufacturers offer **telephone support**, through which users can ask questions directly of the manufacturer's employees. The quality of phone support can vary dramatically. The time it takes to reach an employee is one issue, and the cost of the call is another. Some companies have 800 numbers, so the call is free. Others do not charge for the support, but you must pay for the phone call. Still others have 900 numbers, so you must pay directly for the phone call and support.

Bugs

Upgrades. The software market is constantly evolving. As years go by, word processors, spreadsheet software, and database management systems add features and become more sophisticated. When one software company adds features to its product, companies with related products feel pressure to add similar features to their own packages. This phenomenon leads software companies to create upgrades to their existing software. An **upgrade** is simply a new version of the software, generally with additional features.

The **version** of a piece of software is generally indicated by a number; an upgrade has a higher number than the previous version. For example, in 1992, Autodesk upgraded its computer-aided drafting program, AutoCAD, from Release 11 to Release 12. Many companies signal a major change by adding a whole unit to the version number; they signal a minor change by increasing the version number by one tenth or one hundredth. For example, when Microsoft made minor improvements to its integrated package, Works 2.0, it released version 2.01. When it upgraded Windows 3.0, the new version became Windows 3.1. The company's 1991 upgrade to Word for Windows changed the program from Word for Windows 1.1 to Word for Windows 2.0.

When looking at a company's policy concerning upgrades, the most important consideration is the price charged users of the previous version. Once you own one version of a software program, most companies offer you upgrades for a fraction of the cost of the original program. A few companies even offer upgrades for free. Others, however, charge the full cost of the software for each upgrade.

Purchase and Installation

Once you finally choose a product and purchase it, there are still a few important steps.

Register Your Copy. First, as soon as you take a new piece of software out of the box, you should register your copy with the software manufacturer. Usually this step requires filling out and mailing a 3"x5" card. The purpose of registering your copy is to inform the software company that you own a legal copy of its software. Once you register, the company will inform you by mail of upcoming upgrades and other products. In some cases, you will not be able to obtain phone support unless you have registered.

Make a Backup Copy. The next step after registering your copy is to make a backup copy of the software because disks can become damaged. The best way to safeguard your valuable

Figure 4-23
This user is installing a new application onto his computer's hard disk.

new software is to create an extra copy of the original diskettes before you install the program on your hard disk. Most software manuals remind you to do this as part of the installation process.

Install the Software. With software, **installation** means copying the program files from the original diskettes to the computer's hard disk (Figure 4-23). In years past, this process was done manually, issuing copy commands to move the files. Now the process is often automated by an installation program. The user simply types "INSTALL" or "SETUP" or selects an icon with a mouse and then answers the questions asked by the installation program. In any case, the software usually comes with an installation guide that tells you what to do.

Read the Manual. When you are learning a new program — especially one with an intuitive GUI — there is a natural temptation to dive right in and try to accomplish your goals without any guidance. Exploring and experimenting is a valuable way to learn about software. Nevertheless, it is almost always worth your while to read at least the first few chapters of the software manual immediately after you purchase the software. There are two good reasons for doing so. First, time is money. In most cases, reading how a task is supposed to be accomplished is less time consuming than attempting to figure it out on your own. Second, there are often multiple methods for accomplishing the same task. Most of the time, one method is better than the others. If you experiment and find a way to do what you want, you will probably stick with that method, even though better options may be available. The manual is more likely to point you in the right direction the first time.

Software Piracy

When trying to solve a problem, it is often tempting to borrow someone else's software. **Software piracy** is the illegal copying or duplication of software. Software pirates cost the software industry billions of dollars every year and drive up the cost of the software to consumers.

Most software is licensed for use on a particular type of computer. Software is protected by the same type of copyright that protects this book. A copyright is a right that an author has to protect the expression of an idea and to control its publication. With respect to software, a copyright means that software cannot be shared. The problem is that software is very easy to copy and share, and the copy works just as well as the original (except that the person with the copy can't register with the company and doesn't have the documentation). The Software Publishers Association is a group of software companies that have joined together to protect software copyrights and to fight software piracy. The group conducts audits of computers in organizations and files lawsuits if it finds examples of software theft.

Copy Protection. Some software companies have tried to curb software piracy by modifying the software so that it will not run properly unless an authorized copy of the software is being used. By requiring that a special diskette is used or that a device is installed into the computer, these companies are attempting to combat software piracy. These systems are called **copy-protected software**. One problem with copy-protected software is that it makes it very difficult for legitimate users to create a legal backup copy of the software.

Site Licenses. Many organizations ask software companies to sell them site licenses to simplify the process of obtaining copies of software for a number of computers (Figure 4-24). A **site license** is a written document detailing the purchasers' right to copy and use a software product on a specified number of computers at a single time. For example, a school may purchase a 20-copy license of WordPerfect so it can install the program on all 20 computers in its computer lab. Such a site license is less expensive than purchasing 20 separate copies of the software. The advantage of the site license is that the purchaser can make an honest attempt to curb software piracy by purchasing, at a discount, a relatively large number of copies. This also provides software tools to many individuals in the organization and creates a standard for a particular application.

Figure 4-24
Many businesses purchase site licenses so they can use the same program on a set number of machines.

Shareware and Public Domain Software. A relatively new concept in the purchase of software is the notion of shareware. **Shareware** is reasonably priced software that is distributed free of charge or for a nominal fee. If after using the software you find it useful, you are asked to send in a payment. There are thousands of shareware titles encompassing applications from games to accounting systems.

There are also programs that are in the public domain. **Public domain software** is very similar to shareware in that you can obtain it legally without paying for it. When something is in the public domain, that indicates that the item can be used by the public without a fee. In some cases, the author of the public domain software will list a name and address and request a fee, but users are not required by law to pay.

Comprehension Questions

1. Which is probably a more significant upgrade, version 3.01 to 3.10 or version 2.2 to 3.0?

2. If you operated a computer lab at a school and needed 25 copies of WordPerfect, what type of license would you buy?

3. Who do you think are the main targets of Software Publishing Association lawsuits? Why?

Using What You Know

1. Of the sources of information given in this chapter, which is most valuable to you as president of BVOS? Why?

2. Say you own a piece of software and a new version has just been released. What factors will affect your decision whether to buy the new upgrade?

3. What do you think are the advantages and disadvantages of distributing a program as shareware?

Summary Points

Common Applications

Most users have similar computing needs, including collecting and analyzing data and communicating ideas.

Database Software
- ☐ A database is a collection of related data, organized into fields, records, and files.
- ☐ Modern DBMSs allow the user to sort records, create queries, and secure data.

Spreadsheet Software
- ☐ A spreadsheet is a grid of columns and rows used to perform calculations on sets of numbers.
- ☐ The what-if capability of spreadsheet software allows the user to ask hypothetical questions related to numerical data.
- ☐ Most modern spreadsheet packages include graphing capabilities.

Word Processing Software
- ☐ A word processor makes it possible to edit text, because the printing process is separate from the process of creating the document.

Desktop Publishing Software
- ☐ DTP software shares many of the same capabilities as word processing software, but it specializes in advanced formatting features and the ability to integrate text and graphics.

Graphics Software
- ☐ Analytic graphics are used to display numerical information.
- ☐ Presentation graphics packages combine analytic graphics with sophisticated formatting capabilities.
- ☐ Draw programs, including CAD software, use vector graphics to create images with sets of straight lines called vectors.
- ☐ Paint programs use raster graphics to create bitmapped images.

Communications Software
- ☐ Communications programs manage the transmission and receipt of data using a modem.
- ☐ Communications software allows the user to upload and download files, access bulletin boards, subscribe to information services, and send electronic mail.
- ☐ With a fax modem, some communications packages allow the user to send and receive faxes via computer.

Integrated Application Packages
- ☐ Integrated packages combine several applications into one package that has a common interface.
- ☐ Applications in integrated packages usually include word processing, spreadsheets, databases, communications, and graphics.
- ☐ Integrated packages are generally less expensive than buying each application separately, but they do not provide all of the advanced capabilities.

Hypermedia
☐ Hypermedia is a subset of the database family that incorporates the advantages of multimedia.

Artificial Intelligence and Expert Systems
☐ Artificial intelligence attempts to endow computers with the ability to think and reason like humans.

☐ Expert systems mimic the human decision-making process in a narrow problem area.

Utility Software
Utility software programs supply software functionality that is not included in the set of applications that run on the computer.

Utility Packages
☐ Utility packages include a set of popular utilities.

Backup Systems
☐ Backing up data consists of copying the contents of a hard disk and storing the copy in a safe place.

☐ Software companies have created backup software to simplify the process of backing up data.

☐ Most backup programs include data compression techniques that pack the data together and save storage space.

Data Compression Software
☐ Data compression software is used to pack as much data onto a hard disk as possible.

☐ Data compression can slow down a computer system.

Antivirus Software
☐ A virus is a program that automatically copies itself from one host program to another. Viruses can be benign or dangerous.

☐ Antivirus software detects and eradicates viruses.

Font Managers
☐ A typeface is the complete set of printed characters that conform to a particular style; a font is a typeface of a specific size.

☐ Font managers work to match screen fonts and printer fonts.

Screen Savers
☐ Screen savers protect display monitors by replacing, after a specified interval, a still screen with a blank screen or a screen showing moving images.

Selecting Software
The process of selecting a piece of software conforms to our problem-solving model.

Sources of Information
☐ There are several valuable sources of information, but the most extensive are computer industry periodicals.

Magazines and Newspapers
☐ Worthwhile publications include *PC Magazine, PC World, Macworld, MacUser, Byte, PC Week,* and *Computerworld.*

Friends and Associates
☐ Word-of-mouth advice is free, can include candid opinions, and can help ensure compatibility.

Computer User Groups
☐ Organizations of users share free information and advice about a particular software product.

Other Sources of Information
☐ Consulting firms are available for computer advice.

Evaluation Criteria

Compatibility
☐ Most programs will run on only one type of machine; if you own hardware, your software choices are already narrowed.
☐ Plenty of software is available for most hardware platforms.

Software Features
☐ Every competing program has a slightly different set of features.

User Interface
☐ If the user interface has not already been determined by your operating system or environment, you should take it into account when comparing products.

Reputation
☐ Each software manufacturer has a reputation; as you come to know them, they will affect your choices.

Software Support
☐ The value of a given program's software support is determined by the documentation that comes with the product, the on-line help features, and the telephone support offered by the manufacturer.

Upgrades
☐ A company's pricing policy on upgrades should be considered when buying a package.

Purchase and Installation

Register Your Copy
☐ Registering your ownership of a program with the manufacturer will keep you informed of upgrades and, in some cases, allow you to obtain telephone support.

Make a Backup Copy
☐ Just in case your original program disks become damaged, you should make a backup copy of them.

Install the Software
☐ Installing the software consists of copying the files to the system's hard disk.
☐ Many modern packages have installation programs that automate the installation process.

Read the Manual
☐ Reading the manual saves time in the long run and ensures that you use the most efficient method to perform tasks.

Software Piracy
☐ The illegal copying of software hurts the software industry and raises the costs of software.

Copy Protection
☐ Some software companies protect their copyrights by requiring that a special disk is used or that a device is installed into the computer.

Site Licenses
☐ Site licenses allow customers to purchase the rights to run a program on a set number of machines.

Shareware and Public Domain Software

☐ Shareware is distributed free; if users continue to use the software, they are asked to send a fee to the owner.

☐ Programs in the public domain are free; the programmer can request a fee, but there is no legal responsibility for users to pay.

Knowing the Facts

True/False

1. The advantage of data compression is that it speeds up your use of the computer.
2. Sending a file to another user through the phone lines is called downloading.
3. Artificial intelligence is an attempt to endow computers with the ability to think and reason.
4. Hypermedia software is a subset of the database family.
5. Most spreadsheet packages include analytical graphics programs.
6. Expert systems are able to mimic the human decision-making process, but only in a narrow problem area.
7. VisiCalc was the first electronic spreadsheet.
8. Every computer system should have antivirus software, because viruses occur naturally in data.
9. Paint programs use vectors to create graphics, while draw programs use bitmaps.
10. Text used in a DTP program is generally created in a word processing program.

Short Answer

1. What are the three types of software support?
2. In a spreadsheet, a _____ is the intersection of a row and a column.
3. The formal term for a piece of database software is a _____.
4. When considering a company's policy concerning _____, the most important factor is the price they charge to users of the previous version.
5. Name three magazines that report on the computer industry.
6. Name three advantages of asking friends and business associates for advice about software products.
7. CAD stands for _____.
8. The _____ capability of spreadsheets allows users to obtain answers to hypothetical questions involving numbers.
9. _____ is the term used to describe a specific size of a typeface.
10. Most backup utilities employ _____ techniques that minimize the amount of space required by the data being backed up.

Answers

True/False

1. F
2. F
3. T
4. T
5. T
6. T
7. T
8. F
9. F
10. T

Short Answers

1. help features, documentation, phone support
2. cell
3. database management system, or DBMS
4. upgrades
5. *PC Magazine, PC World, Byte, MacWorld, Mac User,* etc.
6. it's free; you can ask specific questions; you'll get candid answers
7. computer-aided design
8. what-if
9. Font
10. data compression

Challenging Your Understanding

1. When patients go to a doctor, they often complain that they have to wait too long to see the physician, but fully expect the doctor to spend a great deal of time with them in the examination room. The same phenomenon occurs in telephone support. What can a software company do to provide cost-effective telephone support in a timely fashion?

2. Spreadsheet programs are becoming very powerful. What are the characteristics of a problem that can be effectively addressed using a spreadsheet? What kinds of problems are ill suited for spreadsheets?

3. What are the key distinctions between word processing and desktop publishing? As word processing software becomes more powerful, will there be much of a distinction?

4. How do electronic mail, faxes, and bulletin boards differ? It would seem that they all serve very similar purposes.

5. Do you think that in the future the difference between artificial intelligence and natural intelligence will be noticeable?

6. How often should you back up your data? How often do you want your bank to back up data concerning your balance? Where should you store your backed up data?

7. Is utility software just a type of application software? What kinds of problems does it solve?

8. What kind of person do you think creates computer viruses? Are these people criminals? If so, what laws are they breaking?

9. What are some good sources to consult before buying application software? What are some bad sources?

10. List the important factors to consider when purchasing software. Rank these factors from most important to least important.

11. Would you bet your business on shareware or public domain software? Why or why not?

Programming and Programming Languages

Key Terms

Ada
alpha version
analog device
ANSI
ASCII
assembly language
BASIC
beta version
binary code
binary numbering
   system
bit
bug
byte
C
COBOL
code
compiler
data
digital device
EBCDIC
executable file
debugging
fifth-generation
   language (5GL)

file
first-generation
   language
flowchart
FORTRAN
fourth-generation
   language (4GL)
high-level language
information
instruction explosion
interpreter
kilobyte (K)
knowledge
logic error
logic structure
loop structure
low-level language
machine language
megabyte (MB)
natural language
   processing (NLP)
nonprocedural
   language
object code

object-oriented
   programming
Pascal
portability
program
programming
pseudocode
query
second-generation
   language
selection structure
sequence structure
source code
spaghetti code
SQL
structured
   programming
subroutines
syntax error
third-generation
   language
top-down design
transistors

Objectives

In this Chapter you will learn to:

- Differentiate among data, information, and knowledge
- Describe how a binary device can represent data
- Compare an analog device to a digital device
- Name and define the units used to measure binary data
- List the three most common alphanumeric codes used by computers
- Differentiate between low-level and high-level languages
- Briefly explain the characteristics of each of the five software generations
- List six high-level languages and describe each of them
- Draw parallels between the programming process and the problem-solving process
- Describe three techniques of structured programming
- Name and define the three basic logic structures
- Compare a compiler to an interpreter
- Describe the two main types of errors that the debugging process tries to eliminate

When Is Programming Necessary?

As we saw in the last chapter, you will solve several of your business problems by purchasing application software. Sometimes, though, you will run into a problem that could be solved using a computer, but no application software exists to help you do so. At this point, you may have to create the software yourself or have it made for you. To know what this process entails, you need to understand what computer programming is, how programmers create software, and what programming languages they use.

Before we delve into these topics, however, you must first understand how data differs from information, and how information differs from knowledge. The distinction is vital to your appreciation of programming — and even of software in general — because computers can work only with data, but people generally want to gain information or knowledge. Once this distinction is clear, we can move on to describing first how the computer represents data, and finally to the process of programming.

As president of a small company, you might ask why you need to know anything about programming. One reason is that, as president, part of your job is to provide the best tools for your employees so they can work efficiently. For the problems we are addressing in this book, the tools are pieces of application software. Since all software is the product of programming, it is important to have some notion of programming in order to understand software; software simply makes more sense if you know something about the process of creating it.

Another reason for knowing about programming is that programmers from the head office are going to visit your branch. Using the programming capabilities of dBASE IV, they will tailor your application software to meet the needs of your inventory database. By doing so, these programmers will save you and your employees countless hours of work. As president, you don't need to know how to create these programs yourself, but you do need to know why the company programmers are coming and what they are doing.

Data, Information, and Knowledge

A computer is a device for processing data. A computer user, however, is generally interested in obtaining information, with the ultimate goal of increasing knowledge. Understanding the differences between data and information, and between information and knowledge, will help you get the most out of your computer.

Data is facts without a context. Data can come in many forms: Numbers, letters, sounds, images, smells, and tastes are all data. Humans derive an overall impression of the world around them (reality) by obtaining data through the senses (sight, sound, touch, taste, and smell). By combining the data we get through our senses, we add meaning to the data and thereby turn the data into **information**. For example, yellow, sphere, and fuzzy, taken individually, are pieces of data. Put this data together and you have information about a tennis ball. In short, information is data plus meaning, or data in context.

Here's another example. The number .357 is a piece of data. Taken alone, it has no meaning — it's just a number. We don't know if it refers to a gun (a .357 Magnum) or the humidity of the air. But if .357 is data found in a table of batting averages, it becomes information about a batter. In this context .357 means that the batter has gotten a hit almost 36 percent of the times that he has been to bat.

When found in a table of batting averages, .357 is information. Understanding the significance of this batting average is **knowledge**. In other words, knowledge is information plus significance. We gain knowledge by collecting information over time and assimilating it with what we already know. If you have a knowledge of baseball, you know that .357 is an excellent batting average and might well earn a player several million dollars a year. Knowledge provides a perspective on how to use information and data, as illustrated in Figure 5-1.

Another way to compare data, information, and knowledge is to look at how much each is worth. In general, data isn't worth anything. After all, what good are numbers, words, or sounds if we don't know what they refer to? As soon as this data is put in context, though, it

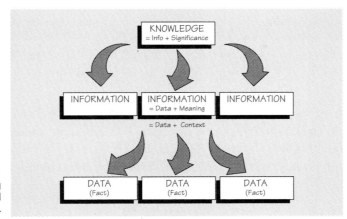

Figure 5-1
The relationship among data, information, and knowledge.

can have value. If you find a post-it note on your floor that says 4:30 P.M., it probably isn't worth anything. But if that same post-it is stuck to your calendar next to a note that says "Meet with bank loan officer," that post-it could be worth thousands. Thus, information is value-added data. Knowledge, however, is generally worth even more than information, because knowledge represents an entire body of information.

When you think about how a computer works, it's important to remember that humans tend to work with information and knowledge. The data we receive is almost invisible to us because it is usually received in context. Thus, data becomes information for us before we even think about it. A computer, on the other hand, works exclusively with data (though it does its work incredibly well). If the computer is used properly, it can present data in such a way that the data has immediate meaning for the user and is perceived as information. But the computer is none the wiser (Figure 5-2).

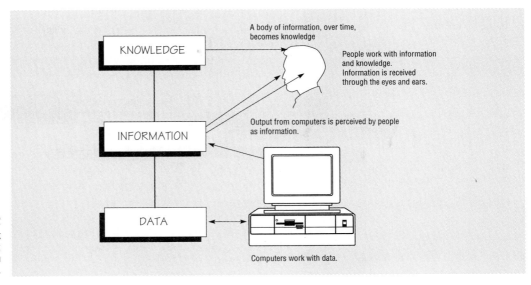

Figure 5-2
Computers work exclusively with data; humans tend to work with information and knowledge.

Comprehension Questions

1. From the user's point of view, what is the purpose of processing data?
2. Is a photograph a piece of information or a piece of data? Explain your answer.
3. Of data, information, and knowledge, which can be owned? Which is easiest to sell?

Using What You Know

1. List 10 types of data that you might keep in your customer database.
2. List five pieces of information that might prove useful in your efforts to make a profit in your new enterprise.
3. Name three areas of knowledge you will look for when hiring delivery drivers.

How the Computer Represents Data

A computer is an electronic device that processes and stores data in the form of electricity. It contains millions of **transistors**, which are tiny electronic switches. These transistors recognize only two states: on and off. Thus, all the data that is held in the computer must be represented by a series of switches that are either on or off. Computers are referred to as **binary** because they use only two electrical states.

Over time, computers will probably evolve from using electrical charges to using units of light called photons. Theoretically, at least, photon-based computing can be far more powerful and efficient than electron-based computing. As technology catches up with theory, the computer industry will move in this direction.

Analog and Digital Data

You might think that there is not much you can do with a series of on and off switches. As it turns out, though, you can create an approximate representation of just about anything, provided you have enough switches.

Base 10	Binary Code
0	0000
1	0001
2	0010
3	0011
4	0100
5	0101
6	0110
7	0111
8	1000
9	1001

Table 5-1
Counting from 0 to 9 using base 10 and binary code.

Because the computer is a binary device, we can use a **binary numbering system** to represent any series of switches. The binary numbering system works the same way as our base-10 numbering system, but instead of having 10 digits (0 through 9), we have only two (0 and 1). In this system, a 0 represents a switch that is off, and a 1 represents a switch that is on. Thus, any data that is held in the computer can be represented by base-2 numbers (see Table 5-1). **Binary code** is the term used to refer to computer data that is represented using a series of binary numbers. Because all data in a computer is represented with numbers, a computer is referred to as a **digital device**.

The opposite of a digital device is an **analog device**. An analog device is one that represents data with continuously variable physical quantities. The human ear, for example, is described as an analog device because it translates the physical phenomenon of sound using the physical movement of the eardrum.

The simplest example to illustrate the difference between the terms *analog* and *digital* is to look at the difference between an analog watch and a digital watch. The analog watch represents the rotation of the earth with rotating hands. The method of representation is directly related to the phenomenon being represented. A digital watch, however, displays the time in numbers by breaking the time it takes the earth to rotate into numbered intervals of hours and minutes. At any given instant, the time shown on the digital watch is just an approximation, because the numbers display an exact time for a whole second or a whole minute. The digital watch can display more accurate times by breaking the time into smaller units, but the time shown is always an approximation.

Another way to explain the difference between analog and digital is to compare a phonograph record to a compact disk. On a phonograph record, which is an analog device, sound is translated into a wavy line, which is etched into the record as a groove (see Figure 5-3a). The waves in the groove correspond directly to the frequency of the sound that is recorded. In theory at least, any frequency of sound can be represented accurately by the physical characteristics of the groove.

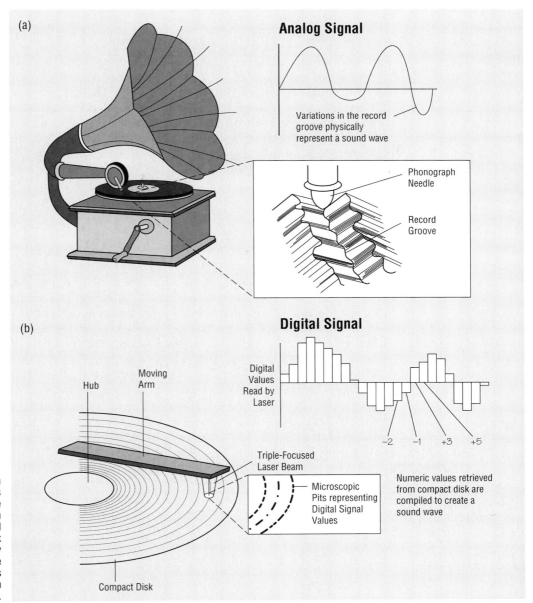

(a)

Analog Signal

Variations in the record groove physically represent a sound wave

Phonograph Needle

Record Groove

(b)

Digital Signal

Digital Values Read by Laser

−2   −1   +3   +5

Hub

Moving Arm

Triple-Focused Laser Beam

Microscopic Pits representing Digital Signal Values

Numeric values retrieved from compact disk are compiled to create a sound wave

Compact Disk

Figure 5-3
(a) The phonograph, an analog device, records sound with a groove, the shape of which corresponds to the sound wave; (b) a compact disk breaks the sound into very short intervals, the average frequency of which is recorded as a number on the disk.

A compact disk, on the other hand, represents sound as numbers, and is therefore a digital device. To do this, the compact disk must divide the sound into discrete intervals and then use a number to represent the average frequency of the sound within that interval (see Figure 5-3b). Even though the sound is constantly changing, the compact disk can store an excellent approximation of the sound with a very rapid sequence of numbers.

Bits and Bytes

When discussing computers, it is often important to talk about quantities of data: How much data can a computer hold? How much data can a computer process in one second? Because data in a computer consists of electrical switches, the smallest quantity of data is a single electrical on-off switch. The name for a single switch is one **bit**, which is a contraction of **bi**nary digi**t**.

Because a single bit can't represent very much data, bits are grouped into sets of eight. Eight bits together comprise one **byte**. When discussing quantities of data, bytes are actually a much more useful standard of measurement than bits, because it takes one byte to represent each character on the keyboard. For example, on a microcomputer, the uppercase letter "A" is usually represented by the following byte of data: 01000001.

As you can see, one byte still isn't a very big unit of measurement, especially when you consider that a single software program or data file can consist of thousands or even millions of bytes. For this reason, computer users often refer to kilobytes and megabytes. One **kilobyte** (abbreviated **K**) equals 1,024 bytes, and one **megabyte** (abbreviated **MB** or **meg**) equals 1,024 kilobytes, or 1,048,576 bytes. For extremely large measurements, one billion bytes is a gigabyte (one gig), and one trillion bytes is a terabyte.

ASCII

As noted above, it takes one byte to represent a single keyboard character. However, the system one uses to represent letters as numbers is entirely arbitrary. In other words, each computer maker could devise a different system. If they did, though, transferring data between one type of computer and another would be difficult. Over time, computer makers saw the advantage of a standard code for representing characters. The one used in micro-computers is called **ASCII** (pronounced *ask-ee*), which is an acronym for the American Standard Code for Information Interchange. A portion of the ASCII table, translating keyboard characters into bytes of binary code, is shown in Table 5-2.

The most widely used encoding scheme outside of ASCII is called **EBCDIC** (pronounced *eb-see-dick*), an acronym for Extended Binary Coded Decimal Interchange Code. This scheme is used primarily on large IBM computers. A third and increasingly popular code, produced by the American National Standards Institute, is called **ANSI** and is used in programs such as Microsoft Windows and Word. ANSI codes are very similar to ASCII codes; in fact, the first 128 characters are almost identical. The remaining characters, which are used for graphics, indentations, and other formatting characters, are different.

Normally, the difference between ASCII (or ANSI) and EBCDIC is not very important because so many of us only use microcomputers. However, if we want to send information from a microcomputer to an IBM mainframe, the difference can be troublesome. For example, on a PC, the character "L" is 01001100, which, when sent to a mainframe, is interpreted as "<". In order to transfer the data, it must be translated using a device or software package called a protocol converter.

	EBCDIC	ASCII		EBCDIC	ASCII		EBCDIC	ASCII
A	193	65	a	129	97	0	240	48
B	194	66	b	130	98	1	241	49
C	195	67	c	131	99	2	242	50
D	196	68	d	132	100	3	243	51
E	197	69	e	133	101	4	244	52
F	198	70	f	134	102	5	245	53
G	199	71	g	135	103	6	246	54
H	200	72	h	136	104	7	247	55
I	201	73	i	137	105	8	248	56
J	209	74	j	145	106	9	249	57
K	210	75	k	146	107			
L	211	76	l	147	108			
M	212	77	m	148	109			
N	213	78	n	149	110			
O	214	79	o	150	111			
P	215	80	p	151	112			
Q	216	81	q	152	113			
R	217	82	r	153	114			
S	226	83	s	162	115			
T	227	84	t	163	116			
U	228	85	u	164	117			
V	229	86	v	165	118			
W	230	87	w	166	119			
X	231	88	x	167	120			
Y	232	89	y	168	121			
Z	233	90	z	169	122			

Table 5-2
ASCII and EBCDIC
equivalents for numbers
and letters.

Files

A set of data that the user has given a name to is called a **file**. Files can consist of text (alphanumeric characters), pictures, or sound. Anything that can be represented with binary code can be a file. Normally, a file is a group of data that goes together (see Figure 5-4).

A **program** is a special kind of file that the computer can execute. For this reason, programs are sometimes referred to as **executable files**.

```
D:\>cd dos

D:\DOS>dir

 Volume in drive D is JACK STRAW
 Volume Serial Number is 18F6-523A
 Directory of D:\DOS

 .            <DIR>      12-07-92  12:14a
 ..           <DIR>      12-07-92  12:14a
 APPEND   EXE     10774 04-09-91   1:00p
 ASSIGN   COM      6399 04-09-91   1:00p
 ATTRIB   EXE     15796 04-09-91   1:00p
 BACKUP   EXE     36092 04-09-91   1:00p
 CHKLIST  CPS       297 12-07-92  12:17a
 DISKCOMP COM     10652 04-09-91   1:00p
 DISKCOPY COM     11793 04-09-91   1:00p
 NLSFUNC  EXE      7052 04-09-91   1:00p
       10 file(s)       98855 bytes
                      3919872 bytes free

D:\DOS>
```

Figure 5-4
A directory of files listed
using DOS. The column
on the far left lists the
names of each file; the
next column lists the file
extensions (files with
extensions COM or EXE
are executable files).

Comprehension Questions

1. Why is it more logical that a byte is composed of 8 bits, rather than some round number such as 5 or 10 bits? (*Hint:* The computer is a binary device.)

2. Why do you think ASCII code is not widely used by microcomputer software in Japan?

3. Is a glass thermometer that you use to take a person's temperature a digital device or an analog device? Why?

Using What You Know

1. Of the three coding schemes discussed in the last section, which one will be used the most by BVOS computers? Justify your answer.

2. How many bits of data does it take to spell out Buena Vista Office Supply?

3. If a double-spaced page of text includes about 250 words that average six characters each (including spaces), how many kilobytes of memory are required to hold the 10-page status report to headquarters that you have written?

What Is Programming?

All data and software must be reduced to binary code for a computer to be able to use them. In order for software to be understood, the instructions that make up each program must be stored in **machine language**, a particular kind of binary code, illustrated in Figure 5-5. **Programming** is the process of creating the instructions that the computer can use. Most of this process is done by programmers who write software using programming languages. A second part is done by interpreters and compilers, which are pieces of software that convert programming languages into machine language that the computer can understand.

There are two ways to translate a program (known in this context as **source code**) into machine language. The first way is to use a **compiler**, which translates the language all at once into machine language. After one pass, the compiler will inform the user of pieces of code that it cannot understand. When the programmer has solved all of the problems, the compiler generates what is called **object code**, which is just a machine language version of the program.

Some computer languages use interpreters instead of compilers. Rather than creating the object code in advance, an **interpreter** translates the language while the program is running. For this reason, an interpreted language must always be accompanied by the interpreter program. To fix errors in the program, the programmer must attempt to run it. When the interpreter runs into a line of code that it can't interpret, it stops, and the programmer fixes that line (or whatever line caused the problem).

As you might expect, programs written with interpreted languages are slower than those written in compiled languages. Just as a diplomat must speak more slowly when an interpreter is standing next to him, the interpreted program runs more slowly because the interpreter must first translate the program, then carry out its instructions.

The Five Generations of Programming Languages

Programming languages have evolved as the languages have become less like machine language and more like the languages we use in speech and writing.

Low-Level Languages

Programming languages are referred to as low level or high level, depending on how similar the language is to machine code. **Low-level languages** are all the first- and second-generation languages. Machine language is considered the lowest level of programming language because it is closest to the actual requirements of the hardware platform. Sometimes this is called "programming on the bare metal." Machine languages are known as **first-generation languages** because they were the first to be used by programmers. Although common in the 1940s, machine language is still written today, though sparingly.

```
58 10 C 054
58 40 1 024
D2 02 4 011 C 00D
50 10 D 234
92 00 D 234
96 80 D 234
41 10 D 234
D2 03 D 060 C 06A
58 F0 C 010
05 EF
58 10 C 054
D2 03 D 060 C 06E
58 F0 C 010
05 EF
58 70 D 200
58 10 C 054
18 21
D2 03 2 098 C 024
58 F0 2 0C8
05 EF
95 00 2 088
58 20 C 040
07 72
50 10 D 200
58 70 D 200
58 50 C 028
07 F5
92 E8 6 000
58 00 D 22C
50 00 D 228
58 00 C 02C
50 00 D 22C
58 20 C 030
95 E8 6 000
07 82
58 10 C 01C
07 F1
58 00 D 228
50 00 D 22C
58 10 C 054
```

Figure 5-5
An example of machine code that can be understood by the computer.

In **second-generation languages**, programmers began using mnemonics or symbols (usually words) to represent commonly used strings of machine language. All languages from the second generation forward are referred to as symbolic languages. The symbols are translated into machine language using an assembler. A hallmark of the 1950s, **assembly language** is widely used today because it allows programmers to better control the operation of the computer. Many high-level programs use portions of assembly language programs to speed processing. An example of assembly language is shown in Figure 5-6 on the next page.

Low-level languages require a great deal of programming experience because the languages have very few English-like statements and most of the instructions are in very detailed code. Although they are very fast, low-level languages have a disadvantage: They have almost no **portability** between computers. In other words, there is a different machine language and assembly language for each type of microprocessor. Thus, if a programmer writes an assembly language program for a particular model of PC, it will not work on any model that uses a different CPU, much less on a Macintosh or a NeXT computer.

High-Level Languages

The third, fourth, and fifth generations of computer languages are all referred to as **high-level languages**. Three features of these languages distinguish them as high level. First, the code used in high-level languages is much more like English than the code used in low-level languages. High-level languages

```
START     EQU    *
          L      1,054(0,12)              DCB=1
          L      4,024(0,1)
          MVC    011(3,4),00D(12)                          V(ILBOEXT1)
          ST     1,234(0,13)              SAV3
          MVI    234(13),X'00'            SAV3
          OI     234(13),X'80'            SAV3
          LA     1,234(0,13)              SAV3
          MVC    060(4,13),06A(12)        WC=01            LIT+10
          L      15,010(0,12)             V(ILBOQIO0)
          BALR   14,15
          L      1,054(0,12)              DCB=1
          MVC    060(4,13),06E(12)        WC=01            LIT+14
          L      15,010(0,12)             V(ILBOQIO0)
          BALR   14,15
          L      7,200(0,13)              BL =1
          L      1,054(0,12)              DCB=1
          LR     2,1
          MVC    098(4,2),024(12)                          GN=01
          L      15,0C8(0,2)
          BALR   14,15
          CLI    088(2),X'00'
          L      2,040(0,12)              GN=08
          BCR    7,2
          ST     1,200(0,13)              BL =1
          L      7,200(0,13)              BL =1
```

Figure 5-6
An example of assembly
language.

use words like WHILE, IF, THEN, ELSE, FOR, IN, DO, and END. Second, high-level languages are machine independent, meaning that their programs are much more portable than those of low-level languages. The compiler or interpreter is, of course, machine dependent, since the machine language is not portable. Third, high-level languages exhibit **instruction explosion**. This means that when an assembly program is translated into machine language, each line of assembly — each instruction — becomes one machine language instruction. A single line of a high-level language, however, may be compiled or assembled into several (or many) machine language instructions. Often a good compiler or interpreter can be judged by how few lines of machine language it creates from single lines of the high-level code.

There are scores of high-level programming languages. Each of these languages was created to address a certain set of programming problems. For example, there are languages designed to help teach other languages. Some languages are most often used in business data processing, and others are most often used in scientific work. Table 5-3 contains a list of some popular high-level programming languages and their strengths. As you can see, there is no shortage of programming languages. You might also note that most of the names of programming languages, such as FORTRAN, are capitalized because they are acronyms.

Most high-level languages are **third-generation languages**. All of the languages listed in Table 5-3 are of the third generation. In general, a third-generation language is a general-purpose symbolic language that is machine independent.

Fourth-generation languages are often called **4GLs**. As we move from the third generation to the fourth and fifth generations, computers become easier and easier to use. 4GLs are more English-like than previous languages and allow users to concentrate more on what they want the computer to do rather than how to do it (Figure 5-7). This is what makes fourth- and future-generation languages **nonprocedural languages**. The result is that users with little computer training can become effective programmers. Fourth-generation

Language	Strengths
Ada	A multipurpose, structured language used by the U.S. government.
BASIC	An easy-to-learn, yet relatively powerful language used in home computers as well as in business. (Beginner's All-Purpose Symbolic Instruction Code)
C	Creates very portable, structured programs in a variety of areas. C is widely held as the most popular programming language in the world.
COBOL	A language suited to business data processing and sophisticated file processing. More business programs are currently written in COBOL than in any other language. (COmmon Business-Oriented Language)
FORTRAN	A language created for complex mathematical computations. FORTRAN is the programming language of choice for many scientific and engineering application. (FORmula TRANslator)
Pascal	A language used to create structured programs. Pascal was designed to teach structured programming and as such is very popular among student programmers.

Table 5-3
Some popular high-level languages and their strengths.

languages are often less flexible than third, because most 4GLs are created for specific purposes. Some products that are usually considered application packages, such as dBASE, are also considered 4GLs because they can be programmed to carry out specific kinds of tasks.

Fifth-generation languages, or **5GLs**, combine the easy-to-use aspects of 4GLs with artificial intelligence and expert systems to make the computer even easier to use. Although very few 5GLs are available, one of their primary characteristics is **natural language processing (NLP)**. Natural language processing allows the user to instruct the computer just as he or she would instruct a human assistant. For example, an instruction to display yesterday's sales for the southeast region, organized by sales territory, can be typed "DISPLAY YESTERDAY'S SALES FOR THE SOUTHEAST REGION, ORGANIZED BY SALES TERRITORY". As you can see, there is no difference between what we wanted to do and how we told the computer to do it. It is predicted that future 5GLs will help create computers that we can actually talk to.

Figure 5-7
Instructions written in SQL, a 4GL used to query databases.

```
SELECT LAST_NAME FIRST_NAME FROM EMPLOYEE_FILE
      WHERE SSN IS IN
            (SELECT SSN FROM JOB_LIST, PROJECTS
            WHERE JOB_LIST.JOB_NUMBER = PROJECTS.JOB_NUMBER
            AND PROJECTS.TYPE = "SOFTWARE")
```

Comprehension Questions

1. Why are symbolic languages easier to use than machine languages?
2. Of the three differences cited between low- and high-level languages, which do you think is most important to software manufacturers?
3. Why do you think students learning programming are more likely to be trained in a third-generation language than a fourth-generation language?

Using What You Know

1. As president of BVOS, if you were to learn a programming language, what type would you learn and why?
2. From the evolution of programming languages described in this section, what might you expect from sixth-generation languages?
3. For what types of jobs would it be useful to know first-generation languages? Why?

Common Programming Languages

Although many programming languages exist, there are several that are frequently encountered in business. These languages are used to create programs that help users solve business and other kinds of problems.

BASIC

One of the easiest programming languages to learn is **BASIC** (**B**eginner's **A**ll-Purpose **S**ymbolic **I**nstruction **C**ode). BASIC was developed in 1964 at Dartmouth College by John Kemeny and Thomas Kurtz to teach students the logic of programming without the programming complications that often came with other languages of the day. At one time, the BASIC programming language was a standard feature that came with the IBM PC. Although BASIC was conceived as a tool to help students learn another programming language (FORTRAN), today it is a powerful, well-supported language in its own right. There are different versions of BASIC depending on the computer being used. BASIC is commonly implemented using an interpreter. Figure 5-8 shows a short BASIC program.

FORTRAN

FORTRAN (**FOR**mula **TRAN**slator) is a third-generation language known for being able to perform extensive mathematical manipulations. Developed in 1957 by John Backus, FORTRAN is the oldest high-level programming language. Prior to its creation, programs were written in assembly or machine language. FORTRAN was the first programming language that could be used to write programs on one computer for subsequent use on another computer. Program portability has since become a standard feature of high-level programming languages. A short FORTRAN program is shown in Figure 5-9.

```
'December 8, 1992
'File:  HILOW.BAS
'Programmer:  D. Adams
'
'This program reads in a set of test scores from the file  STU-
DENT.DAT.
'It then print the largest and smallest test scores and the students
'who earned those scores.
'
'INPUT variables:  std$        is the student's name
'                  grade       is the student's test score
'OUTPUT variables: highest     is the highest test score
'                  lowest      is the lowest test score
'                  hstd$       is the student with the highest test
score
'                  lstd$       is the student with the lowest test
score
'
OPEN "STUDENT.DAT" FOR INPUT AS #1
highest = 0                              'Initialize the variables
lowest = 100
ON ERROR GOTO printit
DO UNTIL EOF(1)
        INPUT #1, std$, grade        'Read data
        IF grade  highest THEN       'Check for the largest value
             highest = grade         'Remember the highest grade
             hstd$ = std$            ' and the corresponding student
        END IF
        IF grade  lowest THEN        'Check for the smallest value
             lowest = grade          'Remember the lowest grade
             lstd$ = std$            ' and the corresponding student
        END IF
LOOP
'
'Print out the values.
'
printit:
PRINT "The highest grade was"; highest; "earned by "; hstd$; "."
PRINT "The lowest  grade was"; lowest; "earned by "; lstd$; "."
CLOSE (1)
END
```

Figure 5-8
A short but complete program written in BASIC.

```
      REAL GPA
      CHARACTER STDNAME*20
      INTEGER I
      OPEN(5,"STUDENT.DAT"
 100 READ (5,200,EOF=500)NAME, GPA
 200 FORMAT(A20,F4.3)
      IF (GPA .GE. 3.0) WRITE (6,400) NAME, GPA
 400  FORMAT(IX,A20,7X,F5.2)
     GOTO 100
 500 CONTINUE
     CLOSE
     STOP
     END
```

Figure 5-9
The same program as Figure 5-8, but written in FORTRAN.

Figure 5-10
Grace Murray Hopper, the "mother of modern programming."

COBOL

COBOL (**CO**mmon **B**usiness-**O**riented **L**anguage) is a language frequently used for developing business applications. COBOL was formally defined in 1959 by Grace Hopper. Hopper, who retired as a Rear Admiral from the U.S. Navy (see Figure 5-10), is affectionately known as the "mother of modern programming." COBOL, the first language developed specifically with portability in mind, was a consortium effort among business, government, and academia. COBOL's portability caused the price of software to decrease because a software company could write a payroll program, for example, then sell it to several companies. The buyer was able to purchase a program without the substantial development costs normally associated with software, and the seller was able to recoup development costs and make a profit. COBOL encouraged business use of computers. A sample COBOL program is depicted in Figure 5-11.

```
IDENTIFICATION DIVISION.
PROGRAM-ID.            GRADES.
ENVIRONMENT DIVISION.
CONFIGURATION SECTION.
SOURCE-COMPUTER.    IBM-370.
OBJECT-COMPUTER.    IBM-370.
INPUT-OUTPUT SECTION.
FILE-CONTROL.
    SELECT INPUT-FILE ASSIGN TO UT-S-SYSIN.
DATA DIVISION.
FILE SECTION.
FD  INPUT-FILE
        LABEL RECORDS ARE STANDARD
        RECORD CONTAINS 80 CHARACTERS
        DATA RECORD IS INPUT-CARD.
01      INPUT-CARD.
        05  STUDENT-NAME    PIC X(20).
        05  GPA             PIC 9V999.
        05  FILLER          PIC X(56).
WORKING-STORAGE SECTION.
77      EOF                 PIC X VALUE 'N'.
01      OUTPUT-LINE.
        05  STUDENT-NAME    PIC X(20).
        05  FILLER          PIC X(10) VALUE SPACES.
        05  GPA             PIC 9.999.
PROCEDURE DIVISION.
        READ INPUT-FILE AT END MOVE 'Y' TO EOF.
        PERFORM PRINT-DATA UNTIL EOF = 'Y'.
        CLOSE INPUT-FILE.
        STOP RUN
PRINT-DATA.
        IF GPA GREATER THAN OR EQUAL TO 3.0 THEN
            MOVE CORRESPONDING INPUT-CARD TO OUTPUT-LINE
            DISPLAY OUTPUT-LINE.
        READ INPUT-FILE AT END MOVE 'Y' TO EOF.
```

Figure 5-11
The same program as Figure 5-8, but written in COBOL.

Pascal

Developed in the early 1970s by Swiss scientist Niklous Wirth, **Pascal** is a general-purpose high-level language named after the French mathematician Blaise Pascal. Pascal uses the principles of structured programming, which require that a program be written according to a logical structure. Larger routines are broken down into smaller ones (called "modules"), each of which performs a specific activity.

Pascal first gained popularity in academic circles as a teaching tool. It has strongly influenced other structured languages such as Ada and dBASE. Figure 5-12 shows a short Pascal program.

```
program students;
type      student_rec   = record
              name       : string[20];
              gpa        : real;
          end;
          student_file = file of student_rec;
var       student       : student_rec;
          datafile      : student_file;

begin
          assign(datafile,"STUDENT.DAT");
          reset(datafile);
          while(not Eof(datafile)) do
                  begin
                          if (student.gpa = 3.0) then begin
                                  writeln(student.name, stu-
dent.gpa);
                                  Read(datafile,student);
                                  end;
                      end;
          end;
          close(datafile);
end.
```

Figure 5-12

The same program as Figure 5-8, but written in Pascal.

C

In 1972 Dennis Ritchie of Bell Laboratories created a programming language that was designed, like COBOL, to be portable across several types of computers. The difference between COBOL and **C** was the way the programmer controlled the structure of the program. Programmers use a set of rules to help them create programs that will be easy to read, understand, and fix. The C programming language specifically incorporates these constructs of "structured programming"; other languages such as COBOL do not. C has been called the most portable programming language available. Therefore, many application packages have been written in C. The C language is one of the most popular programming languages in the world. (As an aside, the predecessor of C was B, a low-level assembly-like programming language; the predecessor of B was an assembly language.) A sample C program is shown in Figure 5-13 on the next page.

SQL

SQL (**S**tructured **Q**uery **L**anguage) was developed in the 1970s at IBM San Jose Research Laboratories by D. Chamberlain and others. SQL is a 4GL that allows users to ask questions

```
#include <stdio.h>
#include <conio.h>

void main()
{
    FILE *s_file;
    char student_name[20];
    float gpa;
    s_file=fopen("STUDENT.DAT","r");
    while (! feof(s_file)) {
        fscanf(s_file, "%20s %e",&student_name, &gpa);
        if (gpa >= 3.0)
            printf("%s\n",student_name);
    }
    fclose(s_file);
}
```

Figure 5-13
The same program as
Figure 5-8, but written in C.

of, or **query**, a database. SQL also lets users put data into a database and change data that is already in a database. A database query is created when a user has a question that needs to be answered or a problem to be solved. SQL is also called "structured English" because of the way it "forces" users to write its commands. SQL is the standard language for interacting with a database.

SQL can be incorporated directly into some third-generation languages to increase the power of these older languages. SQL is used in dBASE IV as a standard interface language for creating dBASE programs. Figure 5-14 shows an SQL query of a database.

Figure 5-14
A database query written in
SQL.

```
SELECT STUDENT_NAME GPA FROM STUDENT_RECORDS WHERE GPA = 3.0
```

Ada

The United States government has long been in the business of establishing standards for computer hardware and software. Collectively, the federal government is the largest consumer of computer hardware and software. The government writes programs to fly missiles, print paychecks, audit tax forms, monitor jet fighters, conduct air-traffic control, monitor satellites in space, launch space shuttles, and keep track of the citizenry. **Ada** was originally developed for and by the U.S. Department of Defense. The government selected the Ada programming language to be the standard programming language for all major federal systems projects. Ada is a high-level, third-generation programming language that was designed to work well in both real-time and batch systems. Figure 5-15 shows a short Ada program.

Ada was named after Ada Byron King, the Countess of Lovelace (Figure 5-16). Ada Lovelace, daughter of the English romantic poet, Lord Byron, was a contemporary of Charles Babbage, the "father of computers." Babbage was a mathematician at Cambridge University who developed the "analytical engine," a calculating device that used punched cards as input data. In 1842, at the age of 27, Lovelace began working with Babbage and making significant changes to the control sequences of the engine. Ada Lovelace is credited for being the first programmer, because she described programming concepts that are the heart of all computer programs today.

```
with TEXT_IO;
use TEXT_IO;
with SEQUENTIAL_IO;
procedure STUDENT_READ is
        type STUDENT_RECORD is
                record
                        STUDENT_NAME : STRING(1..20);
                        GPA          : FLOAT;
                end record;
        package STUDENT_IO is new SEQUENTIAL_IO(STUDENT_RECORD);
        use STUDENT_IO;
        SRECORD : STUDENT_RECORD;
        SFILE   : STUDENT_IO.FILE_TYPE;
begin
        OPEN(SFILE,IN_FILE,"STUDENT.DAT");
        READ(SFILE,SRECORD);
        while not END_OF_FILE(SFILE)
                loop
                        if SRECORD.GPA not  3.0 then
                                PUT(SRECORD.STUDENT_NAME);
                                NEW_LINE;
                        end if;
                        READ(SFILE,SRECORD);
                end loop;
        CLOSE(SFILE);
end STUDENT_READ;
```

Figure 5-15

The same program as Figure 5-8, but written in Ada.

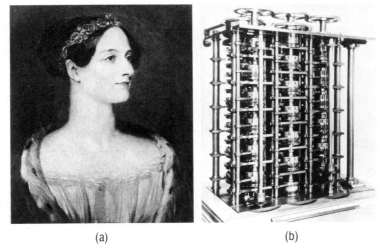

(a)   (b)

Figure 5-16

(a) Ada Byron King, the Countess of Lovelace; (b) Charles Babbage's analytical engine.

Other Languages

It is at times difficult to separate a programming language from application software. For example, the database package dBASE is an application package that allows users to design and use databases (which will be discussed later). However, dBASE has a programming language that will allow a programmer to create an application to solve a problem. Likewise, the spreadsheet program Lotus 1-2-3 is an application that allows users to analyze data in spreadsheet form. However, Lotus 1-2-3 contains a kind of programming language called a **macro** that allows programmers and users to create Lotus 1-2-3-based applications (see

```
A1: [W11] ^\G                                                          READY

              A          B            C          D       E      F      G    ◀
1    \G                {GOTO}{NAME 2}                   Press GOTO then NAME twi  ▶
2                                                                              ▲
3                                                                              ▼
4    \S                {D 19}{U 19}                     Shift current row to top ?
5
6
7    \D                {PANELOFF}{WINDOWSOFF}            Freeze screen
8                      /rfd1~                           Format current cell as D
9                      @NOW{CALC}~                      Type @NOW, convert formu
10                     {WINDOWSON}{PANELON}             Unfreeze screen
11
12
13   \R                {GETLABEL "Round to how many decimal places? ",PLACE}
14   R_LOOP            {EDIT}{HOME}@ROUND(
15                     {END},{PLACE})~
16                     {DOWN}
17                     {IF @CELLPOINTER("type")="v"}{BRANCH R_LOOP}
18                     {QUIT}
19
20   PLACE          2
07-Dec-92  01:44 AM            UNDO                             NUM
```

Figure 5-17
A Lotus 1-2-3 macro, an example of programming with an application.

Figure 5-17). As programming languages become more English-like, the difference between a program and a programming language will be difficult to pinpoint.

Object-Oriented Programming

Traditional programming focuses on the function of a program. Creating the program is a process of emulating how people carry out a task, and data is organized so the computer can execute the instructions as quickly as possible. **Object-oriented programming**, which has gained popularity in the past few years, is an alternative to the traditional programming strategy. Rather than seeing a task purely as a means for accomplishing an end, object-oriented programming looks at the various elements as having certain attributes and as performing certain actions.

For example, a programmer creating the BVOS customer billing system might create "customer" and "account" objects. The attributes of each customer object are its name, address, and so on. The attributes of each account object include its balance and date due. A customer object that needs an account balance could send a message to the account object that reads "tell balance."

The strategies used in object-oriented programming allow programmers to create, use, and reuse programs more easily than do more traditional strategies. Object oriented programming therefore decreases programming costs and increases the quality of programs. Symantec's C++ and Borland's Pascal with Objects are two well-known object-oriented languages.

Comprehension Questions

1. Which language is more likely to be used to calculate satellite orbital paths, FORTRAN or COBOL?
2. What language might be best for developing accounting software?
3. Name an advantage of learning Pascal rather than BASIC.

Using What You Know

1. Use computer magazines to find five companies that market programming software. What are the companies and what languages do they use?

2. Find at least two competing prices for C compilers. How much do they cost?

3. If you had only one programmer at BVOS, what language would you want him or her to learn, and how might you use that person's skills?

The Programming Process

The very first computing machines were entirely hardware; no software was needed. Computing devices were the tools of mathematicians and engineers who needed to calculate mathematical equations quickly. A hardware approach to computing systems is very limiting, however, because this inflexible device affects the way problems are viewed. As the old saying goes, "If all you have is a hammer, soon all your problems begin to look like nails."

Through the work of legendary figures in computing such as John Von Neumann and Grace Murray Hopper, we began to focus on the sets of instructions that control the computer. This software approach, which only became popular in the 1940s and 1950s, is far more flexible for solving problems. It allows a single computer to be used for a wide range of tasks. It also means that the process of creating a set of instructions — a program — is completely separated from designing the hardware.

When a programmer sets out to create a program, all he or she is really doing is solving a problem. The process for creating a program, therefore, is just a special case of the problem-solving process. The two processes, programming and problem solving, are compared in Figure 5-18.

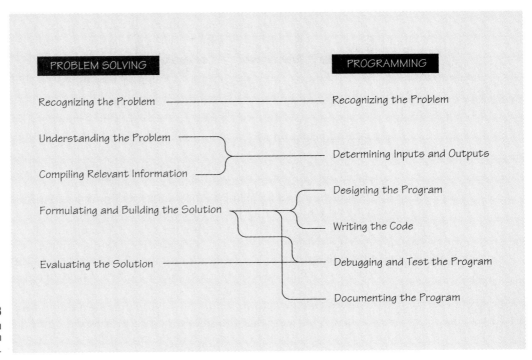

Figure 5-18
The steps involved in programming and problem solving are very similar.

Recognizing the Problem

As with all problem solving, programming begins with recognizing that there is a problem. Often this step occurs when a computer user realizes that a problem cannot be solved with any software products that are currently available. Once the user has come to this conclusion and decides that a program must be created, the final part of this step is to create a clear statement of the objectives that the program needs to meet.

Determining Inputs and Outputs

Step 2 is to determine what output is desired and what input is necessary to produce that output. This step can be thought of as "pre-design." As you can see from Figure 5-18, specifying input and output is a combination of understanding the problem and compiling relevant information. In this step, the programmer may also decide on the programming language that will be used.

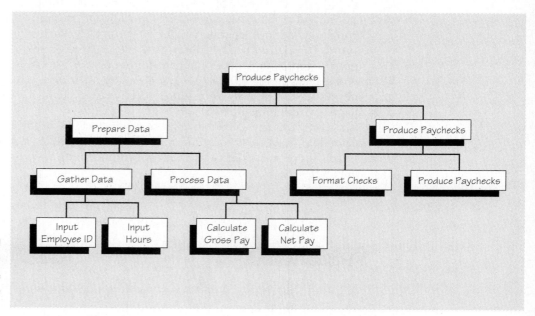

Figure 5-19
Top-down design involves breaking the overall problem into a set of subroutines, which can be programmed separately.

Designing the Program

Next we come to the all-important design step. For the most part, the longer a programmer spends on the design step, the less time he or she will spend writing the program. The object of this stage is to create the most efficient method for producing the desired output from the available input, given the types of processing that the computer is capable of.

During the past few decades, a great deal of attention has been paid to how programs are designed. Over the years, programmers have found that the most effective way to make good software is to build a logical framework for the program. This general approach and the techniques that are used in it are known as **structured programming**.

Top-Down Design. The most fundamental technique used in structured programming is to break the overall objective into smaller tasks and keep doing this until the smaller tasks are relatively simple. This "divide and conquer" approach is called **top-down design**. The result of top-down design is that programming consists of writing a series of **subroutines**, which can be put together to accomplish the original objective (Figure 5-19). Subroutines are also sometimes called modules, procedures, functions, or routines.

Pseudocode. One relatively informal method for creating a top-down design is to write **pseudocode**. Pseudocode gets its name because it looks like code that has been written in a real computer language, but it isn't. Pseudocode is a way for the programmer to go through the motions of writing a program without worrying about the exact syntax of the computer language. This allows the programmer to concentrate on the logic of a program.

The degree of detail incorporated into the pseudocode is entirely up to the programmer. He or she may, in fact, start with a very rough pseudocode that summarizes the entire program in just a few lines. The programmer might then develop and polish his or her work until it is very similar to the actual language in which the program will be written. Figure 5-20 shows pseudocode for part of the top-down design developed in Figure 5-19.

```
Produce paychecks

Enter employee ID number
Enter hours worked by employee.
Calculate employee's net pay
Calculate employee's gross pay.
Ensure that information has been entered
    and calculated for all employees.
Format paychecks.
Print paychecks.
```

Figure 5-20
Pseudocode written to address part of the top-down design shown in Figure 5-19.

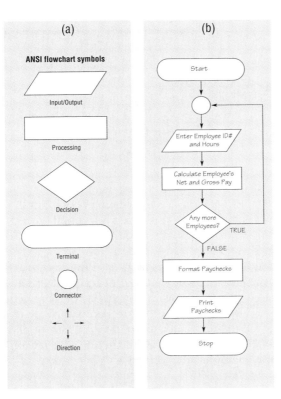

Figure 5-21
(a) The standard ANSI flowchart symbols; (b) a flowchart, a formal representation of the top-down design shown in Figure 5-19.

Flowcharting. Another, more formal, technique for structured programming is to create a logical **flowchart** of the desired program. Figure 5-21 shows a flowchart of the same top-down design you saw in Figures 5-19 and 5-20. Notice the different shapes used in different steps of the chart. Each of these shapes tells you something about the function of that step.

Logic Structures. Unlike pseudocode, the flowchart provides a graphic representation of how the input data becomes output. Notice that the program does not always move in a straight line down through the chart. In addition to sequential steps, there are branches where selections must be made, and there are loops that force the program to repeat a series of steps. These are the three basic **logic structures** that are used in programs: sequence, selection, and loop.

The **sequence structure** is, of course, the simplest (see Figure 5-22). When the program gets done with one step or one subroutine, it moves on to the next. Because the computer reads the steps of the program in sequential order unless it is told to do otherwise, no special statement needs to be made to create a sequential structure.

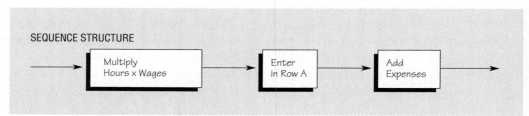

Figure 5-22
A sequence structure.

A **selection structure** (Figure 5-23) is used when the type of processing depends on the nature of the input data. Selection structures are sometimes referred to as IF-THEN-ELSE structures because these are the programming terms normally used to create the structure. The condition, or IF statement, is the one in the diamond-shaped decision box in the flowchart. This is where a certain condition is evaluated. If the condition is true, the program moves to the THEN statement and carries out the processing instructions. If the condition is false, the program moves to the ELSE statement and carries out those processing instructions. The flowchart here shows just two processing possibilities (THEN or ELSE), but there is no reason why there couldn't be more than two.

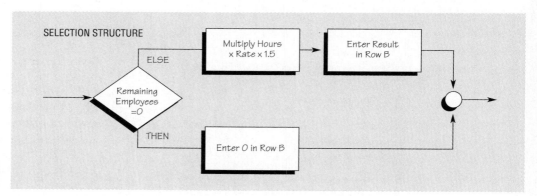

Figure 5-23
A selection structure.

A **loop structure** is similar to a selection structure but uses one of two statements, either DO WHILE or DO UNTIL. In the DO WHILE statement, the loop statement is repeated *while* the condition is true. The program will keep looping back until the condition is no longer true. In a DO UNTIL statement, the loop is repeated *until* the condition is true (see Figure 5-24).

The Opposite of Structured Programming. You might think that giving a program a logical, top-down design is the obvious way to proceed, and all programmers would follow that course. Unfortunately, there are lots of illogical ways to proceed, and there are plenty of bad programs out there to prove it. Often the sign of a badly written program is lots of GOTO statements that tell the computer to jump to a different place in the program. The result of too many GOTO statements is **spaghetti code**. The reason for the term is obvious if you try to create a flowchart of such a program.

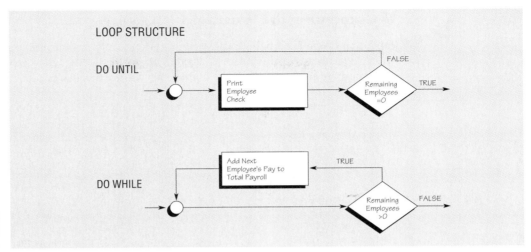

Figure 5-24
The DO WHILE and DO
UNTIL loop structures.

Writing the Code

Once an efficient design has been created for a program, the next step is to sit down at the computer and actually write the instructions, or **code**. In structured programming, writing the code is the process of rebuilding the pseudocode or flowchart within the constraints of the programming language being used.

Debugging the Program

Rarely has a program been written that did not contain errors. An error in a program is known as a **bug**, and fixing errors is known as **debugging**. This quaint term has a perfectly logical explanation. As you've learned, Admiral Grace Hopper was one of the first programmers. In 1945, she was trying to find the source of a problem she was having with an IBM Mark I computer, a 51-foot contraption that weighed 5 tons. She eventually discovered the problem: A moth had been caught in one of the electronic relays. Ever since then, hardware and software malfunctions have been called bugs.

Software errors generally fall into one of two categories. **Syntax errors** are mistakes that violate the rules of whatever program the language is written in. The first phase of debugging is running the program through the compiler or interpreter. One of the responsibilities of the compiler or interpreter is to identify syntax errors.

Logic errors most often occur when the programmer has made an unfounded assumption. When you are creating a program, it is important to remember that a computer is absolutely literal, meaning that it does exactly what the program tells it to do. One common type of logic error is writing an endless loop. A DO WHILE loop might include a condition that is always true, or a DO UNTIL loop a condition that is always false. In either case, the computer will become stuck in the loop.

Once the software has been debugged, it must be tested. For commercial software, the testing process often takes months. The first version of the software, known as the **alpha version**, is usually tested only by an in-house audience. The second, and hopefully last preliminary version, is the **beta version**, which goes to an outside test audience. When a new version of a program is about to be released, you will often see reports on the beta version in trade magazines such as *PC World, Macworld,* and *PC Magazine.*

Documenting the Program

Documentation is a final important step in the programming process. Every program needs to be documented; the process should begin in the design stage. A program's internal documentation should include comments within the code itself, such as a preliminary

```
DECLARE SUB loademup (n, sum)          'This program reads test scores
DECLARE SUB sortem (n)                 'and prints the n, mean, median,
DECLARE SUB variance (n, var, mean)    'variance and standard deviation.
DIM SHARED x(200)

CALL loademup(n, sum)                  'Read STUDENT GRADES
CALL sortem(n)                         'Sort the grades for the median
mean = sum / n                         'Calculate mean
CALL variance(n, var, mean)            'Calculate variance
median = x(INT((n / 2) + .5))             'Locate middle value
PRINT "# tests ="; n
PRINT "mean    ="; mean
PRINT "median  ="; median
PRINT "variance="; var
PRINT "std dev ="; SQR(var)
END

SUB loademup (n, sum)
  sum = 0                              'Initialize sum variable
  n = 0                                'Initialize number of grades
  OPEN "TEST.GRD" FOR INPUT AS #1
  WHILE NOT EOF(1)
      n = n + 1                        'Accumulate number of grades
      INPUT #1, x(n)                   'Read file
      sum = sum + x(n)                 'Accumulate sum of grades
  WEND
  CLOSE (1)
END SUB

SUB sortem (n)                         'This routine uses the common
 flag = 0                              'BUBBLE Sort to sort the grades
 FOR i = 1 TO n - 1                    'in an ascending fashion.
  FOR j = 1 TO n - i
   q = j + 1
   IF x(j)  x(q) THEN                  'This logic swaps the places of
      hold = x(j)                      'two test scores that are out of
      x(j) = x(q)                      'order (i.e. not in ascending order)
      x(q) = hold
   END IF
  NEXT
 NEXT
END SUB

SUB variance (n, var, mean)
 sumvar = 0                                     'Initialize variance sum
 FOR k = 1 TO n
     sumvar = sumvar + (x.k - mean) ^ 2         'Calculate variance
 NEXT
 var = sumvar / (n - 1)
END SUB
```

Figure 5-25
Documentation consists of (a) annotations in the source code and (b) separate printed documents.

(a)

description and line-by-line explanations (Figure 5-25a). External documentation should include flowcharts for use by programmers in understanding the logical structure of the program, and manuals to facilitate use of the program (Figure 5-25b).

(b)

Comprehension Questions

1. Suppose a program is compiled successfully, but the print command causes output to be sent to the monitor. Is this a syntax error or a logic error?

2. Is top-down design part of structured programming, or is it the other way around?

3. Which is the more formal process: creating a flowchart or writing pseudocode? Justify your answer.

Using What You Know

1. Programming software is often much more than just operating an interpreter or a compiler. What might such software packages include to help the programmer?

2. Besides using it as a programming tool, how might you use flowcharting software around the office?

3. How is choosing an application program similar to programming? What parts of each process are related?

Summary Points

Data, Information, and Knowledge
☐ Data is abstract descriptions of reality.
☐ Information is data plus meaning, or data in context.
☐ Knowledge is information plus significance.
☐ Data has no inherent worth. Information and knowledge have value.
☐ Computers process data but cannot create information. If the data is presented well, we can interpret it as information.

How the Computer Represents Data
☐ Today's computers process electrical signals.
☐ Computers are binary because they represent data with on/off switches.

Analog and Digital Data
☐ Computers are referred to as digital devices because they represent all data as numbers.
☐ Analog devices represent data with continuously variable physical quantities that are related to the phenomenon being represented.
☐ A digital device can only approximate a physical phenomenon.

Bits and Bytes
☐ A bit, which is the smallest quantity of digital data, represents one on/off switch.
☐ Eight bits make a byte.
☐ It takes one byte to represent each character on the keyboard.
☐ A kilobyte is 1,024 bytes. A megabyte is 1,024 kilobytes.

ASCII
☐ The most common binary coding scheme used on microcomputers is called ASCII.
☐ EBCDIC is used on mainframes.
☐ ANSI is similar to ASCII and is gaining popularity on microcomputers.

Files
☐ A group of data that the user has given a name to is called a file.
☐ Programs are also files.

What Is Programming?
☐ Programming is the process of creating instructions that the computer can understand and execute.
☐ Compilers and interpreters are programs that translate the instructions written by the programmer into machine language instructions.
☐ A compiler translates the code all at once and reports syntax errors.
☐ An interpreter translates the code while the program is running.
☐ Programs written in interpreted languages are slower than those written in compiled languages.

The Five Generations of Programming Languages

Low-Level Languages
☐ Low-level languages include the first and second generations.
☐ The first generation is machine language.
☐ The second generation, assembly languages, uses mnemonics to stand for sets of machine language instructions.
☐ Low-level languages have almost no portability between machines.

High-Level Languages

- ☐ The third through fifth generations are high-level languages.
- ☐ High-level languages look more like English, are machine independent, and exhibit instruction explosion.
- ☐ Third-generation languages are general-purpose symbolic languages, also known as procedural languages.
- ☐ Fourth-generation languages (4GLs) are nonprocedural, are easier to use than third-generation languages, and are created for specific purposes.
- ☐ Fifth-generation languages combine 4GLs with artificial intelligence, expert systems, and natural language processing.

Common Programming Languages

BASIC

- ☐ BASIC was originally developed as a tool to teach programming.

FORTRAN

- ☐ FORTRAN is the oldest high-level language; it is the first portable language.
- ☐ FORTRAN is used for mathematical manipulations.

COBOL

- ☐ Developed by Admiral Grace Hopper, COBOL was a consortium effort among business, academia, and government.
- ☐ COBOL is popular for business applications.
- ☐ COBOL was designed with portability in mind, a feature that made software development economically feasible.

Pascal

- ☐ Pascal is noted for its structured programming.
- ☐ It was initially popular in academia.

C

- ☐ C includes the constructs of structured programming.
- ☐ It is known as the most portable language and is one of the most popular languages in the world.

SQL

- ☐ SQL is a 4GL that allows the user to ask questions of a database.

Ada

- ☐ The government selected Ada as the standard language used in federal programs.

Other Languages

- ☐ Application packages such as Lotus 1-2-3 and dBASE include 4GLs to tailor the application. It can be difficult to distinguish a flexible application from a programming language.

Object-Oriented Programming

- ☐ Object-oriented programming represents a departure from the strategies of traditional programming. The programmer's focus is on the elements of the program and what they do; the result is a reuseable code.

The Programming Process

- ☐ The programming process is a special case of the problem-solving process.

Recognizing the Problem

- ☐ This step begins with recognizing that existing software will not meet a given need; it ends with a clear statement of the program's objectives.

Determining Inputs and Outputs

- ☐ This "pre-design" phase combines understanding the problem with compiling relevant information.

☐ The programmer picks the programming language in this phase.

Designing the Program

☐ Proper design uses the techniques of structured programming.

☐ Top-down design is a "divide and conquer" strategy. The result is that programming consists of writing a series of subroutines.

☐ Pseudocode is a strategy in which the programmer writes the logic of the program without worrying about the syntax of the language.

☐ Flowcharting diagrams the logic of the program.

☐ The logic of a program can include sequence, selection, and loop structures.

☐ Unstructured programming is characterized by numerous GOTO statements.

☐ The result of unstructured programming is spaghetti code.

Writing the Code

☐ In structured programming, writing the code is the process of rebuilding the pseudocode or flowchart within the constraints of the language's syntax.

Debugging the Program

☐ Debugging the program consists of eliminating syntax and logic errors from the instructions.

☐ Commercial software goes through a long process of debugging that includes preliminary alpha and beta versions of the software.

Documenting the Program

☐ Documenting the program, both within the code and in print, is often considered a part of the programming process.

Knowing the Facts

True/False

1. Programs written in third generation languages tend to be more portable than those written in assembly language.

2. Compilers and interpreters are pieces of software.

3. The most common code used for representing alphanumeric characters on a microcomputer is ANSI.

4. Only high level languages exhibit instruction explosion.

5. The result of top-down design is that programming consists of writing a series of subroutines.

6. The simplest logic structure is the selection structure.

7. Information can be thought of as data plus meaning.

8. BASIC, C, and FORTRAN are third-generation languages.

9. Programs that use an interpreter tend to be faster than those that use a compiler.

10. A digital device represents data as a series of numbers.

Short Answer

1. IF THEN ELSE statements initiate _____ structures.

2. Name a 4GL that allows users to ask questions of a database.

3. A _____ translates a program into machine language while the program is running.

4. An endless loop is a common type of _____ error.

5. Computers are referred to as _____ devices because they use only two electrical states.

6. _____ bytes equals approximately one megabyte.

7. _____ is a language originally created by Admiral Grace Hopper for developing business applications.

8. _____ is a language that was originally created to help teach programming.

9. _____ is the process of creating instructions that the computer can execute.

10. DO WHILE and DO UNTIL are used in _____ structures.

Answers

<table>
<tr><td>True/False</td><td>Short Answer</td></tr>
<tr><td>1   T</td><td>1.   selection</td></tr>
<tr><td>2.   T</td><td>2.   SQL</td></tr>
<tr><td>3.   F</td><td>3.   interpreter</td></tr>
<tr><td>4.   T</td><td>4.   logic</td></tr>
<tr><td>5.   T</td><td>5.   binary</td></tr>
<tr><td>6.   F</td><td>6.   One million</td></tr>
<tr><td>7.   T</td><td>7.   COBOL</td></tr>
<tr><td>8.   T</td><td>8.   BASIC</td></tr>
<tr><td>9.   F</td><td>9.   programming</td></tr>
<tr><td>10. T</td><td>10. loop</td></tr>
</table>

Challenging Your Understanding

1. Do cassette tapes that store music encode the music as analog data or digital data? If you answered "analog," is it possible to store music on tape digitally? If you answered "digital," is it possible to store music on tape analogically?

2. The prefix "kilo" means 1,000. Why do you think a kilobyte equals 1,024 bytes rather than 1,000 bytes?

3. When we get to the point where we can talk to computers, will we need programmers?

4. Programs go through many, many revisions. When do you think a program is ready to be used? Who makes that determination?

5. Some research indicates that workers in an already stressful environment can be further stressed out when they use a computer program that does not adequately solve the user's problem. Should programmers be held accountable for the programs they write or is it the responsibility of the user to make appropriate use of the software?

6. Some estimates indicate that maintaining a program can cost as much as developing a program. What can programmers do to make maintaining a program as inexpensive as possible?

7. Give an example of a syntax error and a logic error arising from writing a short paragraph.

Unit II Project

Comparing Leading Word Processors for Gonzalez Legal Services

After graduating from a secretarial school as a legal secretary, Marcia Gonzalez was hired by Lopez, Nguyen and Porra, a well-established legal firm in a large city. Marcia started out as a filing clerk and over an eight-year career progressed from that position to senior legal secretary for Patricia Stokowski, a junior partner in the firm.

Marcia had learned the legal business quite well. She noted that a great deal of the day-to-day work in a law office involved the formatting and creation of standard legal documents. It occurred to her that Lopez, Nguyen and Porra could save a lot of money if they outsourced much of the secretarial support to an outside company whose business was the creation of legal documents. Marcia eventually got up the courage to present her idea to Patricia, who thought it was a great idea and encouraged Marcia to seriously consider it.

Patricia put up part of the seed money and Gonzalez Legal Services was formed. Patricia convinced the other junior partners to send as much work to Marcia as possible. In ten months, Lopez, Nguyen and Porra were able to reduce personnel costs by $35,000. On the anniversary of the partnership formation, Marcia got a contract with Lopez, Nguyen and Porra to handle all the routine legal transactions for the firm for the next five years. Soon three other large firms were also using Gonzalez.

Now Marcia had a problem. Her labor costs were beginning to significantly climb. Each additional work order actually was decreasing the after tax profit she made. Something had to be done to automate her business. The natural place to start was to computerize the creation of the legal documents.

You have been hired by Gonzalez Legal Services to help select a word processing system to support the creation, storage, retrieval and printing of large legal documents. Use whatever resources are available to you, but keep in mind that the system must be able to work in a legal environment and must have the ability to create and implement standard legal documents and form letters. Provide Ms. Gonzalez with a list of three word processing packages that would suit her needs. You should detail the strengths and weaknesses of each.

Hardware and Operating Systems

So far, we've said a great deal about software without saying much about hardware. We wanted to discuss software first because, when buying a new computer system, the hardware should be chosen to support the applications you have purchased and will purchase in the future. Compatibility between present and future applications is vital; you don't have the luxury of buying a new computer when you need a new application! Now that you know how to purchase software, we need to look at the equipment that supports it.

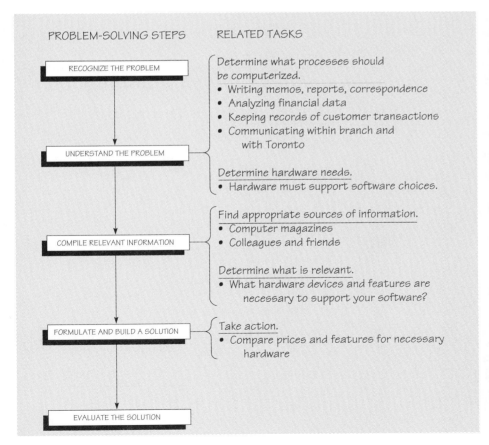

Figure III-1 In this unit, you will again be executing steps 2, 3, and 4 of the problem-solving process. This time, you will focus on hardware and operating systems.

Purchasing Hardware

In setting up your branch of BVOS, you have followed steps 2, 3, and 4 of the problem-solving methodology with respect to software. You have taken measures to understand the varied needs of your staff, your customers, and the central office in Toronto. You isolated important applications, used computer magazines to compare them, and selected appropriate programs. Now it's time to repeat these steps to choose the right hardware. Figure III-1 on the previous page shows what steps 2, 3, and 4 will include this time around.

Kinds of Hardware

As we explained in Unit I, computer systems are made up of hardware, software, data, and people. Software is a set of instructions and procedures that tell the computer what to do. Hardware is the physical manifestation of the computer system. If you can touch it, it is hardware. Thus a diskette is hardware, but the program contained on it is software. Often when users think about computer systems, they visualize the hardware that makes up the system.

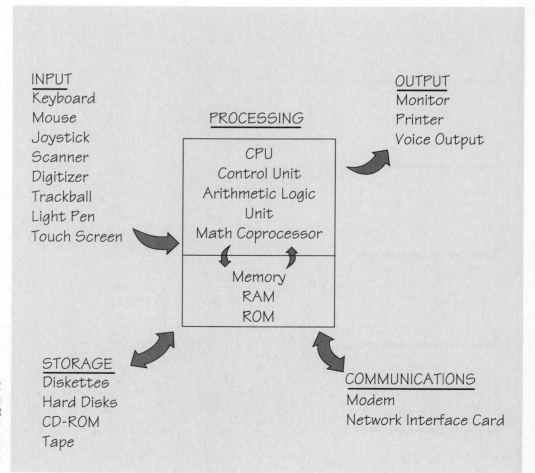

Figure III-2
A standard input-processing-output diagram, with storage and communication added. The most common devices are listed under the function they serve.

INPUT
Keyboard
Mouse
Joystick
Scanner
Digitizer
Trackball
Light Pen
Touch Screen

PROCESSING
CPU
Control Unit
Arithmetic Logic Unit
Math Coprocessor
Memory
RAM
ROM

OUTPUT
Monitor
Printer
Voice Output

STORAGE
Diskettes
Hard Disks
CD-ROM
Tape

COMMUNICATIONS
Modem
Network Interface Card

Microcomputer hardware consists of a collection of electronic devices that can help the user process data. These devices are broadly categorized into two functions: processing and input/output (I/O). Processing devices enable the computer to evaluate, manipulate, and store data for the user. Memory chips and CPUs are examples of processing devices. I/O supports communication between the processing devices and the world outside. I/O devices (1) provide interfaces so humans can interact with computers; (2) allow for the long-term storage of data; and (3) facilitate communication with other computers.

Although all three of these functions are part of I/O, we typically refer to input devices and output devices as those hardware components that serve the first function, that is, input from users and output to users. A mouse and a scanner are examples of input devices. Monitors and printers are output devices. Components that serve the second I/O function, allowing for the storage of data, are commonly referred to as storage devices. The third function, communication, is served by modems, fax modems, and network hardware. Figure III-2 summarizes the relationships among input, processing, output, storage, and communication devices.

Processing Devices

Key Terms

286
386
486
arithmetic logic unit (ALU)
bit
bus
byte
cache memory
central processing unit (CPU)
chassis
chip
clock speed
clones
compatibles
control unit
data bus
desktop model
expansion board
expansion slot
footprint
kilobyte (K)
math coprocessor

megabyte (MB)
megahertz (MHz)
memory
memory chip
MIPS
motherboard
nonvolatile memory
parallel port
peripheral
port
power supply
RAM
register
resistor
ROM
serial port
SIMM
surge suppresser
system unit
tower model
transistor
upward compatibility

Objectives

In this chapter you will learn to:

■ Define the two main parts of the central processing unit (CPU) and describe the purpose of each

■ Differentiate between the most common CPUs used on IBMs and compatibles

■ Name two important factors that affect the processing speed of the CPU

■ Explain the purposes of RAM and ROM and explain why ROM is nonvolatile and RAM is volatile

■ Describe how the CPU and RAM work together to compute simple arithmetic problems.

■ Explain how to calculate the amount of memory a computer requires

■ Differentiate between the two types of cache memory

■ Identify the main choices that are available when buying a chassis for a system unit

■ Name the main computer components found within the system unit

■ Explain how peripherals are connected to the CPU using expansion slots, expansion boards, data buses, and ports

■ Explain the importance of a surge suppresser

Processors: The Computer Engine

Each family of computer— Mac, IBM, NeXT, and so on — has a different set of processing equipment. In fact, more than their brand names, their processing differences are what separate computers into these families. So, choosing what type of computer to buy is really a processing decision. Even within a particular family, deciding which model computer to buy is a processing decision, because each model a company makes has different processing capabilities.

In this chapter, you will learn about the two basic processing components: microprocessors and memory chips. In addition, you will learn about the way the processing components are connected to the rest of the hardware devices. At the end of the chapter, you will look at computer magazines for new products, their processing capabilities, and their prices.

The System Unit: All the Hardware You Need

In most microcomputers, all of the processing components, including the central processing unit (CPU) and memory chips, are part of the **system unit** (Figure 6-1). The primary components of the system unit are the ports, the power supply, and the **motherboard**, which contains the bus, the CPU, all of the chips for controlling system peripherals, and slots for additional circuit boards. We will discuss these components in the sections that follow.

In addition, the system unit may include one or more storage devices, such as diskette drives or a hard disk drive. It can even include the display monitor. Therefore, the system unit itself is not a processing device; it is a catch-all term for the set of components that are housed together.

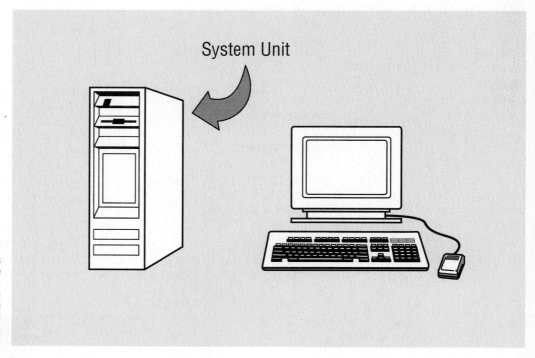

Figure 6-1
The system unit of this computer houses the motherboard with the CPU, memory chips, expansion slots, and bus. It also includes the ports, the hard disk, one diskette drive, and the power supply.

When speaking to computer users or even salespeople, it is important to realize that many people refer to the entire system unit as the CPU. This usage is not accurate, because the CPU is just a small part of the system unit. Nevertheless, the usage is common and you should be familiar with it.

The Computer Chip: The Computer's Core

At the heart of every microcomputer is a set of integrated circuits, usually called *chips*. A **chip** is a small piece of silicon, often no bigger than your smallest fingernail, that is etched with electrical pathways (Figure 6-2).

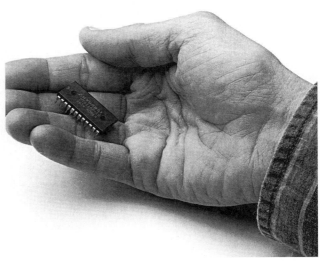

Figure 6-2
A computer chip.

As you learned in Chapter 5, computers represent data with a series of on-off switches called *transistors*. The earliest computers — those created before 1947, when the transistor was invented — used vacuum tubes instead of transistors. A vacuum tube is an electronic device that controls the flow of electrons in a vacuum. Each vacuum tube, which was several inches tall and an inch or more in diameter, acted as a single switch. Computers made with vacuum tubes, such as the one shown in Figure 6-3 on the next page, were gigantic and often weighed several tons. The ENIAC (Electronic Numerical Integrator and Calculator), developed for the U.S. Army in 1946, occupied 1800 square feet and contained 18,000 vacuum tubes (Figure 6-4 on the next page).

In 1947, researchers at AT&T's Bell Laboratories invented the **transistor**, a semiconductor device that operates as an electronic switch. When activated, it opens a circuit, bridges the gap between two wires, and allows current to flow. The transistor was made of solid materials instead of hollow tubes: This was the birth of "solid-state" electronics. During the 1950s, the size of computers shrank dramatically because the transistors used were much smaller than vacuum tubes (Figure 6-5b on the next page). Nevertheless, each transistor had to be individually soldered onto a circuit board, and a powerful computer of the day needed thousands of transistors.

Figure 6-3
A vacuum tube can act as a single electronic switch.

Figure 6-4
The ENIAC computer was big enough to fill a medium-sized house.

About 10 years after the invention of the transistor, Jack Kirby and Robert Noyce invented the integrated circuit, which combined a set of transistors and **resistors** (electronic components that resist the flow of current) on a single chip. Since that time, the size of the integrated circuit, or chip, has steadily shrunk, and the number of transistors on a single chip has multiplied. Modern chips like the one shown in Figure 6-5 pack millions of transistors onto a piece of silicon that is smaller than the earliest transistor.

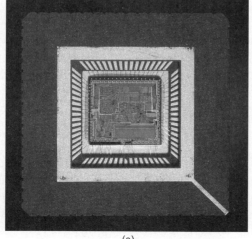

Figure 6-5
(a) The tiny chip on the right contains millions of electronic switches; (b) the transistor is a single switch.

(a)

(b)

The CPU

There are actually many types of computer chips. The two types that make up the processing components of a microcomputer are called microprocessors and memory chips. **Memory chips** hold programs and data. Memory will be discussed later in this chapter.

The term *microcomputer* comes from the fact that processing is controlled by a microprocessor. The main microprocessor in a microcomputer is the **central processing unit** or **CPU**. The CPU, known as the computing part of the computer, is responsible for controlling the flow of data throughout the computer and for executing program instructions (Figure 6-7).

CPU

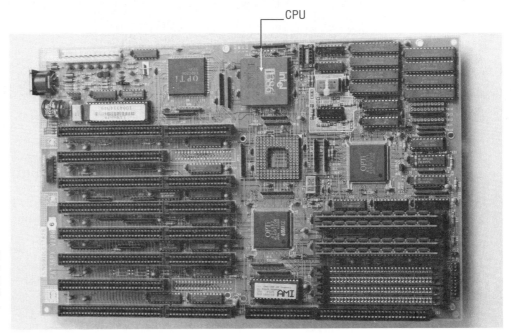

Figure 6-6
The CPU controls the flow of data on the motherboard and thoughout the computer.

Every CPU has at least two parts: a control unit and an arithmetic-logic unit (Figure 6-7 on the next page). The **control unit** retrieves program instructions from memory, evaluates them, and retrieves data from memory. It then coordinates the processing that takes place in other parts of the CPU. The control unit is the "switchboard" of the computer, making connections between other hardware components.

The **arithmetic-logic unit**, or **ALU**, works in conjunction with the control unit by handling all of the arithmetic and logical functions required by the control unit. Numbers are transferred from memory to the ALU for calculation, and the results are sent back to memory. The ALU performs addition, subtraction, division, and multiplication, and it evaluates equality or inequality. Actually, the ALU performs addition to do all of this. For example, to determine the product of 4 and 3, the computer starts with 0 and adds 4 three times (4 + 4 + 4) to get 12. **Registers**, part of the ALU, are high-speed memory circuits. Small sets of data are moved from memory to the registers when the ALU is to perform arithmetic or logical operations on the data.

A **math coprocessor**, an optional extension to the control unit and the ALU, can help speed up processing. Some mathematical computations can be very time consuming for an ALU to handle (see Figure 6-8 on page CF 128). Although we can easily look up a logarithm

Figure 6-7
A typical CPU contains a
control unit and an
arithmetic logic unit.

in a table, the computer must calculate, to the desired numerical precision, the value. Because the CPU was designed to manipulate a wide variety of data types (numbers, text, and graphics), it could not be tuned to perform a single type of activity. However, by adding a math coprocessor to the CPU, we add a special purpose chip that will perform mathematical routines extremely quickly. This speeds up programs that use mathematics or sophisticated, vector-generated graphics.

We should note, however, that the software must be able to detect the presence of the math coprocessor in order to use it. Some microprocessors, such as the 486DX, have incorporated a math coprocessor in them. With others, it is possible to add a coprocessor.

Popular Microprocessors

Microcomputers are often differentiated by the type of CPU they use. For example, the IBM PC, first sold in 1981, used the 8088 chip, manufactured by Intel Corporation. As software requirements have grown and computer manufacturers compete with more powerful and faster machines, more advanced chips have been packaged with new computers. Today, the most popular IBMs use 80286, 80386, and 80486 chips, also manufactured by Intel. A machine with one of these CPUs is commonly referred to as a **286**, **386**, or **486**. Software is constantly getting faster, easier to use, and more powerful. Processing power races to keep pace with the ever-improving software. Because of these proven patterns, it is safe to say that the 386 microprocessor has become a business standard. Of course, as soon as anything becomes a standard in the computer industry, change can't be far behind. The 386 should probably be a minimum for all machines at BVOS.

If you plan to run DOS programs or Windows programs, a 386SX processor is sufficient, although a 386DX is faster and not much more expensive. The difference between these two CPUs is the speed with which the CPU can send and receive data. If you run a lot of Windows programs and want good performance, get at least a 486SX. However, if you plan to run CAD programs, spreadsheets, and anything else that would work better with a math coprocessor, a 486DX performs best.

In addition to the computers actually constructed by IBM, a large number of **clones** or **compatibles** are made by other companies and conform to the design standards of IBM machines. The compatibles market grew during the 1980s, primarily because (1) the microprocessors used by IBM machines were made by another company (Intel), and (2) because the IBM did not prosecute companies that copied its design. By the mid-1980s, IBMs and compatibles were the most common type of microcomputer in the world. As a result, although *PC* can simply mean "personal computer," the term usually means IBMs and compatibles, that is, any machine that conforms to the standards set by the IBM PC. Intel was the first, but is no longer the only, company to develop CPUs for IBM-compatible PCs. Advanced Micro Devices (AMD) chips cost PC makers less (enabling them to pass on consumer savings), plus AMD's top-of-the-line 386 chip outperforms Intel's highest rated 386 chip.

Unlike the IBMs and compatibles, the Macintosh line of computers, made by Apple Computer, Inc., uses chips made by Motorola. The original Macintosh used the Motorola 68000. More recent Macintosh machines use the 68020, the 68030, and the 68040. As with Intel's 286, 386, and 486, higher numbers translate into more processing power and speed (Table 6-1).

Manufacturer	Chip number	Computers using the chip
Intel	8088	IBM Personal Computer
	8086	AT&T Personal Computer 6300
	80286	IBM PC/AT, Compaq Portable II
	80386	IBM Personal System/2 Model 80
		Compaq Deskpro 386
	80486	IBM PS/2 Model 70
Motorola	68000	Apple Macintosh
	68010	AT&T Personal Computer 7300
	68020	Apple Macintosh II
	68030	Apple Macintosh IIcx
		NeXT computer
	68040	Hewlett-Packard workstations

Table 6-1
Chip manufacturers, numbers, and computer users.

Measuring the Speed of a CPU

All microprocessors are not created equal. They vary most in the speed at which they carry out their tasks and the volume of tasks they can do. The speed of the CPU is controlled by the electronic clock that is connected to it. This clock generates electrical "ticks" millions of times per second. The number of ticks is called the **clock speed** of the computer. Because one tick is actually an electrical cycle, clock speeds are measured in millions of cycles per second, or **megahertz (MHz)**.

The best way to think about clock speed is to remember that one cycle is the amount of time it takes to turn a transistor on and off again. Therefore, the faster the clock speed of a computer, the faster the computer can process data. All other factors being equal, a microprocessor working at 50 MHz operates twice as fast as one operating at 25 MHz.

The original IBM PC, which used the Intel 8088 chip, operated at 4.77 MHz. Most 286 computers operate at 16 MHz, though some run slower. 386 chips can operate at 16, 20, 25, or 33 MHz. 486 machines usually operate at 25, 33, 50, or 66 MHz, or even faster. By the time

Figure 6-8
A motherboard and the
math coprocessor.

you read this book, the 486DX2 may be available, at 100 MHz. Clock speed is a central factor affecting the performance of the computer, so there is constant pressure from consumers who want computers operating at faster clock speeds.

Because these CPUs can operate with different system clocks, the clock speed is often included with the CPU number to indicate the type of machine. For example, someone might tell you, "I use a 386 25," meaning the person uses a 386 processor operating at 25 MHz.

Note that, although the higher the number of MHz the better (faster), you can't compare speeds from different generations of CPUs. A 486 running at 25 MHz is faster than a 386 running at 33 MHz, for example. At the time this book was written, the fastest IBM-compatible performance on the market was the 486 CPU running at 66 MHz.

Another unit of measure used when talking about microprocessors is the number of instructions per second the chip can execute. The unit used to measure instructions per second is **MIPS**, which stands for Millions of Instructions Per Second. An **instruction** is a statement that specifies what operation a CPU is to perform. In this case, the term *instruction* refers to a machine language instruction, so each one is very rudimentary. For example, a single instruction might tell the control unit only to access a byte of data in memory and give the data to the ALU. A subsequent instruction might tell the ALU what to do with the data. The number of instructions per second that a computer can execute is a more difficult figure to determine than the clock speed, because several factors are taken into account. MIPS, however, is a more accurate gauge of the computer's processing speed than clock speed.

Word Size

Before discussing word size, let's review the definitions of bit and byte. Computer input is converted into binary members (0 or 1), and a **bit** is one of these digits. Eight bits make a **byte**, which is the common unit of computer storage and is equivalent to one alphanumeric character.

Most microprocessors in use today are 16-bit or 32-bit processors. The number of bits refers to the microprocessor's **word size**, which is the amount of data it can accept at one time. A 16-bit microprocessor, such as Intel's 8088 or 80286, accepts data two bytes (16 bits) at a time. A 32-bit microprocessor, such as Intel's 80386 or 80486 and Motorola's entire 68000 line, accepts data four bytes at a time. All other factors being equal, a 32-bit microprocessor processes data twice as fast as a 16-bit microprocessor. Word size is another factor affecting a computer's MIPS rating. Table 6-2 summarizes the clock speeds and word sizes of the most popular CPUs from Intel and Motorola.

Chip number Intel	Clock Speed	MIPS	Word size
8088	5 Mhz	.33	16
	8 Mhz	.75	
8086	8 Mhz	.66	16
	10 Mhz	.75	
80286	10 Mhz	1.5	16
	12 Mhz	2.66	
80386SX	16 Mhz	2.5	32
	20 Mhz	4.2	
80386DX	16 Mhz	5-6	32
	20 Mhz	6-7	
	25 Mhz	8.5	
	33 Mhz	11.4	
80486SX	25 Mhz	20	32
	33 Mhz	27	
80486DX	25 Mhz	20	32
	33 Mhz	27	

Table 6-2 Clock speeds and word sizes for Intel and Motorola processors.

Comprehension Questions

1. If the only arithmetic function the ALU really uses is addition, how is it able to compute division problems?
2. Why is it acceptable to speak of a PC made by Compaq when the original PC was created by IBM?
3. Using only the information we have provided regarding word size and clock speed, how much faster is a 386 operating at 32 MHz than a typical 286?

Using What You Know

1. On which computer systems in the new Buena Vista Office Supply branch will it be most advantageous to have a math coprocessor? Why?
2. When a word processing program performs a word search, the user types in a word, and the computer tells the user where that word occurs in the current document. What type of operation is the ALU performing to accomplish this task?
3. Why is it not possible for MIPS to be greater than MHz?

Memory

In addition to the type of CPU, its clock speed, and its word size, the other major factor affecting the processing power of a computer is the amount of memory it has. **Memory** (sometimes called primary storage) is the set of electronic "cubbyholes" where data and program instructions are stored when the CPU needs quick access to them (Figure 6-9). Each one-byte cubbyhole is assigned a unique address so that the CPU can store and retrieve data by location.

There are two kinds of memory chips in every microcomputer: ROM chips and RAM chips.

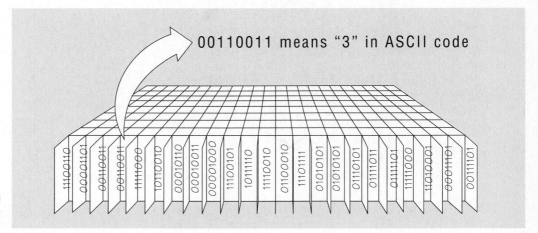

00110011 means "3" in ASCII code

Figure 6-9
Each cubbyhole in memory can hold one byte of data.

ROM

ROM stands for read-only memory (you'll catch some people saying "ROM memory," but the term is redundant). ROM permanently stores data and instructions frequently needed by the computer. It includes the basic instructions needed to start the computer and utility programs needed to maintain the computer. ROM is referred to as **nonvolatile memory** because the user cannot change what is stored there. Nonvolatile memory retains the data and instructions it contains, even when the computer's power is turned off. That way, when the computer is turned on again, those instructions and data are ready and waiting to tell the computer what to do.

RAM

ROM represents only a small fraction of the total memory in a computer. The computer needs far more space to hold all of the other items that the CPU needs ready access to: The operating system, the application program being used, and data that the application program is manipulating are all stored in memory (Figure 6-10). These programs and data are held in another type of memory called **RAM**, which stands for random-access memory. All program execution and data processing take place in RAM. Other common terms for RAM are *memory*, *main memory*, *primary storage*, and *read/write memory*.

The usefulness and the dangers of RAM lie in the fact that RAM stores data as tiny electrical charges, which must be kept alive by the computer's power supply. The advantage of storing

Figure 6-10
ROM and RAM on the
motherboard.

data in this way is that it can be processed very quickly, and it can be changed. Thus, when a program or data is no longer needed, the RAM holding it can be erased, allowing space for new programs and data to be loaded. The danger of RAM is that all data and instructions held there must receive a constant supply of current. If the power supply is interrupted for even a fraction of a second, the data and instructions in RAM disappear. This is why RAM is referred to as **volatile memory**. Because RAM doesn't "remember" once you turn off the power to your computer, it's important to save your work frequently. When you do this, your work is saved to a storage device, which we will discuss in Chapter 8.

Like the other parts of the CPU, memory is also compared in terms of speed. However, memory is not regulated by the electronic clock that governs the ALU and control unit. Instead, the speed of memory is discussed in terms of how quickly the specific memory contents can be located and transmitted to the CPU. Because memory chips are extremely fast, retrieval time is usually measured in nanoseconds. (One nanosecond equals one billionth of a second.) The smaller the value, the faster the memory can be used. Memory speed is another factor affecting the MIPS rate. You should look for a memory speed of 60 to 80 nanoseconds. Another factor is the wait state, the amount of time that passes before an operation takes place.

How the CPU and RAM Work to Process Data

To give you an idea of just how the CPU and RAM work together to process data, let's look at a short set of instructions you might use at BVOS. Say you have used your spreadsheet software to set up the electronic spreadsheet shown in Figure 6-11 on the next page, which calculates total revenue and total expenditures for a one-month period. The last cell in the spreadsheet calculates total profit by subtracting total expenditures from total revenue. You have entered a formula in this cell, so the calculation is performed automatically.

As shown in Figure 6-12 on the next page, to calculate total profit the computer must execute the cell formula, which is held in memory, step by step:

1. The control unit of the CPU finds the memory address of the data held in the cell linked to the "Total Revenue" label and sends the data to a register in ALU. The ALU is then holding the number $40,903.

2. The control unit finds the address of the data held in the cell linked to the "total expenditures" label and sends the data to another register in the ALU. The ALU is now also holding the number $36,934.

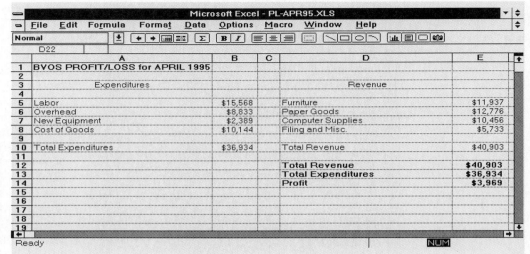

Figure 6-11

You created this spreadsheet at BVOS to calculate total revenue and total expenditures for a one-month period. The last cell contains a formula that automatically calculates total profit by subtracting total expenditures from total revenue.

3. The control unit tells the ALU to subtract 36,834 from 40,903.

4. Because the ALU computes all arithmetic with addition, it adds the opposite of 36,834 to 40,903 and returns the result, 3,969, to the control unit.

5. The control unit stores 3,969 in the memory address that is linked to the cell next to the "Total Profit" label.

6. The control unit sends $3,969 to the monitor with instructions about where to place the data. The result of the calculation is displayed on the screen.

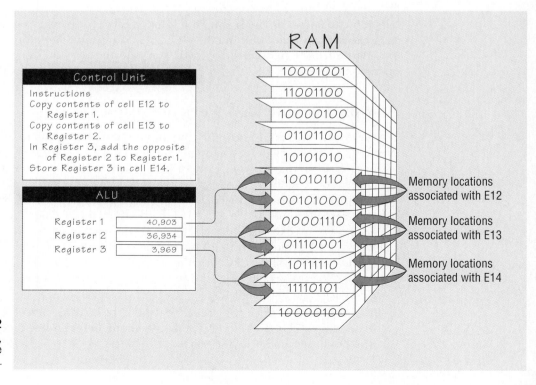

Figure 6-12

How the control unit, ALU, and RAM process a simple formula.

Measuring RAM

The amount of memory in your computer is a crucial factor affecting what software you will be able to run. During the early and mid-1980s, most of the IBM PCs sold were packaged with a maximum of 640 kilobytes (K) of RAM. (A **kilobyte** is equal to 1024 bytes.) At that time, 640 K was sufficient to run most of the programs that were on the market, and memory was generally measured in kilobytes.

As software became more powerful, however, it required more and more available RAM. To meet the requirements, microcomputers started being packaged with more RAM, and RAM is now often measured in megabytes (MB). (A **megabyte** is equal to a million bytes.) Today, it is difficult to find a computer with less than 1 MB of RAM. Even laptop and notebook models are more often sold with at least 2 MB. Many desktop models come with much more: They range from 1 to 64 MB of RAM.

The total amount of memory that a computer can access is dependent on the CPU. Some microprocessors can manipulate or address millions or billions of bytes of memory, while others can address only thousands. For example, most of the PCs that came with 640 K of RAM could address only 1 MB of memory. 386 and 486 computers, however, can address 4 gigabytes (about 4 billion bytes). Figure 6-13 shows the maximum addressable memory for the most popular PC microprocessors.

Figure 6-13
Maximum addressable memory for Intel's most popular CPUs.

Chip	Addressable Memory
8086	1 megabyte
8088	1 megabyte
80286	16 megabytes
80386SX	16 megabytes
80386DX	4 gigabytes
80486SX	4 gigabytes
80486DX	4 gigabytes

Cache

Cache is a reserved section of high-speed memory that can run up to five times the speed of RAM. It stores the most recently used information in fast memory (cache) on the assumption that the most recently accessed information will be used next. This is true 85 percent of the time. The CPU, which moves the data back and forth between cache and RAM, can access the data faster when it's in cache.

Most systems with cache have 64 K of it, but some come with 256 K or more. However, the incremental benefit is negligible once you pass 256 K. All 486 CPUs come with an 8 K cache, and many are designed to supplement that. If you want cache, you must buy a machine that's designed for it.

A disk cache is a portion of RAM that acts as a buffer between the CPU and the disk and thereby minimizes the time required by programs that frequently require storage.

Deciding How Much Memory to Buy

How much RAM is enough? Quite often the amount of RAM needed is related to how fast you want your computer to operate. With many software packages, when enough RAM is not available, disk storage is used. Using disk storage slows down processing because it cannot be accessed as quickly as RAM. Check the applications that you will be running to see how much memory they can take advantage of.

To decide how much memory to buy when you purchase a computer, you should first estimate your minimum memory requirements. To determine the minimum memory requirements, you must look at the RAM requirements for the largest program you are going to use, then you must add enough bytes to fit the largest data file that you might need to access through your largest piece of software. These numbers, however, are just your minimum requirements. You will probably want to buy significantly more memory for some machines for several reasons:

- Upgrades of software almost always require more memory than the previous version. For example, WordPerfect 4.2, the best-selling word processing software during the late 1980s, required 256 K of RAM. WordPerfect 5.1, however, requires 384 K of RAM, and WordPerfect for Windows takes up 2 MB of RAM. If you want to keep up with the current versions of your software, you may need more memory with each upgrade.

- Microcomputer users tend to accessorize their systems with helpful utility programs, such as screen savers, virus protection, font managers, and so on. While such programs can be helpful, they take up space in RAM. Consequently, it's a good idea to plan on some extra space to handle any utility programs you might want to install.

- If you buy an IBM or compatible and want to keep open the option of running Windows or OS/2, you will need much more memory than you would for a DOS machine. Just to run Lotus 1-2-3 for Windows on the Windows 3.1 platform requires 3 MB of RAM, as opposed to 512 K to run Lotus 1-2-3 R2.2 on a pure DOS platform.

If you can afford it, it is always a good idea to buy extra memory. The pace of software innovation is staggering, and the only way to factor it in is to buy a computer that gives you room to grow. If necessary, you can expand your RAM with **SIMMs** (single in-line memory modules), which are narrow printed circuit boards that hold memory chips (Figure 6-14).

Figure 6-14
A SIMM, used to add memory to a microcomputer.

SIMMs come in 1, 2, 4, 8, and 16 MB increments and connect to the motherboard. Some motherboards have room for as many as 16 SIMMs — that's a maximum of 256 MB of extra RAM.

Comprehension Questions

1. Explain why the basic instructions used to start the computer can't be held in RAM.
2. Briefly explain why memory speed affects the MIPS rate.
3. Explain how the CPU and RAM might process the problem of determining which is larger, 3 or 4.

Using What You Know

1. Using newspaper advertisements, find two comparable computers with different amounts of memory. Using the information you have found, how much more would you say it costs to have 8 MB of RAM rather than 4 MB?

2. What is the minimum memory requirement to run Windows NT and Lotus 1-2-3 for Windows?

3. Compare the memory requirements for the following products:
    - The latest version of WordPerfect on the Mac
    - The latest version of WordPerfect for Windows
    - The latest version of WordPerfect for DOS

Connecting Peripherals

The CPU and memory comprise the computer's processing components, but they need a way to communicate with the other hardware components. Both the CPU and the memory chips are mounted on the motherboard. The other hardware devices are connected to the motherboard through expansion slots, ports, and the data bus.

Ports

A **port** is an I/O device interface in which an external peripheral can be plugged into the system unit. Ports can be connected directly to the motherboard or to expansion boards. A computer uses ports to communicate with its peripherals (Figures 6-15 and 6-16).

There are many types of ports that a computer can use. On IBMs and compatibles, you will usually find two types of ports mentioned in computer literature and ads: parallel ports and serial ports. While both of these types transfer data using circuits, they differ in the way the data is transferred. In a **parallel port**, a series of parallel wires allow a group of bits to be transmitted at once. Parallel ports are sometimes called *centronics ports* after the connector that is often used to attach printers to expansion boards. Parallel ports are most often used to connect output devices, especially printers.

A **serial port** transmits data one bit at a time. Serial ports generally have fewer wires in their connectors than do parallel ports. Modems are always attached to serial ports, mice often are, and printers sometimes are.

Figure 6-15 Parallel, serial, and SCSI ports.

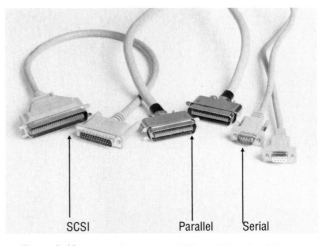

SCSI   Parallel   Serial

Figure 6-16 Cable connectors for SCSI, parallel, and serial ports.

Both types of ports have advantages. Parallel ports are able to transmit faster, while serial ports are better suited to transmit over long distances.

Macintosh computers use a special type of port interface known as a **SCSI** (pronounced "scuzzy"). SCSI stands for Small Computer System Interface. In the Mac, the SCSI design is built into the motherboard. SCSI boards can also be installed in PCs. A SCSI design allows peripherals to be connected in sequence, creating a daisy chain.

Expansion Slots and Boards: Built-in Flexibility

Peripherals are hardware devices, such as modems, printers, and so on, that connect to the computer. Many peripherals require an expansion board, which plugs into an **expansion slot** on the motherboard (Figures 6-17 and 6-18). **Expansion boards** are printed circuit boards similar to the motherboard. They provide a hardware interface between the peripheral and the motherboard. On one edge of an expansion board, there is a gold strip. This strip is the part that fits into the expansion slot on the motherboard.

Expansion boards are used to add many types of devices, including additional disk drives or RAM, communication devices such as modems or fax boards, input devices such as scanners, or output devices such as printers or display adapters. The number of expansion slots on your motherboard determines the maximum number of expansion boards that can fit in your computer. PCs have from three to eight slots. What's important is the number of slots left over after your system is configured. If you run out of slots, you can no longer expand your system.

Data Buses

The motherboard uses electronic pathways called **data buses** to transfer data between the CPU and the peripherals, as well as between the CPU and the memory chips (Figure 6-19).

Figure 6-17 Expansion slots on the motherboard.

Figure 6-18 Expansion boards plugged into expansion slots on a motherboard.

Figure 6-19
The data bus on the motherboard.

The kind of bus used in a computer is important for two reasons. First, the size of the bus affects how fast data can flow through it. The CPU determines what size bus can be built onto the motherboard. For example, the 8088 chip uses an 8-bit bus, the 286 uses a 16-bit bus, and the 386DX and 486 use 32-bit buses (Figure 6-20). The wider the bus, the more data can move through it in a given amount of time.

Second, the way a motherboard and its buses are constructed also affects the computer's capabilities. Among IBMs and compatibles, there are four competing architectures. It's important to know which bus architecture a computer has before purchasing any peripherals. The Industry Standard Architecture (ISA) type of bus was the first and dates to the original IBM PC. The ISA architecture allows for 8-bit and 16-bit bus lines. When IBM began making machines with 386 processors, it needed a new architecture that could handle the 32-bit bus. IBM created the MicroChannel Architecture (MCA), which requires special, more sophisticated peripheral expansion boards. The problem with MCA was that the old 8-bit and 16-bit boards wouldn't work. The companies that manufactured those boards were understandably upset, since IBM had broken the trend of upward compatibility. **Upward compatibility** means that new machines can use the same software and hardware used in older, less powerful machines. Without upward compatibility, every advancement in hardware would require users who want to take advantage of the advancement to buy an entirely new system.

Figure 6-20
Intel and Motorola have gradually expanded their bus sizes.

Chip	Bus size
8088	8 bits
8086	16 bits
80286	16 bits
80386SX	16 bits
80386DX	32 bits
80486SX	32 bits
80486DX	32 bits

To solve the problems created by MCA, a group of hardware manufacturers came up with the Extended Industry Standard Architecture (EISA), which is compatible with ISA-based peripherals, but can transfer 32 bits (Figure 6-21 on the next page). Under certain circumstances, EISA is not as fast as MCA, but only EISA is upward compatible.

The newest bus architecture is called the *local bus*. A machine with the new 32-bit local bus architecture is faster than those with MCA, ISA, or EISA. A computer with a local bus and a 33 MHz CPU can transfer 132 MB of data per second. MCA with 33 MHz transfers at 40 MB per second, EISA at 33 MB per second, and ISA at 8.33 MB per second.

Power Supplies

A critical component in all computers is the power supply (Figure 6-22). The **power supply** is the device that takes ordinary household AC power and transforms it into DC current, on which the computer operates. It is important to match the power supply with the power consumption of the peripherals and the motherboard. In some older PCs, it is not possible, for example, to install a second hard disk, because the power supply is insufficient to power the device.

For many computers, the power cable is the only electronic pathway between the computer and the outside world. Unfortunately, the quality of electrical power to your home or office can vary substantially. Unlike refrigerators and incandescent lamps, computers cannot easily withstand such environments. If a power surge (a wave of voltage) or spike (a very short, sharp blast of voltage) hits your computer, it can burn out the power supply, burn through the connections between the power supply and the motherboard, and destroy the motherboard. From the motherboard, the electrical surge or spike can proceed to the monitor, the disk drives, and keyboard. This short burst of electricity could reduce your computer to a high-tech paper weight.

Consequently, computers need devices that protect them from electrical problems associated with blackouts, brownouts, sags, and other power level inconsistencies. A **surge suppressor** (or surge protector) will keep electrical surges and spikes from passing from the electrical system to the power supply. A surge suppressor, such as the one illustrated in

Figure 6-21
ISA and EISA expansion boards. ISA boards can fit into EISA slots.

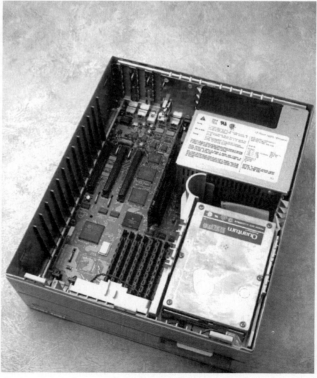

Figure 6-22
An open system unit showing the power supply.

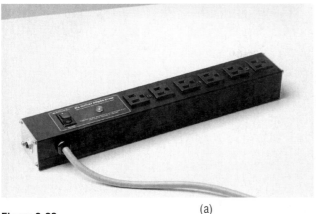

(a)

Figure 6-23
(a) A surge suppressor;
(b) an uninterruptable
power supply.

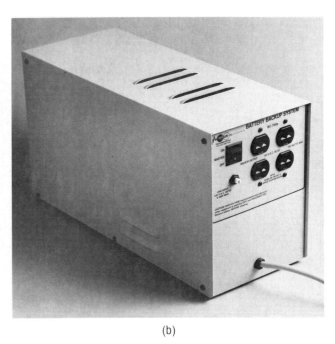

(b)

Figure 6-23a will detect an unusual increase in the level of electricity and then immediately break the electrical connection. The faster it breaks this connection, the better the protection.

Other power protection devices, such as **uninterruptable power supplies**, can keep the computer operating several minutes after the loss of power, giving you time to save your files and power down (Figure 6-23b). Because of the tremendous amount of electrical power, no power protection mechanism can protect against a lightning strike. There are two types of uninterruptible power supplies: one switches to a battery supply when the power goes out; the other runs the computer off a battery and is always recharging the battery, so there is no switching delay.

Always make sure the outlets you use to plug in your computer and peripherals are three-pronged, grounded outlets. An electrician can tell you whether an outlet is grounded.

The power supply in the computer generates heat, which requires the chassis to contain a fan for cooling the computer. The chassis has air holes through which cooler air outside the computer is drawn and warmer air inside is pushed out. It is critical that these airways remain open when the computer is on. It is also important to remember that having too many air holes in a computer is undesirable. While installing a peripheral device in a computer, it is tempting to leave the cover of an expansion slot open. When this happens, however, the air flow that was created in the chassis design is disrupted, and the computer becomes improperly cooled because the air does not flow over the appropriate parts of the motherboard. In addition, having too many open airways encourages dust and moisture to accumulate in the microcomputer.

The Chassis

The outside of the system unit is called the system cabinet or **chassis**. A chassis must conform to certain Federal Communicatons Commission regulations regarding the amount of radio interference that emanates from the computer. These regulations (termed the Class B rule) are designed to provide reasonable protection against electrical interference in a residential installation. A device that did not conform to this rule might cause interference with radios

Figure 6-24
Desktop models in the
Macintosh line. The
compact machine on the
right has a smaller
footprint than the one on
the left.

and televisions. In addition, just as radio waves can escape from a computer, these same waves can intrude on the computer. When this happens, data loss can occur.

When you purchase the system unit of a computer, you may have to decide on a chassis design. During the early and mid-1980s, most of the computers sold were **desktop models**, meaning that the chassis was designed to lie flat on a desk. Whether the monitor was an integral part of the chassis or not, it tended to sit on top of the system unit. These chassis were often compared by the size of their **footprint**, or the amount of space they occupied on the desk. For example, the less expensive models in the Macintosh line — the Mac Plus, the SE, and later the Mac Classic — featured a small footprint, with the monitor built into the chassis (Figure 6-24). The more powerful machines in the line — the Mac II, the LC, and several others — had separate monitors and chassis with larger footprints. This configuration was typical for PCs.

Gradually, chassis started appearing in another configuration, the tower model, which provided an alternative to the desktop model. **Tower models** stand on one end, as shown in Figure 6-25. This design frees desk space, either by allowing the chassis to stand on the floor (either under or next to a desk) or simply by taking less space on the desk. Tower models often come in three sizes: full towers, mid-towers, and mini-towers.

The chassis design of a computer can affect the number of expansion boards that can be connected to the motherboard. Full tower and large desktop models generally provide the most room for expansion boards. Mini-towers and small footprint models usually have fewer slots to fit boards into. When shopping for a computer, it is always important to think about what peripherals you may want to attach and how much room a given model or chassis gives you for growth. Also, be aware that some expansion boards are longer than others. Some are full length; others are half length. When you compare two computer designs, look at the number of full-length and half-length boards that will fit in the system unit.

Some companies, such as Apple and IBM, tend to package the system unit, monitor, keyboard, and mouse together in a few different configurations. When purchasing one of

Figure 6-25
Chassis designs for PCs.

these packages, you often don't choose the type of chassis — it's determined by the model you want. When purchasing a clone, however, you can often determine the exact specifications of your computer and can choose whatever chassis design you prefer.

Comprehension Questions

1. Why is the difference between MCA and EISA less relevant for new computer users than for experienced users who are upgrading to new processing equipment?

2. Describe a situation in which you might want to purchase a mini-tower model for your system unit.

3. Why does a printer require a parallel port, while a modem requires a serial port?

Using What You Know

1. You have decided to buy a full tower system unit for the network server. You have the choice of putting it in the stockroom, the sales room, or a small closet off of the sales room. Which would you choose and why?

2. Why must a 286 have a 16-bit bus rather than a 32-bit bus?

3. What type of chassis is most appropriate for the computers in the stockroom and why?

Summary Points

Processors: The Computer Engine

☐ Choosing what type of computer to buy is a decision about processing.

The System Unit: All the Hardware You Need

☐ The system unit includes the motherboard, the ports, and the power supply. It often includes the disk drives, and it sometimes includes a monitor.

☐ Many users say *CPU* when they mean *system unit*.

The Computer Chip: The Computer's Core

☐ A computer chip is a piece of silicon etched with electrical pathways.

☐ The invention of the transistor in 1947 allowed computer makers to replace vacuum tubes with solid-state electronics.

☐ Millions of transistors now fit on a chip that is smaller than the earliest transistor.

The CPU

☐ The two main types of chips found in microcomputers are microprocessors and memory chips.

☐ The main microprocessor in a microcomputer is the CPU.

☐ The CPU consists of the control unit and the ALU.

☐ A math coprocessor may also be added to the CPU to speed up mathematical processing. A 486 CPU includes a math coprocessor.

Popular Microprocessors

☐ Today, the most popular PCs use the 286, 386, and 486 CPUs.

☐ The term *PC* includes both IBMs and compatibles or clones.

☐ Macs use the 68000 line of Motorola chips.

Measuring the Speed of a CPU

☐ The speed of a CPU is controlled by an electronic clock; the number of ticks per second is measured in MHz.

☐ MIPS is a more complete measurement of the computer's speed because more factors are included.

Word Size

☐ Word size, which measures the number of bits that a computer can accept at once, is another factor affecting MIPS.

Memory

☐ The speed of memory also affects the MIPS rate.

ROM

☐ ROM, which is nonvolatile, stores the basic instructions needed to start the computer.

RAM

☐ All of the programs and data to which the CPU needs ready access are stored in RAM, which is volatile.

How the CPU and RAM Work to Process Data

☐ The control unit passes data back and forth between RAM and the ALU.

Measuring RAM

☐ Most early PCs had 640 K of RAM.

☐ Today, RAM is often measured in megabytes because the requirements of modern software have pushed manufacturers to supply more RAM with new computers.

Cache
- ☐ Cache can speed up processing by providing a buffer between the CPU and RAM.
- ☐ A disk cache can speed up certain types of processing that require storage by providing a buffer between the CPU and storage.

Deciding How Much Memory to Buy
- ☐ Minimum memory requirements are figured by adding the memory requirements of your operating system, your largest application program, and the largest data file you will access with your largest application program.
- ☐ You may need to buy more than your minimum requirements to allow for software upgrades, utilities, or moving from DOS to a GUI.

Connecting Peripherals

Ports
- ☐ Ports are the I/O device interface into which peripherals are plugged; they can be directly connected to the motherboard or connected to an expansion board.
- ☐ Parallel ports allow a group of bits to be transmitted at one time.
- ☐ Serial ports allow data to be transferred only one bit at a time.

Expansion Slots and Boards: Built-in Flexibility
- ☐ Many peripherals require expansion boards, which are plugged into expansion slots on the motherboard.

Data Buses
- ☐ The CPU is connected to memory and all the peripherals through the data bus.
- ☐ The size of the data bus affects the MIPS rate.
- ☐ The design, or architecture, of the data bus also affects performance.

Power Supplies
- ☐ The power supply converts household AC current to DC current.
- ☐ Surge suppressors protect computer equipment from electrical surges and spikes.

The Chassis
- ☐ The box that forms the outside of the system unit can come in several different configurations.
- ☐ Chassis models are compared by their footprints, by whether they are desktop or tower models, or by what size tower model they are.

Knowing the Facts

True/False

1. The ALU uses addition to perform multiplication, division, subtraction, and comparison.
2. MCA motherboards cannot be connected to expansion boards that are designed for ISA motherboards.
3. Data can be transmitted more quickly through parallel ports than through serial ports.
4. A computer operates on DC current.
5. One way to help keep your system cool is to remove as many of the expansion slot covers as possible.
6. RAM stores programs needed to start the computer.
7. The size of the data bus affects the MIPS rating.
8. Modems usually require parallel ports.
9. The data bus connects the CPU to the RAM chips.
10. In some computers, the monitor is inside the system unit.

Short Answer

1. A memory cache is a buffer between _____ and the CPU.
2. What are the two basic types of computer chips used in processing?
3. The processing components of the computer are mounted on the _____.
4. ROM is referred to as _____ memory, because it retains its contents even when the computer is turned off.
5. What 1947 invention eventually led to the development of the computer chip?
6. What are the two main components of the CPU?
7. Hardware devices connected to the motherboard through expansion slots or ports are known as _____.
8. The word size of the 386 and 486 chips is _____ bits.
9. The most accurate measurement of a computer's processing speed is _____.
10. IBMs and compatibles are collectively referred to as _____.

Answers

True/False

1. T
2. T
3. T
4. T
5. F
6. F
7. T
8. F
9. T
10. T

Short Answer

1. RAM
2. memory chips and microprocessors
3. motherboard
4. nonvolatile
5. the transistor
6. the control unit and the ALU
7. peripherals
8. 32
9. MIPS
10. PCs

Challenging Your Understanding

1. Using whatever resources are available to you, find prices for a Dell 486 33 MHz with 8 MB of RAM. Find the price for the same configuration from IBM. How do you explain the difference?

2. On ISA-bus PCs, the 8 MHz data bus is the slowest device on the motherboard. It is slower than RAM and slower than the CPU. What are the implications of this (if any) for computer users?

3. It is generally possible to upgrade a PC by purchasing additional memory. Find out approximately how much it costs to add each MB of RAM.

4. After using a Mac LC with 2 MB of RAM for a year, your accountant wants to increase the RAM to 8 MB. Is this change possible? If so, how much does it cost?

5. If BVOS is immediately successful, you may need to hire a secretary to handle some of your correspondence and cover general work around the office. This person's computer needs would be strictly limited to word processing. What kind of processing components would you buy for this new employee, and why?

6. Say you are buying computers with 386 microprocessors running at 16 MHz with 2 MB of RAM for each of the stockers and salespeople. Use a popular computer magazine, such as *PC Magazine* or *PC World*, to find the minimum that you will be able to spend for each of these computers.

Input and Output Devices

Key Terms

alphanumeric keys
bar-code readers
cathode ray tube (CRT)
CGA
characters per second (cps)
click
cursor (text cursor)
cursor-movement keys
digitizer tablet
dot matrix printer
dot pitch
double-click
drag
EGA
ergonomics
flat-panel display
function keys
gray scale
hard copy
impact printer
ink-jet printer
internal fonts
laser printer
letter-quality print

light pen
liquid crystal display (LCD)
monitor
monochrome
mouse
near letter-quality (NLQ) print
numeric keypad
optical character recognition
   (OCR)
pages per minute (ppm)
pixel
pointing device
PostScript
printer driver
QWERTY
resolution
scanners
soft copy
soft fonts
SVGA
toggle switch
touch screen
trackball
VGA

Objectives

In this chapter you will learn to:

- Define the four major areas of the keyboard
- Explain the importance of keyboarding skills
- Name and describe the three common mouse techniques
- Explain the differences among the mouse, the trackball, and the pen
- Describe how scanners differ from manual input devices
- Define the capability of OCR software
- Explain why voice input is difficult and how it is currently accomplished
- Name the two basic types of monitor and differentiate between them
- Name the three types of flat-screen monitor
- Explain how monitors create multiple shades of gray or colors
- Describe the most important factors to consider when purchasing a monitor
- Name the four types of graphics card used on the PC and explain the differences among them
- Name the three most common types of printers and describe how each works
- Compare the three types of printers in terms of resolution and speed

Getting Data "In" and Information "Out"

Input refers to data being retrieved by processing devices from peripherals, such as a disk drive, modem, or keyboard. *Output* means data sent from processing to a peripheral. This is the formal, and more technically accurate, use of these terms. However, an *input device* more often means a device that a computer user employs to give data to the computer. *Output device* usually means the monitor or the printer, that is, a device that is used to present processed data to the user. When people need only to see processed data, it is sent to the monitor. When people want printed output, it goes to the printer. These are the meanings that we use in this chapter.

This chapter covers several types of input devices, including keyboards, pointing devices, and scanners. The second half of the chapter covers monitors and printers.

The Keyboard and Its Parts

The most widely used input device for microcomputers is the keyboard. In fact, the first microcomputers to gain widespread acceptance in the market used keyboards as the sole input device. As processing power and user interfaces became more sophisticated, other devices were added. The keyboard, however, remains the most versatile input device, though it isn't always the easiest one to use.

As shown in Figure 7-1, a keyboard can include as many a five separate areas: the alphanumeric keys, the function keys, the cursor-movement keys, the numeric keypad, and the toggle-switch lights.

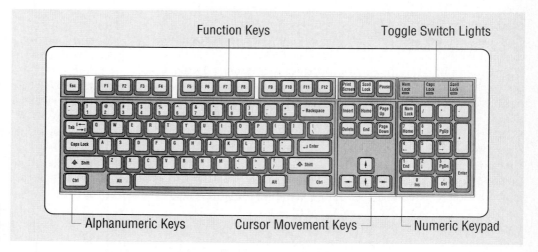

Figure 7-1
The IBM 101 keyboard, the standard for many PCs.

Alphanumeric Keys.   The area of the keyboard that includes all the letters of the alphabet consists of the **alphanumeric keys** (Figure 7-2). The term *alphanumeric* comes from the fact that this part of the keyboard includes all of the ALPHAbet and all of the NUMERICal digits. This area looks very similar to the keyboard of a standard typewriter. Like a typewriter, this area includes punctuation marks, the Tab key, Backspace key, Spacebar key, Enter key (usually called the Return key on a typewriter), and the Shift and Caps Lock keys. This part of the keyboard is sometimes called the **QWERTY** (pronounced "kwer-tee") keyboard, a name derived from the first six characters on the left in the top row of letters.

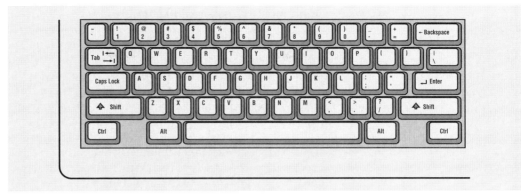

Figure 7-2
The alphanumeric keys, also known as the QWERTY keyboard.

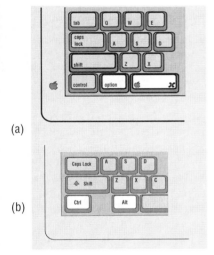

(a)

(b)

Figure 7-3
Modifier keys on
(a) the Mac keyboard and
(b) the IBM keyboard.

In addition to the typewriter keys, the alphanumeric area of a keyboard usually includes two other keys (actually four, since both keys are found on both sides of the keyboard). On the Apple keyboards used with the Macintosh (Figure 7-3a), they are the Command and Option keys. The Command key usually has a four-petaled, flowerlike image on it, as well as an apple symbol on it. On the IBM keyboard (a keyboard design, not necessarily made by IBM), the two extra keys are the Ctrl and Alt keys, which stand for "control" and "alternate" (Figure 7-3b). All of these keys are used in the same way as the Shift key. The user holds down one of these keys while typing another alphanumeric, function, or cursor-movement key. The function of these additional keys is determined by the program being used.

Function Keys. IBM and compatible computers all have **function keys** that enable a software developer to assign a specific software function to a single key (Figure 7-4). Once again, the function of the particular key, or key combination, varies with the program being used. For example, the F3 key in WordPerfect for the PC tells the computer to display the Help menu. In DOS, F3 tells the computer to repeat the last command typed at the keyboard.

A few special keys are located in the same row as the function keys. To the left of the function keys on most keyboards, you will find the Escape (Esc) key. The Escape key allows you to cancel a command that is about to be executed. To the right of the function keys are Print Scrn, Scroll Lock, and Pause or Break. If your printer is set up to do so, Print Scrn will print everything that appears on your monitor. Scroll Lock holds the cursor in one place on the screen as the text scrolls by. In some programs, Pause or Break allows you to cancel a command that is currently being processed.

Figure 7-4
The function keys. On older IBM keyboards, they are located to the left of the alphanumeric keyboard.

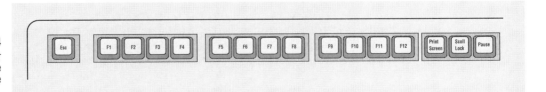

Cursor-Movement Keys. The **cursor** is the point on the screen where letters, numbers, or punctuation symbols typed at the keyboard will be entered. The **cursor-movement keys** (Figure 7-5) allow the user to use the keyboard to move the cursor around the screen. The

Figure 7-5
The cursor movement keys.

Figure 7-6
The numeric keypad.

arrow keys simply move the cursor one character, cell, or field to the right, left, up, or down. The Home and End keys can be used to move the cursor to the beginning or end of a document, but their functions vary depending on the program. Page Up and Page Down (PgUp and PgDn) cause the cursor to jump to the top of the previous or subsequent screen or page. The Delete key works just like the Backspace key, except it deletes the character at the cursor (or to the right of the cursor when it is displayed as a vertical line), rather than the character to the left of the cursor. Finally, the Insert key is a **toggle switch**, meaning that pushing it once turns the Insert mode on, and pushing it again turns the feature off. When Insert mode is on, new characters typed in the middle of a line of text will make room for themselves and will not erase existing characters. When Insert Mode is off, the keyboard is in Overwrite mode, also called Typeover. With Typeover on, new characters typed in the middle of a line of text will overwrite existing characters.

The Numeric Keypad.   The **numeric keypad** (Figure 7-6), located on the right side of the keyboard, allows for quick entry of numbers. The keypad is more useful than the numbers across the top of the alphanumeric keyboard for entering a large set of numerals. The numeric keypad includes arithmetic function keys (+, –, *, and /), a well as an Enter key. The cursor-movement keys may be combined with, or repeated on, the keypad. To use the cursor control keys on the keypad, turn off the numbers by pressing the Num Lock key.

Lights on the Keyboard.   Keyboards often have three toggle-switch lights on them: Num Lock, Caps Lock, and Scroll Lock (Figure 7-7). Each light is connected to a toggle switch on the keyboard. The Num Lock light is controlled by the Num Lock key on the numeric keypad. When the light is on, typing the keys on the numeric keypad will display numbers. When the light is off, the keys on the keypad can be used for cursor movement. The Caps Lock key is connected to the Caps Lock key on the alphanumeric keyboard. When it is on, alphabetic characters you type will appear capitalized. The Scroll Lock light is connected to the Scroll Lock key,

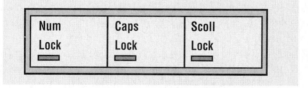

Figure 7-7
Toggle-switch lights.

which is located in the same row as the function keys. In some programs, turning on Scroll Lock will hold the cursor in one place on the screen and force the data to scroll past the cursor. When Scroll Lock is off, you can move the cursor around the screen.

Data Entry with the Keyboard

When business people speak of *data entry*, they usually mean typing numbers and letters at the keyboard. A data entry job at a company usually entails typing documents or entering numbers into a company database. But data entry personnel are not the only ones entering data at the computer. Financial analysts, department managers, and other company personnel also enter data at computers. Therefore, virtually every microcomputer user needs to know how to use a keyboard (Figure 7-8). This means that typing or keyboarding skills have become more and more important as computer use has grown. Learning to type with all 10 fingers without looking at the keyboard has become a valuable asset in the job market.

You probably already know how painfully slow keyboarding can be if you can't type. To make you feel better, you should know that there is a historical reason for the level of dexterity required for typing. The QWERTY keyboard was designed when the manual, nonelectric typewriter was the only kind that existed. If two keys are pressed at the same time on a manual typewriter, the arms that reach up and hit the paper tend to get stuck. The QWERTY keyboard was originally designed to slow typists down and thereby keep typewriters from getting jammed. Those of us who have learned to type on QWERTY keyboards don't want to learn again. As a result, no redesign of the standard layout has ever gained acceptance.

Figure 7-8
Being able to type with all 10 fingers and not look at the keyboard has become a valuable skill for all business people.

A Few Words About Ergonomics: The Human Factor

Most of the keyboard illustrations in this chapter show keyboards we're all familiar with. However, there is a special kind of keyboard that folds in the middle in order to angle the user's hands into what is, for some people, a more comfortable and natural position. This keyboard was developed in response to a marked increase in chronic wrist and hand injuries suffered by people who spend a lot of time at the keyboard.

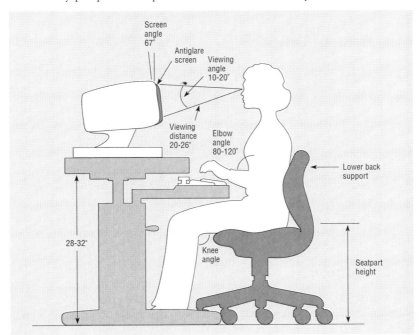

Figure 7-9
Proper body position when working at a computer can help prevent strain and injury.

The keyboard is an ergonomically designed product. **Ergonomics** is the study of people-machine relationships. An ergonomically designed product accommodates a person's body or actions. There are optimum kinds of equipment and optimum ways to adjust this equipment. Adjusting your sitting position so that you are comfortable is important as well. Figure 7-9 on the previous page shows a good posture for sitting at the keyboard, along with proper heights and distances for equipment. Additional ergonomic equipment can include wrist rests, an adjustable desk chair, and a foot rest. Bear in mind that regardless of how ergonomically designed your work area is, you may need to take periodic brief breaks to stretch your neck, shoulders, and back muscles.

Comprehension Questions

1. Some keyboards, such as those that came with the original Macintoshes, don't have numeric keypads. Who at BVOS would appreciate a keyboard with a numeric keypad?
2. Within a given program, how many different actions can be assigned to a single function key on the computer?
3. What kinds of application programs absolutely require input devices other than the keyboard?

Using What You Know

1. Are there any computers at BVOS that do not need keyboards? If so, which ones? Why?
2. Which of your employees need typing skills the most? Why?
3. From the advertisements you can find in magazines, see if you can tell whether keyboards are typically included when you buy a computer or are typically purchased separately. What does an average computer keyboard cost?

Pointing Devices

The keyboard provides one important way to interact with the computer. However, as anyone who can't type knows, the keyboard can be an unnatural mechanism for human interaction. Another family of devices, which attempts to make up for the shortcomings of the keyboard, is broadly classified as pointing devices. A **pointing device** allows the user to interact with the computer simply by pointing to parts of the screen.

Some form of pointing device — most often a mouse — is a standard component of almost every prepackaged microcomputer available today. The reason is that more and more programs are incorporating graphical user interfaces (GUIs). In a GUI, commands can be executed by selecting the command name using the pointer (though there are often keyboard methods for doing the same thing). In addition to GUIs, which are generally easier to use with a pointing device, modern graphics software virtually requires the use of one.

The Mouse

A **mouse** (Figure 7-10) is a pointing device that enables the user to identify a position on the screen by moving a tool around on a horizontal surface, such as a desktop or a mouse pad.

As the mouse is moved across the surface, the cursor on the screen moves correspondingly. The mouse can be used to select icons or commands on a menu, to move text and data in a program, or to move the text cursor around the document. A mouse is used in graphics programs to mark parts of graphic images and to create illustrations. Many programs — especially those that incorporate a graphical user interface — are beginning to require the use of a mouse.

The mouse was developed at the Stanford Research Institute. Apple popularized the device by packaging it with the Macintosh, beginning with the first Macs sold in 1984. The mouse, in fact, was a major part of Apple's original advertising campaign. In the ad they used, they encouraged users to "test drive" the Mac. Their claim that the mouse made the Mac easier to use than the PC was hotly contested by PC users, but the Mac and its mouse-dependent GUI were a big hit. Over time, many developers of software for the PC began to tap into the popularity of the mouse in an effort to make the PC more user friendly.

Figure 7-10
A Mac mouse, a trackball,
and a PC mouse.

A mouse controls a mouse pointer, or mouse cursor, on the screen. To use the mouse, you push it around the desktop or mouse pad to move the mouse pointer to the desired position on screen. You then initiate some action with a mouse button. A mouse has one, two, or three buttons on it. To select something on the screen, such as a command, a graphic object, or a GUI icon, you move the mouse pointer to the command, object, or icon, then **click** once with the main mouse button (with two- and three-button mice, this is usually the leftmost button). To move an item across the screen, you move the pointer to the item, press and hold the mouse button, and **drag** the item to the new location. Finally, you can **double-click** (click twice in rapid succession) to select an item and initiate an action at the same time. Clicking, dragging, and double-clicking are the three basic techniques used with a mouse.

A **trackball** is a device that provides the functionality of a mouse, but doesn't roll around on the desk. A trackball is like an upside down mouse. It is a ball that rolls around in a base, and it controls the pointer on the screen. Buttons, which work much like mouse buttons, are located on the side of the unit.

Trackballs are especially popular with portable and laptop computers like the one shown in Figure 7-11, because an appropriate surface for a mouse is not always available when using a laptop or portable computer.

Light Pens and Digitizer Tablets

A **light pen** (Figure 7-12) is a light-sensitive, pen-shaped instrument that is connected to a video terminal. The user puts the light pen against the desired point on the screen and presses a button on the pen to identify the screen location. Pressing this button causes the pen to sense light. The place being illuminated identifies the screen location. Light pens are used in place of keyboards to select menu items and to draw. They are especially popular in environments such as auto shops, where dirt and grease make keyboards impractical.

Some other systems use a pen that is connected by a wire to a **digitizer tablet**, which acts as a surface for the pen to "write" on while the screen cursor creates a corresponding image. The digitizer tablet allows the user to write, draw, select command choices, or just replace the cursor with the pen. This technology is used in point of sale entries, warehouse inventory, and with graphics software (Figure 7-13).

Touch Screens

Touch screens can only loosely be defined as pointing devices, because the "pointing device" is actually the user's finger. Such screens permit the user to touch certain areas of a monitor to give commands. For example, instead of typing a command to view market information, the user can simply touch a menu item called MARKET INFORMATION with a finger. Touch screens are important components in the new technology called multimedia, where computers incorporate video, voice, graphics, and text into applications. Although few software packages currently utilize touch screens, they are gaining popularity quickly

Figure 7-11 The Macintosh PowerBook includes a built-in trackball.

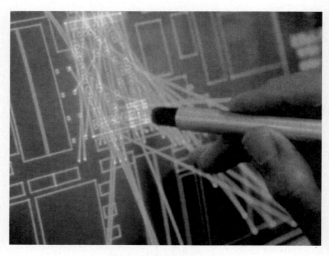

Figure 7-12 A light pen.

for applications in retail stores. They help customers find items, receive coupons and information about products, access bridal registries, take blood pressure, and even buy lottery tickets (Figure 7-14).

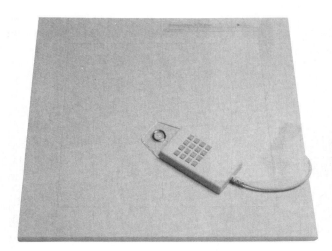

Figure 7-13   A digitizer tablet used as part of a graphics workstation.

Figure 7-14   Touch screens like this one are becoming common in department stores, supermarkets, and other retail stores.

Comprehension Questions

1. Can you think of a reason why mice are more popular than trackballs, even though trackballs take up less room on the desk?
2. Why are function keys used less often than they used to be?
3. What arguments can be made for using keyboard commands rather than mouse commands?

Using What You Know

1. On which computers at BVOS would it be most advantageous to have a mouse? On which would the mouse be dispensable?
2. Why is a pointing device an important part of a desktop publishing system?
3. How might a pen and digitizer tablet be used to streamline data entry in a stockroom?

Scanning Devices: Automating the Input Process

Both keyboards and pointers are used when data must be entered manually. Sometimes, though, the data that we need to input already exists on paper or in some other printed form. **Scanners** automate the process of data entry by reading an image and translating it into digital code. They do this by shining a light at the image and recording the intensity of the light that is reflected. With this technique, scanners can be used to digitize text, photographs, graphics, and bar codes to create binary code.

Figure 7-15
The results of digitizing a photo with a flat-bed scanner.

Most of the scanners used with microcomputers are two-dimensional image scanners. The images most frequently digitized are pages of text and graphic images. These scanners are classified as flat-bed or hand-held, and as color or gray-scale. With a flat-bed scanner, the image is placed on a flat piece of glass in much the same way a piece of paper is placed on a photocopier (Figure 7-15). Hand-held scanners are much smaller, with scanning fields usually no wider than 4½ inches. Gray-scale scanners reduce both color and black-and-white images to shades of gray. Color scanners are able to record the color of the image being scanned.

Optical Character Recognition

Using a scanner requires application software that can interpret the image that is created. Normally, when an image is scanned, graphics software is used to save the image as a bitmap file. If text is scanned, however, the computer requires software with **optical character recognition (OCR)** capabilities to regenerate text from a bit-mapped image that was created by a scanner. Once the text is read by the OCR software, it can be manipulated, edited, and printed by word processing or DTP software. The IRS uses OCR to convert the bit-mapped files created from scanning completed 1040 forms back to text.

As OCR software becomes more advanced, more and more types of print can be recognized. Advanced OCR software is becoming better and better at recognizing handwriting and converting it into ASCII text. Thus, a page of notes that you take for class can be turned into a document without your retyping the text.

Bar-Code Readers

Although the most common type of scanner used with microcomputers is the image scanner, bar-code readers are actually much more prevalent items, though they are generally used with larger computer systems. **Bar-code readers**, such as the one shown in Figure 7-16, are used to read bar codes, such as the universal product code, or UPC, symbol used on products in grocery and retail stores. Bar-code readers are faster than human data entry and are far more accurate. Using bar codes, a photo-electric scanner converts the succession of stripes into a code. The code identifies the product and data related to it. In the supermarket, the data is usually a brief description of the item and the price. Because the point of sale software that interprets the bar code is normally connected to an inventory database, this data can be used to track inventory. Thus, when an item is purchased, the item is automatically deducted from the store's inventory. When a number of items have been purchased, the software can automatically order new stock and relay financial data to the store's accounting system.

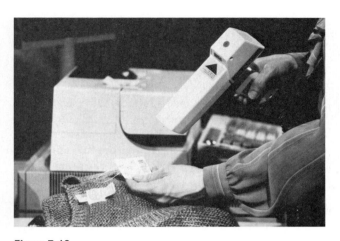

Figure 7-16
The most common type of scanner is the bar-code reader.

Voice Input

Science fiction writers have been writing for half a century about machines that can understand our spoken commands. Today fact is meeting fiction. **Voice input** systems scan the sound of your voice, digitize the data, and compare the digitized sound to a set of commands. If there is a match, the action associated with that sound is performed. With voice input, you can quickly and easily accomplish tasks such as telling the computer to save your current document. Voice input systems are invaluable to people whose physical handicaps would otherwise prevent them from using computers.

Interpreting digitized sound is a difficult problem. There are vast differences in the way people pronounce words. Consequently, we need to train the computer to understand how we say certain sounds. To do this, we initialize the voice system by saying certain key words and sounds into a microphone when the computer tells us to. This information is captured in a voice template that is then used to interpret what we say. Each subsequent statement is compared to the template before it is converted into text.

Comprehension Questions

1. What do you think are the most important sounds to record on a voice template? Why?
2. What skill is no longer required by sales clerks in stores that have bar-code readers?
3. If OCR software is not used, what type of application is most likely to use scanned images?

Using What You Know

1. How is optical character recognition like scanning your voice?
2. If headquarters printed bar codes on all their packaging, which of the BVOS computers would you want to equip with bar-code readers?
3. How might a gray-scale flat-bed scanner with OCR software be used at BVOS?

Monitors

A **monitor** is simply a device that displays output on a screen. The monitor in a microcomputer is generally the default output device. In other words, if you don't tell the CPU to send data somewhere else, it sends the data to its monitor and the output is displayed on your computer screen. There are a wide variety of monitors available, varying in type, size, resolution, ability to display color, and several other factors.

Monitor screens are made up of pixels, which are tiny dots (Figure 7-17). A **pixel**, which stands for *picture element*, is the smallest graphic unit on the screen. A pixel consists of one dot on a monochrome screen and three dots (red, green, and blue), or clusters of these dots, on a color screen. The density of the pixels on the screen determines the resolution of the

Figure 7-17 A computer screen contains a grid of pixels similar to the ones shown here but much smaller and closer together. In a color monitor, each pixel is composed of three dots: one blue, one red, and one green. The shade of each pixel is determined by combining these three colors.

monitor. **Resolution** refers to the degree of sharpness and clarity of the images displayed. Factors affecting the resolution include the overall dimensions of the screen, the total number of pixels, and, for color monitors, the **dot pitch**, the distance between the three colored dots that make up a single pixel. (Dot pitch does not apply to monochrome monitors.) The lower the dot pitch the sharper the image. For example, if you see an ad for a monitor that reads "15-inch, .28mm, 1024 x 768," this monitor measures 15 inches diagonally, the dot pitch is .28 mm, and there are 768 rows of pixels, with 1024 pixels in each row.

Types of Monitors

There are two main types of monitors: CRT monitors and flat-panel monitors. The types are differentiated by the methods they use to display an image.

CRT Monitors.   The **cathode ray tube,** or **CRT**, works just like your television. As shown in Figure 7-18, a special type of vacuum tube sprays a stream of electrons, which are directed onto a piece of glass that is coated with phosphor. When the electrons hit the phosphor, the phosphor glows.

The phosphor on the piece of glass, or screen, is organized into pixels. The phosphor in each pixel quickly fades after the electron beam passes. Consequently, the pixels need to be refreshed frequently by the beam. If they are not refreshed frequently enough, the screen appears to flicker. To give you an idea of how noticeable flicker is, manufacturers sometimes list how many times the screen is refreshed each second. The unit provided is Hertz (Hz), which measures cycles per second. Monitors generally operate at at least 60 Hz.

CRT monitor manufacturers go to great pains to eliminate flicker. The most popular method currently available for reducing flicker is a noninterlaced screen. Televisions use interlaced screens, which means that the electron beam starts at the top of the screen and scans every other row in each vertical pass — the odd rows on the first pass and the even rows on the second. The screen appears to be refreshed

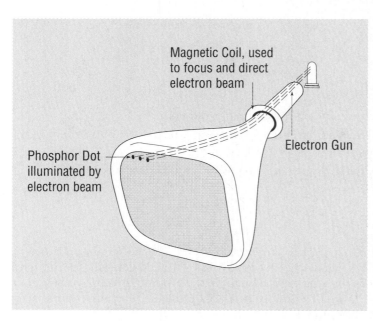

Magnetic Coil, used to focus and direct electron beam

Electron Gun

Phosphor Dot illuminated by electron beam

Figure 7-18
How an image is created by a cathode ray tube.

about 60 times per second. But in fact, each line of pixels is refreshed only 30 times per second; each line is refreshed every other cycle. Noninterlaced screens refresh every row with every pass. A computer can more easily refresh every other row because each pass requires only half as much information. Noninterlacing requires more data, but flicker is less noticeable. Monitor ads usually indicate if a screen is noninterlaced, or NI, because the reduced flicker is a selling point. Noninterlacing can add significantly to a monitor's price.

Flat-Panel Monitors. The main limitation of CRT screens is that they must be at least several inches deep and often weigh several pounds. Furthermore, CRTs require a lot of power. As a result, they cannot be used in laptop computers, where everything must be light, compact, and energy efficient. These machines use **flat-panel displays** (Figure 7-19). There are currently three competing technologies in flat-panel monitors.

The most popular form of flat-panel display so far is the LCD monitor, which uses the same technology as digital watches. **LCD** stands for **liquid crystal display**. The pixels in an LCD are composed on liquid crystal and are suspended between two panes of glass with wires running through them, as shown in Figure 7-20. Usually, there is a light behind the back glass. In its normal state, the liquid crystal material is clear, and the light shines through. But when current shoots through the wire that runs through a pixel, the liquid becomes solid looking, and the light is blocked.

The two other techniques used in flat-panel displays are *gas-plasma* and *electroluminescence* (EL). Both tend to be easier to read than LCD monitors because, like a CRT, the screen itself emits light and therefore does not need to be backlit. **Gas-plasma displays** use gas that glows when it is electrically charged. **Electroluminescent displays**, like CRT displays, use phosphor, but they cause the phosphor to glow with perpendicular sets of wires (Figure 7-21 on the next page).

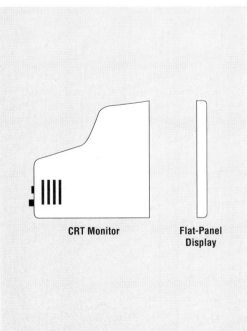

CRT Monitor   **Flat-Panel Display**

Figure 7-19 CRT monitors are at least several inches deep and often weigh several pounds. Flat-panel monitors are thinner, lighter, and require less power.

Glass panels

Charged wire   Chambers filled with Liquid Crystal material   Uncharged wire

Figure 7-20 How an image is created with an LCD monitor.

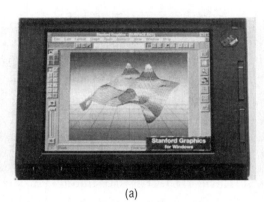 

Figure 7-21
The two leading types of flat-panel monitors: (a) LCD; (b) gas-plasma.

(a)   (b)

Monitor Size

Just like the televisions in our homes, monitors differ in size. Some monitors have very small screens; others can display two full pages of information at a time. Studies show that the bigger the screen, the less eye strain accompanies computer work. Large screens are becoming popular in graphical user interface environments and in desktop publishing applications.

Single-page monitors do not vary much in size. The average CRT screen for PCs is 14 inches, measured diagonally. Increasingly, users are choosing 16-inch or larger monitors. If you're planning to use your computer for desktop publishing, graphic design, or large spreadsheets, you should consider a screen that is larger than 14 inches. A 20-inch monitor, for example, allows you to display two facing 8-inch pages. Unfortunately, large screen monitors are significantly more expensive than their 14-inch counterparts. Be sure that your software can adjust the amount of information it places on the screen to take advantage of the larger screen. Figure 7-22 compares some of the monitors available with the Macintosh.

Monochrome and Color Monitors

The first characteristic that buyers usually consider when purchasing a monitor is whether or not they need the screen to display color. A **monochrome** monitor displays images in one color against a background of a different color. The most common colors are black, amber, or green characters on white or black backgrounds. Amber is considered easiest on the eyes. Many early PC monitors could display only 25 lines of type at one time, with 80

(a)   (b)   (c)   (d)

Figure 7-22   Macintosh monitors: (a) the compact 9-inch screen; (b) the 13-inch screen, standard on the Mac II and other large footprint models; (c) the full-page monitor; and (d) the dual-page monitor.

characters in each line. However, today most monochrome monitors can display graphics, too. Resolution tends to be better on monochrome monitors than on color monitors. They are very suitable for many home or office applications. By linking more than one bit to each pixel, **gray-scale** monitors are able to create varying darknesses in a single pixel. Monitors that are not gray-scale approximate shading with a checkerboard (or some other pattern) of light and dark pixels.

Color monitors provide more variation in the way information is presented. After all, color has a significant impact on the way information is perceived by the user. In addition, because human eyes differ in their ability to see certain colors, allowing the user to change the color of information that is presented can improve productivity and decrease eye strain.

A color monitor creates all other colors by combining red, green, and blue. For this reason, color monitors are sometimes referred to as *RGB monitors*. Color monitors are similar to gray-scale monitors in that each pixel must be linked to a number of bits. The number of colors a pixel can display is determined by the number of bits linked to each pixel. The most primitive color monitors can display only four colors (red, green, blue, and black), using just two bits for each pixel. At the other end of the scale, 24-bit color monitors can display over 16 million colors with each pixel.

Graphic Cards for the PC

When using a PC or compatible, the type of graphics adapter or graphics card (the expansion board that must accompany the monitor) distinguishes monitors from each another. Macintosh machines all come with high-quality, high-resolution graphics capability and do not require an additional graphics adapter. A PC or compatible monitor, however, may be labeled CGA, EGA, VGA, or SVGA.

The Color Graphics Adapter (**CGA**) was the first type of color graphics monitor that was released with the IBM PC. CGA systems display 320 x 200 pixels (320 horizontally and 200 vertically) in four colors on the screen when the monitor is in graphics mode. CGA provides relatively primitive graphics capability, at least by today's standards. Enhanced Graphics Adapters (**EGA**) were the next generation: They can produce 16 colors on the screen, with 640 x 350 resolution. Video Graphics Array (**VGA**) monitors create even more vivid and clear images. As the name indicates, they are ideal for video graphics because they allow the user to choose from among over 200,000 different colors in 640 x 480 resolution, though only 16 colors can be displayed on the screen at once. With their high resolution, VGA monitors are appropriate for computer-aided design applications, business graphics, and video games. Super VGA, or **SVGA**, is capable of 1024 x 768 resolution, with 16 colors on the screen at any given time. At lower resolutions, SVGA adapters can display much higher numbers of colors at once.

The minimum standard resolution for IBM-compatible systems is 640 x 480. This standard is VGA. However, more users are turning to SVGA, which is 800 x 600 or 1024 x 768, depending on the software. SVGA is priced competitively with VGA. For 14-inch color monitors, the dot pitch should be .28 mm or lower.

Trying to select a video card can be perplexing. In general, the newer technology in VGA cards can produce sharper images more quickly than CGA or EGA cards, though the older monitors can be obtained for much less money. The more you use the monitor, the more you should be concerned with how the text and graphics look. If they are sharp and easy to read, then your eyes will tire less quickly. Moving to a graphical user interface will certainly encourage the use of higher resolution color monitors.

When purchasing a VGA or SVGA adapter card, it is important to make sure that it has enough internal memory. If you are using Windows or any graphics programs, insufficient memory may cause your system to slow down. Modern adapter cards often contain 1 MB of their own memory. If the memory on your card is not sufficient, it may be possible to buy an accelerator card to speed up your system.

Purchasing a Monitor

When purchasing a monitor, you must decide what kind of resolution and color you want, then select the hardware that will support those specifications. If you are planning to use your computer primarily for word processing and some spreadsheet work, a medium-resolution monitor will do. If you plan to perform desktop publishing and will be using multiple fonts and graphics, a screen with higher resolution will display those fonts and graphics more accurately.

The decision whether to purchase a color or monochrome monitor is based upon personal preference and economics. For example, GUIs can be easier to interpret in color, but the added convenience may not warrant the added cost. Although color is very desirable when doing graphics work on the screen, it is of little use when you print the graphics if you don't have a color printer.

Buying a monitor involves the purchase of two pieces of equipment: the monitor itself and the video graphics card that goes inside the computer. You should make sure that the card and the monitor are compatible, because some cards cannot communicate with some monitors. In general, a VGA card can communicate only with a VGA-compatible monitor.

When you shop for a monitor, ask the dealer to demonstrate how it displays text and graphics in several applications. Check the clarity of small type; this is an important test for a monitor.

Comprehension Questions

1. How many bits must be connected to each pixel to display 256 colors or 256 shades of gray?

2. When you do graphics work, why might it still be appropriate to have a color monitor even though you don't have a color printer?

3. How many more pixels are there on an SVGA screen than on an EGA screen?

Using What You Know

1. Who at BVOS (or which group) will be least concerned with the resolution and color on the screen?

2. Compare the cost of a high-resolution (1024 x 768) monochrome monitor with that of a high-resolution color monitor. If you were using the monitor on a daily basis, would the difference in cost deter you from buying the color monitor? Why or why not?

3. Describe, in detail, the kind of monitor you, as president of BVOS, have on your laptop. More important, why do you have such a monitor?

Printers

Besides monitors, the only other standard output device is the printer. Printing is the creation of text or graphic images on paper. Printed output is often referred to as **hard copy**, while output on the screen is known as **soft copy**.

There are three types of printers to which microcomputers are commonly connected: dot matrix printers, ink-jet printers, and laser printers.

Dot Matrix Printers

The most prevalent type of printer used with microcomputers is the dot matrix printer. **Dot matrix printers** create images with a set of pins that push an inked ribbon against the paper. Dot matrix printers are often compared by the number of pins they use to impact the paper. The most common kinds are 9-pin and 24-pin printers. The larger the number, the higher the print quality. As shown in Figure 7-23, a 24-pin printer creates characters that are smoother and more fully formed than a 9-pin printer. A popular dot matrix printer is shown in Figure 7-24.

Although dot matrix printers do not produce the highest quality print, they are very popular, primarily because they are the least expensive type of printer. Another advantage is that, among the three main printer types, dot matrix printers are the only ones to physically strike the paper. As a result, they are called **impact printers**. The only other type of impact printer is the daisy wheel printer, which works like some typewriters, with letters on a spinning wheel that are pushed against the paper. Daisy wheel printers are still found in many schools and offices, though few are now being sold. Impact printers are necessary when printing on multicopy forms, such as bills and receipts. One disadvantage of impact printers is that when in operation, they are louder than other types.

Similar to a dot matrix printer is a thermal printer. This printer burns small dots onto special paper to create an image. Again, the more dots, the better the print. Thermal dot matrix printers are also popular in fax machines.

INTERNATIONAL

INTERNATIONAL

Figure 7-23
Magnified letters from 9-pin and 24-pin dot matrix printers.

Figure 7-24
A popular dot matrix printer.

Ink-Jet Printers

Ink-jet printers create images by shooting tiny droplets of ink at the paper (Figure 7-25). The aim of the spray is much more precise than the pins of a dot matrix printer, so the resolution of the image is far better. Color ink-jet printers are able to create color images by combining red, green, blue, and black ink. Ink-jet printers are usually about twice as fast as dot matrix printers. However, they often require coated paper; even good-quality bond paper makes the ink look fuzzy.

Laser Printers

The preferred printer among microcomputer users is the laser printer. A **laser printer** uses laser beams to project an image onto a photosensitive drum, where powdered ink called *toner* is bonded to the paper with heat (Figure 7-26). The technology used is very similar to that used in photocopiers.

Although laser printers cannot achieve the quality of print normally found in books, their output is more than sufficient for most business and personal applications. When used at the office, a laser printer is generally shared by several employees due to its cost. However, the cost of laser printers is dropping. Figure 7-27 shows a popular laser printer.

Color laser printers combine colored toner to create their images. Color printers are used primarily for desktop publishing. Base your selection of a color printer on speed, resolution, the number of colors needed, and the ease and cost of ink replacement.

Comparing Printers

There are several factors to take into account when comparing printers. Printers vary in the quality of print, speed, software compatibility, available fonts, and of course, cost.

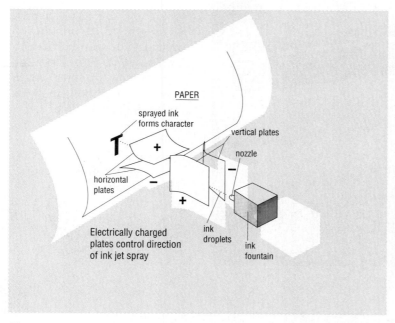

Figure 7-25   Ink-jet printers create images by spraying tiny drops of ink onto the paper.

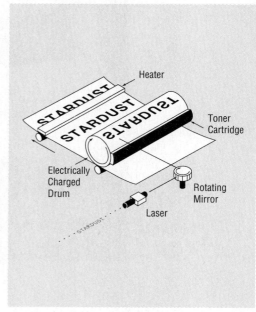

Figure 7-26   How a laser printer creates an image.

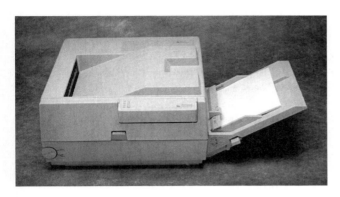

Figure 7-27
A typical laser printer.

Quality of Print. Print quality is measured in various ways. The simplest comparison is between letter-quality and near letter-quality print. A printer that can produce **letter-quality print** creates characters that are comparable in quality to typewriter print. Printers that produce **near letter-quality (NLQ) print** create characters that are less sharp. Dot matrix and thermal printers are known for being near letter quality, while laser and ink-jet printers are known for their letter-quality type. Figure 7-28 shows the difference between near letter-quality and letter-quality output.

As mentioned, the near letter-quality output of a dot matrix printer is measured by how many pins the printer uses. Letter-quality printers are often compared by the number of dots per inch (dpi) they create. A higher number means higher quality text. Typically, laser printers operate at a minimum of 300 dpi, though 600 dpi is common and much higher numbers are available. Ink-jet printers are able to print up to about 300 dpi.

Dot matrix printers are often purchased when the user is concerned with the content of what the computer produces rather than how the printed copy looks. Dot matrix printers are also necessary for printing on multiple-copy forms. They will provide adequate output for most users. In addition to being less expensive than a laser printer, a dot matrix printer requires less periodic maintenance. Also, those with a large number of pins and fresh ribbons can produce near letter-quality output. However, when presentation of the output is a major concern, such as a presentation to a client, letter-quality printers are more desirable.

Printer Speed. Another major factor distinguishing one printer from another is the speed with which it creates characters or images. There are two methods for measuring printer speed, depending on how the printer creates a page of text. Dot matrix and ink-jet printers print one character at a time and are therefore measured in terms of **characters per second (cps)**. Dot matrix printers commonly print about 100 cps, though modern ones may print faster. Ink-jet printers often print twice that fast. Cps figures are useful for comparison, but

(a)   (b)   (c)

made his
work
basis for
from the

made his
work
basis for
from the

made his
work
basis for
from the

Figure 7-28   (a) A close-up of NLQ output from a 24-pin dot matrix printer; (b) output from a 300 dpi ink-jet printer
(c) output from a 600 dpi laser printer.

are often misleading, because they are calculated based on the time it takes to print one line. The figure does not take into account the time it takes to move the paper to the next line.

Laser printers use a more reliable figure, known as **pages per minute**, or **ppm**, because they lay out an entire page and print it with a rolling drum that is as wide as the page. Laser printers range between 4 and 25 ppm, though most operate at about 6 ppm. By comparison, ink-jet printers can print about three pages per minute. In general, the faster the printer, the more expensive it is, regardless of how the letters are printed on the page. Naturally, the speed of a printer becomes more of an issue if several people are going to share a single printer.

When considering the speed of any printer, you must remember that the figures given by the manufacturer are for printing pages of text and for printing in black and white. As soon as you begin to add graphics and color to your document, your printing speeds will drop dramatically. This is because graphics and color require far more memory than text. For example, one page of text, even if it is dense and complicated, is not likely to require more than 10 K of memory. One page of bit-mapped graphics, however, can occupy more than 200 K. The length of time it takes the printer to print the page is closely related to the amount of memory that the page requires.

Software Compatibility. When you use a printer, you have to make sure that your application or operating system software knows what kind of printer you want to use, because different printers are controlled with different codes. To use a printer, your software needs a **printer driver**, which is a small piece of software that translates the CPU's output into codes that the printer understands.

With so many printers on the market, creating and maintaining drivers can be over-whelming. Adobe Systems has attempted to solve this problem by suggesting that printers be supplied with special purpose CPUs that can do the work of the printer driver. The computer is then able to send the printer a standard set of control codes, so all software can send the same output to any printer. The Adobe standard is called **PostScript** (Figure 7-29). PostScript printers are usually more expensive because of the increased processing capabil-ities of the printer. Some non-PostScript printers can be converted by installing a PostScript printer cartridge into the printer. Although not as prevalent, another standard for laser printers is Hewlett-Packard's Printer Control Language, PCL.

Figure 7-29
Three standard PostScript fonts: Times, Palatino, and Helvetica, all in 16-point type.

TIMES   PALATINO   HELVETICA

Available Fonts. A printer needs instructions about how to print various fonts. These instructions may come from software that is stored in the computer, or they may come from a ROM chip in the printer. Fonts that are built into the printer are called **internal fonts**. Fonts that are downloaded from the computer are called **soft fonts** (because they come from software). You can increase the number of soft fonts by purchasing additional fonts, either individually or as font libraries. Internal fonts can be supplemented by adding a cartridge to the printer.

The number of fonts available to you will affect the versatility of the printer. For most business and personal applications, you can get by with just a few fonts. However, if your work involves DTP, you might always be pushing for new fonts. In this case, you should consider buying a printer with a large supply of internal memory; each font that you need to download will take up space in your printer's memory. Having a PostScript printer can solve some of your font problems because many PostScript printers come with 35 internal fonts, each of which can be scaled to different point sizes.

Comprehension Questions

1. Of dot matrix, ink-jet, and laser printers, which type prints the fastest?
2. Are thermal printers useful for printing on multiple-copy forms? Why or why not?
3. Say a dot matrix printer can print at 100 cps. How long would it take the printer to generate a page with 250 words of six characters each? How many pages per minute is this? Does this figure seem believable?

Using What You Know

1. Which is higher resolution, a 300 dpi laser printer or a 1024 x 768 SVGA monitor?
2. Which computers at BVOS should be linked to dot matrix printers and why?
3. Does anyone at BVOS need a laser printer? Why or why not?

Summary Points

Getting Data "In" and Information "Out"

☐ In common usage, an input device is hardware that the user employs to give data to the computer, and an output device is hardware used to present information to the user.

The Keyboard and Its Parts

☐ The keyboard was the first input device widely used with microcomputers.
☐ It remains the most versatile input device.

Alphanumeric Keys

☐ The alphanumeric keys form the QWERTY keyboard, which resembles the standard typewriter keyboard.

Function Keys

☐ The function keys accomplish tasks that are determined by the program being used.

Cursor-Movement Keys

☐ The cursor-movement keys are used to move the cursor around the screen or document.

The Numeric Keypad

☐ The numeric keypad is a convenient alternative to the numbers that run across the top of the alphanumeric keys.

Lights on the Keyboard

☐ Many keyboards have three lights to indicate the condition of three toggle switches: the Num Lock, Scroll Lock, and Caps Lock keys.

Data Entry with the Keyboard

☐ *Data entry* can refer to a job that requires typing or entering numbers, or it can simply refer to keyboard input.

A Few Words About Ergonomics: The Human Factor

☐ There are optimum kinds of equipment and optimum ways to adjust the equipment to maximize your comfort and minimize the risk of injury when you use the computer.

Pointing Devices

☐ Pointing devices have become more common as GUIs have gained popularity.

The Mouse

☐ The three basic mouse techniques are clicking, dragging, and double-clicking.
☐ The Macintosh popularized the mouse.
☐ A trackball is essentially an upside-down mouse that is especially useful in laptop computers.

Light Pens and Digitizer Tablets

☐ A pen is applied directly to the screen or a digitizer tablet to write, draw, or select command choices.

Touch Screens

☐ Touch screens, which allow the user to use a finger as a pointing device, are becoming popular in many retail stores.

Scanning Devices: Automating the Input Process

☐ Scanners automate data entry by reading a printed image.
☐ Scanners can be color or gray-scale, hand-held or flat-bed.

Optical Character Recognition

☐ OCR software enables the computer to regenerate text by scanning a printed document.

Bar-Code Readers

☐ Bar-code readers are used primarily in point of sale systems to keep track of inventory and speed sales.

Voice Input

☐ Voice input systems are becoming more adept at understanding spoken commands.

Monitors

☐ The monitor is usually the default output device.

Types of Monitors

CRT Monitors

☐ The cathode ray tube is the same technology as used in televisions.
☐ The resolution is determined by the density of pixels.
☐ The amount of flicker is determined by the refresh rate and whether the screen is interlaced or non-interlaced.

Flat-Panel Monitors

☐ Flat-panel displays are useful in portables and laptops because they use less power, weigh less, and take up less space than standard monitors.
☐ The three common types of flat-panel displays are LCD, gas-plasma, and electroluminenscent.

Monitor Size

☐ Bigger screens are useful in DTP work and cause less eye strain.
☐ The average monitor is 14 inches, measured diagonally.

Monochrome and Color Monitors

☐ Monitors can generate shades of gray or color by linking each pixel to more than one bit.

☐ Color monitors generate all other colors by combining red, green, and blue.

Graphic Cards for the PC

☐ Graphics monitors require a CGA, EGA, VGA, or SVGA graphics card that is compatible with the monitor.

Purchasing a Monitor

☐ The kind of monitor you purchase should depend on economics and how you will use it.

Printers

Dot Matrix Printers

☐ Dot matrix printers create an image by striking the paper with inked pins; the number of pins determines the resolution.

☐ Because their pins strike the paper, dot matrix printers can be used for multiple-copy forms.

☐ Thermal printers burn small dots onto special paper.

Ink-Jet Printers

☐ Ink-jet printers shoot tiny drops of ink at the paper.

Laser Printers

☐ Laser printers work much like photocopiers.

Comparing Printers

Quality of Print

☐ Dot matrix and thermal printers can be NLQ, while ink-jet and laser printers can be letter quality.

☐ Letter-quality printers measure their resolution in dpi.

Printer Speed

☐ Dot matrix and ink-jet printers measure speed in cps.

☐ Laser printers measure speed in ppm, a more accurate measurement than cps.

☐ Printing graphics and color will slow down any type of printer.

Software Compatibility

☐ Printers require printer drivers.

☐ PostScript printers have extra processing power built in to alleviate the need for printer drivers.

Available Fonts

☐ Internal fonts are built into the printer.

☐ Soft fonts are downloaded from the computer.

Knowing the Facts

True/False

1. OCR is capable of reading handwriting but not printed text.
2. In a color monitor, each pixel is controlled by a single bit.
3. Bar-code readers are most often used in point of sale systems.
4. The layout of the keys on the keyboard was originally designed to slow down typists.
5. Strictly speaking, the numeric keypad on a keyboard is not a necessity, because it provides no additional functionality.
6. Cps is a more accurate measurement than ppm.
7. Interlaced screens are less prone to flicker than non-interlaced screens.
8. Color monitors create all other colors by combining red, yellow, and blue.
9. Because of the popularity of GUIs, the keyboard is quickly being replaced by the mouse.
10. The mouse is the most common pointing device packaged with laptops because of the limited space available on the keyboard.

Short Answer

1. PostScript printers help alleviate the need for including a wide variety of _____ with each software package.
2. _____ fonts are downloaded from the computer to the printer each time they are used.
3. Refresh rate is measured in cycles per second, also known as _____.
4. LCD monitors are popular in _____ computers because they require less space and power than CRT monitors.
5. A _____ provides the functionality of a mouse, but doesn't need to roll around on a horizontal surface.
6. _____ printers create an image with a technique similar to that of a photocopier.
7. _____ printers are effective for printing on multiple-copy forms.
8. The Caps Lock, Scroll Lock, and Insert keys are referred to as _____ because they control features that can be turned either on or off.
9. What family of computers popularized the mouse?
10. To translate a printed page into ASCII text, a scanner must be used with _____ software.

Answers

True/False

1. F
2. F
3. T
4. T
5. T
6. F
7. F
8. F
9. F
10. F

Short Answer

1. printer drivers
2. Soft
3. Hertz or Hz
4. laptop or portable
5. trackball
6. Laser
7. Dot matrix
8. toggle switches
9. Macintosh
10. OCR

Challenging Your Understanding

1. Look at *PC Magazine* or *PC World*. What is the price of laser printers? How does this compare with a dot matrix printer that can print near letter quality?

2. Laser printers use toner cartridges. How much do they cost? Does their price affect your laser printer decision? How long do they last?

3. If we could talk to computers, would we need any of the input devices discussed in this chapter? Why?

4. Try to determine how much a printer should cost as a percentage of the cost of the entire computer system. What types of applications require the cost of the printer to be a higher percentage of the total?

5. What are some of the legal and ethical issues associated with using image scanners?

CHAPTER 8

Storage Devices

Key Terms

CD-ROM
directories
disk crash
diskette
diskette drive
folder
formatted (initialized)
hard disk
hard disk drive
nonremovable storage
optical disk
read-write head
removable storage
storage device
storage media
subdirectories
tape drive
write protect

Objectives

In this chapter you will learn to:

- Differentiate between storage devices and storage media
- Describe how diskettes are formatted
- List the storage capacities of double-density and high-density diskettes
- Explain how diskettes can be write protected
- Understand important ways to take care of diskettes
- Describe what happens in a disk crash
- Describe two advantages of hard disks over diskettes
- Name the most important advantage diskettes have over hard disks
- Name and describe two common schemes for creating hierarchical file structures
- Define the three magnetic alternatives to internal hard disks
- Describe how tape drives can be used to back up hard disks
- Define CD-ROM and name three other emerging storage technologies

Storage Devices and Storage Media

All of the hardware components we have talked about up to this point have been "devices": processing devices, input devices, and output devices. In this chapter we discuss storage devices, but we will also be discussing storage *media*. **Storage devices** are used to put the data on and take the data off of storage media. **Storage media** are passive pieces of hardware that merely hold data. For example, as shown in Figure 8-1, a diskette *drive* is a storage device. It is connected, via the data bus, to the CPU, and is therefore an I/O device. It is used to read data from and write data to a diskette, which is a storage medium. (*Medium* is the singular form of *media*.)

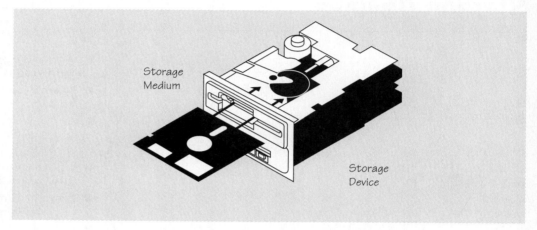

Storage
Medium

Storage
Device

Figure 8-1
A diskette drive is a
storage device. A diskette
is a storage medium.

Diskettes and Drives

The first type of storage device widely used with microcomputers was the diskette drive, and the first storage medium was the diskette. A **diskette**, sometimes called a floppy disk, is a round piece of mylar (plastic) coated with a magnetic substance called ferrous oxide and encased in a square plastic envelope or shell. The first standardized diskette was 8 inches in diameter. Today there are two common kinds of diskette: the 5¼-inch diskette and the 3½-inch diskette (Figure 8-2). The older of the two is the 5¼-inch diskette, which is encased in a flexible plastic envelope. This type is gradually being replaced by the 3½-inch diskette, which comes in a hard plastic case with a sliding cover. The 3½-inch type is winning the popularity contest not just because it is smaller, but because it can hold more data and, because of its case, is less vulnerable to damage and loss of data.

A **diskette drive** (also known as a floppy disk drive or

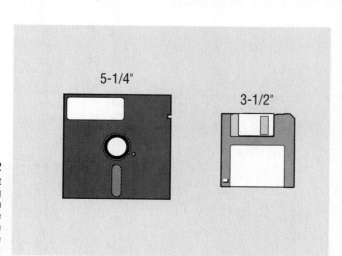

5-1/4"

3-1/2"

Figure 8-2
The 5¼-inch diskette at
left is gradually being
replaced by the 3½-inch
diskette. The 3½-inch type
is smaller, holds more
data, and is less vulnerable
to damage.

floppy drive) is the I/O device used to access the data on a diskette. The diskette drive (Figure 8-3) consists of a drive bay, where the diskette is inserted; the drive, which rotates the disk; and the most important part, the read-write head. A **read-write head** works like the recording and play heads of a cassette tape recorder. It reads the magnetic charges on the disk, records new charges when necessary, and erases old charges.

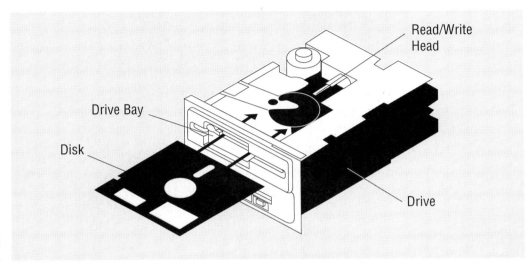

Figure 8-3
A 5¼-inch diskette drive.

How Data Is Organized on a Diskette

When you buy a new diskette, it is just what we have described: a piece of plastic with magnetic material on it. In order to be used, the diskette must be formatted. **Formatting** (**initializing** is the Mac term for the same process) is the process of mapping the magnetic surface into an arrangement of tracks and sectors that would look something like a dartboard if the arrangement were visible (Figure 8-4). First, the read-write head creates concentric circular tracks. Then the drive divides each track into sectors. This mapping enables the diskette drive to quickly locate any spot on the diskette.

Early diskettes held data on only one side. All modern diskettes, however, use both sides. The total number of tracks, sectors, and therefore bytes, on a diskette depend on the size of the diskette, the quality of the diskette material, and the capabilities of the diskette drive.

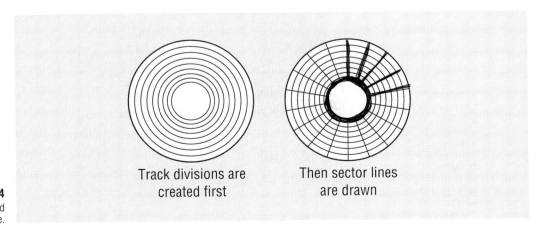

Track divisions are
created first

Then sector lines
are drawn

Figure 8-4
Organization of a formatted
diskette.

FLOPPY DISK CAPACITIES

Macintosh	5 1/4"	3 1/2"
Double Density	N/A	800 KB
High Density	N/A	1.44 MB
IBM		
Double Density	360 KB	720 KB
High Density	1.2 MB	1.44 MB
Extra Density*		2.88 MB

*requires Extra Density drive

Table 8-1

Summary of diskette capacities for PCs and Macs.

Most 5¼-inch diskettes hold either 360 K or 1.2 MB, depending on whether the diskette is double density or high density. Double-density diskettes have less capacity than high density. If used on a Macintosh, 3½-inch diskettes hold either 800K or 1.44 MB. On a PC or compatible, 3½-inch diskettes hold 720 K or 1.44 MB (Table 8-1).

Even with 3½-inch diskettes, PCs and Macs format diskettes differently. As a result, a PC cannot read a diskette that has been initialized on a Mac unless the PC has a special device that lets it do so. To address this compatibility problem, some Macs are equipped with a SuperDrive. With a utility program, the Mac can use the SuperDrive to read 3½-inch diskettes formatted on a PC.

Protecting Data: Just in Case

Although in general diskettes can be read or written to, it is possible to protect the data on the diskette from being written over by the read-write head. As shown in Figure 8-5, 5¼-inch diskettes have write-protect notches, and 3½-inch diskettes have write-protect tabs. If the notch is covered with a piece of tape or the tab is pushed so that a hole shows through the case, the drive's read-write head will not write data to the diskette. The data can then be read but not changed. The diskette is said to be **write protected**.

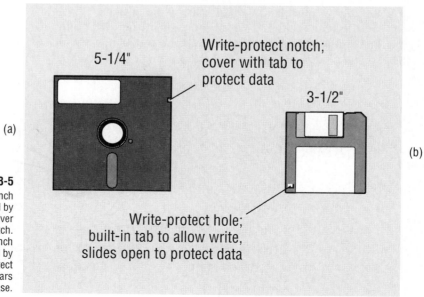

(a)

(b)

Figure 8-5

Data on 5¼-inch diskettes is protected by putting a piece of tape over the write protect notch. Data on 3½-inch diskettes is protected by pushing the write protect tab so a hole appears through the case.

Taking Care of Diskettes

When data is moved from memory to storage, it is translated from electrical charges into magnetic charges. The data is therefore more durable, because it no longer requires current from the power supply. It is by no means permanent, however. Not only can data be written over by the drive's read-write head, it can be destroyed by any number of environmental hazards. The following is a list of dos and don'ts for taking care of your diskettes:

- Do not touch the surface of the diskette. This is a common danger with 5¼-inch diskettes, because some part of the diskette is always visible. With 3½-inch diskettes, it's best simply to avoid sliding the protective cover.

- Don't remove a diskette from a drive when the drive light is on. The drive light tells you that the diskette is spinning and the read-write head may be reading or writing to the diskette. Removing the diskette when this is happening is likely to damage the data currently held on the diskette. It can also damage the head.

- Don't expose diskettes to any magnetic fields. In addition to real magnets, common problem items include paper clips, poorly insulated wires, and music speakers.

- Don't expose diskettes to excessive heat or excessive moisture.

- Do store diskettes upright when they are not being used.

- Do use diskette labels and label your diskettes carefully with descriptive names. It often helps to include the date that data was written on a diskette, and, if appropriate, the program that was used to create the files. If it isn't already obvious, you should also include the storage capacity of the diskette.

In addition to the above rules, 5¼-inch diskettes need added care because they do not have a hard protective shell. With 5¼-inch diskette

- Use only felt-tip pens when writing on diskette labels that are already attached to the diskette. Pencils, erasers, and ball-point pens require too much pressure and can damage the diskette surface.

- Do not stack anything on top of the diskette. The pressure may damage the data surface.

- When not in use, keep the diskette in a paper or plastic diskette envelope. The plastic envelopes that come with 3½-inch diskettes don't add much protection, but the 5¼-inch envelopes protect the exposed diskette surface.

- Don't ever force the diskette into the drive. If it doesn't fit easily, something is in the way.

- Don't bend or fold the diskette, and don't try to attach it to anything with a clip or staple.

With proper care, diskettes can last a long time, though you should never rely heavily on a diskette. If data is important, make sure there are at least two copies of it — more than two, if the data is truly vital.

Purchasing Diskette Drives

Computers used in homes and businesses generally have either one or two diskette drives. Having two drives is common on PCs because of the conflict between 3½ and 5¼-inch diskettes. Many IBMs now come with a single 3½-inch drive. Clones, however, tend to have one of each size. Although the 3½-inch drives are gaining popularity, there are still a lot of 5¼-inch drives out there. If you need to trade diskettes with someone who has only the older type of drive, you must have that kind of drive as well. Moreover, some PC software is provided only on 5¼-inch diskettes, though most developers make their products available on both sizes. If you are buying a PC with only one drive, you probably want the 3½-inch drive. If you are getting two, it's safest to have one of each.

When purchasing a Mac, the decision of how many drives to have installed is a simple one, since all Mac diskettes are 3½ inches. If you want to copy data between two diskettes in one step, you might want two drives. Otherwise, one is usually sufficient.

If you ever find that you need another diskette drive, you can probably add it. If there is room in your system unit, PCs can generally be upgraded with an additional internal drive. If there isn't room, you may be able to attach an external diskette drive like the one shown in Figure 8-6.

Figure 8-6
If you want to add another diskette drive but there is no room in your system unit, you can add an external drive like the one shown here.

Comprehension Questions

1. Diskette drives tend to be upward compatible. What does this tell you about high-density drives?
2. Is a RAM chip a device, a medium, or both?
3. Why can a paper clip be a hazard around a diskette?

Using What You Know

1. What is the difference in cost between a 10-diskette box of high-density 3½-inch diskettes and a 10-diskette box of double-density 3½-inch diskettes?

2.   What is the difference in cost between an external and an internal 3½-inch drive?

3.   For what kind of data is it a good idea to write protect your diskettes? What kind of data is best left on unprotected diskettes?

Hard Disks and Hard Disk Drives

Although most microcomputers made during the early 1980s relied on diskette drives as their sole storage device, it didn't take computer manufacturers long to realize that a more convenient method was needed. With entirely diskette-based systems, users had to switch diskettes in and out of drives constantly. First the diskette containing the operating system was inserted, the data was read into memory, and the diskette was removed. Then the application diskette was inserted. If a second diskette drive was available, a diskette could be put in the second drive to store data. Otherwise, the data diskette and application diskette had to be swapped in and out of the single drive as needed.

The solution to the problem was the internal **hard disk**, a large magnetic storage area built into the system unit (Figure 8-7). The **hard disk drive** is the I/O device that accesses data on the hard disk. The hard disk is sealed inside the hard disk drive. As a result, hard disks are known as **nonremovable storage**. By contrast, diskettes are **removable storage**, because the diskette can be taken out of the drive and placed in a different one.

Although it is often important to distinguish between diskettes and drives, the terms *hard disk* and *hard disk drive* are often used interchangeably. This rarely causes any confusion, since the disk is nonremovable.

In their early days, hard disks allowed users to keep at least the operating system and the application packages in one handy place. The diskette drive was always free for data files. Early hard disks were often 20 MB, which seemed like a lot when users were accustomed to nothing but diskettes. As program size grew and users began keeping their data files on the hard disk, however, 20 MB became

Figure 8-7
An internal hard disk inside the system unit

woefully inadequate. Today, hard disks of 10 times that size are becoming the norm. As an example, consider that Windows 3.1, a popular graphical user interface for PCs, takes up 10 MB, and you need to add another 4 to 15 MB for each application. And that's just for the software programs; you also need to store data, of course, and that requires more memory.

Hard Disks Compared to Diskettes

A hard disk is actually not one but a stack of rigid aluminum disks, called platters (Figure 8-8 on the next page). The hard disk is able to store more data than diskettes can because several disks are used, and because data can be packed on the metal far more densely than on mylar. The hard disk drive works the same way as the diskette drive, though there are some important differences in design.

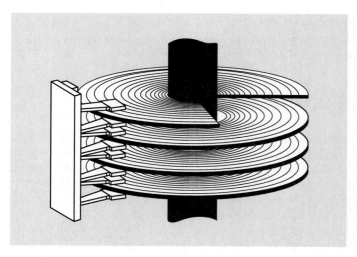

Figure 8-8
A hard disk is usually a stack of aluminum platters. The same tracks on different platters define a cylinder. Locations on the hard disk are defined by cylinder, side (which side of which platter), and sector.

First, there are a number of read-write heads, one for each side of each platter. Second, the drive and read-write heads are attached to the disk differently because the disk is never removed from the drive. Third, and most important, the read-write heads travel very close to the disk surface, but never touch the disk. Diskette drive read-write heads are designed to touch the diskette surface. If any contact occurs between a hard disk and the head, the system experiences a **disk crash** (also called a head crash). In a disk crash, data is lost and the disk and head often have to be replaced. Sometimes it's cheaper to just buy a whole new hard disk.

Preventing a disk crash is a tricky business, considering the disk spins at about 3000 revolutions per minute — about 45 miles per hour — and the head travels only 15 millionths of an inch above the platter. On a diskette, the residue from a fingerprint might be enough to obscure the data so the diskette drive's read-write head can't read it. But on a hard disk, a fingerprint can actually bridge the gap between the disk and the head and cause a crash. Figure 8-9 gives an idea of how close together the head and disk are. Now you know why the hard disk has to be sealed in a metal case.

Figure 8-9
Hair, dust, even a fingerprint is enough to cause a hard disk crash.

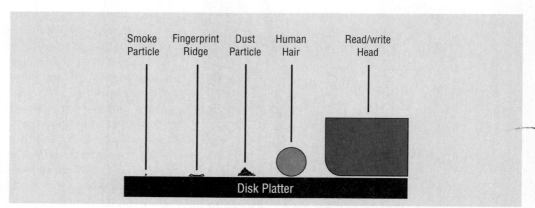

There are two major advantages of hard disks over diskettes: lots of storage capacity and fast access times. On the other hand, diskettes have the advantage of easy portability. Let's look at these factors one at a time.

Capacity.   Hard disks can have several hundred times the storage capacity of diskettes. With respect to data files, this added capacity is a huge convenience. With respect to modern applications packages, a hard disk's capacity is a necessity.

Access Time.   Hard disk drives work like common compact disk players. When we want to listen to song number seven on a CD, we must instruct the CD player to play the song. After receiving the command, the player must position the laser over the correct spot on the CD (Figure 8-10). In computer terms, this is called a *seek*. Next, we have to wait for the beginning of the song to rotate under the laser. This is called *rotational delay*. Finally, we wait while the player reads the digital data off the CD using the laser and sends it to the amplifier. This is the *transfer time*. Therefore, a hard disk's access time is the sum of the seek time, the rotational delay, and the transfer time.

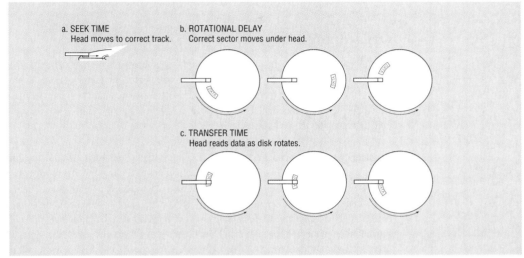

Figure 8-10
Access times for disk drives are the sum of (a) seek time, (b) rotational delay, and (c) transfer time.

In a hard disk, speed is the second most important feature, after storage capacity to consider. The speed at which your hard disk stores and retrieves data greatly affects your system's performance.

Portability.   The biggest advantage of diskettes over hard disks is easy portability. Data can be copied to a diskette and then taken home, passed to another user at the office, or even sent through the mail. Although programs are usually installed on a hard disk, they are originally supplied on diskettes because buyers must purchase them and bring them home before they can be installed. Software developers, in fact, are some of the biggest consumers of diskettes.

No matter how much a user may plan to depend on a hard disk, having a diskette drive is still a necessity for a standalone machine, because it's the usual way to get new software onto the hard disk.

Formatting a Hard Disk

Despite the differences in design, a hard disk is used just like a diskette. Before a hard disk can be used, it needs to be formatted. Formatting a hard disk divides it into tracks and sectors. With some computers, it is possible to partition the hard disk so that it can be treated as two or more smaller disks. This technique is just a method for organizing data, though, because the disk is still a single physical unit. As with diskettes, different operating systems format hard disks in different ways. This is generally not an issue, however, because hard disks are not normally exchanged between systems.

Types of Hard Disks

The least expensive and most popular hard disk is the IDE (integrated drive electronics). Some users who need a large-capacity drive or who want to expand their system with CD-ROM or tape drives prefer the SCSI (small computer systems interface, pronounced "scuz-ee") drive.

Organizing Files

Besides losing data from a disk crash, the biggest pitfall when using a hard disk is lack of good organization. On a disk, whether diskette or hard, files are listed in **directories**. The problem is that a large hard disk can easily store several thousand files. Without organization, all of these files would be listed in a single directory. Finding a single file among thousands could be almost impossible.

Subdirectories and Folders.   To solve the problem of disk organization, operating systems allow users to create hierarchical file structures. With a hierarchical structure, the user can break down the main directory (often called the root directory) into a group of **subdirectories**. In some operating systems, these subdirectories are referred to as **folders** because they are used in much the same way file folders are used in a filing cabinet. Each subdirectory or folder can contain files, other folders, or both. Except that they take up disk space, there is no logical limit to the number of subdirectories, so the user is free to create as intricate a hierarchy as he or she needs.

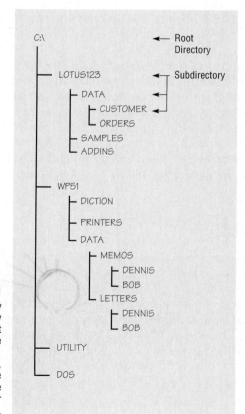

Figure 8-11
A hard disk directory structure, organized by application. The root directory contains the subdirectories LOTUS123, WP51, UTILITY, and DOS. The first two of these directories contain their own subdirectories.

Common Organizational Models.   On computers used in businesses, there are two common organizational models for storing files. The first could be called "organization by application" (Figure 8-11). When applications are installed on a hard disk, all the program files (the factory-created files that come with the software) for a single package are generally put in one subdirectory. Some users like to organize their data files according to the structure that these applications create, so that all of the documents created using a given application can be found in subdirectories within that application's subdirectory. For example, say you typically use two programs, WordPerfect and Lotus 1-2-3. The WordPerfect subdirectory might contain subdirectories called "Letters" and "Memos." The Letters and Memos subdirectories could, in turn, be subdivided according to the addressees of the letters and memos. Likewise, the Lotus 1-2-3 subdirectory might contain subdirectories for "Budgets" and "Forecasts."

Another popular organizational model might be called "organization by project" or "organization by client." In this scheme, an

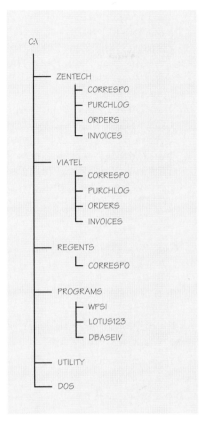

Figure 8-12
A hard disk directory structure, organized by client

example of which is shown in Figure 8-12, the program files for each application are still placed in their own directories, but no other files are stored there. Instead, data file subdirectories are created for each client or each project in progress. For example, at BVOS, the main directory of a disk might contain subdirectories with the names of companies that often buy supplies from you, such as Zentech, Viatel, and Regents. Each of these subdirectories could contain several types of application documents. Rather than being organized by application, they are grouped according to the nature of four smaller subdirectories: "Correspondence," "Purchase Logs," "Orders," and "Invoices."

These two organizational schemes are the most common, but there are plenty of others some perhaps even more effective or more efficient. Every user has different needs. Above all else, the structure should fit the need.

Alternatives to Internal Hard Disks

Throughout this section we have described the internal hard disk. There are, however, several other options for high-volume magnetic storage devices. An older computer that doesn't have an internal hard disk and doesn't have room to have one installed can be upgraded with an external hard disk (Figure 8-13). External disks work exactly the same way as internal ones, except that they are outside the system unit and are therefore somewhat more portable. An external hard disk can also be used to supplement the storage space of a computer that has an internal hard disk that is not large enough for the user's needs.

A second option is the hard card (Figure 8-14). Every disk drive requires a disk controller card, which is just a special type of expansion board connected to the motherboard. A hard

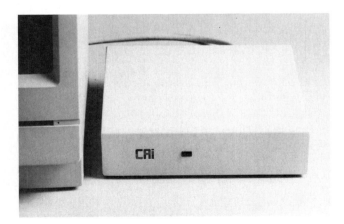

Figure 8-13 An external hard disk.

Figure 8-14 A hard card, which is plugged into an expansion slot in the motherboard.

Figure 8-15 A hard disk cartridge.

card combines the disk drive and the card by mounting a small hard disk directly on the controller board. Hard cards are now available as large as 105 MB, and they are growing quickly. They allow users with extra expansion slots to add storage without taking up space anywhere else.

A third option is the removable hard disk cartridge (Figure 8-15). The cartridge bridges the gap between the hard disk and the diskette by allowing the hard disk to be removed from the system unit. Disk cartridges allow the user to have virtually unlimited storage space, divided into large chunks of, say, 40 MB.

Comprehension Questions

1. Data access for CD players and disk drives requires the same three steps. So what is the basic difference between these two types of devices?

2. A hard disk cartridge is not truly a removable storage medium. What does this tell you about what is inside the cartridge?

3. In addition to transporting data, what other uses can you think of for diskettes?

Using What You Know

1. How large are hard disk cartridges now, and how much do they cost?

2. Compare the cost of a 200 MB hard disk and a comparable amount of hard disk cartridges.

3. What is the difference in price between a 200 MB external hard disk and a 200 MB hard internal disk?

Magnetic Tape

When you've got all your programs and data on one hard disk, one perpetual fear is that you'll experience a disk crash and lose everything. The fear is not unfounded; disk failures are regrettably common, and every user should back up his or her hard disk. As we explained when we covered utilities, software is available to make the process easier.

If you are backing up data onto diskettes, the process can be painful. Backing up a 100 MB hard disk, even with data compression techniques, can require 50 diskettes and take a great deal of time. To cure this inconvenience, hardware manufacturers have adapted cassette tape technology to computer storage needs. Using a cassette that looks very much like a music cassette, a **tape drive** (Figure 8-16) can copy the contents of an entire hard drive onto one tape. With such a device, you can tell your system to back itself up on the tape drive and then leave your computer to finish the process on its own. As with diskettes, you

Figure 8-16
Magnetic tape and a tape drive used for backup purposes.

can also back up designated files or groups of files — by name or by date created, for example — rather than backing up the entire hard disk.

Backing up with tape drives still requires backup utility software, but the software gives you added flexibility. Some software for tape drives allows you to schedule a backup when you aren't even present. As long as the computer is on and the cassette is in the drive, the tape drive will start backing up at a specified time. On the other hand, you might want to back up your hard disk while you continue to work with some other program. This may also be possible.

You might ask, "If cassettes can hold so much information, why don't we use them instead of hard disks?" The answer lies in the difference between sequential media and random-access media. A backup tape, like a cassette music tape, is a sequential medium. To find a particular piece of data on the tape, the tape drive must scan the tape sequentially, in forward or reverse, until it encounters the data. If you have ever looked for a song on a cassette, you know this can take some time.

A hard disk, however, is like a CD in that it is a random-access medium. When a CD player looks for a song, it only takes a second or two. The CD is mapped (formatted), and the player can use the map to jump directly to the right spot. After all, the distance between any two places on a CD can't be more than about five inches, whereas two spots on a cassette can be 100 yards apart. A hard disk is like a CD: Its surface is mapped and the read-write head can move to any point very quickly.

Other Forms of Tape

Cassettes are by far the most common type of tape used with microcomputers. Other types of tape are available, however. If you watch movies from the 1960s and 1970s, scientific and governmental computers are often shown with reel-to-reel tapes. Although reel-to-reel tape is not often used with microcomputers, it is still the standard means for backing up large amounts of data on minis and mainframes and for transferring data between the two.

How Often Should I Back Up?

Think about how much time and money you will spend if you cannot get a computer back to the state it was in before a hard disk failure in a reasonably short time. For example, if you spent three days creating a spreadsheet for a class or for work, would you mind spending another three days recreating that spreadsheet? What is that time worth to you? If you were writing a report that was printed two weeks ago, but was changed several times since the last time you printed it, how important were those changes?

No one is going to force you to back up your data. You have to decide how often to back up based upon how valuable your time is. Keep in mind that backing up is not a costless activity. It takes a while to back up a large disk drive. If you don't have the time to spare, this could be a tough decision. The answer to the question "How often should I back up?" is "Just often enough."

Also consider what you need to back up and when. You may not need to back up the entire hard disk every time you do a backup.

Optical Storage Technology

A disk that is written to and read by light is an **optical disk**. Although optical disks can store 600 MB or more of data and software, they are removable, like ordinary diskettes. The increased capacities of these devices are encouraging software manufactures to incorporate many more features into their systems than they did previously. In addition, users of small computers have access to a substantial amount of data that they previously could not store. Although optical disk technology is now considerably slower than its magnetic counterpart, changes in technology will improve this problem.

Some optical disks, like compact disk read-only memory, or **CD-ROM**, can only be read from. As the name implies, CD-ROM is a read-only media. CD-ROM disks can be read by a laser in the CD-ROM drive (Figure 8-17), but they cannot be written to — at least not yet. The advantage of CD-ROM technology is the amount of data that can be stored on a single disk. One disk can hold as much as 650 MB of data.

CD-ROMs are used to store data that rarely, if ever, changes. For example, a CD-ROM that contains zip codes and road maps would not need to be updated as frequently as a file with payroll information. Entire encyclopedias are available on a single disk, as are complete sets of street maps for the major (and not-so-major) metropolitan areas of the United States. CD-ROM is also used to store multimedia presentations, which require vast amounts of memory. Despite the storage capacity of a CD-ROM disk, however, one disk can hold only about 10 minutes of full-motion video with sound.

Other optical disks can be written on a single time and then read many times. These are called write-once, read many, or **WORM**, disks. These disks are used to store archival information such as end-of-the-year financial data for a business. Once this data has been created, legally it cannot be changed, so WORM technology is a perfect storage medium for it.

Floptical disks (removable optical diskettes) are optical disks that can be written to and read over and over again. This gives users the ability to store and use millions and millions of bytes of data and software. The NeXT computer was one of the first computers to incorporate the optical disk.

Figure 8-17
A CD-ROM disk and drive.

Comprehension Questions

1. Is it seek time, rotational delay, or transfer time that makes cassette tapes slower than hard disks?
2. Is a diskette a sequential medium or a random-access medium?
3. Why can't a microcomputer back up to a CD-ROM disk?

Using What You Know

1. What data might headquarters provide to BVOS branches on CD-ROM?
2. If you had a 200 MB hard disk, can you think of any reason that you might want two 100 MB cassettes or even four 50 MB cassettes for backing up?
3. Since the time this book was published, what new storage media have emerged?

Summary Points

Storage Devices and Storage Media

☐ Storage devices are I/O peripherals used to write to and read from storage media.

Diskettes and Drives

☐ Diskettes, which are made of flexible mylar, come in two sizes: 3½ inches and 5¼ inches.
☐ The 3½-inch model is becoming more prevalent than the 5¼- inch model.
☐ A diskette drive consists of the drive bay, the drive, and the read-write head.

How Data Is Organized on a Diskette

☐ To be used, new diskettes must be formatted, a process that maps the surface into tracks and sectors.
☐ 5¼-inch diskettes store either 360 K or 1.2 MB, depending on whether they are double density or high density.
☐ 3½-inch diskettes initialized on a Mac can store either 800 K or 1.44 MB.
☐ 3½-inch diskettes formatted using DOS can store either 720 K or 1.44 MB.

Protecting Data: Just in Case

☐ Both sizes of a diskette can be write protected by covering the write-protect notch or sliding the write-protect tab.

Taking Care of Diskettes

☐ Diskettes must be protected from pressure, heat, and magnetic fields.
☐ Diskettes must not be removed from the drive while the drive light is on.

Purchasing Diskette Drives

☐ If you are buying a PC with one drive, you should probably get a 3½-inch drive; if you are getting two drives, get one of each size.

Hard Disks and Hard Disk Drives

☐ The hard disk allows the user to have access to a large, nonremovable storage device.

Hard Disks Compared to Diskettes

☐ A hard disk consists of a set of aluminum platters.
☐ In a hard disk drive, the read-write head never touches the media; if it does, the system experiences a disk crash.

Capacity

☐ Hard disks can store hundreds of times more data than a single diskette.

Access Time

☐ Though seek time and rotational delay are negligible factors, transfer time is much better with hard disks than with diskettes.

Portability

☐ Diskettes are portable; hard disks — especially internal ones — are much less so.

Formatting a Hard Disk

☐ To be used, a hard disk must be formatted — a process of dividing the disk into tracks and sectors.

Types of Hard Disks

☐ Two available hard disks are the IDE and the SCSI.

Organizing Files

☐ Operating systems list files on disks in directories.

Subdirectories and Folders

☐ Operating systems allow users to establish hierarchical file systems by creating subdirectories or folders.

Common Organizational Models

☐ The two most common ways to organize files are organizing by application and organizing by client or project.

Alternatives to Internal Hard Disks

☐ Other types of hard drives include external hard disks, hard cards, and hard disk cartridges.

Magnetic Tape

☐ Tape drives adapt cassette tape technology to the process of backing up hard disks.

☐ Tape drives cannot replace hard disks because they are a sequential medium, which is inherently slower than a random-access medium.

Other Forms of Tape

☐ Minis and mainframes use reel-to-reel tapes for backup and data transfer.

How Often Should I Back Up?

☐ Backing up is a time trade-off between the time it takes to perform the backup and the time it takes to replace lost work.

Optical Storage Technology

☐ CD-ROM uses the same optical technology as music CDs.

☐ A single CD-ROM disk can store up to 650 MB of data.

Knowing the Facts

True/False

1. A CD-ROM drive is a storage medium.
2. 5¼-inch diskettes are made of mylar, and 3½-inch diskettes are made of aluminum.
3. One reason that 3½-inch diskettes have become more popular than 5¼-inch diskettes is that the smaller diskettes can hold more data.
4. A single hard disk can have several platters.
5. Diskettes should not be removed from the drive unless the drive light is on.
6. The magnetic field around a magnetized paper clip is enough to damage a diskette.
7. The read-write head of a hard disk should never touch the disk surface.
8. *Subdirectory* and *folder* are synonymous terms.
9. Though hard disks have greater capacity, access times for diskettes are less.
10. Hard cards are removable hard disks that can be changed in much the same way as diskettes.

Short Answer

1. Finding data on _____ media is much more time consuming than on random-access media.
2. _____ tape is used for backup and data transfer on minis and mainframes.
3. Some optical media, such as _____ disks, can be read but not written to.
4. _____ allow the user to perform unattended backups of the hard disk onto a single storage unit.
5. On a hard card, the disk is mounted directly on the _____.
6. A hierarchical file structure can be created on a disk using the _____.
7. Though a fingerprint can obscure data on a diskette, it is thick enough to cause a _____ in a hard disk drive.
8. What size diskettes do Macintoshes use?
9. What does the drive light on a diskette drive tell you?
10. Only a _____ should be used to write on a 5½-inch diskette.

Answers

True/False

1. F
2. F
3. T
4. T
5. F
6. T
7. T
8. T
9. F
10. F

Short Answer

1. sequential
2. Reel-to-reel
3. CD-ROM
4. Tape drives
5. controller card or expansion board
6. operating system
7. disk crash
8. 3½-inch diskettes
9. "The diskette is spinning" or "Don't remove the diskette."
10. felt-tip pen

Challenging Your Understanding

1. As technology improves, we will be able to store more and more data on our storage devices. What is the down side of this phenomenon?

2. Look in a computer magazine and determine the cost per megabyte for five hard disks. What are the characteristics that seem to affect the price of a hard disk? What is the best deal you can find?

3. Discuss ways in which the way you use your computer affects how often you should back up your data.

4. Backing up an entire hard disk can take a long time — sometimes hours, if the hard disk is large and you are backing up to diskettes. Under what circumstances might you back up only part of your data? Would these circumstances occur often? See if you can describe a strategy for minimizing the amount of data that you have to back up.

5. Why is CD-ROM becoming such a popular medium? What are the limitations of CD-ROM, and how do these limitations affect the uses for the medium?

Communication Devices

Key Terms

acoustic coupler
baud
bits per second (bps)
bulletin board service (BBS)
bus network
client/server computing
   (cooperative processing)
communication error
data bits
diskless workstation
enterprise wide network
fax modem
file server (network server)
full duplex
half duplex
handshake
Hayes-compatible

hierarchical network
host computer
information service
local area network (LAN)
metropolitan area network (MAN)
modem
network interface card (NIC)
node
parity bit
printer server
protocol
ring network
star network
stop bit
terminal
wide area network (WAN)

Objectives

In this chapter you will learn to:

- Identify the four necessary elements of communication and explain the importance of protocol
- Describe how a modem works
- Identify the two types of modem and the speeds at which they can operate
- Describe the settings that must be agreed upon before users communicate via modem
- Explain how a fax is used
- List the advantages and disadvantages of using a fax modem, as opposed to a stand alone fax
- Explain the advantages of networks and the differences among a LAN, a MAN, and a WAN
- Describe the advantages of having a file server and a printer server
- Name and describe four network configurations
- Identify the hardware and software required by computers in a network

Communicating at BVOS

The lifeblood of any healthy enterprise is communication. BVOS is no different. In planning your branch, there is much to consider. Your first priority will be to establish fast, orderly communication systems within your new branch. Only then can you serve your customers with maximum efficiency. You must then establish a link with the main BVOS office in Toronto. A large part of the main office activities concern getting sales data from all of the branches on a daily basis. By getting up-to-the-minute information, the main office personnel can manage inventory levels carefully so that cash is not tied up in overstocked merchandise and customers are not sent away because of underestimated demand.

As you can see, planning your communication systems properly is essential. This chapter will provide important information that will help you make the most of your own personal and professional needs.

What Happens When Communication Occurs?

Before we begin discussing the technology involved with communication systems, it is important that you have a clear understanding of the communication process. A communication system requires four elements: the message, the sender, the receiver, and the channel (Figure 9-1). The message is the picture, words, or data that a sender is trying to deliver to the receiver. The sender is the originator of the message, and the receiver is the intended recipient. The channel consists of the assorted communication devices over which the message is transmitted.

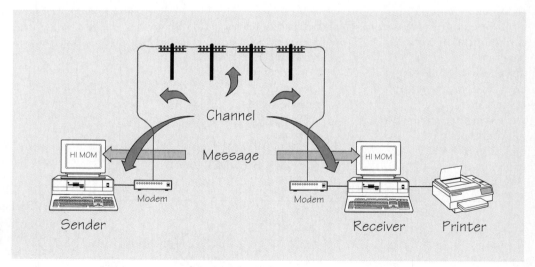

Figure 9-1
The sender transmits the message through the channel to the receiver.

Standards: The Backbone of Computer Communication

One vital ingredient that lets these four elements work together is a set of procedural standards for communication, known as a **protocol**. When people use vocal communication, both the sender and receiver need to use the same language. Likewise, when a sender and a receiver communicate with computers, the receiving computer needs to know in what format the data is being sent.

The Importance of Standards. One of the reasons that protocol is so important in data communication is that it enables errors to be caught and fixed. A **communication error** occurs when the data that was received is not identical to the data that was sent. Just as voice communication is difficult in a noisy room, data communication is error-prone when the channel is experiencing noise. We have all had a telephone conversation interrupted by a click or hum or squeal, or even by the voice of some other person on the same line. These problems in telephone lines can be caused by a device failure, by someone starting a car, by a sun spot, by a water cooler turning on, or by any number of other causes. If a media problem occurs when we are speaking on the phone, the error is usually reported immediately with a simple "Excuse me?" or "Could you repeat that?" If the problem occurs when transmitting data over phone lines, the receiving computer must catch the error. Whatever channel is being used, with proper protocol, the receiving computer should realize that it has received an error and ask the sending computer to repeat the signal.

The Speed of Transmission

When media problems occur in data communication, the errors caused can be huge. The size of a communication error is dependent upon both the amount of time the media problem occurs and the rate at which the data is being transmitted. The speed of transmission is measured either in **baud** or **bits per second (bps)**, two terms that are often used interchangeably though they are technically different. Baud is the number of changes in the electrical state of the line in one second. Modern transmission techniques pack multiple bits into every change of state, so bps can now be a lot higher than baud.

To get an idea of how big errors can be, let's say we are transmitting data at 19,200 bits per second (bps). When talking on the telephone, if you hear a "tick" on the line that is caused by an error in the phone system, you are hearing something that has a duration of approximately 1/100th of a second. During that 1/100th of a second, 192 bits, or 28 bytes, are being destroyed by the error. *That's this sentence's size!*

Communication Via Modem

When two computer users who are not in close proximity want to communicate or share data, they often do so using phone lines with the help of a modem. A **modem** is a hardware device that, in conjunction with communication software, allows a computer to send or receive data through a telephone system.

How the Modem Works

The word *modem* is actually an acronym for MOdulator/DEModulator. The telephone system was designed to transmit analog voice signals, because that's the way we talk. Computers, however, use digital signals to communicate. To enable computers to use these lines, a device was needed to change a digital signal into an analog signal. That's a modulator. At the receiving end, the data must be changed from analog back to digital — the job of the demodulator. The modem can do both of these functions, but there must be a modem attached to both the sending and receiving computers. Figure 9-2 (on the next page) summarizes how modems are used to transmit data over phone lines.

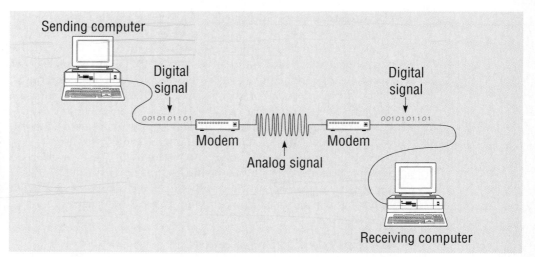

Figure 9-2
The sender's modem
modulates the data into an
audible (analog) signal. The
receiver's modem
demodulates the audible
signal back into a digital
signal that the computer
can understand.

Types of Modems

A modem can be internal or external — inside or outside the system unit. An internal modem is mounted on an expansion card that is attached to the motherboard (Figure 9-3a). At one end of the card is a phone jack, into which a standard phone cable can be plugged. An external modem is attached to the motherboard via a serial port (Figure 9-3b). In general, internal modems are less expensive than external modems because the latter require their own power supply, whereas internal modems run off the power supply inside the system unit. External modems are popular with users who don't have available expansion slots in their computers. External modems are also more easily shared among a group of users who need only occasional access to a modem.

Most modems are attached directly to the telephone system using common modular jacks; some use **acoustic couplers** to transmit over the standard telephone handset. The telephone handset is placed into the coupler, which is attached to a serial port on the computer. Modems with acoustic couplers transmit at slower speeds than those that are directly connected. However, they are useful for portable computers that may have to go where there is no modular jack.

Modems can transmit at a variety of speeds. Older models operate at 300, 1200, or 2400 bits per second. Newer models work at 4800, 9600, 14,400, or 19200 bps. As telephone companies install more advanced equipment, even greater speeds may become practical. Most users purchase modems that will operate at at least 2400 bps, and many are now buying much faster models. Your need for speed depends on how you will be using your modem. If you are going to use it only once in a while, or if you are transferring files of moderate size, buying a high-speed modem is probably a waste of money. Speed becomes more valuable if you are transferring graphics or if you will be using the modem every day. As with many types of hardware, if you are not looking for the latest technology, finding used equipment can be extremely cost efficient.

Using a Modem

Modems are programmable, controllable devices that must be used with a piece of communication software. Many modems for microcomputers are **Hayes-compatible**. Hayes is a long-time manufacturer of modems and has designed a language that controls its modems.

(a)

(b)

Figure 9-3

(a) An internal modem;
(b) an external modem.

The Hayes command set has been adopted by other modem manufacturers. No matter what type of modem you buy, make sure it is Hayes-compatible.

To use a modem, you must first load your modem or communication software. Next, you need to make sure that your modem is set up in the same way as the modem that you want to communicate with. There are several settings that you need to check. Figure 9-4 shows the Settings menu for ProComm Plus, a popular communication package.

The Transmission Rate. Both sending and receiving modems need to transmit at the same speed. Often this is not an issue, because most modem software can automatically detect the transmission rate of incoming signals. However, you may need to set your modem to send at a slower speed than it is capable of if the receiver's modem has a maximum baud rate that is less than yours. Most modems are downward-compatible, so you usually don't need to worry about not being able to communicate just because the other user's modem can operate faster or slower. For instance, a 9600-bps modem can send or receive at 2400-bps if that is the maximum the other modem can use.

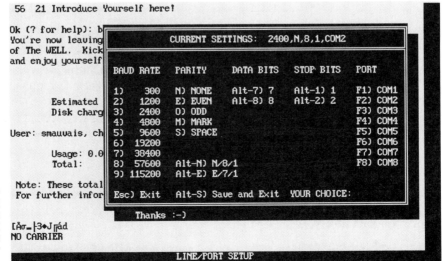

Figure 9-4

This menu controls several important communication settings. The sender and receiver's settings must be the same before proper communication can occur.

Transmission Modes.   Modems transmit in two modes. **Half duplex** mode refers to the transmission of data in both directions, but only one direction at once. **Full duplex** refers to the ability to send and receive simultaneously.

Data Bits.   The number of **data bits** tells the software how many bits of data to send in each set. Normally, microcomputers send either seven or eight bits of data in a string.

Stop Bits.   At the end of each string of data, the modem sends either one or two stop bits. The **stop bit** simply signals the receiving computer that the sequence of bits has ended.

The Parity Bit.   The **parity bit** provides a way for the receiving computer to know if there were any errors in communication. If the parity bit is used, it is set to either **even parity** or **odd parity**. With even parity, the sending computer manipulates the parity bit so that each string of data has an even number of 1s. For example, the sequence of bits, 10001100, has an odd number of 1s. The sending computer would set the parity bit to 1 to bring the total number of 1s up to four, an even number. If a computer receives a string of data for which the parity bit is not correct, it asks the sending computer to repeat the string.

Making the Call.   Once you have made sure that the settings are the same for both modems, you are ready to connect. To do so, you simply instruct your modem software to dial the phone number of the receiving computer. When the other modem answers, each of the two modems sends a small set of data called a **handshake**. The handshake formally establishes the link by testing the settings and ensuring a valid connection.

What happens next depends on the computer you have called. Often, the modem software of the receiving computer prompts you for identification. Then you may be presented with a menu of choices. Menu interfaces are common with modem software. The most common actions performed with modem software are sending and receiving files. To send a file to another user, computer system, information service, or bulletin board, you generally choose "Upload" from a menu. To obtain (receive) a file, you choose "Download." After telling the other computer that you want to upload or download a file, you use your own modem software to initiate the transfer. The transfer itself must adhere to a particular protocol. Common data transfer protocols for microcomputers include Xmodem, Ymodem, Kermit, and many others. Most modem software is capable of adhering to several different protocols.

Using a Bulletin Board Service

Through their modems, users can connect and communicate with bulletin board services (BBSs) and information services such as Prodigy and CompuServe. A **bulletin board service**, or **BBS,** is a forum in which users can trade information on a certain subject. The BBS is run from a central computer, which users call and connect to. To access a BBS, you simply adjust your communication software to the correct line settings and call the service's phone number. Once the connection is made and the user is on-line, he or she can read messages sent by others or leave new messages. Some services have a flat subscription rate that you pay each month; others bill by the amount of time you stay on-line.

Some BBS's allow you to read and participate in on-line conferences on a myriad of subjects. Other bulletin boards focus on specific subjects, ranging from Star Trek to electrical engineering.

Using an Information Service

Information services are on-line companies that allow you to do many things, from shopping and banking to booking an airline reservation or searching for certain types of news. Information services often include their own bulletin boards and conferencing capabilities. Electronic mail (E-mail) is available with many information services. Connecting to an information service and paying for your connect time is much like connecting to a bulletin board. Because the range of services offered is usually much broader, information services generally cost more than bulletin board services.

Table 9-1 lists a few of the well-known BBSs and information services, the type of service they offer, and their connection settings. The column labeled PDS tells you the type of parity (E = even, O = odd, N = none), the number of data bits, and how many stop bits they use. For example, "N81" indicates that you should set your modem for no parity bit, eight data bits, and one stop bit.

PROCOMM PLUS (tm) Dialing Directory

NAME		NUMBER	BAUD	PDS	D P	SCRIPT	PROTOCOL	TERMINAL	MODEM
1- DEANS OFFICE	NJ	201-279-7048	2400	N81	F 0			ANSI	MODEM
2- PC CONNECTIONS	DC	202-547-2008	2400	N81	F 0			ANSI	MODEM
3- BRUCE'S BAR &GRILL	CT	203-236-3761	2400	N81	F 0			ANSI	MODEM
4- HH-INFONET	CT	203-246-3747	2400	N81	F 0			ANSI	MODEM
5- ROCKY ROAD	CT	203-791-8838	2400	N81	F 0			ANSI	MODEM
6- GOLDEN SPRINGS BBS	AL	205-238-0012	2400	N81	F 0			ANSI	MODEM
7- PRO-TECH BBS	AL	205-452-3897	2400	N81	F 0			ANSI	MODEM
8- CYCLONE BBS	AL	205-974-5123	2400	N81	F 0			ANSI	MODEM
9- ARCHMAGE BBS	WA	206-493-0401	2400	N81	F 0			ANSI	MODEM
10- 28 BARBARY LANE	WA	206-525-2828	2400	N81	F 0			ANSI	MODEM
11- BARBEQUED RIBBS	WA	206-676-5787	2400	N81	F 0			ANSI	MODEM
12- NORTHERN LIGHTS	ME	207-766-5808	2400	N81	F 0			ANSI	MODEM
13- COASTAL DOS USER	ME	207-797-4975	2400	N81	F 0			ANSI	MODEM
14- GREATER BOISE BBS	ID	208-332-5227	2400	N81	F 0			ANSI	MODEM
15- INVENTION FACTORY	NY	212-431-1194	2400	N81	F 0			ANSI	MODEM
16- FRIENDS TOO	NY	212-489-0516	2400	N81	F 0			ANSI	MODEM
17- DATACOM	NY	212-496-7946	2400	N81	F 0			ANSI	MODEM
18- MAC HACers	NY	213-546-9640	2400	N81	F 0			ANSI	MODEM
19- NEWTOWN SQUARE	PA	215-356-8623	2400	N81	F 0			ANSI	MODEM
20- NEXUS BBS=	PA	215-364-5662	2400	N81	F 0			ANSI	MODEM
21- THE HARBOR	PA	215-372-2788	2400	N81	F 0			ANSI	MODEM
22- PHILLY GAMERS=	PA	215-544-3757	2400	N81	F 0			ANSI	MODEM
23- KUTZTOWN CONN=	PA	215-683-9038	2400	N81	F 0			ANSI	MODEM
24- TMC BBS	PA	215-694-1534	2400	N81	F 0			ANSI	MODEM
25- THE CORE	PA	215-XXX-8113	2400	N81	F 0			ANSI	MODEM
26- PC-OHIO	OH	216-381-3320	2400	N81	F 0			ANSI	MODEM
27- AMCOM	OH	216-526-9840	2400	N81	F 0			ANSI	MODEM
28- RUSTY & EDIE'S	OH	216-726-0737	2400	N81	F 0			ANSI	MODEM
29- ASK FRED'S BBS	OH	216-783-9632	2400	N81	F 0			ANSI	MODEM
30- RIVER CITY NETWORK	IN	219-237-0651	2400	N81	F 0			ANSI	MODEM

Copyright (C) 1987,91 Datastorm Technologies, Inc.

Table 9-1
Some popular information services and BBSs.

Fax Modems

The facsimile machine, or fax, has become an indispensable part of modern business. A modern stand alone fax machine (sometimes called a Group III fax) is like a scanner and a printer attached to a modem. To use a fax machine (Figure 9-5 on the next page):

1. The sender types in the telephone number of the receiving fax.

2. The sender feeds the printed pages that need to be sent into the fax machine.

3. The sender's fax scans the document, and the modem in the sender's fax modulates the dark and light spots on the paper into audible signals.

4. The receiver's fax machine demodulates the data and recreates the image.

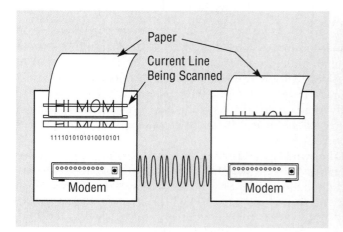

Figure 9-5   The process of faxing a document includes scanning an image line by line and then sending the results of the scan via modem.

Figure 9-6   A stand alone fax machine.

The scanning, transmission, and printing stages happen in such rapid succession that the receiver's fax machine prints the document at almost the same time it is scanned. Fax technology has come a long way in the past 20 years. It continues to advance with better resolution output and faster transmission. A modern stand alone fax machine is shown in Figure 9-6.

A **fax modem**, also called a fax board, is a computer peripheral that accomplishes the same goal as the stand alone fax. Rather than sending printed documents, however, you are able to send data files. Like a modem, the fax modem must be controlled by fax software that is loaded into RAM.

To send a fax using a fax modem, you generally begin by opening a document using a standard application program, such as a spreadsheet or a word processor. You then "print" the document to the fax rather than the printer (Figure 9-7). The fax software creates a bitmap of the document and sends the data to the fax modem line by line. The receiving fax interprets

Figure 9-7
This dialog box appears when you "print" to a fax modem using WINFAX, a fax program for Windows.

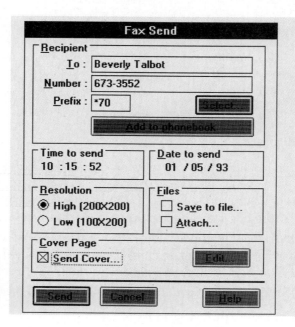

the data the same way it would a fax from a stand alone machine. If the fax modem is receiving a fax, it accepts the data and creates a bitmap of the page. The user can then view the file on screen or print it with whatever printer is attached to the system. Like modems, fax modems can be either internal or external.

There are both advantages and disadvantages to fax modems compared to stand alone fax machines. The biggest advantage of the fax modem is the price. Fax modems start at less than $100. In addition, the resolution of a fax that is created directly from an electronic file is generally better than one that is scanned from a piece of paper. Finally, you can save time and paper by not having to print out a document before faxing it.

The advantage of a stand alone fax is primarily that most print faster than fax modems, although fax modems are catching up. Printing a bit-mapped image through your computer can be very slow. Some of the more expensive fax software programs include OCR capabilities, so you can recreate a text document before you print. The text document you create will print much faster than the bitmap. The stand alone fax, however, prints as it receives the data. In addition, you will sometimes need to send a document that exists only on paper. A fax modem must be accompanied by a scanner to send hard copy.

Comprehension Questions

1. If you are transmitting data at 2400 bps and your communication is interrupted for .05 seconds, how much data needs to be retransmitted?

2. What information must be included in the pamphlet that CompuServe (a popular information service) gives to users who want to become subscribers of the service?

3. What style of chassis is least likely to accommodate an internal modem?

Using What You Know

1. Compare prices for a 2400-bps and a 9600-bps modem. What is the difference in price for otherwise comparable capabilities?

2. In addition to taking orders over the telephone, BVOS will take orders by fax. Does it make more sense to have a stand alone fax or a fax modem? Why?

3. Under what circumstances would it be helpful to have both a fax modem and a stand alone fax?

Networks: Communicating Without Phone Lines

Modems are used for communicating via telephone lines, but a different technology is used for communication at closer distances. A **local area network** (**LAN**) is used to connect computers that are located within the same room, building, or complex. Each of the computers attached to a LAN is called a **node**. With a LAN, a company can buy a single expensive printer or a scanner that everyone can share without having to purchase individual peripherals for every machine. Another advantage of LANs is that they can be used to help people work together. Networks allow users to schedule meetings more efficiently, share documents more rapidly, and simply communicate, either one to many or many to one, instantaneously.

Hardware Connections: What Networks Are Made Of

The reason that computers within a LAN can communicate so much more quickly is that they are directly connected to each other. The most common way to connect computers in a LAN is with special wires or cables. A variety of types of wire or cable are used, including twisted-pair wires (such as standard telephone wire), coaxial cables (such as those used by cable television companies), and fiber-optic cables. These three types of cables are shown in Figure 9-8.

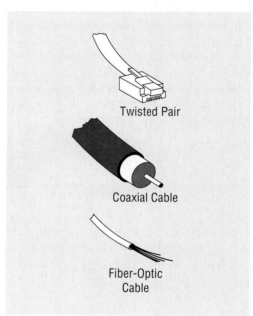

Various types of media have different characteristics that affect their capacity for data. Twisted pair wires are the cheapest medium, but standard telephone wire can carry only two signals simultaneously — one signal in each direction. Coaxial cables, on the other hand, can carry almost 100 signals at once, and fiber-optic cables can carry thousands.

In addition to "hardwired" LANs that use wires or cables, there is a trend toward wireless LANs that transmit data using electromagnetic waves, including visible light, infrared, and microwaves. The advantage of such media is simply that no wires are needed, so a major cost of setting up or modifying a LAN can be eliminated. The disadvantage is that, so far, transmission speeds are not as high as with hardwired systems.

As they eliminate the need for hardwired networks, communication by electromagnetic waves is also expanding the LAN to the point that it can no longer be described as local. In the past, LANs usually operated within a single office building. Networks that spanned greater distances required telephone lines and were called **wide area networks**, or **WANs**. WANs are capable of spanning the globe, because they use communication satellites to transmit across large distances (Figure 9-9).

Twisted Pair

Coaxial Cable

Fiber-Optic Cable

Figure 9-8
The three most common types of cables used in LANs.

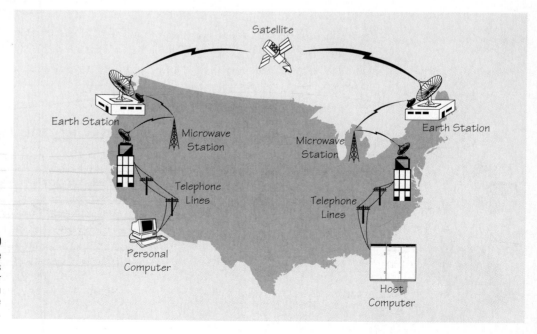

Figure 9-9
Using satelite communications, users attached to LANs, or merely using modems, can communicate around the world.

Similar technology, when combined with electromagnetic waves such as microwaves, can transmit signals across town. For example, a company with two buildings one mile apart can use antennas or dishes, similar to the dishes used to receive cable television signals. With a dish on top of each building pointed at the other building (Figure 9-10), the company can expand its LAN into an **enterprise wide network** (also called a **metropolitan area network**, or **MAN**).

File Servers: The Network's Electronic File Cabinet

A **file server**, also called a **network server**, is a fast computer with a large amount of secondary storage, to which all of the other computers in a network have access for data storage and retrieval. A typical file server is shown in Figure 9-11. The file server stores programs and data files shared by the users on the network. File servers can substantially reduce the cost of personal computers on a network, because each computer need not have its own large hard drive. In addition, use of a file server facilitates sharing data, because the data is stored centrally. A single change to a file stored on a file server allows everyone on the LAN to use the most current version of the data. Finally, file servers also provide a single point of backup of user data. Because most of the data will be stored on a file server, a single backup procedure will protect the data resources of all LAN users.

Nodes connected to a file server can be diskless workstations. A **diskless workstation** has its own processing components and generally a keyboard (possibly a mouse or some other input device as well) and a monitor, but it lacks any storage device of its own. When this type of computer is turned on, it looks to the file server for the operating system. All of the applications and data files used by a diskless workstation are also held on the file server.

Increasingly, file servers are replacing mainframes. They perform many of the same functions and are less expensive to purchase and maintain. However, a file server can cause legal problems if it is abused. It is tempting to buy a single copy of a program, place it on a file server, and allow all of the LAN users to share the single copy. This practice is illegal. Most software is licensed to run on a single processor, so only one copy of the program can be running at a time. To address the problem, many software companies sell LAN packages that allow users to buy the right for a fixed number of users to use a single copy of the software. Site licenses are also gaining popularity for similar reasons. A site license authorizes the copying, distributing, and use of software within a single designated facility or jurisdiction.

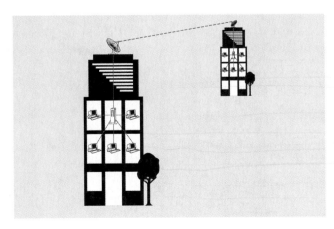

Figure 9-10 Wireless communications have led to the development of the enterprise wide network, in which employees in different buildings can communicate as if their computers were hardwired together.

Figure 9-11 A network file server

Client/Server Computing

Client/server computing, also known as **cooperative processing**, involves using two or more networked computers to perform an application task. For example, one computer might contain a database, while another computer might have the user interface that allows users to manipulate the database. By segregating the activities of these computers, each can be optimized for that particular activity. The database computer (the server) can have a large, fast hard disk, while the user computer (the client) has a high-resolution color graphics monitor and a mouse. This approach to networking allows the strengths of each system to complement the other. As computers become more and more powerful and are interconnected with other kinds of computers, client/server computing may become the standard application architecture.

Printer Servers

Another common type of server is the **printer server**. A printer server (or network printer) allows multiple users to take advantage of a single printing device. High-speed printers, printers with large amounts of RAM, printers with special fonts or paper stock, and color printers are often used as printer servers. This is a cost-effective way to provide the maximum flexibility of printer support while purchasing just a few expensive devices.

The greatest disadvantage of printer servers is that, because of their frequent use, they often require more maintenance than their desktop counterparts. Also, accessing the printer can be a challenge. If users on three floors of a building are sharing a laser printer, the users whose offices are not on the same floor as the printer must leave their desks to retrieve their output. Also, sensitive documents can be compromised when printed on a network printer, because of the easy access afforded to users of the printer.

Network Configurations

Local area networks can be set up in a number of configurations. The most popular are the bus, star, hierarchical, and ring networks.

Bus Networks.   The oldest form of LAN is the **bus network**. The microcomputers in a bus network are connected to a common wire, called the **bus**, through which each computer can transmit and receive data. This arrangement is especially common in relatively small networks. It is a simple, noncentralized way to share peripherals and data in an office. A diagram of the bus network is shown in Figure 9-12.

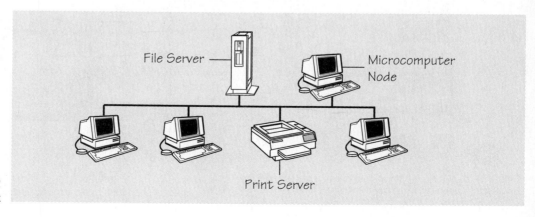

Figure 9-12
A bus network

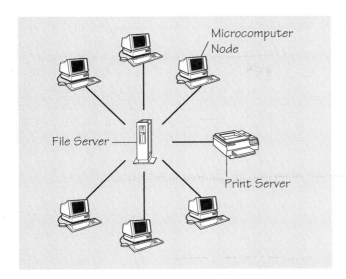

Figure 9-13
A star network.

Star Networks. In a **star network**, each node is connected directly to a central device called a *hub*. As shown in Figure 9-13, all network traffic is routed through the hub to each network node. The hub can be a simple routing device or a centralized host computer.

With a centralized network organized around a host computer, it is also common for the nodes to be terminals, rather than computers. A **terminal** is simply an input and output device that relies entirely on the host computer for processing. Terminals are especially common on mainframe systems.

If the central computer is a mini, mainframe, or even a powerful microcomputer that is heavily relied on for processing, it is referred to as the **host computer**. If the central computer is used primarily as a storage device, it is a file server.

The star network is especially well suited for a small company with a relatively large database to which many employees need access. In this case, the file server is sometimes called the *database server*. Each of the computers in the network can run the database software, and yet all can share the central database.

It is not necessarily true that all of the peripherals in a star network are connected to the host computer or file server. Often, less expensive peripherals, such as dot matrix printers and modems, are connected directly to the node computer.

Hierarchical Networks. Larger computer networks sometimes use another centralized arrangement, called a **hierarchical network** (Figure 9-14). This arrangement is similar to the star network, except that there are more than two levels in the system. In other words, the host computer has several smaller computers linked to it, and these are hosts to yet smaller computers or terminals. These mid-level computers could be specialized computers that help control the terminals, or general purpose minicomputers. For example, a large company's mainframe might be linked to several minicomputers, and these might be connected to micros, diskless workstations, and terminals.

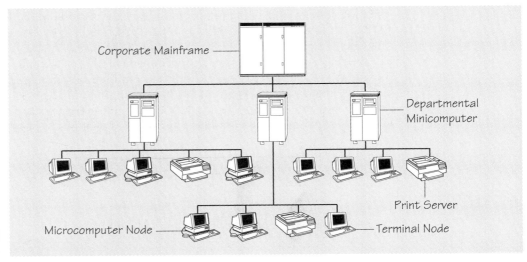

Figure 9-14
A hierarchical network.

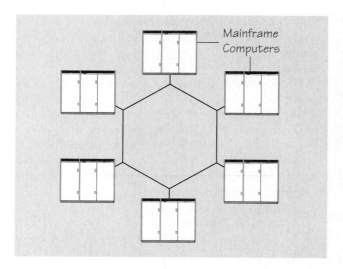

Mainframe Computers

Figure 9-15

A ring network. Each of the mainframes in this ring could be the host computer of a smaller, centralized LAN.

Ring Networks. The fourth arrangement for a network, shown in Figure 9-15, is a decentralized system called a **ring network**. As the name implies, each of the computers in a ring network is connected to two others, so that data can be passed all the way around in a circle. In a ring network, a message sent by one computer must travel around the ring until it reaches the correct destination.

Network Software and Interface Boards

As with communication over the phone lines, communication in a network requires an expansion board within each computer, plus software to control the communication. The expansion board is called a **network interface card**, or **NIC**. The NIC performs the tasks of sending and receiving data through whatever wires or cables are used in the network. The NIC generally has a port at one end for attaching the wire or cable.

The NIC is controlled by the computer's CPU with the help of network software. In general, network software adheres to one of the major network protocols, such as Ethernet, Token Ring, or LocalTalk. These protocols are also referred to as *access methods*. The most widely used pieces of network software are made by Novell. Macs, however, come with AppleTalk, which adheres to LocalTalk access methods, though it can be adapted to Ethernet or Token Ring systems.

Wireless Computers

Wireless computers are not new. Police vehicles have long had computers that allow police officers instantaneous access to information about people and vehicles. These systems are attached to a radio that sends and receives data through the airways. Now this type of technology is moving into the office in the form of wireless LANs.

Local area networks do not always require a wire to connect nodes on the network. New telecommunications technologies allow users to connect to a LAN without installing wire. These computers exchange information using either infrared or radio frequencies. Infrared LANs are located in a room where an infrared receiver can be "seen" from each computer. This line-of-sight access, however, is not required for radio connectivity. For radio LANs, each node in a network contains a small transmitter that is tuned to frequencies received by the host computer. Data is broadcast from both the host and each node. Special rules are needed to make sure that two or more computers don't try to transmit at the same time. For both infrared and radio LANs, the speed of data transmission is almost equivalent to that of wired LANs, although the error rate may be a bit higher.

Comprehension Questions

1. Which is likely to need greater processing speed, a host computer or a file server?
2. Does the use of telephone cable mean that you are using a WAN?
3. What aspect of a MAN makes it similar to a WAN?

Using What You Know

1. Which network configuration is most appropriate for connecting the computers at BVOS?
2. Which computers at BVOS could be diskless workstations? How would this arrangement work?
3. If BVOS were to use a star network, how might this configuration be linked to headquarters to form a hierarchical network?

Summary Points

Communicating at BVOS
- Your branch of BVOS requires both internal communication and communication with the central office in Toronto.

What Happens When Communication Occurs?
- Communication requires a sender, a receiver, a message, and a medium.

Standards: The Backbone of Computer Communications
- A set of standards for communication is called a protocol.

The Importance of Standards
- A communication error occurs when the data received is not the same as the data sent.

The Speed of Transmission
- Communication speed is measured in baud or bits per second.
- The size of a communication error is determined by the duration of the problem and the speed of transmission.

Communication Via Modem
- A modem allows computers to communicate through the phone lines.

How the Modem Works
- A modem modulates digital signals and demodulates analog signals.

Types of Modems
- Modems can be internal or external.
- Modems operate at 300, 1200, 2400, 4800, 9600, or 14,400 bps.

Using a Modem
- Modems can connect directly to a telephone wire or use an acoustic coupler.
- Modems should be Hayes-compatible.

The Transmission Rate

☐ After the modem software is loaded, the bps rate must be set to agree with the bps rate of the other computer.

Transmission Modes

☐ In half duplex communication, data goes in only one direction at a time; in full duplex, data travels back and forth simultaneously.

Data Bits

☐ The number of data bits tells the software how many bits to send in each set.

Stop Bits

☐ The stop bit informs the receiving computer of the end of each set of data bits.

The Parity Bit

☐ The parity bit provides a check for communication errors.

Making the Call

☐ When the modem reaches another modem, they establish communication with an audible handshake.
☐ Uploading is sending a file to another computer; downloading is retrieving a file from another computer.

Using a Bulletin Board Service

☐ Bulletin board services are electronic forums in which users can share information.

Using an Information Service

☐ Information services are similar to BBSs, except that they tend to include a broader range of services, such as news, electronic shopping, and E-mail.

Fax Modems

☐ A fax allows one person to send a scanned image to another.
☐ A fax modem works like a stand alone fax but transmits files rather than hard copy to another fax.
☐ Fax modems cost less than stand alone faxes and have better resolution.
☐ A stand alone fax prints faster and accepts printed pages.

Networks: Communicating Without Phone Lines

☐ LANs allow users in an office to collaborate closely.

Hardware Connections: What Networks Are Made Of

☐ LANs are usually linked with twisted-pair wires, coaxial cables, or fiber optic cables.
☐ Some LANs use electromagnetic waves to communicate, and therefore do not require wires.
☐ Networks that include telecommunication are called WANs.
☐ Networks that transmit data across town using electromagnetic signals are called MANs.

File Servers: The Network's Electronic File Cabinet

☐ File servers offer an economical way for a group of computers to have access to a large storage device.
☐ Use of a file server can pose a legal problem if users do not purchase network versions or site licenses for software.

Client/Server Computing

☐ The client/server design allows the various parts of a network to cooperate in accomplishing tasks by taking advantage of the strengths of each part.

Printer Servers

☐ A printer server offers an economical way for a group of computers to share an expensive printing device.

Network Configurations

Bus Networks

☐ Computers in a bus network are all attached to a common wire, called the *bus*.

Star Networks

☐ Star networks are a centralized configuration with a host computer or file server.
☐ Diskless workstations in a star network can operate without storage devices.
☐ Terminals are nodes that rely entirely on the host computer for their processing needs.

Hierarchical Networks

☐ Hierarchical networks have more than one level of host computer.

Ring Networks

☐ A ring network requires that messages travel around the ring to the desired destination.

Network Software and Interface Boards

☐ A microcomputer attached to a network requires a network interface card.
☐ The NIC is operated by network software, which usually adheres to one of the common protocols.

Wireless Computers

☐ Networks can now transfer data through infrared waves or radio frequencies and thereby avoid the problems of installing wires around an office.

Knowing the Facts

True/False

1. A modem is capable of converting analog signals to digital, and vice versa.
2. A modem can be part of a network.
3. Modems are internal devices; fax modems are external.
4. Both a modem and a fax modem require software.
5. A file server is an economical way to share a large storage device.
6. For one computer to fax a message to another, each would need a fax modem.
7. When used by computers, telephone signals are digital.
8. A bus network is the most complicated network design.
9. Each node of a network requires processing devices.
10. The ring network is the most common configuration for microcomputers.

Short Answer

1. What does LAN stand for?
2. A set of standard rules for communication is called a _____.
3. Communication requires four elements: a sender, a receiver, a message, and a _____.
4. The most efficient centralized network for a small company is the _____ configuration.
5. A monitor and keyboard linked to a host computer is called a _____.
6. In hardwired networks, _____ cables can carry more data than either coaxial cables or twisted-pair wires.
7. What does NIC stand for?
8. To convert a faxed image into text, a computer must have _____ software.
9. To _____ is to send a file to a remote computer; to _____ is to receive a file from a remote computer.
10. The _____ bit provides a way for a receiving computer to know if there was a communication error.

Answers

<table>
<tr><td colspan="2">

True/False

1. T
2. T
3. F
4. T
5. T
6. T
7. F
8. F
9. F
10. F

</td><td colspan="2">

Short Answer

1. local area network
2. protocol
3. channel
4. star
5. terminal
6. fiber optic
7. network interface card
8. OCR
9. upload; download
10. parity

</td></tr>
</table>

Challenging Your Understanding

1. Why aren't modems used to communicate on a local area network?

2. A network interface card can cost about $400, a network operating system can cost $3,000, a file server can cost $5,000, wiring for 20 computers can cost $2,000, and a printer server and printer can easily cost $1,000. How do you think business managers justify the expense of creating a local area network?

3. If data is transmitted at 2400 bps and the data travels at the speed of light (186,000 miles per second), how long is a single byte, in miles?

4. A popular saying in the computer business is "The most secure computer is the one that does the least I/O." In a telecommunications network, security is often a problem. How can you make a network as secure as possible?

5. Is a cable television network similar to a local area network, a wide area network, or a metropolitan area network? Why?

Operating Systems

Key Terms

access privileges
BIOS
compatible
cooperative multitasking
device
DOS
Finder
middleware
multitasking
multithreading
operating system (OS)
OS/2
portable
preemptive multitasking
System file
Unix
Windows
Windows NT
workstation

Objectives

In this chapter you will learn to:

- Name and describe the three primary responsibilities of an operating system
- Explain the purpose of BIOS
- Describe how file fragmentation occurs
- Define multitasking
- Describe the two main capabilities of a multiuser OS
- Explain the difference between compatibility and portability
- Describe the advantages and disadvantages of using DOS, the Macintosh operating system, Windows NT, Unix, and OS/2 2.0

Operating Systems at BVOS

Turning back to the scenario we have followed throughout this book, this chapter completes the process of purchasing hardware and software for Buena Vista Office Supply. If you have been completing the exercises, you will have made critical purchasing decisions related to all major aspects of the computer system by the time you finish this chapter.

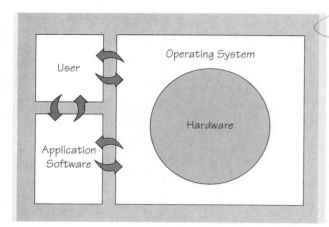

Figure 10-1

The operating system provides an interface between the hardware, which is the core of the computer, and both the user and the applications.

Primary Responsibilities of the Operating System

Today's operating systems provide a wide variety of convenient user tools and advanced capabilities. Many operating systems have adopted the most popular utility programs and included them in the OS files. Nevertheless, these programs and capabilities are add-ons, and it is important to know the core responsibilities of an operating system.

An **operating system**, or **OS**, is a set of programs that run the computer and provide an interface between the application programs — such as word processors and spreadsheets — and the hardware, as well as between the hardware and the user (Figure 10-1). All applications must communicate with the computer through the operating system. Because it is fundamental to the operation of the computer, the operating system must always be the first set of programs loaded into a microcomputer's memory. The programs that make up an operating system can be grouped into one of three primary responsibilities:

- device management
- file management
- memory management

Device Management

Each peripheral (the monitor, the keyboard, and so on) that is attached to the CPU, whether through the motherboard or a port, is called a **device**. Device is just a synonym for peripheral that we use when talking about the operating system.

The CPU of a microcomputer doesn't know how to use all the devices that are attached to it — in fact, it doesn't necessarily even know the devices exist. In order for the CPU to use these devices and use them properly, it needs some instructions.

Some of the instructions that the CPU needs are located in a special program called **BIOS**, which stands for Basic Input/Output System. On a PC, BIOS is located in a ROM chip. When the computer is turned on, BIOS performs diagnostic procedures to test the system resources. First, BIOS tests to see if the RAM chips are functioning properly. Next, BIOS searches for devices and tells the computer where they are. Finally, as shown in Figure 10-2, BIOS provides instructions for interpreting keyboard characters and sending them to the monitor or to the storage devices.

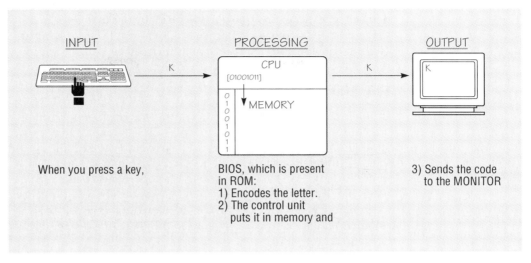

INPUT

When you press a key,

PROCESSING

CPU
[01001011]

MEMORY

BIOS, which is present
in ROM:
1) Encodes the letter.
2) The control unit
   puts it in memory and

OUTPUT

3) Sends the code
   to the MONITOR

Figure 10-2
One of the functions of
BIOS is interpreting input
from the keyboard.

Although BIOS tells the CPU where the devices are, the CPU still needs instructions to use the devices properly. Some of these instructions are included in the operating system's device management programs. The amount of device management provided by the OS varies dramatically from one OS to another. On the Macintosh, the devices are centrally controlled by the OS. DOS, however, provides a minimal amount of device management. Because device management isn't tightly controlled by DOS, developers of application software for DOS systems are forced to include the rest of the device management that is required. So, although one of the responsibilities of an OS is device management, the whole responsibility is spread among the BIOS program, the OS, and the application software.

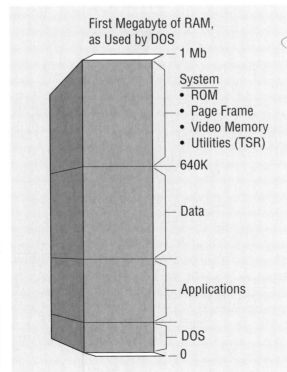

First Megabyte of RAM,
as Used by DOS

1 Mb

System
• ROM
• Page Frame
• Video Memory
• Utilities (TSR)

640K

Data

Applications

DOS

0

Figure 10-3
When using DOS, the first
megabyte of memory can
be thought of as a stack.
DOS is at the bottom
because it is loaded first;
then comes the
application, and finally the
data. Software to access
the monitor, plus several
small utility programs, are
kept in a separate area
above 640 K.

Memory Management

In addition to BIOS, the computer's ROM chip includes a "bootstrap" routine that tells the CPU to look for the operating system in storage and load it into RAM. After the bootstrap routine is completed, the OS takes sole responsibility for telling the CPU how to use RAM for holding all of the data and programs that are needed (Figure 10-3). For example, if the user wants to load an application program, he or she issues an appropriate command to the OS. The OS finds the application program and identifies where in RAM the program should be put. The program can't be put just anywhere; the OS is already occupying some part of RAM, and more space is necessary for loading data files or other programs. Once the application file is loaded, the operating system must keep track of data files that are loaded and modified from within the application. When the user quits a program or closes a data file, the OS clears that area of RAM.

File Management

Besides managing memory, the OS must keep track of everything in storage. Each disk that the computer accesses has a set of files on it. The files may be organized into a directory structure. The directory structure and the location of each file is located in a special place on the disk. If the disk was formatted on a PC using DOS, the location of each file is contained in the FAT, or File Allocation Table. The operating system creates this table on every disk when the disk is formatted (actually, DOS creates two of them, just to be safe), accesses the information in it whenever a file needs to be retrieved from storage, and updates the information anytime data is written to the disk. In essence, the operating system acts as a librarian for the CPU.

Knowing where files are stored on disk can be extremely difficult, especially if a file has been modified a number of times. Say a data file consisting of a letter to a client is originally stored in three adjacent sectors on a disk. Over time, other files are stored on the disk, until there are no more empty areas next to where the letter is stored. Then the user modifies the letter. The modifications don't fit with the rest of the file, so they are placed somewhere else on the disk. The operating system then has to keep track of two separate areas for the same file. Every time the file is modified, the same process can take place. Keeping track of such fragmented files is subject to error, and accessing them is time consuming for the computer. A disk maintenance (or optimizer) utility can be used to reorder the files properly or "defragment" them. Figure 10-4 shows the results of defragmenting a hard disk using Norton Utilities.

Comprehension Questions

1. Which one of the operating system's primary responsibilities is in charge of sending data to a modem?
2. Why must BIOS be read by the computer before the operating system is?
3. What do you think a defragmentation utility does?

Using What You Know

1. What types of computers might not need operating systems?
2. Does the operating system for a diskless workstation require storage management programs? Why or why not?
3. In the top screen of Figure 10-4, why are there unused disk areas between areas that are being used?

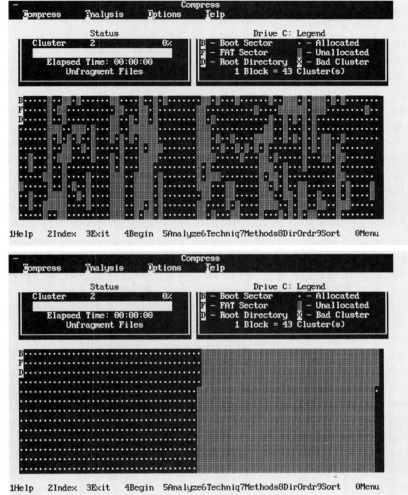

Figure 10-4
When you use a defragmentation program, you are shown a diagram of the disk. The top screen shows the diagram before defragmentation, and the bottom screen after.

Types of Operating Systems

Operating systems have evolved over the years in response to changes in user demands and hardware capabilities. Not only have many utilities been layered on top of the programs that handle the essential responsibilities of the operating system, but new programs have also been added to handle more advanced capabilities. Some of these capabilities have existed on mainframe computers for many years . As microcomputers have become more powerful, the operating systems designed for them have adopted capabilities traditionally associated with mainframe computers. Whether or not you actually need these capabilities will depend on how you intend to use your computer.

Singletasking and Multitasking Operating Systems

One of the biggest buzzwords in the current battle for the operating system throne is multitasking. **Multitasking**, which used to be called multiprogramming, is the ability to run several programs at the same time.

Multitasking is made possible by the differences between processing speed and input or output speed. The microprocessor works very quickly, while I/O devices tend to operate more slowly. When you are typing, for example, the time between each letter you press seems like ages to the CPU. During that interval, it may be able to execute thousands of machine instructions in some other program. Even much faster I/O operations, such as writing data to a disk, allow the CPU plenty of time to execute other instructions. Multitasking operating systems take advantage of these gaps by focusing the power of the CPU on several programs at once.

Multitasking operating systems are further broken down into cooperative multitasking and preemptive multitasking. These are highly technical differences, but they make it possible to distinguish between one OS and another. Essentially, **preemptive multitasking** is more efficient than cooperative multitasking, because the former allows whichever program needs the microprocessor must to go ahead and use it. **Cooperative multitasking** simply divides the CPU's time equally among the programs that are using it. Windows 3.1, shown in Figure 10-5, performs cooperative multitasking.

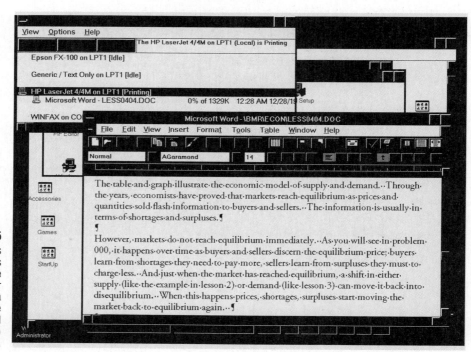

Figure 10-5
Windows 3.1 allows certain types of computers to perform cooperative multitasking. Here the user continues to work with a word processor, while the Print Manager (displayed at the top of the screen) processes a printing job.

Single- and Multiple-User Operating Systems

Some computers can interact with only a single user, while other computers can support multiple users. Single-user operating systems have relatively simple device management programs because they can concentrate on a single keyboard and a single monitor. Multiple-user operating systems are more complicated because they must keep track of all the requests each user makes. For example, one user may be entering an inventory request at the same time another user is reading an E-mail message. As shown in Figure 10-6, the operating system must keep track of input from one and output from the other. A host computer, especially one with terminal nodes, needs to handle multiple-user requests.

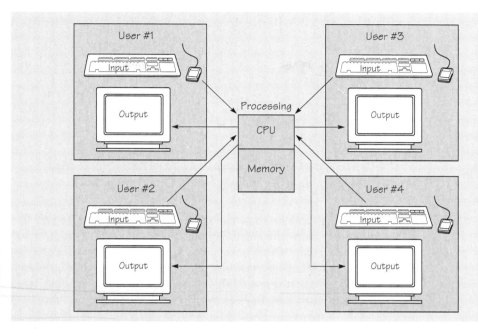

Figure 10-6
A multiuser operating system must keep track of input, processing, and output from more than one user at the same time.

Another important function of a multiuser operating system is managing the **access privileges** afforded to each user. On a multiuser computer, each user normally must enter the system with a "logon" command, such as the one shown in Figure 10-7. The computer then prompts the user for an identification number and possibly a password. The computer associates this identification with certain privileges: Often the user is allowed a fixed amount of storage space and access to specific files or programs. Controlling access privileges thus allows a company to limit the use of valuable resources and protect sensitive files. A network file server's operating system must be able to manage access privileges.

Figure 10-7
On this Novell network, users must issue the LOGIN command followed by their name. The operating system then prompts the user for an identification number, which does not appear on the screen when it is typed. If the identification number is correct, the user is given specific access privileges.

```
Running on DOS V5.00

Attached to server FS-ZA
01-21-93     12:22:27 PM

C:\>f:login brad
Enter your password:
Device LPT1: re-routed to queue PRINTQ_TOP on server FS-ZA.

Shell version: 3.22 Std
Previous setting: SHOW DOTS=OFF    Changed to ON

H:\HOME\BRAD>
```

Single- and Multiple-Processor Operating Systems

Although it is rare for microcomputers, minis and mainframes can have many central processing units. In fact, some very large computers, such as those used to predict the weather or explore for oil, can have thousands of CPUs. These sets of chips are called *multiprocessors* or *parallel processors*. A parallel operating system is used to coordinate the parallel processors and provide communication between them. Each of the processors also has a small operating system.

Portable and Nonportable Operating Systems

With respect to hardware, software can be judged by its compatibility and its portability. A program that is **compatible** with a given machine will run on that machine. A machine that is compatible with another machine can run the same software. Compatibility has been an issue among hardware manufacturers for years, especially in the IBM-compatibles arena. Traditionally, software was written to run on a certain type of machine, and manufacturers of similar machines had to worry about compatibility.

A program that is **portable** can be run on many different machines. Whereas compatibility is often an issue for hardware manufacturers, portability is becoming an issue with software developers. This issue is likely to grow in importance, especially as the Unix operating system gains a foothold in the microcomputer operating system market.

In the late 1960s, a programmer named Ken Thompson, who worked at Bell Laboratories, wanted to move a program from an expensive General Electric computer to a less expensive minicomputer made by Digital Equipment Corporation. Although the DEC equipment offered a good hardware environment for running Thompson's program, it lacked the kind of software support needed to continue his work. Thompson created **Unix** as a set of routines to support the DEC system.

Although the original Unix system was written in assembly language, a subsequent version used a language called "B," which Thompson developed in 1970. B was extended and refined by Dennis Ritchie, another Bell Labs programmer. The resulting language was C. Unix was rewritten in C in 1973.

The major reason for rewriting Unix in C was the desire to move it to a wider range of machines. Only a small portion of Unix is written specifically for a certain computer. The rest — the part written in C — is easily transferred from one machine to another. This portability requires changing the small parts of the program that are written for a particular computer and then recompiling the C portion of the operating system.

Today, efforts to create portable operating systems are in full swing. In addition to the work that has occurred and continues to occur on Unix, Microsoft and IBM are working on operating systems that are portable. There is a greater advantage than simply being able to move the operating system from one type of machine to another. Portability in an OS makes application programs more portable as well. For example, right now it is not possible to use a word processor like Microsoft Word for the Mac on a PC. If Word was written for a portable OS, however, it would run on any computer that could run the portable OS.

Middleware

A new type of software, called **middleware**, attempts to shield users from the complexity of computer systems by providing a layer of software between the application and the operating system. Middleware is a layer of software that integrates disparate technologies. Some people use the analogy of a glue that binds certain pieces of software together.

Middleware simplifies the process of connecting various software products, regardless of whether or not these products compete with or adhere to a given set of standards. As a result, developers and users don't have to deal with all the diversity that results from multivendor configurations and can instead focus on their own technology or applications.

Comprehension Questions

1. Some operating systems accomplish multitasking by allocating short, successive blocks of time to each program that is running. What type of multitasking do you think this is — cooperative or preemptive?
2. Do the computers attached to a file server need a multiuser operating system? Why or why not?
3. Say you already own a set of application programs and hardware devices. Now you need an OS. Is your primary concern the compatibility or the portability of the OS?

Using What You Know

1. Would the stockroom workers at BVOS benefit from a multitasking OS? Why or why not?
2. Which computer at BVOS requires a multiuser OS?
3. As president, how important is the portability of the OS you use at BVOS?

Popular Operating Systems

During the 1980s, two operating systems got most of the attention. DOS was the overwhelming market leader because it had become the standard operating system for all PCs (IBMs and compatibles). The operating system for the Mac also got a lot of attention because it won users by pioneering the possibilities of the user-friendly graphical user interface.

Today, the operating system market is in much greater disarray. While still popular, the Macintosh doesn't command much more or less of the market than it did several years ago, but the DOS market has fragmented. To some extent, this fragmentation has been the result of the Mac's popular operating system. PC users made it clear that they wanted a GUI. More important, however, DOS was designed for the PCs of the 1980s, most of which used the 8088 or 286 chip. Both of these are 16-bit chips, and DOS is a 16-bit operating system. The 386 and 486, however, are 32-bit chips. A 16-bit operating system cannot take full advantage of their capabilities.

Several contenders are vying for the gap created by DOS's shortcomings. The first to enter the race was IBM's OS/2, which first hit the market in 1987. The early versions didn't gain widespread use, but IBM is pressing hard with version 2.0, released in 1992. Another competitor is Unix, which has moved from being a minicomputer OS down to the micro level with the introduction of the 32-bit chip. Finally, Windows NT, which, with Windows 3.1, already has a significant market share, is trying to dominate the market as Microsoft's 32-bit replacement for DOS.

Let's look more closely at each of these operating systems, beginning with the old standard, DOS.

DOS

Microsoft's Disk Operating System, or **DOS**, was developed for IBM and released in 1981. Microsoft Corporation got its start a few years earlier when Bill Gates dropped out of Harvard to form the company with his high school friend Paul Allen (Figure 10-8). They began their business by writing versions of BASIC for the first microcomputers. In 1980, IBM decided to hire the young company to create an operating system for entry into the microcomputer market. When the IBM PC came out a year later, it was an immediate success, and the operating system became a success with it.

As the compatibles market grew, two nearly identical versions of the operating system emerged: PC-DOS was the version licensed by IBM to be packaged on its machines; MS-DOS was Microsoft's proprietary version that was sold to compatibles vendors. Largely through the sales of DOS, Microsoft established itself as the most influential software company. Paul Allen has since left Microsoft to form his own software company, the Asymetrix Corporation. Bill Gates, still the head of Microsoft, has gone on to become the richest man in the United States. In 1992, Mr. Gates, in his mid-thirties, was worth about $8 billion.

Over the years, DOS has matured. It started as a minimalist operating system — what you needed in order to run a PC (Figure 10-9). It grew to include a wide array of utilities. It also grew to keep up with hardware developments, such as the hard disk and 3½-inch diskettes. Today, DOS still represents the minimum requirements of an operating system. The reason, though, is that DOS remains the market-share leader. To beat the leader, an operating system must offer more in terms of features, portability, and compatibility.

```
B:\>format b:
Insert new diskette for drive B:
and press ENTER when ready...

Checking existing disk format.
Saving UNFORMAT information.
Verifying 1.44M
Format complete.

Volume label (11 characters, ENTER for none)?

    1457664 bytes total disk space
    1457664 bytes available on disk

       512 bytes in each allocation unit.
      2847 allocation units available on disk.

Volume Serial Number is 3F34-07EC

Format another (Y/N)?
```

Figure 10-9
Most users access DOS
from the command line.
Here, the user has entered
the FORMAT command to
reformat the disk.

Here are a few of the advantages and disadvantages of using DOS:

Advantages

- *A huge market base.* For more than 10 years, DOS has been the market-share leader. If you use DOS, you are part of the biggest microcomputer community in the world. In addition, DOS is the industry standard. Even though DOS is losing its lead in the market, new operating systems for PCs still try to make their systems DOS-compatible. New users of other OSs can still use their old DOS applications and files, and DOS users are never cut off from the movement toward more powerful operating systems.

- *The most applications to choose from.* Because DOS dominated the market for so long, thousands of applications and utilities have been written for it. This situation gives users a great deal of flexibility when choosing the right tool for the job.

- *A fast platform for text-based work.* Most of the recently developed operating systems are built around a graphical user interface (GUI). DOS, however, is a text-based system, meaning that it is meant to manage text characters rather than graphical elements. For users who do not want a GUI — whether because of a personal preference or because their systems slow down under the added requirements of a graphical system — DOS is fast and efficient.

- *Can be used with 16-bit chips.* Although the vast majority of the computers sold today include the 386 and 486 32-bit architecture, there are plenty of 286, and even 8088, machines still in the workplace. The reason is that these machines are more than adequate for basic, everyday word processing and spreadsheet needs. If this is all you intend to do with a computer, you can pick up a used machine and a copy of DOS for very little money.

Disadvantages

- *Limited memory management.* One of the major complaints about DOS is that it cannot access more than 1 MB of memory without special software. Many of today's applications require more. Using Windows 3.1 alone requires far more than 1 MB.

- *Lack of a fully integrated GUI.* Confirmed DOS users will tell you that DOS has a GUI, the DOS Shell, which can be run in either graphics mode or text mode (Figure 10-10).

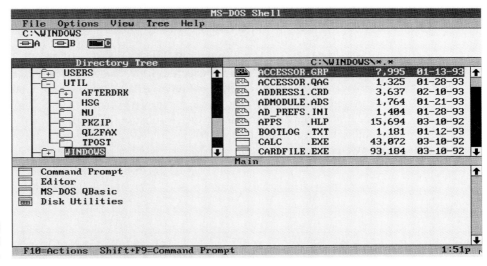

Figure 10-10
The DOS Shell, an optional graphics environment.

This is true, and the DOS Shell is significantly more intuitive, and therefore easier to learn, than the original command-line interface. The operating system as a whole, however, is not graphically based, but text based; the GUI is just an add-on feature. This means that applications running under DOS are usually text based, though they may have graphics modes. This aspect of DOS cannot be called a flaw, because many users prefer the speed and efficiency of text based applications. New users, however, seem to prefer working in graphic environments.

- *Lack of a standard interface.* Ever since the Mac gained a foothold in the market, there has been a move toward interfaces that have a standard look to them. The advantage here is that users can learn new programs more quickly because many aspects of using each program are the same. Windows and Windows NT are perfect examples of how PC interfaces have followed the Mac's lead. DOS, however, remains much more open-ended. A software developer creating a DOS application can create any type of interface. This freedom makes it more difficult to move from one application to another.

- *Cannot perform multitasking.* By itself (without the addition of a graphic environment such as Windows or Deskview 386), DOS is a single-tasking operating system. For many types of computer use, this limitation may not be a problem. However, users who want to either run one program in the background while they use another or load several applications at once so they can switch quickly between them will find DOS cumbersome.

Users frustrated with DOS have been predicting the demise of the operating system for years. Ironically, some aspects of this highly volatile industry don't change nearly as quickly as the experts expect. The reason is the stability of the "installed base," that is, the existing computer systems. There are more computers running DOS than any other operating system in the world. Even though most of the new equipment may be better served by a more powerful OS, DOS will maintain a major presence in the market for several more years.

The Macintosh's System Software

Although the operating system for the Macintosh is called the **System file**, many Mac users aren't even aware of it. The reason is that the System file, a 32-bit operating system, works in conjunction with the **Finder**, an extremely well-designed GUI that insulates the user from the real responsibilities of the operating system (Figure 10-11). The Finder manages the System by using a series of graphical images. For instance, to delete a file from the Macintosh, you simply drag the file into an icon representing a trash can. The Finder manages applications and controls the icons, Clipboard, and Scrapbook functions.

The Macintosh, which was released in 1984, has maintained a similar interface throughout its history. The most recent version of the operating system, System 7, looks very much like the original system, although the recent version is far more powerful. Operating system advancements on the Macintosh have closely paralleled those on the PC. The reason is that the Mac remains a major competitor to the PC, even though the two systems are, in many respects, incompatible.

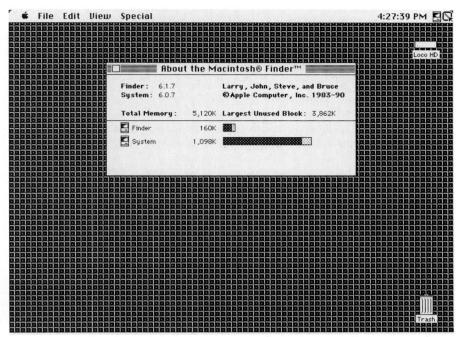

Figure 10-11
The Macintosh and its
operating system, which is
controlled by the System
file and the Finder.

Here are some of the advantages and disadvantages to using the Macintosh and its resident operating system.

Advantages

- *A consistent, "friendly" interface.* The Mac's operating system forces the applications that run under it into a familiar look. As shown in Figure 10-12 on the next page, each one has a set of pull-down menus across the top of the screen, and many of the menus are the same. Consequently, Mac applications are relatively easy to learn, at least in comparison to DOS applications. Historically, ease of use has been the Mac's biggest selling point.

- *A fully integrated graphics interface.* Every program that runs on the Mac is in graphics mode all the time. This feature is an added level of consistency that sets the System apart from DOS, where you can be unexpectedly switched into and out of graphics mode.

- *Continuing efforts at compatibility with DOS machines.* DOS-based machines are not able to run Macintosh applications, but the opposite is less and less true. In recent years, Apple has worked hard to accommodate business users by building in the ability to run PC software. The first step was to include the SuperDrive, which can read DOS-formatted disks. More recently, Apple has made it possible to install PC boards in the Mac and thereby run DOS applications.

- *Multitasking.* Recent versions of the System are able to perform cooperative multitasking, though they are not capable of full, preemptive multitasking.

- *Simplicity of moving data between applications.* Another feature that the Mac's operating system pioneered was the "Clipboard." The Clipboard is a holding pen for data that has been cut or copied from an application. Once the data is in the Clipboard, it can be pasted into another application. This capability makes it possible, for

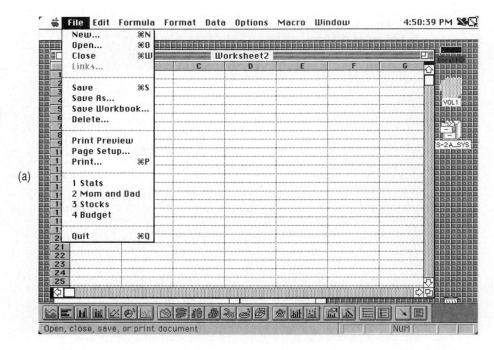

(a)

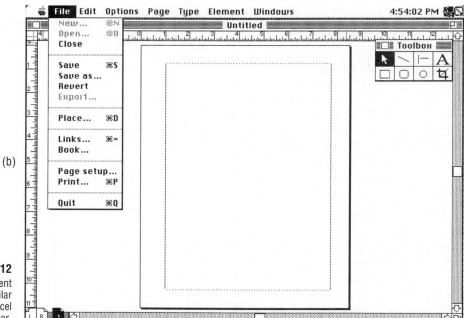

(b)

Figure 10-12
Two very different
programs with a similar
look: (a) Microsoft Excel
and (b) Aldus PageMaker.

instance, to copy a graph created in a spreadsheet into a business report created with a word processor (Figure 10-13 on the next page). With subscribe and publish features, it is also possible to create dynamic links on the Mac. With a dynamic link, material that has been copied into another document will change if the original document is altered. For example, say you create a bar graph showing the amount of your power bill each month. You then copy the graph into a memo to your employees about saving

(a)
(b)

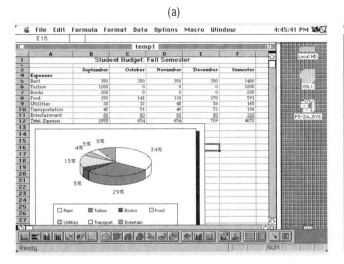
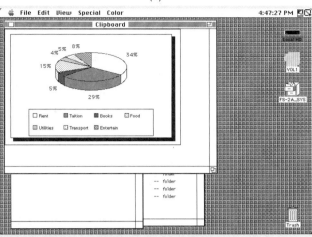

(c)

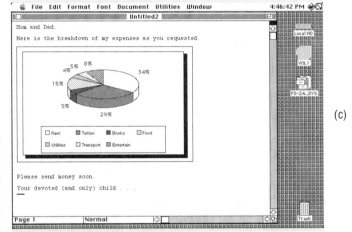

Figure 10-13

(a) A graph is created in Microsoft Excel.
(b) The graph is copied into the Clipboard.
(c) The graph is pasted into a memo written in Claris MacWrite II.

electricity. Before you give the memo out, you get another power bill and add it to your spreadsheet, which automatically adds it to your graph. If you had created a dynamic link, the graph in your memo would be updated automatically as well.

- *High-quality on-screen graphics.* Creating and manipulating graphic images is made easy by the Mac's high-quality video output.

Disadvantages

- *Inability of PCs to run Mac software.* Despite Apple's efforts to accommodate DOS software, most PC machines cannot run Mac software. For the Mac user, this means that the majority of the business community cannot access Mac software and, more important, data that is formatted for the Mac. Incompatibility has been Apple's biggest stumbling block with the Mac.

- *Expense.* The other major drawback of using the Mac is the price of the machine. Because of the competition from compatibles, the cost of technology on the PC has steadily declined. The same is not true of the Macintosh, where compatible machines are not available. As a result, for a given amount of processing power, storage capacity, and input and output devices, it is cheaper to buy a PC than a Mac.

Looking at the disadvantages mentioned above, you can see that they aren't directly related to the Mac's operating system. The operating system is difficult to fault: It has always been ahead of its time.

Microsoft Windows 3.1 and Windows NT

In 1985, Microsoft released **Windows** as a way to give DOS a Mac-like interface. The name Windows comes from the program's ability to maintain different viewing areas on the screen (Figure 10-14). Each window can contain a different application. Users can switch back and forth between windows with the click of a mouse button.

Windows gives DOS users the ability to work in a graphic environment and still have access to all of the regular DOS applications. They can also use Windows applications, programs specifically designed to operate under Windows. Like the programs designed for the Mac, Windows programs all have a similar look (Figure 10-15). Another advantage of Windows over DOS alone is the ability to move data quickly between applications. Finally, Windows permits a certain level of multitasking. The level of multitasking that is possible depends on the type of machine being used and the mode that Windows is run in.

The problem with Windows is that it must run under DOS. Therefore, Windows is still largely limited to a 16-bit system, and it cannot directly address more than 1 MB of memory. To take advantage of the true power of the 32-bit chips, Microsoft is finalizing **Windows NT** (NT stands for "New Technology"). Windows 3.1 is really just a high-powered shell for DOS but Windows NT is a true operating system. NT is still compatible with DOS because it can use any DOS applications, but DOS is not present in the system. Thus, NT will be Microsoft's replacement for DOS in the 32-bit market.

When purchasing software related to these products, it is critical to distinguish between Windows and Windows NT. You can rely on NT to run applications designed for DOS-dependent Windows, but not vice versa. Also, programs written specifically for NT will generally be faster and more efficient than those written for DOS-dependent Windows.

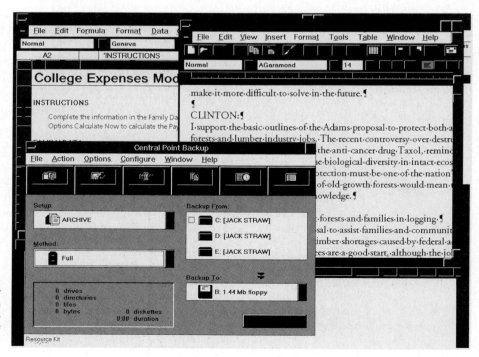

Figure 10-14
In Windows, the user can keep several applications visible on the screen at the same time.

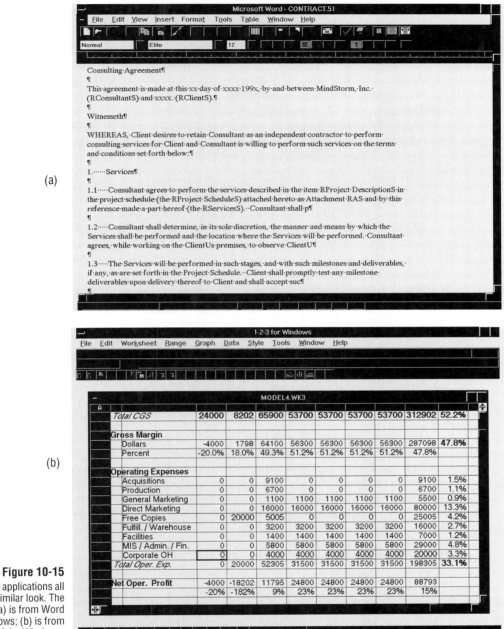

Figure 10-15
Windows applications all have a similar look. The screen in (a) is from Word for Windows; (b) is from Lotus 1-2-3 for Windows.

Here are some of the potential advantages and disadvantages of Windows NT.

Potential Advantages

- *32-bit processing.* The biggest advantage of NT over DOS is that the operating system is designed to take advantage of the 32-bit processing capabilities of 386 and 486 chips.

- *Full preemptive multitasking.* NT is able to perform the highest level of multitasking, allowing applications to use the CPU when they need it most. This is a step up from DOS-dependent Windows, which could perform only cooperative multitasking.

- *Direct access to 4 gigabytes of memory.* Like the other 32-bit operating systems, NT is not subject to the 1 MB barrier under which DOS suffers. NT memory access is therefore faster and more efficient.

- *Excellent data exchange capabilities.* As with the versions of Windows that run under DOS, NT is able to move data between applications quickly and easily. Windows and Windows NT are even able to create dynamic links between files using Windows' OLE (Object Linking and Embedding).

- *The ability to use DOS applications and DOS-dependent Windows applications.* NT is upward-compatible, so users can keep their old Windows programs, as well as their old DOS programs. DOS is, after all, a Microsoft product. The company is likely to make every possible effort not to leave its old customers out in the cold, no matter how much it wants to sell new versions of its application software.

Potential Disadvantages

- *Extensive hardware requirements.* The biggest complaint about NT is the amount of memory that it requires. Prior to the new 32-bit operating systems, few microcomputers for business had more than 4 MB of memory. Because of software like NT, old users are being forced to add memory, and machines with 8 or 16 MB are becoming the norm.

- *A complicated GUI.* Although the complaint is subjective, many users say that NT, like Windows before it, is more difficult than it needs to be. Perhaps the most specific criticism is that the File Manager is not a fully integrated part of the interface. Users must first open the File Manager before they can move, copy, or delete files. Other software vendors have responded to these complaints by creating shells for NT. The Norton Desktop for Windows NT, for example, is one of these shells.

Windows NT has a big advantage in the battle over 32-bit systems, simply because of the success of Windows 3.0 and 3.1. The program does face formidable challengers. Nevertheless, the installed base has shown its force before in the OS war, and Microsoft's presence in the market may be more important than any technical issues.

Unix

The oldest operating system competing for today's market is actually not DOS but Unix. For years, Unix has been touted as "the operating system of the future," but it has yet to gain a large portion of the PC or Macintosh market.

As noted before, Unix was originally developed at AT&T for one of its minicomputers. AT&T licensed the software to universities, and the students at these schools modified and improved the code. The University of California at Berkeley was especially influential in the evolution of the operating system. Some of the improvements were integrated back into AT&T's version of Unix, while others became part of other versions. The number of developers involved with Unix is one of the factors that has made the system so powerful.

Although Unix has yet to gain a large following among business microcomputer users, it does command the lion's share of the workstation market. A **workstation** is a high-powered microcomputer (or a single-user minicomputer) that is used for scientific, engineering, or technical applications. Many workstations are equipped with top-of-the-line graphics capabilities to meet the needs of today's computer-assisted design (CAD) software. Currently, more than three quarters of all workstations use some version of Unix. Figure 10-16 shows one version.

Here are the advantages and disadvantages of using Unix:

Advantages

- *32-bit processing.* Like its competitors and unlike DOS, Unix is a 32-bit operating system.

- *Portability.* Unix is currently the most portable operating system available for micro-computers. With relative ease, a given version of Unix can be adapted to any number of micros, minis, or mainframes.

- *Multitasking.* Like the other 32-bit OSs, Unix is capable of multitasking.

- *Multiuser capabilities.* Unlike Windows NT or OS/2, Unix is able to manage multiple-user requests. This may prove to be a powerful advantage for Unix as more small businesses adopt sophisticated networks.

- *Well-developed networking capabilities.* Because it has always had multiuser capabilities, Unix's networking features are well developed and standardized.

- *Direct access to 4 gigabytes of memory.* Like NT and OS/2 2.0, Unix is not burdened by the 1 MB DOS barrier.

- *Fewer system requirements than Windows NT or OS/2 2.0.* Some versions of Unix will run reliably on systems with 4 MB of RAM. NT and OS/2 both require at least 6 MB for full functionality.

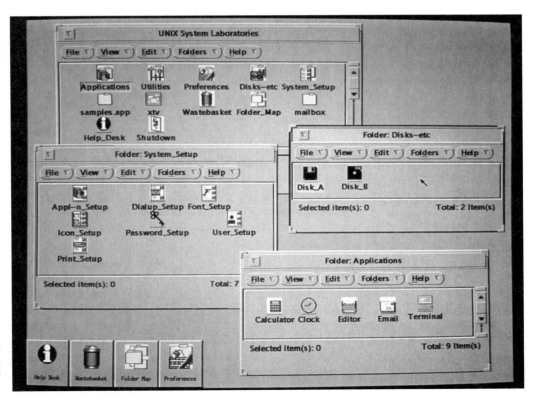

Figure 10-16

Unix System V, by Unix Software Laboratories (a division of Bell Labs).

Disadvantages

- *Competing versions of the software.* Although the number of developers made Unix a powerful operating system, it also led to multiple versions. Unix was originally an AT&T product, but many other companies now market versions of Unix. These companies include such major computer vendors as Sun Microsystems, IBM, Hewlett-Packard, and NeXT. Standards are beginning to emerge, but they are not yet sufficiently stable to satisfy the business community, where compatibility is a high priority.

- *Lack of compatible application software.* Perhaps the biggest disadvantage of using Unix is the lack of business application software that has been written for it. This problem is compounded by the number of versions of Unix, since a program written for one version will not necessarily work on any other version. As standards emerge for Unix, this disadvantage could eventually disappear.

It remains to be seen whether Unix is really the OS of the future. The largest factors in Unix's success are likely to be the existence of top-quality applications for business and compatibility with the DOS and Windows software that is currently so prevalent.

OS/2

In 1987, IBM, with help from Microsoft, released the first version of **OS/2**, the operating system specifically designed to take advantage of the newer Intel chips, beginning with the 286. OS/2 was heralded as a great leap forward because it brought multitasking to the PC. Some industry experts predicted the quick demise of DOS in the face of competition that had superior capabilities. OS/2's reception in the market, however, was lukewarm, to a large extent because of the program's size and lack of applications developed to take advantage of its advanced features.

With OS/2 2.0, IBM made its entrance into the 32-bit OS market (Figure 10-17). IBM is now in a head-to-head race with Windows NT. Unix is in the race as well, so we can safely assume that this market will be unstable for quite some time.

Here are the advantages and disadvantages of using OS/2 2.0:

Advantages

- *32-bit processing.* Like NT and Unix, OS/2 takes advantage of the 32-bit Intel chips, the 386 and the 486.

- *Ability to perform preemptive multitasking.* Like Unix and Windows NT, OS/2 is able to do the highest form of multitasking.

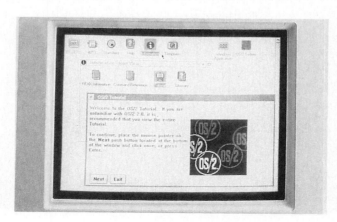

Figure 10-17
OS/2 2.0, IBM's competitor in the 32-bit operating systems market

- *Ability to run DOS and DOS-dependent Windows applications.* To tap into the DOS and Windows markets, IBM has made it possible to run all DOS applications, as well as DOS-dependent Windows applications. OS/2 was the first to include this feature; the software came out a year before NT.

- *Mac-like GUI.* The OS/2 GUI more closely resembles the Mac interface than the NT GUI does. Many of the most common tasks, such as deleting and printing files, can be done simply by moving icons on the screen, a technique called "drag and drop." For example, a file can be deleted by moving its icon to a trash icon.

- *Ability to run applications in "protected mode."* Starting with the 286, it is possible to set up areas in RAM that will not interfere with each other. Using this feature is known as *running applications in protected mode.* In protected mode, if there is a problem with one application, it can be restarted without restarting the whole computer. Although Windows has now adopted this feature, OS/2 incorporated it years before with the first version of the software.

- *No 1 MB barrier.* Like NT and Unix, OS/2 is not subject to the DOS 1 MB barrier.

Disadvantages
- *Few existing 32-bit applications.* IBM's biggest hurdle is a lack of software that will take advantage of the new 32-bit system. Thousands of developers are working on programs for 32-bit OS/2, but it takes time to build up a substantial arsenal.

- *Extensive system requirements.* Like NT, OS/2 2.0 needs at least 6 MB of RAM to run reliably. This requirement is forcing users to add memory to their existing systems or purchase new computers.

- *Difficult installation.* Many early adopters of OS/2 2.0 have complained that the installation process is a headache. Once it is accomplished, however, most users seem more than satisfied with the software's performance.

- *Training old users to operate a new interface.* To win the OS war, IBM needs to convince DOS and Windows users that they should switch to OS/2. Where Windows is already entrenched, this is a difficult feat, because the path of least resistance is to switch to NT.

OS/2 beat Microsoft in the race to release a 32-bit operating system — a wise tactical move. Moreover, OS/2 2.0 is a vast improvement over the earlier versions of the software. But while OS/2 was being revamped, Windows 3.0 and 3.1 took a huge share of the high-end PC market. Now IBM is faced with the formidable task of winning those users over to its OS. As we have said before, the excellence of IBM's product may not be as big a factor as the simple fact that Microsoft dominates the OS market. Time will tell.

Comprehension Questions

1. What aspect of DOS has led to the war among NT, OS/2, and Unix?
2. Which company is the biggest player in the PC software market?
3. What two factors made it imperative that OS/2 2.0 could run DOS and DOS-dependent Windows applications?

Using What You Know

1. Our discussion of 32-bit operating systems is necessarily tentative because this book went to print before the final version of Windows NT was released. Who appears to be winning the war over the 32-bit systems?

2. Compare prices between OS/2 and Windows NT. Make sure the prices you find are for the start-up version of the software, rather than for the upgrade.

3. With the previous purchasing decisions you have made in mind, which operating system would you choose for BVOS?

Summary Points

Operating Systems at BVOS

☐ This chapter completes the process of buying hardware for BVOS.

Primary Responsibilities of the Operating System

☐ The minimum requirements of an operating system are device, file, and memory management.

Device Management

☐ Before the OS is loaded, BIOS checks the RAM chips and looks for devices.
☐ After the BIOS is read, device management is handed over to the OS, though some of this responsibility may be shared with the application software.

Memory Management

☐ After the bootstrap routine tells the CPU to load the OS into RAM, all memory management is handled by the OS.

File Management

☐ The OS acts as a librarian for the CPU, keeping track of where files are stored on the disk.
☐ File management becomes much more complicated when modifications to files causes them to be fragmented.

Types Of Operating Systems

☐ Operating systems for micros are now able to accomplish some of the same capabilities as those of mainframes.

Singletasking and Multitasking Operating Systems

☐ The ability to run more than one program at once is made possible by the difference between processing speed and I/O speeds.
☐ Multitasking OSs are broken down into preemptive and cooperative systems; preemptive systems are more efficient.

Single- and Multiple-User Operating Systems

☐ Multiple-user OSs must keep track of multiple and simultaneous I/O requests.
☐ Most multiple-user OSs also manage the access privileges of the users.
☐ A file server's multiuser OS must be able to manage access privileges.

Single- and Multiple-Processor Operating Systems

☐ Some large computers have many CPUs in them and require a parallel operating system to handle the parallel processors.

Portable and Nonportable Operating Systems

☐ A compatible program can run on a given machine; a compatible machine can run the same software as another machine.

☐ A portable program can be used on different machines.

☐ Unix, which was first developed at AT&T, was the first portable operating system.

Middleware

☐ Middleware establishes an interface between the operating system and the applications.

Popular Operating Systems

☐ The dominance that DOS held in the OS market during the 1980s is giving way to a period of intense competition between the 32-bit operating systems for the PC.

DOS

☐ Microsoft became the biggest player in the software industry by creating the operating system for IBM's first PC and the compatibles market.

Advantages

☐ DOS has the advantage of having the largest market base, having the most applications to choose from, being a fast platform for text-based applications, and not requiring 32-bit chips.

Disadvantages

☐ DOS can only directly address 1 MB of RAM; it lacks a fully integrated GUI and a standard interface; and it cannot perform multitasking without the help of other software.

The Macintosh's System Software

☐ The Mac is most popular with users seeking a computer that is easy to operate and with "power users" who need high-quality graphics.

Advantages

☐ The Mac has a consistent, friendly GUI; it is capable of multitasking and trading or sharing information between applications; and it has high-quality video output.

☐ Apple makes it as simple as possible to use DOS-based data and programs on the Mac.

Disadvantages

☐ The major disadvantages of purchasing a Mac are its expense and the inability of most PCs to run Mac programs or load Mac-formatted data.

Microsoft Windows 3.1 and Windows NT

☐ DOS-dependent Windows was originally created as a GUI shell for the PC.

☐ Windows NT is Microsoft's 32-bit replacement for DOS.

Potential Advantages

☐ NT performs 32-bit processing and preemptive multitasking; it eliminates the 1 MB barrier; it has excellent data exchange capabilities; and it can run DOS and DOS-dependent Windows applications.

Potential Disadvantages

☐ NT requires more memory than most older machines have.

☐ Some users complain that Windows is harder to use than it needs to be.

Unix

☐ Unix is touted as the OS of the future, but it has yet to command a large portion of the business market.

☐ Over three quarters of all workstations use some form of Unix.

Advantages

☐ Like NT and OS/2, Unix is multitasking and is not hindered by the 1 MB DOS memory barrier.

☐ Unix is also a portable, multiuser system; it does not require as much RAM as NT or OS/2; and it has well-developed and standardized networking capabilities.

Disadvantages

☐ Competing versions of Unix make compatibility a problem.

☐ Unix does not yet have as formidable an arsenal of business applications as the other OSs.

OS/2

☐ The early versions of OS/2 were not a great success, but OS/2 2.0 is now in the race for the lead of the 32-bit operating systems.

Advantages

☐ OS/2 2.0 has advantages similar to those of NT, though its interface may be easier to use.

Disadvantages

☐ Compared to NT, the disadvantages of OS/2 are mainly difficult installation, lack of software designed specifically for it, and the fact that much of its target market is already using DOS-dependent Windows.

Knowing the Facts

True/False

1. BIOS must be read before the operating system can be loaded into RAM.
2. BIOS is stored permanently on the RAM chip.
3. DOS can perform preemptive multitasking; OS/2 can perform cooperative multitasking.
4. Multitasking is the modern term used to describe multiprogramming.
5. Unix was originally developed at AT&T.
6. The many developers who worked on Unix have made it a highly compatible operating system.
7. Prior to Windows NT, Windows required DOS to be running in the background.
8. The Macintosh's System file is the core of a 16-bit operating system.
9. A PC is more likely to be able to run Mac software than the other way around.
10. Software designed for Windows NT will run on DOS-dependent Windows, but the opposite is not true.

Short Answer

1. What are the three primary requirements of an operating system?
2. What is the term used to describe a file that is located in nonadjacent sectors on a disk?
3. What capacity must the operating system of a host computer on a network have?
4. What was the first major portable operating system?
5. What operating system is used by more than 75 percent of today's workstations?
6. What operating system pioneered the possibilities of being user friendly?
7. The existence of _____ has made it cheaper to buy a PC than a Macintosh of similar power.
8. One complaint with OS/2 and Windows NT is the amount of _____ required to run these pieces of software.
9. The Mac allows the user to create dynamic links using the publish and subscribe features. A similar capability is possible with Windows using _____.
10. Historically, the biggest factor in the OS war has been _____.

Answers

True/False

1. T
2. F
3. F
4. T
5. T
6. F
7. T
8. F
9. F
10. F

Short Answer

1. device, file, and memory management
2. fragmented
3. It must be a multiuser OS or have the ability to manage multiple I/O requests.
4. Unix
5. Unix
6. The Mac's System
7. compatibles
8. memory
9. OLE (Object Linking and Embedding)
10. market share, or the installed base

Challenging Your Understanding

1. Is it possible to select the wrong operating system for a computer? What are the most important things to think about when choosing an operating system?

2. Should an operating system come standard with a computer when you buy it? Why or why not?

3. Why must all multiuser operating systems be multitasking?

4. What does a multiprocessing operating system have to do that is different from a multitasking operating system?

5. Why is the user interface often a concern for the operating system rather than the application software?

Unit III Project

Tracking Computer Prices for the LAT Newsletter

Los Alamos Technology (LAT) is a business that monitors developments in the computer industry. Companies around the world use the services of LAT analysts to anticipate changes in the computer industry and to help make plans for incorporating new technologies that are being developed into their strategic plans. For example, a large express mail company used information provided by LAT to incorporate hand-held computers into their delivery business and gain a substantial edge over their competition.

Lisa Bunker is the lead analyst for the microcomputer industry focus group. The purpose of this group is to analyze and forecast developments specifically related to desktop microcomputers used in business. While browsing through reams of data that LAT routinely collects concerning developments in microcomputers, it occurred to Lisa that there must be hundreds of small businesses that would pay for information about the current prices and capabilities of microcomputers. She formulated the idea of producing and selling a newsletter that detailed the prices and capabilities of microcomputers and microcomputer components. Lisa presented her ideas to the LAT board of directors and was encouraged to create a prototype newsletter to present to the board at its next monthly meeting. The board authorized Lisa to assign you for the next month to gather data and help produce the prototype.

Using popular microcomputer magazines such as *PC Magazine* and *Byte*, your job is to find the price and feature list of the "average" microcomputer for sale over the past twelve months. What does it include? How much does it cost? What is the average cost per component if the components were purchased independently? Use a graph to depict your findings and then, using this information, help Lisa anticipate developments in microcomputers a year from now.

Organizational Solutions

With the end of Unit III you have put your major purchasing decisions behind you. As president of your BVOS branch, you have bought the necessary hardware and software for your new business. You have already hired most of your employees. Now it is time to build your computer system.

Building a computer system at a business means much more than setting up the hardware and loading the software onto a hard disk. The real work of building the system is creating the information systems that serve the information needs of the company. This is a complex process that involves designing the databases that will store data related to a company's operation and establishing the means for getting raw data into and processed data out of the database.

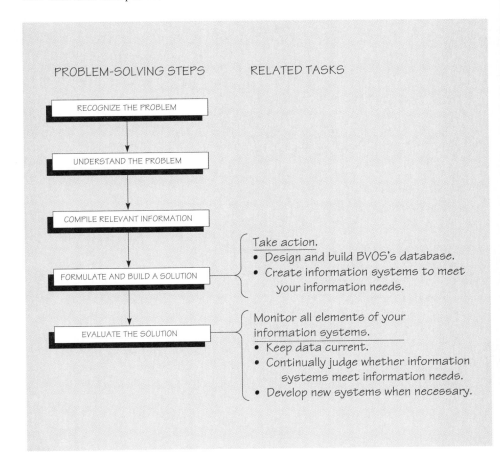

Figure IV-1   In this unit, we will focus on steps 4 and 5 of the problem-solving process.

To demonstrate how information systems are established, we begin with a close look at databases, the core of data around which most information systems are built. Then, we define and categorize the many information systems that use the database, as well as a few that do not. Finally, we examine the steps involved in developing an information system.

In the two previous units, we focused on steps 2, 3, and 4 of the problem-solving methodology. In this unit, our primary emphasis will be on step 4, though we will have a few things to say about step 5, evaluating the solution. Figure IV-1 illustrates how this unit fits into the problem-solving process.

Managing Databases

Key Terms

alphanumeric field
binary field
button
database
database administrator
data dictionary
date field
field
field name
field type
file
flat-file database
graphic field
hierarchical database
hypermedia database
indexing
logical field
memo field
network database
numeric field
query
record
query language
relation
relational database
report
sorting
stack
time field

Objectives

In this chapter you will learn to:

- Describe the differences between how a paper-based office organizes data and how a computerized office organizes data
- Explain the relationships among the three elements that make up a database
- Name the five main types of fields
- Explain the importance of database structure
- Describe each of the five common database structures
- Explain the advantage of a relational structure over a hierarchical, network, or flat-file structure
- Describe how a hypermedia database differs from a traditional database
- Differentiate between sorting and indexing
- Give examples of how a database can be queried
- Name and describe the five goals of a database
- Describe the role of the database administrator
- Describe how databases can affect personal privacy

Managing Data at BVOS

With this chapter, we turn our attention to the fourth element of the computer system: data. The BVOS inventory database is the living core of the business. It is a record of all daily transactions, including items in stock, items ordered by customers, and items on order from the regional distributor. In this chapter, we look at the concept of a database: how it is created, how it can be structured, and how software can be used to manage it.

Managing Data in a Paper-Based Office

Before the proliferation of computers in business, data was kept in the form of written records. Organization of data was largely determined by the ubiquitous file cabinet: Data was stored on forms and other documents, which were organized into folders, which were grouped into hanging folders, which fit into file drawers.

Maintaining this organizational system required the continual creation and proper storage of paper records. For example, if BVOS were a paper-based office, every new customer who ordered supplies would need to fill out a new customer form. One copy of the form would be filed, as shown in Figure 11-1. Another copy would have to go to the inventory manager, who would use the data for accounting purposes. Still another copy would go to the stockroom workers so they could fill the order and give it to the delivery drivers.

Finding a given piece of data in such a system would require finding the right piece of paper. If you were to look in the file cabinet, you would have to look through the hierarchy of drawer, hanging folder, file folder, and documents, and hope the document had been correctly filed. Collecting a set of data that wasn't all filed together might mean finding each desired element separately. If two people needed access to the same data, they had to either share it or make duplicates of it.

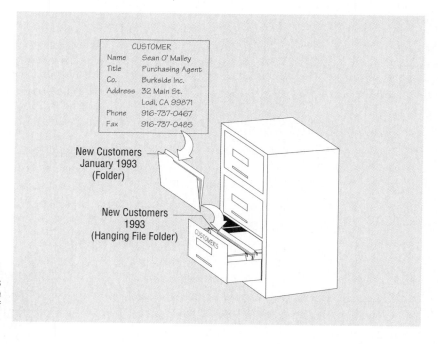

Figure 11-1
The paper-based office is heavily dependent on the organizational structure of the filing cabinet.

Managing Data in the Computer Age

The introduction of the computer allowed for the creation of the **database**, in which data is stored and organized electronically. Managing data with a computer is less time consuming, more reliable, and more flexible than managing data with a file cabinet. Rather than writing or typing data onto forms that are then filed, office workers key data into a computer. The data is organized automatically according to how the database has been set up. Finding a given piece or set of data is often just a matter of asking the computer program for it.

For example, in the computer-based BVOS office, entering data about a new customer is easy. When a new customer calls with an order, BVOS salespeople can take the order, just as they would take any other order. The only difference is that, in a computerized database, when the salesperson enters a business name that has not been entered before, the database management system prompts the salesperson for data that usually appears on the order form automatically, such as the business address and the telephone number (Figure 11-2).

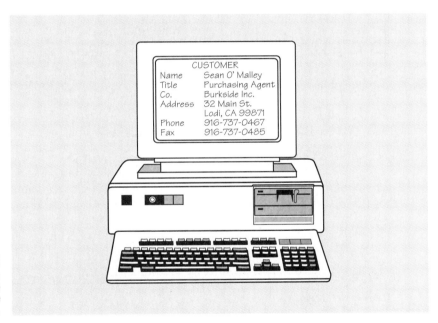

Figure 11-2
The filing cabinet has been surpassed by the capabilities of the electronic database.

Once the data is in the database, it can be available to different workers at the same time. If the inventory manager is doing billing at the same time that a stockroom worker is filling the order, no problem: The data from the order can appear on both computers simultaneously. What's more, if the inventory manager needs to find out how many boxes of paper have been ordered during the past month, she can simply ask the database management system to display the information. The organization of data can be flexible enough to answer that question, and many others, immediately.

Creating a Database

The most critical phase of database management is setting it up. Perhaps the most powerful capability of a good database is the user's ability to write queries to it. A **query** is simply a question. A database query, such as the one shown in Figure 11-3, is a request for data that meets certain criteria. If a database limits the kinds of queries the user can write, it also limits the accessibility of data.

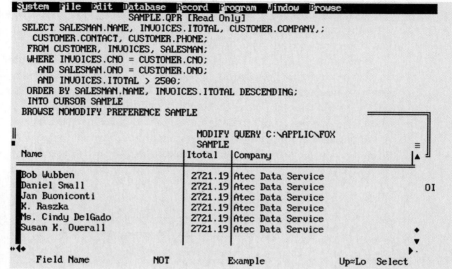

Figure 11-3

The command that begins "Select..." is a database query. The lines at the bottom of the screen are the results, that is, the records that meet its conditions.

The Three Basic Elements of a Database

Recall from Chapter 4 that a database is organized into files, records, and fields. A database is composed of related files. Each **file** holds a set of related records. Each **record** contains data about a thing or an event (Figure 11-4). Within a record, data is organized into **fields** that describe the thing or event. Records about things often refer to a person, a product, or a company. Records containing data about an event often refer to a business transaction. For example, each of the records in a CUSTOMER file at BVOS might contain data about one of

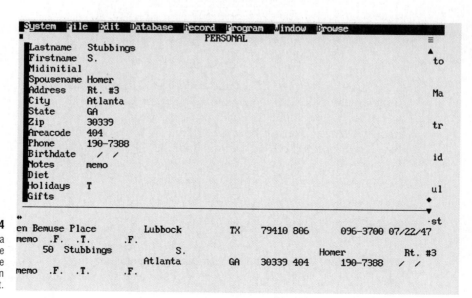

Figure 11-4

A single record in a database shown at the bottom of the screen are multiple records in columnar format.

the businesses that has ordered office supplies. Another file named STOCK might contain data about each order that has been placed with the regional distributor.

Within a database file, each of the records has the same set of fields (Figure 11-5). For example, each record in the CUSTOMER file would contain fields for the name of the business, the street address, the telephone number, a contact name, and the BVOS business account number.

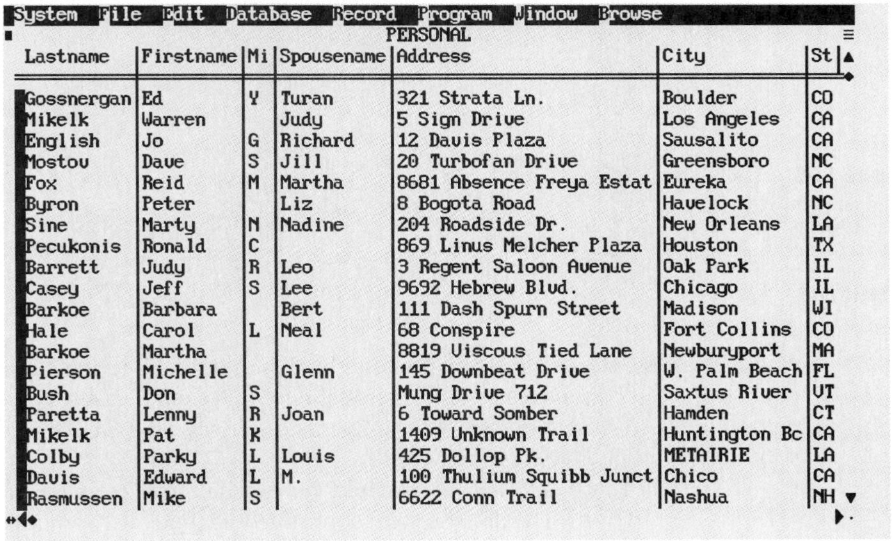
System File Edit Database Record Program Window Browse

PERSONAL

Lastname	Firstname	Mi	Spousename	Address	City	St
Gossnergan	Ed	Y	Turan	321 Strata Ln.	Boulder	CO
Mikelk	Warren		Judy	5 Sign Drive	Los Angeles	CA
English	Jo	G	Richard	12 Davis Plaza	Sausalito	CA
Mostov	Dave	S	Jill	20 Turbofan Drive	Greensboro	NC
Fox	Reid	M	Martha	8681 Absence Freya Estat	Eureka	CA
Byron	Peter		Liz	8 Bogota Road	Havelock	NC
Sine	Marty	N	Nadine	204 Roadside Dr.	New Orleans	LA
Pecukonis	Ronald	C		869 Linus Melcher Plaza	Houston	TX
Barrett	Judy	R	Leo	3 Regent Saloon Avenue	Oak Park	IL
Casey	Jeff	S	Lee	9692 Hebrew Blvd.	Chicago	IL
Barkoe	Barbara		Bert	111 Dash Spurn Street	Madison	WI
Hale	Carol	L	Neal	68 Conspire	Fort Collins	CO
Barkoe	Martha			8819 Viscous Tied Lane	Newburyport	MA
Pierson	Michelle		Glenn	145 Downbeat Drive	W. Palm Beach	FL
Bush	Don	S		Mung Drive 712	Saxtus River	VT
Paretta	Lenny	R	Joan	6 Toward Somber	Hamden	CT
Mikelk	Pat	K		1409 Unknown Trail	Huntington Bc	CA
Colby	Parky	L	Louis	425 Dollop Pk.	METAIRIE	LA
Davis	Edward	L	M.	100 Thulium Squibb Junct	Chico	CA
Rasmussen	Mike	S		6622 Conn Trail	Nashua	NH

Figure 11-5
This database file is displayed as a list. Each row is one record. The column headings indicate the fields that appear in every record.

Defining the Fields

Before any data can be entered into a database file, each of the fields that make up a record must be defined. Figuring out which fields to include can be critical. Unnecessary fields should be avoided; they waste both disk space and the time it takes to key data into them. At the same time, it is important not to omit any essential fields and to divide compound fields into their principal parts.

For example, say you are setting up the CUSTOMER database at BVOS (Figure 11-6 on the next page). In doing so, you find that some of the businesses that order from Buena Vista have P.O. boxes, and some do not. Rather than enter the P.O. box in an ADDRESS field, you decide to create a separate POBOX field. You reason that correspondence and billing should go the P.O. box, while deliveries should go to the street address. Besides, if BVOS ever needs to use a third-party delivery service, such as Federal Express or UPS, they will not be able to deliver to the P.O. box. Another important decision you make is to break up ADDRESS into STREET, CITY, STATE, and ZIP. After all, P.O. boxes still require the city, state, and ZIP code. Also, there may be instances in which BVOS wants to sort customers by ZIP code to save on postage fees (the Post Office charges less for bulk mail that is presorted by ZIP code).

After deciding which fields need to be included in the database, you need to decide on each field's name, size, and type. The **field name** is the label linked to a field. It should accurately describe the data that will go in that field. At the same time, a field name should be as short as possible without compromising the descriptiveness of the name. As an example, in a PERSONNEL database, LAST may be a better field name than LAST_NAME, simply because it is shorter. LN, however, might leave someone wondering what data is supposed to go in the field.

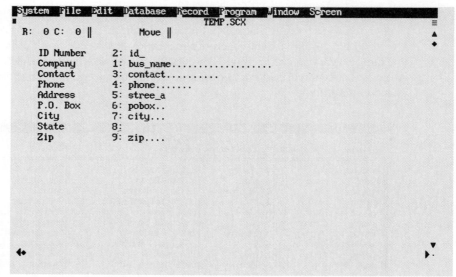

Figure 11-6
A blank form for your
CUSTOMER file. To set up
the file, you must define
the name, length, and type
of each field.

The next step is to define the length of each field. In general, a field should be just long enough to accommodate the longest data entry. In some cases, you will know exactly how long the field should be. STATE, for instance, can always be two characters long. With other fields, you will have to guess.

The third step is to define the **field type**, which indicates how the data in the field can be processed by the DBMS. The most common field types are numeric, alphanumeric, logical, date, and time. In addition, memo and binary fields are sometimes included. The INVOICE file shown in Figure 11-7 includes several of these types .

Numeric Fields. **Numeric fields** contain numbers that can be used in calculations. For example, a PRICE field would be defined as numerical so that the data in it could be added or subtracted from other prices or dollar amounts. A QUANTITY field in an inventory database is another example of a numeric field.

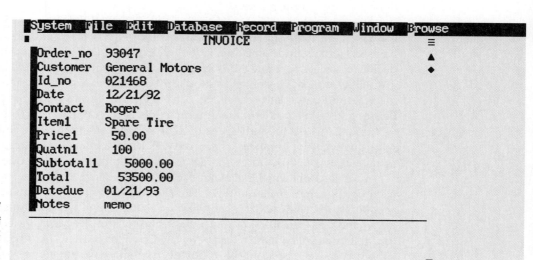

Figure 11-7
This file includes four of
the major field types:
numeric, alphanumeric,
date, and memo.

Alphanumeric Fields.   An **alphanumeric field** can contain virtually any symbol on the keyboard: numbers, letters, punctuation, and so on. Fields such as NAME and ADDRESS would be defined as alphanumeric. In addition, a field like ID# (which contains a Social Security number or business identification number) would also be defined as alphanumeric, even though it consists entirely of numbers, because the numbers would never be used in calculations.

Logical Fields.   **Logical fields** consist of a single character, which is used to specify a logical condition true or false. For example, PAID? might be a logical field on an electronic purchase order. The field would accept one of only two characters, Y or N (for *yes* or *no*). The contents of the field could be used in if-then conditions to figure total billing for a customer at the end of the month.

Date and Time Fields.   **Date fields** and **time fields** allow users to enter a date or time in a standard format. The computer converts the date or time to a number that it can use to make comparisons. Thus, the contents of a DATE_PURCH (date purchased) field can be subtracted from a DATE_PAID field to determine if a customer owes a late payment charge.

Other Fields.   **Memo fields** are text-based fields that allow users to enter notes. **Binary fields** and **graphic fields** can contain someone's photograph or fingerprints. Databases used by state motor vehicle departments often include these two fields.

Creating a Data Dictionary.   Setting up a data dictionary for your database management system helps ensure data integrity and accuracy. A **data dictionary**, according to Freedman's *The Computer Glossary*, is itself a database — one that contains the name, type, range, source, and authorization access for every data element in another database or set of databases. It also provides information about which applications use the data and how. The data dictionary can be used as an information system for management and documentation, or it can be used to actually control the operation of the database management system.

Designing the Database Structure

After you decide which fields to include in a database, give them names, and decide their size and type, your next step is to decide on the structure of the database. This decision may be the most important one in the entire set-up process, because it will have a profound affect on the accessibility of the data. The decision should go hand in hand with the database software (the DBMS) that you choose. Database packages have very different capabilities in terms of creating various types of structures.

There are five common database structures: hierarchical, network, relational, flat-file, and hypermedia.

Hierarchical Databases.   The **hierarchical database**, the oldest and simplest structure, most closely resembles the file cabinet system of organization. The structure, when diagrammed, looks like a family tree (Figure 11-8 on the next page). Each record and file can be related to only one parent, though it can be related to many children. This structure is the most rigid type of database: It is difficult to change and difficult to query. Setting up such a database requires defining all the hierarchical relationships in advance by linking the records in different files. Retrieving a piece of data requires either knowing where the data is stored in the hierarchy or wading through a lengthy search process.

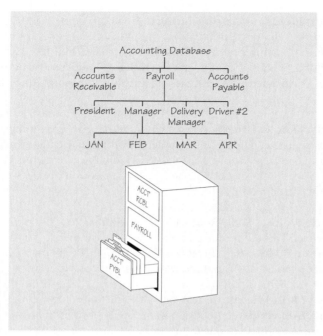

Figure 11-8
A hierarchical database is organized in much the same way as files in a file cabinet.

The hierarchical structure is no longer as widely used as it once was, and it is most often found on mainframe databases. Nevertheless, it is appropriate for certain types of data, such as personnel databases in large corporations, where each employee has a specific place within a group, department, and division. To access data about a specific employee, you would first identify the division, department, and group in which the person works. However, storing data in this way would make it difficult to search for all of the employees that, for example, had salaries over $30,000 per year. Doing so would require searching through every branch of the hierarchical tree.

Network Databases.   The network structure is related to the hierarchical structure but is slightly more flexible. In the **network database**, which is shown in Figure 11-9, records in one file can be linked to several records of another file. This arrangement works well for systems in which people or events belong to several groups simultaneously. For example, in a database that keeps track of student scheduling at a school, each student might be enrolled in six different classes. Using a network arrangement would allow you not only to ask what students are in a particular class, but also to ask what classes a particular student is in. Nevertheless, other types of queries, such as finding all students with a 3.0 minimum grade-point average, would still be difficult to complete.

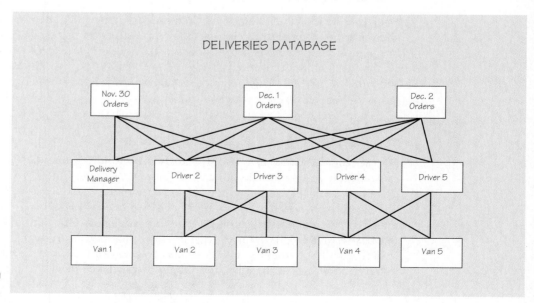

Figure 11-9
A network database.

Relational Databases.   To overcome the accessibility problems associated with hierarchical and network databases, many modern databases adhere to the relational model, an example of which is diagrammed in Figure 11-10. The relational database was developed at IBM by E. F. Codd in 1971. In a **relational database**, data is stored in tables, which are called **relations**. Each relation equals a single file. The fields in the file make up the columns of the table, and the records make up the rows. The data in any two tables that share a common field can be compared, and the data in each is accessible from the other. For example, the key field that links data about people in many government databases is the Social Security number.

Customer File

BUS #	NAME	CONTACT	ADDRESS	ADDRESS	CITY	ST	ZIP	PHONE
0011	Asym	M. Fong	1 Broad	1 Broad	SF	CA	941212	726-3400
0012	Attas	Z. Zimmer	17 Market	17 Market	SF	CA	94118	713-2233
0013	Bayre	S. Payne	456 16th	456 16th	SF	CA	94118	655-0220
0014	Best	M. Stiles	72 Taylor	72 Taylor	SF	CA	94123	456-0020

Orders File

ORDER #	DATE	NAME	ITEM 1	QTY 1	ITEM 2	QTY 2	ITEMS
0723	11-28	Vacco.	00231	1	26135	25	—
0724	11-28	Storm	01462	10	02217	1	—
0725	11-28	Bayre	07220	1	05146	1	77335
0726	11-28	Westl.	07220	5	23440	10	74096
0727	11-28	Transi.	11420	50	72435	1	—
0728	11-28	Force	51173	1	01105	10	00223

Figure 11-10
The relational model. Files are organized into tables. Data from two files with the same field can be compared and used at the same time.

The relational database offers many capabilities that were not possible with previous structures. Let's use the BVOS inventory database to demonstrate just one of these possibilities (Figure 11-11 on the next page). Say you have created the CUSTOMER file, which contains the names and addresses of all businesses that buy supplies from BVOS. Next you create the ORDERS file, which contains a record of each customer order, including the items ordered, their prices, the date and time of the order, and the name of the company making the order. A record in the ORDERS file is created by a salesperson each time a new order is received. When the printed order is created to accompany the delivery, the printed form contains the data in the order record, plus the name and address of the company so the delivery driver knows exactly where to take the order. The salesperson does not need to fill out the address of the business, however, because the ORDERS file can be compared to the CUSTOMER file through the field that specifies the name of the business. The address that accompanies that business in the CUSTOMER file is then automatically copied onto the printed order form for the customer.

Most of the major DBMS packages marketed for the microcomputer, such as dBASE IV, Paradox, and FoxBase, are capable of creating relational databases.

Flat-File Databases.   The flat-file model is a subset of the relational database model, with limited functionality. **Flat-file databases** are organized into tables, but there are no capabilities for comparing the data in common fields between tables (Figure 11-12 on the next page). In other words, flat-file databases are relational databases that consist of a single file.

Customer File

BUS #	NAME	CONTACT	ADDRESS	ADDRESS	CITY	ST	ZIP	PHONE
0011	Asym	M. Fong	1 Broad	1 Broad	SF	CA	941212	726-3400
0012	Attas	Z. Zimmer	17 Market	17 Market	SF	CA	94118	713-2233
0013	Bayre	S. Payne	456 16th	456 16th	SF	CA	94118	655-0220
0014	Best	M. Stiles	72 Taylor	72 Taylor	SF	CA	94123	456-0020

Orders File

ORDER #	DATE	NAME	ITEM 1	QTY 1	ITEM 2	QTY 2	ITEMS
0723	11-28	Vacco.	00231	1	26135	25	—
0724	11-28	Storm	01462	10	02217	1	—
0725	11-28	Bayre	07220	1	05146	1	77335
0726	11-28	Westl.	07220	5	23440	10	74096
0727	11-28	Transi.	11420	50	72435	1	—
0728	11-28	Force	51173	1	01105	10	00223

DELIVERY STATEMENT

Bayrest Mattress
456 16th
San Francisco, CA 94118
(415) 655-0220

Order #: 0725
Date of order: Nov. 28, 1993

Item		Qty.	Price
Desklamp	07220	1	12.95
File Cab.	05146	1	45.50
File Fold	77335	50	22.75
Sub tot.			81.20
Tax			6.54
Total			87.74

Figure 11-11
The DELIVERY STATEMENT combines data from two relations, the CUSTOMER file and the ORDER file.

Flat-file DBMSs are common among integrated software packages, such as Microsoft Works and Claris Works. In addition, many spreadsheet packages include database capabilities, but these capabilities are limited to creating flat-file structures.

There are many cases in which a flat-file structure is sufficient. For example, if you wanted to create an inventory of the valuable items in your home, you could create it with a flat-file structure. The file could contain one record for each item, with fields for the item name, where it was purchased, the purchase date, and the cost.

Employees

Soc. Sec. #	L. Name	F. Name	Phone	Address	City	Zip
523-41-0727	Lee	Tory	253-7720	5 Blue Ct.	Sausalito	94252
711-73-2486	Yep	Lisa	741-0231	42A Greer	Fremont	95110
141-71-5901	Sorensen	Scott	741-5960	103 Pleasant	San Mateo	94335
224-05-9207	Malecki	Gwen	525-6609	9230 48th Ave.	San Francisco	94116
293-21-7720	Vasquez	Raul	821-5137	4320 Mission	Daly City	94017
566-02-5572	Drobnis	Gloria	741-5532	2 Glenellen	Daly City	94012

Figure 11-12
The flat-file model is similar to the relational model, but only one file is accessible at a time.

Hypermedia Databases.   Hypermedia software is actually a form of DBMS, although there are significant differences between **hypermedia databases** and the other structures we have mentioned. The most well-known hypermedia package is HyperCard, a version of which is supplied with every Macintosh. A similar package available for the PC is Linkway.

In HyperCard, each file consists of a set of cards called a **stack**. A card is therefore the HyperCard equivalent of a record, but there are many important differences. Rather than being a group of fields, a card is a graphical area that can include fields, text, or graphic images.

In addition to the freedom afforded the person creating each card, the flexibility of a HyperCard database is enhanced by the ability to create buttons. A **button** links one card to another card in the same stack or a different stack. When a user clicks on a button with the mouse, the card that it is linked to is immediately displayed. It is even possible to link a button to a sound file that plays a recording.

The uses for hypermedia software are many and varied. One of the most popular is in education; hypermedia databases can be used as teaching tools that allow maximum freedom for the student. For instance, Broderbund Software publishes a geometry tutorial written in HyperCard. The student steps through the stack, clicking on buttons to request examples or to watch animated graphic displays. The software can test the student's knowledge and automatically reteach concepts that were not mastered.

Macintosh software manuals are now often provided in the form of HyperCard stacks. Users can look up subjects in an electronic index and click on the subject they need help on. When reading a definition on screen, users can click on highlighted words to get help on terms they don't understand or of which they aren't sure.

Comprehension Questions

1. What basic fact about database structure guarantees that a table in a relational database is always neatly rectangular?
2. In what way is a hypermedia database similar to a relational database?
3. Are date and time fields more like alphanumeric fields or numeric fields? Why?

Using What You Know

1. Describe two flat-file databases that you could set up for your personal use at BVOS (that is, not connected to the central inventory database).
2. The PERSONNEL file at BVOS contains the following fields: LAST, FIRST, MI, M/F, POBOX, STREET, CITY, STATE, ZIP, AREACODE, TEL#, DOB (date of birth), and SSN (Social Security number). Name the field type for each and give a brief justification (one sentence) for each answer.
3. Describe one way that you might use a hypermedia database at BVOS.

Using a Database

Knowing how to use a database to obtain information is a valuable skill. Unfortunately, there are so many database models and so many methods for getting information out of them that covering this topic completely is beyond the scope of this book. There are, however, a few techniques that you should know about: sorting and indexing, querying, and generating reports.

These three techniques are most appropriate for relational and flat-file databases. They do not apply directly to hypermedia databases.

Sorting and Indexing

One valuable capability of a database is the user's ability to obtain lists of related data. With a database, you could generate such a list in a matter of seconds.

The danger in generating a list is that, unless you specify otherwise, the database will list the records in the order in which they were entered. Often, this order is not particularly useful. A more appropriate list order can be generated by sorting or indexing the records.

In **sorting** the records in a database, you are actually changing their sequence. Say you add a record to the CUSTOMER database file each time a new customer orders supplies. When you enter the new customer, the DBMS adds the new record to the end of the file. If you were to sort the file alphabetically by the names of the businesses, the order of the records in the file would change. The DBMS actually rewrites the file onto the storage medium in the new order.

Indexing is a more flexible method for rearranging the appearance of records, because indexing does not actually change the order of the records. Instead, an indexed group of records represents a temporary order created according to the alphabetical or numerical order of one or more fields. To avoid rewriting the data file, the DBMS creates a second file, which stores the indexed field in the desired order, with pointers that tell the location of each record in the actual data file. Most DBMSs are capable of maintaining several indexes, so the user can quickly display a number of arrangements.

Querying the Database

Querying a database allows the user to obtain specific information that meets desired criteria. The simplest type of data query is the search. In a search, the user asks the DBMS to find a specific record or data item. More complicated queries generally involve collecting a set of records that are related in some way.

The best way to understand the possibilities of a data query is to see a few examples. The example shown in Figure 11-13a is written for dBASE in the fourth-generation query language that is used with DBMSs. A **query language** is any high-level language that is built into a DBMS for the purpose of interacting directly with the database. Figures 11-13b and 11-13c demonstrate creating a query by example in Approach, a Windows-based DBMS.

Generating Reports

A database cannot be printed as simply as a document created in a word processor. Printing a database requires generating a **report** using the DBMS's report writer (Figure 11-14 on page 252). Before a report can be printed, the user must state exactly what information should appear in it and how it should be arranged. Often, the creation of a report is done in conjunction with data obtained using an index (or sort), a query, or both.

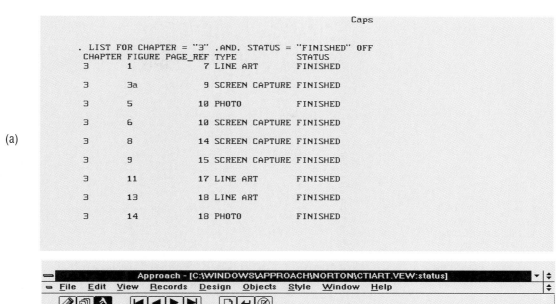

(a)

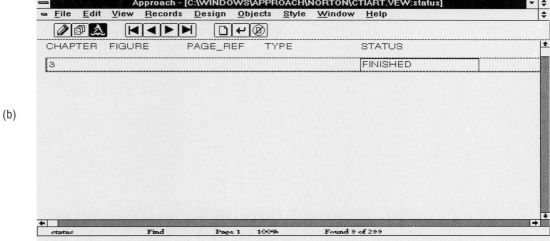

(b)

(c)

Figure 11-13

(a) The query language built into dBASE IV is a relatively intuitive 4GL. Each of these screens shows (b) a query and (c) its results.

CHAPTER 7 ART FIGURES STATUS REPORT

CHAP#	FIG#	PAGE	TYPE	STATUS	DESCRIPTION
7	1	46	LINE ART	FINISHED	IBM 101 keyboard.
7	2	46	LINE ART	FINISHED	Alphanumeric keys.
7	3a	47	LINE ART	FINISHED	Mac SHIFT, OPTION and COMMAND keys.
7	3b	47	LINE ART	FINISHED	IBM 101 SHIFT, CONTROL and ALTERNATE keys.
7	4	48	LINE ART	FINISHED	Function keys.
7	5	49	LINE ART	FINISHED	Cursor control keys.
7	6	49	LINE ART	FINISHED	Numeric keypad.
7	7	50	LINE ART	FINISHED	Keyboard lights.
7	8	50	PHOTO	FINISHED	Data entry employee.
7	9	51	PHOTO	FINISHED	TONY ergonomic keyboard.
7	10	51	LINE ART	FINISHED	Person at computer showing healthy position.
7	11	53	PHOTO	FINISHED	Some mice.
7	13	55	PHOTO	FINISHED	Powerbook.
7	14	55	PHOTO	FINISHED	Light pen.
7	15	55	PHOTO	FINISHED	Digitizer tablet.
7	16	56	PHOTO	FINISHED	Customer using touch screen.
7	17	58	PHOTO	FINISHED	Flatbed scanner.
7	18	59	PHOTO	FINISHED	Bar code reader.
7	20	62	LINE ART	FINISHED	Schematic of screen as grid of pixels.
7	21	62	LINE ART	FINISHED	Cathode ray tube diagram.
7	22	63	LINE ART	FINISHED	Side views of CRT and flat-panel.
7	23	64	LINE ART	FINISHED	LCD pixels with and without current.
7	24	64	PHOTO	FINISHED	Various monitors.
7	25	65	PHOTO	FINISHED	Some Mac monitors.
7	26	71	LINE ART	FINISHED	9 pin vs. 24 pin print.
7	27	71	PHOTO	FINISHED	A common dot-matrix printer.
7	28	72	LINE ART	FINISHED	Ink-jet printer.
7	29	72	LINE ART	FINISHED	Laser printer.
7	30	72	PHOTO	FINISHED	Laser printer.
7	31	73	PHOTO	FINISHED	Close-up of outputs of 24-pin NLQ dot matrix, 300 dpi ink-jet and 600 dpi inkjet.
7	32	76	TEXT FIG	FINISHED	The word PostScript in various fonts.

Figure 11-14

To create a report, the user of a database manager must identify exactly what the report should include and how it should be formatted.

The Goals of a Database

With the ability to sort, index, query, and generate reports, the electronic database provides the user with a vastly improved solution over the paper-based office for five major reasons. It improves:

- Data efficiency
- Data integrity
- Access flexibility
- Data independence
- Data security

These advantages are the goals of database management systems. However, not all DBMSs achieve them equally well. For example, the mainframe databases of the 1960s did not provide nearly the same access flexibility as the relational databases that can be created on today's powerful microcomputers using a modern DBMS. Let's examine each of these goals more closely.

Data Efficiency

The first advantage of a database over paper records is that the database can eliminate the replication of information. People in an organization often need the same data at the same time. For example, at BVOS, the inventory manager might be using all of the current month's orders from a certain customer to create an invoice for billing. At the same time, the stockroom might be filling the latest order. The sales office might also need a copy of the latest order to answer questions from the customer. Without an electronic database, every order taken by the sales force would have to be copied immediately so that records could be kept in the sales office, orders could be filled by the stockroom, and billing and inventory could be managed by the inventory manager.

Creating so many copies is both wasteful and time consuming. By storing all records in a central database, multiple copies can be eliminated. The same data can be accessed simultaneously by all departments.

Data Integrity

Beyond being wasteful, keeping multiple copies of data in an office is dangerous. If there are three copies of an order floating around the office, which one is the master copy? If the customer calls back to make a minor change to the order and the copies are already dispersed around the office, should the salesperson find all the copies and make the change to each of them? The biggest problem with data redundancy is that it leads to incorrect, inconsistent, and outdated data.

With a centralized database, however, the salesperson making the change to the order could make the change to the only copy that exists — the master copy in the database. If the order had already been filled by the stockroom, that information would be apparent in the database, and the salesperson would have access to this up-to-date information so that the customer could be informed.

Access Flexibility

A third advantage of using an electronic database is the flexibility with which data can be retrieved. If BVOS were a paper office, the data related to customer orders would be on the order forms filled out by the salespeople. To keep track of how many reams of copier paper had been ordered in the last week, the inventory manager would have to look at all the orders that had been filled out. With a database and a DBMS, however, the inventory manager can retrieve data in whatever form she needs it. If she needs to know how many reams of paper have been ordered, she should be able to determine exactly that, without having to go through all of the other data related to each individual order. In fact, finding such data might require just a few keystrokes.

The biggest improvements in DBMSs over the past 30 years have been toward the goal of access flexibility. As you have seen, the design of the relational database is especially conducive to flexibility. Older hierarchical databases were much less flexible.

Data Independence

Related to the advantage of data flexibility is data independence. Data independence means that the data itself is independent of the database application that uses it. This simply means that the database is not the same thing as the DBMS. The database is the data itself and its organizing structure. The DBMS is the management software and all of the programs that have been created with it to access the database. Data independence allows the user to add, delete, and change data within a database, without affecting the programs that have been written to access the database.

Data Security

The final goal of the DBMS is the ability to control who can access data. This ability is valuable in keeping data from being intentionally or inadvertently changed and in keeping sensitive data hidden from view. For example, the only people who should be allowed to create or change a customer order at BVOS are the salespeople. Allowing anyone else to change an order could lead to errors in filling the order. As another example, you and your inventory manager should be the only people who have access to employee wages. By limiting access privileges, employees could access an employee database to find out someone's phone number, but they could be prevented from seeing that person's salary. Today, organizations can be held financially or criminally liable if sensitive data about employees or customers is stolen or misused.

The Role of the Database Administrator

In the information age in which we live, the database of a company can be its most valuable asset. Therefore, a database needs to be managed and cared for as a critical component of the business. Large companies that can afford a full-time employee for the job often hire a **database administrator** (Figure 11-15). Even smaller businesses find it valuable to appoint the role of database administrator to a single person.

Figure 11-15
The database administrator must document systems, train employees, keep the database running smoothly, administer changes, and guide the development of new databases.

One of the major responsibilities of this job is documenting the various database systems used in the organization. This documentation lists what data is available, how it is accessed, how it is formatted, and what programs use it. The database administrator also provides training to employees who need to use the database.

In addition to documentation and employee support, the database administrator is charged with monitoring and tuning the database to keep it running smoothly and quickly. Databases, especially those with high transaction volumes, can become cluttered with old data fields. In most database systems, when a record is deleted, it is simply marked as being deleted, but the space that the record took up on the hard disk is still reserved. Periodically, the database administrator must repack and reindex the database to improve performance. If this is not done, it takes longer and longer for data to be retrieved from the system.

Any major changes that need to be made to the database are either handled or supervised by the database administrator. Supervising changes involves investigating what programs or departments will be affected by the change and notifying the relevant users. If someone requests a change that will adversely affect certain programs or the work of certain employees, the database administrator must arbitrate the conflicts.

Finally, the database administrator guides the development of new databases and new database applications. It is always important for new applications to make the best possible use of an existing database. When it comes to creating new databases, the administrator's knowledge is a valuable resource, and this person should be consulted in creating the most efficient and accessible design.

Database Threats to Personal Privacy

The power of the database has unleashed an incredible array of business opportunities. The ability to keep track of large amounts of data and the ability to link database files in a relational structure has spawned — among other ventures — the mailing list industry. Mailing lists are incredibly valuable to businesses because they can help target customers. On the other hand, the same industry is often abhorred by consumers because it is responsible for a large percentage of all junk mail and unsolicited phone calls.

People often find getting onto a mailing list a mysterious phenomenon. Consumers may suddenly receive a barrage of solicitations without knowing why. Often, it is because they have subscribed to a magazine, filled out an application for a commercial product or service, or completed a warranty card for a new product. Many consumers believe that filling out the warranty registration card included with many products is the only way to guarantee service. In fact, however, if a warranty exists, it is in effect when you purchase a product, and the bill of sale or receipt acts as proof of purchase. The purpose of warranty cards is to help companies collect data about who is buying their products. Once they have collected this data, they can sort, query, and even sell it to other companies without the consumer's knowledge.

The availability of information can affect your life in much more serious ways than mere junk mail and phone calls. Some companies keep credit histories on virtually every adult in the country. When you apply for a loan or a credit card or try to rent a house, you can be sure that someone will check your credit history. Employers run credit checks and criminal history investigations to judge the honesty of potential employees. Doctors can see if a patient has ever sued another doctor for malpractice. Landlords can check a database to see if another landlord has ever filed a complaint against a prospective tenant.

Minor data entry errors or slight misunderstandings can make these records grossly inaccurate, but they are nevertheless used to make important decisions. Though it is difficult to avoid mailing lists and corporate databases completely, it is worthwhile to monitor new developments. Infringements on personal privacy are a growing concern, and privacy law is expanding to keep up with advancements in database technology. There is even some momentum toward creating a fundamental right to privacy with an amendment to the Bill of Rights. Professor Lawrence Tribe, a noted legal scholar at Harvard University, has proposed just such an amendment (Table 11-1).

Table 11-1
Lawrence Tribe's proposed amendment to the Constitution.

Professor Lawrence Tribe's proposed 27th amendment:
This Constitution's protections for the freedoms of speech, press, petition, and assembly, and its protections against unreasonable searches and seizures and the deprivation of life, liberty, or property without due process of law, shall be construed as fully applicable without regard to the technological method or medium through which information content is generated, stored, altered, transmitted, or controlled.

Comprehension Questions

1. What are the pros and cons of filling out a registration card for a new piece of software?

2. What steps must be taken to print an alphabetical list of customers whose ZIP code is 94121?

3. Are programming skills required of the database administrator? Why or why not?

Using What You Know

1. What major field of study in college would qualify a person to be a database administrator?

2. How does the growing power of LAN servers help to make advanced database capabilities more feasible for small businesses?

3. Describe three ways in which data security will be a critical issue for the BVOS inventory database.

Summary Points

Managing Data at BVOS

☐ The BVOS inventory database is a vital record of daily transaction for the business.

Managing Data in a Paper-Based Office

☐ Data in a paper-based office is organized in files that are placed in folders within a file cabinet.

Managing Data in the Computer Age

☐ The computer allows data to be organized in databases, which are more flexible, more reliable, and require less labor than a paper-based system.

Creating a Database

☐ A database that has been set up well will come close to achieving the five goals.

The Three Basic Elements of a Database

☐ A database is subdivided into files, records, and fields.

☐ Each record contains data about a thing or an event, and every record in a file contains the same fields.

Defining the Fields

☐ A balance must be struck to include all necessary fields without wasting space or time.

☐ Field names should be both descriptive and short.

☐ Fields should be just long enough to accommodate the longest entry.

Numeric Fields

☐ Numeric fields contain numbers that can be used in calculations.

Alphanumeric Fields

☐ Alphanumeric fields can contain any keyboard symbol and cannot be used in calculations.

Logical Fields

☐ Logical fields contain a single character to specify a true or false condition.

Date and Time Fields

☐ Date and time fields allow data to be entered in their standard formats, but also allow the data in the fields to be compared.

Other Fields

☐ Memo fields and binary or graphic fields allow notes, photos, and graphics to be entered.

Creating a Data Dictionary

☐ A data dictionary is a database that helps organize another database.

Designing the Database Structure

☐ The structure of a database has a profound effect on the accessibility of the data.

Hierarchical Databases

☐ The hierarchical structure is the most rigid, following the file-cabinet model.

Network Databases

☐ The network structure is similar to the hierarchical, but multiple links to records in other files are allowed.

Relational Databases

☐ Relational databases organize files into tables; tables with common fields can be compared so that data in one is accessible to another.
☐ Most modern DBMS packages adhere to the relational model because it is more flexible than previous models.

Flat-File Databases

☐ The flat-file structure also relies on tables of data, but no comparisons can be made between files.

Hypermedia Databases

☐ Hypermedia software packages, such as HyperCard, are used to create stacks of cards, which can include fields, text, or graphics.
☐ Cards in a stack can be linked with buttons.

Using a Database

Sorting and Indexing

☐ Sorting a file rearranges the actual order of the records in the file.
☐ Indexing a file creates an index that lists an alternate arrangement that can be displayed.

Querying the Database

☐ Data is selectively displayed with a query, which finds data that meets certain criteria.

Generating Reports

☐ For a database to be printed, the user must generate a report.
☐ Reports are often created in conjunction with indexes and queries.

The Goals of a Database

☐ The goals of a DBMS are maximizing the five advantages that the database has over a paper-based system.

Data Efficiency

☐ A database allows for a single electronic copy of data, which can be shared among users, thus reducing data redundancy.

Data Integrity

☐ The centralization of data in a database leads to more correct, consistent, and current data.

Access Flexibility

☐ A good DBMS allows data to be retrieved in the form in which it is needed.

☐ The biggest improvements in DBMSs have been in access flexibility.

Data Independence

☐ Data independence is the separation of the data from the programs that use it.

Data Security

☐ A DBMS should enable the person who sets up the database to control who has access to it.

The Role of the Database Administrator

☐ An organization's database administrator manages and maintains the company's databases.

☐ The administrator's duties often include documenting the database, training employees, repacking and fine-tuning the database, making employees aware of changes, arbitrating conflicts, and helping with the development of new databases.

Database Threats to Personal Privacy

☐ The power of the database has spawned the direct mail industry, as well as other information-dependent businesses.

☐ The availability of information about people can dramatically affect their lives, and the field of privacy law is growing to keep up with increasing database power.

Knowing the Facts

True/False

1. Maximizing data integrity means ensuring that data is correct, consistent, and current.
2. Greater redundancy of data leads to greater data integrity.
3. The size of a field should represent the average between the largest and smallest data items that will be entered in that field.
4. Access flexibility with a relational database is generally better than with a network database.
5. In a large company, all reports should be generated by the database administrator to ensure data integrity.
6. The simplest type of data query is the search.
7. Filling out a warranty registration card has no effect on whether or not a product is under warranty.
8. A flat-file database may contain any number of files.
9. Sorting is more cumbersome than indexing, because sorting creates a second file that contains the field being sorted.
10. For a database to be printed, a query must be generated.

Short Answer

1. _____ databases are a type of relational database that does not allow comparisons between tables.
2. E. F. Codd developed the _____ for IBM in 1971.
3. A version of _____, a hypermedia software package, comes with every Macintosh.
4. The _____ industry has been spawned by the capabilities of modern DBMSs.
5. Improvements in data integrity are possible with reductions in data _____.
6. Limiting access privileges is one way to improve data _____.
7. The field type of a field containing a street address should be _____.
8. A _____ field (indicate type) lists whether a condition is true or false.
9. What database structure most closely resembles the organization of a file cabinet?
10. A _____ is a data search or a request for data that meets a given criteria or set of criteria.

Answers

True/False

1. T
2. F
3. F
4. T
5. F
6. T
7. T
8. F
9. F
10. F

Short Answer

1. Flat-file
2. relational database
3. HyperCard
4. mailing list
5. redundancy
6. security
7. alphanumeric
8. logical
9. hierarchical
10. query

Challenging Your Understanding

1. One of the most challenging problems facing data processing managers is the question of when to remove data from a database. After all, you cannot keep data around forever. It becomes too difficult to manage and it eventually becomes irrelevant. What rules would you use to remove data from a database?

2. Can you think of any data that should not be collected in a database? Give some examples and the consequences of storing that data.

3. The relational database design creates a flexible database that can be used to answer questions that may arise in the future, as well as those at hand. Why is this advantage important? Why can't users specify all of the required information before a database is constructed?

4. Sorting is the most common activity performed on a business computer. Why is sorting more common than querying?

5. Your telephone number is not your property. The number is "owned" by the telephone company. A company can own database hardware and software, but the ownership of the data is less clear. Think about a database that contains information about consumer purchase behaviors. Who owns the data in that database — the consumers or the company that collected the data? Why?

Information Systems for Business

Key Terms

accounts payable
accounts receivable
computer-aided design (CAD)
computer-aided manufacturing (CAM)
decision support system (DSS)
demand reports
downsizing
E-mail
exception reports
flaming
general ledger
information system
job displacement
job enlargement
just-in-time (JIT) manufacturing
management information systems (MIS)
middle-level managers
operations managers
outsourcing
payroll
performance monitoring
scheduled reports
quality control
upper-level managers
voice mail

Objectives

In this chapter you will learn to:

- Define the term *information system*
- Identify the three levels of management and describe the types of information required by each
- Describe operational information systems and give examples of them in production and accounting departments
- Describe management information systems and decision support systems
- Explain how E-mail works and identify its advantages and disadvantages
- Describe voice mail
- Explain how computerized information systems relate to quality control, job displacement, job enlargement, and performance monitoring
- Identify the advantages of downsizing and outsourcing

Information Systems in Large Businesses

Throughout this book, we have focused on the needs of Buena Vista Office Supply to explain how computers are used in business. In these last two chapters, we look more closely at larger businesses. Corporations and large organizations are complex enough to require highly developed information systems to coordinate their activities. In this chapter, we look at the full range of information systems that exist to give you a better idea of how computers and technology support all aspects of a large company.

What Is an Information System?

The term **information system** has two meanings, depending on who you ask for the definition. If you ask computer users in business, they may give you the more narrow definition. Users tend to think of an information system is a means of obtaining information from a company's database. The information system includes the database itself, the means for getting data into the database, and the application programs that get data out in a useful format. If you ask an information systems (IS) professional, however, he or she may give you a more general definition: An information system is a path or set of established paths along which data travels through an organization.

For the most part, these two groups — general business users and IS professionals — are talking about the same thing. The most talked-about kinds of information system are those in which data is generated at the operations level of a business, collected in a database, and processed so that managers can glean information from it and make decisions. The broader definition, however, also includes information systems, such as electronic mail, in which data and information do not necessarily move up through the levels of management. Most of this chapter addresses information systems as defined by the first group. At the end of the chapter, however, we discuss these other types of information system that do not fit into the narrower definition.

Levels of Management and Their Needs for Information

To understand the purpose of an information system, it is helpful to see a standard diagram showing the levels of management in a company. A large business can be thought of as a pyramid, resting on a large foundation (Figure 12-1). This foundation represents the operations level of the company, which consists of workers organized into departments. There are five basic departments in many companies:

- The production department produces goods.
- The marketing department sells the goods that the production department makes, or it sells services.
- The research department develops new products or services and improves old ones.
- The personnel department hires new employees.
- The accounting department coordinates the financial needs of the company, including billing customers, paying for raw materials, and paying employees.

The pyramid that sits on top of this base of departments and their employees are the managers that run the company. The pyramid is divided into three levels:

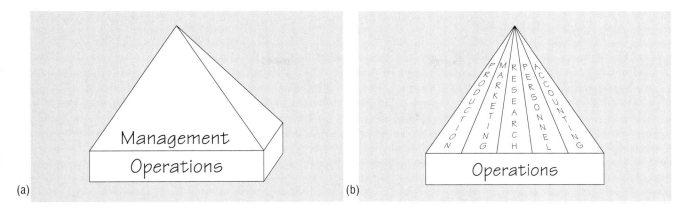

(a)

(b)

Figure 12-1
(a) Management is like a pyramid resting on the foundation of operations.
(b) The operations and management levels are divided into departments.

- **Operations managers** supervise the daily operation of the company.
- **Middle-level managers** track operations over time and develop tactical plans to meet the objectives of upper-level management.
- **Upper-level managers**, or executives, oversee the entire company, monitor profits and losses, and determine the company's future by developing business strategies.

Each type of manager needs different kinds of information. Operations managers need information systems that allow them to keep track of details. Operations managers in production departments need to keep track of inventory (or availability of personnel, in the case of a service organization). Operations managers in accounting departments need to watch cash flow. The information systems that support these and other operations managers focus on the present and the immediate future. These managers make relatively structured decisions; certain sets of data require certain decisions. For example, when an operations manager in a production department finds that the inventory of raw materials has shrunk to a certain level, the manager orders new raw materials.

Middle-level managers need information systems that give them more long-term data. They do not need to monitor every minute aspect of their departments, but they need to synthesize a wide range of factors to make tactical decisions. Middle-level managers often require reports that summarize operational conditions or track them over time. They make more open-ended, less structured decisions than those made by operations managers. They combine facts, gained from the information systems that serve them, with their own expertise to carry out the strategies dictated by executives.

Upper-level managers make relatively unstructured decisions; they require more intangible factors, such as personal experience and company goals and strategies, so their need for information can vary greatly. They must always be concerned with long-term growth. Upper-level managers also tend to be more concerned with the relationships between departments than are middle-level managers, who still function at the departmental level.

As you move up the pyramid, managers need an increasing amount of data from outside the organization — data about competitors, customers, markets, and the economy — as well as more and more summarized information from within the organization.

Comprehension Questions

1.   If the whole country were considered one company, how could the U.S. Postal Service be considered an information system?

2. Would the Postal Service fit the narrow or broad definition of an information system?

3. What level of manager is likely to use information about the sales strategies of competitors?

Using What You Know

1. Describe where the various employees of BVOS fit into the business model described in the previous section.

2. You might say that BVOS has two main departments. What are they, and who works in them?

3. We named the five most common business departments, but there are many others. Name three other types of departments.

Information Systems for Operations Managers

The information systems that exist for operations managers, which are sometimes called transaction processing systems or electronic data processing systems, are as many and as varied as the managers' departments and the duties. To give you a general sense of what operational information systems do, let's look at two types and how they use computers.

Production Systems

When a production department generates a tangible good such as shoes or airplane engines, as opposed to a service such as advertising, the department performs a manufacturing process. Manufacturing a product involves the movement of raw materials through a process that transforms them into finished goods. For some products, the process can be incredibly complex. Imagine the production process in manufacturing an automobile. Computers are integrated into the manufacturing process at three levels: design, manufacturing, and inventory control.

CAD. **Computer-aided design**, or **CAD,** programs are used in both production and research departments to create electronic models of products before they are produced. CAD is often performed by users at expensive workstations with advanced input devices, such as light pens and digitizer tablets. With a CAD system, a designer can draft a product, create specifications for each part, and even test its functionality and strength (Figure 12-2). The result of a CAD design is a set of working drawings, a database that describes every dimension of every part of the product, and even a list of materials needed to make the product.

CAM and Robotics.   Once a product has been designed using a CAD system, the database created by CAD can be used by a **computer-aided manufacturing**, or **CAM**, system. CAM actually has two meanings. The more colorful type of CAM is robotics: numerical control devices and process control devices. Recall that a robot is a computer that uses numerical input to create physical output. The simplest types of robots are actually numerical control devices. These are standard pieces of machinery, such as drills and lathes, that can be controlled with numerical input — sometimes coming directly from a CAD system — rather than operated manually (Figure 12-3). More advanced industrial robots are specifically designed to perform such duties as packing boxes, painting cars, and welding metal parts.

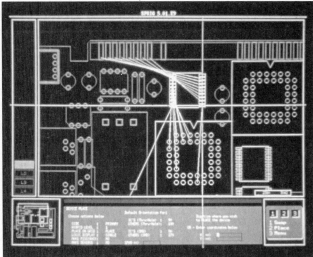

Figure 12-3   This drill is referred to as a numerical control device because it is controlled with CAM software rather than operated manually.

Figure 12-2   This electrical diagram was drawn using CAD software. The model is held in memory as a database.

Process control takes automation one step further by controlling a series of manufacturing steps, such as stages along an assembly line, with the help of a computer.

CAM and Inventory Management.   The other meaning of CAM involves using a computer to manage inventory. This type of CAM isn't as colorful as industrial robots, but it fits the strict definition of the term *information system* rather than the broad one. In some manufacturing processes, where computers have been extensively integrated, a CAM system can use the CAD database and list of materials to manage the inventory of raw materials needed for production and finished goods.

The most critical component of inventory management is forecasting when the inventory of raw materials will be depleted. Raw materials for the production process don't just appear on the delivery dock of a company. Someone must order them and schedule delivery. Raw materials that are not ordered on time or not delivered on time can jeopardize an entire production process.

The traditional method for dealing with this problem was to keep plenty of raw materials in inventory at all times. However, the more inventory a company has on its shelves, the more capital investment it has tied up in the production process. One alternative to keeping lots of raw materials inventory in stock is a technique mastered by Japanese companies called **just-in-time (JIT) manufacturing**. With a well-managed JIT system, a company runs out of raw materials just as the new supply arrives.

Accounting Systems

Computers were first used in business as tools for accounting. In fact, the machine that Hollerith created to help tabulate the 1890 census results was later manufactured and sold as an accounting device. Modern accounting information systems affect every part of the company and every level of management. Every accounting information system includes at least four databases:

- **Accounts receivable** keeps track of who owes the company money, how much they owe, and when the money is due.
- **Accounts payable** keeps track of who the company owes money to, how much is owed, and the terms of the debt.
- **Payroll** keeps track of the wages owed to each employee, plus insurance and retirement deductions, Social Security, and tax withholdings. The payroll system is actually a type of accounts payable that recognizes the company's short-term debt to employees.
- The **general ledger** integrates and summarizes the data in the other three systems.

Every one of these subsystems can be made more efficient with the help of computers. In fact, software is available to help businesses set up each of them. At the operations level, this software helps organize the information to aid in data entry and routine payments and billing. At higher management levels, the systems are used to create a number of accounting reports, including balance sheets, profit and loss records, and reports indicating the true cost of goods sold.

Information Systems for Middle and Upper Management

Middle-level and upper-level managers deal less with data input and more with process output and summaries of data entered at the operational level. In large corporations, the information systems designed to meet the needs of middle-level managers are sometimes called *management information systems*, although the same term is also used to mean any information system. Upper-level managers rely on *decision support systems* to help them generate business strategies.

Management Information Systems

A **management information system (MIS)** is an established process for generating reports that serve the needs of middle-level managers. Very little data goes into a company's database at this level of management. Middle managers obtain data from the databases in an effort to monitor and steer the company.

The role of the middle manager is served by three types of reports. **Scheduled reports** (Figure 12-4a) are generated regularly to keep middle managers abreast of the routine operations of the business. **Exception reports** (Figure 12-4b) are created in response to an unusual event or set of circumstances. Finally, **demand reports** (Figure 12-4c) are requested by middle managers when they want to see a specific set of data that is not displayed in other reports.

Decision Support Systems

Because upper-level managers make relatively unstructured decisions, the information systems that support them, called **decision support systems (DSS)**, tend to be oriented less toward reports and more toward generating answers to open-ended questions, such as questions about the efficacy of closing a factory or opening a new one. Like middle managers, executives get data out of a database rather than putting it in. But the data that upper-level managers get out of the database is not typically presented in standard formats. The format is more often tailored to answer the question being asked.

(a)

```
*********************************************************************************
DATE:  2/05/93                UNITED TECHNOLOGIES INC                PAGE:  1
                         J O B   C O S T  /  M E M O   A C C O U N T I N G

BRANCH:  SAN FRANCISCO                                    DATES:  1/01/93 - 1/31/93
*********************************************************************************

FILE NUMBER        REVENUE              ACTUAL COST            PROFIT
-----------        -------              -----------            ------
0048700            349.83                 299.83               50.00
0048701            232.00                 143.70               88.30
0048702            437.64                 322.64              115.00
0048703            833.07                 431.91              401.16
0048704            328.58                 313.99               14.59
0048705            374.51                 324.51               50.00
0048706            409.79                 359.79               50.00
0048707            981.31                 931.31               50.00
0048708            687.86                 637.86               50.00
0048709          1,103.40                 921.97              181.43
0048710          3,389.78               3,025.80              363.98
0048711            876.99                 755.99              121.00
0048712            494.00                 345.50              148.50
0048713            760.78                 642.29              118.49
0048714            474.63                 359.63              115.00
0048715            496.35                 391.35              105.00
0048716            360.56                 344.03               16.53
0048717              0.00                 180.44              180.44-
0048718            325.80                 311.58               14.22
0048719          1,111.90               1,153.22               41.32-
0048720            144.00                  31.15              112.85
0048721          1,002.58                 844.08              158.50
0048722            373.88                 225.38              148.50
0048723          2,713.46               2,570.11              143.35
0048724            510.16                 460.20               49.96
0048725            326.73                 276.73               50.00
0048726            318.41                 268.41               50.00
0048727            435.53                 302.53              133.00
```

(b)

```
*********************************************************************************
DATE:  2/05/93                UNITED TECHNOLOGIES INC                PAGE:  1
                         J O B   C O S T  /  M E M O   A C C O U N T I N G

BRANCH:  SAN FRANCISCO        EXCEPTION:  PROFIT < 0      DATES:  1/01/93 - 1/31/93
*********************************************************************************

FILE NUMBER        REVENUE              ACTUAL COST            PROFIT
-----------        -------              -----------            ------
0048717              0.00                 180.44              180.44-
0048719          1,111.90               1,153.22               41.32-
0048734           1278.85                1328.90               50.05-
0048737            278.18                 293.97               15.79-
0048749            129.52                 284.52              155.00-
0048776          1,200.04               1,347.21              147.17-
0048781             76.55                 199.55              123.00-
0048782            172.41                 222.00               49.69-
0048801          1,500.32               1,506.75                6.43-
0048822             16.80                 185.30              168.50-
0048835              0.00                 186.40              186.40-
0048849            293.23                 473.00              180.77-
0048855            150.00                 225.33               75.33-
0048861            457.25                 460.45                3.20-
0048891            889.59                1010.80              121.21-
0048897            135.76                 235.70               99.94-
```

(c)

```
*********************************************************************************
DATE:  2/05/93                UNITED TECHNOLOGIES INC                PAGE:  1
                              A / R   A G I N G   R E P O R T

CUSTOMER TYPE:  TRADE CUSTOMER       FOR PERIOD ENDING:  02/93            TIME:  15:36:42
*********************************************************************************

CUSTOMER CODE & NAME       PHONE#        CREDIT LIMIT
                                                                    AGED BALANCE
    INVOICE # & DATE   INVOICE AMOUNT    BALANCE         0-30        31-60          61-90
--------------------------------------------------------------------------------

ABM341  ABM SYSTEMS       2124985983     5,000
    2345     1/13/93       568.34        568.34          568.34
    2467     1/18/93       345.87        345.87          345.87
    2491     1/23/93       448.43        448.43          448.43

         ****CUSTOMER TOTALS             1362.64         1362.64
              PERCENT OF TOTAL                           100

AHM656  A & H MANUFACTURING 4153459438   20,000
    1945     12/20/92       431.35        431.35                        431.35

         ****CUSTOMER TOTALS             431.35                         431.35
              PERCENT OF TOTAL                                          100

BRA198  BRAMBLEBUNT INC    2138476377    5,000
    1533     11/15/92        20.00         20.00                                     20.00
    1562     11/15/92       200.00-       200.00-                                   200.00-
    1961     12/20/92       635.64        635.64                        635.64
    1974     12/21/92       513.17        513.17                        513.17

         ****CUSTOMER TOTALS             968.81                        1148.81      180.00
              PERCENT OF TOTAL                                          118.6        18.6-

BRS233  BRANT SHIPPING     7072927689    17,000
    2231     1/6/93         476.50        476.50          476.50
    2301     1/8/93         261.23        261.23          261.23

         ****CUSTOMER TOTALS             747.73          747.73
              PERCENT OF TOTAL                           100

BTC346  BUILDTECH          2128476398    4,000
    1550     11/15/93       602.94        602.94                                    602.94

         ****CUSTOMER TOTALS             602.94                                     602.94
              PERCENT OF TOTAL                                                       100
```

Figure 12-4

Examples of (a) a scheduled report, (b) an exception report, and (c) a demand report.

Decision support systems provide a user-friendly interface so that upper-level managers can obtain specific data without having to use the programming capabilities of the DBMS. In addition to the company's databases, the DSS may also have access to spreadsheet programs, statistical analysis programs, and analytical graphics software.

Comprehension Questions

1. What level of manager is likely to use a report comparing advertising costs to sales levels?

2. CAD is often used by both production and research departments. Can the same be said of CAM? Why or why not?

3. Why is JIT manufacturing more difficult to manage than traditional methods of inventory control?

Using What You Know

1. Describe what transactions are recorded in accounts receivable and accounts payable at BVOS.

2. Why do you think the user interface for a DSS tends to be friendlier than that of an MIS?

3. If you wanted a DSS for your work at BVOS, what kinds of information would you want to be able to get out of it?

Enterprise-Wide Information Systems

As we noted earlier in the chapter, not all information systems fit the narrow definition. The information systems we have discussed so far serve to automate business functions and to provide data so that managers can make informed decisions. With these types of systems, data is input at the operations level and travels up the pyramid to be used by managers. There are, however, less structured types of information systems that are used simply to communicate information. The most common types of information systems for communication are electronic mail and voice mail.

E-Mail

If a company has a network, it can be more efficient and more convenient for employees to communicate using the network rather than using memos and other paper-based methods of communication. Electronic mail, commonly called **E-mail**, is an information system that allows computer users to write, send, and read messages, such as the one shown in Figure 12-5, using a computer network. Local area networks allow workers within a business to send messages around the office. Wide area networks allow computer users at opposite ends of the country to trade messages.

Using E-Mail.   To use E-mail, the person with whom you want to communicate must also have access to an E-mail system. Quite often, a user begins by entering a log-in identification and perhaps a system address, rather than his or her name. (Other systems require the user's

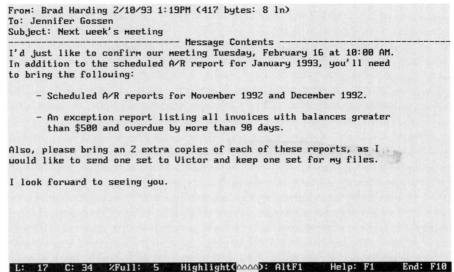

From: Brad Harding 2/10/93 1:19PM (417 bytes: 8 ln)
To: Jennifer Gossen
Subject: Next week's meeting
------------------------------- Message Contents -------------------------------
I'd just like to confirm our meeting Tuesday, February 16 at 10:00 AM.
In addition to the scheduled A/R report for January 1993, you'll need
to bring the following:

    - Scheduled A/R reports for November 1992 and December 1992.

    - An exception report listing all invoices with balances greater
      than $500 and overdue by more than 90 days.

Also, please bring an 2 extra copies of each of these reports, as I
would like to send one set to Victor and keep one set for my files.

I look forward to seeing you.

L: 17   C: 34   %Full: 5   Highlight(△△△△): AltF1   Help: F1   End: F10

Figure 12-5

E-mail systems make cooperation and communication around the office much easier.

password.) The system address is a set of numbers and letters that identifies the electronic location of the user. As soon as you log in, the E-mail system tells you whether you have any messages waiting. If you do, you can read them, print them, save them, delete them, or forward them to another person.

To send a message, you must know the name or user ID and perhaps address of the person to whom you are sending the message (Figure 12-6). Some E-mail systems have directories that let you look up a person's address by looking up a last and first name. You type your message after you address it. If several people need to read the message, you can send the same message to several users simultaneously.

Advantages of E-mail. E-mail has many advantages. Probably the most important is the speed of communication and the quality of detail that such a system permits. E-mail messages

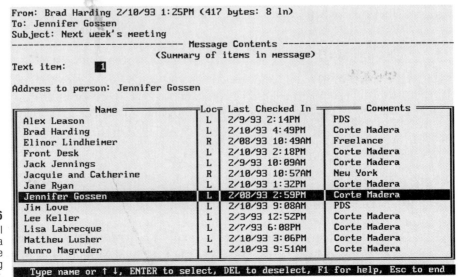

From: Brad Harding 2/10/93 1:25PM (417 bytes: 8 ln)
To: Jennifer Gossen
Subject: Next week's meeting
------------------------------- Message Contents -------------------------------
                         (Summary of items in message)

Text item: 1

Address to person: Jennifer Gossen

Name	Loc	Last Checked In	Comments
Alex Leason	L	2/9/93 2:14PM	PDS
Brad Harding	L	2/10/93 4:49PM	Corte Madera
Elinor Lindheimer	R	2/08/93 10:49AM	Freelance
Front Desk	L	2/10/93 2:18PM	Corte Madera
Jack Jennings	L	2/9/93 10:09AM	Corte Madera
Jacquie and Catherine	R	2/10/93 10:57AM	New York
Jane Ryan	L	2/10/93 1:32PM	Corte Madera
Jennifer Gossen	L	2/08/93 2:59PM	Corte Madera
Jim Love	L	2/10/93 9:08AM	PDS
Lee Keller	L	2/3/93 12:52PM	Corte Madera
Lisa Labrecque	L	2/7/93 6:08PM	Corte Madera
Matthew Lusher	L	2/10/93 3:06PM	Corte Madera
Munro Magruder	L	2/10/93 9:51AM	Corte Madera

Type name or ↑↓, ENTER to select, DEL to deselect, F1 for help, Esc to end

Figure 12-6

Sending an E-mail message is merely a matter of composing the message and knowing where you want to send it.

can be sent across the country cheaply and in a matter of seconds. They also tend to eliminate "telephone tag" because the recipient does not need to be present for the message to be sent. In businesses, this capability allows managers to react quickly to changes both within the business and in the marketplace. In addition, E-mail increases the amount of useful information that can be exchanged. Finally, E-mail messages tend to be more complete and accurate than voice communication. If an employee can sit down and thoughtfully compose a message rather than convey the message verbally, the message is more likely to contain all of the information that the sender needs to convey.

Disadvantages of E-mail.   E-mail can also cause problems. Because it is so easy to send an E-mail message, users sometimes write messages hastily, without developing their messages fully or considering the consequences of their messages. For example, say a company announces a pay raise that is lower than employees are expecting. A disgruntled worker may fire off a message to a manager saying things that he or she would not say in a face-to-face discussion. This is an example of a phenomenon called **flaming**.

The tendency toward flaming points to the differences between the dynamics of E-mail and those of face-to-face communication. It's easier to tell someone how you really feel when you don't have to deal directly with the person's reaction. And because the two people are not face to face, they are less able to gauge the effect of their words on each other. They cannot transmit and interpret important communication cues, such as tone of voice and body language. Certain forms of communication, such as sarcasm and humor, often do not travel well in E-mail. But remember that once you send an E-mail message, it's irretrievable, just like the letter you drop in a mailbox. And also remember that, in the workplace at least, you will have to face your E-mail correspondents sooner or later.

Another concern about the use of E-mail is that of privacy. Because messages are stored temporarily in a central database, the individuals that manage the database can have access to the messages. Several lawsuits have been filed against companies for alleged invasion of privacy in e-mail. The companies often contend that the E-mail system, like other computer technology, is the property of the company, and the company has a right to regulate its use. The plaintiffs believe that their rights to privacy and free speech have been violated. With public E-mail systems, the federal government now requires that the carrier maintain the privacy of the communication. However, no clear mandate has been set for private communication systems. Thus it is best to avoid intimate revelations in E-mail. Delete sensitive messages when you no longer need them.

Voice Mail

A **voice mail** (sometimes called V-mail) system is a computer-based system by which the user of a standard telephone can send, receive, store, or redirect voice messages. A voice mail system is more than an answering machine. When coupled with an automatic call distribution system, callers can control the direction of their calls through an organization. Voice menus are often used to provide options from which the caller can select. A voice mail menu might say: "Press 1 for new orders; press 2 for billing inquiries; press 3 for shipment status; or press 4 to talk to an operator." When calling a specific person who is not at his or her desk, the caller is able to either leave a message or redirect the call to an operator or another employee. Voice mail systems also allow users to forward their incoming calls to phones in other offices.

The primary advantage of voice mail is that it provides an efficient method for a business to communicate with the rest of the world. Anyone with a push-button phone can call in and generally either reach who they want or leave a message without involving an operator. In addition to providing customers and clients easy channels for communication, a voice mail system saves the company the labor costs of manually handling every incoming phone call.

One disadvantage of some voice mail systems is not being able to edit a message as you can with E-mail. With some systems, you can, however, erase a message that you have just recorded and start over. A more important disadvantage is the impersonal nature of the system in comparison to operator-directed calls. Many people prefer to have a human being help them get through to the right person at a company and take their messages.

Related Business Issues

The use of information systems in both small and large businesses has had a profound effect — both good and bad — on employment, consumer products, and, of course, the way that companies manage their affairs. In this section, we look at a few of the most important effects of information systems.

Quality Control

The basic idea of **quality control** is to measure and compare goods and services. Information systems related to quality control maintain current and historical data about such factors as sales or production targets, failure and reject rates of manufactured parts, and customer satisfaction. Managers use these kinds of data to make judgments about the effectiveness of production and marketing techniques, as well as about their employees.

Total quality management, or TQM, is a methodology for establishing, measuring, and implementing quality performance measures from one end of the production process to the other. TQM looks not only at the production systems, but also at the human systems. From customer service to the factory floor, the focus is on the use of top-quality parts, processes, and people.

Job Displacement and Job Enlargement

From the business's point of view, one of the most persuasive arguments for automating a business function is the reduction in the workforce. For example, between 1972 and 1977, computerization at AT&T allowed the company to eliminate 50,000 workers from the payroll, even though demand for telephone service was increasing.

Job displacement as a result of computer technology has both positive and negative effects. The obvious negative effect is the unemployment that can result from automating business functions. If you look more closely at this phenomenon, however, you will find that not as many jobs are lost as you might think. When systems are automated, jobs are created at computer hardware, software, and services companies. Jobs are also created for information systems professionals who create and manage the new systems. The key to keeping or getting a job often depends on the computer skills you have and your ability to learn new ones.

Another effect of computerization is the changing responsibilities of the workforce. In general, reducing the workforce at a company requires more of the employees who are not displaced, an effect called **job enlargement**. Computers allow fewer managers to supervise more workers and fewer workers to produce more goods. Companies are finding that as new computer systems are introduced, the companies must provide effective retraining so their workers learn to handle their increased responsibilities. This effect can be either good or bad, depending on the nature of the change, the feelings of the employees, and how employers manage the change. Some people resent having their job descriptions change to include a host of new responsibilities. Others find that, with automation, their jobs include less drudgery and more interesting work.

Finally, one of the leading benefits of computerization is the decreased cost of consumer goods. When a company can save money by automating some processes, some of the savings pass on to consumers in the form of lower prices.

Performance Monitoring

Computers are multifaceted. While allowing a clerk to electronically file documents, a computer can also track how many documents per hour the clerk is filing. By comparing the output from each employee, operations and middle-level managers can distribute awards or mete out warnings or punishment.

This **performance monitoring** can happen with or without the worker's knowledge. In some cases, performance monitoring can be an effective way to boost productivity. In other cases, however, it can have severe effects on the social and psychological reactions of the employee because it is so intrusive. At a warehouse owned by a large grocery chain, for example, employees were monitored according to how long it took them to bend over and move one box! If workers begin to resent the monitoring system, the system can decrease morale and, in turn, decrease productivity.

Downsizing and Outsourcing

When considering the benefits of automating a process or creating an information system, the central question asked by executives is whether or not the new system justifies its own cost. This is a tough question. Analyzing return on investment requires calculating the profit that a system makes relative to its costs. If the rate of return is greater than the prevailing interest rate, the system is deemed a success. Computerized information systems, however, are difficult to cost justify. The cost of hardware and software is easy to figure, but the benefit is much more difficult to pinpoint.

One of the ways companies are decreasing their information systems costs is reducing, or **downsizing**, the function of the central information system. Downsizing involves distributing the computer resources throughout an organization and then coordinating information exchange in a centralized fashion. For example, before downsizing, a marketing department's information system is stored in the company's mainframe. After downsizing, it is stored in a smaller departmental computer, which is often a file server. (A file server is a high-speed computer in a local area network that stores programs and data files shared by users on that network.)

In a downsizing situation, telecommunications systems are used to share data between departments. Downsizing reduces the cost of a centralized information systems department by moving the costs onto the departments that use the systems. Downsizing is therefore one way to make users more responsible for the resources they use.

Another popular technique for decreasing the costs of computing is **outsourcing**. Instead of employing a full-time, in-house computer operations staff, a company hires a computer service company to manage, maintain, and service a networked computer system. The client company owns the hardware and software but outsources the service and support. Outsourcing makes sense for companies that do not require a full-time network manager but find it impractical to expect an employee with other responsibilities to handle such a specialized job.

Comprehension Questions

1. How does sending a file via modem differ from sending a message across the country using an E-mail system?

2. Describe an information system that accomplished both performance monitoring and quality control.

3. In the short term, which do you think saves a company more money, downsizing or outsourcing?

Using What You Know

1. Describe a voice mail menu for customers and clients who call BVOS.

2. Describe the ways in which BVOS might use an E-mail system.

3. Describe how information systems could be used at BVOS to maintain quality control.

Summary Points

Information Systems in Large Businesses

☐ Complex organizations require highly developed information systems to coordinate their activities.

What Is an Information System?

☐ The narrow definition of an information system is that it provides a means for managers to obtain information from a company's database.

☐ The more general definition is that an information system is an established path or set of paths along which information can travel through an organization.

Levels of Management and Their Needs for Information

☐ A company can be diagrammed as a pyramid of managers on top of a foundation of operations-level workers.

☐ Workers are often organized into five basic departments: production, marketing, research, personnel, and accounting.

☐ Managers are divided between three levels: operations managers, middle-level managers, and upper-level managers.

☐ Each level of management needs different kinds of information to make different kinds of decisions.

☐ Operations managers make structured, immediate decisions; middle-level managers make less structured, tactical decisions; and executives make unstructured, strategic decisions.

Information Systems for Operations Managers

Production Systems

☐ Manufacturing is performed by a production department that creates a tangible good.

CAD

☐ CAD is used by production and research departments to design and test products.

CAM and Robotics

☐ One meaning of CAM is the use of a CAD database for robotics, numerical control, and process control.

CAM and Inventory Management

☐ Another meaning of CAM is the use of a computer to manage inventories of raw goods and finished products.

☐ Just-in-time manufacturing is a technique for keeping just enough stock of raw materials on hand.

Accounting Systems

☐ Accounting systems include at least four databases: accounts receivable, accounts payable, payroll, and the general ledger.

Information Systems for Middle and Upper Management

Management Information Systems

☐ Management information systems generate scheduled, exception, and demand reports to help middle-level managers make tactical decisions.

Decision Support Systems

☐ Decision support systems allow upper-level managers to obtain information in a variety of formats, depending on the requiremets of the decision being made.

Enterprise-Wide Information Systems

☐ Some types of information systems, rather than serving the specific needs of managers, simply create communication channels in an organization.

E-Mail

☐ E-mail allows users connected to a WAN or LAN to send written messages to each other.

Using E-Mail

☐ Using E-mail may or may not require specifying a system address of your own computer and knowing the address of the receiving computer.

☐ E-mail messages are stored in a database until the recipient accesses the system, at which time they can read, print, save, delete, or forward each message.

Advantages of E-mail

☐ E-mail is fast, cheap, and effective.

Disadvantages of E-mail

☐ E-mail can be subject to invasions of privacy.

☐ The medium can lead to flaming or other inappropriate types of messages because of the different dynamics of face-to-face and on-line communication.

Voice Mail

☐ Voice mail systems act as electronic operators, allowing callers to direct their own calls and leave answering-machine-type messages. They also provide flexibility to users through call-forwarding and other features.

☐ The primary advantage of voice mail is its efficiency for the business.

☐ The primary disadvantage is the impersonal nature of the system.

Related Business Issues

Quality Control

☐ Managers use computerized quality control techniques to make judgments about production and marketing techniques and about employees.

Job Displacement and Job Enlargement

☐ Job displacement can add to unemployment. It can also save money for a business and thereby raise profitability and lower consumer prices.

☐ Computer skills can help decrease your chances of being displaced and increase your job opportunities.

☐ When employees are displaced by computers, remaining employees find their jobs enlarged.

Performance Monitoring

☐ Performance monitoring systems can boost productivity or deter it by demoralizing workers.

Downsizing and Outsourcing

☐ Determining return on investment for computer systems is difficult because the benefits are difficult to quantify.

☐ One way for companies to save money on computer systems is downsizing, which is the process of moving applications from mainframes to file servers and to other more local computer, thus distributing computing costs more equitably.

☐ Outsourcing involves hiring outside computer specialists to manage, service, and support the computer system when it is not cost effective to maintain that level of expertise in-house.

Knowing the Facts

True/False

1. Personnel departments usually handle the accounting systems of large companies.

2. Middle-level managers make strategic decisions; upper-level managers make tactical decisions.

3. Middle-level managers need data that spans a greater period of time than the data required by operations managers.

4. Executives tend to make decisions that are more structured than those made by operations managers.

5. CAM can mean either robotics or computerized inventory control.

6. Payroll is a type of accounts payable that recognizes a company's short-term debt to employees.

7. Decision support systems are used to generate scheduled, exception, and demand reports.

8. Using E-mail requires that both the sender and the receiver of a message are connected to the same network.

9. Analyzing return on investment requires calculating the profit that a system makes relative to its costs.

10. Forcing departments to buy their own minicomputers, rather than using the company's mainframe, is an example of outsourcing.

Short Answer

1. _____ can lead to a phenomenon called flaming, in which one person insults another when he or she would not ordinarily do so in face-to-face contact.

2. _____ often have user-friendly interfaces that allow executives to obtain specific data without having to use the programming capabilities of a DBMS.

3. Most data that enters a company's database comes in at the _____ level and is analyzed at the management level.

4. An accounting database called the _____ _____ integrates and summarizes the data in payroll and accounts receivable and payable.

5. The first use of computers in business was as tools for _____.

6. With a fully automated manufacturing systems, a _____ database can be used as input by CAM systems to control industrial robots or manage inventory.

7. In _____, a company sells its centralized computer system to a computer services company.

8. _____ manufacturing is a technique used to minimize the amount of inventory that a company keeps.

9. The purpose of _____ is to measure and compare goods and services to make judgments about the effectiveness of production and marketing techniques.

10. Scheduled reports are generated regularly; _____ reports are generated in response to an unusual event or set of circumstances.

Answers

True/False

1. F
2. F
3. T
4. F
5. T
6. T
7. F
8. T
9. T
10. F

Short Answer

1. E-mail
2. Decision support systems
3. operations
4. general ledger
5. accounting
6. CAD
7. outsourcing
8. Just-in-time
9. quality control
10. exception

Challenging Your Understanding

1. When voice mail was first becoming popular, callers frequently complained about leaving messages on computers and not interacting with humans. Now, many callers would prefer to leave a message on a machine rather than talk directly to a human. Can you explain this dramatic shift?

2. Some experts maintain that very few people actually lose jobs to computers. Rather, computers allow fewer workers to do more things, so workers are displaced and not replaced by computers. What do you think?

3. In a JIT system, the manufacturer carries the optimal amount of inventory in stock. Just when the inventory is running out, the new shipment arrives. This requires good relationships with suppliers and substantial information systems resources to coordinate the orders. Given the costs involved, why is this a popular idea?

4. Which level of manager requires the most information from outside the company? Why?

Developing Information Systems

Key Terms

computer-aided software engineering (CASE)
data flow diagram
economic feasibility
feasibility study
garbage in, garbage out (GIGO)
legal feasibility
obsolescence
operational feasibility
prototyping
request for proposal (RFP)
request for quote (RFQ)
schedule feasibility
system flowchart
system analyst
system designer
system development life cycle
technological feasibility

Objectives

In this chapter you will learn to:

■ Name and describe the seven steps of the system development life cycle

■ Compare the system development life cycle to the programming process and the problem-solving process

■ Describe how CASE tools are used in system development

■ Identify the importance of user involvement in system development

■ Explain the purpose and process of prototyping

■ List the ethical responsibilities of the information systems professional

■ Describe three common misconceptions about information systems

The System Development Life Cycle

Because they serve the needs of people in a changing environment, information systems act like living organisms. They are conceived and born, they mature and grow old, and they eventually die and are replaced with newer information systems. The **system development life cycle** is typically described as having seven stages:

1. Recognizing the problem
2. Analyzing the current system
3. Designing the new system
4. Developing the new system
5. Installing the new system
6. Evaluating and maintaining the system
7. Recognizing obsolescence

This sequence of stages closely resembles two other sets of stages we have covered: programming and problem solving (Figure 13-1). The resemblance is logical, because an important part of system development is programming, and programming is a means for solving a problem. The resemblance between development of an information system and problem solving makes sense for another reason. Throughout this book, we have used problem solving as a structured method for creating a computer system. Now we are describing an information system rather than just a computer system. The computer system is the heart of an information system, so the processes for establishing both are similar.

Recognizing the Problem

The life cycle of a system begins when the users of a mature information system begin to identify problems in it. For example, say an operations manager for an accounting department is analyzing an accounts receivable system. In doing so, he finds that, on average, account balances go unpaid for 10 weeks. From working at other companies and from knowing the goals of his middle-level manager, he knows that this delay is too long. Unfortunately, the operations manager is unable to simply bill sooner, because the number of orders processed every week is already pushing the limits of the hardware and software currently being used.

This type of problem recognition, in which the user identifies the need for change, is the most common scenario. It generally ends with users writing a formal request to initiate the development of a new system (Figure 13-2). However, problem recognition can come from other sources. If upper managers discover that a competitor has developed an advanced information system to gain a competitive advantage, they may institute a similar change as a competitive necessity.

Once management agrees to initiate a new development cycle, the last step of problem recognition — sometimes considered a separate stage — is often to write a **feasibility study**. This study is a preliminary investigation of the problem to see if the benefits of solving it outweigh the costs of developing a solution. Several kinds of feasibility must be looked at, including technological, economic, legal, operational, and scheduling.

- **Technological feasibility** determines whether the problem can be solved using current technology. Technological feasibility is not always a "yes or no" question. Sometimes, technological innovation may be worth the risks, especially when management is pursuing a competitive advantage.

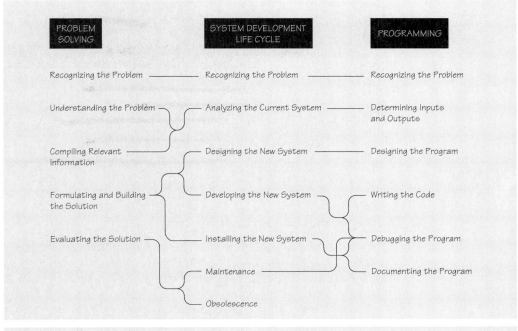

Figure 13-1
The system development life cycle is closely related to the problem solving steps and the programming process.

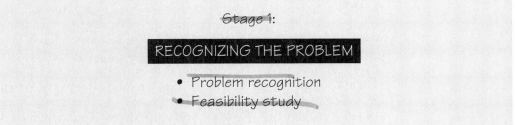

Figure 13-2
The most important phases of stage 1.

- **Economic feasibility** is easy to understand but difficult to determine. The question is simply whether the new system will be worth the money. Unfortunately, it is much easier to determine the costs of a new system than to put a dollar amount on the benefits.

- Business laws and regulations change frequently. As a result, a company must consider the **legal feasibility** of a new information system solution. Because computer applications are always growing, you can expect to see increased legislation affecting the use of computers in business.

- **Operational feasibility** helps determine whether the proposed system will function in the organization. The new system may require restructuring a department. The company might need to hire additional personnel, or the system may displace employees from their current positions. If the new system will be too disruptive, it may not be pursued.

- Finally, **scheduling feasibility** ascertains when the system will be ready for implementation. If the information systems department cannot develop the system in the required time, management may consider an outside vendor. The price of hiring another vendor may, in turn, undermine the economic feasibility of solving the problem.

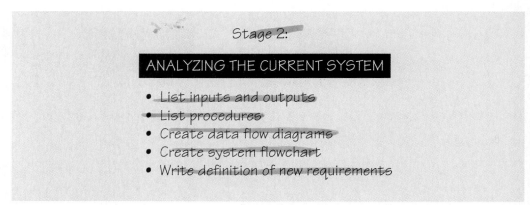

Figure 13-3
Stage 2 of the system
development life cycle.

Analyzing the Current System

If a feasibility study shows that a new system will be cost effective, the company begins a detailed analysis of the current information system. At some companies, professionals called **system analysts** specialize in this kind of work. At smaller companies, users of the current system can take on this role.

The analysis stage has several goals, as shown in Figure 13-3. First, the inputs and outputs of the current system are listed; the person doing the analysis documents each type of data that the system requires and the reports or other processed data that the system generates. After documenting inputs and outputs, the system analyst next lists all of the procedures for using the current system. A third goal of the analysis stage is to use the inputs, outputs, and procedures to create data flow diagrams and systems flowcharts, both of which show graphically how data moves through an information system. The difference between the two is that the **data flow diagram** is a broad view of the whole system, including the people who use it. **System flowcharts** detail how data moves through the computer system. These diagrams closely resemble the flowcharts created in programming.

System analysts use several common methods to gather data about the current system. Four of the most common are:

- Interviewing users
- Distributing written questionnaires
- Observing operations
- Collecting output documents and system documentation

In smaller companies, or when a user is doing the system analysis, these methods may not all be necessary. In a larger company, however, the system analyst may have little experience with the work carried on at the operations level of a given department. In this case, the analyst needs to establish as many channels of communication with the users as possible.

The result of the analysis stage is a written, detailed definition of the new system requirements. Like the feasibility study, this report is generally submitted to middle- or upper-level managers before the next stage begins.

Designing the New System

Once the old system has been thoroughly analyzed, the new system must be designed to meet the new requirements. The design stage of the system development life cycle, summa-

Figure 13-4
Stage 3 of the system
development life cycle.

Stage 3:

DESIGNING THE NEW SYSTEM

- Propose design solutions
- Second feasibility study

rized in Figure 13-4, is similar to the design stage of the programming process. Designing a system, however, is a broader problem because it includes not only software, but hardware, people, and procedures. At this point, an information systems professional, known as the **system designer**, heads the project. The designer may be the same person as the analyst or a new professional with specific experience in this field.

The techniques used in this stage borrow from the previous stages. Normally, the first thing the system designer must do is propose several designs. Each of these is described with the help of data flow diagrams and system flowcharts. In some cases, the system designer uses pseudocode to rough out the design for programs that need to be written or purchased. As you can see, system developers adhere to the principles of structured programming, even though programming is just part of the problem.

After the various proposed alternatives are designed, they are presented to middle or upper managers, who must again consider the feasibility of each solution. Like the feasibility study mentioned in the first stage, this design report must reconsider certain kinds of feasibility, especially economic, operational, and scheduling. The design report should also make a recommendation about which design offers the best solution.

It is possible for this second feasibility study to reveal that the benefits of creating any solution do not outweigh the costs. Despite significant investment in the project at the end of the design stage, it is still better to scrap a design that is too technically difficult, too expensive, or too time consuming than to proceed to the development stage.

Developing the New System

When a final design has been approved, it is time to develop the new system. Development consists of buying necessary hardware and programming or purchasing software (Figure 13-5).

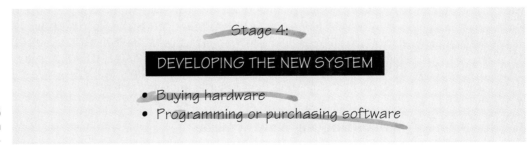

Figure 13-5
Stage 4 of the system
development life cycle.

Stage 4:

DEVELOPING THE NEW SYSTEM

- Buying hardware
- Programming or purchasing software

Buying Hardware.   Many new information systems require the purchase of hardware. If a company is moving from a manual to a computerized system, development includes purchasing all of the hardware for the new system. If a company is replacing one computerized system with another, much — if not all — of the old hardware may still be useful. Additional hardware may be required, however. For example, if an inventory control system is being improved with bar-code readers, the existing company or departmental computer may handle this change just fine. In terms of hardware, the company may need to purchase only the bar-code readers themselves.

You are already familiar with most of the issues involved in purchasing hardware, because we covered them in Unit III. When you purchase relatively small or inexpensive equipment, such as bar-code readers or even microcomputers, the techniques and sources you have used throughout this book will serve you well.

In large companies, however, a new information system may require a mainframe or a large number of smaller hardware devices. In such cases, the purchaser has a great deal of money to spend and therefore has some leverage among hardware manufacturers. The developer should send out several **requests for proposal**, or **RFPs**. An RFP is exactly what its name implies: It is a request for a vendor to send a bid offering a hardware solution to the requirements specified in the RFP. The bid includes the description of the solution and the price that the vendor will charge the business developing the system. A company will normally send out several RFPs so that it can compare competing bids and pick the best one.

If a company knows exactly what it wants in the way of a hardware solution, it may send out **requests for quote**, or **RFQs**, rather than RFPs. RFQs identify a specific product and ask for the price at which the vendor is willing to sell it. Judging the best quote is a relatively simple process; however, judging the best proposal requires deciding who best satisfies the requirements as well as offering the best value.

Programming or Purchasing Software.   Unlike hardware, which is almost always bought when needed, software can be either bought or created. We have already discussed the program vs. purchase decision in Unit II, so we won't go into detail again here. As with hardware, when purchasing software, a company may want to send out RFPs or RFQs. If the company needs software that is not available in the market, it is more likely to send out RFPs. If the software already exists and the company needs a site license or support service or help with installation, it is more likely to send RFQs.

If a company decides that it is more efficient to develop the software in-house (with programmers who are already employees), the development follows the sequence of the programming cycle.

Structured programming is extremely important here. In all likelihood, the person who writes the program will not be the one who maintains or reworks it later on. If the program is not logically structured and well documented, the second programmer will waste countless hours trying to understand its design. Another reason for structured programming is the ease with which program modules and subroutines can be used in other systems throughout the company. The ability to reuse parts of programs is obviously more cost efficient for a company than building every program from scratch.

Installing the New System

Installing a new information system in a large company (Figure 13-6) is a period of high visibility for information systems professionals. This stage should be approached cautiously and the job carried out thoroughly. To a large degree, the quality of work during installation can determine the long-term worth of the system.

The installation stage has five parts:

- Setup

- Testing

- Documentation

- Conversion

- Training

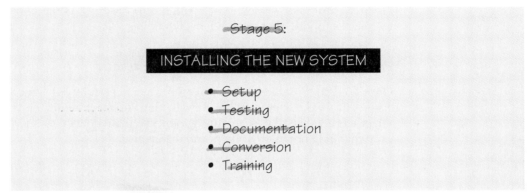

Figure 13-6
Stage 5 of the system
development life cycle

These are not steps; they can take place simultaneously or they can overlap.

Setup. Setting up the new system is a matter of putting together the various parts that have been purchased or developed on site. It can have many aspects, depending on the nature of the new system. In addition to connecting hardware and loading software, setup can include construction to accommodate new hardware or users, rewiring, configuring software to run efficiently on hardware, and many other tasks.

Testing. The biggest part of testing a new system is often testing software developed in-house. This includes debugging the code as well as having employees perform the alpha and beta testing. In addition to testing software, hardware must be checked to see if it works properly, and new procedures should be carried through to see that they produce the desired results.

Documentation. Like a software program, an information system must be thoroughly documented. The internal and external documentation of the programs is part of the development process. The documentation that is part of installation tells how employees are to use all parts of the system. It should cover every procedure the system is designed to perform, how data is entered and by whom, and how and in what form data is retrieved.

Conversion. If the new system requires data from the old system, that data may have to be converted so the new system can understand it. Converting data from a manual system to a computerized system can require a massive amount of data entry. Converting from one software package to another or from one hardware platform to another usually means translating the format. The growth of portable software — especially operating systems — will lessen the difficulty of this type of conversion.

How you execute the conversion from one system to another can spell the difference between success and failure of the new system. If you rip out the old system on Friday and plan to start with the new system Monday morning, you will have problems. Instead, phase the new system in one department at a time or one function at a time.

Training.   Perhaps the most critical part of installation is training the employees who will use the system. Motivating people to learn the system is crucial for successful implementation. The training can be performed by one of several groups: representatives of the vendor that sold the system or parts of it; employees from the information systems department who designed and developed the system; or the users who first learned the system and helped test it. In any case, someone or some group must act as the expert and be available for technical support, even after the initial training.

Evaluating and Maintaining the System

Once you have installed the information system, it is fully developed and normal operations can begin as you enter the stage of evaluating and maintaining the system (Figure 13-7). You might expect that all that remains is periodic maintenance to keep the system serving the ever-changing needs of workers and managers.

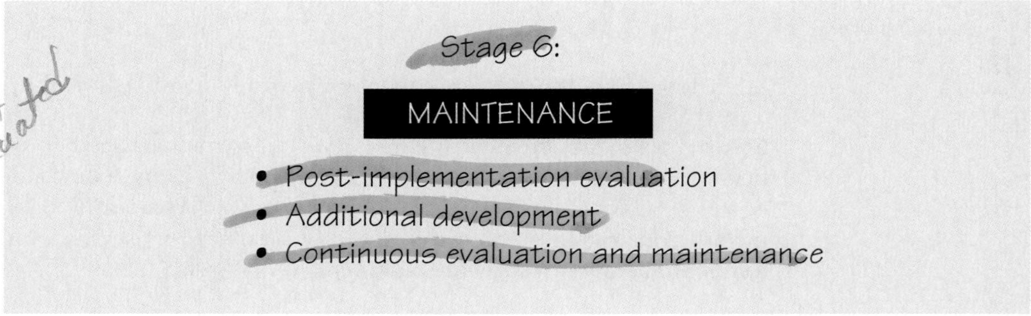

Stage 6:

MAINTENANCE

- Post-implementation evaluation
- Additional development
- Continuous evaluation and maintenance

Figure 13-7
Stage 6 of the system
development life cycle.

Actually, though, the maintenance stage begins with a post-implementation evaluation, which is written by users of the new system. In this report, users compare performance with the goals that were identified early in the development process. If the goals were not met, some additional development may be required.

Throughout the normal operating life of the system, other evaluations may be written. Problems that arise are handled by a maintenance group. The cost of maintenance has led companies to realize the value of proper design and development and of this formal developmental process. Simply speaking, a well-designed system is easier and therefore less costly to maintain. And it may save you a lot of money. According to some experts, the cost of maintenance over the entire life of a system roughly equals the cost of development.

Recognizing Obsolescence

No matter how well an information system is designed, the cost of periodic maintenance gradually increases. Each "patch" that a maintenance group adds to a system makes it more cumbersome. Eventually, like an old car, it is no longer worth fixing. Even if the system has not been continually repaired, the advent of new technology may make it more cost efficient to scrap the system than bring it up to date. This is the stage of **obsolescence** (Figure 13-8), when new feasibility studies begin to initiate a new system development life cycle.

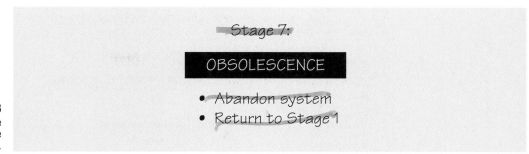

Figure 13-8
The obsolescence stage leads back to stage 1 of the cycle.

Comprehension Questions

1. What stage in the system development life cycle has no counterpart in the problem-solving process? Why?

2. Why is the life of a system described as a cycle?

3. Why must data flow diagrams contain symbols that differ from those used in system flowcharts?

Using What You Know

1. At BVOS, who would most likely act as the system analyst in the development of an accounting system?

2. If a company is changing from a manual to computerized accounting system, what do you think is the most costly part of the installation stage?

3. Why is it not necessary to send out an RFP for the LAN server you intend to use at BVOS?

Tools and Techniques for Developing Information Systems

A variety of tools and techniques have been created to help in the analysis and design of information systems.

CASE Tools

One of the most promising tools used to aid system analysts and programmers is called **computer-aided software engineering**, or **CASE**, tool. CASE tools are software packages that help programmers write programs.

CASE packages can include several different tools (Figure 13-9 on the next page). They can help create flowcharts, keep track of program specifications, and generate reports and program documentation. Most also include third- or fourth-generation languages, as well as libraries in which to store subroutines and modules that can be reused. In general, CASE tools support as many facets of the programming process as possible and promote the creation of top-down, structured programs.

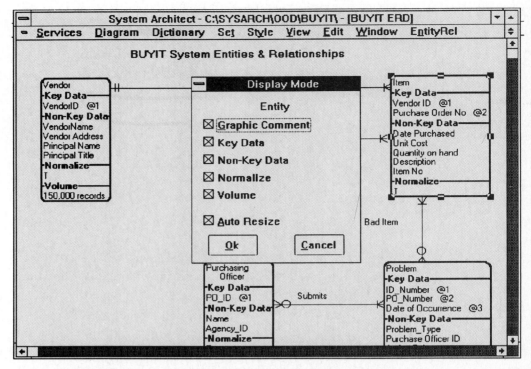

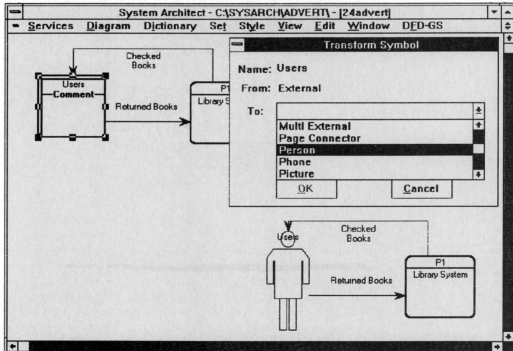

Figure 13-9
These screens show just a few of the tools that have been developed for CASE packages.

User Involvement

The importance of user involvement in the system development process should not be underestimated (Figure 13-10). It is critical that an information systems professional realize he or she is working for users. These users are generally knowledgeable about the specific application area for which the program is being written. They also have a vested interest in the quality of the system that the information system professional creates. The perspective and interest of the users can be a valuable resource for the IS professional, who, after all, has experience in the fields of programming and system development but may know very little about the complexity of the users' jobs.

Figure 13-10
Perhaps the most crucial ingredient of successful system development is user involvement.

In addition to the users' worth as a resource, users are also customers. In many cases, if they have doubts about the quality of work coming from the information systems department, or if they are displeased with the IS department's responsiveness to their concerns, they can take their problem to an outside vendor. This type of competition can motivate systems professionals to excel at their jobs.

Information system development in Europe is especially oriented toward the involvement of the user. There, users are encouraged to define and even solve system problems. The participative methods they use also tend to be less structured than the system development life cycle described in this chapter.

Prototyping

No matter how hard an analyst may try, sometimes the system that is delivered does not meet the users' expectations. One way of assuring that the user's needs are met is by **prototyping**. This technique involves the creation of a simple program that mimics the operations the user desires. In general, the system evolves through a series of interim steps, with a tremendous amount of user involvement during the process. The first prototype is not a totally functional system, but includes the major system components, so that users see what the new system will do. As the interim steps are carried out, users give their feedback and aid in the evolution of the system. In some cases, the prototype itself grows into the actual system. In others, it is just an increasingly complex model that is rebuilt when the actual system is developed. Today, prototypes can be developed quickly using special programming tools, such as CASE tools. Sometimes, users themselves create the prototype.

Unfortunately, a prototype can give the user an unrealistic view of the complexity of the project. Typically a programmer will create a prototyped system without many of the components required for a corporate information system. For example, a prototyped system may have no security or error-checking routines built in. These components are often some of the most difficult elements of a system to build. Also, if a user is helping to create the prototype, the user will probably get an inaccurate picture of how hard it is to write a program. This can cause some disregard for the efforts of the programmer and analyst.

Ethics and the Information System Professional

Richard Mason, a noted researcher of ethical uses of information technology, states that the information systems professional is responsible for four ethical agendas: privacy, accuracy, property, and access. Privacy is the right of an individual or organization to control the collection, use, and dissemination of identifiable information. The information systems professional is responsible for maintaining the privacy of those whose data is in his or her control. The IS professional is charged with assuring that the data in corporate databases is as accurate as possible and remains secure while it is in the possession of the organization. Property refers to the ownership of intellectual property such as software. Users of information systems are charged with making sure that all software they use is properly licensed. Finally, access refers to access to information technology and data. The IS professional is charged with removing technological barriers between authorized users and the information technologies and data that will help them do their jobs.

Misconceptions About the Information System

There are three prevalent myths surrounding the use of computing technology in business.

The first myth is that computerization always improves efficiency. There are many ways to design an information system. If a system exactly mimics the manual system it replaces, there is no substantive change to the nature of the work, only to who is carrying it out. A better way to design a system is to determine if the business process can be re-engineered using computer technology. In this case, the business function can be improved rather than simply automated. But just as we are able to improve a function with a computer, we can likewise harm a function. The misdiagnosis of a problem or a poor implementation of the design can severely limit the success of the system and even disrupt the operation of the business function.

A common mistake analysts make when designing information systems is failing to take into account the human systems in the organization. When this happens, the most technically perfect solution to a problem may be doomed to failure. Hence, the second myth is that every problem in a system has a purely technological solution. The successful computer analyst wears many hats when designing a system. He or she might be a computer consultant one moment, a business consultant another, and a rhetorical sounding board another. The idea is that the installation of an information system requires the modification of human systems. The modification may be entirely computerized, but it can also be a hybrid of computer systems and manual systems. These hybrid solutions are often the most efficient because they do not force the limitations of the computer onto every systems problem.

Finally, many computer users act as if the computer is always correct. To some individuals, if some piece of information came from a computer, it must be right. These people ascribe to the computer certain characteristics that border on science fiction. Even knowledgeable computer users often feel very confident about the way the technology works. Neither group challenges the assumptions under which the program was designed or the system runs.

In part, this misconception comes from the fact that the use of a computer can add a certain credibility to one's argument. Desktop publishing, presentation graphics, and sophisticated computer models can make an impressive statement during a presentation. Often, though, the style of presentation is more persuasive than the facts. When faced with supposed facts from a computer, remember the most important computer adage: *Garbage in, garbage out,* or *GIGO.* The saying means that the worth of what comes out of the computer is only as valuable or accurate as the data that went in.

Comprehension Questions

1. Does prototyping tend to encourage or discourage user involvement? Why?
2. Why is managing access the sole responsibility of the information systems professional?
3. Explain why protecting intellectual property is not solely the responsibility of the information systems professional.

Using What You Know

1. Compare prototyping to generating pseudocode.
2. Invent three scenarios related to daily operations at BVOS that illustrate each of the common misconceptions about computers.
3. If there is no full-time information systems professional at BVOS, who should oversee the four ethical responsibilities related to that role?

Summary Points

The System Development Life Cycle

☐ The seven stages of the system development life cycle closely resemble the stages in the programming process and the problem-solving process.

Recognizing the Problem

☐ The life cycle typically begins when users run into problems with the existing system.

☐ The cycle can begin with middle- or upper-level managers who are looking for a competitive advantage.

☐ The stage ends with a feasibility study that examines the technological, economic, legal, operational, and scheduling feasibility of finding a solution to the problem.

Analyzing the Current System

☐ The goals of the analysis stage are to list inputs, outputs, and procedures, and to create system flowcharts and data flow diagrams.

☐ The system analyst may use several techniques to gather information, including interviews, questionnaires, observations, and existing documents.

☐ A detailed list of the new system requirements should be written at the end of the analysis stage.

Designing the New System
- [ ] The system design stage resembles the design stage of the programming process.
- [ ] Several alternative designs should be developed by the system designer.
- [ ] Another feasibility study focusing on the feasibility of the solutions is written at the end of this stage.

Developing the New System

Buying Hardware

- [ ] In a large company, if a detailed solution has not been developed, the company may send out RFPs.
- [ ] If the company knows exactly what it is looking for, it will send out RFQs.

Programming or Purchasing Software

- [ ] If a company wants to buy software that does not yet exist, it will send out RFPs.
- [ ] If the company wants a special deal on existing software, it will send out RFQs.
- [ ] If the software is being programmed in-house, structured programming is extremely important.

Installing the New System

Setup

- [ ] Setup can include such jobs as construction and software configuration, in addition to putting hardware together and loading software.

Testing

- [ ] Testing includes testing the hardware, software, and procedures.

Documentation

- [ ] The documentation tells the users how to operate the system.

Conversion

- [ ] Conversion involves moving existing data, work, and procedures from the old system to the new system.

Training

- [ ] Training of new users can be carried out by programmers, vendors, or other users who helped test the system.

Evaluating and Maintaining the System
- [ ] Maintenance begins with a post-implementation evaluation that reports whether the system meets the requirements.
- [ ] Evaluations of a system are written throughout its life, and a maintenance group takes care of problems.

Recognizing Obsolescence
- [ ] As a system ages, maintenance becomes gradually more expensive, until the system is obsolete.

Tools and Techniques for Developing Information Systems

CASE Tools
- [ ] CASE tools are sets of programs that help the programmer write programs.

User Involvement
- [ ] The users' experience and interest in the success of the system should be used as a resource by the information systems professionals.
- [ ] IS professionals may also be motivated by the fact that users can go to outside vendors.
- [ ] Companies in Europe tend to use more highly participative and less structured methods in systems development than those in the United States.

Prototyping

☐ Prototyping is a means for more accurately meeting the needs of users by creating a model that mimics the design and function of the desired system.

☐ The model is successively revised with the help of user feedback.

Ethics and the Information Systems Professional

☐ Information systems professionals should be responsible for four ethical agendas: privacy of information, accuracy of data, rights to intellectual property, and appropriate access to the system.

Misconceptions About the Information System

☐ Professionals tend to believe that computerization always improves efficiency.

☐ Computers only improve efficiency if the computer solution is better engineered than the manual solution.

☐ People tend to think that system problems always have computer solutions.

☐ Often, the best solution is a hybrid of manual and computerized systems.

☐ People tend to think that the computer is always right.

☐ Remember: "Garbage in, garbage out."

Knowing the Facts

True/False

1. At small companies, users often play the role of the system analyst.

2. Responses to RFPs are more difficult to evaluate than responses to RFQs.

3. According to some experts, the long-term cost of maintenance roughly equals the cost of development.

4. Training employees to use a new system must be carried out by the programmers who developed the software for it.

5. Prototype systems are developed by users and gradually evolve into the working system.

6. The first feasibility study focuses on the problem, while later ones focus on proposed solutions.

7. The internal and external software documentation generated during the programming process acts as the documentation for the whole information system.

8. Hybrid systems can be more efficient than fully computerized systems.

9. The participative development methods used in Europe tend to be more structured than methods used in the United States.

10. Technological feasibility identifies whether a solution is worth the money it will cost.

Short Answer

1. _____ often include programs for creating documentation, flowcharts, and even module libraries.

2. _____ involves creating a model of the proposed system; the model is presented to users for their feedback.

3. The problem with determining _____ feasibility is that it is much easier to measure the costs of a new system than to put a dollar amount on the benefits.

4. Portable software will lessen the difficulties in the _____ part of the installation stage when one computerized system is being replaced with another.

5. The system flowchart shows how data moves through the computer system; the _____ shows how data moves through the entire information system.

6. The belief that the computer is always right is refuted with the adage "_____."

7. One part of the installation stage, _____, can include construction, rewiring, and configuring software.

8. Companies that have defined system requirements but have not developed a detailed design are likely to send out _____ to potential vendors.

9. Feasibility studies are often conducted at the ends of the "recognizing the problem" stage and the _____ stage.

10. If a company wants to purchase software that is already on the market, it is likely to send out _____.

Answers

True/False

1. T
2. T
3. T
4. F
5. F
6. T
7. F
8. T
9. F
10. F

Short Answer

1. CASE tools
2. Prototyping
3. economic
4. conversion
5. data flow diagram
6. garbage in, garbage out
7. setup
8. RFPs
9. "designing the new system," or design
10. RFQs

Challenging Your Understanding

1. Compare the steps involved in writing a research paper to the steps of the system development life cycle.

2. Some people maintain that the four responsibilities of information system professionals are actually *everybody's* responsibilities. Explain how each of the four could be construed as a responsibility of the BVOS sales force.

3. How does the system development life cycle differ from the problem-solving process?

4. The system development life cycle is ideally suited for creating management information systems, but not quite as well suited for setting up something like an E-mail system. Descibe how the steps of the life cycle might differ for setting up an E-mail system.

Unit IV Project

Selecting an Integrated Accounting System for Michelman Fine Furniture

In 1923 Peter Michelman emigrated to the United States. Peter, a cabinet maker, moved to San Antonio, Texas, to open a cabinetry shop. Peter worked hard, learned the language of business, and prospered. When his sons were teenagers, Peter decided to expand his business to include the sale and manufacture of home furniture. By the late 1950s, Michelman Fine Furniture was one of the leading domestic furniture makers in the country. The company manufactured furniture in Texas, California, Alabama, and South Carolina, and shipped products to retailers in every state in the nation.

Peter retired in 1961 and turned operations over to his eldest son, Erik, who managed the company for 25 years, maintaining its commitment to quality. Erik's daughter, Alyssa, became president and presided over the modernization of the company. She wants to create a microcomputer-based accounting system and to replace the six-year-old minicomputer. The current system is used by six accounting clerks and provides accounting reports and on-line data access to Michelman management.

The new system must run on microcomputers attached to a local area network. The integrated accounting system should have a general ledger, payroll, accounts receivable, accounts payable, and inventory modules. As a chief consultant for a computer services company, you have been hired to evaluate three integrated accounting systems and to suggest which best meets the needs of Michelman Fine Furniture. Using information found in computer magazines, prepare a report detailing your findings for Alyssa. You should assume that Michelman Fine Furniture has no microcomputers and will need to purchase and install them, too. However, before the computers are purchased, Alyssa wants your opinion so that she can purchase the computers after selecting the application software. Consequently, your report should also detail the kinds of computers the system will run on and the operating systems that are supported. Package your report as a total, turnkey solution to the accounting system problem at Michelman Fine Furniture.

Glossary

286 A PC (IBM or compatible) built around the 80286, a 16-bit processor from Intel.

386 A PC built around the 80386, a 32-bit processor from Intel.

486 A PC built around the 80486, a 32-bit processor from Intel.

access privileges Refers to the ability of a multi-user system to control which users can read and write which data.

accounts payable Accounting system that keeps track of who the company owes money to, how much is owed, and the terms of the debt.

accounts receivable Accounting system that keeps track of who owes the company money, how much they owe, and when the money is due.

acoustic coupler A device attached to a modem that sends and receives signals through a standard telephone handset.

Ada The standard programming language for all major federal systems projects. Ada was originally designed for the U.S. Department of Defense. It works well in real-time and batch systems.

alpha version The first version of a software program that is released to a select group of users for testing.

alphanumeric field A type of database field that can contain letters, numbers, punctuation symbols, and other typewriter characters. Data in an alphanumeric field cannot be used in calculations.

alphanumeric keys The area of a computer keyboard that looks like the standard typewriter keyboard.

analog device A machine that represents data with continuously variable physical quantities.

analytic graphics Charts and graphs used to summarize numerical data.

ANSI American National Standards Institute. ANSI code is a popular alternative to ASCII.

antivirus software Utility software used to detect and eradicate computer viruses.

Apple Computer Company Hardware and software company founded by Steve Jobs and Steve Wozniak in 1976. Apple is best known for developing the Macintosh computer.

Apple II Apple Computer's first big success, released in 1977. The Apple II had an open architecture and was released in several different models.

application A task required by a computer user.

application package A piece of application software. The term generally refers to proprietary software.

application software A program that is used to accomplish a specific type of task required by the user.

arithmetic logic unit (ALU) The part of the CPU that works in conjunction with the control unit by handling arithmetic and logical processing.

artificial intelligence A broad field that attempts to endow computers with the ability to think and reason in ways similar to humans.

ASCII American Standard Code for Information Interchange, the most common character code used by microcomputers.

Automated Teller Machine (ATM) A special purpose computer that allows a bank's customers to perform banking transactions.

backing up (archiving) Copying data and software from a computer's hard disk, usually to diskettes or tape, and storing the copy in a safe location.

bar-code reader A scanner capable of reading bar codes, such as the universal product code (UPC) symbol.

BASIC Acronym for Beginner's All-Purpose Symbolic Instruction Code, a third-generation language popular with microcomputer users. Originally created by John Kemeny and Thomas Kurtz.

batch processing Refers to a computer system that stores input for a period of time before processing it in large sets.

baud A unit for measuring the speed of data transmission. Baud measures the number of times that the signal changes electrical states in a single second.

beta version The last pre-final version of a program, which is released to a large group of users for testing.

binary Consisting of only two possible states.

binary code The term used to refer to computer data that is represented using a series of binary numbers.

binary field A type of database field that contains a bitmap; a graphic field.

binary numbering system (Base 2). A numbering system with only two symbols, 1 and 0.

BIOS Basic Input/Output System. A program, usually stored in ROM, that is loaded before the operating system. BIOS controls how the CPU interacts with I/O devices.

bit A binary digit, represented using a single transistor. The smallest unit of computer data.

bitmap An image stored as a grid of dots that represent the pixels on the screen.

bits per second (bps) A unit for measuring the speed of data transmission. Contrast with baud.

bug An error in software or malfunction in hardware.

bulletin board service (BBS) An electronic forum, normally accessed with a modem, in which users trade information by reading and leaving messages.

bus An electronic pathway. The two most common types of bus are the data bus and the address bus.

bus network A network configuration in which all of the computers and peripherals are connected to a single transmission line.

byte Eight bits, grouped together. The byte is a useful unit for measuring data, because it takes one byte to signify a single alphanumeric character.

C A powerful programming language designed by Dennis Ritchie to be portable across several types of computers.

cache A high-speed memory device. A disk cache is a reserved section of RAM that speeds up operations requiring frequent reading and writing to disk. A memory cache is a high-speed buffer between the CPU and memory.

CAM Computer-assisted manufacturing. CAM can refer to the use of robotics and numerical control devices or the use of computers to monitor inventory during manufacturing.

CASE tool A computer-aided software engineering software package that helps programmers write programs.

cathode ray tube (CRT) A special type of vacuum tube that sprays a stream of electrons, which are directed onto a piece of glass that is coated with phosphor. The term CRT is also used to refer to a monitor built around such a vacuum tube.

CD-ROM Compact Disk-Read Only Memory. An optical disk that uses the same laser technology as musical compact disks.

central processing unit (CPU) The part of a computer responsible for controlling the flow of data throughout the computer and for executing program instructions. Sometimes called the brain of the computer.

CGA Color Graphics Adapter. The first type of color graphics adapter that was released with the IBM PC. CGA systems display 320 x 200 pixels (320 horizontally and 200 vertically) in four colors on the screen when the monitor is in graphics mode.

characters per second (cps) A unit for measuring printer speed. The number of alphanumeric characters printed in one second.

chassis The box that houses the system unit.

chip A small piece of silicon that is etched with electrical pathways.

client/server computing A computer information system strategy that uses two or more networked computers to perform an application task.

click A mouse technique of pointing to a place on the monitor and pressing once on the mouse button.

clock speed The number of electronic cycles per second, measured in megahertz. One cycle is the amount of time is takes to turn a transistor on and off again.

clone A microcomputer that is similar in design to the IBM PC and PS/2 and is capable of running the same software.

COBOL Acronym for COmmon Business-Oriented Language, a programming language frequently used for developing business applications. COBOL was formally defined in 1959 by Grace Hopper.

code Programming instructions.

command-line interface A type of user interface in which the user controls the program by typing commands at the keyboard.

communications device A hardware component that enables one computer system to share data with another. Connecting communications devices requires a communications medium, the most common of which are telephone lines, electromagnetic waves, and coaxial, twisted-pair, and fiber-optic cable.

communications error A problem that occurs when the data received is not identical to the data sent.

communications software Application software that manages the transmission of data between one computer and another.

Compaq The first major manufacturer of IBM compatible computers. Compaq remains an important player in the compatibles market.

compatible With respect to programs, the ability to run on a given machine. With respect to hardware, the ability of one machine to run the same software as another machine. Also, see clone.

competitive advantage A business strategy that relies on innovation to gain an edge over the competition.

competitive necessity A technique that is required of a business in order to remain competitive.

compiler A program that translates programming code into machine language. A compiler translates all the code at once before the program can be run.

computer An electronic device for processing data.

computer information systems An organized means of collecting and processing data that makes the data useful to a company.

computer system A collection of hardware, software, data, and people that work together.

computer-assisted design (CAD) Use of a computer system to create high-quality electronic models and exact scaled images.

context-sensitive help Software features that automatically display the relevant help screen depending on the command or procedure that the user is trying to execute.

control unit The part of the CPU that retrieves program instructions from memory, evaluates them, and retrieves data from memory.

cooperative multitasking A multitasking strategy in which the CPU executes different programs by alternating between them at an even rate. Contrast with preemptive multitasking, a more advanced strategy.

copy protected Refers to software that includes safeguards against software piracy.

cursor The point on the screen where letters, numbers, or punctuation symbols typed at the keyboard will be entered.

cursor-movement keys Keys that allow the user to move the cursor around the screen with the keyboard. They include the arrow keys, as well as other keys, such as End, Home, Page Up, and so on.

data Raw, unprocessed facts that, for a computer, consist of numbers, letters, images, and sounds. The computer accepts data as input.

data bits A modem setting that tells the software how many bits of data to send in each set. Normally, microcomputers send either seven or eight bits of data in a string when communicating via a modem.

data bus An electronic pathway between the CPU and other hardware devices, including memory and all peripherals. It is used for transferring data throughout the computer system.

data compression The use of logical and mathematical methods to minimize the amount of storage space that software or data occupies.

data dictionary A database that contains data about the fields and access privileges of another database.

data flow diagram A diagram of an entire information system. In addition to computing steps, such as processing and storage, it includes the users of the system and the data that travels through it.

database An organized collection of data that allows users to sort entries and query the database manager for data that meets certain criteria.

database administrator An employee who manages a corporate database.

database file A group of related records, each of which has the same set of fields.

database management system (DBMS) A program that allows users to create a database, as well as sort, query, and create reports with it.

date field A type of data field that contains a date. Data can be entered into a date field in standard date formats (for example, 12/31/93).

debugging The process of eliminating errors from programming code.

decision support system (DSS) An information system for executives, which tends to be oriented less toward reports and more toward generating answers to open-ended questions.

desktop model A computer chassis that is designed to lie flat on a desktop.

desktop publishing (DTP) Using a computer to create high-quality documents that are ready to be sent to a printer. Although desktop publishing software shares many of the same capabilities as modern word processing software, DTP software specializes in the most advanced features, especially the ability to incorporate a wide variety of typefaces and the ability to combine text and graphics.

device A peripheral.

digital device A machine that represents all data as numbers.

Digital Equipment Corporation (DEC) A hardware company founded in 1957 by Kenneth Olsen. DEC is most famous for the PDP and VAX series of computers.

digitizer tablet An input device used in conjunction with an electronic stylus. As the user points to places on the tablet with the stylus, the corresponding point on the screen is selected.

directory An organized listing of files on a disk.

disk crash Contact between the read-write head and the disk surface in a hard disk. A disk crash results in loss of data where the head touched the disk.

diskette A round piece of mylar (plastic) coated with ferrous oxide and encased in a square plastic envelope or shell.

diskette drive The I/O device that is used to access the data on a diskette.

diskless workstation A networked computer that has its own processing components and generally a keyboard (possibly a mouse or some other input device as well) and a monitor, but lacks any storage device of its own. When this type of computer is turned on, it looks to the file server for the operating system.

documentation The print material that comes with a piece of proprietary software. Also, print material and explanations of programming code that are created as part of the programming process.

DOS Microsoft's Disk Operating System, designed for PCs. DOS is the most widely used operating system in the world.

dot matrix printer An output device that creates images with a set of pins that push an inked ribbon against paper.

dot pitch The distance between the three colored dots that make up a single pixel on a color monitor.

double-click A mouse technique of pointing to a place on the monitor and pressing the mouse button twice in rapid succession.

downloading Retrieving a file from another computer.

downsizing Reducing the function of the central information systems department and distributing computer resources throughout an organization.

drag A mouse technique of holding down the mouse button while moving the pointer on the screen.

dynamic link A cross-reference between data files that allows a single data item to be used in several different files. When the data is changed in one file, the change is reflected in all linked files.

E-mail An information system that allows computer users to write, send, and read messages using a computer network.

EBCDIC Extended Binary-Coded Decimal Interchange Code, a character code used by IBM mainframes.

edit Make changes to a document

EGA Enhanced Graphics Adapter, a system for displaying graphics images on a PC monitor. EGA can produce 16 different colors on the screen, with 640 x 350 resolution.

enterprise-wide network A communications network that includes a group of the computers that are used in the same company, even if the computers are located in separate buildings.

ergonomics The study of the physical relationship between people and machines.

evaluation copy A piece of software that a dealer has provided to customers so they can judge the software before they buy it.

executable file A program.

expansion board A printed circuit board that provides a hardware interface between a peripheral and the motherboard.

expansion slot An electronic connection on the motherboard that allows the user to plug in an expansion board.

expert system A software package that has been created to mimic the human decision-making process in a narrow problem area.

fax modem A computer peripheral that accomplishes the same goal as the standalone fax, except that the user is able to send only files, rather than hard copy.

feasibility study A preliminary investigation of a problem to see if the benefits of solving it outweigh the costs of developing a solution.

field A unit of data, the type of which has been predefined. In most databases (excluding hypermedia databases) all records in a file have the same set of fields.

field name The label linked to a field in a database. If the database is viewed as a table, the field names are usually displayed as the column headings.

field type Describes the kind of data that can be held in a given field. The field type determines the ways in which the database manager can process the data in that field.

fifth-generation language A programming language that combines the easy-to-use aspects of a fourth-generation language with artificial intelligence and expert systems to make the computer even easier to use. Although very few 5GLs are available, one of their primary characteristics is natural language processing (NLP).

file A set of data that the user has given a name to.

file management The process of organizing software and data

in a meaningful way on a hard disk, making frequent backups, and eliminating old files.

file server A fast computer with a large amount of secondary storage to which all of the other computers in a network have access for data storage and retrieval.

Finder A Macintosh operating system file that manages files.

first-generation language A machine language.

flaming Creating an inappropriate or overly emotional message on an E-mail system.

flat-file database A database structure in which data is organized as tables, but only one table can be accessed at a time.

flat-panel display Compact, energy-efficient monitors that are only one or two inches thick. Most often used with laptop computers.

flowchart A structured programming tool that shows the logical progression of processing in a program.

folder Same as subdirectory. The Mac displays subdirectories as folders, which are represented by icons that look like file folders.

font A specific typeface, in a specific size. Some font managers use font to mean typeface.

font manager A utility program used to control what fonts are available for use, which ones can be displayed, and which ones can be printed.

footprint The amount of horizontal space that a computer's chassis occupies.

formatted Refers to a disk that has been mapped into tracks and sectors. A disk is not useable until it has been formatted.

FORTRAN Acronym for FORmula TRANslator, a third-generation language known for being able to perform extensive mathematical manipulations. Developed in 1957 by John Backus.

fourth-generation language A programming language that is more intuitive than a third-generation language. 4GLs are often more specialized than third-generation languages. Some people consider object-oriented languages to be 4GLs.

full duplex Refers to the ability to send and receive data simultaneously.

function keys Keyboard keys marked F1, F2, and so on. Their function is determined by the software being used.

game software A type of application software that allows the computer to be used to play video games.

garbage in, garbage out (GIGO) Saying meaning that the worth of computer system or information system output is only as valuable or accurate as the input.

general ledger Accounting system that integrates and summarizes the data in accounts receivable, accounts payable, and payroll.

general purpose computer A computer designed to solve a variety of problems.

graphic field See *binary field*.

graphic user interface (GUI) A type of user interface in which the program is controlled by using a mouse, trackball, or stylus and digitizer tablet to select items shown on the screen. In addition to text and menus, a graphical user interface usually includes icons that represent programs, data files, and commands.

graphics software Application software that allows the user to create illustrations, diagrams, graphs, or charts.

gray scale Refers to a monochrome monitor that can create varying intensities of the single color.

half duplex Refers to the transmission of data in both directions, but only one direction at a time.

handshake A set of data that formally establishes a communications link by testing the line settings and thereby ensuring a valid connection.

hard copy Printed output. Contrast with *soft copy*, which is displayed on a monitor.

hard disk A large magnetic storage medium, consisting of stacked aluminum platters.

hard disk drive The I/O device that reads and writes data from and to a hard disk.

hard disk management See file management.

hardware The machinery of the computer system. Hardware consists of input, processing, output, storage, and communication components.

Hayes-compatible Refers to a modem that uses the standard command language created by Hayes Microcomputer Products, Inc., the oldest manufacturer of modems for microcomputers.

help features Files, built into the software package, that the user can access while using the software.

Hewlett-Packard A company best known in the computer business for the LaserJet series of printers. HP also makes computers, ranging in size from micros to mainframes.

hierarchical database A database structure in which each record is related to a single parent record, though each can be related to many child records. When diagrammed, the hierarchical structure looks like a family tree.

hierarchical network A network configuration in which the host computer has several smaller computers linked to it, each of the smaller computers can have other computers linked to it, and so on.

high level language A third-, fourth-, or fifth- generation language.

host computer A central network computer that is relied on heavily by the other nodes for processing.

hypermedia database A database structure in which data is organized by cards, each of which can contain fields of any data type, and each of which can be linked to any other card in any other stack.

hypermedia software A subset of the database family that incorporates the advantages of multimedia for conveying information.

IBM Corporation International Business Machines, the largest producer of mainframe machines and one of the major microcomputer manufacturers. Most notably, the manufacturer of the IBM PC, XT, AT, and PS/2, as well as the mainframe System/360 and the OS/2 operating system.

icon A small on-screen picture that represents a program, data file, or command.

impact printer An output device that creates hard copy by striking the paper with an inked element.

indexing Creating an alternate order for the records in a database file. Unlike a sort, an index is not a permanent reordering.

information Processed data; data in context; data plus meaning.

information service An on-line company that allows the subscriber access to a number of services. Information services often include their own bulletin boards and conferencing capabilities. Electronic mail (E-mail) is available with many information services.

information system A set of established paths along which data travels through an organization.

initialized The Mac's term for formatted.

ink-jet printer An output device that creates hard copy images by shooting tiny droplets of ink at the paper.

input device A hardware component that accepts data from the person or machine using the computer and transmits it to the processing devices.

installation With proprietary software, the process of copying software from diskettes to a hard disk. With an information system, the process of setting up the new hardware and software and training the users of the new system.

instruction explosion The increase that occurs in the number of lines of code when a program is translated into machine language.

integrated application package Software that combines a collection of applications in one package with a common interface. Common applications found in an integrated package include a word processor, a database, a spreadsheet, a graphics system, and a communications system.

interactive program Software that requires user input to guide processing. Real-time processing is usually accomplished with interactive programs.

internal font A font built into the printer.

interpreter A program that translates code into machine language while the program is running.

job displacement A forced change in employment as a result of the increased use of computers.

job enlargement Expansion of job responsibilities as a result of computer technology. Often a byproduct of job displacement.

just-in-time manufacturing (JIT) A manufacturing technique that minimizes inventory by supplying new materials just as the old materials are used up and by supplying just enough output to meet demand.

kilobyte (K) 1,024 (210) bytes.

knowledge Represented by an understanding of the significance of information.

knowledge engineer A generic term for an expert systems programmer.

laptop A portable microcomputer that weighs less than 10 pounds and folds down to the size of a two-inch thick pad of paper. Often used interchangeably with notebook.

laser printer An output device that uses laser beams to project an image onto a photosensitive drum, where powdered toner is bonded to the paper with heat. The process is similar to that used by photocopiers.

letter-quality print Refers to a printer that creates characters comparable in quality to typewriter print.

light pen A light-sensitive, pen-shaped input device that is connected to a video terminal.

liquid crystal display (LCD) A type of flat-screen monitor that contains a film of liquid crystal between two panes of glass. Wires running through the crystal can make the pixels opaque or transparent.

local area network (LAN) A group of computers that are located within the same room, building, or complex and connected to each other through cabling or some other method.

logic error A mistake in a program that does not violate the syntax rules of the language but causes unexpected results.

logic structure One of several techniques for processing data. The three most common logic structures are the sequence, selection, and loop structures.

logical field A type of database field that contains a single character, which indicates a logical condition, true or false. There are only two possibilities in a logical field.

loop structure Also called a DO WHILE or DO UNTIL structure. A logic structure in which a set of processing steps is repeated until a given condition is true or false.

Lotus 1-2-3 The most widely used spreadsheet program, made by the Lotus Development Corporation.

low-level language Any first- or second-generation language (machine language or assembly language).

machine language Binary code that is understandable by the computer.

Macintosh Apple Computer's most successful line of computer. The first Mac was released in 1984. All Macintosh models use the 68000 series of chips from Motorola.

mainframe A class of large, general purpose computers capable of handling the input, output, and processing needs of many users simultaneously.

management information systems (MIS) An established process for generating information that serves the needs of middle-level managers.

math coprocessor An extension to the control unit and the ALU that can help speed up processing of complex calculations.

megabyte (MB) 1,048,576 (220) bytes.

megahertz (MHz) A unit measuring millions of cycles per second.

memo field Text-based database fields that allow users to enter notes.

memory The set of electronic cubbyholes where data and program instructions are stored when the CPU needs quick access to them.

memory chip An integrated circuit that holds memory and data that is readily available to the CPU.

menu-driven interface A type of user interface in which the user can control the software by choosing from lists of options that are presented on screen.

metropolitan area network (MAN) *See enterprise-wide network.*

microcomputer The smallest class of computers, its CPU consists of a single microprocessor. The majority of microcomputers are intended to be used by only one person at a time.

microprocessor A computer chip, such as the CPU of a microcomputer, that is capable of processing data.

Microsoft Corporation The largest and most powerful software company in the world. The developer of DOS, Windows, and several popular application packages, including Microsoft Works, Word, and Excel.

middle-level managers Managers who track operations over time and develop tactical plans to meet the objectives of upper-level management.

middleware Software that establishes an interface between application software and the operating system. Middleware shields the user from the complexity of the system.

minicomputer A class of general purpose computers that are smaller than mainframes but perform similar tasks. They are usually capable of handling the input, output, and processing needs of at least several users simultaneously.

MIPS Millions of instructions per second. A unit used to measure the processing speed of a computer.

modem Contraction of "modulator-demodulator." A hardware device that allows a computer to send and receive data through a telephone system.

monitor An output device that displays output on a screen.

monochrome Refers to a monitor that displays only one color.

motherboard An electronic circuit board that includes the bus, the CPU, all of the chips for controlling system peripherals, and slots for additional circuit boards. Also called the *system board*.

mouse A pointing device that enables the user to identify a position on the screen by moving a tool around on a horizontal surface, such as a desktop or a mouse pad.

multimedia Refers to the use of several communicative media within a single presentation.

multitasking The ability to run several programs at the same time.

near letter-quality (NLQ) print Refers to a printer that creates characters that are not as sharp as typewriter print but are sharper than standard, 9-pin, dot-matrix print.

network database A database structure in which each record can be related to multiple parent records and multiple child records.

network interface card (NIC) An expansion card that acts as the device interface between a computer and the rest of the network.

network server See file server.

node Refers to each of the computers or terminals in a network.

non-procedural language Flexible programming languages that require less training of the programmer than more traditional procedural languages.

nonremovable storage A storage medium that cannot be removed from the storage device. Most hard disks are nonremovable.

nonvolatile memory A type of memory, the contents of which are not erased when the power supply is shut off.

notebook A light laptop. Laptop and notebook are now often used interchangeably.

numeric field A type of database field that contains numbers, which can be used in calculations.

numeric keypad A group of keys, normally located at the right side of the keyboard, that allow for convenient entry of numbers and mathematical symbols.

object code A machine language version of a program.

operating system A set of programs that run the computer, providing an interface between the programs and the hardware, as well as between the hardware and the user.

operations manager A member of the lowest level of management in a company who supervises its daily operation.

optical character recognition (OCR) A software technique that allows text to be regenerated from a bit-mapped image of alphanumeric characters.

optical disk A storage medium that can be written to and read with light. A CD-ROM disk is an optical disk that can be read from but not written to.

OS/2 A 32-bit operating system from IBM.

output device A hardware component that accepts processed data from the processing devices and returns it as information to the person or machine using the computer.

outsourcing Hiring an outside consulting company to handle responsibilities that were traditionally managed by an internal information systems department.

pages per minute (ppm) A unit for measuring printer speed. The unit measures how many pages of text can be printed in one minute.

palmtop A hand-held microcomputer designed to offer a limited number of features. To date, palmtops do not offer the full functionality of notebook computers.

parallel port A device interface that allows simultaneous transmission of several bits.

parity bit A single bit used in data communications that allows the receiving computer to know if there were any errors in transmission.

payroll An accounting system that keeps track of the wages owed to each employee, plus insurance and retirement deductions, Social Security, and tax withholdings. The payroll system is actually a type of accounts payable that recognizes the company's short-term debt to employees.

PC Although *PC* stands for *personal computer*, the term usually refers to IBM computers and compatibles.

performance monitoring Measuring the output of employees through systems built into the computers they use at work.

peripheral Hardware devices, such as modems, mice, and external disk drives, that connect to the system unit.

pixel Contraction of *picture element*. A pixel, which appears as a dot on a monitor, is the smallest graphic unit on the screen.

point of sale (POS) computer Special purpose computers that were developed to make it easier for large stores to keep track of inventory. They are usually housed in cash registers and attached to scanning devices, such as bar-code readers.

pointing device An input device, such as a mouse, that allows the user to interact with the computer simply by pointing to parts of the screen.

port An I/O device interface, in which an external peripheral can be plugged into the system unit.

portability The ability of programming code to be used on different types of computers.

portable A microcomputer that can be folded up to the size of a briefcase, or smaller.

PostScript A standard, developed by Adobe Systems, for translating CPU output into data that the printer can understand.

power supply A hardware component in the system unit that takes ordinary household AC power and transforms it into DC current, on which the computer operates.

preemptive multitasking A multitasking strategy in which several programs can share the CPU, and the tasks being executed are prioritized, so the most important tasks are executed first. Contrast with cooperative multitasking.

presentation graphics High-quality analytic graphics that use color, multiple typefaces, and 3-D effects.

printer driver A piece of software that translates the CPU's output into codes that the printer understands.

printer server A shared printer in a network.

procedural language A programming language that requires the programmer to be trained in the proper order of actions that the language allows.

processing devices Electronic circuits, the purpose of which are to manipulate data using a written set of instructions.

program A series of instructions that tell a computer how to perform a task. Used interchangeably with *software* or a *piece of software*.

programming The process of creating the instructions the computer can use.

protocol Standards for communication.

prototyping A technique involving the creation of a simple program that mimics the operations desired by the user of an information system.

pseudocode A structured programming technique in which the programmer writes the code without worrying about proper syntax.

public domain Refers to software to which nobody claims a copyright.

quality control Measuring and comparing the output of goods and services to ensure customer satisfaction.

query Literally, *question*. A request for data from a database that meets certain criteria.

query language A high-level language that is built into a DBMS for the purpose of interacting directly with the database.

QWERTY Term used to describe the alphanumeric keys on a keyboard or the way in which the keys are arranged. The term QWERTY comes from the first six characters in the upper-left row of letters.

random access memory (RAM). Volatile memory used to store data and programs to which the CPU needs immediate access.

read-write head The part of a disk drive that reads the magnetic charges on the disk and records new charges when necessary.

real-time processing Refers to a computer system that processes input as soon as it is received.

record A set of fields containing data about a person, place, or event.

register A high-speed memory circuit within the CPU.

relation A table of data. Each column in the table is a field, and each row is a record.

relational database A database structure in which data is organized into tables. If one table contains the same data item as another table, data from both can be accessed at the same time. The relational structure is more flexible than the hierarchical, network, or flat-file structures.

removable storage A storage medium, such as a diskette, that can be removed from a storage device.

report Output from an information system. The most common types are scheduled, exception, and demand reports.

request for proposal (RFP) A request for vendors to send bids offering hardware solutions to a given problem.

request for quote (RFQ) A request for vendors to indicate the price at which they will sell specified hardware or software.

resistor An electronic component that resists the flow of current.

resolution The degree of clarity of images displayed on a monitor or a printed page.

ring network A network configuration in which each computer is linked to two others, so that data can be passed all the way around in a circle.

read-only memory (ROM) Nonvolatile memory that is permanently stored on the motherboard of a microcomputer.

scanner An input device that automates the process of data entry by reading an image and translating it into digital code.

screen saver A utility that, after a specified number of minutes during which no input has been received, causes the screen to go blank or display geometric patterns or moving pictures. As soon as input is received, the screen redisplays whatever was on it before the screen saver was activated.

second-generation language An assembly language. The lowest level of symbolic language.

selection structure Sometimes called an IF-THEN-ELSE structure. A branching structure in which the processing that occurs depends on the outcome of a logical decision that is based on the condition of data.

sequence structure A logic structure in which data is passed from one programming step to the next.

serial port A device interface capable of transmitting only one data bit in each direction at a time.

shareware Software that is distributed free of charge or for a nominal fee. If, after using the software, the customer finds it useful, the customer is required to pay for it.

single in-line memory module (SIMM) Circuit boards that hold memory chips.

simulation software A type of application software that uses the computer to imitate some other device, such as a car, jet, or forklift.

site license The right to copy and use a software product on a specified number of computers.

soft copy Output displayed on a monitor. Contrast with hard copy, which is printed output.

soft fonts Fonts downloaded from the computer to the printer.

software The part of a computer system that tells the hardware how to perform a job.

software piracy Illegal duplication or use of software.

sorting Reordering the records in a database file.

spaghetti code The opposite of a structured program. Spaghetti code is typified by many GOTO statements.

special purpose computer A computer designed to address just one kind of problem.

spreadsheet A grid of rows and columns used to perform calculations on large sets of numbers. Often used to mean spreadsheet software, a program that allows the user to create electronic spreadsheets.

SQL Acronym for structured query language, a fourth-generation language designed for managing databases.

star network A network configuration in which each node is connected directly to a central device called a hub.

stop bit In data communication, a single bit used that signals the receiving computer of the end of a sequence of bits.

storage device A hardware component that accesses magnetic or optical data. A disk drive is a storage device.

storage media Passive pieces of hardware that hold data. Data held on storage media is nonvolatile. A diskette is a storage media.

structured programming An approach to programming in which a logical framework is developed before any code is written.

subdirectory A directory within another directory. A subdirectory can contain files or other subdirectories.

subroutine A set of code in a program that accomplishes a limited task.

supercomputer A class of powerful computers designed to solve large, complex mathematical problems.

surge suppresser A hardware device that keeps electrical surges and spikes from passing from the electrical source (usually a wall socket) to the power supply.

SVGA Super VGA, a graphics system for the PC capable of 1024 x 768 resolution, with 16 colors on the screen at any given time. At lower resolutions, SVGA adapters can display much higher numbers of colors at once.

syntax error A mistake in program code that violates the rules of whatever language the program is written in.

System file The core of the Macintosh's operating system.

system flowchart Detailed diagram showing how data moves through the computer systems that are used in an information system.

system unit The main hardware unit of a microcomputer. It includes the motherboard, ports, and power supply, and frequently the disk drives and sometimes the monitor.

systems analyst Professional who specializes in the detailed analysis of existing and planned information systems.

systems designer Professional who manages the design of a new information system.

systems development life cycle Phases through which an information system goes during its design, development, installation, maintenance, and obsolescence.

tape drive An I/O device for accessing magnetic tape. A tape drive is commonly used for making backup copies of a hard disk.

telephone support A service offered by a software developer through which users can ask questions directly to employees of the manufacturer.

terminal An I/O device that relies entirely on the host computer for processing and storage. The most common type of terminal is just a remote keyboard and monitor.

third-generation language A general purpose symbolic language that is machine independent.

time field A type of database field that contains a time of day. Data can be entered into a time field in standard time formats (for example, 3:45 PM).

timesharing Multiple users sharing the central processing unit of a computer.

toggle switch A key that turns a feature, such as Insert mode, on and off.

top-down design A divide-and-conquer approach to programming in which the programmer breaks the overall objective into smaller and smaller tasks until each is relatively simple.

touch screen A monitor that also accepts input. Users make choices by touching different parts of the screen.

tower model A computer with a chassis designed to stand on one end so it takes up less space on a desk or on the floor.

trackball A pointing device that provides the functionality of a mouse, but doesn't roll around on the desk.

transistor An on/off switch that controls the flow of electricity.

tutorial software A type of application software that teaches a subject by having the student step through a series of screens. Good tutorial software is highly interactive.

typeface A complete set of printed characters that are created with a single style.

Unix A multiuser operating system originally developed by Ken Thompson at Bell Laboratories. Today, Unix is the most popular OS used on workstations.

upgrade A new version of an existing piece of software, generally with additional features.

uploading Sending a file to another computer through a modem or a network.

upper-level managers Also known as executives, they oversee the entire company, monitor profits and losses, and determine the company's future by developing business strategies.

upward compatibility A strategy in the design of hardware that allows new equipment to be attached to the same hardware devices and use the same software as old equipment.

user The person operating the computer system. Sometimes defined as the recipient of processed data or information.

user friendly Referring to a computer or computer software that is easy to use.

user interface A facet of any computer program that controls how the computer accepts data and commands as input, and to some degree, how it presents data as output.

utility A program that aids the internal functioning of the computer. Sometimes classified as a type of application software.

vector A straight line that is designated by its end points.

version One iteration in the evolution of a software package, generally indicated by a number that follows the name of the program.

VGA Video Graphics Array, a graphics system for the PC capable of displaying 200,000 different colors in 640 x 480 resolu-

tion, though only 16 colors can be displayed on the screen at once.

virus A rogue program that attaches itself to a legitimate program and automatically copies itself into other programs.

voice input Refers to computer systems capable of accepting spoken commands or data.

voice mail A computer-based system by which the user of a standard telephone can send, receive, store, or redirect voice messages.

volatile memory Memory that loses its contents when the power supply is shut off. Volatile memory is sometimes called read and write memory.

what-if capability The ability to ask a hypothetical question and consider alternatives simply by entering new data or changing a formula.

wide area network (WAN) A group of computers that are connected through communications devices but are not in close proximity.

Windows A graphic user interface designed by Microsoft for DOS-based computers. Although Windows acts like an operating system, it requires DOS to be running at the same time.

Windows NT Microsoft's 32-bit operating system for computers using Intel's 386 or 486. Unlike Windows, Windows NT is a full-fledged operating system and does not require DOS.

word processing The process of creating text documents on a computer.

word size The number of bits that a computer can process at once. The word size of a CPU is the same as the size of its registers.

WordPerfect The most widely used word processing package, made by the WordPerfect Corporation.

workstation A powerful microcomputer, often designed for scientific research or for architectural or engineering design. Many workstation CPUs are designed around RISC (Reduced Instruction Set Computing) architectures.

write protected Refers to a diskette that can be read but not written to.

Index *

A

access
> flexibility of databases, 253
> methods and protocols, 206
> privileges, 217
> time on hard disks, 180-181

accounting systems, described, 265-266

accounts receivable/payable, accounting systems, 266

acoustic couplers, described, 196

Ada language
> compared, 97f
> described, 102

addressable memory,
> Intel CPU, 133f

Adobe Systems, makes PageMaker and PostScript, 166

After Dark, screen saver, 74f

Aldus PageMaker, 224f

Allen, Paul, founder of Microsoft, 28-29, 220f

alphanumeric fields, described, 245

alphanumeric keys
> keyboard, 148
> (*see also* QWERTY)

alpha version of software, 109

Altair 8800 computer, Micro Instrumentation and
> Telemetry Systems, 28

Altair, microcomputers, 15f

Alternate (Alt) key, on IBM keyboards, 149

ALU (*see* arithmetic-logic unit compared)

Amdahl, mainframe manufacture, 15

American Airlines' Sabre System, described, 32-33

American Express, computer industry, 34

American Hospital Supply Corp., ASAP system described,
> 33

American National Standards Institute, described, 92

AMEX (*see* American Express)

analog data, computers, 90-92

analog device, described, 90

analytic graphics, described, 65

Analytic Systems Automatic Purchasing, system by
American Hospital Supply Corp., 33

analyzing current system, life cycle, 280, 282

Anderson Consulting, computer services, 35

ANSI (*see* American National Standards Institute)

antivirus software, described, 72, 73f

Apple Computer, Inc.
> Apple I/II computers, 26, 27f
> computer evolution, 27f
> computers, 25-28
> Mac, 27f
> Mac II, 27f

Macintosh computers, 127
> PowerBook, 27f

printer production, 30

AppleTalk, by Macintosh, Inc., 206

application packages (*see* application software)

applications, many for DOS, 221-222

application software, 60-86
> compatibility lacking in Unix, 230

described, 47-48
> operating systems, 18
> user groups, 77f

archiving data (*see* backup entries)

arithmetic-logic unit, control unit compared, 125

arrow keys, described, 149

artificial intelligence, described, 69-70

ASAP (*see* Analytic Systems Automatic Purchasing)

ASCII
> described, 92-93
> and OCR, 156

Ashton-Tate, acquired by Borland International, 31

Assembly language
> described, 95
> used in Unix, 218

Asymetrix Corp., created by Paul Allen, 220

AT&T Corp.
> Bell Laboratories invent transistor, 123
> Unix development, 228
> Unix Software Laboratories subsidiary, 229

ATM (*see* automated teller machine)

AutoCAD, microcomputer use, 66f

automated teller machine, described, 11

B

Babbage, Charles, "father of computers," 102

Backspace key, described, 150

backup
> frequency, 186
> making copies, 79-80
> process, 71f
> systems described, 71-72
> tape drives used, 185f

Backus, John, developed FORTRAN language, 98

banks
> ATMs use real-time processing, 54f
> use batch processing, 55

bar-code readers, described, 156

Basic Input/Output System (*see* BIOS)

BASIC language
> compared, 97f
> described, 98

BASIC program, compared with FORTRAN program, 99f

batch processing, described, 54-55

baud, described, 195

DOS Tutorials

Tutorial 1

Introduction to DOS

Before You Begin

Before you begin this tutorial, make sure you have the following items:

- **A blank, unformatted diskette.** This should be either a 5¼-inch or 3½-inch diskette, to match the size of the diskette drive(s) on your computer.

- **A blank diskette label and a felt-tip pen**.

- **A diskette known as the Systems Disk**. This diskette is prepared in a special way and contains the DOS software. If your computer has a hard disk, the hard disk will serve as your Systems Disk, and you won't need a separate Systems Disk. If your computer has one or two diskette drives and no hard drive, you'll need a Systems Disk that matches the size of drive A of your computer. Check with your technical support person about the Systems Disk.

- **Your DOS Data Diskette**. See the beginning of this book for instructions on how to create this diskette.

After you collect these items, you will use your DOS data diskette to help you work through DOS Tutorials 1 and 2.

OBJECTIVES

In this tutorial you will learn to:

- Start your computer and the disk operating system (DOS)

- Recognize the DOS prompt and execute DOS commands

- Set the date and time of the computer clock

- Clear the screen

- Check the DOS version

- Change the default drive

- List the names of the files on a diskette and recognize correct DOS filenames and common filename extensions

- Name, copy, rename, and delete files

- Format and write-protect a diskette

- Copy and check an entire diskette

- Use wildcard characters in DOS commands

- Turn off your computer

What Is DOS?

Often likened to an air-traffic controller, the **disk operating system**, usually called **DOS** (rhymes with boss), is a set of programs that controls the fundamental activities of your computer. For example, DOS starts the computer, prepares the diskettes so they can store data, copies the contents of one diskette to another, and manages the flow of data from the keyboard into the CPU, from the CPU to the monitor, from the CPU through the ports to the printer, and so forth.

Some of these activities — such as managing the flow of data from the CPU to the monitor — occur automatically. Other activities — such as preparing and copying diskettes — occur only when you instruct DOS to perform those activities. Whether you use a computer to write letters, prepare financial reports, manage client information, or perform any other type of task, you need to know how to use DOS.

Starting Your Computer and DOS

The procedure of turning on your computer and starting DOS is commonly referred to as **booting** the computer or booting the system. You can't boot your system unless you use a hard disk or diskette that contains DOS. Such a disk is called the **Systems Disk** because it contains the software essential for your computer to work.

Now let's see how to boot a computer. If you're using a computer in a classroom laboratory, consult with your technical support person before starting the following procedure. Complete this procedure only if you are using your own computer or your instructor or technical support person tells you to do so.

If you have *two diskette drives*, the drives are called drive A and drive B. If your drives are next to each other, drive A is on the left and drive B is on the right. If the drives are stacked, drive A is on the top and drive B is on the bottom. If you have *one diskette drive*, the drive is called drive A. Figures 1-1 and 1-2 illustrate how to insert disks into your disk drives.

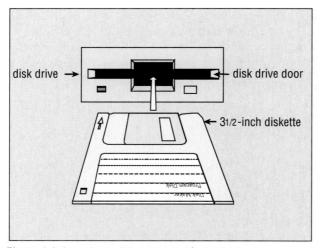

Figure 1-1: Inserting a diskette into a 3½-inch drive

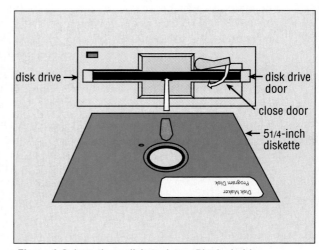

Figure 1-2: Inserting a diskette into a 5¼-inch drive

In the procedures in this and subsequent tutorials, a word or symbol within brackets refers to a key on the keyboard. For example, [Enter] refers to the Enter key on the right side of the main keyboard.

To boot a computer:

① If you have a *two-diskette system*, insert the Systems Disk in drive A. See Figures 1-1 and 1-2.

If you have a *hard-disk system* or if your computer is part of a network, make sure no diskette is in drive A and the door, if any, to drive A is open.

If you're not sure which disk drive is drive A, check with your technical support person.

② Be sure to turn on the monitor and any other peripherals you are going to use.

For example, if you are going to print a file, turn on your printer as well as your monitor.

③ If your computer is off, turn it on.

Usually the switch has a 0 or a circle for "off" and 1 or a line for "on" and is often found on the right side of your computer. Flip the switch to 1. You'll see the disk drive light go on while DOS and perhaps other programs are loaded into the computer.

If your computer has a built-in clock/calendar, the booting process is complete. If your computer doesn't have a clock/calendar, the screen displays two messages similar to those shown in Figure 1-3. The first line usually is the date 01-01-1980 (January 1, 1980). The second line is a **prompt,** that is, a message that requests information and waits for you to type that information into the computer. In this particular case the prompt requests you to type in a new date.

Figure 1-3
Prompt for the
new date

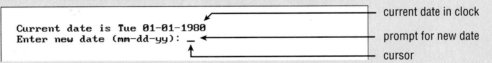

Current date is Tue 01-01-1980 ——— current date in clock
Enter new date (mm-dd-yy): _ ◄——— prompt for new date
                           ↑
                        cursor

④ Enter today's date and press **[Enter]**.

You must type the date as numbers, with hyphens separating the month, day, and year. For example, if today were March 16, 1993, you would type 3-16-93.

If you make a mistake while typing the date, press [Backspace] (the key marked with a left arrow and located in the upper right corner of the main keyboard) to delete the mistake, then type the correct information.

After you enter today's date, you'll see two additional messages, as shown in Figure 1-4 on the next page. The first message is the time, given in hours, minutes, and seconds (to the nearest one-hundredth of a second), that has elapsed since you turned on your computer. The second message is a prompt asking you to enter the current time.

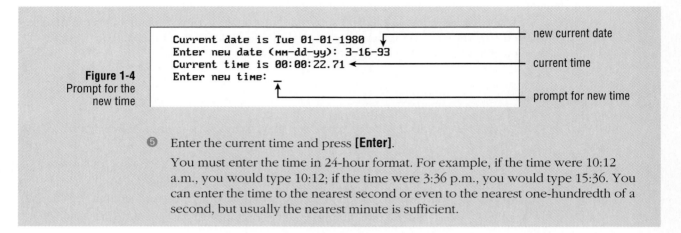

Figure 1-4
Prompt for the
new time

⑤ Enter the current time and press **[Enter]**.

You must enter the time in 24-hour format. For example, if the time were 10:12
a.m., you would type 10:12; if the time were 3:36 p.m., you would type 15:36. You
can enter the time to the nearest second or even to the nearest one-hundredth of a
second, but usually the nearest minute is sufficient.

This completes the procedure for booting your computer. You will probably see a message
telling you what version of DOS you are using, similar to what you see in Figure 1-5. The **version**
is a number (such as 2.1, 3.0, 3.3, or 5.0) that indicates a particular variation from the original
DOS. Each update of DOS is assigned a new version number. The higher the number, the later
the release date, and the newer and more improved the features.

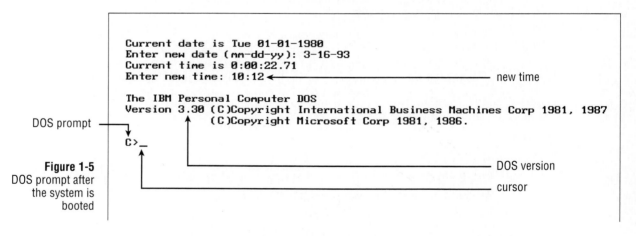

Figure 1-5
DOS prompt after
the system is
booted

The DOS Prompt

After you have booted your computer, the DOS prompt appears on the screen. The DOS prompt
is a letter such as C or A, usually followed by a greater-than sign (>), similar to the prompt in
Figure 1-5. When the DOS prompt first appears, the letter indicates the drive that contains the
Systems Disk. For example, if you booted your computer using a hard disk, the DOS prompt is
probably C>. If you booted your computer using a diskette in drive A, the DOS prompt is A>. If
you booted your computer and logged into a network, the DOS prompt may be F> or something
else. On some computers the DOS prompt may appear as C:\> or A:\>.

Immediately to the right of the DOS prompt is the **cursor**, usually a blinking underscore
(_) character, which shows where the next character you type will appear on the screen.
The DOS prompt and the cursor indicate that the computer is ready for you to give it
instructions.

If your computer is not part of a network, go to the section "DOS Commands" on the next page.

Logging into a Network

If the computer you use is part of a network, you may have to log into the network. To **log in** or **log on** means to identify yourself as an authorized user and to gain access to the network resources. The following procedure describes how to log into a Novell network. You would follow similar steps for other commonly used networks. Consult your technical support person for your procedure.

To log into a Novell network:

❶ At the DOS prompt type the log-in command and your group name or user name (if required) and press **[Enter]**.

For example, if your group name is simply your course title and section, you might type something like LOGIN BUS101-12. Type the log-in command and the group name supplied by your instructor or your technical support person.

The network software now prompts you to type the **password**, a secret code or word that you must know to log into the network.

❷ Type the password supplied by your instructor or technical support person and press **[Enter]**.

The monitor usually doesn't display a password as you type it. This keeps other people from seeing the password on the screen and gaining illegal access to the network. If you see a message such as "Access denied," you may have made a mistake in typing the password. If this happens, retype the password. If you still are denied access, check with your instructor or technical support person.

If you have used the correct group name and password, you will be able to use the DOS programs and the applications software to which your group name (or user name) and password give you access. As you follow the steps in this and the next tutorial, some DOS commands might not be available on your network. Consult your technical support person if you have questions about access to DOS commands.

If your computer is part of a network, follow the steps in this book identified as those for a hard-disk system. Whenever this book refers to drive C or DOS prompt C>, substitute drive F or DOS prompt F> or whatever prompt is on your network.

DOS Commands

Once you have booted your computer, you can issue DOS commands. A **command** is an instruction that you enter into the computer to accomplish a specific task. Figure 1-6 on the following page lists the most commonly used DOS commands. "Internal" and "External" are explained in a later section. As you work through this tutorial and DOS Tutorial 2, you will learn how to execute these commands.

DOS Command	Description	Type
CHDIR (CD)	Change default directory	Internal
CHKDSK	Check disk	External
CLS	Clear the screen	Internal
COPY	Copy file(s)	Internal
DATE	Set or change date of DOS calendar	Internal
DEL	Delete file(s) (see also ERASE)	Internal
DIR	List the contents of a directory	Internal
DISKCOPY	Copy an entire disk	External
ERASE	Erase file(s) (see also DEL)	Internal
FORMAT	Format a disk	External
MKDIR (MD)	Make a new directory	Internal
PROMPT	Change appearance of DOS prompt	Internal
RENAME (REN)	Rename a file	Internal
RMDIR (RD)	Remove (erase) a directory	Internal
TIME	Set or change time of DOS clock	Internal
VER	Display the DOS version number	Internal

Figure 1-6
Commonly used
DOS commands

To execute a DOS command, you must first be sure that the DOS prompt (C>, A>, or F>, for example) appears on the screen and that the cursor is to the right of the prompt. If you don't see the DOS prompt, consult your technical support person.

If you make a mistake while typing a command and have not yet pressed [Enter], you can press [Backspace] to delete the mistake and then type the correct information. If you make a mistake and then press [Enter], DOS displays the error message "Bad command or file name." If this occurs, retype the DOS command correctly.

Setting the Date and Time (DATE, TIME)

Let's execute a DOS command by using the commands DATE and TIME. Some computers have an internal clock run by a battery. If the clock's battery runs down or the clock is not set to the correct time, these commands let you set the correct date and time. Having the correct date and time in the computer is important because DOS records the date and time whenever you save your computer work to a disk. Knowing the date and time of your work helps you, for example, keep track of which draft of a report you did first or when you wrote a certain letter.

First let's use the DATE command to set the correct date on your computer.

To execute the DATE command:
1. Make sure the DOS prompt and the cursor appear on your screen.
2. Type **date** and press **[Enter]**.

You can type the name of this or any DOS command in uppercase or lowercase letters or a mixture of both. DOS displays the message "Current date is" followed by a date (such as 1-01-1980) and then displays a prompt for you to enter the new date, as shown in Figure 1-7.

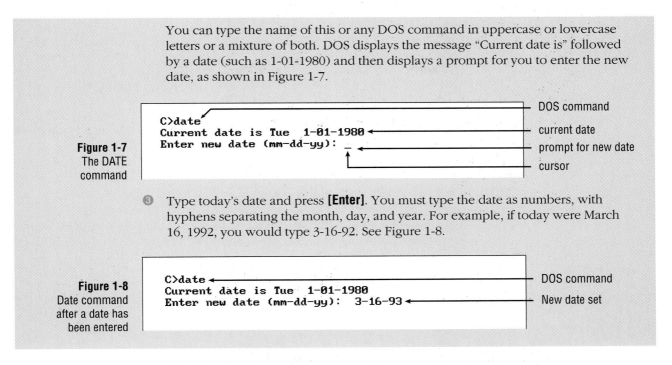

Figure 1-7
The DATE
command

❸ Type today's date and press **[Enter]**. You must type the date as numbers, with hyphens separating the month, day, and year. For example, if today were March 16, 1992, you would type 3-16-92. See Figure 1-8.

Figure 1-8
Date command
after a date has
been entered

Next let's use the TIME command to set the correct time on your computer.

To execute the TIME command:

❶ Type **time** and press **[Enter]**.

DOS displays the messages shown in Figure 1-9.

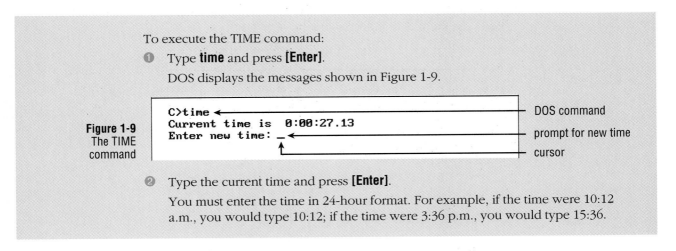

Figure 1-9
The TIME
command

❷ Type the current time and press **[Enter]**.

You must enter the time in 24-hour format. For example, if the time were 10:12 a.m., you would type 10:12; if the time were 3:36 p.m., you would type 15:36.

From now on until you turn it off, your computer will keep the correct date and time. You might have to reset the date and time whenever you turn on your computer.

Clearing the Screen (CLS)

Another commonly used DOS command is **CLS**, which stands for **cl**ear **s**creen. You use this command to clear your screen of unwanted output, such as you now have. Let's clear the screen.

To clear the screen:

❶ Make sure the DOS prompt and the cursor appear on your screen.

❷ Type **cls** and press **[Enter]**.

Remember, you can type a command in uppercase or lowercase letters or both.

DOS clears the screen and then displays the DOS prompt and the cursor in the upper left corner.

Checking the DOS Version (VER)

Another DOS command is **VER**, which checks the version of your DOS. You should know which version of DOS you are using, since some versions of DOS have commands not found in earlier versions.

To check the DOS version:

❶ Make sure the DOS prompt and the cursor appear on your screen.

❷ Type **ver** and press **[Enter]**. The version of DOS running on your computer appears on the screen (see Figure 1-10). Instead of version number 3.30, you may see the number 2.10, 3.20, 5.00, or some other number. If the number is less than 2.1, consult your technical support person. Some of the DOS commands explained in this book require version 2.1 or higher.

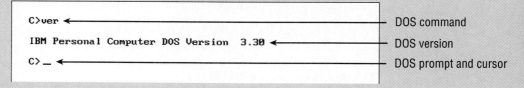

Figure 1-10
The VER command

```
C>ver ←                                              ── DOS command

IBM Personal Computer DOS Version   3.30 ←           ── DOS version

C> _ ←                                               ── DOS prompt and cursor
```

Changing the Default Drive

When you boot your computer, the DOS prompt displays the letter of the boot drive, for example, A, C, or F. This letter designates the **default drive**, which is the disk drive that DOS will use for any DOS command you issue, unless you specifically designate a different drive. You can change the default drive by typing the letter of the disk drive that you want to be the default drive, typing a colon (:), and then pressing [Enter]. In the following steps, you'll change the default drive so you can work with the DOS data diskette you created at the beginning of this tutorial.

To change the default drive using a two-diskette system:

❶ Insert the DOS data diskette into drive B (see Figures 1-1 and 1-2 on page DOS 4).

❷ Type **b**: and press **[Enter]**.

Notice that the DOS prompt now indicates that the new default disk drive is B.

To change the default drive using a hard-disk system:

❶ Insert the DOS data diskette into drive A (see Figures 1-1 and 1-2 on page DOS 4).

❷ Type **a**: and press **[Enter]**.

Notice that the DOS prompt now indicates that the new default disk drive is A.

You'll now be able to check the contents of the DOS data diskette by executing the appropriate DOS command.

Listing the Files on a Disk (DIR)

The contents of a disk are collected into groups of data or into sets of instructions called **files**. Each file contains the data from a particular application or the instructions for a particular computer program. For example, suppose you were writing a letter to a customer. The word processing program that you would use to write the letter would be in one or more files. The data (in this case, the words and punctuation marks) for the letter would be in another file. If you then wrote a second letter, the data for that letter would be stored in still another file.

To distinguish among the various files, DOS uses a different filename for each file. A **filename** is a unique name, composed of up to eight characters, that identifies a particular file on a diskette. A filename may also include a **filename extension**, which is composed of up to three characters. Filename extensions are optional, but when they are used, a period [.] separates the filename from the filename extension. Filename extensions are described in more detail later.

You can obtain a list of the filenames and other information about the files by using the **DIR** command, which stands for "directory listing." A **directory listing** is a list of information about the files on a diskette. The information in the directory listing usually includes the filename, the size of the file, and the date and time that the file was created or last modified.

Listing the Files on the Default Drive

We'll first list the files on the default drive, which should be drive B if you're using a two-diskette system or drive A if you're using a hard-disk system.

To list the files on the default drive:

❶ Make sure that the DOS prompt indicates the default disk drive letter where the DOS data diskette is located.

If you're using a *two-diskette system*, the DOS prompt should be B, indicated by B> or B:\>.

If you're using a *hard-disk system*, the DOS prompt should be A, indicated by A> or A:\>.

❷ Type **dir** and press **[Enter]**.

Your screen should look similar to Figure 1-11. The DOS data diskette actually has more files than can fit on one screen.

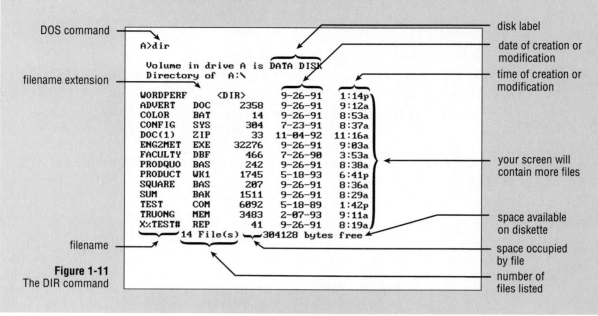

DOS command

filename extension

filename

Figure 1-11
The DIR command

```
A>dir

    Volume in drive A is DATA DISK
    Directory of   A:\

WORDPERF    <DIR>        9-26-91   1:14p
ADVERT      DOC    2358  9-26-91   9:12a
COLOR       BAT      14  9-26-91   8:53a
CONFIG      SYS     304  7-23-91   8:37a
DOC(1)      ZIP      33 11-04-92  11:16a
ENG2MET     EXE   32276  9-26-91   9:03a
FACULTY     DBF     466  7-26-90   3:53a
PRODQUO     BAS     242  9-26-91   8:38a
PRODUCT     WK1    1745  5-18-93   6:41p
SQUARE      BAS     207  9-26-91   8:36a
SUM         BAK    1511  9-26-91   8:29a
TEST        COM    6092  5-18-89   1:42p
TRUONG      MEM    3483  2-07-93   9:11a
X%TEST#     REP      41  9-26-91   8:19a
        14 File(s)    304128 bytes free
```

disk label

date of creation or modification

time of creation or modification

your screen will contain more files

space available on diskette

space occupied by file

number of files listed

DOS first lists the volume label or tells you that the disk has no label. If you have DOS version 5.0 or later, DOS also indicates the volume serial number. Then DOS provides information about each file on the default drive: the filename and filename extension, the size of the file in bytes, and the date and time that the file was created or last modified. At the end of the directory, DOS lists the number of files on the disk, displays the amount of free storage space on the disk (in bytes), and redisplays the DOS prompt and cursor at the end of the directory listing.

Listing the Files on Another Drive

Suppose you want to list the files on a drive other than the default drive. You can do this by using the DIR command with the drive designation. In the following steps, you'll leave the default drive, where the DOS data diskette is located, and list the directory of the boot drive.

To list the files on a disk other than the default drive on a *two-diskette system*:

❶ Make sure the DOS data diskette is still in drive B and the default drive is drive B.

❷ Make sure the Systems Disk is still in drive A.

❸ Type **dir a:** and press **[Enter]**.

In this DOS command *a:* is a **parameter**, that is, it specifies the object of the DIR command. In this case, the object of the DIR command is the disk drive for which you want a directory listing. Be sure to type a space between *dir* and its parameter, *a:*. A listing of the files on the diskette in your drive A appears on the screen.

To list the files on a disk other than the default drive using a *hard-disk system*:

❶ Make sure the DOS data diskette is still in drive A and the default drive is drive A.

❷ Type **dir c:** and press **[Enter]**.

In this DOS command *c:* is a **parameter**, that is, it specifies the object of the DIR command. In this case, the object of the DIR command is the drive for which you want a directory listing. Be sure to type a space between *dir* and its parameter, *c:*. A listing of the files on your hard disk appears on the screen.

The directory listing you see is in the same format as Figure 1-11, but the actual filenames listed will be different.

Pausing the Directory Listing (/P)

You probably noticed that when you used DIR to get a directory listing of the files on the DOS data diskette not all the file information fit on the screen at once. Those files at the beginning of the listing disappeared from the screen before you could read the information. To solve this problem, you can use the **/P** (pause) option with the DIR command. An **option** specifies how you want DOS to carry out a command and is usually represented by a slash (/) and a letter. In this case, the /P option, when used with the DIR command, instructs DOS to pause the directory listing after each screenful. This pause allows you to look at the screen; when you're ready, you press a key to view the next and any subsequent screenfuls one at a time. Let's see how the /P option works.

To pause the directory listing using the /P option:

❶ Make sure the DOS data diskette is still in drive B if you're using a *two-diskette system* or in drive A if you're using a *hard-disk system*.

❷ Make sure the default drive is where the DOS data diskette is located.

❸ Type **dir/p** and press **[Enter]**.

In this DOS command, */p* is the option. You can type the /P option with an uppercase or a lowercase P. You may include a space between *dir* and the option, but you don't need one. DOS displays one screenful of files and then displays a message such as "Strike a key when ready . . ." at the bottom of the screen. See Figure 1-12 on the following page.

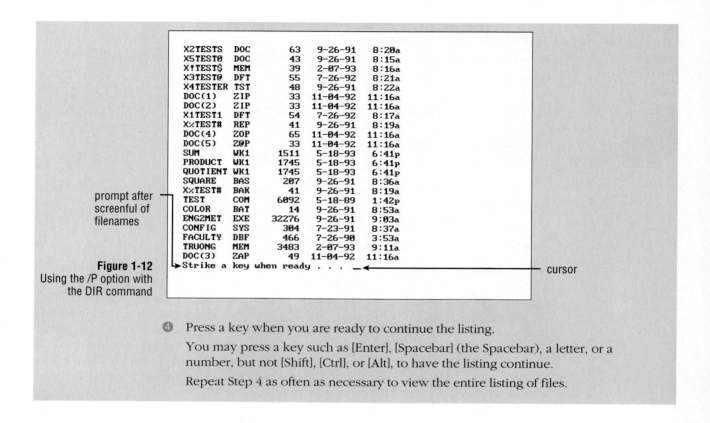

```
         X2TESTS    DOC       63    9-26-91    8:20a
         X5TEST0    DOC       43    9-26-91    8:15a
         X!TEST$    MEM       39    2-07-93    8:16a
         X3TEST@    DFT       55    7-26-92    8:21a
         X4TESTER   TST       48    9-26-91    8:22a
         DOC(1)     ZIP       33   11-04-92   11:16a
         DOC(2)     ZIP       33   11-04-92   11:16a
         X1TEST1    DFT       54    7-26-92    8:17a
         X%TEST#    REP       41    9-26-91    8:19a
         DOC(4)     ZOP       65   11-04-92   11:16a
         DOC(5)     Z@P       33   11-04-92   11:16a
         SUM        WK1     1511    5-18-93    6:41p
         PRODUCT    WK1     1745    5-18-93    6:41p
         QUOTIENT   WK1     1745    5-18-93    6:41p
         SQUARE     BAS      207    9-26-91    8:36a
         X%TEST#    BAK       41    9-26-91    8:19a
         TEST       COM     6092    5-18-89    1:42p
         COLOR      BAT       14    9-26-91    8:53a
         ENG2MET    EXE    32276    9-26-91    9:03a
         CONFIG     SYS      304    7-23-91    8:37a
         FACULTY    DBF      466    7-26-90    3:53a
         TRUONG     MEM     3483    2-07-93    9:11a
         DOC(3)     ZAP       49   11-04-92   11:16a
       ➔ Strike a key when ready . . .  ◄───────────── cursor
```

prompt after screenful of filenames

Figure 1-12
Using the /P option with the DIR command

④   Press a key when you are ready to continue the listing.

You may press a key such as [Enter], [Spacebar] (the Spacebar), a letter, or a number, but not [Shift], [Ctrl], or [Alt], to have the listing continue.

Repeat Step 4 as often as necessary to view the entire listing of files.

Displaying Only Filenames (/W)

Another way to display a long directory listing is to use the **/W** (wide) option. When you include this option in the DIR command, DOS lists only the filenames (including the filename extensions) across the width of the screen, five filenames per line. The file size and other information about the file are not listed. Let's use the /W option to get a directory listing of the DOS data diskette.

To use the /W option:

①   Make sure the DOS data diskette is in the default drive, as before.

②   Type **dir/w** and press **[Enter]**. A listing like the one in Figure 1-13 appears on the screen.

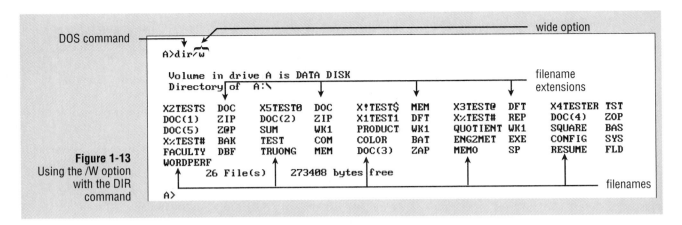

Figure 1-13
Using the /W option
with the DIR
command

For extremely long listings, you can combine the /P and /W options. If you typed *dir/p/w*, for example, DOS would display five filenames per line and pause after each screen. You can also combine parameters and options. For example, by typing *dir b:/p/w*, you would get a directory listing of the diskette in drive B that displays five filenames per line and pauses after each screen.

Filenames and Filename Extensions

As mentioned earlier, each file has a name by which you can identify the file on the disk. The name of a file usually has two parts: the **filename**, which should reflect the specific contents of the file, and the **filename extension**, which often reflects the general type of file. For example, the filename extension EXE indicates that a file is an executable file, in other words, a file that contains instructions the computer can execute.

Rules for Naming Files

You should know the DOS rules for naming files, because you'll have to name the files that you create when you use applications programs. Whenever you name a file, follow these rules:

- The filename must consist of one to eight characters.
- The filename may (but doesn't have to) include a filename extension, with a period separating the filename from the filename extension. A filename extension consists of one to three characters.
- A filename or filename extension may contain any of the letters A through Z in uppercase (although you may enter the letters in either uppercase or lowercase), the digits 0 through 9, and any of the following keyboard characters:

  $ & # @ ! % ' ` ~ ( ) { } − _ ^

  These letters, numbers, and characters are said to be valid.
- A filename or filename extension may not contain any of the following characters:

  ? . " / \ [ ] : | < >+ = ; , *

  These characters are said to be invalid. A space is also invalid. A period (.) is valid only to separate the filename and the filename extension.

The following examples of filenames follow these naming rules. Such filenames are said to be *legal*.

LETTER.2	The filename has eight or fewer characters, the filename extension has three or fewer characters, and all the characters are valid.
93REPORT.{3}	The filename consists of eight valid characters, and the filename extension consists of three valid characters.
W63&9%	The filename consists of six valid characters; using no filename extension is legal.

The following examples of filenames do *not* follow the DOS naming rules. Such filenames are said to be *illegal.*

JONESLETTER.2	The filename contains more than eight characters. If you tried give a file this name, DOS would automatically shorten the filename to eight characters: JONESLET.2
REPORT.1993	The filename extension contains more than three letters. DOS would automatically shorten the filename extension to three characters: REPORT.199
MY REP.[5]	The filename contains an invalid character (a space), and the filename extension contains two invalid characters, [and]. DOS would not allow this filename.

Common Filename Extensions

Although files may have *any* filename extension that follows the above rules, some filename extensions are used more frequently because they have special meanings. Figure 1-14 lists some of these common filename extensions and their usual meanings. Some of these filename extensions are required; for example, all executable files must have the extension EXE or COM. Others are not required; for example, your backup files don't have to have the extension BAK. They could have the extension OLD or something else.

Filename Extension	Usual Meaning
BAK	Backup file — contains a copy of another file
BAS	BASIC file — contains instructions in the BASIC programming language
BAT	Batch file — contains multiple DOS commands
COM	Command file — contains computer instructions
DBF	Database file — contains data from dBASE
EXE	Executable file — contains computer instructions
SYS	System file — provides information for DOS
WK1	Spreadsheet file — contains data from Lotus 1-2-3

Figure 1-14
Common filename
extensions

Renaming a File (RENAME or REN)

Choosing meaningful, descriptive names for your files is not easy. Sometimes you'll find that your choice of a filename is not the best, and you want to change it. For example, suppose you created a file that contained a memo to your coworker Sergio Pelota, and you named the file MEMO.SP. You then realized that the name of the file was not as descriptive as it could be because after a week or two you might forget what MEMO.SP contains. You could solve the problem by changing the filename from MEMO.SP to PELOTA.MEM, a more descriptive name. Let's try this now.

To rename a file:

❶ Make sure the DOS data diskette is still in drive A or B, as before, and the default drive is the drive that contains the DOS data diskette.

❷ Type **dir/w** and press **[Enter]** to get a directory listing. Then verify the file MEMO.SP is on the diskette.

❸ Type **rename memo.sp pelota.mem** and press **[Enter]**.

Instead of typing *rename*, you could type *ren*, the shortened version of the command to rename a file.

The RENAME command always requires two parameters, the first one specifying the original filename and the second one specifying the new filename. See Figure 1-15.

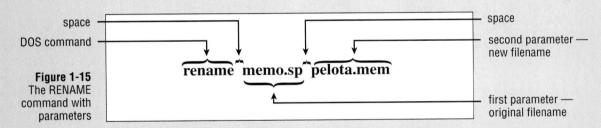

Figure 1-15
The RENAME command with parameters

space
DOS command

space
second parameter — new filename

first parameter — original filename

rename memo.sp pelota.mem

If the file has been renamed successfully, DOS displays no message; it simply displays the DOS prompt. Usually DOS displays a message only when an error occurs.

❹ Type **dir/w** again to view the directory listing to see that the filename has been changed from MEMO.SP to PELOTA.MEM. See Figure 1-16 on the following page.

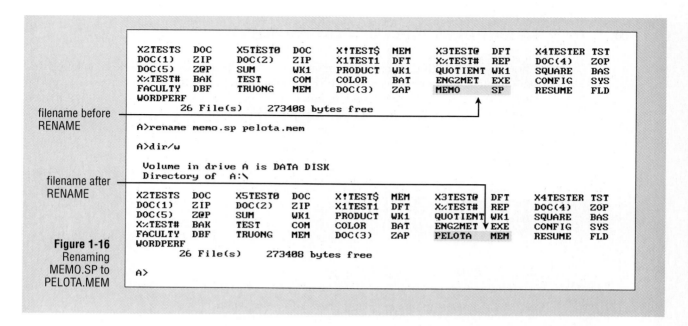

filename before RENAME

```
X2TESTS   DOC    X5TEST0   DOC    X!TEST$   MEM    X3TEST@   DFT    X4TESTER  TST
DOC(1)    ZIP    DOC(2)    ZIP    X1TEST1   DFT    X%TEST#   REP    DOC(4)    ZOP
DOC(5)    Z@P    SUM       WK1    PRODUCT   WK1    QUOTIENT  WK1    SQUARE    BAS
X%TEST#   BAK    TEST      COM    COLOR     BAT    ENG2MET   EXE    CONFIG    SYS
FACULTY   DBF    TRUONG    MEM    DOC(3)    ZAP    MEMO      SP     RESUME    FLD
WORDPERF
        26 File(s)       273408 bytes free

A>rename memo.sp pelota.mem

A>dir/w

 Volume in drive A is DATA DISK
 Directory of  A:\
```

filename after RENAME

```
X2TESTS   DOC    X5TEST0   DOC    X!TEST$   MEM    X3TEST@   DFT    X4TESTER  TST
DOC(1)    ZIP    DOC(2)    ZIP    X1TEST1   DFT    X%TEST#   REP    DOC(4)    ZOP
DOC(5)    Z@P    SUM       WK1    PRODUCT   WK1    QUOTIENT  WK1    SQUARE    BAS
X%TEST#   BAK    TEST      COM    COLOR     BAT    ENG2MET   EXE    CONFIG    SYS
FACULTY   DBF    TRUONG    MEM    DOC(3)    ZAP    PELOTA    MEM    RESUME    FLD
WORDPERF
        26 File(s)       273408 bytes free

A>
```

Figure 1-16
Renaming
MEMO.SP to
PELOTA.MEM

The RENAME (or REN) command changes the filename but does not modify the contents of the file.

Deleting a File (ERASE or DEL)

Suppose that a month after writing your memo to Sergio you no longer needed to keep the file on your disk. You could use the DOS command **ERASE** or **DEL** (delete) to remove the file from the disk. In fact, it is good practice to periodically erase files that you no longer need. This maximizes your disk capacity and keeps your disk from becoming cluttered. To see how ERASE and DEL work, you'll now erase the file PELOTA.MEM from your DOS data diskette.

If you are working on a network system, do not do the following steps unless your instructor tells you to do so.

To erase a file from the diskette:

❶ Make sure the DOS data diskette is in drive A or B, as before, and the default drive is the drive that contains the DOS data diskette.

❷ Type **erase pelota.mem** and press **[Enter]**.

Instead of typing *erase*, you could type *del* (for "delete"). The functions of ERASE and DEL are identical, so it doesn't matter which of the two commands you use. Both commands require one parameter, the filename of the file you want to delete.

❸ Type **dir/w** to view the directory listing and to verify that PELOTA.MEM is no longer on the diskette. See Figure 1-17.

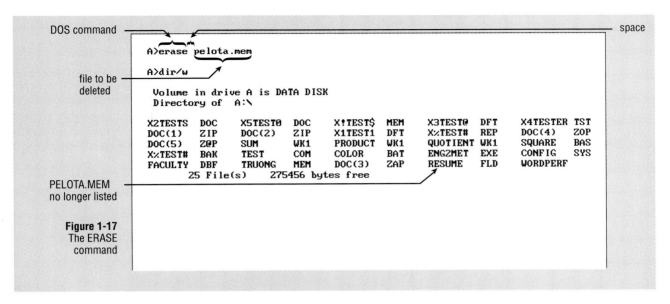

Figure 1-17
The ERASE
command

When you use the ERASE or DEL command, DOS removes the file from the disk and frees up the space on the disk. Files that you subsequently save to the disk can use the space previously occupied by the deleted file.

Be careful when you use ERASE or DEL. Once you delete a file, you *cannot* restore it, unless you have access to a specialized "undelete" program. Always double-check the name of the file you use with ERASE or DEL before you press [Enter].

Internal vs. External DOS Commands

Up to this point in the tutorial, all the commands you've used have been internal DOS commands. An **internal command** is built into DOS and can be executed without the Systems Disk in a disk drive. You can execute an internal command any time after you boot your computer, regardless of what diskettes are in a drive.

In the next section, you'll use an external DOS command. An **external command** is a program file that resides on the DOS Systems Disk. The program file has a filename that corresponds to the name of the command and a filename extension of COM or EXE. For example, in the next section, you'll use the FORMAT command. This is an external DOS command that uses the program file FORMAT.COM. This file, therefore, must be on your hard drive or on the Systems Disk in a diskette drive for you to use the FORMAT command. If you try to execute this or any other external command without the Systems Disk, DOS will give you the error message "Bad command or file name." To avoid this error or to correct it, make sure the file corresponding to the command is on a diskette and then try to execute the command again. If you're not certain about the availability of an external command, consult your technical support person.

Figure 1-6 shows the command type, internal or external, of the most commonly used DOS commands.

Formatting a Diskette (FORMAT)

A new diskette is like a phonograph record with no grooves; it can't receive or store any files. Before you can use a new diskette, you must **format** it, that is, prepare the diskette to receive files. If you were to use the DIR command, for example, with an unformatted diskette, DOS would display the error message shown in Figure 1-18. If you ever encounter such an error message, replace the unformatted diskette with a formatted one and then press A (abort) to stop the action and return to the DOS prompt.

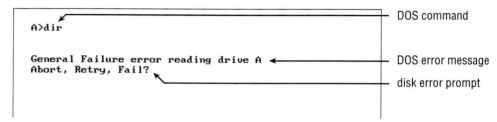

Figure 1-18
DOS error message when you execute the DIR command on an unformatted diskette

You can think of a formatted diskette as having magnetic grooves called **tracks** on which DOS can store files. Formatting creates tracks in concentric circles around the center of the diskette and divides each track into **sectors**. Each side of a 1.44M 3½-inch diskette, for example, contains 80 tracks divided into 18 sectors (Figure 1-19). Diskettes of lower capacity have fewer tracks and fewer sectors. For example, each side of a 360K 5¼-inch diskette contains 40 tracks divided into nine sectors.

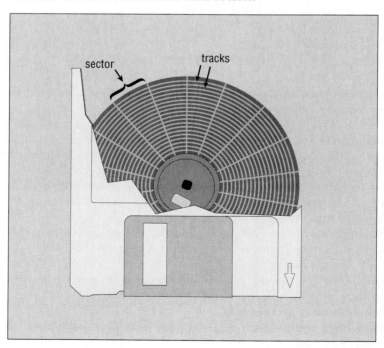

Figure 1-19
Tracks and sectors on a formatted 3½-inch diskette

Before you continue, ask your instructor or technical support person for permission to format diskettes.

In the following steps, you'll use the FORMAT command to format a diskette. *Be sure you do not format your hard disk or any diskette that contains important information.* Formatting a used diskette destroys all data on that diskette. To avoid problems, check with your technical support person, then carefully perform the following steps.

To format a diskette on a *two-diskette system*:

❶ Make sure the Systems Disk is in drive A, then type **a:** and press **[Enter]** to make drive A the default drive.

❷ Type **format b:** and press **[Enter]**.

This command instructs DOS to format a diskette in drive B. The message shown in Figure 1-20 appears on the screen. If you see any other message on the screen, consult your technical support person immediately.

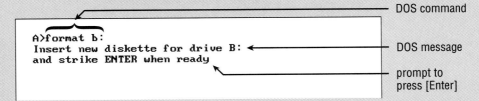

DOS command

DOS message

prompt to press [Enter]

Figure 1-20
Prompt after you execute the FORMAT command on a two-diskette system

```
A>format b:
Insert new diskette for drive B:
and strike ENTER when ready
```

❸ Insert an *unformatted* diskette into drive B.

Make sure the unformatted diskette matches the size and the capacity of the disk drive.

Now go to Step 5 on the next page.

To format a diskette using a *hard-disk system*:

❶ Remove the DOS data diskette from drive A.

❷ Type **c:** and press **[Enter]** to make drive C the default drive.

❸ Type **format a:** and press **[Enter]**.

This command instructs DOS to format a diskette in drive A. A message similar to the one in Figure 1-21 appears on the screen. If you see any other message on the screen, consult your technical support person immediately.

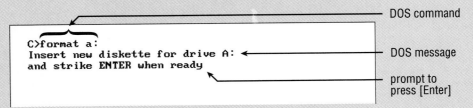

DOS command

DOS message

prompt to press [Enter]

Figure 1-21
Prompt after you execute the FORMAT command on a hard-disk system

```
C>format a:
Insert new diskette for drive A:
and strike ENTER when ready
```

❹ Insert an *unformatted* diskette into drive A.

Make sure the unformatted diskette matches the size and the capacity of the disk drive.

For either a *two-diskette system* or a *hard-disk system*:

⑤ Press **[Enter]** to initiate the formatting process.

While the diskette is formatting, a DOS message tells you what is happening. The particular message you see depends on the version of DOS you're using.

After the formatting is complete, DOS displays the message "Format complete." Depending on which version of DOS you are using, DOS may then display the message "Volume label (11 characters, ENTER for none)?" A **volume label** is a name recorded electronically on a diskette. Whenever you use DIR to view the contents of your diskette, the volume label will appear. Using a volume label helps you identify and manage your diskettes.

⑥ If you see the volume label prompt, type a volume name and press **[Enter]** or just press [Enter] without typing a volume name.

DOS now displays a message giving you the disk space and the technical information about how DOS uses that space. See Figure 1-22. It then displays a final message asking if you want to format another diskette.

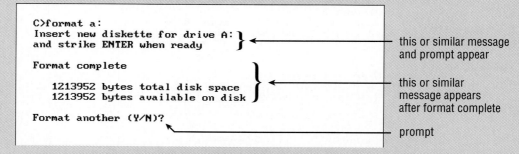

Figure 1-22
Screen after you format a diskette

```
C>format a:
Insert new diskette for drive A:
and strike ENTER when ready          }  this or similar message
                                         and prompt appear
Format complete
                                     }  this or similar
    1213952 bytes total disk space       message appears
    1213952 bytes available on disk      after format complete

Format another (Y/N)?                   prompt
```

⑦ Press **n** (*no*) and press **[Enter]** to indicate that you don't want to format another diskette.

⑧ Remove the newly formatted diskette from the disk drive. If it is a 5¼-inch diskette, place it into a diskette sleeve.

⑨ On an adhesive diskette label, write a description of what you plan to store on the diskette, such as "Data diskette," and the date. Attach the label in the upper left corner of the diskette. See Figure 1-23.

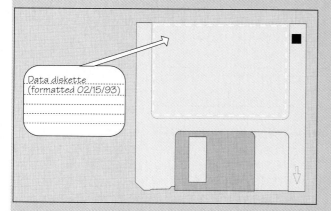

Figure 1-23a: Applying an adhesive label to a 3½-inch diskette

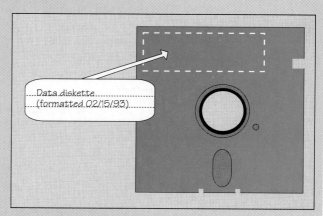

Figure 1-23b: Applying an adhesive label to a 5¼-inch diskette

Be sure to write the description on the label *before* you attach it to the diskette to avoid damaging the diskette.

This completes the steps for formatting a diskette. You can now store information on the diskette.

Write-Protecting a Diskette

When you save important files or store valuable programs on a diskette, you may want to ensure that no one can alter these data or programs. You can **write-protect** the diskette, which means you can prevent anyone from writing more information onto the diskette, renaming the files on the diskette, or erasing information from the diskette. You can load files from a write-protected diskette into your computer's memory so you can use the files, but you can't modify the contents of the diskette in any way.

To write-protect a 5¼-inch diskette, you attach a write-protect tab — a piece of plastic tape — across the write-protect notch. To write-protect a 3½-inch diskette, you open the write-protect window.

If you try to erase a file from a write-protected diskette, DOS displays the error message shown in Figure 1-24. If you still want to erase the file, you have to take the diskette out of the drive, remove the write-protect tab or close the write-protect window, reinsert the diskette into the drive, and press *R* (*retry*). If you decide not to erase the file from the diskette, you press *A* (*abort*) to cancel the command.

Figure 1-24
DOS error message when you try to erase a file from a write-protected diskette

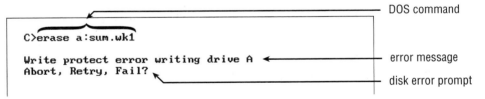

Even though write-protection helps safeguard files, you shouldn't write-protect a diskette as soon as you save information to it. For example, if you're in the middle of writing a report, you don't want to write-protect the diskette, because you'd have to remove the write-protection to save an updated version of the report.

Copying Files (COPY)

You can also safeguard files by making backups. A **backup** file is a copy of a file that you can keep as a safeguard against accidental deletion, damage, or loss of the original file. Having a backup when something goes wrong saves you considerable time, effort, and anguish.

Another reason to copy files is to create different versions of similar files. For example, suppose you're looking for a job in sales and have decided to apply for positions in field sales and telemarketing. You might want to create two versions of your résumé, each one emphasizing different skills. After using a word processor to create the first version, called RESUME.FLD (the résumé emphasizing field sales skills), you could copy it using a different filename, such as RESUME.TEL, then modify the copy to create a new version that emphasizes telemarketing skills.

Copying a File from One Disk to Another

In the following steps, you'll copy the file RESUME.FLD from drive A to drive B if you're using a two-diskette system, or from drive A to drive C if you're using a hard-disk system. Follow the steps appropriate for your computer system.

To copy a file from one drive to another on a *two-diskette system*:

① Insert the DOS data diskette into drive A, then type **a:** and press **[Enter]** to set the default drive to drive A.

② Insert a blank, formatted diskette, such as the one you formatted earlier in this tutorial, into drive B.

③ Type **copy a:resume.fld b:** and press **[Enter]**.

This command says, "Copy the file RESUME.FLD from drive A to drive B." In this command the first parameter, *a:resume.fld*, specifies the **source**, which is the file you're going to copy. The second parameter, *b:*, specifies the **target**, which is the diskette onto which the copy will be made. See Figure 1-25.

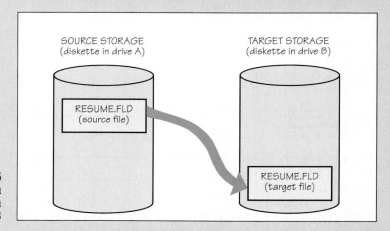

SOURCE STORAGE
(diskette in drive A)

TARGET STORAGE
(diskette in drive B)

RESUME.FLD
(source file)

RESUME.FLD
(target file)

Figure 1-25
Copying a file from a
diskette in drive A to a
diskette in drive B

Make sure you do not type a space between the disk designation, *a:*, and the filename, *resume.fld*. You must, however, type a space between the source filename and the target drives. In this example, you could also type *copy resume.fld b:* without specifying the drive of the source file, since the source file is on a diskette in the default drive. Your screen should now look similar to Figure 1-26. A message indicates that DOS has copied one file.

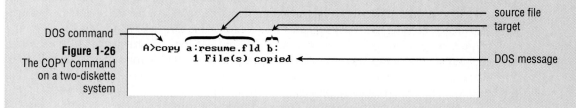

DOS command

Figure 1-26
The COPY command
on a two-diskette
system

source file
target

A>copy a:resume.fld b:
    1 File(s) copied

DOS message

④ Type **dir b:/p** and press **[Enter]** to verify that RESUME.FLD was in fact copied to drive B.

To copy a file from one drive to another on a *hard-disk system*:

① Insert the DOS data diskette into drive A.

② Type **copy a:resume.fld c:** and press **[Enter]**.

This command says, "Copy the file RESUME.FLD from drive A to drive C." In this command, the first parameter, *a:resume.fld*, specifies the **source**, that is, the file that you're going to copy. The second parameter, *c:*, specifies the **target**, which is the disk onto which the copy will be made. See Figure 1-27.

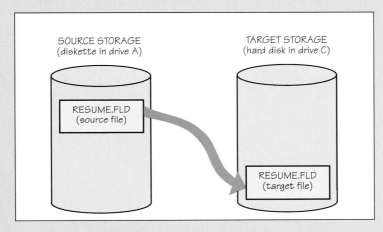

Figure 1-27
Copying a file from a
diskette in drive A to a
hard disk

Make sure you do not type a space between the disk designation, *a:*, and the filename, *resume.fld*. You must, however, type a space between the source filename and the target drive. In this example, you could also type *copy a:resume.fld* without specifying the target drive, since in this case the target drive is the default drive. Your screen should now look similar to Figure 1-28. A message indicates that DOS has copied one file.

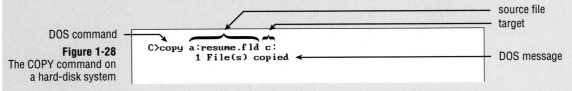

Figure 1-28
The COPY command on
a hard-disk system

③ Type **dir c:/w/p** and press **[Enter]** to verify that RESUME.FLD was in fact copied to drive C.

In these steps, you have made a backup copy of the file RESUME.FLD on a disk other than the DOS data diskette. It is always a good idea to keep backup files of important files.

Copying a File Using a New Filename

Besides using the COPY command to make backups of important files, you can also use COPY to help create two versions of a file on the same disk. In the following steps, you'll copy the file RESUME.FLD, the field sales résumé, to the file RESUME.TEL, which you can then modify to create a telemarketing résumé.

To copy a file using a new filename on a *two-diskette system*:

❶ Make sure your formatted diskette containing RESUME.FLD is still in drive B.

❷ Type **b:** and press **[Enter]** to change the default drive to drive B.

❸ Type **copy resume.fld resume.tel** and press **[Enter]**. See Figure 1-29.

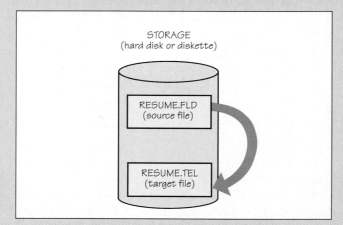

Figure 1-29
Copying a file to the same diskette with a new filename

This command says, "Make a copy of the file RESUME.FLD on the same diskette but name the copy RESUME.TEL." The first parameter of the command is the source file, that is, the file that you want to copy. The second parameter is the target file, that is, the file that you want to create. See Figure 1-30. Since you haven't specified a drive with either the source file or the target file, DOS uses the default drive (in this case, drive B) to find the source file RESUME.FLD and to copy the target file RESUME.TEL.

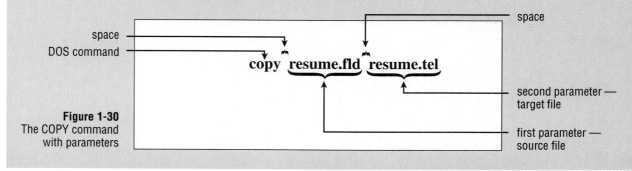

Figure 1-30
The COPY command with parameters

④ Type **dir/w/p** and press **[Enter]** to verify that RESUME.TEL is now on the diskette in drive B.

To copy a file using a new filename on a *hard-disk system*:

❶ Type **c:** and press **[Enter]** to change the default drive to the hard disk, where a copy of the file RESUME.FLD is located.

❷ Type **copy resume.fld resume.tel** and press **[Enter]**. See Figure 1-29.

This command says, "Make a copy of the file RESUME.FLD on the same disk but name the copy RESUME.TEL." The first parameter of the command is the source file, that is, the file you want to copy. The second parameter is the target file, that is, the file you want to create. See Figure 1-30. Since you haven't specified a drive with either the source file or the target file, DOS uses the default drive (in this case, drive C) to find the source file RESUME.FLD and to copy the target file RESUME.TEL.

❸ Type **dir/w/p** and press **[Enter]** to verify that RESUME.TEL is now on the disk in drive C, that is, the hard disk.

After you make a copy of the original field sales résumé, you can use your word processor to modify the copy to emphasize your telemarketing skills.

Copying a Diskette (DISKCOPY)

Sometimes you want to copy an entire diskette, not just one or two files, to another diskette. For example, when you purchase applications software, you should copy all the original diskettes to backup diskettes and then use the backups in your day-to-day computer work. If you have a diskette with extremely important data, you should make a backup of the entire diskette to safeguard against accidental deletions, damage, or loss. If you need to give a colleague all your files on a particular diskette, you could copy the entire diskette.

To copy an entire diskette, you use the DISKCOPY command. The diskette you want to copy is called the source diskette, and the diskette that will be the copy is called the target diskette (Figure 1-31 on the following page). In the following steps, you'll copy the DOS data diskette to a blank diskette.

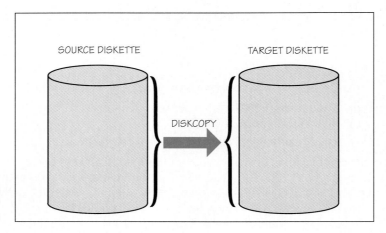

Figure 1-31
Copying an entire
diskette to another
diskette

Follow the appropriate steps for your system. If you have a two-diskette system with drives of equal size, that is, both are 5¼-inch drives or both are 3½-inch drives, and you use diskettes of equal capacity, you can copy from drive A to drive B. If you have a two-diskette system with drives of unequal size, that is, one is a 5¼-inch drive and one is a 3½-inch drive, you will have to use just drive A or just drive B to make diskette copies. If you have questions about your disk drive capacities or the method for using DISKCOPY, consult your technical support person.

To copy a diskette using a two-diskette system with drives of equal size:

❶ Insert a Systems Disk that contains the file DISKCOPY.COM into drive A and make drive A the default drive.

Since DISKCOPY is an external DOS command, you need the program file available to execute the command. If you have questions about the availability of DISKCOPY.COM, consult your technical support person.

❷ Type **diskcopy a: b:** and press **[Enter]**.

Make sure you type a space between the a: and the b:. This command says, "Copy a source diskette in drive A to a target diskette in drive B." The first parameter of DISKCOPY specifies the drive that contains the source diskette and the second parameter specifies the drive containing the target diskette. The DOS messages instruct you to insert the source diskette into drive A and the target diskette into drive B. See Figure 1-32 on the following page.

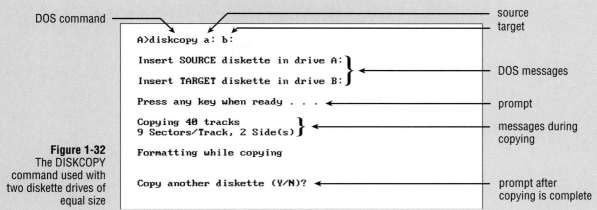

Figure 1-32
The DISKCOPY command used with two diskette drives of equal size

DOS command

source
target

```
A>diskcopy a: b:

Insert SOURCE diskette in drive A:

Insert TARGET diskette in drive B:

Press any key when ready . . .

Copying 40 tracks
9 Sectors/Track, 2 Side(s)

Formatting while copying


Copy another diskette (Y/N)?
```

DOS messages

prompt

messages during copying

prompt after copying is complete

❸ Remove the Systems Disk and insert the source diskette — in this case, the DOS data diskette — into drive A.

❹ Insert the target diskette — a blank diskette — into drive B.

Make sure that your target diskette is blank or that you no longer need the information on it. (You can use the diskette you formatted earlier in this tutorial.) Any data currently on the target diskette will be destroyed when you execute the DISKCOPY command. DOS prompts you to press any key when you are ready.

❺ Press **[Enter]** to start the copying process.

If soon after you start the copy process, DOS displays the error message "Drive types or diskette types not compatible," follow the steps below for copying with drives of unequal size.

While copying is occurring, messages similar to those in Figure 1-32 appear on the screen. If your blank diskette was already formatted, you won't see the message "Formatting while copying."

After the source diskette has been copied, DOS asks if you want to copy another diskette.

❻ Press **n** (no) to instruct DOS that you don't want to copy another diskette.

To copy a diskette using a two-diskette system with drives of unequal size:

❶ Insert a Systems Disk that contains the file DISKCOPY.COM into drive A and make drive A the default drive.

Because DISKCOPY is an external DOS command, you need the program file available to execute the command. If you have questions about the availability of DISKCOPY.COM, consult your technical support person.

❷ Type **diskcopy a: a:** and press **[Enter]**.

Make sure you type a space between the first a: and the second a:. This command says, "Copy a source diskette in drive A to a target diskette also in drive A." The first parameter of DISKCOPY specifies the drive that contains the source diskette, and the second parameter specifies the drive that contains the target diskette. You could also type diskcopy b: b: and press [Enter].

Assuming that you're using drive A, DOS next prompts you to insert the source diskette into drive A. You will use the same drive for both the source diskette and the target diskette since DISKCOPY does not allow you to copy using two drives of unequal size or capacity.

❸ Remove the Systems Disk and insert the source diskette — that is, the DOS data diskette — into drive A.

DOS prompts you to press any key when ready.

❹ Press **[Enter]** to start the copying process.

❺ When prompted to do so, remove the source diskette from drive A and insert the target diskette — that is, a blank diskette — in drive A.

Make sure that your target diskette is blank or that you no longer need the information on the diskette. (You can use the diskette you formatted earlier in this tutorial.) Any data currently on the target diskette will be destroyed when you execute the DISKCOPY command. DOS again prompts you to press any key when ready.

❻ Press **[Enter]** to continue the copy process.

❼ Continue to respond to the DOS prompts to insert the source diskette or the target diskette until the copying process is complete.

While copying is taking place, messages similar to those in Figure 1-33 appear on the screen. If you are using an unformatted diskette as the target diskette, you'll also see the message "Formatting while copying."

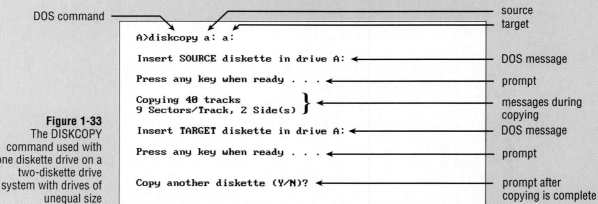

Figure 1-33
The DISKCOPY command used with one diskette drive on a two-diskette drive system with drives of unequal size

After the source diskette has been copied, DOS asks if you want to copy another diskette.

❽ Press **n** (no) to tell DOS that you don't want to copy another diskette.

To copy a diskette on a hard-disk system:

❶ Make sure drive C is the default drive.

Since DISKCOPY is an external DOS command, you need the program file available to execute the command. If you have questions about the availability of DISKCOPY.COM, consult your technical support person.

❷ Type **diskcopy a: a:** and press **[Enter]**.

This command says, "Copy a source diskette in drive A to a target diskette also in drive A." The first parameter of DISKCOPY specifies the drive that contains the source diskette, and the second parameter specifies the drive that contains the target diskette. See Figure 1-34.

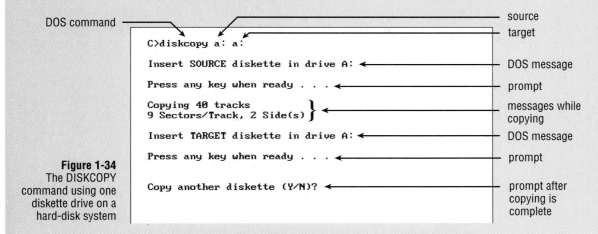

DOS command

source
target

```
C>diskcopy a: a:

Insert SOURCE diskette in drive A:          DOS message

Press any key when ready . . .              prompt

Copying 40 tracks
9 Sectors/Track, 2 Side(s)                  messages while
                                            copying

Insert TARGET diskette in drive A:          DOS message

Press any key when ready . . .              prompt

Copy another diskette (Y/N)?                prompt after
                                            copying is
                                            complete
```

Figure 1-34
The DISKCOPY command using one diskette drive on a hard-disk system

DOS then prompts you to insert the source diskette into drive A.

❸ Insert the source diskette — that is, the DOS data diskette — into drive A.

DOS prompts you to press any key when ready.

❹ Press **[Enter]** to start the copying process.

❺ When prompted to do so, remove the source diskette from drive A and insert the target diskette — that is, a blank diskette — into drive A.

Make sure that your target diskette is blank or that you no longer need the information on the diskette. (You can use the diskette you formatted earlier in this tutorial.) Any data currently on the target diskette will be destroyed when you execute the DISKCOPY command. DOS again prompts you to press any key when ready.

❻ Press **[Enter]** to continue the copying process.

❼ Continue to respond to the DOS prompts to insert the source diskette or the target diskette until the copying process is complete.

While copying is taking place, messages similar to those in Figure 1-34 appear on the screen. If you are using an unformatted diskette as the target diskette, you'll also see the message "Formatting while copying."

After the source diskette has been copied, DOS asks if you want to copy another diskette.

❽ Press **n** (no) to tell DOS that you don't want to copy another diskette.

Now you have two exact copies of the same diskette. Be sure to write a brief description of the diskette, in this case, "Backup DOS data diskette," and the date on an adhesive label. Then attach the label to the backup diskette.

Checking a Disk (CHKDSK)

After you format or copy a diskette, it is a good idea to use the CHKDSK (check disk) command to check the diskette for possible problems and to get a report on the status of your diskette and your computer's memory. The CHKDSK command tells you if the files on the diskette are properly stored. It also tells you the capacity of the diskette, the amount of free space available on the diskette, the capacity of your computer's memory, and the amount of free space available in memory.

To use the CHKDSK command on a *two-diskette system*:

❶ Insert a Systems Disk that contains the file CHKDSK.COM or CHKDSK.EXE into drive A and make drive A the default drive.

Because CHKDSK is an external DOS command, you need the program file available to execute the command. If you have questions about the availability of CHKDSK, consult your technical support person.

❷ Insert the diskette that you want to check into drive B. In this case, insert your backup DOS data diskette into drive B.

❸ Type **chkdsk b:** and press **[Enter]**.

The parameter b: specifies the diskette that you want to check. DOS produces messages similar to those in Figure 1-35.

DOS command

Figure 1-35
The CHKDSK command to check the diskette in drive B on a two-diskette system

information about diskette

information about computer memory

To use the CHKDSK command on a *hard-disk system*:

❶ Make drive C the default drive.

Because CHKDSK is an external DOS command, you need the program file available to execute the command. If you have questions about the availability of CHKDSK, consult your technical support person.

❷ Insert the diskette that you want to check into drive A. In this case, insert your backup DOS data diskette into drive A.

❸ Type **chkdsk a:** and press **[Enter]**.

The parameter a: specifies the disk that you want to check. DOS produces messages similar to those shown in Figure 1-36.

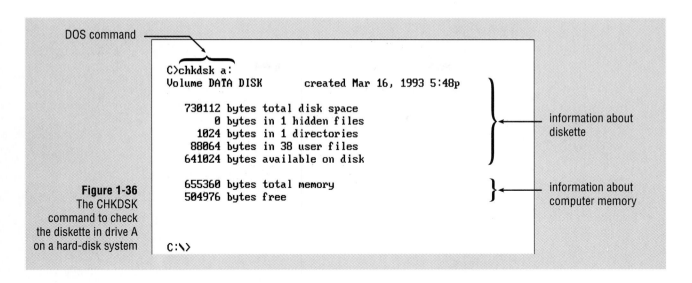

DOS command

```
C>chkdsk a:
Volume DATA DISK        created Mar 16, 1993 5:48p

  730112 bytes total disk space
       0 bytes in 1 hidden files
    1024 bytes in 1 directories
   88064 bytes in 38 user files
  641024 bytes available on disk

  655360 bytes total memory
  504976 bytes free


C:\>
```

information about diskette

information about computer memory

Figure 1-36
The CHKDSK command to check the diskette in drive A on a hard-disk system

As you can see, CHKDSK gives you helpful information about your diskettes and your computer's memory.

Using Wildcards in DOS Commands

Sometimes you might want to use the same DOS command on more than one file. For example, suppose you want to delete all the files on a disk. Or suppose you want to copy several files on one disk to another disk. You can use the ERASE (DEL) or COPY command to perform this task on one file at a time — or you can use wildcards. Wildcards are symbols that represent characters common to the filenames of a group of files. The two DOS wildcards are the asterisk (*) and the question mark (?). In a DOS command the asterisk means "match any number of characters," and the question mark means "match any single character." Because a wildcard tells DOS to act on several files at once, you must exercise extreme caution in using wildcards with ERASE or DEL, since you could easily delete valuable files by accident.

First let's see how to use wildcards with the DIR command. Suppose you had 26 files on a diskette and three of them had the filename extension WK1. WK1 is the standard filename extension for worksheet files created with the spreadsheet program Lotus 1-2-3. Suppose also that you wanted to view a listing of only the worksheet files and you didn't have time to search through the entire list of 26 files. You could use the * wildcard in your DIR command to create a directory listing of only those files with the extension WK1. Let's try this now.

To use the * wildcard:

❶ Make sure the DOS data diskette is in drive A, then type **a:** and press **[Enter]** to make A the default drive.

❷ Type **dir *.wk1** and press **[Enter]**.

This command means, "Give a directory listing of all files that have any filename and that have the filename extension WK1." DIR can take a parameter that specifies the filename or set of filenames for which you want a listing.

DOS lists the files that satisfy the command's requirements. See Figure 1-37 on the following page. As you can see, the DOS data diskette has three files with the filename extension WK1.

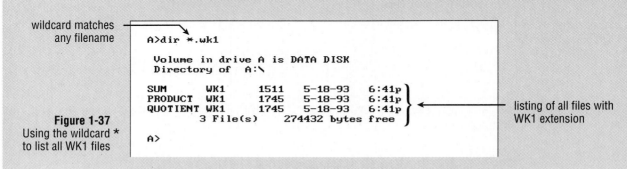

wildcard matches any filename

listing of all files with WK1 extension

Figure 1-37
Using the wildcard *
to list all WK1 files

Now suppose that among the 26 files on your diskette, several files had the closely related filenames X1TEST1, X5TEST0, X!TEST$, and so forth, and had different filename extensions, such as DFT and DOC. You could use the ? wildcard to get a listing of only this particular group of files without having to look through all the other files on your diskette.

To use the ? wildcard:

❶ Make sure the DOS data diskette is in drive A and drive A is the default drive.

❷ Type **dir x?test?.*** and press **[Enter]**.

This command means, "Give a directory listing of all the files that begin with an X, have any character (letter, digit, or special character) after the X, then have the word TEST followed by any character, and then have any filename extension." DOS lists the files X1TEST1.DFT, X5TEST0.DOC, X!TEST$.MEM, and so forth. See Figure 1-38.

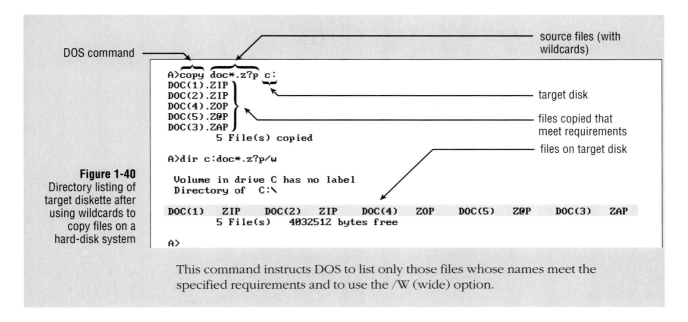

Figure 1-40
Directory listing of target diskette after using wildcards to copy files on a hard-disk system

This command instructs DOS to list only those files whose names meet the specified requirements and to use the /W (wide) option.

You can also use wildcards to delete a group of files. For example, suppose you no longer wanted the TEST*.Z?P files on the disk to which they were just copied. You could use ERASE or DEL with wildcards to delete only those files and no others.

To delete a group of files using a *two-diskette system*:

❶ Make sure your formatted diskette from the previous steps is still in drive B.

❷ Type **del b:doc*.z?p** and press **[Enter]**.

DOS deletes all the files on drive B that meet the requirements. If the deletions are successful, DOS gives no message. You can use the DIR command to verify that DOS has in fact deleted the files.

To delete a group of files using a *hard-disk system*:

❶ Make sure drive A is still the default drive.

❷ Type **del c:doc*.z?p** and press **[Enter]**.

DOS deletes all the files on drive C that meet the requirements. If the deletions are successful, DOS gives no message. You can use the DIR command to verify that DOS has in fact deleted the files.

Remember to be especially cautious about using wildcards to delete files, since you can easily delete valuable files by accident.

Turning Off Your Computer

If you are in a computer lab, check with your instructor or technical support person before proceeding.

After you have finished a session on your computer or at the end of a day's work, you may want to turn it off. The following guidelines will help you to know when and how to turn off your computer:

- Before you turn off your computer, make sure the cursor is at the DOS prompt. In general, don't turn off your computer from within an applications program. Exit the application first.

- If you're going to be away from your computer for a short time — less than two hours, for example — just leave your computer on. In these situations, it causes more wear on your computer system to turn it off and then back on than it does just to leave it on.

- Never flip the computer back on immediately after you have turned it off. If you turn off your computer and then decide to turn it back on, wait about 30 seconds. This gives the circuitry time to discharge properly and avoids damage to the computer chips. Some computers have a delay mechanism that prevents you from turning them back on without a short waiting period.

- Never turn off a computer connected to a network unless instructed to do so by your technical support person.

If appropriate, turn off your computer now. Make sure that the peripherals — the monitor, the printer, and so forth — are also turned off. Remove any diskettes that might be in the drives.

Exercises

1. What is the purpose of the disk operating system (DOS)?

2. List five tasks that you can instruct DOS to do.

3. What is the DOS prompt? Why is it important?

4. What is the difference between an internal and an external DOS command? Why is it important to know this difference?

5. What keys would you press to change the default drive from C to A? Why would you want to change the default drive from C to A?

6. Why do you have to format a diskette before you use it the first time?

7. Explain the purpose of each of the following DOS commands and write the keys you would press (including parameters, if necessary) to execute each command.
   a. VER   d. DIR
   b. CLS   e. DEL
   c. DATE   f. TIME

8. What is another name for each of the following commands?
   a. RENAME
   b. ERASE

9. Explain each of the following terms:
   a. boot
   b. logging in
   c. password
   d. filename extension
   e. tracks
   f. sectors
   g. source disk
   h. target disk
   i. write-protect
   j. wildcards
   k. parameter
   l. option

10. What is the function of the following DIR options?
    a. /W
    b. /P

11. What are the two DOS wildcards? Why would you use them?

12. Explain how you would perform the following tasks, including the keys you would press:
    a. Format a diskette.
    b. Copy a file named INFO.FIL from drive A to drive B.
    c. Copy all the files with the filename extension LET from drive A to drive B.
    d. Get a listing of all the files on a disk that have the filename extension EXE.
    e. Check the capacity and the free space on a disk and in the computer's memory.
    f. Copy the entire contents of a diskette.

13. Which of the following characters are valid for a DOS filename? Which are invalid?
    a. /
    b. &
    c. +
    d. {
    e. [
    f. *
    g. @
    h. space

14. Which of the following filenames are legal? Which are illegal? For each illegal filename, state why it is illegal.
    a. MYFILE.001
    b. BOB CALL.LET
    c. 1993REP.Q2
    d. CHPT_02.DOC
    e. WP{FIL}.%%%
    f. PARKCITY.FILE
    g. QUARTER-2.REP
    h. $HAPPY$
    i. MOM+DAD.LET

Tutorial Assignments

Perform the following activities and answer the following questions while at your computer. You may have to use one or more DOS commands to answer a question.

1. Immediately after you boot your system and get to the DOS prompt, what does your DOS prompt look like?

2. What version of DOS is your computer running?

3. Clear your computer screen.

Get a directory listing of your DOS data diskette, then answer the following questions.

4. How many files are on the diskette?

5. Which file is the oldest, that is, has the earliest date and time of creation or modification? What is the date and time of that file?

6. Which file is the largest, that is, takes up the greatest amount of space in bytes? What is the size (in bytes) of that file?

7. How many files on the DOS data diskette have the filename extension WK1? *Hint:* Use a wildcard with DIR to answer this question.

Use the DOS data diskette to perform the following exercises and to answer the following questions:

8. Check the DOS data diskette using the CHKDSK command.
   a. What is its capacity (in bytes)?
   b. How much free space (in bytes) is available?
   c. What is the memory capacity of the computer you're using?
   d. How much free memory is available in your computer at this time?

9. Copy the file SUM.WK1 with the new filename ADD.WK1 so that both files reside on the DOS data diskette.

10. Delete all the files with the filename extension BAK.

Tutorial 2

Working with Directories

Before You Begin

Before you begin this tutorial, make sure you have the following items:

- **The diskette that you formatted in DOS Tutorial 1 or any other newly formatted diskette**. We'll call this the "work diskette" because you will work with it in learning and using the DOS commands explained in this tutorial. Using a felt-tip pen, write "Work Diskette" on the diskette label.
- **The Systems Disk**. If you have a two-diskette system, the Systems Disk is the diskette that contains DOS. If you have a hard-disk system, the hard disk is the Systems Disk, so you don't need a separate Systems Disk.
- **The DOS data diskette**.

What Is a Directory?

Suppose you worked in an office and wanted to find the 1992 annual sales report that you wrote several weeks ago. You'd go to your file cabinet, open the appropriate file drawer, and find the hanging folder labeled "Reports." You'd then take out the manila folder labeled "Sales," open the folder, and remove the document titled "1992 Annual Sales Report" (Figure 2-1). The document wouldn't be hard to find if you had filed it away in the correct file drawer, the correct hanging folder, and the correct manila folder. But imagine how hard the report would be to find if you had filed it randomly in the file drawer among dozens or even hundreds of other documents.

Managing your computer files works the same way, but instead of using a file cabinet, you store your computer files on a disk. Instead of using hanging folders and manila folders, you use directories. A **directory** is a division of a disk in which a group of files can be stored.

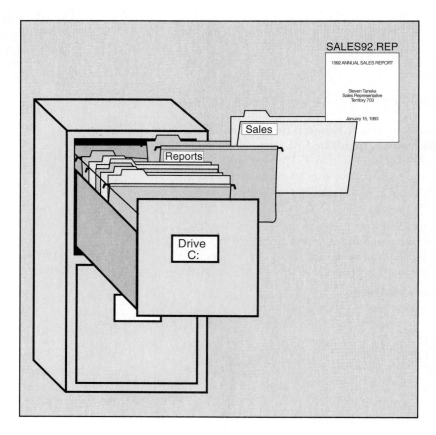

Figure 2-1
File organization

DOS allows you to have directories within directories within other directories and so forth, enabling you to have a complete **tree** of directories (Figure 2-2). The directory tree begins with the **root directory**, which is the disk itself and which is usually represented by the disk letter followed by a colon and a backslash (\), for example, C:\ or A:\. All the other directories on the disk branch from the root directory. Directories found within other directories are sometimes called **subdirectories**. Actually DOS commands don't differentiate between directories and subdirectories — they treat all levels of branches on the directory tree as directories. Although we use the term *subdirectories*, keep in mind that subdirectories are simply directories within other directories.

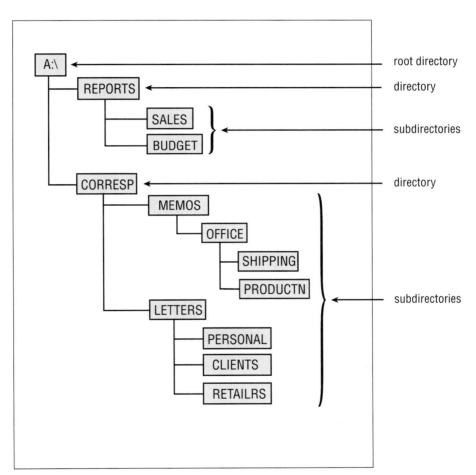

Figure 2-2
A sample
directory tree

What Is a Path?

Suppose you had to tell a colleague how to find the 1992 Annual Sales Report shown in Figure 2-1. You'd say, "Open drawer C, get out the hanging folder named REPORTS, remove the manila folder named SALES from the REPORTS hanging folder. There you'll find the Annual Sales Report."

Similarly, when you want to access a file on a disk — so you can copy the file, delete it, rename it, or do something else with it — you have to tell DOS where the file is located. The complete specification of a file — including disk, directories (if any), and filename — is called the complete **path** to the file. For example, the complete path to the file SALES92.REP in Figure 2-1 is C:\REPORTS\SALES\SALES92.REP. In this path, "C:\" is the root directory on drive C, "REPORTS" is the directory REPORTS within the root directory, "SALES" is the subdirectory SALES within REPORTS, and "SALES92.REP" is the file that contains the annual sales report. Backslashes separate directories and subdirectories within a path.

Besides complete paths, you can use partial paths. For example, if the default drive were C, you could leave off the C: and just use the path \REPORTS\SALES\SALES92.REP to access the file SALES92.REP. In this case, the initial backslash takes the place of "C:\."

You can also specify paths to directories and subdirectories. For example, if you wanted to get a directory listing of the files within the directory REPORTS, you would type the DIR command and then use the path A:\REPORTS (or just \REPORTS if A were the default drive) to indicate the directory you wanted to list.

Making a Directory (MKDIR or MD)

Suppose you wanted to use your computer to prepare quarterly, annual, and special reports. Rather than saving all the files of your reports in the root directory of a disk, you could create a directory called REPORTS as in Figure 2-2. Furthermore, suppose that you also used your computer to write letters and other types of correspondence. Rather than saving all those files in the root directory or mixing them with the report files, you could create a separate directory called CORRESP (for "correspondence"). Finally, you could create another separate directory called MEMOS, in which you would save your memo files. By creating those three directories within the root directory and saving your files within the appropriate directory, you could keep your reports, letters (correspondence), and memos well organized.

You can create a directory within the root directory or within another directory by using the DOS command MKDIR, or MD for short. Let's use the MD command to create the three directories — REPORTS, CORRESP, and MEMOS — on the diskette that you formatted in DOS Tutorial 1 or on some other newly formatted diskette. MD and all the other DOS commands used in this tutorial are *internal* commands, so you don't have to have the Systems Disk to execute the commands.

To make a new directory:

1. If you have a *two-diskette system*, insert the Systems Disk into drive A, turn on your computer, and get to the DOS prompt A>. After the DOS prompt appears on the screen, remove the Systems Disk from the drive.

   If you have a *hard-disk system*, turn on your computer and get to the DOS prompt C>.

   If you're using a computer on a network, make sure the computer is on, that you are logged into the network, and that the DOS prompt (for example, F>) is on the screen.

2. Insert the work diskette (the diskette you formatted in DOS Tutorial 1) or some other newly formatted diskette into drive A.

3. Make sure drive A is the default drive.

   If necessary type **a:** and press **[Enter]** to make A the default drive.

4. Type **md reports** and press **[Enter]**.

   The DOS command MD requires one parameter, the name of the new directory you want to create. DOS makes the new directory REPORTS, which in this case is a subdirectory of the root directory.

5. Type **md corresp** and press **[Enter]** to create a directory for holding letters and other correspondence.

   DOS creates a second directory within the root directory.

6. Type **md memos** and press **[Enter]** to create a directory for holding memo files.

   DOS creates a third subdirectory of the root directory. Now REPORTS, CORRESP, and MEMOS are all subdirectories within the root directory (Figure 2-3).

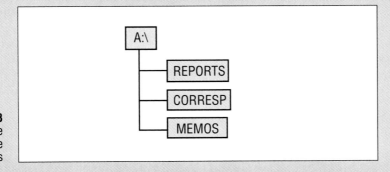

Figure 2-3
a directory tree
with the three
new directories

⑦ To verify that the directories have been created, type **dir** and press **[Enter]**. Your screen should look similar to Figure 2-4.

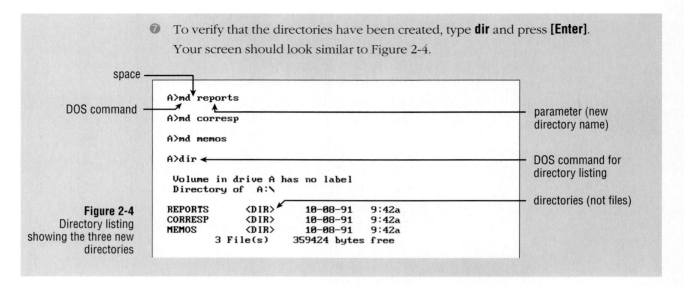

space

DOS command

parameter (new directory name)

DOS command for directory listing

directories (not files)

```
A>md reports

A>md corresp

A>md memos

A>dir

 Volume in drive A has no label
 Directory of  A:\

REPORTS       <DIR>      10-08-91   9:42a
CORRESP       <DIR>      10-08-91   9:42a
MEMOS         <DIR>      10-08-91   9:42a
         3 File(s)     359424 bytes free
```

Figure 2-4
Directory listing showing the three new directories

Notice that in the directory listing, "<DIR>" appears to the right of the names of the directories REPORTS, CORRESP, and MEMOS to indicate that these are directory names, not filenames.

Naming a Directory

Since you'll have to create directories on your own disks to keep your personal and business files organized, you must learn the rules for naming directories. Fortunately the rules for naming a directory are the same as those for naming a file. A directory name consists of one to eight characters, and may have an extension of up to three characters. Most computer users, however, don't use extensions in directory names. The characters in directory names may be the letters A through Z, the digits 0 through 9, and any other keyboard characters except the symbols ? . " / \ [ ] : | < > + = ; , and *. A space is not allowed in a directory name.

Removing a Directory (RMDIR or RD)

Once you no longer need a directory, you can use the DOS command RMDIR or RD to remove it from the disk. Suppose, for example, you realized that memos are actually a type of correspondence and thus decided to remove the MEMOS directory. (Later you'll see how to make it a subdirectory in CORRESP.) In the following steps, you'll remove the MEMOS directory using the RD command.

To remove a directory:

❶ Make sure the work diskette is still in drive A and A is the default drive.

❷ Type **rd memos** and press **[Enter]**.

DOS deletes the directory from the diskette.

❸ Type **dir** and press **[Enter]** to verify that MEMOS is no longer on the diskette. See Figure 2-5.

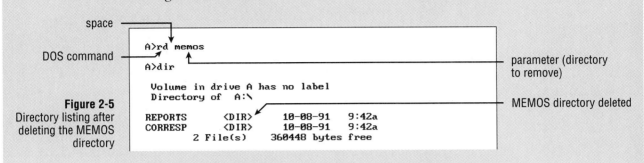

space — ┐
DOS command — ┐
parameter (directory to remove)
MEMOS directory deleted

Figure 2-5
Directory listing after deleting the MEMOS directory

```
A>rd memos

A>dir

     Volume in drive A has no label
     Directory of  A:\

REPORTS         <DIR>       10-08-91    9:42a
CORRESP         <DIR>       10-08-91    9:42a
          2 File(s)      360448 bytes free
```

A directory must be completely empty before you can delete it. Usually you will have to use the ERASE or DEL command to erase all the files in the directory before you remove the directory. Let's see what happens if you try to remove a directory that isn't empty.

To try to remove a directory that isn't empty:

❶ Remove the work diskette from drive A and insert the DOS data diskette into drive A. Make sure drive A is still the default drive.

❷ Type **dir *.** and press **[Enter]**.

Notice that this command uses the wildcard * for the filename but no wildcard for the filename extension. This tells DOS to list only those files or directories with no extension in their names. Since most filenames but few directory names have extensions, this command gives you a listing of only the subdirectories of the A drive root directory. In this case, you'll see a directory listing similar to the one in Figure 2-6.

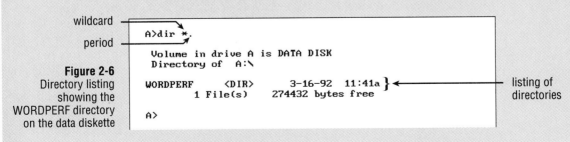

wildcard —
period —
listing of directories

Figure 2-6
Directory listing showing the WORDPERF directory on the data diskette

```
A>dir *.

     Volume in drive A is DATA DISK
     Directory of  A:\

WORDPERF        <DIR>        3-16-92   11:41a
          1 File(s)      274432 bytes free

A>
```

❸ Type **rd wordperf** and press **[Enter]**.

This command tells DOS that you want to remove the directory named WORDPERF. However, because the directory is not empty, a DOS error message appears on the screen. See Figure 2-7.

attempt to remove
nonempty directory

Figure 2-7
DOS message when
you try to remove a
directory that isn't
empty

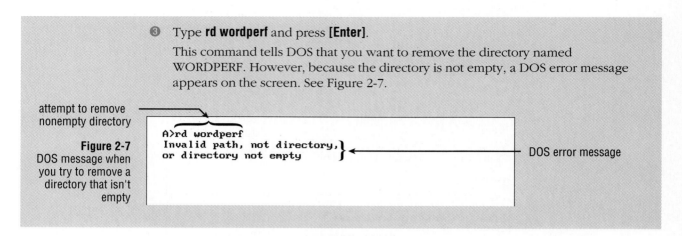

A>rd wordperf
Invalid path, not directory,
or directory not empty

DOS error message

In these steps, you didn't really want to remove the WORDPERF directory, of course. When you actually do want to remove a directory that isn't empty you should then use the ERASE or DEL command to erase all the files in the directory and then use the RD command again to remove the directory. As always, be extremely careful not to delete any file that might be valuable.

Changing the Information in the DOS Prompt (PROMPT)

If immediately after you boot your computer, your DOS prompt appears as C:\> rather than C> or as A:\> rather than A>, you don't need to use the DOS command PROMPT. Consult your instructor or technical support person on whether you need to read this section.

The usual DOS prompt, such as A> or C>, indicates the default drive but not the default directory. The **default directory** is the directory, such as C:\REPORTS, that DOS uses when you issue any DOS command, unless you specifically instruct DOS to use a different directory. The default directory includes not only the default root directory, such as C:\ or A:\, but also the directory or subdirectory, such as REPORTS. When you issue the DIR command, for example, without specifying a drive or a directory, DOS gives you a listing of files and directories within the default directory. Thus, if you execute the DIR command when A:\REPORTS is the default directory, you'll see a listing of the files within the directory REPORTS. The next section explains how to change the default directory.

The DOS command PROMPT PG lets you modify the DOS prompt so it includes not only the default drive but also the default directory (Figure 2-8 on the next page). With the name of the default directory path as part of the DOS prompt, you'll always know where DOS is in the directory tree and whether you have to change the default directory or specify the path to access a file or another directory. Let's use the PROMPT PG command to change the DOS prompt so that it shows the default directory.

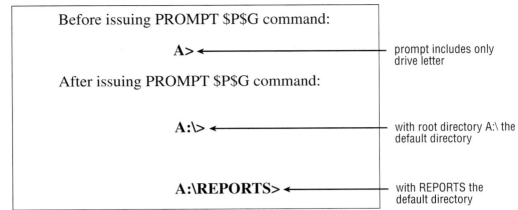

Figure 2-8
The DOS prompt
before and after you
issue the PROMPT
command

Before issuing PROMPT PG command:

A> ←——————————————— prompt includes only
drive letter

After issuing PROMPT PG command:

A:\> ←——————————————— with root directory A:\ the
default directory

A:\REPORTS> ←——————————————— with REPORTS the
default directory

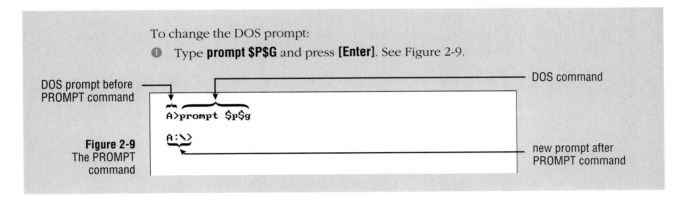

To change the DOS prompt:
1. Type **prompt PG** and press **[Enter]**. See Figure 2-9.

DOS prompt before
PROMPT command

DOS command

A>prompt pg

A:\>

Figure 2-9
The PROMPT
command

new prompt after
PROMPT command

In the parameter PG of the PROMPT command, $P instructs DOS to include the path in the prompt, and $G tells DOS to include a greater-than sign (>). If the default directory is the root directory in drive A, then the DOS prompt will look like this: A:\>. If you changed the default directory to REPORTS, for example, the DOS prompt would look like this: A:\REPORTS>.

Changing the Default Directory (CD)

Suppose you wanted to view a listing of the files in a subdirectory, delete a file within that subdirectory, and perform other activities with files in the subdirectory. The simplest way to work with files in a subdirectory is to change the default directory to that subdirectory. This allows you to use only filenames as parameters to DOS commands, rather than having to use complete paths.

To change the default directory, you use the CHDIR or CD command. Let's practice this command by first changing the default directory from the root directory A:\ on the DOS data diskette to the WORDPERF directory.

To change the default directory:

❶   Make sure the DOS data diskette is still in drive A and A is the default drive.

❷   Type **cd \wordperf** and press **[Enter]**. See Figure 2-10.

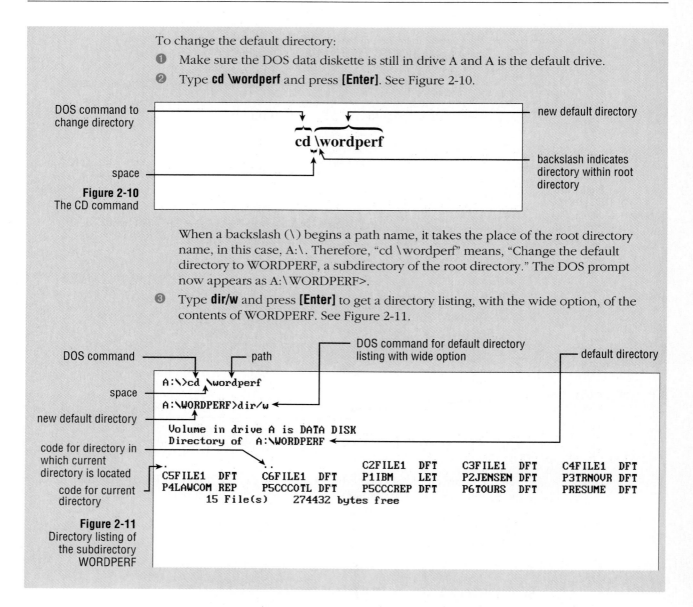

DOS command to change directory

new default directory

cd \wordperf

space

backslash indicates directory within root directory

Figure 2-10
The CD command

When a backslash (\) begins a path name, it takes the place of the root directory name, in this case, A:\. Therefore, "cd \wordperf" means, "Change the default directory to WORDPERF, a subdirectory of the root directory." The DOS prompt now appears as A:\WORDPERF>.

❸   Type **dir/w** and press **[Enter]** to get a directory listing, with the wide option, of the contents of WORDPERF. See Figure 2-11.

DOS command   path

DOS command for default directory listing with wide option

default directory

space

new default directory

code for directory in which current directory is located

code for current directory

```
A:\>cd \wordperf

A:\WORDPERF>dir/w

Volume in drive A is DATA DISK
Directory of  A:\WORDPERF

.                     ..                  C2FILE1   DFT    C3FILE1   DFT    C4FILE1   DFT
C5FILE1   DFT    C6FILE1   DFT    P1IBM     LET    P2JENSEN  DFT    P3TRNOVR  DFT
P4LAWCOM  REP    P5CCCOTL  DFT    P5CCCREP  DFT    P6TOURS   DFT    PRESUME   DFT
         15 File(s)     274432 bytes free
```

Figure 2-11
Directory listing of the subdirectory WORDPERF

Because WORDPERF is now the default directory and because the DIR command doesn't specify a path to another directory, DOS gives a directory listing of only those files within the WORDPERF directory, not a listing of all the files on the diskette. The file listing in Figure 2-11 includes two codes: one period (.) means the current directory; two periods (..) mean the directory in which the current subdirectory is located. In this case, therefore, the single-period code stands for WORDPERF, and the double-period code stands for the root directory A:\.

Now let's use the CD command to change the default directory on the work diskette.

To change the default directory:

❶ Remove the DOS data diskette from drive A and insert the work diskette.

❷ Type **cd \reports** and press **[Enter]** to change the default directory to REPORTS.

Now the default directory is REPORTS, and the DOS prompt is A:\REPORTS>.

❸ Type **dir** and press **[Enter]** to get a directory listing of the contents of REPORTS. See Figure 2-12.

DOS command —

new default directory —

Figure 2-12
Directory listing of
the subdirectory
REPORTS (empty)

— path

— no files, two codes

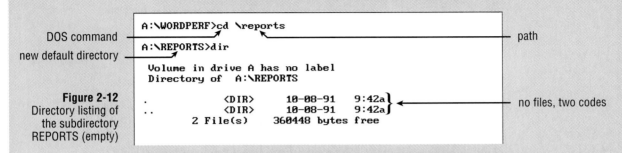

Since REPORTS is currently empty, no filenames appear in the directory listing; only the single-period and double-period codes appear.

❹ Type **cd \corresp** and press **[Enter]** to change the default directory to CORRESP.

The DOS prompt is now A:\CORRESP>.

❺ Type **cd ** and press **[Enter]** to change the default directory back to the root directory.

By typing a backslash (\) without a directory name in the CD command, you instruct DOS to make the root directory the default directory. The DOS prompt now appears as A:\>.

As you can see from these examples, you can go from any directory, such as the root directory A:\, to any other directory or subdirectory, such as REPORTS, by typing the command CD, a space, a backslash (\), and then the name of the directory.

Making a Subdirectory within a Directory

Up until now, the only directories you've made are subdirectories of the root directory. Now let's see how to make a subdirectory within another directory or subdirectory. In this case, we'll change the default directory to CORRESP and then make the subdirectories MEMOS and LETTERS within CORRESP. Furthermore, we'll create three subdirectories within the subdirectory LETTERS (Figure 2-13).

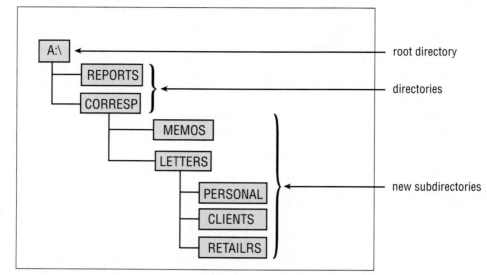

Figure 2-13
Directory tree of the work diskette with the new subdirectories

To make a subdirectory within a directory:

❶ Make sure the work diskette is still in drive A.

❷ Type **cd \corresp** and press **[Enter]** to change the default directory to CORRESP.

The DOS prompt should now appear as A:\CORRESP>, indicating that the default directory is CORRESP, which is a subdirectory of the root directory A:\.

❸ Type **md memos** and press **[Enter]**.

The command MD makes a subdirectory within the current default directory. The default directory in this case is CORRESP. Therefore, the command *md memos* creates the subdirectory MEMOS within the directory CORRESP.

❹ Type **md letters** and press **[Enter]**.

This command creates the subdirectory LETTERS within the directory CORRESP.

❺ Type **dir** and press **[Enter]** to get a directory listing of the files and subdirectories within the directory CORRESP. See Figure 2-14.

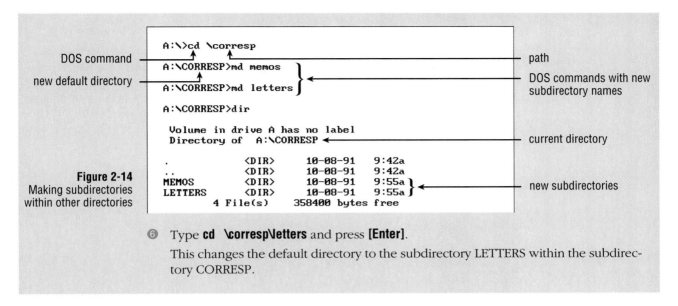

Figure 2-14
Making subdirectories within other directories

DOS command

new default directory

path

DOS commands with new subdirectory names

current directory

new subdirectories

```
A:\>cd \corresp

A:\CORRESP>md memos

A:\CORRESP>md letters

A:\CORRESP>dir

 Volume in drive A has no label
 Directory of  A:\CORRESP

 .              <DIR>      10-08-91    9:42a
 ..             <DIR>      10-08-91    9:42a
 MEMOS          <DIR>      10-08-91    9:55a
 LETTERS        <DIR>      10-08-91    9:55a
          4 File(s)    358400 bytes free
```

6 Type **cd   \corresp\letters** and press **[Enter]**.

This changes the default directory to the subdirectory LETTERS within the subdirectory CORRESP.

If you use your computer to type a lot of letters, you'll want to keep them organized on your disk. Suppose, for example, that you write three types of letters: personal letters to friends and relatives, letters to clients, and letters to retailers. It makes sense, therefore, to create a subdirectory of \CORRESP\LETTERS for each of these three types of letters. Let's create the three subdirectories PERSONAL, CLIENTS, and RETAILRS.

To create new subdirectories:

1 Type **md personal** and press **[Enter]**.
2 Type **md clients** and press **[Enter]**.
3 Type **md retailrs** and press **[Enter]**.

You can't use the word *retailers* for a directory name because it has nine letters. Instead, you have to use the shortened name *retailrs*.

The commands in these steps created the subdirectories PERSONAL, CLIENTS, and RETAILRS within the LETTERS directory. Now your work diskette has the directory tree shown in Figure 2-13.

Using Paths with DOS Commands

You can use paths with any DOS command that accepts a drive letter or a filename as a parameter. For example, you can get a directory listing of all the files in the WORDPERF subdirectory of the DOS data diskette even when the default directory is the root directory A:\ by including the path \WORDPERF as the parameter of DIR. Using a path with DIR saves you time when you want to see what is in a directory but you don't necessarily want to work with the files in that directory.

Using a Path with DIR

First let's see how to use a path to get a directory listing of the files in a directory other than the default directory.

To use a path to get a directory listing:

❶ Remove the work diskette and insert the DOS data diskette into drive A.

❷ Type **cd** \ and press **[Enter]** so the root directory becomes the default directory. The DOS prompt should appear as A:\>.

❸ Type **dir a:\wordperf/w** and press **[Enter]**.

DOS gives you a directory listing similar to Figure 2-15.

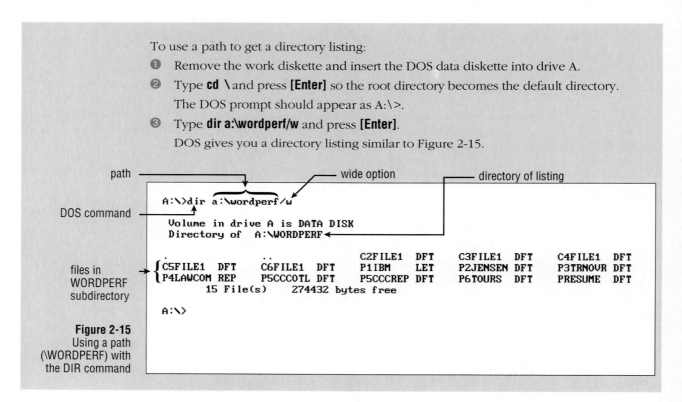

path ─────────────── wide option ───── directory of listing

DOS command ─────

```
A:\>dir a:\wordperf/w

Volume in drive A is DATA DISK
Directory of   A:\WORDPERF

  .                    ..                  C2FILE1  DFT   C3FILE1  DFT   C4FILE1  DFT
 C5FILE1  DFT   C6FILE1  DFT   P1IBM    LET   P2JENSEN DFT   P3TRNOUR DFT
 P4LAWCOM REP   P5CCCOTL DFT   P5CCCREP DFT   P6TOURS  DFT   PRESUME  DFT
        15 File(s)     274432 bytes free

A:\>
```

files in WORDPERF subdirectory

Figure 2-15
Using a path (\WORDPERF) with the DIR command

As this example demonstrates, you can list the files in a directory other than the default directory.

Using Paths to Copy Files

You can also use paths to copy files from one subdirectory to another. For example, suppose you wanted to save all your spreadsheet files that you created with the spreadsheet program Lotus 1-2-3 in a separate subdirectory called 123FILES, but they were currently stored in the root directory. You would then create a new subdirectory named 123FILES, copy the spreadsheet files from the root directory into the subdirectory, and then delete the copy of the files from the root directory. Recall from Tutorial 1 that Lotus 1-2-3 files have the filename extension WK1. Let's perform these commands on the DOS data diskette.

To use paths to copy files from one directory to another:

❶ Make sure the DOS data diskette is still in drive A and the root directory A:\ is the default directory.

❷ Type **md 123files** and press **[Enter]**.

This creates a new directory on the DOS data diskette where you can save your Lotus 1-2-3 spreadsheet files.

❸ Type **copy *.wk1 \123files** and press **[Enter]** to copy the WK1 files into the directory 123FILES. See Figure 2-16.

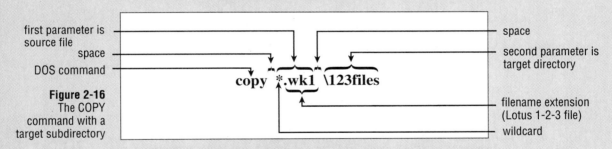

first parameter is source file
space
DOS command

Figure 2-16
The COPY command with a target subdirectory

space
second parameter is target directory

filename extension (Lotus 1-2-3 file)
wildcard

In this command, the parameter *.WK1 specifies that the target files are all the files within the default directory (in this case, the root directory) that have the filename extension WK1. The parameter \123FILES specifies that the target directory is 123FILES.

❹ Type **dir \123files** and press **[Enter]** to verify that the WK1 files were copied. See Figure 2-17. (*Note:* The file ADD.WK1 will appear on your screen only if you completed the Tutorial Assignments at the end of DOS Tutorial 1.)

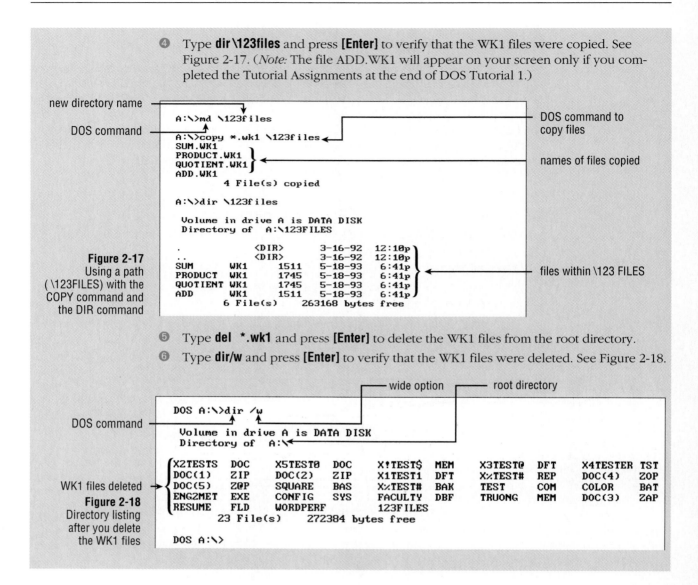

Figure 2-17
Using a path
(\123FILES) with the
COPY command and
the DIR command

❺ Type **del *.wk1** and press **[Enter]** to delete the WK1 files from the root directory.

❻ Type **dir/w** and press **[Enter]** to verify that the WK1 files were deleted. See Figure 2-18.

Figure 2-18
Directory listing
after you delete
the WK1 files

You can also copy files from one subdirectory to another subdirectory when neither subdirectory is the default directory. Suppose, for example, that the root directory A:\ were the default directory and you wanted to copy a file from the subdirectory 123FILES into the subdirectory WORDPERF using a new filename. In the following steps, you'll copy the file QUOTIENT.WK1 from the subdirectory 123FILES into the subdirectory WORDPERF using the new filename DIV.WK1.

To copy a file from one subdirectory to another:

❶ Make sure the DOS data diskette is still in drive A and the root directory A:\ is the default directory.

❷ Type **copy \123files\quotient.wk1 \wordperf\div.wk1** and press **[Enter]**. See Figure 2-19.

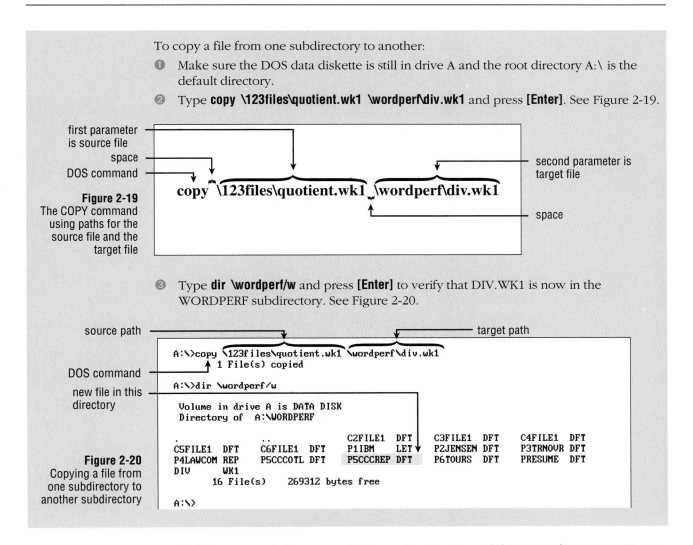

Figure 2-19
The COPY command using paths for the source file and the target file

❸ Type **dir \wordperf/w** and press **[Enter]** to verify that DIV.WK1 is now in the WORDPERF subdirectory. See Figure 2-20.

Figure 2-20
Copying a file from one subdirectory to another subdirectory

In this command, the source file is specified by the path \123FILES\QUOTIENT.WK1, and the target file is specified by the path \WORDPERF\DIV.WK1. Because you have included a filename in the second parameter and not just a directory name, DOS knows that you want to use a new filename for the copy of the source file. Notice that in these examples, you don't have to include "A:" because drive A is the default. You could, however, include the entire paths — A:\123FILES\QUOTIENT.WK1 and A:\WORDPERF\DIV.WK1.

These steps have demonstrated the power of paths. Using paths, you can access any directory or any file from within any other directory.

Exercises

1. Define or describe the following:
   a. directory
   b. subdirectory
   c. default directory
   d. root directory
   e. directory tree

2. List and explain the step(s) to make a directory.

3. What are the rules for naming a directory?

4. List and explain the step(s) to change the default directory.

5. List and explain the step(s) to remove a directory from a disk.

6. What is the purpose of the DOS command PROMPT PG?

7. What is a path? What is a pathname?

8. Suppose you wanted to delete the file CHECKING.WK1 from the subdirectory 123FILES on the diskette in drive A when A:\ is the default directory. List the instructions you would issue to DOS to delete CHECKING.WK1 from 123FILES without changing the default directory.

9. Suppose you wanted to copy the file JONES.LET from the subdirectory COMPANY within the directory LETTERS on drive C to the subdirectory CORRESP within the directory WPFILES on the diskette in drive A. List the instructions you would issue to DOS to perform this operation.

Tutorial Assignments

Perform the following activities using the work diskette from this tutorial.

1. Within the directory REPORTS, make the subdirectories SALES and BUDGET.

2. Within the directory MEMOS, which is found within the directory CORRESP, make the subdirectory OFFICE.

3. Within the directory OFFICE from Assignment 2, make the subdirectories SHIPPING and PRODUCTN.

4. Draw a directory tree of the organization of the directories and subdirectories on the work diskette.

Perform the following activities using the DOS data diskette (not the work diskette):

5. From the root directory, make a subdirectory named WPFILES in which you will store your word processing document files.

6. Copy the document files that have the filename extension DOC from the root directory into the WPFILES subdirectory. Delete the DOC files in the root directory.

7. From the root directory, get a directory listing of the files in the WPFILES subdirectory.

8. Change the default directory to WPFILES and get a directory listing of the files in that directory.

9. Change the default directory back to the root directory.

10. From the root directory, rename the file ADVERT.DOC in the directory WPFILES with the new name INVEST.DOC. *Hint:* Use the path to the file ADVERT.DOC in the first parameter of the RENAME command, but use only the new filename in the second parameter.

Index

WordPerfect 5.1 Tutorials

- Tutorial 1 **Creating a Document**

- Tutorial 2 **Formatting and Editing a Document**

- Tutorial 3 **Using Additional Editing Features**

- Tutorial 4 **Formatting Multiple-Page Documents**

- Tutorial 5 **Using Special Word-Processing Features**

- Tutorial 6 **Merging Documents**

Tutorial 1

Creating a Document

Requesting Information on Training Materials

Case: Clearwater Valve Company

Andrea Simone recently received a degree in business management with a specialty in operations and production. She has just been hired as the executive assistant to Steve Morgan, the operations manager for Clearwater Valve Company. Clearwater designs and manufactures specialty valves for industrial sprinkler, cooling, and plumbing systems.

One of Steve's responsibilities as operations manager is to train employees at Clearwater's production plant on safety procedures. He decides to purchase training videos so he can conduct safety training easily and inexpensively. After looking through several catalogs, Steve determines that Learning Videos Inc., of Pecos, Texas, publishes a video that seems appropriate, but he has several questions about the video. Steve asks Andrea to write a letter to request further information. He gives her a handwritten note with his questions.

In this tutorial you'll complete Andrea's assignment. You'll learn how to plan a letter and then how to use WordPerfect to write the letter to Learning Videos Inc.

OBJECTIVES

In this tutorial you will learn to:

- Start WordPerfect

- Use the pull-down menus, the function keys, and the function-key template

- Get help on WordPerfect features

- Clear the document screen

- Delete text

- Use word wrap

- Move the cursor

- Save and retrieve a document

- Preview and print a document

- Exit WordPerfect

Writing with WordPerfect

Before you begin you need to learn three key terms that WordPerfect users frequently use: document, document screen, and document file. In WordPerfect terminology, the letter that you'll write is called a document. A **document** is any written item, such as a memo, letter, or report. You use the document screen to create and edit documents. The **document screen** is the visual display on the computer monitor where you see the text you type and the changes you make to the document that you are creating and editing. You save your WordPerfect documents in a **document file**, which is stored on a hard disk or a diskette and which contains the text and formatting information about your document. You'll then print the document (Figure 1-1).

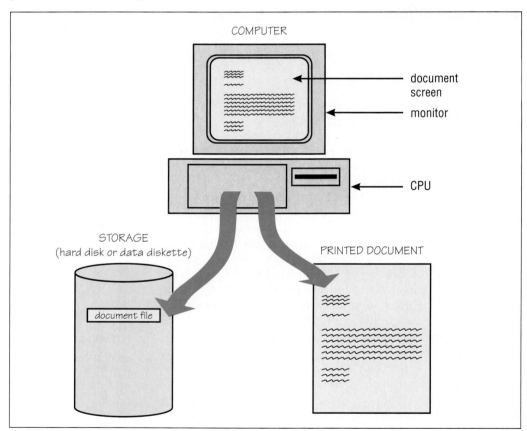

Figure 1-1
Document screen on the monitor, document file on disk, and printed document

Let's now begin with the first step in writing with WordPerfect — planning a document.

Planning a Document

Planning a document before you write it increases the quality of your writing, makes your document more attractive and readable, and, in the long run, saves you time and effort. You can divide your planning into four parts: content, organization, style, and format.

Content

Begin your planning by first determining what you want to say in the document, that is, the content. The content should clearly convey your purpose and should be appropriate for your reader(s). Are you writing to obtain information, to persuade, to inform, or to motivate? If you don't have all the information necessary to accomplish your purpose, gather additional details from such sources as notes, memos, letters, reports, and colleagues.

After you have assembled the necessary information, you should determine the scope of the document. Usually you won't use all the information you've gathered. Include enough information to achieve your objective but not so much that your reader may become overwhelmed or bored. Keep your message simple, yet complete.

As Andrea considers her purpose and her reader, she focuses on the handwritten note from Steve Morgan (Figure 1-2). The note lists Steve's questions and contains the catalog information about the training video. Andrea decides that the questions will be the primary content of her letter and that the catalog information will help her reader identify the correct video. She knows that this is all the information she needs to plan the content and that she should keep the letter to a few short paragraphs.

> Andrea, please write and find out the following:
>
> Does the video cover the most recent OSHA, HAZCOM, and EPA regulations on chemical safety?
>
> What instructor materials are available?
>
> The video is catalog number LV18427, "Safety in the Work Place." Our customer service rep is Peter Argyle. His address is Learning Videos Inc., 862 Pinewood Road, Suite #210, Pecos, TX 79772.

Figure 1-2
Handwritten note
from Steve Morgan
to Andrea Simone

Organization

After you have determined the content of your document, you should decide how to organize the information so that your ideas appear in a logical and coherent sequence. For example, if you're telling a story, you might want to recount the events in chronological order. If you're giving instructions on a procedure, you should give step-by-step directions. If you're sending a message that might upset your reader, you could begin with an explanation or with positive or neutral statements before you deliver the bad news.

For a short letter or memo, you can organize the information in your head; for a longer document, you should create a complete outline before you begin writing.

How should Andrea organize her letter? She decides to use the standard organization for a business letter, which begins with the date, the inside address, and the salutation, then presents the body or text of the letter, and concludes with a complimentary closing and the writer's name and title. For the body of the letter, Andrea decides to include four paragraphs. The first paragraph will identify the video and express Clearwater's interest in the video. The second and third paragraphs will include Steve's questions about the video, and the fourth paragraph will close the letter and request a prompt reply.

Style

After you have settled on the content and the organization of your document, you should next begin writing, using an appropriate style that satisfies your purpose and meets the needs of your audience. In business documents the style should be simple and direct. You can achieve this style by using simple words, direct sentences, and short paragraphs so your reader can easily grasp the meaning of the text and read at a brisk, natural pace. Simplicity and directness are the hallmarks of a good business writing style.

Your style can be simple and direct yet still have variety in writing tones. A report to your company's board of directors, for example, might be formal and reserved. A memo to a colleague, on the other hand, might be informal and conversational. In all documents, however, you should avoid trite expressions, overstatements, euphemisms, inappropriate jargon, and sexist language. Make your ideas concrete, specific, and exact.

In the case of Andrea's letter to request information, her style should be clear, simple, and direct. She should also make the tone of her letter positive and pleasant, to encourage a quick response from Learning Videos.

Format

Finally you should make your documents visually appealing. An attractive document is a readable document. Such formatting features as ample white space, sufficient line spacing, and appropriate headings make your document readable and your message clear. Your reader will spend less time trying to understand your message and more time acting on it. Usually the longer and more complex a document is, the more attention you'll need to pay to its format.

Since Andrea's letter to Learning Videos is short and simple, she decides to use the standard business letter format provided by WordPerfect. This format includes single-spaced lines and one-inch margins around all four edges of the page.

■   ■   ■

Having planned what she's going to write, Andrea is ready to use WordPerfect to write the letter to Learning Videos Inc. In this tutorial, you'll create Andrea's letter as shown in Figure 1-3.

Before you start this tutorial, make sure WordPerfect is installed on your computer system. If you're using a computer in a lab, check with your instructor or technical support person. If you're using your own computer, install WordPerfect by following the installation instructions that came with your copy of the software.

November 2, 1992

Mr. Peter Argyle
Learning Videos Inc.
862 Pinewood Road, Suite #210
Pecos, TX 79772

Dear Mr. Argyle:

I have read the catalog description of your training video number
LV18427, entitled "Safety in the Work Place." The video seems
appropriate for our training needs at Clearwater Valve Company, but
I would like additional information.

Specifically, please answer these questions:

1.   Does the video cover the most recent OSHA, HAZCOM, and EPA
regulations on handling hazardous chemicals?

2.   What instructor materials are available for testing and
documenting student performance?

Your attention to this matter is appreciated. I hope to hear from
you soon.

Sincerely yours,

Andrea Simone

Andrea Simone
Executive Assistant

Figure 1-3
Letter from Andrea
Simone to Learning
Videos Inc.

Starting WordPerfect

To use WordPerfect to create documents, you have to start the WordPerfect software. Let's start WordPerfect now.

To start WordPerfect:

❶ Make sure you have the WordPerfect data diskette ready. If you haven't already created the WordPerfect data diskette, see the beginning of this book for instructions.

❷ If necessary, turn on your computer.

If a menu of programs appears on the screen and WordPerfect is listed as one of those programs, you can run WordPerfect simply by selecting that menu item. If the menu doesn't list WordPerfect, exit from the menu. If you don't know how to exit the menu or how to select WordPerfect, consult your technical support person. Steps 3 through 6 assume that your computer can't start WordPerfect directly from a menu program.

❸ Make sure the DOS prompt and the cursor appear on the screen.

❹ If necessary, change the default disk drive to the drive where WordPerfect is installed by typing the letter of the disk drive and a colon (:) and then pressing **[Enter]**.

For example, if WordPerfect is installed on disk drive C, type **C:** and press **[Enter]**. If WordPerfect is installed on disk drive F, type **F:** and press **[Enter]**. Check with your technical support person if you are not sure how to change drives.

❺ Change the default directory to where WordPerfect is installed. For example, if your WordPerfect program was installed in the subdirectory WP51, you would type **cd\wp51** and press **[Enter]**. This changes the current default directory to the subdirectory called WP51.

If the message "Invalid directory" appears on the screen, WordPerfect is probably installed in a different directory, in which case you have to change the default directory to the one on which WordPerfect is located. If necessary, check with your technical support person for the directory containing WordPerfect.

❻ Type **wp** and press **[Enter]**.

This starts WordPerfect. You'll first see the WordPerfect title screen, then after another moment or two, the WordPerfect document screen. See Figure 1-4.

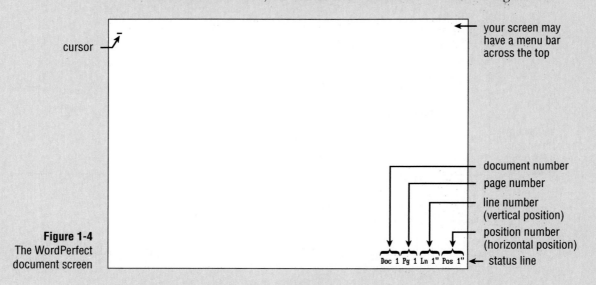

cursor

your screen may have a menu bar across the top

document number
page number
line number (vertical position)
position number (horizontal position)

Doc 1 Pg 1 Ln 1" Pos 1" ← status line

Figure 1-4
The WordPerfect document screen

Sometimes when you start WordPerfect, you may see the message "Are other copies of WordPerfect currently running?" This message indicates that you may be running WordPerfect from a network and using the same directory as other users. If you see this message and you are on a network, ask your technical support person how to proceed. If you see this message and you're not on a network, press **n** ("no").

WordPerfect may then display the message "Old backup file exists. 1 Rename; 2 Delete." Press **2** to delete the old backup file.

You have now completed the procedure for starting WordPerfect.

The Document Screen and the Status Line

Figure 1-4 shows the blank WordPerfect document screen on which you create and edit WordPerfect documents. As you type words and phrases, they become part of the document that appears on the document screen. Notice the blinking cursor in the upper left corner. The cursor marks the spot where the next character that you type will appear in the document.

The bottom line of the screen is called the **status line**. It tells you the document number, the page number, the line number, and the position number where the cursor is located.

Document Number

WordPerfect allows you to have two documents in your computer memory at a time. *Doc 1* on the status line means that the cursor is currently in document 1; *Doc 2* would mean that the cursor is currently in document 2. (You'll see how to use the second document screen in WordPerfect Tutorial 5.)

Page Number

Pg 1 means that the cursor is currently on page 1 — the first printed page — of your document. If your document has more than one page, this message will change as you move the cursor to other pages of the document.

Line Number

The line number is the distance from the top of the page to the current location of the cursor. *Ln 1"* means that the text you type will be one inch from the top of the page when you print the document. As you add lines of text to the document, the cursor moves farther down on the screen and the line number increases.

Unless you specify otherwise, your document will automatically have a one-inch margin at the top and the bottom of each page.

Position Number

The position number is the distance from the left edge of the page to the current location of the cursor. *Pos 1"* means that the text that you type at Pos 1" will be one inch from the left edge of the printed page when you print the document. As you type each character along a line of text, the cursor moves to the right and the position number increases.

Unless you specify otherwise, your document will automatically have a one-inch margin along the left and right edges of the page.

The word "Pos" on the status line also gives information about the keyboard and the appearance of the characters at the cursor. For example, if Caps Lock is on (so that typed letters appear in uppercase), "Pos" appears as "POS." If Num Lock is on, "Pos" first appears as blinking characters. These characters stop blinking once you start to use WordPerfect or you press [Num Lock]. You'll learn the other features of the status line later.

The Default Settings

Part of planning a document is deciding the document format, including the width of the margins, the line spacing, and the justification (how the text is aligned along the left and right margins). WordPerfect provides a set of standard format settings that you can use with most documents. These standard settings are called the **default** format settings because they automatically specify a format for your document unless you specifically change them. Figure 1-5 lists common WordPerfect default format settings. Your setup of WordPerfect may have different default settings. Some of these settings may not make sense to you now, but they will become clear as you work through the tutorials. You won't change any format settings in this tutorial.

Default Format Settings	
Left margin	1 inch
Right margin	1 inch
Top margin	1 inch
Bottom margin	1 inch
Justification	Full
Line spacing	1 (single)
Paper size	8.5 x 11 inches
Tabs	Every 0.5 inch
Page numbering	None
Hyphenation	Off
Repeat value	8
Date format	Month Day, Year
Widow/orphan	Off
Units of measure	" (inches)

Figure 1-5
Some WordPerfect default format settings

Executing WordPerfect Commands

Now that you have started WordPerfect, you are ready to use it by executing WordPerfect commands. A **command** is an instruction you issue to WordPerfect to perform a specific task, such as set the size of the margins, change the line spacing, or underline text.

You can issue a command using two general methods: pull-down menus or function-key commands. A **pull-down menu** is a list of commands that appears to be "pulled down" from the top of the document screen. You can then select the command you want from the list. A **function-key command** is a command you issue by pressing a function key, sometimes alone and sometimes in combination with a modifier key ([Shift], [Ctrl], or [Alt]).

In the steps that follow, you'll use a pull-down menu, with and without a mouse, and a function-key command to insert the date into the text.

Using the Keyboard with Pull-Down Menus

First let's see how to use the keyboard with the pull-down menus.

To use the keyboard to pull down a menu:

❶ Press **[Alt][=]**.

This key combination means that you press [Alt] and hold it down; while you are holding it down, press [=] (the equal sign). Then release both keys.

This key combination causes the WordPerfect menu bar to appear across the top of the screen. See Figure 1-6. You'll learn the meaning of each of the nine items in the menu bar later.

menu bar →

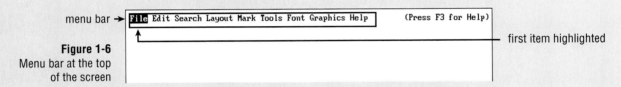

first item highlighted

Figure 1-6
Menu bar at the top
of the screen

With the menu bar on the screen, you can press [→] to move the cursor to the right and [←] to move it to the left to highlight the menu items.

❷ Press **[→]** five times to move the cursor to Tools.

Notice that each time you press [→], the cursor moves and highlights the next item to the right.

❸ Press **[↓]** or **[Enter]** to pull down the Tools menu.

This menu lists the various Tools options. See Figure 1-7.

Tools highlighted

first option highlighted

menu of options
and their equivalent
function-key
commands

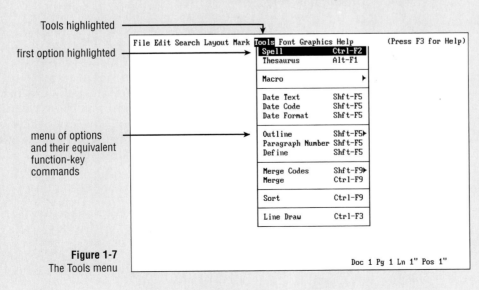

Figure 1-7
The Tools menu

❹ Press [→] to pull down the Font menu, then press [←] to return to the Tools menu. This step demonstrates how you can move from one pull-down menu to another by pressing the arrow keys.

❺ Press **[Esc]** twice to close the menu bar.

Pressing [Esc] once closes the Tools pull-down menu; pressing [Esc] a second time closes the menu bar. You also could have pressed [F1] or [Space] (the spacebar), but don't do so now — you have already closed the pull-down menu and the menu bar. All three keys work the same in closing menus.

Now that you know how to pull down a menu, move from one menu to another, and close a pull-down menu and the menu bar, you are ready to execute a WordPerfect command. In the following steps, you will use the Date Text command, which automatically inserts the current date into the document. Using the Date Text command saves you the keystrokes of typing the date and ensures that the date is accurate. Let's execute the Date Text command using the keyboard and the pull-down menu.

To execute the Date Text command from a pull-down menu:

❶ Press **[Alt][=]** to display the menu bar.

❷ Press [→] five times to highlight Tools, then press **[Enter]**. The Tools menu appears on your screen.

❸ Press [↓] three times to highlight Date Text and press **[Enter]**.

The menu bar disappears from the screen, and the current date appears on the document screen. See Figure 1-8. The document you are creating now contains the current date.

cursor

Figure 1-8
Document screen
after date inserted

November 2, 1992_

date inserted using current
Date Text option (your
date will be different)

❹ Press **[Enter]** to move the cursor to the next line.

You can use an alternative keyboard method to select an option from a pull-down menu. In this method, you press the highlighted letter of the command you want to execute. The highlighted letter is called the **mnemonic letter** because it is usually the first letter of the command and is easy to remember. In the following steps, you'll use this alternative method to insert the date again into the document. Later you'll erase the extra date.

To use the mnemonic letters to pull down a menu and execute a command:

❶ Press **[Alt][=]** to display the menu bar.

❷ Press **T** or **t** to select Tools.

Notice that the *T* in the word *Tools* on the menu bar is highlighted. This means you can select the menu item simply by pressing that letter. You can use either an uppercase or a lowercase letter to select a menu item. *In this book, we'll show the letter that you should press in uppercase, but you can press an uppercase or lowercase letter to execute the command.*

❸ Press **T** again to select Date Text.

The *T* in *Date Text* in the pull-down menu is highlighted and thus is the mnemonic letter. Now the current date appears again on the screen.

❹ Press **[Enter]** to move the cursor to the next line.

Using the mnemonic-letter method of selecting an option rather than pressing [↓] to highlight the option and then pressing [Enter] almost always requires fewer keystrokes. With mnemonic letters you had to use only four keystrokes to insert today's date: [Alt][=], T, and T. With the cursor keys, you had to use 12 keystrokes.

Using the Mouse with Pull-Down Menus

WordPerfect also allows you to use the mouse pointer and the mouse button to select items on the pull-down menu. If your computer doesn't have a mouse, go to the next section.

Using a mouse involves moving the mouse pointer, clicking a button, and dragging the mouse. To move the mouse pointer, which in WordPerfect appears as a rectangular box on the screen, move the mouse along a hard surface until the mouse pointer is at the desired location. To **click** on an item means to move the mouse pointer to the desired location and then to press and immediately release either the left mouse button (found on the left side of the mouse) or the right mouse button (located on the right side of the mouse). To **drag** the mouse means to move the mouse pointer to the desired location on the screen; press the left button and hold it down; while still holding down the button, move the mouse pointer to a new location on the screen; then release the mouse button.

Now that you know how to use a mouse, let's use it to insert the date once again into the document.

To use the mouse to pull down a menu:

❶ Press the right mouse button. This displays the menu bar at the top of the screen, just as if you'd pressed [Alt][=]. (If you accidentally press the right mouse button while working in WordPerfect — that is, you don't want the menu bar to appear — just press [Esc] or the right mouse button again to close the menu bar.)

❷ Click on Tools in the menu bar.

This means move the mouse pointer to any letter in the word Tools and then press and immediately release the *left* mouse button. The Tools menu appears on the screen.

❸ Click on Date Text.

This means move the pointer to any letter in Date Text; then press and immediately release the left mouse button. This operation selects Date Text, and inserts today's date again into the document.

❹ Press **[Enter]** to move the cursor to the next line.

In this book, we assume that you are using the keyboard to pull down menus and to select menu options. Feel free, however, to use the mouse if you have one.

Using the Function Keys and the Template

In addition to using the menu bar and pull-down menus, you can execute WordPerfect commands by pressing function keys. The commands available with the function keys are listed on the function-key templates (Figure 1-9).

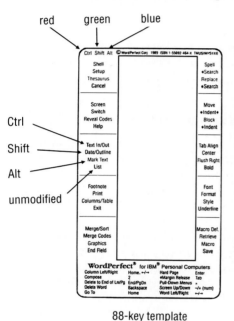

88-key template

The **template** is a plastic sheet that sits on the keyboard over the function keys and lists the names of the WordPerfect function-key commands, also called simply **WordPerfect keys**. The names of the WordPerfect keys are color coded to indicate which modifier key, if any, you have to press with the function key to issue the command. A command name in black indicates no modifier key; green indicates [Shift]; blue indicates [Alt]; and red indicates [Ctrl]. Thus, to execute the command for Date/Outline, which appears in green next to the function key [F5], you would press [Shift][F5]. In these tutorials, when you are to issue any WordPerfect command using the function keys, the modifier and the function key will be in boldface and in separate brackets, for example, [Shift][F5]. Following the modifier and the function key will be the name of the WordPerfect key in parentheses, for example, (Date/Outline). In the following steps you'll use the template and the function keys to insert the current date into the document for the third time.

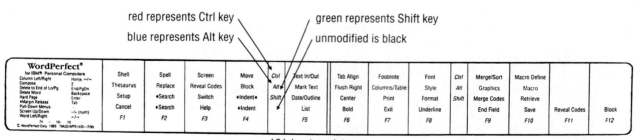

101-key template

Figure 1-9
The WordPerfect function-key templates

To insert today's date using the function keys:

❶ Press **[Shift][F5]** (Date/Outline). The Date/Outline menu appears on the status line. See Figure 1-10.

Date/Outline menu on status line

Figure 1-10
The Date/Outline menu

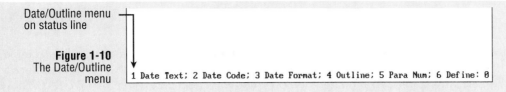

```
1 Date Text; 2 Date Code; 3 Date Format; 4 Outline; 5 Para Num; 6 Define: 0
```

Remember that [Shift][F5] means that you press and hold down the [Shift] key, press the [F5] key, and then release both keys. This WordPerfect key is called Date/Outline because it displays a menu of items that include date features and outline features. You'll learn more about the outline features in Tutorial 5.

❷ Select **1** (Date **T**ext).

You can select this option by pressing 1, which is the option number, or by pressing T, which is the option mnemonic. WordPerfect inserts today's date into the document. At this point, if you have followed all the previous examples, including those with mouse commands, the current date appears four times on your screen.

❸ Press **[Enter]** to move the cursor to the next line.

In most cases, when you press a function key with one of the modifier keys, WordPerfect displays a menu, such as the one shown in Figure 1-10. You can then select an option from the menu by pressing the number that corresponds to the menu item you want or by pressing the mnemonic letter (the highlighted letter in the menu item).

Pull-Down Menus vs. Function Keys

You've seen various ways of executing WordPerfect commands using pull-down menus, both with the keyboard and with the mouse. You've also seen how to execute the same WordPerfect commands using the function keys and the function-key template. But which method is better, pull-down menus or function keys?

The answer depends on your level of experience and your personal preference. Most commands require fewer keystrokes if you use the function keys rather than the pull-down menus with the keyboard, but the pull-down menus are usually easier to learn. Using pull-down menus with the mouse is sometimes easier than using the function keys. Even when it is more time consuming, some people simply prefer using the pull-down menus to using the function keys. In these WordPerfect tutorials, we give you a choice of how to execute a command. You can follow whichever method you prefer or whichever method your instructor requires.

When we ask you to execute a command, we first instruct you how to issue the command from a pull-down menu, which you can select using the keyboard or the mouse. We then tell you how to issue the same command using a function key. For example, an instruction to execute the Date Text command would be "Select Date Text from the Tools menu or press [Shift][F5] (Date/Outline) and select 1 (Date Text)." To execute this command using pull-down menus, you would press [Alt][=] or press the right mouse button to display the menu bar, pull down the Tools menu, and then select Date Text. To execute this command using the function keys, you would press [Shift][F5] (Date/Outline) and then either press 1 (or T) or click the mouse pointer on Date Text. In those operations where you can use only the keyboard but not the mouse, we will just tell you what keys to press.

Getting Help

How do you know which menu item to select or which function key to press, for example, to change the margins, to number pages, or to perform any other WordPerfect command? The best way is through training and continued experience in using WordPerfect. These WordPerfect tutorials will give you the training and the experience you need to perform the most important WordPerfect operations.

But WordPerfect provides another way for you to learn what commands are available and how to execute them: the WordPerfect Help feature. Both the main menu bar and the template list the Help feature. When you select Help from the menu bar or press [F3] (Help), WordPerfect displays a help screen and waits for you to do one of the following:

- Press a letter to get an alphabetical list of features whose names start with that letter
- Press [F3] (Help) again to display an illustration of the function key template
- Press any other function key or any cursor-movement or deletion key to get a description of that key
- Click the right mouse button or press [Enter] to exit Help and return to the document screen

Let's use each of these commands to get help with WordPerfect features.

Getting Help with a List of Features

Suppose you forget how to execute the WordPerfect command for inserting the date into a document. You can use the Help feature to get information on "Date" by using the alphabetical list of features. Let's do that now.

To get an alphabetical list of features that start with the letter D:

1 Select Help from the menu bar or press **[F3]** (Help). WordPerfect displays the Help screen. See Figure 1-11.

```
Help                                        WP 5.1   09/25/91

      Press any letter to get an alphabetical list of features.

          The list will include the features that start with that letter,
          along with the name of the key where the feature is found.  You
          can then press that key to get a description of how the feature
          works.

      Press any function key to get information about the use of the key.

          Some keys may let you choose from a menu to get more information
          about various options.  Press HELP again to display the template.




Selection: 0                               (Press ENTER to exit Help)
```

WordPerfect version

version release date

Figure 1-11
The Help screen

❷ Press **D**.

WordPerfect displays a list of the features that start with the letter D, including "Date Format," "Date/Time," "Default Codes," "Delete," and "Document Format." See Figure 1-12. The list gives the name of the feature, the name of the WordPerfect key on the function-key template, and the keystrokes you would press to execute the command.

features that start with D →

names of WordPerfect keys on template

function-key commands and other keystrokes

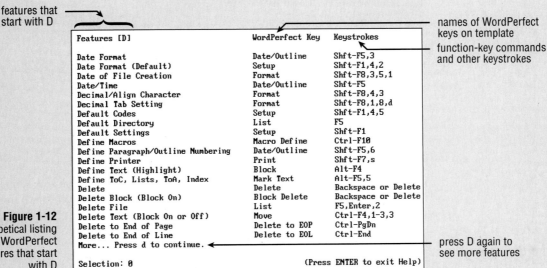

```
Features [D]                        WordPerfect Key   Keystrokes

Date Format                         Date/Outline      Shft-F5,3
Date Format (Default)               Setup             Shft-F1,4,2
Date of File Creation               Format            Shft-F8,3,5,1
Date/Time                           Date/Outline      Shft-F5
Decimal/Align Character             Format            Shft-F8,4,3
Decimal Tab Setting                 Format            Shft-F8,1,8,d
Default Codes                       Setup             Shft-F1,4,5
Default Directory                   List              F5
Default Settings                    Setup             Shft-F1
Define Macros                       Macro Define      Ctrl-F10
Define Paragraph/Outline Numbering  Date/Outline      Shft-F5,6
Define Printer                      Print             Shft-F7,s
Define Text (Highlight)             Block             Alt-F4
Define ToC, Lists, ToA, Index       Mark Text         Alt-F5,5
Delete                              Delete            Backspace or Delete
Delete Block (Block On)             Block Delete      Backspace or Delete
Delete File                         List              F5,Enter,2
Delete Text (Block On or Off)       Move              Ctrl-F4,1-3,3
Delete to End of Page               Delete to EOP     Ctrl-PgDn
Delete to End of Line               Delete to EOL     Ctrl-End
More... Press d to continue. ◄

Selection: 0                                   (Press ENTER to exit Help)
```

Figure 1-12
An alphabetical listing of WordPerfect features that start with D

press D again to see more features

❸ Press **[Shift][F5]** (Date/Outline). WordPerfect displays information about Date/Outline, including a menu of the features you can select after you issue the Date/Outline command. See Figure 1-13. To get an explanation of any feature in this menu, select that item. In this case, you want an explanation of WordPerfect's Date Text option, so you will select Option 1 (Date Text).

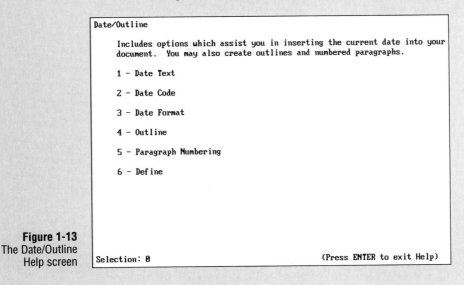

```
Date/Outline

    Includes options which assist you in inserting the current date into your
    document.  You may also create outlines and numbered paragraphs.

    1 - Date Text

    2 - Date Code

    3 - Date Format

    4 - Outline

    5 - Paragraph Numbering

    6 - Define




Selection: 0                                   (Press ENTER to exit Help)
```

Figure 1-13
The Date/Outline Help screen

④ Select **1** (Date **T**ext) from the menu. WordPerfect displays a detailed explanation of the feature you selected, namely, Date Text. See Figure 1-14.

```
Date Text/Code

    Inserts the date and time into your text at the current cursor location.
    The date and time used is the "system" date and time.  You specify how the
    date and time should be displayed with Date Format (Shift-F5,3).

    Date Text - Inserts the current date and time as text.

    Date Code - Inserts the current date and time as a WordPerfect code.   The
        code will always print the current date and time.
```

Figure 1-14
The Date Text/Code
Help screen

⑤ Press **[Enter]** when you are ready to exit Help and return to the document screen.

Getting Help with the Function-Key Templates

If you don't have a WordPerfect function-key template on your computer keyboard, you can use Help to see the template. In the following steps, you'll view the enhanced and the standard keyboard templates.

To use Help to display the function-key templates:

① Select Help from the Help menu or press **[F3]** (Help) to display the Help screen.

② Press **[F3]** (Help) again to display the function-key template for a 101-key enhanced keyboard. See Figure 1-15.

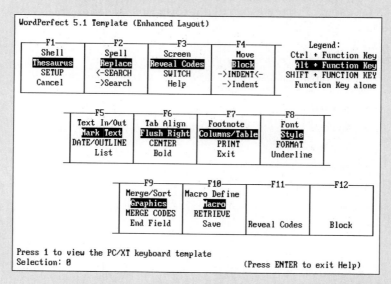

Figure 1-15
The 101-key
template shown on a
Help screen

This screen template lists the function keys (with and without modifier keys) that you would press to execute WordPerfect commands.

❸ Press **1** to display the function-key template for an IBM PC/XT-style keyboard. See Figure 1-16.

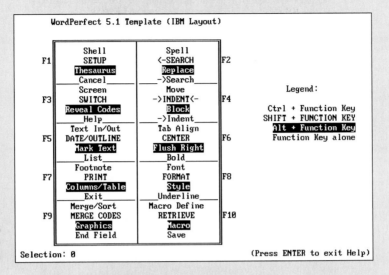

Figure 1-16
The 83-key template shown on a Help screen

```
       WordPerfect 5.1 Template (IBM Layout)

              Shell          Spell
        F1    SETUP          <-SEARCH        F2
              Thesaurus      Replace
              Cancel         ->Search
              Screen         Move                    Legend:
        F3    SWITCH         ->INDENT<-      F4
              Reveal Codes   Block              Ctrl + Function Key
              Help           ->Indent           SHIFT + FUNCTION KEY
              Text In/Out    Tab Align          Alt + Function Key
        F5    DATE/OUTLINE   CENTER          F6    Function Key alone
              Mark Text      Flush Right
              List           Bold
              Footnote       Font
        F7    PRINT          FORMAT          F8
              Columns/Table  Style
              Exit           Underline
              Merge/Sort     Macro Define
        F9    MERGE CODES    RETRIEVE        F10
              Graphics       Macro
              End Field      Save

       Selection: 0                    (Press ENTER to exit Help)
```

❹ Press **[Enter]** when you are ready to exit Help and return to the document screen.

Getting Help with Special Keys

Suppose you wanted information on using the right arrow key [→]. You could again use the Help feature for assistance.

To get help on a cursor-movement key or any other special key (such as [Backspace], [Del] or [Tab]):

❶ Select Help from the Help menu or press **[F3]** (Help).

❷ Press the key you want an explanation of, in this case, **[→]**. WordPerfect explains how to use the left arrow [←] and the right arrow [→] keys alone and with the [Home], [Esc], and [GoTo] keys. See Figure 1-17 on the next page. Your screen might look slightly different depending on your version of WordPerfect.

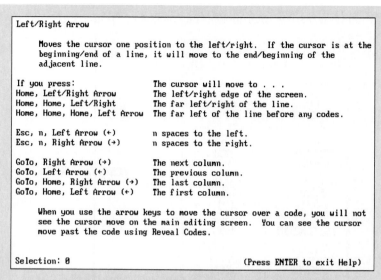

```
Left/Right Arrow

    Moves the cursor one position to the left/right.  If the cursor is at the
    beginning/end of a line, it will move to the end/beginning of the
    adjacent line.

If you press:                    The cursor will move to . . .
Home, Left/Right Arrow           The left/right edge of the screen.
Home, Home, Left/Right           The far left/right of the line.
Home, Home, Home, Left Arrow     The far left of the line before any codes.

Esc, n, Left Arrow (←)           n spaces to the left.
Esc, n, Right Arrow (→)          n spaces to the right.

GoTo, Right Arrow (→)            The next column.
GoTo, Left Arrow (←)             The previous column.
GoTo, Home, Right Arrow (→)      The last column.
GoTo, Home, Left Arrow (←)       The first column.

    When you use the arrow keys to move the cursor over a code, you will not
    see the cursor move on the main editing screen.  You can see the cursor
    move past the code using Reveal Codes.

Selection: 0                           (Press ENTER to exit Help)
```

Figure 1-17
The Help screen for
left/right arrow key

❸ Press **[Enter]** when you're ready to exit Help and return to the document screen.

Correcting Errors

Beginners and experienced WordPerfect users alike make mistakes. One of the advantages of using a word processor is that when you make a mistake, you can correct it quickly and cleanly. The following steps show you several ways to correct errors when you're entering text or executing a command. First, you'll learn how to use the Backspace key to correct typing errors.

To use [Backspace] to correct typing errors:

❶ Make sure the cursor is on the blank line below the last date text you entered in the previous sections.

❷ Type **Andria**. See Figure 1-18. This is a misspelled version of Andrea Simone's first name.

```
November 2, 1992
November 2, 1992
November 2, 1992
November 2, 1992
Andria_
```

misspelling ——   —— cursor

Figure 1-18
Document screen with
misspelled *Andria*

❸ Press **[Backspace]** twice to erase the last two letters. See Figure 1-19.

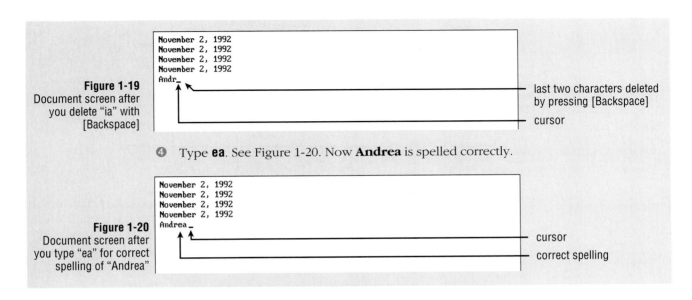

Figure 1-19
Document screen after
you delete "ia" with
[Backspace]

last two characters deleted
by pressing [Backspace]

cursor

❹ Type **ea**. See Figure 1-20. Now **Andrea** is spelled correctly.

Figure 1-20
Document screen after
you type "ea" for correct
spelling of "Andrea"

cursor

correct spelling

These steps demonstrate that if you discover a typing error soon after you have made it, you can press [Backspace] to erase the characters to the left of the cursor, back to and including the error, and then type the correct characters. You can also eliminate unwanted space. For example, if you accidentally press [Enter] or [Space], you can use [Backspace] to return the cursor to where you want it. If you make an error and discover it some time later, you can use the arrow keys ([←], [→], [↑], and [↓]) to move the cursor to the error, delete the error, and type the correct characters.

To use the left arrow key to correct a typing error:

❶ Press **[Space]** and type **Semone**. This is a misspelled version of Andrea Simone's last name.

❷ Press **[←]** until the cursor is at the first "e" in "Semone." See Figure 1-21.

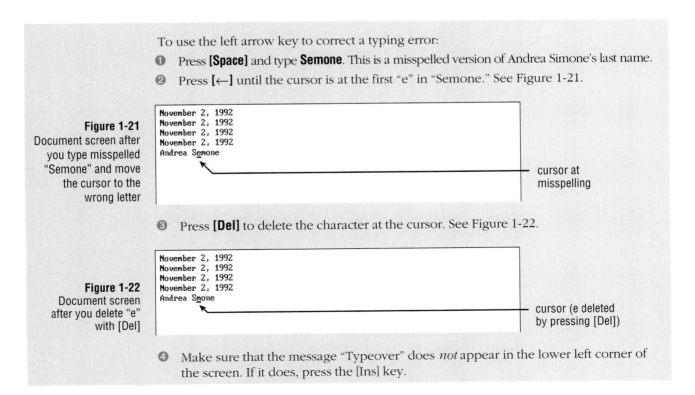

Figure 1-21
Document screen after
you type misspelled
"Semone" and move
the cursor to the
wrong letter

cursor at
misspelling

❸ Press **[Del]** to delete the character at the cursor. See Figure 1-22.

Figure 1-22
Document screen
after you delete "e"
with [Del]

cursor (e deleted
by pressing [Del])

❹ Make sure that the message "Typeover" does *not* appear in the lower left corner of the screen. If it does, press the [Ins] key.

⑤   Type **i** to insert the correct letter. See Figure 1-23.

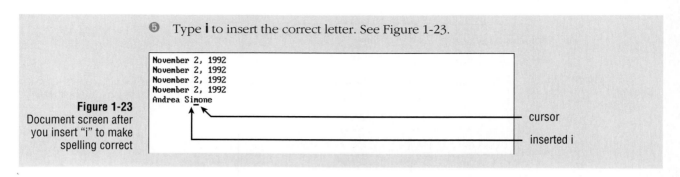

Figure 1-23
Document screen after
you insert "i" to make
spelling correct

cursor

inserted i

You'll learn other methods of correcting typing errors later in this tutorial and in future tutorials. Another mistake that all WordPerfect users make is pressing the wrong function key. In the following steps, you'll learn two ways to correct this kind of mistake: by pressing [F1] (Cancel) and by using a menu option to close a menu and return to the document screen.

To use the [F1] (Cancel) key to close a menu and return to the document screen:

❶   Press **[Shift][F5]** (Date/Outline).

WordPerfect displays a one-line menu on the status line at the bottom of the screen. Let's assume now that you really didn't want to press [Shift][F5] (Date/Outline), but you meant to press something else.

❷   Press **[F1]** (Cancel) to close the menu and return to the document screen.

Sometimes you may have to press [F1] (Cancel) more than once to get back to the document screen.

Now let's try the second way to correct pressing the wrong function key.

To use an option to close a menu and return to the document screen:

❶   Press **[Shift][F5]** (Date/Outline). A zero (0) appears on the far right side of the one-line menu on the status line. See Figure 1-24.

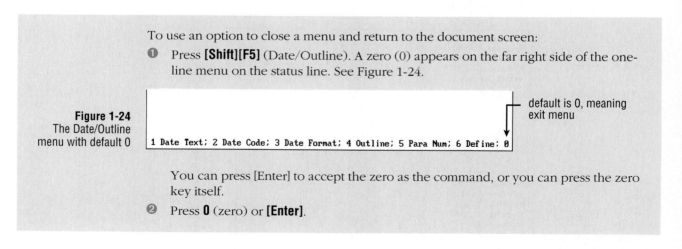

Figure 1-24
The Date/Outline
menu with default 0

1 Date Text; 2 Date Code; 3 Date Format; 4 Outline; 5 Para Num; 6 Define: 0

default is 0, meaning
exit menu

You can press [Enter] to accept the zero as the command, or you can press the zero key itself.

❷   Press **0** (zero) or **[Enter]**.

Most WordPerfect menus display a zero as an option. You can press the zero key or [Enter] to close the menu and return to the document screen.

Clearing the Document Screen

You are now ready to begin typing Andrea's letter to Learning Videos. But before you can type the letter, you must be sure that the WordPerfect document screen is clear. If you don't clear the screen before starting the letter, all the text that now appears on the document screen will be part of the document when you print it. Let's clear the screen now.

To clear the document screen:

① Select Exit from the File menu or press **[F7]** (Exit).

WordPerfect displays the prompt "Save document?" at the bottom of the screen and pauses for you to answer "yes" or "no." See Figure 1-25.

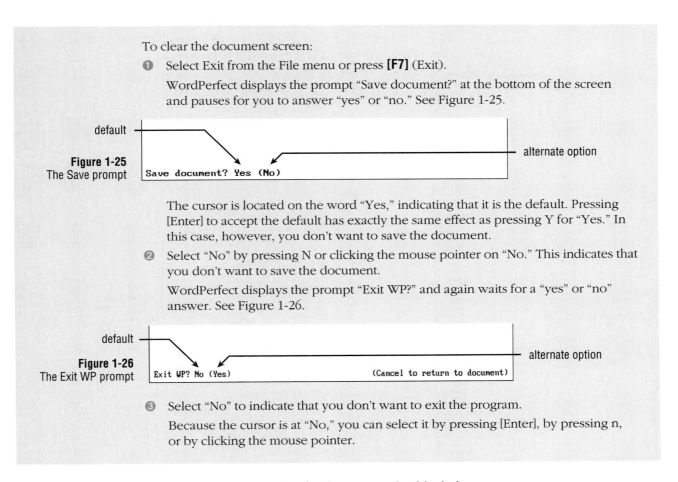

Figure 1-25
The Save prompt

default

alternate option

`Save document? Yes (No)`

The cursor is located on the word "Yes," indicating that it is the default. Pressing [Enter] to accept the default has exactly the same effect as pressing Y for "Yes." In this case, however, you don't want to save the document.

② Select "No" by pressing N or clicking the mouse pointer on "No." This indicates that you don't want to save the document.

WordPerfect displays the prompt "Exit WP?" and again waits for a "yes" or "no" answer. See Figure 1-26.

Figure 1-26
The Exit WP prompt

default

alternate option

`Exit WP? No (Yes)                    (Cancel to return to document)`

③ Select "No" to indicate that you don't want to exit the program.

Because the cursor is at "No," you can select it by pressing [Enter], by pressing n, or by clicking the mouse pointer.

You are still in WordPerfect but now with a blank document screen.

Entering Text

With a blank document screen on your computer monitor and the cursor at Ln 1" Pos 1", you're ready to type Andrea's letter (Figure 1-3). Let's begin by typing the date, the inside address, and the salutation of the letter.

To type the date, the inside address, and the salutation:

❶ Press **[Enter]** six times.

This moves the cursor down one inch from the top margin, giving a total of about two inches of space at the top of the page and allowing room for the Clearwater Valve Company letterhead. The line number on the status line should read Ln 2" (or some number close to 2), indicating that the cursor is two inches from the top of the page. See Figure 1-27. If you pressed [Enter] too many times, just press [Backspace] to delete the extra blank lines. If the line number on your screen has a slightly different value, like Ln 1.95 or Ln 2.12, don't worry. Different printers produce slightly different measurements when you press [Enter].

Andrea is now ready to insert the date.

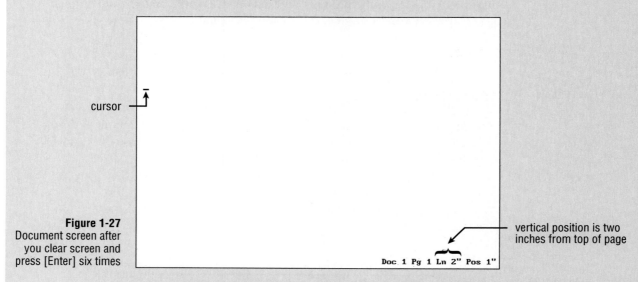

cursor

Figure 1-27
Document screen after you clear screen and press [Enter] six times

vertical position is two inches from top of page

Doc 1 Pg 1 Ln 2" Pos 1"

❷ Select Date Text from the Tools menu or press **[Shift][F5]** (Date/Outline) and select **1** (Date **T**ext). (The date that appears in your document most likely will differ from the date in Figure 1-3.)

❸ Press **[Enter]** twice to insert a double space between the date and the inside address.

Next Andrea enters the inside address, which she got from Steve's note.

❹ Type **Mr. Peter Argyle** and press **[Enter]**. Type **Learning Videos Inc.** and press **[Enter]**. Type **862 Pinewood Road, Suite #210** and press **[Enter]**. Finally, type **Pecos, TX 79772** and press **[Enter]** twice, once to end the line and once to add an extra blank line. See Figure 1-28.

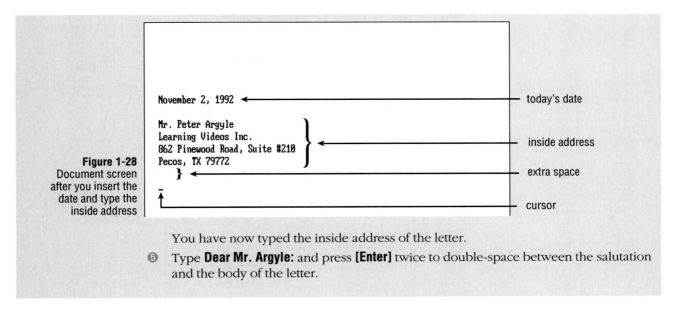

Figure 1-28
Document screen
after you insert the
date and type the
inside address

You have now typed the inside address of the letter.

⑤ Type **Dear Mr. Argyle:** and press **[Enter]** twice to double-space between the salutation and the body of the letter.

Andrea has now completed the date, the inside address, and the salutation of her letter, using a standard format for business letters. See Figure 1-29.

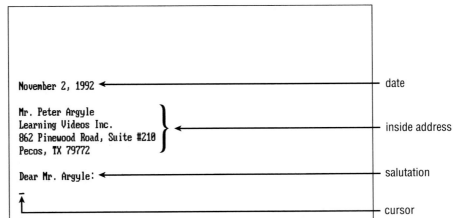

Figure 1-29
Document screen
after you type the
salutation

Saving a Document

The letter that you're typing is currently stored in your computer's memory but not on a disk. If you were to exit WordPerfect without saving your letter, turn off your computer, or experience an accidental power failure right now, the information you have typed would be lost. You should get in the habit of frequently saving your document to a disk. Unless a document is very short, don't wait until you've typed the whole document before saving it. As a rule of thumb, save your work about every 15 minutes.

Although Andrea hasn't been working on this letter for 15 minutes yet, she decides, just to be safe, to save the document now.

To save a document:

❶ Insert the WordPerfect data diskette into drive A and close the drive door.

This tutorial assumes that you have a hard disk — drive C — and at least one diskette drive.

❷ Select Save from the File menu. See Figure 1-30. Alternatively you can press [F10] (Save).

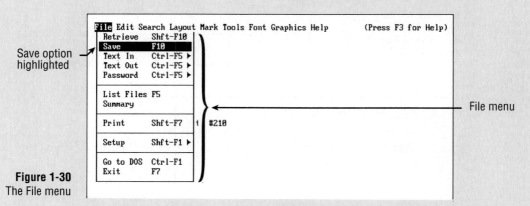

Save option highlighted →

Figure 1-30
The File menu

← File menu

WordPerfect displays the prompt "Document to be saved:" on the status line and waits for you to type a name for the document.

❸ Type **a:\s1file1.dft**. See Figure 1-31. Press **[Enter]**.

save prompt —

Figure 1-31
The Save prompt
with the filename

filename

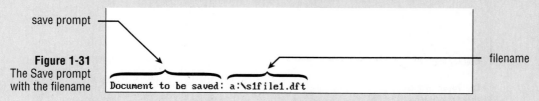

WordPerfect saves the document file to the diskette in drive A. If the error message "Drive not ready reading drive A. 1 Retry; 2 Cancel" appears, make sure the diskette in drive A is positioned properly and the drive door is completely closed. Then select 1 (Retry). If the error message "General failure reading drive A. 1 (Retry); 2 (Cancel)" appears, your diskette is probably not formatted. Remove it from the drive, insert a formatted diskette, close the drive door, and select 1 (Retry).

Figure 1-32 shows the process that occurs when you save a document. WordPerfect copies the file in the computer's memory to your computer's disk storage. Now identical copies of the file exist both in computer memory and on the diskette.

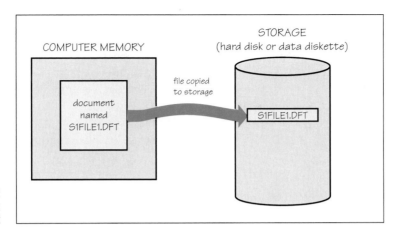

Figure 1-32
Process of saving a
document

After you save the document to the diskette, the path and filename of the document, "A:\S1FILE1.DFT," appear on the screen (Figure 1-33).

Figure 1-33
Status line showing
the path and the
document name

Document Filenames

Besides saving your documents frequently, another good habit to follow is to use descriptive filenames that help identify the contents of your files. Document filenames can be any legal DOS filename and may contain the path (such as "a:\" or "c:\wpfiles\"). The filename may contain from one to eight characters and may include a filename extension of one to three characters. In S1FILE1.DFT the filename extension DFT stands for "draft," indicating that this is Andrea's first draft of the letter.

Eight characters in the filename and three in the filename extension often don't allow you to use complete names, but you can at least create meaningful abbreviations. For example, since Andrea is writing a letter to Learning Videos Inc., she could save the final version of her letter with the filename LVI.LET, where LVI is an abbreviation of the name of the company, and LET reminds her that the document is a letter. If she were to write a memo to Clearwater employees about the 1992 budget, she might name the memo 92BUDGET.MEM, where the filename extension MEM stands for memo.

In this book, the six tutorials on WordPerfect involve many files. Therefore, we use filenames that will help you and your instructor recognize the origin and the content of the various documents. To name these files so you can recognize their contents, we have categorized them as follows:

File Category	Description
Tutorial Cases	The files you use to work through each tutorial
Tutorial Assignments	The files that contain the documents you need to complete the Tutorial Assignments at the end of each tutorial
Case Problems	The files that contain the documents you need to complete the Case Problems at the end of each tutorial
Saved Document	Any document you have saved

Let's take the filename S1FILE1.DFT, for example. At first glance this filename might appear to have no meaning, but it does contain meaningful abbreviations. The first character of the filename identifies the file as one of the four categories given above, as shown next:

If the first character is:	The file category is:
C	Tutorial **C**ase
T	**T**utorial Assignment
P	Case **P**roblem
S	**S**aved Document

Thus, S1FILE1.DFT is a document that you have saved.

The second character of the document filename identifies the tutorial from which the file comes. Thus, S1FILE1.DFT is a file you saved from Tutorial 1. The remaining six characters of the filename identify the specific file. All documents in the tutorials are named FILE, followed by a number. Each time you save a file, you will increase the number after FILE by 1. The filename extensions also help identify the file. A letter has the filename extension LET, a memo MEM, a report REP, and a draft of a document DFT. Thus, the filename S1FILE1.DFT tells you that this is the first draft that you saved in Tutorial 1.

The file T1FILE1.LET is the first document (a letter) found in the Tutorial Assignments from WordPerfect Tutorial 1, and C4FILE1.REP is the report you will use in a Tutorial Case for WordPerfect Tutorial 4. Files that you retrieve or save in the Tutorial Assignments and the Case Problems have a word or an abbreviation (other than FILE) to help identify the document. For example, P1IBM.LET is the filename of the Case Problem "Letter to IBM" from WordPerfect Tutorial 1.

Word Wrap

Having saved the first part of your document, you are now ready to complete the letter. As you type the body of the letter, do not press [Enter] at the end of each line. Instead allow WordPerfect to determine where one line ends and the next one begins. When you type a word that extends into the right margin, WordPerfect automatically moves the cursor and the word to the next line. This automatic movement of the cursor and a word to the next line is called **word wrap**. Word wrap ensures that each line of text is the proper length to fit between the left and right margins and eliminates the need for you to press [Enter] at the end of each line, as you would on a typewriter. If you happen to press [Enter] before word wrap occurs, press [Backspace] until the cursor moves back to the previous line, then continue typing. Let's see how word wrap works as you type the body of the letter.

To observe word wrap while you are typing a paragraph:

❶ Be sure the cursor is at the left edge of the screen and two lines below the salutation of the letter.

❷ Type **I have read the catalog description of your training video number**, press **[Space]**, and then slowly continue to type **LV18427**. As you type, notice that the cursor and LV18427 automatically jump to the next line. See Figure 1-34.

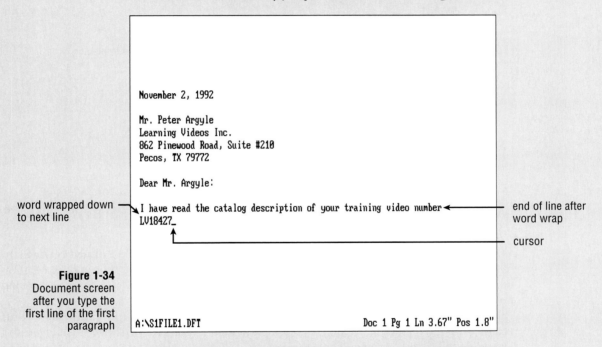

November 2, 1992

Mr. Peter Argyle
Learning Videos Inc.
862 Pinewood Road, Suite #210
Pecos, TX 79772

Dear Mr. Argyle:

word wrapped down to next line → I have read the catalog description of your training video number ← end of line after word wrap
LV18427_

cursor

A:\S1FILE1.DFT   Doc 1 Pg 1 Ln 3.67" Pos 1.8"

Figure 1-34
Document screen after you type the first line of the first paragraph

Because different printers have different sized letters and numbers, the word at which word wrap occurs in your document may be different.

❸ Type the rest of the first paragraph of the body of the letter. See Figure 1-35.

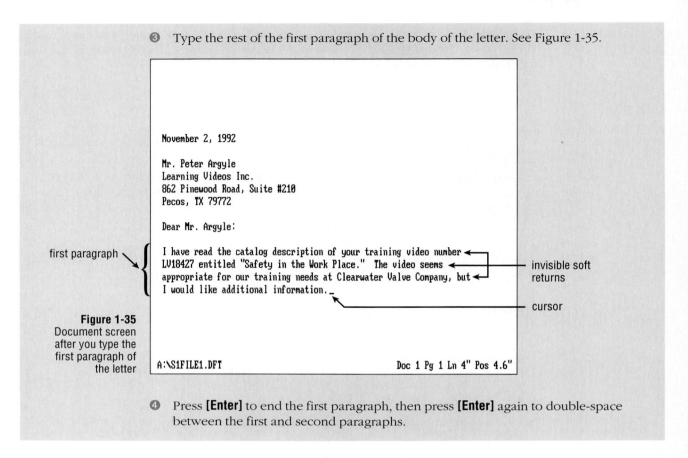

first paragraph

November 2, 1992

Mr. Peter Argyle
Learning Videos Inc.
862 Pinewood Road, Suite #210
Pecos, TX 79772

Dear Mr. Argyle:

I have read the catalog description of your training video number ◄——
LV18427 entitled "Safety in the Work Place." The video seems ◄——
appropriate for our training needs at Clearwater Valve Company, but ◄——
I would like additional information. _

invisible soft returns

cursor

Figure 1-35
Document screen after you type the first paragraph of the letter

A:\S1FILE1.DFT   Doc 1 Pg 1 Ln 4" Pos 4.6"

❹ Press **[Enter]** to end the first paragraph, then press **[Enter]** again to double-space between the first and second paragraphs.

When you press [Enter], WordPerfect inserts an invisible code called a **hard return** into the document to mark the end of a line or the end of a paragraph. The word or punctuation immediately preceding a hard return always ends a line, regardless of how long or short the line is.

When a line ends with a word wrap, WordPerfect inserts an invisible code called a **soft return** into the document to mark the end of the line (Figure 1-35). The words before and after a soft return are not necessarily permanent — if you later add text to or delete text from the line, the word at which word wrap occurs may change.

Remember the following rule: As you type, press [Enter] only at the end of a paragraph or where you want a line to definitely end. This allows WordPerfect to automatically insert soft returns so that each line of a paragraph fits between the left and right margins.

Let's continue entering the text of the letter.

To enter the second paragraph of the letter:
❶ Type the first line of the second paragraph. See Figure 1-36.

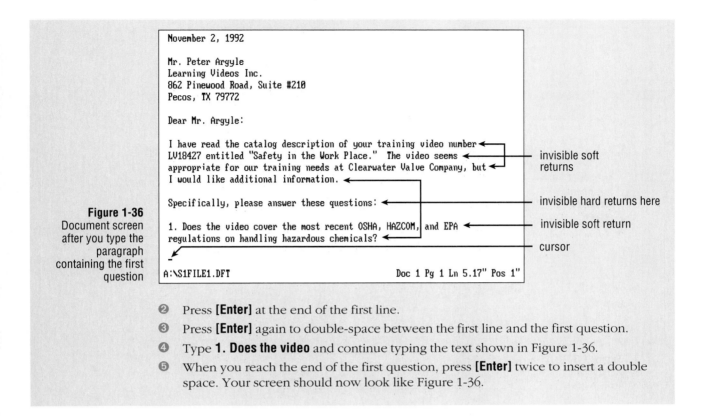

Figure 1-36
Document screen after you type the paragraph containing the first question

② Press **[Enter]** at the end of the first line.

③ Press **[Enter]** again to double-space between the first line and the first question.

④ Type **1. Does the video** and continue typing the text shown in Figure 1-36.

⑤ When you reach the end of the first question, press **[Enter]** twice to insert a double space. Your screen should now look like Figure 1-36.

Scrolling

As you can see in Figure 1-36, the cursor is at the bottom of the screen and the screen is essentially filled with text. In the steps that follow, you will see that as you continue typing the letter, the text on the screen will shift up, so that the beginning lines of the letter disappear off the top of the screen. This shifting up or down of text, called **scrolling**, allows you to see one screenful at a time of a long document. The entire document is still in the computer's memory and available for editing; you just can't see it all at once (Figure 1-37 on the next page). Let's see the effect of scrolling as you insert the next several lines of text into Andrea's letter.

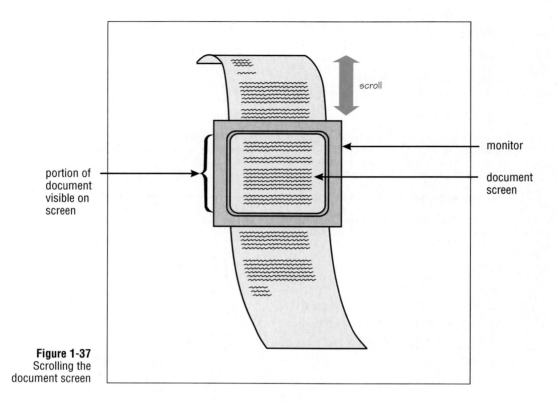

Figure 1-37
Scrolling the
document screen

To observe scrolling while you are entering text:

1. Make sure the cursor is at the bottom of the screen, two lines below the end of the first question.

2. Type the second question, shown in Figure 1-38, but stop before you press [Enter].

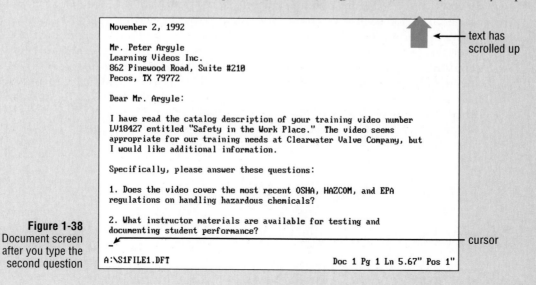

Figure 1-38
Document screen
after you type the
second question

❸ With the cursor just to the right of the question mark in question 2, press **[Enter]** twice and watch what happens to the date at the top of the screen. See Figure 1-38. Your screen might not scroll at this point but will later.

❹ Type **Your attention to this matter** and continue typing to the end of the paragraph, then press **[Enter]** twice. See Figure 1-39.

Figure 1-39
Document screen
after the date has
scrolled off the top
of the screen

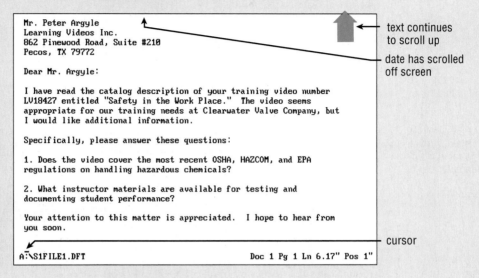

```
Mr. Peter Argyle
Learning Videos Inc.
862 Pinewood Road, Suite #210
Pecos, TX 79772

Dear Mr. Argyle:

I have read the catalog description of your training video number
LV18427 entitled "Safety in the Work Place."  The video seems
appropriate for our training needs at Clearwater Valve Company, but
I would like additional information.

Specifically, please answer these questions:

1. Does the video cover the most recent OSHA, HAZCOM, and EPA
regulations on handling hazardous chemicals?

2. What instructor materials are available for testing and
documenting student performance?

Your attention to this matter is appreciated.  I hope to hear from
you soon.

A:\S1FILE1.DFT                              Doc 1 Pg 1 Ln 6.17" Pos 1"
```

text continues
to scroll up

date has scrolled
off screen

cursor

As you can see in Figure 1-39, the date no longer appears on the document screen. When you pressed [Enter] at the bottom of the screen, the text above the cursor scrolled up so that the date is no longer in view.

You are now ready to type the complimentary close of Andrea's letter, as well as her signature block.

To finish typing the letter:

❶ Make sure the cursor is two lines below the last paragraph, which ends with "hear from you soon." See Figure 1-39.

❷ Type **Sincerely yours,** (including the comma).

❸ Press **[Enter]** four times to allow space for the signature.

❹   Type **Andrea Simone**, press **[Enter]**, and type **Executive Assistant**. See Figure 1-40.

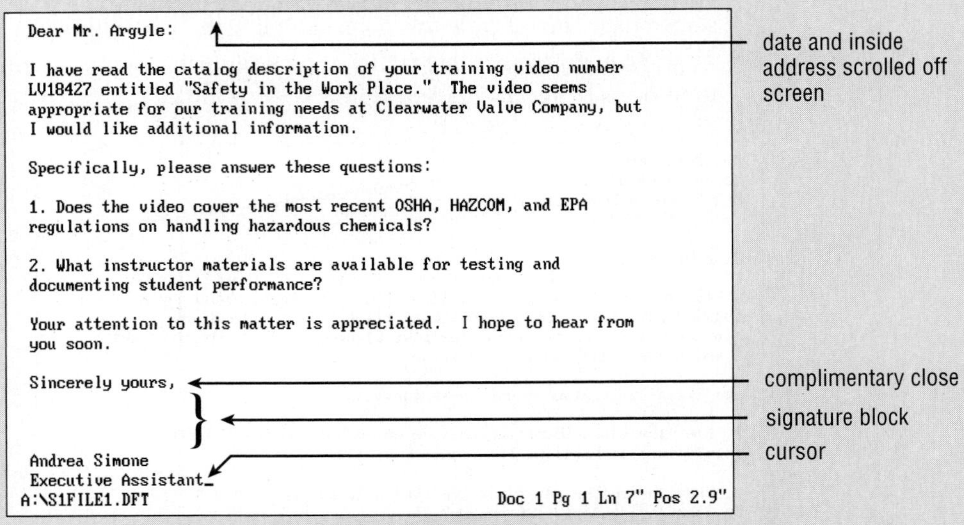

```
Dear Mr. Argyle:              ↑

I have read the catalog description of your training video number
LV18427 entitled "Safety in the Work Place."  The video seems
appropriate for our training needs at Clearwater Valve Company, but
I would like additional information.

Specifically, please answer these questions:

1. Does the video cover the most recent OSHA, HAZCOM, and EPA
regulations on handling hazardous chemicals?

2. What instructor materials are available for testing and
documenting student performance?

Your attention to this matter is appreciated.  I hope to hear from
you soon.

Sincerely yours,  ←

                  }  ←

Andrea Simone
Executive Assistant
A:\S1FILE1.DFT                              Doc 1 Pg 1 Ln 7" Pos 2.9"
```

date and inside
address scrolled off
screen

complimentary close

signature block

cursor

Figure 1-40
The document
screen after you type
the complimentary
close and the
signature block

As you type the last paragraph, the complimentary close and the signature block of the letter, the beginning lines of the letter scroll off the top of the screen so you can't see them any longer.

To see the beginning of the letter, you can use the arrow keys to scroll the text back into view.

To scroll the text using arrow keys:

❶   Press and hold down **[↑]** until the cursor is at the beginning of the letter and the line number reads Ln 1".

Notice that as you press **[↑]** when the cursor is at the top of the screen, the text of the letter scrolls down, so that the lines at the end of the letter disappear from the screen and the lines at the beginning reappear. When the cursor gets to the beginning of the document, scrolling stops because the cursor can't go any higher.

❷   Press and hold down **[↓]** until the cursor is at the end of the letter, on or below the line "Executive Assistant."

As you can see, the arrow keys allow you to scroll the document so you can move the cursor to part of the document that doesn't currently appear on the screen.

Take a few minutes to read over the letter you've just typed and compare it with Figure 1-3. Your letter should have the same text, but yours won't include the Clearwater letterhead, probably won't have the same date, and may have a different number of words on each line. Use the arrow keys ([↑], [↓], [→], and [←]) to move the cursor to various locations within the letter. If you find any errors, make the necessary corrections now.

Saving the Completed Letter

Having completed her letter, Andrea now wants to save the document to a diskette. Although she saved the letter earlier, the version currently on her diskette is incomplete. You must remember to save a document after you complete it, even though you've saved the document one or more times while you were creating it. Let's save the completed letter now.

To save the completed letter:

❶ Make sure the diskette you used earlier to save the partial letter is still in drive A.

It doesn't matter where the cursor is on the document screen when you save a document.

❷ Select Save from the File menu or press **[F10]** (Save).

WordPerfect displays the prompt "Document to be saved: A:\S1FILE1.DFT." Since you've already saved the file previously, WordPerfect displays the complete path and filename of the document.

❸ Press **[Enter]** to accept the given path and filename.

WordPerfect asks you if you want to replace the old version on the diskette with the new version on the screen. This is a helpful reminder that the filename you're using to save the document already exists on the diskette. If you didn't want to replace the current file on the diskette with the document file in memory, you would select "No" and then save the document using a new filename. In this case, however, you want to replace the old version with the new version.

❹ Select "Yes" to replace the old version with the new version.

The complete letter now exists as a document file on your diskette.

Previewing a Document

Andrea has completed her letter and is pleased with its content, organization, and style, but she really can't see the overall format of the letter. The document screen displays the text, but it doesn't show the margins or how the letter will fit onto the printed page.

Before Andrea prints the letter, she wants to make sure it has the proper format. WordPerfect provides a method for her to preview the letter before she prints it. Let's preview the letter you've just typed.

To preview a document:

❶ Select Print from the File menu or press **[Shift][F7]** (Print). WordPerfect displays the Print/Options menu. See Figure 1-41.

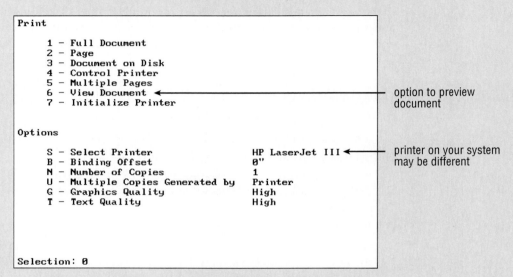

```
Print

        1 - Full Document
        2 - Page
        3 - Document on Disk
        4 - Control Printer
        5 - Multiple Pages
        6 - View Document          ◀─────   option to preview
        7 - Initialize Printer              document


Options

        S - Select Printer              HP LaserJet III  ◀──  printer on your system
        B - Binding Offset              0"                    may be different
        N - Number of Copies            1
        U - Multiple Copies Generated by    Printer
        G - Graphics Quality            High
        T - Text Quality                High



Selection: 0
```

Figure 1-41
The Print/Options menu

The Print command is found in the File menu because printing is an operation that deals with the entire document file.

❷ Select **6** (**V**iew Document).

A picture of the document appears on the screen with a one-line menu at the bottom of the screen. See Figure 1-42. If your monitor doesn't support graphics mode, WordPerfect displays an error message, since the View Document command works only with graphics monitors.

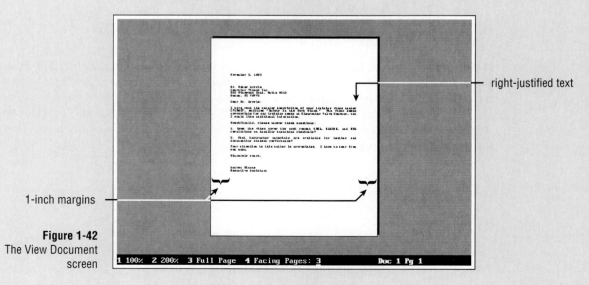

right-justified text

1-inch margins

Figure 1-42
The View Document screen

```
1 100%  2 200%  3 Full Page  4 Facing Pages: 3          Doc 1 Pg 1
```

❸ If you can't see the entire page of the letter, as shown in Figure 1-42, select **3** (Full Page).

Now you can see the one-inch margins on the left and right edges of the page. You can also see that the body of the letter will be printed with justified text, that is, the right edge of the text lines are aligned along the right margin.

The Full Page view lets you see how the entire page will look, but you can't actually read the text. To get a closer view of the document, you can select 1 (100%) to see the document in its actual size or 2 (200%) to see the document in twice its actual size.

❹ Select **1** (100%) to see the document in approximately its actual size.

Even in actual size the document is still hard to read on a graphics screen. For example, some of the commas may look like periods. Don't worry about this. When you print the document, it will be very readable.

❺ Press **[↓]** several times and **[↑]** several times to see how the page scrolls on the screen.

❻ Press **[F7]** (Exit) when you are ready to exit the *View Document* option and return to the normal document screen.

Andrea is satisfied with the format of the letter.

Printing a Document

Having typed, saved, and previewed the document, Andrea is now ready to print it. Let's print the letter now.

To print a document currently on the document screen:

❶ Make sure your printer is turned on and the paper is properly adjusted in the printer. If you have questions about setting up your printer for use with WordPerfect, see your technical support person.

❷ Select Print from the File menu or press **[Shift][F7]** (Print).

❸ Select **1** (**F**ull Document) to print the entire document.

WordPerfect prints the entire letter. Your printed letter should look similar to Figure 1-3, but without the letterhead.

Exiting WordPerfect

Andrea has now finished typing and printing her letter to Learning Videos Inc., so she is ready to exit WordPerfect. She knows that she should never just turn off the computer without first properly exiting WordPerfect. Let's see how to exit WordPerfect properly.

To exit WordPerfect:

❶ Select Exit from the File menu or press **[F7]** (Exit).

WordPerfect displays the prompt "Save document?" and waits for you to select "Yes" or "No." Since you have saved the document since the last modification, the message "(Text was not modified)" appears on the right side of the status line.

❷ Since you've already saved the completed document to the disk, select "No." (If you hadn't saved your document yet, you would select "Yes," type the document name, and press [Enter].) WordPerfect displays the prompt "Exit WP?" and again waits for you to select "Yes" or "No."

❸ Select "Yes" to exit WordPerfect. If you select "No" by accident, WordPerfect clears the document screen but leaves you in WordPerfect. In that case, repeat Steps 1 through 3.

You have now exited WordPerfect. The cursor returns to the DOS prompt if you entered WordPerfect from DOS or to a menu program if you entered WordPerfect through a menu.

Retrieving a Document

After Andrea types, saves, and prints the draft version of the letter to Learning Videos Inc., she gives the printed copy of the letter to her supervisor, Steve Morgan. Steve reads the letter and makes a note to Andrea to include a question about volume discounts (Figure 1-43). After she adds this question, Andrea will print the letter and mail it.

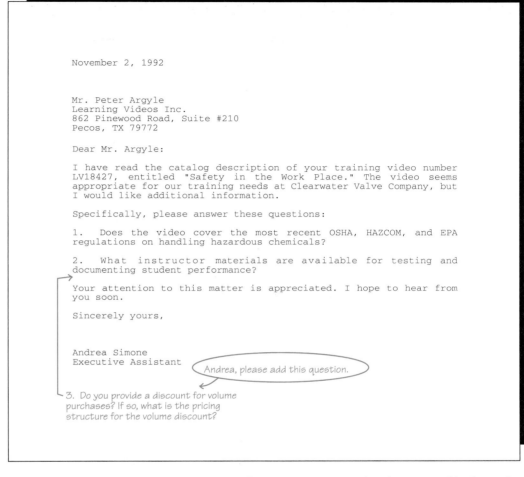

Figure 1-43
Andrea's draft with
Steve's addition

Andrea now needs to start WordPerfect again, retrieve the document file from the diskette into computer memory, add a third question to the letter, save the revised letter, and print the final version of the letter.

To retrieve a document file onto the document screen:

❶ Start WordPerfect as you did earlier, in the section "Starting WordPerfect."

❷ Make sure the document screen is blank.

   If necessary, clear the screen as explained in the section "Clearing the Document Screen."

❸ With a blank document screen, select Retrieve from the File menu or press **[Shift][F10]** (Retrieve).

   WordPerfect displays the prompt "Document to be retrieved:" and waits for you to type the document name.

❹ Make sure the diskette on which you saved the letter is in drive A.

❺ Type **a:\s1file1.dft** and press **[Enter]**.

WordPerfect retrieves the document from the diskette onto the document screen. See Figure 1-44.

cursor →

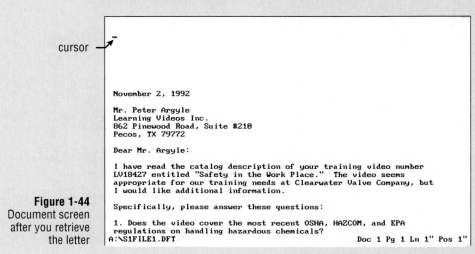

```
November 2, 1992

Mr. Peter Argyle
Learning Videos Inc.
862 Pinewood Road, Suite #210
Pecos, TX 79772

Dear Mr. Argyle:

I have read the catalog description of your training video number
LV18427 entitled "Safety in the Work Place."  The video seems
appropriate for our training needs at Clearwater Valve Company, but
I would like additional information.

Specifically, please answer these questions:

1. Does the video cover the most recent OSHA, HAZCOM, and EPA
regulations on handling hazardous chemicals?
A:\S1FILE1.DFT                                    Doc 1 Pg 1 Ln 1" Pos 1"
```

Figure 1-44
Document screen
after you retrieve
the letter

When you retrieve a document from the diskette, WordPerfect copies the document file into the computer's memory (Figure 1-45). A copy of the document file remains on the diskette.

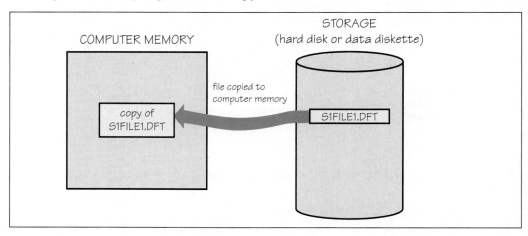

Figure 1-45
The process of
retrieving a file

Now that she has retrieved the file, Andrea is ready to make the addition to the letter as Steve requested. Let's modify the letter now.

To modify the letter:

❶ Press [↓] and [→] to move the cursor to the end of question 2, immediately after the phrase ". . . documenting student performance?"

❷ Make sure "Typeover" doesn't appear in the lower left corner of the screen. If it does, press [Ins].

❸ Press [**Enter**] twice to insert a double space after question 2.

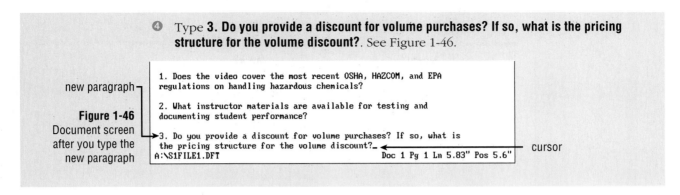

❹ Type **3. Do you provide a discount for volume purchases? If so, what is the pricing structure for the volume discount?**. See Figure 1-46.

new paragraph ⌐

Figure 1-46
Document screen
after you type the
new paragraph

```
1. Does the video cover the most recent OSHA, HAZCOM, and EPA
regulations on handling hazardous chemicals?

2. What instructor materials are available for testing and
documenting student performance?

3. Do you provide a discount for volume purchases? If so, what is
the pricing structure for the volume discount?_
A:\S1FILE1.DFT                               Doc 1 Pg 1 Ln 5.83" Pos 5.6"
```

cursor

The letter is now modified the way Steve wants it. Andrea looks over the letter one last time for any errors. She is ready to print the final version. But before she prints the letter, she realizes that she has to save this new, final version since the letter on the screen is different from the one on the diskette. Let's save the final version now.

To save the final version of the letter with a new filename:

❶ Select Save from the File menu or press **[F10]** (Save).

WordPerfect displays the prompt "Document to be saved: A:\S1FILE1.DFT." Remember, the name of the file of the document on the screen automatically appears in the prompt. But because this is the second time you're saving the letter and because you want to keep the previous version of the letter, now saved in S1FILE1.DFT, you'll use a new filename.

❷ Type **a:\s1file2.let** and press **[Enter]**.

Now a copy of the final letter on the screen is saved on the diskette as S1FILE2.LET. See Figure 1-47.

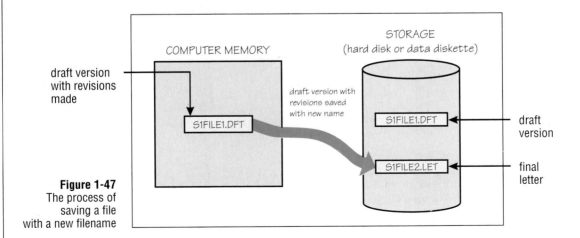

Figure 1-47
The process of
saving a file
with a new filename

This completes Andrea Simone's letter to Learning Videos Inc. She can now print the final copy of the letter.

❸ Print the document. See Figure 1-48.

will not appear on your document →

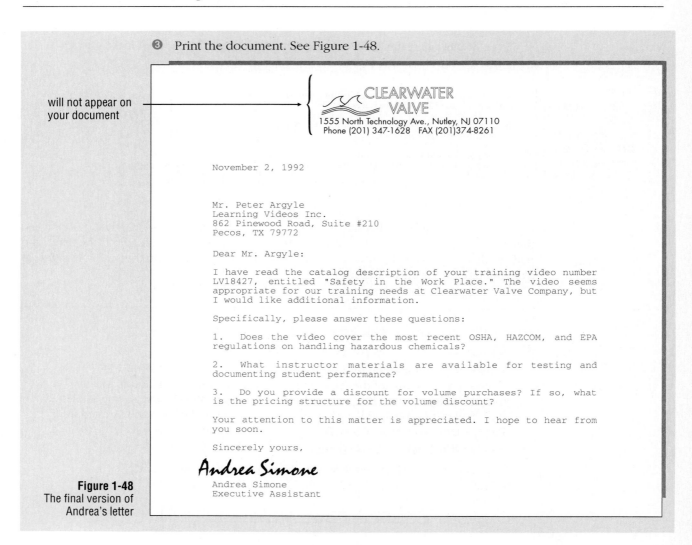

CLEARWATER VALVE
1555 North Technology Ave., Nutley, NJ 07110
Phone (201) 347-1628   FAX (201)374-8261

November 2, 1992

Mr. Peter Argyle
Learning Videos Inc.
862 Pinewood Road, Suite #210
Pecos, TX 79772

Dear Mr. Argyle:

I have read the catalog description of your training video number
LV18427, entitled "Safety in the Work Place." The video seems
appropriate for our training needs at Clearwater Valve Company, but
I would like additional information.

Specifically, please answer these questions:

1.   Does the video cover the most recent OSHA, HAZCOM, and EPA
regulations on handling hazardous chemicals?

2.   What instructor materials are available for testing and
documenting student performance?

3.   Do you provide a discount for volume purchases? If so, what
is the pricing structure for the volume discount?

Your attention to this matter is appreciated. I hope to hear from
you soon.

Sincerely yours,

Andrea Simone

Andrea Simone
Executive Assistant

Figure 1-48
The final version of
Andrea's letter

Exercises

1. If the cursor is at the DOS prompt and in the directory where the WordPerfect program is located, what do you type to start WordPerfect?

2. What does the status line message Ln 2" mean?

3. What does the status line message Pos 3.5" mean?

4. List two ways you can automatically insert today's date into a WordPerfect document.

5. How would you find out information on using [Del] (delete key) in WordPerfect?

6. What are the default margin settings in WordPerfect?

7. With the cursor in the document screen, what key(s) would you press to do the following?
   a. Display the menu bar
   b. Clear the WordPerfect document screen
   c. Double-space between paragraphs
   d. Move the cursor one character to the left
   e. Print the document that is on the document screen
   f. Exit WordPerfect

8. Define the following WordPerfect terms:
   a. Word wrap   f. Pull-down menu
   b. Retrieve   g. Scrolling
   c. Default format settings h. Mnemonic letter
   d. Function-key template   i. Hard return
   e. Document screen   j. Soft return

9. Name and describe four steps in planning a document.

10. Why should you usually save a document to your disk several times even before you finish typing it?

Tutorial Assignments

Be sure your WordPerfect data diskette is in drive A and clear the document screen. Then retrieve the file T1FILE1.DFT and do the following:

1. Delete the current date at the beginning of the letter, then use WordPerfect's Date Text command to insert today's date into the document.

2. Save the letter as S1FILE1.LET.

3. Preview the document to see what it will look like before you print it.

4. Print the document.

Clear the document screen, retrieve the letter T1FILE2.DFT from your data diskette and do the following:

5. In the body of the memo delete the space between "Clear" and "Water," and then delete the "W" and insert "w" so the word reads "Clearwater" instead of "Clear Water."

6. Save the document as S1FILE2.MEM.

7. Print the document.

Use Figure 1-49 to complete Assignments 8 through 12.

Date: November 13, 1992

To: Andrea Simone, Executive Assistant, Operations

From: Roberta Caldwell, Human Resources Manager

Re: Safety Training

Thanks for your help in setting up the safety training for our employees. Your care and
attention to detail in selecting training videos, scheduling, instructors, and keeping training
records has been extremely beneficial to Clearwater Valve Company.

cc: Steve Morgan

Figure 1-49

8. Type the memo, pressing [Space] twice after "Date:," "To:," "From:," and "Re:." For now
    use the date shown in the memo.

9. Delete the date in the memo and use WordPerfect's Date Text feature to insert today's date.

10. Save the memo as S1FILE3.MEM.

11. Preview the memo before printing it.

12. Print the memo.

Case Problems

1. Letter to IBM

Joseph Cardon is the manager of information systems for the public accounting firm of
Armstrong, Black & Calzone. One of his responsibilities is to recommend which brand of
personal computers employees should use. After reading an advertisement in which IBM
Corporation offers a free copy of the book *How To Buy a Personal Computer for Your Small
Business*, Joseph decides to write a letter requesting the book. He has already written the
body of the letter and now needs only to insert the date, the inside address, the salutation,
the complimentary close, and his name and title.

Retrieve the document P1IBM.LET from your data diskette and do the following:

1. Move the cursor to the beginning of the document and press [Enter] six times to insert
    sufficient space for a letterhead.

2. Use WordPerfect's Date Text feature to insert today's date.

3. Insert four blank lines after the date and, using the proper business-letter format, type the inside address: **IBM Corporation, P.O. Box 92835, Rochester, NY 14692**.

4. Insert a blank line after the inside address, then type the salutation **Dear Company Officers:**. Then insert another blank line.

5. Move the cursor to the end of the document and type the complimentary close and your name and title.

6. Save the letter as S1IBM.LET.

7. Preview the letter.

8. Print the letter.

2. Memo to Congratulate a Colleague

One of your colleagues at Clearwater Valve Company, Debora Stern, was recently given a company award as sales representative of the year.

1. Write a memo to Debora Stern congratulating her on receiving the award. Remember to use the four-part planning process. You should plan the content, organization, and style of the memo, and use the standard memo format shown in Figure 1-50.

Date:	*(today's date)*
To:	*(the name of the person to whom you are writing this memo)*
From:	*(your name)*
Re:	*(a brief description of the subject of the memo)*

Figure 1-50

2. Save the document as S1STERN.MEM.

3. Preview the memo.

4. Print the memo.

3. Letter of Introduction to a Prospective Client

Suppose you're a sales representative for Clearwater Valve Company. You have a list of prospective clients, one of whom is Mr. Ken Kikuchi of CryoTech Pharmaceuticals, 891 Avocado Avenue, Escondido, CA 92925.

1. Write a letter introducing yourself to Mr. Kikuchi and request the opportunity to visit him and others at CryoTech Pharmaceuticals.

2. Save the letter as S1CRYO.LET.

3. Preview the letter.

4. Print the letter.

Tutorial 2

Formatting and Editing a Document

Writing a Product Information Memo for an Ad Launch

Case: Decision Development Corporation

David Truong is an assistant product manager at Decision Development Corporation (DDC), a company that specializes in business software tools. David reports to Liz Escobar, the product manager. One of David's responsibilities is to write product description memos to the DDC advertising group explaining the key features and benefits of new products. The advertising group uses these memos to help them prepare for the launch meetings, at which the advertising campaigns for new products are planned.

Liz has just stopped by David's office and asked him to write a product description memo to the ad group about DDC's newest product, InTrack, an investment tracking program. Liz reminds David that, as usual, she wants him to submit his first draft to her for comments and corrections. After she returns the draft to him, he should make the necessary changes and print three copies of the memo — one for the advertising group, one for her, and one for the InTrack product file.

In this tutorial you'll plan, write, and edit David's memo for the ad launch.

OBJECTIVES

In this tutorial you will learn to:

- Make large-scale cursor moves
- Change margins
- Justify text
- Boldface and underline text
- Reveal hidden format codes
- Indent a paragraph
- Delete words and lines of text and undo deletions
- Use the insert and typeover modes
- Insert a hard page break
- Use the speller and the thesaurus
- Print multiple copies of a document

Planning the Document

First David plans the four components of the document. He considers content, organization, style, and format.

Content

David has kept notes on the key features of InTrack and has a copy of the program specifications produced by the company software design team. His notes contain information he can use for the content of his product description memo. As he reads these notes, David realizes that they contain much more information than he needs to put in the memo. He decides to distill this information so the advertising group will understand the product and still have the necessary details to write the text of the advertisements, commonly called ad copy. He assumes that the ad group is familiar with computer software, so he feels free to use computer jargon.

Organization

Because the product description is a memo, David knows that his document will begin with the standard memo heading. He decides that the body of the memo will be a numbered list of the key features of InTrack.

Style

David assumes that the ad group will adapt and edit his information to a style that suits the needs of the ad campaign. His style, therefore, will be clear and straightforward, the best way to convey product information.

Format

David decides that in his first draft he will use WordPerfect's default format settings, which include one-inch margins and text aligned along the right margin. He knows that Liz might suggest format changes, but for now he'll use the defaults.

■   ■   ■

Having planned the document, David creates the rough draft of the memo. He submits it to Liz, who later returns the draft with her editing marks and notes (Figure 2-1). David looks over her comments and is ready to create the final draft of the InTrack product description memo.

Indent to 1.5" for 3-ring binder holes

DATE: January 15, 1993

TO: Advertising Group

FROM: David Truong, Assistant Product Manager
RE: *Product Description of InTrack*

turn off justification to make more informal

Liz has asked me to provide you the following list of key features of **InTrack** to help you plan the advertising campaign:

indent all para-graphs

run speller!

1. **InTrack** is a sophisticated yet easy-to-use investemnt management system. Customers will use the software to post all of their investment transactions; track commissions, dividends, and interest; create value projections; create tax information; and print reports on investment performance, portfolio values, capitol gains, investment income, and so forth. The mouse-supported menu-driven user interface is powerful and easy to learn.

repetitious; use better words

2. **InTrack** helps customers ~~keep~~ track ~~of~~ mutual funds, bonds, stocks, money market funds, certificats of deposit (CDs), real estate, annuities, trusts, and almost any other type of investment. ~~Customers can use the program to keep track of any kind of investment they want.~~

3. **InTrack** can be customized for any type of investment. Customers can print reports using built-in forms or can design their own reports.

4. **InTrack** is ideal for managing IRAs and Keog Plans. The the program will forecast the potential monthly and annual retirement income derived from IRAs and Keogh Plans.

5. **InTrack** provides internal telecommunications support. CUstomers can use the program to get on-line financial information from most of the electronic information services. Customers can also carry out transactions with their broker directly from within **InTrack**. *Dave, doesn't broker have to own InTrack?*

6. **InTrack** pays easily for itself within the first year of use, because (a) the program costs less than other products of this type on the market, (b) the cost of the program is tax deductible, (c) the program simplifies tax preparation, and (d) the program provides the necessary information to make smart investment decisions and allows customers to get the most return on their investment dollar.

3.0 (or higher)

7. **InTrack** runs on any IBM-compatible personal computer under DOS 3.2 (or higher) or under Windows. The program does not require a hard disk drive, but one is highly recommended. The fully installed program, with all features and auxiliary files, requires about 3.4 megabytes of disk space.

wasn't this lower?   *Dave, what about other hardware options?*

Figure 2-1
The ad launch memo with Liz's edits and notes

In the instructions on editing the memo, you'll be given a choice of whether to use pull-down menus (with the keyboard or with the mouse) or to use the function-key template and the function keys to execute WordPerfect commands. You'll remember from Tutorial 1 that to use the pull-down menus you press [Alt][=] or the right mouse button to display the menu bar at the top of the document screen. Then you select a menu item by pressing the highlighted mnemonic key, by using an arrow key to highlight the menu item and pressing [Enter], or by clicking on the menu item. To use the template and a function key to execute a command, you press a modifier key ([Shift], [Alt], or [Ctrl]), if any, and a function key. We'll tell you the function-key combination to press and the name of the WordPerfect command listed on the function-key template. When a pull-down menu option or function-key command causes WordPerfect to display a menu, you select the appropriate option from that menu by pressing the number or mnemonic letter corresponding to the desired option or by clicking the mouse on that option.

Retrieving the Document

David begins by retrieving the first draft of his memo, which has the filename C2FILE1.DFT. The filename extension .DFT stands for "draft." Let's retrieve the memo now.

To retrieve the document:

❶ Start WordPerfect (if you haven't done so already) and make sure the document screen is clear. If necessary, refer to Tutorial 1 to see how to clear the document screen.

❷ Insert your WordPerfect data diskette into drive A and close the disk drive door.

❸ Select Retrieve from the File menu or press **[Shift][F10]** (Retrieve). The prompt "Document to be retrieved:" appears on the status line at the bottom of the screen.

❹ Type **a:\c2file1.dft** and press **[Enter]**. The rough draft of David Truong's memo appears on the screen. See Figure 2-2.

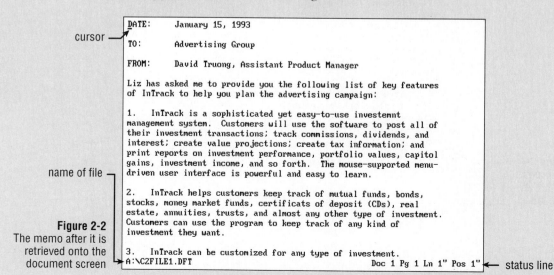

cursor ⟶

name of file ⟶

Figure 2-2
The memo after it is retrieved onto the document screen

status line ⟵

```
DATE:      January 15, 1993

TO:        Advertising Group

FROM:      David Truong, Assistant Product Manager

Liz has asked me to provide you the following list of key features
of InTrack to help you plan the advertising campaign:

1.   InTrack is a sophisticated yet easy-to-use investemnt
management system.  Customers will use the software to post all of
their investment transactions; track commissions, dividends, and
interest; create value projections; create tax information; and
print reports on investment performance, portfolio values, capitol
gains, investment income, and so forth.  The mouse-supported menu-
driven user interface is powerful and easy to learn.

2.   InTrack helps customers keep track of mutual funds, bonds,
stocks, money market funds, certificats of deposit (CDs), real
estate, annuities, trusts, and almost any other type of investment.
Customers can use the program to keep track of any kind of
investment they want.

3.   InTrack can be customized for any type of investment.
A:\C2FILE1.DFT                            Doc 1 Pg 1 Ln 1" Pos 1"
```

Making Large-Scale Cursor Moves

You're already familiar with the arrow keys ([→], [←], [↑], and [↓]) to move the cursor one character to the right or left or one line up or down. Now you'll see how to move the cursor more than one character or one line at a time. You should make an effort now to learn and remember these large-scale cursor moves because they will save you considerable time and energy when you have to move the cursor around to different parts of your documents.

In the following steps, you'll see how to move the cursor quickly from one place to another within the document.

Also, as you work through the following steps, you may notice several typographical and spelling errors. Don't correct the errors at this time. They appear in the document to help you learn various ways of editing the text and correcting the spelling.

To make large-scale cursor moves:

❶ Press **[Home]**, **[Home]**, and **[↓]**.

This sequence of keystrokes is separated by commas, meaning that you should press each key separately but don't type the commas. Notice that pressing these keys moves the cursor to the end of the document.

❷ Press **[Home]**, **[Home]**, and **[↑]** to move the cursor to the beginning of the document.

❸ Press **[↓]** enough times to move the cursor to the "1" in the first numbered paragraph of the memo. See Figure 2-3.

```
DATE:      January 15, 1993

TO:        Advertising Group

FROM:      David Truong, Assistant Product Manager

Liz has asked me to provide you the following list of key features
of InTrack to help you plan the advertising campaign:

1.   InTrack is a sophisticated yet easy-to-use investemnt
management system.  Customers will use the software to post all of
their investment transactions; track commissions, dividends, and
interest; create value projections; create tax information; and
print reports on investment performance, portfolio values, capitol
gains, investment income, and so forth.  The mouse-supported menu-
driven user interface is powerful and easy to learn.

2.   InTrack helps customers keep track of mutual funds, bonds,
stocks, money market funds, certificats of deposit (CDs), real
estate, annuities, trusts, and almost any other type of investment.
Customers can use the program to keep track of any kind of
investment they want.

3.   InTrack can be customized for any type of investment.
A:\C2FILE1.DFT                              Doc 1 Pg 1 Ln 2.5" Pos 1"
```

cursor →

Figure 2-3
The cursor position at
paragraph 1

❹ Press **[End]** to move the cursor to the end of the current line. This method is much faster in moving the cursor to the end of the line than if you repeatedly press [→] until the cursor gets to the end of the line.

❺ Press **[Home]** and **[←]** to move the cursor to the beginning of the current line.

❻ Press **[Ctrl][→]** (Word Right) three times to move your cursor to the word "a," then press **[Ctrl][←]** (Word Left) three times to move the cursor back to the "1."

As you can see, [Ctrl][→] moves the cursor one word to the right, and [Ctrl][←] moves the cursor one word to the left.

❼ With Num Lock off, press **[+]** (Screen Down) on the numeric keypad once to move the cursor to the bottom of the screen. Press it again to move the cursor down another screen. See Figure 2-4. Your screen may look different due to differences in font size.

cursor ⌐

```
the program simplifies tax preparation, and (d) the program
provides the necessary information to make smart investment
decisions and allows customers to get the most return on their
investment dollar.

7.   InTrack runs on any IBM-compatible personal computer under DOS
3.2 (or higher) or under Windows.  The program does not require a
hard disk drive, but one is highly recommended.  The fully
A:\C2FILE1.DFT                               Doc 1 Pg 1 Ln 8.83" Pos 1"
```

Figure 2-4
The cursor after you use the Screen Down command

Pressing [+] on the keypad with Num Lock off moves the cursor to the bottom of the current screen. When you press it again, the cursor moves to the bottom of the next screenful of text. You must remember to use the plus-sign key [+] *on the keypad* and to have Num Lock off. If you press the plus key on the typewriter section of the keyboard or on the keypad with Num Lock on, a plus character will be inserted into the document.

❽ Press **[−]** (Screen Up) on the numeric keypad twice.

Pressing [−] on the keypad once moves the cursor to the top of the current screen. Pressing it again moves the cursor up another screenful. See Figure 2-5. Your cursor might be in a slightly different position because of differences in font size.

cursor at beginning of document ⌐

```
DATE:      January 15, 1993

TO:        Advertising Group

FROM:      David Truong, Assistant Product Manager

Liz has asked me to provide you the following list of key features
of InTrack to help you plan the advertising campaign:

1.   InTrack is a sophisticated yet easy-to-use investemnt
management system.  Customers will use the software to post all of
their investment transactions; track commissions, dividends, and
interest; create value projections; create tax information; and
print reports on investment performance, portfolio values, capitol
gains, investment income, and so forth.  The mouse-supported menu-
```

Figure 2-5
The cursor after you use the Screen Up command

The cursor-movement keys demonstrated in the preceding steps are only a few of the many ways you can move the cursor in WordPerfect. Figure 2-6 lists most of the WordPerfect cursor-movement commands. You'll use some of the other cursor-movement keys in later tutorials.

Cursor Key	Movement
[←]	Left one character
[→]	Right one character
[↑]	Up one line
[↓]	Down one line
[Ctrl][←]	Left one word
[Ctrl][→]	Right one word
[Home], [←]	Far left side of screen
[Home], [→]	Far right side of screen
[Home], [Home], [←]	Beginning of line (even when the line extends beyond the left edge of the screen)
[Home], [Home], [→] or [End]	End of line (even when the line extends beyond the right edge of the screen)
[Home], [↑] or keypad [-]	Top of screen, then up one screen at a time
[Home], [↓] or keypad [+]	Bottom of screen, then down one screen at a time
[PgUp]	First line of previous page
[PgDn]	First line of next page
[Home], [Home], [↑]	Beginning of document (after any formatting codes)
[Home], [Home], [↓]	End of document (after any formatting codes)

Figure 2-6
WordPerfect
cursor-movement
keys

As you move the cursor through a document, you'll discover that the cursor won't move to a region of the screen not occupied by text. If the cursor were at the end of a document, for example, and you pressed [+] (Screen Down), the cursor wouldn't move, since it couldn't go down lower than the end of the document. Similarly if the cursor were at the end of a short line of text and you pressed [→], the cursor wouldn't go any farther to the right, but would move to the first character of the next line.

Sometimes as you move the cursor through a document, you'll see WordPerfect reformat the screen by shifting text left or right, wrapping words from one line to another, and so forth. This happens because some format changes don't actually appear on the screen until you move the cursor through the affected text.

Changing Margins

David's first task in editing the memo is to increase the left margin to 1.5 inches. Because the left margin affects the length of text lines, David will use the Line menu to change the margin. Let's change the margin now.

To change the left margin:

❶ Press **[Home]**, **[Home]**, **[↑]** to make sure the cursor is at the beginning of the document.

If you want to change a margin for an entire document, you must move the cursor to the beginning of the document before you set the new margin value. If you were to change a margin or other format value when the cursor was in the middle of the document, the change would be in effect only from the location of the cursor to the end of the document.

❷ Select Line from the Layout menu (Figure 2-7).

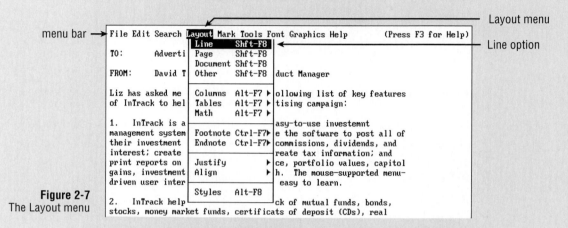

Figure 2-7
The Layout menu

Alternatively, press **[Shift][F8]** (Format) to display the menu shown in Figure 2-8, and select **1** (**Line**).

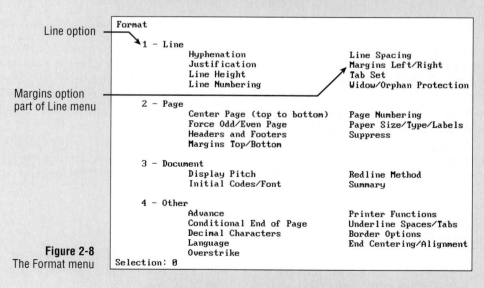

Figure 2-8
The Format menu

The Format: Line menu now appears on the screen. See Figure 2-9. You'll learn the meaning of the many Line commands as you go through these tutorials. For now you are interested only in option 7 (Margins). To the right of this option WordPerfect displays the current margins: Left 1" and Right 1". You want to change the value for the left margin.

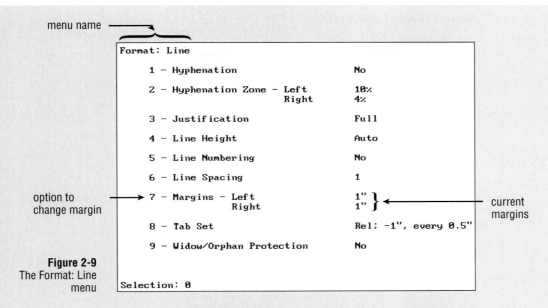

menu name

```
Format: Line

    1 - Hyphenation                        No

    2 - Hyphenation Zone - Left            10%
                          Right            4%

    3 - Justification                      Full

    4 - Line Height                        Auto

    5 - Line Numbering                     No

    6 - Line Spacing                       1

    7 - Margins - Left                     1"
                 Right                     1"  }

    8 - Tab Set                            Rel; -1", every 0.5"

    9 - Widow/Orphan Protection            No


Selection: 0
```

option to change margin

current margins

Figure 2-9
The Format: Line menu

③ Select **7** (**M**argins).

To select this option you can press 7, press M, or click the mouse pointer on "7 - Margins." The cursor moves to the right of the Margin option. You can now type the new value for the left margin.

As Figure 2-1 shows, Liz asked David to make the left margin 1½ inches.

④ Type **1.5** and press **[Enter]**.

The cursor moves to the value for the right margin. If you wanted to change that value, you would type a new number. But in this case, you want to leave the right margin at 1 inch, because Liz didn't ask David to change the right margin.

⑤ Press **[Enter]** to accept the current value.

As a general rule in WordPerfect, you just press [Enter] to accept a current setting, value, or name.

⑥ Press **[F7]** (Exit) to exit the Format: Line menu and return to the main document.

The text along the left margin moves to the right. See Figure 2-10. Your screen may not show the full effect of changing the margin until you move the cursor down through the text or you tell WordPerfect to "rewrite" the screen, that is, to show you what the entire screen looks like with any changes.

margin increased by 0.5 inch

cursor

1.5 inches from left edge of paper

Figure 2-10
Document screen after you change the left margin

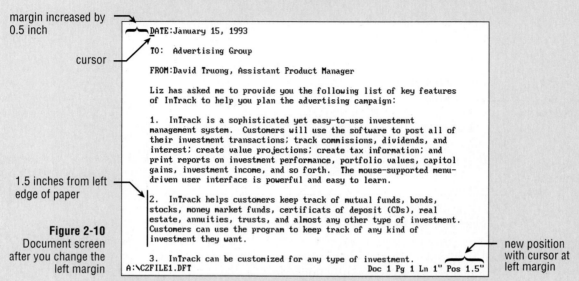

new position with cursor at left margin

⑦ Make sure the cursor is on the "D" in "DATE," and press **[Ctrl][F3]** (Screen) and select **3** (**R**ewrite). See Figure 2-11.

margin still at 1.5 inches but shifted on screen

cursor

Figure 2-11
Document screen after you execute the Rewrite command

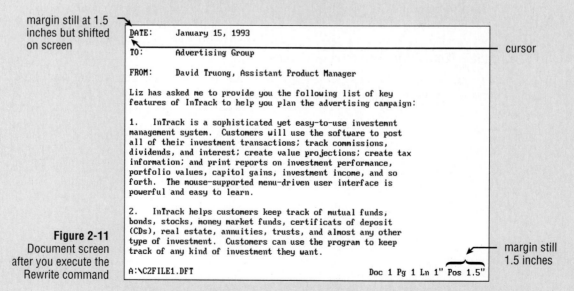

margin still 1.5 inches

This command causes WordPerfect to rewrite the screen to show the effect of changing the margin. In most cases you won't have to use the Rewrite command because WordPerfect automatically reformats the screen when you move the cursor into that region of the screen.

As you can see, when you want to change the margins or any other format setting, you first move the cursor to the position where you want the new format to begin and then set the new format feature. The new format setting takes effect from that point in the document to the end of the document, unless you change the format setting later. In our example, David and Liz wanted the left margin to be 1.5 inches for the entire document, so you moved the cursor to the beginning of the document before you changed the margin.

Justifying Text

Justification usually means adjusting the spacing between characters so that text is aligned along the right margin as well as along the left margin. Modern word processors and desktop publishing software, however, define justification to mean more than right-aligned margins. Specifically WordPerfect allows for four types of justified text: left, center, right, and full (Figure 2-12).

```
Full Justification
This paragraph is an example of full justification. The lines
of  text  are  aligned  along  the  left  and  the  right
margins.  This gives an ordered look to the document but is
generally more difficult to read than left-justified text.
Full justification is the default setting in WordPerfect.


Left Justification
This paragraph is an example of left justification. The
lines of text are aligned along the left margin but are
"ragged" along the right margin.  This gives a less
ordered look to the document but is generally easier to
read than fully justified text.


Right Justification
     This paragraph is an example of right justification. The
        lines of text are aligned along the right margin but
     ragged along the left margin.  You would never use right
      justification in the body of a normal document, but you
                          might use it for special effects.


Center Justification
            This paragraph is an example of center
        justification. The lines of text are centered
        between the left and the right margins.  You
        would never use center justification in the
          body of a normal document, but you would
            frequently use it in creating title pages.
```

Figure 2-12
Examples of justification

The WordPerfect default format setting is full justification, and that is how David formatted the first draft of his product description memo. But Liz has suggested that he change the format setting to left justification to make the memo appear less formal. David can do this by using the Format: Line menu, which you have already used. Let's change the justification of the memo that appears on your screen.

To change text justification using the pull-down menus:

❶ Press **[Home]**, **[Home]**, **[↑]** to make sure the cursor is at the beginning of the document.

Remember that since you want to change justification for the entire document, you must move the cursor to the beginning of the document before you change the format setting. Otherwise, justification will be in effect only from the current location of the cursor to the end of the document.

❷ Press **[Shift][F8]** (Format) and select **1** (**L**ine); then from the Format: Line menu, select **3** (**J**ustification). WordPerfect displays the one-line Justification menu at the bottom of the screen. See Figure 2-13.

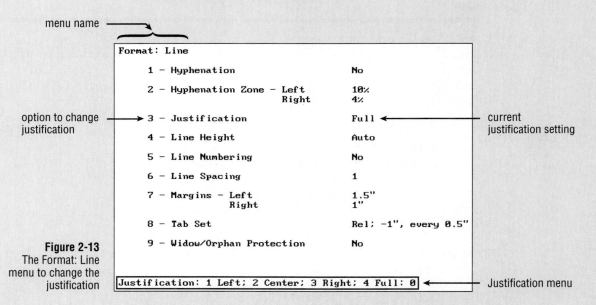

menu name

option to change justification

current justification setting

Figure 2-13
The Format: Line menu to change the justification

Justification menu

❸ Select **1** (**L**eft) to set the document to left justification.

❹ Press **[F7]** (Exit) to exit the menu and return to the document screen.

To use the pull-down menus to set left justification, you would select Justify from the Layout menu and then select Left from the Justify menu. See Figure 2-14.

menu name

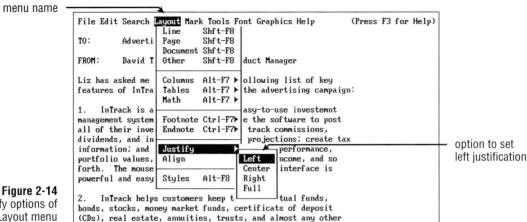

option to set
left justification

Figure 2-14
The Justify options of
the Layout menu

From the cursor's current location — the beginning of the memo in this instance — to the end of the document, the text is now left-justified. Since the document screen looks the same for full and for left justification, you will not see any changes until you use View Document to preview the document or until you print it. Let's preview the document to see what the left justification looks like.

To preview the document:

❶ Select Print from the File menu or press **[Shift][F7]** (Print) to display the Print/Options menu.

❷ Select **6** (**V**iew Document) to see what the document will look like when you print it. See Figure 2-15.

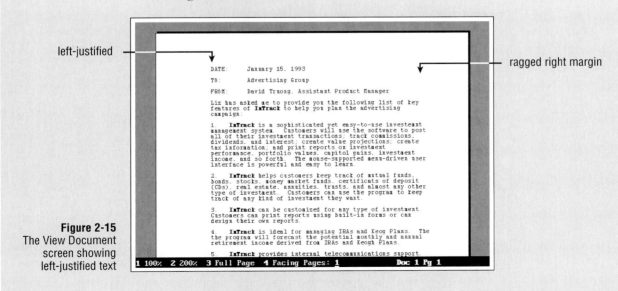

left-justified

ragged right margin

Figure 2-15
The View Document
screen showing
left-justified text

❸ Press **[F7]** (Exit) when you are ready to return to the document screen.

The document is left-justified, that is, aligned along the left margin but ragged along the right margin.

Using Tabs

As Figure 2-1 shows, David's next task in revising the memo is to insert the "RE," or reference, line below the "FROM" line. In the following steps you'll use [Enter] to insert new lines and then use the [Tab] key to insert space between the word "RE:" and the word "Product," as was already done between "TO:" and "Advertising" (Figure 2-16).

tab

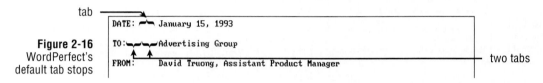

Figure 2-16
WordPerfect's
default tab stops

two tabs

The [Tab] key indents text by inserting space from the current cursor location to the next tab stop. **Tab stops** are precise locations on the text lines; WordPerfect's default settings of the tab stops are every one-half inch from the left margin. Tabs are useful in aligning text vertically in your document. In the case of David's memo, the tab stops after "DATE:," "TO:," and "FROM:" keep the text precisely aligned (Figure 2-17). You should not use [Space] to align text; the text might appear aligned on the document screen, but when you print the document, the text might not be aligned. Let's use [Tab] to insert space between "RE:" and the word "Product."

aligned

Figure 2-17
Using [Tab] to
align text

space produced
by using tabs

To use [Tab] to insert space:

❶   Move the cursor to the "F" in "FROM" on the third line of text in the memo.

❷   Press **[End]** to move the cursor to the end of the line, after the word "Manager."

❸   Press **[Enter]** twice to double space after the "FROM" line.

❹   Type **RE:** and press **[Tab]** twice.

   Pressing [Tab] twice inserts space between "RE:" and the tab stop at Pos 2.5". The cursor is now directly beneath the word "David."

❺   Type **Product Description of** and press **[Space]**.

You're now ready to type the word "InTrack" in boldface.

Boldfacing Text

One way to highlight a word in your document is to use boldfacing. **Boldfaced text** is text with thicker characters than normal text. Let's now type the word "InTrack" in boldfaced text in David's memo.

To boldface text:

❶ Make sure the cursor is to the right of the space after the phrase "Product Description of" that you typed in the previous section.

❷ Press **[F6]** (Bold).

After you press **[F6]** (Bold), the position number after "Pos," on the far right side of the status line, appears in bold. With bold turned on, whatever text you type will appear as bold on the screen and in your printed document.

❸ Type **InTrack** and press **[F6]** (Bold) again to turn off bold. See Figure 2-18.

Figure 2-18
Document screen
after you type
boldfaced "InTrack"

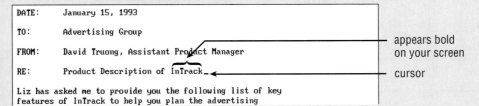

```
DATE:       January 15, 1993

TO:         Advertising Group

FROM:       David Truong, Assistant Product Manager         appears bold
                                                            on your screen
RE:         Product Description of  InTrack                 cursor

Liz has asked me to provide you the following list of key
features of InTrack to help you plan the advertising
```

When you press [F6] (Bold) the second time, bold is turned off. The "Pos" number on the status line returns to normal text.

As you can see from these steps, [F6] (Bold) is a toggle key. A **toggle key** is any key that turns on a feature the first time you press the key and turns off the feature the next time you press the key. Thus, pressing [F6] once turns bold on, and pressing [F6] again turns bold off.

You can also turn on or turn off bold by selecting Appearance from the Font menu and then selecting Bold from the Appearance menu (Figure 2-19 on the next page). This method, however, would require five keystrokes — [Alt][=], O, A, and B — instead of just one, [F6].

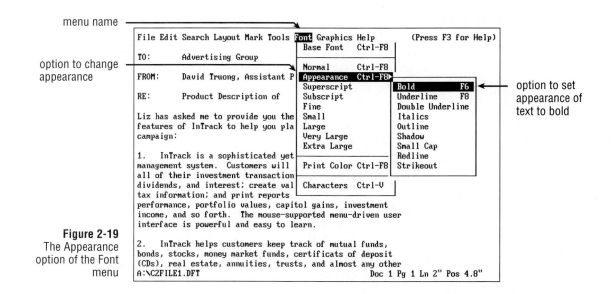

menu name

option to change appearance

option to set appearance of text to bold

Figure 2-19
The Appearance option of the Font menu

Underlining Text

David next wants to address Liz's question at the end of paragraph 5 in the memo. David decides to insert a note explaining that brokers must also have InTrack to use this option. He wants the note to be in parentheses, with the word "Note" underlined.

To underline text:

❶ Move the cursor to the end of paragraph numbered 5, after the phrase ". . . directly from within InTrack."

❷ Press **[Space]** twice to insert two spaces at the end of the sentence and type **(** (left parenthesis).

❸ Press **[F8]** (Underline).

The position number on the status line indicates underline mode. See Figure 2-20. On a color monitor the position number changes colors or appears in reverse video. On most monochrome monitors the position number is underlined. With underline turned on, whatever text you type will be underlined, color-coded, or in reverse video on the screen and underlined in your printed document. [F8] (Underline) is a toggle key.

Figure 2-20
Document screen just before you type with underlining on

```
5.    InTrack provides internal telecommunications support.
CUstomers can use the program to get on-line financial
information from most of the electronic information
services.  Customers can also carry out transactions with
their broker directly from within InTrack.  (
A:\C2FILE1.DFT                                Doc 1 Pg 1 Ln 7.5" Pos 6"
```

cursor

underline on

❹ Type **Note** and then press **[F8]** (Underline) to toggle off underlining.

Notice that the position number no longer indicates underlining and that the word "Note" is underlined, color-coded, or in reverse video, depending on your type of monitor. See Figure 2-21.

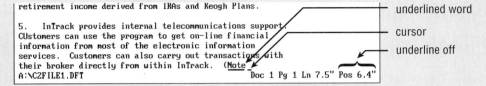

Figure 2-21
Document screen
after you type
underlined "Note"

⑤ Type a colon (:), press **[Space]** twice, then type **Their broker must also have** and press **[Space]**.

⑥ Press **[F6]** (Bold) to turn on boldfacing for the word "InTrack."

⑦ Type **InTrack** and press **[F6]** (Bold) to toggle off boldfacing.

⑧ Press **[Space]** and type **to use this option.)**. See Figure 2-22.

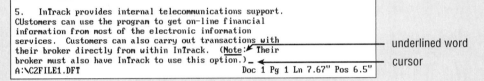

Figure 2-22
Document screen
after you type the
note

You can also turn on or turn off underlining by selecting Appearance from the Font menu and then selecting Underline from the Appearance menu. This method, however, would require five keystrokes — [Alt][=], O, A, and U — instead of just one, [F8].

Saving an Intermediate Version of the Document

David has now worked on the document for over 15 minutes and feels that it's time to save his changes. Let's save the document now.

To save the document:
① Make sure your WordPerfect data diskette is still in drive A.
② Select Save from the File menu or press **[F10]** (Save).

WordPerfect displays the prompt "Document to be saved: A:\C2FILE1.DFT" on the status line.

If you wanted to save the document using the old name, you would press [Enter] to accept the default filename, C2FILE1.DFT. In this case, however, you want to keep the original version on your diskette and save the file to a new filename.

③ Type the new filename **a:\s2file2.dft** and press **[Enter]**.

WordPerfect saves the edited memo to your data diskette using the filename S2FILE2.DFT.

Revealing Format Codes

Whenever you execute a WordPerfect format command (for example, to left-justify text) or change the text appearance (for example, to boldface or underline text), WordPerfect inserts an invisible format code into your document. These codes tell WordPerfect how to format the document on the screen and how the document will appear when you print it.

When you are typing a document, you usually don't need to see these format codes. But every once in a while — such as when you've pressed the wrong key or you want to change one of the format codes — you need to reveal these codes. In the following steps, you'll move the cursor to the beginning of the document and reveal the format codes.

To reveal the format codes:

❶ Move the cursor to the beginning of the document by pressing **[Home]**, **[Home]**, **[↑]**.

❷ Select Reveal Codes from the Edit menu (Figure 2-23) or press **[Alt][F3]** or **[F11]** (Reveal Codes). (The [F11] key is found only on an enhanced 101-key keyboard, not on a standard 83-key keyboard.)

menu name ──────

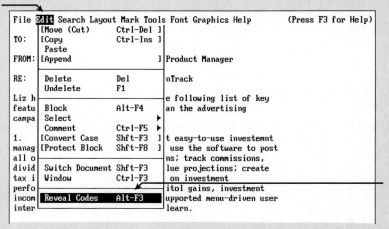

Figure 2-23
The Reveal Codes
option of the Edit
menu

option to display
format codes

The screen is now divided in half. The top half is the document window and the bottom half is the Reveal Codes window. See Figure 2-24.

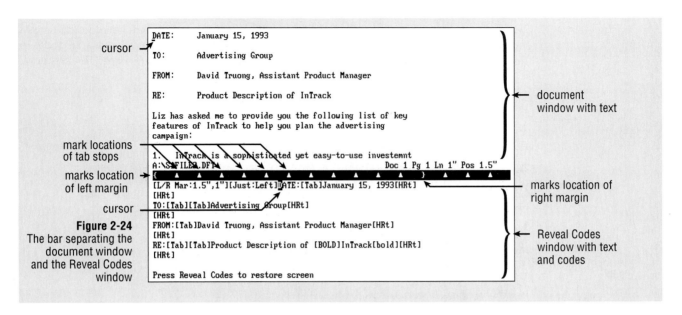

cursor →

DATE: January 15, 1993

TO: Advertising Group

FROM: David Truong, Assistant Product Manager

RE: Product Description of InTrack

→ document window with text

Liz has asked me to provide you the following list of key features of InTrack to help you plan the advertising campaign:

mark locations of tab stops

marks location → of left margin

cursor

1.   InTrack is a sophisticated yet easy-to-use investemnt
A:\SAFILES.DFM   Doc 1 Pg 1 Ln 1" Pos 1.5"

← marks location of right margin

[L/R Mar:1.5",1"][Just:Left]DATE:[Tab]January 15, 1993[HRt]
[HRt]
TO:[Tab][Tab]Advertising Group[HRt]
[HRt]
FROM:[Tab]David Truong, Assistant Product Manager[HRt]
[HRt]
RE:[Tab][Tab]Product Description of [BOLD]InTrack[bold][HRt]
[HRt]

Press Reveal Codes to restore screen

← Reveal Codes window with text and codes

Figure 2-24
The bar separating the document window and the Reveal Codes window

The bar separating the document window and the Reveal Codes window contains a left brace ({) to mark the left margin, a right brace (}) to mark the right margin, and triangles (▲) to mark the tab stops.

You can tell the location of the cursor in the Reveal Codes window because the code or character at the cursor is highlighted. For example, in Figure 2-24 the cursor is on the "D" in "DATE", so the "D" is highlighted in the Reveal Codes window. Since both the document window and the Reveal Codes window have a cursor, the screen actually shows two cursors. Let's move the cursor to demonstrate how the two cursors move together.

To move the cursor with Reveal Codes on:

❶ Move the cursor down to the 3 at the beginning of paragraph 3.

As you press [↓], the text in the document window and the information in the Reveal Codes windows scroll up.

❷ Press and hold down [→] for two or three seconds to watch how the two cursors move across the screen.

As you can see, the two cursors always move together through the document.

❸ Press **[Home]**, **[Home]**, **[↑]** to return to the top of the document.

In the Reveal Codes window, the highlighted words in square brackets are the format codes (Figure 2-25). Notice that the first code is [L/R Mar:1.5",1"]. This code was inserted into the document when you changed the margin settings earlier in this tutorial. The next code is [Just:Left], to indicate that you have specified left justification.

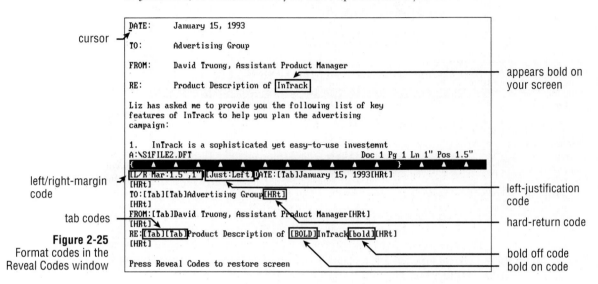

cursor

appears bold on your screen

left/right-margin code

left-justification code

tab codes

hard-return code

Figure 2-25
Format codes in the
Reveal Codes window

bold off code
bold on code

Other format codes include [Tab] to mark where you pressed [Tab] to move the text to the next tab stop on the RE line of the heading, [HRt] for the hard returns, and the paired codes [BOLD] to mark the beginning of boldfaced text and [bold] to mark the end of boldfaced text.

Figure 2-26 is a list of common WordPerfect format codes. Some of these codes won't make sense to you now, but their meanings will become clear as you work through this and later tutorials.

Codes	Meaning
[ ]	Hard space
[-]	Hyphen
-	Soft hyphen
/	Cancel hyphenation
[Dec Tab]	Decimal align in Tab
[BOLD][bold]	Bold begin and end
[Block]	Block begin
[Center]	Center
[Flsh Rgt]	Flush right
[HPg]	Hard page break
[HRt]	Hard return
[Hyph On/Off]	Hyphenation on or off
[→Indent]	Indent
[→Indent←]	Left/Right indent
[Just:Left]	Left justification
[L/R Mar:n,n]	Left and right margin values
[Ln Spacing:n]	Line spacing
[SPg]	Soft page break
[SRt]	Soft return
[SUBSCPT][subscpt]	Subscript begin and end
[SUPRSCPT][suprscpt]	Superscript begin and end
[Tab]	Tab (move to next tab stop)
[T/B Mar:n,n]	Top and bottom margin values
[UND][und]	Underline begin and end
[W/O On/Off]	Widow/orphan protection on or off

Figure 2-26
Common WordPerfect format codes — n represents the number you type

Keep Reveal Codes on, because in the next section you'll use the Reveal Codes window to help you edit the document.

Indenting a Paragraph

The Reveal Codes window will help David perform his next task. One of Liz's suggestions for the product description memo is to indent the numbered paragraphs. David realizes that he can't use tabs to do this because a tab inserts space only on the line where [Tab] was pressed. Instead, he must use the [F4] (Indent) command, which indents not just the first line of the paragraph but all subsequent lines until the end of the paragraph, which is marked by a hard return. David's task, therefore, is to change the [Tab] format code to the [→Indent] format code at the beginning of each numbered paragraph.

To change [Tab] codes to [→Indent] codes:

❶ Make sure the Reveal Codes window appears on the screen.

If necessary, select Reveal Codes from the Edit menu or press [Alt][F3] or [F11] (Reveal Codes).

❷ Move the cursor to the "1" of the first numbered paragraph. You can now see a **[Tab]** code to the right of the 1.

❸ Press **[→]** twice to put the cursor on the [Tab] code. See Figure 2-27.

cursor

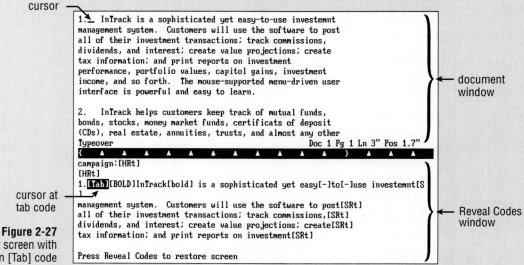

Figure 2-27
Document screen with
cursor on [Tab] code

cursor at
tab code

document
window

Reveal Codes
window

❹ Press **[Del]** to delete the [Tab] code. (Remember that if you use the [Del] key on the numeric keypad, Num Lock must be off.)

The [Tab] code disappears and the text beginning with "InTrack is a . . ." moves next to the 1.

❺ Press **[F4]** (Indent). The [→Indent] code is inserted into the document. See Figure 2-28.

As you can see, the [→Indent] code appears in the Reveal Codes window, and the paragraph is fully indented. If you don't see the entire paragraph indented, press [Ctrl][F3] (Screen) and select 3 (Rewrite) to tell WordPerfect to reformat the screen.

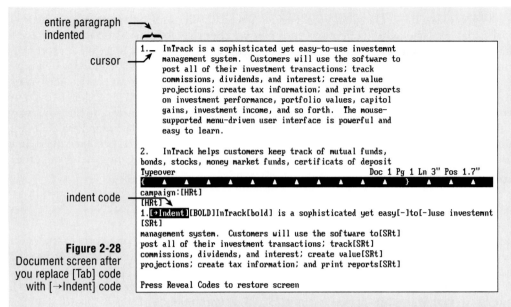

entire paragraph indented

cursor

indent code

Figure 2-28
Document screen after you replace [Tab] code with [→Indent] code

The amount of space that the text is indented depends on the location of the tab stops. Since WordPerfect's default format settings have a tab stop at every 0.5 inch, the paragraph is indented 0.5 inch from the left margin, or 2 inches from the left edge of the page.

⑥ Move the cursor to the [Tab] code at the beginning of the next numbered paragraph, delete the code, and press **[F4]** (Indent) to insert the [→Indent] code at that location. Repeat this step until you have indented all seven paragraphs.

⑦ Select Reveal Codes from the Edit menu or press **[Alt][F3]** or **[F11]** (Reveal Codes) to close the Reveal Codes window and display a full document screen.

The document screen should now look similar to Figure 2-29. As you can see, Reveal Codes is a toggle key: selecting it a first time opens the Reveal Codes window and selecting it a second time closes the Reveal Codes window.

indented paragraphs

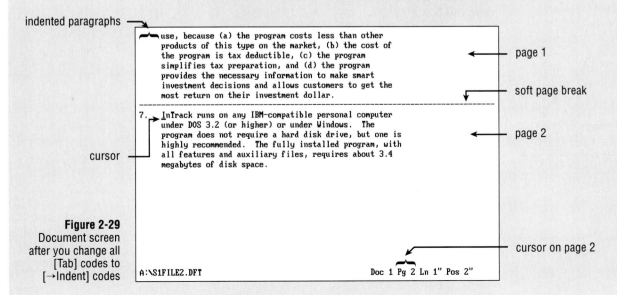

page 1

soft page break

page 2

cursor

Figure 2-29
Document screen after you change all [Tab] codes to [→Indent] codes

cursor on page 2

As you made these changes, WordPerfect automatically inserted a **soft page break** — a code that indicates where one page ends and another page begins. The location of a soft page break is shown as a broken line across the screen (Figure 2-29). It is called a *soft* page break because if you add or delete text before the break, the page break location may change.

In this section, you've learned how to reveal format codes, delete the codes, and insert other codes. You've also seen how to indent a paragraph using the [F4] (Indent) key. You can use these methods to change any format code. For example, if you decide that you want to change some boldfaced text back to normal appearance, you could turn on Reveal Codes, move the cursor to the code that marks the beginning or the end of the boldfaced text, and delete the code. When you delete either code, WordPerfect automatically deletes the other.

Deleting Words and Lines of Text

David is already familiar with using [Backspace] to delete a character or a code to the left of the cursor and with using [Del] to delete a character or a code at the cursor. But WordPerfect also provides ways for you to delete larger chunks of text.

For example, on the first line of paragraph 2 in the product description memo, Liz suggested that the phrase "keep track of" be simplified to "track." David will use WordPerfect's [Ctrl][Backspace] (Delete Word) to delete the words "keep" and "of." Let's make the change in your document.

To delete a word from the text:

❶ Move the cursor to the first letter of the word "keep" in the first line of paragraph 2 in the product description memo.

To use the [Ctrl][Backspace] (Delete Word) command, you can move the cursor anywhere within the word or to the space just to the right of the word that you want to delete.

❷ Press **[Ctrl][Backspace]** (Delete Word). The word and the space after it disappear from the document.

❸ Press **[Ctrl][→]** (Word Right) to move the cursor past "track" and to the word "of."

❹ Press **[Ctrl][Backspace]** (Delete Word). The word and the space after it disappear from the document. See Figure 2-30.

Figure 2-30
Document screen
after you use
[Ctrl] [Backspace]
(Delete Word)

```
on investment performance, portfolio values, capitol
gains, investment income, and so forth.  The mouse-
supported menu-driven user interface is powerful and
easy to learn.                                              ———— words deleted

2.   InTrack helps customers track mutual funds, bonds,
     stocks, money market funds, certificats of deposit
A:\S1FILE2.DFT                              Doc 1 Pg 1 Ln 4.67" Pos 5"
```

Another valuable deletion command is [Ctrl][End] (Del to EOL), which instructs WordPerfect to "delete from the cursor to the end of the current line." You can use this command to delete a complete or partial line of text. In the product description memo, Liz wants David to delete the last sentence of paragraph 2, since the sentence is redundant. Let's use [Ctrl][End] (Del to EOL) to delete this sentence.

To delete from the cursor to the end of a line:

❶　Move the cursor to the end of the first sentence in paragraph 2. See Figure 2-31.

Figure 2-31
Document screen
before you use
[Ctrl][End]
(Del to EOL)

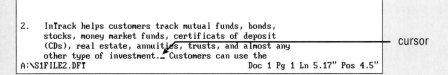

❷　Press **[Ctrl][End]** (Del to EOL).

The text from the cursor to the end of the line is deleted, and the remaining text in the sentence moves into the place of the deleted text. See Figure 2-32.

Figure 2-32
Document screen
after you press
[Ctrl][End]
(Del to EOL)

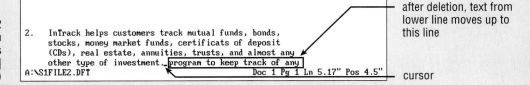

❸　Press **[Ctrl][End]** (Del to EOL) until you finish deleting the sentence.

In addition to [Ctrl][Backspace] (Delete Word) and [Ctrl][End] (Del to EOL), you can use the keystrokes shown in Figure 2-33 to delete text. As you become more familiar with WordPerfect, you'll be able to use these other delete commands in your own documents.

Figure 2-33
WordPerfect
deletion keystrokes

Key(s)	Deletion
[Del]	Character at the cursor
[Backspace]	Character to the left of the cursor
[Ctrl][Backspace]	Word at the cursor
[Ctrl][End]	From the cursor to the end of the line
[Ctrl][PgDn]	From the cursor to the end of the page
[Home], [Backspace]	From the cursor to the beginning of the word
[Home], [Del]	From the cursor to the end of the word

Undeleting Text

Whenever you delete text from a document, WordPerfect temporarily saves the deleted text, just in case you want to **undelete**, or restore, it later. WordPerfect doesn't store all your deletions, *only the last three*. Let's use WordPerfect's Undelete capability to delete and then restore the word "investment."

To undelete text:

❶ Make sure the cursor is still at the end of paragraph 2 in the product description memo.

❷ Press **[Ctrl][←]** (Word Left) to move the cursor to the beginning of the word "investment."

❸ Press **[Ctrl][Backspace]** (Delete Word) to delete the word "investment" and the period.

Let's suppose that now you want the word and the period back in your document.

❹ Select Undelete from the Edit menu or press **[F1]** (Cancel).

WordPerfect immediately restores the most recent deletion to the screen, keeps the undeleted text highlighted, and displays the Undelete menu on the status line. See Figure 2-34. To see the next-to-the-last deletion, you would select 2 (Previous Deletion); to see the deletion before that, you would select 2 (Previous Deletion) again.

Figure 2-34
The Undelete menu

```
    gains, investment income, and so forth.   The mouse-
    supported menu-driven user interface is powerful and
    easy to learn.

2.   InTrack helps customers track mutual funds, bonds,
    stocks, money market funds, certificats of deposit
    (CDs), real estate, annuities, trusts, and almost any
    other type of investment.
Undelete: 1 Restore; 2 Previous Deletion: 0
```

undeleted text

Undelete menu

❺ Select **1** (**R**estore). The deleted word "investment" and the accompanying period are restored to the document as if they had never been deleted.

After deleting text, you can type new text, move the cursor, or execute other commands before you undelete the deleted text. For example, if you pressed [F1] (Cancel) and selected 1 (Restore), WordPerfect would restore the deleted text at the current location of the cursor, not where the deleted text originally appeared. David can, therefore, use Undelete to move a word or a phrase from one location to another. Let's try this by deleting the word "pays" in paragraph 6 and restoring it after the word "easily" to switch the order of the words, as Liz suggested.

To use Undelete to move a word:

❶ Move the cursor to the word "pays" on the first line in paragraph 6.

❷ Press **[Ctrl][Backspace]** (Delete Word) to delete the word.

❸ Press **[Ctrl][→]** (Word Right) to move the cursor past "easily" to the "f" in the word "for."

❹ Select Undelete from the Edit menu or press **[F1]** (Cancel) and select **1** (**R**estore). See Figure 2-35.

Figure 2-35
Document screen after you delete, then restore a word

```
    information from most of the electronic information
    services.  Customers can also carry out transactions
    with their broker directly from within InTrack.   (Note:
    Their broker must also have InTrack to use this
    option.)

6.   InTrack easily pays for itself within the first year of
    use, because (a) the program costs less than other
A:\S1FILE2.DFT                           Doc 1 Pg 1 Ln 8.33" Pos 4"
```

position of word after being deleted, then restored

cursor here

Now the phrase reads "InTrack easily pays for itself," as Liz suggested.

Using Typeover Mode

When you start WordPerfect, the document screen starts out in **insert mode**, which means that the characters you type are inserted into the document at the cursor and existing characters move to the right.

If you press [Ins] (Insert), the document screen changes from insert mode to **typeover mode**, which means that the characters you type replace existing text at the cursor. When typeover mode is on, the word "Typeover" appears on the left side of the status line at the bottom of the screen. The filename of the document no longer appears on the status line.

As shown in Figure 2-1, Liz wants David to add "3.0 or higher" to the second line of paragraph 7. Let's use insert mode to insert "3.0 or higher" and then use typeover mode to change "3.4" to "2.5" in the last line of the same paragraph.

To use insert mode:

❶ Move the cursor to the period (.) after the word "Windows" at the end of the first sentence in paragraph 7.

❷ Make sure "Typeover" does *not* appear on the status line. If it does, press **[Ins]** to return to insert mode.

❸ Press **[Space]** and type **3.0 (or higher)**.

When you type this short phrase, watch as the sentence "The program does not require . . ." is pushed to the right and then wrapped to the next line.

Next let's use typeover mode to change "3.4" to "2.5".

To use typeover mode:

❶ Move the cursor to the "3" in "about 3.4 megabytes" in the last line of paragraph 7.

❷ Press **[Ins]**. The word "Typeover" appears on the left side of the status line at the bottom of the screen, replacing the document name.

❸ Type **2.5**. With typeover mode on, the new characters replace, or type over, the original characters at the cursor. In this case "2.5" replaces "3.4." See Figure 2-36.

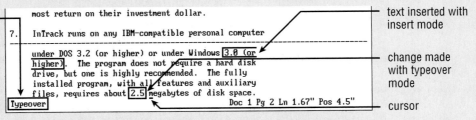

indicates typeover mode

Figure 2-36
Document screen after you use insert mode and typeover mode

text inserted with insert mode

change made with typeover mode

cursor

```
          most return on their investment dollar.

   7.     InTrack runs on any IBM-compatible personal computer
          ----------------------------------------------------
          under DOS 3.2 (or higher) or under Windows 3.0 (or
          higher). The program does not require a hard disk
          drive, but one is highly recommended. The fully
          installed program, with all features and auxiliary
          files, requires about 2.5 megabytes of disk space.
   Typeover                                Doc 1 Pg 2 Ln 1.67" Pos 4.5"
```

❹ Press **[Ins]** to turn off typeover mode and return to insert mode.

As you can see, [Ins] is a toggle key: pressing it once changes the document screen from insert mode to typeover mode; pressing it a second time changes the document screen from typeover mode back to insert mode.

Inserting a Hard Page Break

Look at Liz's question at the bottom of Figure 2-1: "Dave, what about other hardware options?" In response to this question, David decides to add a paragraph at the end of the product description.

To add a paragraph to the memo:

❶ Press **[Home]**, **[Home]**, **[↓]** to move the cursor to the end of the document.

❷ Press **[Enter]** twice to double-space between paragraph 7 and the new paragraph you're about to type.

❸ Type **8.** (the number 8 and a period) and press **[F4]** (Indent) to indent the new paragraph.

❹ Press **[F6]** (Bold) to turn on bold, type **InTrack**, press **[F6]** (Bold) again to turn off bold, and press **[Space]**.

❺ Type the remainder of the paragraph: **supports, but does not require, the following hardware items: VGA color graphics, Microsoft-compatible mouse, and Hayes-compatible modem.** See Figure 2-37.

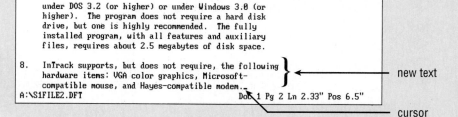

Figure 2-37
Document screen
after you type
paragraph 8

```
under DOS 3.2 (or higher) or under Windows 3.0 (or
higher).  The program does not require a hard disk
drive, but one is highly recommended.  The fully
installed program, with all features and auxiliary
files, requires about 2.5 megabytes of disk space.

8.   InTrack supports, but does not require, the following
     hardware items: VGA color graphics, Microsoft-
     compatible mouse, and Hayes-compatible modem._
A:\S1FILE2.DFT                          Doc 1 Pg 2 Ln 2.33" Pos 6.5"
```

new text

cursor

This last paragraph completes the text of the memo. But notice that paragraph 7 is split between page 1 and page 2. On your screen paragraph 7 might not be split between two pages. Even if it is not split, continue reading and follow the next set of steps. David doesn't want a page break within a numbered paragraph, so he decides to use what is called a hard page break just before paragraph 7. A **hard page break** is a format code that forces all text after it onto the next page. Regardless of how much text you might add or delete before a hard page break, the text on the page will end at that point, and the text that follows will go onto the next page. WordPerfect marks the location of a hard page break with a horizontal line of double dashes that extend across the width of the screen.

Let's insert a hard page break to force paragraph 7 and the text that follows it onto the next page.

To insert a hard page break:

❶ Move the cursor to the "7" at the beginning of paragraph 7.

❷ Press **[Ctrl][Enter]** (Hard Page) to force paragraph 7 onto the next page. The hard page break appears on the screen. See Figure 2-38.

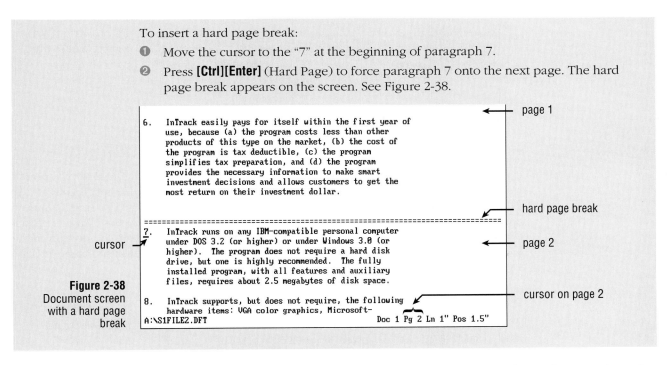

Figure 2-38
Document screen with a hard page break

The format code for a hard page break is [HPg]. You can use this code as you have the other codes you've already learned about. For example, to delete a hard page break, you would move the cursor to the location of the page break, turn on Reveal Codes, move the cursor to the [HPg] code, and press [Del] to delete it.

Checking the Spelling in a Document

David's product description memo still contains misspelled words and other typographical errors, commonly called "typos." You can catch most misspellings and typos by running the **speller** — a WordPerfect feature that checks the spelling within a document — as Liz suggested to David in the first paragraph of the memo. When you run the speller, WordPerfect checks each word in your document against the WordPerfect **dictionary**, a file on the disk that contains a list of correctly spelled words.

Let's correct the spelling errors in David's memo by using the speller.

Running the Speller

To run the speller:

❶ Select Spell from the Tools menu or press **[Ctrl][F2]** (Spell). WordPerfect displays the one-line speller menu on the status line. See Figure 2-39.

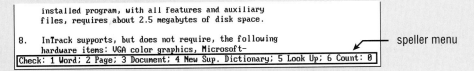

Figure 2-39
The speller menu

❷   Select **3** (**D**ocument) to check the spelling of the entire document. WordPerfect automatically starts checking from the beginning of the document, no matter where the cursor is.

Skipping a Word Not Found in the Dictionary

The first "misspelled" word detected by WordPerfect is "Truong" (Figure 2-40). Although "Truong" is spelled correctly, it's not in WordPerfect's dictionary. WordPerfect highlights the word to flag it as a potential error and divides the screen in two, with the document window on top and the dictionary window on bottom. A list of suggested "correct spellings" appears in the dictionary window, and the one-line Not Found menu appears at the bottom of the screen. Since we don't want to change "Truong" to any of the suggested spellings, let's tell WordPerfect to skip this word from now on.

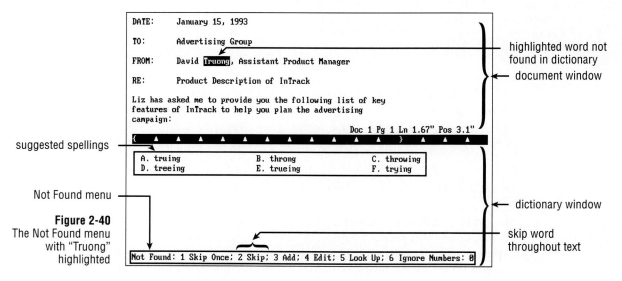

suggested spellings

Not Found menu

Figure 2-40
The Not Found menu
with "Truong"
highlighted

highlighted word not
found in dictionary

document window

dictionary window

skip word
throughout text

To skip a word not found in WordPerfect's dictionary:

❶   Select **2** (Skip). This option tells WordPerfect to skip all occurrences of the word "Truong" here and in the remainder of the document.

WordPerfect next stops at "InTrack." This is another example of a correctly spelled word that isn't in WordPerfect's dictionary.

❷   Select **2** (Skip) to skip this and all future occurrences of "InTrack."

WordPerfect continues checking words in the document against words in the dictionary until it comes to the next word not found in the dictionary.

Selecting a Suggested Spelling

The first word that David actually misspelled is "investemnt." WordPerfect highlights the word, gives a suggested spelling ("investment"), and displays the Not Found menu at the bottom of the screen (Figure 2-41).

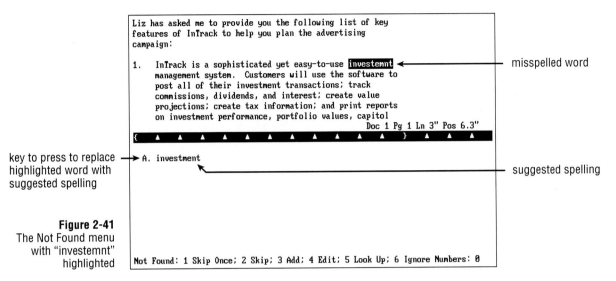

misspelled word

key to press to replace highlighted word with suggested spelling

suggested spelling

Figure 2-41
The Not Found menu with "investemnt" highlighted

In the following steps, you'll select a replacement word from the dictionary window. WordPerfect will then replace the misspelled word in the document with the selected word from the dictionary window.

To select a suggested spelling from the dictionary window:

❶ Press the letter next to the correct word in the dictionary window. In this example, press **A** or **a**. WordPerfect immediately replaces the misspelled word with "investment" and continues the spell checking.

The next misspelled word is "certificats." WordPerfect displays two suggested words in the dictionary window. See Figure 2-42.

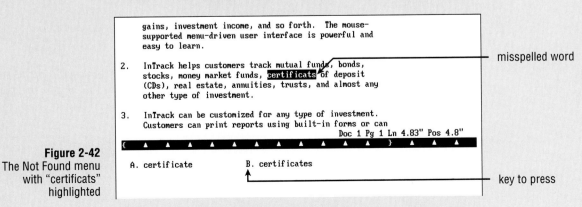

misspelled word

Figure 2-42
The Not Found menu with "certificats" highlighted

key to press

❷   Press **B** (or **b**) to select "certificates" from the dictionary window.

Skipping a Word Once

WordPerfect next stops at the word "CDs," an abbreviation for "certificates of deposit," and presents a long list of possible words in the dictionary window (Figure 2-43). Since none of these words is correct, let's tell WordPerfect to skip this word once but to flag any later occurrence of "CDs" or "cds" in the document.

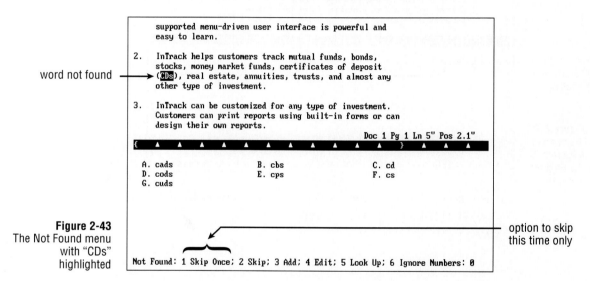

word not found →

option to skip
this time only

Figure 2-43
The Not Found menu
with "CDs"
highlighted

To skip a word once:

❶   Select **1** (Skip Once). This option tells WordPerfect that you want to skip the word this time only.

The next "misspelled" word is "IRAs."

❷   Select **2** (Skip) to skip this and all future occurrences of "IRAs" in the document.

As a general rule, select 1 (Skip Once) if there's a chance that the flagged word may actually be a misspelling later in the document. Select 2 (Skip) if you know that the word will appear again later in the document but you don't want the speller to flag it.

Editing a Misspelled Word

WordPerfect next stops at the word "Keog" and displays several suggested words in the dictionary window (Figure 2-44). The correct word is "Keogh," which is the name of a retirement investment plan. In this case, "Keog" is not a correct spelling, but the correct spelling is not found in the WordPerfect dictionary either. Thus, you need to edit the word, that is, change the word so that it is spelled correctly.

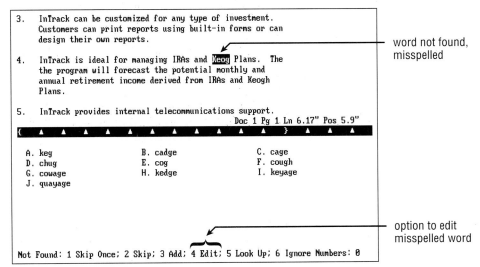

Figure 2-44
The Not Found menu with "Keog" highlighted

word not found, misspelled

option to edit misspelled word

To edit a misspelled word:

❶ Select **4** (Edit). The cursor moves into the document window at the beginning of the misspelled word, and the dictionary window disappears.

❷ Move the cursor to the space after "Keog," type **h** to make the word "Keogh," and press **[F7]** (Exit) to exit the document window and return to the speller.

The word is now spelled the way you want it. However, it's still not in the WordPerfect dictionary, so it remains highlighted.

❸ Select **2** (Skip) to skip this and all future occurrences of the word "Keogh" in the document.

Correcting Double Words

WordPerfect next stops at the double words "The the" and displays the Double Word menu on the status line (Figure 2-45).

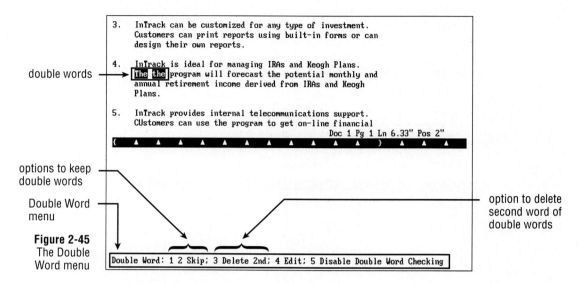

double words

options to keep double words

Double Word menu

option to delete second word of double words

Figure 2-45
The Double Word menu

To correct double words:

❶ Press **3** (Delete 2nd) to delete the second occurrence of the word "the."

You would select option 1 or 2 if you wanted to skip the double words and leave both words in your document.

Your document now has only "The" instead of "The the" at that location in the document.

Correcting Irregular Case

The next typo that WordPerfect encounters is an irregular case error. An "irregular case" error is a word that has some lowercase letters and one or more uppercase letters after the initial letter. When David typed the rough draft of the memo, he accidentally held the [Shift] key down too long and typed "CUstomer" instead of "Customer." When such an error occurs, WordPerfect highlights the erroneous word and displays the Irregular Case menu (Figure 2-46).

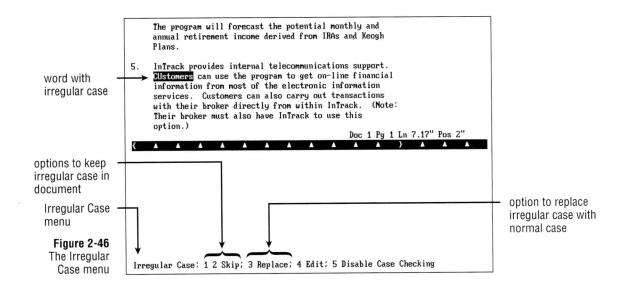

word with
irregular case

options to keep
irregular case in
document

Irregular Case
menu

Figure 2-46
The Irregular
Case menu

option to replace
irregular case with
normal case

To correct irregular case:

❶ Select **3** (Replace) to replace the irregular case word "CUstomer" with correct word "Customer."

❷ When the speller stops at any other word not found in the dictionary (such as "VGA" or "Microsoft"), select 1 (Skip Once) or 2 (Skip). Repeat this step until the speller reaches the end of the document and displays the word count.

You have now completed the spell checking of the document. WordPerfect displays the number of words (355) in the document. You are ready to exit the speller.

To exit the speller:

❶ Press any key to exit the speller and return to the normal document screen.

Checking for Misused Words

Keep in mind that the WordPerfect speller checks only spelling, not meaning or usage. For example, in paragraph 1 of the product description memo, David used the word "capitol," which means a building in which a legislature convenes, instead of "capital," which means assets or wealth. WordPerfect doesn't have a program to help you catch this type of error, so you must carefully proofread your document for correct usage. Let's correct the error now.

To correct a misused word:

❶ Move the cursor to the "o" in "capitol" in paragraph 1 of the memo.

❷ Press **[Ins]** to turn on typeover mode.

❸ Type **a** to change "capitol" to "capital."

❹ Press **[Ins]** to turn off typeover mode and return to insert mode.

Using the Thesaurus

David is now ready to address Liz's last suggestion. In paragraph 1, David used the verb "create" twice in the same series of items. Liz thinks this is repetitious and suggests he choose better words. He agrees but isn't sure what words to use in their place. He realizes that WordPerfect's thesaurus can help him with his problem. The **thesaurus** is a WordPerfect file that contains a list of words and their synonyms and antonyms. In the following steps, you'll see how to use the thesaurus.

To use the thesaurus:

❶ Move the cursor to the first occurrence of "create" on the fourth line of the first numbered paragraph.

The cursor can be anywhere in the word or at the space just after the word.

❷ Select Thesaurus from the Tools menu or press **[Alt][F1]** (Thesaurus). WordPerfect displays a list of the synonyms and antonyms of "create" in the thesaurus window. See Figure 2-47.

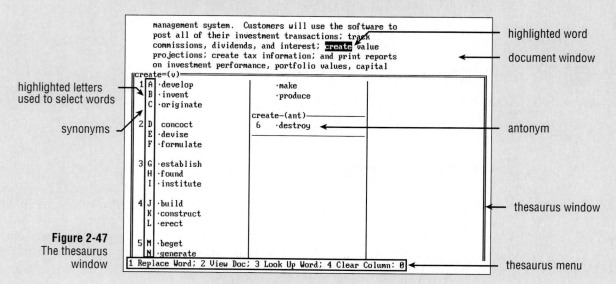

Figure 2-47
The thesaurus
window

David looks over the words and decides that the word "make" is the best choice. Notice that "make" is in the second column of synonyms, but the uppercase highlighted letters you use to select a word are in the first column. Let's move the highlighted letters to the second column so we can choose a word from that column.

❸ Press [→] to move the highlighted letters to the second column. See Figure 2-48.

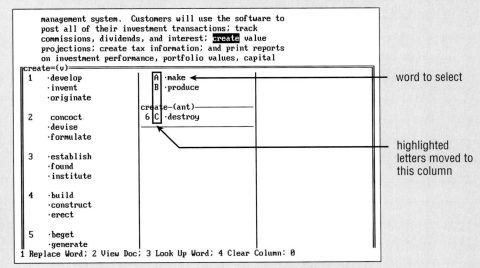

Figure 2-48
The thesaurus window after you move selection letters to second column

❹ Select **1** (Replace Word) and press **A** or **a** to replace "create" with "make." WordPerfect makes the replacement and closes the thesaurus window.

David wants to replace the second occurrence of "create" with the word "generate." Because WordPerfect closes the thesaurus window after an option is selected from the thesaurus menu, David has to reissue the Thesaurus command.

❺ Move the cursor to the second occurrence of "create" and execute the Thesaurus command.

❻ Select **1** (Replace Word) and press **N** to replace "create" with "generate."

As you can see, the thesaurus is a powerful tool for helping you choose synonyms and antonyms for words in your document.

Saving the Final Version of the Document

David has now completed all the changes in the document that Liz suggested. Your document should now look like Figure 2-49 on the following pages.

DATE: January 15, 1993

TO: Advertising Group

FROM: David Truong, Assistant Product Manager

RE: Product Description of **InTrack**

Liz has asked me to provide you the following list of key
features of **InTrack** to help you plan the advertising
campaign:

1.   InTrack is a sophisticated yet easy-to-use investment
      management system. Customers will use the software to
      post all of their investment transactions; track
      commissions, dividends, and interest; make value
      projections; generate tax information; and print
      reports on investment performance, portfolio values,
      capital gains, investment income, and so forth. The
      mouse-supported menu-driven user interface is powerful
      and easy to learn.

2.   **InTrack** helps customers track mutual funds, bonds,
      stocks, money market funds, certificates of deposit
      (CDs), real estate, annuities, trusts, and almost any
      other type of investment.

3.   **InTrack** can be customized for any type of investment.
      Customers can print reports using built-in forms or can
      design their own reports.

4.   **InTrack** is ideal for managing IRAs and Keogh Plans.
      The program will forecast the potential monthly and
      annual retirement income derived from IRAs and Keogh
      Plans.

5.   **InTrack** provides internal telecommunications support.
      Customers can use the program to get on-line financial
      information from most of the electronic information
      services. Customers can also carry out transactions
      with their broker directly from within **InTrack.** (Note:
      Their broker must also have **InTrack** to use this
      option.)

6.   **InTrack** easily pays for itself within the first year of
      use, because (a) the program costs less than other
      products of this type on the market, (b) the cost of
      the program is tax deductible, (c) the program
      simplifies tax preparation, and (d) the program
      provides the necessary information to make smart
      investment decisions and allows customers to get the
      most return on their investment dollar.

Figure 2-49
Page one of the
final version of the
document
(continued on next
page)

7. **InTrack** runs on any IBM-compatible personal computer under DOS 3.2 (or higher) or under Windows 3.0 (or higher). The program does not require a hard disk drive, but one is highly recommended. The fully installed program, with all features and auxiliary files, requires about 2.5 megabytes of disk space.

8. **InTrack** supports, but does not require, the following hardware items: VGA color graphics, Microsoft-compatible mouse, and Hayes-compatible modem.

Figure 2-49
Page two of the final version of the document (continued from previous page)

After editing any document, you should save it to the diskette; otherwise, the diskette copy of the document will still be the previous version without any of the corrections you made since your last save. In this case, let's assume David wants to keep a record of his original rough draft (C2FILE1.DFT) and the most recently saved version (S2FILE2.DFT). He saves the final version of the memo as S2FILE3.MEM.

To save the final version of the document:

❶ Make sure your WordPerfect data diskette is still in drive A.

❷ Select Save from the File menu or press **[F10]** (Save). WordPerfect displays the prompt "Document to be saved: A:\S2FILE2.DFT" on the status line.

❸ Type the new filename **a:\s2file3.mem** and press **[Enter]**.

WordPerfect saves the final version of the memo to your diskette using the filename S2FILE3.MEM. See Figure 2-50.

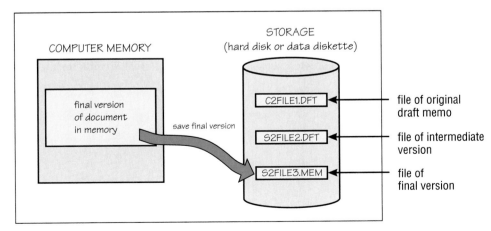

Figure 2-50
Saving the final version

Printing Multiple Copies of a Document

David's last task is to print three copies of the memo. He could simply execute the print command three times, but there is an easier way. Let's use WordPerfect's Number of Copies feature to print three copies of the memo.

To print multiple copies of a document:

❶ Select Print from the File menu or press **[Shift][F7]** (Print) to display the Print/Options menu. See Figure 2-51.

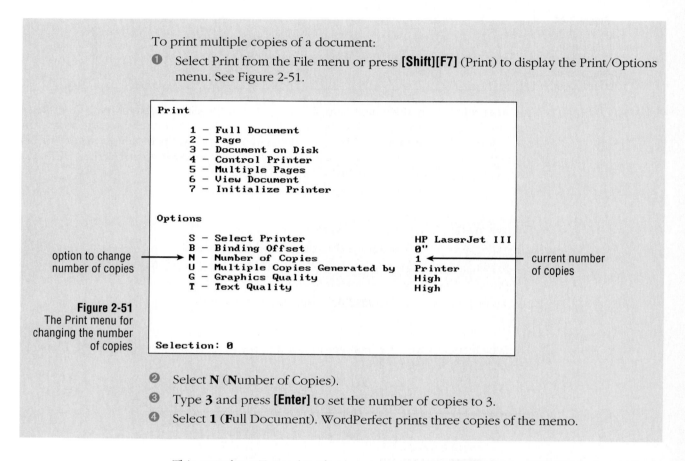

option to change
number of copies

current number
of copies

Figure 2-51
The Print menu for
changing the number
of copies

❷ Select **N** (**N**umber of Copies).

❸ Type **3** and press **[Enter]** to set the number of copies to 3.

❹ Select **1** (**F**ull Document). WordPerfect prints three copies of the memo.

This completes Tutorial 2. If you want to exit WordPerfect, press [F7] (Exit), then N (No), and then Y (Yes).

Exercises

1. Which key(s) do you press to move the cursor in the following directions?
    a. To the left side of the screen
    b. To the right side of the screen
    c. To the beginning of the document
    d. To the end of the document
    e. One word to the left

2. Describe what you would do to change the right margin of a document to 1.5 inches.

3. What key(s) would you press to do the following?
   a. Turn on boldfacing
   b. Turn off boldfacing
   c. Turn on underlining
   d. Turn off underlining

4. What would you do to see the format code that marks the location where you changed the margins within a document?

5. What is the WordPerfect code for each of the following?
   a. Soft return
   b. Hard return
   c. Soft page break
   d. Hard page break
   e. Tab

6. What is the difference between a soft return and a hard return?

7. Explain the meaning of each of the following WordPerfect terms:
   a. Full justification
   b. Left justification
   c. Right justification
   d. Center justification

8. Explain the difference between [Tab] and [F4] (Indent).

9. Explain the difference between insert mode and typeover mode. What key do you press to change from one mode to the other?

10. What key(s) do you press to force a page break? Why would you want to force a page break?

11. What key(s) do you press to delete the following portions of a document? *Hint:* See Figure 2-33.
    a. The word at the cursor
    b. From the cursor to the end of the line
    c. From the cursor to the beginning of a word
    d. From the cursor to the end of a word

12. After you've deleted a word or a phrase, how do you undelete, or restore, the word or phrase?

13. How many groups of deleted text does WordPerfect save for future undelete operations?

14. Name at least three types of errors that the WordPerfect speller can find.

15. If you type the sentence "That is just to bad!" and then run the speller, why won't the speller detect the incorrect usage of the word "to"?

16. Besides synonyms what does the WordPerfect thesaurus list?

17. What procedure would you follow to print five copies of a memo?

18. Define the word "toggle" as it is used in WordPerfect.

Tutorial Assignments

> In the following Tutorial Assignments, make sure you clear the document screen before retrieving each file.

Retrieve the file T2FILE1.DFT and do the following:

1. Change the justification from full to left for the entire document.

2. In the numbered paragraphs change the tabs to indents.

3. Use the WordPerfect speller to correct misspelled words, double words, and irregular case words.

4. Carefully read the document and make a list of the words that are "misspelled" or incorrectly used but that the speller failed to flag. Edit the document to correct these words.

5. Save the document as S2FILE1.MEM.

6. Print the document.

Retrieve the file T2FILE2.DFT and do the following:

7. Use the thesaurus to substitute the word "plethora" for a simpler word that has the same meaning.

8. Use the thesaurus to list the antonym(s) of the word "abstruse," then reword the entire sentence using an antonym.

9. Save the document as S2FILE2.MEM.

10. Print three copies of the document by changing the Number of Copies option on the Print and Options menu.

Retrieve the file T2FILE3.DOC and do the following:

11. Insert a hard page break after the company telephone number, so the first six lines become a title page and the rest of the document is on a separate page.

12. At the beginning of the second page, just after the page break, change the justification to left.

13. Save the document as S2FILE2.DOC.

14. Print one copy of the document.

Retrieve the file T2FILE4.DFT and do the following:

15. After the first paragraph to the right of the colon, type "InTrack can really help improve the return on your investments." Put "InTrack" in boldfaced type.

16. Use typeover mode to change the number "4,827.29" to "5,216.41."

17. Run the speller to correct the typos in the document.

18. Save the document as S2FILE4.MEM.

19. Print one copy of the document.

Retrieve the file T2FILE5.DOC and do the following *in the order given*:

20. Turn on Reveal Codes and make a handwritten list of all the format codes you can see in the document.

21. Clear the document screen, then type the list of format codes you found. Type only one code per line.

22. Number each code in the list and indent ([F4]) after each number.

23. After each format code, type a colon (:), then type the meaning of the code.

24. Save the document as S2CODES.DOC.

25. Print the document.

Case Problems

1. CompuLearn Inc.

Sharon Pincus is a computer consultant working for CompuLearn Inc. of Biloxi, Mississippi. One of CompuLearn's potential clients is Mr. Michael Jensen, the office manager of Boyer and Stephenson Law Offices, 841 Magnolia Avenue, Jackson, MI 93204. Mr. Jensen has requested information from CompuLearn about the experience and the qualifications of the computer trainer who would be assigned to his office. Sharon has been assigned to this account, so she has to write Mr. Jensen to tell him about her experience and qualifications.

Retrieve the file P2JENSEN.DFT and do the following:

1. Set the entire document to left justification.

2. Change the margins to 1.5 inches on the left and the right.

3. Insert today's date, the inside address, and the salutation at the beginning of the document.

4. Number the three paragraphs that explain Sharon's qualifications. Indent all the lines of the paragraph *after* the paragraph number.

5. At the end of the third numbered paragraph, add: **I also know all aspects of <u>WordPerfect</u>, including basic document editing, graphics, styles, macros, and desktop publishing**.

6. Run the speller to correct any typos and spelling errors. Proofread the document for errors that the speller may have missed.

7. Since the use of the word "aspect" twice in the third numbered paragraph is repetitive, use the thesaurus to replace the second occurrence of "aspects" with a synonym. After you make the replacement, be sure to make the synonym plural.

8. Save the document as S2JENSEN.LET.

9. Print two copies of the letter.

2. Z & Z Electronics Product Description

Carlos Gallegos is the product manager of Z & Z Electronics. Carlos has to prepare a brief description of a new computer cabinet manufactured by Z & Z. The product description must include a cover sheet (Figure 2-52a on the next page) and, on a separate sheet, the body of the document (Figure 2-52b on the following page).

Z & Z COMPUTER CABINET

Product Description

Z & Z Electronics
3256 South Saratoga Road
Walla Walla, WA 99362
(509) 882-4756

Figure 2-52a

The Z & Z Computer Cabinet

Dimensions: 6 ft. wide, 5 ft. 6 in. tall, 2 ft. 8 in. deep

Material: Composition board with walnut or maple veneer

Features: Retractable keyboard drawer, 4-inch high monitor stand, printer shelf (large enough to accommodate any laser printer), four book shelves, three drawers for office supplies and for computer paper, built-in power strip and separate on/off switch for the computer and each peripheral.

Price: $285.00 (suggested retail)

Figure 2-52b

Do the following:

1. Type the cover sheet of the document with center-justified text.

2. Insert a hard page break after the cover sheet.

3. For the body of the product description, set the margins to 2.0 inches on the left and 1.0 inch on the right.

4. Make the document left-justified.

5. Type the body of the product description as shown in Figure 2-52. Notice that the descriptive text on the right is indented and that some of the words and phrases are boldfaced or underlined.

6. Save the document as S2COMCAB.DOC, where COMCAB stands for computer cabinet.

7. Print a copy of the document.

3. Celebrity Management Corporation Statement of Goals

Cecilia Jordon is president of Celebrity Management Corporation, a small Los Angeles company that manages the personal appearances, endorsements, and investments of actors, radio personalities, and sports figures. Cecilia is preparing a memo listing proposed goals for the company. She first writes a rough draft of the memo (Figure 2-53).

```
                                          November 9, 1992

MEMORANDUM TO:   Members, Executive Committee
                 Celebrity Management Corporation

                 Jim Aguilar
                 Samantha Clark
                 Ellen Inouye
                 George Koerner

FROM:            Cecilia Jordon, President

SUBJECT:         Company Goals

In advance of our executive meeting on November 16,
1992, please consider the following list of tentative
annual company goals. Keep in mind that our goals
should be aggressive, measurable, and attainable.

     1.   Increase the number of clients by 20%.
     2.   Increase the average income/dividend per
          client by 5%.
     3.   Develop a company culture.
     4.   Expand our current office space by 14,000
          square feet.
     5.   Hire four new agents.

If you have comments or questions prior to the planning
meeting, please contact me.
```

Figure 2-53

Do the following:

1. With a clear document screen, set the margins to 1.5 inches on the left and

2. Set the document to left justification.

3. Type the rough draft of the document as shown in Figure 2-53.

4. Save the document as S2CMC1.DFT.

5. Print the document.

   Cecilia has her assistant proofread and edit the document. Cecilia then appr
   changes (Figure 2-54) and has her assistant make them.

```
                                              November 9, 1992

                MEMORANDUM TO:   Members, Executive Committee
                                 Celebrity Management Corporation

                                 Jim Aguilar
                                 Samantha Clark
                                 Ellen Inouye
                                 George Koerner

                FROM:            Cecilia Jordon, President

                SUBJECT:         Company Goals
                                          planning
                In advance of our executive meeting on November 16,
                1992, please consider the following list of tentative    for 199
                annual company goals. Keep in mind that our goals
                should be aggressive, measurable, and attainable.

                    1.   Increase the number of clients by 20%.
                    2.   Increase the average income/dividend per
                         client by 5%.
                    3.   Develop a company culture.  (not measurable)
                    3.   Expand our current office space by 14,000
                         square feet.
                    4.   Hire four new agents.

                If you have comments or questions prior to the planning
                meeting, please contact me.
```

Figure 2-54

6. Revise the document according to the editing marks shown in Figure 2-54.

7. Save the new version of the memo as S2CMC2.MEM.

8. Print three copies of the memo.

Tutorial 3

Using Additional Editing Features

Writing an Inventory Observation Memo

OBJECTIVES

In this tutorial you will learn to:

- Align text flush right

- Center a line of text

- Search and replace text

- Use block operations to move, delete, and copy text

- Use block operations to change the appearance of existing text

- Use block operations to convert existing text to all uppercase

Case: Sorority Designs Inc.

Melissa Walborsky graduated last June with a degree in accounting and has earned her C.P.A. certificate. She recently began work on the audit staff at McDermott & Eston, an accounting firm in Syracuse, New York. One of Melissa's first assignments is an audit of Sorority Designs Inc. (SDI), a clothing company that markets stylish apparel designed for college-age women. As a member of the audit team, she observed the inventory at SDI's warehouse in Syracuse. Susan Guttmann, Melissa's manager, has asked her to write the inventory observation memo for the audit working papers (documents that verify the nature of an audit and the results). Melissa will write a first draft of the memo. Then based on her own analysis and proofreading, she will revise it. Finally she will submit her draft to Susan for approval, in accordance with the established policy for all McDermott & Eston documents.

Planning the Document

Before writing the memo, Melissa looks at her own notes, the audit working papers, and several other inventory observation memos to help her determine the content, organization, style, and format of her document.

Content

Melissa decides to base the content of her memo primarily on her notes (Figure 3-1) and her personal recollection of the inventory.

Inventory Observation, Syracuse warehouse, June 30, 1993

– Arrived 7:20 a.m.
– No merchandise shipped that day.
– Slow moving and damaged merchandise: shipped to
  Ithaca outlet.
– Periodic test counts on 31% of inventory.
– Cutoff controls: noted apparel received on June 28 and noted
  no merchandise shipped on June 29.

Figure 3-1
Notes Melissa took
during inventory
observations

Organization

Melissa's document will follow the standard organization for an inventory observation memo, with the headings "Observation of Inventory Taking," "Slow Moving and Damaged Merchandise," "Test Counts," "Cutoff Controls," and "Conclusions." She determines that the memo needs only one or two paragraphs under each heading.

Style

Melissa decides to use a straightforward writing style but also to include the usual auditing jargon, since she knows that her audience will be other accountants at McDermott & Eston.

Format

Melissa decides not to change any of WordPerfect's default format settings. She leaves the margins at one inch on the left, right, top, and bottom and keeps the default of full justification. Melissa will modify the format of the heading, however, so that the document follows the standard McDermott & Eston format for inventory observation memos.

Retrieving the Document Using List Files

Let's begin by retrieving Melissa's rough draft of her inventory observation memo. But instead of using the Retrieve feature, let's use WordPerfect's List Files feature. List Files allows you to list the files on a disk or in a directory and to retrieve, delete, rename, or print the document files. The advantage of List Files in retrieving a document is that you don't have to remember the exact name of a document file — you can look over the list of filenames and select the one you want.

To retrieve the document using List Files:

1 Insert your WordPerfect data diskette into drive A and make sure the document screen is clear.

2 Select List Files from the File menu. See Figure 3-2. Alternatively press **[F5]** (List). WordPerfect displays the word "Dir" followed by the name of the default directory on the status line.

You can now type a root directory or a directory path to get a directory listing.

menu name →

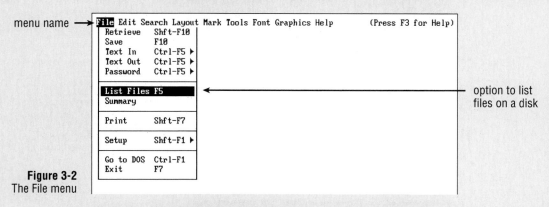

option to list
files on a disk

Figure 3-2
The File menu

3 Type **a:** and press **[Enter]**. WordPerfect displays a List Files menu, similar to the one in Figure 3-3.

option to
retrieve file

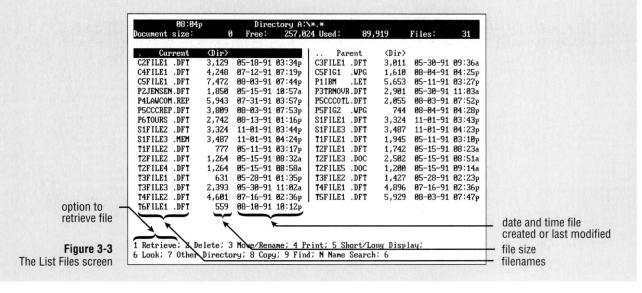

date and time file
created or last modified
file size
filenames

Figure 3-3
The List Files screen

❹ Move the cursor so the filename C3FILE1.DFT is highlighted.

You can use the mouse pointer to click on the filename C3FILE1.DFT or use the keyboard cursor-movement keys to move the cursor to C3FILE1.DFT.

❺ Select **1** (**R**etrieve). If WordPerfect displays the prompt "Retrieve into current document?", your document screen already contains a document. You should select "No," press **[F7]** (Exit) to return to the document screen, clear the screen, and return to Step 1.

The rough draft of the inventory observation memo appears on the WordPerfect document screen. Your screen will look similar to Figure 3-4.

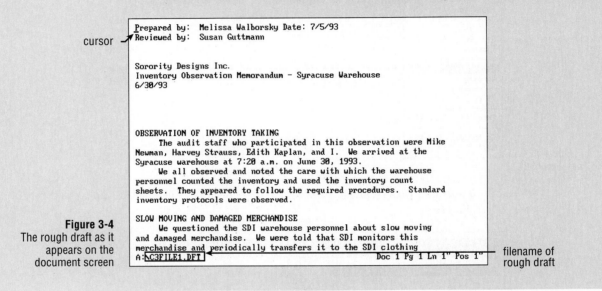

cursor →

```
Prepared by:  Melissa Walborsky Date: 7/5/93
Reviewed by:  Susan Guttmann


Sorority Designs Inc.
Inventory Observation Memorandum - Syracuse Warehouse
6/30/93



OBSERVATION OF INVENTORY TAKING
     The audit staff who participated in this observation were Mike
Newman, Harvey Strauss, Edith Kaplan, and I.  We arrived at the
Syracuse warehouse at 7:20 a.m. on June 30, 1993.
     We all observed and noted the care with which the warehouse
personnel counted the inventory and used the inventory count
sheets.  They appeared to follow the required procedures.  Standard
inventory protocols were observed.

SLOW MOVING AND DAMAGED MERCHANDISE
     We questioned the SDI warehouse personnel about slow moving
and damaged merchandise.  We were told that SDI monitors this
merchandise and periodically transfers it to the SDI clothing
A:\C3FILE1.DFT                         Doc 1 Pg 1 Ln 1" Pos 1"
```

Figure 3-4
The rough draft as it appears on the document screen

filename of rough draft

Remember that this is Melissa's *rough draft*, which she has not yet revised. It contains formatting, spelling, and other errors. In the following section Melissa will revise the memo before she submits it to Susan. Take time now to read through the entire document to familiarize yourself with its content and some of its problems (Figure 3-5).

Prepared by: Melissa Walborksy Date: 7/5/93
Reviewed by: Susan Guttmann

Sorority Designs Inc.
Inventory Observation Memorandum - Syracuse Warehouse
6/30/93

OBSERVATION OF INVENTORY TAKING
    The audit staff who participated in this observation were Mike
Newman, Harvey Strauss, Edith Kaplan, and I. We arrived at the
Syracuse warehouse at 7:20 a.m. on June 30, 1993.
    We all observed and noted the care with which the warehouse
personnel counted the inventory and used the inventory count
sheets. They appeared to follow the required procedures. Standard
inventory protocols were observed.

SLOW MOVING AND DAMAGED MERCHANDISE
    We questioned the SDI warehouse personnel about slow moving
and damaged merchandise. We were told that SDI monitors this
merchandise and periodically transfers it to the SDI clothing
outlet store in Ithica. We observed a holding area wherein such
merchandise is stored until the next shipment to Ithica. Thus, we
did not include the slow moving and damaged merchandise in the
count.

TEST COUNTS
    We made test counts on approximately 31% the inventory. We
recorded our findings in our work papers and noted that these
counts substantiated SDI's counts.

CUTOFF CONTROLS
    We took time to gain access to and examine the Receipt Log and
the Shipping Log for this warehouse. We noted the merchandise
received on June 28, 1993; we also noted that no merchandise was
shipped on June 29, 1993. We used the June 28 numbers for our
subsequent purchases and sales cutoff tests.

Conclusions
    I believe we made an accurate count of all saleable
merchandise in the Syracuse warehouse on June 30, 1993, because the
SDI personnel followed all required procedures and because the
merchandise held for delivery to the Ithica outlet store was not
counted.

Figure 3-5
Melissa's rough draft

Using Flush Right

Melissa begins by observing that in most of the other company memos the date on the top line of the document appears flush against the right margin. She decides, therefore, to use WordPerfect's Flush Right feature to move the date to the right margin. Let's use Flush Right to position the date on the right margin.

To move existing text flush right:

❶ Move the cursor to the "D" in "Date" on the first line of the document.

Whenever you use this feature, move the cursor to the first letter of the group of words that you want flush right.

❷ Select Flush Right from the Align option of the Layout menu. See Figure 3-6. Alternatively press **[Alt][F6]** (Flush Right).

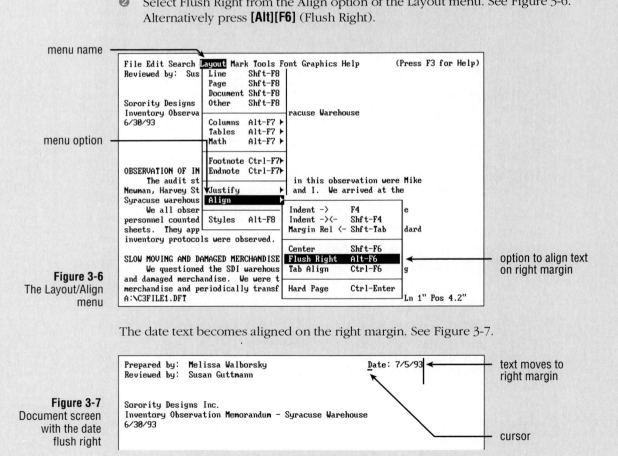

Figure 3-6
The Layout/Align menu

The date text becomes aligned on the right margin. See Figure 3-7.

Figure 3-7
Document screen with the date flush right

Melissa then decides to add the date that she thinks Susan Guttmann will review the memo, knowing that the date may change.

To type flush-right text:

❶ Move the cursor to the end of the second line, after "Susan Guttmann."

❷ Select Flush Right from the Align option of the Layout menu or press **[Alt][F6]** (Flush Right). The cursor is now at the far right margin of the document.

❸ Type **Date: 7/9/93**.

Notice that as you type the cursor stays in the same place, rather than moving from left to right. Instead the characters move from right to left, away from the right margin. See Figure 3-8.

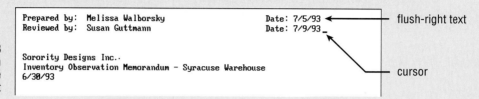

Figure 3-8
Document screen
with second date
flush right

Centering Text

Melissa realizes that the three title lines in the inventory observation memo — starting with "Sorority Designs" and ending with the date of the audit, "6/30/93" — should be centered between the left and the right margins. Let's use WordPerfect's Center command to format these three lines of text.

To center text:

❶ Move the cursor to the "S" in "Sorority," at the beginning of the third line of the document.

To center any line of text, you first place the cursor at the beginning of that line.

❷ Select Center from the Align option of the Layout menu or press **[Shift][F6]** (Center). As soon as you select the Center command, WordPerfect centers the line of text between the margins. See Figure 3-9.

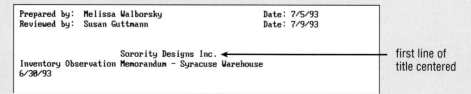

Figure 3-9
Document screen with
first title line centered

❸ Move the cursor to the beginning of the next line.

❹ Select Center from the Align option of the Layout menu or press **[Shift][F6]** (Center).

⑤ Use the same procedure to center the next line of text. See Figure 3-10.

Figure 3-10
Document screen
with all three title
lines centered

```
Prepared by:  Melissa Walborsky              Date: 7/5/93
Reviewed by:  Susan Guttmann                 Date: 7/9/93


                    Sorority Designs Inc.
        Inventory Observation Memorandum - Syracuse Warehouse    ⎫
                         6/30/93                                  ⎭ ◄─── all three lines
                                                                         centered
```

⑥ Turn on Reveal Codes to see the [Flsh Rgt] and the [Center] format codes that
WordPerfect inserted into the document in this and the previous set of steps. (You
will have to move the cursor up near the beginning of the document to see the
[Flsh Rgt] codes.) After you have viewed the codes, turn off Reveal Codes.

As a general rule, when you want to center many lines of text, such as all the lines on a
title page of a report, use the Center Justification command, which you learned in
WordPerfect Tutorial 2. When you want to center only a few lines of text, use the Center
command.

Searching for Text

When you're working with a short document — a half page in length, for example — you
can find a specific word or phrase or move the cursor to a specific location just by using the
cursor-movement keys. But when you're working with a longer document, the best way to
find a specific word or phrase or to move to a specific location may be with the Search
command. A **search** is an operation you use to position the cursor at a specified sequence
of characters or codes, called the **search string**. The search string may include a single
character, such as "T" or "4"; a format code, such as [→Indent] or [HRt]; a word or group of
words, such as "inventory" or "shipping log"; or any combination of characters, codes, or
words.

Let's look at an example of how you would use the Search command. Melissa notices
that in her inventory observation memo she left out the word "of" after "31%" in the first line
under "TEST COUNTS." She decides to use WordPerfect's Search command to move the
cursor quickly to that location in the memo.

To search for text:

❶ Move the cursor to the beginning of the document.

Since you will tell WordPerfect to search forward from the cursor toward the end
of the document, you want to move the cursor to the beginning of the document
to make sure that you find the specified search string.

❷ Select Forward from the Search menu. See Figure 3-11. Alternatively press **[F2]**
(Search).

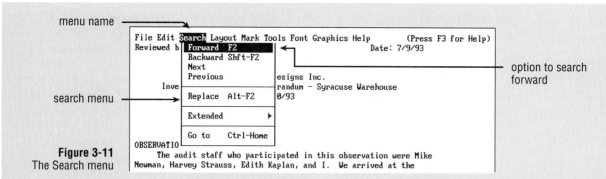

Figure 3-11
The Search menu

menu name

search menu

option to search
forward

WordPerfect displays the prompt "-> Srch:" and waits for you to type the search string. The "->" in the prompt represents a forward arrow, meaning that WordPerfect will search from the cursor toward the end of the document.

③ Type **31%** and press **[F2]** (Search).

Do *not* press [Enter], because that would insert a hard-return code [HRt] into the search string, and WordPerfect would search for the string "31%[HRt]" instead of just "31%." If you accidentally pressed [Enter] and have not yet pressed [F2], just press [Backspace] to erase the [HRt] code. Similarly be careful not to type a space or a period as part of the search string. In other words, type *only* the characters that you want WordPerfect to search for. WordPerfect searches through the document until it finds the next occurrence of the search string — "31%" — and then positions the cursor immediately after the string. In Melissa's inventory observation memo the string "31%" occurs only once, so the cursor moves to just after "31%."

④ Press **[Space]** and type **of** to add the missing word. See Figure 3-12.

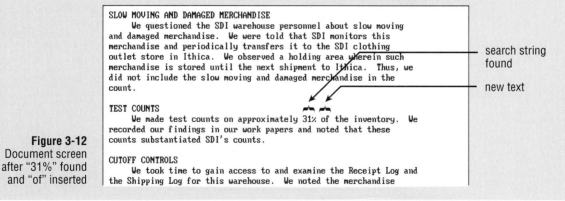

search string
found

new text

Figure 3-12
Document screen
after "31%" found
and "of" inserted

After you have had some practice, you'll find that using the Search command to move the cursor to specific locations within your document is usually much faster than using only the cursor-movement keys.

Searching and Replacing

Search and replace, sometimes simply called **replace**, is an operation that searches through a document for a search string and then replaces one or more occurrences of that search string with another specified string, called the **replacement string**. The replacement string, like the search string, can be any combination of characters, codes, or words. You can use search and replace to change one word to another word, one phrase to another phrase, one set of format codes to another set of format codes, and so forth, throughout your document.

Let's use search and replace to change an incorrect word in the inventory observation memo to the correct word. For example, Melissa notices that she misspelled "Ithaca" throughout the document. She can't use WordPerfect's speller to make the correction, because "Ithaca" is not in the speller dictionary. She decides, therefore, to use WordPerfect's Replace feature to search for all occurrences of "Ithica" and replace them with "Ithaca."

To search and replace a string of text:

❶ Move the cursor to the beginning of the document.

The Replace feature works from the position of the cursor to the end of the document. Thus, to perform the operation for an entire document, you need to move the cursor to the beginning of the document.

❷ Select Replace from the Search menu or press **[Alt][F2]** (Replace). WordPerfect displays the "w/Confirm?" prompt. See Figure 3-13.

Figure 3-13
The "w/Confirm" prompt

prompt to select search and replace with or without confirmations

```
inventory protocols were observed.

SLOW MOVING AND DAMAGED MERCHANDISE
    We questioned the SDI warehouse personnel about slow moving
and damaged merchandise.  We were told that SDI monitors this
merchandise and periodically transfers it to the SDI clothing
w/Confirm? No (Yes)
```

Selecting "Yes" instructs WordPerfect to pause at every occurrence of the search string and wait for you to decide whether you want that occurrence of the search string replaced.

❸ Select "No" by pressing **N** or by pressing **[Enter]** (since "No" is the default), or by clicking the mouse pointer on "No."

Selecting "No" tells WordPerfect that you don't want to confirm the replacements. That is, WordPerfect will automatically replace every occurrence of the search string, "Ithica", with the replacement string, "Ithaca", throughout your document, without pausing to ask for confirmation.

The "-> Srch:" prompt appears on the status line followed by the previous search string. See Figure 3-14.

Figure 3-14
The "-> Search" prompt with previous search string

prompt for search string

```
SLOW MOVING AND DAMAGED MERCHANDISE
    We questioned the SDI warehouse personnel about slow moving
and damaged merchandise.  We were told that SDI monitors this
merchandise and periodically transfers it to the SDI clothing
-> Srch: 31%
```

previous search string

❹ Ignore the previous search string and type **Ithica**, then press **[F2]** (Search). "Ithica" becomes the new search string. The prompt "Replace with:" appears on the status line.

❺ Type **Ithaca** and press **[F2]** (Search). "Ithaca", the correct spelling of the city, becomes the replacement string.

WordPerfect carries out the search and replace, changing all occurrences of "Ithica" to "Ithaca." If you scroll the screen up to the first occurence of "Ithaca", your screen will look like Figure 3-15.

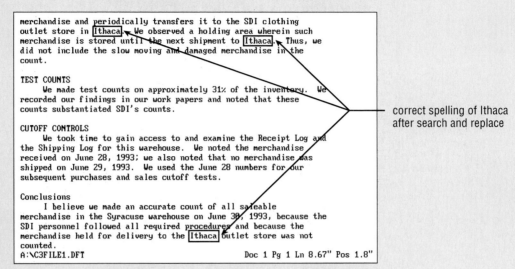

correct spelling of Ithaca
after search and replace

Figure 3-15
Document screen
after the Replace
operation

As Melissa reads through her draft of the memo, she realizes that she has used the word "merchandise" excessively. She decides that in some places she could use the word "apparel" instead, since apparel is the only type of merchandise that SDI sells. To avoid the repetitive use of "merchandise," she performs a search and replace *with confirmation*. This means that at each occurrence of "merchandise" in the document, WordPerfect will stop and ask her if she wants to replace "merchandise" with "apparel."

In this example, we'll use the search string "merchandise" in all lowercase letters. This instructs WordPerfect to stop at *all* occurrences of "merchandise" with either uppercase or lowercase letters, such as "Merchandise" or "MERCHANDISE." When you use uppercase letters in a search string, WordPerfect searches only for a string with those uppercase letters. For example, if "Ithica" were the search string, WordPerfect would stop at "Ithica" and "ITHICA" but not at "ithica."

Let's use search and replace with confirmation to change some of the occurrences of "merchandise" to "apparel." In the following steps, the choice of when to change a word and when to leave it unchanged is based on whatever seems better to Melissa, not on any rules.

To search and replace with confirmation:

❶ Move the cursor to the beginning of the document and select Replace from the Search menu or press **[Alt][F2]** (Replace).

❷ At the prompt "w/Confirm?" select "Yes."

Selecting "Yes" instructs WordPerfect to stop at all occurrences of the search string and to prompt for confirmation before replacing the text.

❸ Type **merchandise** and press **[F2]** (Search). The word "merchandise" becomes the search string.

❹ Type **apparel** and press **[F2]** (Search).

The word "apparel" becomes the replacement string. The cursor now stops at the first occurrence of "merchandise," located in the second heading, and WordPerfect waits for you to accept or decline the replacement. See Figure 3-16.

Figure 3-16
The confirmation prompt with the cursor on "MERCHANDISE"

```
SLOW MOVING AND DAMAGED MERCHANDISE◄───────────────────────── cursor
      We questioned the SDI warehouse personnel about slow moving
and damaged merchandise.  We were told that SDI monitors this
merchandise and periodically transfers it to the SDI clothing
outlet store in Ithaca.  We observed a holding area wherein such
merchandise is stored until the next shipment to Ithaca.  Thus, we
did not include the slow moving and damaged merchandise in the
count.

TEST COUNTS
      We made test counts on approximately 31% of the inventory.  We
recorded our findings in our work papers and noted that these
counts substantiated SDI's counts.
Confirm? No (Yes)◄──────────────────  Doc 1 Pg 1 Ln 4.33" Pos 3.5"──── confirmation prompt
```

❺ Select "Yes" to replace "merchandise" with "apparel" in the second heading. The cursor then continues to move to each occurrence of "merchandise," stopping each time for you to accept or decline the replacement.

❻ The word "merchandise" occurs four times in the paragraph following the second heading. Select "Yes" to accept the replacement in the first sentence of the paragraph, select "No" to decline the replacement in the second sentence, select "No" again to decline replacement in the third sentence, and select "Yes" to accept the replacement in the last sentence.

❼ Select "No" twice to decline replacement of both occurrences of "merchandise" in the paragraph under "CUTOFF CONTROLS."

❽ Select "Yes" to accept replacement of the first occurrence of "merchandise" in the final paragraph, then select "No" to decline replacement of the last occurrence of "merchandise" in the document.

The search and replace operation is now complete. Your printed document will look similar to Figure 3-17. The word "Apparel" in the second heading isn't in all uppercase letters, as it should be, but you'll fix that problem later. The first letter of "Apparel" is uppercase because, in a search and replace, WordPerfect automatically capitalizes the first letter of the *replacement* word when the first letter of the *replaced* word is uppercase.

```
Prepared by:  Melissa Walborksy              Date:  7/5/93
Reviewed by:  Susan Guttmann                 Date:  7/9/93

                     Sorority Designs Inc.
       Inventory Observation Memorandum - Syracuse Warehouse
                          6/30/93


OBSERVATION OF INVENTORY TAKING
   The audit staff who participated in this observation were Mike
Newman, Harvey Strauss, Edith Kaplan, and I. We arrived at the
Syracuse warehouse at 7:20 a.m. on June 30, 1993.
   We all observed and noted the care with which the warehouse
personnel counted the inventory and used the inventory count
sheets. They appeared to follow the required procedures. Standard
inventory protocols were observed.

SLOW MOVING AND DAMAGED Apparel
   We questioned the SDI warehouse personnel about slow moving
and damaged apparel. We were told that SDI monitors this
merchandise and periodically transfers it to the SDI clothing
outlet store in Ithaca. We observed a holding area wherein such
merchandise is stored until the next shipment to Ithaca. Thus, we
did not include the slow moving and damaged apparel in the count.

TEST COUNTS
   We made test counts on approximately 31% of the inventory. We
recorded our findings in our work papers and noted that these
counts substantiated SDI's counts.

CUTOFF CONTROLS
   We took time to gain access to and examine the Receipt Log and
the Shipping Log for this warehouse. We noted the merchandise
received on June 28, 1993; we also noted that no merchandise was
shipped on June 29, 1993. We used the June 28 numbers for our
subsequent purchases and sales cutoff tests.

Conclusions
   I believe we made an accurate count of all saleable apparel in
the Syracuse warehouse on June 30, 1993, because the SDI personnel
followed all required procedures and because the merchandise held
for delivery to the Ithaca outlet store was not counted.
```

Figure 3-17
Melissa's revised draft of the memo

Saving and Printing the Document

Melissa now feels that the inventory observation memo is ready to save to the disk and to print for review by her manager, Susan.

To save and print the document:

❶ Make sure your data diskette is in drive A.

❷ Save the document using the path and filename A:\S3FILE2.DFT.

Melissa uses the filename extension .DFT to signify that this is still a draft of the memo. Before saving and printing the final version, she wants Susan to read it.

❸ Make sure your printer is turned on and ready to print, then print the document.

After she prints the document, Melissa gives it to Susan, who notes errors and makes other changes. Susan returns the edited document to Melissa and asks her to make the changes before printing a copy for the file (Figure 3-18). Because Susan did, in fact, review the memo on 7/9/93, she doesn't tell Melissa to change that date.

Block Operations

One of the most powerful editing features in WordPerfect is the Block command, which executes block operations. A **block operation** is a set of commands that allows you to modify or otherwise act on an existing unit of text. The unit of text may be any portion of your document — a single character, a phrase, a sentence, a paragraph, a page, or a group of pages.

Block operations are powerful because they allow you to change a block of text all at one time instead of changing each word individually. For example, you could change all the text in a paragraph from normal to boldfaced, from left-justified to centered, or from uppercase and lowercase to all uppercase. You can also use block operations to delete a block of text, save a block of text to a disk, or move a block of text from one location to another within your document.

Prepared by: Melissa Walborksy   Date: 7/5/93
Reviewed by: Susan Guttmann   Date: 7/9/93

                        Sorority Designs Inc.   *bf*   *underline*
        Inventory Observation Memorandum - Syracuse Warehouse
                              6/30/93

OBSERVATION OF INVENTORY TAKING
     The audit staff who participated in this observation were Mike
Newman, Harvey Strauss, Edith Kaplan, and I. We arrived at the
Syracuse warehouse at 7:20 a.m. on June 30, 1993.
     We all observed and noted the care with which the warehouse
personnel counted the inventory and used the inventory count
sheets. They appeared to follow the required procedures. Standard
inventory protocols were observed.
                                              uppercase
SLOW MOVING AND DAMAGED Apparel
     We questioned the SDI warehouse personnel about slow moving
and damaged apparel. We were told that SDI monitors this
merchandise and periodically transfers it to the SDI clothing
outlet store in Ithaca. We observed a holding area wherein such
merchandise is stored until the next shipment to Ithaca. Thus, we
did not include the slow moving and damaged apparel in the count.

TEST COUNTS
     We made test counts on approximately 31% of the inventory. We
recorded our findings in our work papers and noted that these
counts substantiated SDI's counts.

CUTOFF CONTROLS   *d*
     We took time to gain access to and examine the Receipt Log and
the Shipping Log for this warehouse. We noted the merchandise
received on June 28, 1993; we also noted that no merchandise was
shipped on June 29, 1993. We used the June 28 numbers for our
subsequent purchases and sales cutoff tests.

Conclusions   *capitalize entire word*
     I believe we made an accurate count of all saleable apparel in
the Syracuse warehouse on June 30, 1993, because the SDI personnel
followed all required procedures and because the merchandise held
for delivery to the Ithaca outlet store was not counted.

Figure 3-18
Melissa's revised draft with Susan's edits

Figure 3-19 shows the many block features that are available in WordPerfect. Some of these features are familiar to you (such as Bold, Delete, and Flush Right), but many of them may be unfamiliar (such as Append, Comment, and Convert Case). You'll learn many of these features as you complete this and future tutorials.

Features	Description
Append	Add block to the end of an existing file
Bold	Boldface blocked text
Comment	Convert block to a document comment
Convert Case (Switch)	Switch all characters in block to uppercase or lowercase
Center	Center block horizontally
Copy	Make copy of block at another location in the document
Cut	Remove block and paste it into another location in document
Delete	Erase block
Flush Right	Align block against the right margin
Font	Change the size or appearance of blocked text
Macro	Macro acts upon block
Mark Text	Mark block for lists, index, table of contents
Move	Move block to another location in document
Print	Send block of text to the printer
Protect	Keep block of text together on same page to protect against page break
Replace	Search and replace words, phrase, or codes within block
Save	Save block of text to disk
Search	Search for text or codes within block
Shell	Append or save block of text to clipboard
Sort	Sort lines or records within block
Spell	Check spelling within block
Style	Insert style-formatting codes within block
Table	Convert block of text to table
Text In/Out	Save block as text file
Underline	Underline block

Figure 3-19
WordPerfect's
block features

Block operations involve first selecting, or highlighting, the block of text that you want to modify and then executing the appropriate WordPerfect command to act on the block of text. Let's illustrate this procedure by boldfacing an existing phrase in Melissa's inventory observation memo.

Boldfacing Existing Text

Look at Figure 3-18 and notice that Susan's first suggested change is to boldface the client's name in the document title. This is a common practice at McDermott & Eston.

Melissa already knows how to use [F6] (Bold) to boldface *new* text that she hasn't typed yet, but to boldface *existing* text, she has to use the Block feature. Let's use WordPerfect's Block command to boldface the client's name.

To boldface a block of existing text:

❶ Move the cursor to the "S" in "Sorority" in the document title.

In most block operations you first move the cursor to the beginning of the block of text that you want to modify.

You are now ready to turn on Block, that is, begin marking a block of text.

❷ Select Block from the Edit menu. See Figure 3-20. Alternatively press **[Alt][F4]** or **[F12]** (Block).

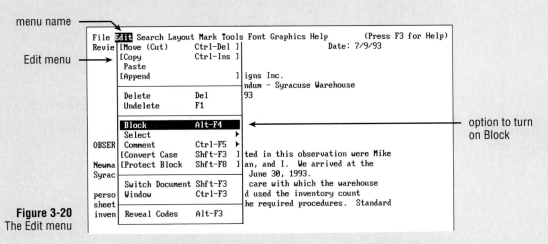

menu name

Edit menu

option to turn on Block

Figure 3-20
The Edit menu

WordPerfect displays the blinking message "Block on" at the bottom of the screen on the left side of the status line, to indicate that Block is on, and highlights the position number on the right side of the status line. See Figure 3-21 on the next page.

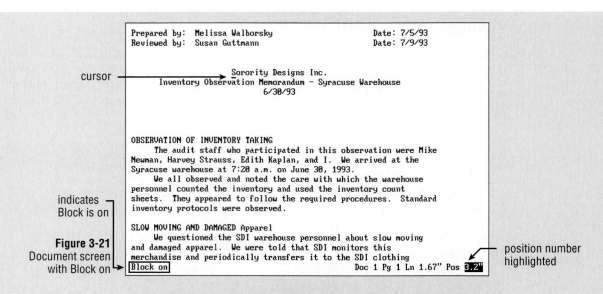

cursor

indicates
Block is on

Figure 3-21
Document screen
with Block on

position number
highlighted

③ Move the cursor to the end of the phrase "Sorority Designs Inc."

In most block operations you select the block by moving the cursor to the end of the block of text that you want to modify. WordPerfect then highlights the selected block of text. See Figure 3-22.

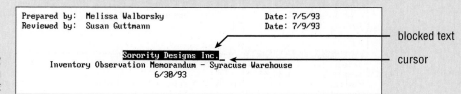

Figure 3-22
Document screen
with blocked text

blocked text

cursor

You can also use the mouse to highlight a block of text. Move the mouse pointer to the beginning of the block of text that you want to modify, press and hold down the left mouse button, drag the mouse pointer — that is, move the mouse pointer while you are still holding down the left button — to the end of the block of text, and release the mouse button. You can now use the mouse or the keyboard to execute other commands.

④ Select Bold from the Appearance menu of the Font menu. See Figure 3-23. Alternatively press **[F6]** (Bold). The block of text becomes boldfaced, and Block is automatically turned off.

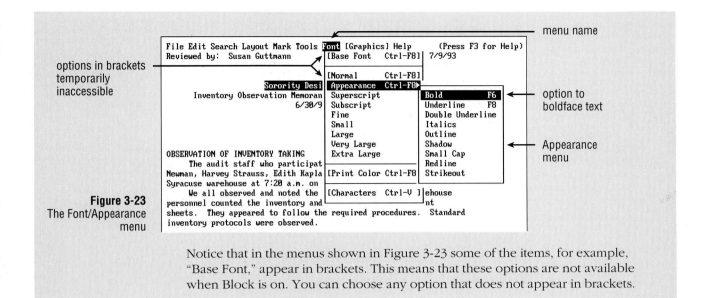

menu name

options in brackets
temporarily
inaccessible

option to
boldface text

Appearance
menu

Figure 3-23
The Font/Appearance
menu

Notice that in the menus shown in Figure 3-23 some of the items, for example, "Base Font," appear in brackets. This means that these options are not available when Block is on. You can choose any option that does not appear in brackets.

As you have seen, WordPerfect's Block feature allows you to change the appearance of a blocked section of text to boldfaced, underlined, double underlined, and so forth.

If you accidentally boldface a block of text that you want in normal appearance, turn on Reveal Codes, move the cursor to the [BOLD] or [bold] code, and delete the code. When you delete either [BOLD] or [bold], WordPerfect automatically removes both codes from the document.

Underlining a Block of Text

Again look at Figure 3-18. Susan's next suggested change is to underline "Syracuse Warehouse" in the second line of the memo title. Let's use a block operation to underline this existing text.

To underline a block of existing text:
❶ Move the cursor to the "S" in "Syracuse," which is the beginning of the block of text that you want to highlight.
❷ Select Block from the Edit menu, press **[Alt][F4]**, or press **[F12]** (Block).

WordPerfect displays the blinking message "Block on" and highlights the position number on the status line.

❸ Move the cursor to the end of "Syracuse Warehouse." The selected block of text becomes highlighted. See Figure 3-24.

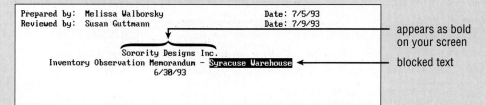

Figure 3-24
Document screen
with blocked text

Instead of using the keyboard to execute Steps 1 through 3, you could drag the mouse pointer over the text that you want to modify.

❹ Select Underline from the Appearance menu of the Font menu or press **[F8]** (Underline).

The block of text becomes underlined, and Block is automatically turned off.

Deleting a Block of Text

Another time-saving block feature is deleting a block of text. If you want to delete more than two or three words, you can save time by using Block. For example, in Figure 3-18 in the paragraph headed "CUTOFF CONTROLS," Susan suggests that Melissa delete the unnecessary and wordy phrase "took time to gain access to and". Let's use a block operation to delete this phrase.

To delete a block of text:

❶ Highlight the phrase "took time to gain access to and" by moving the cursor to the "t" in "took," just below the heading "CUTOFF CONTROLS," turning on Block, then moving the cursor to the "d" in "and". Alternatively you can highlight the phrase by dragging the mouse pointer over it.

❷ Press **[Backspace]** or **[Del]**. WordPerfect displays the prompt "Delete Block?" See Figure 3-25.

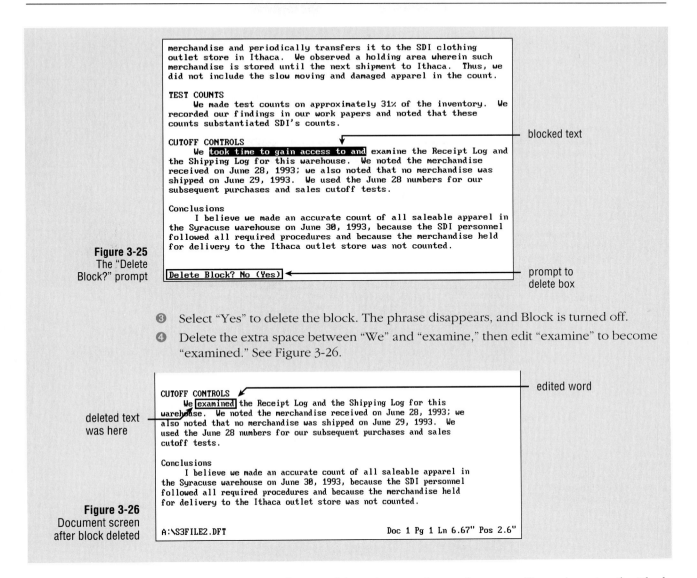

Figure 3-25
The "Delete Block?" prompt

blocked text

prompt to delete box

③ Select "Yes" to delete the block. The phrase disappears, and Block is turned off.

④ Delete the extra space between "We" and "examine," then edit "examine" to become "examined." See Figure 3-26.

edited word

deleted text was here

Figure 3-26
Document screen after block deleted

The more text you have to delete, the more keystrokes you will save by using the Block feature.

If you accidentally delete the wrong block of text, you can restore it by selecting Undelete from the Edit menu or by pressing [F1] (Cancel) and then selecting 1 (Restore).

Converting a Block of Text to All Uppercase

In Figure 3-18 Susan's next editing mark is in the second heading. When Melissa used search and replace to change "merchandise" to "apparel," she forgot to change "Apparel" to all uppercase in the heading. Melissa knows that she can use a block feature to convert case.

To convert the case of a block of text:

❶ Highlight the word "Apparel" in the first heading using the keyboard or the mouse.

❷ Select To Upper in the Convert Case menu of the Edit menu. See Figure 3-27. Alternatively press **[Shift][F3]** (Switch) and select **1** (**U**ppercase).

menu name

option to convert case

Figure 3-27
The Edit/Convert Case menu

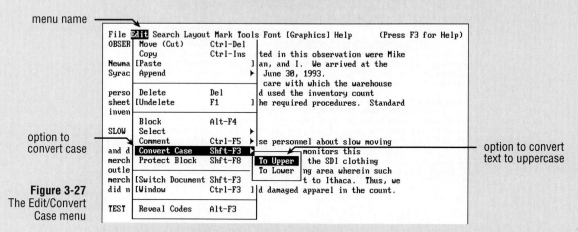

option to convert text to uppercase

The word "Apparel" is converted to the all uppercase "APPAREL," and Block is turned off. See Figure 3-28.

Figure 3-28
Document screen with text converted to all uppercase

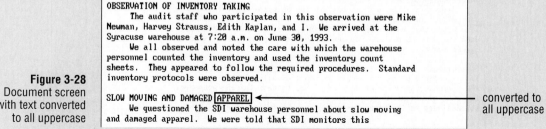

converted to all uppercase

Susan also noted that the last heading, "Conclusions," should also be in all uppercase letters. Let's correct this error as well using a block operation.

❶ Highlight the word "Conclusions" just above the last paragraph of the memo.

❷ Select To Upper in the Convert Case menu of the Edit menu or press **[Shift][F3]** (Switch) and select **1** (**U**ppercase).

The word "Conclusions" becomes "CONCLUSIONS." Your document screen should now appear similar to Figure 3-29.

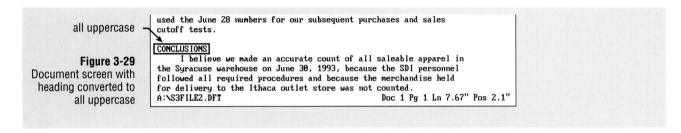

all uppercase

Figure 3-29
Document screen with
heading converted to
all uppercase

You can also use the Convert Case feature to convert a block of text to all lowercase characters.

Moving a Block of Text

One of the most important uses of Block is to move text. Suppose, for example, you have typed a paragraph into a document but then realize the paragraph is in the wrong place. You could solve the problem by deleting the paragraph and then retyping it at the new location. But a much more efficient approach would be to use a block operation to move the paragraph. This is sometimes called "cut and paste," because after highlighting the block of text that you want to move, you cut (delete) it from the text and then paste (restore) it back again (Figure 3-30).

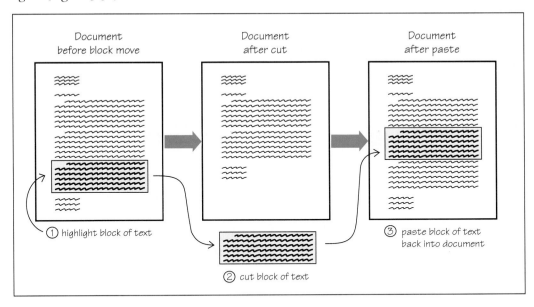

Figure 3-30
The cut and paste
operation

In Figure 3-18 Susan suggests that Melissa move the "TEST COUNTS" section so that it is the second section in the memo instead of the third. Melissa knows that instead of deleting and retyping the paragraph she can use the Block and Move commands to move the entire section. Let's do this now. You can move the text using either the keyboard or a mouse.

To move a block of text using the keyboard:

❶ Move the cursor to the first "T" in "TEST COUNTS," turn on Block, then move the cursor to the "C" in "CUTOFF" to highlight the entire block that you want to move.

Because you want to move the entire section of text, you block from the beginning of one heading to the beginning of the next heading to include the blank line after the paragraph. The blank line is not highlighted, because Block highlights only existing text. See Figure 3-31.

blocked text →

```
         We questioned the SDI warehouse personnel about slow moving
and damaged apparel.  We were told that SDI monitors this
merchandise and periodically transfers it to the SDI clothing
outlet store in Ithaca.  We observed a holding area wherein such
merchandise is stored until the next shipment to Ithaca.  Thus, we
did not include the slow moving and damaged apparel in the count.

TEST COUNTS
         We made test counts on approximately 31% of the inventory.  We
recorded our findings in our work papers and noted that these
counts substantiated SDI's counts.

CUTOFF CONTROLS
         We examined the Receipt Log and the Shipping Log for this
warehouse.  We noted the merchandise received on June 28, 1993; we
also noted that no merchandise was shipped on June 29, 1993.  We
```
← cursor

Figure 3-31
Document screen with blocked text for moving

❷ Select Move (Cut) from the Edit menu. See Figure 3-32.

menu name →   option to move block

```
File Edit Search Layout Mark Tools Font [Graphics] Help     (Press F3 for Help)
and d | Move (Cut)        Ctrl-Del | that SDI monitors this
merch | Copy              Ctrl-Ins | fers it to the SDI clothing
outle | [Paste                   ] | ed a holding area wherein such
merch | Append                   ▶ | xt shipment to Ithaca.  Thus, we
did n |                             | d damaged apparel in the count.
      | Delete             Del
TEST  | [Undelete          F1     ] | inately 31% of the inventory.  We
      |                             | papers and noted that these
recor | Block             Alt-F4
count | Select                    ▶
      | Comment           Ctrl-F5 ▶
CUTOF | Convert Case      Shft-F3 ▶
      | Protect Block     Shft-F8   | nd the Shipping Log for this
wareh |                             | se received on June 28, 1993; we
also  | [Switch Document  Shft-F3 ] | shipped on June 29, 1993.  We
used  | [Window           Ctrl-F3 ] | ubsequent purchases and sales
cutof |
      | Reveal Codes      Alt-F3
```

Figure 3-32
The Edit menu with Move highlighted

Alternatively press **[Ctrl][F4]** (Move) to display the Move menu and select **1** (**B**lock), then **1** (**M**ove). See Figure 3-33.

```
         I believe we made an accurate count of all saleable apparel in
the Syracuse warehouse on June 30, 1993, because the SDI personnel
followed all required procedures and because the merchandise held
for delivery to the Ithaca outlet store was not counted.
Move: 1 Block; 2 Tabular Column; 3 Rectangle: 0
```
← move menu

Figure 3-33
The Move menu

This cuts, or deletes, the selected block of text from the document. The prompt "Move cursor; press Enter to retrieve" appears on the status line. See Figure 3-34. This prompt tells you to move the cursor (using the cursor-movement keys or a search operation) to the position where you want to move the deleted text and then to press [Enter] to restore the text into the memo.

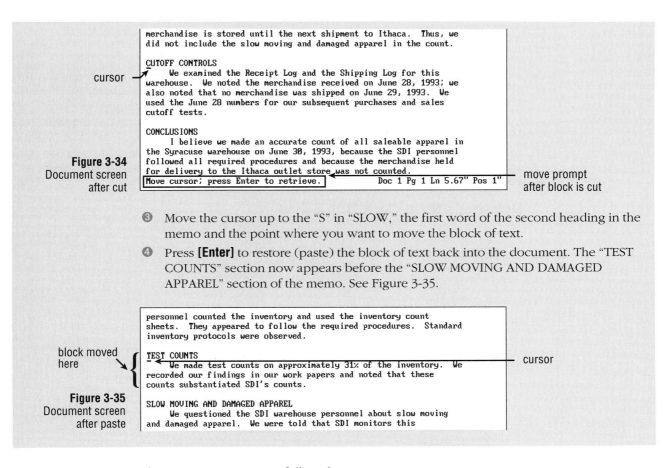

Figure 3-34
Document screen
after cut

cursor

move prompt
after block is cut

Figure 3-35
Document screen
after paste

block moved
here

cursor

❸ Move the cursor up to the "S" in "SLOW," the first word of the second heading in the memo and the point where you want to move the block of text.

❹ Press **[Enter]** to restore (paste) the block of text back into the document. The "TEST COUNTS" section now appears before the "SLOW MOVING AND DAMAGED APPAREL" section of the memo. See Figure 3-35.

If you are using a mouse follow these steps.

To move a block of text using the mouse:

❶ Move the mouse pointer to the "T" in "TEST COUNTS," press and hold down the left mouse button, move the mouse pointer to the "C" in "CUTOFF," and release the mouse button. This highlights the entire block that you want to move.

Because you want to move the entire section of text, you block from the beginning of one heading to the beginning of the next heading to include the blank line after the paragraph.

❷ Select Move (Cut) from the Edit menu.

This cuts, or deletes, the selected block of text from the document. The prompt "Move cursor; press Enter to retrieve" appears on the status line.

❸ Move the mouse pointer to the "S" in "SLOW," the first word of the second heading in the memo and the point where you want to move the block of text, then click the left mouse button.

❹ Select Paste from the Edit menu. The "TEST COUNTS" section now appears before the "SLOW MOVING AND DAMAGED APPAREL" section of the memo. See Figure 3-35.

The Select Command

As you saw in the previous section, you can use the Block command to highlight any unit of text. WordPerfect provides another method, called Select, for highlighting specific units of text. Select, however, allows you to highlight only sentences, paragraphs, and pages, but not other groups of text such as partial sentences or multiple paragraphs. Using Select you can move the cursor to any location within a sentence, paragraph, or page, execute the Select command to highlight the desired unit of text, and then perform the desired operation, such as Move or Delete. This procedure is usually faster than using Block to highlight text.

Deleting a Sentence Using Select

Melissa will use the Select command to delete the unnecessary sentence at the end of the second paragraph in the document, as Susan suggests.

To delete a sentence using the Select command:

❶ Move the cursor anywhere within the sentence "Standard inventory protocols . . ."

With the Select command, you can move the cursor to anywhere in the sentence or to the punctuation mark at the end of the sentence.

❷ Select Sentence from the Select menu of the Edit menu. See Figure 3-36. Alternatively you can press **[Ctrl][F4]** (Move) and select **1** (**S**entence).

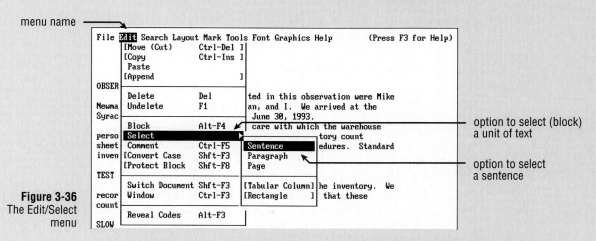

menu name

Figure 3-36
The Edit/Select
menu

option to select (block)
a unit of text

option to select
a sentence

The entire sentence is highlighted, just as if you had used the Block command, and a one-line menu appears at the bottom of the screen. See Figure 3-37.

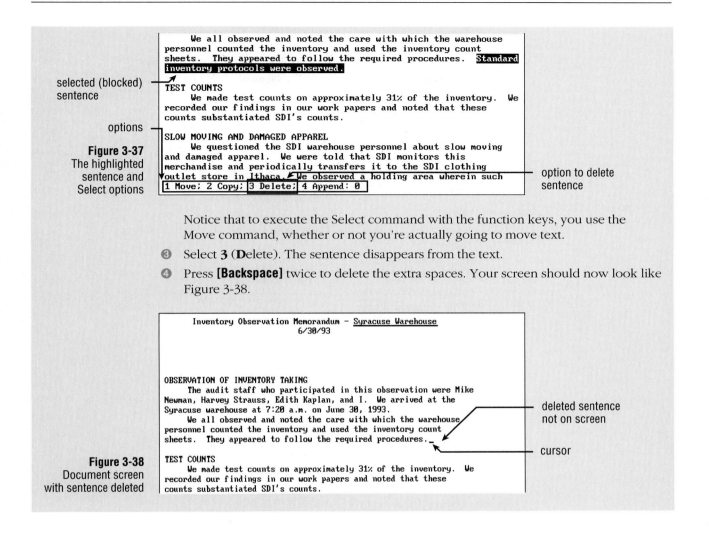

selected (blocked) sentence

options

Figure 3-37
The highlighted sentence and Select options

option to delete sentence

Notice that to execute the Select command with the function keys, you use the Move command, whether or not you're actually going to move text.

❸ Select **3** (**D**elete). The sentence disappears from the text.

❹ Press **[Backspace]** twice to delete the extra spaces. Your screen should now look like Figure 3-38.

Figure 3-38
Document screen with sentence deleted

deleted sentence not on screen

cursor

Copying a Paragraph Using Select

You can also use the Move command to copy a sentence, a paragraph, or a page. Although Melissa has no reason to copy text in her memo, let's copy the second paragraph to the end of the memo, for illustration purposes only, and then use Select to delete the copy.

To copy a paragraph:

❶ Leave the cursor to the right of the period following "required procedures," or move the cursor anywhere within the second paragraph of the memo.

❷ Select Paragraph from the Select menu of the Edit menu or press **[Ctrl][F4]** (Move) and select **2** (**P**aragraph). The entire paragraph that you want to copy is highlighted. See Figure 3-39.

selected (blocked)
paragraph

options

Figure 3-39
The selected
paragraph to copy

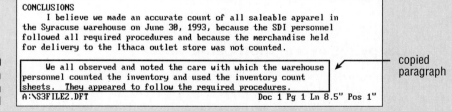

```
Newman, Harvey Strauss, Edith Kaplan, and I.  We arrived at the
Syracuse warehouse at 7:20 a.m. on June 30, 1993.
        We all observed and noted the care with which the warehouse
personnel counted the inventory and used the inventory count
sheets.  They appeared to follow the required procedures.
TEST COUNTS
        We made test counts on approximately 31% of the inventory.  We
recorded our findings in our work papers and noted that these
counts substantiated SDI's counts.

SLOW MOVING AND DAMAGED APPAREL
        We questioned the SDI warehouse personnel about slow moving
and damaged apparel.  We were told that SDI monitors this
merchandise and periodically transfers it to the SDI clothing
outlet store in Ithaca.  We observed a holding area wherein such
1 Move; 2 Copy; 3 Delete; 4 Append: 0
```

option to copy
paragraph

❸ Select **2** (**C**opy). WordPerfect leaves the selected paragraph intact, turns off the highlight, and displays the prompt "Move cursor; press Enter to retrieve" on the status line.

Now you need to move the cursor to the location where you want the second copy of the paragraph.

❹ Move the cursor to the end of the document.

❺ Select Paste from the Edit menu or press **[Enter]** to insert the copy of the paragraph into the text. Press **[Enter]** twice to insert hard returns so that the new copy of the paragraph appears two lines below the preceding paragraph. A copy of the original paragraph appears at this new location in the text. See Figure 3-40.

Figure 3-40
Document screen
after paragraph
copied

```
CONCLUSIONS
        I believe we made an accurate count of all saleable apparel in
the Syracuse warehouse on June 30, 1993, because the SDI personnel
followed all required procedures and because the merchandise held
for delivery to the Ithaca outlet store was not counted.

        We all observed and noted the care with which the warehouse
personnel counted the inventory and used the inventory count
sheets.  They appeared to follow the required procedures.
A:\S3FILE2.DFT                          Doc 1 Pg 1 Ln 8.5" Pos 1"
```

copied
paragraph

Deleting a Paragraph with Select

Just as you can delete a sentence using Select, you can also delete a paragraph using Select. To demonstrate this feature, let's delete the paragraph that we just copied to the end of the memo.

To delete a paragraph with Select:

1. Make sure the cursor is somewhere in the paragraph beginning "We all observed and noted" at end of the document.

2. Select Paragraph from the Select menu of the Edit menu or press **[Ctrl][F4]** (Move) and select **2** (**P**aragraph). The entire paragraph that you want to delete is highlighted. See Figure 3-41.

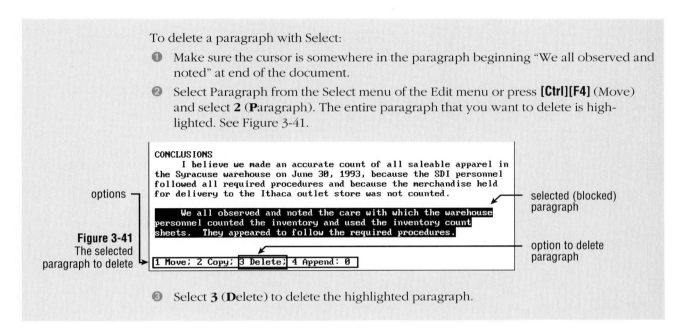

options —

Figure 3-41
The selected
paragraph to delete ►

— selected (blocked)
paragraph

— option to delete
paragraph

```
CONCLUSIONS
     I believe we made an accurate count of all saleable apparel in
the Syracuse warehouse on June 30, 1993, because the SDI personnel
followed all required procedures and because the merchandise held
for delivery to the Ithaca outlet store was not counted.
     We all observed and noted the care with which the warehouse
personnel counted the inventory and used the inventory count
sheets.  They appeared to follow the required procedures.

1 Move; 2 Copy; 3 Delete; 4 Append: 0
```

3. Select **3** (**D**elete) to delete the highlighted paragraph.

The final version of your document should now look similar to Figure 3-42 on the next page.

Prepared by: Melissa Walborksy   Date: 7/5/93
Reviewed by: Susan Guttmann   Date: 7/9/93

Sorority Designs Inc.
Inventory Observation Memorandum - <u>Syracuse Warehouse</u>
6/30/93

OBSERVATION OF INVENTORY TAKING
    The audit staff who participated in this observation were Mike
Newman, Harvey Strauss, Edith Kaplan, and I. We arrived at the
Syracuse warehouse at 7:20 a.m. on June 30, 1993.
    We all observed and noted the care with which the warehouse
personnel counted the inventory and used the inventory count
sheets. They appeared to follow the required procedures.

TEST COUNTS
    We made test counts on approximately 31% of the inventory. We
recorded our findings in our work papers and noted that these
counts substantiated SDI's counts.

SLOW MOVING AND DAMAGED APPAREL
    We questioned the SDI warehouse personnel about slow moving
and damaged apparel. We were told that SDI monitors this
merchandise and periodically transfers it to the SDI clothing
outlet store in Ithaca. We observed a holding area wherein such
merchandise is stored until the next shipment to Ithaca. Thus, we
did not include the slow moving and damaged apparel in the count.

CUTOFF CONTROLS
    We examined the Receipt Log and the Shipping Log for this
warehouse. We noted the merchandise received on June 28, 1993; we
also noted that no merchandise was shipped on June 29, 1993. We
used the June 28 numbers for our subsequent purchases and sales
cutoff tests.

CONCLUSIONS
    I believe we made an accurate count of all saleable apparel in
the Syracuse warehouse on June 30, 1993, because the SDI personnel
followed all required procedures and because the merchandise held
for delivery to the Ithaca outlet store was not counted.

Figure 3-42
The final version of the memo

Select vs. Block

You might not know whether it's better to use Select or Block when you want to modify some existing text. Keep in mind the following information. You can use Select or Block to move, copy, or delete text, but you can use only Block, not Select, to perform other operations such as changing the case, converting from normal text to boldfaced text, or centering the text. Furthermore, Select works only with a clearly defined unit of text — namely, a sentence, a paragraph, or a page — while Block can work with any section of text, such as a word, a phrase, or a group of adjacent paragraphs. Therefore, to move, copy, or delete a sentence, a paragraph, or a page, it would probably be better to use Select. If, on the other hand, you want to do anything else — such as change the case of a phrase or a sentence, delete two adjacent sentences, boldface a paragraph, or copy two adjacent paragraphs — you should use the Block command.

Saving and Printing the Memo

Melissa has completed all the corrections that Susan suggested and can now save and print the finished memo. Melissa should also run the speller before she prints the final copy of her memo. She might also want to use View Document to see how the memo will look on the printed page before she prints it. We'll assume that she's already done these things, and so we won't do them here.

To save and print the memo:

1. Make sure your data diskette is still in drive A.
2. Save the document as A:\S3FILE3.MEM.

   The .MEM filename extension signifies that this is the final version of the memo. WordPerfect saves the final version of the memo to the diskette.
3. Make sure your printer is on and ready to print, then print the document.

Exercises

1. What keys(s) would you press to do the following?
   a. Move a phrase flush against the right margin of the page
   b. Center a line of text between the left and the right margins
   c. Search for the first occurrence of the word "payment" in a document
   d. Search for a previous occurrence (that is, earlier in the document than where the cursor is currently located) of the word "audit" in a document

2. Describe an example of when you would use each of the following function-key commands.
   a. [Alt][F4] or [F12] (Block)   c. [Shift][F2] (Search Left)
   b. [Ctrl][F4] (Move)   d. [Alt][F2] (Replace)

3. List five common commands that you can execute with Block on.

4. Describe how you would boldface text as you type it and then describe how you would boldface text that already exists in a document.

5. What happens when you press the following key(s) with Block on? *Hint:* Look at Figure 3-19.
   a. [Ctrl][F2] (Spell)   c. [Del]
   b. [Shift][F3] (Switch), 2 (Lowercase)   d. [F10] (Save)

6. How would you copy a sentence in your document?

7. For which of the following operations would you use the Block command? For which would you use the Select command?
   a. Deleting three adjacent paragraphs of text
   b. Deleting an entire page of text
   c. Deleting a sentence
   d. Copying a paragraph
   e. Copying a page
   f. Copying a phrase

8. Under what conditions could you safely carry out a search and replace operation without confirmation? Under what conditions would you need to carry out search and replace with confirmation?

Tutorial Assignments

> For the following Tutorial Assignments, make sure the document screen is clear before you retrieve a document.

Retrieve the file T3FILE1.DFT and do the following:

1. Center the first three lines of text. Do not use the center-justification feature.

2. Without retyping the title, change it to all uppercase letters.

3. Boldface the title.

4. Do a search and replace operation to change all occurrences of "SDI" to "Sorority Designs."

5. Save the document as S3MISSON.DOC.

6. Print the document.

Retrieve the file T3FILE2.DFT and do the following:

7. Use Flush Right to right-justify the date in the top line of the memo.

8. Center the title lines, the two lines under Melissa Walborsky's name.

9. Make the title "Solving the Inventory Reduction Problems" uppercase and bold.

10. Move paragraph number 3 above paragraph number 2, then renumber the paragraphs.

11. Without retyping them, underline the words "surprise" in paragraph 3 and "ink" in paragraph 4.

12. Copy the current paragraph 3 to the end of the document and change its paragraph number to 5.

13. In the new paragraph 5, change "audits of their inventories" to "observations of trash cans and dressing rooms." In the second sentence of paragraph 5, change "audits" to "observations."

14. In paragraph 1, move the second sentence, which begins "These beginning figures," to the end of the paragraph.

15. Save the document as S3INVCON.MEM.

16. Print the document.

Retrieve the file T3FILE3.DFT and do the following:

17. Use [Alt][F2] (Replace) to replace all occurrences of the invisible [Tab] code with the code [→Indent]. *Hint:* In the search and replace operation, press **[Tab]** to create the search string and **[F4]** (Indent) to create the replacement string. You may want to turn on Reveal Codes here, but you can execute the command with Reveals Codes off.

18. Use search and replace with confirmation to change all occurrences of "Ithaca Clothing Outlet Store" to "ICOS" in the body of the report but not in the title.

19. Save the document as S3ICOS.MEM.

20. Print the document.

Case Problems

1. Employee Turnover Memo

Aisha Kadar, the director of human resources for the public accounting firm of Armstrong, Black & Calzone (ABC), sends a report each month to the senior partners to summarize employee turnover. The data on turnover rates, including comparisons with previous periods and with industry averages, appear in a Lotus 1-2-3 spreadsheet that accompanies the memo. The main purpose of this quarter's memo is to summarize and explain a higher than normal employee turnover rate.

Do the following:

1. Retrieve the file P3TRNOVR.DFT.

2. In the first line make the date (including the word "Date") flush against the right margin.

3. Center the two title lines of the memo.

4. Boldface the title line "Employee Turnover Memorandum."

5. Change the three headings (which start "Turnover during," "Reasons for," and "Items to") to all uppercase characters.

6. Use a block move operation to switch around reasons number 2 and 3. Revise the paragraph numbers so they are consecutive.

7. Move the first sentence of the last paragraph to the end of the paragraph.

8. Where such changes wouldn't cause an error in the meaning of the text, carry out a search and replace operation to change all occurrences of "the firm" to "ABC."

9. Carry out a search and replace with confirmation to change the tabs ([Tab] codes) after the numbers in the numbered paragraphs to indents ([→Indent] codes).

10. Save the document as S3TRNOVR.MEM.

11. Print the memo.

2. Restaurant Review for *Restaurant Happenings*

Gene Marchand is a freelance writer for *Restaurant Happenings*, a weekly magazine published nationally whose audience is restaurant owners and managers. His editor has asked him to write an article on Pizza Now!, a new chain of drive-in pizza franchises. Figure 3-43 shows the first five paragraphs of Gene's rough draft of the article.

Do the following:

1. Clear the document screen and type the header lines, as shown in Figure 3-43, at the beginning of the document. This header is a standard format used by freelance writers.
    a.   On the left type the author's name, address, and phone number.
    b.   Flush right on the first line, type the word count for the article.
    c.   Flush right on the second line, type the rights that the author is offering: "First North American Serial Rights."

2. Type the title in boldface type and centered between the left and the right margins.

3. Type the author's byline centered between the left and right margins.

4. Type the rest of the article as shown in Figure 3-43.

5. Save the article as S3PIZZA.DOC.

6. Print the document.

```
Gene Marchand                        Word Count (approx):  1800
315 Eastern Parkway #921        First North American Serial Rights
Brooklyn, NY 11201
(718) 812-4875


                     Can Food Be Fast and Good?
                        Pizza Now! Says Yes


                          by Gene Marchand




     Phillip Goldman is the founder and CEO of Pizza Now! Inc., a
franchiser of drive-through fast-food pizza restaurants. He knows
he has a tough job convincing the public that fast-food pizza can
taste good, but he's convinced me.
     I'll take that back. He didn't convince me. His pizza did.
     When I drove through one of his Pizza Now! restaurants in
Pheonix, Arizona, I was in for a pleasant surprise. Not only did I
get my two slices of pizza and a small tossed salad in less time
that it takes to get a Big Mac at McDonald's, but I also found the
pizza to be good tasting. Very good tasting.
     If you like Pizza Hut's, Domino's, or Little Caesar's pizza,
you'll love Pizza Now!'s pizza.
     So what is Goldman's secret to high quality pizza in record
time? I recently talked with him at his company headquarters in
Mesa, just outside of Phoenix. He had some interesting views about
his franchise business and about his pizza.
```

Figure 3-43

3. Life Success Inc.

Michael Thompson is director of Life Success Inc. This nonprofit organization gives one-day training seminars in major cities across the United States to help high school students improve their self-esteem and to realize their full potential as responsible family members, employees, and citizens. Michael is planning the program for the Life Success seminar to be held March 27, 1993, at the Balboa Park Auditorium in San Diego, California. A copy of his tentative program is shown in Figure 3-44 on the next page.

```
                         Life Success Seminar
                  Balboa Park, San Diego, California
                          March 27, 1993



   Welcome . . . . . . . . . . . . . . . . . . Michael Thompson
                                   Director, Life Success Inc.

   Musical Number . . . . . . . . . . . . . La Jolla Youth Chorus
       "The Wind Beneath My Wings" by Larry Henley and Jeff Silbar
                    Directed by Patricia Wilson

   Speaker . . . . . . . . . . . . . . . Alisha Whiting Robinson
                                   Professor of Sociology, UCSD
                  "Finding Role Models"

   Musical Number . . . . . . . . . . . . . La Jolla Youth Chorus
            "From a Distance" by Julie Gold
                Directed by Patricia Wilson

   Introduction of Guest Speaker . . . . . . . . Michael Thompson

   Guest Speaker . . . . . . . . . . . . . . . . . . . Bruce Hurst
                               Star Pitcher, San Diego Padres
                  "Living Up to Your Potential"
```

Figure 3-44

Do the following:

1. Clear the document screen and type the three title lines of the program.

2. Center and boldface all of the title lines.

3. Type the first three items in the program. Press **[Alt][F6]** (Flush Right) *twice* after the first item on each line to produce text that is flush right, with dot leaders.

4. To create the fourth item in the program (the second musical number), use a block operation to copy the second item (the first musical number), then edit the song title rather than retype the entire text.

5. Save the document as S3LIFE.DOC.

6. Print the document.

Tutorial 4

Formatting Multiple-Page Documents

Writing a Sales Report

Case: Camino Office Equipment Corporation

Steven Tanaka is a sales representative for the Camino Office Equipment Corporation (COEC), which sells photocopy machines, fax machines, dictaphones, telephone answering equipment, and other high-technology office equipment. At the end of every year, Steven writes a report that summarizes his sales results, compares these results with previous years' sales, and discusses strategies for future sales. Steven is currently working on his 1992 annual sales report.

Planning the Document

Steven wrote his first annual sales report in 1989. At that time he was trained by company personnel on how to write reports, and he read several reports by successful COEC sales representatives. He now plans his annual report throughout the year by filing notes and data on his sales activities and results. At the end of the year, he organizes and analyzes this information and uses the company guidelines for the content, organization, style, and format of his report.

Content

The main contents of Steven's annual report, besides his own notes and observations, are the quarterly sales figures for the current year and the previous two years. He obtains prior-year sales figures from previous annual reports and total annual sales figures from COEC's main office.

OBJECTIVES

In this tutorial you will learn to:

- Change line spacing
- Center a page from top to bottom
- Change tab settings
- Number pages
- Create headers and footers
- Suppress headers, footers, and page numbers
- Create and use styles
- Create tables
- Set Conditional End of Page
- Set Widow/Orphan Protection

Just as important as the data are his interpretations of the data. Steven knows that a good sales report includes analysis and recommendations.

Organization

Steven organizes his report according to company policy, with a title page, an introduction, a presentation and interpretation of the gross sales for the current and the previous two years, an analysis and summary of the year's sales effort, and recommendations for improved sales in the future.

Style

The report follows established standards of style, emphasizing clarity, simplicity, and directness.

Format

In accordance with COEC policy, Steven's report will include a title page, with each line of text centered between the left and the right margins and the entire text centered between the top and the bottom margins. The lines of text in the body of the report will be double-spaced. Every page, except the title page, will include a header and a page number. Tabs at the beginning of each paragraph will be 0.3 inch. Some information will be presented in a table.

Changing the Line Spacing

Steven has already written and edited the body of his report, but he has yet to type the title page and format the report as COEC requires. He marks a copy of his document with the changes he needs to make (Figure 4-1). As he looks over his copy, Steven decides that first he should retrieve the document and double-space the text. Let's change the line spacing in Steven's report.

To change the line spacing:

❶ Retrieve the document C4FILE1.DFT from your data diskette in drive A.

❷ Make sure the cursor is at the beginning of the document.

Remember that WordPerfect's formatting features take effect from the point in the document where you make the change to the end of the document. If you want to set new line spacing for the entire document, you must move the cursor to the beginning of the document before you change the line spacing.

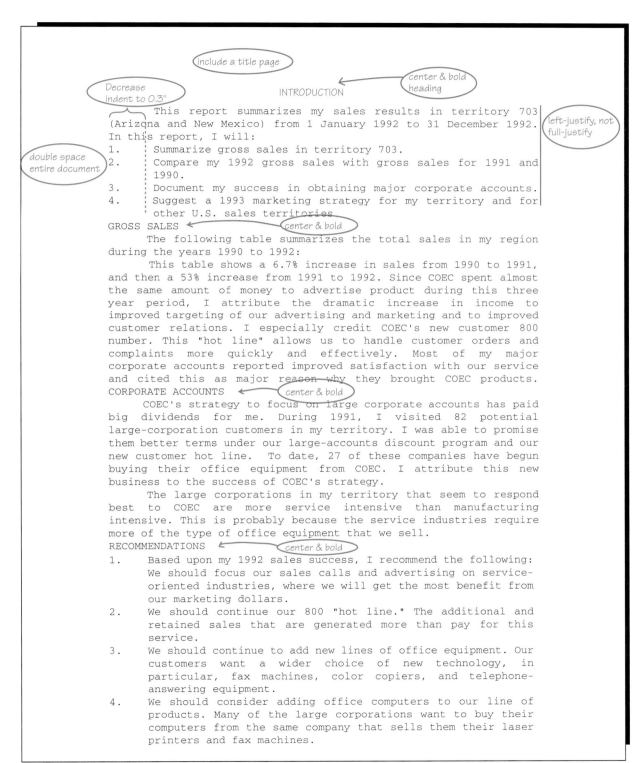

include a title page

center & bold heading

INTRODUCTION

Decrease indent to 0.3"

left-justify, not full-justify

This report summarizes my sales results in territory 703 (Arizona and New Mexico) from 1 January 1992 to 31 December 1992. In this report, I will:

double space entire document

1. Summarize gross sales in territory 703.
2. Compare my 1992 gross sales with gross sales for 1991 and 1990.
3. Document my success in obtaining major corporate accounts.
4. Suggest a 1993 marketing strategy for my territory and for other U.S. sales territories.

GROSS SALES ← center & bold

The following table summarizes the total sales in my region during the years 1990 to 1992:

This table shows a 6.7% increase in sales from 1990 to 1991, and then a 53% increase from 1991 to 1992. Since COEC spent almost the same amount of money to advertise product during this three year period, I attribute the dramatic increase in income to improved targeting of our advertising and marketing and to improved customer relations. I especially credit COEC's new customer 800 number. This "hot line" allows us to handle customer orders and complaints more quickly and effectively. Most of my major corporate accounts reported improved satisfaction with our service and cited this as major reason why they brought COEC products.

CORPORATE ACCOUNTS ← center & bold

COEC's strategy to focus on large corporate accounts has paid big dividends for me. During 1991, I visited 82 potential large-corporation customers in my territory. I was able to promise them better terms under our large-accounts discount program and our new customer hot line. To date, 27 of these companies have begun buying their office equipment from COEC. I attribute this new business to the success of COEC's strategy.

The large corporations in my territory that seem to respond best to COEC are more service intensive than manufacturing intensive. This is probably because the service industries require more of the type of office equipment that we sell.

RECOMMENDATIONS ← center & bold

1. Based upon my 1992 sales success, I recommend the following: We should focus our sales calls and advertising on service-oriented industries, where we will get the most benefit from our marketing dollars.
2. We should continue our 800 "hot line." The additional and retained sales that are generated more than pay for this service.
3. We should continue to add new lines of office equipment. Our customers want a wider choice of new technology, in particular, fax machines, color copiers, and telephone-answering equipment.
4. We should consider adding office computers to our line of products. Many of the large corporations want to buy their computers from the same company that sells them their laser printers and fax machines.

Figure 4-1
The rough draft of Steven's report with his editing marks

❸   Select Line from the Layout menu. See Figure 4-2. Alternatively, press **[Shift][F8]** (Format) and select **1** (**L**ine).

menu name

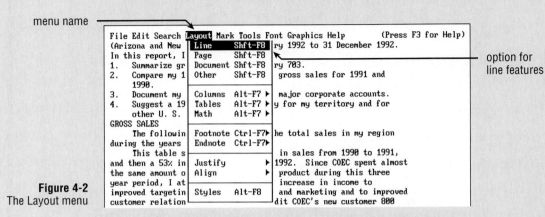

option for
line features

Figure 4-2
The Layout menu

WordPerfect displays the full-screen menu shown in Figure 4-3.

option to change
line spacing

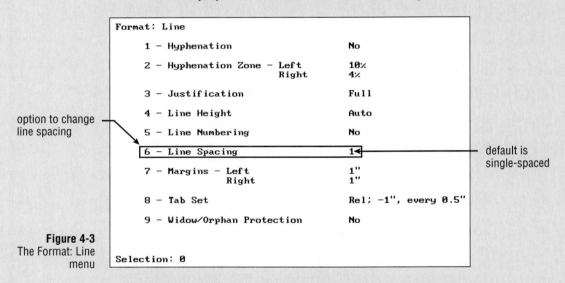

default is
single-spaced

Figure 4-3
The Format: Line
menu

Notice that option 6 is Line Spacing and that to the right of the option is the current line spacing. If you want to make the document double-spaced, you have to change this value from 1 (single spacing) to 2 (double spacing).

❹   Select **6** (Line **S**pacing). The cursor moves to the current value of the line spacing.

❺   Type **2** and press **[Enter]** to set the spacing to 2.

❻   Press **[F7]** (Exit) to return to the document screen. The text of the report is double-spaced. See Figure 4-4.

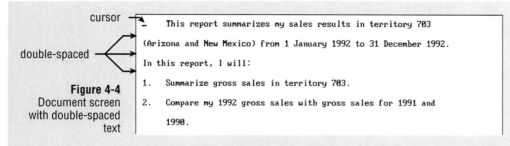

Figure 4-4
Document screen
with double-spaced
text

cursor

double-spaced

❼ Turn on Reveal Codes to view WordPerfect's format code for double spacing and then turn off Reveal Codes.

The code for double spacing is [Ln Spacing:2]. This code is a signal to WordPerfect to double-space the text from that point until the end of the document or until the next [Ln Spacing] code.

You can set the line spacing to any value you want, from 0.01 to 255.99 inches. The most common line spacings, however, are 1 for single spacing, 1.5 for one and one-half spacing, 2 for double spacing, and 3 for triple spacing.

Centering a Page Top to Bottom

Steven next decides to create the title page. He will first insert a hard page break at the beginning of the document, instruct WordPerfect to center the lines between the left and the right margins, and then type the title page.

To create the title page:
❶ Make sure the cursor is at the beginning of the document, just to the right of the [Ln Spacing:2] code.

If necessary turn on Reveal Codes to make sure the cursor is in the right place, and then turn off Reveal Codes.

❷ Press **[Ctrl][Enter]** (Hard Page) to force a hard page break.

The hard page break mark appears on the screen, and the status line indicates that the cursor is now on page 2. See Figure 4-5. You have now created a separate page where you'll type the title of the report.

hard page break

cursor

Figure 4-5
Document screen
after you insert a hard
page break to create a
separate title page

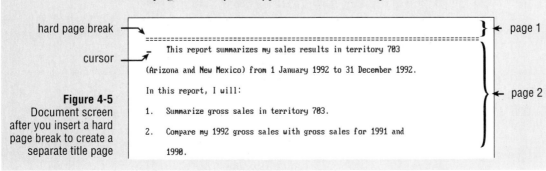

page 1

page 2

③ Set the document to left justification by selecting Left from the Layout/Justify menu. See Figure 4-6. Alternatively press **[Shift][F8]** (Format); select **1** (**L**ine), **3** (**J**ustification), and **1** (**L**eft); and press **[F7]** (Exit).

menu name

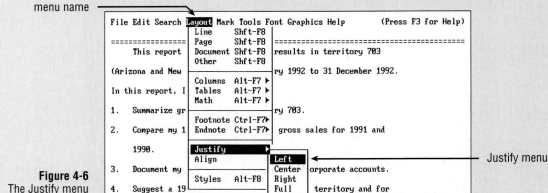

Figure 4-6
The Justify menu

Justify menu

Setting left justification accomplishes two things. First, it sets the body of the report to left justification, which Steven wants. Second, it prevents a problem later on when you set the beginning of the title page to center-justify the title. The problem is that when you set center justification, WordPerfect automatically strips all [Tab] codes from the center-justified text. By setting left justification here, WordPerfect won't center-justify the body of the text when you center-justify the title page.

④ Move the cursor back to the first page.

⑤ Execute the Center Justification command, using the menus or keystrokes similar to those for setting left justification. This causes all the text on the title page (page 1) to be center-justified.

⑥ Type the text of the title page, as shown in Figure 4-7. After you type the title ("1992 ANNUAL SALES REPORT") in boldfaced characters, turn off bold and press **[Enter]** four times to insert four blank lines. Then type the next block of text (name, title, territory) and press **[Enter]** five times to insert five more blank lines. Finally insert today's date using WordPerfect's Date Text command. Your screen should look similar to Figure 4-7.

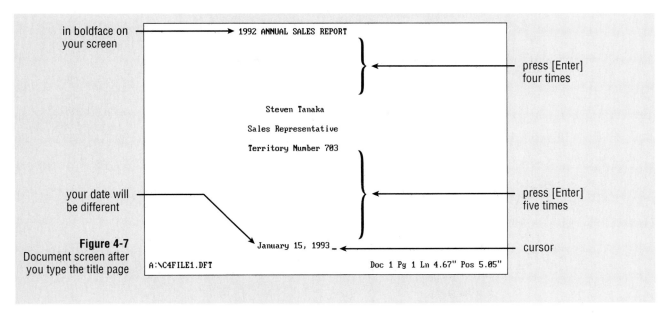

in boldface on
your screen

1992 ANNUAL SALES REPORT

press [Enter]
four times

Steven Tanaka

Sales Representative

Territory Number 703

your date will
be different

press [Enter]
five times

Figure 4-7
Document screen after
you type the title page

January 15, 1993

cursor

A:\C4FILE1.DFT   Doc 1 Pg 1 Ln 4.67" Pos 5.05"

These steps create the title page, but COEC requires that the text of the page be centered between the top and bottom margins on the page. As you can see from the View Document screen (Figure 4-8), the text of the title page is too high up on the page. You could insert hard returns at the beginning of the page until the text is centered. But WordPerfect provides an easier, more accurate method to center text on a page — a feature called Center Page Top to Bottom. Once Steven sets this feature at the beginning of a page, the text will stay centered between the top and the bottom margins, regardless of how much or how little text is on the page.

Let's center the title page now.

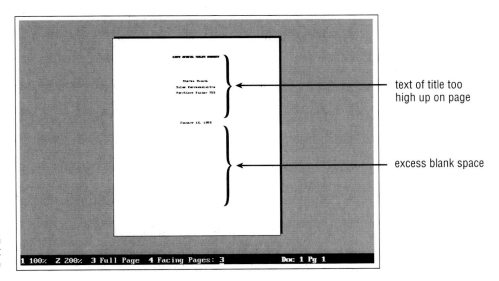

text of title too
high up on page

excess blank space

Figure 4-8
View Document
screen of title page

1 100%   2 200%   3 Full Page   4 Facing Pages: 3   Doc 1 Pg 1

To center the page top to bottom:

❶ Press **[Home]**, **[Home]**, **[Home]**, **[↑]** to move the cursor to the very beginning of the document, prior to any format codes.

For the Center Page Top to Bottom feature to work, the cursor must be located before any text on the page and before any format code that affects the appearance of the first line of text on the page, such as [HRt], [Tab], or [BOLD]. Pressing [Home] three times prior to pressing [↑] moves the cursor before all text and all codes in the document.

❷ Select Page from the Layout menu or press **[Shift][F8]** (Format) and select **2** (**P**age). The Format: Page menu appears on the screen. See Figure 4-9.

menu name

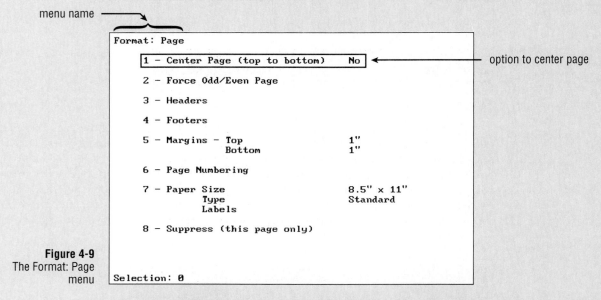

```
Format: Page

     1 - Center Page (top to bottom)      No        ◄──  option to center page

     2 - Force Odd/Even Page

     3 - Headers

     4 - Footers

     5 - Margins - Top                    1"
                   Bottom                 1"

     6 - Page Numbering

     7 - Paper Size                       8.5" x 11"
                Type                       Standard
                Labels

     8 - Suppress (this page only)



Selection: 0
```

Figure 4-9
The Format: Page
menu

❸ Select **1** (**C**enter Page top to bottom), select "Yes" to verify that you do want to center the page, and press **[F7]** (Exit) to return to the document screen. WordPerfect inserts the [Center Pg] code into your document at the location of the cursor, as you can see if you turn on Reveal Codes. Turn off Reveal Codes before going to Step 4.

❹ Select View Document from the Print/Options menu to see how the page is centered. See Figure 4-10. After you have viewed the document, press **[F7]** (Exit) to return to the document screen.

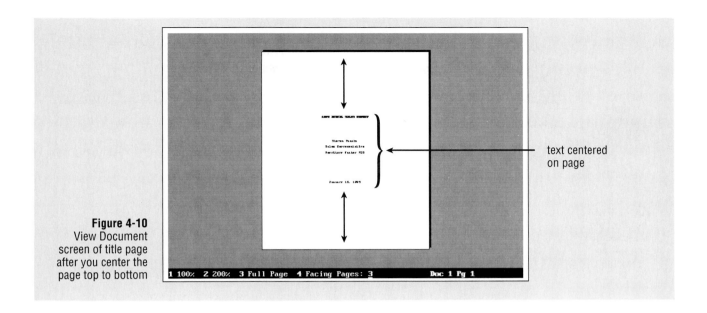

Figure 4-10
View Document
screen of title page
after you center the
page top to bottom

text centered
on page

Changing the Tab Stops

Steven looks over his edited report (Figure 4-1) and decides to next change the amount of indented space at the beginning of each paragraph from 0.5 inch to 0.3 inch, according to COEC requirements.

When Steven wrote the draft of his report, he pressed [Tab] at the beginning of each paragraph. This created a 0.5-inch space at the beginning of each paragraph, because the first tab stop to the right of the left margin was at 0.5 inch. A **tab stop** is a location (usually specified in inches) along each text line to which the cursor will move when you press [Tab] or [Indent] (Figure 4-11). In WordPerfect the default setting of the tab stops is every 0.5 inch from the left margin. With a 1-inch left margin and the cursor located at the left margin (Pos 1", as indicated on the status line), pressing [Tab] will move the cursor and all text to the right of the cursor to the tab stop at Pos 1.5".

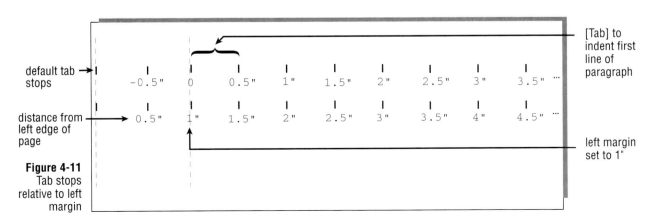

default tab
stops

distance from
left edge of
page

Figure 4-11
Tab stops
relative to left
margin

[Tab] to
indent first
line of
paragraph

left margin
set to 1"

To create the numbered paragraphs, Steven typed a number and a period, which positioned the cursor at about Pos 1.2", and then he pressed [F4] (Indent). This caused the entire paragraph to be indented to the next tab stop at Pos 1.5" (Figure 4-12). The cursor will return to the left margin at Pos 1" after you press [Enter] at the end of the paragraph.

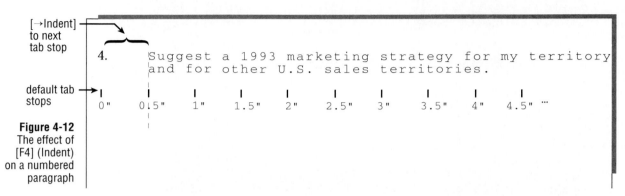

[→Indent] to next tab stop

default tab stops

Figure 4-12
The effect of [F4] (Indent) on a numbered paragraph

4.   Suggest a 1993 marketing strategy for my territory and for other U.S. sales territories.

0"   0.5"   1"   1.5"   2"   2.5"   3"   3.5"   4"   4.5" ...

Because the COEC format calls for the first line of each paragraph to be indented 0.3 inch, Steven has to change the tab stops. Let's first instruct WordPerfect to display the Tab menu, which indicates the location of the current tab stops.

To display the Tab menu:

❶   Make sure the cursor is at the beginning of the document so that the change in location of tab stops will affect the entire document, from beginning to end.

❷   Select Line from the Layout menu or press **[Shift][F8]** (Format) and select **1** (**Line**). WordPerfect displays the Format: Line menu, as shown in Figure 4-13.

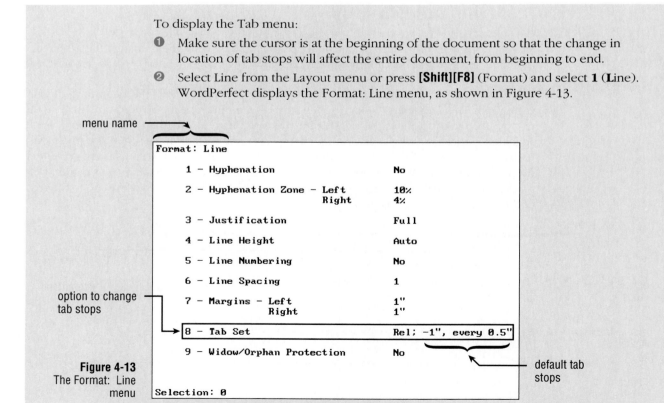

menu name

option to change tab stops

Figure 4-13
The Format: Line menu

default tab stops

```
Format: Line

    1 - Hyphenation                         No

    2 - Hyphenation Zone - Left             10%
                           Right            4%

    3 - Justification                       Full

    4 - Line Height                         Auto

    5 - Line Numbering                      No

    6 - Line Spacing                        1

    7 - Margins - Left                      1"
                  Right                     1"

    8 - Tab Set                             Rel; -1", every 0.5"

    9 - Widow/Orphan Protection             No

Selection: 0
```

❸   Select **8** (**T**ab Set). The Tab menu appears at the bottom of the screen. See Figure 4-14.

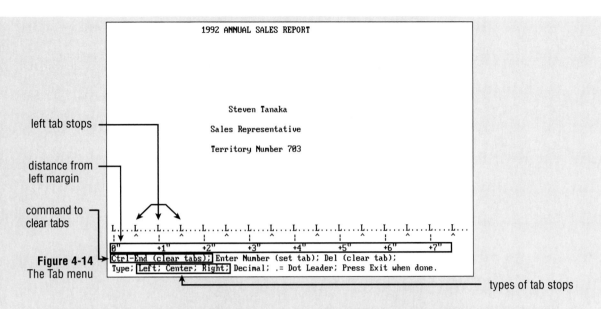

Figure 4-14
The Tab menu

The menu consists of a tab scale, usually labeled in inches, that indicates the location of each tab stop. Each tab stop is marked with the letter L, which stands for left tab stop. A left tab stop allows you to align words and phrases along their left edges, as shown in Figure 4-15, which also demonstrates center and right tabs.

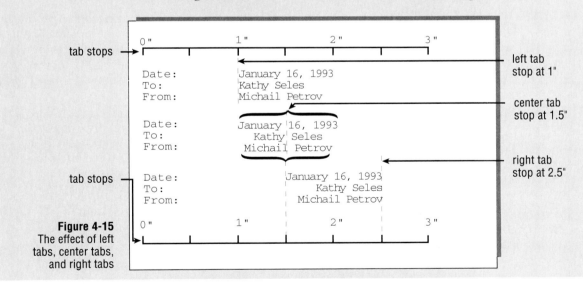

Figure 4-15
The effect of left tabs, center tabs, and right tabs

Next let's clear the current tab stops so we can set new ones.

To clear the tab stops:

❶ Make sure the cursor is located at 0" on the tab scale.

You can use **[←]** and **[→]** to move the cursor, or you can type the value (in this case, 0 or zero) and press **[Enter]**, to position the cursor on the tab scale. The 0" means that the cursor is zero inches from the left *margin* of the page, not from the left edge of the page.

❷ Press **[Ctrl][End]** (Del to EOL) to delete the tab stops from the cursor to the end of the line. See Figure 4-16.

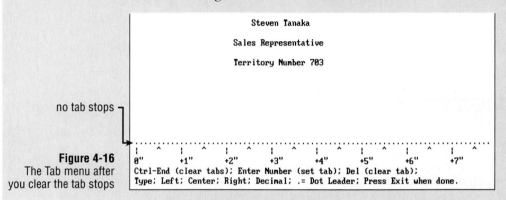

no tab stops

Figure 4-16
The Tab menu after
you clear the tab stops

With all the old tab stops cleared, you are ready to set the new tab stops. You can set tab stops one at a time by moving the cursor to the desired location and pressing [Tab], or you can set several evenly spaced tabs in one operation. Let's begin by setting a tab stop at 0" and then set evenly spaced tabs, starting at 0.3" and continuing every 0.5" after that.

To set the tab stops:

❶ Press **[Tab]** to set the tab at the current cursor position. In this case the cursor is at 0", so an "L" (for left tab) appears on the tab scale at that location. You can also press L to set a left tab.

A tab stop at 0" is required in case you release the left margin (by pressing [Shift][Tab] (Left Margin Release) so the cursor moves into the left margin); you then can press [Tab] to get back to the left margin. You would need tab stops to the left of 0" if you planned to type text inside the left margin in your document.

Next let's set the evenly spaced tabs. In WordPerfect, to set evenly spaced tabs, you first type the distance from the left margin where you want the tabs to begin, type a comma, and then, without typing a space after the comma, type the spacing between the tabs.

❷ Type **0.3,0.5** and press **[Enter]**.

Be sure to include the 0 (zero) in front of the decimal when you type these numbers. The command **0.3,0.5** tells WordPerfect to set a tab stop at 0.3 inch from the left margin and subsequent tabs at every 0.5 inch from that location. The new tab settings appear on the tab scale. See Figure 4-17.

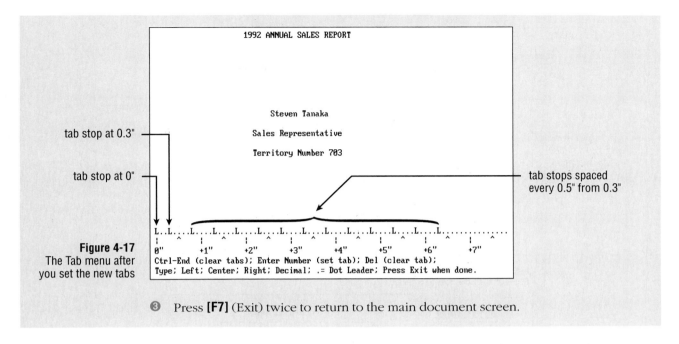

tab stop at 0.3"

tab stop at 0"

tab stops spaced
every 0.5" from 0.3"

Figure 4-17
The Tab menu after
you set the new tabs

❸   Press **[F7]** (Exit) twice to return to the main document screen.

Now scroll down through the body of the document. Notice that the first line of each paragraph is indented 0.3 inch from the left margin rather than 0.5 inch.

Numbering Pages

Since the report is longer than one page, Steven wants to number the pages. He can do this automatically with the Page Numbering feature. The COEC standard format requires that reports have page numbers centered at the bottom of each page.

To set page numbering:

❶   Make sure the cursor is at the beginning of the document before any text and before any code that affects the first line of text. This ensures that page numbering is turned on for the entire document. You may need to turn on Reveal Codes and move the cursor to the right of [Ln Spacing:2] and on [Just:Center].

❷   Select Page from the Layout menu or press **[Shift][F8]** (Format) and select **2** (**P**age). The Format: Page menu appears on the screen.

❸   Select **6** (Page **N**umbering). The Format: Page Numbering menu appears on the screen. See Figure 4-18 on the next page.

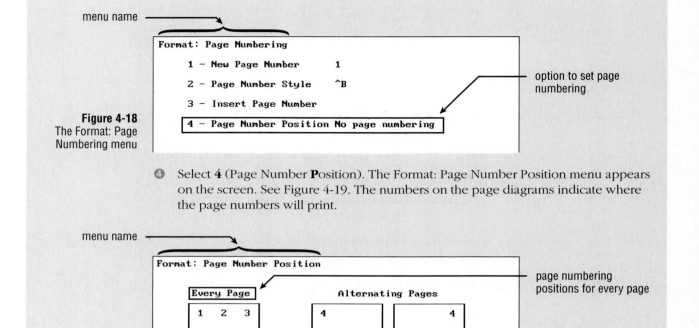

Figure 4-18
The Format: Page
Numbering menu

Figure 4-19
The Format: Page
Number Position
menu

❹ Select **4** (Page Number **P**osition). The Format: Page Number Position menu appears on the screen. See Figure 4-19. The numbers on the page diagrams indicate where the page numbers will print.

Remember that Steven wants his page numbers centered at the bottom of each page, so you should select option 6.

❺ Select **6** and then press **[F7]** (Exit) to return to the document screen.

This instructs WordPerfect to print a page number at the bottom center of every page, below the last line of text and just above the bottom margin. Page numbers do not appear on the document screen.

Creating Headers and Footers

Steven next wants to instruct WordPerfect to print the title of his report and his name at the top of every page. Text printed at the top of each page is called a **header**. Most books have headers on each page to guide the reader. Headers contain, for example, the page number and the name of the book or the chapter name or number. Similarly a **footer** is one or more lines of text printed at the bottom of each page that serve the same purpose as the header.

When you create a header, WordPerfect prints it just below the top margin and then inserts a blank line between the header and the first line of text on the page. Similarly

WordPerfect prints a footer just above the bottom margin and inserts a blank line between the footer and the last line of text on the page.

Let's create a header that includes the name of the report and Steven's full name.

To create a header:

❶ Make sure the cursor is still at the beginning of the document before any text or code that affects the first line of text.

❷ Invoke the Format: Page menu by selecting Page from the Layout menu or pressing **[Shift][F8]** (Format) and selecting **2** (**P**age).

❸ Select **3** (**H**eaders).

WordPerfect lets you define up to two different headers at a time, Header A and Header B. In this report you'll use only one header. In other documents, you might want two headings — one heading, such as the title, on odd-numbered pages, and another heading, such as the author's name, on even-numbered pages.

❹ Select **1** (Header **A**). The one-line menu shown in Figure 4-20 appears at the bottom of the screen. You'll use this menu to select the pages on which the report should have headers. This menu also allows you to discontinue any current header or to edit an existing header.

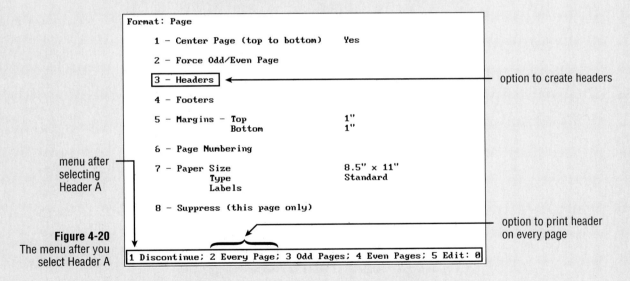

Figure 4-20
The menu after you
select Header A

❺ Select **2** (Every **P**age). WordPerfect displays the header edit screen.

❻ Type **1992 ANNUAL SALES REPORT**, press **[Alt][F6]** (Flush Right), type **Steven Tanaka**, and press **[Enter]**. See Figure 4-21 on the next page. Because WordPerfect automatically inserts one blank line between the header and the body of the page text, pressing [Enter] here inserts an additional blank line after the header.

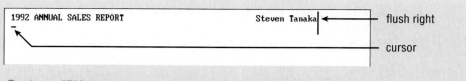

Figure 4-21
The Header Edit
screen

❼ Press **[F7]** (Exit) twice to return to the document screen.

You can't see the header on the document screen, but you can see it on the View Document screen.

To create a footer, you use the same procedure except that in step 4, you select 4 (Footers) instead of 3 (Headers). To edit a header or a footer, select 5 (Edit) in Step 5.

If you want the page numbers to be part of headers or footers, do *not* set page numbering. Instead, include the page number in the definition of the headers or footers by pressing [Ctrl][B] to insert the ∧B code into the text of the header or footer. Then when you print the document, the page numbers will appear where ∧B appears in the definition of the header or footer. In his report Steven put page numbering at the bottom of the page, so it won't interfere with the headers.

Suppressing Page Numbering, Headers, and Footers

Steven has inserted the codes for page numbering and a header, but he doesn't want these page features to appear on the title page. To eliminate headers, footers, and page numbering on any particular page, you can use the Page Suppress feature. Let's use this feature now.

To suppress the page numbering and the header on the current page:

❶ Make sure the cursor is at the beginning of the title page, just after the format code for Header A. Use Reveal Codes to position the cursor properly.

❷ Invoke the Format: Page menu and select **8** (Su**p**press). WordPerfect displays the Format: Suppress (this page only) menu. See Figure 4-22.

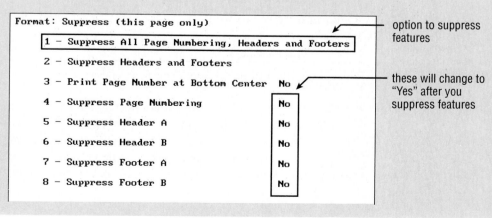

Figure 4-22
The Format:
Suppress menu

❸ Select **1** (**S**uppress All Page Numbering, Headers and Footers). As you do, notice how options 4 through 8 change to indicate "Yes," so that no page numbering, header, or footer will be printed on the current page.

❹ Press **[F7]** (Exit) to return to the document screen.

Now when Steven prints his annual report, no page number or header will appear on the title page.

Setting a New Page Number

Even though a page number won't appear on the title page when Steven prints the report, the title page is still page 1 of the document, and the body of the report begins on page 2. But Steven wants the body of the report to begin on page 1. This requires that he change the page numbering for the document beginning on the page after the title page. Let's use WordPerfect's Page Numbering feature to set a new page number.

To set a new page number:

❶ Move the cursor to the beginning of page 2, so that the cursor is just after the [HPg] code and on the [Just:Left] code. You may have to turn on Reveal Codes to position the cursor properly, and then turn off Reveal Codes.

❷ Invoke the Format: Page menu and select **6** (Page **N**umbering). As before, WordPerfect displays the Format: Page Numbering menu.

❸ Select **1** (**N**ew Page Number). The cursor moves to the right of the New Page Number option, and WordPerfect waits for you to type the new page number.

❹ Type **1** and press **[Enter]**.

❺ Press **[F7]** (Exit) to return to the document screen. WordPerfect inserts the [Pg Num:1] code into the document.

Now when Steven prints the document, the beginning of the body of the report will be page 1, the page after that will be page 2, and so forth.

Viewing and Saving the Document

There is no way of seeing headers, footers, or page numbers on the document screen, but you can see these features on the View Document screen. Let's see how Steven's document looks now.

To view the document:

❶ Make sure the cursor is still on the first page of the body of the report.

❷ Select Print from the File menu or press **[Shift][F7]** (Print) to display the Print/Options menu.

❸ Select **6** (**V**iew Document), then select **3** (Full Page) so you can see the entire page at once. See Figure 4-23.

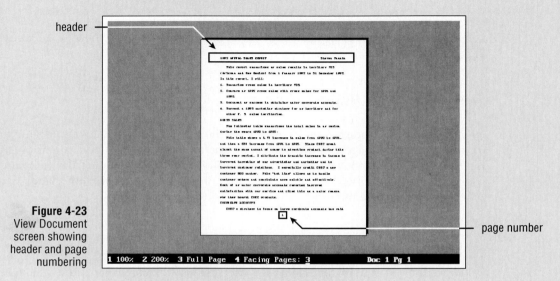

Figure 4-23
View Document screen showing header and page numbering

Even though the words are too small to read, you can see the position of the header at the top of the page and the page number at the bottom of the page.

❹ Select **1** (100%) so you can read the header at the top of the page. Then scroll the screen so you can read the page number at the bottom of the page.

❺ Press **[PgDn]** to view a subsequent page of the document or **[PgUp]** to view a previous page of the document.

❻ Press **[F7]** (Exit) when you are ready to return to the main document screen.

Having worked on this version of his report for about 15 minutes, Steven decides to save the document with the changes he's made so far. Let's save the document.

To save the document:

❶ Select Save from the File menu or press **[F10]** (Save).

❷ Type **a:s4file2.dft** and press **[Enter]** to save this draft of the report.

WordPerfect Styles

One of the most powerful features in WordPerfect is the Styles feature. A WordPerfect **style** is a set of format codes or other codes and text that you can apply to words, phrases, paragraphs, or even entire documents to change their appearance or format. Once you define the format codes of a particular style, WordPerfect saves the style as part of the document so you can use the style over and over again to specify a particular format without having to go through the formatting keystrokes each time. For example, Steven wants to use a style in his report to specify the format for section headings within his document. He can create a style that tells WordPerfect to insert an extra blank line just before each heading and to center and boldface the text in the heading.

The advantages of using styles to format titles, headings, and other elements of your document include the following:

- **Efficiency**. Once you specify the format codes within a style, you can use the style in every similar element of the document. For example, when Steven creates the style for the headings in his annual report, he has to set center and bold only once; he can then use that style with all the headings in his document.

- **Flexibility**. If you later decide to change the style, you have to change the style only once, and the format of all the headings throughout the document will automatically change. For example, if Steven decided that he wanted all headings to be underlined instead of boldfaced, he could go through the entire document and change each heading individually. With a style he would have to make the change only once, in the style itself.

- **Consistency**. Without styles you can sometimes forget exactly how you formatted a document element. With styles the same format codes apply to every instance. For example, Steven can be confident that his report will follow the required COEC style and that all headings will have the same format.

Once you understand how to create and use styles, you'll want to create styles for document titles, headings, numbered lists, and other features within your document that require special formatting.

Creating a Style

Steven notices that the headings in his report don't follow the required COEC format. He decides to create a style to format all the headings efficiently and consistently. Let's create the heading style now.

To create a style:

❶ With the cursor anywhere in the document screen, select Styles from the Layout menu or press **[Alt][F8]** (Style). WordPerfect displays the Styles menu. See Figure 4-24. Your Styles menu may already include one or more existing styles.

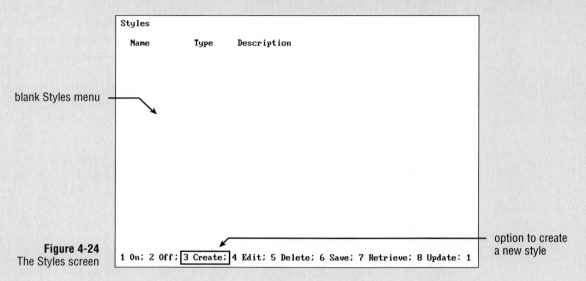

blank Styles menu

option to create a new style

Figure 4-24
The Styles screen

Creating a style doesn't insert a code into the document, so the cursor can be anywhere in the document when you define the style.

❷ Select **3** (**C**reate). The Styles: Edit menu, where you create and edit styles, now appears on the screen. See Figure 4-25.

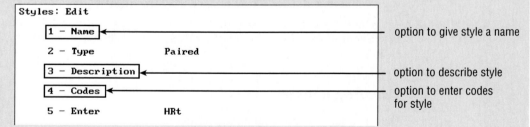

option to give style a name

option to describe style

option to enter codes for style

Figure 4-25
The Styles: Edit menu

Next you want to name the style that you're going to create. Let's call the style "Heading."

❸ Select **1** (**N**ame), type **Heading**, and press **[Enter]**.

Notice on the Styles: Edit menu that option 2 is Type. WordPerfect allows three types of styles: paired, open, and outline. "Paired" means that when you turn the style on, the new formatting features begin, and when you turn it off, these features end. "Open" means that when you turn the style on, the new formatting features begin and remain turned on until the end of the document or until the formatting features are changed. "Outline" means that the style is part of outlining or paragraph numbering. Steven wants to keep the Heading style paired, so you won't change the default setting for Type.

Next you'll give the style a description so you can remember the style's purpose.

④ Select **3** (**D**escription), type **Heading of a section of text**, and press **[Enter]**.

You'll next enter the format codes for the Heading style.

⑤ Select **4** (**C**odes) to display the Style Codes screen. See Figure 4-26.

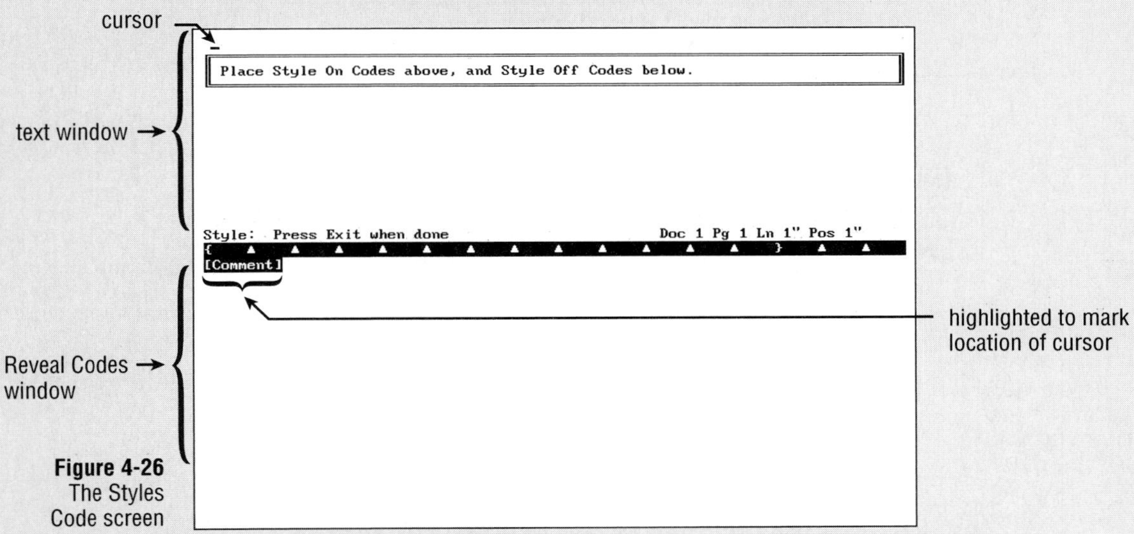

cursor

text window →

Place Style On Codes above, and Style Off Codes below.

Style: Press Exit when done   Doc 1 Pg 1 Ln 1" Pos 1"
{ ▲   ▲   ▲   ▲   ▲   ▲   ▲   ▲   ▲   ▲   }   ▲   ▲
[Comment]

highlighted to mark
location of cursor

Reveal Codes →
window

Figure 4-26
The Styles
Code screen

The top half of the Styles Code screen is a text window, where you see any text that you enter as part of the style. The bottom half of the screen is the Reveal Codes window, where you see any format codes that you enter as part of the style. The text window contains a comment box with the message "Place Style On Codes above, and Style Off Codes below." The [Comment] code indicates the location of the comment box in the Reveal Codes window. The purpose of the comment box is to mark the location of the text to which you will apply the style. For example, if you're going to apply the style to your major headings, imagine that the comment box is one of those headings. Any code that precedes the comment box will turn on the specified format or appearance for that heading. Any code that comes after the comment box will turn off the specified format or appearance.

You'll now add the format codes to the codes screen. In the next two steps you'll instruct WordPerfect to insert a blank line, to center the text, and to boldface the text to which the style is applied.

To add format codes to the Styles Code screen:

❶ Make sure the cursor is above the comment box in the text window. The [Comment] code in the Reveal Codes window should be highlighted.

Now let's instruct WordPerfect to insert a blank line and to center and boldface the text.

❷ Press **[Enter]**, **[Shift][F6]** (Center), and **[F6]** (Bold). These keystrokes insert the codes [HRt] (hard return), [Center], and [BOLD] before the comment in the Reveal Codes window.

❸ Move the cursor below the comment box in the text window, which is to the right of [Comment] in the Reveal Codes window, and press **[F6]** (Bold). This inserts the code [bold] to turn off bold after the heading. See Figure 4-27.

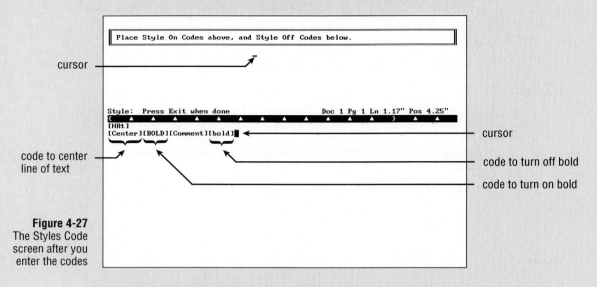

cursor

Figure 4-27
The Styles Code
screen after you
enter the codes

You have now inserted the desired codes into the style.

❹ Press **[F7]** (Exit) to exit the Styles Code screen and return to the Styles: Edit screen.

Normally, when you press [Enter] while using a style, WordPerfect inserts a hard return; but in this style, we want to instruct WordPerfect that pressing [Enter] should turn off the style.

❺ Select **5** (**Enter**) and select **2** (**Off**).

❻ Press **[F7]** (Exit) twice to return to the main document screen.

You have finished creating the style named "Heading," which contains the codes that Steven wants for the headings. In the next section you use the style to format the headings in the report.

Using a Style

Steven is now ready to use the Heading style to create a heading for a section of text.

To use the Heading style:

❶ Turn on Reveal Codes and move the cursor to the right of the [Just:Left] code at the beginning of the second page. The cursor should highlight the [Tab] code at the beginning of the first paragraph.

❷ Press **[Enter]** to create a blank line for the heading, then move the cursor back to the blank line. The cursor should be on the [HRt] code.

③ Select Styles from the Layout menu or press **[Alt][F8]** (Style) to display the Styles menu. The Styles menu displays the name and the description of the Heading style that you just created. See Figure 4-28.

new style
(highlighted)

Figure 4-28
The Styles screen
after you create the
"Heading" style

```
Styles

  Name        Type      Description

  Heading     Paired    Heading of a section of text
```

④ Make sure "Heading" is highlighted and select **1 (On)**. This turns on the style and returns you to the document screen. Any text that you type will be centered and boldfaced until you turn off the style by pressing [Enter].

⑤ Type **INTRODUCTION** and press **[Enter]** to end the style.

You can see how this page of your document will appear by executing the View Document command (Figure 4-29). The first line below the top margin is the header, and four lines below that is the heading, centered and boldfaced. After you have viewed the page, return to the main document screen.

Figure 4-29
The INTRODUCTION
heading formatted
with the Heading style

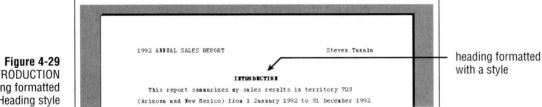

heading formatted
with a style

Using a Style with Existing Text

Steven has already typed the other headings of the report: "GROSS SALES," "CORPORATE ACCOUNTS," and "RECOMMENDATIONS." He can apply his Heading style to these headings without retyping them, just as you can apply WordPerfect's bold feature to a phrase without retyping it.

To use a style with existing text:

① Move the cursor to the beginning of the next heading, to the "G" in "GROSS SALES."

To apply a style, you first block the text you want in that style.

② Select Block from the Edit menu or press **[Alt][F4]** or **[F12]** (Block).

③ Press **[End]** to move the cursor to the end of the heading. This blocks (highlights) the heading.

④ Select Styles from the Layout menu or press **[Alt][F8]** (Style).

⑤ Make sure "Heading" is highlighted and select **1 (On)**. This turns on the style at the beginning of the blocked text and turns it off at the end of the blocked text. The heading immediately moves down one line and becomes centered and boldfaced.

⑥ Repeat these steps for the other two headings, "CORPORATE ACCOUNTS" and "RECOMMENDATIONS."

The headings within the report now all have the same format.

WordPerfect Tables

Steven decides to include in his report a table of data that summarizes the gross sales for the previous three years. Before modern word processors were available, typists faced a tedious process when they had to create tables. But with WordPerfect's Tables feature, creating a table is relatively simple. You can specify the number of columns and rows, insert or delete columns and rows, change the width of columns, draw or remove lines between columns and rows, change the format of text and numbers within the table, and perform other tasks to make the table attractive and readable, without having to retype the table's data.

Creating a Table

Steven will use the Tables feature to produce a table of his annual sales (Figure 4-30). Let's make this table now as part of the report.

TERRITORY 703 GROSS SALES (in dollars)					
Year	Qtr. 1	Qtr. 2	Qtr. 3	Qtr. 4	TOTAL
1990	542,197	591,287	588,841	498,276	2,220,601
1991	562,422	681,647	584,892	540,699	2,369,660
1992	891,322	904,498	896,217	934,228	3,626,265

Figure 4-30
Data table for
Steven's report

To create a table:

❶ Move the cursor to the end of the first line of the section "GROSS SALES," just after the colon at the end of the phrase "during the years 1990 to 1992." This moves the cursor to the location in the document where you want the table to appear.

❷ Press **[Enter]** to insert a line between the text and the table. See Figure 4-31.

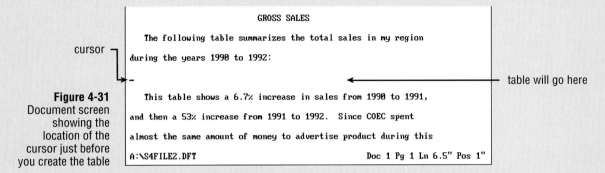

Figure 4-31
Document screen showing the location of the cursor just before you create the table

❸ Select Create from the Tables menu of the Layout menu. See Figure 4-32. Alternatively press **[Alt][F7]** (Columns/Tables), select **2** (**T**ables), then **1** (**C**reate).

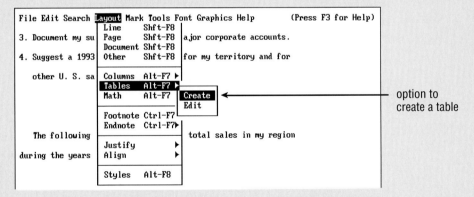

Figure 4-32
The Tables menu

WordPerfect prompts you for the number of columns in the table. Steven's table has six columns.

❹ Type **6** and press **[Enter]**.

WordPerfect prompts you for the number of rows in the table. Steven's table has five rows.

⑤ Type **5** and press **[Enter]**. The Table Edit menu appears on the screen, with the table cursor in cell A1. See Figure 4-33. This menu allows you to create new tables and edit existing tables.

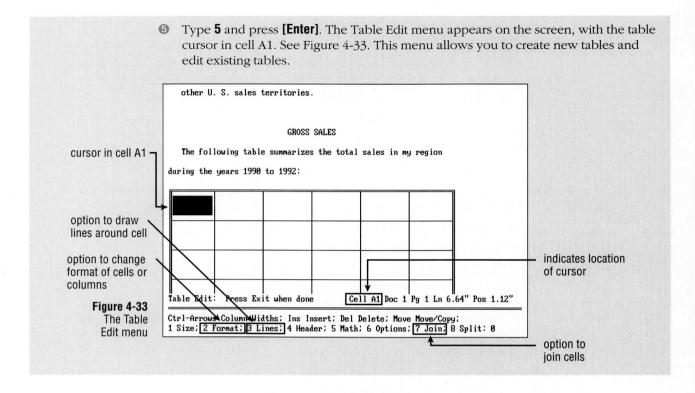

cursor in cell A1

option to draw lines around cell

option to change format of cells or columns

indicates location of cursor

option to join cells

Figure 4-33
The Table
Edit menu

In a WordPerfect table, a **cell** is a single box into which you can type a number or text. To identify a specific cell within a table, WordPerfect assigns letters to the columns of the table, with the first column on the far left named column "A," the next column "B," and so on in alphabetical order. WordPerfect numbers the rows of a table from top to bottom, starting with row 1. Each cell, therefore, is designated by a letter and a number. The cell in the upper left corner is A1; the cell to its right is B1; the cell below A1 is A2; and so forth, as shown in Figure 4-34.

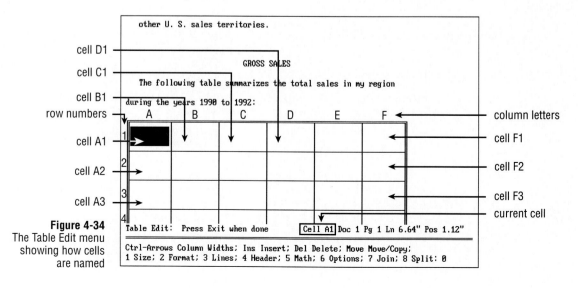

cell D1

cell C1

cell B1
row numbers

cell A1

cell A2

cell A3

column letters

cell F1

cell F2

cell F3
current cell

Figure 4-34
The Table Edit menu
showing how cells
are named

While the Table Edit menu is active, you can move the cursor from cell to cell by using the arrow keys ([→], [←], [↑], [↓]), [Tab] (to move right), or [Shift][Tab] (to move left). You can use [End] to move to the far right column and [Home], [←] to move to the far left column. Practice using these cursor-movement keys to move the cursor around the table.

Formatting a Table

Steven realizes that he'll have to modify the format of his table to make it attractive and readable. First he'll join the cells in the top row into one large cell so it can contain the title of the table, as shown in Figure 4-30.

To join cells in a table:

❶ Make sure the cursor is in cell A1, the first cell in the group of cells we want to join.

❷ Press **[Alt][F4]** or **[F12]** (Block) and **[End]** to highlight the top row of cells.

You can't use the pull-down menus to turn Block on while the Table Edit menu is active. If you accidentally press the right mouse button, WordPerfect will exit the Tables menu. To return to the Tables menu, make sure the cursor is in one of the table cells and press **[Alt][F7]** (Columns/Tables).

❸ Select **7** (**J**oin) to display the prompt "Join cells?" See Figure 4-35.

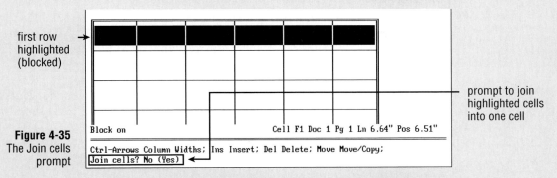

first row highlighted (blocked)

prompt to join highlighted cells into one cell

Figure 4-35
The Join cells prompt

❹ Select "Yes" to join the top row of cells into one cell. The top row is now a single cell in which you can type the title of the table.

Next Steven decides to draw double lines under the top row to separate the title from the rest of the table.

To draw a double line under a cell:

❶ Make sure the cursor is still in cell A1.

❷ Select **3** (**L**ines), **4** (**B**ottom), and **3** (**D**ouble) to draw a double line at the bottom of the top cell.

Steven next wants to draw a double line below each cell of row 2. As shown in Figure 4-30, these double lines will separate the column labels from the data in the columns.

To draw a double line under a row of cells:

❶ Move the cursor to cell A2.

❷ Press **[Alt][F4]** or **[F12]** (Block) and **[End]** to highlight the second row, then use the same keystrokes given in the previous Steps to draw a double line across the bottom of this row.

Next Steven decides that the labels and the numbers in the columns should be right-justified, that is, aligned flush against the right side of the cells. Let's change the format of the columns to be right-justified.

To right-justify text in columns of cells:

❶ Move the cursor back to cell A2.

❷ Block the entire row of cells as you did before.

❸ Press **2** (**Format**), **2** (**Column**), **3** (**Justify**), and **3** (**Right**) to set right justification for all the columns of the table. Any text that you type into the table will be flush right in the cells. Notice how the cursor now appears in the upper right corner of cell F2.

Having set all the columns to right justification, Steven realizes that he wants the title, in cell A1, to be centered between the left and the right edges of the table, as shown in Figure 4-30. Let's set center justification for cell A1.

To center-justify a cell:

❶ Move the cursor to cell A1.

❷ Press **2** (**Format**), **1** (**Cell**), **3** (**Justify**), and **2** (**Center**) so any text typed in that cell will be centered.

By changing only this cell to center justification, the other cells stay set to right justification.

Steven now wants to decrease the width of column A, the Year column. The key combination to decrease the width of a column is [Ctrl][←]. Let's decrease the column width now.

To decrease the width of a column:

❶ Move the cursor to cell A2 to position the cursor in the column whose width you want to change.

❷ Press **[Ctrl][←]** twice to decrease the width of the column.

Steven now wants to increase the width of column F, the Totals column. This column has to be wider to accommodate the larger numbers of the totals. The key combination to increase the width of a column is [Ctrl][→]. Let's increase the column width now.

To increase the width of a column:

❶ Move the cursor to cell F2.

❷ Press **[Ctrl][→]** twice to increase the width of the column.

Now that he has completed the format changes of the table, Steven can exit the Table Edit menu, return to the document screen, and enter the text and data into the tables.

To exit the Table Edit menu:

❶ Press **[F7]** (Exit) to exit the Table Edit menu and to return to the document screen.

Your screen should now look similar to Figure 4-36. You can't change the format of the table when the cursor is in the document screen. You can only enter, edit, or delete information in the cells of the table.

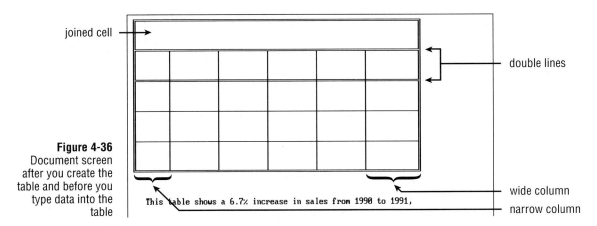

Figure 4-36
Document screen after you create the table and before you type data into the table

joined cell · double lines · wide column · narrow column

This table shows a 6.7% increase in sales from 1990 to 1991,

Entering Labels and Data into the Table

Having created and formatted the table, Steven is now ready to enter data into the table. Entering data is not difficult, since you can use most of the standard WordPerfect cursor-movement keys and deletion keys. Besides those keys, you can use [Tab] to move the cursor to the right one cell (without inserting a [Tab] code) and [Shift][Tab] moves the cursor to the left one cell. Let's enter the labels and the data into the table now.

To enter data into the table:

❶ Move the cursor to cell A1 and type the title of the table as shown in Figure 4-30.

❷ Type the data into the other cells of the table as shown in Figure 4-30.

Your screen should now look like Figure 4-37.

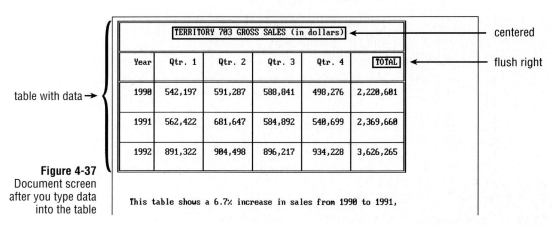

table with data →

TERRITORY 703 GROSS SALES (in dollars)						centered
Year	Qtr. 1	Qtr. 2	Qtr. 3	Qtr. 4	TOTAL	flush right
1990	542,197	591,287	588,841	498,276	2,220,601	
1991	562,422	681,647	584,892	540,699	2,369,660	
1992	891,322	904,498	896,217	934,228	3,626,265	

Figure 4-37
Document screen
after you type data
into the table

This table shows a 6.7% increase in sales from 1990 to 1991,

Editing the Table Format

After completing the table, Steven decides that the "TOTAL" label in column F should be centered in the column rather than right-justified. Thus, he needs to edit the table.

To edit the table:

❶ Move the cursor anywhere within the table. The current-cell designation (letter and number) appears on the status line.

❷ Press **[Alt][F7]** (Columns/Tables). The Table Edit menu appears on the screen. You can now select any of the options in the menu.

❸ Move the cursor to cell F2.

❹ Press **2** (**F**ormat), **1** (**C**ell), **3** (**J**ustify), and **2** (**C**enter).

The text ("TOTAL") becomes centered in the cell.

❺ Press **[F7]** (Exit) to return to the document screen.

You have now completed the table. Your screen should look like Figure 4-38.

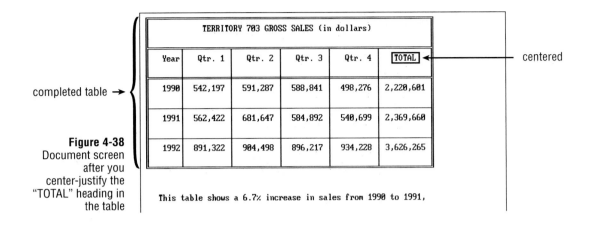

Figure 4-38
Document screen
after you
center-justify the
"TOTAL" heading in
the table

TERRITORY 703 GROSS SALES (in dollars)					
Year	Qtr. 1	Qtr. 2	Qtr. 3	Qtr. 4	TOTAL
1990	542,197	591,287	588,841	498,276	2,220,601
1991	562,422	681,647	584,892	540,699	2,369,660
1992	891,322	904,498	896,217	934,228	3,626,265

completed table →

centered

This table shows a 6.7% increase in sales from 1990 to 1991,

Setting a Conditional End of Page

After he has created the table, Steven looks over the document and notices a serious formatting problem: the heading "RECOMMENDATIONS" is isolated at the bottom of page 2 (Figure 4-39). (Because of differences in type size among printers, your document might not have the heading isolated at the bottom of the page. Do the steps in this section anyway.)

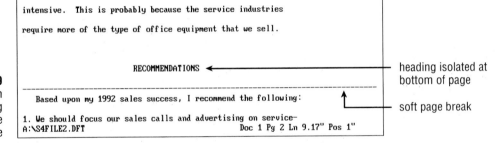

Figure 4-39
Document screen
with a heading
isolated at the
bottom of the page

intensive. This is probably because the service industries

require more of the type of office equipment that we sell.

                        RECOMMENDATIONS

  Based upon my 1992 sales success, I recommend the following:

1. We should focus our sales calls and advertising on service-
A:\S4FILE2.DFT   Doc 1 Pg 2 Ln 9.17" Pos 1"

heading isolated at
bottom of page

soft page break

One solution to the problem would be to press [Ctrl][Enter] (Hard Page) to insert a hard page break just before the heading. The drawback of this solution is that if Steven later adds or removes text anywhere before the hard page break, the location of the page break probably would be unacceptable. For example, if Steven adds three or four lines on page 2, one or two of the lines would spill over to page 3, the rest of page 3 would be blank, and "RECOMMENDATIONS" would start on page 4, as shown in Figure 4-40.

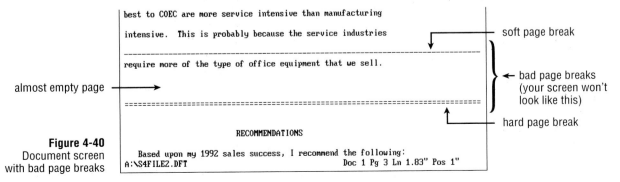

almost empty page →

Figure 4-40
Document screen
with bad page breaks

best to COEC are more service intensive than manufacturing

intensive. This is probably because the service industries

----
require more of the type of office equipment that we sell.

==

                        RECOMMENDATIONS

  Based upon my 1992 sales success, I recommend the following:
A:\S4FILE2.DFT   Doc 1 Pg 3 Ln 1.83" Pos 1"

soft page break

bad page breaks
(your screen won't
look like this)

hard page break

A better solution would be to use WordPerfect's Conditional End of Page feature. Conditional End of Page is a command that allows you to specify the number of lines of text that should be kept together on one page. For example, if you specify that six lines of text should be kept together, WordPerfect inserts a soft page break if the six lines would otherwise be split between two pages (Figure 4-41).

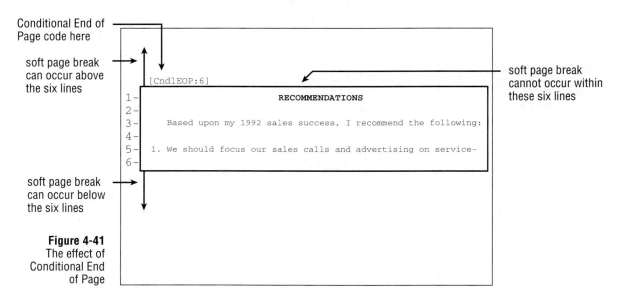

Conditional End of
Page code here

soft page break
can occur above
the six lines

soft page break
cannot occur within
these six lines

soft page break
can occur below
the six lines

[CndlEOP:6]

RECOMMENDATIONS

Based upon my 1992 sales success, I recommend the following:

1. We should focus our sales calls and advertising on service-

Figure 4-41
The effect of
Conditional End
of Page

Steven decides to use the Conditional End of Page code above the "RECOMMENDATIONS" heading. That way, regardless of any changes he makes to the document, the heading will never be isolated at the bottom of a page.

To set Conditional End of Page:

❶ Move the cursor on the blank line below the paragraph that ends "office equipment that we sell" and above the heading "RECOMMENDATIONS."

When you specify Conditional End of Page, move the cursor to the line *above* the text that you want kept together.

❷ Select Other from the Layout menu or press **[Shift][F8]** (Format) and select **4** (**O**ther) to display the Format: Other menu. See Figure 4-42.

menu name

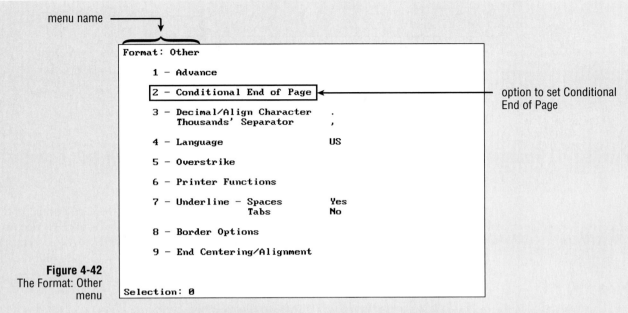

option to set Conditional
End of Page

Figure 4-42
The Format: Other
menu

❸ Select **2** (**C**onditional End of Page). A prompt asks you for the number of lines that you want kept together. See Figure 4-43.

Figure 4-43
The prompt after you
select Conditional
End of Page

prompt after selecting
Conditional End of Page

The number of lines requested includes the blank lines in double-spaced text. So if you want the heading and the first two lines of text in the paragraph under the heading to be kept together, you should specify six (three lines of double-spaced text) as the number of lines to keep together.

❹ Type **6** and press **[Enter]**.

❺ Press **[F7]** (Exit) to exit the Format: Other menu and return to the document screen. WordPerfect has inserted the format code [Cndl EOP:6], which you can see by turning on Reveal Codes.

❻ Rewrite the screen by pressing **[Ctrl][F3]** (Screen) and selecting **3** (**R**ewrite). WordPerfect inserts a soft page break above the heading so that the heading is on page 3. See Figure 4-44 on the next page.

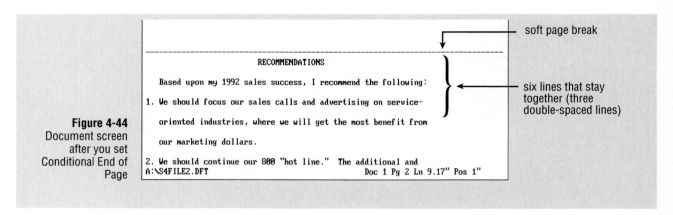

soft page break

six lines that stay
together (three
double-spaced lines)

Figure 4-44
Document screen
after you set
Conditional End of
Page

Steven realizes that every heading in the document should have the Conditional End of Page command, so that no heading ever gets isolated at the bottom of a page. It occurs to Steven that he really should put the Conditional End of Page code in the Heading style. The code would then take effect at every heading automatically. Let's insert the Conditional End of Page code into the Heading style.

To set Conditional End of Page in the style:

❶ Select Styles from the Layout menu or press **[Alt][F8]** (Style) to display the Styles screen.

❷ With "Heading" highlighted, select **4** (**E**dit) and **4** (**C**odes), so you can edit the "Heading" style in the codes screen.

❸ With the cursor at the beginning of the style codes, select Other from the Layout menu or press **[Shift][F8]** (Format) and select **4** (**O**ther) to display the Format: Other menu.

❹ Select **2** (**C**onditional End of Page), type **6**, and press **[Enter]**, and press **[F7]** (Exit). The code [Cndl EOP:6] appears in the style.

❺ Press **[F7]** (Exit) until you return to the main document screen.

With Conditional End of Page in the heading style, you don't need the code that you inserted above the "RECOMMENDATIONS" heading, although the extra code won't hurt anything. (If you like, you can turn on Reveal Codes and delete the [Cndl EOP:6] code above "RECOMMENDATIONS.") Because the code is in the Heading style, everywhere the style is applied, six lines of text after the start of the style will move as one inseparable block of text.

Setting Widow/Orphan Protection

Steven now notices another formatting problem: underneath the table at the bottom of page 1 is a single line of text isolated from the rest of its paragraph. Because of differences in type sizes, your document might not have this line under the table at the bottom of page 1. This is called an **orphan** — the first line of a paragraph appearing alone at the bottom of a page. Similarly a **widow** is the last line of a paragraph appearing alone at the top of a page. Widows and orphans detract from the appearance and readability of a document. Fortunately you can solve the problem of widows and orphans by using WordPerfect's Widow/Orphan Protection. Let's set widow/orphan protection in Steven's report.

To set widow/orphan protection:

❶ Move the cursor to the beginning of the document before any text.

❷ Select Line from the Layout menu or press **[Shift][F8]** (Format) and select **1** (**L**ine). The Format: Line menu appears on the screen.

❸ Select **9** (**W**idow/Orphan Protection). WordPerfect displays the prompt shown in Figure 4-45.

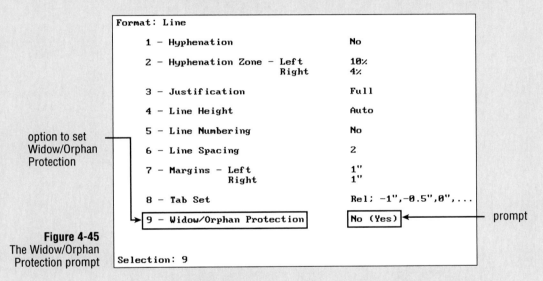

option to set Widow/Orphan Protection

prompt

Figure 4-45
The Widow/Orphan Protection prompt

```
Format: Line

      1 - Hyphenation                        No

      2 - Hyphenation Zone - Left            10%
                            Right            4%

      3 - Justification                      Full

      4 - Line Height                        Auto

      5 - Line Numbering                     No

      6 - Line Spacing                       2

      7 - Margins - Left                     1"
                    Right                    1"

      8 - Tab Set                            Rel; -1",-0.5",0",...

      9 - Widow/Orphan Protection            No (Yes)

Selection: 9
```

❹ Select "Yes" to verify that you do want Widow/Orphan protection turned on.

❺ Press **[F7]** (Exit) to return to the document screen. WordPerfect inserts the code [W/O On] into the document.

Now move the cursor to the bottom of page 1 and then to the top of page 2. If there was an orphan before, the orphan is gone. The first line of the paragraph has moved below the soft page break, to page 2.

Saving and Printing the Report

Save Steven's report as S4FILE3.REP, view the document, and then print the report. Your final copy of the report should look like Figure 4-46 on the following pages.

1992 ANNUAL SALES REPORT

Steven Tanaka
Sales Representative
Territory Number 703

January 15, 1993

1992 ANNUAL SALES REPORT   Steven Tanaka

INTRODUCTION

   This report summarizes my sales results in territory 703
(Arizona and New Mexico) from 1 January 1992 to 31 December 1992.
In this report, I will:

1.   Summarize gross sales in territory 703.

2.   Compare my 1992 gross sales with gross sales for 1991 and
     1990.

3.   Document my success in obtaining major corporate accounts.

4.   Suggest a 1993 marketing strategy for my territory and for
     other U. S. sales territories.

GROSS SALES

   The following table summarizes the total sales in my region
during the years 1990 to 1992:

TERRITORY 703 GROSS SALES (in dollars)					
Year	Qtr. 1	Qtr. 2	Qtr. 3	Qtr. 4	TOTAL
1990	542,197	591,287	588,841	498,276	2,220,601
1991	562,422	681,647	584,892	540,699	2,369,660
1992	891,322	904,498	896,217	934,228	3,626,265

1

Figure 4-46
The final version of
Steven's annual
sales report

1992 ANNUAL SALES REPORT   Steven Tanaka

    This table shows a 6.7% increase in sales from 1990 to 1991,
and then a 53% increase from 1991 to 1992. Since COEC spent
almost the same amount of money to advertise product during this
three year period, I attribute the dramatic increase in income to
improved targeting of our advertising and marketing and to
improved customer relations. I especially credit COEC's new
customer 800 number. This "hot line" allows us to handle
customer orders and complaints more quickly and effectively.
Most of my major corporate accounts reported improved
satisfaction with our service and cited this as a major reason
why they bought COEC products.

                        CORPORATE ACCOUNTS
    COEC's strategy to focus on large corporate accounts has paid
big dividends for me. During 1991, I visited 82 potential large-
corporation customers in my territory. I was able to promise
them better terms under our large-accounts discount program and
our new customer hot line. To date, twenty-seven of these
companies have begun buying their office equipment from COEC. I
attribute this new business to the success of COEC's strategy.
    The large corporations in my territory that seem to respond
best to COEC are more service intensive than manufacturing
intensive. This is probably because the service industries
require more of the type of office equipment that we sell.

                              2

1992 ANNUAL SALES REPORT   Steven Tanaka

                        RECOMMENDATIONS
    Based upon my 1992 sales success, I recommend the following:
1. We should focus our sales calls and advertising on service-
    oriented industries, where we will get the most benefit from
    our marketing dollars.
2. We should continue our 800 "hot line." The additional and
    retained sales that are generated more than pay for this
    service.
3. We should continue to add new lines of office equipment. Our
    customers want a wider choice of new technology, in
    particular, fax machines, color copiers, and telephone-
    answering equipment.
4. We should consider adding office computers to our line of
    products. Many of the large corporations want to buy their
    computers from the same company that sells them their laser
    printers and fax machines.

                              3

Figure 4-46
(continued)

■   ■   ■

Exercises

1. Define or describe the following terms:
   a. line spacing
   b. style (for formatting)
   c. page numbering
   d. header
   e. footer

2. How would you create a header that prints your name in the upper left corner of every page?

3. How would you create a footer that prints your name in the lower right corner of every page?

4. Why would you use each of the following features?
   a. Conditional End of Page
   b. Widow/Orphan Protection
   c. Line Spacing
   d. Tables
   e. Suppress (this page only)
   f. Style

5. What are the advantages of using a WordPerfect style to format the headings in your documents?

6. How would you set tabs every one-fourth inch from the left margin of a document?

7. When you use WordPerfect's Tables feature to create or edit a table, how would you do each of the following?
   a. Draw double lines at the bottom of a cell
   b. Set the alignment (justification) to Center
   c. Create a single horizontal box that spans the entire width of the table

Tutorial Assignments

Retrieve the file T4FILE1.DFT from the data diskette and do the following:

1. Center the title page between the top and the bottom margins.

2. Change the line spacing to triple spacing.

3. Number all the pages of the document in the top right corner of each page.

4. Suppress page numbering on the title page.

5. Change the tabs from 0.5-inch intervals to 0.3-inch intervals (from the left margin).

6. Save the file as S4FILE1.DOC and print it.

Retrieve the file T4FILE2.DFT from the data diskette and do the following:

7. Create a header that prints your name in the upper left corner of each page and prints the page number in the upper right corner of the page. *Hint:* Within a header, press [Ctrl][B] to insert the code ^B for page numbers.

8. Create a style that centers a title page top to bottom, centers the lines of the title between the left and the right margins, and suppresses page numbering and your

header. Then use the style to create a title page with the title "Preparing for Sales Calls," your name, and the current date.

9. Create a style that formats the headings. Each heading should include a Conditional End of Page code (with six lines kept together) and a blank line. The text of the heading should be underlined and centered. Apply this style to the three headings in the document.

10. Save the file as S4FILE2.DOC and print it.

Clear the document screen and do the following:

11. Create an empty table that has four columns and six rows.

12. Make the top row of cells into one cell, change its justification to center, and type the heading **New Clients in Territory 703**.

13. In the second row of cells type the following headings (one heading per cell): **Company Name**, **Purchasing Agent**, **Phone Number**, and **City**. Adjust the widths of the cells so that each heading fits neatly on one line within the cell.

14. In the other four rows of the table type the data in Figure 4-47.

Figure 4-47

> Kaibab Construction Co., Matt Bringhurst, (602) 834-1763, Tucson
> Sandia Electronics Corp., Megan Tartakov, (602) 418-8930, Mesa
> Santa Fe Travel, Inc., Bertha Lopez, (505) 128-4747, Santa Fe
> White Sands Manufacturing Corp., Carl Wilson, (505) 311-4800, Las Cruces

15. Adjust the width of the columns so that the information fits neatly in each cell.

16. Save the file as S4FILE3.TAB and print it.

Case Problems

1. Report on Computer Use in a Law Firm

Laura Eisel is the office manager for Orehoski, Donaldson & McAllister, Attorneys at Law, a large law firm headquartered in Seattle. When Laura joined the firm 18 months ago, she began updating the office computer system with IBM-compatible machines networked together using Novell NetWare. Now after the office has used the updated system for a full year, she has been asked to write a report to the senior partners of the firm on how the computer system has affected the firm and to make recommendations on updating the computer system at the firm's Portland, Oregon, office.

Do the following:

1. Retrieve the body of Laura's report (P4LAWCOM.REP) from the data diskette.

2. Change the line spacing to double spacing.

3.   Prepare a title page for the document as follows:
  a.   The title is "PCs in the Law Office."
  b.   The subtitle is "Report on the New Computer System at Orehoski, Donaldson & McAllister."
  c.   The author is Laura Eisel.
  d.   The date is the current date.
  e.   Format this title page to improve its appearance.

4.   Add page numbering to the document, so that WordPerfect prints the page number in the lower right corner of every page except the title page.

5.   Include a header that prints on every page except the title page. On the left margin of the header, insert "REPORT ON COMPUTER USE" and insert the author's name flush right on the same line.

6.   Make sure the report has no isolated headings, widows, or orphans.

7.   Save the file as S4LAWCOM.REP and print it.

2.   Financial Information on Professional Basketball Teams

Catarina Calderon is the assistant marketing manager for NBAHoops of Durham, North Carolina, a major publisher of basketball collection cards. She recently read a report on the worth of America's professional sports teams in *Financial World* magazine and has decided to write a memo to marketing and sales personnel in her company summarizing key information on the top National Basketball Association (NBA) teams.

Do the following:

1.   Type a standard memo heading with the following information: **DATE: January 16, 1992; TO: Marketing and Sales Personnel; FROM: Catarina Calderon, Asst. Marketing Manager.**

2.   For the body of the memo type the following sentence: **The following table summarizes financial data about the top ten NBA teams in order of estimated franchise value.**

3.   Below the sentence create the following table. Your table should look as much like the one in Figure 4-48 as possible.

4.   Save the file as S4NBATAB.MEM and print it.

TOP TEN NBA TEAMS IN FRANCHISE VALUE (All values in millions of dollars)			
Team Name	Annual Revenues	Player Salaries	Franchise Value (Est.)
Los Angeles Lakers	62.2	12.6	200
Boston Celtics	30.7	10.5	180
Detroit Pistons	47.3	10.9	150
Chicago Bulls	27.4	9.3	100
New York Knicks	25.6	13.3	100
Phoenix Suns	20.7	8.8	99
Philadelphia 76ers	20.4	9.8	75
Cleveland Cavaliers	22.6	9.0	61
Orlando Magic	22.5	13.3	61
Portland Trailblazers	21.4	11.2	60

Figure 4-48

3. Report on Advantages of Word Processing in Business

Write a three- to four-page report, including a title page, on the advantages of using a word processor in business. Compare writing letters, memos, and reports with a typewriter versus a computer. Include the major time-saving features of a word processor.

As part of the report, do the following:

1. Include a table showing the amount of time required to produce various types of document with a typewriter and with a word processor. The table should look like Figure 4-49.

Estimated Time (Minutes) to Type a Document		
Type of Document	Typewriter	WordPerfect
memo	8	6
letter	15	10
sales report	120	70
financial report	240	140

Figure 4-49

2. Double-space the report.

3. Include a header with the name of the report and your name.

4. Include page numbering in the bottom right corner of every page.

5. Create a WordPerfect style that you'll use to create headings within the report. Use the style to create three or more headings that divide the report into sections.

6. Save the file as S4WP.REP and print it.

Tutorial 5

Using Special Word Processing Features

Writing a Feasibility Report

Case: Connolly/Bayle Publishing Company

Since graduating last year with a degree in business management, Jonathan Lew has worked in outside sales for Connolly/Bayle (C/B) Publishing Company, which publishes computer magazines. Recently Jonathan took an in-house job as an assistant to Ann McMullen, the business manager for C/B Publishing. The company's cofounders, Stephen Connolly and John Bayle, have asked Ann to head a task force to investigate the feasibility of starting a new magazine aimed at graphic designers who use personal computers. The task force consists of Ann, Jonathan, two marketing managers, and two editors who manage other magazines at C/B Publishing.

The task force first met to map out strategies for the feasibility study. They decided to send out questionnaires, conduct interviews, and make financial projections with David Palermo, an accountant at C/B Publishing. After completing the study, the task force met again to analyze the information, draw conclusions, and make recommendations. Ann asked Jonathan to draft the outline for the final report and to distribute copies of the outline to the other task members for their approval. Once the outline has been approved, Ann will write the main body of the actual report and Jonathan will prepare the report for final distribution by adding footnotes, section headings, and other features.

OBJECTIVES

In this tutorial you will learn to:

- Use the Outline feature
- Switch between two documents
- Use split-screen windows
- Create and use macros
- Create footnotes
- Use hyphenation

Planning the Document

The responsibility for planning the document rests with all members of the task committee, even though Ann will write the actual body of the report.

Content

The content of the feasibility report will come from the results of the feasibility study, from the financial analysis, and from notes that Ann and Jonathan took in the task force meetings.

Organization

Jonathan will organize the feasibility report by creating an outline. He decides to have an introduction section, which states the purposes of the report and explains how the data for the report were gathered. He will then include sections on the target audience, expenses, and projected income for the magazine. The report will conclude with a summary and the recommendation of the task force.

Style

Jonathan wants the feasibility report to be like any other business document and follow a straightforward, clear style.

Format

C/B Publishing has no policy on how to format reports. Jonathan will use WordPerfect's default settings for margins, tabs, and justification and the standard format he learned in college for titles, headings, and page numbering.

■   ■   ■

The Outline Feature

Jonathan's task is to organize the data collected in the feasibility study and to outline the report. He decides to use WordPerfect's Outline feature. Each paragraph in an outline is preceded by a paragraph number. **Paragraph numbers** in a WordPerfect outline are Roman numerals (I, II, III, etc.), Arabic numerals (1, 2, 3, etc.), uppercase letters (A, B, C, etc.), and lowercase letters (a, b, c, etc.) that label the paragraphs and the subparagraphs of an outline to show the relationships between ideas and information. To show these relationships, the paragraph numbers represent **levels**: level-1 paragraphs (major ideas) are usually preceded by Roman numerals, level-2 paragraphs (supporting ideas) by uppercase letters, level-3 paragraphs by Arabic numerals, level-4 paragraphs by lowercase letters, and so forth (Figure 5-1). WordPerfect's Outline feature allows up to eight levels of paragraph numbers.

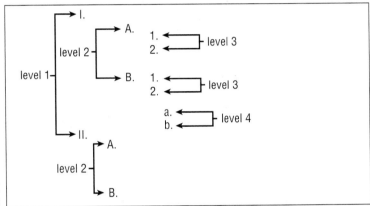

Figure 5-1
Outline levels

The advantage of WordPerfect's Outline feature is that paragraph numbering is automatic. When Outline is on and you press [Enter] to end one paragraph and start a new one, WordPerfect automatically inserts the next paragraph number of the outline. With a simple keystroke, you can change a paragraph number from a higher level to a lower level or from a lower level to a higher level. When you move a paragraph or a group of paragraphs in the outline, WordPerfect automatically renumbers the paragraphs.

Creating an Outline

The first draft of Jonathan's outline is shown in Figure 5-2. In the following steps you'll use WordPerfect's Outline feature to create this outline.

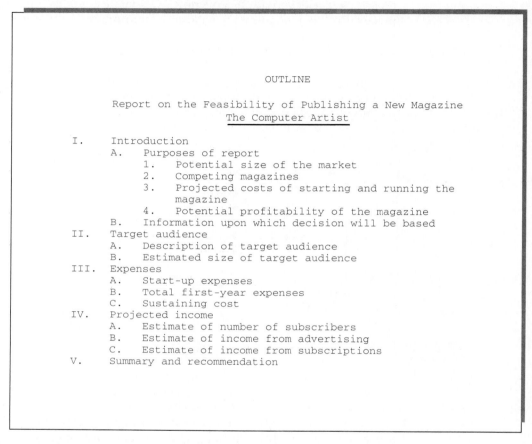

Figure 5-2
Jonathan's outline
of the report

First, however, you have to create the title of the outline.

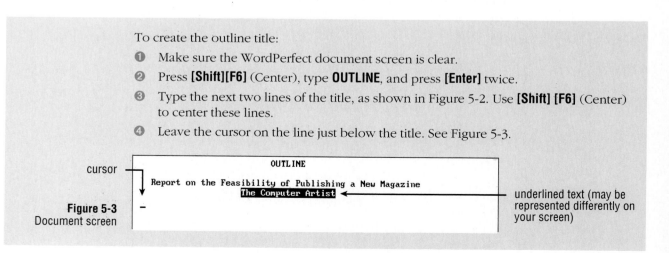

To create the outline title:

1. Make sure the WordPerfect document screen is clear.
2. Press **[Shift][F6]** (Center), type **OUTLINE**, and press **[Enter]** twice.
3. Type the next two lines of the title, as shown in Figure 5-2. Use **[Shift] [F6]** (Center) to center these lines.
4. Leave the cursor on the line just below the title. See Figure 5-3.

Figure 5-3
Document screen

Now you're ready to turn on WordPerfect's Outline feature and to create the outline. With Outline on, whenever you press [Enter], WordPerfect automatically inserts a new paragraph number into the document. You can then press [F4] (Indent) and type the text of the paragraph; change the paragraph number from a higher level to a lower level (for example, from II to A) by pressing [Tab] or from a lower level to a higher level (for example from A to II) by pressing [Shift][Tab] (Left Margin Release); or delete the paragraph number entirely by pressing [Backspace]. As you work through the following steps, you'll see how these commands work to help you create an outline quickly and efficiently.

To create an outline:

❶ With the cursor at the left margin on the first line after the title, select Outline from the Tools menu, then select On to turn on Outline. See Figure 5-4.

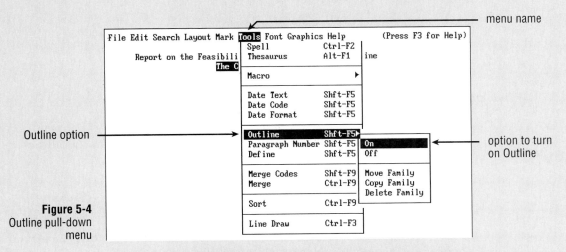

Figure 5-4
Outline pull-down menu

Alternatively press **[Shift][F5]** (Date/Outline) and select **4** (**O**utline) to display the Outline menu. See Figure 5-5. Select **1** (**O**n) from the Outline menu to turn on Outline. The message "Outline " appears on the left side of the status line at the bottom of the screen.

Figure 5-5
Turning Outline on

❷ Press **[Enter]**. WordPerfect inserts a paragraph number (in this case, a Roman numeral I) and a period at the beginning of this new line. With Outline on, every time you press [Enter], a new paragraph number appears on the screen.

❸ Press **[F4]** (Indent). This command indents after the paragraph number so you can type the text of the paragraph.

Pressing [F4] (Indent) keeps the same paragraph number. If you accidentally pressed [Tab], WordPerfect would indent and change the paragraph number from

"I" to "A." If this happens, press [Shift][Tab] (Left Margin Release) to "unindent" and to instruct WordPerfect to change from a lower level (A) back to the next higher level of paragraph number (I).

❹   Type **Introduction**. See Figure 5-6.

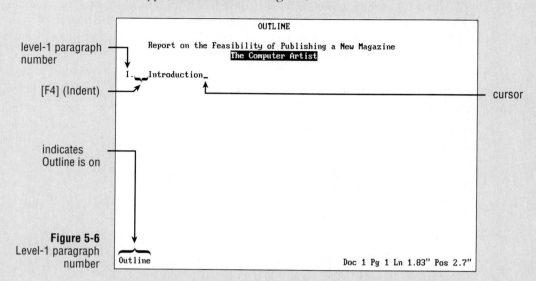

Figure 5-6
Level-1 paragraph
number

❺   Press **[Enter]** to move the cursor to the next line. WordPerfect automatically inserts the next level-1 paragraph number (II).

As you can see from Figure 5-2, you want the level-2 paragraph number A, not paragraph number II, on this line. To indent and change the paragraph number, you press [Tab].

❻   Press **[Tab]** to change from the level-1 paragraph number I to the level-2 paragraph number A and indent to the next tab stop.

❼   Press **[F4]** (Indent) to indent without changing the paragraph number, then type **Purposes of report**. See Figure 5-7.

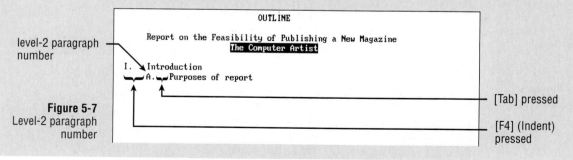

Figure 5-7
Level-2 paragraph
number

Now let's continue creating the outline shown in Figure 5-2.

To continue the outline:

❶ Press **[Enter]** to move to the next line and to insert the next paragraph number (B) into the text.

❷ Press **[Tab]** to change from a level-2 to a level-3 paragraph number and to indent to the next tab stop. The paragraph number "B" changes to "1."

❸ Press **[F4]** (Indent) and type **Potential size of the market**.

❹ Press **[Enter]** to move to the next line and to insert the next paragraph number (the level-3 paragraph number 2), press **[F4]** (Indent), and type **Competing magazines**.

❺ Press **[Enter]** to insert the next paragraph number (3), press **[F4]** (Indent), and type **Projected costs of starting and running the magazine**.

❻ Press **[Enter]**, press **[F4]** (Indent), and type **Potential profitability of the magazine**.

You have now completed four items at level-3 paragraph numbering (Figure 5-8). In the next steps, you'll instruct WordPerfect to change a lower-level paragraph number to a higher-level paragraph number.

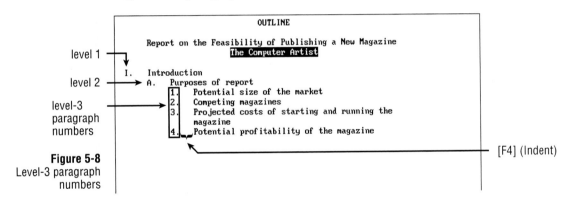

Figure 5-8
Level-3 paragraph numbers

To change from a lower-level to a higher-level paragraph number:

❶ Press **[Enter]**. WordPerfect inserts the level-3 paragraph number 5, which you don't want.

To change from a level-3 to a level-2 paragraph number, you press [Shift][Tab] (Left Margin Release).

❷ Press **[Shift][Tab]** (Left Margin Release) to return to the next higher level of paragraph numbering.

③ Press **[F4]** (Indent) and type **Information upon which decision will be based**. Your screen should now look like Figure 5-9.

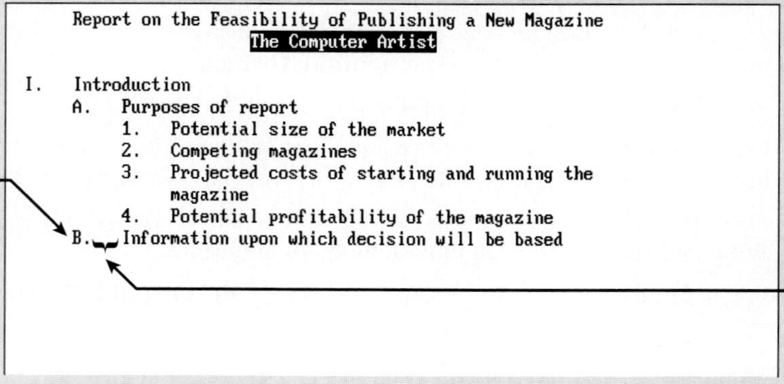

```
        Report on the Feasibility of Publishing a New Magazine
                         The Computer Artist

    I.   Introduction
         A.   Purposes of report
              1.   Potential size of the market
              2.   Competing magazines
              3.   Projected costs of starting and running the
                   magazine
              4.   Potential profitability of the magazine
         B.   Information upon which decision will be based
```

pressed
[Shift] [Tab]
(Margin Release)

[F4] (Indent)

Figure 5-9
Outline after you
type item I.B.

④ Complete the outline shown in Figure 5-2.

⑤ Save this intermediate version of the outline as S5OUTLIN.DFT. Follow the same steps you would use to save any other document.

Editing an Outline

Jonathan gives the task force members a copy of the outline at their next meeting. The task force decides to add a new section on competing magazines, as shown in Figure 5-10. They also suggest that current items III ("Expenses") and IV ("Projected income") be switched, so that projected income is discussed before expenses. Finally they suggest that items B and C under "Projected income" be switched, so that the estimate of income from subscriptions comes immediately after the estimate of the number of subscribers. Jonathan decides to use WordPerfect's powerful outline editing features to make these changes.

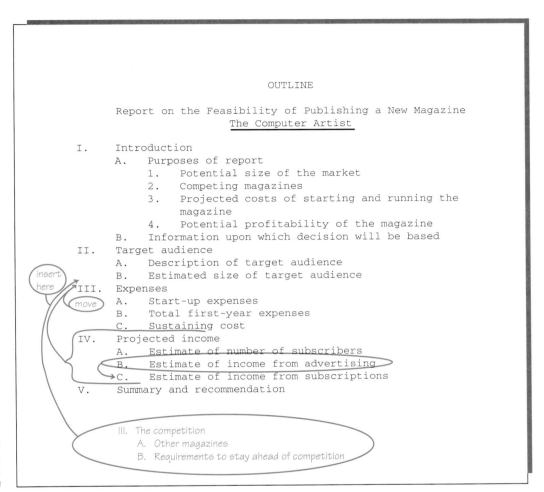

Figure 5-10
The task force's
suggested changes
to the outline

Moving the Cursor through an Outline

You can use all the standard WordPerfect cursor-movement commands in an outline, but WordPerfect also provides four special cursor-movement commands, shown in Figure 5-11. These special commands require an enhanced keyboard with separate cursor-movement keys. (If you don't have an enhanced keyboard, go to the next section.) Let's practice using the special cursor-movement commands.

Keys	Description
[Alt] [→]	Move cursor to next paragraph number.
[Alt] [←]	Move cursor to previous paragraph number.
[Alt] [↓]	Move cursor to next paragraph number at same outline level or higher.
[Alt] [↑]	Move cursor to previous paragraph number at same outline level or higher.

Figure 5-11
Special outline
cursor-movement
keys

To use the special cursor-movement commands to move the cursor through the outline:

❶ Make sure the intermediate version of the outline, S5OUTLIN.DFT, is on the WordPerfect document screen.

❷ Use the standard cursor-movement keys to move the cursor to the "I" in "Introduction," to the right of Roman numeral I.

❸ Press **[Alt][→]** several times and then **[Alt][←]** several times. Observe the behavior of the cursor.

As you can see, the cursor moves forward to the next paragraph number each time you press [Alt][→] and backward to the previous paragraph number each time you press [Alt][←].

❹ Press **[Alt][↓]** several times and **[Alt][↑]** several times. Observe the behavior of the cursor.

As you can see, pressing [Alt][↑] moves the cursor backward to the previous paragraph number of the same level or higher, and pressing [Alt][↓] moves the cursor forward to the next paragraph number of the same level or higher.

With these special cursor-movement commands, you can move the cursor quickly from one place to another within an outline.

Inserting New Paragraph Numbers into an Outline

After the task force meeting Jonathan returns to his office and edits a copy of the outline according to the committee's suggestions (Figure 5-10). Let's first insert the text on competing magazines, which begins with outline paragraph number III.

To insert new paragraph numbers into an outline:

❶ Move the cursor to the end of item II.B., "Estimated size of target audience," that is, to the end of the line above the paragraph number that you want to insert.

❷ Press **[Enter]**. WordPerfect inserts a hard return, moves the cursor down a line, and inserts the paragraph number "C" under the "B."

Because Jonathan wants a level-1 paragraph number (III) here, he must change the paragraph number "C" from a lower to a higher level.

③ Press **[Shift][Tab]** (Left Margin Release) to change the paragraph number from a lower to a higher level.

The "C" disappears, the cursor moves one tab stop to the left, and "III" appears on the screen. WordPerfect automatically increments the subsequent level-1 paragraph numbers.

④ Press **[F4]** (Indent) and type **The competition** to insert the level-1 paragraph.

Next you'll insert the two level-2 paragraphs of the revised outline.

⑤ Press **[Enter]** to insert a hard return and insert a new paragraph number, press **[Tab]** to change to a lower level of paragraph number (A), press **[F4]** (Indent), and type **Other magazines**.

⑥ Press **[Enter]**, press **[F4]** (Indent), and type **Requirements to stay ahead of competition**.

Your screen should now look like Figure 5-12. Jonathan has inserted the section on competing magazines, as suggested by the other members of the task force.

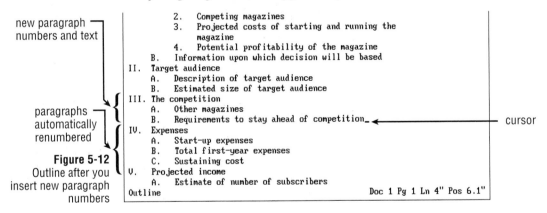

new paragraph numbers and text

paragraphs automatically renumbered

Figure 5-12
Outline after you insert new paragraph numbers

cursor

```
              2.   Competing magazines
              3.   Projected costs of starting and running the
                   magazine
              4.   Potential profitability of the magazine
         B.   Information upon which decision will be based
    II.  Target audience
         A.   Description of target audience
         B.   Estimated size of target audience
    III. The competition
         A.   Other magazines
         B.   Requirements to stay ahead of competition_
    IV.  Expenses
         A.   Start-up expenses
         B.   Total first-year expenses
         C.   Sustaining cost
    V.   Projected income
         A.   Estimate of number of subscribers
    Outline                              Doc 1 Pg 1 Ln 4" Pos 6.1"
```

Moving an Outline Family

Jonathan's next task is to move an outline **family**, which is a group of paragraph numbers and accompanying text that includes the level where the cursor is located and all subordinate levels under that level (Figure 5-13) on the next page. In this case the outline family that you want to move is paragraph number V ("Projected income") and all subordinate paragraphs.

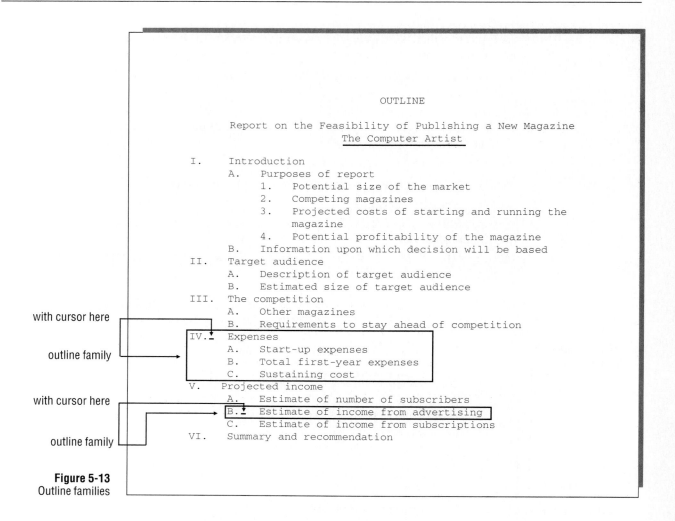

with cursor here

outline family

with cursor here

outline family

Figure 5-13
Outline families

To move an outline family:

❶ Move the cursor to the right of the paragraph number that heads the family you want to move. In this case move the cursor to the right of Roman numeral V, after the period and to the left of the "P" in "Projected income."

❷ Select Move Family from the Tools/Outline menu or press **[Shift][F5]** (Date/Outline), select **4** (**O**utline), and select **3** (**M**ove Family). The family you want to move becomes highlighted. See Figure 5-14.

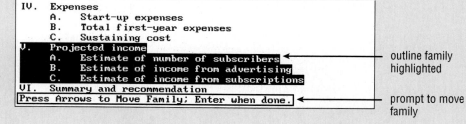

Figure 5-14
Highlighted outline
family before move

outline family
highlighted

prompt to move
family

❸ Press [↑] and then **[Enter]**. The highlighted family moves above the previous family, so the moved family begins with paragraph number IV instead of V. At the same time the old family that begins with "IV. Expenses" becomes the new family "V. Expenses."

You have now moved the "Projected income" family above the "Expenses" family. Your next task is to move the item "B. Estimate of income from advertising" underneath the item "C. Estimate of income from subscriptions." Let's use the Move Family command again to make the move.

❹ Move the cursor just to the right of "B." underneath "IV. Projected income."

❺ Select Move Family from the Tools/Outline menu or press **[Shift][F5]** (Date/Outline), select **4** (**O**utline), and select **3** (**M**ove Family). The line "B. Estimate of income from advertising" becomes highlighted.

❻ Press [↓] and then **[Enter]** to move the highlighted text down one line, as suggested by the task force committee.

You have now moved "Estimate of income from advertising" under "Estimate of income from subscriptions."

Turning Off Outline Mode

If your document doesn't contain any text after the outline, you do not have to turn off Outline mode. But if you want to insert additional text below the outline, you must turn off Outline mode.

To turn off Outline:

❶ Move the cursor to the end of the outline.

❷ Select Outline from the Tools menu, then select Off to turn off Outline. Alternatively press **[Shift][F5]** (Date/Outline) and select **4** (**O**utline) to display the Outline menu. Select **2** (**O**ff) from the Outline menu. The message "Outline" disappears from the status line.

❸ Save the outline as S5OUTLIN.DOC, print it, and clear the document screen.

The final version of your outline should now look like Figure 5-15 on the next page.

```
                              OUTLINE

        Report on the Feasibility of Publishing a New Magazine
                         The Computer Artist

    I.    Introduction
          A.    Purposes of report
                1.    Potential size of the market
                2.    Competing magazines
                3.    Projected costs of starting and running the
                      magazine
                4.    Potential profitability of the magazine
          B.    Information upon which decision will be based
    II.   Target audience
          A.    Description of target audience
          B.    Estimated size of target audience
    III.  The competition
          A.    Other magazines
          B.    Requirements to stay ahead of competition
    IV.   Projected income
          A.    Estimate of number of subscribers
          B.    Estimate of income from subscriptions
          C.    Estimate of income from advertising
    V.    Expenses
          A.    Start-up expenses
          B.    Total first-year expenses
          C.    Sustaining cost
    VI.   Summary and recommendation
```

Figure 5-15
Final version of
outline

Using the Two Document Screens

After approving Jonathan's revised outline, the task force agrees that Ann should begin writing the first draft of the report.

Retrieving a Document into the Second Document Screen

Ann wants to have the approved outline handy at all times without cluttering her desk; therefore, she decides to use WordPerfect's dual document feature. The **dual document feature** allows you to have two different documents in WordPerfect at once. You can then easily switch back and forth between the two documents. This is helpful if you want to read one document while creating another, copy text from one document to another, or edit two documents together. In this case Ann will write her report on document screen 1 (labeled "Doc 1" on the status line) and keep the outline on document screen 2 (labeled "Doc 2" on the status line). In that way she will always have access to the approved outline in WordPerfect. Let's use WordPerfect's dual document feature to begin writing the report.

To use document screen 2:

❶ Make sure you have saved the final version of the outline document as S5OUTLIN.DOC and cleared the document screen.

❷ Press **[Shift][F3]** (Switch) to switch from document screen 1 to document screen 2. The right side of the status line shows "Doc 2" instead of "Doc 1." See Figure 5-16.

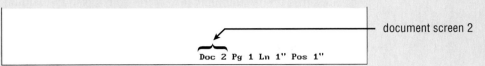

Figure 5-16
Status line of
document screen 2

❸ Retrieve S5OUTLIN.DOC. Now the outline is in Doc 2.

Copying Text between Doc 1 and Doc 2

Ann can now view the outline in Doc 2 whenever she wants and then return to Doc 1, where she will write the report. She uses [Shift][F3] (Switch) to switch between the two documents. So that she doesn't have to retype the title in creating her report, Ann will use dual documents to copy the title of the outline from Doc 2 to Doc 1. Let's copy the title from Doc 2 to Doc 1 using a block operation.

To copy text from Doc 2 to Doc 1:

❶ Make sure the current document screen is Doc 2, then move the cursor to the left margin of the line that begins "Report on the Feasibility." The cursor should be at Pos 1".

❷ Turn Block on by selecting Block from the Edit menu or by pressing **[Alt][F4]** or **[F12]** (Block).

❸ Move the cursor to the end of the line, after "The Computer Artist," to highlight the title.

❹ Select Copy from the Edit menu or press **[Ctrl][F4]** (Move) and select **1** (**B**lock) and **2** (**C**opy). The prompt "Move cursor; press Enter to retrieve" appears on the status line.

❺ Press **[Shift][F3]** (Switch) to switch to Doc 1, then press **[Enter]** to insert a copy of the title into the report. A copy of the title appears in Doc 1. See Figure 5-17.

Figure 5-17
Document screen 1
after you copy
title from
document screen 2

If "Outline" appears on the status line of Doc 1, you have accidentally copied the Outline code for Doc 2. You should then turn on Reveal Codes in Doc 1, delete [Outline], and turn off Reveal Codes.

These steps demonstrate that you can use the familiar copy and cut-and-paste operations to copy and move text not only within a document but also between documents.

Using Split-Screen Windows

Ann decides that she would really like to be able to see the outline while she is typing her report. Using [Shift][F3] (Switch) she can easily switch between the two documents, but she can't see them both on the screen at once. To see both documents on the screen at once, she will use the Window feature.

To use the Window feature to see both Doc 1 and Doc 2:

➊ Make sure that Doc 1 is still on your screen.

➋ Select Window from the Edit menu or press **[Ctrl][F3]** (Screen) and select **1** (**W**indow). The prompt "Number of lines in this window" appears on the status line. The default value, usually 24, appears with the prompt.

The total number of text lines on a document screen is normally 24. When you use split-screen windows, each document must have at least two lines; therefore, you can type any value from 2 to 22 as the number of lines in this window. In most cases, you'll want approximately the same number of lines in each window, that is, about 12 lines of text.

➌ Type **12** and press **[Enter]**. WordPerfect splits the screen into two windows, with Doc 1 on the top and Doc 2 on the bottom. See Figure 5-18.

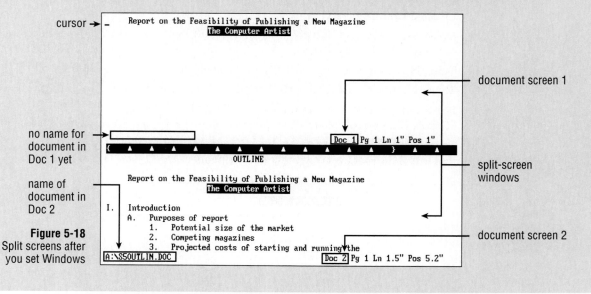

cursor →

document screen 1

no name for document in Doc 1 yet

name of document in Doc 2

Figure 5-18
Split screens after you set Windows

split-screen windows

document screen 2

Now Ann will be able to see both documents on the screen at once. She can edit only one document at a time, however, so the cursor will be in either one window or the other. She can move the cursor between the two windows by pressing [Shift][F3] (Switch).

Ann decides that her report should be double-spaced, so her next task is to set double spacing for the document in Doc 1. Let's insert the format code for double spacing.

To double-space the document in Doc 1:

❶ Make sure the cursor is at the beginning of the document in Doc 1.

❷ Select Line from the Layout menu or press **[Shift][F8]** (Format) and select **1** (**L**ine). The Format: Line menu appears on the screen.

❸ Select **6** (Line **S**pacing), type **2** for double spacing, and press **[Enter]**.

❹ Press **[F7]** (Exit) to return to the document screen.

Next Ann wants to type a heading for the first section of her report.

❺ Move the cursor to the end of the document title, to the right of "The Computer Artist," after the Underline code, and press **[Enter]** to double-space after the title.

❻ Press **[F6]** (Bold) to turn on boldfacing, type **Introduction**, press **[F6]** (Bold) again to turn off boldfacing, and press **[Enter]**.

With the outline in Doc 2, Ann continues to type the report in Doc 1. Except for copy and cut-and-paste operations, WordPerfect commands performed in one document don't affect the other document.

In the next steps, you'll retrieve the remainder of Ann's draft of the report and then turn off split-screen windows.

To retrieve the report and turn off split-screen windows:

❶ With the cursor underneath the first heading ("Introduction") and with the WordPerfect data diskette in drive A, select Retrieve from the File menu or press **[Shift][F10]** (Retrieve), type **a:\c5file1.dft**, and press **[Enter]**.

❷ Take a few minutes to read the report so you'll be familiar with its contents. Notice that the title of the magazine is missing from the first paragraph of the report. You'll fix that problem later.

❸ Select Window from the Edit menu or press **[Ctrl][F3]** (Screen) and select **1** (**W**indows).

④ Type **24** and press **[Enter]** to tell WordPerfect that you want the current window to be 24 lines, or the entire screen. WordPerfect removes the split-screen windows so that Doc 1 and Doc 2 are on different screens. Your screen should look similar to Figure 5-19.

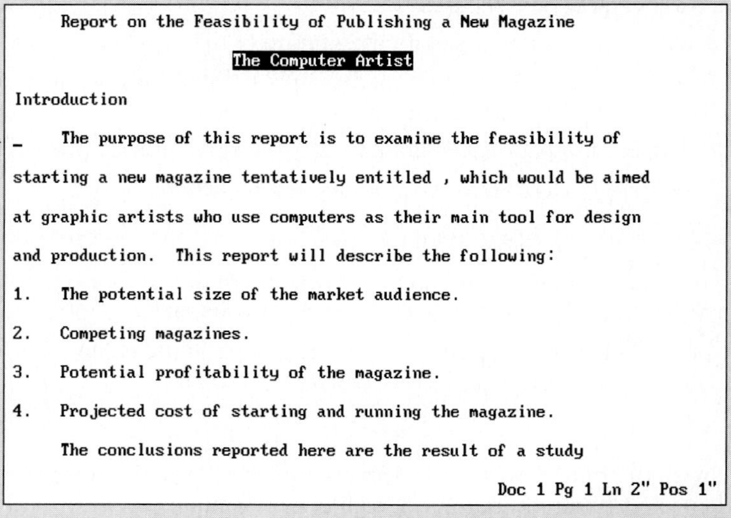

cursor ➔

Figure 5-19
Document screen
after you retrieve
report

Macros

Ann knows that while writing the feasibility study she will have to type the name of the proposed magazine, "The Computer Artist," several times. For any word-processing procedure that you have to repeat several times — a series of WordPerfect commands, a word, a phrase, or a combination of commands and text — you can create a macro to perform the procedure for you. A **macro**, in its simplest sense, is a "recording" of keystrokes that you can "play back" at any time by pressing just a few keystrokes.

Creating a macro to execute frequently pressed keystrokes has several advantages:

• Macros save time. By executing a macro, you can save many keystrokes, which means you can prepare your document faster.

• Macros are accurate. When you execute a macro, you don't have to worry about typos or other mistakes. If you created the macro correctly, every time you use it, the keystrokes are executed without error.

• Macros are consistent. Macros that insert text and formatting features create the same text and format each time.

Creating a Macro

Creating a macro requires five steps (Figure 5-20):

1. Turn on the "recording," that is, turn on macro definition.

2. Name the macro.

3. Describe the macro.

4. Record the keystrokes.

5. Turn off the "recording," that is, turn off macro definition.

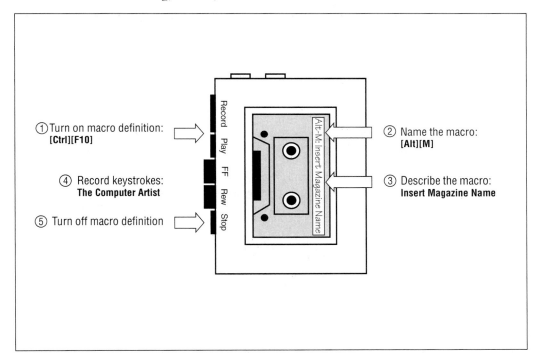

Figure 5-20
Five steps to create
a macro

When you create a macro, you can select one of three ways of naming the macro. An **Alt macro** is a macro you name by pressing [Alt] and a letter, for example, [Alt][M]. You can use any one of the 26 letters of the alphabet, but you can't use any other type of character, that is, no digits or symbols. To execute an Alt macro, that is, to "play back" the recorded keystrokes, you press [Alt] and the letter.

A **named macro** is a macro you name by typing a legal DOS filename. To execute a named macro, you issue the [Alt][F10] (Macro) command, type the filename of the named macro, and press [Enter].

An **Enter macro** is a macro without a name or a description. When WordPerfect asks you for the macro name to create or execute the macro, you just press [Enter]. In the steps that follow, you'll create and execute each of these three types of macros.

Before you create any macros, you should instruct WordPerfect about the disk and the directory where you want the macros saved. Since you will want WordPerfect to save your macros to your data diskette, let's specify drive A as the location of the macros.

To specify the location of macros:

❶ Insert your WordPerfect data diskette into drive A.

❷ Select Location of Files from the File/Setup menu. See Figure 5-21.

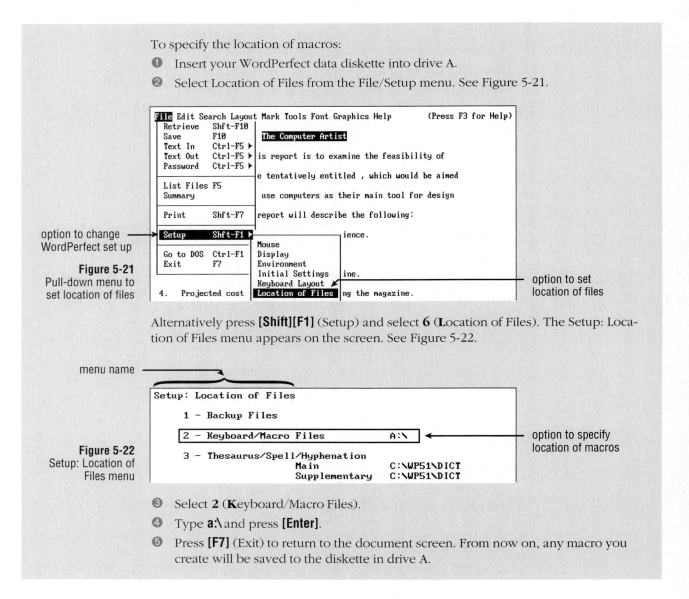

option to change
WordPerfect set up

Figure 5-21
Pull-down menu to
set location of files

option to set
location of files

Alternatively press **[Shift][F1]** (Setup) and select **6** (**L**ocation of Files). The Setup: Location of Files menu appears on the screen. See Figure 5-22.

menu name

Figure 5-22
Setup: Location of
Files menu

option to specify
location of macros

❸ Select **2** (**K**eyboard/Macro Files).

❹ Type **a:** and press **[Enter]**.

❺ Press **[F7]** (Exit) to return to the document screen. From now on, any macro you create will be saved to the diskette in drive A.

In the following steps you'll define a macro that inserts the name of the proposed magazine.

To define a macro:

❶ Move the cursor to the comma after "tentatively entitled" in the second line of the first paragraph. When you create a macro, the keystrokes you record are executed in the document. If the macro will insert text, move the cursor to the position in the document where you want that text.

❷ Press **[Ctrl][F10]** (Macro Define) to turn on macro definition. The prompt "Define macro:" appears on the status line, and WordPerfect waits for you to give the macro a name.

For this macro, we'll create an Alt macro. And because this is a macro to insert the name of a magazine, we'll use "M" for "magazine."

❸ Press **[Alt][M]** to name the macro. This creates an Alt macro, which WordPerfect will save using the filename ALTM.WPM.

The prompt "Description:" appears on the status line. Let's type a description that will remind us of the macro's function.

❹ Type **Insert magazine name** and press **[Enter]**.

WordPerfect displays the message "Macro Def" in blinking bold characters on the left side of the status line. From this point on, until you turn off macro definition, WordPerfect will record every keystroke or mouse command that you execute. Now let's record the keystrokes for the Alt-M macro.

❺ Press **[F8]** (Underline), type **The Computer Artist**, and press **[F8]** (Underline). These keystrokes, which create the underlined title of the proposed magazine, are now recorded in the Alt-M macro.

Now that you have recorded the keystrokes for the Alt-M macro, you'll turn off macro definition.

❻ Press **[Ctrl][F10]** (Macro Define) to turn off macro definition. The message "Macro Def" disappears from the status line. WordPerfect saves the completed macro as ALTM.WPM.

You can use essentially the same procedure to record any sequence of keystrokes, such as your company name, your own name and address, or the keystrokes for setting double spacing.

Correcting an Error in a Macro

Take a moment to look at your document. Did you spell "The Computer Artist" correctly? Is it underlined? If you made a mistake, you can define the macro again. Let's assume you made an error and have to redefine the Alt-M macro.

To correct an error in a macro:

❶ Delete any text you typed while creating the macro and move the cursor to where you want to insert the text of the macro. In this case completely delete "The Computer Artist," including the underline code, that you inserted while creating the macro.

❷ Press **[Ctrl][F10]** (Macro Define) to turn on macro definition.

③ Press **[Alt][M]** to name the macro. WordPerfect displays a prompt that a macro named ALTM.WPM already exists. See Figure 5-23.

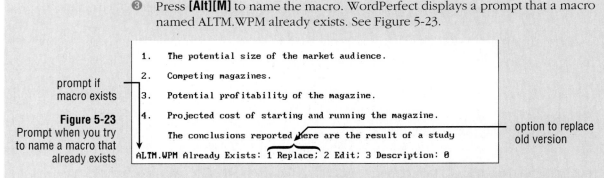

prompt if macro exists

Figure 5-23
Prompt when you try to name a macro that already exists

option to replace old version

```
1.   The potential size of the market audience.

2.   Competing magazines.

3.   Potential profitability of the magazine.

4.   Projected cost of starting and running the magazine.

     The conclusions reported here are the result of a study

ALTM.WPM Already Exists: 1 Replace; 2 Edit; 3 Description: 0
```

④ Select 1 (**R**eplace) to instruct WordPerfect that you want to replace the existing (erroneous) macro with a new one with the same name. WordPerfect displays the prompt "Replace A:\ALTM.WPM?"

⑤ Select "Yes" to delete the old macro and to begin defining the new one. WordPerfect displays the prompt "Description:" on the status line.

⑥ Type **Insert magazine name** and press **[Enter]**.

⑦ Type the correct keystrokes that you want to record in the macro, that is, press **[F8]** (Underline), type **The Computer Artist**, and press **[F8]** (Underline).

⑧ Press **[Ctrl][F10]** (Macro Define) to turn off macro definition.

In general any time you make a mistake while you are creating a simple macro, just press [Ctrl][F10] (Macro Define) to turn off macro definition and then start over.

Executing an Alt Macro

Now that you've correctly created an Alt macro, you're ready to use the Alt-M macro to insert the magazine name into the document. To execute an Alt macro, you press [Alt] and, while holding it down, press the letter you used to create the macro.

To execute an Alt macro:

① Move the cursor to the location in your document where you want the macro executed. In this case move the cursor just to the right of the phrase "target audience" on the first line under the heading "The Target Audience."

② Press **[Space]**, type **of**, and press **[Space]**.

Now you're ready to insert the underlined name of the magazine. But instead of using the Underline command and typing the text, you'll execute the macro you just created.

③ Press **[Alt][M]**. The underlined magazine title appears in the document.

④ Now move the cursor after "The potential audience" at the beginning of the second sentence of the next paragraph.

⑤ Insert the phrase "for The Computer Artist" using the Alt macro. Your screen should look similar to Figure 5-24.

```
Graphic Designers, we estimated that over 95,000 graphic designers

------------------------------------------------------------------------
work within the United States and Canada.

    Our analysis of the questionnaires to graphic artists

suggested that 69% of them use personal computers and that an

additional 13% plan to purchase and use a personal computer within

the next 18 months.  The potential audience for The Computer Artist ◄────

is therefore 82% (69% + 13%) of 95,000, or a total of 78,000
```

Figure 5-24
Document screen
after you use macro
to insert magazine
name

underlined magazine
name inserted with
macro

Although Ann created and used the Alt-M macro while writing her feasibility report, the macro is not associated exclusively with the report but is saved to the disk as a separate file. She can use the Alt-M macro in this report and in any future documents she writes using the disk on which she saved the macro.

Creating a Named Macro

Ann knows that in this report and in other documents, she frequently will have to type the abbreviated name for Connolly/Bayle Publishing Company — C/B Publishing — so she decides to create a macro.

As you create the macro, you'll insert the name "C/B Publishing" into the document at the beginning of the title; later you'll use the macro to insert the name elsewhere in the document. First you'll have to prepare the report to insert a new title line.

To insert a new title line:

❶ Move the cursor to the beginning of the document so that the cursor is located after the initial formatting codes but before the title. You may have to turn on Reveal Codes to make sure that the cursor is on the first [Center] code. Turn off Reveal Codes after you position the cursor.

❷ Press **[Enter]** to insert a blank line at the beginning of the document, move the cursor back to the blank line, and press **[Shift][F6]** (Center).

You're now ready to create the macro to insert the abbreviated company name. Ann decides to define a named macro using the name "CB," which stands for "C/B Publishing." In a named macro you can use any legal DOS filename without a filename extension. WordPerfect automatically adds the .WPM extension. Let's create the named macro. Remember, if you make a mistake while recording keystrokes in the macro, turn off macro definition and start again.

To create a named macro:

❶ Press **[Ctrl][F10]** (Macro Define) to turn on macro definition. The prompt "Define macro:" appears on the status line, and WordPerfect waits for you to give the macro a name.

❷ Type **cb** and press **[Enter]** to name the macro. The prompt "Description:" appears on the status line.

❸ Type **Insert company name** and press **[Enter]** to describe the function of the macro. WordPerfect displays the message "Macro Def" in blinking bold characters on the left side of the status line.

❹ Type **C/B Publishing** but do *not* press [Enter]. If you did press [Enter], the macro would record the [Enter], and every time you executed the CB macro, a hard return would be inserted into the document. If you made a mistake, turn off macro definition and start over, replacing the original CB macro with the correct version.

❺ Press **[Ctrl][F10]** (Macro Define) to turn off macro definition. The message "Macro Def" disappears from the status line, and WordPerfect automatically saves the macro as CB.WPM.

Your screen should now look like Figure 5-25.

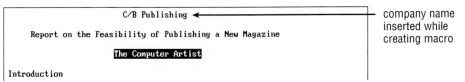

company name
inserted while
creating macro

Executing a Named Macro

To prepare for executing the CB macro or any other macro that inserts format codes or text, you have to move the cursor to the location in your document where you want the code or text.

To execute a named macro:

❶ Move the cursor to the right of the words "will help" just above the heading "The Target Audience" and press **[Space]**. This places the cursor where you want the name "C/B Publishing" inserted.

❷ Press **[Alt][F10]** (Macro). The prompt "Macro" appears on the status line for you to enter the name of the macro.

❸ Type **cb** and press **[Enter]**. The macro inserts the name of the company into the document at the location of the cursor.

Next let's use the CB macro to insert the company name elsewhere in the document.

❹ Move the cursor to the "b" at the beginning of "board of directors" in the middle of the paragraph under the heading "The Competition."

❺ Press **[Alt][F10]** (Macro), type **cb**, and press **[Enter]**. Press **[Space]** to leave a space after the company name.

Ann has now completed her work on this draft of the document and is ready to save the intermediate version to the disk.

⑥ Save the document as S5FEAS1.DFT.

So far you have seen how to define two types of macros, Alt macros and named macros. The advantage of a named macro over an Alt macro is that the named macro is mnemonic, meaning that you can use easy-to-remember names for the macro. The advantage of the Alt macro is that it takes fewer keystrokes to execute than a named macro. For example, to execute the CB macro, you have to press [Alt][F10] (Macro), type "CB," and press [Enter] — a total of five keystrokes. To execute the Alt-M macro, you just press [Alt][M] — two keystrokes.

Creating an Enter Macro

Ann gives Jonathan a diskette that contains a copy of the file S5FEAS1.DFT and asks him to make any formatting changes that he feels would improve the appearance of the document. Jonathan decides that each heading should be preceded by three blank lines (not just the two lines currently in the double-spaced document) and that to simplify editing a Conditional End-of-Page command should be inserted just before each heading. Making these changes for the six headings would require many keystrokes, so Jonathan decides to create a macro to make the changes quickly and accurately.

Such a macro is applicable only to this report, because Jonathan doubts he would use it in future documents. He therefore decides to create an Enter macro instead of an Alt or a named macro. Unlike an Alt and a named macro, an Enter macro doesn't have a name or a description. To define or execute an Enter macro, you just press [Enter] when WordPerfect prompts you for the macro name.

Let's create an Enter macro to format the headings of Ann's report. As you create the macro, you'll record the keystrokes for formatting the first heading. Later you'll use the macro to format the other headings in the document.

As you create a macro, *the keystrokes are executed as you enter them*, thus modifying your document. If you press the wrong keys, your document could be altered *beyond repair*. Therefore, always save your document before you create or execute a complex macro. Make sure you have saved this document as S5FEAS1.DFT.

To create an Enter macro:

❶ Move the cursor to the beginning of the document. Because this Enter macro will search for the first occurrence of a heading, we'll start the macro at the beginning of the document.

❷ Press **[Ctrl][F10]** (Macro Define) to initiate the definition of the macro.

❸ Press **[Enter]**. This creates an Enter macro, with no name and no description. The blinking message "Macro Def" appears on the status line.

You're now ready to record the keystrokes of the macro. Because the headings contain the only boldfaced characters in the report, you'll begin the macro by searching for the [BOLD] code.

❹ Press **[F2]** (Search), then **[F6]** (Bold), then **[F2]** (Search).

The cursor moves to the first occurrence of boldfaced text, which is the heading "Introduction," just after the invisible [BOLD] code. The Pos value on the status line indicates that bold is on. To format the heading, you want the cursor before the [BOLD] code. In the keystrokes that follow, you'll move the cursor to the left of the [BOLD] code, then set conditional end of page.

⑤ Press [←] to move the cursor to the left of the [BOLD] code, press **[Shift][F8]** (Format), select **4** (**O**ther), select **2** (**C**onditional End of Page), type **6** (the number of lines that you want kept together), and press **[Enter]**. Keep the cursor on the Format: Other menu.

Next you want to add the codes necessary to insert one blank line just above the heading. You can't just press [Enter], because with the line spacing set to double, the [Enter] would insert two blank lines. Therefore, you must first set the spacing to single, press [Enter], then reset the spacing back to double.

⑥ Press **[Enter]** to return to the Format menu, select **1** (**L**ine), select **6** (Line **S**pacing), type **1** (for single spacing), and press **[Enter]**. Press **[F7]** (Exit) to return to the document screen. Press **[Enter]** to insert one blank line.

Now you have to set the spacing back to double.

⑦ Press **[Shift][F8]** (Format), select **1** (**L**ine), select **6** (Line **S**pacing), type **2** for double spacing, and press **[Enter]**. Press **[F7]** (Exit) to return to the document screen.

Now you have to move the cursor below the heading so that when you execute the macro, the cursor will be past the heading you've just edited and will find the next occurrence of a heading.

⑧ Press **[↓]** to move the cursor below the heading.

This sequence of keystrokes is long and tedious, which is why you want to do it only once, not at every heading.

⑨ Press **[Ctrl][F10]** (Macro Define) to turn off macro definition.

Executing an Enter Macro

Having formatted the first heading while he was creating the Enter macro, Jonathan is now ready to use the macro to format the other five headings. Since the only boldfacing in this document is in the headings, the macro will find and modify only headings. Don't use this macro in documents that may have boldfacing other than in headings.

To execute an Enter macro:
❶ Press **[Alt][F10]** (Macro). WordPerfect displays the "Macro" prompt.
❷ Press **[Enter]**.

The macro finds the next [BOLD] code, which occurs only in headings in this document, and inserts the desired formatting codes.

---

❸   Repeat Steps 1 and 2 to format the other four headings in the report.

Your screen should now look like Figure 5-26.

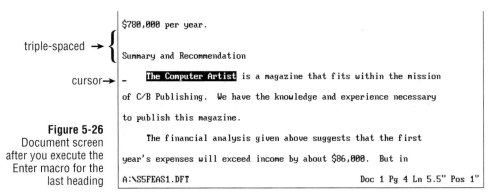

triple-spaced →

cursor →

Figure 5-26
Document screen
after you execute the
Enter macro for the
last heading

```
$780,000 per year.

Summary and Recommendation

-    The Computer Artist is a magazine that fits within the mission

of C/B Publishing.  We have the knowledge and experience necessary

to publish this magazine.

    The financial analysis given above suggests that the first

year's expenses will exceed income by about $86,000.  But in

A:\S5FEAS1.DFT                              Doc 1 Pg 4 Ln 5.5" Pos 1"
```

Footnotes

Jonathan printed and distributed a copy of the feasibility report to the members of the task force, who then suggested some minor revisions. They felt that the report should include three footnotes: the first giving the source of the data published by the American Society of Graphic Designers, the second explaining how the task force arrived at the proposed subscription rate of $55, and the third giving the source of the expenses required to start up the proposed magazine.

Creating a Footnote

The three footnotes suggested by the task force are shown in Figure 5-27. Let's create them now.

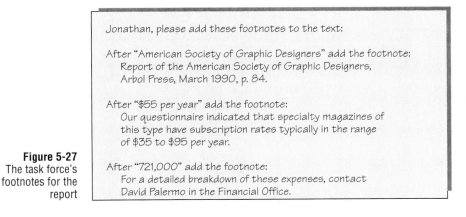

Figure 5-27
The task force's
footnotes for the
report

Jonathan, please add these footnotes to the text:

After "American Society of Graphic Designers" add the footnote:
    Report of the American Society of Graphic Designers,
    Arbol Press, March 1990, p. 84.

After "$55 per year" add the footnote:
    Our questionnaire indicated that specialty magazines of
    this type have subscription rates typically in the range
    of $35 to $95 per year.

After "721,000" add the footnote:
    For a detailed breakdown of these expenses, contact
    David Palermo in the Financial Office.

To create a footnote:

❶ Move the cursor to the location where you want the footnote number to appear in the text. In this case move the cursor to the right of the comma that follows the phrase "American Society of Graphic Designers" in the paragraph under "The Target Audience."

❷ Select Create from the Layout/Footnote menu. See Figure 5-28.

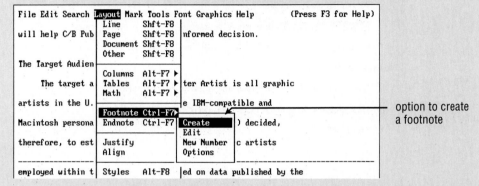

Figure 5-28
Pull-down menu to
create a footnote

Alternatively press **[Ctrl][F7]** (Footnote) to display the one-line menu shown in Figure 5-29, then select **1** (**F**ootnote) to display the menu shown in Figure 5-30, and select **1** (**C**reate).

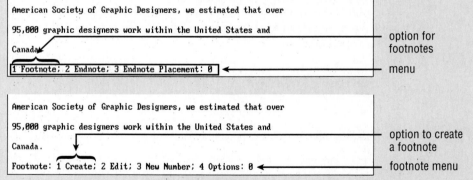

Figure 5-29
The menu after
pressing **[Ctrl][F7]**
(Footnote)

Figure 5-30
The Footnote menu

The blank Footnote Edit screen appears. See Figure 5-31. The screen contains an automatic tab and a superscript footnote number.

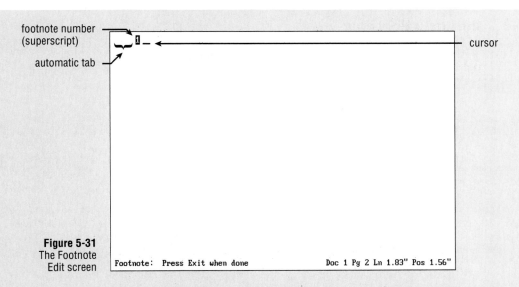

footnote number
(superscript)

automatic tab

cursor

Figure 5-31
The Footnote
Edit screen

Footnote: Press Exit when done   Doc 1 Pg 2 Ln 1.83" Pos 1.56"

❸ Without pressing [Space] or [Tab], type the text of the first footnote as shown in Figure 5-27.

❹ Press **[F7]** (Exit) to return to the document screen.

WordPerfect automatically inserts the correct footnote number into the body of the report and formats the text of the footnote at the bottom of the page.

❺ Select View Document from the Print/Option menu, set the view to 100%, and scroll the screen so you can see the bottom of the page. See Figure 5-32.

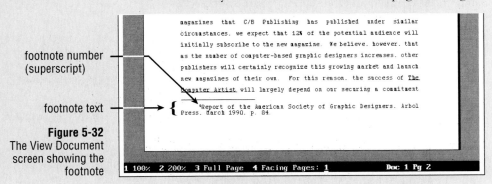

footnote number
(superscript)

footnote text

Figure 5-32
The View Document
screen showing the
footnote

The text of the footnote appears at the bottom of the page with a horizontal line separating the footnote from the body of the text.

❻ Exit the View Document screen and return to the document screen.

Editing a Footnote

After typing the first footnote, Jonathan remembers that the report cited in the footnote was published in 1991, not in 1990. The footnote from the task force was incorrect. Thus, he needs to edit the footnote to make this correction.

To edit a footnote:

❶ Select Edit from the Layout/Footnote menu or press **[Ctrl][F7]** (Footnote), select **1** (**F**ootnote), and select **2** (**E**dit). WordPerfect displays the prompt "Footnote Number?" with a default footnote number, either 1 or 2, depending on where your cursor is in the document.

❷ If the default number is 1, you can press **[Enter]** to accept the default. Otherwise, type the number of the footnote (in this case **1**) and press **[Enter]**. The footnote edit screen appears with the footnote text that you previously typed.

❸ Using the normal WordPerfect cursor-movement and edit keys, change "1990" to "1991."

❹ Press **[F7]** (Exit) to return to the document screen.

The text of footnote 1 is now correct.

Adding a New Footnote

Jonathan now wants to add the second and third footnotes.

To add a footnote:

❶ Move the cursor to the space after the final "r" in the phrase "$55 per year" in the second paragraph under "Projected income."

❷ Select Create from the Layout/Footnote menu or press **[Ctrl][F7]** (Footnote), select **1** (**F**ootnote), and select **1** (**C**reate). The cursor is now in a blank Footnote Edit screen, with footnote number 2 in the upper left corner of the screen.

❸ Type the text of the second footnote, as shown in Figure 5-27. Your screen should now look like Figure 5-33. Then press **[F7]** (Exit) to return to the document screen.

footnote number ⟶

Figure 5-33
The Footnote Edit
screen with
footnote 2

> **2**Our questionnaire indicated that specialty magazines of
> this type have subscription rates typically in the range of $35
> to $95 per year.

❹ Use Steps 1 through 3 to help you create the third footnote shown in Figure 5-27. Put this footnote after the period following the number "$721,000" in the paragraph headed "Expenses."

Benefits of the Footnotes Feature

As you have seen, the Footnotes feature provides three benefits:

- WordPerfect automatically numbers the footnotes. If you add a footnote anywhere in the document, delete a footnote, or move a footnote, WordPerfect automatically renumbers all the footnotes so they appear consecutively.
- WordPerfect automatically formats the footnote text at the bottom of the page.
- WordPerfect allows you to edit the footnote.

What is true of footnotes is also true of **endnotes**, which are notes printed at the end of the document rather than at the bottom of each page. You can create and edit endnotes the same way you created and edited footnotes, except that you would select Endnotes rather than Footnotes from the Layout menu or from the menu that appears after you press [Ctrl][F7] (Footnote).

To delete a footnote, you move the cursor to the footnote and use the normal deletion keys to delete the footnote code. When you delete a footnote, WordPerfect automatically renumbers the footnotes to keep them in order.

To move a footnote, you move the cursor to the footnote, turn on Reveal Codes, block the footnote code, and use a normal cut-and-paste block operation to move the footnote to another point in your document.

Using Hyphenation

When text is fully justified, WordPerfect inserts small spaces between words and characters to keep the lines of text aligned along the right margin. Sometimes this causes unsightly "rivers," or blank regions, through the text. When text is only left-justified, an extremely ragged right edge may occur (Figure 5-34 on the next page). To solve these problems, you can use WordPerfect's automatic hyphenation feature. With hyphenation on, long words that would otherwise wrap to the next line are divided in two, so that part of the word stays on the original line. Thus, the number of "rivers" or the amount of raggedness along the right margin in decreased.

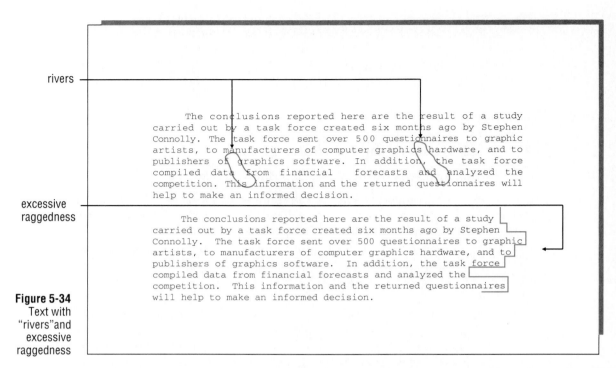

rivers

excessive
raggedness

Figure 5-34
Text with
"rivers"and
excessive
raggedness

When you turn on hyphenation and then move the cursor through your document, WordPerfect analyzes each word that falls at or near the end of a line and checks to see if it should be wrapped to the next line, kept on the same line without hyphenation, or hyphenated. If WordPerfect needs help in deciding how to hyphenate a word, a prompt appears on the status line to ask you where or if you want the word hyphenated.

As the final step in formatting his document, Jonathan decides to turn on hyphenation. You should turn on hyphenation as the *last step* in the final version of a document; otherwise, WordPerfect will constantly interrupt you with hyphenation prompts as you type and modify the text of your document.

To turn on hyphenation:

❶ Move the cursor to the beginning of the document.

Hyphenation occurs only from the point in the document where you turn on hyphenation to the end of the document. Since you want to hyphenate the entire document, you should move the cursor to the beginning of the document.

❷ Select Line from the Layout menu or press **[Shift][F8]** (Format) and select **1** (**L**ine). The Format: Line menu appears on the screen.

❸ Select **1** (**H**yphenation), select "Yes" to verify that you want to turn on hyphenation, and press **[F7]** (Exit) to return to the document screen.

❹ Press **[Home]**, **[Home]**, **[↓]** to move the cursor to the end of the document, forcing WordPerfect to format the entire document.

As the cursor moves through the document, WordPerfect automatically hyphenates some words. If WordPerfect doesn't know how to hyphenate a word that needs hyphenation, it will stop and ask you for help in positioning the hyphen. You can then instruct WordPerfect where to hyphenate or not to hyphenate the word at all. For example, WordPerfect may stop at the word "approximately" and display the prompt shown in Figure 5-35. Depending on the size of type used by your printer, WordPerfect may stop at other words.

prompt

Figure 5-35
The Position
hyphen prompt

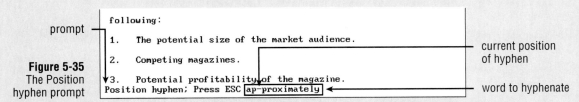

current position
of hyphen

word to hyphenate

⑤   Press [→] or [←] to change the location of the hyphen in the prompt and then press **[Esc]**.

For example, if WordPerfect stopped at "approximately," you would press [→] to move the hyphen so the word in the prompt is "approx-imately" and then press [Esc]. WordPerfect would accept this suggested position for the hyphen only if "approx-" could fit on the current line. If WordPerfect can't hyphenate a word in the suggested position, the hyphen automatically jumps back to the original position, and the "Position hyphen" prompt is displayed again.

⑥   If WordPerfect displays a "Position hyphen" prompt and you want to accept WordPerfect's suggested position of the hyphen, press **[Esc]**. If you don't want to hyphenate the word, press **[F1]** (Cancel).

⑦   If WordPerfect stops at any other words in the document, use your best judgment to position the cursor with **[→]** and **[←]**, then press **[Esc]** when you're satisfied with the position of the hyphen. Press **[F1]** (Cancel) to instruct WordPerfect not to hyphenate the word.

The words that WordPerfect selects for hyphenation depend on the size of the font (typeface). If you make a mistake in hyphenating a word, move the cursor to the word and delete the hyphen.

This completes the feasibility report, as shown in Figure 5-36 on the following pages. Your document may look slightly different because of differences in font size and positions of the hyphens. You can now save and print the document and exit WordPerfect. Exiting WordPerfect with documents on both document screens (Doc 1 and Doc 2) requires some additional steps.

To save and print the document and exit WordPerfect:

❶   Save the document as S5FEASIB.REP and print it.

❷   Exit WordPerfect by pressing **[F7]** (Exit). The prompt "Save document?" appears on the screen.

❸   Select "No." WordPerfect displays the prompt "Exit doc 1?"

❹   Select "Yes." The cursor is now in Doc 2.

❺   Press **[F7]** (Exit) again, select "Yes" or "No" (depending on whether you want to save the document in Doc 2. WordPerfect displays the "Exit WordPerfect" prompt.

❻   Select "Yes" to exit WordPerfect.

C/B Publishing

Report on the Feasibility of Publishing a New Magazine

<u>The Computer Artist</u>

Introduction

The purpose of this report is to examine the feasibility of starting a new magazine tentatively entitled <u>The Computer Artist</u>, which would be aimed at graphic artists who use computers as their main tool for design and production. This report will describe the following:

1.   The potential size of the market audience.

2.   Competing magazines.

3.   Potential profitability of the magazine.

4.   Projected cost of starting and running the magazine.

The conclusions reported here are the result of a study carried out by a task force created six months ago by Stephen Connolly and John Bayle. The task force sent over 500 questionnaires to graphic artists, to manufacturers of computer graphics hardware, and to publishers of graphics software. In addition, the task force compiled data from financial forecasts and analyzed the competition. This information and the returned questionnaires will help C/B Publishing to make an informed decision.

The Target Audience

The target audience of <u>The Computer Artist</u> is all graphic artists in the U.S. and Canada who use IBM-compatible and Macintosh personal computers. We (the task force) decided, therefore, to estimate the total number of graphic artists employed within the

---

target area. Based on data published by the American Society of Graphic Designers,[1] we estimated that over 95,000 graphic designers work within the United States and Canada.

Our analysis of the questionnaires to graphic artists suggested that 69% of them use personal computers and that an additional 13% plan to purchase and use a personal computer within the next 18 months. The potential audience for <u>The Computer Artist</u> is therefore 82% (69% + 13%) of 95,000, or a total of 78,000 artists. We expect that this number will increase in the coming years because nearly 100% of the new graphic artists coming into the field will use computers on the job, while those retiring tend to be the artists who don't use computers. In the next five years, the target audience could number over 100,000.

The Competition

About eight trade magazines regularly cover the subjects of graphics software, desktop publishing, and graphic design, but no magazine published today focuses specifically on graphic design using personal computers. From experience with other professional magazines that C/B Publishing has published under similar circumstances, we expect that 12% of the potential audience will initially subscribe to the new magazine. We believe, however, that as the number of computer-based graphic designers increases, other publishers will certainly recognize this growing market and launch new magazines of their own. For this reason, the success of <u>The Computer Artist</u> will largely depend on our securing a commitment

---

[1]Report of the American Society of Graphic Designers, Arbol Press, March 1991, p. 84.

Figure 5-36
Pages one and two
of the final version
of the report

from the C/B Publishing board of directors to aggressive marketing
and adherence to high publication standards. We must secure this
commitment if we hope to increase or even maintain our subscription
level two or three years into circulation. Being the first
magazine to tap this market will help us, but we must be ever
vigilant of the competition.

Projected Income

Our income from The Computer Artist has two sources, subscriptions and advertising.

From the estimated size of the potential audience (78,000
graphic designers in the U.S. and Canada) and the expected
percentage of subscribers (12%), we project that we will have
9400 subscribers within the first year of publication. Assuming
a subscription rate of $55 per year[2] and 9400 subscribers, the
potential income from subscriptions will be $517,000.

Results of the questionnaires sent to manufacturers of
computer graphics hardware and to publishers of graphics software
were very encouraging. We have verbal commitments for full-page,
half-page, and quarter-page advertisements from several large
hardware and software companies who market graphics programs, laser
printers, plotters, soft fonts, printer cartridges, and optical
character recognition software. The marketing members of the task
force are confident that with effort and focus, they can sell all of
our advertisement space in The Computer Artist.

---

[2]Our questionnaire indicated that specialty magazines of this
type have subscription rates typically in the range of $35 to $95
per year.

We have budgeted 16 of the 64-page issues for ad space. If we
fill all 16 pages in 12 issues per year, and if we assume an
average gross income per page of $4000, the total revenues from
page advertisements will be approximately $768,000 per year.

The total projected income from publication of the magazine
will, therefore, be approximately $1,285,000 per year.

Expenses

The cost of starting the magazine (including hiring six new
staff members, renovating office space, meeting additional office
expenses and other overhead costs, marketing expenses for the
first two issues, and producing the first two issues) will be approximately $721,000.[3] Continued marketing expenses will be ap-
proximately $21,000 per month. Editorial and production expenses
(based on our experience with our other magazines of similar size
and format) will be approximately $44,000 per month. The total
expense the first year will, therefore, be about $1,371,000, and
the repeating expense after the initial investment will be about
$780,000 per year.

Summary and Recommendation

The Computer Artist is a magazine that fits within the mission
of C/B Publishing. We have the knowledge and experience necessary
to publish this magazine.

The financial analysis given above suggests that the first
year's expenses will exceed income by about $86,000. But in
subsequent years, the income will exceed expenditures by about

---

[3]For a detailed breakdown of these expenses, contact David
Palermo in the Financial Office.
$505,000.

Figure 5-36
Pages three and
four of the final
version of the report

```
$505,000
        Based on the above analysis, we recommend publication of the
new magazine The Computer Artist.
```

Figure 5-36
Page five of the
final version of the
report

Exercises

1. Define or describe each of the following terms:
    a. paragraph number in an outline
    b. outline level
    c. outline family

2. How would you begin an outline?

3. How would you create a footnote?

4. How would you turn on hyphenation?

5. List the five steps in creating a macro.

6. Describe how to execute each of the following types of macros:
    a. Alt macro
    b. Named macro
    c. Enter macro

7. What is an advantage and a disadvantage of each of the three types of macros?

8. What would you do to be able to view two different documents on the screen simultaneously?

9. Suppose you needed to copy several nonconsecutive sentences and paragraphs from one document to another. How would you perform that task?

10. If WordPerfect needs help in positioning the hyphen when hyphenation is on, the "Position hyphen" prompt appears on the screen with a suggested position for the hyphen. What would you do to change the position of the hyphen and instruct WordPerfect to continue checking through the document?

Tutorial Assignments

Retrieve the file T5FILE1.DFT from your WordPerfect data diskette and do the following:

1. With T5FILE1.DFT in Doc 1, write an outline of the report in Doc 2, switching between your outline and the report as needed and using WordPerfect's outline feature. Use the headings and subheadings of the report to help in preparing the outline.

2. Save the outline as S5PUBLSH.OTL.

3. Print the outline.

4. In the report in Doc 1, turn on automatic hyphenation. Move the cursor to the end of the document to reformat the document, and respond to any hyphenation prompts that WordPerfect might display.

5. Create a macro named TITLE.WPM that boldfaces a heading and switches it to all upper-case letters (for example, "Introduction" to "**INTRODUCTION**"). *Hint:* To boldface or capitalize existing text, you have to use a block operation.

6. Use the macro you just created to boldface and capitalize the other three major headings in the report.

7. Save the report as S5PUBLSH.DFT.

8. Print the report.

9. Move the cursor to the right of the comma after the word Publish! in the first paragraph of the report. Insert the following footnote:

    Publish! is published monthly by PCW Communications, Inc., 501 Second St., San Francisco, CA 94107.

10. Move the cursor to the right of the article title "The Big Scan" (after the quotation mark) and insert the following footnote:

    Erik Holsinger and Bob Weibel, "The Big Scan," Publish!, March 1990, pp. 56–64.

11. Move the cursor to the right of the article title "Keep It In Color" (after the quotation mark) and insert the following footnote:

    Peter Vanags and Keith Baumann, "Keep It In Color," Publish!, March 1990, pp. 69–78.

12. Save the document as S5FILE1.REP.

13. Print the final version of the document.

Case Problems

1. Hartwell Pharmaceuticals' Corporate Fitness Program

Kawika Hemuli is an assistant business manager for Hartwell Pharmaceuticals Corporation, a 6,500-employee research and development company in Dubuque, Iowa. He wants to write a justification report, in memorandum format, to propose that the company create a corporate fitness program. His short report is shown in Figure 5-37.

Do the following:

1. Write a short outline of the contents of the report.
2. Save the outline as S5FITNES.OTL.
3. Print the outline.
4. Type the report until you get to the first occurrence of the phrase "corporate fitness program" in the SUBJECT of the memo.

Hartwell Pharmaceuticals Corporation

March 19, 1993
MEMO TO:Pablo Iquique
FROM:Kawika Hemuli
SUBJECT:Proposal to create a corporate fitness program

Purpose. To save money by improving employee morale and retention and lowering employee absenteeism.

Description of the Program. A corporate fitness program would allow employees (for a nominal fee of, for example, $25 per year) to enjoy the benefits of a fitness center--including exercycles, weight-lifting equipment, etc.--and fitness counseling--including exercise prescriptions and weight-loss programs. We would hire a fitness counselor (who has a degree in commercial fitness[1]) to set up and manage the program. We would renovate part of our current activity center to include the additional exercise equipment, and we would create five miles of paths for jogging, walking, or biking in the woods on the north and east ends of the company land.

Cost and Savings. The initial cost of setting up an employee fitness program would be approximately $280,000[2]--which includes consulting services, renovation of the activity center, creation of the jogging paths, printing of notices and program materials, and hiring a fitness counselor. The annual cost to the company would be approximately $35,000 in the beginning (a gross cost of $110,000 less about $75,000 in annual membership fees from employees). The company is currently losing an estimated $185,000 per year because of absenteeism and employee turnover. Other companies have experienced up to a 25% drop in absenteeism and turnover upon establishing a similar fitness program. Assuming that our program does the same, we would save $46,250. The net savings to the company would therefore be about $11,000 per year. The savings to the company would rise as more employees joined the program.

Proposal. I propose that Hartwell do the following:

1. Retain a consulting firm to make recommendations regarding a fitness program and to design the fitness center and jogging trails.
2. Hire a fitness counselor soon after the consulting firm provides its initial report. The fitness counselor could then help in the planning of facilities and programs.

---

[1]Bachelor's degrees in commercial fitness are given by many large universities. The training usually includes exercise physiology, nutrition, and business management.

[2]This and all figures in this proposal are rough approximations only. The consulting firms who will help us plan the fitness program will be able to provide us with more realistic numbers.

Figure 5-37

```
     3.     Charge the fitness counselor with the task of signing up as
            many employees as possible, with the goal of eventually making
            the program self-sustaining.
     4.     Begin the renovation and construction of facilities.
     5.     Print information about the fitness program, and send it to
            all employees.
     6.     Recruit employees to participate in the fitness program.

     Conclusion.  A corporate fitness program would not only improve
     physical health and morale of our employees but, in the long run,
     would save the company money.  In addition, such a program would
     help in recruiting top personnel to our company.
```

Figure 5-37
(continued)

5. Create an Enter macro that inserts the phrase "corporate fitness program" into the document. Use the macro each time you need to type that phrase in the report.

6. Create a macro, named Alt-H, that formats the first heading ("Purpose") as shown in Figure 5-37. Use the macro to help you create subsequent headings in the report.

7. Finish typing the report, including footnotes, as shown in Figure 5-37.

8. Save the report as S5FITNES.REP.

9. Print the report.

2. Computer Consultants Corporation: Improving Office Efficiency

Robert Smith, who graduated with a bachelor's degree in business finance five years ago, works as a junior consultant for Computer Consultants Corp. (CCC), headquartered in New York City. He has just finished a study of the office automation needs of Central Park Medical Offices, a consortium of 12 physicians.

1. Retrieve into Doc 2 the outline of Robert's report, P5CCCOTL.DFT, from your WordPerfect data diskette.

2. Create a macro named Alt-U (for "up") that moves an outline family up one family (for example, from "4" to "3" or from "b" to "a").

3. Use the Alt-U macro to move the outline family that begins "2. CCC classes" up one family so that it is "1" instead of "2."

4. Use the Alt-U macro to move the item "D. Computerized accounting system" up one family so that it is "C" instead of "D."

5. Save the outline to the disk using the filename S5CCC.OTL.

6. Print the outline.

7. Retrieve Robert's report, P5CCCREP.DFT, into Doc 1.

8. Turn on hyphenation.

9. Add the following footnote at the end of recommendation number 1: To obtain a catalog of WordPerfect training tapes, write or phone LearnKey, Inc., 93 S. Mountain Way Dr., Orem, UT 84058, (800) 937-3279, which produces a wide selection of effective but inexpensive tapes.

10. Add the following footnote after the phrase "transcription costs" in recommendation number 2: "Prescription for Transcription," <u>WordPerfect Magazine</u>, July 1990, pp. 15–17.

11. Save the report to the file S5CCC.REP.

12. Print the report.

3. Report on Computers in Business

Write a double-spaced, three- to four-page report (700–1,000 words) on some facet of computers in business. Make the topic as narrow as possible to adequately cover the subject in three to four pages. Possible titles include:

- "Challenges in Learning to Use a Computer in Business"
- "How Computers Have Changed Small Businesses"
- "Using Computers in a Home Business"
- "The Advantages of a Local-Area Network in a Business Office"
- "Using a Word Processor to Make Money in Your Spare Time"
- "The Future of Computers in the Office"
- "How Computers Waste Time and Money"
- "How Computers Save Time and Money"

Possible sources of information include your own experience, interviews with business managers and owners, magazine articles, newspaper articles, and books.

If you have difficulty deciding on a topic or gathering information for your paper, consult a librarian at your university or municipal library or see your instructor.

Do the following:

1. Write an outline before you write the report, then revise the outline after you have completed your report. Submit both versions of the outline with this case problem.

2. Double-space the report.

3. Create a title page that contains the title of your article, your name, the title of your course, the date, and any other information your instructor wants you to include.

4. Turn on hyphenation for your report.

5. Include a header and page numbering.

6. Include at least two footnotes giving the sources of information for your report.

7. Create at least two macros to help you write the report. Make sure copies of the macro files are on the diskette that you submit to your instructor.

Tutorial 6

Merging Documents

Writing a Sales Form Letter

Case: Sanders Imports, Inc.

Immediately after graduating from high school, Whitney Sanders began working as a clerk in an import store owned by International Products, Ltd. (IPL), a large corporation with franchises throughout the United States. During the next six years, Whitney worked her way up to international buyer within IPL. Her job entailed traveling to foreign countries, especially Central and South America, to purchase specialty items such as rugs, wood carvings, picture frames, ceramics, and cast-iron furniture.

Although she enjoyed her job and was successful at it, Whitney wanted to go back to school and earn a degree in business administration. She felt such a degree would improve her professional opportunities. So after seven years with IPL, Whitney resigned and went back to school full time. Four years later she received a B.S. with a major in business administration and a minor in international relations from Howard University in Washington, D.C.

With degree in hand Whitney started her own import business called Sanders Imports, Inc. (SII), headquartered in Gaithersburg, Maryland, just outside Washington, D.C. Within 18 months her business was healthy and growing. Among her successes are several large contracts with three major discount department stores and over 20 specialty shops throughout the United States. Whitney markets to these clients by publishing a quarterly catalog that contains color photographs and descriptions of the items she imports.

Last week Whitney added two major items, Mexican iced-tea glass tumblers and Ecuadorian hand-carved chess sets, to her catalog. She is not scheduled to publish another catalog for two months, but she wants to advise her customers immediately about these highly marketable products. She decides to write a letter to her clients (Figure 6-1).

OBJECTIVES

In this tutorial you will learn to:

- Create primary and secondary merge files

- Merge files

- Sort a secondary file

- Create address labels

Sanders Imports, Inc.
429 Firstfield Road, Gaithersburg, MD 20878
Phone (301) 590-1000 Fax (301) 590-1825
Orders 1-800-IMPORTS

                                                    Date

First Name   Last Name
         Company
         Street Address
   City,   State   Zip

Dear NickName:

     I am writing to let you know about two exciting new SII
products that I'm certain will appeal to your customers.

     ICED TEA GLASS TUMBLERS, 16oz., finely painted patterns,
imported from Mexico, suggested retail price $4.95 per set of four
tumblers, your price $2.18 per set. These drinking glasses have
heavy glass bottoms and clear glass sides and come in six different
patterns. Sold in attractive cardboard carrying box. Because they
are attractive yet inexpensive, these tumblers will sell well.

     HAND-CARVED CHESS SETS, Staunton pattern, weighted and felted
bases, detailed knights, natural grain, U.S. Chess Federation
approved, imported from Quito, Ecuador, suggested retail price
$38.95, your price $16.68 per set. These sets are almost identical
in appearance to the sets imported from India that sell for twice
this amount.

     I have enclosed photographs of these products.

     NickName   , please call me for more information or to
receive samples of either of these items. As always, it is a
pleasure doing business with   Company   .

                                   Sincerely yours,

                                   Whitney Sanders

                                   Whitney Sanders
                                   President, SII

Enclosures

Figure 6-1
Whitney's form
letter

The Merge Feature

Whitney wants to write a **form letter**, which is a letter that contains information pertinent to a large number of people (in this case, Whitney's clients) but that also contains information specific to the addressee. The specific information in Whitney's form letter is an inside address and salutation for each client and in the body of the letter the client's first name and the company's name.

To achieve these objectives efficiently, Whitney will use WordPerfect's Merge features. In general a **merge** is an operation that combines information from two documents to create several slightly different final documents.

Merge Documents

The merge operation employs two documents: a primary file and a secondary file. A **primary file** is a document — such as a letter or a contract — that, in addition to text, contains merge commands to mark where data — such as a name or an address — will be inserted. In Whitney's case, the primary file will be like Figure 6-1, except that instead of blanks the document will contain merge commands to mark the location for individualized names, addresses, and other data.

A **secondary file** is a document that contains specific information — such as names, street addresses, cities, states, and zip codes — that will be merged into the primary file. In Whitney's case, the secondary file will be an address list, similar to Figure 6-2, except that the file will have a slightly different format and will also contain merge commands to help WordPerfect merge the information into a primary file.

Malone, Rebecca C. (Becky)
415-825-1585
Compton Novelty Shop
8415 El Arbol Street
Compton, CA 90220

McArdy, Gregory P. (Paul)
719-448-0025
Paul's Imports
854 North Pike's Peak Road
Colorado Springs, CO 80902

Sorenson, Mary Beth (Mary)
218-968-1593
North Star Emporium
51 West Center Street
Bemidji, MN 56601

Pilar, F. Emilio (Emilio)
602-433-8878
Grand Canyon Imports
4851 Caibab Highway Suite 210
Flagstaff, AZ 86001

Gutanov, Mikhail Ivonov (Mike)
404-921-3722
Peachtree Emporium
88 Peachtree Plaza
Atlanta, GA 30304

Figure 6-2
Client data for
Whitney's
secondary file

The final document(s) produced by merging information from the secondary file into the primary file is called the **merged document** (Figure 6-3).

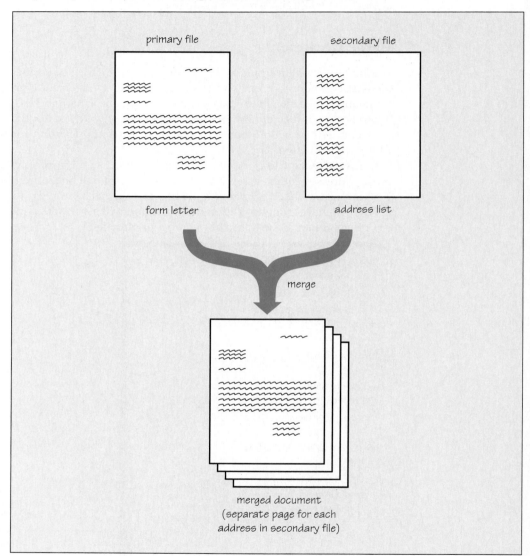

Figure 6-3
Merging a primary
file and secondary
file to create the
merged document

Merge Operations

During a merge operation, the merge commands in the primary file instruct WordPerfect to fetch specific information from the secondary file. For example, one merge command in the primary file might fetch a name, while another merge command might fetch a street address. For each name and street address in the secondary file, WordPerfect usually creates a separate page in the merged document. Thus, if Whitney's secondary file has, for example, five names and addresses of clients, the merge will produce five different letters, each with a different name and address and each on a separate page in the merged document (Figure 6-4).

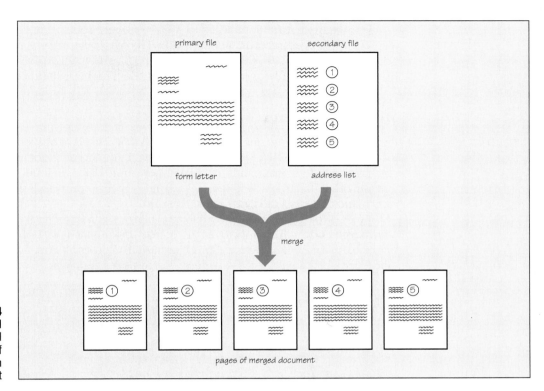

Figure 6-4
Pages of merged
document equal
number of
addresses in
address list

Records and Fields

The set of data on one individual in the secondary file is called a **record**. In Whitney's secondary file each record contains information about one client (Figure 6-5). Each item within a record is called a **field**. One field might be the client's name; another field, the client's street address; another field, the client's city; and so forth. For a merge operation to work properly, every record must have the same set of fields.

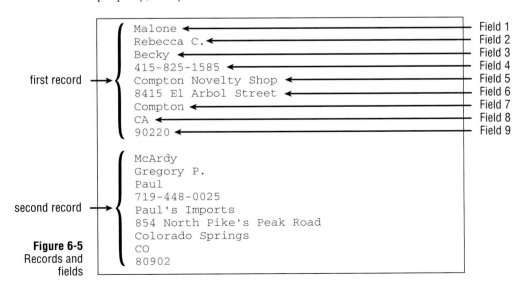

Figure 6-5
Records and
fields

Secondary files are not limited to records about clients. You could create a secondary file with employee records, another with records of suppliers, another with records of equipment, and so forth. Once you understand how to manage and manipulate the records in secondary merge files, you'll be able to use them for many different types of applications.

Merge Commands

Primary files usually contain merge commands that instruct WordPerfect which fields of each record to fetch and where to place those fields in the merged document. Primary files may also contain merge commands that insert the current date, get input from the keyboard, and perform other functions. Secondary files contain merge commands that mark the end of each record and that label the fields in each record.

Figure 6-6 is a table of the most common merge commands. Each merge command consists of a **merge code**, which appears in the primary document as an uppercase word enclosed in braces (curly brackets), such as {FIELD} or {DATE}. You don't actually type the characters in a merge code but rather use WordPerfect's Merge Codes command to insert the codes.

Merge Command	Action
{DATE}	Insert current date
{FIELD}FieldName~	Fetch data from field named *FieldName* in secondary file
{FIELD NAMES}*FieldName1~* *FieldName2~* *FieldName3~~*	List names of fields in secondary file
{END FIELD}	Mark end of the field
{END RECORD}	Mark end of the record

Figure 6-6
Common merge
commands

Some merge commands also require a parameter. For example, the {FIELD} command requires a parameter that names a particular field within a record. The end of a parameter is marked with a tilde (~). Hence, a primary document that contained the merge command {FIELD}FirstName~ would instruct WordPerfect to fetch the field named "FirstName" from a record in the secondary file (Figure 6-7). In the {FIELDNAME} command a tilde marks the end of each field name and another tilde marks the end of the entire list of field names. The {DATE} command, which inserts the current date into the document, doesn't require a parameter.

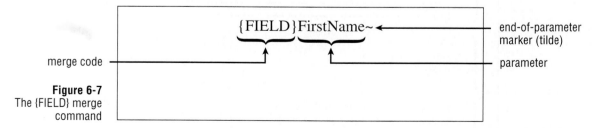

merge code

Figure 6-7
The {FIELD} merge
command

Whitney's primary file, including the merge codes, is shown in Figure 6-8. Your task in the following section will be to create this primary file.

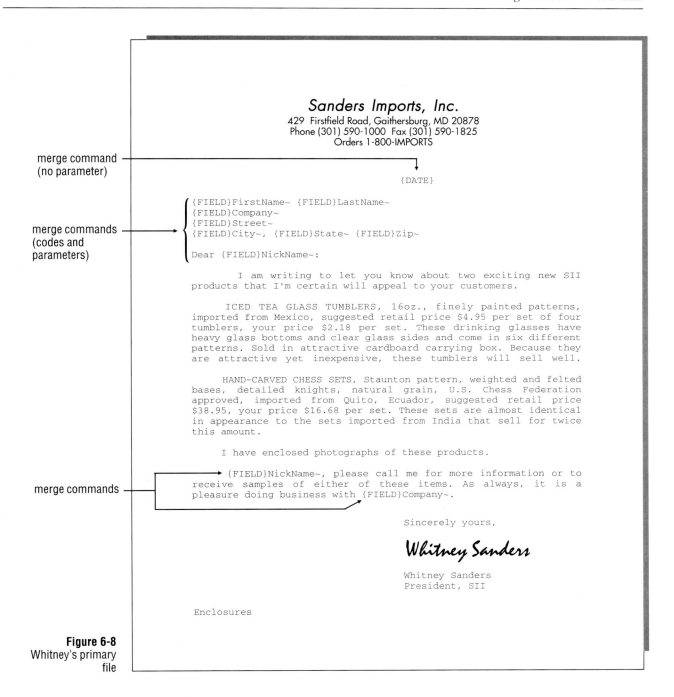

merge command (no parameter)

merge commands (codes and parameters)

merge commands

Figure 6-8
Whitney's primary file

Creating a Primary File

A primary file contains text and merge commands. Creating a primary file is similar to creating any other type of WordPerfect document, except that you use [Shift][F9] (Merge Codes) to insert the merge commands into the primary file. You'll begin by inserting the {DATE} command.

To insert {DATE} into the primary file:

❶ Make sure the document screen is clear and press **[Enter]** until the cursor is at Ln 2.5" or lower.

This leaves room for the company letterhead at the top of the page. If your paper doesn't have a letterhead, the blank space will keep the text of the letter from being too high up on the page.

❷ Press **[Tab]** until the cursor is at Pos 4.5", where Whitney wants to put the date in the letter.

Now you're ready to instruct WordPerfect to insert the {DATE} code.

❸ Select More from the Tools/Merge Codes menu. See Figure 6-9.

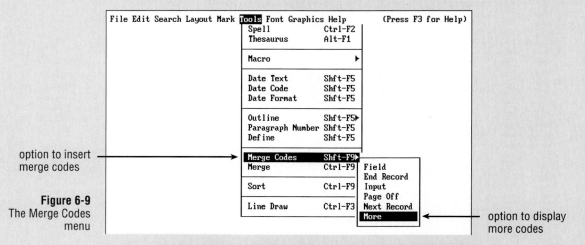

option to insert merge codes →

Figure 6-9
The Merge Codes menu

← option to display more codes

Alternatively press **[Shift][F9]** (Merge Codes) to display the one-line menu shown in Figure 6-10.

Figure 6-10
Menu to select merge codes

option to display more codes

1 Field; 2 End Record; 3 Input; 4 Page Off; 5 Next Record; 6 More; 0

Then select **6** (**M**ore). Because the merge code {DATE} doesn't appear on the pull-down menu or on the one-line menu, you must select More to get a listing of more merge codes. A window of merge codes appears in the upper right corner of the screen. See Figure 6-11. The window displays only a few of the many merge codes at any one time. You can use the arrow keys to scroll the contents of the window to display other codes.

Merge Codes window →

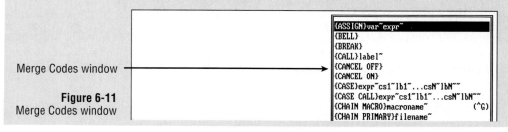

Figure 6-11
Merge Codes window

④ Use the cursor-movement keys or the mouse to move the cursor so that {DATE} is highlighted, then press **[Enter]**. You can also press **D** to tell WordPerfect to immediately move the cursor to the merge codes that begin with D, then you can use an arrow key to move the cursor to {DATE}. WordPerfect inserts the {DATE} code into the document, closes the Merge Codes window, and returns the cursor to the document screen.

Later, when Whitney executes the merge, WordPerfect will insert the current date at the location of the {DATE} code on each copy of the letter in the resulting merged document.

In the following steps, you'll insert the {FIELD} command into the primary file.

To insert the {FIELD} command into the primary file:

① Press **[Enter]** three times to triple space between the date and the inside address.

② Select Field from the Tools/Merge Codes menu or press **[Shift][F9]** (Merge Codes) and select **1** (**F**ield).

WordPerfect displays the prompt "Enter Field:" and waits for you to type the name of the field. The field name in the primary file must correspond to a field name in the secondary file. Since Whitney hasn't created the secondary file yet, she can use any field name she wants at this point. She'll have to remember these field names when she creates her secondary file.

③ Type **FirstName** and press **[Enter]**. WordPerfect inserts the {FIELD} command, the name of the field, and a tilde (~), which marks the end of the field name. See Figure 6-12.

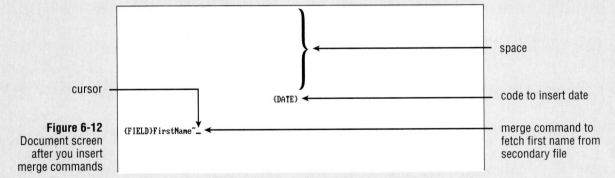

Figure 6-12
Document screen
after you insert
merge commands

(labels in figure:)
cursor
space
{DATE} — code to insert date
{FIELD}FirstName~ — merge command to fetch first name from secondary file

When Whitney executes the merge, WordPerfect will fetch the first name — which will include the first name and a middle name or a middle initial — from the secondary file and insert it into the document at that location.

④ Press **[Space]** to insert a space after the first name(s), then select Field from the Tools/Merge Codes menu or press **[Shift][F9]** (Merge Codes) and select **1** (**F**ield).

⑤ Type **LastName** and press **[Enter]**. See Figure 6-13.

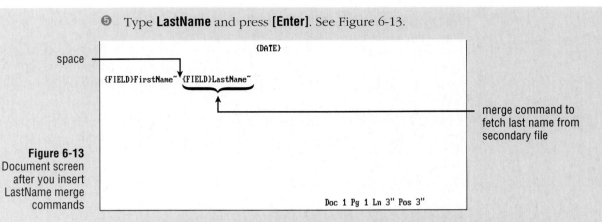

Figure 6-13
Document screen
after you insert
LastName merge
commands

⑥ Press **[Enter]** to move the cursor to the next line and insert the {FIELD} code with the field name "Company," as shown in Figure 6-8.

⑦ Continue typing the merge codes to insert the inside address and the salutation, until your screen looks like Figure 6-14. Remember, never *type* a merge code, such as "{FIELD}"; always use the Merge Codes command to insert the codes.

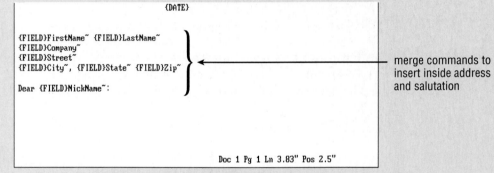

Figure 6-14
Document screen
after you insert
merge commands
for address and
salutation

Carefully check over your document to make sure all the field names are spelled correctly.

⑧ Press **[Enter]** twice to double-space after the salutation.

The {FIELD}NickName~ command in the salutation tells WordPerfect to fetch a name that might be the same as the first name but is usually different. For example, the secondary file might list a client's first name as "Rebecca C." but her nickname as "Becky."

You'll now retrieve the rest of the form letter (the primary file) from the WordPerfect data diskette and insert two other merge commands.

To retrieve the file and insert merge commands:
① Insert the data diskette into drive A.

Because you will frequently use the diskette in drive A to save and retrieve files, you will now change the default directory to A:.

❷ Press **[F5]** (List), and then press **[=]** (equal sign). At the prompt "New directory = ," type **a:** and press **[Enter]**. Then press **[F1]** (Cancel) to cancel the directory listing.

❸ Retrieve the file C6FILE1.DFT from the data diskette in drive A.

WordPerfect may ask, "Retrieve into current file? No (Yes)." This is to help prevent you from accidentally combining an existing file with the file you presently have loaded. In this case, you *want* to combine them, so answer Yes.

❹ Move the cursor to the comma that begins the last paragraph of the letter.

❺ Insert the command {FIELD}NickName~.

❻ Move the cursor to the period at the end of the last paragraph.

❼ Insert the command {FIELD}Company~. See Figure 6-15. The merge commands in the last paragraph of the document will tell WordPerfect to insert the nickname and the company name of the client at these locations in the letter. By placing these merge commands in the body of the form letter, Whitney is able to personalize the letter.

Figure 6-15
Document screen after you insert merge commands in last paragraph

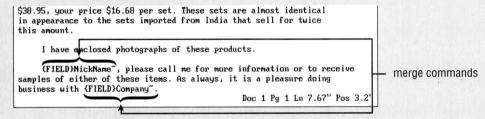

merge commands

❽ Save the file as S6SLSLET.PF.

The abbreviation "SLSLET" stands for "sales letter," and the filename extension "PF" stands for "primary file," to remind you that this is the primary file used in a WordPerfect merge operation.

Creating a Secondary File

As Whitney acquires new and potential clients, she types information about them into a WordPerfect secondary file. She can then merge the secondary file with a primary merge file to generate her sales letters.

Figure 6-16 on the next two pages shows the first five records of Whitney's secondary file. As you can see, the file contains merge codes that specify the names of the fields and that mark the ends of fields and records.

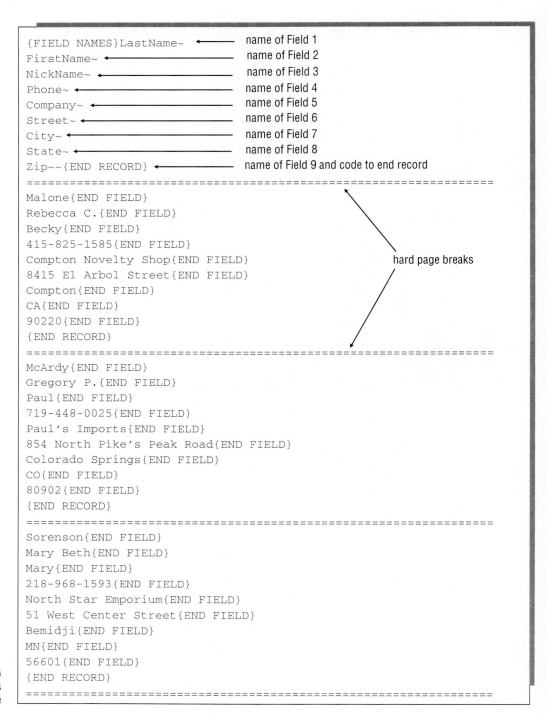

```
{FIELD NAMES}LastName~         name of Field 1
FirstName~                     name of Field 2
NickName~                      name of Field 3
Phone~                         name of Field 4
Company~                       name of Field 5
Street~                        name of Field 6
City~                          name of Field 7
State~                         name of Field 8
Zip~~{END RECORD}              name of Field 9 and code to end record
=================================================================
Malone{END FIELD}
Rebecca C.{END FIELD}
Becky{END FIELD}
415-825-1585{END FIELD}
Compton Novelty Shop{END FIELD}         hard page breaks
8415 El Arbol Street{END FIELD}
Compton{END FIELD}
CA{END FIELD}
90220{END FIELD}
{END RECORD}
=================================================================
McArdy{END FIELD}
Gregory P.{END FIELD}
Paul{END FIELD}
719-448-0025{END FIELD}
Paul's Imports{END FIELD}
854 North Pike's Peak Road{END FIELD}
Colorado Springs{END FIELD}
CO{END FIELD}
80902{END FIELD}
{END RECORD}
=================================================================
Sorenson{END FIELD}
Mary Beth{END FIELD}
Mary{END FIELD}
218-968-1593{END FIELD}
North Star Emporium{END FIELD}
51 West Center Street{END FIELD}
Bemidji{END FIELD}
MN{END FIELD}
56601{END FIELD}
{END RECORD}
=================================================================
```

Figure 6-16
Whitney's
secondary file

```
Pilar{END FIELD}
F. Emilio{END FIELD}
Emilio{END FIELD}
602-433-8878{END FIELD}
Grand Canyon Imports{END FIELD}
4851 Caibab Highway Suite 210{END FIELD}
Flagstaff{END FIELD}
AZ{END FIELD}
86001{END FIELD}
{END RECORD}
===================================================================
Gutanov{END FIELD}
Mikhail Ivonov{END FIELD}
Mike{END FIELD}
404-921-3722{END FIELD}
Peachtree Emporium{END FIELD}
88 Peachtree Plaza{END FIELD}
Atlanta{END FIELD}
GA{END FIELD}
30304{END FIELD}
{END RECORD}
===================================================================
```

Figure 6-16
(continued)

To create a secondary file, you must follow certain procedures:

1. **Name the fields.** WordPerfect internally numbers each field within a record, but to make merge commands easier, you can tell WordPerfect the name of each field. In Figure 6-16, for example, the name of Field 1, the first field in each record, is "LastName." Wherever the primary file contains the merge command {FIELD}LastName~, WordPerfect will insert the information from the first field of the secondary file.

2. **Mark the end of the field names.** After you name all the fields, WordPerfect automatically inserts the {END RECORD} code to indicate that there are no more field names and inserts a hard page break.

3. **Insert data into the secondary file.** You type the text of a field and then insert the code {END FIELD} to mark the end of the field. You must follow exactly the format you used when you named the fields. For example, the first field of every record must be the last name; the second field of every record must be the first name; and so forth. If you change the order of entering information into the secondary file, Word-Perfect will insert the wrong information into the merge document during the merge operation. If the information for a particular field isn't available — for example, if you don't have a telephone number — you must still insert the Phone field by marking the end of the field with the {END FIELD} code. At the end of each record, you must insert the {END RECORD} code.

Let's create the secondary file of information about Whitney's clients. First we'll insert the merge command {FIELD NAMES}, which names the fields.

To insert the {FIELD NAMES} command:

❶ Clear the document screen.

❷ Select More from the Tools/Merge Codes menu or press **[Shift][F9]** (Merge Codes) and select **6** (**M**ore).

❸ Move the cursor to {FIELD NAMES} in the Merge Codes window and press **[Enter]**. WordPerfect displays the prompt "Enter Field 1:," as shown in Figure 6-17.

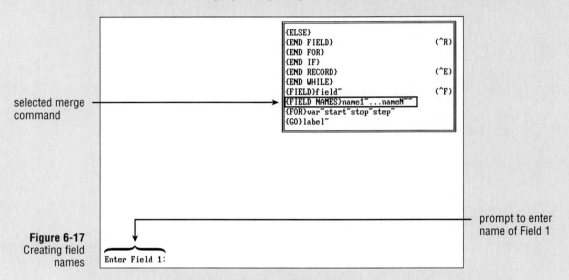

selected merge command

```
{ELSE}
{END FIELD}                          (^R)
{END FOR}
{END IF}
{END RECORD}                         (^E)
{END WHILE}
{FIELD}field~                        (^F)
{FIELD NAMES}name1~...nameN~~
{FOR}var~start~stop~step~
{GO}label~
```

prompt to enter name of Field 1

Figure 6-17
Creating field names

`Enter Field 1:`

❹ Type **LastName** and press **[Enter]** to specify that the first field in each record will contain the last name of the client.

Now WordPerfect prompts for the field name of Field 2, that is, the name of the second field of each record.

❺ Type **FirstName** and press **[Enter]**. WordPerfect displays the prompt for the name of Field 3.

❻ Type **NickName** and press **[Enter]**. This tells WordPerfect that the third field in each record will contain the client's nickname.

❼ Continue to type field names at the prompts, referring to Figure 6-16. The names of Fields 4 through 9 are "Phone," "Company," "Street," "City," "State," and "Zip."

WordPerfect automatically prompts you for the next field name until you tell WordPerfect to end the field names.

❽ After you have typed the last field name (Field 9, "Zip") and the prompt "Enter Field 10:" appears on the screen, press **[Enter]** without typing a name.

This signals WordPerfect that you have completed all the field names. The field names now appear across the top of the screen. See Figure 6-18. The {END RECORD} code and a hard page break appear after the last field name.

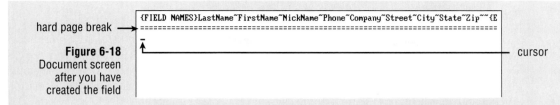

hard page break →

Figure 6-18
Document screen
after you have
created the field

cursor

If you made a mistake typing a field name, use the normal WordPerfect edit keys to fix the error.

You can't see all the field names at once because the line is wider than one screen line. Let's insert a hard return at the end of each field name so each name appears on a separate second line.

To place the field names on separate lines:

❶ Move the cursor to the right of the first tilde (~), just after "LastName," and press **[Enter]**. The subsequent field names move to the next line.

❷ Move the cursor to the right of the tilde after each of the other field names and press **[Enter]**; then move the cursor below the page break. See Figure 6-19.

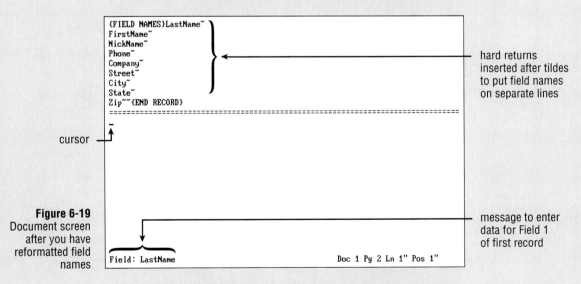

cursor

hard returns
inserted after tildes
to put field names
on separate lines

Figure 6-19
Document screen
after you have
reformatted field
names

message to enter
data for Field 1
of first record

❸ Save the intermediate version of the secondary file as S6ADDR.INT. "ADDR" indicates that the file contains addresses, and the filename extension "INT" stands for "intermediate version" of the file.

The secondary file you have just created contains no records yet. You'll now enter the data for each record.

Entering Data into a Secondary File

After you create the {FIELD NAMES} command at the beginning of a secondary file, WordPerfect automatically inserts a hard page break after the {END RECORD} code, moves the cursor below the page break, and displays the current field on the left side of the status line at the bottom of the screen (Figure 6-19). Whitney is now ready to enter client information into the file, as shown in Figure 6-16. Let's begin by entering data into the first record.

To enter a record into a secondary file:

❶ With the cursor positioned just below the page break, type **Malone** and press **[F9]** (End Field). (If you pressed [Enter] instead of [F9] (End Field), press [Backspace] to delete the invisible [HRt] code.)

WordPerfect allows more than one line of text in a field. For example, you may want to include a department name and the company name on two separate lines in the Company field. In this particular file we will include only one line per field. WordPerfect inserts the merge code {END FIELD} to the right of "Malone" and automatically inserts a hard return to move the cursor to the next line. The message "Field: FirstName" appears on the status line. See Figure 6-20.

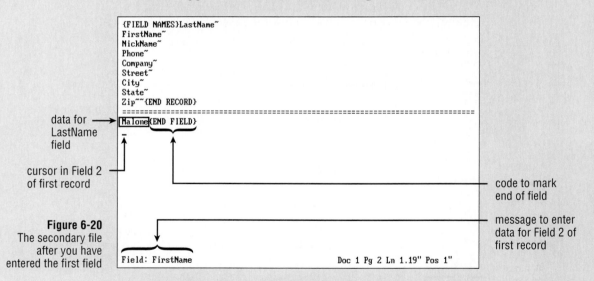

data for → LastName field

cursor in Field 2 of first record

Figure 6-20
The secondary file after you have entered the first field

code to mark end of field

message to enter data for Field 2 of first record

❷ Type **Rebecca C.** and press **[F9]** (End Field) to insert the client's first name. Notice that this field also contains any middle name or middle initial of the client. WordPerfect inserts the {END FIELD} code and a hard return. The message "Field: NickName" appears on the status line.

❸ Type **Becky** and press **[F9]** (End Field) to insert the client's nickname. The NickName field contains only one name, the name that the client goes by. The nickname will often be the same as the client's first name.

WordPerfect displays the message "Field: Phone" on the status line. See Figure 6-21.

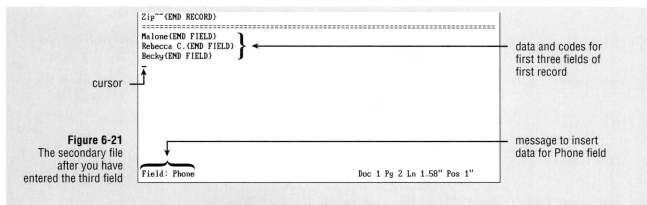

Figure 6-21
The secondary file
after you have
entered the third field

cursor

data and codes for
first three fields of
first record

message to insert
data for Phone field

④ Type **415-825-1585** and press **[F9]** (End Field) to enter the client's phone number. WordPerfect inserts the {END FIELD} code and displays the message "Field: Company" on the status line.

⑤ Type **Compton Novelty Shop** and press **[F9]** (End Field) to enter the client's company name and the {END FIELD} code. WordPerfect displays the message "Field: Street" on the status line.

⑥ Type **8415 El Arbol Street** and press **[F9]** (End Field) to enter the street address and the {END FIELD} code.

⑦ Type **Compton** and press **[F9]** (End Field) to enter the city and the {END FIELD} code.

⑧ Type **CA** and press **[F9]** (End Field) to enter the two-letter code of the state into the record.

⑨ Type **90220** and press **[F9]** (End Field) to insert the zip code into the record. See Figure 6-22.

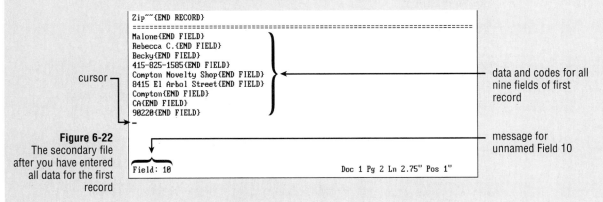

Figure 6-22
The secondary file
after you have entered
all data for the first
record

cursor

data and codes for all
nine fields of first
record

message for
unnamed Field 10

You have now entered all the data for the first record. The status line displays the message "Field: 10" instead of a field name, because the secondary file has only nine named fields. You now must mark the end of this record.

To mark the end of a record:

❶ Select End Record from the Tools/Merge Codes menu or press **[Shift][F9]** (Merge Codes) and select **2** (**E**nd Record). WordPerfect inserts the {END RECORD} command and a hard page break. See Figure 6-23.

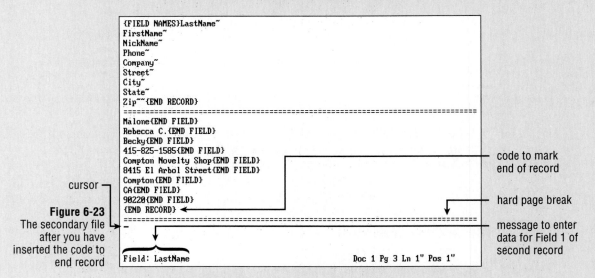

cursor

Figure 6-23
The secondary file after you have inserted the code to end record

code to mark end of record

hard page break

message to enter data for Field 1 of second record

Having created the first record in the secondary file, you can now enter the next four records of Whitney's client list, as shown in Figure 6-16.

❷ Finish entering the other four records into the secondary file. Your screen will look like Figure 6-24.

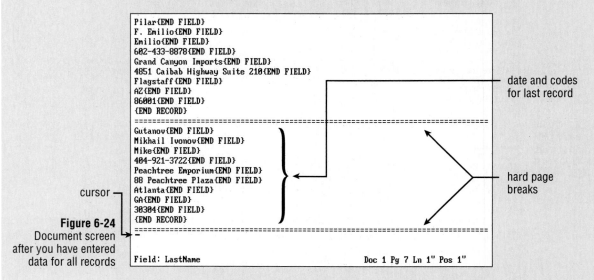

date and codes for last record

cursor

Figure 6-24
Document screen after you have entered data for all records

hard page breaks

It's easy to make mistakes as you enter information for each record. Make sure you enter each item (last name, first name, nickname, phone number, company name, street, city, state, and zip code) into a separate field. Remember to press [F9] (End

Field) after you enter an item into a field and to select End Record at the end of each record.

After you have entered the final record, WordPerfect prompts you for the last name of another record (Figure 6-24). Ignore this prompt.

❸ After you have entered the data and double-checked it for accuracy, save the document as S6ADDR.SF. The filename extension "SF" stands for "secondary file."

Although Whitney's secondary file will eventually contain numerous records (one for each of her many clients), S6ADDR.SF contains only five records, a sufficient number to demonstrate WordPerfect's merge features.

Merging Primary and Secondary Files

Now that she has created her form letter (primary file) and her address list (secondary file), Whitney is ready to merge the two files to create individual letters to send to her clients. Let's merge S6SLSLET.PF (the primary file) with S6ADDR.SF (the secondary file).

To merge a primary file and a secondary file:

❶ Clear the document screen.

Because the results of the merge will appear in the document screen, you must clear the screen before you execute the merge.

❷ Select Merge from the Tools menu or press **[Ctrl][F9]** (Merge/Sort) and select **1** (**M**erge). The prompt "Primary file:" appears on the status line.

❸ Type **s6slslet.pf** and press **[Enter]**. This is Whitney's primary file, which contains her form letter. The prompt "Secondary file:" appears on the status line.

❹ Type **s6addr.sf** and press **[Enter]**. This is Whitney's secondary file, which contains her address list. WordPerfect merges the primary and secondary files to create the merged document.

The end of the merged document now appears on the document screen (Figure 6-25).

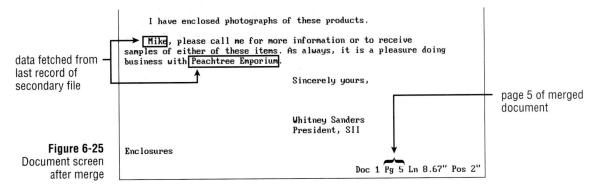

Figure 6-25
Document screen after merge

data fetched from last record of secondary file

page 5 of merged document

```
        I have enclosed photographs of these products.

     →  Mike, please call me for more information or to receive
        samples of either of these items. As always, it is a pleasure doing
        business with Peachtree Emporium.

                               Sincerely yours,


                               Whitney Sanders
                               President, SII

Enclosures


                                         Doc 1 Pg 5 Ln 8.67" Pos 2"
```

During the merge operation, WordPerfect extracted information from one record in the secondary file and inserted it into the primary file according to the merge commands in the primary file to create a letter. After each letter, WordPerfect inserted a hard page break so that each letter will print on a separate page. You can use the cursor-movement keys to move through the resulting merged document. As you can see, it contains five pages, one page for each of the five records in the primary file. The first page of the merged document, the letter to Rebecca Malone, appears in Figure 6-26.

this will not be on
your document

Sanders Imports, Inc.
429 Firstfield Road, Gaithersburg, MD 20878
Phone (301) 590-1000 Fax (301) 590-1825
Orders 1-800-IMPORTS

May 11, 1993

Rebecca C. Malone
Compton Novelty Shop
8415 El Arbol Street
Compton, CA 90220

Dear Becky:

I am writing to let you know about two exciting new SII products that I'm certain will appeal to your customers.

ICED TEA GLASS TUMBLERS, 16oz., finely painted patterns, imported from Mexico, suggested retail price $4.95 per set of four tumblers, your price $2.18 per set. These drinking glasses have heavy glass bottoms and clear glass sides and come in six different patterns. Sold in attractive cardboard carrying box. Because they are attractive yet inexpensive, these tumblers will sell well.

HAND-CARVED CHESS SETS, Staunton pattern, weighted and felted bases, detailed knights, natural grain, U.S. Chess Federation approved, imported from Quito, Ecuador, suggested retail price $38.95, your price $16.68 per set. These sets are almost identical in appearance to the sets imported from India that sell for twice this amount.

I have enclosed photographs of these products.

Becky, please call me for more information or to receive samples of either of these items. As always, it is a pleasure doing business with Compton Novelty Shop.

Sincerely yours,

Whitney Sanders

Whitney Sanders
President, SII

Enclosures

Figure 6-26
First page of
merged document

Sorting a Secondary File

As Whitney looks through the merged document with the letters to her clients, she observes one problem. She is going to use bulk mailing rates to send her letters, but the U.S. Postal Service requires bulk mailings to be divided into groups according to zip code. Currently the letters are in the order in which she added the client information to her secondary file. She must, therefore, sort the secondary file.

In WordPerfect, to **sort** means to arrange a list or a document in some specified order. WordPerfect allows you perform three types of sort: merge, line, and paragraph. A **merge sort** allows you to sort the records in a secondary file, as you'll see shortly. A **line sort** allows you to sort lines within a document (Figure 6-27). A **paragraph sort** allows you to sort the paragraphs within a document. You have to tell WordPerfect which type of sort you want to carry out.

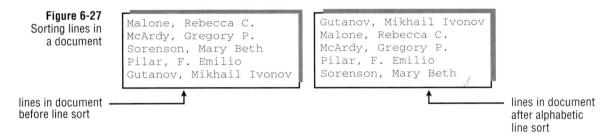

Figure 6-27
Sorting lines in a document

lines in document before line sort

lines in document after alphabetic line sort

You also need to tell WordPerfect whether the sort involves only numbers, called a **numeric sort**, or numbers and letters, called an **alphanumeric sort**. For a merge sort, you need to instruct WordPerfect to sort by last name, by company name, by zip code, or by one of the other fields in the records. You also need to tell WordPerfect which word in the field to sort by. For example, if Whitney wanted to sort her secondary file by FirstName, which includes not only the first name but also any middle name or middle initial, she must tell WordPerfect to sort using the first word in the FirstName field.

Whitney decides that before printing the letters, she will sort the secondary file by zip code and then execute the merge again so that the letters are in order of zip code number. Let's do that now.

To sort the secondary file:

❶ Clear the merged document from the document screen and retrieve S6ADDR.SF, the secondary file with client information.

❷ Select Sort from the Tools menu or press **[Ctrl][F9]** (Merge/Sort) and select **2** (**S**ort). WordPerfect asks for the input file to sort. The input file is the file that you want to sort. The screen file is listed as the default. See Figure 6-28.

```
90220{END FIELD}
{END RECORD}
==================================================================
McArdy{END FIELD}
Gregory P.{END FIELD}
Paul{END FIELD}
Input file to sort: (Screen)
```

default input file

prompt to enter input file

Figure 6-28
Prompt for input file to sort

❸ Press **[Enter]** to select the default input file (the screen). In other words, you want to sort the file currently on the document screen. If you wanted to sort a file on the disk, you would type the filename as the input file. WordPerfect now asks for the output file, that is, the file where the results of the sort will be saved. The input file and the output file may be the same file or different files. The screen is the default location for the output file.

❹ Press **[Enter]** to select the default output file (the screen). WordPerfect displays the Sort menu in the window on the bottom half of the screen. See Figure 6-29. You will use this menu to specify the details of how you want WordPerfect to sort the file on the document on the screen.

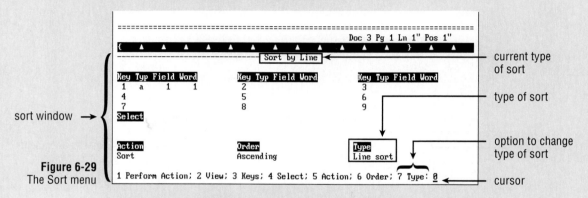

Figure 6-29
The Sort menu

First, let's instruct WordPerfect that you want to carry out a merge sort, not a line sort or a paragraph sort.

❺ Select **7** (**T**ype) and **1** (**M**erge) to change the type of sort to merge. Now the title of the Sort menu is "Sort Secondary Merge File." See Figure 6-30.

Next you'll tell WordPerfect whether the sort is alphanumeric or numeric and specify the field and word by which you want to sort. You will enter this information into the **sort keys**, regions of the sort menu that instruct WordPerfect how to carry out the sort. Let's use the sort keys (Figure 6-30) to tell WordPerfect that we want to sort by Field 9 ("Zip").

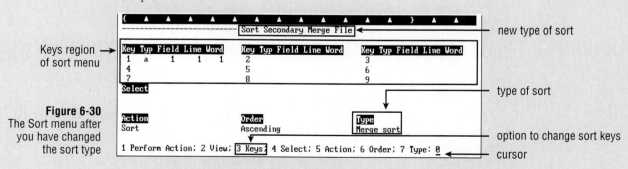

Figure 6-30
The Sort menu after you have changed the sort type

❻ Select **3** (**K**eys) to move the cursor to the "a" in the Keys region of the Sort menu, under the "Typ" heading. See Figure 6-31.

cursor →

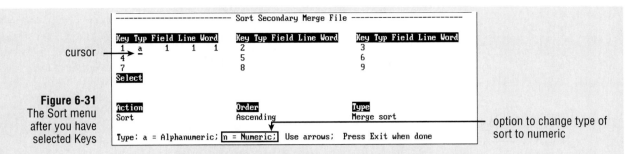

Figure 6-31
The Sort menu
after you have
selected Keys

option to change type of
sort to numeric

Because you want to sort according to a number — the zip code — you'll tell
WordPerfect to carry out a numeric sort rather than an alphanumeric sort.

⑦ Press **n** to change the sort type from alphanumeric to numeric. The cursor automatically moves to the right of "1" under the "Field" heading.

⑧ Type **9** to select Field 9 ("Zip"). See Figure 6-32.

Field 9 ("Zip") →

cursor →

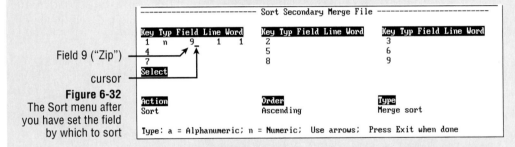

Figure 6-32
The Sort menu after
you have set the field
by which to sort

Since the Zip field is a number, you don't need to specify a word within the field. The
Keys region of the Sort menu allows you to specify up to nine sort keys. You would
use these other keys if, for example, your secondary file had many clients with the
same zip code and you wanted WordPerfect to sort all records having the same zip
code by the client's last name. You'd then move the cursor to the next key and specify
the appropriate information to sort alphabetically on Field 1. In Whitney's secondary
file, however, the order of the records having the same zip code doesn't matter, so she
doesn't set any other sort keys.

⑨ Press **[F7]** (Exit) to leave the Keys region of the Sort menu.

You have now specified all the information that WordPerfect needs to sort the secondary file by zip code. The Sort menu should look like Figure 6-33. Notice that the Order setting is "Ascending," which means that the sort will be from lowest to highest zip code number. If you wanted the sort to be "Descending," that is, to go from highest to lowest zip code number, you would select 6 (Order) and then 2 (Descending).

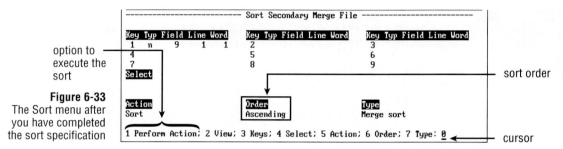

Figure 6-33
The Sort menu after you have completed the sort specification

option to execute the sort

sort order

cursor

```
------------------------- Sort Secondary Merge File -------------------------

Key Typ Field Line Word    Key Typ Field Line Word    Key Typ Field Line Word
 1   n    9    1    1        2                          3
 4                           5                          6
 7                           8                          9
Select

Action                     Order                      Type
Sort                       Ascending                  Merge sort

1 Perform Action; 2 View; 3 Keys; 4 Select; 5 Action; 6 Order; 7 Type: 0
```

You're now ready to perform the sort operation. You'll then save the secondary file, merge the primary and secondary files, and save and print the resulting merged document.

To perform the sort:

❶ Select **1** (**P**erform Action) to execute the sort.

WordPerfect sorts the secondary file, outputs the results to the document screen, exits the Sort menu, and returns the cursor to the document screen. The screen contains the secondary file with its records sorted according to zip code. See Figure 6-34. Use your cursor keys to move through the document to see that the first record is Mikhail Gutanov, with a zip code of 30304 (Georgia), and that the last record is Rebecca Malone, with a zip code of 90220 (California). You should now save the sorted secondary file.

```
{FIELD NAMES}LastName~
FirstName~
NickName~
Phone~
Company~
Street~
City~
State~
Zip~~{END RECORD}
================================================================
Gutanov{END FIELD}
Mikhail Ivonov{END FIELD}
Mike{END FIELD}
404-921-3722{END FIELD}
Peachtree Emporium{END FIELD}
88 Peachtree Plaza{END FIELD}
Atlanta{END FIELD}
GA{END FIELD}
30304{END FIELD}
{END RECORD}
================================================================
Sorenson{END FIELD}
Mary Beth{END FIELD}
Mary{END FIELD}
A:\S6ADDR.SF                                    Doc 1 Pg 1 Ln 1" Pos 1"
```

lowest zip code number

Figure 6-34
Document screen after sort

❷ Save the secondary file as S6ADDR2.SF.

❸ Clear the document screen and merge S6SLSLET.PF and S6ADDR2.SF.
❹ Save the merged document as S6MERGED.DOC.
❺ Print all five pages of the merged document.

As you can see, the letters print in order of zip code number, starting with the letter to Mike Gutanov, whose zip code is 30304, and ending with Becky Malone, whose zip code is 90220.

Printing Address Labels

Whitney wants to mail the form letters and accompanying photographs in 9-by-12-inch manila envelopes. Rather than typing the address on each envelope, she will use WordPerfect's labels and merge features to create mailing labels.

Creating the Labels Primary File

Whitney's first task is to create a primary file that specifies the format of the mailing label. The contents of the labels primary file is shown in Figure 6-35. As you can see, this primary file contains {FIELD} commands similar to those in Whitney's form letter. Let's create the labels primary file.

Figure 6-35
The primary file
to create labels

```
{FIELD}FirstName~ {FIELD}LastName~
{FIELD}Company~
{FIELD}Street~
{FIELD}City~, {FIELD}State~ {FIELD}Zip~
```

To create a primary file for labels:
❶ Clear the document screen.
❷ Create a document exactly like Figure 6-35. Use the Merge Codes command to enter the {FIELD} codes and then type the appropriate field names as shown.
❸ Save the file using the filename S6LABELS.PF.

Because the mailing labels contain only the names and addresses of the clients, this labels primary file includes no other text.

Merging the Labels Primary File with the Address List

Whitney's next task is to merge the labels primary file she has just created with the secondary file (the address list) she created earlier.

To merge the files:
❶ Clear the document screen.

❷ Select Merge from the Tools menu or press **[Ctrl][F9]** (Merge/Sort) and select **1** (**M**erge).

❸ Type **s6labels.pf** and press **[Enter]** to specify the name of the primary file.

❹ Type **s6addr2.sf** and press **[Enter]** to specify the name of the secondary file. WordPerfect carries out the merge to yield the merged document with one page for each record in the secondary file. See Figure 6-36.

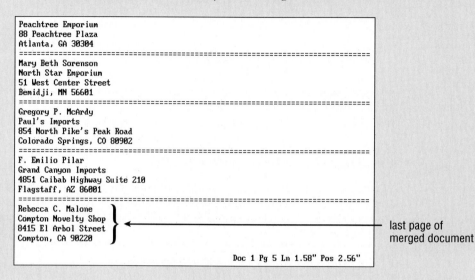

Figure 6-36
Document screen
of labels merged
document

If Whitney were to print the merged document as it appears now, she would get one address in the upper left corner of each printed page. She really wants the addresses to be printed on a standard sheet of gummed labels. Fortunately WordPerfect provides a method for creating a document that prints on gummed labels.

Creating the Labels Document

To format the merged document for labels, you need to change the page definition. WordPerfect's **page definition** is a set of instructions that specifies the page type and page size. By telling WordPerfect that the page definition is for labels and by specifying certain measurements about the labels, you can create a page definition for printing the clients' names and addresses on gummed labels.

Whitney has purchased Avery Laser Printer Labels number 5161/5162 from a local office supply store. She measures one of the labels and decides how she wants the addresses formatted on the labels (Figure 6-37). She also measures the distance between labels and the margins around the labels (Figure 6-38). If you use a different type of gummed label, set up your own page definition by measuring the size of the labels, the margins that you want within each label, the distances between labels, and the space between the labels and the edges of the labels page, as shown in Figures 6-37 and 6-38. You are now ready to define a labels page so that WordPerfect will format the merged document for the sheets of gummed labels.

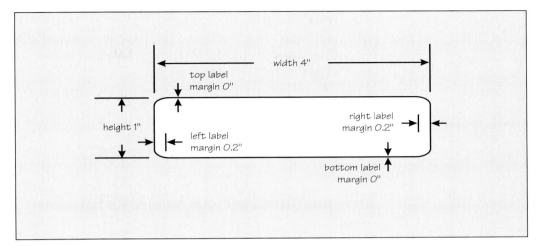

Figure 6-37
Data for defining
a label

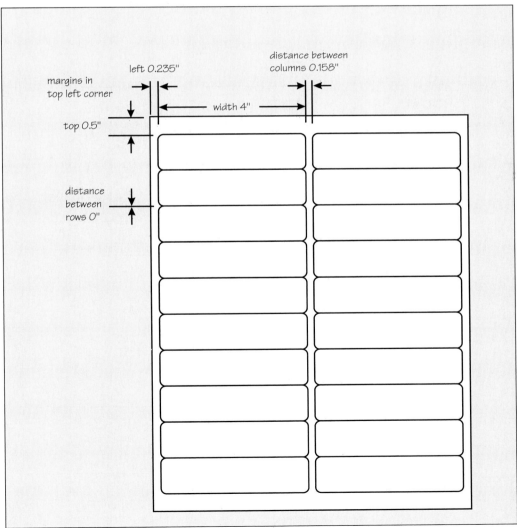

Figure 6-38
Data for defining
the labels page

To create a labels page definition:

❶ Move the cursor to the beginning of the merged document and select Page from the Layout menu or press **[Shift][F8]** (Format) and select **2** (**P**age). The Format: Page menu appears on the screen.

❷ Select **7** (Paper **S**ize). The Format: Paper Size/Type menu appears on the screen. See Figure 6-39.

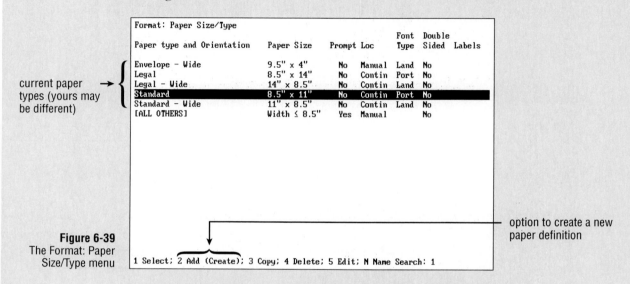

current paper types (yours may be different)

option to create a new paper definition

Figure 6-39
The Format: Paper Size/Type menu

❸ Select **2** (**A**dd) to display the Format: Paper Type menu. This menu allows you to select a page type.

❹ Select **4** (**L**abels) to display the Format: Edit Paper Definition menu. See Figure 6-40.

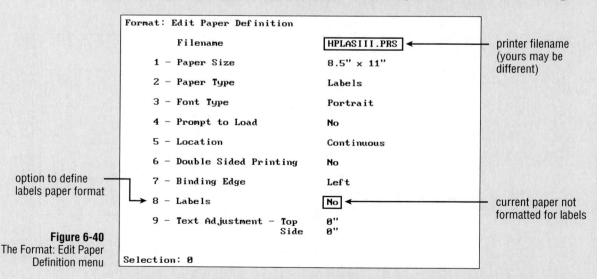

printer filename (yours may be different)

option to define labels paper format

current paper not formatted for labels

Figure 6-40
The Format: Edit Paper Definition menu

❺ Select **8** (**L**abels) and select "Yes." The Format: Labels menu appears on the screen. See Figure 6-41.

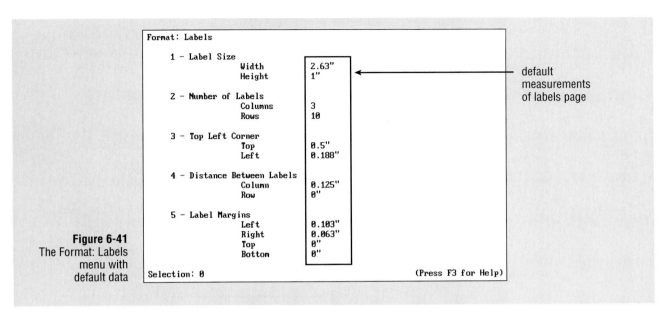

```
Format: Labels

    1 - Label Size
                  Width         2.63"          ◄─────        default
                  Height        1"                           measurements
                                                             of labels page
    2 - Number of Labels
                  Columns       3
                  Rows          10

    3 - Top Left Corner
                  Top           0.5"
                  Left          0.188"

    4 - Distance Between Labels
                  Column        0.125"
                  Row           0"

    5 - Label Margins
                  Left          0.103"
                  Right         0.063"
                  Top           0"
                  Bottom        0"

Selection: 0                                    (Press F3 for Help)
```

Figure 6-41
The Format: Labels
menu with
default data

The menu shown in Figure 6-41 allows you to specify the measurements of the labels shown in Figures 6-37 and 6-38. In the following steps you will enter the measurements for Whitney's labels (if you are using a different type of gummed label, enter your own measurements).

To specify the dimensions of the labels:

❶ Select **1** (Label **S**ize), type **4**, and press **[Enter]** to set the width to 4". Type **1** and press **[Enter]** to set the height to 1".

❷ Select **2** (**N**umber of Labels), type **2**, and press **[Enter]** to set the number of columns to 2, since the labels page has two columns of labels. Type **10** and press **[Enter]** to set the number of rows to 10, since the labels page has 10 rows of labels.

❸ Select **3** (**T**op Left Corner) and enter the data shown in Figure 6-38: Top 0.5" and Left 0.235".

❹ Select **4** (**D**istance Between Labels) and enter the data shown in Figure 6-38: Column 0.158" and Row 0".

❺ Select **5** (**L**abel Margins) and enter the data shown in Figure 6-37: Left 0.2", Right 0.2", Top 0", and Bottom 0".

Your screen should now look like Figure 6-42. Check all the data to make sure they are correct. If you find a mistake, select the appropriate menu item and retype the information. Once all the data are correct, you are ready to exit the Format: Labels menu.

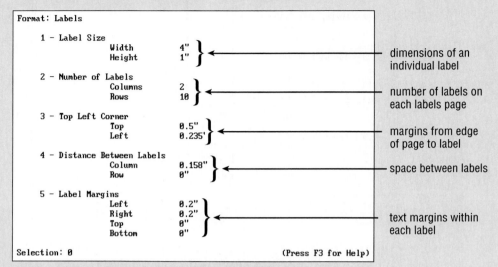

Figure 6-42
The Format: Labels menu after you have entered data

⑥   Press **[F7]** (Exit) twice to exit the Format: Labels menu and return to the Format: Paper Size/Type menu.

⑦   With Labels highlighted, press **1** (**S**elect). This selects the Labels page definition that you just created.

⑧   Press **[F7]** (Exit) to return to the document screen. The document is now ready for printing onto a sheet of gummed labels.

Defining the Labels page is a tedious process, but once you've done it, WordPerfect saves the definition for later use. Whitney will be able to use the Labels page definition whenever she prints mailing labels.

Printing the Labels

You can now view the document to see how it will look before you print it. Then you should save the document and print it.

To view, save, and print the labels document:
❶   Select Print from the File menu or press **[Shift][F7]** (Print).
❷   Select **6** (**V**iew Document). See Figure 6-43.

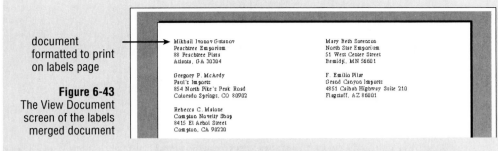

document
formatted to print
on labels page

Figure 6-43
The View Document
screen of the labels
merged document

③ Press **[F7]** (Exit) to return to the document screen.

④ Save the document as S6LABELS.DOC.

If you don't have a sheet of labels, you can print the screen document to an ordinary blank sheet of paper. If you're using an actual sheet of labels, consult your technical support person on how to feed the labels page into the printer.

⑤ Print the labels document.

Whitney now has the letters and the labels necessary to send her sales letters. She attaches the gummed labels to the manila envelopes, inserts the sales letters and product photographs, and mails them.

Exercises

1. Define or describe each of the following:
   - a. primary file
   - b. secondary file
   - c. merge code
   - d. merged document
   - e. record
   - f. field
   - g. sort key

2. Explain how you would insert the {DATE} merge command into a primary file.

3. Suppose during a merge you wanted to insert a field named Company into a primary file. Explain how you would do this.

4. How would you initiate a merge between a primary and a secondary file?

5. When entering data into a secondary file, how do you mark the end of a field? the end of a record?

6. What is the purpose of the {FIELD NAMES} merge code in a secondary file?

7. How would you sort a secondary file using the last name as the sort key? Assume the last name is Field 1, named "Last," in the secondary file.

8. Explain in general (without listing keystrokes) how you would use a secondary file to create mailing labels.

Tutorial Assignments

Retrieve the file T6FILE1.DFT and do the following:

1. To the right of "DATE:" in the memo, press **[Tab]** and insert the {DATE} merge code.

2. To the right of "MEMO TO:," press **[Tab]** and then insert {FIELD} merge commands for the fields First (for the first name) and Last (for the last name).

3. At the beginning of the body of the memo, before the word "please," insert the {FIELD} code for the field First, followed by a comma and a space.

4. Save the file as S6MEMO.PF.

Clear the document screen and do the following:

5. Insert the {FIELD NAMES} merge code to create the following field names: Last, First, and HomePhone.

6. Create a record for each of the following Sanders Imports employees. Enter the records in the order given:
Sanders, Whitney, 285-2857
Zayas, Gerry, 489-7765
Creer, Paul, 288-8104
Colón, Mario, 489-9147
Ballentyne, Marsha, 384-0108
Allen, Rachel, 285-9144
Marchant, Philipe, 489-1215

7. Save the file as S6EMPL1.SF.

8. Sort the file by last name.

9. Save the sorted file as S6EMPL2.SF.

Clear the screen and do the following:

10. Merge the files S6MEMO.PF and S6EMPL2.SF.

11. Save the merged document as S6MEMO.MRG.

12. Print the file S6MEMO.MRG.

Case Problems

1. Ad Letter for White Water Tours

Peter Crow, a graduate in business management from the University of Arizona, is founder of White Water Tours. This small company allows Peter to combine his training in business with his love of travel and white-water rafting. He has obtained names of potential customers from many sources, such as sporting goods stores and outdoor clubs. Peter wants to send a form letter to these potential customers to announce his new Colorado River rafting tours. He will enclose with each letter a color brochure that explains the tours in more detail.

Do the following:

1. Retrieve P6TOURS.DFT, the body of Peter's ad letter from your data diskette.

2. Insert {FIELD} codes at the beginning of the document for the date, the inside address, and the salutation. You will create the secondary file later, so you may choose the names you give to each field. The secondary file will contain the following data: last name, first name, street address, city, state, and zip code.

3. At the beginning of the next to the last paragraph, insert the merge code to mark where you want WordPerfect to insert the first name.

4. Save the primary file as S6TOURS.PF.

5. Clear the screen and create a secondary file from the following information:
   Mikkelson, Aubry, 8551 Sun Valley Drive, Boise, ID 83708
   Wolfgramm, Stephen, 184 Atlantic Avenue, Stamford, CT 06904
   Sigimoto, Ken, 911 North Bradley Street, Greensboro, NC 27420
   Almaraz, Humberto, 591 West Black Hills Drive, Sioux Falls, SD 57101
   Cundick, Cole, 11821 Smokey Mountains Avenue, Kingsport, TN 37662
   Johnson, Tyrell, 841 South Pacific Drive, Redmond, WA 98052

6. Save the secondary file as S6CLIENT.SF.

7. Sort the secondary file by zip code and save the results using the same filename, S6CLIENT.SF.

8. Merge the files to create the final ad letters.

9. Save the merged document as S6TOURS.MRG.

10. Print the first three pages of S6TOURS.MRG.

2. Form Letter to Friends and Relatives

Do the following:

1. Write a one-page form letter — a primary merge file — to your friends and relatives. Include in the letter one or more of the following types of information:
   a. What you have learned about word processing from this class
   b. Your current class schedule, with a brief description of each class
   c. Your professional plans after graduation
   d. Your ideas for setting up your own business
   e. Merge codes to specify where names and addresses will be inserted into the merged document

2. Save the letter as S6PERLET.PF.

3. Create a secondary merge file containing the names and addresses of some of your friends and relatives. You may use fictitious names and addresses if you choose.

4. Sort the secondary file alphabetically by last name.

5. Save the sorted secondary file as S6FAMILY.SF.

6. Merge S6PERLET.PF and S6FAMILY.SF.

7. Save the merged document as S6FAMILY.MRG.

8. Print the first three pages of the merged document.

3. Managing a Collection

WordPerfect can help you manage lists of items such as client records, employee records, names and addresses of family members and friends, collections, and many other things. Your task is to create a secondary merge file for a collection. The collection can be compact discs, cassettes, wine, sports cards, coins, stamps, books in your personal library, or anything else you desire.

Do the following:

1. Create the secondary file with the following field names:
    a. "Item" for the name of item
    b. "Value" for the cost at the time of purchase or the current estimated cost
    c. "Source" for the name of the publisher or the location of the acquisition
    d. "Date" for the date of acquisition or the date of publication
    e. "Note" for a comment about the item

2. Include 10 records in the secondary file. If your collection doesn't have 10 items, include fictitious data.

3. Sort the file alphabetically, in ascending order, using Item as the sort key.

4. Save the file as S6COLLCT.SF.

5. Create a primary file that will generate a list of the 10 items in your collection.

6. Save the primary file as S6COLLCT.PF.

7. Merge the primary and secondary files.

8. Change the page breaks to hard returns in the merged document, so the list of all 10 items fits on one page.

9. Save the merged document as S6COLLCT.MRG.

10. Print S6COLLECT.MRG.

11. Sort the secondary file using Value as the sort key and going from highest value to lowest value. *Hint*: Set Order to Descending.

12. Save the resulting secondary file as S6COLLC2.SF.

13. Merge S6COLLC2.SF with S6COLLCT.PF.

14. Save the merged file as S6COLLC2.MRG.

15. Print S6COLLC2.MRG.

WordPerfect Index

E

F

M

M filename extension   WP 195
macros
    Alt macros   WP 193-95
    corrections   WP 193-94
    creating   WP 191-93, WP 195-98
    defined   WP 190
    Enter macros   WP 197-99
    executing   WP 194-99
    named macros   WP 195-97
mailing labels. *See* address labels
making. *See* creating
margins
    changing   WP 53-57
    marking   WP 65
MEM filename extension   WP 27
menu bar   WP 11-12
merge codes   WP 220, WP 222, WP 228
merge commands   WP 220-21
Merge feature   WP 216-17
merge sort   WP 235, WP 240
merging documents
    concepts/terminology   WP 217-20
    defined   WP 218
    primary/secondary files   WP 233-34
messages, typeover   WP 21
minus (–) sign   WP 52
misspellings. *See* spell checking
mistakes. *See* errors/mistakes
mnemonic letters   WP 12-13, WP 50
modifier keys   WP 14, WP 15
modifying. *See* changing
mouse pointer   WP 13-14, WP 50, WP 119
moving
    blocks of text   WP 117-19
    footnotes   WP 203
    outline family   WP 183-85

N

named macros   WP 191, WP 195-97
[NUM LOCK]   WP 9, WP 52

numbers
    document pages   WP 143-44, WP 146-47, WP 147
    paragraphs in outlines   WP 175, WP 182-83
numeric sort   WP 235

O

on-line help. *See* help, getting
open style   WP 150
orphan (and widow) protection   WP 164-65
Outline feature
    concepts/terminology   WP 175
    creating   WP 176-80
    cursor movement through   WP 181-82
    editing   WP 180-81
    inserting new paragraphs   WP 182-83
    moving outline family   WP 183-85
    split screens and   WP 188-90
    turning off   WP 185
outline style   WP 150

P

page breaks   WP 70
page definition, address labels   WP 240
Page Numbering feature   WP 143-44
Page Suppress feature   WP 146
pages
    centering top to bottom   WP 135-39
    conditional end of   WP 161-64
    numbering   WP 9, WP 143-44, WP 146-47
paired style   WP 150
paragraph sort   WP 235
paragraphs
    copying   WP 121-22
    deleting   WP 123
    indenting   WP 67-70
    numbers in outlines   WP 175, WP 182-83
parameters   WP 220
[PgDn]   WP 53
[PgUp]   WP 53
plus (+) sign   WP 52
position number   WP 9

T

[Tab] WP 60
[TAB] format code WP 66
Tab menu WP 140-41
tab stops WP 60, WP 65, WP 139-43
tables
  creating WP 154-57
  editing WP 160-61
  entering labels/data WP 159-60
  formatting WP 157-59
Tables feature WP 154
templates WP 14-15, WP 18-19, WP 50
text
  boldfacing WP 61-62, WP 111-13
  centering WP 101-2
  converting to uppercase WP 115-17
  copying WP 121-22, WP 187-88
  deleting WP 70-71, WP 114-15
  entering in documents WP 23-25,
    WP 28-31
  justifying WP 57-60
  moving WP 100-101, WP 117-19
  replacing WP 103-6
  restoring WP 115
  searching WP 102-6
  undeleting WP 71-72
  underlining WP 62-63, WP 113-14
Thesaurus command WP 82-83
tilde (~) sign WP 220
titles
  named macros WP 195
  outlines WP 176-77
toggle keys WP 61
Tools menu WP 11-12
triangle symbols WP 65
typeover mode WP 21, WP 40, WP 73-74

U

undeleting. *See* restoring
underlining text WP 62-63, WP 113-14
uppercase characters WP 115-17. *See* also
  case sensitivity

V

View Document command WP 36, WP 59
View Document screen WP 147-48
viewing documents WP 147-48

W

widow (and orphan) protection WP 164-65
widths, columns/tables WP 158-59
windows WP 188-90
word wrap WP 28-31
WordPerfect
  changing documents WP 40-42
  concepts/terminology WP 4
  correcting errors WP 20-22
  default format settings WP 10
  dictionary WP 75
  document screen/status line WP 9
  entering text WP 23-25
  executing commands WP 10-15
  exiting WP 37-38
  filenames WP 27-28
  function-key commands WP 14-15
  getting help WP 16-20
  previewing documents WP 35-37
  printing WP 37
  retrieving documents WP 38-40
  saving documents WP 25-27, WP 35
  scrolling WP 31-34
  starting WP 7-8
  Styles feature WP 149-54
  Tables feature WP 154-61
  word wrap WP 28-31
words, misspelled. *See* spell checking

Lotus 1-2-3
Tutorials

- **Using Spreadsheets in Business**

- **Tutorial 1   An Overview of Lotus 1-2-3**

- **Tutorial 2   Creating a Worksheet**

- **Tutorial 3   Modifying a Worksheet**

- **Tutorial 4   Working with Larger Worksheets**

- **Tutorial 5   Designing Professional Worksheets**

- **Tutorial 6   Creating and Printing Graphs**

- **Tutorial 7   Using a 1-2-3 Database**

- **Tutorial 8   Creating and Using Macros**

Using Spreadsheets in Business

Generations of frustrated people who worked with numbers using only pencils and erasers would envy you. They added long columns of numbers, and if a figure changed, they had to erase and recalculate. Or they multiplied to determine percentages and erased and multiplied again if a mistake crept in. The arrival of the calculator saved time, but until computers became available, people remained subject to the tyranny of pencil and eraser.

With Lotus 1-2-3, the computer automatically erases and re-calculates for you, saving countless hours. Projects whose complexity could eat up pencils and erasers can now be accomplished in minutes. When you learn how to use 1-2-3, imagine how much easier it will be to create a budget, prepare an invoice, or calculate interest on a loan. Instead of one option, you can evaluate several, for example, "What if advertising costs average $2,000 instead of $1,500 per month?" "What if this year's bonus is 4 percent, 6 percent, or 8 percent?"

Not surprisingly, businesses are enthusiastic users of spreadsheet software. That's because in almost any department of a company, spreadsheets can help people do their jobs more quickly and more effectively.

TOPICS

This chapter covers the following topics:

- What Is a Business?

- Computers in Business

- What Is a Spreadsheet?

- How Are Spreadsheets Used in Business?

  Using Spreadsheets in Accounting

  Using Spreadsheets in Marketing

  Using Spreadsheets in Finance

  Using Spreadsheets in Human Resource Management

- What You Will Learn About Spreadsheets in Business

What Is a Business?

Your local drugstore is a business, as are the neighborhood cleaner, florist, market, and restaurants. So are Sears, General Motors, and Kodak. All of these businesses provide products and services people need; in return, they earn money to compensate employees and owners for their hard work and money invested. Thus, we can say that a *business* is an organization that seeks profit by providing goods or services.

You may be planning a business career as, for example, a store owner, stockbroker, accountant, or manager. Even if you are not a business major, you engage in business activities. If you earn money, you have to decide how to spend it, how to save it, and what taxes to pay. If you become a lawyer or a doctor, you will have to pay rent for your office and compensate your employees; you may have to market your skills to prospective clients or patients. If you become an artist, you will have to acquire materials and sell your works. So even if you don't decide on a traditional business career, you can still use a spreadsheet program to help you make wise business decisions.

Computers in Business

People — employees — are an important resource in any business. To be effective employees, people need information. Information is sometimes described as a company's most valuable resource. It enables employees to review past business decisions and activities, and learn from their mistakes. It provides an accurate picture of the company's present position and a basis for forecasting the future. Decisions made throughout a company reflect the quality of information available to its employees.

In every department of a company, data accumulate — on sales volume and promotion costs, for example, on customers, and on expenses for furniture, supplies, and entertainment. The challenge faced by all businesspeople is to transform data into meaningful information, to process data by creating structured reports. When this is done well, employees can rely on accurate information and thus provide better products and services for customers.

Pencils and erasers, even calculators and filing cabinets, are of little help in managing and organizing large quantities of data. Fortunately, computers have dramatically improved companies' ability to process data, to pull information together, and to provide reports on all aspects of their operations.

Spreadsheets are one of the most valuable computer tools for producing usable information. The availability of spreadsheet software made businesses recognize the speed and flexibility of the microcomputer. With 1-2-3 on microcomputers throughout a company, decision makers at every level can analyze past experience, forecast the future, and, even more importantly, test assumptions by posing "what if?" questions and studying the results. Let's define spreadsheets and then see how they can be used in various business settings.

What Is Spreadsheet Software?

To understand what a spreadsheet is, we must first look at the language of accounting. If you have ever seen a budget, listing months across the top of a page and income and expense items vertically along the left, you have seen a type of accounting worksheet, or ledger (Figure 1). A **worksheet** is a grid of intersecting vertical **columns** and horizontal **rows** that organizes data in an easily understandable way. With this grid organization, data are entered

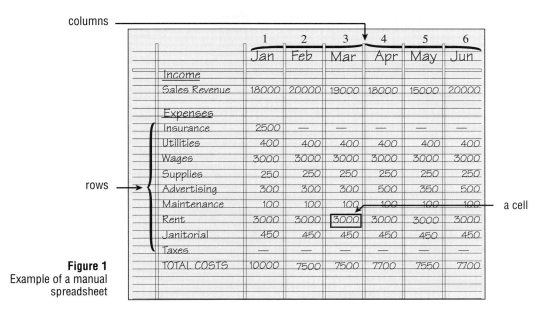

Figure 1
Example of a manual spreadsheet

into the appropriate **cells**, the intersections of rows and columns. Until recently, you would have to use a calculator and a pencil to calculate totals and place them in the proper cells.

With the advent of the microcomputer came the *electronic* worksheet. This computer software, called **spreadsheet software**, creates a similar grid or worksheet on your computer screen (Figure 2) and instructs the computer to perform the calculations for you.

```
B4: [W8] 15000                                                          READY

         A        B       C       D       E       F       G       H
               Jan      Feb     Mar     Apr     May     Jun
1 ·
2  Income
3  --------------
4  Sales Revenue 15000   20000   19000   10000   15000   20000
5
6  Expenses
7  --------------
8  Insurance    2500
9  Utilities     400     400     400     400     400     400
10 Wages        3000    3000    3000    3000    3000    3000
11 Supplies      250     250     250     250     250     250
12 Advertising   300     300     300     500     350     500
13 Maintenance   100     100     100     100     100     100
14 Rent         3000    3000    3000    3000    3000    3000
15 Janitorial    450     450     450     450     450     450
16 Taxes
17               ----------------------------------------------
18 Total Costs 10000    7500    7500    7700    7550    7700
19
20
26-Jun-91  02:14 PM        UNDO
```

Figure 2
Example of an electronic worksheet

You don't have to be a computer expert to use a spreadsheet. You simply tell the software what result you want in certain cells, and the software adds the numbers in rows or columns, multiplies the contents of one cell by another, or applies formulas.

What if you want to see what happens if sales, salaries, or supplies vary? What if you simply change your mind or make a mistake? To consider another option or to correct an error, you enter the appropriate numbers and instructions. The computer recalculates and changes all relevant cells for you. You can print various versions of a worksheet, store them, and study their meanings at your convenience before you make a decision. You can even display the results in graphic form, for example, as a pie chart or a bar graph (Figure 3).

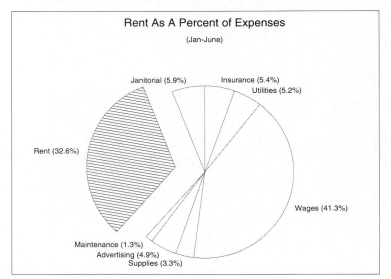

Figure 3
Example of a pie
chart generated by
Lotus 1-2-3

You can use 1-2-3 not only to produce a visual aid to clarify information, but also to produce reports that search for and extract specific data. With its data management function, for example, you can instruct 1-2-3 to list all employees at a certain salary level or to prepare a report showing all invoices that are 30 days overdue. The graphing and data management functions of 1-2-3 provide additional tools for interpreting, displaying, and reporting data.

How Are Spreadsheets Used in Business?

Although businesses depend on spreadsheets to summarize numerical data and to keep records, spreadsheets are most powerful as a decision-making tool. The spreadsheet's ability to answer the question "What if?" helps businesspeople make sound decisions. For example, suppose you are planning to start your own business. The "what if" feature of 1-2-3 enables you to measure the effects on profit of paying one employee or two, of renting a more or a less expensive space, and of obtaining loans at different interest rates. What if sales the first six months are 100 units? 250 units? What if you pay employees a straight salary? Salary plus commission? 1-2-3 helps you see the whole picture and eliminates much of the guesswork.

This "what if" ability makes spreadsheets essential throughout an organization — in accounting, marketing, finance, and human resources management. Let's first define these basic business functions and then use a real example to demonstrate the use of spreadsheets in each. The people who contributed examples to this book are enthusiastic about their spreadsheet projects. Spreadsheets have enabled them to organize and display information and to make instant calculations. For entry-level employees all the way to top management, spreadsheets are an invaluable tool.

Using Spreadsheets in Accounting

Called "the language of business," accounting communicates information about the financial well-being of a company. Accountants classify transactions — for example, as purchases, sales, or entertainment costs — then record and summarize the financial data and help interpret the data for decision makers. They help managers find answers to questions like, "Will the company have enough cash to pay the bills next quarter?" "Which of our products is least profitable?" People outside the firm, such as potential investors or bankers, look to the financial statements prepared by accountants to learn about a company's debt or cash surplus.

As organizations expand and grow more complex, the practice of accounting becomes more sophisticated. Thus, accounting is becoming increasingly dependent on computers to measure, analyze, and report information that is so essential in business today. For example, Veronica Villarreal's project at Mesilla Valley Mall illustrates the power of spreadsheets to record accounting information and produce reports. After Veronica earned an associate's degree in business, she began working in the business office of the mall. When she arrived, gift certificates good for merchandise in mall stores were recorded and totaled by hand (Figure 4). This was a time-consuming job because it was done twice — once when a certificate was issued and again when it was redeemed.

Figure 4
A sample gift certificate

Veronica's manager asked her to use 1-2-3 to design a worksheet for tracking gift certificates, which were sold to customers, issued as special promotions, and presented as employee-of-the-month awards. The manager wanted to keep track of how many certificates in each category were issued each month. Furthermore, he wanted his staff to have a reliable way of recording which certificates were redeemed and which were still outstanding.

Veronica designed a worksheet that made keeping track of the gift certificates quicker and easier. A simplified version of her worksheet appears in Figure 5 on the following page.

```
A1: [W2]                                                    READY

       A    B      C         D        E       F       G        H
1                        Mesilla Valley Mall Gift Certificate
2
3
4
5    Cert #                Customer                  Cert    Cert Not
6                  Amt       Sale    Promo    EOM   Cleared  Cleared
7                 ------    ------   ------  ------  ------   ------
8     668          50                         50      50
9     669          10        10                                10
10    670          25        25                       25
11    671          25        25                                25
12    672          50                 50                        50
13    673          50                 50              50
14    674          15        15                       15
15    675          50        50                                50
16               ------    ------   ------  ------  ------   ------
17   Subtotal     275       125      100      50     140      135
18
19
20
CERTIF.WK1                      UNDO
```

Figure 5
A simplified version of
Veronica Villarreal's
worksheet

By eliminating tedious repetitive calculations, spreadsheets provide time for creative problem solving. They are essential for recording, summarizing, and analyzing data and producing accounting information such as monthly income statements, cash flow reports, budgets, and, as we've seen, even gift certificates.

Using Spreadsheets in Marketing

Building a better mousetrap won't earn profits for a company unless people need and want a better mousetrap. *Marketing* involves ensuring that a company's products or services satisfy customers' needs. When people find what they want and need, they will pay the company for its products or services, thus generating profits for that company.

To provide this important link between the company and its customers, market research identifies target customers by their age, income, lifestyle, and so on; it then attempts to determine the wants and needs of these target customers. Through advertising, the company strives to inform consumers about what it has to offer them. A systematic marketing effort depends on accurate information for planning a successful strategy and measuring sales results.

At Rauh Good Darlo & Barnes Advertising Agency, Kelly Seelig uses a spreadsheet for planning and scheduling advertising campaigns for her clients. She develops a budget for ads in newspapers and magazines, and for radio and television commercials. Then she schedules these ads over a period of months for maximum effectiveness. Kelly finds a spreadsheet ideal for creating her media plan.

A portion of her media schedule worksheet for magazine advertising shows expenditures for each publication by month and calculates totals by month and by publication (Figure 6). The printed worksheet helps Kelly and her client, in this case a hotel, to see when and where the dollars will be spent. What if they schedule more or fewer ads? The impact on the budget is immediately clear.

Media Schedule							
Publication	Jan	Feb	Mar	Apr	May	Jun	Subtotal
HOTEL & TRAV		$6,094			$6,094		$12,188
Calif Sect.		Spr Is			Sum Is		
Circ: 63,795		4-color			4-color		
CALIF MAG		$3,600	$3,330				$6,930
Trav. Planner		1/4 pg	1/4 pg				
Circ: 356,438							
LOS ANGELES					$6,525		$6,525
Issued annually					1/2 pg		
Circ: 222,629					4-color		
SUNSET	$2,695				$1,348		$4,043
Entire circ.	1/4 pg				1/4 pg		
Circ:1,400,000	w/copy				w/copy		
SUBTOTALS	$2,695	$9,694	$3,330	$0	$13,967	$0	$29,686

Figure 6
A portion of the printout for Kelly Seelig's media schedule worksheet

Spreadsheets have many applications in marketing, not only in advertising but also in market research, product management, and sales. Marketing personnel rely on spreadsheets to analyze past experience, forecast future results, and test various assumptions. Spreadsheets help marketing personnel collect and interpret data about customers and measure the company's effectiveness in communicating with its customers. 1-2-3 can be the vital ingredient in a successful marketing effort.

Using Spreadsheets in Finance

In any business, you must consider not only your customers and what products they need and want, but also where to obtain funds for materials, manufacturing, and employee compensation. Sales of your product can vary from month to month, so you must be certain that you have cash on hand to pay the bills, including taxes, and that you can control expenses.

Finance is the business function of planning how to obtain funds and how to use them to achieve the company's goals. In addition to sales dollars, companies can obtain funds by selling shares in ownership (stocks and bonds), attracting venture capital, and borrowing money. Accountants collect, organize, and present data that the specialists in finance interpret to ensure the financial health of the company. Since forecasting, budgeting, and tax management are among their duties, finance specialists process volumes of numerical data. They rely on computers to transform these data quickly into useful information.

Spreadsheets enable people with a finance background to find creative solutions to problems. At Ungermann-Bass, a computer communications company, Wendy Ray studied this high-tech company's method of paying its bills. She knew that many of the company's suppliers offered discounts for prompt payment of their invoices, but the accounting department at Ungermann-Bass wasn't paying early enough to take advantage of these savings. Wendy decided to use a 1-2-3 worksheet to determine how many discounts were taken and how many were lost. With the data on 1-2-3, Wendy presented well-documented information to a company vice president and recommended a change in payment policy.

Figure 7 is a summary worksheet showing discounts taken for two quarters, the first before Wendy's recommendations were adopted and the second after. Notice that her worksheet analysis enabled the company to increase the number of discounts taken in those quarters from 91.14 percent to 97.95 percent. In a year, the company saved over $100,000, thanks to Wendy's recommendations.

```
A1: [W14]                                                          READY

        A           B         C        D         E        F
1                         Discounts Taken Summary
2
3   Date        Discounts  Discounts  % Taken  Discounts  % Lost
4               Available    Taken              Lost
5
6   October       23,576    19,052    80.81%    4,524    19.19%
7   November      32,149    28,911    89.93%    3,238    10.07%
8   December      36,647    36,225    98.85%      422     1.15%
9   Quarter Total 92,372    84,188    91.14%    8,184     8.86%
10
11
12  January       34,607    33,964    98.14%      643     1.86%
13  February      23,577    23,326    98.94%      251     1.06%
14  March         20,238    19,525    96.48%      713     3.52%
15  Quarter Total 78,422    76,815    97.95%    1,607     2.05%
16
17
18
19
20
DISCOUNT.WK1            UNDO
```

Figure 7
A portion of Wendy
Ray's summary
worksheet

Besides helping to control expenses, finance specialists respond to requests for information coming from different departments of the company. The manufacturing department may ask for monthly reports of actual spending compared to its expense budget. Marketing may want to keep abreast of how its sales results to date compare with forecasts. 1-2-3 can generate these reports and provide comparisons with last year's results.

Without spreadsheets, these analyses and projections would require laborious calculations, subject at every step to errors. The spreadsheet user's ability to ask, "What if?" and have 1-2-3 recalculate all the numbers has significantly improved financial planning and control.

Using Spreadsheets in Human Resource Management

A marketable product and the funds to manufacture it aren't enough. Businesses need people to get the job done. *Human resources management* is the process of determining a company's needs for employees and finding, training, and motivating those employees.

Each unit of a company must concern itself with managing the human resource; many companies also have a human resources or personnel department. Among such a department's tasks is providing job enrichment and compensation incentives to promote employee satisfaction and productivity and to reduce turnover. Human resource specialists are often charged with administering payroll and benefits, keeping salary records, and evaluating various forms of compensation such as profit sharing and bonuses. By facilitating the record-keeping functions, computers free human resource specialists to invest more time in training and motivating employees.

For example, human resource administrator Thalia Ohara of *PC World* magazine uses 1-2-3 to track profit sharing earned by employees. Profit sharing is a system that rewards employees for their role in producing profits by paying them a percentage of those profits.

At *PC World*, the amount of profit-sharing funds each employee earns is a percentage of the employee's gross salary. The profit-sharing worksheet that Thalia created shows each employee's profit sharing earned for the year, which is deposited in the employee's account (Figure 8). When an employee earns a raise in salary, Thalia enters the new salary, and 1-2-3 recalculates the amount of profit sharing and revises the totals. Profit sharing encourages employees to stay with the company for at least seven years. If they leave before seven years, they can withdraw only a percentage of the contribution, called the vesting percentage, based on their years of service.

```
A1: [W1]                                                    READY

      A      B         C        D     E        F        G       H
1
2                         Profit Sharing Plan
3
4     Participant  Vesting     Date  Contrib  Annual  Amount  Pay out
5                     %        Hired    %      Salary  Contrib  Amount
6
7     V. Barnerd    10%    4/10/89   12%  $50,000   $6,000    $600
8     D. Bridges     0%    6/18/90   12%   28,000    3,360       0
9     W. Callaway   20%    8/24/88   12%   35,000    4,200     840
10    G. Chico     100%   11/26/82   12%   42,000    5,040   5,040
11    T. Elia       40%    1/05/87   12%   38,000    4,560   1,824
12    J. Hull        0%    4/02/90   12%   24,000    2,880       0
13    G. Liu        10%    5/22/89   12%   40,000    4,800     480
14
15
16
17
18
19
20
PROFSHAR.WK1                  UNDO
```

Figure 8
A portion of Thalia Ohara's profit sharing worksheet

As shown in this example, Thalia has streamlined and simplified salary and benefits administration, thanks to her worksheet. From tracking parking passes to calculating salaries, profit sharing, and bonuses, 1-2-3 makes human resources management more flexible and efficient.

What You Will Learn About Spreadsheets in Business

Spreadsheets have transformed the business of business by giving people quick access to information vital for doing their jobs. *Lotus 1-2-3 for Business* places this essential software tool in your hands right from the beginning. Through step-by-step tutorials, you will have the opportunity to apply spreadsheet principles to real business problems. As you learn about spreadsheets in business, you will develop business problem-solving skills that you can use in other courses and that you can take with you to whatever career you choose.

Lotus 1-2-3 is recognized as the spreadsheet standard. If you can list 1-2-3 skills on your resume, it will catch an employer's eye. Employers know that 1-2-3 enables employees to perform their jobs more efficiently and effectively. Because 1-2-3 improves your productivity, it increases your chances to get a job, to advance in your job, and to be successful.

In the tutorials and the cases that follow, you will look at 1-2-3 in a business context. *Lotus 1-2-3 for Business* will help you see that business problem solving is more than just collecting and recording data, and that learning to use spreadsheets is more than simply pressing the right keys on your computer. *Lotus 1-2-3 for Business* emphasizes transforming data into information useful for understanding business relationships and for making sound business decisions.

Tutorial 1

An Overview of Lotus 1-2-3

This tutorial introduces you to terms you will use to describe a 1-2-3 worksheet. You will also learn to navigate a worksheet using a keyboard and a mouse. Finally, you will tour 1-2-3 and see some demonstrations of its worksheet, graphics, database, and macro capabilities.

Before you begin, be sure you have initialized 1-2-3 and installed it on your computer, as described in the installation instructions.

How to Follow the Numbered Steps in the Lotus 1-2-3 Tutorials

In the Lotus 1-2-3 tutorials, you will follow step-by-step instructions. These instructions are displayed as numbered lists on a shaded background, as shown in Figure 1-1. Notice in this figure:

- Boldface indicates keys that you should press.
- Function keys, such as **[F2]**, are followed by the 1-2-3 key name in parentheses.
- Key combinations, such as **[Alt][F4]**, mean that you press and hold down the first key, and then while holding the first key, you press the second key. You then release both keys.

To use the UNDO command:

❶ Press **[F2]** (EDIT).

❷ Press **[Backspace]** three times to erase PAY, the incorrect label.

❸ Type **SALARY**, the correct label, and then press **[Enter]**. The new correct label is now in cell C7. See Figure 1-30.

❹ Press **[Alt][F4]** to view the incorrect label once more. Press **[Alt][F4]** again to restore the correct label.

Figure 1-1
Example of step-by-step instructions

Starting 1-2-3

Start your computer. Be certain that the DOS prompt appears. If you are using 1-2-3 in a lab, you might need to ask your instructor or technical support person for instructions.

To start 1-2-3:

❶ If your worksheet files are stored on a hard disk, go to Step 2.

   If your worksheet files are on your data diskette, place the diskette in drive A.

❷ Be sure that the current drive is the drive where you installed 1-2-3. On most systems this is drive C. If 1-2-3 is installed on drive C and if your current drive is not C, then type **C:** and press **[Enter]**.

❸ Now change to the subdirectory where 1-2-3 has been copied. For example, if the name of the subdirectory is "123r23," you would type **cd\123r23** and press **[Enter]** to switch to the directory where 1-2-3 is stored. Check with your instructor or technical support person for the name of the subdirectory.

❹ At the DOS prompt type **123** and press **[Enter]**. The 1-2-3 program is loaded into computer memory. Figure 1-2 shows the usage of computer memory after 1-2-3 has been loaded.

The Worksheet **L 15**

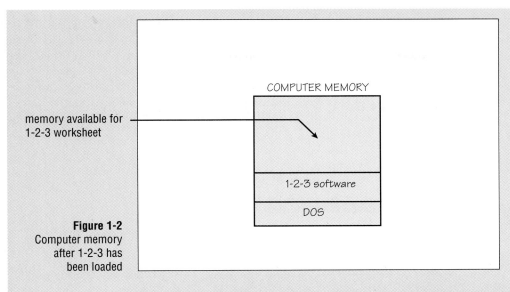

COMPUTER MEMORY

memory available for
1-2-3 worksheet

1-2-3 software

DOS

Figure 1-2
Computer memory
after 1-2-3 has
been loaded

An introductory screen appears, followed by a blank 1-2-3 worksheet. See Figure 1-3. If the blank worksheet does not appear, your copy of 1-2-3 may not be installed correctly. See the instructions in the installation guide or check with your instructor or technical support person.

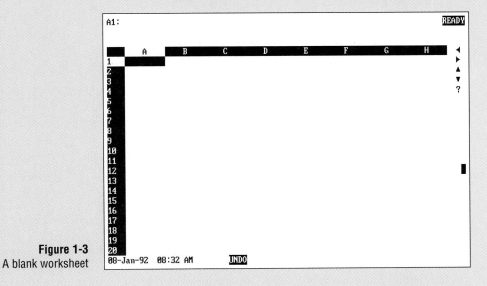

Figure 1-3
A blank worksheet

The Worksheet

The **worksheet** is the basic structure for storing and organizing data when you are using spreadsheet software such as Lotus 1-2-3. In Lotus 1-2-3 the worksheet is a grid made up of columns and rows. The worksheet contains 8,192 rows and 256 columns.

A **row number** in the left border of the worksheet identifies each row (Figure 1-4). Rows are numbered consecutively from 1 to 8192. A **column letter** in the top border of the worksheet identifies each column. Columns are lettered A-Z, then AA-AZ, then BA-BZ, and so on to column IV. A **cell** is a unit of the worksheet that stores data. It is formed by the intersection of a column and a row and is identified by its column letter and row number. For example, the intersection of column B and row 8 is cell B8. B8 is called the **cell address**; whenever you specify a cell address, be sure to name the column letter first and then the row number.

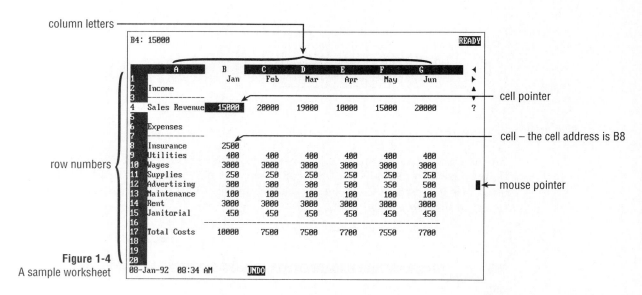

Figure 1-4
A sample worksheet

Notice the highlighted rectangle in cell B4 in Figure 1-4. This is called the **cell pointer**. The cell pointer appears in only one cell of the worksheet, but you can move the cell pointer to any cell of the worksheet. The **current cell** is the cell in which the cell pointer rests and in which you enter data.

The 1-2-3 Screen

The 1-2-3 screen is made up of three areas: the **worksheet area**, the **control panel**, and the **status line** (Figure 1-5). The 1-2-3 screen cannot display all 8,192 rows and 256 columns of a worksheet at one time. Typically a 1-2-3 screen displays 20 rows and eight columns at a time (the number of columns might vary if the width of a column has changed). The rows and columns that appear on your screen are a window into your worksheet and represent the **worksheet area**.

control panel {

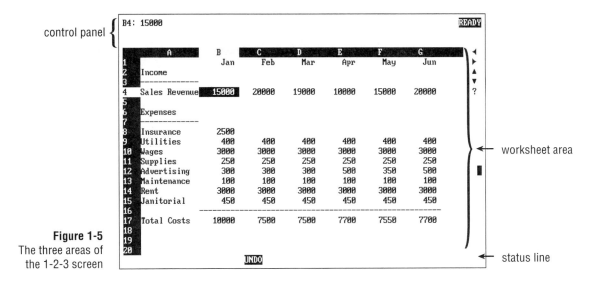

Figure 1-5
The three areas of
the 1-2-3 screen

worksheet area

status line

The top three lines of the 1-2-3 screen contain the control panel. The **control panel** displays information about the current cell and about commands (Figure 1-6).

address of current cell

control panel {

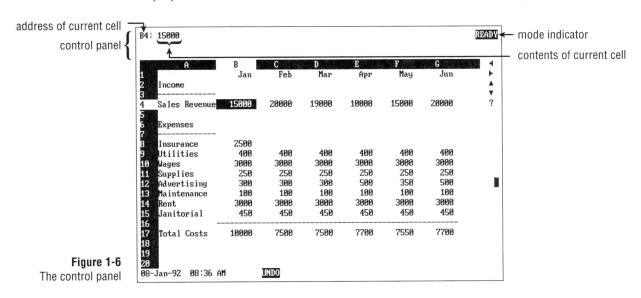

mode indicator

contents of current cell

Figure 1-6
The control panel

The *first line* of the control panel displays information about the current cell and the mode, or state, of 1-2-3. At the far left of the first line, 1-2-3 displays the **address**, or location, of the current cell and its contents.

At the far right of the first line of the control panel, 1-2-3 displays the **mode indicator**, which tells you what **mode**, or state, 1-2-3 is currently in. For example, when 1-2-3 is ready for you to type or select a command, 1-2-3 is in READY mode. When you are performing a task in 1-2-3, the mode indicator changes to show the current status of the task. Figure 1-7 on the following page lists some of the mode indicator messages.

Mode Indicator	Meaning
EDIT	You pressed (F2) [EDIT] to edit an entry or entered a formula incorrectly.
ERROR	1-2-3 is displaying an error message. Press (F1) [HELP] to display a Help screen that describes the error or press [Esc] or [enter] to clear the error message.
FILES	1-2-3 is displaying a menu of filenames in the control panel. Press (F3) [NAME] to display a full-screen menu of filenames.
FIND	You selected /Data Query Find or pressed (F7) [QUERY] to repeat the last /Data Query Find you specified, and 1-2-3 is highlighting a database record that matches your criteria.
FRMT	You selected /Data Parse Format-Line Edit to edit a format line.
HELP	You pressed (F1) [HELP], and 1-2-3 is displaying a Help screen.
LABEL	You are entering a label.
MENU	You pressed / (Slash) or < (Less-than symbol), and 1-2-3 is displaying a menu of commands.
NAMES	1-2-3 is displaying a menu of range names, graph names, or attached add-in names.
POINT	1-2-3 is prompting you to specify a range, or you are creating a formula by highlighting a range.
READY	1-2-3 is ready for you to enter data or select a command.
STAT	You selected /Worksheet Status or /Worksheet Global Default Status, and 1-2-3 is displaying the corresponding status screen.

Figure 1-7
Mode indicator
messages

The *second line* of the control panel displays the current entry when you are creating or editing the entry. It can also display the **main menu**, which is a list of commands, and the submenus that appear after you make a selection from the main menu. The rectangular highlight that appears on a command in the menu is called the **menu pointer**.

The *third line* of the control panel displays information about the command highlighted by the menu pointer. 1-2-3 lists either the submenu commands for the highlighted command or a description of the highlighted command.

The **status line** (Figure 1-8) is the bottom line of the screen. It displays the date-and-time indicator and the status indicators.

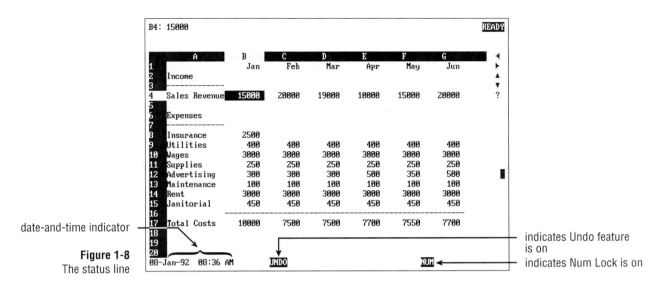

date-and-time indicator

Figure 1-8
The status line

indicates Undo feature is on
indicates Num Lock is on

The **date-and-time indicator** appears in the left corner of the status line. It usually displays the current date and time.

A **status indicator** appears when you use certain 1-2-3 keys and when a particular program condition exists. For example, UNDO indicates you can press the key combination [Alt][F4] (UNDO) to undo your last action, and NUM indicates the [NUM LOCK] key is on.

Moving the Cell Pointer Using the Keyboard

To be able to enter or view data in your worksheet, you need to learn how to move the cell pointer. **Pointer-movement keys** enable you to move the cell pointer from cell to cell within your worksheet. You move the cell pointer up, down, left, and right with the pointer-movement keys on your keyboard. Figure 1-9 lists the most commonly used pointer-movement keys. Let's try moving the cell pointer one cell at a time. As you move it within the worksheet, notice how the location of the cell pointer changes in the status line of the control panel.

Figure 1-9
Commonly used pointer-movement keys

Key	Moves cell pointer
[→]	Right one cell
[←]	Left one cell
[↓]	Down one cell
[↑]	Up one cell
[Tab]	Right one screen
[Shift][Tab]	Left one screen
[Ctrl][→]	Right one screen
[Ctrl][←]	Left one screen
[Home]	To cell A1
[PgDn]	Down one screen
[PgUp]	Up one screen

To move the cell pointer in the worksheet:

❶ Press **[Home]** once to move the cell pointer to cell A1, if it is not currently in cell A1.

❷ Press **[→]** once to move the cell pointer to cell B1.

❸ Press **[↓]** once to move the cell pointer to cell B2.

❹ Press **[PgDn]** once to move the cell pointer down one screen. The cell pointer now appears in cell B22, and rows 21 to 40 appear on the screen. See Figure 1-10.

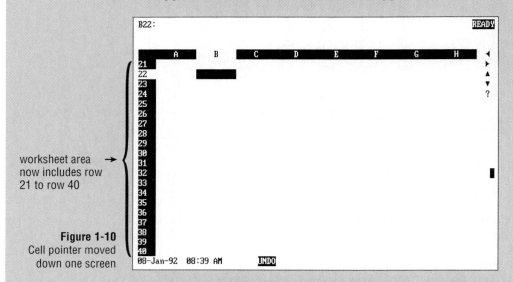

worksheet area →
now includes row
21 to row 40

Figure 1-10
Cell pointer moved
down one screen

Then press **[PgUp]** to move the cell pointer back up one screen. When a pointer-movement keystroke moves the cell pointer into a cell not currently in the worksheet area, 1-2-3 shifts the worksheet area to display a different part of the worksheet.

❺ Press **[Tab]** once to move the cell pointer right one screen. Press **[Shift][Tab]** to move left one screen. Remember that to use the key combinations, such as [Shift][Tab], you press and hold the first key. Then while holding the first key, you press the second key. Then release both.

Moving the Cell Pointer Using the [End] Key

The [End] key allows you to move around the worksheet quickly. If you press a pointer-movement key after pressing [End], the cell pointer jumps to another cell according to the following rules:

• If the cell pointer is currently in an empty cell, the cell pointer moves in the direction of the arrow key pressed to the first *nonblank* cell or the end of the worksheet.

• If the cell pointer is currently in a nonblank cell, the cell pointer moves in the direction of the arrow key pressed to the first *nonblank* cell at the intersection of a blank and a nonblank cell.

- If you press [Home] after pressing [End], the cell pointer moves to the last cell in the worksheet.

To move the cell pointer using the [End] key:

❶ Press **[Home]** to return to cell A1.

❷ Press **[End]**. Notice the indicator END in the status line.

❸ Press **[↓]**. The worksheet scrolls to the last row in the worksheet. The cell pointer should be in cell A8192. See Figure 1-11.

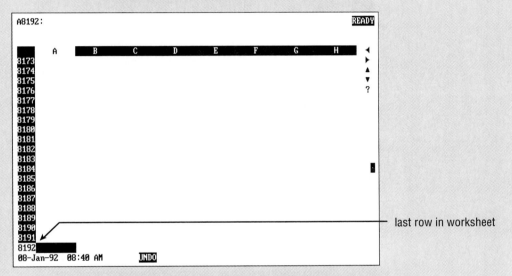

Figure 1-11
Using the [End] key

last row in worksheet

❹ Press **[End]** and then press **[→]** to move to the last column of the worksheet. The cell pointer should be in cell IV8192. See Figure 1-12.

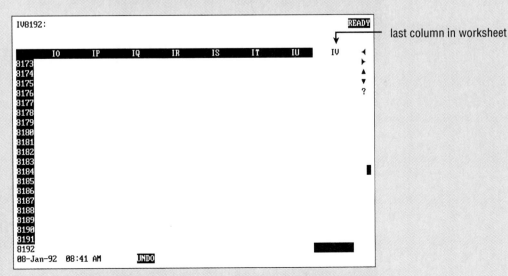

last column in worksheet

Figure 1-12
Using [End] to move
to the last column in
the worksheet

The [Home] key provides a quick way for you to return to the beginning of the worksheet.

⑤   Press **[Home]** to return to cell A1.

Moving the Cell Pointer Using the GoTo Key

The GoTo key, [F5], gives you a way to jump directly to any cell in the worksheet. When you press [F5], 1-2-3 prompts you for the new cell address. You enter a cell address, and 1-2-3 immediately moves the cell pointer to that location. Let's try it.

To move the cell pointer to cell D55 using the GoTo key:

①   With the cell pointer in cell A1, press **[F5]**. You are prompted for the cell location you want to move to. See Figure 1-13.

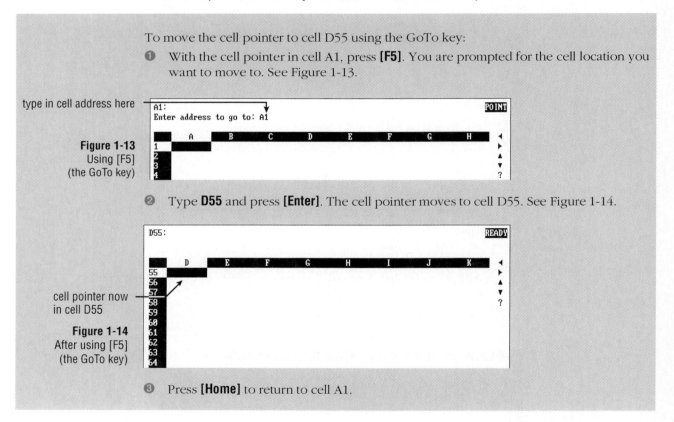

type in cell address here

Figure 1-13
Using [F5]
(the GoTo key)

②   Type **D55** and press **[Enter]**. The cell pointer moves to cell D55. See Figure 1-14.

cell pointer now
in cell D55

Figure 1-14
After using [F5]
(the GoTo key)

③   Press **[Home]** to return to cell A1.

Moving the Cell Pointer Using a Mouse

In 1-2-3 you can also use a mouse for many tasks, including moving the cell pointer. If your computer doesn't have a mouse, go to the next section.

You can tell that your mouse software is loaded if you see a small square block in the middle of your screen when you start 1-2-3 (Figure 1-15). This symbol is called the **mouse pointer**. If you don't see this block and you have a mouse, check with your instructor or technical support person. The mouse pointer moves on the screen exactly as you move the mouse around your desktop. For example, if you move the mouse to the right, the mouse pointer moves to the right.

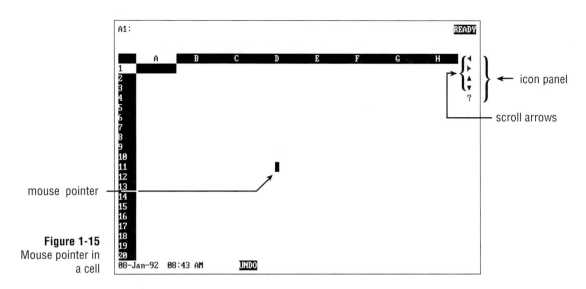

Figure 1-15
Mouse pointer in
a cell

Before you use a mouse, you should be familiar with the following terms: point, click, drag, icon, and icon panel.

Point means to position the mouse pointer on a specific object or area on the screen. You move the mouse in the direction you want the pointer to move.

Click means to press and immediately release the mouse button. Typically you select an object by pointing to that object on the screen and then clicking the mouse button. In most cases you click the left mouse button to select something and click the right mouse button to cancel your selection.

Drag means to press and hold down the left mouse button *while you move* the mouse pointer to another location and then to release the mouse button.

An **icon** is a symbol that represents an action. If a mouse is installed on your computer, five icons — four scroll arrows, facing up, down, left, and right, and a ? — appear on the right side of the screen in an **icon panel** (Figure 1-15). Clicking on one of the scroll arrows has the same effect as pressing one of the arrow keys on the keyboard. The cell pointer moves in the direction indicated by the scroll arrow. Clicking on the ? brings up the Help screen.

There are several ways you can use the mouse to move the cell pointer to another cell when 1-2-3 is in READY mode. The simplest way is to point to a cell on the screen and then click the left mouse button.

To move the cell pointer to cells on the screen:

❶ Move the mouse pointer to cell B5 and click the left mouse button. The cell pointer moves to cell B5.

❷ Move the mouse pointer to cell D10 and click the left mouse button. The cell pointer moves to cell D10.

Another way to use the mouse to move the cell pointer is to use the icons in the icon panel. Pointing to one of the triangles in the icon panel and clicking the left mouse button moves the cell pointer one cell in the direction the triangle points.

To move the cell pointer using the icon panel:

❶ With the cell pointer in cell D10, place the mouse pointer on the down scroll arrow. See Figure 1-16.

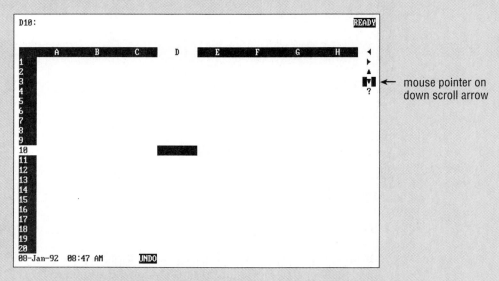

Figure 1-16
Using the icon panel
to move the cell
pointer

mouse pointer on
down scroll arrow

❷ Click the left mouse button. The cell pointer moves to cell D11.

❸ With the mouse pointer pointing to the down scroll arrow in the icon panel, click the left button again. The cell pointer moves to cell D12.

You can also move the cell pointer to a cell not currently displayed on the screen. As you have already learned, 1-2-3 has over two million cells, not all of which appear on the screen at the same time. If a cell does not appear on the screen, you cannot point to it. To move the cell pointer to a cell off the screen using a mouse, you use the icon panel.

To move the cell pointer to a cell off the screen:

❶ Place the mouse pointer on the down scroll arrow and hold down the left mouse button until the cell pointer is in cell D50. When the cell pointer reaches cell D50, release the left mouse button.

Most worksheets have initial instructions on the first screen. To get there quickly, you return to cell A1.

To move the cell pointer to cell A1:

❶ Place the mouse pointer in the small blank area above the first visible row and to the left of the first visible column. See Figure 1-17.

mouse pointer placed in the small blank area above first visible row

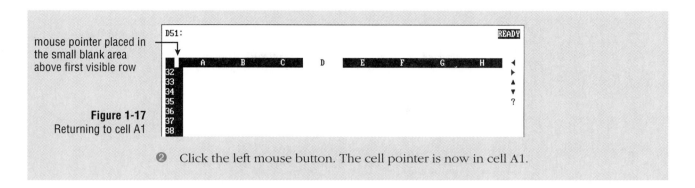

Figure 1-17
Returning to cell A1

❷   Click the left mouse button. The cell pointer is now in cell A1.

In this book we assume that you are using a keyboard to work with 1-2-3, but you should feel free to use a mouse if you have one.

Selecting Commands

To perform operations on the data in a worksheet, you issue commands. These **commands** enable you to accomplish various tasks such as copying, moving, printing, graphing, and saving a worksheet. The commands are displayed as a list of options, called a **menu**, from which you select the command you want to execute.

In 1-2-3 you access the main menu by pressing the slash key (/). Take a second now to locate the slash key in the lower right corner of your keyboard. Whenever you press the slash key, the 1-2-3 main menu appears in the control panel. When a menu is displayed in the control panel, the mode indicator changes to MENU, and the third line of the control panel describes the options for the highlighted command. Then you select a command from the menu to perform the task you desire.

There are two ways to select a command. You can type the first letter or character of the command, or you can press [→], [←], [Spacebar], [Home], or [End] to move the **menu pointer**, the rectangular highlight, to the command and then press [Enter] to select it. Selecting commands by highlighting takes a little more time, but it allows you to view more information about each highlighted command in the menu line. This is especially useful if you are unfamiliar with 1-2-3.

Let's practice using each of these methods for selecting commands by issuing a very common command in 1-2-3 — the command to retrieve a file. To retrieve a data file, you first specify which drive or directory contains the file. As you work through the next steps, remember that you can press [Esc] to back up one step if you make a mistake.

To specify the current data directory:
❶   Press **[/]** (Slash) to display the main menu. See Figure 1-18 on the following page. The Worksheet command is highlighted.

menu pointer→

options for Worksheet command

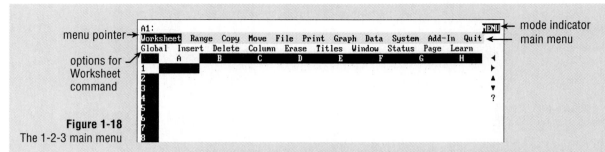

Figure 1-18
The 1-2-3 main menu

mode indicator
main menu

If you have a mouse, you can also display the main menu by moving the mouse pointer into the control panel.

❷ Press [→] four times to highlight File. As you do, notice how the menu line in the control panel changes.

❸ Press **[Enter]** to select File and display the File menu. See Figure 1-19. The Retrieve command is highlighted.

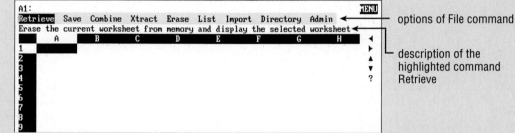

Figure 1-19
The File command menu

options of File command

description of the highlighted command Retrieve

❹ Notice on the menu that the next to last command is Directory. Type **d**, the first letter of Directory, to select it. A prompt then appears on the input line of the control panel asking you to provide specific information. See Figure 1-20.

If you have a mouse, you can also select menu commands and menu options by moving the mouse pointer to the command and clicking the left mouse button.

prompt to indicate where data diskette is located

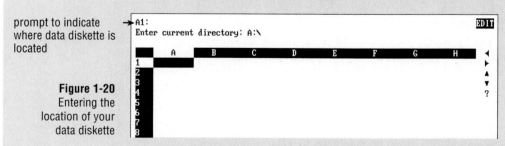

Figure 1-20
Entering the location of your data diskette

❺ If your data diskette is in drive A, type **A:** and press **[Enter]**. If the drive or directory name where you copied your data diskettes is different, type that drive and the directory name.

The prompt and the menu disappear, and the READY mode indicator appears in the upper right corner of your screen.

You are now ready to issue the File Retrieve command. This command lets you bring onto the screen worksheet files that are stored on your data diskette or on your hard disk so you can view and work with them.

To retrieve a file:

❶ Press **[/]** to display the main menu.

❷ Select File either by using the pointer-movement keys to highlight File and then pressing **[Enter]** or by pressing **F**.

❸ Select Retrieve (**R**).

A menu of worksheet filenames from the drive or directory you specified appears on the menu line of the control panel.

❹ The highlight is on the first file, C1TOUR1.WK1. To select it, press **[Enter]**.

The worksheet file C1TOUR1.WK1 appears on the screen (Figure 1-21). This worksheet contains a company's quarterly and year-to-date sales in five international cities. Let's now take a tour of this worksheet and view its data.

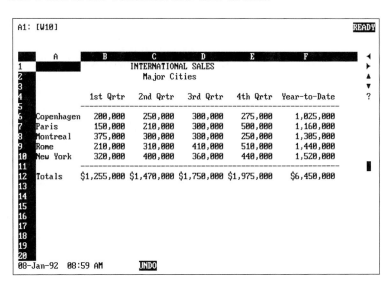

Figure 1-21
Worksheet for C1TOUR1

To view data in the worksheet:

❶ Press **[→]** and **[↓]** as needed to move the cell pointer to B6. Notice that the control panel displays the value contained in B6.

❷ Press **[↓]** until the cell pointer is in B12.

Notice that the control panel shows @SUM(B6..B10) as the contents of the current cell. @SUM is a special 1-2-3 function, or built-in formula, that performs calculations. In this case, @SUM adds the contents of cells B6 through B10 and displays the total in cell B12.

❸ Press **[Home]** to return to cell A1.

Entering Data in a Worksheet

You enter data in a worksheet by moving the cell pointer to a cell, typing the data, and pressing [Enter]. As you type, the mode indicator changes to LABEL or VALUE, depending on how 1-2-3 interprets what you type. In 1-2-3 words are called **labels**. Numbers and formulas are called **values**.

Let's practice entering some data. You will change the data of cell C10 from $400,000 to $350,000. You will then see how 1-2-3 updates the totals automatically. If you make any typing errors and have not yet pressed [Enter], use [Backspace] to erase characters to the left of the cursor. If you have already pressed [Enter], move the cell pointer to the cell with the error. Then retype the entry and press [Enter].

To enter data:

❶ Before you enter any new data, notice that the value in cell C12 is $1,470,000 and that the year-to-date total in cell F12 is $6,450,000.

❷ Move the cell pointer to cell C10.

❸ Type **350000** (four zeros but no comma).

Notice that 1-2-3 displays what you type in the control panel.

❹ Press **[Enter]** and watch how 1-2-3 recalculates all totals that depend on the new value, as shown in Figure 1-22.

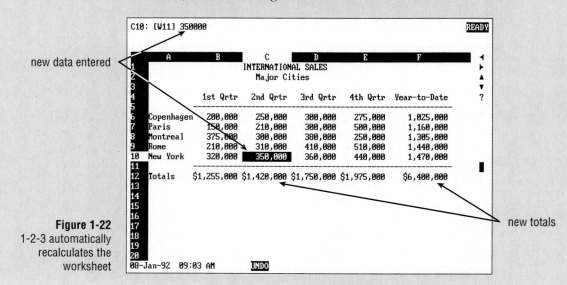

new data entered

new totals

Figure 1-22
1-2-3 automatically recalculates the worksheet

1-2-3 adjusts the first-quarter total in C12 to $1,420,000 and the year-to-date total in F12 to $6,400,000. If 1-2-3 does not adjust the totals on your worksheet, try pressing [F9] (CALC) to recalculate the totals.

1-2-3 Graphics

Whenever you use graphs or charts to present information, you are using **graphics**. Graphing or charting data in a worksheet helps you understand the relationships among the data and helps you analyze your results. Let's tour a few of the types of 1-2-3 graphics that you will learn how to create in the tutorials. To view these graphics, your computer system must have a graphics adapter, so check with your technical support person.

To view a graph of this worksheet's data:

❶ Select /Graph (**/G**) to view the Graph menu and a form called the **Graph Settings dialog box**. See Figure 1-23.

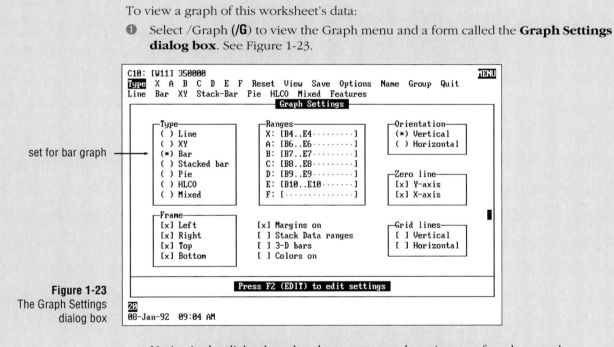

set for bar graph →

Figure 1-23
The Graph Settings
dialog box

Notice in the dialog box that the current graph settings are for a bar graph.

❷ Select View (**V**) to display the graph. See Figure 1-24 on the following page.

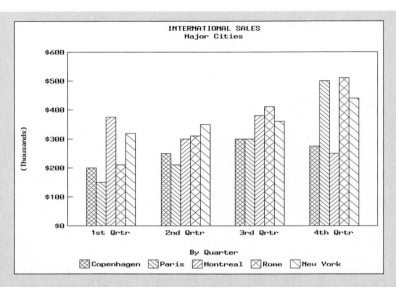

Figure 1-24
A bar graph of the
worksheet data

❸   Press **[Esc]** to return to the Graph menu and the Graph Settings dialog box.

Now let's see how easy it is to create a different type of graph using the same worksheet data.

To view a stacked bar graph of this worksheet's data:

❶   Select Type and then select Stack-Bar (**TS**).

❷   Select View (**V**) to display the new graph.

❸   When you are ready, press **[Esc]** to return to the Graph menu.

❹   Select Quit (**Q**) to quit the graph menu and return to the worksheet.

With 1-2-3 you can create several types of graphs, including bar graphs, pie charts, stacked bar graphs, and line graphs. You can add titles and legends to enhance the appearance and the readability of your graphs.

Using a 1-2-3 Database

A **database** is an organized collection of data. Examples of business databases are a list of customers and the status of their accounts; employee information, such as social security number, salary, and job title; and inventory information, such as stock numbers, quantity in stock, color, and so on. In a list of customers, for example, all the data about each customer are called a **record**, and each individual fact about each customer — name, account status, invoice number, and so on — is called a **field**. In 1-2-3 the columns correspond to the fields and the rows correspond to the records.

Suppose you wanted to create a list of customers who owe your company money, and you wanted to arrange them in order from those owing the most to those owing the least. 1-2-3 can perform several database tasks, such as sorting, to help you organize your data.

To sort a database:

❶ Select /File Retrieve (**/FR**).

When you attempt to retrieve another worksheet without first saving a worksheet that you have modified, the control panel displays the warning "WORKSHEET CHANGES NOT SAVED! Retrieve file anyway?" In this case we do not want to save the worksheet changes, so select Yes (**Y**). A list of worksheet filenames appears on the control panel.

❷ Highlight the filename C1TOUR2.WK1 and press **[Enter]**. Notice that this file contains a database of accounts receivable with paid and unpaid invoice amounts. See Figure 1-25.

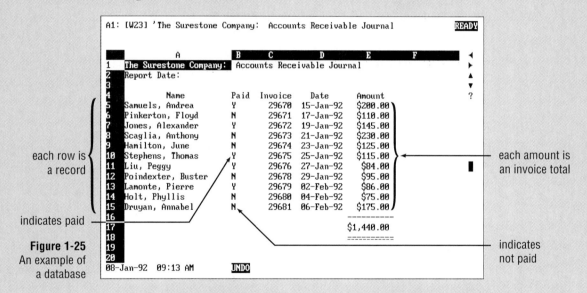

each row is a record

indicates paid

Figure 1-25
An example of a database

each amount is an invoice total

indicates not paid

Each record in this database (from row 5 through row 15) has a number in the Amount field (column E) that represents an invoice total. 1-2-3 can sort these records based on amounts to determine who owes the most money.

❸ Select /Data Sort (**/DS**).

1-2-3 displays a Sort Settings dialog box in which the sort instructions appear. In the Sort Settings dialog box, the primary key is the field 1-2-3 should use to sort the database. In our example, we want the primary-key field to be the Amount field, or column E, and the sort-order setting to be Descending, which instructs 1-2-3 to sort the amounts from the largest to the smallest value. See Figure 1-26 on the following page.

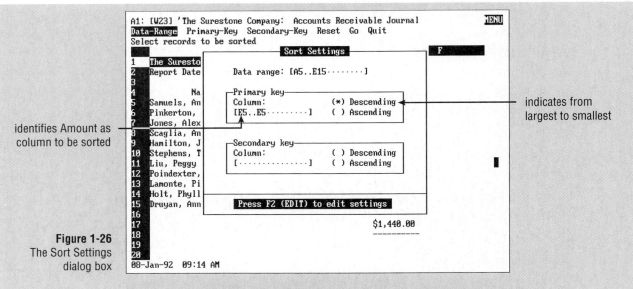

identifies Amount as column to be sorted

indicates from largest to smallest

Figure 1-26
The Sort Settings
dialog box

④   Select Go (**G**). See Figure 1-27.

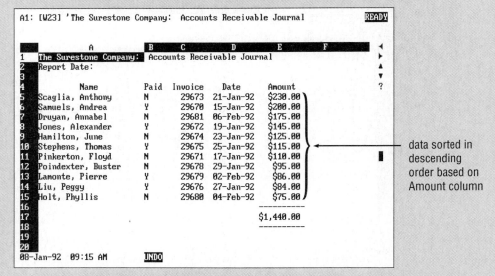

data sorted in descending order based on Amount column

Figure 1-27
Worksheet
after data are
sorted

Watch how quickly 1-2-3 sorts the database according to the invoice amounts in descending order, from largest to smallest. It saves you time and energy and can be a valuable decision-making tool.

Running a 1-2-3 Macro

With 1-2-3 you can create and store *sets* of commands and key strokes called **macro instructions** or **macros**. Macros automate repetitive 1-2-3 tasks, such as entering a date in your worksheet. Suppose, for example, that you must create a weekly report of all customers who have not paid invoices over $100. Once you have created a macro for this task, you can generate the report automatically each week by running the macro.

To run a macro:

❶ Press **[Alt][F3]** (RUN) to begin.

The names of several macros in this worksheet appear. See Figure 1-28.

names of macros →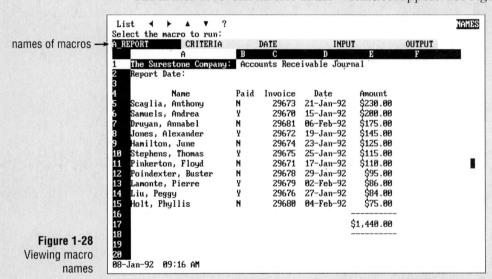

Figure 1-28
Viewing macro names

❷ Press **[→]** twice to move the menu pointer to DATE, then press **[Enter]**.

The DATE macro runs, automatically entering the date in cell D2 of your worksheet. Next let's generate the report.

❸ Press **[Alt][F3]** (RUN).

❹ Since A_REPORT is already highlighted, press **[Enter]** to run this macro.

The A_REPORT macro compares the amount of each unpaid invoice to a specified amount, in this case, $100. 1-2-3 then creates a list of the customers who owe more than $100. See Figure 1-29 on the following page.

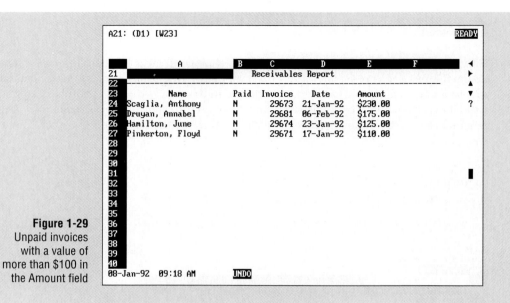

```
A21: (D1) [W23]                                                          READY

                  A              B    C        D          E        F      ◄
21                                     Receivables Report                 ►
22        ------------------------------------------------------------    ▲
23              Name            Paid  Invoice   Date      Amount          ▼
24     Scaglia, Anthony          N     29673  21-Jan-92   $230.00         ?
25     Druyan, Annabel           N     29681  06-Feb-92   $175.00
26     Hamilton, June            N     29674  23-Jan-92   $125.00
27     Pinkerton, Floyd          N     29671  17-Jan-92   $110.00
28
29
30
31                                                                         █
32
33
34
35
36
37
38
39
40
08-Jan-92   09:18 AM            UNDO
```

Figure 1-29
Unpaid invoices
with a value of
more than $100 in
the Amount field

Using On-line Help

If you have difficulty using a 1-2-3 command, you can press [F1] (HELP) at any time while you are using 1-2-3 to get helpful information on many topics. When a Help screen appears, the worksheet on which you are working temporarily disappears.

To use Help:

❶ Press **[F1]** (HELP).

  1-2-3 displays the 1-2-3 Main Help Index. See Figure 1-30.

  If you have a mouse, you can also display the 1-2-3 Main Help Index by clicking the left mouse button on the (?) (the Help icon) located in the top-right portion of your screen.

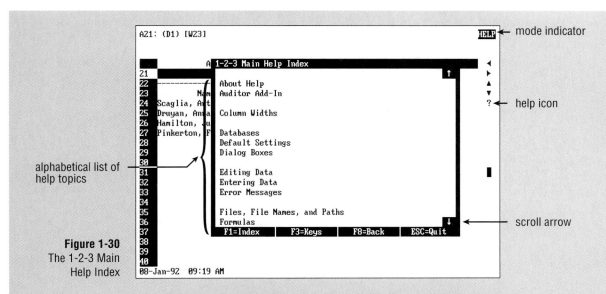

Figure 1-30
The 1-2-3 Main
Help Index

The Help index lists topics you might need help with. If you wanted to see additional help topics, you'd press [PgDn]. If you have a mouse, you can also click the left mouse button on the scroll arrow located in the bottom right corner of the Help window. To select any topic in the Help index, you'd highlight the topic in the index and press [Enter]. Let's try that now.

❷ Highlight the topic Error Messages and press **[Enter]**.

If you have a mouse, you can also click the left mouse button on the topic.

1-2-3 displays a Help screen about error messages. See Figure 1-31. You can use the pointer-movement keys to scroll through the information on error messages.

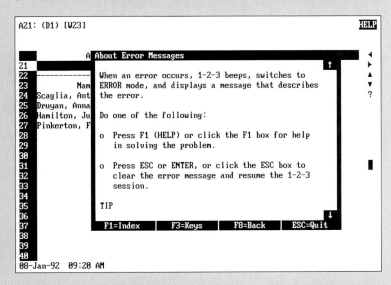

Figure 1-31
Help screen about
error messages

❸ When you are ready to return to the worksheet, press **[Esc]** to return to READY mode.

Quitting 1-2-3

You have completed the tour of 1-2-3. Now it's time to learn how to end, or quit, a 1-2-3 session.

To quit 1-2-3:

❶   Select /Quit Yes (**/QY**).

If you have entered data into the worksheet or changed the data, a prompt appears asking if you want to quit without saving your changes. If this happens, select Yes (**Y**) to quit without saving.

Exercises

1. How many rows are in a 1-2-3 worksheet? How many columns?

2. What keys move the cell pointer one key at a time?

3. How do you move the cell pointer to cell A1 from any other cell in the worksheet?

4. What key do you press to get Help?

5. How do you display the 1-2-3 main menu?

6. How do you exit 1-2-3 and return to DOS?

7. The cell pointer is in cell A1. If you press [PgDn], in what cell will the cell pointer be found?

8. How would you move the cell pointer one full screen to the right?

9. What is the difference between a cell and a cell pointer?

10. What is the cell address of a cell in column C and row 24?

11. Follow the steps on page L 27 to retrieve the file C1TOUR1.WK1. Do the following:
    a. Use the GoTo key to jump immediately to cell C10.
    b. Move to the last cell in the worksheet using the keystrokes that go immediately to that cell. What cell is the last cell in the worksheet?
    c. Return to cell A1 using the fewest number of keystrokes.
    d. Press **[End][↓]**. Where is the cell pointer located now?
    e. Press **[End][↓]** again. Where is the cell pointer located now?
    f. Press **[End][→]**. Where is the cell pointer located now?
    g. Press **[End][↑]**. Where is the cell pointer located now?
    h. Press **[End][←]**. Where is the cell pointer located now?

Setting Up Your Copy of 1-2-3

Default Directories

When you first install 1-2-3, Lotus 1-2-3 automatically stores and retrieves worksheet files from the same directory where the Lotus 1-2-3 programs are stored. This directory is called the **default directory**. Typically your 1-2-3 worksheet files are stored on a different directory or drive than the Lotus 1-2-3 software, so you should change the default drive to the drive/directory where you plan to save your worksheets.

To permanently change the default drive and directory:

❶ Select /Worksheet Global Default Directory (**/WGDD**). The Default Settings dialog box appears. Figure 1 shows that the current default directory is c:\123r24.

enter change here

current directory where 1-2-3 stores or retrieves files

Figure 1
Dialog box showing current default settings

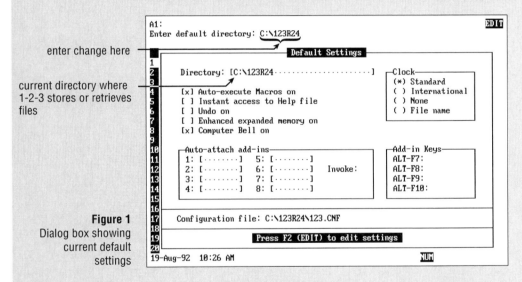

1-2-3 prompts you to enter the letter of the drive or the drive and directory from which you will load and save your worksheet files.

❷ Press **[Esc]** to erase the current directory setting.

Type the drive/directory where you will store your worksheets. Most likely this will be drive A if your worksheet files are stored on a diskette or a directory such as C:\123r23\data if your worksheet files are stored on your hard disk.

❸ If you will be storing your worksheet files on a diskette, place a diskette in drive A before you type **A:** and press **[Enter]**. See Figure 2 on the following page.

If you will be storing your worksheet files on a hard disk, type **C:\123r24\data** and press **[Enter]** or check with your technical support person for the name of the directory in which you will store your data files.

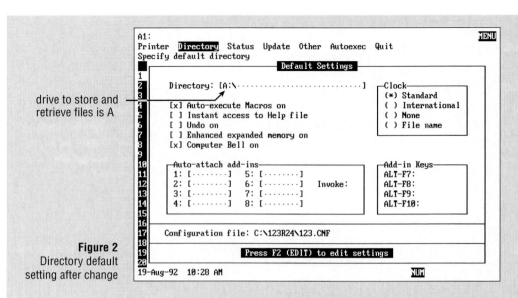

drive to store and retrieve files is A

Figure 2
Directory default setting after change

To change the default directory permanently, so each time you load Lotus 1-2-3, it looks to this new drive or directory:

④ Select Update (**U**).

⑤ To return to the worksheet, select Quit (**Q**).

Displaying Worksheet Filenames on the Worksheet Screen

The name of the worksheet file will appear in the lower left corner of each worksheet displayed beginning in Tutorial 2. If you want to set up your copy of Lotus 1-2-3 so that the name of the worksheet file appears in the lower left corner of your screen, then you need to change the default standard clock setting (date and time) to File name. If you don't change this setting, 1-2-3 displays the date and time in the lower left corner of your worksheet instead of the filename. You can work the tutorials with either the date and time or the filename displayed. It is a matter of personal preference.

To change the default setting so filenames are displayed on the screen:

① Select /Worksheet Global Default Other (**/WGDO**). See Figure 3. The dialog box indicates that the Standard clock setting (date and time) is the current setting.

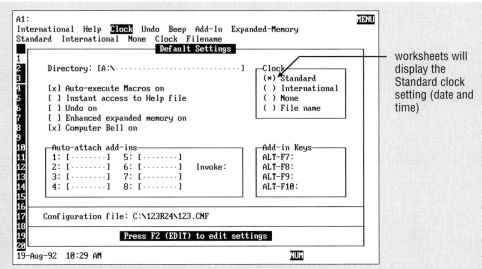

Figure 3
Current Clock
default setting

② Select Clock File name (**CF**) to change the settings to display the filename instead of the date and time. See Figure 4.

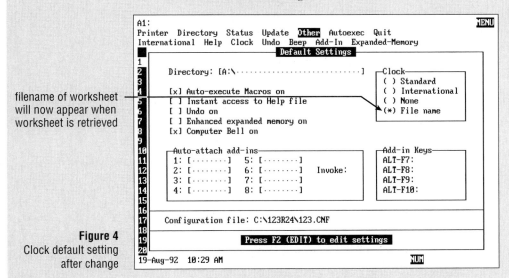

Figure 4
Clock default setting
after change

To save these settings permanently:

③ Select Update (**U**).

④ To return to the worksheet, select Quit (**Q**).

Enabling and Disabling Undo

The Undo feature is an important safeguard against time-consuming mistakes. You can use it whenever the UNDO indicator is displayed on the status line at the bottom of the worksheet screen.

Initially when Lotus 1-2-3 Release 2.4 is installed, the Undo feature is disabled. This means that pressing [Alt][F4] (UNDO) has no effect. To use the Undo feature, you must first turn it on, that is, *enable* it. You should use the following steps to enable Undo when you have no worksheet loaded, for example, immediately after you start 1-2-3.

To enable the Undo feature:

❶ Select /Worksheet Global Default Other (**/WGDO**).

❷ Select Undo Enable (**UE**). See Figure 5. The dialog box indicates Undo is on.

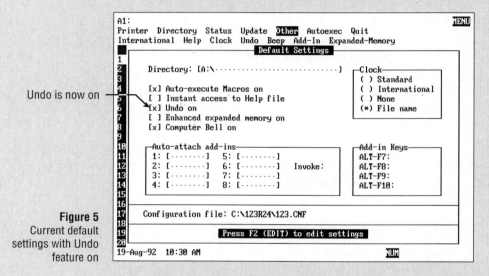

Undo is now on ————→

Figure 5
Current default
settings with Undo
feature on

You may want to save these settings permanently, in which case the Undo feature will automatically be enabled whenever you load 1-2-3.

❸ Select Update (**U**).

❹ To return to the worksheet, select Quit (**Q**).

The Undo feature requires that a portion of memory be reserved to store the previous version of the worksheet. Because of limited computer memory, there may be times when you will have to disable the Undo feature in order to perform other 1-2-3 functions. For example, this situation may occur when you are using a feature of Lotus 1-2-3 called WYSIWYG. If you see the message "out of memory" on your screen, disable the Undo feature.

To disable Undo:

❶ Select /Worksheet Global Default Other (**/WGDO**).

❷ Select Undo Disable (**UD**).

❸ To return to the worksheet, select Quit (**Q**).

Tutorial 2

Creating a Worksheet

Preparing a Simple Payroll

OBJECTIVES

In this tutorial you will learn to:

■ Retrieve and save files

■ Enter numbers, labels, and formulas

■ Correct mistakes and erase entries

■ Edit entries and use the UNDO key

■ Define a range

■ Print a worksheet

■ Erase a worksheet

Case: Krier Marine Services

Vince Diorio is an Information Systems major at the University of Rhode Island. To help pay for his tuition, he works part-time three days a week at a nearby marina, Krier Marine Services. Vince works in the Krier business office, and his responsibilities range from making coffee to keeping the company's books.

Recently Jim and Marcia Krier, the owners of the marina, asked Vince if he could help them computerize the payroll for their four part-time employees. They explained to Vince that the employees work a different number of hours each week for different rates of pay. Marcia does the payroll manually and finds it time consuming. Moreover, whenever she makes errors, she is embarrassed and annoyed at having to take additional time to correct them. Jim and Marcia hope that Vince can help them.

Vince immediately agrees to help. He tells the Kriers that he knows how to use Lotus 1-2-3 and that he can build a spreadsheet that will save Marcia time and reduce errors.

Vince does not begin working with the 1-2-3 software immediately. He knows that effective worksheets are well planned and carefully designed. So he sits down and follows a process he learned in his courses at school.

Planning the Worksheet

Planning the worksheet first is a good habit to establish. If you plan first, your worksheet will be clear, accurate, and useful. Your plan will guide you as you try to solve business problems using 1-2-3.

You can divide your planning into four phases:

- defining the problem
- designing the worksheet
- building the worksheet
- testing the worksheet

Defining the Problem

Begin by outlining what you want to accomplish. Take a piece of paper and a pencil and do the following:

1. List your goal(s).

2. Identify and list the results you want to see in the worksheet. This information is often called *output*.

3. Identify and write down the information you want to put into the worksheet. This information is often called *input*.

4. Determine and list the calculations that will produce the results you desire. These calculations become the *formulas* you will use in the worksheet.

When you finish, you will have completed the first phase of planning. You will have defined the problem and be ready to design the worksheet. Figure 2-1a shows how Vince defined the Krier payroll problem.

My Goal(s):
   Develop a worksheet that calculates the
   Krier Marine Services payroll.

What results do I want to see?
   Weekly Payroll Report

What information do I need?
   Employee name
   Number of hours each employee worked
    during the week
   Employee's rate of pay per hour

What calculations will I perform?
   Gross pay for each employee

Figure 2-1a
Vince's planning
sheet

Designing the Worksheet

Next, on a piece of paper sketch what you think the worksheet should look like. Include titles, row and column headings, totals, and other items of the worksheet. Figure 2-1b shows Vince's sketch.

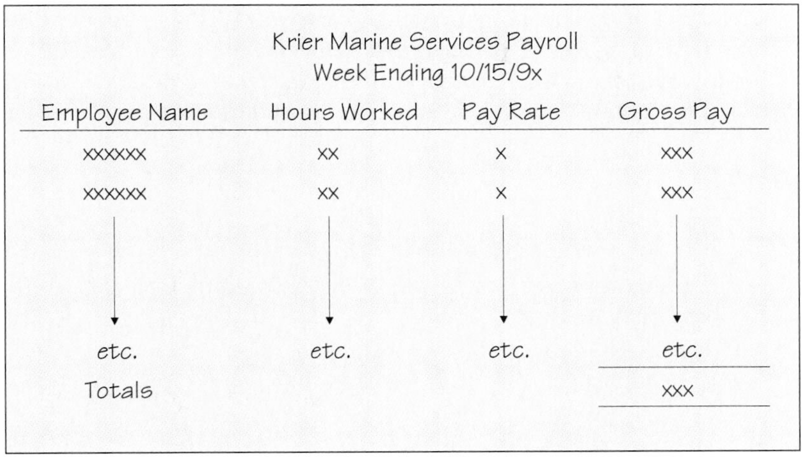

Figure 2-1b
Vince's sketch

Building the Worksheet

After you have defined the problem and sketched the worksheet, you are ready to type your worksheet design into 1-2-3. You enter titles, labels, formulas, input, and other items you listed and sketched when you defined your goal(s) and designed the worksheet.

Testing the Worksheet

After you have built a new worksheet, you should test it before you start to use it. If possible, develop some sample data, also known as test data, and manually calculate the results. Then put the same test data into your 1-2-3 worksheet. Are the results the same? If you discover any differences, you should find the reason(s) and correct any errors in the worksheet.

After completing this fourth phase, you are ready to begin using the worksheet.

■   ■   ■

In Tutorial 2 you will use Vince's problem definition and sketch (Figures 2-1a and 2-1b) as a guide when you build the worksheet for the Krier Marine Services payroll. You will create the worksheet that Vince developed for the Kriers. First you will retrieve a partially completed worksheet, which will serve as your starting point. Next you will enter the payroll data, employee names, hours worked, and rates of pay. Then you will enter formulas to calculate total gross pay for each employee. Finally you will calculate the gross pay for all employees. When the worksheet is complete, you will learn how to print and save it.

Retrieving the Worksheet

Vince Diorio has started working on the spreadsheet for Krier Marine Services. His work-sheet is stored as a file on the Lotus 1-2-3 Data Disk. This file is named C2KRIER1. To use this file, you will retrieve it, that is, read the file into computer memory. Let's retrieve C2KRIER1 now. The file from which you work will either be on a diskette copy of the Sample Files Disk or be a copy of C2KRIER1 that you put on your hard disk. If you want to start over for any reason, such as to recover from a mistake, retrieve C2KRIER1.WK1 again and repeat the steps. You will learn how to correct mistakes as you work through this tutorial.

To retrieve a 1-2-3 worksheet file:

❶ If your data are on a diskette, insert the diskette into drive A. If your data are on the hard disk, go to Step 2.

❷ Start 1-2-3 as you learned in Tutorial 1.

❸ Press **/** (Slash) to activate the 1-2-3 main menu, which shows a list of commands you may choose. See Figure 2-2.

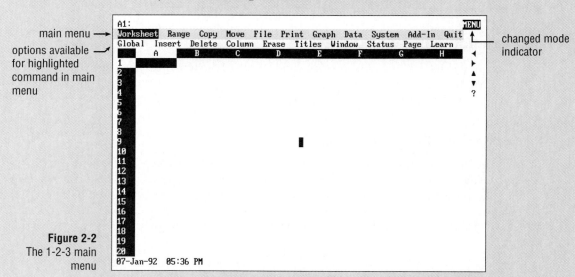

Figure 2-2
The 1-2-3 main menu

The mode indicator in the upper right corner has changed from READY to MENU, and the 1-2-3 main menu appears on the second line of the control panel. This line lists the main actions or commands from which you may select. The third line of the control panel lists the commands available if you select the command currently highlighted in the second line. As you highlight different commands by moving the menu pointer across the menu, a new menu appears as each command is high-lighted.

There are two ways to select a command from the command line:

• You can highlight a menu choice by pressing [→] or [←] to move the menu pointer to the command you want and press [Enter].

- You can type the first character of the command you wish to select. For example, to select File you type F.

④ Select File (**F**). The choices available from the 1-2-3 main menu now appear on the second line of the control panel. See Figure 2-3.

description of the
Retrieve command

Figure 2-3
The control panel

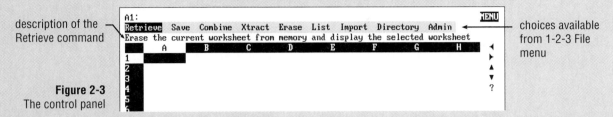

choices available
from 1-2-3 File
menu

⑤ Select Retrieve (**R**) to display the names of the first five worksheet files in the control panel. The files are listed in alphabetical order. The top of your screen should look similar to Figure 2-4.

the drive where
1-2-3 is looking for
files (may be
different on your
system)

Figure 2-4
Retrieving a
worksheet file

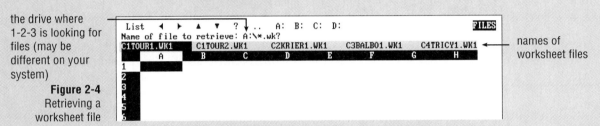

names of
worksheet files

If the filenames do not appear, press [Esc] to return to READY mode. Lotus 1-2-3 may not know where your data are stored. See page L 37 of Tutorial 1 for assistance. If you accidentally press the wrong key and select the wrong command from the menu, you can return to the previous step by pressing the [Esc] key. If you continue to press [Esc], you back up a step at a time until you return to READY mode. You can also press [Ctrl] [Break] to immediately return to READY mode.

If the worksheet filename that you are looking for appears in the control panel, highlight the name and press [Enter]. However, if you don't see the filename on the control panel, you can do one of the following:

- Press [→], [Spacebar], or [←] until you highlight the worksheet filename you desire. Then press [Enter].
- Type the filename of the worksheet file you desire.
- Press [F3] (NAME). 1-2-3 displays a full-screen list of the worksheet files located on the current drive and directory. Select the desired worksheet file by highlighting it, then press [Enter].

⑥ Using the [→] or [←] key, highlight the worksheet file C2KRIER1.WK1. Then press **[Enter]**. 1-2-3 retrieves the file you selected. See Figure 2-5 on the following page.

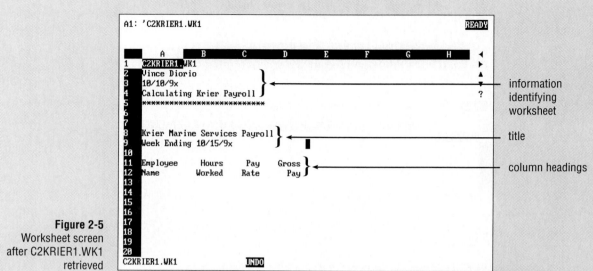

Figure 2-5
Worksheet screen
after C2KRIER1.WK1
retrieved

Your worksheet screen may display the date and time in the lower left corner of the screen instead of the current worksheet filename. You can change your Lotus 1-2-3 setup so the filename appears on the screen. See pages L 38 and L 39 of Tutorial 1 for assistance. Although the worksheet screens in this text display the worksheet filenames, displaying the date and time instead will not affect your worksheet. Whether you display filenames or the date and time is a matter of personal preference.

The worksheet file you retrieved contains the beginning of the worksheet that Vince plans to use in developing the payroll worksheet. Currently the worksheet consists of a title and descriptive column headings. These headings represent the data he will enter or calculate.

You no doubt have noticed that beginning in cell A1 there are four lines of identifying information:

- the name of the worksheet file
- the name of the person who developed the worksheet
- the date the worksheet was created or last modified
- a description of the worksheet.

You should include such a section of identifying information in *every* worksheet you develop, to remind you about what the worksheet contains.

To help you understand what occurs when you retrieve a worksheet file, look at Figure 2-6. When you select File Retrieve and then select the worksheet file C2KRIER1.WK1, 1-2-3 copies the worksheet file from the disk to the computer's memory. C2KRIER1.WK1 is, therefore, in both the computer memory and disk storage.

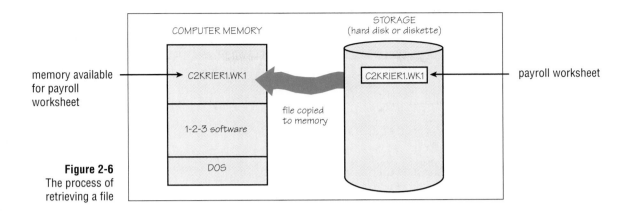

Figure 2-6
The process of
retrieving a file

Entering Labels

Most of the data you enter into a worksheet will be descriptive text, numbers, or formulas. To enter data into a worksheet, you move the cell pointer to the cell where you want the data to appear. You then type the data and press the [Enter] key. 1-2-3 stores what you typed in the cell.

1-2-3 categorizes all entries you type in a cell as either labels or values. **Labels** are descriptive text such as column headings or textual data. If the first character you type is a letter, 1-2-3 assumes you are entering a label in that cell. Also, if you begin typing with one of the four special characters ' ″ ^ \, called **label prefixes**, 1-2-3 will store any characters that follow as a label. As soon as you begin entering a letter or a label prefix, you'll notice that the mode indicator, in the upper right corner of your screen, changes from READY to LABEL.

If you want to enter text that begins with a number, such as the street address *100 Fairgrounds Road*, you must type a label prefix before the street address so that 1-2-3 knows you want this entry treated as a label even though it begins with a number. The most common label prefix is the apostrophe. In other words, you would type *'100 Fairgrounds Road* instead of *100 Fairgrounds Road*, and 1-2-3 would treat this entry as a label. The label prefix does not appear in the cell, but it does appear in the control panel when the cell pointer is in that cell.

If you forget to type the label prefix when entering text that begins with a number, 1-2-3 will beep. You should then press [Esc] to cancel the entry and return to READY mode.

The next step in developing Vince's worksheet is to enter the names of the Krier part-time employees. These entries are labels.

To enter an employee name:

❶ Press [↓] to move the cell pointer to cell A14.

❷ Type **Bramble**. Before you press [Enter], look at the top left of the screen. See Figure 2-7 on the following page.

Bramble appears in
control panel but
not yet in cell A14

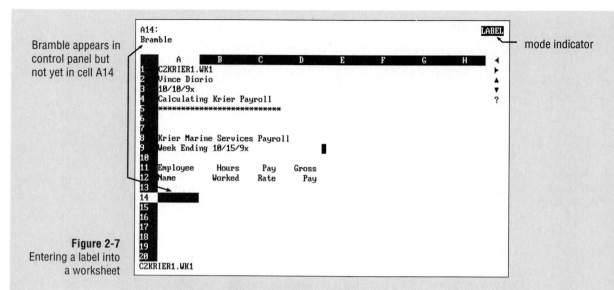

mode indicator

Figure 2-7
Entering a label into
a worksheet

Notice that Bramble appears in the control panel but not in cell A14. Also notice that the mode indicator in the upper right corner of your screen has changed from READY to LABEL mode. This is because when you typed the letter B, 1-2-3 recognized it as a label.

❸   Press **[Enter]**. Bramble now appears in cell A14. See Figure 2-8.

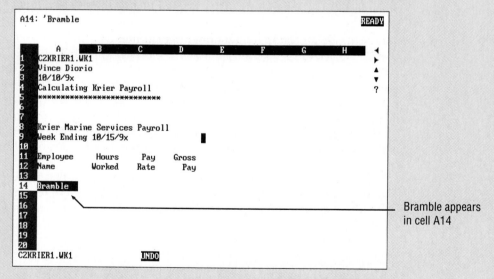

Bramble appears
in cell A14

Figure 2-8
Name of employee
appears in cell

When you press the [Enter] key, the cell pointer remains in cell A14.

To enter the name of the second employee:

❹   Press **[↓]** once to move the cell pointer to cell A15.

❺   Type **Juarez** and then press **[Enter]**.

To enter the third employee:

❻   Press **[↓]** once to move the cell pointer to cell A16.

⑦ Type **Smith** and then press **[Enter]**.

To enter the fourth employee:

⑧ Press **[↓]** once to move the cell pointer to cell A17.

⑨ Type **Diorio** and then press **[Enter]**.

The names of the four employees should now appear on your worksheet. See Figure 2-9.

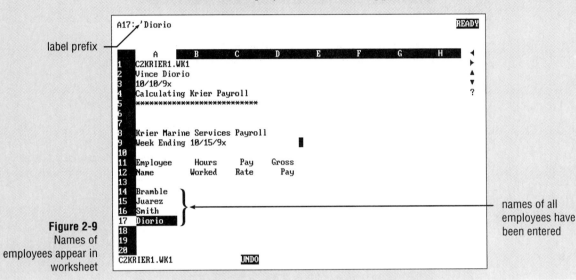

label prefix

names of all employees have been entered

Figure 2-9
Names of employees appear in worksheet

When the cell pointer is in a cell that contains a label, the control panel displays the cell address, an apostrophe, and the label you entered. See Figure 2-9. The apostrophe before the label is the label prefix. 1-2-3 automatically enters a label prefix whenever you enter labels in a worksheet.

Correcting Errors

The following steps show you two of the many ways to correct errors you make when you are entering text or numbers.

To correct errors as you are typing:

① Move the cell pointer to A16 and type **Smiht** but do not press [Enter]. Clearly this label is misspelled. Since you haven't pressed [Enter], you can use [Backspace] to correct the error. On most keyboards, this key is above the [Enter] key.

② Press **[Backspace]** twice to erase the last two characters you typed.

③ Type the correct text — **th** — and press **[Enter]**.

If you notice an error *after* the text or value appears in the cell, you can correct the error by retyping the entry.

To correct errors in a cell:

❶ Be sure the cell pointer is in cell A16 and type **Smiht**. Press **[Enter]**. Smiht appears in cell A16. See Figure 2-10.

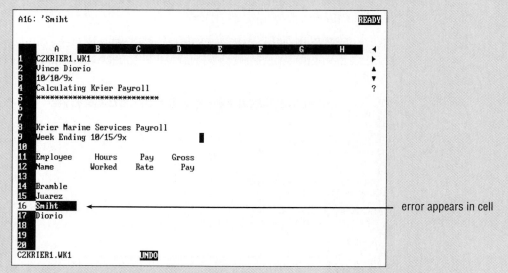

```
A16: 'Smiht                                                    READY

        A         B        C        D        E        F        G        H      ◄
1  C2KRIER1.WK1                                                                 ►
2  Vince Diorio                                                                 ▲
3  10/10/9x                                                                     ▼
4  Calculating Krier Payroll                                                    ?
5  *******************************
6
7
8  Krier Marine Services Payroll
9  Week Ending 10/15/9x                ▌
10
11 Employee      Hours     Pay    Gross
12 Name          Worked    Rate    Pay
13
14 Bramble
15 Juarez
16 Smiht         ◄─────────────────────────────────────────────────  error appears in cell
17 Diorio
18
19
20
C2KRIER1.WK1                  UNDO
```

Figure 2-10
Correcting errors in
a cell

❷ Type **Smith** in cell A16 and press **[Enter]**. As you can see, 1-2-3 enters the new text over the old. This is commonly called *typing over*.

Entering Values

A value in 1-2-3 can be a number or a formula. 1-2-3 interprets an entry in a cell as a **value** if the first character you type is a number (0 through 9) or one of the special characters + – @ . (# $. As soon as you begin entering a number or one of these special characters, you'll notice that the mode indicator changes from READY to VALUE.

When you are entering numbers, keep the following points in mind:

- Numbers cannot contain spaces or commas.
- A number cannot have more than one decimal point.
- Numbers are always right-justified when displayed in cells.
- If you type a plus sign (+) before a number or enter a number in parentheses, the + and the ( ) will not appear in the cell.
- If you enter a number with a percent sign (%), 1-2-3 will automatically divide the number preceding the sign by 100.

Next, enter the hours worked by each employee at Krier Marine Services.

To enter the hours worked:

❶ Move the cell pointer to cell B14, the location of Bramble's hours worked.

Bramble worked 15 hours.

❷ Type **15** and press **[Enter]**. Do not include any symbols or punctuation, such as a comma, when entering values.

❸ Press **[↓]** once to move the cell pointer to cell B15, the location of Juarez's hours worked.

Juarez worked 28 hours.

❹ Type **28** and press **[Enter]**.

❺ Press **[↓]** once to move the cell pointer to cell B16, the location of Smith's hours worked.

Smith worked 40 hours.

❻ Type **40** and press **[Enter]**.

❼ Press **[↓]** to move the cell pointer to cell B17, the location of Diorio's hours worked.

Diorio worked 22 hours.

❽ Type **22** and press **[Enter]**. Your screen should look like Figure 2-11.

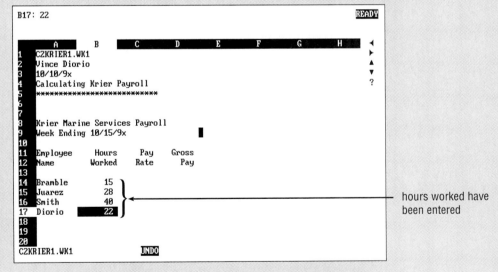

Figure 2-11
Hours worked entered into worksheet

hours worked have been entered

There is another, faster way to enter data. You can enter data in a cell and move the cell pointer to a cell on any side of that cell in one step by pressing a pointer-movement key instead of [Enter]. The **pointer-movement keys** are the directional keys, such as [→], [←], [↑], [↓], [PgDn], and [PgUp], that you press to move the pointer in the worksheet. To learn how to do this, let's enter the hourly pay rates for each employee.

To enter hourly pay rates using pointer-movement keys:

❶   Move the cell pointer to C14, the location of Bramble's pay rate.

Bramble earns $7 an hour.

❷   Type **7** and press [↓] instead of the [Enter] key. Notice that you entered the value in cell C14 and moved the cell pointer to cell C15, the cell immediately below C14. C15 is the location of Juarez's pay rate.

Juarez earns $5 an hour.

❸   With the cell pointer in C15, type **5** and press [↓].

Smith earns $7 an hour.

❹   In cell C16 type **7** and press [↓].

Diorio earns $5 an hour.

❺   In cell C17 type **5** and press **[Enter]**. You have now entered all the data. Your worksheet should be similar to Figure 2-12.

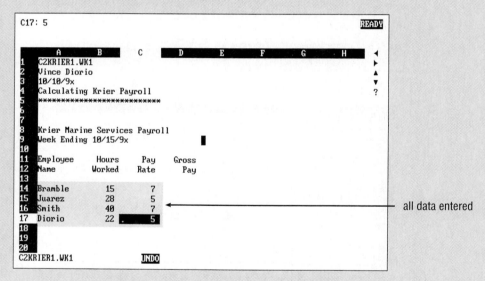

all data entered

Figure 2-12
Pay rates entered
into worksheet

Saving a Worksheet

When you create or modify a worksheet, it is only temporarily stored in the computer's memory. To store your work permanently, you must save the worksheet to your hard disk or data diskette. It is always a good idea to save frequently as you work, rather than to wait until you've finished. Suppose the power goes out or you step away from your computer and someone starts working with another file. Unless you have been saving as you go along, all of your work could be lost.

Next we'll save all the entries you have made so far to a new file named S2KRIER1.WK1. Before you save the file, you should change cell A1 to S2KRIER1.WK1 so the identifying information in the worksheet will be consistent with the new filename.

To change the filename in cell A1 and then save the file:

❶ Press **[Home]** to move the cell pointer to cell A1.

❷ Type **S2KRIER1.WK1** and press **[Enter]**.

❸ Select /File Save (**/FS**). Notice that the mode indicator in the upper right corner changes to EDIT. See Figure 2-13.

1-2-3 prompts you for a filename in the control panel. It also shows the current filename, and the drive from which you retrieved the file.

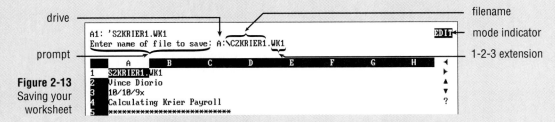

Figure 2-13 Saving your worksheet

❹ Type **S2KRIER1**. Notice that you do not have to erase the current filename.

In 1-2-3 all filenames must consist of not more than eight characters. You can use uppercase or lowercase letters, numbers, and the special characters $ & % ( ) { } – _ to create a filename. 1-2-3 converts any lowercase letters to uppercase letters once you press [Enter]. You cannot use spaces in a filename.

❺ Press **[Enter]** to save the file in the drive and the directory you specified. 1-2-3 will automatically add the file extension .WK1 to the filename.

Figure 2-14 shows the process that occurs when you select File Save and type S2KRIER1. 1-2-3 copies the worksheet file from the computer's memory to your disk storage.

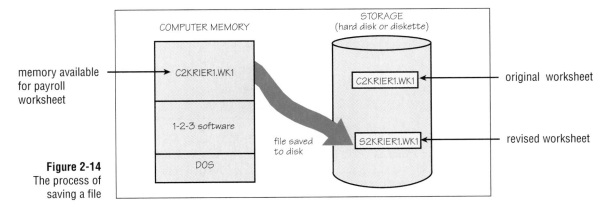

Figure 2-14 The process of saving a file

You have now saved your worksheet, including all the employee data you entered.

Worksheet Filenames in the Lotus 1-2-3 Tutorials

Besides saving frequently, another good habit to follow is to use descriptive names that will help you identify the contents of your files. Worksheet filenames can contain up to eight characters. These characters can be letters, numbers, and all symbols except for spaces, commas, colons, and asterisks. Although eight characters do not often allow you to create complete names, you can create meaningful abbreviations. For example, the Data Disk for Lotus 1-2-3 contains over 50 files. To name these files so that you can recognize their contents, we categorized them as follows:

File Category	Description
Tutorial Case	The files you use to work through each tutorial
Tutorial Assignment	The files that contain the worksheets you need to complete the Tutorial Assignments at the end of each tutorial
Case Problem	The files that contain the worksheets you need to complete the Case Problems at the end of each tutorial or the Additional Cases in Part 3
Saved Worksheet	Any worksheet that you have saved
Module Case	The files you use to work through each module
Exercise Assignments	The files you use to complete the Exercises at the end of each tutorial
Reference Assignments	The files you use to complete the Reference Assignments
WYSIWYG Solutions	All saved worksheets with WYSIWYG enhancements

We used these categories to help name the worksheet files on your data diskette. Let's take the filename C2KRIER1, for example. This name may appear to have no meaning, but it does contain meaningful abbreviations. The first character of every worksheet filename on your data diskette identifies the file as one of the eight file categories discussed above. Thus,

If the first character is:	the file category is:
C	Tutorial **C**ase
T	**T**utorial Assignment
P	Case **P**roblem
S	**S**aved Worksheet
M	**M**odule Case
E	**E**xercise Assignment
R	**R**eference Assignment
W	**W**YSIWYG Solution

Based on these categories, we know that the file C2KRIER1 is a Tutorial Case file.

The second character of every worksheet file identifies the tutorial from which the file comes. Thus, C2KRIER1 is a Tutorial Case from Tutorial 2. The remaining six characters of the filename identify the specific file. All worksheets in tutorials are assigned a name, and the number that follows the name indicates a version number. Thus, C2KRIER1 is the first Tutorial Case worksheet from Tutorial 2. T2KRIER1 is the first worksheet found in the Tutorial Assignments from Tutorial

2, while T2KRIER2 is a second version of that worksheet. As another example, P2TOYS is the filename of the Case Problem "Sales in Toyland" from Tutorial 2.

Using Formulas

In addition to labels and values, you can enter formulas in cells. A formula is an entry in a worksheet that performs a calculation. A **formula** is a mathematical expression that can include numeric constants, cell addresses, arithmetic operators, and parentheses. An **arithmetic operator** indicates the desired arithmetic operation. The arithmetic operators, used in Lotus 1-2-3 are as follows:

Arithmetic Operation	Arithmetic Operator Used in Lotus	Example	Description
Addition	+	10+A15	Add 10 to the value in cell A15 from 10.
Subtraction	–	10–A15	Subtract the value in cell A15.
Multiplication	*	10*A15	Multiply 10 by the value in cell A15.
Division	/	10/A15	Divide 10 by the value in A15.
Exponentiation	^	10^A15	Raise 10 to the value stored in A15.

Using formulas is one way to tap into the power of a spreadsheet like 1-2-3. Once you have entered a formula, 1-2-3 will perform the calculations and make the necessary changes to your data. You will get the new results immediately and with little effort.

Rules of Arithmetic Precedence

The computer performs arithmetic on only one operation at a time. Thus, if a formula contains two or more arithmetic operators, for example 1+.05*1000, the computer performs the operations in a particular sequence, based on the following hierarchy:

Arithmetic Hierarchy	Arithmetic Operation
Calculated first	Exponentiation
Calculated second	Multiplication and division
Calculated third	Addition and subtraction

The sequence in which arithmetic operators are performed is called the **order of precedence.** Exponentiation (raising a number to a power) is performed before all other arithmetic operations; in other words, exponentiation is given precedence over all other operations. Multiplication and division are performed before addition and subtraction.

For example, consider the expression 1+.05*1000. The calculations are performed in the following order:

- First, .05 is multiplied by 1000, since multiplication takes precedence over addition.
- Second, the result of step 1, 50, is added to 1, giving the final result, 51.

Left-to-right Rule

If a formula contains two or more arithmetic operators that have equal precedence, then operations with the same precedence are calculated in order from left to right. For example, in the expression 1+1005–1000 the calculations are performed in the following order:

- First, 1 is added to 1005, since the addition operation appears before the subtraction operation, with which it has equal precedence.
- Second, 1000 is subtracted from the result of step 1, 1006, giving the final result, 6.

Use of Parentheses

Sometimes you want the arithmetic operations to be performed in an order different from that determined by the precedence rules. In those cases you can use parentheses to change the order in which the calculations are performed. Operations inside parentheses are calculated before operations not in parentheses.

For example, suppose you want to calculate the average daily sales of two stores. The first store had sales of $1000, and the second store had sales of $2000; the average sales of the two stores is $1500. If you enter the formula 1000+2000/2, 1-2-3 will give you an incorrect answer, because this formula would be calculated as follows:

- First, 2000 is divided by 2, since division is performed before addition.
- Second, 1000 is added to the result of step 1, 1000. This gives the result of 2000, not the 1500 you expected.

But if you use parentheses in the formula, such as (1000+2000)/2, you can ensure that 1-2-3 will give you the correct result. This formula is calculated as follows:

- First, 1000 is added to 2000, since operations in parentheses are evaluated before operations outside parentheses.
- Second, the result of step 1, 3000, is divided by 2, giving the result 1500.

Entering Formulas

Now that you know how to use formulas, you are ready to calculate the gross pay for each employee. Gross pay is the number of hours worked multiplied by the rate of pay (hours worked × rate of pay). You do not need to do the multiplication yourself; you enter a formula, such as +B14*C14, that tells 1-2-3 which cells to multiply. 1-2-3 performs the calculations immediately and displays the results in the cell that contains the formula. The following steps show you one way to enter a formula.

To enter a formula to compute Bramble's gross pay:
① Move the cell pointer to cell D14, the location of Bramble's gross pay.

❷ Type **+B14*C14**. When the first element in a formula is a cell address, you must begin
the formula with + or –; otherwise, 1-2-3 interprets what you type as a label and
not a formula.

Notice that the formula appears in the control panel as you type and that 1-2-3 is
now in VALUE mode. See Figure 2-15. Remember, if you make a mistake, you can
use [Backspace] if you are still entering the formula, or you can retype the formula
if you have pressed [Enter].

formula to calculate
Bramble's gross pay

mode has
changed

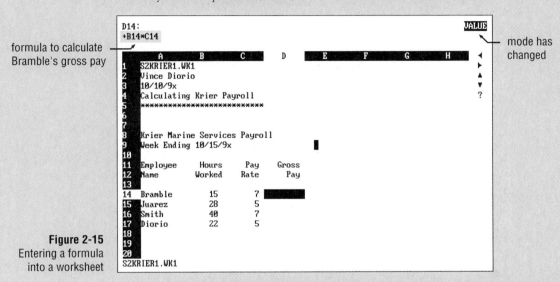

Figure 2-15
Entering a formula
into a worksheet

❸ Press **[Enter]**. 1-2-3 calculates the formula's value, 105, and the result appears in cell
D14. If you get a different result, check the formula or the data values in B14 and
C14. Retype, if you find any errors. See Figure 2-16.

formula appears in
control panel

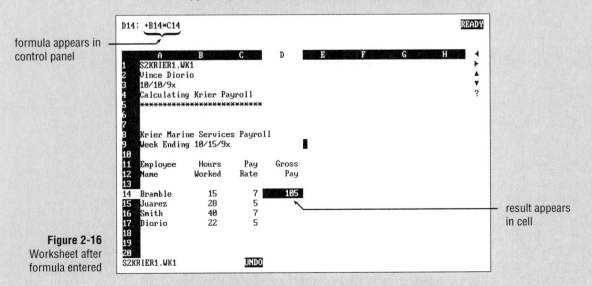

result appears
in cell

Figure 2-16
Worksheet after
formula entered

Now enter the formula in cell D15 to calculate Juarez's gross pay.

④ Move the cell pointer to cell D15. Type **+B15*C15** and press **[Enter]**. The result, 140, appears in cell D15.

Now enter the formula in cell D16 to calculate Smith's gross pay.

⑤ Move the cell pointer to cell D16, type **+B16*C16**, and press **[Enter]**. The gross pay for Smith is 280, which appears in cell D16.

Finally, enter the formula in cell D17 to calculate Diorio's gross pay.

⑥ Move the cell pointer to cell D17, type **+B17*C17**, and press **[Enter]**. Diorio's pay is 110, which appears in cell D17.

Figure 2-17 shows the gross pay calculated for all the employees.

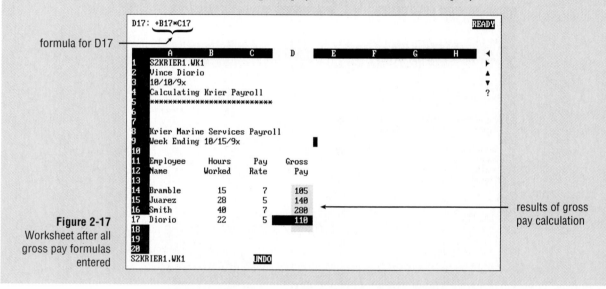

formula for D17

Figure 2-17
Worksheet after all
gross pay formulas
entered

results of gross
pay calculation

Calculating a Sum

Now let's calculate the total gross pay for all employees by adding the gross pay of Bramble, Juarez, Smith, and Diorio, that is, adding the values of cells D14, D15, D16, and D17.

To calculate a sum:

① Move the cell pointer to cell A19. Type the label **Total** and press **[Enter]**.

② Move the cell pointer to cell D19. This is the cell in which we want to put the total gross pay.

The correct formula to calculate gross pay is +D14+D15+D16+D17. But for now, let's intentionally enter an incorrect formula.

③ Type **+D14+D15+C17+D17** and press **[Enter]**. 1-2-3 calculates a total using this formula, and 360 appears in cell D19. See Figure 2-18.

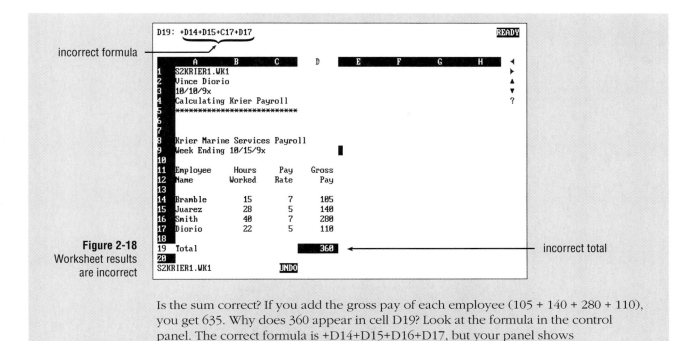

Figure 2-18
Worksheet results
are incorrect

Is the sum correct? If you add the gross pay of each employee (105 + 140 + 280 + 110), you get 635. Why does 360 appear in cell D19? Look at the formula in the control panel. The correct formula is +D14+D15+D16+D17, but your panel shows +D14+D15+C17+D17.

We made this error intentionally to demonstrate that you always run the risk of making errors when you create a worksheet. Be sure to check your entries and formulas. In this case, you would add the results manually and compare them to the value in the worksheet.

Editing Entries in a Cell

If you notice an error in your worksheet, you have already learned that you can move the cell pointer to the cell with the error and retype the entry that contains the error. You can also use EDIT mode to correct the problem. EDIT mode is sometimes faster and easier to use, because you change only the incorrect characters and leave the rest of the entry intact. In 1-2-3 you use [F2] (EDIT) to edit an entry. In the following steps, you'll edit cell D19, which contains the incorrect formula for total gross pay.

To edit the contents of a cell:

❶ Be sure the cell pointer is in cell D19.

❷ Press **[F2]** (EDIT). The formula +D14+D15+C17+D17 appears in the second line of the control panel. The cursor appears at the end of the entry, and you are ready for editing. See Figure 2-19 on the following page.

formula to be edited

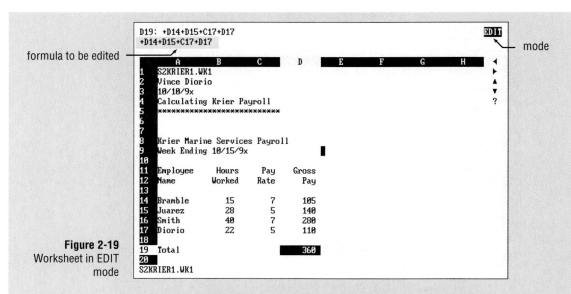

mode

Figure 2-19
Worksheet in EDIT
mode

When you first press [F2], 1-2-3 is in EDIT mode. Any new character you enter is inserted at the cursor, and any characters to the right of the cursor are moved one position to the right. You can activate overtype mode by pressing [Ins]. In this mode any character you type replaces the character directly above the cursor. When 1-2-3 is in overtype mode, you will see the OVR indicator on the status line at the bottom of the screen. Pressing [Ins] again switches 1-2-3 back to insert mode. Figure 2-20 provides a list of keys you can use in EDIT mode.

Key	Action
[→]	Moves cursor one position to right
[←]	Moves cursor one position to left
[Home]	Moves cursor to first position in entry
[End]	Moves cursor one position to right of last character in the entry
[Backspace]	Deletes character to left of cursor
[Del]	Deletes character above cursor
[Ins]	Switches between insert mode and overtype mode
[Enter]	Completes the edit and returns to READY mode
[Esc]	Clears edit line; when pressed again leaves EDIT mode without making changes and returns to READY mode

Figure 2-20
Keys and their
actions in EDIT
mode

❸ Press [←] to position the cursor under the letter C in the formula. Press **[Del]** three times to erase C17, the incorrect portion of the formula.

❹ Type **D16**. Press **[Enter]** and, as you do, notice that the value in D19 changes to 635, the correct total gross pay. Notice also that the correct formula, +D14+D15+D16+D17, appears in the control panel. See Figure 2-21.

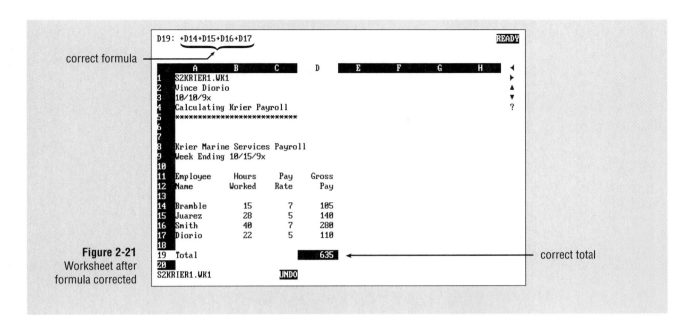

correct formula ⟶

```
D19: +D14+D15+D16+D17                                    READY
          A        B        C        D      E      F      G      H
1  S2KRIER1.WK1
2  Vince Diorio
3  10/10/9x
4  Calculating Krier Payroll
5  ******************************
6
7
8  Krier Marine Services Payroll
9  Week Ending 10/15/9x
10
11 Employee      Hours     Pay     Gross
12 Name          Worked    Rate    Pay
13
14 Bramble         15        7       105
15 Juarez          28        5       140
16 Smith           40        7       280
17 Diorio          22        5       110
18
19 Total                             635    ⟵
20
S2KRIER1.WK1                  UNDO
```

⟵ correct total

Figure 2-21
Worksheet after
formula corrected

Be sure to take advantage of the [F2] (EDIT) key. It is often easier and more efficient to correct mistakes by typing only what needs to be changed.

Entering Lines

Worksheets often contain a row of lines below column headings and above and below subtotals to make the worksheet more readable. In addition, double lines are often used to indicate final totals. You could enter as many minus signs (–) or equal signs (=) as you need to create lines, but 1-2-3 provides a more convenient way. You first type \ (Backslash, not the slash symbol, /) and then type the character you want to use to draw the line. The backslash is a special label prefix that instructs 1-2-3 to repeat the character that follows it until the cell is filled.

To fill a cell with characters:

❶ Move the cell pointer to cell A13. This is a blank cell under a column heading.

❷ Type \ (Backslash) followed by a – (Minus Sign) to fill the cell with minus signs.

❸ Press **[Enter]**. See Figure 2-22 on the following page. Notice how minus signs fill cell A13, producing a line in this cell.

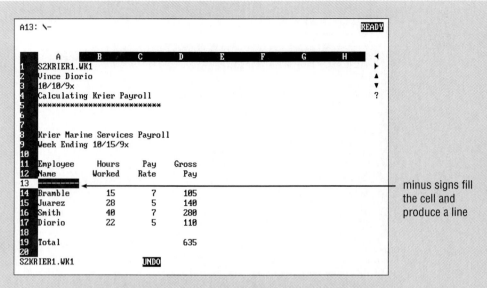

Figure 2-22
Entering lines in a
worksheet

minus signs fill
the cell and
produce a line

④ Move the cell pointer to cell B13, type **\−**, then press **[Enter]**.

⑤ Move the cell pointer to cell C13, type **\−**, then press **[Enter]**.

⑥ Move the cell pointer to cell D13, type **\−**, then press **[Enter]**. You have now entered a line across row 13.

⑦ Move the cell pointer to cell D18, type **\−**, then press **[Enter]**. This enters a line in the gross pay column.

Your screen should be similar to Figure 2-23.

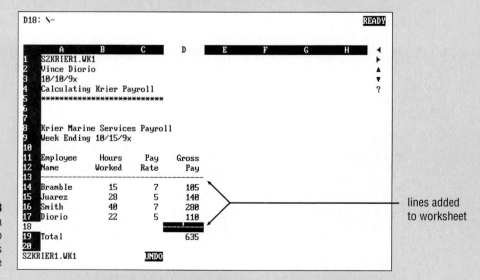

Figure 2-23
Lines added to a
worksheet to
improve its
appearance

lines added
to worksheet

Using UNDO to Correct Mistakes

What would you do if you accidentally typed over or erased a complicated formula? It would probably be a lot of work to figure out the formula again and reenter it. The UNDO feature can help. You can use it to cancel the *most recent* operation you performed on your worksheet.

To use UNDO, two indicators must appear on the screen. The word UNDO must appear in the status indicator at the bottom of your screen. Also, the word READY must appear in the mode indicator in the upper right corner of the screen. This means that your worksheet is in READY mode and can accept a keystroke. If UNDO does not appear in the status line at the bottom of your screen, you cannot do the steps in this section. To load UNDO, see pages L 43 and L 44.

Let's make an intentional mistake and use UNDO to correct it. Instead of typing the label ========= in cell D20, where it belongs, you will type it in cell D19, where it will erase the formula for total gross pay. Then you'll restore the original formula by using the UNDO feature.

To intentionally make a mistake:

❶   Move the cell pointer to cell D19, the cell that contains the formula for total gross pay.

❷   Type \ = and press **[Enter]**. See Figure 2-24.

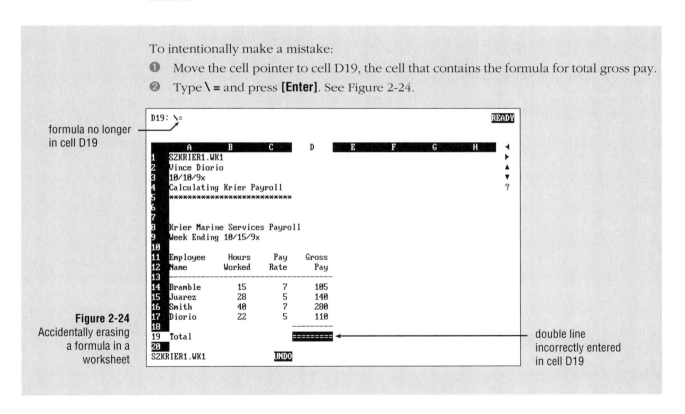

formula no longer in cell D19

double line incorrectly entered in cell D19

Figure 2-24
Accidentally erasing a formula in a worksheet

You have erased the entire formula and replaced it with =========, but don't worry. You can undo the mistake.

To use UNDO to cancel your *most recent* operation:

❶ Press the **[Alt]** key and, while holding it down, press the **[F4]** key ([Alt][F4]). Then release both keys. [Alt][F4] (UNDO) undoes your intentional mistake and restores the formula in D19. The value in D19 should again be 635.

❷ Now move the cell pointer to D20, the cell in which you should enter the double line. Type **\ =** and press **[Enter]**. See Figure 2-25.

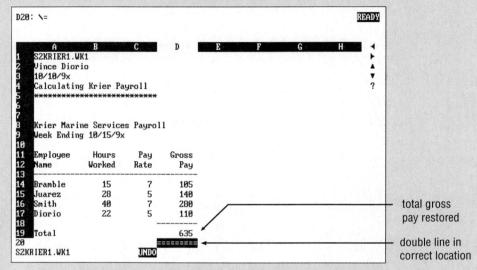

Figure 2-25
The worksheet after
UNDO returns the
formula to the cell

total gross
pay restored

double line in
correct location

Saving a File Using an Existing Filename

As discussed earlier in the tutorial, 1-2-3 does not automatically save your worksheet. You must use the File Save command to make a permanent copy of your worksheet on your data diskette. You used the File Save command earlier; however, since you last issued that command you made several changes to your worksheet. These changes have not been saved. To do that you must update the worksheet file on your data diskette by saving the worksheet again.

To save the worksheet:

❶ Select /File Save (**/FS**). The name of the current worksheet appears in the control panel.

❷ S2KRIER1.WK1, the filename of the current worksheet appears in the control panel. Since you want to update this worksheet by saving the changes, press **[Enter]**.

Because the filename you are saving already exists on your data diskette, 1-2-3 presents you with three options. See Figure 2-26.

options appear in → control panel

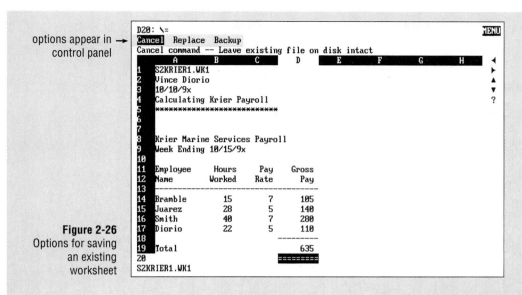

```
D20: \=                                              MENU
Cancel  Replace  Backup
Cancel command -- Leave existing file on disk intact
     A      B      C      D      E      F      G      H
1  S2KRIER1.WK1
2  Vince Diorio
3  10/10/9x
4  Calculating Krier Payroll
5  *****************************
6
7
8  Krier Marine Services Payroll
9  Week Ending 10/15/9x
10
11 Employee     Hours    Pay    Gross
12 Name         Worked   Rate    Pay
13 ------------------------------------
14 Bramble       15       7      105
15 Juarez        28       5      140
16 Smith         40       7      280
17 Diorio        22       5      110
18                             ---------
19 Total                         635
20                             =========
S2KRIER1.WK1
```

Figure 2-26
Options for saving
an existing
worksheet

Cancel – This option returns you to READY mode without saving the current worksheet.

Replace – This option replaces the contents of the worksheet file on your data diskette with the current worksheet in computer memory.

Backup – This option saves the current worksheet and keeps a copy of the previous version of the worksheet. 1-2-3 copies the worksheet file with the same filename but with a BAK extension. The current worksheet is saved with the existing filename and the extension WK1.

Since you want to update the file with the changes, you should use the *Replace* option.

❸   Select Replace (**R**). The updated worksheet file, S2KRIER1.WK1, now contains the current worksheet.

Understanding Ranges

Vince has completed the payroll worksheet for Krier Marine Services. Now he wants to print it. The Print command requires you to identify the range of cells that you want to print. Therefore, you need to understand the term "range" before using the Print command.

A **range** in 1-2-3 consists of one or more cells that form a rectangular shape. A range may be a single cell, a row of cells, a column of cells, or a rectangular block of cells. To define a range, you indicate the upper left corner cell of the rectangle and the lower right corner cell of the rectangle. Two periods [..] separate these entries and represent all the values between the beginning cell and the ending cell, for example, C14..C17. The notation C14..C17 is referred to as a **range address**.

Figure 2-27 illustrates several examples of ranges that you can define in a worksheet.

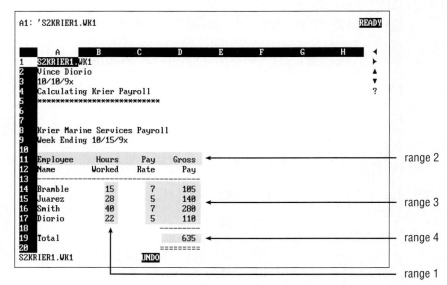

Figure 2-27
Examples of ranges

- The first example, labeled range 1, is identified as B14..B17. This range forms a column of cells located in column B, beginning in row 14 and ending in row 17.

- The second example, range 2, represents a row of cells. The range is defined as A11..D11, which means the range of cells beginning at cell A11 and ending at D11.

- The third example, range 3, represents the rectangular block of cells C14..D17. A block of cells is identified in a worksheet by specifying a pair of diagonally opposite corner cells. C14, the upper left corner, and D17, the bottom right corner, define a block of eight cells.

- The fourth example, range 4, represents the single cell D19..D19. A single cell defined as a range has the same starting and ending cell.

Using the Print Command

You have entered the data, calculated gross pay and totals, saved your worksheet, and learned about ranges. You are now ready to print the Krier payroll worksheet and learn the basics of using the Print command. In 1-2-3 you print by first specifying a range to print and then printing the worksheet. You can print all or part of your worksheet by first defining a rectangular range of cells that you want to print. Vince wants to print the payroll report using the range A8 through D20.

To specify the print range A8..D20:

❶ Select /Print Printer (**/PP**). 1-2-3 displays a menu with eight options and a Print Settings dialog box. See Figure 2-28.

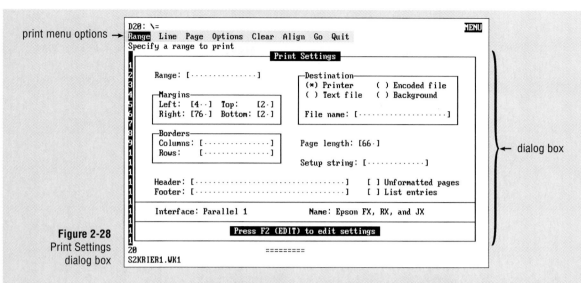

Figure 2-28
Print Settings
dialog box

As you learned in Tutorial 1, a dialog box is a box of options. Besides showing the options for saving an existing worksheet, Figure 2-28 also shows the Print Settings dialog box. This box displays the current print settings. You can select your print settings by making menu selections or by making selections directly from the dialog box. Module 1 contains more information about the use of dialog boxes.

Anytime you print, the printed output will be formatted according to the specifications indicated in the dialog box. If you want to see the worksheet instead of the Print Settings dialog box, you can press the function key [F6]. Press [F6] again, and the Print Settings dialog box reappears.

❷   Select Range (**R**). The worksheet reappears.

To define the print range, you must specify two cell addresses that are diagonally across from each other. Usually the upper left corner and the lower right corner cells define the range.

❸   Move the cell pointer to A8, the upper left corner cell in the print range. See Figure 2-29.

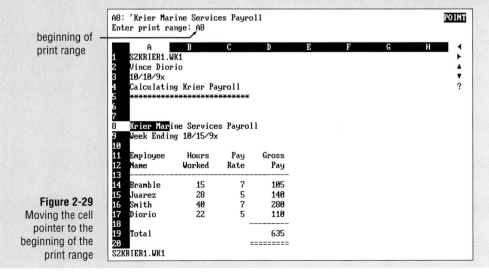

beginning of
print range

Figure 2-29
Moving the cell
pointer to the
beginning of the
print range

❹ Type **[.]** (Period). This fixes, or **anchors**, the cell pointer in the current cell. Whenever you want to specify a range, you should move the cell pointer to the top left corner cell of a range and anchor this position by pressing [.] (Period). See Figure 2-30 and compare it to Figure 2-29. Notice how 1-2-3 indicates that the cell pointer is anchored.

.. indicates range is anchored

Figure 2-30
Anchoring the cell
pointer

```
A8: 'Krier Marine Services Payroll                              POINT
Enter print range: A8..A8
         A         B         C         D         E         F         G         H    ◄
1 S2KRIER1.WK1                                                                      ►
2 Vince Diorio                                                                      ▲
3 10/10/9x                                                                          ▼
4 Calculating Krier Payroll                                                         ?
5 ******************************
6
```

Once the cell pointer is anchored, pressing the pointer-movement keys expands the highlighted range.

❺ Press **[↓]** and **[→],** as needed, to highlight the range A8..D20. The address of the highlighted range appears in the control panel. See Figure 2-31.

print range defined

Figure 2-31
Highlighting the
print range

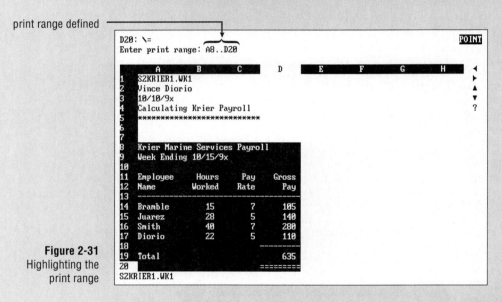

```
D20: \=                                                         POINT
Enter print range: A8..D20
         A         B         C         D         E         F         G         H    ◄
1 S2KRIER1.WK1                                                                      ►
2 Vince Diorio                                                                      ▲
3 10/10/9x                                                                          ▼
4 Calculating Krier Payroll                                                         ?
5 ******************************
6
7
8 Krier Marine Services Payroll
9 Week Ending 10/15/9x
10
11 Employee     Hours     Pay     Gross
12 Name        Worked    Rate      Pay
13 ------------------------------------
14 Bramble       15        7       105
15 Juarez        28        5       140
16 Smith         40        7       280
17 Diorio        22        5       110
18                                -----
19 Total                            635
20                                =====
S2KRIER1.WK1
```

❻ Press **[Enter]**. This completes the definition of the range, which now appears in the Print Settings dialog box. See Figure 2-32.

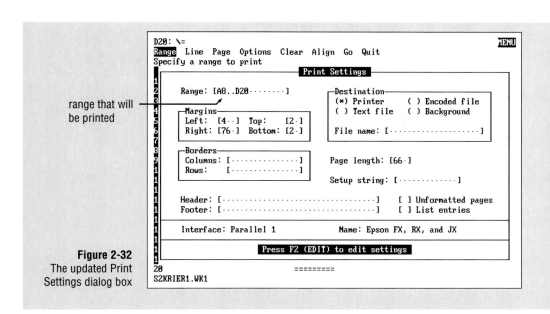

range that will
be printed

Figure 2-32
The updated Print
Settings dialog box

Now that you've instructed 1-2-3 what cells you want to print, you are ready to print the worksheet.

To print a specified range:

❶ Make sure your paper is positioned properly in your printer and the printer is on-line.

❷ Select Align (**A**) to tell 1-2-3 that the paper is correctly positioned at the top of the page and ready for printing. You should always choose Align before beginning to print.

❸ Select Go (**G**) to print the specified range. If the range does not print, your copy of 1-2-3 may not be installed correctly.

❹ Select Page (**P**). You need not wait for the printing to finish before you select Page. The Page command tells 1-2-3 to advance the paper to the top of the next page when it is finished printing. See Figure 2-33 on the following page.

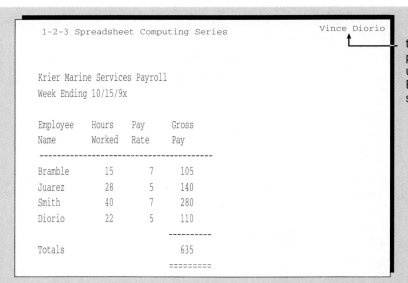

this line appears in
printout if you are
using Student
Business Series
software

Figure 2-33
Printout of Krier
Marine Services
payroll worksheet

If you are having trouble printing, you may need to check with your technical support person for the proper printing procedures in your lab.

⑤   Select Quit (**Q**) to leave the Print menu and return to READY mode with your worksheet displayed on your screen.

⑥   Save your worksheet as S2KRIER1 one last time (**/FS**). Press **[Enter]** and select Replace (**R**). This saves the print settings with the worksheet.

Erasing the Entire Worksheet

Once you have completed a worksheet, you may wish to start a new one. You can do this easily, but always remember to save your current worksheet. Then you can clear the worksheet from memory by using the Worksheet Erase command. You can also use this command if you begin a worksheet but decide you don't want it and have to start over. Let's erase the Krier payroll worksheet.

To erase a worksheet:

❶   Select /Worksheet Erase (**/WE**).

1-2-3 displays a prompt to give you a chance to change your mind. If you select "No," the worksheet will *not* be erased. If you select "Yes," the worksheet will be erased from computer memory.

❷   Type **Y** (Yes) if you are sure you want to erase the worksheet. After you type Y, the worksheet disappears from the screen. See Figure 2-34. 1-2-3 does *not* erase the worksheet from your data diskette, only from the computer's memory.

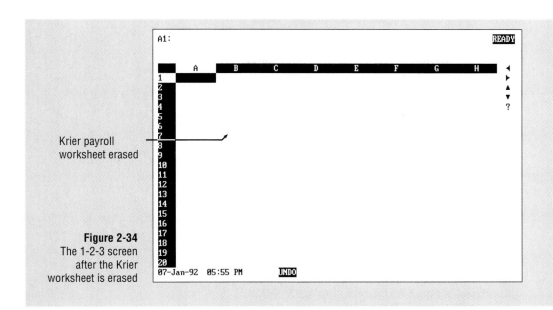

Krier payroll
worksheet erased

Figure 2-34
The 1-2-3 screen
after the Krier
worksheet is erased

If you attempt to erase a worksheet without first saving a new or modified worksheet, the control panel will display the following warning: "WORKSHEET CHANGES NOT SAVED! Erase worksheet anyway?"

If you did not want to save the worksheet, you would select "Yes" and your worksheet would be erased. However, if you did want to save your worksheet but forgot, you would type "No" and you'd return to READY mode. Then you would issue the /File Save command to save your worksheet. After saving your worksheet, you could then issue the Worksheet Erase command.

Quitting 1-2-3

When you are ready to quit 1-2-3, you choose the Quit command. You are then returned to the operating system prompt.

To quit a 1-2-3 session:

❶ Select /Quit (**Q**).

You are given the chance to change your mind. If you select "No" in response to the prompt, 1-2-3 returns to READY mode. If you select "Yes," you end the 1-2-3 session and return to DOS.

❷ Select Yes (**Y**). You are returned to the DOS prompt.

If you have changed the worksheet since the last time you saved it, 1-2-3 displays another Yes/No prompt. If you do not want to save the worksheet, select "Yes" and you leave 1-2-3. However, if you forgot to save your worksheet, type "No" and you return to READY mode. Then issue the /File Save command. After you save your worksheet, you can issue the Quit command.

Exercises

1. Would you enter the following data items as labels or values?
   a. 227-3541   (phone number)
   b. 6.45   (pay rate)
   c. 02384   (zip code)
   d. 46 Main Street   (address)
   e. 25   (units on hand)

2. Load 1-2-3 and enter the following numbers and labels in your worksheet. If you have a problem after any entry, press [Esc] to return to READY mode. For each entry, explain why you got the result you did.
   a. In cell A1 type the street address **1 Main Street**
      In cell A2 type **'1 Main Street**
   b. In cell A5 type the phone number **755-5122**
      In cell A6 type **'755-5122**
   c. In cell A10 type the zip code **02892**
      In cell A11 type **'02892**
   d. In cell A14 type **.25**
      In cell A15 type **25%**
   e. In cell A17 type **6000**
      In cell A18 type **6,000**
   f. Print the worksheet.

3. Create a new worksheet by entering the following values: 10 in cell A1, 20 in cell B1, and 3 in cell C1. For each formula, first calculate the result by hand. Then enter each formula in the specified cell and compare the results.

	Cell	Formula	Hand-calculated result	1-2-3 calculated result
a.	D3	+A1+B1-C1		
b.	D4	+A1-C1+B1		
c.	D6	+A1+B1/C1		
d.	D7	+(A1+B1)/C1		
e.	D9	+A1/B1*C1		
f.	D10	+A1/(B1*C1)		
g.	D13	+B1/A1^C1		
h.	D14	(B1/A1)^C1		

   i. Print the worksheet.

4. Which of the following ranges defines a row of cells? Which range defines a block of cells?
   a. B1..B7
   b. B1..D7
   c. B1..E1
   d. B1..B1

5. You want to display a series of plus signs, +++++++++, in a cell. How do you accomplish this task?

6. Which of the following filenames can be used to name a 1-2-3 worksheet?
   a. Q1.WK1
   b. 1991.WK1
   c. ACCTREC.WK1
   d. ACCT REC.WK1
   e. ACCT_REC.WK1
   f. ACCT.REC.WK1

7. What key(s) would you press to accomplish the following tasks?
   a. get to the Command menu
   b. back up one step in the 1-2-3 menu system
   c. move to cell A1
   d. edit a formula in a cell

Tutorial Assignments

1. Retrieve the file T2KRIER1, find the error, and correct it. (When 1-2-3 displays the list of worksheet files, press [PgDn] several times to find the worksheet file T2KRIER1.) What do you think the person who created the worksheet did when entering the gross pay formula for Bramble? Print the worksheet.

2. Retrieve the file T2KRIER2. Why isn't total gross pay adding correctly? Correct the worksheet and print it.

3. Retrieve the file T2KRIER3. Why is Bramble's gross pay zero? Hint: Think about how labels and values are stored in 1-2-3. Correct the error and print the worksheet.

Retrieve the file T2KRIER4 and do the following:

4. Juarez worked 30 hours for the week, not the 28 hours that was entered. Correct this.

5. Smith's name is actually Smythe. Change the name.

6. In cell B19, write a formula to calculate total hours worked.

7. Add a single line in cell B18 and a double line in cell B20.

Continue using the file T2KRIER4 to complete the following problems on federal withholding tax (FWT). FWT is the amount of money that an employer withholds from an employee's paycheck to pay federal taxes.

8. Assume that the amount withheld from an employee's pay check is 15 percent (.15) of gross pay. Use column E in your worksheet to display FWT. Include the column heading FWT in cell E12. Enter the formula for withholding tax for each employee (gross pay × .15) in cells E14, E15, E16, and E17.

9. Net pay is the gross pay less deductions (gross pay − FWT). Use column F to display the net pay for each employee. Enter the column label Net in cell F11 and the column label Pay in cell F12. Enter the net pay formula for each employee in cells F14, F15, F16, and F17.

10. Calculate the total FWT and the total net pay for all employees. Display these totals in cells E19 and F19, respectively.

11. Add single and double lines where appropriate.

12. Change cell A1 to S2KRIER4.WK1. Now save your worksheet as S2KRIER4.WK1.

13. Print the entire worksheet, including the identifying data at the top of the worksheet. Your print range is A1..F20.

Case Problems

1. Sales in Toyland

An article in the *Wall Street Journal* focusing on sales in the toy industry for 1990 presented the data shown in Figure 2-35.

Toy Companies Nine-month Sales 1990 (in millions)		
Company	**1990**	**1989**
Galoob	105	169
Hasbro	1027	993
Matchbox	140	156
Mattel	1042	878
Tonka	541	625
Tyco	334	269

Figure 2-35

Retrieve the worksheet P2TOYS and do the following:

1. Calculate total sales for the toy industry for 1989 and 1990.

2. Calculate the change in sales from 1989 to 1990. Place this result in column D. Label the column heading Change and use the following formula:

   Change = 1990 sales – 1989 sales

3. Save the worksheet as S2TOYS.

4. Print the worksheet.

2. Travel Agency Survey

A travel industry association conducted a study of American travel habits. Figure 2-36 shows the amount of passenger miles traveled in the United States by various modes of transportation.

U.S. Travel Habits

Mode of Transportation	Passenger Miles (billions)
Cars	1586.3
Airlines	346.5
Buses	45.2
Railroad	18.7

Figure 2-36

Retrieve the worksheet P2TRVL and do the following:

1. Enter the formula to compute total U.S. passenger miles.

2. Enter the formula to compute the percent that each mode of transportation represents of the total U.S. passenger miles. (Divide the passenger miles for each mode of transportation by total passenger miles and then multiply by 100.)

3. Save your worksheet as S2TRVL.

4. Print your worksheet.

3. A Trend Toward More Bankruptcies

Ms. Ganni is a lawyer who administers bankruptcy filings. In the last few years she has seen a rapid increase in the number of bankruptcy cases. She states, "I know the number of bankruptcy cases I've handled has increased enormously. I don't have time for lunch anymore, much less time to analyze all the cases. We need more staff; our system is overloaded!"

As her assistant you must help Ms. Ganni make a case to her bosses for additional resources.

Retrieve the worksheet file P2BNKRPT and do the following:

1. Calculate the total number of bankruptcies in 1989 and 1990.

2. Calculate the percent change in bankruptcies this year compared to last year for each type of bankruptcy as well as the overall percent change. The formula to calculate percent change in bankruptcies for each bankruptcy type in 1990 is

$$\left(\frac{(Bankruptcies\ in\ 1990 - Bankruptcies\ in\ 1989)}{Bankruptcies\ in\ 1989} \right) \times 100$$

3. Save the worksheet as S2BNKRPT.

4. Print the worksheet.

4. Calculating Commissions at Esquire's Clothing

Esquire's Clothing pays its salesforce their commissions every three months. Commissions are based on sales for the previous three months.

Do the following:

1. Retrieve the worksheet file P2COMM.

2. Include the following calculations in your worksheet:
    a. the quarterly sales for each salesperson
    b. the quarterly commission for each salesperson based on the following formula:

    quarterly sales for each salesperson × *salesperson's commission rate*

    c. the quarterly net sales (the amount remaining after commission is deducted) for each salesperson based on the following formula:

    quarterly sales for each salesperson − salesperson's commission amount

    d. totals for each column except the Commission Rate column.

5. Save the worksheet as S2COMM.

6. Print the worksheet.

Tutorial 3

Modifying a Worksheet

Pricing a Mutual Fund

OBJECTIVES

In this tutorial you will learn to:

- Use the @SUM function

- Change the way numbers are displayed

- Change column widths

- Adjust text alignments

- Insert rows

- Move a group of rows or columns to another worksheet area

- Erase a group of cells

Case: Allegiance Incorporated

Pauline Wu graduated last June with a degree in finance. Today she is beginning her new job as a portfolio accountant with Allegiance Incorporated, an investment company. Pauline is excited about getting this job, not only because Allegiance is reputed to be one of the best mutual fund companies in the United States, but also because Allegiance is known for the superior training it provides its new employees.

People who have money to invest but who do not want to manage the investment themselves invest their money with Allegiance. Allegiance employs trained professionals to manage the money in what are called mutual funds. In these funds the money is invested in stocks, bonds, and other publicly traded securities and managed by Allegiance employees, often called portfolio managers.

For example, a portfolio manager might manage a $10 million fund that was started by selling one million shares at $10 a share to people who then became the shareholders of the fund. The manager of this fund then invests the $10 million by buying shares in companies such as IBM, AT&T, and Coca-Cola. The goal of the portfolio manager and the shareholders is that the shares purchased will increase in value so the shareholders will make money.

As a portfolio accountant, Pauline will be responsible for reporting correct information to portfolio managers so they will be able to track how well a fund is performing. One of Pauline's responsibilities in her new job is each day to calculate the value of the Balboa Equity Fund and to report this information to the national newspapers so shareholders can know the value of a share in this fund. Pauline knows that is an important responsibility. Even a minor error in her calculations could cause Allegiance to lose substantial amounts of money. She is eager to begin the new employee training program because it will help her to perform these important calculations accurately.

Pauline first meets the other new portfolio accountants and her training supervisor, Rochelle Osterhaut. Rochelle begins the training by discussing their daily responsibility to calculate the value of a mutual fund share. She hands out a fact sheet (Figure 3-1) that lists details about the Balboa Equity Fund. Rochelle explains that their first assignment is to use this information to calculate the value of a share of the Balboa Fund. She also reminds them that in college they probably learned that the value per share of a fund is usually called the *net asset value*, or *NAV*.

```
Balboa Equity Fund   -   Fact Sheet

Mutual Fund Shares        2000

Net Asset Value            ?


Company Name        Shares Purchased        Current Price

IBM                      100                      91
Coca-Cola                 50                      69 1/4
Texaco                   100                      58 3/4
Boeing                   150                      44 1/2
```

Figure 3-1
Balboa Equity Fund
fact sheet

Rochelle explains that to calculate the NAV they must first determine the market value of each investment owned by the fund. To do this, they multiply the current price of each company share owned by the fund by the total number of shares of this company that the fund purchased. For example, Balboa Equity Fund owns 100 shares of IBM, whose current price is $91 per share. Thus, the market value of these shares in the Balboa Fund is $9,100. After the market value of each security is determined, the accountants add together the market value of each investment and other assets owned by the fund, such as cash on hand. After calculating this total they divide it by the number of shares owned by the fund's shareholders. The result is the NAV. In other words,

$$NAV = \frac{(current\ price \times shares\ of\ company\ A\ owned\ by\ fund) + (current\ price \times shares\ of\ company\ B\ owned\ by\ fund) + \ldots}{number\ of\ shares\ of\ the\ mutual\ fund\ owned\ by\ fund's\ shareholders}$$

Pauline is eager to begin the assignment. She decides to use Lotus 1-2-3 to help make the calculations and to produce a professional-looking report. First, however, she thinks about the project; she outlines her thoughts on a planning sheet and sketches the worksheet (Figures 3-2a and 3-2b).

Planning Sheet
My Goal:
 Calculate Net Asset Value for Balboa Equity Fund each day

What results do I want to see?
 Net Asset Value (Price/Share) of Balboa Equity Fund
 Breakdown of company's that make up the fund along with the
 market value of company's stock

What information do I need?
  For each company stock owned by the fund
   Name of the company
   Number of shares of the company's stock owned by fund
   Current price company's stock is selling for

What calculations will I perform?
 Calculate market value of each stock in the fund
 Calculate total value for all stock in the fund
 Calculate Net Asst Value

Figure 3-2a
Pauline's planning
sheet

	Mutual Fund Shares Price per share (NAV)		
Company Name	# of Shares	Current Price	Market Value
XXXX	XX	XX.XXX	XXXX.XX
XXXX	XX	XX.XXX	XXXX.XX
.			
.			
.			
Totals			XXXX.XX

Figure 3-2b
Pauline's
worksheet sketch

   In this tutorial, you will create the same worksheet that Pauline creates. You will experience the power of the specialized @functions, which speed and simplify the use of formulas, learn more about entering and editing data quickly, and learn how to make changes in the appearance of the worksheet.

Retrieving the Worksheet

Let's begin by retrieving the worksheet.

To retrieve the worksheet:

❶   Select /File Retrieve (**/FR**) and highlight C3BALBO1.WK1. Press **[Enter]**. See Figure 3-3a.

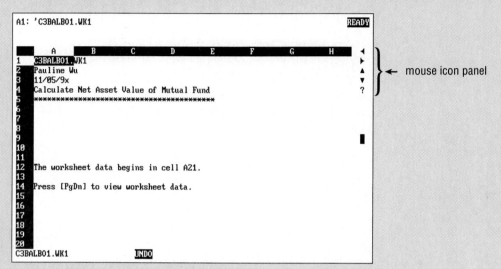

Figure 3-3a
Initial screen from
C3BALBO1.WK1

The initial screen contains documentation about the worksheet and instructions to go to cell A21 to view the worksheet data.

❷   Press **[PgDn]**. See Figure 3-3b.

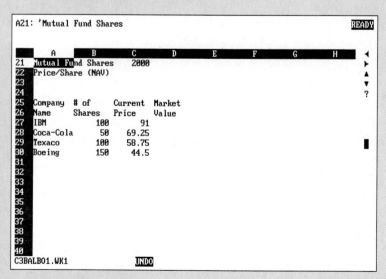

Figure 3-3b
Data on Balboa Equity
Fund

This worksheet contains the Balboa Equity Fund Portfolio data. It includes the company names and the number of shares of each company's stock that the fund purchased. It also shows the current day's stock market price for a share of each company that is part of the Balboa Fund Portfolio. In addition, the worksheet shows the number of mutual fund shares owned by people who have invested in the Balboa Fund.

Entering Formulas

Now that you have the basic data entered in the worksheet, your first step in pricing the mutual fund is to calculate the market value of each company's stock in the fund. The market value is calculated by multiplying the number of shares owned of each company's stock by the current market price of that company's stock, that is,

$$market\ value = number\ of\ shares \times current\ market\ price$$

To calculate the market value for each company:

First calculate the market value for IBM.

❶ Move the cell pointer to D27. Type **+B27*C27** and press [↓].

To calculate the market value for Coca-Cola:

❷ In cell D28 type **+B28*C28** and press [↓].

To calculate the market value for Texaco:

❸ In cell D29 type **+B29*C29** and press [↓].

To calculate the market value for Boeing:

❹ In cell D30 type **+B30*C30** and press **[Enter]**. See Figure 3-4.

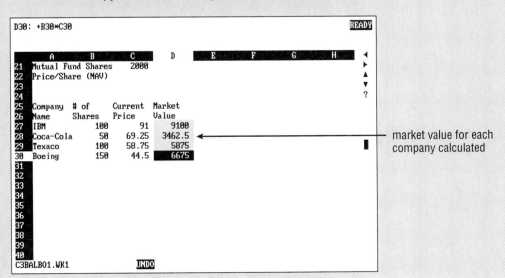

market value for each
company calculated

Figure 3-4
Worksheet after
market value formula
entered

Using the @SUM Function

Now that you have calculated the market value of each company's stock in this fund, you need to calculate the total market value of the fund. The total market value of the fund is the sum of the market values of all the companies in the fund, that is,

total market value = market value of IBM + market value of Coca-Cola + ...

Remember that in Tutorial 2 you summed the total gross pay by specifying the cell location of each employee's gross pay. Similarly you could calculate the total market value by entering the formula +D27+D28+D29+D30, but this would be tedious. It would be especially tedious if the fund had perhaps 75 different companies instead of just 4. To make the process much easier, you'll use 1-2-3's @SUM (pronounced "at sum") function. This function allows you to total the values in a range of cells.

What Is an @Function?

An **@function** is a predefined routine that performs a series of operations or calculations and then gives you a result. It can be thought of as a *predefined formula* that is built into 1-2-3. Functions save you the trouble of creating your own formulas to perform various arithmetic tasks.

Many functions are available in 1-2-3. They are divided into eight categories: mathematical, statistical, database, financial, logical, string, date/time, and special.

Each function begins with the @ (at) symbol followed by the name of the function. The name of the function suggests its purpose. In parentheses following the function name, you put any information the function needs to perform its tasks. The information in parentheses is referred to as the **arguments** of the function. Depending on the @function, the arguments may be values, references to cells or ranges, range names, formulas, and even other @functions. The general format of a function in 1-2-3 is

---

@FUNCTION(arguments)

where:

@ is the symbol that indicates that a function follows.

FUNCTION is the name of the function.

arguments represents the required information that the function needs to do its tasks.

Example:

@SUM(D27..D30)

Pauline is ready to calculate the total market value of the Balboa Equity Fund. To do this, she will use the @SUM function. Remember, the @SUM function adds a range of numbers. You specify the addresses of the first and the last cell of the range you want to add. In other words, @SUM(D27..D30) is equivalent to +D27+D28+D29+D30. The expression in parentheses, D27..D30, is the argument, representing the range of cells that will be added.

To use the @SUM function to calculate total market value:

① Move the cell pointer to A31 to enter the label. Type **[Spacebar] [Spacebar] Totals**. Press **[Enter]**.

② Now move the cell pointer to D31, where you will enter the formula to total the company market values.

③ Type **@sum(** to begin the formula. You may use either uppercase or lowercase when typing the function name SUM.

④ Press **[↑]** to move the cell pointer to D27, the starting point for adding the market values of all companies in this fund. See Figure 3-5.

first cell to be added to obtain total

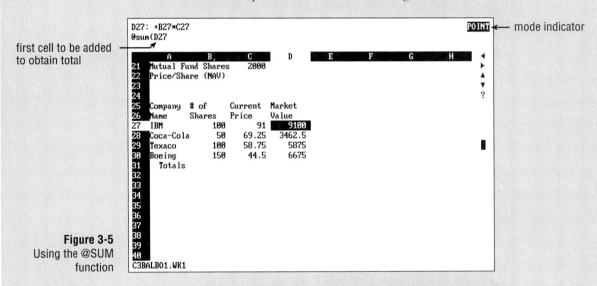

Figure 3-5
Using the @SUM
function

⑤ Type **[.]** (Period) to anchor the cell. Two periods appear in the control panel to indicate that the cell is now anchored.

⑥   Press [↓] to highlight the range D27..D30. See Figure 3-6.

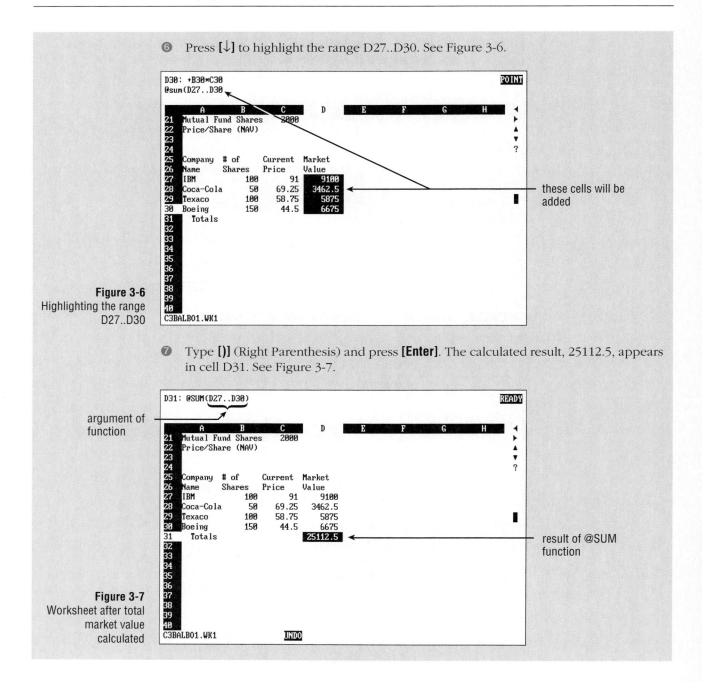

Figure 3-6
Highlighting the range
D27..D30

⑦   Type **[)]** (Right Parenthesis) and press **[Enter]**. The calculated result, 25112.5, appears
   in cell D31. See Figure 3-7.

Figure 3-7
Worksheet after total
market value
calculated

You have now calculated the market value for the Balboa Equity Fund.

The final calculation to determine the NAV is to divide the total market value of the fund
by the number of shares of the fund that have been sold. In other words,

$$NAV = \frac{total\ market\ value\ of\ mutual\ fund}{number\ of\ shares\ of\ fund\ owned\ by\ investors}$$

To calculate the NAV:

❶   Move the cell pointer to C22, where the NAV will be calculated.

❷   Type **+D31/C21** and then press **[Enter]**.

The / (Slash) symbol represents division when used in a formula.

You've now completed the calculations of the NAV. Figure 3-8 shows the worksheet with the NAV calculated. Each share is worth $12.55625.

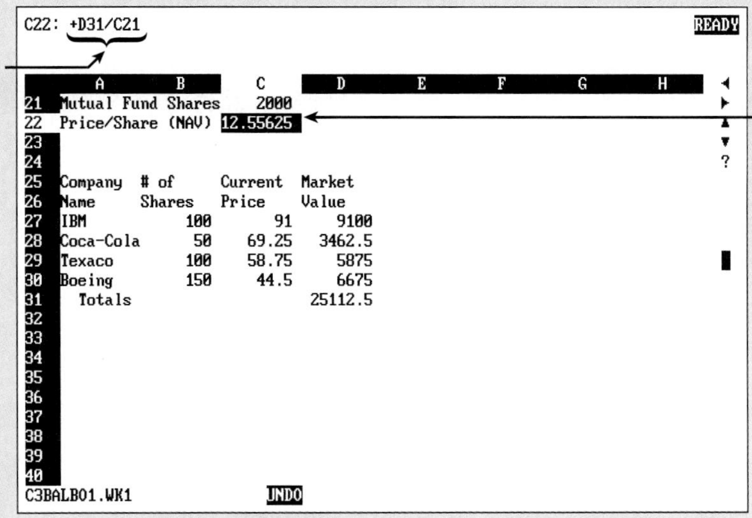

formula to calculate NAV

result of formula to calculate NAV

Figure 3-8
The NAV calculated

Improving the Appearance of the Worksheet

Although Pauline has completed the calculations for pricing the mutual fund, she is not pleased with the appearance of the worksheet. For instance, the numbers in the current price and market value columns are not aligned at the decimal point. In addition, the monetary values do not show dollar signs, and the column headings are not aligned over the numbers in the columns. Some improvements are needed to make the worksheet easier to read and use.

In the next several sections of this tutorial, you will learn to improve your worksheet's appearance. Figure 3-9 shows how the worksheet will look when you are finished.

```
A21: [W32] 'Balboa Equity Fund                                          READY

                A              B      C        D        E      ◄
21 Balboa Equity Fund                                                 ►
22 Net Asset Value for November 5, 199x                               ▲
23                                                                    ▼
24                                                                    ?
25 Company                              # of   Current   Market
26 Name                                Shares   Price     Value
27 ------------------------------------------------------------
28 International Business Machines       100   $91.00   $9,100.00
29 Coca-Cola                             50     69.25    3,462.50    ▌
30 Texaco                               100     58.75    5,875.00
31 Boeing                               150     44.50    6,675.00
32 ------------------------------------------------------------
33   Totals                                             $25,112.50
34
35
36 Mutual Fund Shares                            2000
37 Price/Share (NAV)                          12.55625
38
39
40
S3BALB01.WK1              UNDO
```

Figure 3-9
Final version of
worksheet

Formatting Numbers

You probably found the numeric values in your worksheet difficult to read, because the lists of current prices and market values are not aligned at the decimal point. Unless you instruct 1-2-3 otherwise, it displays numbers with a minus sign for negative values, no thousand separators, and no trailing zeros to the right of the decimal point. This is called the **General format**, and it is 1-2-3's default format. *Default* refers to a format or setting that 1-2-3 automatically uses unless you specifically change it. You can change how 1-2-3 displays data by using the Format command. 1-2-3 provides several alternative formats that you can use to change the way numbers appear in your worksheet.

Figure 3-10 shows some of the types of numeric formatting available in 1-2-3. These formats allow you to alter the number of decimal places displayed with a number. They may include dollar signs and commas with numbers; they can place parentheses around negative numbers; and they can add percent signs to numbers representing percentages.

Format Type	Description	Examples
General	This is the default format; 1-2-3 stores numbers in this format when you first enter them.	0.5 −125
Fixed	This displays numbers to a fixed number of decimal places that you specify.	0.50 1200.57
Currency	Numbers are preceded by dollar signs, and commas are inserted after the thousands and millions places. Negative numbers appear in parentheses.	$1,200.57 ($125.00)
, (Comma)	Commas are inserted after the thousands and millions places. Negative numbers appear in parentheses.	1,200.57 (125.00)
Percent	This multiplies the value by 100 and inserts the percent sign to the right of the value.	50% 14.1%
Scientific	Numbers are displayed as a power of 10. For example, the number 120000000 is displayed as 1.2E+08. The number 1.2E+08 is interpreted as "1.2 times 10 to the power of 8," or 1.2 times 100000000.	1.2E+08

Figure 3-10
Numeric formats

You can format all the cells in your worksheet using the Worksheet Global Format command, which treats all the cells similarly. Or you can format a block of cells, a column, a row, or a single cell using the Range Format command. In the next steps, you will change the format of the current price and market value columns. To do this, you will use the Range Format command.

Pauline decides to include dollar signs for the first value in columns that contain dollar values as well as for cells that contain totals. She will format all the other values in columns that contain dollar values using the Comma format to two decimal places. Let's first format the Current Price and Market Value columns beginning in cell C28 using the Comma format.

To format the current prices and market values in Comma format with two decimal places:
1. Move the cell pointer to C28, the first cell of the column Current Price to be formatted with the Comma format.

❷   Select /Range Format (**/RF**). The second line of the control panel lists all the formats available in 1-2-3. See Figure 3-11.

format commands in 1-2-3

description of Fixed format

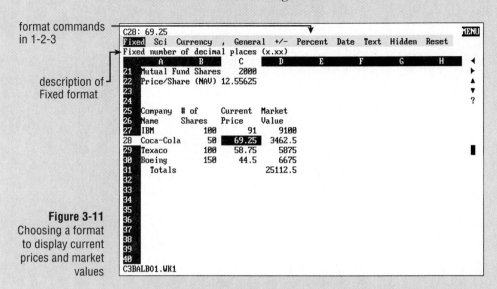

Figure 3-11
Choosing a format to display current prices and market values

Select the Comma format.

❸   Select **[,]** (Comma).

At this point, 1-2-3 asks you to enter the number of decimal places.

❹   Type **2** and press **[Enter]**. Since 2 is the default, it is not necessary to type 2. If you wanted zero decimal places, you'd type 0 before pressing [Enter].

❺   At the range prompt highlight the range C28..D30. Press **[Enter]**. See Figure 3-12.

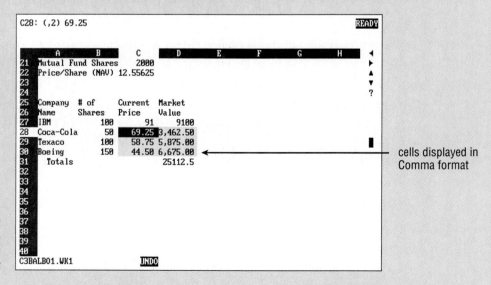

cells displayed in Comma format

Figure 3-12
Formatting the worksheet with the Comma format

Notice that 1-2-3 displays (,2) in the control panel, which means this cell is formatted with the Comma format and two decimal places. In general whenever the cell pointer is in a cell whose format has been changed with a Range Format command, the control panel displays the first character of the cell format name and the number of decimal places the cell will display.

Formatting Considerations

You should be aware of the following when you are formatting numbers:

- If you reduce the number of decimal places of a number, 1-2-3 rounds the number that appears in the cell. For example, if you type the value 25.6273 into a cell but decide to display the number with only two decimal places, the rounded number 25.63 appears in the cell. If you decide to display three decimal places, the number 25.627 appears in the cell.

- For all calculations 1-2-3 uses the value stored in the cell rather than the value that appears in the cell. Thus, for an entry stored as 25.6273 but appearing as 25.63, 1-2-3 uses 25.6273 for all calculations.

- Numeric formatting commands affect the way numbers are displayed on the screen, but they do not alter the cell's actual contents. If you want 1-2-3 to use a rounded number in a calculation, you can use the @ROUND function. The format of this function is @ROUND(*value,places*), where *value* is the number that you want to round and *places* is the number of decimal places that you want in the result. For example, @ROUND(10.131,0) rounds 10.131 to the nearest whole number, that is, 10. Thus, in the formula @ROUND(10.131,0)*2 1-2-3 uses the value 10, not 10.131, when multiplying by 2. The value displayed is 20.

Now let's format the first values in the columns Current Price and Market Value, using Currency format with two decimal places.

To change the first values in the columns Current Price and Market Value columns to Currency format:

1. Move the cell pointer to C27, the first cell under Current Price.
2. Select /Range Format Currency (**/RFC**).
3. At the prompt for the number of decimal places, press **[Enter]**.

4 At the range prompt, press **[→]** to highlight the range C27..D27. Press **[Enter]**. See Figure 3-13.

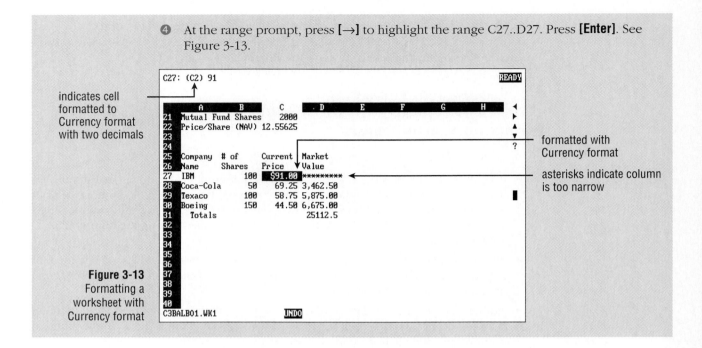

indicates cell formatted to Currency format with two decimals

formatted with Currency format

asterisks indicate column is too narrow

Figure 3-13
Formatting a worksheet with Currency format

Changing Column Widths

What happened to the first value in the column Market Value? Why do asterisks appear in cell D27? The asterisks indicate that the column is not wide enough to display the value. 1-2-3 measures column width by the number of characters displayed in a column. A single column can be up to 240 characters wide. 1-2-3 has a default width of 9 characters in a cell. In this case, therefore, the values do not fit. The asterisks indicate that the market value formatted using Currency format requires more than a 9-character-wide column. You must, therefore, increase the width of the Market Value column.

You can change the widths of all the columns in a worksheet at one time. We use the term **global** to describe a change that involves the *entire* worksheet. You can also make a single column wider or narrower. In the next steps you will widen a single column.

To change the width of column D:
1 Make sure the cell pointer is in any cell in column D.
2 Select /Worksheet Column Set-width (**/WCS**). See Figure 3-14.

preparing to change → column width

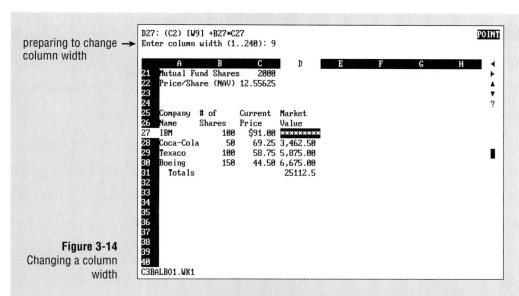

Figure 3-14
Changing a column
width

You can use two methods to enter a new column width: using the pointer-movement keys or typing a number. First, let's use the pointer-movement keys.

❸ Press [→] until the column is wide enough to display the values.

Notice how the column width increases by one character each time you press the key. See Figure 3-15.

column width
is 10

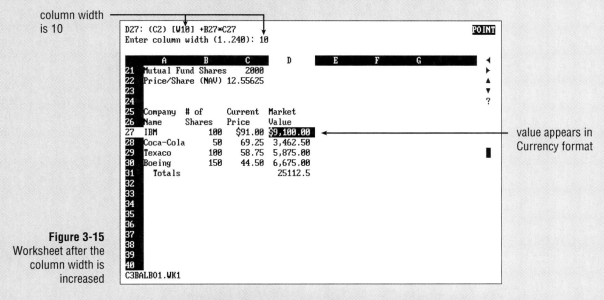

value appears in
Currency format

Figure 3-15
Worksheet after the
column width is
increased

❹ Press **[Enter]**.

Now let's try the second method to widen a column: typing a number. Let's widen the column to 12 characters so it can accommodate an even larger number.

❺ Select /Worksheet Column Set-width (**/WCS**).

⑥   Type **12** and press **[Enter]**. See Figure 3-16.

indicates cell formatted with Currency format and 2 decimal places

indicates width of column is 12 characters

column is 12 characters wide

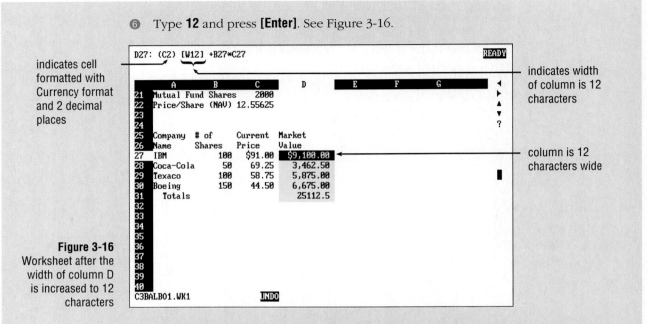

Figure 3-16
Worksheet after the width of column D is increased to 12 characters

Notice that [W12] appears in the control panel, indicating that the current width of the column is 12 characters.

Remember that all columns have a default width of nine characters. You can change the column width to accommodate labels and numbers that are longer than the column's width. Sometimes you might find nine characters too large. In such cases, you can reduce the width of a column by following the same steps you did to widen it. Just remember to choose a number less than 9 or press [←] to lessen the column width.

As Pauline looks at the worksheet, she realizes she still needs to format the cell that contains the total market value. She will format this cell using the Currency format so a dollar sign will appear with the total.

To format the cell containing the total market value:

❶   Move the cell pointer to cell D31, the cell where the total market value is displayed.

❷   Select /Range Format Currency (**/RFC**).

❸   At the prompt for number of decimal places, press **[Enter]**.

❹   Since you are formatting only cell D31, the desired range is already highlighted. Press **[Enter]**. See Figure 3-17.

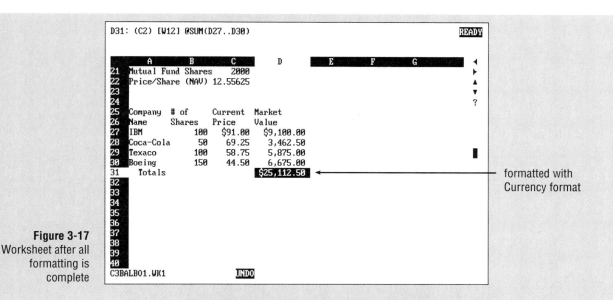

Figure 3-17
Worksheet after all
formatting is
complete

This time no asterisk appears in the cell because the width of the Market Value column (column D) has been expanded to display 12 characters.

Long Labels

Another reason to change the width of a column is to accommodate labels that are longer than nine characters. Often text entered into a cell is longer than the column's width. For example, the company name Hewlett-Packard requires more than nine characters. These text items are called **long labels.** If the cell to the right of the cell containing a long label is blank, the long label extends into the adjacent cell. However, if the cell to the right is not blank, then only the characters that fit into the column's current width will appear. Because the default column width is nine characters, only the first nine characters will appear in the cell unless you change the width.

Let's suppose that Pauline does not want to abbreviate the names of the companies in the fund. Let's enter the full name for IBM, International Business Machines, and observe the result.

To enter a long label:

❶ Move the cell pointer to A27.

❷ Type **International Business Machines** and press **[Enter]**. Since the default column width for column A is 9, only the first nine characters appear — Internati. Look at the control panel; notice that the entire label appears there. This indicates that 1-2-3 has stored the entire label in the cell, but since the width of the column is 9 and the cell to the right of the company name is not blank, only the first nine characters appear on your screen. See Figure 3-18 on the following page.

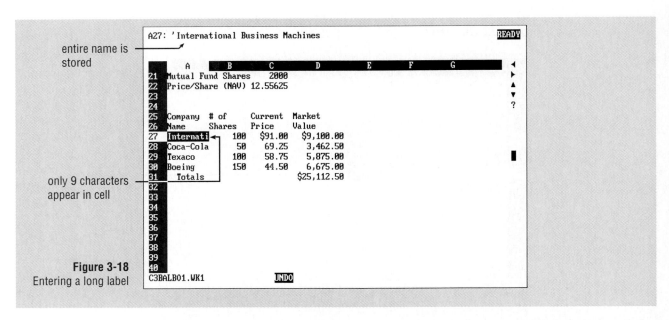

entire name is stored

only 9 characters appear in cell

Figure 3-18
Entering a long label

Pauline wants the entire name of the company to appear, so we must increase the column width.

To increase the column width:

❶ Select /Worksheet Column Set-width (**/WCS**).

❷ Type **32** to allow enough characters for the entire name to appear on the screen.

❸ Press **[Enter]**. See Figure 3-19.

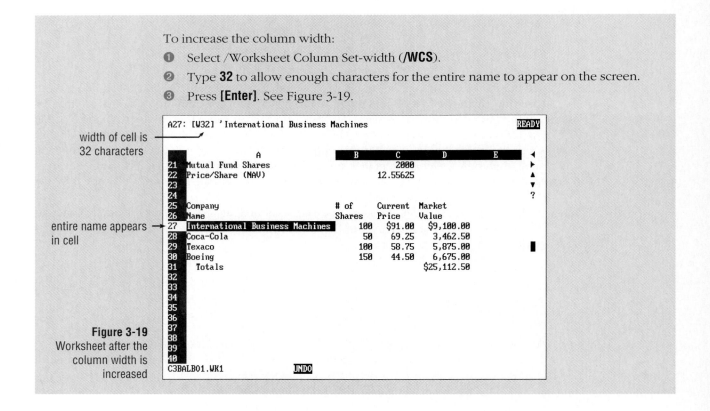

width of cell is 32 characters

entire name appears in cell

Figure 3-19
Worksheet after the column width is increased

Adjusting Labels within a Cell

As you have seen, when you enter a label, 1-2-3 places it by default against the left edge of the cell. Such a label is said to be **left-justified** and has an apostrophe (') label prefix. You can easily change the alignment of labels, that is, center or right-justify them, to suit your needs.

Let's learn how to right-justify the labels in Pauline's worksheet so the headings are over the data in each column.

To right-justify the column headings for the number of shares, the current price, and the market value:

❶ Move the cell pointer to B25.

❷ Select /Range Label Right (**/RLR**). See Figure 3-20. Notice that 1-2-3 automatically anchors the range at cell B25 because the prompt in the control panel indicates a range address rather than a cell address.

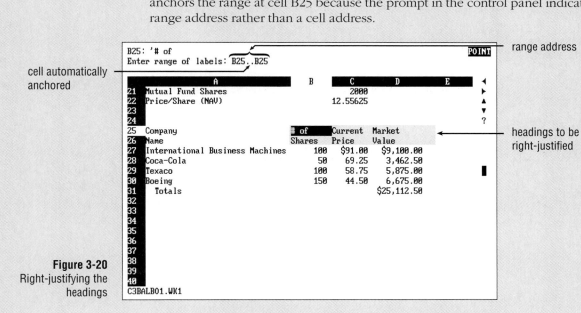

cell automatically anchored

range address

headings to be right-justified

Figure 3-20
Right-justifying the headings

❸ Move the [→] and [↓] keys until the cell range B25..D26 is highlighted. Press **[Enter]**. See Figure 3-21.

" label prefix means the label is right-justified in the cell

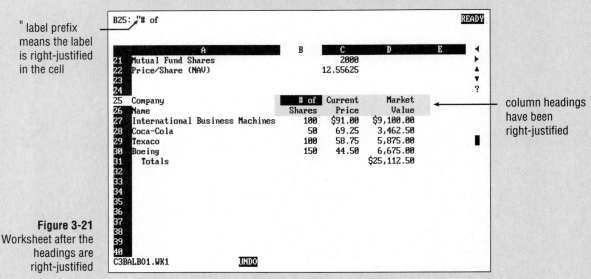

column headings have been right-justified

Figure 3-21
Worksheet after the headings are right-justified

The headings in columns B, C, and D are now right-justified.

Notice in the control panel that a " (Quote) character now precedes the label. The " character is the label prefix 1-2-3 uses to indicate a right-justified label.

To center the labels, you would select Range Label Center in Step 2.

You can also control label alignment as you type labels. For example, to center a label, type the ∧ (Caret) character (found on the [6] key) in front of any label. To right-justify a label, type a "(Quote) character in front of the label.

Before going on, let's save the worksheet.

To save the worksheet:
❶ Press **[Home]** to move the cell pointer to cell A1. Type **S3BALBO1.WK1** and press **[Enter]**. This changes the identifying information in cell A1 so it will be consistent with the new filename.
❷ Save your worksheet (/**FS**), using the name S3BALBO1.

Inserting Rows

You could improve the worksheet's appearance by inserting a line between the column heading and the first company name. In addition, it would look better with a line between the last company name and the row Totals. But there isn't any room. Running out of room often happens when you are in the process of creating a worksheet. Fortunately, with 1-2-3 you can insert or delete one or more rows between adjacent rows. You can also insert one or more columns between adjacent columns. You use the Insert command to insert new rows or columns into your worksheet.

To insert a blank row between A26 and A27 in the worksheet:

① Move the cell pointer to A27, the first row above which you want new rows inserted.

② Select /Worksheet Insert Row (**/WIR**).

The prompt "Enter row insert range: A27..A27" appears on the control panel. Since you are adding only one row, do not change the range. If you wanted to insert more rows, you would press [↓] for every row you wanted to insert.

③ Press **[Enter]**. 1-2-3 inserts one blank row. All the other rows are pushed down below the blank row. Notice also that 1-2-3 adjusts all formula relationships. See Figure 3-22.

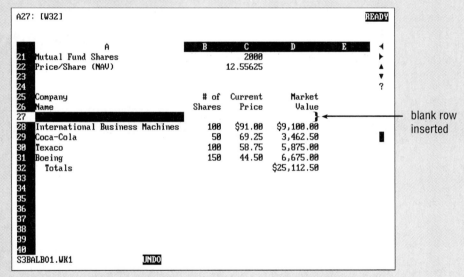

Figure 3-22
Inserting rows into the worksheet

To insert a blank row after Boeing and before the total value row:

④ Move the cell pointer to A32.

⑤ Select /Worksheet Insert Row (**/WIR**).

⑥ Press **[Enter]**. A blank row is inserted between Boeing and the label Totals.

Now let's add some lines to improve the worksheet's appearance. Often in worksheets a single line is inserted between the column headings and the data to help users read the worksheet. To insert such a line you can type \ – to fill each cell with a dashed line. Let's do that now.

To underline the column headings:

❶ Move the cell pointer to A27. Type \ – and press **[Enter]**.

❷ Repeat Step 1 for cells B27, C27, and D27.

To add a row of lines to row 32:

❸ Move the cell pointer to A32. Type \ – and press **[Enter]**.

❹ Repeat Step 3 for cells B32, C32, and D32. See Figure 3-23.

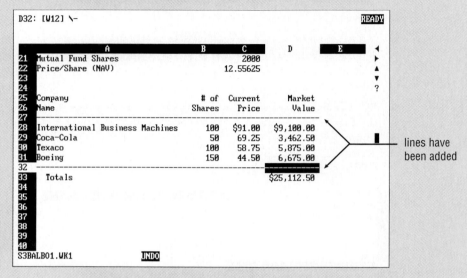

Figure 3-23
Adding dashed
lines to separate
headings and total
from the data

Moving Data

Pauline has made several changes that have improved the appearance of her worksheet. However, after reviewing the current worksheet, Pauline decides that she wants to make additional changes to improve it even more. First, she wants the summary data on mutual fund shares and net asset value to follow the company data. She feels the companies that make up the fund should be placed before the summary information on the NAV. (Report layout often is a matter of personal preference.) In addition, she realizes the report is actually incomplete because the company sells many different mutual funds. The worksheet does not indicate that these data are only for the Balboa Equity Fund. Also, she prices the fund at the end of each day, but the worksheet doesn't indicate the date of this report. Thus, Pauline decides to add the following two lines to the worksheet:

Balboa Equity Fund
Net Asset Value for November 5, 199X

She wants to place this title above the column headings, exactly where the Mutual Fund Shares label is now. How can she rearrange the worksheet without starting over?

Fortunately Lotus 1-2-3 has a Move command. Its function is to move data from one part of the worksheet to another part of the same worksheet. The data that are moved from one location to another disappear from the first location. The Move command is a powerful tool for creating and designing worksheets. Let's move the information on the number of shares owned and the NAV to begin in cell A36, so this information appears after the individual companies in the fund.

To move the range A21..C22 to a new location:

① Move the cell pointer to A21, the upper left corner of the range you want to move.

② Select /Move (**/M**). A21..A21 appears on the control panel as the "Move what?" range. The two periods mean the range is already anchored in cell A21. See Figure 3-24.

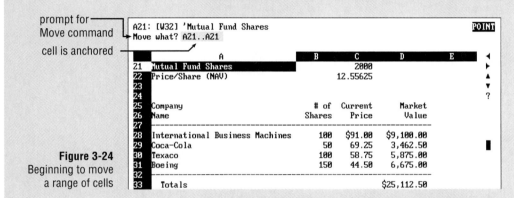

prompt for
Move command

cell is anchored

Figure 3-24
Beginning to move
a range of cells

You next identify the entire range you want to move (A21 to C22):

③ Highlight A21..C22. The highlighted area will be moved. See Figure 3-25.

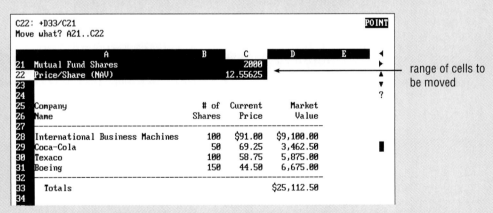

range of cells to
be moved

Figure 3-25
Highlighting the
range of cells to be
moved

④ Press **[Enter]**.

Now you identify where you want to move this block of cells. Specify the upper left corner of the new location for this block of cells:

⑤ Move the cell pointer to A36, the first cell of the "To where?" range. This is the cell where you want the label "Mutual Fund Shares" to begin.

⑥   Press **[Enter]**. The block of cells moves to its new location. See Figure 3-26. Notice that A21..C22 is empty.

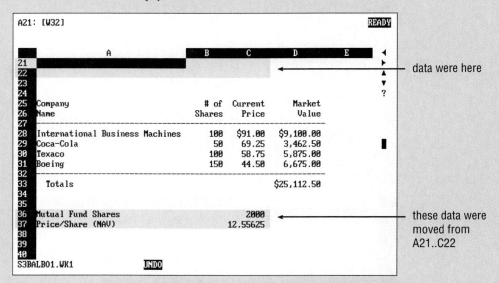

Figure 3-26
Worksheet after
range is moved

When you move part or even all of your worksheet, the worksheet retains all the functional relationships. 1-2-3 automatically adjusts all the formulas in "Move what?" range.

If the UNDO feature is enabled, you can remove the effects of a Move command by pressing [Alt][F4] before executing another command.

When you have completed moving the data, the cell pointer returns to the cell where you started the command.

⑦   Move the cell pointer to the cell that contains the NAV, C37, and examine the formula in the control panel. The formula is now +D33/C36. When the formula was in cell C22, the formula was +D33/C21. 1-2-3 automatically adjusted the formula when the data were moved.

Now you are ready to enter the two-line title: Balboa Equity Fund and Net Asset Value for November 5, 199X.

To enter the title:
❶   Move the cell pointer to cell A21.
❷   Type **Balboa Equity Fund** and press [↓].
❸   In cell A22 type **Net Asset Value for November 5, 199x** and press **[Enter]**. See Figure 3-27.

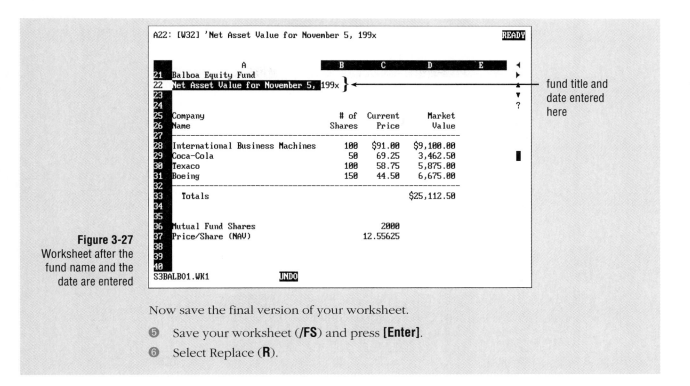

```
A22: [W32] 'Net Asset Value for November 5, 199x                    READY

            A                      B    C      D        E       ◄
21  Balboa Equity Fund                                            ►
22  Net Asset Value for November 5, 199x }◄────────────────────── ▲
23                                                                ▼
24                                                                ?
25  Company                      # of  Current   Market
26  Name                        Shares  Price    Value
27  ──────────────────────────────────────────────────
28  International Business Machines  100  $91.00  $9,100.00        ▌
29  Coca-Cola                         50   69.25   3,462.50
30  Texaco                           100   58.75   5,875.00
31  Boeing                           150   44.50   6,675.00
32  ──────────────────────────────────────────────────
33    Totals                                     $25,112.50
34
35
36  Mutual Fund Shares                   2000
37  Price/Share (NAV)                   12.55625
38
39
40
S3BALB01.WK1              UNDO
```

fund title and
date entered
here

Figure 3-27
Worksheet after the
fund name and the
date are entered

Now save the final version of your worksheet.

⑤ Save your worksheet (**/FS**) and press **[Enter]**.

⑥ Select Replace (**R**).

Erasing a Range of Cells

Now that the worksheet is complete, Pauline thinks about how she will use it on a daily basis. Each day Pauline will enter the current day's price for each company's stock. To make sure that she doesn't accidentally use a price from the previous day, she wants to erase all the prices in the Current Price column before she enters the prices for each day. To erase the prices, she will use the Range Erase command.

To erase the current prices in column C:

❶ Move the cell pointer to C28, the first cell to be erased.

❷ Select /Range Erase (**/RE**). The control panel reveals the address of the current cell and prompts you to specify the range you want to erase.

❸ Press **[↓]** to highlight the range C28..C31. See Figure 3-28 on the following page.

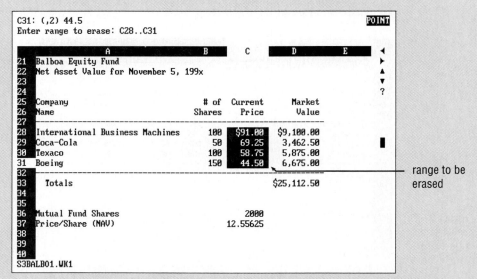

Figure 3-28
Erasing a range of cells

➍ Press **[Enter]**. 1-2-3 erases the entries in C28 to C31. The cell pointer returns to C28, the first cell in the range. See Figure 3-29.

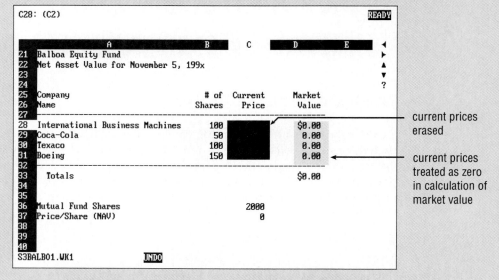

Figure 3-29
Worksheet after the prices are erased

Notice that the market values are now zero. That is because their values are based on the daily prices, which are blank. 1-2-3 treats the blank cells as zero for any calculations that reference these cells.

Another way to clear a cell is with the [Del] key. You would place the cell pointer in the cell you want to erase and press [Del].

Do not use [Spacebar] to erase the contents of a cell. Use the Range Erase command or the [Del] key.

The worksheet is now ready for Pauline to enter the prices for the next day.

> Now that you have completed Tutorial 3, you can read Module 2, *Using WYSIWYG to Enhance and Print 1-2-3 Worksheets* and Module 4, *Using SmartIcons*. Check with your instructor.

Exercises

1. Suppose that you have a worksheet in which cells F6, F7, F8, and F9 have values stored in them. Write two different formulas to calculate the total of these four cells.

2. Which formula adds six entries in row 3?
   a. +A3+A4+A5+A6+A7+A8
   b. @SUM(B3..E3)
   c. @SUM(D3..I3)
   d. +M3+N3+O3+P3

3. Suppose you type the value 1005.254 in cell A5. What format type would you select to have the following values appear in the cell?
   a. $1,005.25
   b. 1,005.3
   c. 1005

4. Figure 3-30 shows a worksheet you started typing. You typed the company name, Allied Freight, in cell A3, and the address, 227 Mill St Canton Ohio 13456, in B3. Why does the complete address appear in cell B3 but only Allied Fr in A3?

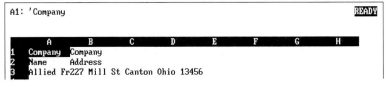

Figure 3-30

5. Figure 3-31 shows part of a worksheet. How would you improve the appearance of this worksheet?   What command(s) would you use?

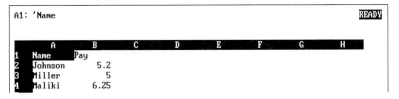

Figure 3-31

6. Retrieve the file E3FILE1.WK1. All the values are currently displayed in the General format. Use the Range Format command to answer 6a through 6d.
   a. Format the values in column C with Fixed format and two decimal places.
   b. Format the values in column D with Fixed format and zero decimal places.
   c. Format the values in column E with Comma format and one decimal place.
   d. Format the values in column F with Currency format and two decimal places.
   e. How are negative numbers displayed for each type of format?

7. Retrieve the file E3FILE2.WK1.
    a. What value was entered in cell A4? B4? C4? D4? E4?
    b. How have the values in the range A4..A6 been formatted? In B4..B6? In C4..C6? In D4..D6? In E4..E6?
    c. Multiply by hand the values displayed in A4 and A5; B4 and B5; C4 and C5; D4 and D5; and E4 and E5.
    d. Compare the results from 7c with the corresponding values in A6, B6, C6, D6, and E6. What conclusion can you draw about how 1-2-3 performs its calculations?

Tutorial Assignments

1. Retrieve the worksheet file T3BALBO1.WK1. The formula in cell C37 is not correct. Price/Share (NAV) shows "ERR" when the worksheet is retrieved.
    a. Explain why ERR is displayed as the value for NAV.
    b. Correct the error.
    c. Save the corrected worksheet as S3BALBO2.
    d. Print the corrected worksheet.

Retrieve the worksheet file T3BALBO2.WK1 and do the following:

2. Adjust two of the labels — Mutual Fund Shares and Price/Share (NAV) — so they are right-justified in their cells, A36 and A37, respectively.

3. Move the values associated with the labels in Tutorial Assignment 2 from cells C36 and C37 to B36 and B37.

4. Format NAV in cell B37 to two decimal places using the Currency format.

5. Print the revised worksheet. Use the print range A21..D37.

6. Save this worksheet as S3BALBO3.

7. Erase the entire worksheet.

8. Retrieve the worksheet file S3BALBO3.WK1.

9. Erase the current prices in the worksheet and then enter the following prices for November 6, 199X: 92, 68.50, 59, and 49. Remember to change the date in the worksheet. Save the worksheet as S3BALBO4. Print the worksheet.

The following exercises involve the worksheet developed in Tutorial 2. Retrieve the file T3KRIER1.WK1 and do the following:

10. In cell B19, use the @SUM function to calculate total hours for all employees.

11. Format the pay rate and gross pay columns to two decimal places using the Currency format.

12. A new employee, Jalecki, has been hired. Insert this name between the names Bramble and Juarez.

13. Save the revised worksheet as S3KRIER1.

14. Print the revised worksheet.

Case Problems

1. Z & Z Electronics Performance Report

Craig Keifer is the general manager of the manufacturing division of Z & Z Electronics. Each year Craig prepares estimated costs for manufacturing cabinets for computers and other electronic equipment. Manufacturing costs include wages/salaries, raw materials, utilities, supplies, and other costs. Craig also prepares a monthly performance report to measure his division's monthly performance compared to his estimate. This report compares the estimated costs with the actual costs for the month just ended and the year-to-date (YTD) cumulative costs. Craig also calculates the difference between estimated and actual costs, called the *variance,* for both the monthly and the cumulative periods. He does this by subtracting estimated costs from the actual costs, in other words,

$$variance \; = \; actual \; costs \; - \; estimated \; costs$$

Retrieve the P3PERFRM.WK1 worksheet. This worksheet contains the cost data for the month of March 1992, as well as cumulative costs since the beginning of the year.

1. Calculate the total costs for both the estimated and the actual cost columns (columns B, C, E, and F).

2. Calculate the variances for each cost for both monthly and year-to-date periods (columns D and G).

3. Improve the appearance of the worksheet. Add titles and lines under headings, format values, increase column widths, and make any other changes that will make the report more readable.

4. Save your worksheet as S3PERFRM.

5. Print your worksheet.

WYSIWYG Assignments

1. Attach WYSIWYG.

2. Add the following enhancements:
   a. Remove any dashed lines before you insert solid lines under column headings and above and below totals.
   b. Use a 14-point Swiss font for the report title line(s).
   c. Boldface the column headings.

3. Save your worksheet as W3PERFRM.

4. Print the entire worksheet on one page.

2. Ford Motor Company Car Sales

A Ford executive is preparing a presentation for a local Chamber of Commerce. The executive asks his assistant, Steve Duncan, to prepare a 1-2-3 worksheet with Ford's sales history (units sold) from 1985 to 1988. Steve starts to summarize the data for Ford's three divisions, Ford,

Mercury, and Lincoln, but he becomes ill and cannot finish the assignment. His worksheet file, P3FORD.WK1, is incomplete:

- He has not entered data for the Mercury division, which is shown in Figure 3-32. The data for the Mercury division should be placed between the Ford and the Lincoln divisions.
- Each division's sales need to be subtotaled, and then all three divisions' sales should be added to provide total sales for Ford Motor Company for each year. Only the labels for the subtotals appear in the worksheet.
- Finally, the worksheet must be more professional in appearance before the executive distributes it to the Chamber of Commerce.

Units Sold—Mercury Division				
Mercury Division	**1985**	**1986**	**1987**	**1988**
Topaz	73554	65498	63217	85936
Sable	879	91314	103399	118117
Cougar	118554	112812	110112	102415
Grand Marquis	134139	118364	119015	115141

Figure 3-32

Complete Steve's worksheet by doing the following:

1. Retrieve the worksheet file P3FORD.WK1.
2. Add the data for the Mercury division between the Ford and the Lincoln divisions.
3. Calculate subtotals for each division.
4. Calculate total sales for all the divisions.
5. Improve the appearance of the worksheet. Include a title, the date, and lines under the column headings, align the column headings, and make any other changes you feel are appropriate.
6. Save your worksheet as S3FORD.
7. Print the worksheet.

WYSIWYG Assignments

1. Attach WYSIWYG.
2. Add the following enhancements:
   a. Remove any dashed lines before you insert solid lines under column headings and above and below totals.
   b. Use a 14-point Swiss font for the report title line(s).
   c. Enclose the report title in a box.
   d. Shade the row containing the totals for Total Ford Division.
3. Save your worksheet as W3FORD.
4. Print the entire worksheet on one page.

3. Calculating the Dow Jones Industrial Average

The Dow Jones Industrial Average (DJIA) is the best-known indicator of how stock prices fluctuate on the New York Stock Exchange (NYSE). The DJIA represents the average price of 30 large, well-known industrial corporations considered leaders in their industry. All the companies are listed on the NYSE.

Each day the DJIA is calculated by summing the closing price of each of the 30 companies and dividing by a divisor. The formula for calculating the DJIA is

$$DJIA = \frac{sum\ of\ daily\ closing\ prices\ for\ 30\ companies}{divisor}$$

On December 31, 1991, the DJIA was 3168.83. The divisor was .5593.

Retrieve the file P3DOW.WK1 and do the following:

1. Finish the calculation of the DJIA (cell B43). (Your answer will be within ± .25 of 3168.83.)

2. Experts suggest that changes in higher-priced stocks have a greater impact on the DJIA than changes in lower-priced stocks. For example, if Merck, a high-priced stock, were to increase by 10% (assume no other stock prices change), the new DJIA would change more than if Bethlehem Steel, a low-priced stock, were to increase by 10%.
    a. In column C, labeled Merck's Adjmt, increase Merck's price by 10% (1.10 × current price) and calculate the new DJIA (cell C43).
    b. In column D, the Bethlehem Steel column, increase Bethlehem Steel's price by 10% and calculate the DJIA (cell D43).
    c. Compare the new averages against the original average by calculating the percent change. Use the following formulas:

    For the percent change in column C:

    $$percent\ change = \frac{(\ Merck\ adjusted\ DJIA\ -\ original\ DJIA)}{original\ DJIA}$$

    For the percent change in column D:

    $$percent\ change = \frac{(Bethlehem\ Steel\ adjusted\ DJIA\ -\ original\ DJIA)}{original\ DJIA}$$

    Note that the original DJIA is in cell B43. How do these new averages compare to the original average?

3. Format your worksheet so it is more readable. Consider formatting values, centering or right-justifying column headings, adding descriptive labels, and making any other changes you think will improve the appearance of your worksheet.

4. Save your worksheet as S3DOW.

5. Print your final worksheet.

WYSIWYG Assignments

1. Attach WYSIWYG.

2. Add the following enhancements:
    a. Remove any dashed lines before you insert solid lines under column headings and above and below totals.

b. Use a 14-point Swiss font for the two lines of the report title.
c. Change the font of the range A10..D60 to 12-point Dutch font.
d. Use a drop shadow to enhance the row containing the DJIA.

3. Save your worksheet as W3DOW.
4. Print the entire worksheet on one page.

4. Cash Budgeting at Foreman's Appliances

Jason Ballentine, the business manager for Foreman's Appliances, a small retail appliance store, is in the process of preparing a cash budget for January. The store has a loan that must be paid the first week in February. Jason wants to determine if the business will have enough cash to make the loan payment to the bank.

Jason sketches the projected budget so that it will have the format shown in Figure 3-33.

Projected Cash Receipts and Disbursements		
January 199x		
Cash balance, January 1, 199x		xxxx
Projected receipts during January:		
Cash sales during month	xxxx	
Collections from credit sales	xxxx	
Total cash receipts		xxxx
Projected disbursements during January:		
Payments for goods purchased	xxxx	
Salaries	xxxx	
Rent	xxxx	
Utilities	xxxx	
Total cash disbursements		xxxx
Cash balance, January 31, 199x		xxxx

Figure 3-33

Next Jason determines that he must perform the calculations in Figure 3-34 to prepare the cash budget.

1. Total cash receipts during January is sum of cash sales and collections from credit sales.
2. Total cash disbursements during month is the sum of payments for goods purchased, salaries, rent, and utilities.
3. Cash balance at the end of the month equals the cash balance at beginning of month plus total cash receipts less total cash disbursements.

Figure 3-34

Finally, Jason plans to use the inputs shown in Figure 3-35 to prepare the cash budget.

Cash balance at beginning of month	32000
Cash sales during month	9000
Collections from credit sales	17500
Payments for goods purchased	15000
Salaries	4800
Rent	1500
Utilities	800

Figure 3-35

Do the following:

1. Prepare a cash budget worksheet based on Jason's information. Enter labels, input values, and formulas.

2. Format the values in the worksheet using the Currency format with zero decimal places.

3. Save your worksheet as S3BUD.

4. Print the projected cash budget.

5. After printing the first budget, Jason remembers that starting this month rent will increase to $1650 a month. Modify the projected cash budget. Print the worksheet with the revised projected cash budget.

WYSIWYG Assignments

1. Attach WYSIWYG.

2. Add the following enhancements:
   a. Remove any dashed lines before you insert solid lines under column headings and above and below totals.
   b. Use a 24-point Swiss font for the first report title line. Use a 14-point Swiss font for the second line.
   c. Boldface the rows with the labels Projected Receipts and Projected Disbursements.
   d. Shade the last row, Cash Balance, January 31, 199X.

3. Save your worksheet as W3BUDGT.

4. Print the entire worksheet on one page.

Tutorial 4

Working with Larger Worksheets

Preparing a Revenue Report

Case: TriCycle Industries

Nick Theodorakis is the assistant sales manager for TriCycle Industries, a recycling center serving the tri-state area of Kentucky, Indiana, and Illinois. For the last two years, TriCycle's sales were not high enough to generate a profit. This year, however, TriCycle has been profitable and has come very close to achieving its sales goals.

As assistant sales manager, Nick services 15 customer accounts, scouts for new accounts, and provides administrative assistance to the TriCycle sales manager, Kay Schilling. At the end of each quarter, Nick assists Kay in preparing a quarterly sales report. Kay then formally presents the report to top management at TriCycle's quarterly meeting.

OBJECTIVES

In this tutorial you will learn to:

- Copy the contents of cells to other locations in the worksheet

- Copy relative cell references

- Copy absolute cell references

- Assign names to cell ranges

- Print with compressed type

Kay meets with Nick to discuss this quarter's report. She shows him the data she has compiled:

TriCycle Industries
1992 Revenue
(000 Omitted)

Recycled Material	First Quarter	Second Quarter	Third Quarter	Fourth Quarter
Plastics	2890	2942	3378	3837
Glass	2701	2862	2869	3601
Aluminum	2247	2282	2489	2602

Kay points out that these data represent the revenue for all four quarters of 1992. She wants to include totals and some additional information to help the top executives compare 1992 revenues to previous years. She asks Nick to create a worksheet using the data she's collected thus far and also showing the following items:

- total revenue by quarter
- total revenue for the year 1992 by recycled material
- total 1992 revenue
- contribution of revenue from each material as a percentage of total 1992 revenue
- average quarterly sales for each material

Nick agrees and offers to give special attention to the appearance of the worksheet, because he knows how important this report will be. Nick spends time thinking about the project and develops a planning sheet and a sketch to assist him in completing the worksheet (Figures 4-1a and 4-1b).

Planning Sheet

My Goal:
  Prepare the sales Report for TriCycle management

What results do I want to see?
  Sales Revenue Report including totals by quarter and recycled material
  Contribution of each recycled material to total revenue

What information do I need?
  Quarterly sales revenue for each recycled material

What calculations will I perform?
  Calculate total revenue for each quarter
  Calculate total revenue for each recycled material for the year
  Calculate total revenue for year
  Calculate percent contribution of each recycled material to total revenue
  Calculate average quarterly sales for each material

Figure 4-1a
Nick's planning
sheet

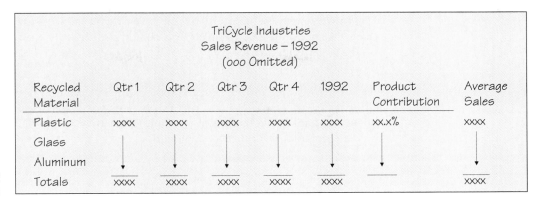

Figure 4-1b
Nick's worksheet
sketch

In this tutorial you will use Kay's data to create Nick's report. You will learn how to copy formulas, a process that saves a great deal of time in creating a worksheet. You will also put to use several valuable 1-2-3 features, such as how to name ranges. You will also learn more about printing with 1-2-3, specifically how to use compressed type to print more data on one line.

Retrieving the Worksheet

Your first step in this tutorial is to retrieve the worksheet that Nick has started based on Kay's data.

To retrieve the worksheet:

❶ Retrieve the file C4TRICY1.WK1. See Figure 4-2.

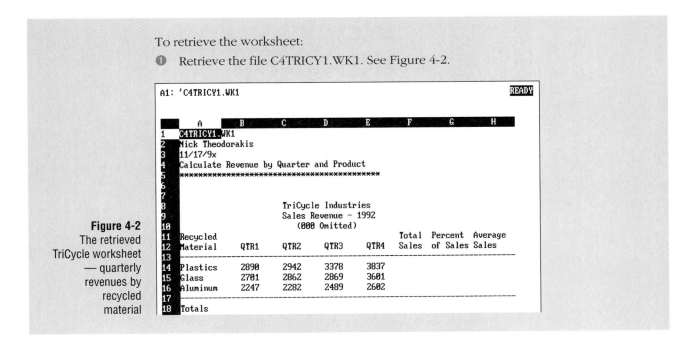

Figure 4-2
The retrieved
TriCycle worksheet
— quarterly
revenues by
recycled
material

This file contains the quarterly revenues of TriCycle Industries categorized by the material they recycle. Titles have been entered, as have revenue amounts for each material for each quarter.

How did TriCycle perform in each quarter? Let's calculate total revenues for each quarter to summarize TriCycle's revenue picture. In Tutorial 3 you used the @SUM function to calculate the total market value of a mutual fund. Now you will use the @SUM function to calculate the total revenue for each quarter.

To calculate total revenue for the first quarter:

❶ Move the cell pointer to B18.

❷ Type **@sum(** to begin the formula.

❸ Move the cell pointer to B14 and then type **[.]** (Period) to anchor the cell pointer.

❹ Press **[↓]** to highlight the range B14..B16. See Figure 4-3.

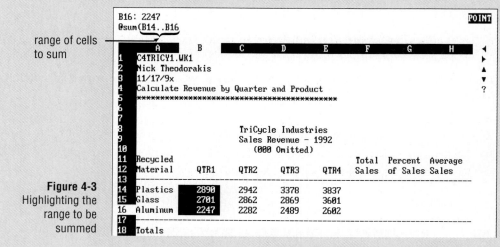

range of cells to sum

Figure 4-3
Highlighting the range to be summed

❺ Type **[)]** (Right Parenthesis) and press **[Enter]**. The total revenue in quarter 1, 7838, appears in cell B18. See Figure 4-4.

formula to calculate total revenue in quarter 1

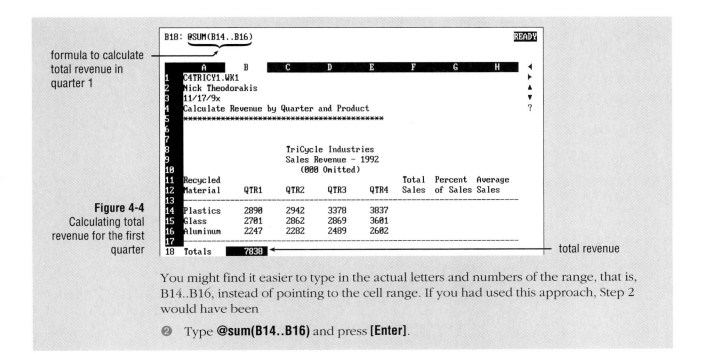

Figure 4-4
Calculating total revenue for the first quarter

total revenue

You might find it easier to type in the actual letters and numbers of the range, that is, B14..B16, instead of pointing to the cell range. If you had used this approach, Step 2 would have been

② Type **@sum(B14..B16)** and press **[Enter]**.

Copying Formulas

You can continue to use the @SUM function to calculate total revenues for the remaining quarters. A faster approach, however, is to use the Copy command. Experienced 1-2-3 users rely on the Copy command because it saves time and decreases the likelihood of errors. Let's calculate total revenues for quarters 2, 3, and 4 by copying the formula in cell B18 to cells C18, D18, and E18.

To copy a formula to cells C18, D18, and E18:

First specify the cell or range you want to copy.

① With the cell pointer in B18, the cell whose formula will be copied, select /Copy **(/C)**.

The control panel displays B18..B18 as the "Copy what?" range, meaning cell B18 is the cell you want to copy to other cells. See Figure 4-5 on the following page.

formula to
be copied

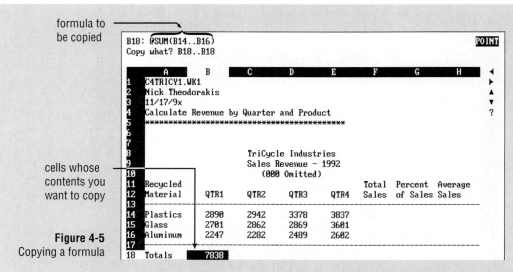

cells whose
contents you
want to copy

Figure 4-5
Copying a formula

❷   Press **[Enter]**, because B18 is the only cell formula you want to copy. Notice that the control panel text changes and requests the range of cells where the formula is to be copied. See Figure 4-6.

formula to
be copied

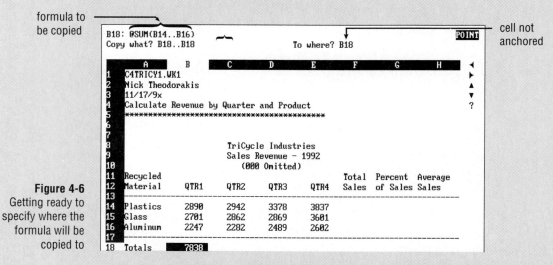

cell not
anchored

Figure 4-6
Getting ready to
specify where the
formula will be
copied to

❸   Move the cell pointer to C18, the first cell in the range to which you are copying the formula.

Now anchor this cell pointer.

❹   Press **[.]** (Period) to anchor the cell pointer. This designates C18 as the first cell in the "To where?" range. See Figure 4-7.

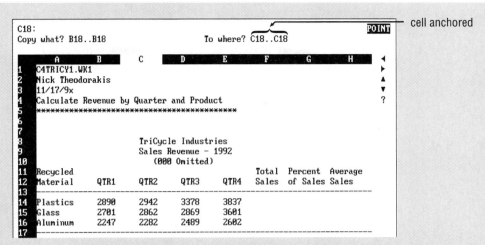

Figure 4-7
Anchoring the cell pointer

⑤ Press [→] as needed to highlight the range C18 to E18. This is the entire "To where?" range. See Figure 4-8.

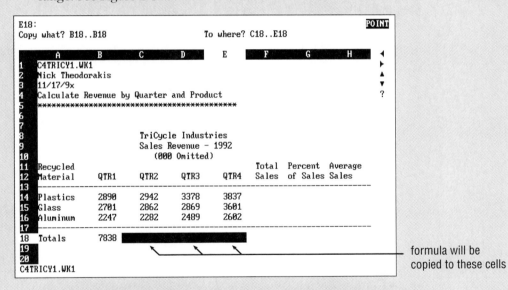

Figure 4-8
Highlighting the cells where the formula will be copied

formula will be copied to these cells

⑥ Press **[Enter]** to complete the command. See Figure 4-9 on the following page.

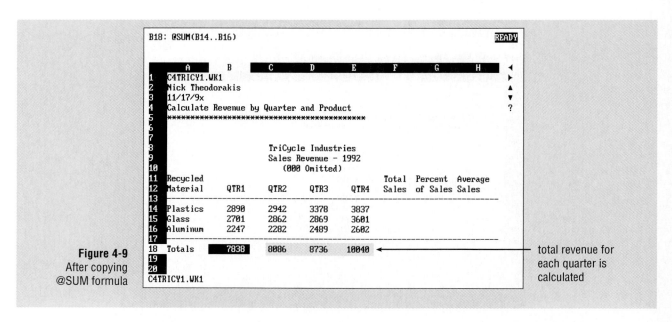

```
B18: @SUM(B14..B16)                                                    READY

        A         B        C        D        E        F       G       H    ◄
 1  C4TRICY1.WK1                                                            ►
 2  Nick Theodorakis                                                       ▲
 3  11/17/9x                                                               ▼
 4  Calculate Revenue by Quarter and Product                              ?
 5  **********************************************
 6
 7
 8                         TriCycle Industries
 9                        Sales Revenue - 1992
10                           (000 Omitted)
11  Recycled                                      Total  Percent  Average
12  Material    QTR1     QTR2     QTR3     QTR4    Sales  of Sales Sales
13  ------------------------------------------------
14  Plastics    2890     2942     3378     3837
15  Glass       2701     2862     2869     3601
16  Aluminum    2247     2282     2489     2602
17  ------------------------------------------------
18  Totals      7838     8086     8736    10040 ◄────
19
20
    C4TRICY1.WK1
```

Figure 4-9
After copying
@SUM formula

total revenue for
each quarter is
calculated

Total revenue for each quarter has now been calculated. You entered the formula for the first quarter and then used the Copy command to copy that formula to the cell locations for quarters 2, 3, and 4.

Understanding Relative Cell References

How 1-2-3 copies a formula depends on whether you use relative cell references or absolute cell references in the formula. The concept of relative and absolute cell references is extremely important to your work with 1-2-3.

A **relative cell reference** is a cell or range of cells in a formula that 1-2-3 interprets as a location relative to the current cell. For example, in cell B18 you have the formula @SUM(B14..B16). 1-2-3 interprets this formula as "add the contents of three cells starting four cells above the formula cell." When you copy this formula to a new location, to cell C18, for example, you copy the relationship between the formula and the cell or range to which it refers. 1-2-3 automatically adjusts the addresses in the copied formulas to maintain the relationship. For example, if you copy the formula @SUM(B14..B16) to cell C18, 1-2-3 would interpret the formula as "add the contents of three cells starting four cells above the formula cell" and would adjust the formula automatically to @SUM(C14..C16).

1-2-3 treats cell references as relative references unless you specify that they are absolute. You will learn about absolute cell references later in this tutorial.

Naming Ranges

Kay also wants to know how much revenue TriCycle earned from recycling each material during 1992. To calculate yearly revenue, you will continue to use the @SUM function. Instead of using cell addresses inside the @SUM function, however, you will use range names in the formulas. Whenever you are working with a large worksheet, you should use descriptive words instead of cell addresses for ranges in a formula. Descriptive words are more meaningful in a formula, since they remind you of the purpose of the calculation. Thus, the formulas are easier to read and understand. 1-2-3 lets you assign descriptive names to individual cells and to cell ranges. You can then use these names in place of cell references when building formulas. For example, the formula @SUM(PLASTICS) is easier to understand than @SUM(B14..E14).

Let's assign range names to the range of cells representing quarterly sales for each recycled material: plastics, glass, and aluminum. Let's also assign a range name to the range of cells representing the four quarterly totals (B18..E18).

To assign the range name PLASTICS to the range B14..E14:

❶ Move the cell pointer to B14, the revenue from recycled plastics in the first quarter.

❷ Select /Range Name Create (**/RNC**).

You can now enter a range name of up to 15 characters.

❸ Type **plastics** and press **[Enter]**. See Figure 4-10.

range name →

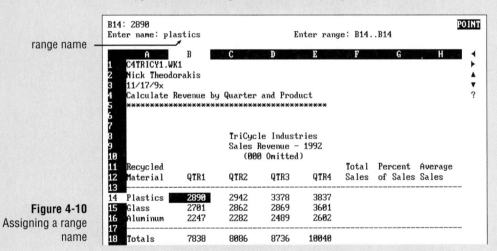

Figure 4-10
Assigning a range
name

You can use lowercase or uppercase letters. 1-2-3 automatically converts lowercase to uppercase.

❹ Press **[→]** to highlight the range B14..E14. You don't need to anchor the cell pointer, because it is automatically anchored when you use the Range Name command.

❺ Press **[Enter]**. You have just named the range B14..E14 PLASTICS.

Next, assign the range name GLASS to the revenue earned from recycling glass during the four quarters.

To assign the range name GLASS to the range B15..E15:

❶ Move the cell pointer to B15, the revenue from glass during the first quarter.

❷ Select /Range Name Create (**/RNC**).

❸ Type **glass** and press **[Enter]**.

④ Press [→] to highlight the range B15..E15.

⑤ Press **[Enter]**. You have just named the range B15..E15 GLASS.

Now assign the range name ALUMINUM to the revenue received from recycling aluminum materials during the four quarters.

To assign the range name ALUMINUM to the range B16..E16:

① Move the cell pointer to B16, the revenue from aluminum in the first quarter.

② Select /Range Name Create (**/RNC**).

③ Type **aluminum** and press **[Enter]**.

④ Press [→] to highlight the range B16..E16.

⑤ Press **[Enter]**. You have just named the range B16..E16 ALUMINUM.

Finally, assign the range name QTR_SALES to the revenue received from recycling all materials during the four quarters.

To assign the range name QTR_SALES to the range B18..E18:

① Move the cell pointer to B18, the revenue from all products during the first quarter.

② Select /Range Name Create (**/RNC**).

③ Type **qtr_sales** and press **[Enter]**.

Notice the use of the [_] (Underscore) to connect words; spaces and hyphens are not recommended in range names, because 1-2-3 might misinterpret these symbols.

④ Press [→] to highlight the range B18..E18.

⑤ Press **[Enter]**. You have just named the range B18..E18 QTR_SALES.

If you select the Range Name Create command and then realize you want to highlight a range that starts in another location, press [Esc] to unanchor the cell pointer. Then move the cell pointer to the appropriate starting cell and press [.] (Period) to reanchor the cell pointer.

Range names can be up to 15 characters long, but they should not include spaces or the characters + * – / & { @ and #. The underscore character is often used to connect words together. Do not use range names such as Q1, because 1-2-3 will interpret these names as cell locations instead of range names.

Using Named Ranges in Formulas

Now you are ready to calculate total revenue earned by TriCycle Industries during 1992. In the previous steps, you created the range names PLASTIC, GLASS, ALUMINUM, and QTR_SALES. Assigning names to a range of cells makes formulas easier to create and interpret. You can use range names in formulas two ways: by choosing the one you want from a list of the previously named ranges or by typing the name of the range directly into the formula.

To obtain a list of range names while you are entering a formula, press [F3] (NAME) to display a list of range names created in the current worksheet. Highlight the range name you want and press [Enter]. The range name then is entered into the formula.

To use a range name in an @SUM formula by choosing from a list of range names:

① Move the cell pointer to F14, the cell in which you want total revenues from plastics for 1992 to appear.

② Type **@sum(**.

③ Press **[F3]** (NAME). This function key displays a list of all range names you have created for this worksheet. See Figure 4-11.

list of range names you've created and from which you can choose

Figure 4-11
Listing the range names by using the [F3] key

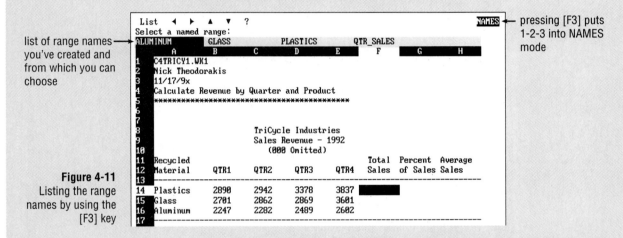

pressing [F3] puts 1-2-3 into NAMES mode

④ Move the cursor to the range name you want, PLASTICS, and press **[Enter]** to select it. Your entry should now look like that in Figure 4-12.

Figure 4-12
Selecting a range name to include in @SUM function

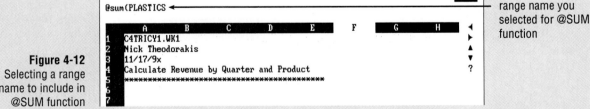

range name you selected for @SUM function

⑤ Complete the formula by typing **[)]** (Right Parenthesis).

⑥ Press **[Enter]**. 1-2-3 calculates the result, 13047, in cell F14. This is the sum of revenues earned from recycling plastics during 1992.

Alternatively, you could have typed in the range name, PLASTICS, directly after the left parenthesis in Step 2 and then omitted Steps 3 through 6. In Step 2 you would have typed **@sum(plastics)** and then pressed [Enter].

Now let's enter the @SUM formulas for glass, aluminum, and quarterly sales.

To continue entering @SUM formulas using the [F3] key:

❶ Move the cell pointer to F15, the cell in which you want total revenues from glass for 1992 to appear.

❷ Type **@sum(**.

❸ Press **[F3]** (NAME). This function key displays a list of all range names you have created for this worksheet.

❹ Move the cursor to the range name you want, GLASS, and press **[Enter]** to select it.

❺ Type **[)]** (Right Parenthesis) and press **[Enter]**. 1-2-3 calculates the result, 12033, in cell F15. This is the sum of revenues earned from recycling glass during 1992.

❻ Move the cell pointer to F16. Repeat steps 2 through 5 to enter an @SUM formula using the range name ALUMINUM to total revenue from aluminum in 1992. The result in F16 should be 9620. See Figure 4-13.

❼ Move the cell pointer to F18. Repeat Steps 2 through 5 to enter an @SUM formula using the range name QTR_SALES to total revenue from all products in 1992. The result in F18 should be 34700. See Figure 4-13.

@SUM function using range name as argument

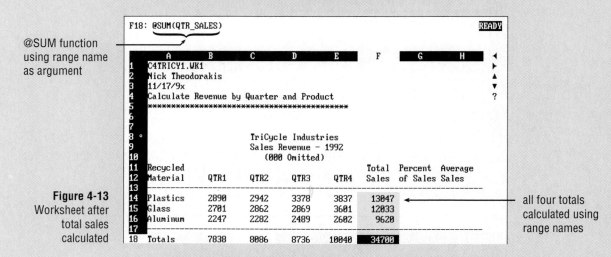

Figure 4-13
Worksheet after total sales calculated

all four totals calculated using range names

If you accidentally press [Enter] before typing the right parenthesis, 1-2-3 automatically beeps and moves to EDIT mode. You should then type [ )] (Right Parenthesis) and press [Enter].

Creating a Table of Range Names

If your worksheet contains several range names, a table containing each range name and its location might be helpful. You use the Range Name Table command to perform this task.

To create a table of range names, you move the cell pointer to the location where you want the range name table to begin. You then select /Range Name Table (/RNT) and highlight the range that will contain the table. Finally, you press [Enter] to complete the command. The range names and their corresponding addresses appear in the worksheet.

Be aware that the range name table is not updated automatically. If you add additional range names after you create the table, you must use the /Range Name command again to update the table.

Deleting Range Names

If you create a range name and then want to delete it, select /Range Name Delete (/RND). A list of the current range names appears in the control panel. Move the menu pointer to the name you want to delete from the list and press [Enter].

Copying Formulas with Absolute References

Nick has now calculated total revenue earned by TriCycle Industries during 1992, as well as individual revenues from plastics, glass, and aluminum. Next, Nick plans to calculate each material's percentage of total 1992 revenue. To calculate each material's contribution to total revenue, you divide the 1992 revenue for each material by total company revenue for 1992. For example,

$$percent\ contribution\ of\ plastics\ to\ total\ revenue = \frac{1992\ revenue\ for\ plastics}{total\ TriCycle\ 1992\ revenue}$$

To calculate the percent contribution of plastics to total revenue:

❶ Move the cell pointer to G14.

❷ Type the formula **+F14/F18** and press **[Enter]**. The result, 0.375994, appears in cell G14. See Figure 4-14.

symbol for division

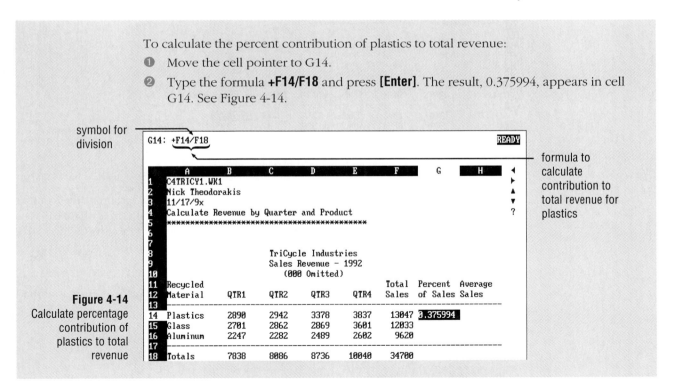

formula to calculate contribution to total revenue for plastics

Figure 4-14
Calculate percentage contribution of plastics to total revenue

Now that you have entered the formula +F14/F18 in cell G14, you can use the Copy command to copy this formula to other cells.

The steps that follow illustrate an approach that leads to incorrect results. We show these steps to demonstrate a common mistake made by many beginning students of 1-2-3, in the hopes of helping you avoid it.

To demonstrate a common mistake:

❶ Be sure the cell pointer is in G14, the cell that contains the formula to be copied. Select /Copy (**/C**). The control panel shows G14..G14 as the "Copy what?" range.

❷ Press **[Enter]**, since G14 is the only cell you want to copy.

❸ Move the cell pointer to G15, the first cell in the range to which you are copying.

❹ Press **[.]** (Period) to anchor the cell pointer. G15 is now the first cell in the range to which you are copying the formula.

❺ Highlight the range G15..G16 and press **[Enter]** to complete the command. Notice that ERR appears in cells G15 and G16. See Figure 4-15.

Figure 4-15
Common error in
copying formulas

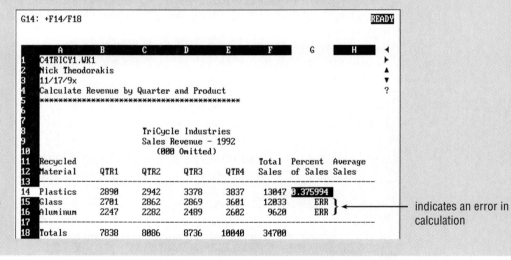

indicates an error in calculation

Move the cell pointer sequentially to each cell that contains ERR and examine the formula in the control panel. Do you see what happened? The formula in cell G15 is +F15/F19, but what you want in G15 is the formula +F15/F18. You also have an incorrect formula in G16, +F16/F20 instead of +F16/F18. All the copied formulas have resulted in ERR appearing in the respective cells.

Why does ERR appear in these cells? When you copied the formula (+F14/F18) in cell G14, 1-2-3 assumed relative addressing and *adjusted* the cell references in the copied formula. The following formulas resulted:

Cell	Formula
G15	+F15/F19
G16	+F16/F20

When 1-2-3 calculated the glass and aluminum contributions using the formulas in G15 and G16, it tried to divide by zero (the values in cells F19 and F20 are both zero). Since division by zero is undefined, the message ERR appears in cells G15 and G16.

To calculate percentage contribution of each material, you need to use the following formulas:

Recycled Material	Formula	Description
Plastic	+F14/F18	$\dfrac{\textit{1992 revenue for plastic}}{\textit{total TriCycle 1992 revenue}}$
Glass	+F15/F18	$\dfrac{\textit{1992 revenue for glass}}{\textit{total TriCycle 1992 revenue}}$
Aluminum	+F16/F18	$\dfrac{\textit{1992 revenue for aluminum}}{\textit{total TriCycle 1992 revenue}}$

Notice that the cells in the numerators vary (F14, F15, F16), while the cells in the denominators are always the same, F18. When you copy the formula for percentage contribution to other cell locations, the cell addresses of the numerator should change relative to the cell formula. On the other hand, when you copy the cell address of the denominator to other cell locations, the cell address should remain unchanged. Thus, using relative referencing for the entire formula doesn't work. This is an example of a situation that requires absolute cell references.

Absolute Cell References

When you copy a formula, you sometimes want 1-2-3 to keep the original cell addresses in the copied formula. You do *not* want 1-2-3 to adjust the cell references for you. To keep the original cell or range reference constant, no matter where in the worksheet the formula is copied, you use an absolute reference. An **absolute cell reference** is a cell address or range name that *always* refers to the same cell, even if you copy the formula to a new location. To designate an absolute cell reference, you use [$] (Dollar Sign) to precede both the column letter and the row number or range name of the cell you want to remain unchanged. Thus, $F$18 is an absolute cell reference, whereas F18 is a relative reference. Initially, both reference the same cell location; however, if you copy the cell location $F$18 to another cell, the cell address in the new location remains unchanged, whereas if you copy the cell location F18 to another cell, the cell address in the new location is automatically adjusted to reflect its position relative to the original cell location.

To specify absolute cell references, you can either type the $ character before the column letter and row number when you enter (or edit) a formula, or you can use another of the 1-2-3 function keys, [F4] (ABS), the Absolute key. When you press the [F4] key while in EDIT mode, 1-2-3 inserts a $ character at the cursor location in the cell address in the control panel. You could also retype the formula using the $ symbol in the appropriate places, but using the [F4] key is usually faster and helps avoid entry errors.

Before you try using the absolute reference in your formula, let's erase the incorrect formulas in cells G15 and G16 that cause ERR to be displayed. When you type or copy an entry into the wrong cell, you can erase the contents of a single cell by moving the cell pointer to the cell you want to erase and pressing [Del].

To erase a cell using [Del]:

❶ Move the cell pointer to G15, the first cell to be erased, and press **[Del]**.

❷ Move the cell pointer to G16 and press **[Del]**. The formulas are erased from cells G15 and G16. See Figure 4-16.

cell is empty →

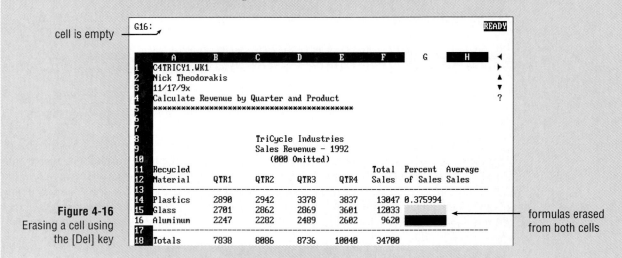

→ formulas erased from both cells

Figure 4-16
Erasing a cell using the [Del] key

Now let's correctly calculate the contributions to total revenue from glass and aluminum.

To use [F4] (ABS) to insert absolute cell references:

❶ Move the cell pointer to G14 and press **[F2]** (EDIT) to display the formula in the control panel. Notice that +F14/F18 appears in the second line of the control panel. See Figure 4-17.

line to be edited →

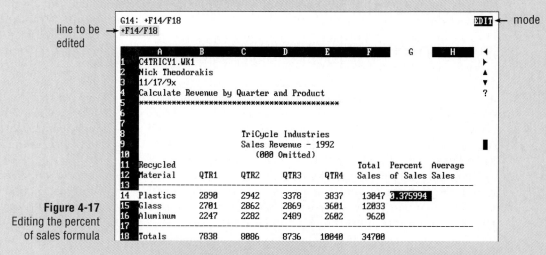

← mode

Figure 4-17
Editing the percent of sales formula

❷ Press **[←]** until the cursor is under the F in F18. Press **[F4]** (ABS) to make the cell reference absolute. Notice that $F$18 appears in the control panel. See Figure 4-18.

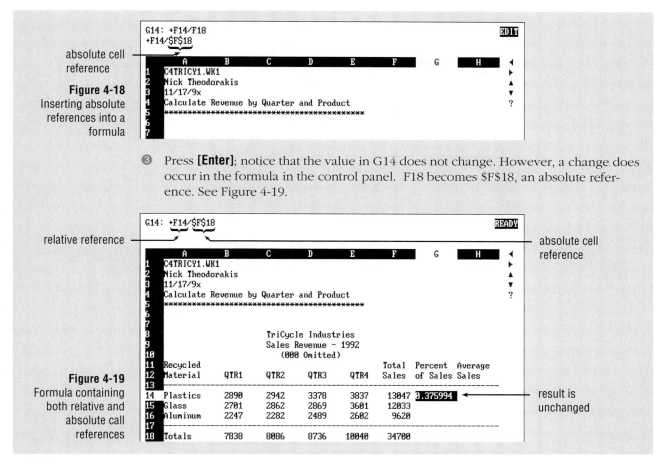

absolute cell
reference

Figure 4-18
Inserting absolute
references into a
formula

❸ Press **[Enter]**; notice that the value in G14 does not change. However, a change does occur in the formula in the control panel. F18 becomes $F$18, an absolute reference. See Figure 4-19.

relative reference

absolute cell
reference

Figure 4-19
Formula containing
both relative and
absolute call
references

result is
unchanged

Now the formula in G14 uses an absolute cell reference to reference total 1992 revenues and a relative reference for each material's revenue. No matter what cell you copy the formula in G14 to, the cell reference $F$18 will not change. To demonstrate this process, let's copy the formula in G14 again to see what happens.

To copy G14 to G15..G16:

❶ Make sure the cell pointer is at G14 and select /Copy (**/C**).

❷ Press **[Enter]**, because G14 is the only cell you want to copy.

❸ Move the cell pointer to G15, the first cell in the range to which you are copying.

❹ Press **[.]** (Period) to anchor the cell pointer. G15 is now the first cell into which you want the formula copied.

❺ Highlight the range G15..G16. This is the range of cells where the formula will be copied.

⑥ Press **[Enter]** to complete the command. The percent contribution of each material to total sales appears in cells G15 and G16. See Figure 4-20.

Figure 4-20
After copying formulas with absolute reference to other cells

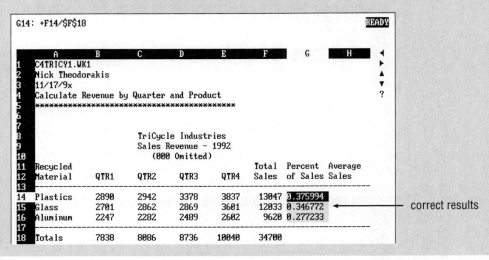

correct results

As a result of the Copy command, the following formulas appear in the control panel when you highlight cells G15 and G16:

Cell	Formula
G15	+F15/$F$18
G16	+F16/$F$18

Normally each material's contribution to total revenue is expressed as a percentage. In the worksheet, however, these values now appear as decimals. Let's change the contribution column so that all values will appear in Percent format. Numbers will then appear as percentages, that is, whole numbers followed by percent signs (%), for example, 15%. 1-2-3 multiplies the decimal number currently in the cell by 100 so that the number becomes a whole number. For example, .05 becomes 5%.

To format a range of cells to Percent format with one decimal place:
① Make sure the cell pointer is in G14 and select /Range Format (**/RF**).
② Select Percent (**P**).
③ Type **1** for the number of decimal places and press **[Enter]**.
④ Highlight the cells G14..G16 and press **[Enter]**. See Figure 4-21.

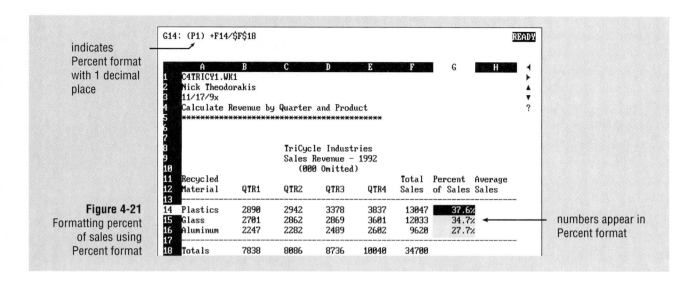

indicates
Percent format
with 1 decimal
place

Figure 4-21
Formatting percent
of sales using
Percent format

numbers appear in
Percent format

Using @AVG to Calculate Average Sales

Nick is ready to calculate the average quarterly sales for each recycled material during the year. To calculate the average, he can use the Lotus 1-2-3 statistical function @AVG. The format for this function is @AVG(*arguments*). The arguments for the @AVG function can be constants, cell references, and ranges.

To calculate the average sales for each material:

❶ Move the cell pointer to cell H14.

❷ Type **@avg(plastics)** and press **[Enter]**. See Figure 4-22. The average quarterly sales for plastics is 3261.75.

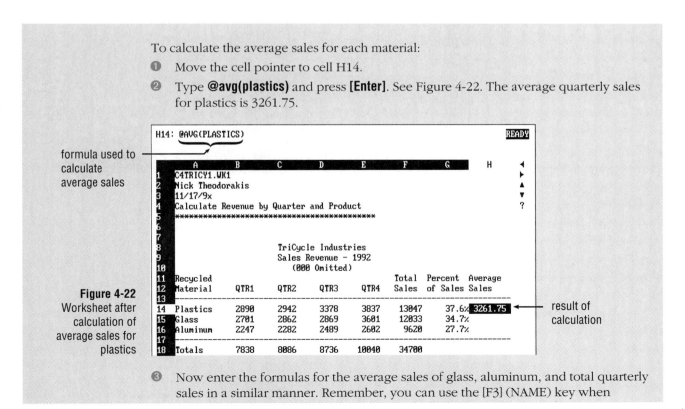

formula used to
calculate
average sales

Figure 4-22
Worksheet after
calculation of
average sales for
plastics

result of
calculation

❸ Now enter the formulas for the average sales of glass, aluminum, and total quarterly sales in a similar manner. Remember, you can use the [F3] (NAME) key when

entering the @AVG function if you can't recall the range name. When you are finished, your worksheet should look like Figure 4-23.

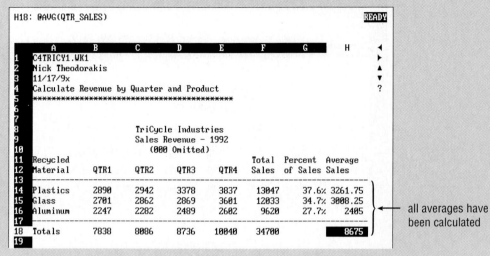

Figure 4-23
Worksheet after
calculation of
average sales for all
products

Finally, let's format the average sales to the nearest dollar.

To format the average sales to the nearest dollar:
1. Move the cell pointer to cell H14.
2. Select /Range Format Fixed (**/RFF**).
3. Type **0** (zero) and press **[Enter]**.
4. Highlight the range H14..H18 and press **[Enter]**. The average sales are displayed to
   the nearest dollar.

The calculations are complete. All that remains is for Nick to save the worksheet and
print the report.

To change the filename in cell A1 and to save the file:
1. Press **[Home]** to move the cell pointer to cell A1.
2. Type **S4TRICY1.WK1** and press **[Enter]**.
3. Select /File Save (**/FS**). Save the worksheet as S4TRICY1.

Printing with Compressed Type

Larger worksheets are often too wide to fit on one printed page. What do you do if you want
to show the entire worksheet on one page for easier interpretation? You can print more data
on a page by instructing your printer to use compressed type. **Compressed type** is a smaller

and more compact type. As a result, your printer can accommodate a 132-character line length instead of the normal 76 characters per line.

Let's adjust the margins and enter a setup string to print with compressed type. A **setup string** is a code sent to the printer to control the characteristics of the printed output.

Many dot-matrix printers use the code \ *015* to designate compressed type. (If you are using an HP LaserJet printer, the code \ *027(s0p16.66H* instructs the HP LaserJet printer to use a smaller type size. This code is case-sensitive, so make sure you enter it exactly as it appears here.) Check your printer manual or ask your instructor or technical support person for the correct code for your printer.

To set up compressed type for Epson printers:

❶ Select /Print Printer (**/PP**).

❷ Select Options Setup (**OS**) to choose the option to enter the code for compressed type.

❸ Type \ (Backslash) **015** and press **[Enter]** to enter the setup string. \015 may not work for your printer. If it doesn't, ask your instructor or lab assistant for the correct code for your printer.

❹ Select Margins (**M**) from the Options menu and then select Right (**R**). The right-margin option sets the maximum number of characters that can print on one line.

❺ Type **132** and press **[Enter]**. Your Print Settings dialog box should look similar to the one in Figure 4-24.

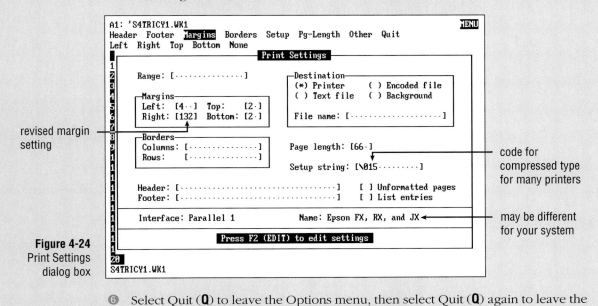

Figure 4-24
Print Settings
dialog box

❻ Select Quit (**Q**) to leave the Options menu, then select Quit (**Q**) again to leave the Print menu.

Now let's print the TriCycle revenue report. Be sure your printer is ready before you begin.

To print the TriCycle report:

❶ Select /Print Printer (**/PP**).

❷ Select Range (**R**).

❸ Move the cell pointer to A8. Press **[.]** (Period) to anchor the cell pointer.

❹ Highlight A8..H18, the cells that contain the report, then press **[Enter]**.

❺ Select Align Go Page (**AGP**) to print the report. See Figure 4-25.

```
1-2-3 Spreadsheet Computing Series                    Nick Theodorakis



                            TriCycle Industries
                            Sales Revenue - 1992
                               (000 Omitted)

Recycled                                    Total   Percent  Average
Material     QTR1    QTR2    QTR3    QTR4    Sales   of Sales Sales
-----------------------------------------------------------------------
Plastics     2890    2942    3378    3837    13047   37.6%    3262
Glass        2701    2862    2869    3601    12033   34.7%    3008
Aluminum     2247    2282    2489    2602    9620    27.7%    2405
-----------------------------------------------------------------------
Totals       7838    8086    8736    10040   34700            8675
```

Figure 4-25
Final TriCycle
revenue report in
compressed type

❻ Select Quit (**Q**) to return to READY mode.

❼ Select /File Save (**/FS**) and save the worksheet again as S4TRICY1.

Printing Checklist

Look at your printed output and check the following:

- **Headings** – Does each listing contain a heading at the top that answers the questions who, what, or where?
- **Columns** – Are all column widths correct? Do any cells contain asterisks, meaning that the values are too wide to appear in the column?
- **Margins** – Are the margins adjusted evenly?
- **Accuracy** – Is all the information correct? Are the numbers accurate? Are all words spelled correctly?
- **Lines** – Do any blank lines appear in unintended places?
- **Appearance** – Is the print legible? Do you need to install a new ribbon or make any adjustments?

Very often you will not be satisfied with your first printing of the worksheet. Fortunately, computers simplify the task of making changes. If necessary, edit your worksheet, save the changes, and print again. Do not hand write corrections.

Printing with Range Names

Range names are often used in printing worksheets. If you are working with a large worksheet and have several different ranges to print, you can assign a range name to each range and then select the appropriate name when specifying the print range.

Clearing the Print Options

There are times when you might want to print more than one report from the same worksheet. For example, in addition to the report just printed, suppose you also wanted to print a summary that included only the total annual sales for each product. This second report would require a different print range and print options. You can use the /Print Printer Clear command to cancel some or all print settings and return the settings to the default settings.

To clear all the print settings:

❶ Select /Print Printer (**/PP**).

Now clear the settings.

❷ Select Clear (**C**).

The *All* option returns all settings to the default settings.

❸ Select All (**A**). See Figure 4-26. Notice that the dialog box indicates all settings have been erased or returned to the default setting.

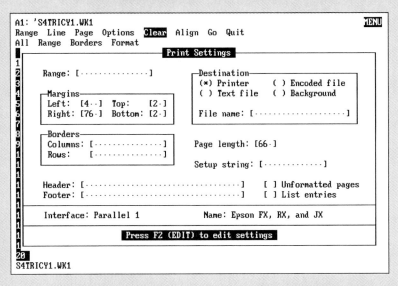

Figure 4-26
All print settings
cleared

❹ Select Quit (**Q**) to leave the Print menu and return to READY mode.

Printing with the Borders Option

Nick decides that he also wants to print a summary report that excludes quarterly sales data. Figure 4-27 is Nick's design of this report.

Recycled Material	1992 Sales	Percent of Sales
Plastics	13047	37.6%
Glass	12033	34.7%
Aluminum	9620	27.7%
Totals	34700	

Figure 4-27
Nick's sketch of summary report

The Borders option of the Print command allows you to add a range from your worksheet to the left side or on top of your print range. You can print row borders, column borders, or both. The column borders let you specify the range that is repeated on the left side of each page. If you specify row borders, the range is repeated at the top of each page.

Remember to exclude the border rows or columns from your print range.

To print the summary report using borders:

1   Select /Print Printer Range (**/PPR**).

2   Move the cell pointer to F11 and press **[.]** to anchor the cell pointer.

3   Highlight the range F11..G18, the range containing total sales, and percent of sales, and press **[Enter]**.

4   Select Option Borders (**OB**).

You want the column labeled Recycled Material to be a border for this report.

5   Select Columns (**C**).

Next, indicate the range you want as a border.

6   Move the cell pointer to A11, press **[.]**, and highlight the range A11..A18. Press **[Enter]**. See Figure 4-28.

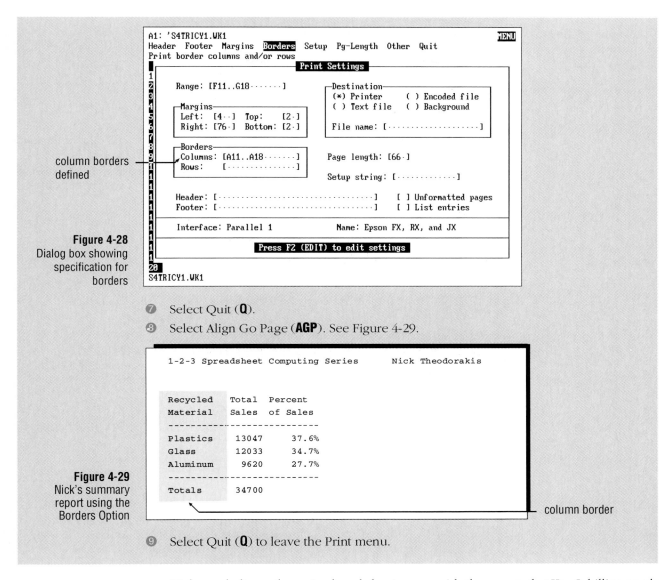

Figure 4-28
Dialog box showing specification for borders

column borders defined

⑦ Select Quit (**Q**).

⑧ Select Align Go Page (**AGP**). See Figure 4-29.

Figure 4-29
Nick's summary report using the Borders Option

column border

⑨ Select Quit (**Q**) to leave the Print menu.

Nick now believes the revised worksheet can provide the reports that Kay Schilling needs to use in her presentations at the quarterly meeting.

■   ■   ■

Exercises

1. Cell D13 contains the formula

   +D10+D11+D12

   After copying this formula to cells E13 and F13, what will the formulas be in cells E13 and F13?

2. Suppose cell D5 contains the formula

    +A5*$B$5+C5

    What are the absolute and relative references in this formula?

3. Suppose you copy the formula in Exercise 2 to cells D6 and D7.
   a. What will the formula be in cell D6?
   b. What will the formula be in cell D7?

4. Suppose cell B10 has been assigned the range name SALES and cell B11 the range name COSTS.
   a. What formula would you enter in cell B12 to calculate profits using cell addresses?
   b. What formula would you enter in cell B12 to calculate profits using range names?

5. Retrieve the file E4FILE1 and do the following:
   a. Copy the column heading in row 1 to row 11. When you're done, the column heading will be in both row 1 and row 11.
   b. Print the range A1..D11.

6. Retrieve the file E4FILE2. Cell D8 contains the formula to calculate the value of the skates in inventory. The formula used is *units in inventory × unit cost* or (+B8*C8).
   a. Use the Copy command to copy the formula in cell D8 to cells D9..D14.
   b. Print the range A1..D14.

7. Retrieve the file E4FILE3 and do the following:
   a. Write a formula in cell C6 to calculate new salaries for employees based on a percentage increase applied to all employees. The percentage increase is stored in cell C1. The formula in cell C6 references the percentage increase stored in cell C1.

      The formula is *current salary × (1 + percentage increase)*.
   b. Use the Copy command to copy the formula in cell C6 to cells C7..C10. Check your results.
   c. Print the worksheet.
   d. Change the percentage increase to 5%. Print the worksheet.

8. Retrieve the file E4FILE4 and do the following:
   a. Print the 12-month forecast, range A3..M12 without changing the print options.
   b. Clear the print settings, then use the borders option to output the 12-month forecast. Use the range A5..A12 as the column border and B3..M12 as the print range.
   c. Clear the settings and use compressed type to print the range A3..M12.

Tutorial Assignments

Retrieve the worksheet T4TRICY1 and do the following:

1. Assign the range name PRINT1 to the range A8..H20. Print this area using the range name to specify the print range.

2. In cell A21 type the label Range Name Table. Beginning in cell A23 create a range name table.

3. Assign the range name PRINT2 to the range A8..H30. Does the range name PRINT2 appear in your range name table? Why or why not?

4. Save this worksheet as S4TRICY2.

5. Print the worksheet. Print the range A8..H30 using the range name PRINT2 to specify the print range.

Retrieve the worksheet T4KRIER1, a version of the final worksheet from Tutorial 2, and do the following:

6. Use the Copy command to copy the gross pay formula in D11 to the cells of the other employees.

7. Use the Copy command to copy the federal withholding formula (cell E11) to the cells of all other employees.

8. Use the Copy command to copy the net pay formula (cell F11) to the cells of the other employees.

9. Assign the following range names:
   a. GROSS_PAY to cells D11..D14
   b. TAXES to cells E11..E14
   c. NET_PAY to cells F11..F14

10. Calculate total gross pay, total taxes withheld, and total net pay using the @SUM function and the range names you assigned in Assignment 9.

11. Print the worksheet.

12. Save the worksheet as S4KRIER1.
    Retrieve the Balboa Equity Fund worksheet, T4BALBO1, and do the following:

13. Assign the range name FUND_SHARES to cell C36, the number of mutual fund shares, and assign the range name TOTAL_VALUE to cell D33, the total value of the mutual fund.

14. Calculate net asset value (NAV) (cell C37) using the range names in the formula instead of the cell locations.
$$NAV = \frac{TOTAL\_VALUE}{FUND\_SHARES}$$

15. Print the results using the *Borders* option. Use A36..C37 as the print range. Assign A21..A22 as row borders. Save your worksheet as S4BALBO1.

Case Problems

1. Employee Turnover Report

Each month the director of human resources for the public accounting firm of Armstrong, Black & Calzone turns in a report summarizing the number of employees who have left the firm. The data in this employee turnover report are valuable information to the senior partners of the firm, because they want to compare their turnover rates with previous periods and industry averages. If their rates are particularly high, they might decide to investigate the cause of the high turnover. Turnover can result from a variety of reasons, such as noncompetitive salaries, poor managers, lack of training, or poor hiring practices.

Do the following:

1. Enter the data from Figure 4-30 into a new worksheet.

Department	Number of Employees	Number of Terminations
Accounting	50	8
Finance	100	3
Marketing	100	5
Systems	50	12
Manufacturing	150	10

Figure 4-30

2. Calculate the number of employees in the company.

3. Calculate the total number of employees who have left the company (number of terminations).

4. Add a column labeled "Dept. Turnover (%)" and calculate the rate of turnover in each department as a percentage of the number of employees in the department. Use the following formula:

$$\textit{rate of turnover} = \frac{\textit{number of employees who left each department}}{\textit{number of employees in each department}}$$

5. Add a column labeled "Company Turnover (%)" and calculate the rate of turnover in each department as a percentage of the number of employees in the company. Use the following formula:

$$\textit{rate of turnover} = \frac{\textit{number of employees who left each department}}{\textit{number of employees in company}}$$

6. Include headings, formatting, and any other changes you think will improve the appearance of the final report.

7. Save the worksheet as S4TRNOVR.

8. Print the worksheet.

WYSIWYG Assignments

1. Attach WYSIWYG.

2. Add the following enhancements:
    a. Remove any dashed lines before you insert solid lines under column headings and above and below totals.
    b. Use a 14-point Swiss font for the report title line(s) and enclose the title in a drop shadow.
    c. Boldface the total row.
    d. Outline the entire report.

3. Save your worksheet as W4TRNOVR.

4. Print the entire worksheet on one page.

2. Leading Restaurant Chains

The managing editor of *Restaurant Happenings*, a weekly magazine, has asked his top writer, Gene Marchand, to research and write a lead article on the sales of U.S. restaurant chains. In researching the story, Gene first determines the U.S. sales for 1988 and 1989 (in millions of dollars) and then totals the number of individual stores in 1989 for each restaurant chain. As the publishing deadline approaches, Gene asks you — the office Lotus 1-2-3 whiz — to help him with this article. Gene wants you to use 1-2-3 to calculate the following four facts:

- industry totals for sales and number of stores
- percentage change in sales between 1988 and 1989 for each restaurant chain
- each restaurant's share of total industry sales in 1989
- average sales per store for each chain in 1989

Do the following for Gene:

1. Retrieve the worksheet file P4RSTAUR.WK1.

2. Calculate the four facts listed above.
   a. Calculate totals for sales in 1988, sales in 1989, and number of stores.
   b. Calculate percentage change in sales for each restaurant chain by using the following formula:

$$percentage\ change\ in\ sales\ = \frac{(chain's\ 1989\ sales - chain's\ 1988\ sales)}{chain's\ 1988\ sales}$$

   c. Calculate each chain's share of total industry sales in 1989 by using the following formula:

$$chain's\ share\ of\ total\ industry\ sales\ in\ 1989\ = \frac{chain's\ sales\ in\ 1989}{total\ industry\ sales\ in\ 1989}$$

   d. Calculate the average sales per store in 1989 by using the following formula:

$$average\ sales\ per\ store\ in\ 1989\ = \frac{chain's\ sales\ in\ 1989}{number\ of\ stores\ in\ chain}$$

3. Add titles and dashed lines and format the numeric values to make the worksheet easier to read.

4. Save the worksheet as S4RSTAUR.

5. Print the results.

WYSIWYG Assignments

1. Attach WYSIWYG.

2. Add the following enhancements:
   a. Remove any dashed lines before you insert solid lines under column headings and above and below totals.
   b. Change the first line of the report title to a 24-point Swiss font. Use a 14-point Swiss font for the remaining report title lines.
   c. Boldface and italicize the row that contains totals.

3. Save your worksheet as W4RSTAUR.

4. Print the entire worksheet on one page.

3. Panther Oil Service, Inc.

Evonne Manfred is the owner and bookkeeper at Panther Oil Service, Inc., a small oil delivery and service company. Evonne keeps track of cash receipts using Lotus 1-2-3. Each week Evonne records customers' deliveries and payments in a worksheet.

Do the following:

1. Retrieve the file P4OIL. This worksheet is partially completed. Data on deliveries to customers have been entered, along with column headings for other items to be included in the worksheet.

2. Complete the worksheet by incorporating Evonne's calculations as shown in Figure 4-31.

Calculations

For each customer:

    Amount due = Gallons delivered × cost per gallon

    Balance owed = Amount due − (cash payment + discount taken)

Calculate company totals for:

    gallons delivered

    amount due

    cash payment

    discount taken

    balance owed

Calculate averages for:

    gallons delivered

    amount due

    balance owed

Notes on calculations:

a.   Use the @ROUND function to round the amount due and balance owed to nearest cent.

b.   Discount taken represents a cash discount taken by customer for prompt payment.

c.   Charge per gallon is the same for each customer during the week.

Figure 4-31

3. Enter the customer payment data for the week 2/4/92 to 2/8/92 as shown in Figure 4-32.

Customer	Cash Payment	Discount Taken
Murphy	150.04	3.06
Higgins	50.00	
Belden	178.33	3.64
Breign	80.27	1.64
Connell	206.04	
Sabo	100.00	
Costelle	124.65	2.54
McNeal	163.13	3.33
Williams	191.92	3.92
Dean	54.57	
Daly	144.34	2.95
Walcott	155.84	3.18
Samelson	40.00	
Lishinsky	134.15	2.73
Longo	114.26	2.33

Figure 4-32

4. Improve the appearance of the worksheet: widen the columns, align column headings over numbers, format numeric columns, and add a report title.

5. Save the worksheet as S4OIL.

6. Print a cash receipts report that lists all customer information in the worksheet.

WYSIWYG Assignments

1. Attach WYSIWYG.

2. Add the following enhancements:
   a. Place a box around the Cost per gallon label and amount.
   b. Remove any dashed lines before you insert solid lines under column headings and above and below totals.
   c. Change the font of the first line of the report title to 24-point Swiss.
   d. Change the font of all other lines of the report title to 14-point Swiss.
   e. Boldface the column headings.

3. Save the file as W4OIL.

4. Print the entire report on one page.

4. Exchange Rates and Foreign Operations

As the world becomes "smaller," more and more companies operate in more than one country. A particular challenge for multinational companies is coping with doing business in different currencies. One interesting finance problem involves how to interpret financial results when different currencies are used. Typically, each country reports results in its local currency (dollar, mark, yen, franc, etc.). The challenge is to prepare a report that allows management to compare these results and accurately interpret them. Let's assume that a U.S. publishing company wants all the results of its different divisions converted to U.S. dollars.

Smithson Publishing International has divisions in England, France, Germany, and Italy. Quarterly each division reports data on sales revenue to corporate headquarters in the United States where the data are combined. Each division reports its sales in its local currency (Figure 4-33).

	Sales Revenue (Local Currency)			
Period	**England (pound)**	**France (franc)**	**Germany (mark)**	**Italy (lira)**
QTR1	270197	1943779	1282234	159887439
QTR2	272814	2218784	1385572	213441654
QTR3	346404	2760962	1372975	232303732
QTR4	375395	2711160	1458096	239693192

Figure 4-33

Since the data are reported in the currency of the local country, Smithson's top executives cannot accurately interpret these numbers. They cannot tell, for example, which division has the highest revenue or which division has the lowest. Thus, a staff assistant, Jim Newman, converts these foreign currencies to U.S. dollars. He collects data on exchange rates, which represent the price of one country's currency in terms of another. For example, if the exchange rate between the British pound and the U.S. dollar is 1:1.8505, for every British pound you would receive 1.8505 U.S. dollars.

Jim keeps track of the exchange rates between the United States and each of the four countries in which Smithson has divisions. At the end of each quarter, he enters the exchange rates into a second table (Figure 4-34).

	Exchange Rates			
Period	**England (pound)**	**France (franc)**	**Germany (mark)**	**Italy (lira)**
QTR1	1.8505	0.1672	0.5773	0.0007818
QTR2	1.7445	0.1613	0.5486	0.0007447
QTR3	1.5740	0.1413	0.5062	0.0006993
QTR4	1.6119	0.1568	0.5316	0.0007301

Figure 4-34

Using these two tables, Jim can generate a third table, which shows the sales revenue for Smithson's four divisions converted to U.S. dollars.

To convert the sales data to U.S. dollars, each quarter's sales revenue for a country is multiplied by the corresponding exchange rate. For example, in England sales in the first quarter were 270,197 pounds. At the end of the first quarter, the exchange rate between the British pound and the U.S. dollar was 1:1.8505. Therefore, first-quarter sales in England expressed in U.S. dollars would be

$$revenues \times exchange\ rate = converted\ amount$$

or in this case,

$$270,197 \times 1.8505 = \$500,000$$

Do the following:

1. Retrieve the worksheet P4EXCHNG.WK1. This file contains the data shown in Figures 4-33 and 4-34.

2. Create a third table that shows sales revenue expressed in U.S. dollars categorized by country and by quarter. Use the formula given above for converting currencies.

3. Also include in this table the calculation of total revenue by country.

4. Include in this table the calculation of total revenue by quarter.

5. Add titles and dashed lines, format the values, and make any other changes that will improve the appearance of the worksheet.

6. Save your worksheet as S4EXCHNG.

7. Print the three tables.

WYSIWYG Assignments

1. Attach WYSIWYG.

2. Add the following enhancements:
   a. Create a table (grid) effect for each table.
   b. Draw a double-lined outline around the entire report.

3. Save your worksheet as W4EXCHNG.

4. Print the three tables on one page.

Tutorial 5

Designing Professional Worksheets

Projecting Income

Case: Trek Limited

Hillary Clarke is an accountant at Trek Limited, a manufacturer of fine luggage that has been in business for 55 years. Hillary works in the controller's office and reports to the controller, Stephan Akrawi. Stephan was so impressed with Hillary's work over the 14 months she has worked for him that he selected her to attend Trek's employee development workshop series.

Today is Hillary's first day back at her regular job after attending the workshop series. She is excited about the many skills she has learned, and she tells Stephan that she'd like to use some of them immediately. She is particularly excited about the workshop called "Financial Planning Using Lotus 1-2-3," because she thinks she can use what she learned to help Stephan with some of his projects. Last year Hillary assisted Stephan in updating Trek's Five-Year Plan, a collection of financial projections that help Trek's department managers make decisions about how to run the company. By making certain assumptions, such as that sales will increase 10% next year, the managers can plan, budget, and set goals accordingly. The plan includes the company's forecasts, or "best guesses," on what sales, expenses, and net income will be over the coming years.

In the past Stephan prepared the plan manually, but this year Hillary wants Stephan to use Lotus 1-2-3. She points out how much more helpful the plan would be if the department managers could perform what-if analyses. Department managers could make different assumptions about the financial data to see what results those assumptions would have on the company's finances. For example, what if sales went down 10% next year instead of up? What would the results be on profits or on expenses? What if the price of cowhide increased 5% over the next two years? How would that affect the cost of manufacturing?

OBJECTIVES

In this tutorial you will learn to:

- Freeze titles
- Use the @IF function
- Protect cells
- Use windows
- Document a worksheet
- Print cell formulas
- Use a one-way data table
- Use the Data Fill command

How would it affect profits? What-if analysis using Lotus 1-2-3 could help managers make better decisions. They would not have to face the drudgery of numerous recalculations; they could easily, quickly, and accurately consider different alternatives by changing the data and then having Lotus 1-2-3 recalculate the formulas and totals. Thus, managers would spend more time and creative energy on decision making because they would not have to recalculate formulas and totals every time they asked, "What if?"

Stephan agrees with Hillary about using Lotus 1-2-3. He gives her the latest data that the accounting department prepared for 1992 (Figure 5-1). They agree that Hillary should design a Lotus 1-2-3 worksheet that reflects the Trek planning process. Then together they will perform some what-if analysis and show the department managers how they can use what-if analysis with 1-2-3.

Trek Limited Income Statement

	1992	Percent of Sales
Sales	$150,000	
Variable Costs:		
Manufacturing	75,000	50%
Selling	15,000	10%
Administrative	6,000	4%
Total Variable Cost	96,000	
Fixed Costs:		
Manufacturing	10,000	
Selling	20,000	
Administrative	5,000	
Total Fixed Cost	35,000	
Net income before taxes	19,000	
Income taxes	4,750	
Net income after taxes	$14,250	

Figure 5-1
Trek's accounting department data

Hillary spends time studying the accounting department's data and begins to create her planning sheet (Figure 5-2a). After writing down her goal and her desired results, she considers what information she needs. She knows that, generally, the sales estimate is used as the starting point for projecting income. Why? Because production and selling are geared to the rate of sales activity.

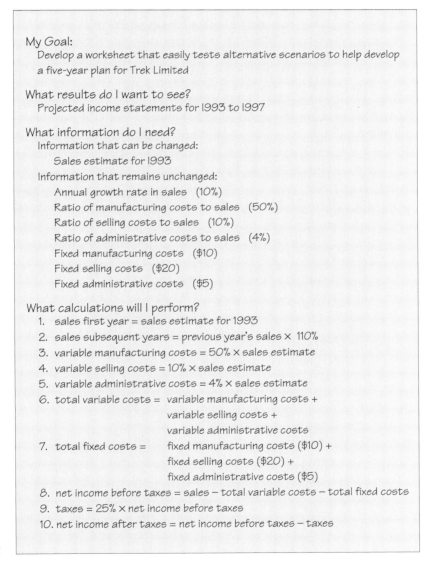

My Goal:
   Develop a worksheet that easily tests alternative scenarios to help develop
   a five-year plan for Trek Limited

What results do I want to see?
   Projected income statements for 1993 to 1997

What information do I need?
   Information that can be changed:
      Sales estimate for 1993
   Information that remains unchanged:
      Annual growth rate in sales   (10%)
      Ratio of manufacturing costs to sales   (50%)
      Ratio of selling costs to sales   (10%)
      Ratio of administrative costs to sales   (4%)
      Fixed manufacturing costs   ($10)
      Fixed selling costs   ($20)
      Fixed administrative costs   ($5)

What calculations will I perform?
   1. sales first year = sales estimate for 1993
   2. sales subsequent years = previous year's sales × 110%
   3. variable manufacturing costs = 50% × sales estimate
   4. variable selling costs = 10% × sales estimate
   5. variable administrative costs = 4% × sales estimate
   6. total variable costs = variable manufacturing costs +
                              variable selling costs +
                              variable administrative costs
   7. total fixed costs =   fixed manufacturing costs ($10) +
                              fixed selling costs ($20) +
                              fixed administrative costs ($5)
   8. net income before taxes = sales − total variable costs − total fixed costs
   9. taxes = 25% × net income before taxes
   10. net income after taxes = net income before taxes − taxes

Figure 5-2a
Hillary's planning
sheet

Hillary decides to start her projections for 1993 sales at the same level as 1992, although she knows the managers will change this during their what-if analysis. Stephan suggests she build in a 10% increase per year in sales for 1994 to 1997. He believes sales will go up 10% annually as a result of a new line of luggage Trek Limited plans to introduce in 1993.

After looking at the sales side, Hillary turns her attention to costs. She must look at both variable costs and fixed costs. Variable costs are those that change in direct proportion to related volume. For instance, as sales volume goes up, variable costs such as materials, assembly labor, and sales commissions also go up. Fixed costs are costs that remain unchanged despite changes in related volume. For example, rent, property taxes, executive salaries, and insurance remain the same even when sales go up.

Once again, Hillary refers to the accounting department data in Figure 5-1. She decides to use the variable-cost percentages as the basis for calculating variable costs. For example, if sales were $200,000, the variable manufacturing costs would be calculated at 50% of sales, or $100,000. She also decides to use the fixed costs shown in the accounting data.

Next, Hillary considers the final group of calculations, net income. To calculate net income before taxes, Hillary calculates the difference between sales and the total of variable and fixed costs. She assumes taxes will be 25% of net income before taxes. Finally, she calculates net income after taxes, that is, net income before taxes minus income taxes.

Figure 5-2b is a sketch of how Hillary wants her worksheet to look. In this tutorial you will use Hillary's planning sheet and sketch to learn how to freeze titles, protect specified data, split screens, design and document your worksheet, and make use of data tables to ask what-if questions.

Trek Limited
Projected Income Statement
(000 omitted)

	1993	1994	1995	1996	1997
Sales	xxx	.	.	.	.
Variable Costs:		.	.	.	.
Manufacturing	xxx	.	.	.	.
Selling	xxx	.	.	.	.
Administrative	xxx	.	.	.	.
Total Variable Costs	xxx	xxx	xxx	xxx	xxx
Fixed Costs:					
Manufacturing	xxx	.	.	.	.
Selling	xxx	.	.	.	.
Administrative	xxx	.	.	.	.
Total Fixed Costs	xxx	xxx	xxx	xxx	xxx
Net Income Before Taxes	xxx	.	.	.	.
Income taxes	xxx	.	.	.	.
Net Income After Taxes	xxx	xxx	xxx	xxx	xxx

Figure 5-2b
Hillary's worksheet
sketch

Retrieving the Worksheet

Before you follow through on Hillary's plan, you will retrieve the worksheet she built based on her planning sheet and worksheet sketch and practice using the what-if capability of 1-2-3.

To retrieve the worksheet:

❶ Select /File Retrieve (**/FR**).

❷ Highlight the file C5TREK1.WK1. Press **[Enter]**.

❸ Press **[PgDn]** to view the Projected Income Statement.

This worksheet contains the projected income statement for Trek Limited for the years 1993 to 1997 (Figure 5-3). All values are shown in thousands. For example, sales in 1993 are shown as 150, which represents $150,000. Also note that to simplify the numbers in this worksheet the cells were formatted to display zero decimal places. As a result, some totals do not appear to be correct. This is because the data are rounded whenever they appear on the screen.

```
                                   Trek Limited
                           Projected Income Statement
                                 (000 omitted)

                         1993      1994      1995      1996      1997
                         -----------------------------------------------
Sales                     150       165       182       200       220
Variable Costs:
   Manufacturing           75        83        91       100       110
   Selling                 15        17        18        20        22
   Administrative           6         7         7         8         9
                         -----------------------------------------------
   Total Variable Costs    96       106       116       128       141

Fixed Costs:
   Manufacturing           10        10        10        10        10
   Selling                 20        20        20        20        20
   Administrative           5         5         5         5         5
                         -----------------------------------------------
   Total Fixed Costs       35        35        35        35        35

Net Income Before Taxes    19        24        30        37        44
Income Taxes                5         6         8         9        11
                         -----------------------------------------------
Net Income After Taxes     14        18        23        28        33
                         ===============================================
```

area of worksheet that appears on your screen

Figure 5-3
Contents of the entire worksheet

Demonstrating the What-If Feature

To demonstrate 1-2-3's what-if capability using Hillary's worksheet, let's suppose that you increase the sales estimate for 1993 from $150,000 (entered as 150) to $175,000 (entered as 175).

To use the what-if capability:

❶ Move the cell pointer to cell B28, sales for 1993.

❷ Type **175** and press **[Enter]**. Watch how the sales, costs, and net incomes change as a result of the change to 1993 sales. See Figure 5-4.

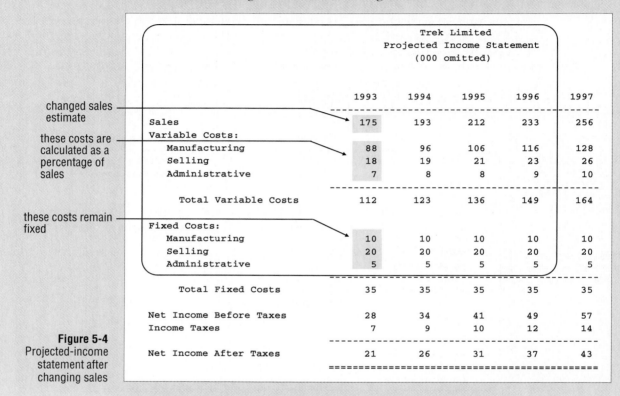

changed sales estimate

these costs are calculated as a percentage of sales

these costs remain fixed

Figure 5-4
Projected-income statement after changing sales

```
                                    Trek Limited
                            Projected Income Statement
                                  (000 omitted)


                            1993      1994      1995      1996      1997
                           ------    ------    ------    ------    ------
Sales                       175       193       212       233       256
Variable Costs:
    Manufacturing            88        96       106       116       128
    Selling                  18        19        21        23        26
    Administrative            7         8         8         9        10
                           ------    ------    ------    ------    ------
        Total Variable Costs 112       123       136       149       164

Fixed Costs:
    Manufacturing            10        10        10        10        10
    Selling                  20        20        20        20        20
    Administrative            5         5         5         5         5
                           ------    ------    ------    ------    ------
        Total Fixed Costs    35        35        35        35        35

Net Income Before Taxes     28        34        41        49        57
Income Taxes                 7         9        10        12        14
                           ------    ------    ------    ------    ------
Net Income After Taxes      21        26        31        37        43
                           ======    ======    ======    ======    ======
```

Since the sales estimate for 1993 increased from 150 to 175, the variable costs, which are calculated as a percentage of sales, also increased. Net income also changed, since both sales and variable costs changed. The fixed costs, however, did not change.

The sales estimates for 1994 through 1997 also increased. Because sales are estimated to grow at 10% each year, changing the starting sales estimate for 1993 changes the sales for 1994 through 1997.

Scrolling on Large Worksheets

Notice that the entire income statement does not fit on the screen — you cannot see the information for 1997. Also, the rows that follow "Administrative" in Hillary's worksheet sketch do not appear on the screen, even though she has typed them into her worksheet. To view this information, you use the cursor-movement keys to scroll down the screen. *Scrolling* is a way to view all parts of a large worksheet that cannot fit on one screen. For example, when you scroll down, a row previously unseen appears at the bottom of the screen and the row at the top disappears.

To scroll Hillary's worksheet:

❶ Press **[PgDn]** until Net Income After Taxes appears on the screen. Note that the column headings no longer appear on the screen. See Figure 5-5.

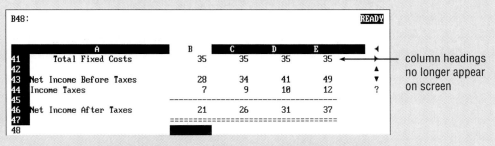

Figure 5-5
Scrolling Hillary's worksheet

❷ Now move the cell pointer to cell A21.

The planning period for the company is 1993 to 1997, but 1997 does not appear on the screen. Let's scroll to the right to view the 1997 projections.

To scroll to the right:

❶ Press **[→]** until the 1997 column appears. Notice that the descriptive labels no longer appear on the left of the screen. This makes the worksheet data difficult to interpret. See Figure 5-6 on the following page.

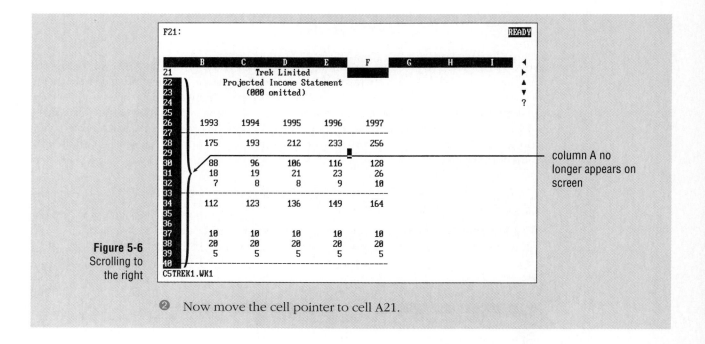

Figure 5-6
Scrolling to
the right

② Now move the cell pointer to cell A21.

Freezing Titles

As you move the cell pointer around a worksheet that is larger than the screen, you may find it difficult to remember row and column labels that may have disappeared. The Title command helps you keep your place on a large worksheet by "freezing" row and column titles on the screen; the titles then remain on the screen as you move within the worksheet. The Titles command allows you to freeze rows, columns, or both. If you choose *Horizontal*, you freeze all rows above the cell pointer on the screen. If you choose *Vertical*, you freeze all columns to the left of the cell pointer. If you choose *Both*, you freeze all rows above and all columns to the left of the cell pointer. In the next steps, you will freeze both the worksheet column headings and the account titles.

To freeze titles:
① Be sure cell A21 is in the upper left corner of the worksheet. Move the cell pointer to cell B28, the location below and to the right of the cells you want to remain on the screen.
② Select /Worksheet Titles (**/WT**). Your control panel should look like Figure 5-7.

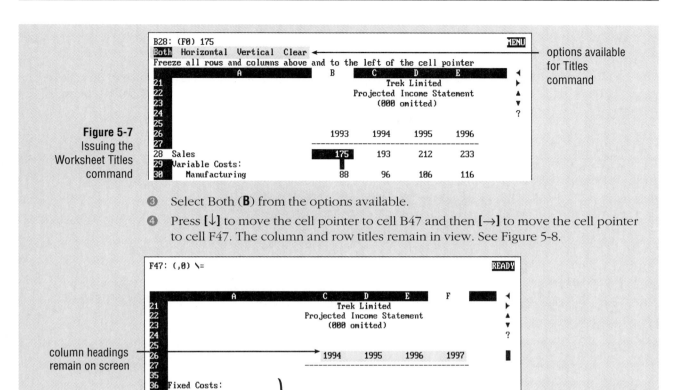

Figure 5-7
Issuing the
Worksheet Titles
command

③ Select Both (**B**) from the options available.

④ Press [↓] to move the cell pointer to cell B47 and then [→] to move the cell pointer to cell F47. The column and row titles remain in view. See Figure 5-8.

Figure 5-8
After issuing the
Titles command

⑤ Press [**Home**].

Notice that the cell pointer returns to cell B28 rather than cell A1. Cell B28, the first unfrozen cell, becomes the upper left corner of the worksheet.

Unfreezing Titles

Once you freeze an area of the worksheet, you cannot move the cell pointer into that area while you are in READY mode. You can, however, use the [F5](GoTo) key to move the cell pointer into the frozen area so you can make any changes to the headings or row labels.

If you need to unfreeze titles, you would select the command /Worksheet Titles Clear (/WTC). You would then be able to move the cell pointer into any area of the worksheet.

@IF Function

Now you are ready to follow Hillary's plan. The first thing Hillary wants to do is to see the effect of a poor sales year on net income. She assumes sales will be $75,000 (entered as 75) instead of $150,000 (entered as 150).

To consider the relationship between poor sales and income:

❶   Be certain the cell pointer is in cell B28.

❷   Type **75**. Press **[Enter]**.

❸   Move the cell pointer to cell B47 and look at the values in the rows for income taxes and net income after taxes. See Figure 5-9.

Figure 5-9
Incorrect
calculations for
income taxes

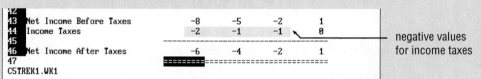

negative values
for income taxes

Notice that income taxes appear as negative values for 1993, 1994, and 1995. This is not correct. Taxes should be zero whenever the net income before taxes is less than zero. How can we correct this?

❹   Move the cell pointer to cell B44. Look at the control panel and observe that the formula for calculating income taxes is +B43*0.25 (25% of net income before taxes). This formula is correct as long as net income before taxes is a positive number. If net income before taxes is a negative number, the worksheet should set income taxes equal to zero, not a negative value. What went wrong? Hillary represented the relationship between net income before taxes and income taxes incorrectly when she built her worksheet.

There are many situations where the value you store in a cell depends on certain conditions, for instance:

• An employee's gross pay may depend on whether that employee worked overtime.

• A taxpayer's tax rate depends on his or her taxable income.

• A customer's charge depends on whether the size of the order entitles that customer to a discount.

In 1-2-3 the @IF function allows you to make comparisons to determine which actions 1-2-3 should take. The @IF function has the following format:

@IF(*condition,true expression,false expression*)

The parenthetic expression can be interpreted to mean that if the condition is true, 1-2-3 is to execute the true expression; otherwise, it is to execute the false expression.

The @IF function has three components:

- A *condition* is a logical expression that represents a comparison between quantities. This comparison results in a value that is either true, indicated by a value of 1, or false, indicated by a value of 0.
- A *true expression* is a value or label stored in a cell if the condition is true.
- A *false expression* is a value or label stored in a cell if the condition is false.

An example may help to illustrate the format of an @IF function. Suppose you needed to determine whether an employee earned overtime pay, that is, whether he or she worked more than 40 hours in a week. This can be expressed as:

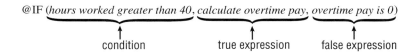

In this example, the condition is the comparison between the hours an employee works and 40 hours. The true expression is executed if an employee works more than 40 hours; then the condition is true and overtime pay is calculated. The false expression is executed if an employee works 40 hours or less; then the condition is false and overtime pay is 0.

The most common condition, a simple condition, is a comparison between two expressions. An **expression** may be a cell or range reference, a number, a label, a formula, or another @function. Besides expressions, a condition contains a comparison operator. A **comparison operator** indicates a mathematical comparison, such as less than or greater than. Figure 5-10 shows the comparison operators allowed in 1-2-3.

Type of Comparison	1-2-3 Symbol
Less than	<
Greater than	>
Less than or equal to	<=
Greater than or equal to	>=
Equal to	=
Not equal to	<>

Figure 5-10
Examples of comparison operators

A comparison operator is combined with expressions to form a condition. For example, say the hours worked are stored in cell D10; then the condition "*the number of hours worked is greater than 40*" would be expressed in 1-2-3 as @IF(D10>40...). Figure 5-11 on the following page illustrates several examples of conditional situations and how they can be expressed in 1-2-3.

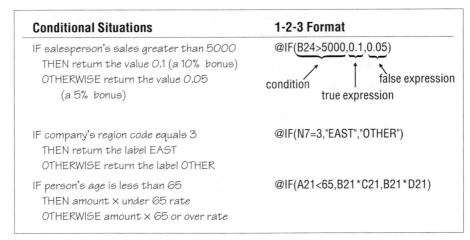

Figure 5-11
Examples of
conditional
situations

Let's now use the @IF function to correct Hillary's worksheet.

To use the @IF function to determine taxes:

❶ Make sure the cell pointer is in cell B44.

❷ Type **@if(b43>0,0.25*b43,0)** and press **[Enter]**. See Figure 5-12.

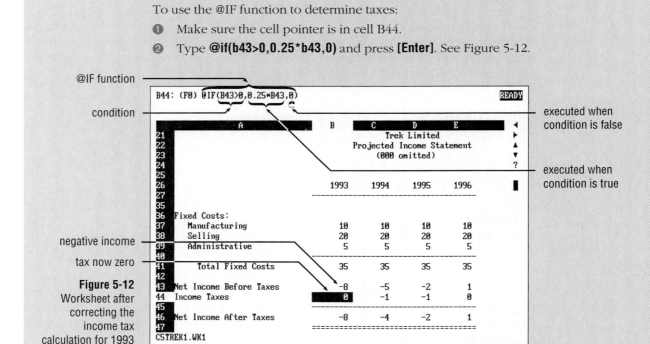

Figure 5-12
Worksheet after
correcting the
income tax
calculation for 1993

Do not include any spaces when you type this or any other @function and be sure
to separate each component with a comma. You can interpret this function as

IF the value in cell B43 is greater than 0
THEN return the value .25*B43 to cell B44
OTHERWISE return the value 0 to cell B44

Now let's copy this function to cells C44 through F44 so the correct formulas to calculate income taxes for the years 1994 to 1997 can be included in the worksheet.

To copy the function to cells C44..F44:

❶ Make sure the cell pointer is in cell B44.

❷ Select /Copy (**/C**). Press **[Enter]** since you are copying only the function in cell B44.

❸ Move the cell pointer to C44 and press **[.]** to anchor the cell pointer.

❹ Highlight the range C44..F44. Press **[Enter]**.

Notice that taxes are now zero. See Figure 5-13.

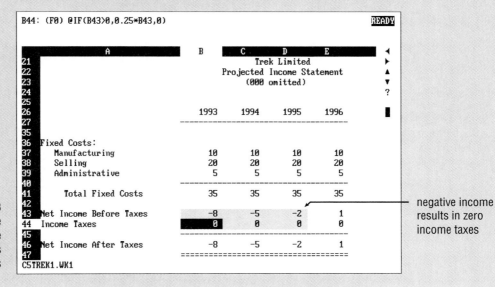

Figure 5-13
Worksheet after the corrected income tax calculation is copied to all cells

In addition to making changes to sales estimates, Hillary decides she wants to see how changes in the ratio of variable manufacturing costs to sales affects net income. To make this change, Hillary must change the formula for each cell that references variable manufacturing costs (B30, C30, D30, E30, F30). For example, she wants to change variable manufacturing costs from 50% to 52% of sales.

To change constants in a formula:

❶ Move the cell pointer to cell B30.

❷ Press **[F2]** (EDIT) to invoke EDIT mode.

❸ Change 0.5 to 0.52 and press **[Enter]**. The formula appears in the control panel as 0.52*B28, and the variable manufacturing costs in 1993 are 39.

Now copy the formula to C30..F30, where the formulas for variable manufacturing costs for the years 1994 to 1997 are located.

To copy the formula to C30..F30:

❶ With the cell pointer in B30, select /Copy (**/C**). Press **[Enter]**.

❷ Move the cell pointer to C30. Press **[.]** to anchor the cell pointer.

❸ Highlight C30..F30. Press **[Enter]**. See Figure 5-14.

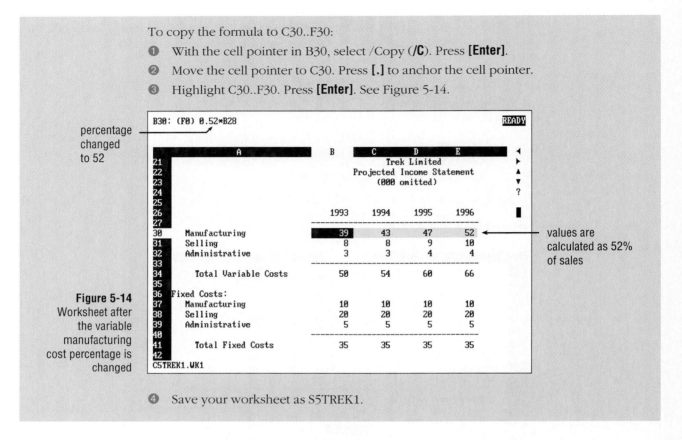

percentage changed to 52

values are calculated as 52% of sales

Figure 5-14
Worksheet after the variable manufacturing cost percentage is changed

❹ Save your worksheet as S5TREK1.

To change variable selling costs from 10% to 11% requires a similar process. But is there a way to change the variable costs that takes less time and avoids the possibility of errors that can occur with so many changes? Hillary thinks about how to revise the worksheet. She realizes that the more she uses numeric constants in her formulas, the less flexibility she has if she wants to change those values. Thus, she decides to completely revise her worksheet. She prepares a new plan and worksheet sketch. Figure 5-15 shows her revised plan, which includes these major changes:

- dividing the worksheet into three sections to clarify tasks — documentation, input, and calculation/output

- providing managers with five variables instead of one on which they can perform what-if analysis

- replacing constants in formulas with range names, such as GROWTH, that reference cells in the input area

- including the @ROUND function in formulas to avoid rounding errors

Now you can retrieve the new worksheet that Hillary has built.

My Goal:
    Develop a worksheet that easily tests alternative scenarios to help
    develop a five-year plan for Trek Limited

What results do I want to see?
    Projected income statements for 1991 to 1995

What information do I need?
    Information that can be changed:
        Sales estimate for 1991
    Information that remains unchanged:
        Annual growth rate in sales   (10%)
        Ratio of manufacturing costs to sales   (50%)
        Ratio of selling costs to sales   (10%)
        Ratio of administrative costs to sales   (4%)
        Fixed manufacturing costs   ($10)
        Fixed selling costs   ($20)
        Fixed administrative costs   ($5)

Hillary now wants to change this information →

What calculations will I perform?
  1. sales first year = sales estimate for 1991

                                                        Sales growth rate
  2. sales subsequent years = previous year's sales × ~~110%~~

                                            ratio of manufacturing costs to sales
  3. variable manufacturing costs = ~~50%~~ × sales estimate

                                    ratio of selling costs to sales
  4. variable selling costs = ~~10%~~ × sales estimate

                                  ratio of administrative costs to sales
  5. variable administrative costs = ~~4%~~ × sales estimate

  6. total variable costs = variable manufacturing costs +
                                 variable selling costs +
                                 variable administrative costs

  7. total fixed costs =   fixed manufacturing costs ($10) +
                                 fixed selling costs ($20) +
                                 fixed administrative costs ($5)

  8. net income before taxes = sales - total variable costs - total fixed costs

Hillary will make this a conditional statement →

              If net income before taxes > 0 then
  9. taxes = 25% × net income before taxes
            Otherwise taxes = 0

  10. net income after taxes = net income before taxes - taxes

Figure 5-15
Hillary's revised
planning sheet

To retrieve a file:

❶ Select /File Retrieve (**/FR**).

❷ Highlight C5TREK2.WK1 and press **[Enter]**.

Notice in Figure 5-16 that Hillary has divided her new worksheet into three sections: documentation, input, and calculation/output. The **documentation section** contains information about the worksheet. Typically this section consists of the title of the worksheet, the filename, the name of the developer, the date it was prepared, the date it was last modified, and the purpose of the worksheet. Additional documentation might include information about the layout of various sections within the worksheet, the names and locations of named ranges, and instructions to the user. The most common location for the documentation section is the top left corner of the worksheet, where the information is immediately displayed when the worksheet is loaded.

A second section, the **input section**, contains the variables used in formulas that are likely to change. Sometimes the input section is said to contain the worksheet's *assumptions*, because the results of the worksheet are based on the values in the input section. For example, in Hillary's worksheet, the input section lists the variables a manager at Trek can change. The manager can ask what-if questions by changing the values in the input section and observing the changes in the projected-income statement. The values in the projected-income statement change because the formulas that calculate projected-income reference the cells in the input area.

A third section, the **calculation/output section**, performs the calculations. This section includes formulas and fixed data. In Hillary's case this section contains the formulas to calculate projected income over the five-year period. The formulas do not contain constants; instead they reference cells in the input area. The formulas often include range names to clarify their meanings.

Some worksheets divide the calculation/output section into separate sections. In those worksheets the output section summarizes the results from the calculation section and places them near the input section. That way you can immediately view the results of changing input values without having to search for this information in a different area of the worksheet.

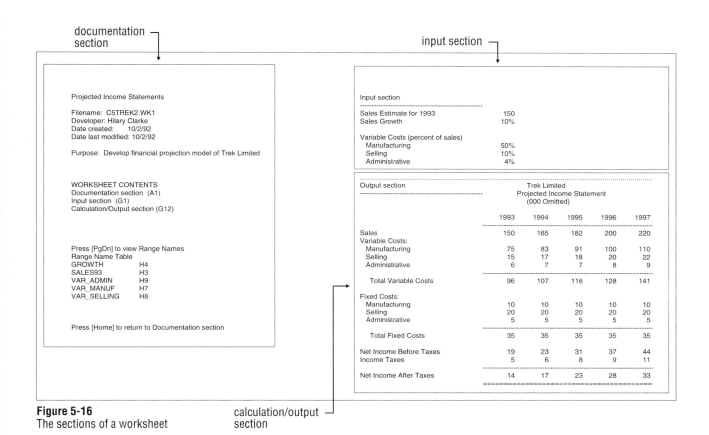

documentation section

input section

Projected Income Statements

Filename: C5TREK2.WK1
Developer: Hilary Clarke
Date created: 10/2/92
Date last modified: 10/2/92

Purpose: Develop financial projection model of Trek Limited

WORKSHEET CONTENTS
Documentation section (A1)
Input section (G1)
Calculation/Output section (G12)

Press [PgDn] to view Range Names
Range Name Table
GROWTH   H4
SALES93   H3
VAR_ADMIN   H9
VAR_MANUF   H7
VAR_SELLING   H8

Press [Home] to return to Documentation section

Input section

Sales Estimate for 1993   150
Sales Growth   10%

Variable Costs (percent of sales)
   Manufacturing   50%
   Selling   10%
   Administrative   4%

Output section		Trek Limited			
		Projected Income Statement			
		(000 Omitted)			
	1993	1994	1995	1996	1997
Sales	150	165	182	200	220
Variable Costs:					
Manufacturing	75	83	91	100	110
Selling	15	17	18	20	22
Administrative	6	7	7	8	9
Total Variable Costs	96	107	116	128	141
Fixed Costs:					
Manufacturing	10	10	10	10	10
Selling	20	20	20	20	20
Administrative	5	5	5	5	5
Total Fixed Costs	35	35	35	35	35
Net Income Before Taxes	19	23	31	37	44
Income Taxes	5	6	8	9	11
Net Income After Taxes	14	17	23	28	33

Figure 5-16
The sections of a worksheet

calculation/output section

A Worksheet Map

A worksheet "map," similar to the one in Figure 5-17, can often accompany the worksheet to inform users about the organization of the worksheet. Such a map is especially helpful in a large worksheet that consists of many sections. The map identifies each section and the cell range of each section. With the worksheet map, users can quickly find different sections of the worksheet.

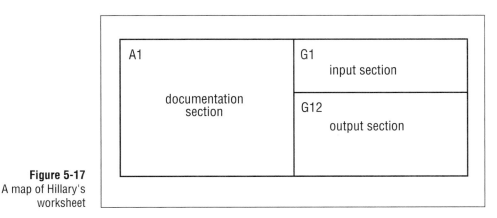

A1

documentation section

G1

input section

G12

output section

Figure 5-17
A map of Hillary's worksheet

Demonstrating What-If with the Revised Worksheet

Remember that Hillary developed this new worksheet because the previous worksheet was difficult to use for what-if questions. Let's try this new worksheet and see if it is any easier to use for this purpose.

To use the revised worksheet to change the variable percentage of manufacturing cost from 50% to 52% of sales:

➊   Press **[Tab]** to move to the input section. Then move the cell pointer to cell H7.

➋   Type **52%**. Press **[Enter]**. See Figure 5-18. You could also enter the value as .52.

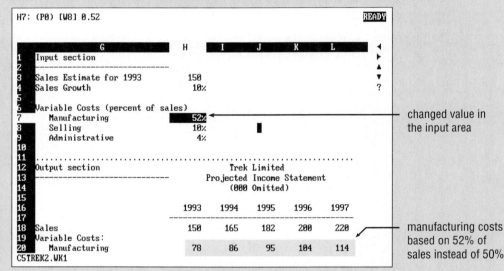

Figure 5-18
Using the revised
worksheet to ask
what-if questions

changed value in
the input area

manufacturing costs
based on 52% of
sales instead of 50%

The variable manufacturing costs change from 75, 83, 91, 100, and 110 to 78, 86, 95, 104, and 114. Notice that we did not have to change formulas when we used this worksheet. When Hillary used the previous worksheet, she had to make changes to the formula every time a variable-cost percentage changed. The new worksheet is designed to transfer the input percentage to the calculation/output section, where the calculations are performed.

➌   Move the cell pointer to cell H20. See Figure 5-19.

no constant in
this formula

reference to the
input section
(cell H7)

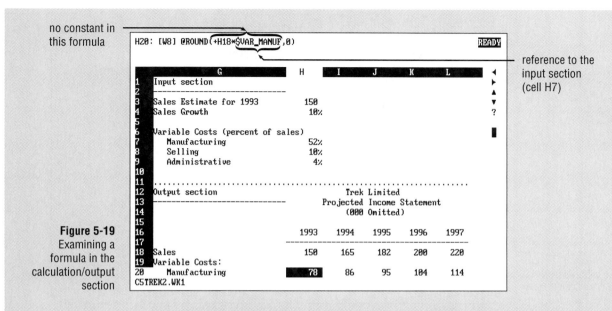

Figure 5-19
Examining a
formula in the
calculation/output
section

Notice that in cell H20 the formula to calculate variable manufacturing costs
uses a range name, VAR_MANUF, to reference the variable manufacturing cost
percentage (cell H7). The variable manufacturing cost formula in cell H20 is
@ROUND(+H18*$VAR_MANUF,0) instead of (.5*B28), which was the formula used
in the previous worksheet. Cell H18 contains the sales estimate for 1993. Now all a
user has to do is change the variable manufacturing-to-sales percentage in the
input area, and the formula in cell H20 will automatically recalculate.

Hillary thinks the revisions she has made to the worksheet will help managers more
easily ask what-if questions. For example, suppose a manager wants to see what would
happen if the growth rate increased from 10% to 15%.

To ask "What if the growth rate for sales increased to 15%?":

➊ Move the cell pointer to cell H4, the input area for the sales growth rate.

➋ Type **15%**. Press **[Enter]**. You can also enter the value as .15.

Observe the results in the output section. See Figure 5-20 on the following page. Notice
how sales in 1994 changed from 165 to 173. The revised sales estimates for 1994 also
affected all the variable costs. The fixed costs, on the other hand, haven't changed. Net
income before and after taxes has also changed. The increased growth rate also affects
sales, variable costs, and income for 1995, 1996, and 1997.

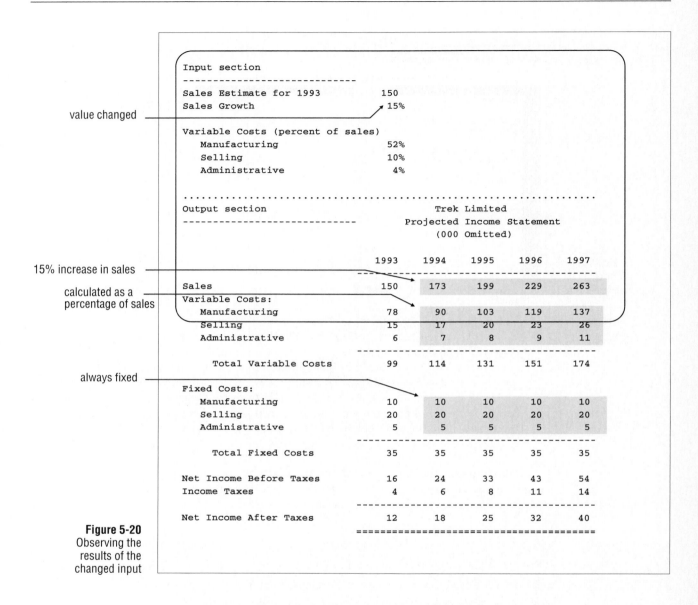

value changed

15% increase in sales

calculated as a
percentage of sales

always fixed

Figure 5-20
Observing the
results of the
changed input

```
Input section
---------------------------------
Sales Estimate for 1993          150
Sales Growth                     15%

Variable Costs (percent of sales)
    Manufacturing                52%
    Selling                      10%
    Administrative                4%

.................................................................
Output section                        Trek Limited
---------------------------     Projected Income Statement
                                      (000 Omitted)

                        1993    1994    1995    1996    1997
                        ----------------------------------------
Sales                    150     173     199     229     263
Variable Costs:
    Manufacturing         78      90     103     119     137
    Selling               15      17      20      23      26
    Administrative         6       7       8       9      11
                        ----------------------------------------
    Total Variable Costs  99     114     131     151     174

Fixed Costs:
    Manufacturing         10      10      10      10      10
    Selling               20      20      20      20      20
    Administrative         5       5       5       5       5
                        ----------------------------------------
    Total Fixed Costs     35      35      35      35      35

Net Income Before Taxes   16      24      33      43      54
Income Taxes               4       6       8      11      14
                        ----------------------------------------
Net Income After Taxes    12      18      25      32      40
                        ========================================
```

Hillary is pleased with her work and decides to ask Stephan to try the revised worksheet. But Stephan wants to ask different what-if questions. He moves the cell pointer to cell I18 in the calculation/output section and changes the sales in 1994 to 200.

Hillary explains to Stephan that all changes to the worksheet must be made in the input section, not the output section. She thinks to herself that she must prevent Stephan or other managers from inadvertently making the same mistake. She remembers from her workshop that she can protect cells. She decides first to correct the error Stephan made and then to protect the formulas in cell I18 and any other appropriate cells from being changed. Let's make the same mistake Stephan made.

To make Stephan's mistake:

❶ Move the cell pointer to cell I18. Notice the formula @ROUND((1+$GROWTH)*H18,0) in the control panel.

❷ Type **200**. Press **[Enter]**. See Figure 5-21.

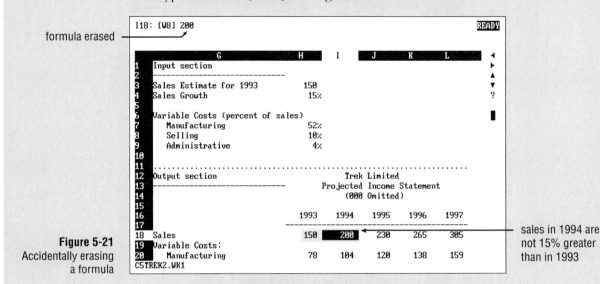

formula erased

Figure 5-21
Accidentally erasing
a formula

sales in 1994 are
not 15% greater
than in 1993

Originally cell I18 contained the formula @ROUND((1+$GROWTH)*H18,0). When Stephan typed 200 in I18, he erased the formula and replaced it with the constant 200. The formula that was originally in this cell instructed 1-2-3 to increase sales for 1994 by the growth rate, currently 15%. Now that the formula is no longer in the cell, sales for 1994 do not reflect the anticipated 15% sales growth. Sales for 1994 are 200 and will remain 200 unless the formula is reentered in this cell.

Fortunately Hillary is able to use the Undo feature and restore the worksheet to its previous state.

❸ Press **[Alt][F4]** (UNDO). Cell I18 now shows 173, and the formula @ROUND((1+$GROWTH)*H18,0) appears in the control panel. If the Undo feature has not worked, type the formula @ROUND((1+$GROWTH)*H18,0) into cell I18.

Protecting and Unprotecting Ranges

Hillary learned in her workshop that what Stephan did is a common mistake. Accidentally erasing worksheet formulas occurs often, so she learned it is a good idea to protect certain areas of a worksheet from accidental changes. She learned a combination of commands with which she can first protect an entire worksheet and then unprotect the range or ranges in which she or other users need to enter or edit data. In the steps that follow, you will begin the process of protecting specific ranges in Hillary's worksheet by first protecting the entire worksheet.

To protect an entire worksheet:

① Select /Worksheet Global (**/WG**) to display the Global Settings dialog box, as shown in Figure 5-22. Notice that the global protection setting is not on.

protection is not on →

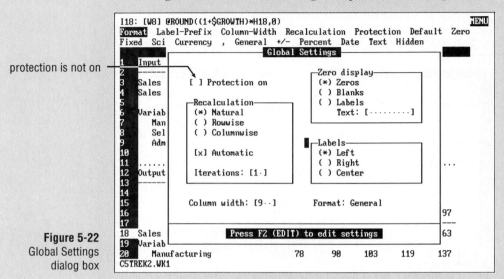

Figure 5-22
Global Settings
dialog box

② Select Protection Enable (**PE**) to turn on global protection. 1-2-3 then returns to the worksheet automatically.

③ With the cell pointer in cell I18, type **200** and press **[Enter]**. You are now prevented from making a change to that cell.

The ERROR indicator in the upper right corner and the message "Protected cell" in the middle of the screen remind you that the cell is protected. Notice the control panel. The letters PR (protected) appear in the control panel whenever the cell pointer is on a protected cell. See Figure 5-23.

indicates this cell
is protected

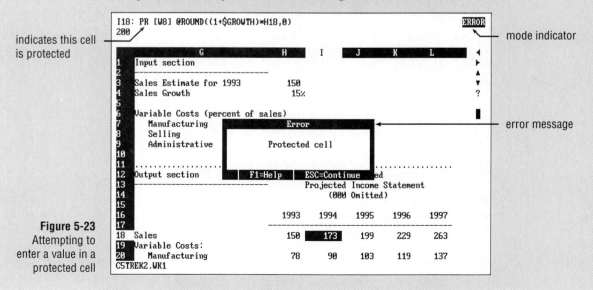

mode indicator

error message

Figure 5-23
Attempting to
enter a value in a
protected cell

④ Press **[Esc]** to return to READY mode.

Move the cell pointer to any other cell in the worksheet and try to enter data or make a change. You'll find that you cannot make a change.

Currently every cell in the worksheet is protected. So what do you do if you need to enter values in some cell? In Hillary's worksheet, for example, we know that managers might want to ask what-if about data in cells H3 through H9. In the next steps, you will learn how to lift the protection, or unprotect, the range of cells that represents the input section of the worksheet.

To unprotect cells in a protected worksheet:

① Press **[Home]**. Press **[Tab]** and move the cell pointer to cell H3, the first cell to be unprotected.

② Select /Range Unprot (**/RU**).

③ Press **[↓]** to highlight the range H3..H9, the range of the input values.

④ Press **[Enter]**. The input area is now unprotected. See Figure 5-24.

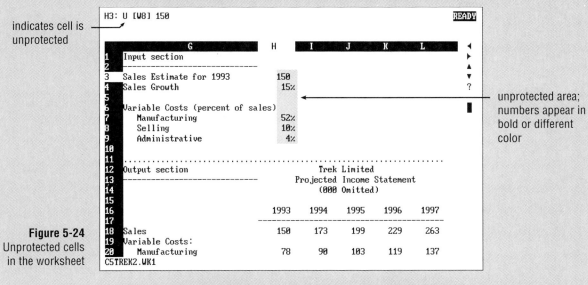

indicates cell is unprotected

unprotected area; numbers appear in bold or different color

Figure 5-24
Unprotected cells in the worksheet

You have now lifted protection from cells H3 to H9. The only area in the worksheet where you can make entries is the input area. Notice that the control panel's first line displays U (unprotected) whenever the cell pointer is in an unprotected cell. Another indication that protection is not in effect for these cells is that the values in these cells appear in boldface or in a different color.

To see if you can enter data in the input section, let's change the variable administrative costs to 5% in cell H9.

To make a change in cell H9:

❶ Move the cell pointer to H9, the cell for the variable administrative-cost percentage.

❷ Type **5%** and press **[Enter]**. You can also enter this value as .05. Notice that data can now be entered in unprotected cells.

❸ Press **[PgDn]** to see the results. Variable administrative costs are now 8, 9, 10, 11, and 13 for the years 1993 through 1997. See Figure 5-25.

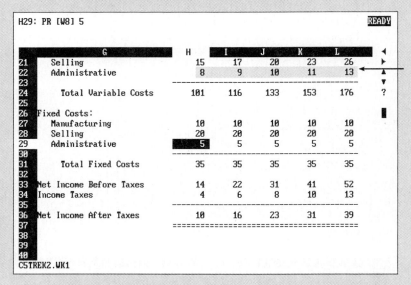

administrative costs increase as a result of increase in administrative-cost percentage

Figure 5-25
Change in administrative-cost percentage

If you decide to modify formulas or labels in the worksheet, remember that you will have to turn off protection. Let's try that.

To turn off protection:

❶ Select /Worksheet Global Protection (**/WGP**).

❷ Select Disable (**D**).

When you have completed the changes, you can turn on protection again by selecting /Worksheet Global Protection Enable (/WGPE). Let's keep the protection feature off for now.

Although adding protection to the worksheet is certainly an improvement, Hillary still is not satisfied. When changes are made in the input section, she has to press [PgDn] to see the results. She must then move the cell pointer back to the input section or press [PgUp] if she wants to make another change. Is there a way to have both the input and output sections appear on the screen at the same time?

Using Windows

To keep separate parts of the worksheet in view at the same time, you can use the Worksheet Window command. This command lets you view two parts of a large worksheet simultaneously, either horizontally or vertically. You can observe the results from one part of a worksheet while you make changes to another. You use [F6] (WINDOW) to move the cell pointer between the two windows.

In the next steps, you will split the worksheet into two windows — one for the input section and the other for the Projected Income Statement.

To split the screen into two windows:

❶ Press **[PgUp]**. Then move the cell pointer anywhere in row 8, the point where you decide to split the worksheet. For a horizontal window the rows above the cell pointer are placed in the top window. For vertical windows the columns to the left of the cell pointer are placed in the left window.

Next let's split the screen horizontally.

❷ Select /Worksheet Window Horizontal (**/WWH**). This command instructs 1-2-3 to split the screen horizontally into two windows, one above and one below the cell pointer. See Figure 5-26.

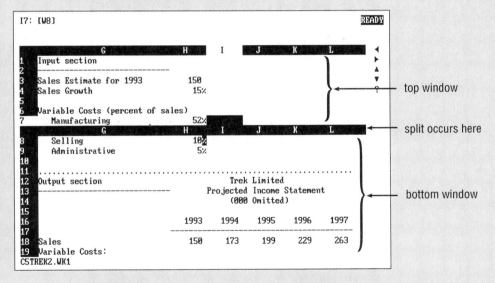

Figure 5-26
Splitting the
screen into two
windows

❸ Press **[F6]** (WINDOW) once to move the cell pointer to the bottom window. Press **[F6]** (WINDOW) again to switch back to the top window.

The Window key switches the cell pointer back and forth between the two windows.

④ If necessary, adjust your view of the worksheet so the cells G3 to H9 are visible in the top window.

⑤ Press **[F6]** (WINDOW) again to switch the cell pointer to the bottom window. Then press **[↓]** until row 37 is visible. Your screen should be similar to Figure 5-27.

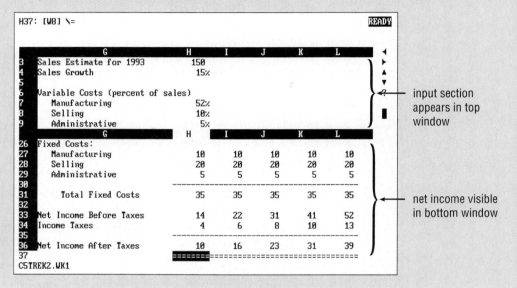

Figure 5-27
Worksheet windows adjusted to view the input section and the net income data

Now you can view, at the same time, part of the worksheet in the top window and part of the Projected Income Statement in the bottom window. Let's change the 1993 sales estimate to 225 and view the results.

To make a change and immediately view the results:

❶ Press **[F6]** (WINDOW) to switch to the top window.

❷ Move the cell pointer to cell H3, the location for the sales estimate.

❸ Type **225** in cell H3. Press **[Enter]** and watch as the results of the change appear immediately. See Figure 5-28.

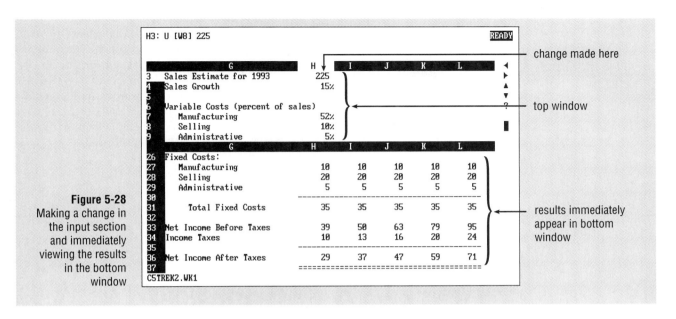

Figure 5-28
Making a change in
the input section
and immediately
viewing the results
in the bottom
window

It will be easier to perform other tasks in this tutorial if you first clear the windows.

To clear the windows:
- ❶ Select /Worksheet Window Clear (/**WWC**).

Hillary now thinks that the worksheet is getting closer to her ideal, but she still is not completely satisfied. Each time she tries new input values, she finds herself writing down the results on a sheet of paper. She wonders if there is a way to make more than one change at a time and see the results. Hillary decides to ask an experienced 1-2-3 user at her company. She explains the problem and is told to try the Data Table command.

Before using this command, Hillary decides to set her worksheet aside. She wants to develop and experiment on a new worksheet so she does not accidentally lose or destroy her current worksheet.

To save the worksheet:
- ❶ Select /File Save (/**FS**). Type **S5TREK2** and press **[Enter]**.

Printing Cell Formulas

So that she will be able to review the formulas in her current worksheet, Hillary prints the cell formulas that make up the current worksheet.

Printing the cell formulas is an option of the Print command. Using this option to create a printout of the cell formulas provides you with a record of the worksheet. It also allows you to see several formulas at once, thereby letting you see how formulas relate to one another. This is especially helpful if you are trying to find a problem in your worksheet. Instead of moving from cell to cell and viewing each formula in the control panel, you have a printout of all the formulas. By attaching this printout to the usual output from your worksheet, you add valuable backup documentation for the worksheet. Let's now use the print-cell-formula option of the Print command to print the worksheet's formulas.

To print the cell formulas:

❶ Select /Print Printer Range (**/PPR**).

❷ Move the cell pointer to G18, the first cell of the print range.

❸ Press **[.]** to anchor the cell pointer. Then highlight G18..L37 and press **[Enter]**.

The print range consists of the cells in the calculation/output area.

❹ Select Options Other Cell-Formulas (**OOC**) to cause the range to print as cell formulas rather than as values. Notice the last setting, "List entries," in the lower left corner of the Print Settings dialog box, which now specifies that cell formulas will be output. See Figure 5-29.

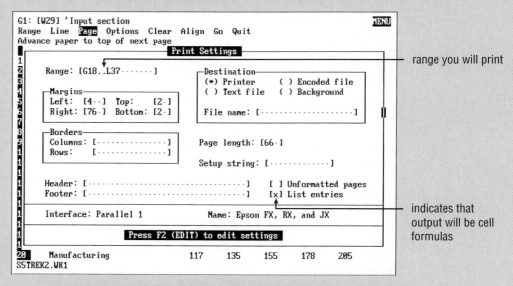

Figure 5-29
The Print Settings
dialog box

❺ Select Quit (**Q**) to leave the Options menu and return to the Print menu. Make sure the printer is ready.

❻ Print the cell formulas. Select Align Go Page (**AGP**). 1-2-3 prints a list of the cell address and cell formula for each cell within the specified range. See Figure 5-30. Notice in this figure that the second column shows the display format and the column width as well as the contents of each cell.

❼ Select Quit (**Q**) to exit the print menu.

display format, column width, and cell formula
cell address

```
G18: (G) [W29] 'Sales
H18: [W8] +SALES93
I18: [W8] @ROUND((1+$GROWTH)*H18,0)
J18: [W8] @ROUND((1+$GROWTH)*I18,0)
K18: [W8] @ROUND((1+$GROWTH)*J18,0)
L18: [W8] @ROUND((1+$GROWTH)*K18,0)
G19: (G) [W29] 'Variable Costs:
G20: (G) [W29] '   Manufacturing
H20: [W8] @ROUND(+H18*$VAR_MANUF,0)
I20: [W8] @ROUND(+I18*$VAR_MANUF,0)
J20: [W8] @ROUND(+J18*$VAR_MANUF,0)
K20: [W8] @ROUND(+K18*$VAR_MANUF,0)
L20: [W8] @ROUND(+L18*$VAR_MANUF,0)
G21: (G) [W29] '   Selling
H21: [W8] @ROUND(+H18*$VAR_SELLING,0)
I21: [W8] @ROUND(+I18*$VAR_SELLING,0)
J21: [W8] @ROUND(+J18*$VAR_SELLING,0)
K21: [W8] @ROUND(+K18*$VAR_SELLING,0)
L21: [W8] @ROUND(+L18*$VAR_SELLING,0)
G22: (G) [W29] '   Administrative
H22: [W8] @ROUND(+H18*$VAR_ADMIN,0)
I22: [W8] @ROUND(+I18*$VAR_ADMIN,0)
J22: [W8] @ROUND(+J18*$VAR_ADMIN,0)
K22: [W8] @ROUND(+K18*$VAR_ADMIN,0)
L22: [W8] @ROUND(+L18*$VAR_ADMIN,0)
H23: [W8] \-
I23: [W8] \-
J23: [W8] \-
K23: [W8] \-
L23: [W8] \-
G24: (G) [W29] '       Total Variable Costs
H24: [W8] +H20+H21+H22
I24: [W8] +I20+I21+I22
J24: [W8] +J20+J21+J22
K24: [W8] +K20+K21+K22
L24: [W8] +L20+L21+L22
G26: (G) [W29] 'Fixed Costs:
G27: (G) [W29] '   Manufacturing
H27: [W8] 10
I27: [W8] 10
J27: [W8] 10
K27: [W8] 10
L27: [W8] 10
G28: (G) [W29] '   Selling
H28: [W8] 20
I28: [W8] 20
J28: [W8] 20
K28: [W8] 20
L28: [W8] 20
G29: (G) [W29] '   Administrative
H29: [W8] 5
I29: [W8] 5
J29: [W8] 5
```

Figure 5-30
A printout of the cell formulas (continued on next page)

```
K29: [W8]  5
L29: [W8]  5
H30: [W8]  \-
I30: [W8]  \-
J30: [W8]  \-
K30: [W8]  \-
L30: [W8]  \-
G31: (G) [W29] '       Total Fixed Costs
H31: [W8]  +H27+H28+H29
I31: [W8]  +I27+I28+I29
J31: [W8]  +J27+J28+J29
K31: [W8]  +K27+K28+K29
L31: [W8]  +L27+L28+L29
G33: (G) [W29] 'Net Income Before Taxes
H33: [W8]  +H18-H24-H31
I33: [W8]  +I18-I24-I31
J33: [W8]  +J18-J24-J31
K33: [W8]  +K18-K24-K31
L33: [W8]  +L18-L24-L31
G34: (G) [W29] 'Income Taxes
H34: [W8]  @ROUND(@IF(H330,H33*0.25,0),0)
I34: [W8]  @ROUND(@IF(I330,I33*0.25,0),0)
J34: [W8]  @ROUND(@IF(J330,J33*0.25,0),0)
K34: [W8]  @ROUND(@IF(K330,K33*0.25,0),0)
L34: [W8]  @ROUND(@IF(L330,L33*0.25,0),0)
H35: [W8]  \-
I35: [W8]  \-
J35: [W8]  \-
K35: [W8]  \-
L35: [W8]  \-
G36: (G) [W29] 'Net Income After Taxes
H36: [W8]  +H33-H34
I36: [W8]  +I33-I34
J36: [W8]  +J33-J34
K36: [W8]  +K33-K34
L36: [W8]  +L33-L34
H37: [W8]  \=
I37: [W8]  \=
J37: [W8]  \=
K37: [W8]  \=
L37: [W8]  \=
```

Figure 5-30
(continued from
previous page)

Data Tables

Now let's see how Hillary can use a data table to make more than one change at a time and see the results. She decides she wants to make several changes to estimated 1993 sales and observe how those changes will affect net income before taxes.

A data table is an area of the worksheet set up to show the results a formula generates each time you change a value in that formula.

Let's illustrate this concept using a bank loan as an example. Suppose you are considering borrowing $100,000 to buy a home. The bank requires monthly payments over 25 years. What if you wanted to know how much your monthly payments would be at various interest rates, such as 9%, 10%, 11%, 12%, and 13%? To show the relationship between the monthly payments and the various interest rates, you could use a data table such as Figure 5-31.

Interest Rate	Monthly Payment
9%	839.20
10%	908.70
11%	980.11
12%	1053.22
13%	1127.84

Figure 5-31
Monthly loan
payments at
different interest
rates

This figure shows how monthly payments increase as interest rates increase. The data table is a valuable tool because it allows you to try out several what-if questions at one time and observe their results. In the case of the monthly payments for the loan, you are saying:

What is the monthly payment *if* the interest rate is 9%?

What is the monthly payment *if* the interest rate is 10%?

What is the monthly payment *if* the interest rate is 11%?

What is the monthly payment *if* the interest rate is 12%?

What is the monthly payment *if* the interest rate is 13%?

Using a data table, you need only one formula to produce a table that shows the different results generated each time a new interest rate is substituted in the formula. When the value of only one variable in a formula is varied, the data table is referred to as a **one-way data table**.

One-Way Data Tables

The components and the layout of a one-way data table are shown in Figure 5-32 on the following page. As you can see, a one-way data table includes an **input cell** and a **table range.** The table range consists of four components: a **blank cell**, a **formula**, **input values**, and a **results area.**

The data table must contain these four components and be laid out as shown in Figure 5-32.

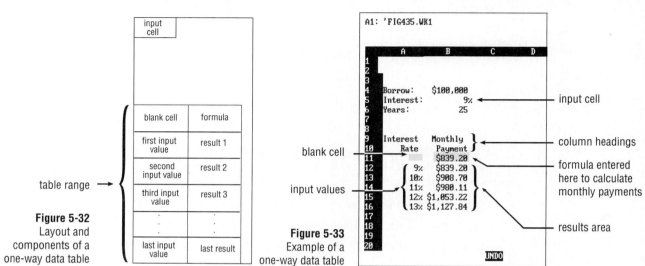

Figure 5-32
Layout and components of a one-way data table

Figure 5-33
Example of a one-way data table

Figure 5-33 illustrates the components of the data table using a bank loan example. (You do not have a worksheet file for this example.) The components are defined as follows:

- The *input cell* is an unprotected cell that can be anywhere in the worksheet. It can be blank or can contain one of the input values. In the bank loan example, cell B5 is the input cell.

- The *blank cell* is a cell that does not contain data and is located at the intersection of the first row and the first column of the table range. In the bank loan example, cell A11 is considered the blank cell.

- The *formula* (or formulas) must be in the first row of the table range, starting at the second cell from the left. The formula contains a **variable**. A variable is a part of the formula for which different values can be substituted. In the bank loan example, the formula to calculate the monthly payments is in B11.

- The *input values* must be in the first column of the table range, starting immediately below the empty cell. The input values are the values that 1-2-3 substitutes for a variable whenever it performs the calculations specified in the formula. In the bank loan example, the interest rates in cells A12 to A16 are the input values that are substituted in the formula to calculate the monthly payments.

- The *results area* is the unprotected area below the formula and to the right of the input values. 1-2-3 enters the results of each calculation next to the input value it used. The results area should be blank when you first set up the data table because 1-2-3 writes over any data in this area when it calculates results. In the bank loan example, the results area is cells B12 to B16.

Setting Up a One-Way Data Table

Hillary now has her list of formulas and she has read how to use the Data Table command in her 1-2-3 reference manual. She draws a sketch that will help her visualize the planned changes in estimated 1993 sales and how these changes affect net income before taxes. Figure

5-34 is her handwritten sketch of how she wants her data table to look. Notice that she has followed the correct layout for a data table and has included all the required components.

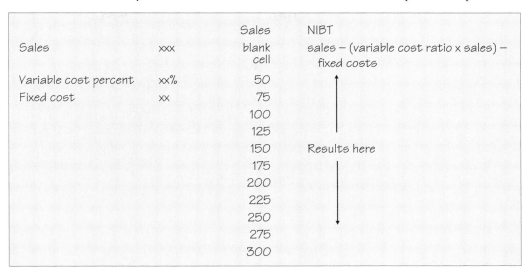

Figure 5-34
Hillary's sketch for
her data table

Now let's construct Hillary's data table. Begin by retrieving the file C5TREK3.WK1.

To retrieve the file:

❶ Select /File Retrieve (**/FR**). Highlight C5TREK3.WK1 and press **[Enter]**.

Your screen should now look like Figure 5-35. Notice that this file contains the input values that Hillary will use. Sales start at $50,000 (remember, the worksheets indicate the number of thousands), and variable costs are 64% of sales. Variable costs are the sum of variable manufacturing (50%), variable selling (10%), and variable administrative (4%) costs. Fixed costs are $35,000, the sum of fixed manufacturing ($10,000), fixed selling ($20,000), and fixed administrative ($5,000) costs.

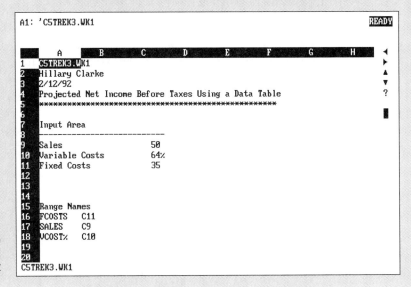

Figure 5-35
Hillary's retrieved
worksheet

Your first step is to select a location in the worksheet to place the data table. The location of a data table can be any blank area of your worksheet. Let's use the cell range E8..F19.

Next, you must enter descriptive headings for the columns in the data table. Headings are *not* part of a data table, but you should enter them because they help you read the values in the data table. Hillary's sketch of the data table contains the headings you will now enter.

To enter headings for the data table:

❶ Move the cell pointer to cell **E7**. Type **"Sales** and press **[Enter]**. Notice that the label, Sales, is right-justified in the cell. That is because you typed the label prefix " (Quotation Mark) before you typed Sales.

❷ Move the cell pointer to F7 and type **"NIBT**, an abbreviation for net income before taxes. Press **[Enter]**.

Using the Data Fill Command

Now that you have entered the headings, let's enter the values in the input value section of the data table. Remember from the worksheet sketch that Hillary wants to see what will happen to NIBT as sales estimates increase in intervals of 25,000, starting at 50,000 and ending at 300,000 (remember, you type only the number of thousands, i.e., 50 for 50,000, 75 for 75,000, and so on).

You could enter each number — 50, 75, 100, and so on, up to 300 — in each appropriate cell, but that would be rather time consuming. Instead you can use a new command, the Data Fill command, to enter all the sales estimates at one time into the input value section of the data table. The Data Fill command lets you enter a sequence of equally spaced values into a range of cells, either in one column or in one row. To use the Data Fill command, you first need to understand four new terms:

- The **fill range** is the range you want to fill with a series of sequential values. In Hillary's case, the fill range is E9..E19.

- The **start value** is the first value you want to enter in the fill range. In Hillary's case, 50 is the start value.

- The **step value** is the increment between the values in the sequence. Hillary wants to increase sales estimates in increments of 25.

- The **stop value** is the value you want to use as a limit for the sequence. Hillary wants her data table to stop at 300. The default limit is 8191.

To use the Data Fill command:

❶ Move the cell pointer to E9. Notice that cell E8, the first cell in the data table, is empty.

❷ Select /Data Fill (/**DF**).

Now let's enter the fill range.

❸ At cell E9, press **[.]** to anchor the cell pointer.

❹ Highlight the cells E9..E19 and press **[Enter]**.

❺ Type **50** to enter the start value and press **[Enter]**.

❻ Type **25** to enter the step value and press **[Enter]**.

❼ Type **300** to enter the stop value. Take a look at the control panel. See Figure 5-36.

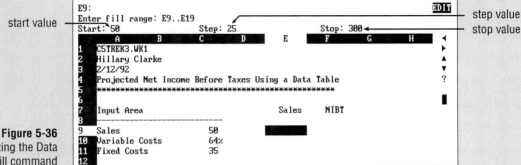

Figure 5-36
Executing the Data
Fill command

❽ Press **[Enter]**. As you do, notice that the input values appear in column E of the data table. See Figure 5-37.

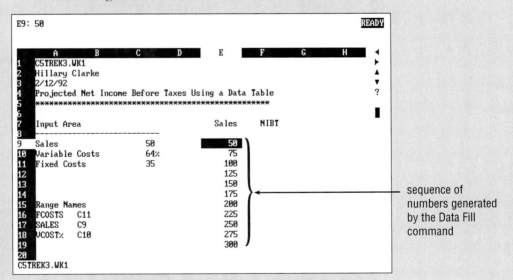

Figure 5-37
The worksheet after
executing the Data
Fill command

Now you should enter the formula to calculate net income before taxes (NIBT) into the formula section of the data table. Checking Hillary's sketch for her data table (Figure 5-34) you can see the formula is

$$sales - (variable\ cost\ ratio \times sales) - fixed\ costs$$

Be sure to enter this formula in cell F8, that is, to the right of the empty cell of the data table.

To enter the formula to calculate net income before taxes:

❶ Move the cell pointer to F8, the first row of the data table.

❷ Type **+sales–(vcost%*sales)–fcosts**. Press **[Enter]** and, as you do, notice that –17, the result of the calculation of this formula, appears in F8. See Figure 5-38.

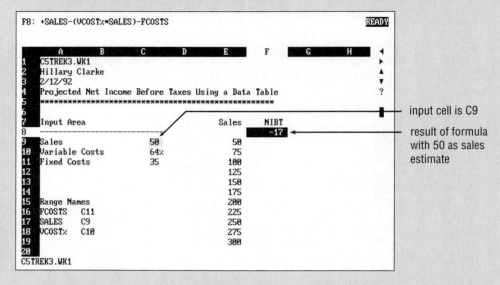

Figure 5-38
Formula to calculate the net income before taxes is entered

The components of the data table have been set up; now it's time to use the Data Table command.

To identify the cells that make up the table range of the data table:

❶ Select the command /Data Table 1 (**/DT1**) to set up a one-way data table. 1-2-3 prompts you to specify the data table range.

❷ Move the cell pointer to E8, the upper left corner of the table range.

❸ Anchor the cell pointer by pressing **[.]**.

❹   Highlight the range E8..F19. See Figure 5-39.

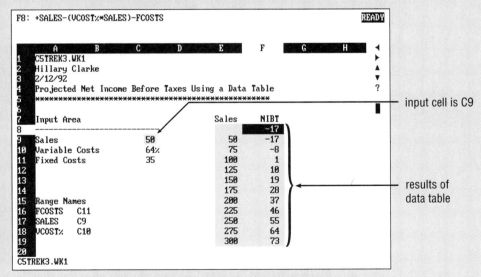

Figure 5-39
The process of
executing the Data
Table command

You have now defined the table range of the data table. Notice that the empty cell, E8, must be included in the range, but we have not included the column headings, which are in E7..F7.

❺   Press **[Enter]**.

Next, 1-2-3 prompts you to specify which cell will be the input cell. The input cell will contain the values from the input value section of the data table.

❻   Type **sales**. Press **[Enter]**. See Figure 5-40.

Figure 5-40
The worksheet
after executing the
Data Table
command

1-2-3 substitutes each value from the input section of the data table (E9..E19) into the input cell (C9), one at a time. Then using the formula in cell F8, 1-2-3 recalculates the formula using these input values and immediately displays the results in the results section of the data table (F9..F19). The data table is now complete, so let's save it.

⑦ Save the worksheet as S5TREK3.

Data tables can provide you even greater flexibility, because you can test the sensitivity of the results to various assumptions. Suppose, for example, that you believe the variable costs will increase from 64% to 66% of sales. With data tables, all you have to do is change the variable cost in cell C10 from 64 to 66 and then press [F8] (TABLE) to recalculate the entire table. Pressing [F8] repeats the last Data Table command you selected, in this case, Data Table 1. 1-2-3 uses the previous setting for the table range and the input cell.

Now let's see how Hillary can quickly change one value using the [F8] (TABLE) key and generate 11 new forecasts of NIBT.

To use [F8] for what-if analysis:

① Move to cell C10, type **66%**, a revised variable cost, and press **[Enter]**. You can also enter the value as .66.

No changes appear in the results area.

② Press **[F8]** (TABLE) to recalculate the table. See Figure 5-41.

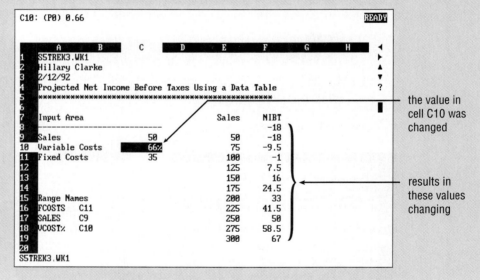

Figure 5-41
Results of data table using [F8] to recalculate results

the value in cell C10 was changed

results in these values changing

Exercises

1. Which of the following @IF functions would work in a 1-2-3 worksheet?
   a. IF(D–40>0,3,7)
   b. @IF(D4–40>0 , 3, 7)
   c. @IFD4–40>0,3,7
   d. @IF(D4–40>0,3,7)

2. Write an English statement that explains what this @IF function says:
   @IF(C15<0,"LOSS","PROFIT")

3. Retrieve the file E5FILE1 and do the following:
   a. Press **[Tab]**. Notice that the names of the countries in column A no longer appear on the screen. This makes it difficult to read the worksheet.
   b. Write down the steps necessary to modify the worksheet so that when you press [Tab] the names of the countries remain on the screen.
   c. Use your answer in (b) to actually modify the worksheet.

4. Retrieve the file E5FILE2 and do the following:
   a. Use the @IF function in cells C4, C5, and C6 to determine a salesperson's commission based on his or her weekly sales. If weekly sales are above 10000, a 12-percent commission rate appears in column C; otherwise, a 7.5-percent commission rate appears in column C.
   b. Print the worksheet and the cell formulas.

5. Retrieve the file E5FILE3 and do the following:
   a. Use the @IF function in cells D3, D4, and D5 to check the value in column B. Display the word MALE or FEMALE in column D, depending on whether the code in column B is M (male) or F (female).
   b. Use the @IF function in cells E3, E4, and E5 to place the phrase UNDER 21 or 21 AND OVER in cells E3, E4, and E5, depending on the age in column C.
   c. Print your worksheet and cell formulas.

6. Identify the command you would use in each of the following situations:
   a. You have a list of 100 customer names, addresses, and phone numbers. As you scroll down the worksheet, the column headings disappear from the screen.
   b. Users of the worksheet keep erasing formulas accidentally.
   c. You want an efficient way to do what-if analysis.
   d. You want to see two different parts of a large worksheet at the same time.
   e. You want to number cells in column A of your worksheet 1 to 500 without typing each number.

Tutorial Assignments

Before you begin these Tutorial Assignments, check your working copy of your data diskette. Be sure you have space to save the additional worksheet files you'll create in these assignments (at least 40,000 bytes). If not, save the files you need for this tutorial to another formatted diskette.

Retrieve the worksheet file T5TREK2 and do the following:

1. Build error checking into the input section. Do this by causing 1-2-3 to display the message "Error in input value" in cell I7 if the value entered for variable manufacturing

costs is greater than 1. Otherwise, be sure that 1-2-3 leaves cell I7 blank. *Hint:* Use the following logic to help you:

> If value entered for variable manufacturing cost greater than 1
>> Display "Error in input value"
> Otherwise
>> Display "   "

2.   Save the worksheet as S5TREK4.

3.   Enter the value 45 in cell H7 as the variable manufacturing costs. Print the input screen.

4.   Enter the value 45% in cell H7 as the variable manufacturing costs. Print the input screen.

Retrieve the worksheet file T5TREK3 and do the following:

5.   Change the fixed costs from 35 to 45 and recalculate the data table. Print your results.

6.   Reduce the variable costs from 64% to 60% and recalculate the data table. Print the results.

7.   Save the worksheet as S5TREK5.

Retrieve the worksheet file from Tutorial 3, T5BALBO1, and do the following:

8.   Protect the worksheet so the only cells that can be changed are the daily stock prices, cells C28..C31.

9.   Attempt to type 125 in cell B28 (you should not be able to). Enter the following prices in cells C28 to C31: 90, 70, 60, and 44, respectively. Save your worksheet as S5BALBO1.

Case Problems

1. Apex Auto Rental

Apex Auto Rental, a local car rental company, rents two types of cars: compact (Pontiac Sunbird) and luxury (Cadillac Seville). The current rental rates are shown in Figure 5-42.

Current Rental Rates

	Compact	Luxury
Charge/day	$38	$50
Charge/mile	$0.22	$0.32

Figure 5-42

1.   Develop a worksheet that calculates and prints customer bills. Your worksheet should be divided into the following sections:
   • A *documentation* section that includes a title, your name, date developed, filename, and purpose.
   • An *input* section to capture the customer billing data in Figure 5-43. Also include in the input area the rental rate table from Figure 5-42.

Figure 5-43

> Name
>
> Type of car (enter 1 if compact, 2 if luxury)
>
> Number of days driven
>
> Miles driven

- A *calculation/output* section in your worksheet for the customer bill. The bill should appear as shown in Figure 5-44.

Figure 5-44

> **Apex Car Rental**
>
> Name: xxxxxxxxxxxxx[1]
>
> Type of car: xxxxxxxxxxx[2]
>
> Days driven: xx[1]
>
> Miles driven: xxx[1]
>
> Amount due: $xxxxx[3]
>
> [1] Reference the data from the input area.
>
> [2] Enter the label Pontiac Sunbird if the code for type of car is a 1; otherwise, enter the label Cadillac Seville.
>
> [3] Amount due is based on the following calculation:
> ($days\ driven \times charge/day$) + ($miles/driven \times charge/mile$)

2. Include features that you think will improve the appearance and use of your worksheet, for example, formatting, range names, cell protection, and more.

3. Use the data in Figure 5-45 to print a bill.

Figure 5-45

Name:	John Connolly
Type of car:	2
Days driven:	4
Miles driven:	525

4. Save your worksheet as P5APEX.

5. Use the data in Figure 5-46 to print a second bill.

Figure 5-46

Name:	Joe Dougherty
Type of car:	1
Days driven:	2
Miles driven:	125

6. Suppose that Apex changes its rates to those shown in Figure 5-47. Update the rate schedule.

New Rental Rates		
	Compact	**Luxury**
Charge/day	$40	$53
Charge/mile	$0.23	$0.35

Figure 5-47

7. Use the data in Figure 5-48 to print a third bill based on the new rates.

Name:	Susan Solomon
Type of car:	1
Days driven:	1
Miles driven:	150

Figure 5-48

WYSIWYG Assignments

1. Attach WYSIWYG.

2. Add the following enhancements:
   a. Remove any dashed lines you might have included in your worksheet. Replace them with solid lines under column headings and above and below totals.
   b. Use a 14-point Swiss font for the report title line(s).
   c. Boldface all descriptive labels in the rental bill in Figure 5-44.
   d. Draw a line around the entire bill.

3. Save your worksheet as W5APEX.

4. Print the entire worksheet on one page.

2. Loan Repayment Schedule

Occasionally businesses need to borrow money for new buildings, equipment, or other large purchases. If a business takes out a term loan, it must pay back the loan in installments over a specified period of time.

For example, assume Lockwood Enterprises borrows $10,000, payable over five years, at an interest rate of 16% per year on the unpaid balance. Each month Lockwood pays $243.18 to cover principal and interest. The principle is the amount of the loan still unpaid, and the interest is the amount paid for the use of the money.

Figure 5-49 is a partial repayment schedule that shows the monthly payments broken out into principal repaid (amount borrowed) and interest paid. If this table were carried out for 60 months (5 years × 12 months per year, or the life of the loan), it would show a remaining balance of 0 at the conclusion of the 60-month period.

Payment Number	Monthly Payment	Interest[1]	Principal Repayment[2]	Remaining Balance
0	0.00	0.00	0.00	10000.00
1	243.18	133.33	109.85	9890.15
2	243.18	131.87	111.31	9778.84
...				
60	243.18	3.20	239.98	0[3]

[1] Interest is equal to the monthly interest rate, .013333 (16% divided by 12 months), times the remaining balance from the previous period. For example, in month 1, interest equals $133.33 (.013333 × 10000). In month 2, interest equals $131.87 (.013333 × 9890.15).

[2] Principal repayment for each period is equal to the monthly payment ($243.18) minus the interest for the period. For example, in month 2, the monthly payment ($243.18) minus the interest ($131.87) equals the principal repaid ($111.31).

[3] Because of rounding, the result will not be exactly zero.

Figure 5-49

Do the following:

1. Develop a worksheet that prepares a complete loan payment schedule for this loan. At the bottom of the payment schedule, calculate the total payments and the total interest.

2. Your worksheet should be divided into the following sections:
   - A *documentation* section that includes a title, your name, date developed, filename, and purpose.
   - An *input* section that includes the amount borrowed, the interest rate, and the monthly payments.
   - A *calculation/output* section consisting of the repayment schedule shown in Figure 5-49.

3. Include features that you think will improve the appearance and use of your worksheet, for example, formatting, range names, cell protection, and other features.

4. Save the worksheet as S5LOAN.

5. Print the input section and the repayment schedule using these data.

6. What if the interest rate is 16.5% and the monthly payment is $245.85 on a $10,000 loan? Print the input section and repayment schedule using these data.

WYSIWYG Assignments

1. Attach WYSIWYG.

2. Add the following enhancements:
   a. Remove any dashed lines you might have included in your worksheet. Replace them with solid lines under column headings and above and below totals.
   b. Shade the input area.
   c. Boldface and italicize the column headings of the repayment schedule.

3. Save your worksheet as W5LOAN.

4. Print the entire worksheet on one page.

3. Predicting Demand for Mars Automobiles

Lynette Spiller, an economist working at HN Motor Company headquarters, has developed the following formula to estimate demand for HN's new line of Mars automobiles:

$$D = 100{,}000 - 100P + 2{,}000N + 50I - 1{,}000G + 0.2A$$

where

D	=	demand for Mars automobiles (in units)
P	=	price of Mars automobile (in dollars)
N	=	population in United States (in millions)
I	=	disposable income per person (in dollars)
G	=	price of gasoline (in cents per gallon)
A	=	advertising expenses by HN for Mars (in dollars)

The senior managers at HN are considering raising the price of Mars, but before they do, they want to determine how increasing the price will affect demand for this car. They ask Lynette to show how increasing the price in $100 increments from $10,000 to $11,000 will affect demand for the Mars.

Assume the following values when estimating demand:

N	=	250
I	=	$14,000
G	=	140 cents (do not enter as 1.40)
A	=	$1,000,000

Do the following:

1. Design a worksheet using the Data Table command to solve this problem. The data table should include a column for possible car prices beginning at $10,000, increasing in $100 increments to $11,000. The second column should show the demand for cars at each price.

2. Your worksheet should be divided into the following sections:
    *   A *documentation* section that includes a title, your name, date developed, filename, and purpose.
    *   An *input* section that includes the following variables: U.S. population, disposable income per person, price of gasoline, and advertising expenses.
    *   A *calculation/output* section consisting of the data table.

3. Include features that you think will improve the appearance and use of your worksheet, for example, formatting, range names, cell protection, and other features.

4. Save your worksheet as S5MARS.

5. Print the input section and the results.

6. What if the gasoline price per gallon is $1.75 (enter as 175 cents) ? Rerun the worksheet using the new price of gasoline. Print your results.

7. What if the gasoline price is $1.75 a gallon and the advertising budget is increased to $1,500,000? Print your results.

WYSIWYG Assignments

1. Attach WYSIWYG.

2. Add the following enhancements:
    a. Remove any dashed lines you might have included in your worksheet. Replace them with solid lines under column headings and above and below totals.
    b. Enclose the input area in a box using the Format Line Outline command.
    c. Boldface the column headings in the data table.

3. Save your worksheet as W5MARS.

4. Print the entire worksheet on one page.

4. Production Planning at QuikNails

QuikNails Manufacturing, makers of artificial fashion fingernails, anticipates selling 42,000 units of QuikNails in May. Currently the company has 22,000 units ready in inventory. The QuikNails plant will produce the additional product (20,000 units) during April to have enough product to meet the sales forecast for May. In addition to meeting May's sales forecast, the plant manager wants to have 24,000 units of QuikNails in inventory at the end of May for anticipated sales at the beginning of June. Thus, the QuickNails production requirement for April is the sum of the QuikNails units necessary to meet May sales estimates (20,000) plus the units needed to meet the desired ending inventory level (24,000).

The major ingredient needed to produce QuikNails is a chemical called Zinex. Assume the production department needs three gallons of Zinex to make one unit of QuikNails. Currently, the company has an inventory of 100,000 gallons of Zinex. The plant will use all of this raw material to meet its production requirement for April. It also needs 110,000 gallons of Zinex on hand at the end of April for production in May.

Sally Dolling is in charge of inventory control for both raw materials and finished products. She needs to inform senior management and the purchasing manager how much Zinex is required for current and future materials production. As Sally's assistant, you will develop a spreadsheet to help calculate the number of gallons of Zinex that she should tell the purchasing manager to buy in April for QuikNails to meet the production requirements. You decide to adapt the form that Sally has been using to develop her estimate for production and material requirements (Figure 5-50).

QuikNails Production:	Units
Monthly sales estimate for QuikNails	xxxx
<u>Less</u> QuikNails currently in inventory	.
Production needed to meet sales forecast	.
<u>Plus</u> QuikNails needed at end of month	.
Total QuikNails production requirement	xxxx
Zinex Purchases:	Gallons
Zinex needed to meet QuikNails production requirement	xxxx
<u>Less</u> Zinex currently in inventory	.
Purchases of Zinex required to meet QuikNails production requirement	.
<u>Plus</u> desired level of Zinex at end of month	.
Total Purchases of Zinex	xxxx

Figure 5-50

Design your spreadsheet so you can easily test alternative plans, such as different sales estimates and different inventory levels for QuikNails and Zinex.

Do the following:

1. Design a worksheet to calculate the production requirements of QuikNails and the amount of Zinex to purchase for the QuikNails manufacturing division.

2. Your worksheet should be divided into the following sections:
    -   A *documentation* section that includes a title, your name, date developed, filename, and purpose.
    -   An *input* section that includes the following variables: monthly sales estimate for QuikNails, QuikNails currently in inventory, QuikNails needed at end of month, Zinex currently in inventory, and desired level of Zinex at end of month.
    -   A *calculation/output* section consisting of the form in Figure 5-50.

3. Include features that you think will improve the appearance and use of your worksheet, for example, formatting, range names, cell protection, and other features.

4. Use the following set of data:

Monthly sales estimate for QuikNails	42,000
QuikNails currently in inventory	22,000
QuikNails needed at end of month	24,000
Zinex currently in inventory	100,000
Desired level of Zinex at end of month	110,000

5. Save your worksheet as S5NAILS.

6. Print the input section and the results.

7. Print the cell formulas.

8. What if the sales estimates of QuikNails for May is revised to 50,000 units? Print your results.

9. What if sales estimates for May is 30,000 units? Print your results.

WYSIWYG Assignments

1. Attach WYSIWYG.

2. Add the following enhancements:
   a. Create a table (grid) effect for the input data.
   b. Draw a double-lined outline around the entire report.

3. Save your worksheet as W5NAILS.

4. Print the entire worksheet on one page.

Tutorial 6

Creating and Printing Graphs

Automobile Industry Sales: A Four-year Summary

Case: McAuliffe & Burns

Carl Martinez majored in human resources in college and was particularly interested in labor relations. Thus, he was delighted when he landed a job as a staff assistant with McAuliffe & Burns (M&B), a leading consulting firm in Washington, D.C. M&B specializes in consulting to unions on labor relations issues.

When Carl began at M&B, his computer skills were not as polished as those of the other staff assistants. He knew how to use a word processor, but his spreadsheet skills were limited. But after M&B sent him to a two-day workshop on Lotus 1-2-3, Carl used Lotus 1-2-3 daily to prepare analyses for M&B's senior consultants. Over time Carl's skills with Lotus 1-2-3 improved dramatically, and he was promoted to a staff associate.

In his new job Carl is working for three senior consultants on a project for the United Auto Workers (UAW) union. Leaders of the UAW hired M&B to help them prepare testimony for upcoming Congressional committee hearings that will investigate whether the United States should establish import quotas for foreign cars.

Carl's first task is to research all automobile sales in the United States and gather data on unit sales by year and by company. After he gathers the data and creates a worksheet, Carl decides that he could present the data more effectively if he used the graphics function of Lotus 1-2-3. Carl is convinced that the data will make more of an impact on the Congressional subcommittee members if the UAW leaders show graphic representations of trends and markets. Carl plans to use a bar graph to show trends and a pie chart to show market shares. Figure 6-1a on the following page shows Carl's planning sheet for preparing his graphs. Figure 6-1b on the following page shows his sketches of the graphs he wants to create with 1-2-3.

OBJECTIVES

In this tutorial you will learn to:

- Start 1-2-3 and PrintGraph

- Create pie, line, bar, and stacked bar graphs

- Add titles, legends, and axis formatting

- Display bar graphs horizontally

- Add 3D effect to bar graphs

- Name and save graph settings

- Save graphs for printing

- Customize and use PrintGraph to print saved graphs

Figure 6-1a
Carl's planning
sheet

My Goal:
    Prepare graphs showing market shares and trends of automobile sales
    in U.S. from 1987 – 1990

What results do I want to see?
    Bar graphs of sales from 1987 – 1990
    Pie chart showing market shares for 1990

What information do I need?
    Number of cars sold by year for General Motors, Ford, Chrysler, Honda,
    Toyota, and Nissan

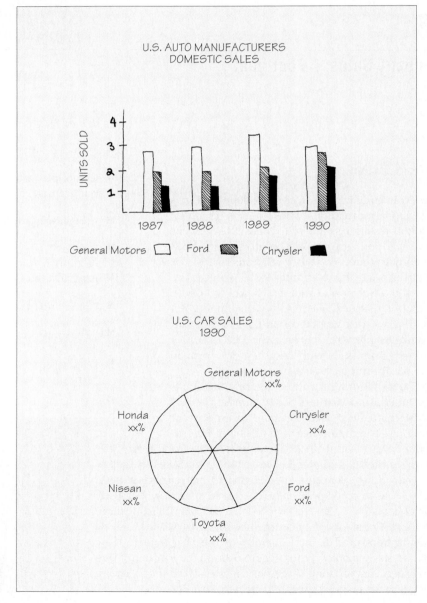

Figure 6-1b
Carl's sketches of
the graphs

This tutorial leads you through Carl's process of using graphs to analyze auto sales in the United States. After starting 1-2-3 from the Access menu, you will create a series of graphs to learn which type of graph is best suited to your data. Finally, you will print the graphs.

Introduction to Graphics

In business, graphics are used to represent one or more data series in a visually appealing and easily understood format. A **data series** is a single set of data represented by a line, a bar, or a pie. For example, a data series may include

- sales of a product by quarter (one data series)
- sales of three products by quarter (three data series)
- daily stock prices of a company over the past month (one data series)
- daily stock prices of two companies over the past month (two data series)

With your computer and 1-2-3, you can create graphs that will help you communicate your ideas quickly and easily. Lotus 1-2-3 includes a variety of graphs: bar graphs, line graphs, stacked bar graphs, pie charts, and XY graphs.

A **bar graph** consists of a series of vertical or horizontal bars. Each bar in the chart represents a single value from a set of values. The length or height of each bar is determined by the size of each value relative to all the other values. A bar graph is used to compare related data items during one time period or over a few time periods, such as four quarters. Bar graphs use the x axis, or horizontal axis, to classify data over regions, over time, over products, and so on. The vertical, or y, axis shows the quantity you are measuring, such as dollars, units sold, weight, or number of employees. For example, revenue at TriCycle Industries (Tutorial 4) could be represented by a bar graph that shows the relationship of sales of recycled materials by quarter (Figure 6-2a).

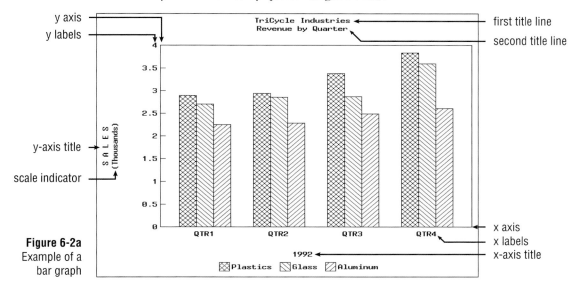

Figure 6-2a
Example of a
bar graph

A **line graph** represents data with points and connects these points with a straight line. Line graphs are effective at showing trends in data over time. Each line represents one set of data, such as the daily stock prices of IBM. A line graph is a better choice than a bar graph to present a large number of data points over time. Figure 6-2b uses a line graph to show quarterly revenue for each recycled material at TriCycle Industries.

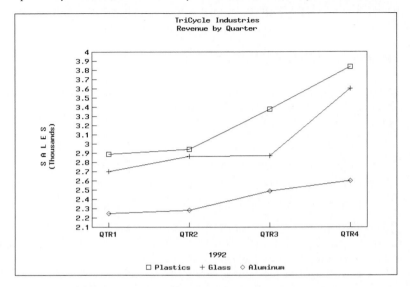

Figure 6-2b
Example of a
line graph

Stacked bar graphs show related data values on top of one another. These graphs show the components of several wholes. They are used to emphasize several totals and a breakdown of their components. For example, sales of each recycled material at TriCycle for the first quarter would appear on one bar, one material on top of the other (Figure 6-2c). A second bar would represent the same data for the second quarter. A third and fourth bar would show the sales of the last two quarters. This graph can compare total sales over several quarters, while also identifying the components that make up each quarterly total.

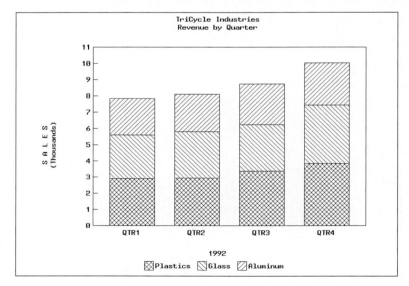

Figure 6-2c
Example of a
stacked bar graph

Pie charts are useful for showing how each value contributes to the whole. For example, the total 1990 sales at TriCycle are divided among plastics, glass, and aluminum (Figure 6-2d), each represented by a slice of the whole. The size of a slice depends on its component's value relative to the whole. When you want to express your data as percentages, consider using pie charts. You can emphasize one or more slices by using a cut, or "exploded," slice to draw the viewer's attention.

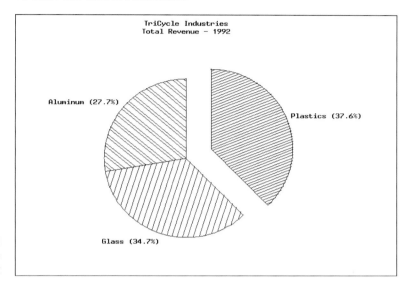

Figure 6-2d
Example of a pie chart

XY graphs, also called scatter graphs, show relationships between two variables. This type of graph shows how a change in one variable relates to another variable. For example, sales management at TriCycle graphed the relationship between the amount of recycled material in tons and sales revenue at TriCycle (Figure 6-2e). We will not cover XY graphs in this tutorial, but you should be aware that Lotus 1-2-3 can produce XY graphs.

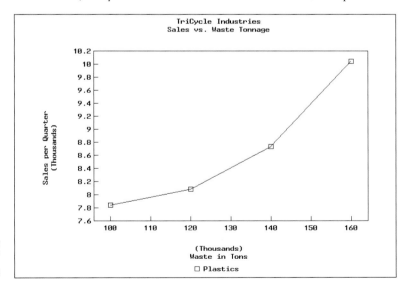

Figure 6-2e
Example of an XY graph

Mixed graphs combine lines and bars in the same graph. Lines are used to accent information in related bars. For example, Figure 6-2f on the following page shows how the quarterly revenue of each of TriCycle Industries' products, shown as bars, can be compared to average quarterly sales, shown as a line.

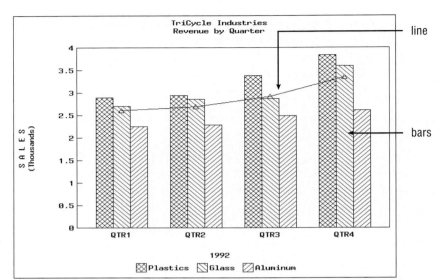

Figure 6-2f
Example of a
mixed graph

Creating a Bar Graph

Now let's retrieve one of Carl's worksheets that contains the number of cars sold in the United States from 1987 to 1990.

To retrieve this file:

● Retrieve the file C6AUTO1.WK1. See Figure 6-3.

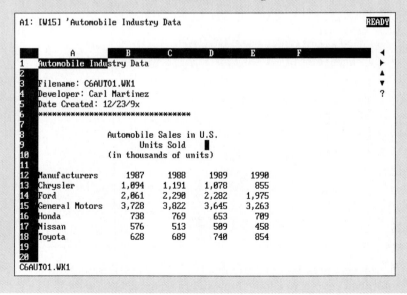

Figure 6-3
Carl's worksheet
showing total
car sales by
manufacturer
by year

Notice that the data in Figure 6-3 contain the number of cars sold annually in the United States from 1987 through 1990, broken down by manufacturer.

According to Carl's sketch, one of the graphs he wants to create is a bar graph showing car sales by manufacturer. Before creating the bar graph, you first need to learn about the Graph menu and the Graph Settings dialog box.

To create any graph in 1-2-3, you must use the Graph command. This command reveals the **Graph Settings dialog box,** in which you specify what data you want to graph and how you want to graph them. As you use the menu options available from the Graph command, 1-2-3 updates the Graph Settings dialog box.

To create a graph, you must specify the following:

- the type of graph you want
- the range of cells that represent the labels for the x axis
- the data series you plan to use in the graph

Carl plans first to compare graphically the total units sold by U.S. manufacturers (Chrysler, Ford, General Motors) over a four-year period (1987 to 1990) and then to compare these total U.S. units to units sold in the United States by Japanese manufacturers. Let's start by creating a bar graph of Chrysler's data that shows unit sales over a four-year period.

To create a bar graph of cars sold by Chrysler:

❶ Select /Graph (**/G**). 1-2-3 displays the Graph Settings dialog box.

❷ Select Type (**T**) and then select Bar (**B**) to indicate the type of graph you want to create — a bar graph. The graph settings now indicate the graph will be a bar graph. See Figure 6-4.

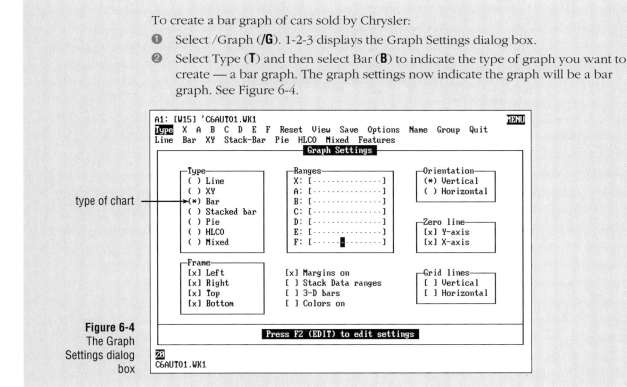

Figure 6-4
The Graph Settings dialog box

Next, specify the X data range, the worksheet range that contains the *labels* you want to place along the *x axis* (horizontal axis). Recall from Carl's sketch (Figure 6-1b) that you are using the years 1987, 1988, 1989, and 1990 as the x-axis labels.

③ Select **X** to specify the X data range. 1-2-3 reveals Carl's worksheet.

④ Move the cell pointer to cell B12, the first label to appear on the x axis. Press **[.]** (Period) to anchor the cell pointer. Then highlight the range B12..E12 and press **[Enter]** to specify the X data range.

Now use the same method to specify the first data series, sales of Chrysler cars from 1987 to 1990, to appear in the graph. The first data series is assigned to the A data range of your 1-2-3 Graph menu.

⑤ Select **A** to specify the A data range from the Graph menu. Move the cell pointer to B13, the cell containing Chrysler's sales data for 1987. Press **[.]** to anchor the cell pointer. Highlight B13..E13. See Figure 6-5a.

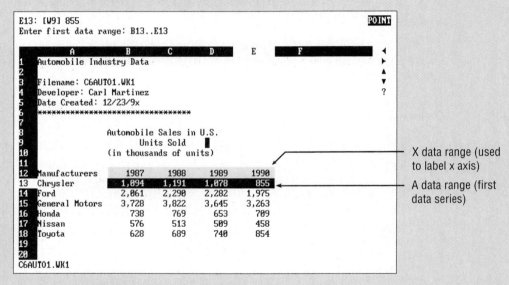

Figure 6-5a
Specifying the
data range

⑥ Press **[Enter]**.

The Graph Settings dialog box now indicates the graph type and the X and A ranges you specified. See Figure 6-5b. You can graph up to six data series at one time. 1-2-3 uses the letters A through F to represent these data series.

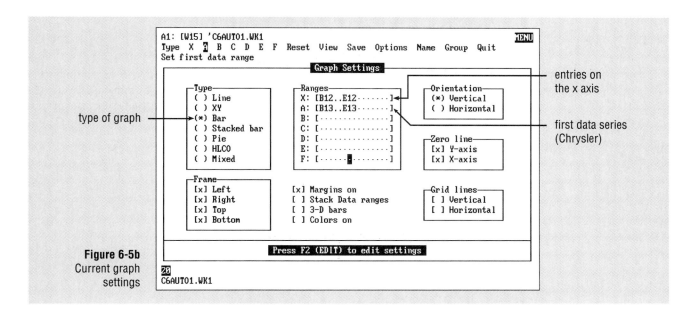

Figure 6-5b
Current graph settings

Viewing the Current Graph

After you have chosen your graph type and specified the data ranges, you can view the graph on the screen.

To view the graph from in the Graph menu:

❶ Select View (**V**). The graph appears on the screen. See Figure 6-6.

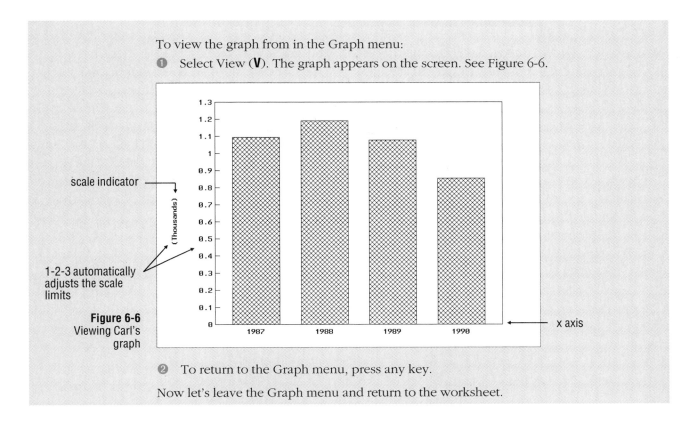

Figure 6-6
Viewing Carl's graph

❷ To return to the Graph menu, press any key.

Now let's leave the Graph menu and return to the worksheet.

❸   Select Quit (**Q**). Now you are in READY mode.

In 1-2-3, the graph that appears on the screen when you enter the View command is called the **current graph**. You can also use [F10] (GRAPH) to display the current graph. This feature allows you to change data in your worksheet and quickly see the results in a graph.

To view the current graph by using the function key [F10]:
❶   Press **[F10]** (GRAPH). The current graph appears.
❷   Press any key to return to the worksheet.

If you press [F10] (GRAPH) when there is no graph type, no A data range, or no X data range specified in the dialog box, your screen will become blank. If that happens, press any key to return to the worksheet.

Adding Multiple Variables

Following Carl's plan, let's continue developing the graph by returning to the Graph menu and then adding the unit sales for Ford and General Motors, that is, the B and C data ranges, to the bar graph.

To add the B and C data ranges to the bar graph:
❶   Select /Graph (**/G**) to return to the Graph menu. The second data series, cars sold by Ford, will be assigned to the second, or B, data range.
❷   Select **B** to specify the B data range from the Graph menu.
❸   Move the cell pointer to B14, the cell containing Ford sales data for 1987. Press **[.]** (Period) to anchor the cell pointer. Highlight B14..E14. Press **[Enter]**.

The Graph Settings dialog box now indicates the graph type and the X, A, and B ranges you have specified.

Now specify the third, or C, data range, sales of General Motors cars from 1987 to 1990.

❹   Select **C**, for the C data range, from the Graph menu. You will assign the data for General Motors to this range.

Move the cell pointer to B15, the cell containing General Motors sales data for 1987. Press **[.]** (Period) to anchor the cell pointer. Highlight B15..E15 and press **[Enter]**.

The Graph Settings dialog box now indicates the graph type and the X, A, B, and C ranges you have specified. See Figure 6-7.

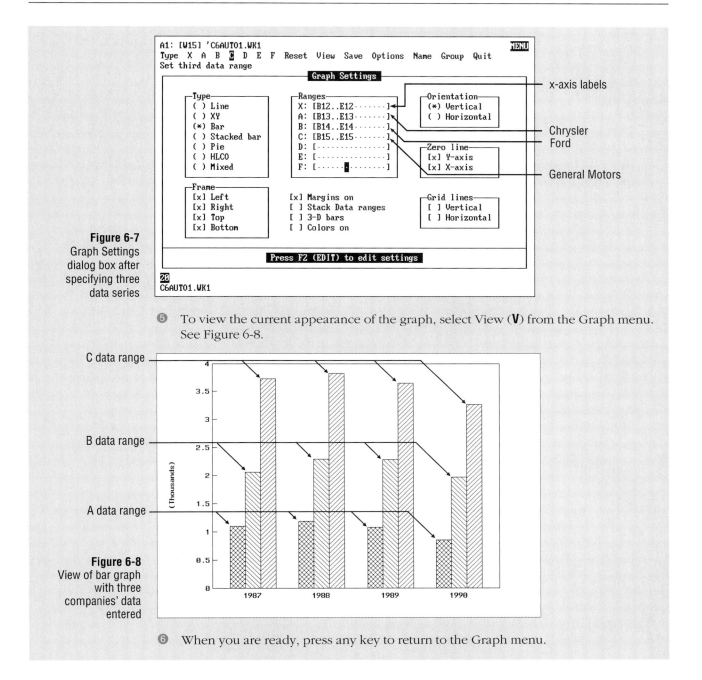

Figure 6-7
Graph Settings
dialog box after
specifying three
data series

⑤ To view the current appearance of the graph, select View (**V**) from the Graph menu. See Figure 6-8.

Figure 6-8
View of bar graph
with three
companies' data
entered

⑥ When you are ready, press any key to return to the Graph menu.

Experimenting with Graph Types

Some types of graphs may be more appropriate for your data than others. You can experiment with types of graphs by simply selecting another graph type from the Graph menu. You can display the same data in different forms and see which form best presents the information. Let's illustrate this concept by changing the graph you just created to a line graph and then to a stacked bar graph.

To change graph type to a line graph:

❶ Select Type Line (**TL**) and then select View (**V**). The data appear as a line graph. See Figure 6-9.

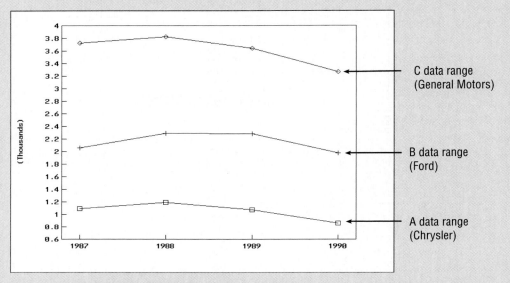

Figure 6-9
View of Carl's data
as a line graph

C data range
(General Motors)

B data range
(Ford)

A data range
(Chrysler)

❷ Press any key to return to the Graph menu.

Now let's see how a stacked bar graph displays the data.

To display a stacked bar graph:

❶ Select Type and Stack-Bar (**TS**).

❷ Select View (**V**). See Figure 6-10.

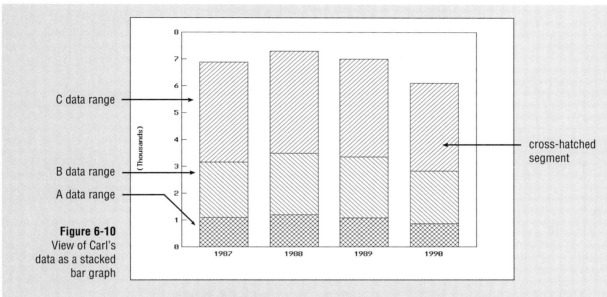

Figure 6-10
View of Carl's
data as a stacked
bar graph

1-2-3 displays the data as a stacked bar graph. This graph has a single bar for every value in the X data range, that is, a bar for each year. Each bar is made up of cross-hatched segments. Each segment of a bar represents the sales that each manufacturer contributed to total domestic sales in that year. Each bar viewed as a whole shows the total domestic sales in each year.

❸ Press any key to return to the Graph menu.

Carl decides that the relationships among the companies over the small number of time periods can best be shown by a bar graph. Let's return the graph settings to a bar graph.

To return the graph settings to those for a bar graph:
❶ Select Type Bar (**TB**).
❷ Select View (**V**). The bar graph appears on your screen.
❸ When you are ready, press any key to return to the Graph menu.

Carl decides not to try another popular type of graph, the pie chart, because it is not appropriate for the type of data with which he is working — data over time. A pie chart is more appropriate to show the relationship of the sales of each automobile company to total sales for a single year. You will create pie charts later in this tutorial.

Adding Titles and Legends

The current form of Carl's graph is difficult to interpret. What information does his graph represent? It has no title or labels to help anyone viewing the graph interpret the information. With 1-2-3 you can include a one- or two-line title and also label your x and y axes. Titles can be up to 39 characters.

Which bar in the graph represents General Motors sales? Ford sales? Chrysler sales? When you graph multiple data series, you should add a **legend** to identify the various lines in a line graph, the bars in a bar graph, or the segments in a stacked bar graph. The legend appears at the bottom of a graph below the x axis. You can add a legend of up to 19 characters for each data series.

Now you will add titles and legends to the bar graph you've created.

To add a title to your graph:

❶ From the Graph menu, select Options Titles First (**OTF**) to indicate you are entering the *first* line of the title. See Figure 6-11. A Graph Legends & Titles dialog box displays the options you specify.

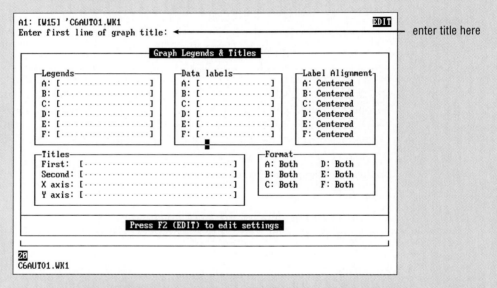

enter title here

Figure 6-11
Graph Legends &
Titles dialog box

❷ Type **U.S. Auto Manufacturers**, the title of Carl's graph, and then press **[Enter]**.

❸ Select Titles Second (**TS**) to indicate you are entering the second line of the title.

❹ Type **Domestic Sales** for the second line of the title, then press **[Enter]**.

Now enter the information for each car company that will be contained in the legend.

To add legends to your graph:

❶ Select Legend A (**LA**) from the Graph menu. Then type **Chrysler** to specify the legend for the A data range. Press **[Enter]** to enter the legend setting.

❷ Select Legend B (**LB**) and type **Ford** for the legend for the B data range. Press **[Enter]**.

❸ Select Legend C (**LC**) and type **General Motors** for the legend for the C data range. See Figure 6-12.

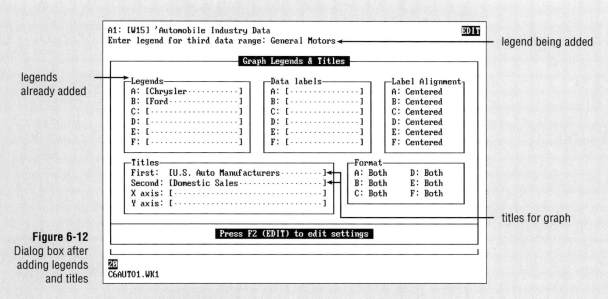

legends already added →

legend being added →

titles for graph →

Figure 6-12
Dialog box after adding legends and titles

④ Press **[Enter]**.

⑤ Select Quit (**Q**) to leave the Options menu.

⑥ Select View (**V**) to display the graph with the title and the legends. See Figure 6-13.

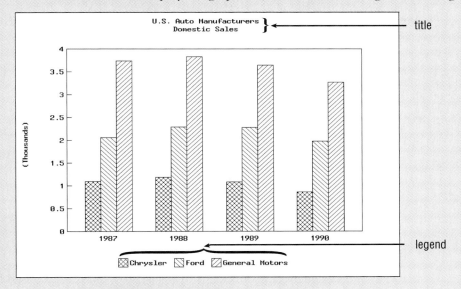

title →

legend →

Figure 6-13
View of Carl's bar graph with title and legends

⑦ Press any key to return to the Graph menu.

Adding Axis Titles

You can add titles for both the horizontal (x) and the vertical (y) axes. In the next steps you will add an axis title to improve the description of the y axis.

To add a y-axis title:

❶   From the Graph menu, choose Options Titles Y axis (**OTY**).

❷   Type **Units Sold**. Press **[Enter]**.

❸   Select Quit (**Q**) to return to the Graph menu.

❹   Select View (**V**) to see the revised graph. See Figure 6-14.

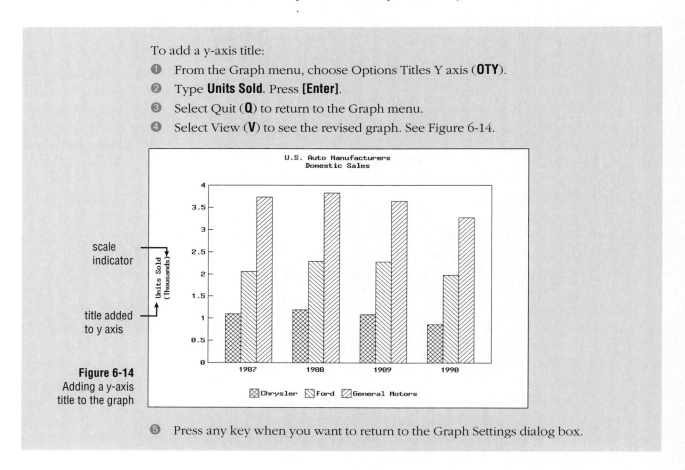

scale indicator

title added to y axis

Figure 6-14
Adding a y-axis title to the graph

❺   Press any key when you want to return to the Graph Settings dialog box.

Axis Scale Indicator

Carl has rounded the numbers in his worksheet to the nearest thousand, as indicated by the line in the worksheet (in thousands of units). For example, the 1990 entry for General Motors of 3,263 actually represents 3,263,000 units sold.

When you create a graph, 1-2-3 automatically scales, or adjusts, the values along the y axis based on the minimum and maximum values from the data series. When any of the y-axis values are above approximately 1,000, 1-2-3 scales the values that appear on the y axis, and automatically displays a scale indicator such as *Thousands* between the y axis and the y-axis title, as in Figure 6-14.

Sometimes the scale indicator may seem confusing. For example, in Figure 6-14, the y-axis title indicates thousands of units sold, but some of the numbers in the worksheet represent millions of units sold. The scale indicator is misleading. One solution is to suppress the display of the scale indicator and revise the y-axis title so it indicates the scale in millions of units sold. Let's do this for Carl's graph.

To remove the scale indicator from the y axis:

❶ Select Options Scale Y-Scale (**OSY**). See Figure 6-15. As the Graph Scale Settings dialog box indicates, the scale indicator is currently on.

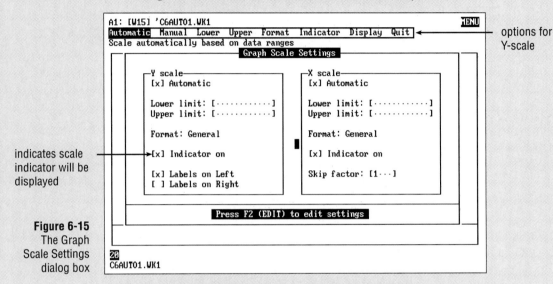

options for Y-scale

indicates scale indicator will be displayed

Figure 6-15
The Graph
Scale Settings
dialog box

A list of eight options appears in the control panel.

❷ Select Indicator (**I**).

To suppress the display of the scale indicator, choose No.

❸ Select No (**N**). The dialog box now shows that the indicator is off.

Now return to the Graph menu and view the graph.

❹   Select Quit Quit View (**QQV**). See Figure 6-16. Notice that the scale indicator no longer appears on the graph.

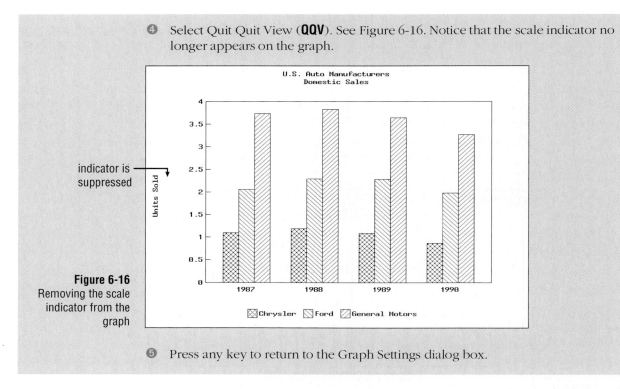

indicator is suppressed

Figure 6-16
Removing the scale indicator from the graph

❺   Press any key to return to the Graph Settings dialog box.

Now revise the y-axis title to include information indicating that the units sold are in millions.

To revise the y-axis title:

❶   Select Options Title (**OT**).

Next you need to change the y-axis title.

❷   Select y axis (**Y**).

The current title, Units Sold, appears in the control panel. Add the text "(in millions)" to the title.

❸   Press **[Spacebar]** and type **(in millions)** and press **[Enter]**.

Now view the graph.

❹   Select Quit View (**QV**). See Figure 6-17.

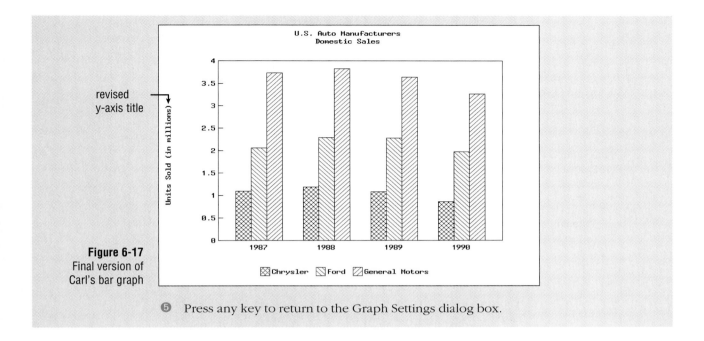

revised
y-axis title

Figure 6-17
Final version of
Carl's bar graph

⑤ Press any key to return to the Graph Settings dialog box.

Naming the Current Graph

Carl plans to create several graphs within his worksheet. To have more than one graph available within your worksheet, you must assign a name to each graph. If you name this bar graph now, 1-2-3 stores all the settings needed to create this graph. Then whenever you want, you can view the graph without having to specify all the settings again.

Let's learn how to create named graphs in 1-2-3 by naming this bar graph BAR3. This name helps to describe the graph as a *bar* graph that compares *3* companies. Note that the bar graph is the current graph, because it is the one you have most recently entered.

To name the current graph:

❶ Select Name Create (**NC**). The Graph Settings dialog box appears on the screen, showing the settings that will be assigned to the named graph.

   Figure 6-18a on the following page illustrates the current worksheet in the computer's memory.

You can enter a name of up to 15 characters. As with range names, spaces and certain characters are not recommended. It's often a helpful reminder to include the type of graph in the name you choose.

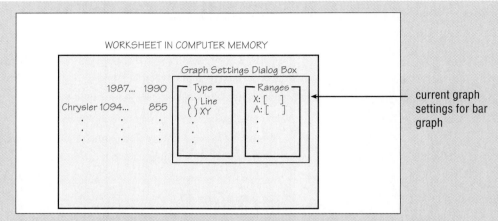

Figure 6-18a
Worksheet in memory immediately before naming the current graph

❷   Type **bar3** as the name of the graph and press **[Enter]**. You won't see any change in the graph settings; this name does not appear in the dialog box, but it does store the information found in the Graph Settings dialog box as part of the worksheet. Figure 6-18b shows that the current graph settings are now named BAR3 and stand as part of the worksheet within the computer's memory.

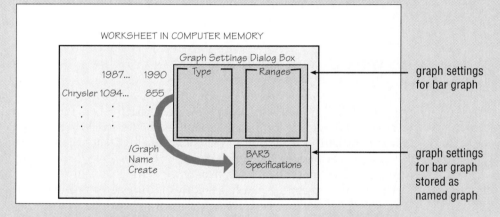

Figure 6-18b
Worksheet in memory after current graph has been named

❸   Select Quit (**Q**) to leave the Graph menu and return to READY mode. It is important to realize that when you name a graph you have not saved the graph specifications to disk. You have modified the worksheet only in the computer memory. To include a named graph as part of a worksheet file on disk, you must use the File Save command.

❹   Save the worksheet file, which includes the named graph BAR3, as S6AUTO1.

Now when you save your worksheet, the settings for each named graph are saved as part of the worksheet. If you haven't named a graph, the settings for that graph will not be saved as part of the worksheet file. For example, earlier in the tutorial you created a line graph and a stacked bar graph. You did not, however, create a named graph for either of these graphs. Therefore, they were not saved as part of S6AUTO1.WK1. See Figure 6-18c.

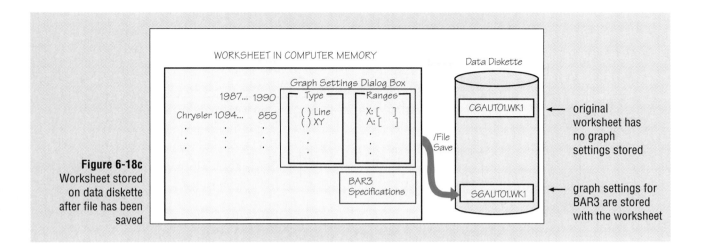

Figure 6-18c
Worksheet stored
on data diskette
after file has been
saved

Resetting Graph Settings

Once you have named a graph, you can define another graph. First, you may need to erase some or all of the current graph settings. You can erase the graph settings for the current graph by using the Graph Reset command.

To erase *all* the current graph settings:

❶ Select /Graph Reset (**/GR**). See Figure 6-19.

You can reset each setting individually, or you can reset the entire graph.

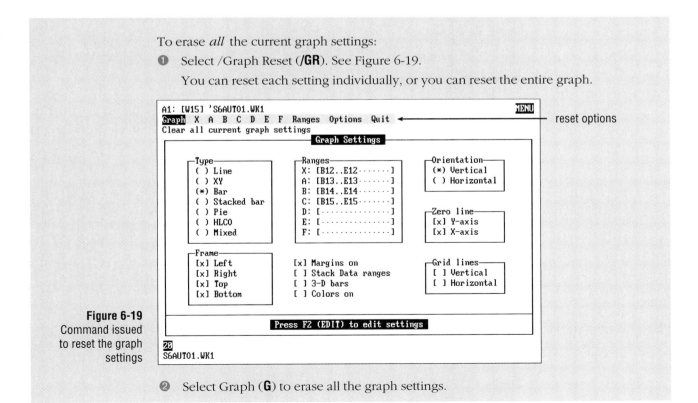

Figure 6-19
Command issued
to reset the graph
settings

❷ Select Graph (**G**) to erase all the graph settings.

The current settings disappear from the Graph Settings dialog box. See Figure 6-20.

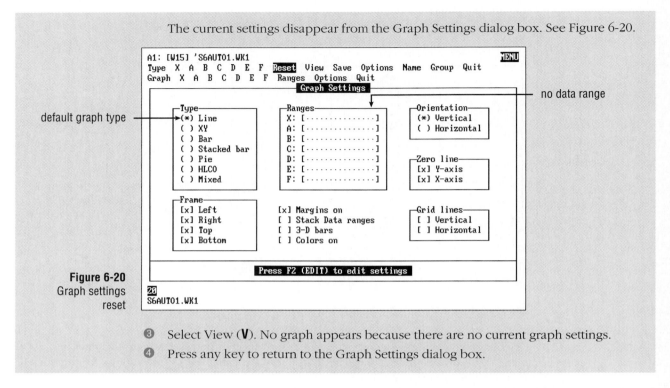

default graph type →

no data range

Figure 6-20
Graph settings
reset

③ Select View (**V**). No graph appears because there are no current graph settings.

④ Press any key to return to the Graph Settings dialog box.

Even though the graph settings are cleared from the screen, the settings for BAR3 are still stored in memory as part of the worksheet. These settings are available by retrieving the named graph BAR3.

Retrieving a Named Graph

You were not able to view the bar graph after you erased the graph settings. However, since you have named your graph, the settings are still part of the worksheet. You can display the bar graph by selecting it from a list of named graph settings.

To view a named graph:

① Select Name Use (**NU**). 1-2-3 displays the names of all the graph settings that are part of this worksheet. In this case, only one graph name appears because you have named only one so far in this tutorial.

② With BAR3 highlighted, press **[Enter]** to view the graph. The bar graph appears on the screen. 1-2-3 has retrieved the graph settings for BAR3 that were stored as part of the worksheet and entered them as the current graph settings.

③ Press any key. The Graph Settings dialog box now contains the settings for the bar graph. See Figure 6-21.

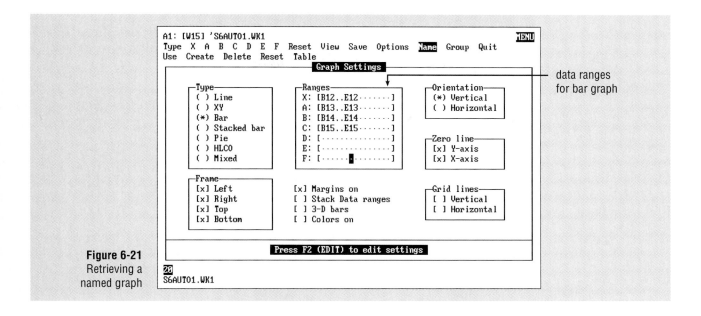

Figure 6-21
Retrieving a
named graph

Defining All Data Ranges Using the Group Command

Now Carl wants to create a bar graph that compares sales for all six companies. To create this graph, he can define each range one at a time as you did when you defined the previous graph. However, he can complete this task much more quickly. If he enters all the data for the graph in one continuous range (adjacent cells), he can use the Group command from the Graph menu to set the X range and all the data ranges for the graph in one step. Let's do this, but before you begin to specify the settings for this graph, let's clear the range settings for the current graph.

To clear the range settings for the current graph:

❶   Select Reset (**R**).

Reset only the range settings.

❷   Select Ranges (**R**). The range settings for X, A, B, and C ranges no longer appear in the Graph Settings dialog box.

❸   Select Quit (**Q**) to return to the Graph menu.

Now you can create the bar graph. Since the data are entered in adjacent cells, you can use the Group command to select a multiple graph range.

To create a bar graph using the Group command:

❶   Select Group (**G**).

Now identify the group range. The data in the first row become the X range, the data in the second row become the A range, the data in the third row become the B range, and so on.

② Move the cell pointer to cell B12.

③ Press **[.]** (Period) to anchor the cell pointer, highlight B12..E18, and press **[Enter]**.

Now 1-2-3 asks how to graph the groups, Columnwise or Rowwise.

If you select Columnwise, the first column within the group will be the X range, and the remaining columns will be used as the data ranges. If you select Rowwise, the first row will be the X range, and the remaining rows will be the data ranges. Let's use Rowwise.

④ Select Rowwise (**R**). See Figure 6-22.

ranges indicate a rowwise selection

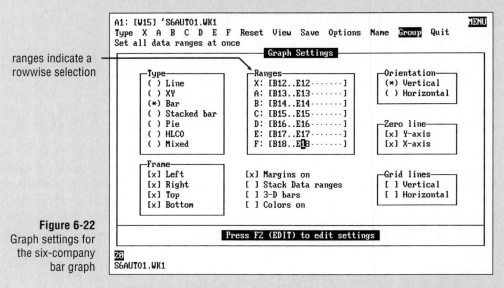

Figure 6-22
Graph settings for the six-company bar graph

Now view the graph.

⑤ Select View (**V**). See Figure 6-23.

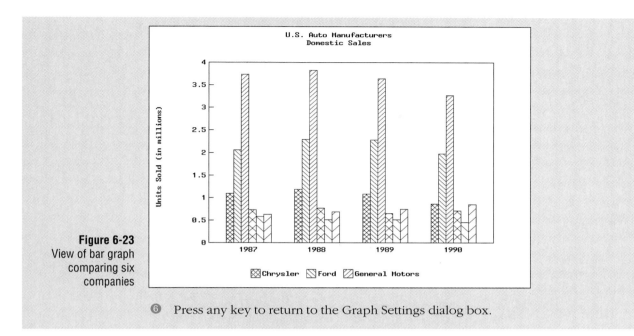

Figure 6-23
View of bar graph
comparing six
companies

⑥   Press any key to return to the Graph Settings dialog box.

Your legend is not accurate; it still reflects the settings from the previous graph. Let's correct the legend.

To add legends for the new graph:

①   Select Options Legend (**OL**).

②   Select Range (**R**).

Now identify the labels you want to use as legends.

③   Move the cell pointer to A13.

④   Press [**.**] (Period) to anchor the cell pointer, highlight the range A13..A18, and press [**Enter**].

Next let's view the graph.

⑤   Select Quit View (**QV**). See Figure 6-24 on the following page. The legends now reflect the six bars.

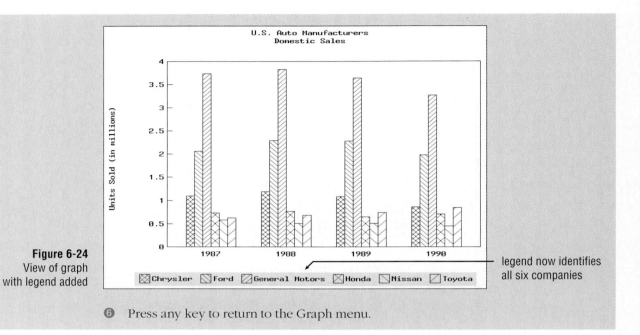

Figure 6-24
View of graph
with legend added

legend now identifies
all six companies

⑥   Press any key to return to the Graph menu.

The Features option from the Graph Type menu also allows you to change the appearance of your graph in other ways. You can use the Horizontal option to rotate the orientation of the graph, and you can use the 3D-Effect option with bar or stacked bar graphs to give an impression of depth in the chart. Let's examine these now.

Horizontal Bar Graphs

You can display a bar graph vertically or horizontally. The standard bar graph is typically displayed vertically. A horizontal bar graph rotates the graph so that it is displayed horizontally on the screen. When you use the Horizontal option, the graph's x axis runs vertically along the left side of the screen and the y-axis labels are along the top. Like a standard bar graph, this graph is used to compare and contrast values. You will use your personal preference to decide on the repositioning of the axes. Let's try the horizontal approach to see how you like it.

To change a vertical bar graph to a horizontal orientation:
❶   Select Type Features (**TF**).
❷   Select Horizontal (**H**).
❸   Select View (**V**). See Figure 6-25.

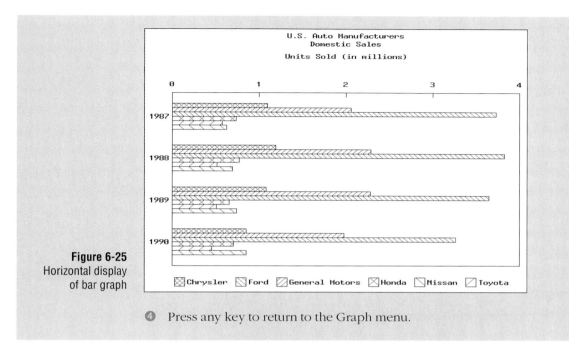

Figure 6-25
Horizontal display
of bar graph

④ Press any key to return to the Graph menu.

After looking at this version of the graph, Carl decides he prefers the vertical orientation. Let's change the graph back to the vertical orientation.

To return to the vertical orientation:
① Select Type Features (**TF**).
② Select Vertical (**V**).
③ Press [**F10**] (GRAPH). Notice that the bar graph is back to standard vertical orientation.
④ Press any key to return to the Graph menu.
⑤ Select Quit (**Q**) to return to the Graph menu.

3D Bar Graphs

1-2-3 allows you to enhance your bar, stacked bar, and mixed graphs to show a three-dimensional effect, which some people prefer to two-dimensional graphs. Let's add a three-dimensional (3D) effect to the current graph.

To add a 3D effect to a bar graph:
① Select Type Features (**TF**).
② Select 3D-Effect Yes (**3Y**).

③ Select Quit View (**QV**). See Figure 6-26.

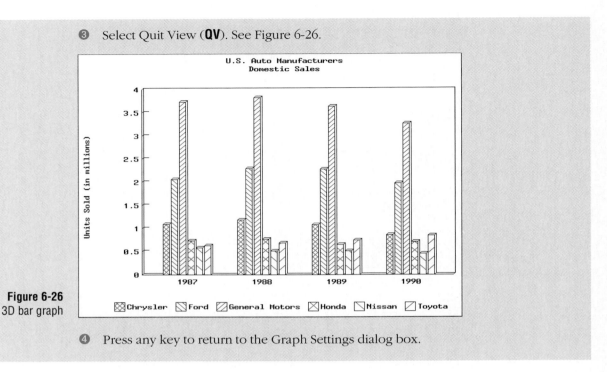

Figure 6-26
3D bar graph

④ Press any key to return to the Graph Settings dialog box.

Which do you think is more attractive? Let's leave Carl's graph in 3D. You have now completed it, so let's name it.

To name the current graph:

① Select Name Create (**NC**). The Graph Settings dialog box appears showing the settings that will be assigned to the named graph.

Let's name the graph BAR6 to describe this file as containing a bar graph comparing the sales of the six companies.

② Type **bar6** as the name of the graph and press **[Enter]**.

③ Select Quit (**Q**) to leave the Graph menu and return to READY mode.

④ Save the worksheet again as S6AUTO1.

Creating a Pie Chart

Now that Carl has looked at automobile sales over time, he decides to focus on sales in a single year — 1990, the last year for which he has complete data. A pie chart is a useful way to visualize data for an entire year, because pie charts typically represent the relative contribution of each part to the whole. The larger the slice, the greater that part's percentage of the whole. When you create a pie chart, you need

- the set of values that represent the slices of the pie
- the set of labels that identify each slice of the pie chart

Before you can enter the settings for the pie chart, you must erase the bar graph settings.

To erase the current graph settings:

❶ Select /Graph (**/G**). Notice that the settings for the bar graph are the current settings.

❷ Select Reset Graph (**RG**). This erases the settings for the bar graph.

Selecting the A Range

Now Carl can begin to enter the settings for the pie chart.

To create a pie chart for the number of cars sold in 1990:

❶ Select Type Pie (**TP**). The pie chart becomes the current graph type. The A data range is used to indicate the set of values that represent the slices of the pie.

❷ Select **A**, the range representing the set of values in the pie chart.

❸ Move the cell pointer to E13, number of cars sold by Chrysler for 1990, and press **[.]** to anchor the cell pointer. Highlight E13..E18 and press **[Enter]**. See Figure 6-27.

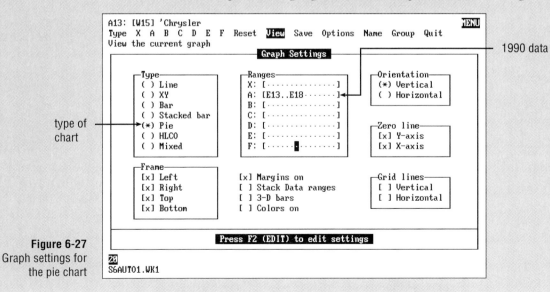

Figure 6-27
Graph settings for
the pie chart

④   Select View (**V**) to view the status of your graph. See Figure 6-28.

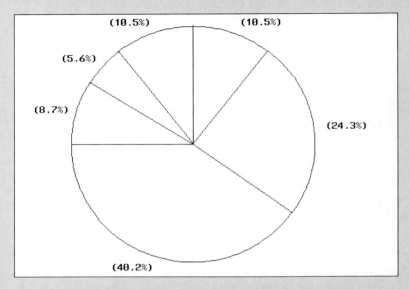

Figure 6-28
A view of Carl's
unlabeled pie
chart

⑤   When you are ready, press any key to return to the Graph menu.

Selecting the X Range

As you viewed the graph, you could not tell which car manufacturer was represented by which slice. Thus, you need to specify in the X range the labels that describe the slices. You will use the names of the car manufacturers in column A of the worksheet as the labels for the slices of the pie chart.

To label each pie slice:

①   Select **X**.

②   Move the cell pointer to A13, the cell holding the label Chrysler. Press **[.]** to anchor the cell pointer. Highlight A13..A18. Press **[Enter]**. Note that the labels in the X range correspond to the elements in the A range, that is, the first label in the X range will be the label of the first slice in the A range, and so on.

③   Press View (**V**) to view the pie chart. See Figure 6-29. Now you can identify each slice in the pie chart with a manufacturer.

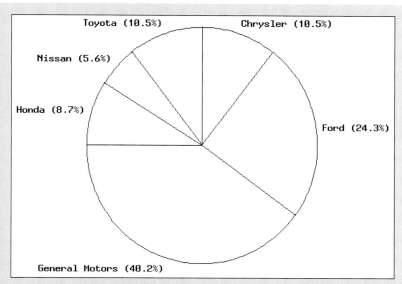

Figure 6-29
Labels added to
Carl's pie chart

❹ When you are ready, press any key to return to the Graph menu.

To help readers interpret your pie chart, you should add a title describing its contents. 1-2-3 allows you to include two title lines in the pie chart. Recall that Carl's sketch of the pie chart had a two-line title: U.S. CAR SALES, 1990.

To add a title to the pie chart:

❶ Select Options Titles First (**OTF**) to add the first line of the title.

❷ Type **U.S. CAR SALES**, then press **[Enter]**.

❸ Select Titles Second (**TS**) to add the second line of the title.

❹ Type **1990** and press **[Enter]**.

❺ Select Quit (**Q**) to leave the Options menu.

❻ Select View (**V**) to see the title you have added to the graph. See Figure 6-30 on the following page.

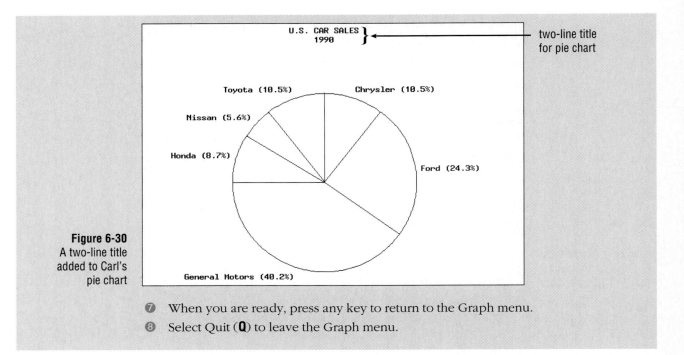

Figure 6-30
A two-line title
added to Carl's
pie chart

⑦ When you are ready, press any key to return to the Graph menu.

⑧ Select Quit (**Q**) to leave the Graph menu.

Selecting the B Range

To make the pie chart easier to read, hatch patterns can be added to shade each slice of the pie chart. You use the B data range to add shading to your pie chart. The B data range is set up in your worksheet to correspond to the elements in the A data range. Each cell in the B range is associated with one cell in the A range. In each cell of the B range, you can enter a number between 1 and 7. 1-2-3 associates these numbers, when used in the B range of the graph settings for a pie chart, with different hatch patterns. A value of 0, 8, or a blank assigned to a cell in the B range indicates you do not want shading in the associated slice.

Let's use cells F13 to F18 to enter the shading codes. The first cell, F13, will identify Chrysler. The second cell, F15, will identify General Motors. The final cell, F17, will identify Nissan. In this graph you will assign shading to the slices for Chrysler, General Motors, and Nissan. The other cells, F14, F16, and F18, are automatically a value of zero, which 1-2-3 interprets to mean "no shading for this slice."

To assign hatch-pattern codes for slices of the pie chart:

❶ Move the cell pointer to cell F13, type **1,** and then press **[Enter]**. This code will assign a pattern to Chrysler's slice.

❷ Move the cell pointer to cell F15, type **2,** and then press **[Enter]**. This code will assign a different pattern to General Motors' slice.

❸ Move the cell pointer to cell F17, type **3,** and then press **[Enter]**. This code will assign yet another pattern to Nissan's slice. See Figure 6-31.

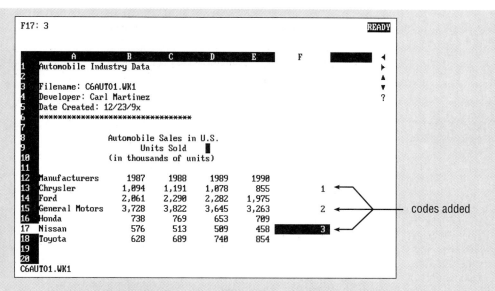

Figure 6-31
Adding codes to
assign patterns to
slices in a pie
chart

Notice that the cells identifying Ford (cell F14), Honda (cell F16), and Toyota (cell F18) are blank. 1-2-3 interprets these blank cells as zero, and no hatched pattern will fill these slices of the pie chart. We have intentionally left these cells blank, because too many patterns make it difficult to distinguish slices.

For the shading to be included in the pie chart, the B range must be included in the graph settings.

To define the B range in the graph settings:

1 Select /Graph B (**/GB**).

2 Move the cell pointer to cell F13, the cell that corresponds to the first cell of the A data range. Press **[.]** [Period] to anchor the cell pointer. Then highlight the range F13..F18 and press **[Enter]**. The B range is now included in the graph settings. See Figure 6-32 on the following page.

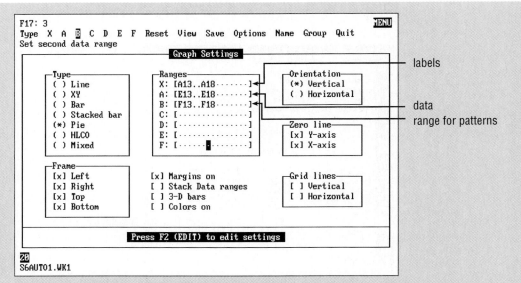

Figure 6-32
Graph Settings
dialog box with
the range for
patterns added

Be sure to highlight all cells in this range even though some may be blank. It's a good idea for the B data range to contain the same number of cells as the pie chart's A data range. This allows the shading assigned to each cell to correspond to the appropriate slice.

❸ Select View (**V**) to display the new pie chart. See Figure 6-33.

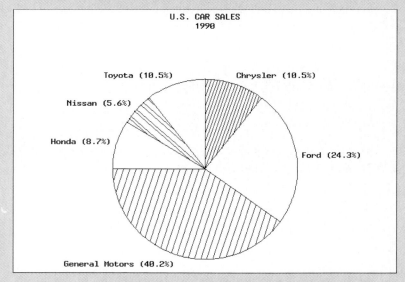

Figure 6-33
Carl's pie chart
with shading

❹ When you are ready, press any key to return to the Graph menu.

You can call even more attention to a slice of the pie chart by "exploding" it, that is, separating it from the rest of the pie. In 1-2-3 you indicate that a slice is to be exploded by adding 100 to whatever the value is in the B range. For example, if the value is 2, you would enter 102 in the B range.

The next steps show you how to set up and use the B data range for exploding a pie slice. Let's explode the slice that represents Chrysler.

First, leave the Graph menu:

➊ Select Quit (**Q**) to return to the worksheet.

➋ Move the cell pointer to F13, type **101,** and press **[Enter]**. See Figure 6-34.

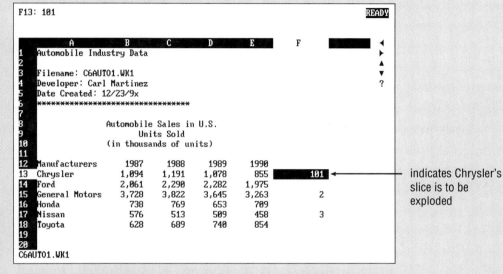

Figure 6-34
Adding the code
to explode a pie
slice

```
F13: 101                                                              READY

          A         B         C         D         E        F         ◀
 1  Automobile Industry Data                                           ▶
 2                                                                     ▲
 3  Filename: C6AUTO1.WK1                                              ▼
 4  Developer: Carl Martinez                                          ?
 5  Date Created: 12/23/9x
 6  ***************************************
 7
 8             Automobile Sales in U.S.
 9                  Units Sold
10            (in thousands of units)
11
12  Manufacturers   1987      1988      1989      1990
13  Chrysler        1,094     1,191     1,078       855           101  ◀── indicates Chrysler's
14  Ford            2,061     2,290     2,282     1,975                     slice is to be
15  General Motors  3,728     3,822     3,645     3,263         2          exploded
16  Honda             738       769       653       709
17  Nissan            576       513       509       458         3
18  Toyota            628       689       740       854
19
20
C6AUTO1.WK1
```

➌ Press **[F10]** (GRAPH) to view the pie chart. See Figure 6-35.

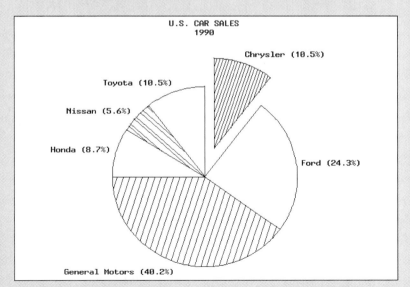

Figure 6-35
Carl's pie chart with
shading and
"exploded" slice

U.S. CAR SALES
1990

Chrysler (10.5%)

Toyota (10.5%)

Nissan (5.6%)

Honda (8.7%)

Ford (24.3%)

General Motors (40.2%)

➍ When you are ready, press any key to return to READY mode.

Let's now assign a name to the pie chart so its settings will be stored with the worksheet.

To assign a name to the pie chart:

❶ Select /Graph Name Create (**/GNC**).

❷ Type **pie90**. Press **[Enter]**. Figure 6-36 shows that the current graph settings are now named PIE90 and are stored as part of the worksheet in the computer's memory.

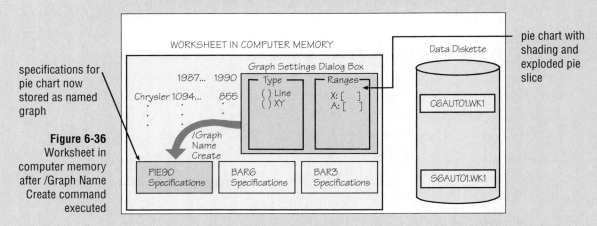

specifications for pie chart now stored as named graph

pie chart with shading and exploded pie slice

Figure 6-36
Worksheet in computer memory after /Graph Name Create command executed

❸ Select Quit (**Q**) to leave the Graph menu.

Save the worksheet file again.

❹ Select /File Save (**/FS**), press **[Enter]**, and select Replace (**R**). The current worksheet replaces the previous version of S6AUTO1.WK1. This saved worksheet now includes three named graphs: BAR3, BAR6, and PIE90. See Figure 6-37.

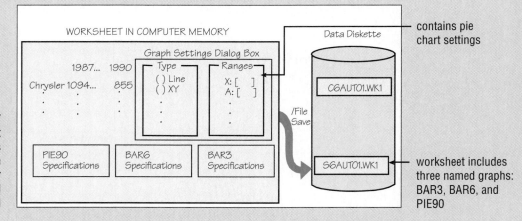

contains pie chart settings

Figure 6-37
Current worksheet replaces S6AUTO1.WK1 on data diskette after /File Save command executed

worksheet includes three named graphs: BAR3, BAR6, and PIE90

The use of the B range for shading and exploding slices applies to pie charts only. For other graph types the B range is used for data. Except for this special use of the B range, pie charts use only the X and A ranges.

Saving Graphs for Printing

In the previous section, you learned how to transform Carl's data into graphs. In this section you will print one of the graphs you created and named. To print a graph, you must take two steps: (1) save the graphs for printing with the Graph Save command and (2) print the graph with the Lotus PrintGraph program.

You must use a special command — the Graph Save command — to save a graph that you want to print. Saving the worksheet by using /File Save saves only *named* graphs for later *viewing*, but not for printing. The /File Save command does *not* create the type of files the PrintGraph program needs to print a graph. To save a graph for printing, *you must use the Graph Save command*. In the next steps you will learn how to save graphs specifically for printing.

To save a graph for printing:

❶ Select /Graph Name Use (**/GNU**) to list the named graphs. Next, retrieve BAR6, the graph you will print.

❷ Highlight BAR6. Press **[Enter]**. The second bar graph you created and named appears on the screen.

❸ Press any key to return to the Graph menu. The graph settings for the bar graph appear in the Graph Settings dialog box.

❹ Select Save (**S**) from the Graph menu. Only the current graph can be saved for printing.

Enter a name for the graph file. DOS limits the filename to eight characters, as it does for worksheet names.

❺ Type **p_bar6** and press **[Enter]**.

1-2-3 saves the graph in a file named P_BAR6.PIC; it automatically adds the extension .PIC. Each graph that you want to print must be saved as a separate .PIC file. See Figure 6-38.

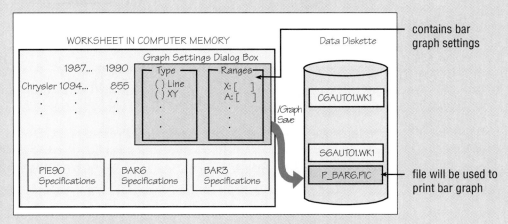

Figure 6-38
P_BAR6.PIC stored on data diskette after /Graph Save command executed

❻ Select Quit (**Q**) to return to READY mode.

❼ Select /File Save (**/FS**), press **[Enter]**, and select Replace (**R**).

Using PrintGraph

The **PrintGraph** program is a separate program that comes with 1-2-3 to enable you to print graphs. With PrintGraph you can print any graph you have previously saved with the Graph Save command.

> *Before continuing, check with your instructor or technical support person to see if PrintGraph is installed on your system. If it is installed, work through this section as usual. If PrintGraph is not installed, it can be installed using your copy of Lotus 1-2-3 software disks. Check with your instructor or technical support person or read the installation instructions that came with the software. If you are using Lotus 1-2-3 in a lab and PrintGraph cannot be installed, read this section, but do not press any keys.*

To start PrintGraph:

❶ Select /Quit Yes (**/QY**) to quit 1-2-3. You are now at the DOS prompt.

❷ Type **pgraph** and press **[Enter]**. The menu of PrintGraph commands appears at the top of the screen, and the current settings of PrintGraph appear below. Your screen should look similar to Figure 6-39.

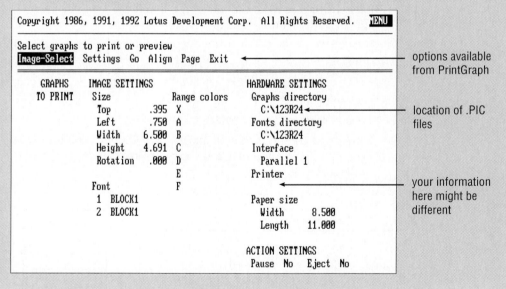

Figure 6-39
PrintGraph settings

If this is the first time you have ever started PrintGraph, the program assumes that your graph (.PIC) files and font (.FNT) files are located either on a PrintGraph disk in drive A or, if you are using a hard-disk system, in your 1-2-3 directory. **Fonts** are the typefaces used to print the graph text.

Look at the rightmost column of the PrintGraph dialog box at the entries under Graphs directory and Fonts directory. You might need to adjust the disk/directory information for your Graph and Font directories and be sure your printer is specified properly. If necessary, ask your instructor or technical support person for assistance. The next steps show you how to change the PrintGraph settings in case the current settings are not correct for your system. Once you make and save these changes, you will not need to go through these steps again unless you make a change in your system.

To adjust the default PrintGraph settings, you first must specify the directory that contains the graph (.PIC) files so PrintGraph knows where to find your graphs:

❶ Select Settings Hardware Graphs-Directory (**SHG**).

❷ Enter the name of the directory or drive where you saved your graph (.PIC) files. Type **a:** (or the name of the drive that contains your graph [.PIC] files) and press **[Enter]**.

Next, specify the directory that contains the font (.FNT) files. PrintGraph needs to access these files to print your graphs.

❸ Select Fonts-Directory (**F**).

❹ Enter the name of the directory or drive where the fonts are stored. Type **c:\123r23** and press **[Enter]** or check with your technical support person for the location of your fonts directory.

Finally, select a graphics printer to print your graphs.

❺ Select Printer (**P**) to display a list of installed printers.

If no printer names appear, rerun the Install program, as described in the Installation Guide.

❻ Follow the on-screen instructions. Press **[↓]** or **[↑]** to highlight the printer you want to use. Press **[Spacebar]** to mark your selection. Then press **[Enter]**. The # sign indicates the printer that you have selected for printing your graphs.

If you have a choice of low and high density, choose low density so your graphs will print more quickly. If you select high density, the quality of the graph will improve, but the graph will take longer to print.

❼ Select Quit (**Q**) to leave the Hardware menu and return to the PrintGraph menu.

❽ Select Save (**S**) to save these settings so they will appear automatically the next time you run PrintGraph.

These settings will remain as the current PrintGraph settings if you decide to print your graphs now.

Now you are ready to print the graph you saved as a .PIC file.

To print a single graph:

❶   Select Image-Select (**I**) from the PrintGraph menu to display an alphabetized list of all the graphs that have been saved for printing. See Figure 6-40.

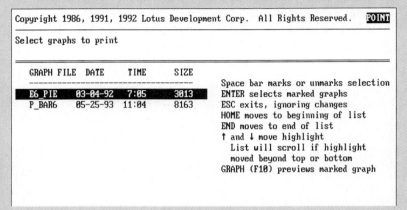

Figure 6-40
Lists of graphs
in the graph
directory

These are the files that you created with the Graph Save command and that 1-2-3 stored with a .PIC extension. Each file stores the description of one graph.

❷   With P_BAR6 highlighted, press **[Spacebar]** to mark your selection. The # sign indicates that a graph has been selected for printing. See Figure 6-41.

graph marked for →
selection

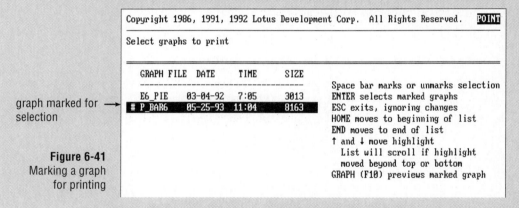

Figure 6-41
Marking a graph
for printing

If you change your mind about which graph to select, you can press [Spacebar] to unmark the selection.

❸   Press **[F10]** (GRAPH) to preview the graph. The bar graph appears on your screen. You should always preview a graph before you print it to make sure you have selected the graph you want to print. Press any key to leave the preview and return to the Select Graphs to Print screen.

❹   Press **[Enter]** to complete the selection process and return to the PrintGraph menu. Notice that a filename appears under the "Graphs to Print" section of the dialog box. See Figure 6-42.

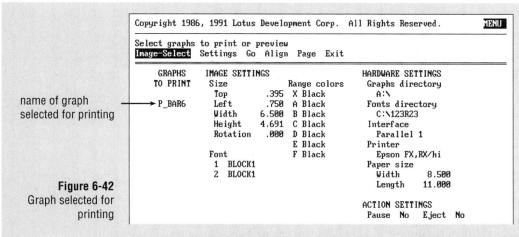

name of graph
selected for printing

Figure 6-42
Graph selected for
printing

⑤ Check that your printer is ready. Then select Align Go (**AG**) to print the first graph. See Figure 6-43.

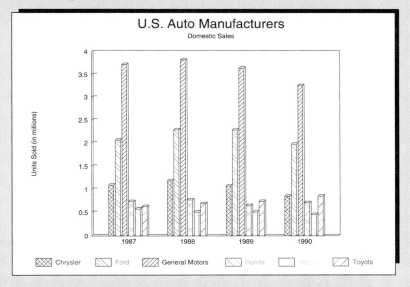

Figure 6-43
Printout of Carl's
final graph

⑥ Select Page (**P**) to advance the printer to the top of the next page.
⑦ Select Exit Yes (**EY**) to leave PrintGraph.

Carl has now finished printing his graph, and he presents it to the senior consultants for their review. They are pleased with his work and decide to use this graph in their upcoming Congressional testimony.

Now that you have completed Tutorial 6, you can read Module 4, *Using WYSIWYG to Print and Enhance Graphs*. Check with your instructor.

Exercises

1. Use Figure 6-44 to identify the following components of a graph:
   a. type of graph
   b. x-axis labels
   c. y-axis title
   d. legends
   e. title
   f. x-axis title
   g. data series for projected sales
   h. scale indicator

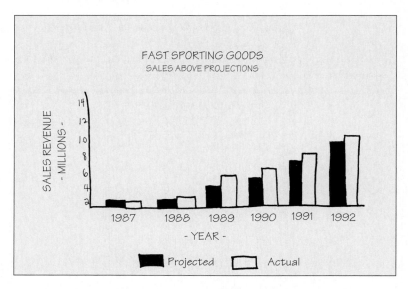

Figure 6-44

Retrieve the worksheet E6FILE1 and do the following:

2. Save the worksheet as S6FILE1.

3. Make the named graph PIE the current graph.

4. Change the value for first-quarter revenue from plastics from 2890 to 4890.

5. View the pie chart again. Did the appearance of the graph change? If yes, how did it change?

6. Make the named graph BAR the current graph. Is this graph based on the original data from the worksheet or the new data you entered in Exercise 4?

7. Save this worksheet as S6FILE1.

8. Erase the worksheet from the screen.

9. Your data diskette contains the file E6_PIE.PIC, which contains the pie chart that you viewed in Exercise 3. If you were to print E6_PIE.PIC, would the graph reflect the original data in the worksheet or the data after the change you made to the worksheet data in Exercise 4?

10.   If you were to retrieve the worksheet S6FILE1.WK1 and view the graph named PIE, would the pie chart be based on the original data or the revised data from Exercise 4?

Tutorial Assignments

Before you begin these Tutorial Assignments, check your data diskette. Be sure you have space to save the additional worksheet files you'll create in these assignments (at least 30,000 bytes). If you do not have enough space, save the files that you need for these assignments to another formatted diskette.

Retrieve worksheet T6AUTO1.WK1 and do the following:

1.   Create a pie chart that illustrates the market share of each of the six auto manufacturers for 1987.

2.   Include a title on the pie chart.

3.   Explode the slice that represents Honda.

4.   Name this graph PIE87.

5.   Save this graph as a .PIC file. Use the name P_PIE87.

6.   Reset all the graph settings in this worksheet.

7.   Prepare a bar graph that shows only the three Japanese companies' sales from 1987 to 1990.

8.   Add a title and legends to this graph.

9.   Name this graph BARJPN.

10.   Save this graph as a .PIC file. Use the name P_BARJPN.

11.   Change the graph to a stacked bar graph.

12.   Name this graph STKJPN.

13.   Save this graph as a .PIC file. Use the name P_STKJPN.

14.   Save your worksheet as S6AUTO2.

15.   Print the graph file P_PIE87.

Case Problems

1. Graphing Health Maintenance Organizations' Membership Data

Medical costs have risen dramatically over the last 10 to 15 years. Health maintenance organizations (HMOs) were created as an alternative to traditional health insurance to help decrease medical costs. HMOs provide a range of comprehensive health care services to people who pay an enrollment fee and become members. By joining an HMO, a member gains access to a team of doctors 365 days a year. Employers, labor unions, government agencies, and consumer groups often provide this type of medical coverage for their employees.

Figure 6-45 shows a table of the enrollment in HMO programs by major insurer.

Enrollment in HMOs	
Insurer	**Millions of members**
Blue Cross	15.5
Cigna	3.6
Aetna	2.5
Metropolitan	2.4
Prudential	2.2
Travelers	1.6

Figure 6-45

Use the data in Figure 6-45 to do the following:

1. Construct a pie chart.
2. Explode the Aetna segment.
3. Add appropriate titles and labels.
4. Name the graph PIEHMO.
5. Save the pie chart as a .PIC file. Use the name P_PIEHMO.
6. Save your worksheet as S6HMO.
7. Print the pie chart.

WYSIWYG Assignments

1. Attach WYSIWYG.
2. Retrieve the worksheet S6HMO.
3. Add the following enhancements:
   a. If your worksheet data do not include the title and the column headings shown in Figure 6-45, add them to your worksheet. Increase the title to 24-point Swiss font.
   b. Boldface the column headings.
   c. Draw a solid line under the column headings.
   d. Insert the current graph below your worksheet data.
4. Save your worksheet as W6HMO.
5. Print the entire worksheet on one page.

2. Sporting Goods Industry Trade Show

The Sporting Goods Manufacturers Association recently held a trade show for sporting goods retailers, where the manufacturers displayed their latest athletic goods. In preparation for the trade show the Sporting Goods Manufacturers Association sent out a press release about the show, including the data shown in Figure 6-46.

Figure 6-46

Sporting Goods Manufacturers' Sales by Category (in millions of dollars)		
	1991	**1992**
Apparel	11600	12645
Footwear	6950	7665
Golf equipment	1350	1285
Exercise	930	975
Camping	825	865

Use the data in Figure 6-46 to do the following:

1. Create a bar graph that compares the sales by category for 1991 and 1992.
2. Enter appropriate titles and a legend.
3. Name the bar graph BARSALES.
4. Create a second bar graph that adds a 3D effect to the bars in the current graph.
5. Name the 3D bar graph BAR3D.
6. Save each graph setting as a .PIC file. Save the bar graphs as P_BARSAL and P_BAR3D.
7. Save your worksheet as S6SPORT.
8. Print your graphs.

WYSIWYG Assignments

1. Attach WYSIWYG.
2. Retrieve the worksheet S6SPORT.
3. Add the following enhancements:
    a. Display the title in a font larger than that used for the text in the worksheet.
    b. Add a solid line under the title as shown in Figure 6-46.
    c. Shade the sales data column for 1992.
    d. Insert the named graph BAR3D to the right of your worksheet data.
4. Save your worksheet as W6SPORT.
5. Print the entire worksheet on one page.

3. Graphing Data on Cellular Telephone Subscribers and Revenues

Many people are using cellular telephones more and more in their business and personal lives. Figure 6-47 on the following page shows the changes in the number of cellular telephone subscribers in the U.S. and the revenue they generated from 1987 through 1991.

	U.S. Cellular Telephones				
	1987	**1988**	**1989**	**1990**	**1991**
Subscribers (millions)	1200	2100	3050	5500	7500
Revenue (billions)	1600	2000	3300	4600	5900

Figure 6-47

Use the data in Figure 6-47 to do the following:

1. Create a horizontal bar graph that shows the growth in number of subscribers from 1987 through 1991.

2. Enter appropriate titles.

3. Name the bar graph BARSUB.

4. Create a second horizontal bar graph that shows the growth in revenue from 1987 through 1991. Enter appropriate titles.

5. Name the graph BARREV.

6. Save each graph setting as a .PIC file. Save the subscriber bar graph as P_BARSUB and the revenue bar graph as P_BARREV.

7. Save your worksheet as S6TELE1.

8. Print your graphs.

9. The 1991 data in Figure 6-47 were estimates. The actual data for 1991 were 8000 subscribers and 6800 in revenue. Change the data in your worksheet.

10. Save the revised .PIC file for the subscriber and revenue bar graphs. Name the files P_BARS and P_BARR, respectively.

11. Save your revised worksheet as S6TELE2.

12. Print your revised graphs.

WYSIWYG Assignments

1. Attach WYSIWYG.

2. Retrieve the worksheet S6TELE2.

3. Add the following enhancements:
   a. Insert the named graph BARSUB under your worksheet data.
   b. Add the comment "Cellular keeps growing" near the bar for 1991.
   c. Include an arrow that draws attention from the text to the 1991 bar on the bar graph.

4. Save your worksheet as W6TELE.

5. Print the entire worksheet on one page.

4. Using Line Charts to Analyze Stock Prices

Levon Smith, a stock analyst for the firm of Morris-Sorensen, specializes in recommending what computer industry stock investors should buy. Levon wants to analyze indexes and stock prices at the end of each month for 1990 to identify any trends. He has collected month-end data (Figure 6-48) on the following indexes and companies: Standard & Poor's 500 stock index, computer industry stock index, Digital Equipment Corporation, IBM, Apple Corporation, and Cray Research.

	S&P 500	Computer Index	Digital Equipment	IBM	Apple	Cray Research
Jan	297	205	118	130	44	64
Feb	289	213	120	130	37	61
Mar	295	195	104	121	34	60
Apr	310	189	97	116	40	59
May	321	191	90	114	49	59
Jun	318	190	86	115	50	58
Jul	346	195	90	116	40	56
Aug	351	193	105	120	45	55
Sep	349	181	104	119	46	54
Oct	340	170	84	110	50	45
Nov	346	164	84	101	47	42
Dec	353	190	80	102	45	40

Figure 6-48
Selected month-end index and stock prices

Retrieve the worksheet P6STOCK.WK1 and do the following:

1. Create a line chart of the month-end Standard & Poor's 500 and computer industry indexes. Remember to include a title and a legend. Name this graph LINE_MARKET.

2. Create a second line chart that includes the month-end stock prices for IBM, Digital, Cray Research, and Apple so Levon can observe the trend in stock prices for these companies. Remember to include a title and legends. Name this graph LINE_COMPANY.

3. Save each line chart as a .PIC file. Save the first line graph as P_LNEMRK and the second graph as P_LNECMP.

4. Save your worksheet as S6STOCK.

5. Print the graphs.

WYSIWYG Assignments

1. Attach WYSIWYG.

2. Retrieve the worksheet S6STOCK.

3. Add the following enhancements:
    a. Insert solid lines under the column headings.
    b. Boldface the column headings.
    c. Insert the named graph P_LNECMP under your worksheet data.
    d. Enclose the legends in a box.
    e. Draw a box around the worksheet data and graph.

4. Save your worksheet as W6STOCK.

5. Print the entire worksheet on one page.

5. The U.S. Airline Industry

During the 1980s, the number of U.S. airline companies decreased. In the 1990s, however, international travel is expected to grow and exceed U.S. travel; thus, the remaining carriers are scrambling to increase their number of international routes. Figure 6-49 shows passenger revenues generated by international routes from 1985 through 1989 for five of the major carriers. These numbers are rounded to the nearest millions.

Carrier	1985	1986	1987	1988	1989
Passenger Revenues International Routes (in millions of $)					
American	400	472	672	884	1858
Continental	249	319	526	743	843
Delta	216	227	410	634	742
Northwest	936	1036	1362	1767	2051
United	114	802	1112	1514	1780

Figure 6-49

Use the data in Figure 6-49 to do the following:

1. Prepare a worksheet that incorporates the data in Figure 6-49 and adds an additional column representing average revenue for each carrier during the five-year period. Also add another row that provides total revenues for each year. Print this worksheet.

2. Prepare a 3D bar graph that compares passenger revenues for all five companies from 1985 through 1989. Remember to include the appropriate titles and legends. Name this graph 3DBAR.

3. Prepare a stacked bar graph showing the same data as Problem 2. Name this graph STACK.

4. Prepare a pie chart of passenger revenues during 1989 that includes all carriers. Name this graph PIE.

5. Save each graph as a .PIC file. Save the bar graph as P_65BAR, the stacked bar as P_65STK, and the pie chart as P_65PIE.

6. Save your worksheet as S6AIRLNE.

7. Print your graphs.

WYSIWYG Assignments

1. Attach WYSIWYG.

2. Retrieve the worksheet S6AIRLNE.

3. Add the following enhancements:
    a. Insert the named graph 3DBAR under your worksheet data.
    b. Add the comment "Big increase" so the text is near the bar for American Airlines 1989.
    c. Include an arrow that draws attention from the text to the 1989 bar on the bar graph.

4. Save your worksheet as W6AIRLINE.

5. Print the entire worksheet on one page.

Tutorial 7

Using a 1-2-3 Database

A Customer/Accounts Receivable Application

Case: Medi-Source Inc.

Medi-Source Inc. distributes supplies to hospitals, medical laboratories, and pharmacies throughout the United States. Files of all Medi-Source customers and accounts receivable data are available to department managers on the company's mainframe computer.

Joan Glazer, the manager of the credit and collection department, was recently reviewing these data and noticed that the outstanding balances of several Massachusetts and Rhode Island customers appeared to be higher than that of the average Medi-Source customer, which is approximately $6,000. She wants to study the accounts in these two states more carefully.

Joan asks Bert Spivak, the manager of the information systems department, to prepare several reports to help her analyze the data. Bert tells her that he and his programming staff are backed up on projects and will not be able to help her for four to six weeks. He suggests instead that he retrieve the Rhode Island and Massachusetts data from the mainframe database and provide her with a Lotus 1-2-3 file. Then she can analyze the data herself. Joan thinks this is a great idea. Bert says he'll have the data to her in two days.

While waiting for the data, Joan thinks about the analysis she will do. She decides to plan her project and makes a list of her goals, output, input, and calculations (Figure 7-1a on the following page). Joan realizes the worksheet will be large and will include several sections. As a part of her planning, she develops a sketch to help organize the overall design of the worksheet (Figure 7-1b on the following page). Note when you look at this figure that each section represents a screenful of information.

OBJECTIVES

In this tutorial you will learn to:

- Define the terms *field*, *record*, and *file*

- Sort a database

- Find records that match specified criteria

- Extract records that match specified criteria

- Use database @functions

My Goals:
  Review the Rhode Island and Massachusetts customer database to
  determine whether balances owed by customers in those states are
  higher than average Medi-Source customers.

What results do I want to see?
  List records in database by:
    customer name
    outstanding balance
    state, and within state by outstanding balance
  List customers with outstanding balances above Medi-Source average.
  Report of outstanding balances by state.

What information do I need?
  Subset of Medi-Source database — all RI and MA customer records

What calculations will I perform?
  Total outstanding balance by state
  Average outstanding balance by state

Figure 7-1a
Joan's planning
sheet

Columns A – H	Columns I – O	Columns P – V	Columns W – AD		
Documentation Section	Customer Data ~~~~~~~~ ~~~~~~~~	Work Section ***Criteria Range ***Output Range: ~~~~~~ ~~~~~~	Report Section Medi-Source Inc. Amount Owed by State		
				RI	MA
			Total	xx	xx
			Average	xx	xx

Figure 7-1b
Joan's sketch of
the sections of her
worksheet

In this tutorial you will learn some new database terms, learn how to arrange data into a meaningful order through sorting, search a database to locate and extract records that meet specific criteria, and use database @functions to perform statistical analysis on selected records within the database.

Introduction to Data File Concepts

Before you retrieve the Medi-Source file, you need to understand important terms that are critical to understanding and using computerized databases. These terms are field, record, and file.

A **field** is an attribute (characteristic) of some object, person, or place. For example, each item of data that Medi-Source tracks is referred to as a field. Customer ID, customer name, balance owed, and year-to-date sales represent attributes about a customer (Figure 7-2). Each represents a field. In 1-2-3 each of these fields is stored in a column of your worksheet.

Figure 7-2
Fields in
Medi-Source's
customer
database

Customer ID
Customer name
Address
City
State
Zip
Type of business
Credit limit
Balance owed
Year-to-date sales
Date of last sale

Related fields are grouped together to form a **record**, a collection of attributes describing a person, place, or thing. In 1-2-3 each record is a single row that contains data for each field. For example, all the data about a customer such as Bristol Pharmacy are referred to as a record.

A collection of related records is called a **data file**. In 1-2-3 a data file is referred to as a **1-2-3 database**. In a 1-2-3 database the top cell of each column contains a **field name** that identifies the contents of the field. Figure 7-3 illustrates a 1-2-3 database. The database has fields for customer number, customer name, type of business, state, sales rep, balance owed, and year-to-date sales. The data about each customer make up a record. The 22 records in their entirety make up the customer database.

field names →

1-2-3 data file →

CUST#	CUSTNAME	TYPE	ST	REP	BAL_OWED	YTD_SALES
1	Bristol Pharmacy	P	RI	4	2,647.10	80,278.87
2	Nepco Labs	L	MA	4	3,274.25	6,866.25
3	EMG & EEG Labs	L	MA	4	12,583.97	31,685.19
4	Oaklawn Pharmacy	P	RI	4	4,513.21	5,176.26
5	St. Josephs Hospital	H	RI	3	47,113.50	4,451.68
6	Cape Psych Center	H	MA	3	31,509.10	44,173.24
7	Bioran Medical Lab	L	MA	3	2,799.12	11,927.84
8	Bayshore Pharmacy	P	MA	3	6,010.36	44,140.87
9	St Anne's Hospital	H	MA	3	1,009.53	2,431.80
10	Landmark Medical Center	H	RI	3	22,630.79	6,494.55
11	Lypho_Med Laboratory	L	RI	2	538.62	3,279.89
12	Gregg's Pharmacy	P	MA	2	2,052.70	3,771.28
13	Bradley Hospital	H	MA	2	9,430.72	32,451.95
14	Braintree Hospital	H	MA	2	36,609.80	75,562.35
15	Miriam Hospital	H	MA	2	14,800.44	24,510.04
16	Forgary Labs	L	MA	1	2,890.08	6,670.41
17	De Bellis Pharmacy	P	RI	1	2,715.35	85,063.85
18	Woman & Infants	H	RI	1	47,915.99	3,415.04
19	Depasquale Pharmacy	P	RI	1	4,214.50	39,727.98
20	Kent Hospital	H	MA	1	1,987.44	4,120.74
21	Butler Hospital	H	RI	1	31,215.67	21,144.05
22	Foster Blood Tests	L	MA	1	2,594.27	4,275.56

field

record

Figure 7-3
Medi-Source Inc.'s
customer data file

Retrieving the Worksheet

To retrieve the Medi-Source customer file (1-2-3 database):

❶   Retrieve the file C7MEDI1.WK1.

❷   Press **[Tab]** to view the 1-2-3 database. See Figure 7-4.

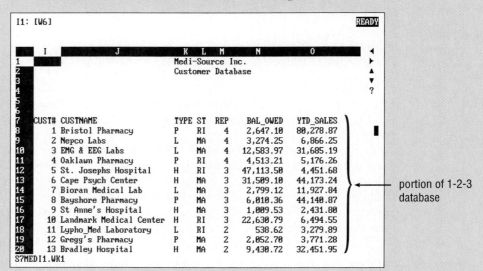

Figure 7-4
Database section
of Joan's initial
worksheet

Notice that each *row* in the database represents a customer record. The first row of the database, row 7, contains the field names. Field names *must* be in the first row of any database you use in 1-2-3 and must be unique.

❸   Press **[PgDn]** to view the remaining records.

❹   Press **[PgUp]** to return to the previous screen.

The field names in the Medi-Source customer database are:

Field	Description
CUST#	Unique identification number assigned to each customer
CUSTNAME	Name of each customer
TYPE	Code indicating the type of business, for example, P = pharmacy, L = laboratory, and H = hospital
ST	State abbreviation: RI = Rhode Island; MA = Massachusetts
REP	ID number of the sales representative assigned to make sales calls on this customer
BAL_OWED	Amount of money customer currently owes Medi-Source
YTD_SALES	Total sales to customer since the beginning of the year

Now that you are familiar with the Medi-Source customer file, you are ready to use it.

Sorting Data

The Data Sort command lets you arrange a 1-2-3 database in an order that you specify. For instance, you could arrange your data alphabetically by customer name or numerically by the amount of money the customer owes to Medi-Source.

Before performing the data sort, you need to understand three terms related to sorting data in 1-2-3: data range, primary key, and secondary key.

Data Range

The **data range** represents the records in the database you want to sort. This range usually includes all the records in the database. The data range does *not* include the field names of the columns, because the field names are merely labels and not part of the data you want to sort. You *must* be sure to include *all* the fields (columns) for the records you specify in the data range; otherwise, you will alter the relationships among data fields in the database.

Primary Key

A field that determines the order in which you sort the database is called a **sort key**. The **primary key** (primary sort key) represents the field (column) you want 1-2-3 to use to determine the new order for the database records. For example, if you want 1-2-3 to arrange the data by the amount customers owe Medi-Source, the primary key is the balance owed field (BAL_OWED).

Secondary Key

The **secondary key** (secondary sort key) represents a second field (column) by which 1-2-3 will determine the sort order within the primary sort key field. It tells 1-2-3 how to arrange the records if two or more records have the same primary key value. In other words, it acts as a tie-breaker. For example, you might select type of customer as the primary sort key and customer name as the secondary sort key. Thus, you could sort the data by customer type (such as hospital, lab, pharmacy) and within each customer type alphabetically by customer name. To explain this example further, all the hospital customers would appear first in alphabetical order, followed by an alphabetized list of laboratory customers, and finally the pharmacy customers would appear arranged in alphabetical order.

Sorting Using the Primary Key

Joan wants to sort the data alphabetically by customer name. Ordering the data by customer name will make it easier for her to locate a particular customer than will the current order of the database, which is by customer number.

To sort a data file by customer name:

❶   Select /Data Sort (**/DS**). 1-2-3 displays the Sort Settings dialog box. See Figure 7-5.

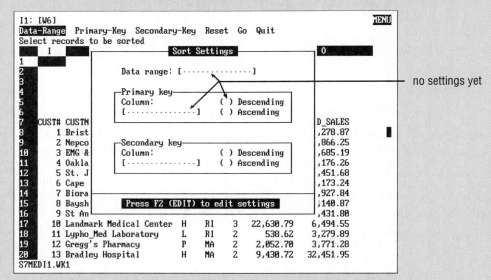

— no settings yet

Figure 7-5
Sort Settings
dialog box

The dialog box indicates the settings for the data range, the primary key, and the secondary key. Currently there are no settings.

Now identify the area of the worksheet to be sorted, which 1-2-3 refers to as the data range.

❷   Select Data-Range (**D**). The worksheet appears on your screen.

❸   Move the cell pointer to the first cell in the data range, I8, and press **[.]** to anchor the cell pointer. Highlight I8..O29 and press **[Enter]**. See Figure 7-6.

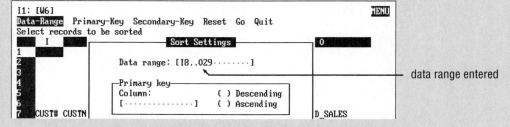

— data range entered

Figure 7-6
Area to be sorted
appears in dialog
box

1-2-3 enters I8..O29 as the data range in the dialog box. Remember that field names are not part of the data range and that every column in your database should be included in the data range.

Joan wants to sort the data by customer name, so next you need to specify CUSTNAME as the primary sort key.

❹   Select Primary-Key (**P**). Move the cell pointer to the first record in the customer name field, cell J8, and press **[Enter]**.

Actually you can move the cell pointer to any cell in column J to indicate that the primary sort key is customer name.

Next you specify the sort order.

⑤   Type **A** to specify ascending sort order and press **[Enter]**. See Figure 7-7.

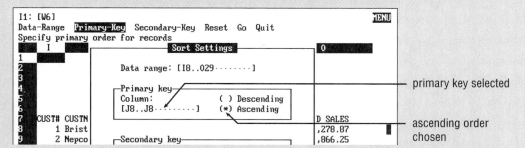

Figure 7-7
Information
about primary
key appears in
dialog box

primary key selected

ascending order
chosen

Ascending order for labels means arranging the data alphabetically from A to Z
and numerically from lowest to highest number. Descending order for labels
means arranging the data alphabetically backward, from Z to A, and numerically
from highest to lowest number.

⑥   Select Go (**G**) to sort the database. When sorting has been completed, your screen
should show the records alphabetized by customer name. See Figure 7-8.

```
I1: [W6]                                                              READY

        I          J              K  L  M      N          O          ◄
1                              Medi-Source Inc.                       ►
2                              Customer Database                      ▲
3                                                                     ▼
4                                                                     ?
5
6
7   CUST# CUSTNAME           TYPE ST REP   BAL_OWED   YTD_SALES
8       8 Bayshore Pharmacy    P   MA   3   6,010.36   44,140.87        █
9       7 Bioran Medical Lab   L   MA   3   2,799.12   11,927.84
10     13 Bradley Hospital     H   MA   2   9,430.72   32,451.95
11     14 Braintree Hospital   H   MA   2  36,609.80   75,562.35
12      1 Bristol Pharmacy     P   RI   4   2,647.10   80,278.87
13     21 Butler Hospital      H   RI   1  31,215.67   21,144.05
14      6 Cape Psych Center    H   MA   3  31,509.10   44,173.24
15     17 De Bellis Pharmacy   P   RI   1   2,715.35   85,063.85
16     19 Depasquale Pharmacy  P   RI   1   4,214.50   39,727.98
17      3 EMG & EEG Labs       L   MA   4  12,583.97   31,685.19
18     16 Forgary Labs         L   MA   1   2,890.08    6,670.41
19     22 Foster Blood Tests   L   MA   1   2,594.27    4,275.56
20     12 Gregg's Pharmacy     P   MA   2   2,052.70    3,771.28
S7MEDI1.WK1
```

Figure 7-8
Records sorted
by customer
name in
ascending order

⑦   Press **[PgDn]** to view the remaining customer records. Press **[PgUp]** to return to the
beginning of the database.

Joan also planned to sort the customer data by balance owed, with customers having
the largest outstanding balance appearing first, that is, in descending order. That way Joan
can quickly identify the customers that have the higher outstanding balances.

To sort a data file in descending order by balance owed:

❶   Select /Data Sort (**/DS**). 1-2-3 displays the Sort Settings dialog box.

Because the range of cells to be sorted was previously entered and still appears in the Sort Settings dialog box, you do not have to select the data range again.

The next step is to change the primary sort key from CUSTNAME to BAL_OWED.

❷   Select Primary-Key (**P**). Move the cell pointer to cell N8 or any other cell in the BAL_OWED column and press **[Enter]**.

❸   Type **D** to specify descending sort order and press **[Enter]**. See Figure 7-9.

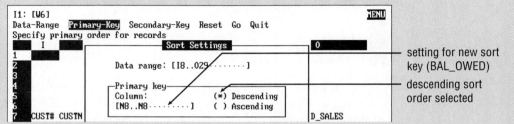

Figure 7-9
Dialog box indicates balance owed field to be sorted in descending order

❹   Select Go (**G**) to sort the database. When sorting has been completed, your screen should look like Figure 7-10. Notice that the customer having the highest balance owed appears first. The customer with the lowest balanced owed is last.

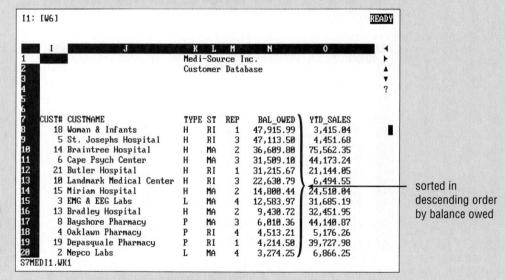

Figure 7-10
Customer records sorted in descending order by balance owed

❺   Press **[PgDn]** to view the remaining customer records. When you have finished viewing the records, press **[PgUp]** to return to the start of the customer database.

Sorting Using a Secondary Key

You can organize data on more than one sort key. For example, Joan wants to organize the customers by state, and within each state she wants to arrange the customers in alphabetical order.

To sort the 1-2-3 database on two sort keys:

❶ Select /Data Sort (**/DS**). The Sort Settings dialog box appears.

Because the range of cells to be sorted was previously entered and still appears in the dialog box, you do not have to select the data range again.

Next specify ST (state) as the primary sort key.

❷ Select Primary-Key (**P**). Move the cell pointer to cell L8, the ST field, and press **[Enter]**.

❸ Type **A** to specify ascending sort order and press **[Enter]**.

Now specify CUSTNAME as the secondary sort key.

❹ Select Secondary-Key (**S**). Move the cell pointer to cell J8, the CUSTNAME field, and press **[Enter]**.

❺ Press **[Enter]** if A (ascending) already appears as the sort order for CUSTNAME. If D appears, type **A** and press **[Enter]**.

❻ Select Go (**G**) to sort the database. See Figure 7-11.

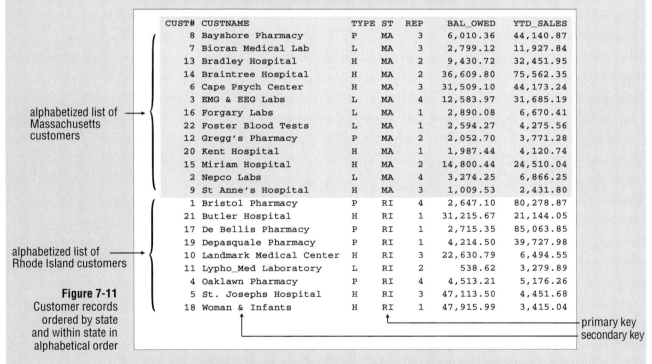

alphabetized list of Massachusetts customers

alphabetized list of Rhode Island customers

Figure 7-11
Customer records ordered by state and within state in alphabetical order

CUST#	CUSTNAME	TYPE	ST	REP	BAL_OWED	YTD_SALES
8	Bayshore Pharmacy	P	MA	3	6,010.36	44,140.87
7	Bioran Medical Lab	L	MA	3	2,799.12	11,927.84
13	Bradley Hospital	H	MA	2	9,430.72	32,451.95
14	Braintree Hospital	H	MA	2	36,609.80	75,562.35
6	Cape Psych Center	H	MA	3	31,509.10	44,173.24
3	EMG & EEG Labs	L	MA	4	12,583.97	31,685.19
16	Forgary Labs	L	MA	1	2,890.08	6,670.41
22	Foster Blood Tests	L	MA	1	2,594.27	4,275.56
12	Gregg's Pharmacy	P	MA	2	2,052.70	3,771.28
20	Kent Hospital	H	MA	1	1,987.44	4,120.74
15	Miriam Hospital	H	MA	2	14,800.44	24,510.04
2	Nepco Labs	L	MA	4	3,274.25	6,866.25
9	St Anne's Hospital	H	MA	3	1,009.53	2,431.80
1	Bristol Pharmacy	P	RI	4	2,647.10	80,278.87
21	Butler Hospital	H	RI	1	31,215.67	21,144.05
17	De Bellis Pharmacy	P	RI	1	2,715.35	85,063.85
19	Depasquale Pharmacy	P	RI	1	4,214.50	39,727.98
10	Landmark Medical Center	H	RI	3	22,630.79	6,494.55
11	Lypho_Med Laboratory	L	RI	2	538.62	3,279.89
4	Oaklawn Pharmacy	P	RI	4	4,513.21	5,176.26
5	St. Josephs Hospital	H	RI	3	47,113.50	4,451.68
18	Woman & Infants	H	RI	1	47,915.99	3,415.04

primary key
secondary key

❼ Press **[PgDn]** to view remaining customer records. When you have finished viewing the records, press **[PgUp]**.

Notice that all Massachusetts customers are grouped together, followed by all customers from Rhode Island. Within each state the customer records are alphabetized.

Data Query Command — Finding Records

Now that Joan has sorted the data, she wants to examine specific customer accounts. While sorting the data, she noticed that customers in the hospital category have outstanding balances that are high compared to customers in the lab and pharmacy categories. So she decides to examine these accounts first.

The Data Query command lets 1-2-3 select records that match certain criteria and finds (highlights) or extracts (copies) these records without examining every record in the database. Before 1-2-3 can find a record in the database, you must specify an input range and set up a criteria range. Let's discuss what we mean by these two ranges.

Input Range

An **input range** is the range of data that 1-2-3 will search when you query a 1-2-3 database. When you specify an input range to use with any Data Query command, you must *include the field names* as part of the range. This is unlike the data range in the Data Sort command, which does *not* include the field names.

You can assign a range name to represent the input range, although 1-2-3 does not require that you do this to execute the Data Query command. A range name allows you to specify the database without having to remember the exact cell locations of your database.

To assign a range name to the database:

1. Move the cell pointer to cell I7, the upper left corner of the database. Remember, when you use the Data Query command, you *must* include the field names in the input range.
2. Select /Range Name Create (**/RNC**).
3. Type the name **database** and press **[Enter]**.
4. Highlight the database cells I7..O29. Press **[Enter]**. The range name DATABASE has been assigned to this range of cells.

   Again, note that the range includes the field names and the data records.

Criteria Range

The **criteria range** is a small area in your worksheet where you tell 1-2-3 which records to search for in the input range. This range must include at least two rows. The first row of the criteria range contains some or all of the field names from the database. The field names in the criteria range *must* be identical to the database field names. The rows below the field names in the criteria range include the search criteria.

The criteria range is often established below or to the right of the input range. Let's use cells P3 to V4. In the first row of the criteria range, you must enter the criteria field names. Because these names must be *identical* to the database field names, it is best to copy the database field names to the criteria range, so no difference can occur between the database field names and the criteria field names.

To copy the database fields names to the criteria range:

① Make sure the cell pointer is in cell I7, the location of the first database field name to be copied.

② Select /Copy (**/C**).

③ Highlight I7..O7. Press **[Enter]**.

④ Now move the cell pointer to cell P3, the location where you will place the field names for the criteria range. Then press **[Enter]**.

⑤ Press **[Tab]** so you can see that the database field names have been copied to the criteria range. See Figure 7-12.

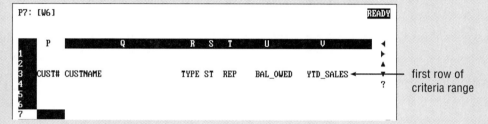

Figure 7-12
Criteria range
field names

Now enter the search criteria into the second row of the criteria range. Joan is searching for all hospital customers. To search for an exact match, enter the value or label you are searching for exactly as it appears in the database. Enter the criterion below the appropriate field name in the criteria range.

To enter the search criteria to find hospital customers:

① Move the cell pointer to cell R4, the location in the criteria range that stores the search criteria for the type of customer.

② Type **H** and press **[Enter]**. 1-2-3 considers lowercase and uppercase characters the same in the criteria range. See Figure 7-13.

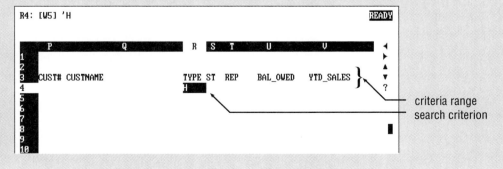

Figure 7-13
Criteria range
completely
specified

You can also assign a range name to the criteria range, although you do not have to do so to use the Data Query command. Assigning a range name allows you to specify the location of the criteria range without remembering the cell locations of the range.

To assign the range name CRITERIA to the criteria range:

❶ Move the cell pointer to P3, the upper left corner of the criteria range.

❷ Select /Range Name Create (**/RNC**).

❸ Type **criteria** and press **[Enter]**. Highlight the criteria range P3..V4. Press **[Enter]**. Now the criteria range P3..V4 has the name CRITERIA.

❹ To document that this range of cells is the criteria range, move the cell pointer to cell P2, type *****Criteria Range**, and press **[Enter]**.

Finding Records Using a Constant

Now that you have set up the input and criteria ranges, you can use the Data Query command to find (highlight) all hospital customers. The Find command is used to activate the search of the database records, finding each record that satisfies the criteria you specified in the criteria range.

To find hospital customers in the database:

❶ Select /Data Query (**/DQ**). The Query Settings dialog box appears. See Figure 7-14.

This dialog box lists the locations of the input, criteria, and output ranges. Currently no query settings are defined.

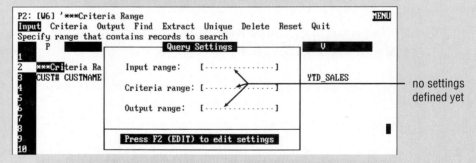

Figure 7-14
Query Settings
dialog box

To use the Find command, you must specify the locations of the input and criteria ranges. First, let's specify the input range.

❷ Select Input (**I**) to indicate the range of cells you want to search.

Enter the name of the input range.

❸ Type **database** and press **[Enter]**.

DATABASE, the range name you assigned to cells I7..O29, appears in the Query Settings dialog box.

Next, specify the criteria range.

❹ Select Criteria (**C**) to indicate the range of cells that contains the search criteria.

Enter the name of the criteria range.

⑤ Type **criteria** and press **[Enter]**.

CRITERIA, the range name you assigned to your criteria range, that is, cells P3..V4, appears in the Query Settings dialog box. See Figure 7-15.

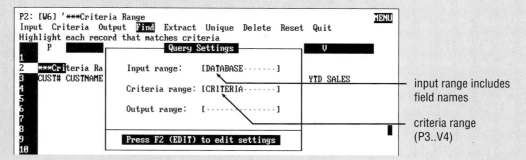

Figure 7-15
Query settings
specified

Now use the Find command to highlight the records that meet the search criteria.

To find all hospital customers:

❶ Select Find **(F)**.

1-2-3 highlights the first record that matches the criterion of TYPE equal to H. See Figure 7-16.

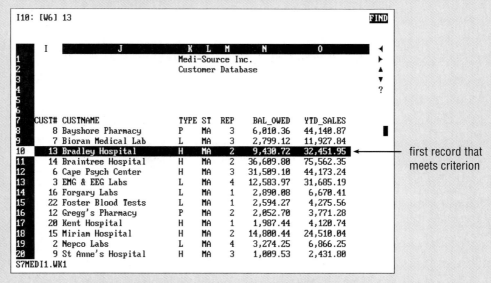

Figure 7-16
Finding all
hospital
customers

❷ Press **[↓]** to find the next hospital customer. Continue to press **[↓]** to find all hospital customers.

You can also press **[↑]** to search the database in the other direction.

❸ Press **[Esc]** or **[Enter]** to return to the Data Query menu.

❹ Select Quit **(Q)** to return to READY mode.

Finding Records Using a Search Formula

Remember that the average customer's outstanding balance is $6,000. This average was based on customers from all states in which Medi-Source does business. Now Joan wants to identify Rhode Island and Massachusetts customers who owe more than the average Medi-Source customer.

This query requires a search formula be included beneath the BAL_OWED field name in the criteria range. When you enter a formula as a criterion, you must begin the formula with a plus sign (+); otherwise, 1-2-3 will consider the entry as a label rather than a search formula. Follow the plus sign with the cell address of the field of the *first record* that appears immediately under the field name in the input range. Next in the formula you must include a comparison operator and a value 1-2-3 will compare against the cell address.

In the following steps, you will enter the search formula +N8>6000. This is the search criterion to find all customers who owe more than $6,000.

First, erase the search criterion from the previous query that still appears in the criteria range.

To erase the search criterion from row 4:

❶ Move the cell pointer to the second line of the criteria range, cell P4.

❷ Select /Range Erase (**/RE**).

❸ Highlight P4..V4 and press **[Enter]**. The row that stores the search criteria is now erased.

Now enter the new search criterion:

❹ Move the cell pointer to cell U4, the cell beneath the criteria field name, BAL_OWED.

❺ Type **+N8>6000** and press **[Enter]**. See Figure 7-17.

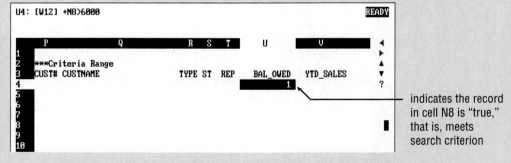

Figure 7-17
Specifying a
formula as the
search criterion

indicates the record
in cell N8 is "true,"
that is, meets
search criterion

Remember, you must place the + sign in front of the cell address; otherwise, 1-2-3 will treat the cell entry as a label. Also remember that you *must reference the first database cell* following the field name in the column you are searching.

Notice that a 1 appears in cell U4. When a condition containing a search formula is assigned to a cell in the criteria range, a 0 or a 1 will appear. The value in U4, the cell with the formula +N8>6000, depends on the value in cell N8. If the value in cell N8 is greater than 6000, the condition is true, and a 1 appears. If the condition is false, a 0 appears.

You can choose to have the formula appear in the criteria range instead of the value 0 or 1. This is often done because the formula is more meaningful to the user than a 1 or a 0. To display the formula in the cell, you use the Range Format Text command.

To display the formula in the cell:

❶ Make sure the cell pointer is at U4.

❷ Select /Range Format Text (**/RFT**).

❸ Cell U4 is the entire range, so press **[Enter]**. The formula for the search criterion now appears in cell U4. See Figure 7-18.

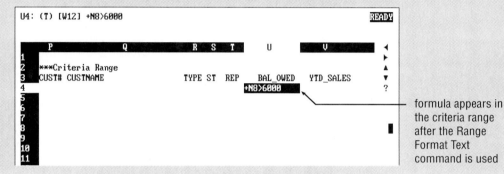

Figure 7-18
Displaying the search formula in the criteria range

formula appears in the criteria range after the Range Format Text command is used

Now Joan uses the Data Query Find command to highlight all customers with a balance above $6,000.

To use the Data Query Find command:

❶ Select /Data Query (**/DQ**).

The same input and criteria ranges that were used earlier in the tutorial now appear in the Query Settings dialog box. Because you defined the input and criteria ranges when you searched for hospital customers, you do not need to define these ranges again.

Once the input and criteria ranges have been defined, you can search the database records by using the Find command.

② Select Find (**F**).

1-2-3 highlights the first record with an outstanding balance greater than $6,000. See Figure 7-19.

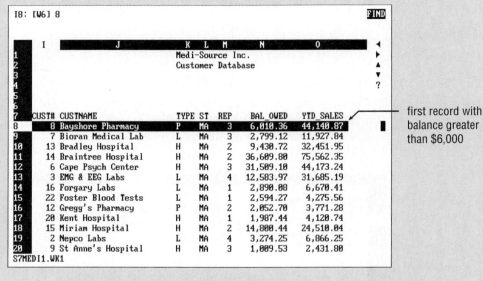

Figure 7-19
Finding customer records with balance owed greater than $6,000

③ Press [↓] to find the next matching record in the database.

Continue to press [↓] to find all customers with a balance above $6,000.

④ Press [**Esc**] and then select Quit (**Q**) to return to READY mode.

Data Query Command — Extracting Records

Joan has been using the Data Query Find command to highlight (locate) all records that meet her search criteria. Now she wants to copy customer records with balances greater than $6,000 to a different part of the worksheet. In this separate area of the worksheet she wants to list only those records that have balances above $6,000. This will make it easier for Joan to print or perform calculations on these records.

The Data Query Extract command lets you copy all records from the input range that match specific criteria in the criteria range to a location in the worksheet called the output range.

Before you use the Data Query Extract command, you must define the input range, the criteria range, and the output range.

Input Range

The input range identifies the location of the 1-2-3 database. This range includes the field names in addition to the records of the database. You specify this range by using the Input option of the Data Query command. The input range was defined when you used the Find command earlier in the tutorial, so you do not need to enter it again.

Criteria Range

The criteria range specifies the criteria you want 1-2-3 to use to extract records from the input range. You specify the criteria range by using the Criterion option of the Data Query command. Joan wants to extract records of customers with balances above $6,000. Because the search criterion is the same as that used earlier in this tutorial, you do not have to enter the search criterion again.

Output Range

The **output range** is an area of the worksheet where records from the input range that meet the search criteria are copied. The first row of the output range must contain field names that are identical to the field names in the input range. The Extract command copies all matching records into the output range beginning in the row below the field names of the output range. Because the Extract command erases all data values that were previously in these cells, it's best to choose an area of your worksheet that contains no data for the placement of the output range. Let's begin the output range in the range P7..V7.

There are two approaches to defining the output range. Usually you specify the row with the field names as the range of the output range. 1-2-3 uses as many rows below the output range as it needs to copy the records to this area. If you defined the output range in this manner, when you issue the Extract command, 1-2-3 automatically erases the contents of every cell below the output range up to the last row in the worksheet. Thus, when locating the output range in your worksheet choose an area that is not above any data.

As an alternative, when defining the output range, you can define its exact size. That is, when defining the output range, include the field names and a range of blank rows. The number of rows in the range depends on the number of records you think you will extract. When you define a *fixed length* output range and the output range is too small to hold all the extracted records, 1-2-3 extracts as many records as can fit in the output range. 1-2-3 also displays the error message "Too many records for Output range." If this occurs, increase the size of the output range and issue the Extract command again. The output range can include some or all of the field names from the input range. When you use the Data Query Extract command, 1-2-3 copies data only to the fields you specified in the output range. Joan wants to copy to the output range the complete record for all customers with balances over $6,000.

To copy the field names from the input range to P7..V7, the first row of the output range:

1. Move the cell pointer to cell I7.
2. Select /Copy (**/C**).
3. Highlight cells I7..O7, then press **[Enter]**.
4. Move the cell pointer to P7 and press **[Enter]**. The database field names appear in P7..V7.
5. Press **[Tab]** to see the copied field names.

⑥ Move the cell pointer to P6, type ***Output Range**, and then press **[Enter]**. This label helps identify this area of the worksheet. See Figure 7-20.

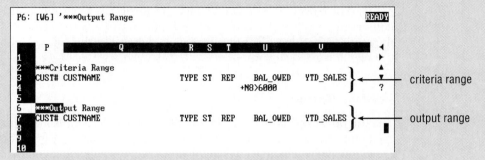

Figure 7-20
Ranges for extract

Although it is not required to extract records, you can assign a range name to the output range P7..V7. This allows you to specify the output range without remembering the cell locations.

To assign the range name OUTPUT to the output range:
① Move the cell pointer to the first field name in the output range, cell P7.
② Select /Range Name Create (**/RNC**).
③ Type **output** and press **[Enter]**.
④ Highlight the field names of the output range, P7..V7, then press **[Enter]**.
The output range now has the name OUTPUT.

Before you can use the Data Query Extract command, you must specify the input, criteria, and output ranges. Because the input and criteria ranges were specified earlier in this tutorial, you do not need to enter them again. However, the output range has not been specified.

To specify the output range for the Data Query command:
① Select /Data Query (**/DQ**).
② Select Output (**O**), press **[F3]** (NAME), and highlight the range name OUTPUT, which is the output range. Press **[Enter]**. See Figure 7-21. The range name of the output range now appears in the Query Settings dialog box.

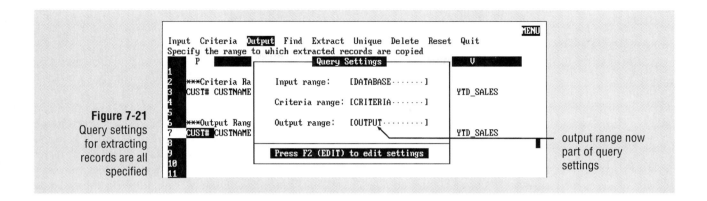

Figure 7-21
Query settings
for extracting
records are all
specified

output range now
part of query
settings

Extracting Records

Now that the input, criteria, and output ranges have been specified, you can use the Extract command. Joan wants to extract customer records with an outstanding balance above $6,000.

To extract records with a balance above $6,000:

❶ Select Extract (**E**).

   1-2-3 copies to the output range all records from the database that meet the search formula you entered, in this case, customers whose balance is greater than $6,000.

❷ Select Quit (**Q**) to return to READY mode.

The extracted records appear below the row containing the output field names. See Figure 7-22. Notice that 1-2-3 has extracted only those records that meet the criterion, that is, only those customers whose outstanding balance is greater than $6,000.

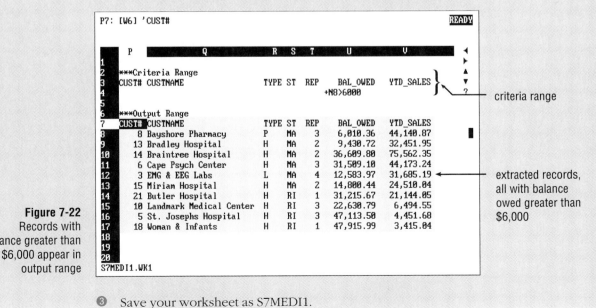

Figure 7-22
Records with
balance greater than
$6,000 appear in
output range

criteria range

extracted records,
all with balance
owed greater than
$6,000

❸ Save your worksheet as S7MEDI1.

Understanding Database @Functions

According to her plan, Joan wants a report that shows the total and average outstanding balances by state. One approach to calculating these statistics is to use the database @functions available in 1-2-3.

Lotus 1-2-3 has seven database @functions: @DAVG, @DSUM, @DMAX, @DMIN, @DCOUNT, @DSTD, and @DVAR. Each function calculates a value based on records in the database that match criteria in the criteria range. The database @functions differ from the corresponding statistical @functions, because the database @functions calculate statistics *only* for the records in a database that match the criteria you specify. For example, you would use @AVG to calculate the average balance owed for all the records in the database. You would use @DAVG to calculate the average balance owed for only those records that meet the criterion of being RI customers.

All 1-2-3 database @functions have the same format:

> *@function(input range, offset, criteria range)*

where *@function* is one of the following: @DAVG, @DSUM, @DCOUNT, @DMAX, @DMIN, @DSTD, or @DVAR and each database function consists of three arguments:

1. *Input range* is the range that contains the database, including the field names in the range definition. The range can be specified as a range name or as cell addresses.

2. *Offset* is the position number of the column in the database that is to be summed, averaged, counted, and so on. 1-2-3 assigns the first field in the database the offset number 0, the second field the offset number 1, and so on. For example, CUST# is the first column in the database and has the offset number 0; CUSTNAME is the second column, so it has the offset number 1; and BAL_OWED is the sixth column in the database, so it has the offset number 5.

3. *Criteria range* is an area of your worksheet where you specify the search criteria to determine which records you will use in the calculations.

Figure 7-23 summarizes the 1-2-3 database @functions.

@Function Name	Description	Example
@DAVG	Averages the values in the offset column that meet specified criteria	@DAVG(A11..G32,6,T25..T26)
@DSUM	Sums the values in the offset column that meet specified criteria	@DSUM(A11..G32,6,T25..T26)
@DMAX	Determines the largest value in the offset column that meets specified criteria	@DMAX(A11..G32,6,T25..T26)
@DMIN	Determines the smallest value in the offset column that meets specified criteria	@DMIN(A11..G32,6,T25..T26)
@DCOUNT	Counts the number of records in the offset column that meet specified criteria	@DCOUNT(A11..G32,6,T25..T26)
@DSTD	Calculates the standard deviation of the values in the offset column that meet specified criteria	@DSTD(A11..G32,6,T25..T26)
@DVAR	Calculates the variance of the values in the offset column that meet the specified criteria	@DVAR(A11..G32,6,T25..T26)

Figure 7-23
Database
@functions

Using Database @Functions

Joan wants to calculate separate statistics for Rhode Island and Massachusetts customers. She wants to know if there is a difference between the total and the average amount owed by customers in each state. Let's now prepare Joan's report. Place this report in the range W1..AB7. The headings and the labels for the report have already been entered in the worksheet.

Now calculate the statistics for the report. To calculate these statistics, you will use the database @functions @DSUM and @DAVG. Each function requires an input range, an offset range, and a criteria range.

The input range identifies the records to be used in calculations. You already defined this range earlier in the tutorial. The input range includes cells I7..O29 and has been assigned the name DATABASE.

You set up separate criteria ranges for each group of records on which you are performing calculations.

Let's first set up a criteria range at AA5..AA6 to use when you search for Rhode Island customers:

❶ Press **[Tab]** to move to the Report section of the worksheet. The title and the headings have already been entered.

❷ Move the cell pointer to cell AA5, the location of the criteria field name.

❸ Type **ST** in uppercase letters and press **[Enter]**.

❹ Move the cell pointer to AA6, the second row of the criteria range.

❺ Type **RI** and press **[Enter]**. The criteria range for Rhode Island customers is complete.

Now assign a range name to the criteria range.

To assign the range name RICRITERIA to the criteria range AA5..AA6:

❶ Move the cell pointer to AA5.

❷ Select /Range Name Create (**/RNC**).

❸ Type **ricriteria** and press **[Enter]**.

❹ Highlight the cells AA5..AA6 and press **[Enter]**.

The criteria range has the name RICRITERIA.

Notice that the criteria range includes only one database field name. The criteria range does not have to include all field names in the database. It needs to include only the field names you intend to search.

Next, set up a separate criteria range at AB5..AB6 to search for customers in Massachusetts:

❶ Move the cell pointer to AB5, the location of the criteria field name of the second criteria range.

❷ Type **ST** in uppercase letters and press **[Enter]**.

❸ Move the cell pointer to AB6, the second row of the criteria range.

❹ Type **MA** and press **[Enter]**. The criteria range for specifying Massachusetts customers is complete. See Figure 7-24.

Figure 7-24
Criteria ranges to be used with database @functions

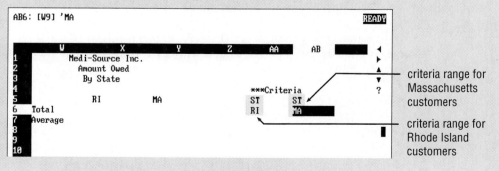

Now assign a range name to the criteria range.

To assign the range name MACRITERIA to the criteria range AB5..AB6:

❶ Move the cell pointer to AB5.

❷ Select /Range Name Create (**/RNC**).

❸ Type **macriteria** and press **[Enter]**.

❹ Highlight the cells AB5..AB6 and press **[Enter]**.

The criteria range has the name MACRITERIA.

Now that you have defined the input and criteria ranges, let's determine the offset number for the balance owed field. You recall that the offset is the position number of the column in the database that is to be summed, averaged, counted, and so on.

To determine the offset number for balance owed:

❶ Move the cell pointer to cell I7, the first field in the database.

❷ Starting with 0 for the first column, CUST#, count the columns to determine the offset number for column N, BAL_OWED. Your answer should be 5. See Figure 7-25.

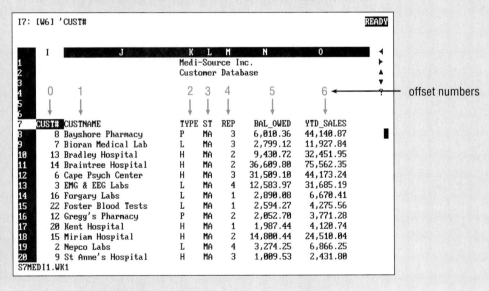

Figure 7-25
Determining the
offset number

Now let's use the database @functions to complete the report.

To use database @functions to calculate the statistics:

❶ Press **[F5]** (GOTO), type **w1**, and press **[Enter]**. The cell pointer is now in the section of the worksheet where you will average and total the outstanding balance by state. See Figure 7-26.

report area →

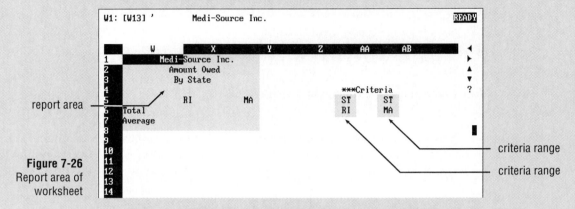

Figure 7-26
Report area of
worksheet

criteria range

criteria range

❷ Move the cell pointer to cell X6, under the cell labeled RI.

❸ Type **@dsum(database,5,ricriteria)** and press **[Enter]** to calculate the total balance owed by Rhode Island customers. The total, 163504.73, appears on the screen.

❹ Move the cell pointer to cell X7.

❺ Type **@davg(database,5,ricriteria)** and press **[Enter]** to calculate the average balance owed by Rhode Island customers. The average balance owed is 18167.192222. See Figure 7-27.

input range →

database →
@function

offset number
criteria range

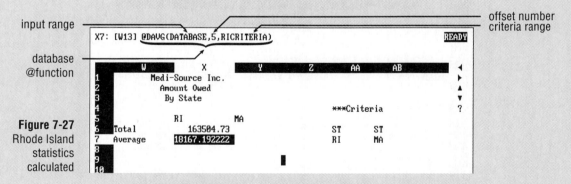

Figure 7-27
Rhode Island
statistics
calculated

❻ Move the cell pointer to cell Y6, under the cell labeled MA.

❼ Type **@dsum(database,5,macriteria)**. Press **[Enter]** to calculate the total balance owed by all Massachusetts customers. Massachusetts customers owe a total of 127551.78.

❽ Move the cell pointer to cell Y7.

❾ Type **@davg(database,5,macriteria).** Press **[Enter]** to calculate the average balance owed by Massachusetts customers. On average, Massachusetts customers owe 9811.675384.

The statistics for the report are complete. Joan, however, wants the amounts in the report displayed to the nearest dollar. Let's now format the values in X6..Y7 using Currency format.

To display the values in the report, using Currency format:

❶   Move the cell pointer to X6.

❷   Select /Range Format Currency (**/RFC**).

❸   Type **0** (zero) and press **[Enter]**.

❹   Highlight X6..Y7. Press **[Enter]**.

Your worksheet should look like Figure 7-28.

Figure 7-28
Joan's calculated information about Rhode Island and Massachusetts customers

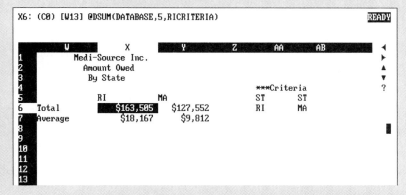

Joan notices that the average outstanding balance for Rhode Island customers is $18,167 — nearly three times more than the Medi-Source customer average nationwide.

❺   Save your worksheet as S7MEDI1.WK1.

Exercises

1. The customer database that you used in this tutorial, C7MEDI1.WK1, contains how many fields? How many records?

2. To sort the customer names in Z-to-A order, you would use which sorting option?

3. Retrieve the file E7FILE1 and do the following:
    a. Assign the range name DATABASE to the range A3..E11.
    b. Sort the data on the field FNAME. Specify the range name DATABASE as the data range for the Data Sort command. Print your results. Explain what happened.

4. Retrieve the file E7FILE2 and do the following:
    a. Assign the range name DATABASE to the range A4..D11.
    b. Print this range.
    c. Sort the data on the field name FNAME in ascending order. Specify the range name DATABASE as the data range for the Data Sort command. Print your results. Explain what happened.

Answer Exercises 5 through 8 using the customer database you used in Tutorial 7.

5. List the steps you would follow to locate Kent Hospital in the customer database using the Find command.

6. List the steps you would follow to extract all Rhode Island customers using the Extract command.

7. What @function would you use to calculate the following statistics?
    a. the average sales for the year for sales representative #4
    b. the highest balance owed by a Rhode Island customer
    c. the number of pharmacies in the database

8. If you had used the database statistical function @DAVG(DATABASE,6, macriteria) in this tutorial, what statistic would you be calculating?

Tutorial Assignments

Before you begin these Tutorial Assignments, check your data diskette. Be sure you have space to save the additional worksheet files you'll create in these assignments (at least 85,000 bytes). If you do not have enough space, save your files for Tutorial 7 to another formatted diskette.

Retrieve the worksheet T7MEDI1.WK1 and do the following:

1. Sort the database by year-to-date (YTD) sales, with the customer having the lowest YTD sales appearing first. The database begins in cell I7. Save the file as S7MEDI2.

2. Sort the database in descending order using the field TYPE (type of customer) as the primary sort key. Save the file as S7MEDI3.

3. Arrange the customer database by type of customer (ascending order); within type of customer arrange the accounts with highest balance owed first. Print the sorted records.

Use the Data Query command for Assignments 4 through 7.

4. Copy the database field names to the first row of the criteria range, P3..V3.

5. Query the database to find all customers located in Rhode Island (code = RI). Save the worksheet as S7MEDI4.

6. Query the database to find all customers with average YTD sales above $50,000. Save the worksheet as S7MEDI5.

7. Query the database to extract and print all customers assigned to sales representative #4. Set up an output range beginning at P7..V7. Save the worksheet as S7MEDI6.

Complete Assignments 8 through 12 using the database statistical function @DAVG. Three criteria ranges have been partially set up in cells Z5, AA5, and AB5.

8.   Calculate the average outstanding balance for hospitals. Complete the criteria range in Z5..Z6. Place your result in cell X6.

9.   Calculate the average outstanding balance for labs. Complete the criteria range in AA5..AA6. Place your result in cell X7.

10.   Calculate the average outstanding balance for pharmacies. Complete the criteria range in AB5..AB6. Place your result in cell X8.

11.   Print this Outstanding Balance Report by Type of Customer.

12.   Save your worksheet as S7MEDI7.

Case Problems

1.   Human Resource Database

The human resource department of a small furniture manufacturer has developed a human resource database. The field names in this database are:

Field	Description
EMP#	Employee number
LNAME	Last name
FNAME	First name
BIRTH	Date of birth (yyyymmdd)
SEX	Code for sex (M = male; F = female)
MAR	Code for marital status (Y = married; N = not married)
DEP	Number of dependents
ANNSAL	Annual salary
HIREDT	Date employee hired (yyyymmdd)
XMPT	Exempt employee (X = exempt; N = nonexempt)
MED	Code for medical plan (F = family plan; I = individual plan; N = not on medical plan)
401K	401K retirement plan (Y = making contributions to plan; N = not making contributions to plan)
DIV	Division where employee works
JOBTITLE	Job title
PER	Payment method (H = hourly; M = monthly)

Retrieve the worksheet P7PERSNL and do the following:

1.   Sort and print the database alphabetically by last name.

2.   Sort and print the database by hire date in ascending order.

3. Sort and print the database by division and, within division, by salary in descending order.

4. Find all employees that have the family medical plan. The code is F.

5. Find all employees with one or more dependents.

6. Extract and print the records of all married employees.

7. Print a summary report showing salaries categorized by sex. Use the database @functions to prepare this report. Format the report as shown in Figure 7-29.

	Salaries — By Sex	
	Females	Males
Average	$ xxxx	$ xxxx
Maximum	$ xxxx	$ xxxx
Minimum	$ xxxx	$ xxxx
Count	xxxx	xxxx

Figure 7-29

8. Save your worksheet as S7PERSNL.

WYSIWYG Assignments

1. Attach WYSIWYG.

2. Add the following enhancements to the summary report:
    a. Replace any dashed lines with solid lines.
    b. Use a 14-point Swiss font for the report title line.
    c. Boldface the column headings.
    d. Draw a box around the entire report.

3. Save your worksheet as W7PERSNL.

4. Print the summary report.

2. The Top 50 U.S. Companies

Every year a leading business magazine publishes a list of the 50 largest U.S. companies and presents financial data about them.

Retrieve the worksheet P7TOP50. The field names in the file containing these data are as follows:

Field	Description
COMPANY	Name of company
INDUSTRY	Industry code
SALES	Sales revenue for the year
PROFITS	Net income
ASSETS	Total assets
EQUITY	Portion of assets owned by stockholders
MKT_VAL	Market value of company

Do the following:

1. Sort and print the database alphabetically by company.

2. Sort and print the database arranged by sales, with the company with the highest sales appearing first.

3. Calculate the rate of return (ROR) for each company. The formula is

$$ROR = \frac{profit}{equity}$$

Place this new field in column H and label the column ROR. Format using the Percent format with one decimal place.

4. Sort the database by ROR, with the company having the highest ROR appearing first. *Hint:* Think about your data range.

5. Print the database, which now includes the ROR field.

6. Extract and print all companies in the computer industry (industry code = 6).

7. Prepare and print a summary report that compares the average, the maximum, and the minimum sales for companies in the oil industry (code = 18) versus companies in the aerospace industry (code = 1). Use the database @functions to prepare this report. Format the report as shown in Figure 7-30.

Figure 7-30

Top 50 U.S. Companies Industry Comparison		
	Oil	Aerospace
Average sales	$ xxx	$ xxx
Minimum sales	xxx	xxx
Maximum sales	xxx	xxx

8. Save your worksheet as S7TOP50.

WYSIWYG Assignments

1. Attach WYSIWYG.

2. Add the following enhancements to the summary report:
   a. Replace any dashed lines with solid lines under column headings.
   b. Change the first line of the report title to a 24-point Swiss font. Use a 14-point Swiss font for the remaining report title lines. Adjust the column widths as appropriate.
   c. Boldface the column headings and report labels.
   d. Draw a box around the entire report.

3. Save your worksheet as W7TOP50.

4. Print the summary report.

3. Inventory of Microcomputer Software

A company that sells microcomputer software has just completed its annual physical inventory prior to preparing its financial statement. The data from this inventory were entered into a 1-2-3 worksheet.

Retrieve the worksheet P7SFTWRE. The field names for this inventory database include the following:

Field	Description
ITEM#	Unique number to identify each product
TITLE	Name of product
CAT	Category of software
COST	Cost to company per unit
QOH	Number of packages on hand (in inventory)
QOO	Number of packages on order
PRICE	Retail price of software package
YTD_SALES	Year-to-date sales

The codes for the category of software (CAT) are:

CO	=	Communications
DP	=	Desktop publishing
DB	=	Database
GR	=	Graphics
SP	=	Spreadsheet
WP	=	Word processing
UT	=	Utility

Do the following:

1. Print a list of current software products arranged by category and, within category, alphabetized by title.

2. Find the software products that have one or more units on order.

3. Extract and print the database (DB) software products.

4. Add two columns to the worksheet, Inventory Value, Cost (column I) and Inventory Value, Retail (column J). Calculate and print the total cost value and the total retail value for each inventory item. (*Hint:* You can use the following formulas: Inventory Value, Cost = QOH × COST and Inventory Value, Retail = QOH × PRICE.) Then total the value of the inventory for the entire company.

5. Calculate and print the total retail value of the inventory by software category. Be sure your report has a separate total for each of the seven category codes. Use database @functions to prepare this report. Format the report as shown in Figure 7-31.

```
              Inventory - Retail Value
               By Software Category

                        Total Retail Value

   Communication            xxxx

   Desktop Publishing        xxxx

   Database                  xxxx

   Graphics                  xxxx

   Spreadsheet               xxxx

   Word Processing           xxxx

   Utility                   xxxx
```

Figure 7-31

6. Prepare a pie chart illustrating the same data that were calculated in Assignment 5. Create a PIC file named PIESOFT.

7. Save your worksheet as S7SFTWRE.

8. Print the pie chart PIESOFT using PGRAPH.

WYSIWYG Assignments

1. Attach WYSIWYG.

2. Add the following enhancements to the software category report:
   a. Change the first line of the report title to a 24-point Swiss font. Use a 14-point Swiss font for the second report title line.
   b. Create a table (grid) effect for the table.
   c. Insert the pie chart in the worksheet to the right of the software category report.
   d. Draw a double-lined box around the entire report and graph.

3. Save your worksheet as W7SFTWRE.

4. Print the revised report, including the graph, using the WYSIWYG Print command.

4. Checkbook Manager

Marvis Frazier wants to develop an electronic checkbook to record all checks and deposits. He decides that the checkbook should have the following columns:

Field	Description
TRANS	Code for transaction: D for deposit; P for payment
CHK_NO	Check number entered for checks; otherwise, blank
TRN_DATE	Date check was written or deposit made
DESCRIPTION	Payee or description of transaction
CAT	Two-character category code: FD = food; OF = office; UT = utilities; CL = clothing; MS = miscellaneous. If this transaction is not a check, leave the field blank.
AMOUNT	Amount of check, charge, or deposit
BALANCE	Running balance in checkbook
CLEARED	Status code: C when check returned with bank statement; O if outstanding (initially assign an O when check is entered in check register). If this transaction is not a check, leave the field blank.

Use the following data for the month of January:

TRANS	CHK_NO	TRN_DATE	DESCRIPTION	CAT	AMOUNT
P	4157	1/3/92	New England Telephone	UT	145.51
P	4158	1/5/92	Stop & Shop	FD	43.02
D		1/5/92	Deposit payroll check		850.28
P	4159	1/6/92	Staples	OF	24.00
P	4160	1/11/92	Federal Express	OF	9.00
P	4161	1/11/92	Narragansett Electric	UT	133.64
P	4162	1/12/92	Stop & Shop	FD	71.43
P	4163	1/16/92	Filene's	CL	79.99
D		1/16/92	Deposit dividend check		125.00
P	4164	1/16/92	O'Neil Oil Service	UT	170.41
P	4165	1/20/92	Stop & Shop	FD	83.83
P	4166	1/25/92	Federal Express	OF	39.00
P	4167	1/25/92	G. Fox	CL	50.00

Set aside a section above the balance column of the checkbook for the beginning balance. The balance at the beginning of the month is $514.25.

Marvis also lists the calculations he needs to perform:

Balance for first transaction:

if TRANS = D then BALANCE = *beginning balance + deposit*
if TRANS = P then BALANCE = *beginning balance – payment*

Balance for all other transactions:

$$\text{if TRANS} = \text{P then BALANCE} = previous\ balance - payment$$
$$\text{if TRANS} = \text{D then BALANCE} = previous\ balance + deposit$$

Do the following:

1. Create the checkbook worksheet.

2. Enter the data into your checkbook worksheet. Remember to assign a code of O (letter O) for all checks written during the month.

3. Marvis received his bank statement for the period ending January 28, 1992. The bank statement shows a balance of $736.61.
   a. There were three items in the bank statement that he has not entered in the check register: a monthly service charge of $6.25, a charge of $20 for new checks, and $3.73 in interest earned for the month. Include these items in the check register. Treat the service charge and the charge for new checks as payments and assign a miscellaneous expense (MS) code. Do not enter any check number in the CHK_NO column. Treat the interest earned as a deposit.
   b. The following checks were also included with the bank statement:

      4157, 4158, 4159, 4161, 4163, 4164, 4165, 4167

      Indicate in your check register that these checks have cleared by placing a code of C in the Cleared column.

4. Use the Data Query Extract command to copy all checks written during the month (CHK_NO greater than zero) to a separate area of the worksheet.

   After extracting the checks, sort them by category code in ascending order and within category code by date in ascending order. Total the checks written for the month.

5. Set aside another area of your worksheet to prepare the following summary report. Use the database statistical function @DSUM to calculate the totals in this report. Use Marvis' sketch shown in Figure 7-32 to help you lay out this report.

Figure 7-32

Expense Summary	
Code	**Total**
CL	xxxx
FD	xxxx
OF	xxxx
UT	xxxx
MS	xxxx
Total	xxxx

6. Include a section of your worksheet for a bank reconciliation report. The format is shown in Figure 7-33.

Bank Reconciliation Report

Ending balance shown on bank statement	xxxx	
Add: deposits made after date of this statement	xxxx[1]	
Subtotal		xxxx
Less: total of outstanding checks	xxxx[2]	
Adjusted balance (should agree with checkbook balance)		xxxx

[1] Check to see if any deposits occurred after statement date. Enter amount. Enter zero for this month.

[2] Use @DSUM to calculate the total outstanding checks (code O).

Figure 7-33

7. Save your worksheet as P7CHECKS.

8. Print the checks-written report (the extracted records).

9. Print the expense summary report.

10. Print the bank reconciliation report.

11. Print the check register.

12. Include a worksheet map that describes the design of your worksheet.

13. Print all the cell formulas as documentation for this worksheet.

WYSIWYG Assignments

1. Attach WYSIWYG.

2. Add the following enhancements to the check register section of your worksheet:
    a. Create a table (grid) effect for the check register.
    b. Draw a box around the check register.
    c. Boldface the column headings.
    d. Remove the dashed lines under the column headings and replace them with solid lines.

3. Save your worksheet as W7CHECKS.

4. Print the revised report.

Tutorial 8

Creating and Using Macros

OBJECTIVES

In this tutorial you will learn to:

■ Plan a macro

■ Create a macro

■ Execute a macro

■ Use LEARN mode

■ Edit and debug a macro using STEP mode

Case: Medi-Source Inc. Revisited

In Tutorial 7 you saw how Joan Glazer used 1-2-3's database capabilities to help her manage the credits and collections department at Medi-Source Inc. Joan has recently learned how to use macros to become an even more productive user of 1-2-3. To her, macros are stored keystrokes. For example, she created a macro to print the Massachusetts and Rhode Island customer database. With that macro she saved herself the time and the trouble of making over 15 keystrokes every time she wanted to print. She pressed only two keys, and Lotus 1-2-3 automatically printed the database.

Joan knows that, in addition to printing, she will need to save her 1-2-3 worksheet. She decides, therefore, that creating a macro to save this worksheet will be useful. Joan also plans to create a macro to create range names, because she frequently assigns range names to use with macros as well as for other 1-2-3 functions.

Joan will continue to use the macro for printing, and she now plans to create additional macros to make it easier for her to use the Medi-Source database. She decides first to prepare her planning sheet on creating these additional macros (Figure 8-1 on the following page).

Planning Sheet

My Goal:
    To simplify the use of the Medi-Source worksheet by creating macros

What results do I want to see?
    Customer database outstanding balance report

What information do I need?
    Customer database
    Macros

What macros do I want?
    Print customer database
    Save worksheet
    Name ranges
    Print Outstanding Balance by State report

Figure 8-1
Joan's planning
sheet

In this tutorial, you will first run a macro from the Medi-Source worksheet. Then you will add several macros to the worksheet. This involves planning, placing, entering, naming, and documenting each macro. Next, you will execute each macro. You will also use an alternative approach to creating macros, the LEARN mode. Finally, you will learn how to find errors in macros using the STEP mode and how to correct them.

What Are Macros?

A **macro** is a series of keystrokes and special commands stored in a worksheet as cell entries. Macros are most often created to automate frequently performed Lotus 1-2-3 tasks, such as printing a worksheet, naming a range, saving a worksheet, or formatting cells. Thus, macros save time. They also help less sophisticated users of 1-2-3 by making the worksheet easier to use.

A macro can be used to carry out a simple task and save a few keystrokes, such as printing a worksheet, or it can be used to help prevent typing or keystroke errors. For example, you can avoid errors by creating a macro that automatically moves the cell pointer to specified cells in a worksheet and automatically enters the date and time. Otherwise, you would have to move the cell pointer to the cells where you want to enter the date and time and then enter this information. A macro can also be designed to accomplish a series of more complex and repetitive tasks, such as preparing a weekly report that (1) lists all receivables over 30 days old, (2) sorts the list alphabetically by account, and then (3) prints three copies using compressed print — all in one macro — all automatically!

Retrieving the Worksheet

Joan has been using macros to make her work at Medi-Source more productive. For instance, she developed a print macro to simplify the printing of the Medi-Source database. Let's retrieve the database worksheet and run Joan's print macro.

To retrieve the worksheet and run the macro:

❶ Select /File Retrieve (**/FR**).

❷ Move the menu pointer to C8MEDI1.WK1 and press **[Enter]**. See Figure 8-2.

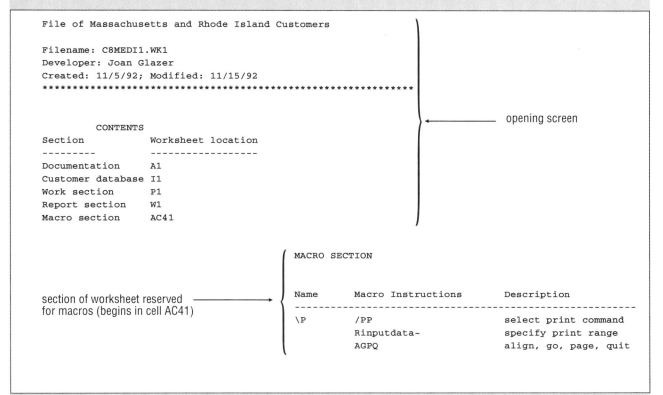

```
File of Massachusetts and Rhode Island Customers

Filename: C8MEDI1.WK1
Developer: Joan Glazer
Created: 11/5/92; Modified: 11/15/92
*************************************************************


          CONTENTS
Section          Worksheet location
---------        ------------------
Documentation    A1
Customer database I1
Work section     P1
Report section   W1
Macro section    AC41
```

opening screen

section of worksheet reserved for macros (begins in cell AC41)

```
MACRO SECTION


Name        Macro Instructions        Description
-----------------------------------------------------------
\P          /PP                       select print command
            Rinputdata~               specify print range
            AGPQ                      align, go, page, quit
```

Figure 8-2
Part of Joan's initial worksheet

Joan named her printing macro \P and saved it with this worksheet. The \P macro automates printing of the customer database.

❸ Turn on your printer and make sure it's ready to print.

❹ Press **[Alt][p]** to run the macro named \P.

To run a macro that consists of a \ (Backslash) and a single letter, you press the [Alt] key in place of the \ (Backslash) and simultaneously press the letter.

⑤ The macro automatically prints the customer database. See Figure 8-3.

CUST#	CUSTNAME	TYPE	ST	REP	BAL_OWED	YTD_SALES
1	Bristol Pharmacy	P	RI	4	2,647.10	80,278.87
2	Nepco Labs	L	MA	4	3,274.25	6,866.25
3	EMG & EEG Labs	L	MA	4	12,583.97	31,685.19
4	Oaklawn Pharmacy	P	RI	4	4,513.21	5,176.26
5	St. Josephs Hospital	H	RI	3	47,113.50	4,451.68
6	Cape Psych Center	H	MA	3	31,509.10	44,173.24
7	Bioran Medical Lab	L	MA	3	2,799.12	11,927.84
8	Bayshore Pharmacy	P	MA	3	6,010.36	44,140.87
9	St Anne's Hospital	H	MA	3	1,009.53	2,431.80
10	Landmark Medical Center	H	RI	3	22,630.79	6,494.55
11	Lypho_Med Laboratory	L	RI	2	538.62	3,279.89
12	Gregg's Pharmacy	P	MA	2	2,052.70	3,771.28
13	Bradley Hospital	H	MA	2	9,430.72	32,451.95
14	Braintree Hospital	H	MA	2	36,609.80	75,562.35
15	Miriam Hospital	H	MA	2	14,800.44	24,510.04
16	Forgary Labs	L	MA	1	2,890.08	6,670.41
17	De Bellis Pharmacy	P	RI	1	2,715.35	85,063.85
18	Woman & Infants	H	RI	1	47,915.99	3,415.04
19	Depasquale Pharmacy	P	RI	1	4,214.50	39,727.98
20	Kent Hospital	H	MA	1	1,987.44	4,120.74
21	Butler Hospital	H	RI	1	31,215.67	21,144.05
22	Foster Blood Tests	L	MA	1	2,594.27	4,275.56

Figure 8-3
Printout of the
customer database
using the print
macro

Now let's look at the section of the worksheet where the print macro, \P, is located.

To examine the \P macro:

❶ Press **[F5]** (GOTO), type **ac41**, and press **[Enter]** to move the cell pointer to the area of the worksheet where Joan plans to store the macros. See Figure 8-4. Joan has labeled cell AC41 MACRO SECTION to identify this section of the worksheet.

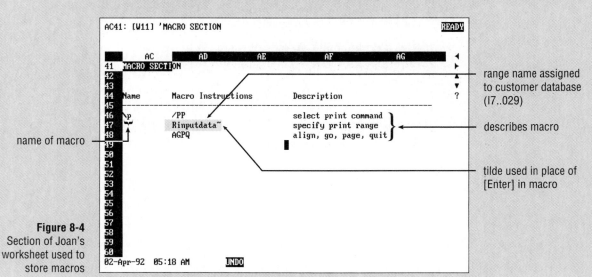

Figure 8-4
Section of Joan's
worksheet used to
store macros

name of macro →

range name assigned
to customer database
(I7..O29)

describes macro

tilde used in place of
[Enter] in macro

2 Move the cell pointer to cell AD46. Here you find the first cell of the actual macro, that is, the stored keystrokes. The complete macro is found in cells AD46, AD47, and AD48. The print macro is a series of keystrokes stored as a label. This macro contains the following stored keystrokes:

/PP	(cell AD46)	/print printer
Rinputdata~	(cell AD47)	Range INPUTDATA (I7..O29) press [Enter]
AGPQ	(cell AD48)	Align Go Page Quit

To run a macro, you must assign a range name to it. Joan has assigned the name \P to her print macro.

The keystroke [Enter] is represented in a macro by the ~ (Tilde). On many keyboards, the tilde is found in the upper left corner of the keyboard, to the left of the "1" key.

3 Move the cell pointer to cell AC46. In this cell Joan has entered the name of the print macro. By including the name of the macro next to the stored keystrokes, she can easily identify the name assigned to the macro.

4 Move the cell pointer to cell AF46, the first line of the description of the macro. The entire description is found in cells AF46, AF47, and AF48. Like cell AC46, these cells serve to document the macro.

As you have seen, the print macro automatically prints the customer database. This saves Joan some time and allows others who may be less familiar with 1-2-3 commands to print the worksheet.

Special Keys

Before you create your own macros, you need to know one more thing about them. Some keys require a special entry to represent the actual keystroke in the macro. As we've just seen, for example, the ~ (Tilde) represents the [Enter] key in Joan's print macro.

Function keys, cursor-movement keys, and other special keys are represented by the name of the key enclosed in braces. For instance, to represent pressing the [→] key in a macro, you would type {right}. To represent pressing the [Home] key, you would type {home}. To represent [F5] (GOTO), you would type {GOTO} followed by the cell address or range name of the location to which you want the cell pointer to jump, and you would type a tilde to end the macro. Figure 8-5 on the following page shows what you should enter in a macro to represent function keys, cursor-movement keys, and other special keys.

Action	Macro Entry
	Cursor-movement keys
Move cursor up one row	{UP} or {U}
Move cursor down one row	{DOWN} or {D}
Move cursor left one column	{LEFT} or {L}
Move cursor right one column	{RIGHT} or {R}
Jump to cell A1	{HOME}
Jump to intersection of first blank and non-blank cells	{END} + (arrow macro key)
Jump up 20 rows	{PGUP}
Jump down 20 rows	{PGDN}
Move left one screen	{BIGLEFT}
Move right one screen	{BIGRIGHT}
	Function keys
F2; edit current cell	{EDIT}
F3; list range names in POINT mode	{NAME}
F4; relative, absolute	{ABS}
F5; move cursor to specified cell	{GOTO}
F6; switch between windows	{WINDOW}
F7; repeat last /Data Query command	{QUERY}
F8; repeat last /Data Table command	{TABLE}
F9; recalculate the worksheet	{CALC}
F10; display current graph	{GRAPH}
	Other special keys
Press the [Enter] key	~
Press the [Esc] key	{ESC}
Press the [Backspace] key	{BS}
Press the [Delete] key	{DEL}

Figure 8-5
Special keys used
for macro
keystrokes

Creating the Macro

It takes time to plan and develop macros, but they can save you a great deal of time and effort.

The process of developing a macro involves several steps:

- planning the macro
- placing the macro
- entering the macro
- naming the macro

- documenting the macro
- saving the worksheet that includes the macro
- running and testing the macro
- debugging, or correcting any problems

Planning the Macro

One way to plan a macro is to write down on paper the keystrokes as you type them. For example, whenever Joan saves the Medi-Source worksheet, she presses the following keys:

Keystroke	Action
/	To call the Command menu
F	To select the File command
S	To select the Save command Prompt appears: "Enter name of file to save: filename"
[Enter]	1-2-3 displays the current file name and the Prompt appears: "Cancel Replace Backup"
R	To select Replace to update file

Thus, Joan writes these keystrokes on a piece of paper:

/FS[Enter]R

This is the macro Joan wants to develop.

Placing the Macro

After planning the macro, you are ready to enter it. First, however, you must decide where to place it in the worksheet. The location of a macro should be in a part of the worksheet that will not be affected by changes made in the rest of the worksheet. One recommendation for the placement of macros is in an unused section of your worksheet, below and to the right of the current worksheet entries. Thus, your macros are not stored in an area that is likely to have data copied to it nor in an area in which you might insert or delete rows (Figure 8-6).

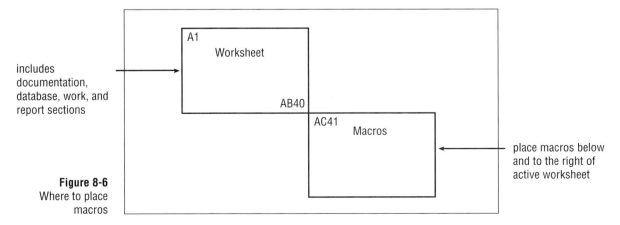

includes documentation, database, work, and report sections

place macros below and to the right of active worksheet

Figure 8-6
Where to place macros

Joan has decided to enter the macros in an area beginning at cell AC41. She has placed the label MACRO SECTION in cell AC41 to identify this area of the worksheet.

Entering the Macro

You can enter a macro in one of two ways:

- By typing the keystrokes that represent the task (macro) as a series of labels directly into the worksheet cells.
- By having 1-2-3 automatically record your keystrokes as you perform the task. You use the LEARN mode, explained later in this tutorial, to do this.

A macro is stored in a cell just like a number, a letter, or a formula. However, in most situations a macro *must* be entered as a label. Thus, you begin a macro with a label prefix, usually the ['] (Apostrophe), and enter the macro in a column of one or more cells. Although a cell can hold up to 240 keystrokes (all 240 keystrokes won't appear in the cell unless the column width is increased, but they are stored in the cell), it is easier to understand a macro if only a small number of related keystrokes are entered in a cell.

Joan has planned her macro. She knows what keystrokes she needs to enter and where to place them. She is now ready to enter the macro by typing it in cell AD50.

To enter the macro worksheet:

❶   Move the cell pointer to cell AD50, the location of the keystrokes for this macro.

❷   Type **'/FS~R** and press **[Enter]**. The keystrokes for this macro appear in cell AD50. See Figure 8-7.

first character in macro is apostrophe

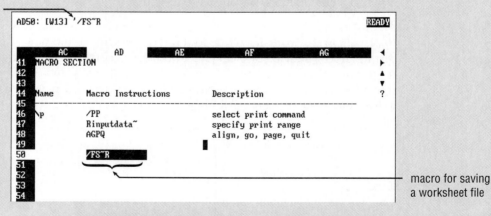

Figure 8-7
Entering the
macro

macro for saving a worksheet file

Because macros are entered as labels, the first entry for a macro is a label prefix. If you do not begin the macro with a label prefix, the 1-2-3 command menu will appear on the screen. If this happens, press [Esc] and retype the macro with an apostrophe as the first character.

If you type the macro keystrokes incorrectly, just reenter the keystrokes or use [F2] (EDIT) to modify the macro entry.

Leave a blank cell below the last macro instruction to indicate the end of the macro.

Naming the Macro

Before you execute a macro, you must assign a range name to it. You can assign two types of range names to a macro:

- A \ (Backslash) and a single letter, such as \P
- A range name consisting of up to 15 characters

With either approach, you give the macro its name by using the Range Name Create (/RNC) command.

When you name a macro, you assign the range name to only the *first* cell of the macro. This is because 1-2-3 reads down the column of macro instructions until it reaches an empty cell; thus, you need name only the first cell.

Joan used the first type of name mentioned (Backslash plus a letter) to name her print macro (\P). For the macros you create in this tutorial, you will use the second approach, a range name with up to 15 characters. Although names such as \P are somewhat simpler to use, they can also be more difficult to remember. If you have several macros in a worksheet, you might forget which letter executes a particular task. By using a more descriptive name, you will be able to remember more about what your macro does.

It is a good practice to start each macro name with a Backslash (\) so you can distinguish the range names that represent macros from other range names you use in your worksheet. Joan decides to name this macro \SAVE; she feels this name should make the macro easy to remember.

To name the save macro \SAVE:

➊ Be sure the cell pointer is in cell AD50, the first cell of the macro. Select /Range Name Create (**/RNC**).

➋ Type the range name **\save** and press **[Enter]**.

➌ Press **[Enter]** to indicate you want to assign the name \SAVE to cell AD50.

Remember that you do not need to assign every cell in the macro to the range name. 1-2-3 will automatically move to the next cell below the current cell in the macro until it finds a blank cell, which indicates the end of the macro.

/Range Name Labels Right   You could also use an alternative method to assign range names to macros. With this method you use the /Range Name Labels Right command to assign the name to the macro. To use this method you would place the cell pointer on the cell immediately to the left of the macro instruction. This is the cell where you'd find the documentation of the macro name. Next you'd use the /Range Name Labels Right (/RNLR) command to assign the range containing the macro names to the cells to the right of this range. The advantage of this method is that it ensures that you include the name of the macro next to the macro instruction for easy identification.

Documenting the Macro

Whenever you create a macro, a good habit is to include a label containing the macro's name in a cell to the *left* of the macro so you can easily see the name when you examine the macro. It is also a good idea to enter a short description of the macro's function to the *right* of the macro. In that way, you can see at a glance what the macro does. Documenting a macro is not required to make it work, but it is a good habit to develop because some macros can be quite complex and difficult to read. Good macro documentation will save you time and help you avoid confusion.

To document Joan's \SAVE macro:

❶   Move the cell pointer to cell AC50 and type the label **' \save**. Press **[Enter]**.

❷   Move the cell pointer to cell AF50 and type **save and replace a worksheet file**, then press **[Enter]**. See Figure 8-8.

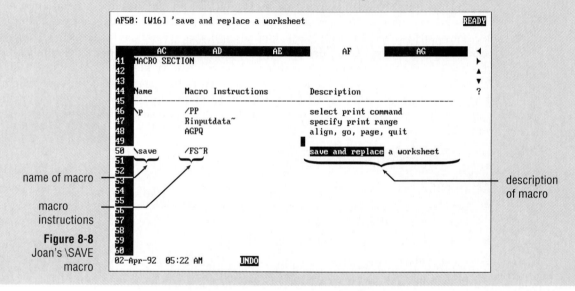

name of macro

macro instructions

Figure 8-8
Joan's \SAVE
macro

description of macro

Running and Testing the Macro

Once you have entered and named your macro, you can run it. How you issue the command to run a macro depends on the type of name you assigned to the macro.

• If you named the macro with a backslash and a letter, you press the [Alt] key while pressing the letter of the macro name. You used this approach to run the print macro.

• If you named the macro with a range name of up to 15 characters, you use [Alt][F3] (RUN) and select the name of the macro you want to execute from a list of names that appears on the control panel.

When you run a macro, 1-2-3 reads the macro keystrokes starting with the first cell of the macro. When all the keystrokes in the first cell have been run, 1-2-3 continues reading down the column of cells, executing all keystrokes in each cell. It continues this process until it encounters an empty cell, which 1-2-3 interprets as the end of the macro.

As a general rule, you should save your worksheet prior to running your macro for the first time. This is a good habit to develop because *running a macro with an error could damage the data in a worksheet.*

Now let's save the current version of the worksheet before you test the macro you just entered.

To save your worksheet as S8MEDI1:

❶ Press **[Home]** and then move the cell pointer to cell A3.

❷ Change the filename in cell A3 from C8MEDI1.WK1 to S8MEDI1.WK1.

❸ Select /File Save (**/FS**).

❹ Type **s8medi1** and press **[Enter]**. The worksheet is saved.

Now you can test the macro to see if it is working correctly.

To run the \SAVE macro :

❶ Press **[Alt][F3]** (RUN) and then press **[F3]** (NAME). See Figure 8-9. A list of range names appears on your screen.

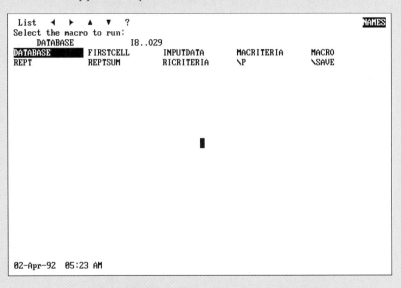

Figure 8-9
List of range
names, including
macros

❷ Make sure the menu pointer highlights the \SAVE macro.

❸ Press **[Enter]** to run the macro.

The macro runs and saves the current worksheet.

Interrupting a Macro

If you need to interrupt a macro during execution, press [Ctrl][Break]. 1-2-3 returns you immediately to READY mode. If the ERROR mode indicator flashes in the upper right corner of your screen when you press [Ctrl][Break], press [Esc]. This clears the error and returns you to READY mode.

Editing a Macro

Don't be surprised if your macro doesn't work the first time you execute it. When you typed the macro, you may have forgotten a tilde, included spaces, or entered the wrong command. The process of eliminating such errors is called **debugging**. If an error message appears when you run a macro, press [Esc] to return to READY mode. Then correct the macro by moving the cell pointer to the cell that contains the macro and do one of the following:

- Type over the current macro.
- Edit the cell of the macro that contains the error by pressing [F2] (EDIT) and changing the necessary keystrokes.

Creating Interactive Macros

Joan also planned to create a macro to create range names, because she frequently assigns range names to use with macros as well as for other 1-2-3 functions. She writes down the keystrokes required for assigning a range name to a range of cells:

Keystroke	Action
/	To call the command menu
R	To select the Range command
N	To select the Name command
C	To select the Create command Prompt appears: "Enter name"
Type range name	
[Enter]	1-2-3 prompts for range
Highlight range	
[Enter]	Indicates end of Range Name command

In looking over her notes, Joan realizes that the macro must pause to allow her to type the range name and the cells that represent the range. You can create macros that prompt you to enter data, enter a range name, or select a 1-2-3 command, and then the macro continues to run. A macro that pauses during its run is called an **interactive macro**.

To create an interactive macro, you use the Pause command, which is represented by {?}. You can enter {?} anywhere in your macro instruction. When 1-2-3 reads the {?} command, it temporarily stops the macro from running so you can manually enter a range name, move the cell or menu pointer, complete part of a command, or enter data for the macro to process. The macro continues processing when you press [Enter].

When you use {?} in a macro, you must complete the cell entry with a ~ (Tilde). This instructs 1-2-3 to accept your input.

Joan writes down the keystrokes required for the range name macro:

/RNC{?}~{?}~

This interactive macro selects /Range Name Create. At the first {?} command, the macro pauses so you can specify the name of the range. When you press [Enter], the macro continues to run. The macro encounters another {?} command and pauses again. This time you highlight the range of cells included in the range name. Press [Enter] again, to indicate that you want to end the pause. 1-2-3 then encounters the tilde and executes [Enter] to store the range. The macro is then complete.

To enter an interactive macro:

❶ Move the cell pointer to the macro area, cell AD52, the location where you will enter the interactive macro.

❷ To enter the macro, type **'/RNC{?}~{?}~** and press **[Enter]**. See Figure 8-10.

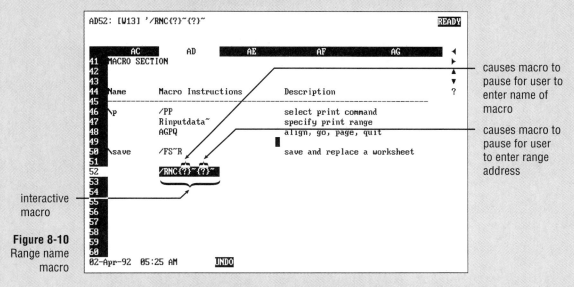

Figure 8-10
Range name macro

Now name the macro \NAME. You will select the Range Name Create command instead of using the \NAME macro, because you are still in the process of creating the \NAME macro.

❸ With the cell pointer at cell AD52, select /Range Name Create (**/RNC**). Type **\name** and press **[Enter]**.

❹ Press **[Enter]** to assign the range name to cell AD52.

Let's document the macro with a name and a description of what it does.

❺ Move the cell pointer to cell AC52, type **'\name**, and press **[Enter]**.

⑥ Move the cell pointer to cell AF52, type **assigns range name** and press **[Enter]**. See Figure 8-11.

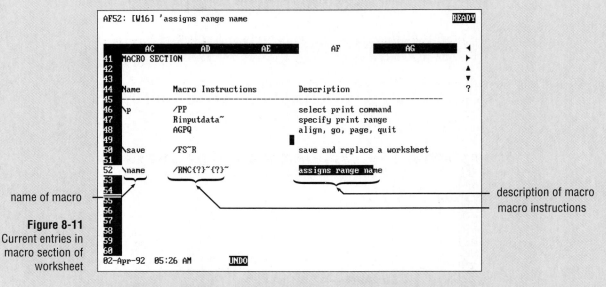

name of macro

Figure 8-11
Current entries in
macro section of
worksheet

description of macro

macro instructions

The \NAME macro is now complete.

Let's determine if the macro works properly. Again you need to save the current version of the worksheet before you run the new macro for the first time. Use the \SAVE macro you created earlier in the tutorial to save your worksheet.

To save your worksheet using the \SAVE macro:
❶ Press **[Alt][F3]** (RUN) and then press **[F3]** (NAME). Highlight \SAVE from the list of range names listed on the screen. Press **[Enter]**. The current version of the worksheet has been saved.

You are now ready to test the \NAME macro. Let's do something that will save us time as we work through this tutorial. Since this is a tutorial on macros, we'll be going to the macro area frequently. Let's assign the name MACROS to cell AC41, so you can use this name with the GOTO key [F5] to move directly to the macro area from any point in the worksheet.

To run the \NAME macro:
❶ Move the cell pointer to cell AC41.
❷ Press **[Alt][F3]** (RUN) and then press **[F3]** (NAME). Highlight \NAME from the list of range names listed on the screen. Press **[Enter]**. See Figure 8-12.

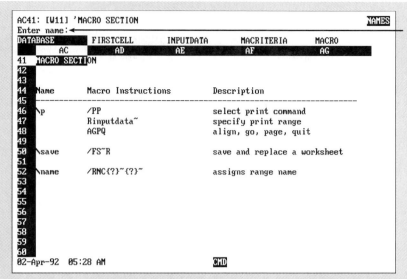

```
AC41: [W11] 'MACRO SECTION                                      NAMES
Enter name: ◄───────────────────────────────────────────────────────
DATABASE         FIRSTCELL      INPUTDATA     MACRITERIA     MACRO
      AC             AD            AE             AF           AG
41 MACRO SECTION
42
43
44 Name          Macro Instructions          Description
45 ─────────────────────────────────────────────────────────────
46 \p            /PP                          select print command
47               Rinputdata~                  specify print range
48               AGPQ                         align, go, page, quit
49
50 \save         /FS~R                        save and replace a worksheet
51
52 \name         /RNC{?}~{?}~                 assigns range name
53
54
55
56
57
58
59
60
02-Apr-92  05:28 AM                   CMD
```

macro pauses
and waits for
you to enter
name of range

Figure 8-12
Running the
\NAME macro

The macro begins to run. When 1-2-3 encounters the first {?}, the macro stops running, and the prompt "Enter name" appears in the control panel.

Notice that the status indicator CMD appears at the bottom of the screen whenever a macro is interrupted.

Now specify the range name.

❸ Type **macros**. Press **[Enter]**.

The macro pauses, waiting for you to highlight the range of cells for the range name.

❹ Press **[Enter]** since the range of the macro is a single cell, AC41.

The macro continues to run until 1-2-3 encounters a blank cell, at which point it stops.

Let's verify that the \NAME macro worked properly.

To test the \NAME macro:

❶ Press **[Home]** to move the cell pointer to cell A1.

❷ Press **[F5]** (GOTO), type **macros**, and press **[Enter]**.

The cell pointer should now be at cell AC41.

LEARN Mode

Joan wants to create a macro that she can use to print a second report — the Outstanding Balance by State report.

As we mentioned earlier, Joan could type this macro directly into worksheet cells or she could use 1-2-3's LEARN mode. In LEARN mode 1-2-3 automatically records the keystrokes as it performs a sequence of 1-2-3 operations. The keystrokes are captured in a separate area of the worksheet called the **learn range**. Joan can then name the learn range and execute it as a macro whenever she chooses.

Let's use LEARN mode to create Joan's macro to print the Outstanding Balance by State report. When you use LEARN mode to create a macro, you must follow these steps:

- Decide where in the worksheet you want to put the learn range. The learn range must be a single column, long enough to contain all the keystrokes of the macro.
- Specify the learn range, using the Worksheet Learn Range command.
- Turn on LEARN mode to start recording all keystrokes.
- Perform the task you want 1-2-3 to record.
- Turn off LEARN mode to stop recording keystrokes.
- Assign a range name to the first cell in the learn range.
- Save the file.
- Run the macro.

Now let's follow these steps and use LEARN mode to create a macro that will print the Outstanding Balance by State report.

First, Joan decides to place the learn range in cells AD54 to AD58.

To specify the learn range and record the macro:

❶ Move the cell pointer to cell AD54 and select /Worksheet Learn Range (**/WLR**).

❷ Press **[.]** to anchor the cell pointer. Highlight the range AD54..AD58 and press **[Enter]**. The learn range is now defined.

Follow the next steps carefully, because once you turn on LEARN mode, every keystroke you make will be recorded. For example, if you press [Backspace] several times to correct typing errors, 1-2-3 will record the [Backspace] keystrokes.

Now turn on LEARN mode.

❸ Press **[Alt][F5]** (LEARN) to turn on LEARN mode. Notice that the status indicator LEARN appears at the bottom of your screen. See Figure 8-13.

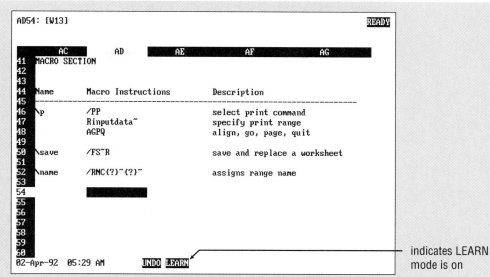

Figure 8-13
Creating a macro
using LEARN
mode

indicates LEARN
mode is on

The next step is to perform the tasks you want to record.

❹ Check to be sure that your printer is on, then select /Print Printer (**/PP**).

❺ Select Range (**R**), type **reptsum**, and press **[Enter]**.

❻ Select Align Go Page Quit (**AGPQ**).

The Outstanding Balance Report begins to print.

Now you should turn off LEARN mode to stop recording the keystrokes.

❼ Press **[Alt][F5]** (LEARN) to turn off LEARN mode. Notice that the status indicator
LEARN no longer appears on the screen. Instead, the CALC indicator appears. If
you don't turn off LEARN mode, 1-2-3 will continue to record your keystrokes and
place them in the macro area.

⑧ Press **[Enter]** so the recorded keystrokes appear in the learn range. The CALC indicator disappears. With the cell pointer in cell AD54, the first cell in the learn range, view the keystrokes that 1-2-3 has recorded. See Figure 8-14.

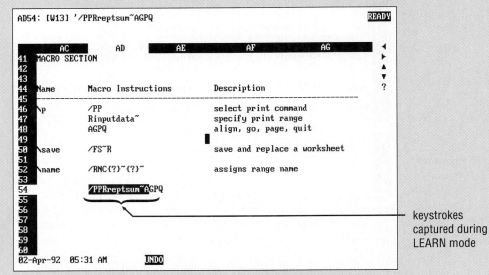

Figure 8-14
Macro created
using LEARN
mode

keystrokes
captured during
LEARN mode

If the macro looks correct, the next step is to specify a range name for it. On the other hand, if the macro needs corrections, you can edit it as you would any other cell.

Let's name the macro \PRINTREPT using the \NAME macro.

To name and document the macro:

① With the cell pointer in cell AD54, press **[Alt][F3]** (RUN) and then press **[F3]** (NAME). Highlight \NAME from the list of range names on the screen. Press **[Enter]**.

② Type **\printrept** and press **[Enter]** to enter the range name.

③ Press **[Enter]** to assign the range name to the first cell of the learn range.

Now let's document the macro.

④ Move the cell pointer to cell AC54. Type **' \printrept**, then press **[Enter]**. Move the cell pointer to cell AF54. Type **prints summary report** and press **[Enter]**. See Figure 8-15.

If you now wanted to create another macro using LEARN mode, you would have to reset the learn range to another range of cells (/Worksheet Learn Range); otherwise, the new macro would be added to the end of the existing macro.

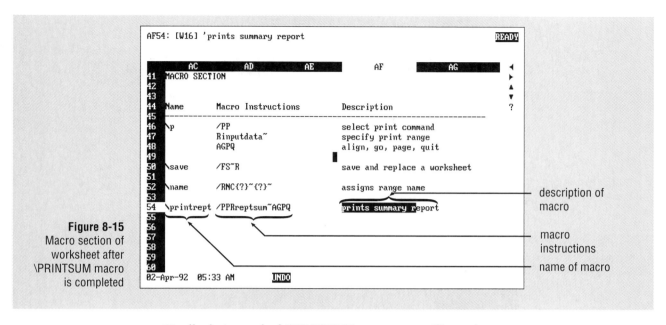

Figure 8-15
Macro section of
worksheet after
\PRINTSUM macro
is completed

Finally, let's run the \PRINTREPT macro to see if it works.

To run the macro:
1. Make sure your printer is on.
2. Press **[Alt][F3]** (RUN) and then press **[F3]** (NAME). Highlight \PRINTREPT from the list of range names on the control panel. Press **[Enter]**.

   The Outstanding Balance by State report is printed.
3. Save your worksheet as S8MEDI1 using the \SAVE macro.

Using STEP Mode to Debug a Macro

The first time you run a macro, it may not work as you intended. In a simple macro, you can easily identify errors by comparing the keystrokes in the worksheet with the keystroke entries you planned. In large macros, however, it is more difficult to identify errors, so Lotus 1-2-3 has a special feature to help you in debugging macros. This feature, called **STEP mode**, allows you to run a macro one keystroke at a time.

To demonstrate the use of STEP mode, let's run the \SAVE macro in STEP mode. First, we'll modify the \SAVE macro so it is intentionally incorrect; then we'll see how STEP mode can help us find the error.

To modify the \SAVE macro and intentionally enter an error:
1. Move the cell pointer to cell AD50, the location of the \SAVE macro.

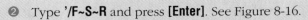 Type **'/F~S~R** and press **[Enter]**. See Figure 8-16.

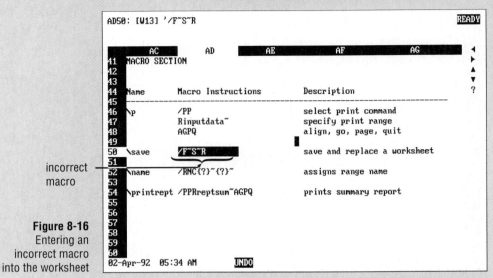

incorrect macro

Figure 8-16
Entering an
incorrect macro
into the worksheet

Notice that a ~ (Tilde) appears between the F and the S. The correct macro is
'/FS~R.

Let's try to use this modified \SAVE macro.

To run the incorrect \SAVE macro:

❶ Press **[Alt][F3]** (RUN) and then press **[F3]** (NAME). Highlight \SAVE from the list of
range names on the screen. Press **[Enter]**. See Figure 8-17.

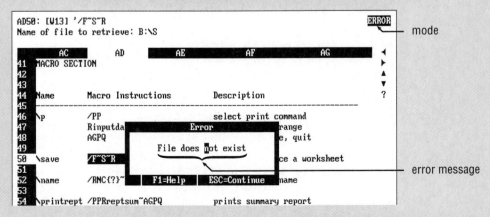

mode

Figure 8-17
Attempting to run
incorrect \SAVE
macro

error message

Notice that the mode indicator in the upper right corner has changed to ERROR
and is blinking. This indicates something is wrong with your macro. In addition,
the message appearing in the middle of your screen says that the "File does not
exist."

❷ Press **[Esc]** to clear the error condition and return to READY mode.

What happened? Why did the macro stop running? If the reason is not obvious to you from looking at the macro keystrokes, you can use STEP mode to help debug the macro.

To use STEP mode:

❶ Press **[Alt][F2]** (STEP). This turns on STEP mode. See Figure 8-18. Notice that the STEP indicator appears in the status line at the bottom of the screen.

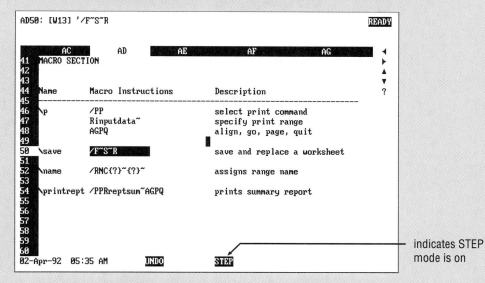

Figure 8-18
Turning on STEP mode

To run a macro in STEP mode, you press any key to run the macro one keystroke at a time. That way, you can see each step the macro takes and perhaps determine the problem with the macro.

Now let's rerun the macro.

❷   Press **[Alt][F3]** (RUN) and then press **[F3]** (NAME). Highlight \SAVE from the list of range names on the screen. Press **[Enter]**. See Figure 8-19.

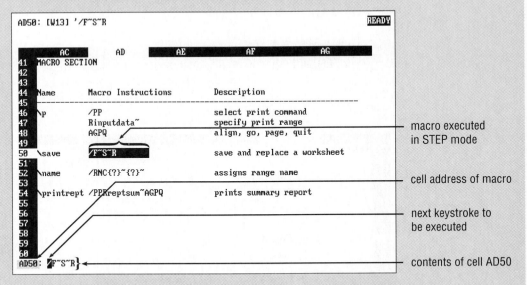

Figure 8-19
Macro appears in
status line

The cell address that contains the macro appears on the status line, along with the contents of that cell. The keystroke to be executed the next time you press a key is highlighted.

❸   Press **[Spacebar]**. This executes the first keystroke of the macro, the / (Slash). See Figure 8-20.

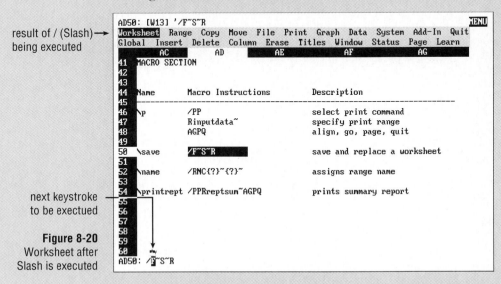

Figure 8-20
Worksheet after
Slash is executed

Notice that the Command menu appears in the control panel. In addition, in the status line, the keystroke that will be executed next, F, is highlighted.

❹   Press **[Spacebar]** once more to execute the next keystroke in the macro. See Figure 8-21.

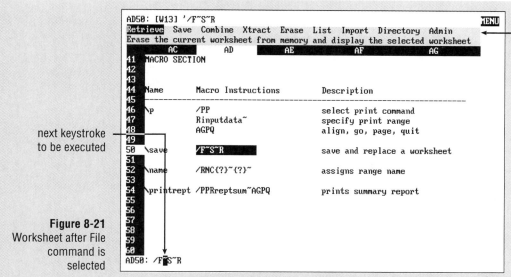

next keystroke
to be executed

result of File
command being
executed

Figure 8-21
Worksheet after File
command is
selected

The File command from the Command menu is selected, and the File command
options appear on the control panel. The Retrieve command is highlighted. Also
notice that the ~ (Tilde) in the status line is highlighted. It is the next keystroke to
be executed.

⑤ Press **[Spacebar]** once again. This runs the ~, that is, the [Enter] keystroke. See
Figure 8-22. Since the Retrieve command was highlighted in the control panel,
pressing [Enter] executes Retrieve rather than Save. The prompt "Name of the file to
retrieve" appears in the control panel. Notice that the next keystroke to be executed, S,
is highlighted in the status line.

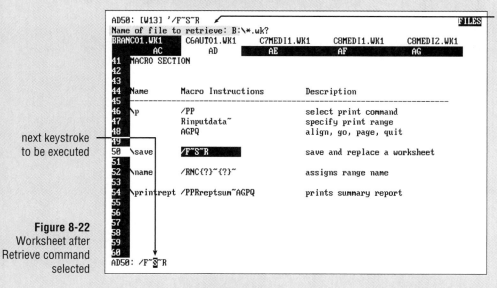

next keystroke
to be executed

Retrieve command
executed as a result
of an erroneous ~
(Tilde)

Figure 8-22
Worksheet after
Retrieve command
selected

⑥ Press **[Spacebar]** again. S is entered as the name of the file to retrieve. See Figure 8-23.

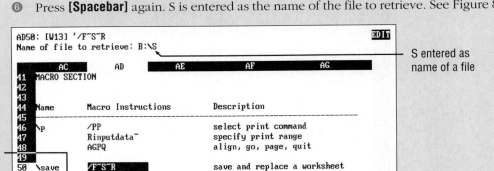

S entered as name of a file

next keystroke to be executed

Figure 8-23
S entered as name of worksheet to retrieve

The status line indicates the ~ (Tilde) will be the next keystroke to be executed.

⑦ Press **[Spacebar]**. 1-2-3 interprets the ~ as the [Enter] keystroke and attempts to retrieve a file named S. See Figure 8-24.

1-2-3 trying to retrieve file S.WK1

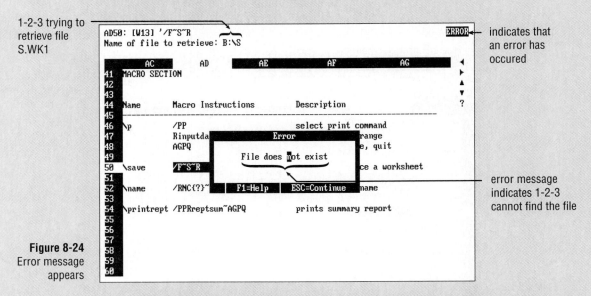

indicates that an error has occured

error message indicates 1-2-3 cannot find the file

Figure 8-24
Error message appears

1-2-3 doesn't find the file S.WK1 on your data diskette. The ERROR indicator appears in the upper right corner of your screen, and the error message "File does not exist" appears in the middle of the screen.

⑧ Press **[Esc]** to clear the error message and return to READY mode.

Once your worksheet is in READY mode, you can edit the macro.

⑨ Be sure the cell pointer is in cell AD50. Type **'/FS~R** and press **[Enter]** to correct the macro.

You are still in STEP mode, which means if you attempt to run another macro, 1-2-3 will continue to run the macro one keystroke at a time.

⑩ Press **[Alt][F2]** (STEP). This turns off STEP mode. Now the macros will run normally. The status indicator STEP disappears from the status line.

The Final Worksheet

As a final step in preparing the worksheet for her staff, Joan decides to create a section of the worksheet that will describe the various options of the worksheet. This section will also provide instructions that walk a user through the various steps to run these options. Figure 8-25 shows Joan's sketch of the instruction sections she plans to enter into her worksheet.

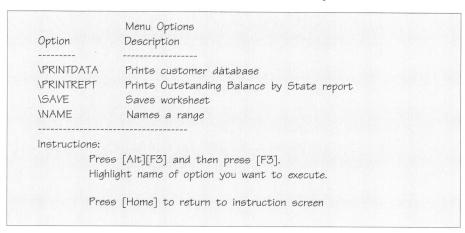

Figure 8-25
Joan's sketch of the instruction section

To retrieve Joan's revised worksheet:

❶ Select /File Retrieve (**/FR**).

❷ Highlight C8MEDI2 and press **[Enter]**. See Figure 8-26 on the following page. The instruction screen appears immediately upon retrieval of the worksheet. This way, the first thing a user sees when retrieving the worksheet will be instructions on how to use the worksheet.

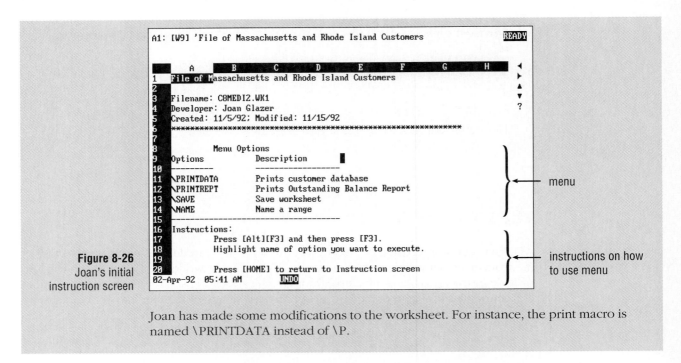

Figure 8-26
Joan's initial
instruction screen

Joan has made some modifications to the worksheet. For instance, the print macro is named \PRINTDATA instead of \P.

Let's try out the revised worksheet.

To print the customer database:

❶ Press **[Alt][F3]** (RUN) and then press **[F3]** (NAME). Highlight \PRINTDATA and press **[Enter]**. The customer database is printed.

Joan is satisfied with the worksheet and is ready to show it to her staff.

■   ■   ■

Exercises

1. What keystrokes are used to do the following?
    a. run a macro
    b. turn STEP mode on and off
    c. turn LEARN mode on and off

2. What do you use in a macro to represent the following?
    a. pressing the [Enter] key
    b. a pause in the running of a macro
    c. pressing [F5] (GOTO) key
    d. the [Up] key

3. What do the following macros do?
    a. {GOTO}macros~ (*Note:* MACROS is a range name.)
    b. /RFF{?}~{?}~
    c. /RFC2~{END}{DOWN}~
    d. /C~{DOWN}~
    e. /PPOOCQQ

Tutorial Assignments

Before you begin these Tutorial Assignments, check your data diskette. Be sure you have space to save the additional worksheet files you'll create in these assignments (at least 30,000 bytes). If you do not have enough space, save your files for Tutorial 8 to another formatted diskette.

Retrieve the worksheet T8MEDI1.WK1. This worksheet contains the four macros created in this tutorial. Make the following additions or modifications to the macro area.

1. First, save this worksheet as S8MEDI2.

2. Modify the \SAVE macro so the cell pointer moves to cell A1 before the worksheet is saved. Save the worksheet using the revised \SAVE macro. What is the purpose of moving the cell pointer to cell A1 before saving the worksheet?

3. Create a macro as follows:
    a. Use the typing method to create a macro to set print settings to compressed print. This macro will set the right margin to 132 and the setup string to the code for compressed print used by your printer. For many printers, the setup string for compressed print is \015.
    b. Name this macro \COMPRESS.
    c. Document the macro.
    d. Save the worksheet as S8MEDI2.
    e. Run the \COMPRESS macro.
    f. Print the customer database using the \PRINTDATA macro.

4. Create a macro as follows:
    a. Use the typing method to create a macro that sets the print settings to normal print. This macro will set the right margin to 76 and the setup string to the code for normal print used by your printer. For many printers, the setup string for normal print is \018.
    b. Name this macro \NORM.
    c. Document the macro.
    d. Save the worksheet as S8MEDI2.
    e. Run the \NORM macro and then run the \PRINTDATA macro.

5. Create an interactive macro to sort the customer database. This macro should include the following steps:
    - Move the cell pointer to the first field name in the customer database. (The range name is FIRSTCELL.)
    - Select the Data Sort command.
    - Reset the sort settings.
    - Select the Data-Range option and assign the range name DATABASE as the data range.
    - Select the Primary-Key option.

- Allow the user to select the primary key. (This step is interactive.)
- Allow the user to type *a* or *d* for sort order. (This step is interactive.)
- Select the Go option to sort the database.

    a.   Use the typing method to enter the sort macro.
    b.   Name this macro \SORT.
    c.   Document this macro.
    d.   Save your worksheet as S8MEDI3.
    e.   Run the \SORT macro and sort the customer database in descending order by balance owed.
    f.   Run the \PRINTDATA macro to print the customer database.

6. Create a macro as follows:
    a.   Use LEARN mode to develop a macro to format a range of cells using Currency format with zero decimal places. Move the cell pointer to the column you want to format before you execute the macro.
    b.   Name this macro \CURRENCY0.
    c.   Document the macro.
    d.   Save the worksheet as S8MEDI3.
    e.   Format the YTD_SALES column (O8..O29) using this macro.

7. Suppose that you want to view widely separated parts of your worksheet at the same time. You can use the Worksheet Windows command to accomplish this. Use LEARN mode to create the following macros. Remember to reset the learn range after creating each macro.
    a.   Develop a macro to set up a horizontal window. Name this macro \WINDOWH. Document this macro.
    b.   Develop a macro to set up a vertical window in your worksheet. Name this macro \WINDOWV. Document this macro.
    c.   Develop a macro to clear the window settings. Name this macro \WINDOWC. Document this macro.
    d.   Save your worksheet as S8MEDI3.

8. Print the macro section of your worksheet.

Retrieve the worksheet file T8MEDI2. This worksheet has two new macros in addition to the four that were originally in the T8MEDI1 worksheet.

9. The first new macro, \COLWIDTH, located in cell AD58, is supposed to change the column width. It doesn't work properly.
    a.   Run the macro.
    b.   Correct the macro.
    c.   Save your worksheet as S8MEDI4.
    d.   Run the corrected macro to increase the column width in column J from 25 to 28 characters.

10. The second macro, \DELRANGE, located in cell AD60, is supposed to allow you to select a range name to delete. When it runs, an error occurs.
    a.   Run the macro.
    b.   Correct the macro so it deletes any existing range name.
    c.   Save your worksheet as S8MEDI4.
    d.   Run the corrected macro and delete the range name \p.

e.   Use the \NAME macro in the worksheet to assign the macro in cell AD48 the name
     \PRINTDATA.
f.   Make the appropriate changes to the macro documentation.
g.   Print the worksheet using the macro \PRINTDATA.
h.   Save the worksheet as S8MEDI4.

Case Problems

1. Reporting on Word Processing Software

A marketing research firm has compiled data on the number of units the top six word
processing software packages have shipped worldwide during 1989 (Figure 8-27).

Product	Units Shipped
WordPerfect	1,400,000
Microsoft Word	500,000
WordStar	345,000
Display Write	300,000
Professional Write	250,000
Multimate	200,000

Figure 8-27

1.   Create a worksheet using the data from Figure 8-27.

2.   Prepare a report that includes all the products and has the format shown in Figure 8-28.

	Add title	
Product	Units shipped	Market share
XXXXXXXXXXX	XXXXX	XX.X%
XXXXXXXXXXX	XXXXX	XX.X%
.	.	.
.	.	.
.	.	.
Total Units	XXXXX	

Figure 8-28

3.   Create a pie chart of shipments by product. Name the graph PIE_SHIP.

4.   Create a bar graph of shipments by product. Name the graph BAR_SHIP.

5. Create a macro to print the report. Name the macro \PRINT.

6. Create a macro to view the pie chart. Name the macro \PIEWP.

7. Create a macro to view the bar graph. Name the macro \BARWP.

8. Include in your worksheet an instruction section that will help anyone who uses the macros in this worksheet. This section should be the first screen that appears when a user retrieves the worksheet.

9. Save your worksheet as S8WORD.

10. Use the macro \PRINT to print the report in Assignment 2.

11. Print the macro section of your worksheet.

WYSIWYG Assignments

1. Attach WYSIWYG.

2. Add the following enhancements:
   a. Replace any dashed lines with solid lines under column headings and above and below totals.
   b. Use a 14-point Swiss font for the report title line(s) and enclose the title in a drop shadow.
   c. Boldface the total row.
   d. Insert the pie chart into the worksheet beneath the report.
   e. Create a macro to print the report and the graph on one page using the WYSIWYG print command. Name this macro \WYSIPRT.

3. Save your worksheet as W8WORD.

4. Print the entire worksheet on one page using the macro \WYSIPRT.

2. Tutorial 3 Revisited

Retrieve the worksheet P8BALBO1, the final version of the Balboa Mutual Fund worksheet from Tutorial 3, and do the following:

1. Modify the worksheet so that the first screen includes the information in Figure 8-29.

Macro Name	Description
\ERASE	Erase a column
\PRINT	Print fund report
\SAVE	Save the worksheet
[*Place instructions on how to run a macro here.*]	

Figure 8-29

2. Create a macro to erase the prices from the Current Prices column. You should be able to select (highlight) the range of cells to erase. Name the macro \ERASE.

3. Create a macro to print the Mutual Fund report. Name the macro \PRINT.

4. Create a macro to save the worksheet. You should be able to name the worksheet that you are saving. Name the macro \SAVE.

5. Save your file as S8BALBO1 using your save macro.

6. Enter the current prices for November 6, 199X, which were as follows:

IBM	92
Coca-Cola	68.50
Texaco	59
Boeing	49

   First, use your macro to erase the Current Price column. Then enter the new prices. Remember also to change the date.

7. Print the Net Asset Value report for November 6, 199X, using your print macro.

8. Print the macro section of your worksheet.

9. Save your file as S8BALBO2.

WYSIWYG Assignments

1. Attach WYSIWYG.

2. Add the following enhancements:
   a. Replace any dashed lines with solid lines under column headings and above and below totals.
   b. Use a 14-point Swiss font for the report title line(s) and enclose the title in a drop shadow.
   c. Boldface the total row.
   d. Shade the NAV and the number of shares components of this report.
   e. Create a macro to print the NAV report using the WYSIWYG print command. Name this macro \WYSIPRT. Include this macro name in your opening screen.

3. Save your worksheet as W8BALBO1.

4. Print the NAV report using the macro \WYSIPRT.

3. Tutorial 6 Revisited

Retrieve the worksheet P8AUTO1, the final version of the Automobile Industry Sales worksheet from Tutorial 6, and do the following:

1. Modify the worksheet so the that first screen includes the information in Figure 8-30.

Macro Name	Description
\BAR	View standard bar graph
\BAR3D	View 3D bar graph
\PIE	View pie chart
\PRINT	Print worksheet data
[Place instructions on how to run a macro here.]	

Figure 8-30

2. Create a macro to view the bar graph BAR3. Name the macro \BAR.

3. Create a macro to view the 3D bar graph BAR6. Name the macro \BAR3D.

4. Create a macro to view the pie chart PIE90. Name the macro \PIE.

5. Create a macro to print the automobile data. Name the macro \PRINT.

6. Save your worksheet as S8AUTO1.

7. Test all your macros.

8. Print the macro section of your worksheet.

WYSIWYG Assignments

1. Attach WYSIWYG.

2. Add the following enhancements:
    a. Insert the pie chart into the worksheet beneath the worksheet data.
    b. Create a macro to print the report and the graph on one page. Name this macro \WYSIPRT.

3. Save your worksheet as W8AUTO1.

4. Print the entire worksheet on one page using the macro \WYSIPRT.

Lotus 1-2-3
Modules

■   ■   ■

- **Module 1** Dialog Boxes

- **Module 2** Using WYSIWYG to Enhance and Print 1-2-3 Worksheets

- **Module 3** Using WYSIWYG to Enhance and Print Graphs

- **Module 4** Using SmartIcons

Module 1

Dialog Boxes

OBJECTIVES

In this tutorial you will learn to:

■ Use dialog box terminology

■ Use a dialog box with a keyboard

Components of a Dialog Box

A **dialog box** is a box in 1-2-3 that contains information about the current settings associated with a particular task. For example, whenever you print in 1-2-3 a Print Settings dialog box appears. You can change the print settings in this dialog box using either a keyboard or a mouse, or you can use the menu that appears above the dialog box to select commands to specify the settings.

If you interact directly with a dialog box (instead of selecting commands from the menu), you select settings by using different objects: option buttons, check boxes, text boxes, command buttons, pop-up dialog boxes, and list boxes. Let's review each of these objects.

Option buttons offer you a set of options, but you can select only one option at a time. You can identify the option buttons in a dialog box by looking for pairs of parentheses ( ). The option that is currently selected is marked by an asterisk in the parentheses. The unselected options have no asterisks in the parentheses. For example, the Graph Settings dialog box in Figure 1-1 on the following page illustrates option buttons and other dialog box features. The section of the dialog box marked Type has seven option buttons. The current selection, the line graph, is marked by an asterisk.

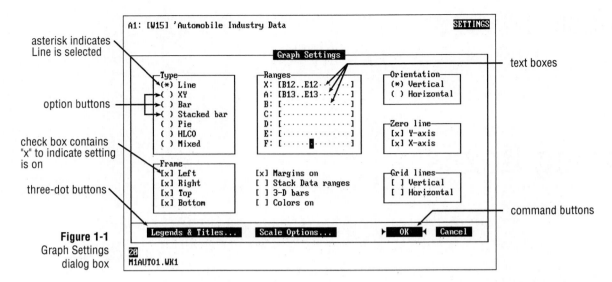

asterisk indicates
Line is selected

option buttons

check box contains
"x" to indicate setting
is on

three-dot buttons

text boxes

command buttons

Figure 1-1
Graph Settings
dialog box

Check boxes are used for settings that can be on or off. A check box appears as brackets [ ]. If an *x* appears in the box, the setting is on. Unlike option buttons, more than one check box in a group can be selected at the same time. For example, as Figure 1-1 illustrates, all the settings that comprise the Frame of the graph are *on*. That means lines will appear on all sides of the graph.

Text boxes are boxes in a dialog box that enclose text in brackets; they are preceded by a descriptive label and a colon. The area within the brackets is where you enter or edit range names, numbers, cell addresses, or text. In Figure 1-1 the section of the dialog box marked Ranges contains several text boxes. When you select any text box in this section of the dialog box, you type in your settings.

Command buttons in dialog boxes are most often labeled OK or Cancel. When you have finished making your choices, you choose OK to accept the settings that currently appear in the dialog box. You choose Cancel if you want 1-2-3 to ignore the settings in the dialog box and continue to use the previous settings. Besides illustrating the OK and Cancel command buttons, Figure 1-1 illustrates an example of another command button that appears in the Graph Settings dialog box. The **three-dot buttons** are command buttons that contain ellipses (...) following the label. These buttons refer you to other dialog boxes that contain related settings. Figure 1-1 illustrates two three-dot command buttons: Legends & Titles and Scale Options, each of which is followed by ellipses.

Some tasks can't fit all their options in one dialog box. In those cases a **pop-up dialog box** appears over the initial dialog box when you select a particular option. A pop-up dialog box leads to further choices that do not appear in the initial dialog box.

List boxes display a list of available choices from which you can choose. If a list is too long to fit on one screen, you can scroll through the list.

Using Dialog Boxes

Before you can use a dialog box, you must activate it by pressing [F2] (EDIT) or by clicking anywhere inside the dialog box with a mouse.

Once a dialog box has been activated, you can select options by using the arrow keys and pressing [Spacebar] or [Enter], by typing the highlighted character of the option you want, or by clicking with the left mouse button.

Selecting Dialog Box Options Using the Keyboard

The Graph command illustrates a variety of settings you can change using the dialog box. You use the Graph command to create a graph. With this command you specify the data you want to graph and how you want to graph them.

The worksheet file M1AUTO1.WK1 contains a line graph of Chrysler's sales from 1987 to 1990. Let's retrieve this worksheet and try using the Graph Settings dialog box to change the line graph to a bar graph.

To retrieve a worksheet:

① Retrieve the worksheet file M1AUTO1.WK1. Select /File Retrieve (**/FR**).

② Highlight the file M1AUTO1.WK1 and press **[Enter]**.

The worksheet contains the settings for a line graph of sales of Chrysler automobiles.

③ Press **[F10]**. A line graph appears. Press any key to continue.

Let's change the current graph to a bar graph.

④ Select /Graph (**/G**). See Figure 1-2.

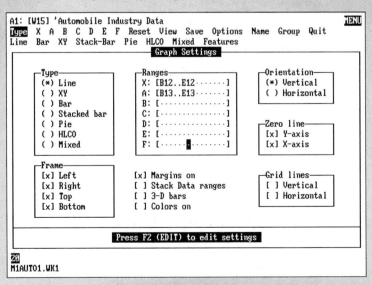

Figure 1-2
Graph Settings
dialog box

In addition to the Graph menu, the Graph Settings dialog box appears. Let's use the dialog box to change the line graph to a bar graph.

When the dialog box first appears on the screen, it is not active. Thus, you cannot make changes to the graph settings using the dialog box. To use the dialog box, you must activate it. Let's do that now.

To activate the dialog box:

❶ Press **[F2]** (EDIT). See Figure 1-3.

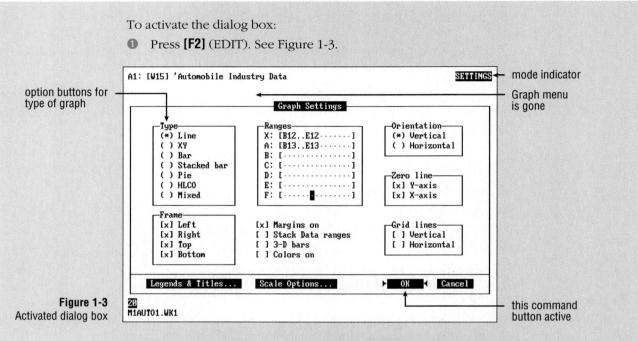

option buttons for type of graph

mode indicator

Graph menu is gone

this command button active

Figure 1-3
Activated dialog box

When the dialog box is active, the mode indicator displays SETTINGS and the Graph menu disappears. The cursor is now positioned on the OK command button near the bottom right corner of the dialog box. This button is active, which we know because it is highlighted or marked by arrows.

To help you distinguish among the options, one letter of each option is displayed in either a different color or a different intensity. To select an option, you either type the highlighted character or use the cursor-movement keys to highlight your choice in the dialog box and then press [Enter] or [Spacebar] to select it.

To change the line graph to a bar graph using the dialog box:

❶ Select Type (**T**). The option buttons within the Type group are activated.

❷ Select Bar (**B**) from the dialog box. See Figure 1-4. The asterisk indicates that you have selected a bar graph.

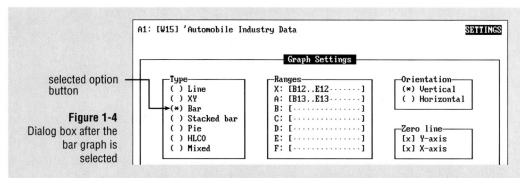

selected option button

Figure 1-4
Dialog box after the bar graph is selected

If you wanted to, you could back out of that command by pressing [Esc]. But don't do that now because that would return you to the previous settings. Instead let's display the bar graph.

❸   Press **[F10]**. A bar graph appears. Press any key to continue.

You can now create a three-dimensional bar graph by turning on the 3-D bars check box.

To turn on the 3-D bars check box:

❶   Type **3**. See Figure 1-5.

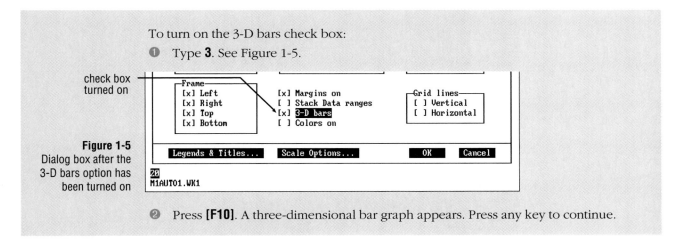

check box turned on

Figure 1-5
Dialog box after the 3-D bars option has been turned on

❷   Press **[F10]**. A three-dimensional bar graph appears. Press any key to continue.

Now let's confirm the settings in the dialog box.

To confirm the settings in the dialog box:

❶   Press **[Tab]** until the command button OK is highlighted. Press **[Enter]**. The Graph menu appears in the control panel.

If you changed your mind, you could move the cursor to the Cancel command button and press [Enter] to reset all current graph settings to the previous settings.

❷   Select Quit (**Q**) to leave the Graph menu.

Dialog boxes provide information on a command's current settings. As you become an experienced 1-2-3 user, you may find using dialog boxes to change settings speeds up work, especially if you use a mouse.

Module 2

Using WYSIWYG to Enhance and Print 1-2-3 Worksheets

OBJECTIVES

In this tutorial you will learn to:

■ Load and activate WYSIWYG

■ Define fonts, typefaces, type sizes, and type styles

■ Enhance worksheets with typefaces, type sizes, and type styles

■ Enhance worksheets with lines and boxes

■ Save worksheets that include WYSIWYG enhancements

■ Print worksheets that include WYSIWYG enhancements

What Is WYSIWYG?

Every day business people read many pieces of paper. If your job is writing those papers, how can you make your work stand out? How can you make the spreadsheets you create catch and keep the reader's attention, be easy to read, and convey your ideas clearly and convincingly?

You can use a new feature of 1-2-3 called WYSIWYG. WYSIWYG enables you to enhance the appearance of your worksheets, databases, and graphs. WYSIWYG, pronounced *wizzy-wig*, stands for "**W**hat **Y**ou **S**ee **I**s **W**hat **Y**ou **G**et." As the acronym says, the worksheet you see on the screen closely resembles what you will see as printed output. WYSIWYG lets you use sophisticated features such as typefaces, type sizes and styles, lines, boxes, and shading to enhance your worksheet, making it easier to read and understand. Compare the worksheets in Figure 2-1 on the following page. Figure 2-1a shows the final version of the worksheet in Tutorial 3, and 2-1b shows the same worksheet enhanced with several WYSIWYG features. By the end of this tutorial you will have modified the worksheet shown in Figure 2-1a so that it looks like the worksheet in Figure 2-1b.

```
Balboa Equity Fund
Net Asset Value for November 5, 1992

Company                              # of   Current      Market
Name                               Shares    Price        Value
-----------------------------------------------------------------


International Business Machines       100   $91.00    $9,100.00
Coca-Cola                              50    69.25     3,462.50
Texaco                                100    58.75     5,875.00
Boeing                                150    44.50     6,675.00
                                                    -------------
   Totals                                           $25,112.50
                                                    ============
Mutual Fund Shares                            2000
Price/Share (NAV)                           $12.56
```

Figure 2-1a
Pauline's
worksheet before
WYSIWYG

Balboa Equity Fund
Net Asset Value for November 5, 1992

Company Name	# of Shares	Current Price	Market Value
International Business Machines	100	$91.00	$9,100.00
Coca-Cola	50	69.25	3,462.50
Texaco	100	58.75	5,875.00
Boeing	150	44.50	6,675.00
Totals			$25,112.50

Mutual Fund Shares	*2000*
Price/Share (NAV)	*$12.56*

Figure 2-1b
Pauline's worksheet
after WYSIWYG
enhancements

You can do several things in WYSIWYG, for example:

- display text and numbers using a variety of typefaces, type styles, and type sizes
- draw lines, boxes, and grids around one or more cells to organize information in sections and blocks to give visual interest
- control the widths of columns and the heights of rows
- print worksheets and graphs on the same page
- annotate graphs with descriptive comments, lines, arrows, rectangles, and ellipses
- preview a worksheet before it is printed

In this module you will learn how to load and activate WYSIWYG; enhance your worksheet with different typefaces, type sizes, and type styles; draw lines and boxes; and print your worksheet using WYSIWYG's print command.

Loading WYSIWYG

When you load 1-2-3 Release 2.3, WYSIWYG is not automatically loaded because it is a separate program called an **add-in program**. WYSIWYG is automatically attached to 1-2-3 Release 2.4. If WYSIWYG is already attached, skip to "Accessing WYSIWYG" on page L 320. Before you can use the WYSIWYG features, you must attach the WYSIWYG program.

Let's attach the WYSIWYG add-in program.

To attach the WYSIWYG add-in program:

① Select /Add-in Attach (**/AA**). A list of add-in programs appears. See Figure 2-2.

WYSIWYG program

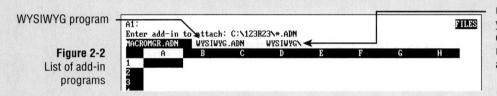

names of programs; if you're using the commercial version, more names will appear

Figure 2-2
List of add-in programs

WYSIWYG.ADN is the program that contains WYSIWYG.

② Highlight WYSIWYG.ADN and press **[Enter]**. The extension ADN stands for **AD**d-i**N**.

Now choose how you want to access the WYSIWYG menu once WYSIWYG is loaded into memory. See Figure 2-3.

options →

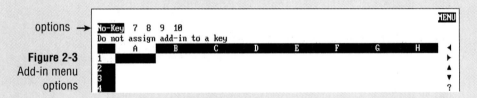

Figure 2-3
Add-in menu options

If you choose *No-Key*, you press [:] to access the WYSIWYG menu.

If you choose *7*, you press [Alt] [F7] to access the WYSIWYG menu.

If you choose *8*, you press [Alt][F8] to access the WYSIWYG menu.

If you choose *9*, you press [Alt][F9] to access the WYSIWYG menu.

If you choose *10*, you press [Alt][F10] to access the WYSIWYG menu.

Pressing the colon key ([:]) is the simplest way to access the WYSIWYG menu.

③ Select No-Key. The WYSIWYG worksheet appears.

④ Select Quit (**Q**) to leave the add-in menu and return to READY mode. WYSIWYG is now attached to 1-2-3.

Like the 1-2-3 program and individual worksheets, the WYSIWYG program takes up computer memory. If you receive an error message when you try to attach WYSIWYG, it may mean that your computer does not have enough available memory to do so. See your instructor or technical support person for help if you are having trouble attaching WYSIWYG.

Accessing WYSIWYG

With WYSIWYG attached, you can access either the 1-2-3 main menu or the WYSIWYG menu. To display the WYSIWYG menu, you press [:] (Colon). To display the 1-2-3 main menu commands, you press [/] (Slash).

Now let's access the WYSIWYG menu.

To access the WYSIWYG menu:

● Press [:]. See Figure 2-4. When you access WYSIWYG, the WYSIWYG command menu appears. Notice that the mode indicator displays WYSIWYG.

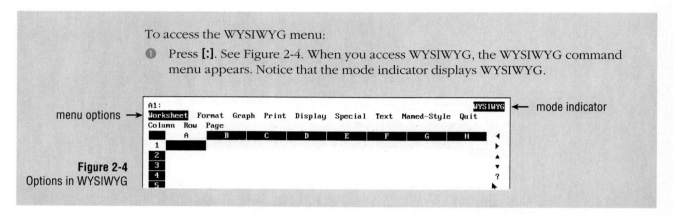

menu options →

Figure 2-4
Options in WYSIWYG

mode indicator

Figure 2-5 summarizes the main menu options in WYSIWYG.

Option	Purpose
WORKSHEET	Sets column widths, row heights, and page breaks
FORMAT	Controls the appearance of your worksheets on screen and when printed
GRAPH	Adds, edits, and saves graphics in a worksheet range
PRINT	Creates printed copies of your worksheet or graph, including all formatting done with the WYSIWYG commands
DISPLAY	Controls how 1-2-3 displays the worksheet on the screen
SPECIAL	Copies and moves WYSIWYG formats from one range to another, imports formats and graphics from another format file, and exports formats and graphics to format files on another disk
TEXT	Enters and edits text in a range of cells as though the words were paragraphs in a word processor
NAMED-STYLE	Assigns names to commonly used formats

Figure 2-5
Summary of
WYSIWYG menu
options

Now return to READY mode.

To leave the WYSIWYG menu and return to READY mode:

● Select Quit (**Q**) from the WYSIWYG menu. You are back at READY mode. WYSIWYG is still attached . To access it again, you simply press [:].

If you are using a mouse, you can also display the WYSIWYG and 1-2-3 menus by moving the mouse pointer into the control panel on your screen. The menu that appears is the last one you used during the current 1-2-3 session. You can switch between WYSIWYG and 1-2-3 menus by clicking the right mouse button while the mouse pointer is in the control panel.

Introduction to Fonts

One way you can improve a worksheet's appearance is to enhance the appearance of the letters, numbers, and symbols. The appearance of letters, numbers, and symbols is determined by their typeface, type size, and type style. First, let's explore the meaning of typeface. The term **typeface** refers to a particular graphical design of letters, numbers, and symbols. Typefaces are designed for readability, to attract attention, or to set a mood. Each typeface has a name, which identifies a specific design of characters and symbols. Figure 2-6 illustrates the four typefaces that are included in the WYSIWYG program: Swiss, Dutch, Courier, and Xsymbol.

Figure 2-6
The typefaces available in WYSIWYG

Typefaces are classified as either serif or sans serif. **Serif** typefaces have small finishing strokes, called serifs, on the ends of the letters, and are often used in the body of a document or a report. **Sans serif** typefaces do not have these finishing strokes at the ends of letters and are commonly used for titles and headings. Dutch and Courier are serif typefaces, while Swiss is a sans serif typeface.

Type size refers to the height of the characters and is usually measured in units called points. A **point** is approximately 1/72 inch; thus, a 72-point typeface is approximately 1 inch high. The higher the point size, the larger the size of the characters. A 6-point type size might be appropriate for a footnote. The main body of text in a book ranges from 9 to 12 points. Headings typically are presented in 18 to 24 points. Figure 2-7 shows the Swiss typeface in three different type sizes: 6, 12, and 24 points.

Figure 2-7
Various type sizes in Swiss typeface

In WYSIWYG the term **font** refers to a typeface (a collection of characters, numbers, and symbols) in one type size. For example, 12-point Swiss is one font, 24-point Swiss is another font, and 12-point Dutch is a third font. WYSIWYG allows you to use up to eight fonts in a worksheet.

Type style is a variation within a font. The typeface remains basically the same, but the width, the weight, or the angle of the characters changes. Boldface, italic, and underline type styles are illustrated in Figure 2-8.

Figure 2-8
Various styles of
Swiss 12-point font

Enhancing a Worksheet with WYSIWYG

Now that you have learned about fonts, you are ready to use several WYSIWYG features to improve the appearance of Pauline's Net Asset Value worksheet. Let's retrieve a modified version of Pauline's final worksheet.

To retrieve Pauline's worksheet:
1. Select /File Retrieve (**/FR**).
2. Type **M2BALBO1** and press **[Enter]**. The worksheet's opening screen appears.
3. Press **[PgDn]** to view the worksheet data. This version of Pauline's worksheet includes the changes requested in the Tutorial Assignments at the end of Tutorial 3, except that the dashed lines used for underlines have been removed. In WYSIWYG you can draw ruled lines without the lines occupying a separate row.

Notice that the worksheet appears in a font different from that in your worksheet in Tutorial 3. When WYSIWYG is attached, the worksheet characters appear in the WYSIWYG default font, which currently is 12-point Swiss.

Changing Typefaces

Many documents use two typefaces, one for headings and one for text. Pauline decides to use the Swiss typeface for her two-line title and then to convert the rest of the worksheet to Dutch typeface.

To change the body of the worksheet to 12-point Dutch font:
1. Move the cell pointer to A25, the first cell in the body of the worksheet.

❷ Select :Format Font (**:FF**). A menu appears listing the eight fonts currently available for use within your worksheet. The fonts consist of Swiss, Dutch, and Xsymbol typefaces in various sizes. The first font that appears in the list is the default font. This font was used for each cell in the worksheet. See Figure 2-9.

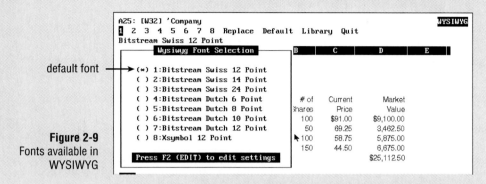

default font →

Figure 2-9
Fonts available in
WYSIWYG

To specify the 12-point Dutch font for a range of cells, you first select the number that precedes the typeface name and size you want.

❸ Type **7**, the number of 12-point Dutch font.

Now specify the cells of the worksheet that will appear in 12-point Dutch font.

❹ Highlight the range A25..D35 and press **[Enter]**. You are returned to READY mode.

The body of the worksheet now appears in 12-point Dutch. See Figure 2-10. Notice that the control panel displays "{DUTCH12}," a format code that indicates the font for the current cell is 12-point Dutch. If no format code appears in the control panel for a specific cell, the default font, font 1, is being used.

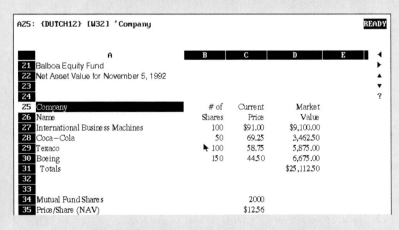

Figure 2-10
Pauline's modified
worksheet

Pauline's worksheet now has two fonts: the titles in 12-point Swiss and everything else in 12-point Dutch. Next, Pauline turns her attention to adjusting the type sizes.

Changing Type Size

Pauline wants the title lines of the worksheet to stand out. To accomplish this, she can display the titles in a larger font. She decides to use a 24-point Swiss font for the first title line. Let's try it.

To change the font of the first line of the title to a 24-point Swiss font:

① Move the cell pointer to A21, the first heading line.

② Select :Format Font (**:FF**). A menu of fonts appears.

③ Type **3** to choose the 24-point Swiss font.

Select the cells you want in this type size.

④ With cell A21 highlighted, press **[Enter]**. The title is displayed in 24-point Swiss, as shown in Figure 2-11. Notice that the height of row 21 is automatically adjusted to fit the size of the 24-point font.

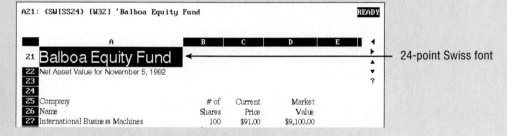

Figure 2-11
Font of the first line of the title is changed

Now let's change the font for the second line of the title to 14-point Swiss. Subtitles normally are displayed in a smaller type size than titles.

To change the font for the second title line:

① Move the cell pointer to A22.

② Select :Format Font (**:FF**). A menu of fonts appears.

③ Type **2** to choose 14-point Swiss.

④ With cell A22 highlighted, press **[Enter]**. The second line of the title is displayed in 14-point Swiss. See Figure 2-12.

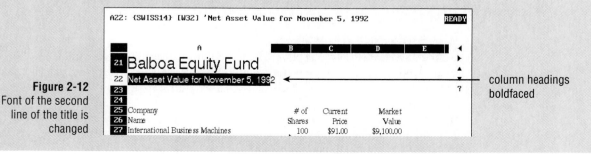

Figure 2-12
Font of the second line of the title is changed

After adjusting the type size Pauline decides to try a type style to draw the reader's attention to various sections of the worksheet.

Changing Styles: Boldface

Several of the :Format commands add styles to a font. For instance, you can add boldface, underline, or italic styles. Pauline decides to set the column heading in a boldface style, to help differentiate the columns from the rest of the worksheet.

To boldface the column headings:

❶   Move the cell pointer to A25, the first cell of the column headings.

❷   Select :Format Bold Set (**:FBS**).

Next indicate the range of cells you want to boldface.

❸   Highlight A25..D26 and press **[Enter]**. In Figure 2-13 notice that the column headings appear in a darker type. Notice that the first line of the control panel indicates the format code for cell A25 is {DUTCH12 Bold} — 12-point Dutch boldface.

format code

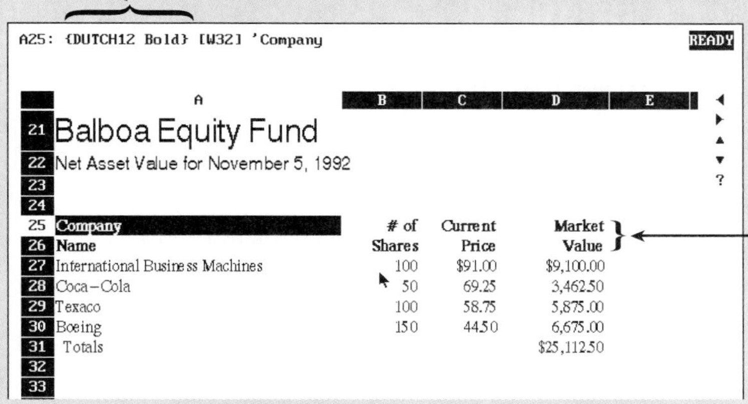

Figure 2-13
Column headings
are boldfaced

column headings
boldfaced

Now that Pauline has boldfaced the column headings, she wants to draw a line under these headings to emphasize them and to make it easier for the reader to read the information contained in the columns.

Drawing Lines

You can add lines, borders, and boxes to your worksheet with the WYSIWYG :Format Lines command. By placing single, double, or thick lines around a cell or a range of cells, you can create different effects. For instance, you can use lines and boxes to add structure in a report, to create tables, or to group related items together. You can put lines on some or all sides of a cell or block of cells.

Pauline believes she can make her worksheet look more professional by adding lines under the column headings and before and after the total. Let's see how.

To draw a line underneath the column headings:

❶   Move the cell pointer to A26, the first cell of the range to be underlined.

❷   Select :Format Lines (**:FL**). See Figure 2-14.

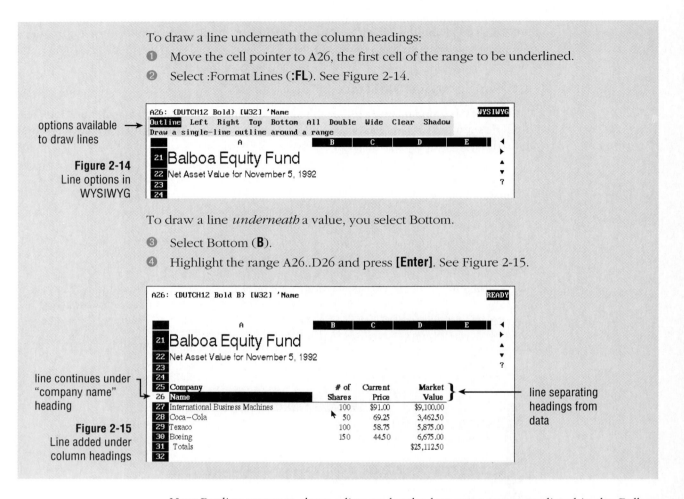

options available → to draw lines

Figure 2-14
Line options in
WYSIWYG

line continues under
"company name"
heading

Figure 2-15
Line added under
column headings

line separating
headings from
data

To draw a line *underneath* a value, you select Bottom.

❸   Select Bottom (**B**).

❹   Highlight the range A26..D26 and press **[Enter]**. See Figure 2-15.

Next Pauline wants to draw a line under the last company name listed in the Balboa Equity Fund to indicate that a total follows.

To draw a line:

❶   Move the cell pointer to A30, the first cell in the row to be underlined.

❷   Select :Format Line Bottom (**:FLB**).

Now specify the cells where the line will be drawn.

❸   Highlight the range A30..D30 and press **[Enter]**.

A common way to indicate a final total in a worksheet is to place a double-ruled line under it.

To add a double-ruled line under the total market value:

➊ Move the cell pointer to D31, the cell where the double-ruled lined will be drawn.

➋ Select :Format Lines Double Bottom (**:FLDB**).

➌ With cell D31 highlighted, press **[Enter]**. See Figure 2-16. A double-ruled line now appears under the total.

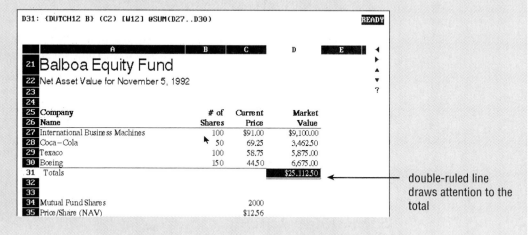

Figure 2-16
Double-ruled line
entered

double-ruled line
draws attention to the
total

Pauline is finished with her revision of the worksheet. She decides to save it.

Saving WYSIWYG Formats

When you save a worksheet that has been enhanced by WYSIWYG, your worksheet consists of two files: a WK1 worksheet file and a FMT format file. Both files have the same filename. Your data and the basic settings, such as column width, cell formats, and range names, are stored in the WK1 file. Your formatting information for the current worksheet, such as fonts, styles, and lines, are stored in a separate worksheet file with an FMT extension. For example, if you save the worksheet file on your screen as W2BALBO1, WYSIWYG automatically saves an associated file, W2BALBO1.FMT, in addition to the W2BALBO1.WK1 file that is saved. Let's save Pauline's worksheet.

To save a worksheet that includes WYSIWYG enhancements:

➊ Press **[Home]** to move to cell A1.

Now enter the filename of the worksheet in cell A1.

➋ Type **W2BALBO1.WK1** and press **[Enter]**.

➌ Select /File Save (**/FS**).

➍ Type **W2BALBO1** and press **[Enter]**. The two worksheet files are saved on your data diskette.

You should be aware of some additional points when you are saving files:

- WYSIWYG must be loaded in computer memory for the formatting information to be saved. If WYSIWYG is not loaded, your formatting changes will not be saved.

- Remember to save your worksheet whenever you make formatting changes, even if you didn't change the data, formulas, or relationships. If you don't, your formatting changes will not be saved.

- When you retrieve a worksheet that has both a WK1 and a FMT file and WYSIWYG is attached, you will see formatting on the screen. If WYSIWYG is not attached when you retrieve the file, you will not see any formatting. It cannot appear until you attach WYSIWYG.

Additional WYSIWYG Formatting

Pauline wants to see how a box with a drop shadow looks around the price/share calculation. Also, she wants to change the style of the text within the box to italic. Finally, she wants to give the stock portfolio section a grid-like look.

Preselecting a Range

Typically you specify a range of cells after issuing a command. However, what happens when you have several commands that affect the same range of cells? For example, suppose for a particular range you wanted to draw a box, change the font, and then italicize the text inside the box. In that case you would find it faster to **preselect the range** of cells before issuing any command. By preselecting a range you can issue several commands without having to respecify the same range each time you issue a new command.

Let's try it.

To preselect a range of cells:

1. Move the cell pointer to A34.

2. Press **[F4]** to anchor the cell pointer.

3. Highlight the range of cells A34..C35. See Figure 2-17. Press **[Enter]**. You are returned to READY mode. The preselected range remains highlighted.

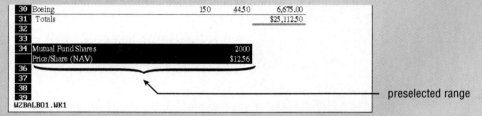

Figure 2-17
Preselecting a range

preselected range

You can now issue a 1-2-3 or a WYSIWYG command, and you will *not* be prompted for a range; the preselected range will be used automatically. After you complete a command, the range remains selected. To cancel a preselected range, you press [Esc] or move the cell pointer to any other cell in the worksheet, but don't do that now.

Drawing a Box

You can use boxes to set off data from the rest of the text. Boxes are often drawn around a complete line of type to draw attention to a piece of information. Let's draw a box around Price/Share (the range that was previously shaded). You use the Lines Outline command to draw boxes.

To draw a box:

● Select :Format Lines Outline (:**FLO**). Remember that the range A34..C35 is pre-selected. A box (outline) appears around the preselected range of cells.

The price/share calculation is now boxed, but Pauline wants to add a drop shadow to the box. Let's see how she can complete this task.

Adding a Drop Shadow

A thick line along the bottom and up the right side of selected cells gives an effect called a **drop shadow** and results in the box having a three-dimensional appearance. You use the :Format Lines Shadow command to create a drop shadow.

To add a drop shadow:

● Select :Format Lines Shadow Set (:**FLSS**).

A drop shadow appears on the box. Next, Pauline decides to change the text inside the box to a different type style.

Changing Style: Italics

To focus attention on particular words or numbers, you can italicize them. Let's see if italics draw your attention to the text within the boxed area.

To italicize text:

● Select :Format Italics Set (:**FIS**). The text within the box is now italicized.

Adding a Grid

Now Pauline wants the section of the worksheet where the individual stocks are listed to appear as a grid, that is, a table with ruled lines. You can create a grid pattern for a table of data by adding lines to all four sides of several cells. Let's try it.

To draw a grid:

❶   Move the cell pointer to A27. As soon as you move the cell pointer in READY mode, 1-2-3 clears the preselected range. From now on you have to specify ranges as part of a command unless you preselect a new range.

You are now ready to add the grid lines.

❷   Select :Format Lines All (**:FLA**).

Next you need to specify the range for the grid.

❸   Highlight the range A27..D30 and press **[Enter]**. See Figure 2-18.

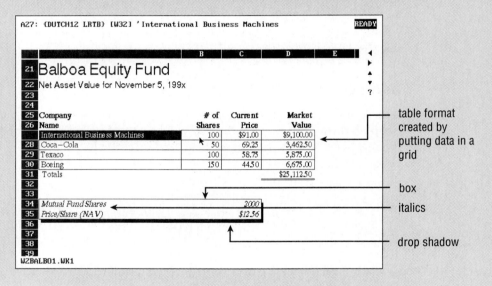

Figure 2-18
Adding a grid

Pauline likes this worksheet and decides to print a hard copy for her supervisor.

Printing with WYSIWYG

If a worksheet includes any WYSIWYG formatting options, you must use the print command *within* WYSIWYG if you want these enhancements to appear in your printout. In other words, WYSIWYG printing is independent of any printing you do using the 1-2-3 /Print commands. If you print using the 1-2-3 /Print command, your WYSIWYG enhancements will not be printed, even if you have attached WYSIWYG. To print your WYSIWYG enhancements, you must access the WYSIWYG printing option with the :Print command. The :Print command lets you print your worksheet exactly as you have formatted it on the screen.

Specifying a Print Range

To print in WYSIWYG, you must specify the range of cells you want printed. Even if you have previously selected a print range using the /Print Range command, you must now specify the print range for WYSIWYG — the print range from the /Print Range command is not transferred to WYSIWYG. Let's print the current version of Pauline's worksheet.

To set the print range:

❶ Select :Print (**:P**). A dialog box appears showing the current settings for WYSIWYG printing.

Next let's specify the range to be printed.

❷ Select Range Set (**RS**).

❸ Move the cell pointer to A21, the first cell in the print range, and press **[.]** to anchor the range.

❹ Highlight the range A21..D35 and press **[Enter]**. The range now appears in the dialog box. See Figure 2-19.

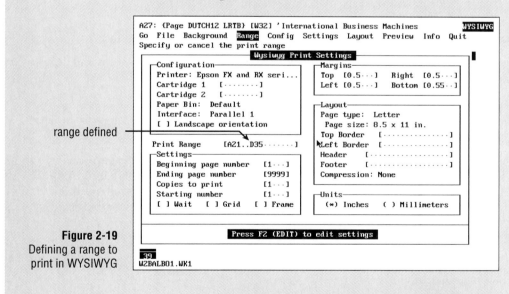

Figure 2-19
Defining a range to
print in WYSIWYG

range defined

You have now specified the print range.

Previewing a Document

Printing in WYSIWYG can take a long time. So before printing, you might want to **preview** the worksheet, that is, see exactly how the printed output will appear on the page before you actually print the worksheet. You use the Preview option to display your print range, one page at a time. The preview screen usually reduces the size of the worksheet. As a result you might not be able to read every character. But you can preview the page design to help you make layout and spacing adjustments. Let's preview Pauline's worksheet.

To preview a page:

❶ Select Preview (**P**). See Figure 2-20. You see the first page of the print range in reduced form on the preview screen. If you have more than one page to preview, you would press [PgDn] or [PgUp] to view the next or previous pages.

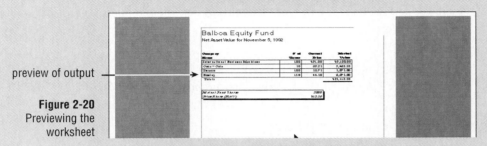

preview of output

Figure 2-20
Previewing the
worksheet

❷ When you're ready to continue, press any key to return to the WYSIWYG print menu.

After previewing the worksheet, Pauline is happy with what she sees and is ready to print it.

Selecting a Printer

You must instruct WYSIWYG which printer to use to print the enhancements. Initially no printer is selected for use.

To select a printer:

❶ Select Config Printer (**CP**). See Figure 2-21. A list of installed printers appears. Depending on the printer you have installed, you may have several choices for the same printer. For example, if you are using an HP laser printer, you have three choices: high density, medium density, or extended capability. Extended capability prints the fastest, while high density gives you better print quality but takes longer to print.

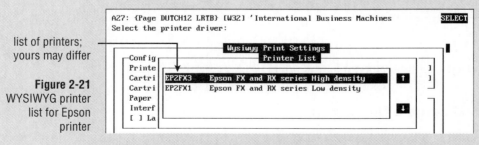

list of printers;
yours may differ

Figure 2-21
WYSIWYG printer
list for Epson
printer

❷ Select the name of the printer that is correct for your current configuration. If you are not sure, check with your instructor or technical support person.

❸ Select Quit (**Q**) to return to the Print menu. You are ready to print.

Printing

Now that you have previewed the worksheet and selected the printer, you are ready to print.

To print the worksheet:

❶ Select Go (**G**). As the document is being printed, the mode indicator flashes "Wait." Depending on the formatting enhancements in your worksheet and the print density you selected, your output may take a few seconds to several minutes to complete. You can see the printing progress on the control panel.

After the worksheet has been printed, you are automatically returned to READY mode. If you have completed the work in this module, save the worksheet again.

To save a worksheet:

❶ Select /File Save (**/FS**) and press **[Enter]**.

❷ Select Replace (**R**). The worksheet replaces the previous version of W2BALBO1.WK1.

Remember that actually two files are replaced: W2BALBO1.WK1 and W2BALBO1.FMT.

Figure 2-22 shows the printed output that Pauline will give to her supervisor.

Balboa Equity Fund
Net Asset Value for November 5, 1992

Company Name	# of Shares	Current Price	Market Value
International Business Machines	100	$91.00	$9,100.00
Coca-Cola	50	69.25	3,462.50
Texaco	100	58.75	5,875.00
Boeing	150	44.50	6,675.00
Total			$25,112.50

Mutual Fund Shares	*2000*
Price/Share (NAV)	*$12.56*

Figure 2-22
Pauline's final
printed worksheet

The Compression Feature

If you want to fit a large worksheet on one page, WYSIWYG can attempt to fit the print range onto one sheet of paper. WYSIWYG will automatically determine how much the worksheet needs to be reduced.

To reduce the size of a worksheet to fit on one page:

❶   Select :Print Layout Compression (**:PLC**).

Now instruct WYSIWYG to automatically compress the print range to attempt to fit it onto one printed page.

❷   Select Automatic (**A**). The dialog box appears, and you can select another option from the WYSIWYG menu.

A worksheet can be reduced to 15 percent of its original size. Very large worksheets, however, may not fit on a single page. If the print range is too large for the maximum reduction allowed, the worksheet will print on multiple pages.

❸   Select Quit (**Q**) to leave the layout menu and return to the WYSIWYG menu.

Design Guidelines

Now that you are ready to use WYSIWYG to enhance your worksheets, you should keep these points in mind:

- Use fonts to enhance your work. But don't overdo it — too many typefaces can make your worksheet confusing. Many users use only one or two typefaces in a document and then vary the type's size and style for emphasis.

- Use a boldface version of the font in your document to make column headings stand out.

- Use lines and shading to enhance legibility and to highlight certain parts of the worksheet.

- Don't cram every bit of data onto one page. Remember, proper use of white space helps make the page easier to read.

Exercises

1.   If you're told to use a 10-point Dutch boldface font, what typeface is that? What type size? What type style?

2.   Which is the larger font: 12-point Swiss or 24-point Swiss?

3.   Is the font used in this sentence serif or sans serif?

4. Assume you have the files M2FILE.WK1 and M2FILE.FMT on your data diskette:
   a. What command would you issue to retrieve the worksheet?
   b. After you retrieve the worksheet, the format enhancements do not appear on your screen. Why would this happen?
   c. You retrieve the worksheet, and the WYSIWYG enhancements appear on the screen. You print the worksheet, but the format enhancements are not printed. Why would this happen?

5. Identify the WYSIWYG enhancements in Figure 2-23.

Quick Food Inc.
Fourth Quarter Sales

Region	Amount
North	$7,565
South	58,245
East	32,655
West	42,123
Total	$140,588

Figure 2-23

6. To activate the WYSIWYG menu, you press what key(s)?

7. Give the commands needed to do the following:
   a. To print your worksheet on one page
   b. To see how your printed output will look before you print
   c. To store your worksheet on your data diskette
   d. To draw a box around a range of cells
   e. To change the font of a title line

8. A worksheet cell contains the title "Sales Summary." This cell has been formatted, but you're not sure what typeface or point size has been used. Where can you look in the worksheet to get this information?

Case Problems

1. Twelve-Month Sales Forecast for International Food Brands, Inc.

International Food Brands, Inc., has completed a forecast of monthly sales for the upcoming year.

Do the following:

1. Attach WYSIWYG.

2. Retrieve the worksheet M2FORE.WK1.

3. Add the following enhancements:

    a.   Use a 14-point Swiss font for the title.
    b.   Boldface the column headings.
    c.   Place a ruled line underneath the column headings.
    d.   Italicize the names of the countries.

4. Save your worksheet as W2FORE.

5. Print the worksheet so the entire worksheet appears on one page.

2. Promotional Coupon for *Weekly Times*

Priscilla Burns is the circulation manager of *Weekly Times*, a newspaper serving three counties in New Hampshire. She has recently arranged for a promotional coupon to be inserted into next month's edition of *New Hampshire Magazine*, which sells in these counties. She has written the coupon, but she still must format it using WYSIWYG.

Do the following:

1. Attach WYSIWYG.

2. Retrieve the worksheet M2COUP.WK1.

3. Add the following WYSIWYG enhancements:
    a.   Draw a box around the entire worksheet.
    b.   Use 14-point Swiss font for the text "Weekly Times."
    c.   Reverse the text "Weekly Times."
    d.   Use 24-point Swiss font for the heading "Super Discount Voucher."
    e.   Place a wide underline under the heading.
    f.   Use 12-point Dutch font for the body of the coupon (A5..G13).
    g.   Boldface the promotional message that begins "now you can receive..."
    h.   Add ruled lines above *NAME, STREET, APT. NO., CITY, STATE,* and *ZIP,* so there is space to enter this information on the coupon. Use 10-point Dutch font for these words.
    i.   Use 8-point Dutch font for the note "Offer good in U.S."
    j.   Put the data about payment terms in a grid format.

4. Save the worksheet as the file W2COUP.

5. Print the formatted worksheet.

Module 3

Using WYSIWYG to Enhance and Print Graphs

OBJECTIVES

In this tutorial you will learn to:

- Insert a graph into your worksheet

- Reduce the size of rows and columns

- Enclose a legend in a box

- Include text on a graph

- Draw arrows

- Print a graph and worksheet data on the same page

Graphs are effective tools for business communications. As you've seen in Tutorial 6, you can select from many different graph types, such as line, bar, stacked bar, pie, and XY graphs. You can add titles, legends, and other text information to a graph. You can also change the appearance of the graph, for example, by displaying bars with a three-dimensional effect or by exploding specific slices of a pie chart.

To communicate the message of your graph even more effectively, you can also use WYSIWYG. With WYSIWYG you can do such things as add boxes, lines, arrows, ellipses, and other shapes. You can prepare a report that contains both the graph and the data that support the graph. You can also print the graph without having to exit 1-2-3 and retrieve the PrintGraph Utility.

Compare the graphs in Figure 3-1 on the following page. Figure 3-1a shows one of the graphs Carl Martinez created while working on his project for M&B Consultants. Figure 3-1b shows the same graph inserted into the worksheet and enhanced with several of WYSIWYG's graphic features. As Figure 3-1b shows, you can use WYSIWYG's Graph commands to:

- display the current graph or a named graph in the worksheet next to the data on which it is based
- add explanatory text to your graph for clarity
- draw arrows to attract the reader's attention
- draw boxes to highlight a portion of the graph
- print graphs from within WYSIWYG

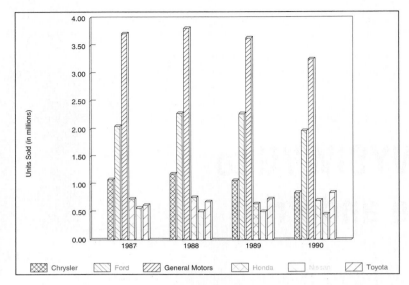

Figure 3-1a
Graph created with
1-2-3's /Graph
commands and
printed using
PGRAPH

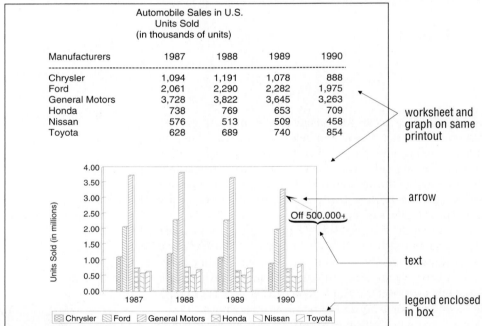

Figure 3-1b
Graph enhanced
with WYSIWYG

Loading WYSIWYG

Remember that when you load 1-2-3, WYSIWYG is not automatically loaded — it is an add-in program. If WYSIWYG has not been loaded, see Module 2, page L 319 for instructions on how to attach WYSIWYG.

Adding a Graph to the Worksheet

Carl Martinez has created several graphs using 1-2-3's /Graph command. He now has WYSIWYG and wants to further improve the appearance of his graph, which will be included in the report being readied for the Senate subcommittee. Carl is ready to enhance one of these graphs using WYSIWYG's :Graph command. Let's retrieve one of the graphs from Tutorial 6, the bar graph that shows unit sales for the six automobile manufacturers from 1987 to 1990.

To retrieve Carl's worksheet:

❶ Select /File Retrieve (**/FR**).

❷ Type **M3AUTO1** and press **[Enter]**.

❸ Press **[F10]** to view the graph.

❹ Press any key to return to READY mode.

Be sure you understand that the WYSIWYG Graph commands *do not create graphs*. You use WYSIWYG commands *once you have already* created a graph using the Graph commands of the 1-2-3 main menu. Furthermore, after you create a graph you must first add the graph to the worksheet before you can enhance the graph using the WYSIWYG Graph commands. You use the Graph Add command to insert the current graph or a named graph into a range in your worksheet.

Carl realizes that he must first add the graph to his worksheet; he wants the graph to appear immediately below the worksheet data in the range A21..E35.

To add a graph to the range A21..E35 in the worksheet:

❶ Select :Graph (**:G**). See Figure 3-2. A list of the 10 options available in the WYSIWYG Graph menu appear.

menu options →

Figure 3-2
Graph options in
WYSIWYG

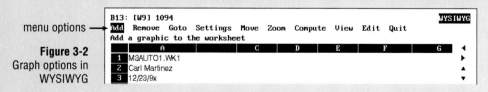

First add the graph to the worksheet.

❷ Select Add (**A**).

You have five choices for the type of graph you can add. You can add the current graph, a named graph, a saved graph with a PIC extension, a special file called a Metafile (CGM extension), or a blank placeholder for a graphic that you can add later.

Add the current graph to the worksheet.

❸ Select Current (**C**).

A graph added to your worksheet can be as large or as small as you want. The size of the range you specify determines the size of the graph in your worksheet. So let's now specify the range A21..E35.

④ Move the cell pointer to cell A21, the location where you want to insert the graph.

⑤ Press **[.]** to anchor the cell pointer. Now highlight A21..E35.

⑥ Press **[Enter]**. WYSIWYG automatically adds the graph to fit into the range you specified.

⑦ Select Quit (**Q**) to leave the WYSIWYG Graph menu and return to READY mode.

⑧ Press **[↓]** until you see the entire graph in the worksheet. See Figure 3-3. The graph appears immediately below the worksheet data.

graph indicator

data →

graph →

Figure 3-3
Viewing the graph
in the worksheet

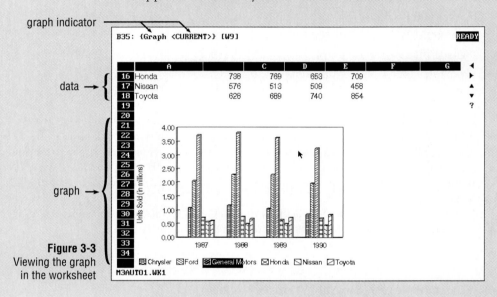

When the cell pointer is in the range occupied by the graph, the control panel displays a graph indicator in curly braces: either the name of the graph or the word CURRENT if a current graph was added to the worksheet.

Changing the Size of Worksheet Cells

You probably have noticed that in 1-2-3 you cannot view a graph and its supporting data on the screen at the same time. With WYSIWYG 1-2-3 can reduce or enlarge worksheet cells *on the screen* so you can see more or fewer rows and columns. The Display Zoom command reduces and enlarges the cells on the screen. Six options are available:

Option	Description
Tiny	Reduces cells displayed to 63% of normal size
Small	Reduces cells displayed to 87% of normal size
Normal	Displays cells at normal size
Large	Enlarges cells displayed to 125% of normal size
Huge	Enlarges cells displayed to 150% of normal size

Figure 3-4

Let's reduce the worksheet so you can view both the data and the graph in the worksheet area.

To reduce the size of the worksheet:

❶ Press **[F5]** (GOTO), type **A13**, and press **[Enter]** to position cell A13 in the upper left corner of the worksheet area.

❷ Select :Display Zoom (**:DZ**).

Select the size reduction.

❸ Select Small (**S**). See Figure 3-5.

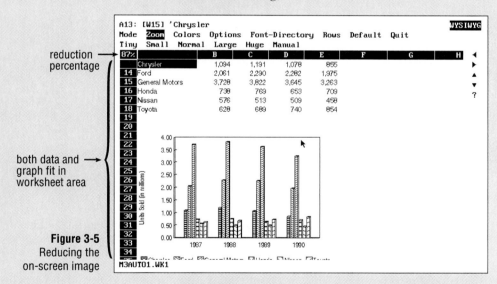

reduction percentage

both data and graph fit in worksheet area

Figure 3-5
Reducing the on-screen image

You are viewing the worksheet at 87 percent of its normal size. Notice that the zoom percentage appears in the upper left corner of your worksheet.

❹ Select Quit (**Q**) to return to READY mode.

To return the worksheet to normal size, use the Display Zoom Normal option.

Changing Worksheet Data and Updating the Graph

If WYSIWYG is attached and you change the data in your worksheet, 1-2-3 automatically redraws the graph in your worksheet to reflect those changes. You don't have to press [F10] (GRAPH) to see the graph, as you would if the graph were not added to the worksheet.

Let's assume an error was made when Chrysler's sales for 1990 were entered. Instead of 855 the value should be 2855. You'll make the change and observe how the graph in the worksheet changes immediately to reflect that change.

To observe how a change to the data affects the graph:

❶ Move the cell pointer to cell E13, the location of Chrysler's 1990 sales.

❷ Type **2855** and press **[Enter]**. Notice how the graph automatically changes to reflect the corrected data. See Figure 3-6.

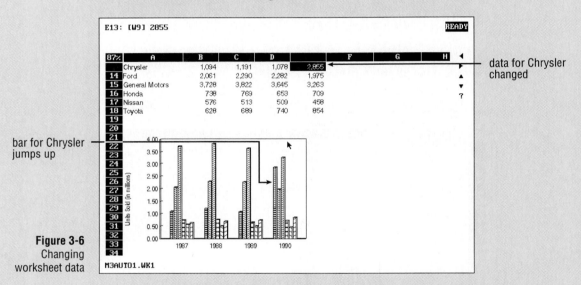

Figure 3-6
Changing
worksheet data

❸ Type **855** and press **[Enter]** to return the value back to its original amount. Notice that the graph is redrawn again.

Carl could now use the WYSIWYG Print command to print the data and the graph on one page, but before he does this he wants to add a few enhancements to the graph.

Using the Graphics Editor

Once the graph has been inserted into the worksheet, you might want to add a variety of design elements, called **objects**, to enhance your graph. Objects include text, lines, arrows, rectangles, ellipses, and polygons. For example, you might want to point out or explain an unusually high or low point on the graph. Or you may want to draw a box around a legend. You can place objects anywhere on your graph.

To add geometric shapes, arrows, and text, you use WYSIWYG's graphics editor. The graphics editor provides a work area in which you can enhance your graph. A major component of the graphics editor is the graphics edit window. You transfer your graph from the worksheet to the graphics edit window. Once the graph is in the graphics edit window, you are ready to add various objects to the graph.

The graphics editor does not allow you to modify any part of the existing graph you created using the 1-2-3 /Graph commands. For example, you cannot modify such items as graph titles, X or Y axis labels, or legend text. To modify those items, you must use 1-2-3's /Graph commands.

Carl decides to draw a rectangle around the legend to help it stand out. He knows that before he can use the graphics editor, he must add the graph to the worksheet. Because he has already added the graph to the worksheet, his next step is to transfer the graph inserted in the worksheet to the graphics editor.

To transfer a graph to the graphics editor:

❶   Select :Graph Edit (**:GE**).

1-2-3 prompts you to identify the graph you want to transfer to the graphics editor.

❷   Move the cell pointer to any cell inside the graph's range, A21..E35, and press **[Enter]**. See Figure 3-7. The worksheet grid disappears and the graph appears in the graphics edit window, below the Graph Edit menu.

Graph Edit menu →

graphics edit → window

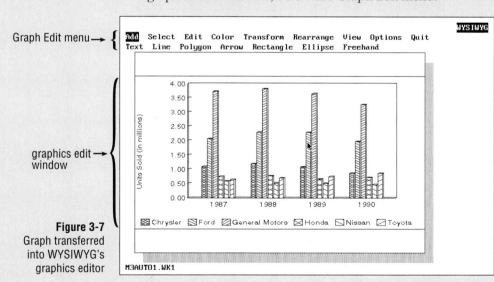

Figure 3-7
Graph transferred into WYSIWYG's graphics editor

You are now ready to edit Carl's graph.

Adding Rectangles

Recall that Carl wants to enclose the legend in a box to make it stand out. To do this, he will add a rectangle to the graph. To draw a rectangle or any other object, you use the Add command from the graphics editor and indicate the upper left and lower right corners of the object.

To help you place the rectangle or any other graphic object exactly where you want it in the graphics edit window, 1-2-3 provides a way for you to know the exact location of the cursor in the graphics edit window. Whenever you add an object to a graph, a cursor appears as a set of crosshairs to indicate exactly where you are in the graphics edit window. In addition to the cursor, the edit window is divided into a grid of very tiny rectangles, 4096 across (X coordinate) by 4096 down (Y coordinate), as shown in Figure 3-8. The upper left corner of the edit window is designated as coordinate X=0, Y=0 and the lower right corner as coordinate X=4095, Y=4095. The X coordinate is always given first. This grid helps you align the object and keep track of its location as you add it to your graph. The X value is the number of tiny rectangles from the left edge of the window, and it helps you measure how far the cursor is from the left side of the window. The Y value is the number of tiny rectangles from the top of the graphics edit window, and it measures how far the cursor is from the top of the window. WYSIWYG reports on the exact location of the cursor as you move it around the graphics edit window.

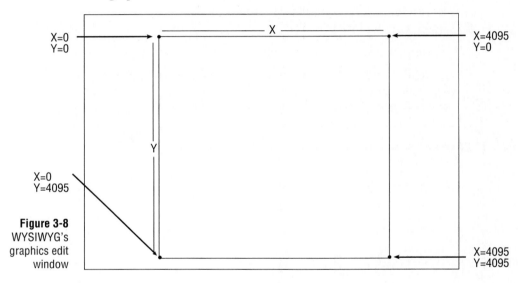

Figure 3-8
WYSIWYG's
graphics edit
window

To add a rectangle to your graph:

❶ Select Add (**A**). A list of objects appears. In this list are all the objects you can add to your graph. You can add text, lines, polygons, arrows, rectangles, ellipses, and freehand objects.

❷ Select Rectangle (**R**). See Figure 3-9.

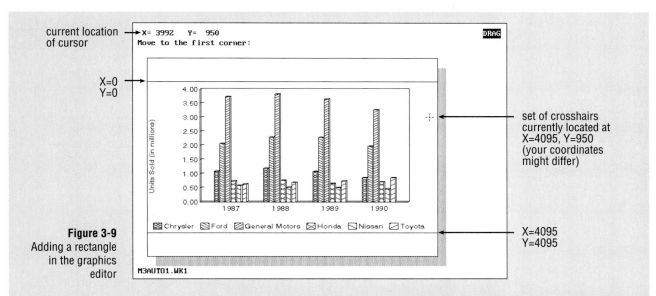

current location of cursor

X=0
Y=0

set of crosshairs currently located at X=4095, Y=950 (your coordinates might differ)

X=4095
Y=4095

Figure 3-9
Adding a rectangle in the graphics editor

The X and Y coordinates that appear in the control panel locate the exact location of the cursor in the graphics edit window.

Next specify the upper left corner of the area where you want the rectangle located.

❸ Press the arrow keys to move the cursor to the left and above the legend symbol for Chrysler. The exact position is indicated by the coordinates X=48, Y=3756. See Figure 3-10. The coordinates on your system may differ slightly from the coordinates listed in this module.

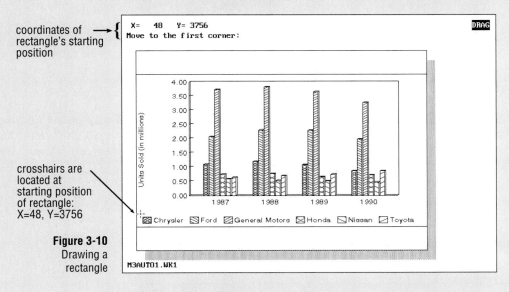

coordinates of rectangle's starting position

crosshairs are located at starting position of rectangle: X=48, Y=3756

Figure 3-10
Drawing a rectangle

❹ Press **[Spacebar]** to anchor the left corner of the rectangle.

Now 1-2-3 prompts you to stretch the box.

➎   Press the arrow keys to move the cursor to the opposite corner of the rectangle, that is, to the right and under the word Toyota (X=3952, Y=4053). As you move the cursor, a rectangle, called a **bounding box**, stretches from the left corner of the rectangle to the position of the cursor. See Figure 3-11.

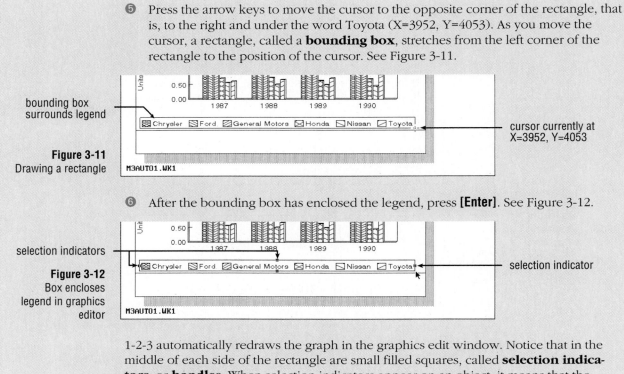

bounding box
surrounds legend

cursor currently at
X=3952, Y=4053

Figure 3-11
Drawing a rectangle

➏   After the bounding box has enclosed the legend, press **[Enter]**. See Figure 3-12.

selection indicators

selection indicator

Figure 3-12
Box encloses
legend in graphics
editor

1-2-3 automatically redraws the graph in the graphics edit window. Notice that in the middle of each side of the rectangle are small filled squares, called **selection indicators**, or **handles**. When selection indicators appear on an object, it means that the object has been *selected* and that changes to the object, such as editing, moving, and rearranging, can be made immediately using other Graph Edit commands.

Carl decides that he doesn't want to make any changes to the lines of the rectangle.

Adding Text

The next enhancement Carl wants to make is to add a text message in the bar graph. Because he wants to focus the reader's attention on General Motors' loss of over 500,000 units, Carl will insert the message "Off 500,000+" next to the bar that represents General Motors' 1990 unit sales.

To add text to your graph, you must again use the graphics editor.

To add text to your graph:

➊   Select Add Text (**AT**). A prompt appears. See Figure 3-13.

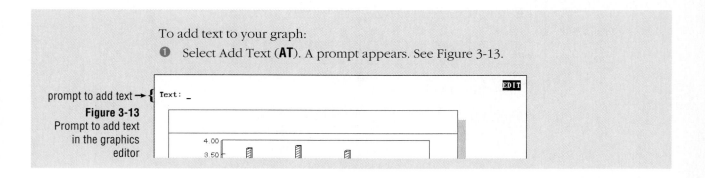

prompt to add text

Figure 3-13
Prompt to add text
in the graphics
editor

Now you can type a single line of text, up to 240 characters, following the prompt for text.

❷ Type **Off 500,000+** and press **[Enter]**. See Figure 3-14 below. 1-2-3 initially places the text in the lower right area of the graphics edit window.

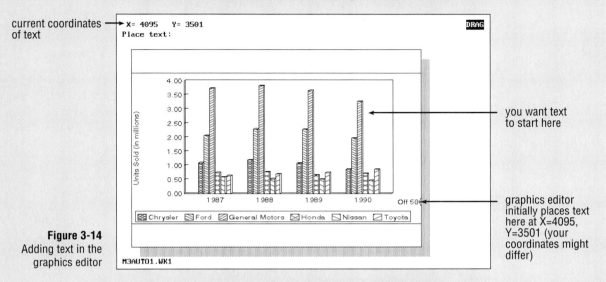

current coordinates of text

you want text to start here

graphics editor initially places text here at X=4095, Y=3501 (your coordinates might differ)

Figure 3-14
Adding text in the graphics editor

Next you need to instruct 1-2-3 where to position the text.

❸ Press the cursor keys until the text appears to the right of the 1990 bar for General Motors (X=3735, Y=1389). Don't worry if you can't locate the exact coordinates. Your results will be the same as long as your coordinates are close to these coordinates.

❹ After positioning the text, press **[Enter]**. See Figure 3-15.

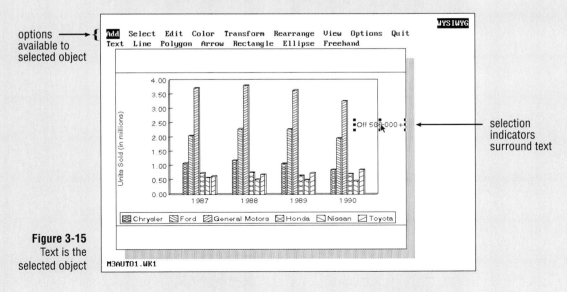

options available to selected object

selection indicators surround text

Figure 3-15
Text is the selected object

The graph is automatically redrawn in the graphics edit window, and selection indicators surround the text. As before, these indicators let you know that the text has been selected and that you can immediately perform another operation on the text such as moving it, editing it, or changing its font.

Adding Arrows

Carl next wants to draw the reader's eye from the message to the bar that shows the decline in General Motors' sales. He decides to add an arrow at the end beside the text message.

To add an arrow to your graph, the graphics editor must be loaded. In this case the graphics editor is already loaded, so you are ready to add the arrow.

To add an arrow to your graph:

❶ With the graph in the edit window of the graphics editor, select Add Arrow (**AA**).

Now move the cursor to the location where the text begins.

❷ Move the cursor to just above the "50" in "500,000" (X=3647, Y=1261), where the end of the arrow will begin. See Figure 3-16.

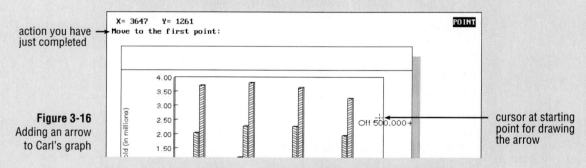

action you have just completed

Figure 3-16
Adding an arrow
to Carl's graph

cursor at starting point for drawing the arrow

❸ Press **[Spacebar]** to anchor the starting point of the arrow.

❹ Press the arrow keys up and to the left to move the cursor toward General Motors' bar for unit sales in 1990. As you press the arrow keys, watch as a line appears, stretching from the first point of the line to the cursor. Position the cursor at the end of the line (X=3335, Y=964). See Figure 3-17.

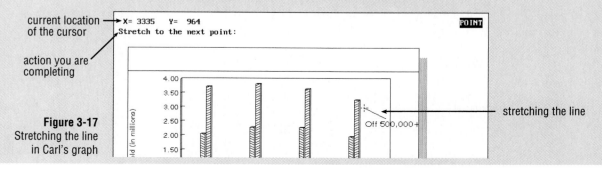

current location of the cursor

action you are completing

Figure 3-17
Stretching the line
in Carl's graph

stretching the line

⑤ Press **[Enter]** to complete the line. The arrowhead is drawn and the Graphic menu appears again. When you draw an arrow, 1-2-3 points the arrowhead toward the last point you specified.

Note the selection indicator on the arrow. As before, this indicates that the arrow is the selected object, and you can immediately make a change to it. For instance, you might change the width of the line.

Carl decides that he likes the arrow just as it is and no changes are needed.

⑥ Select Quit (**Q**) to leave the graphics editor and return to READY mode. See Figure 3-18.

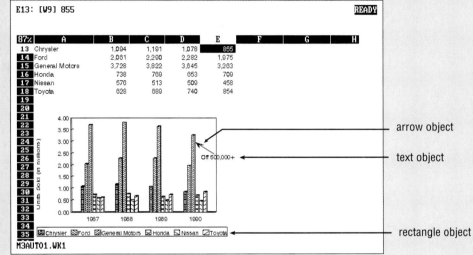

Figure 3-18
Current version of graph in worksheet with three objects added

Saving the Graph

Recall that when you save a worksheet that has been enhanced by WYSIWYG, your worksheet will consist of two files: a WK1 worksheet file and an FMT format file. Both files have the same filename. Your data and basic settings, such as column width, cell formats, and range names, are stored in the WK1 file. Your formatting information for the current worksheet, such as fonts, styles, lines, added graphs, and enhanced graphics, are stored in the FMT file. Let's save Carl's worksheet.

To save a worksheet that includes WYSIWYG enhancements:

❶ Press **[Home]** to move the cell pointer to cell A1.

Enter the name of the file you will use when saving the worksheet.

❷ Type **W3AUTO1.WK1** and press **[Enter]**.

Now save the file.

❸   Select /File Save (**/FS**).

❹   Type **W3AUTO1** and press **[Enter]**. Both the WK1 and FMT files are now saved.

Printing Graphs in WYSIWYG

WYSIWYG provides a way to print your worksheet and graph that is simpler than using 1-2-3's PrintGraph utility. When you add a graph to your worksheet with the Graph Add command, you can use the WYSIWYG Print commands to print a graph by itself or print a graph along with the worksheet data. To print in WYSIWYG, you must specify the range of cells you want printed.

Carl decides to print the bar graph on the same page as the automobile sales data. He looks at the data and the graph, and sees that the range he wants to print is A7..E35.

To set the print range:

❶   Select :Print (**:P**). A dialog box appears showing the current settings for WYSIWYG printing.

❷   Select Range Set (**RS**).

❸   Move the cell pointer to A7, the first cell in the print range, and press **[.]** to anchor the print range.

❹   Highlight the range A7..E35 and press **[Enter]**. The range now appears in the dialog box. See Figure 3-19. You have now specified the print range.

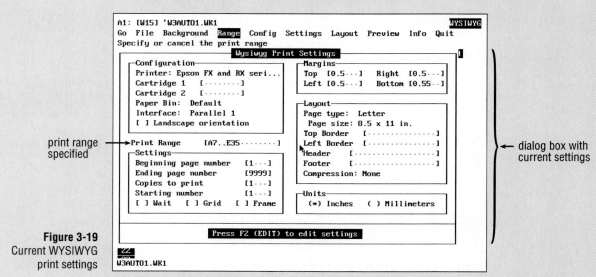

print range specified →

← dialog box with current settings

Figure 3-19
Current WYSIWYG print settings

Next you must instruct WYSIWYG which printer to use to print the graph and the data. If no printer appears in the dialog box, you must select one.

To select a printer:

❶ Select Config Print (**CP**). A list of installed printers appears.

❷ Select the name of the printer you want to use and press **[Enter]**. If you are not sure, check with your instructor or technical support person.

❸ Select Quit (**Q**) to return to the Print menu. You are ready to print.

Printing in WYSIWYG can take a long time. So let's preview the output before actually printing the worksheet.

To preview a page:

❶ Select Preview (**P**). See Figure 3-20.

preview of data
and graph

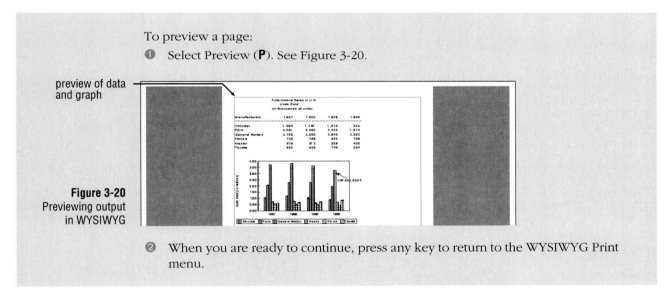

Figure 3-20
Previewing output
in WYSIWYG

❷ When you are ready to continue, press any key to return to the WYSIWYG Print menu.

After previewing the worksheet, Carl is happy with what he sees and is ready to print it.

To print the data and their graph:

❶ Select Go (**G**). As you are printing your document, the mode indicator flashes "Wait." Depending on the formatting enhancements in your worksheet and the printer you selected, your output may take a few seconds to several minutes to complete.

If you are using diskettes to store your data files, you might encounter the message "Error writing file" when you try to print in WYSIWYG. If this happens, place another formatted diskette in the drive and try again.

After the worksheet has been printed, you are automatically returned to READY mode.

Figure 3-21 shows the printed output that Carl will give to his supervisor.

Manufacturers	1987	1988	1989	1990
Chrysler	1,094	1,191	1,078	888
Ford	2,061	2,290	2,282	1,975
General Motors	3,728	3,822	3,645	3,263
Honda	738	769	653	709
Nissan	576	513	509	458
Toyota	628	689	740	854

Automobile Sales in U.S.
Units Sold
(in thousands of units)

Figure 3-21
Carl's final output

Exercises

1. What types of graphs can you add to a worksheet using WYSIWYG?

2. What WYSIWYG commands or actions would you choose to accomplish each of the following?
   a. insert a graph into a worksheet
   b. reduce the size of worksheet cells
   c. add rectangle to a graph
   d. print a hard copy of your data and supporting graph on one page

3. You have just completed a graph using the /Graph command. What steps are necessary to add text inside a box to the graph?

4. You have just added a pie chart to your worksheet using WYSIWYG. Before you have a chance to add some enhancements to the pie chart, you have to stop working. You decide to complete your work tomorrow. What should you do to make sure you can begin your work from the point where you left off today?

5. How would you print each of the following graphs?
   a. a bar graph you added to your worksheet
   b. a bar graph you added to your worksheet but did not enhance with a boxed-in legend

Case Problems

1. Coles Investments

Ian Coles owns an investment research firm. Each month he prepares a newsletter for his clients. This month he is recommending that investors consider investing in pharmaceutical companies. He feels drug companies are recession resistant and offer above-average growth. He is in the process of completing a graph that will be included in his newsletter. Help Ian complete the graph.

Do the following:

1. Attach WYSIWYG.

2. Retrieve the worksheet M3INVEST.WK1.

3. Insert the current graph into the worksheet.

4. Save the worksheet as W3INVEST.

5. Print the data and the graph on one page.

2. Inflation Is Under Control

The Center for Business and Economics at Ashland University publishes a quarterly newsletter about business and economic conditions in the region that is mailed to over 150 businesses. One part of the report deals with consumer prices. Rory Jones is in the process of completing a graph on the U.S. inflation rates since 1981. Help him complete the graph.

Do the following:

1. Attach WYSIWYG.

2. Retrieve the file M3INFLA1.WK1.

3. Use WYSIWYG to insert the current graph to the right of the data in the range D5..H16.

4. Print the data and the graph on one page.

5. Add the following footnote at the bottom left corner of the graph:
    Source: U.S. Department of Labor

6. Display the footnote using an 8-point Dutch font.

7. Add the comment "Inflation Slowed" near the mark for 1991.

8. Include an arrow that draws attention from the text to the 1991 point on the line graph.

9. Save your worksheet as W3INFLA1.

10. Print the graph with its enhancements.

Module 4

Using SmartIcons

What are SmartIcons?

If you are using Lotus 1-2-3 Release 2.4, you can take advantage of a powerful new feature called SmartIcons. **SmartIcons** are graphic images that represent 1-2-3 commands or functions such as retrieving and saving files, formatting data, and printing worksheets. They provide a faster and easier way to access 1-2-3 commands than 1-2-3's menu system.

You can access SmartIcons with a keyboard or a mouse, but mouse users benefit more because complex operations can be executed with one click of the mouse button.

SmartIcons can be used with or without WYSIWYG. Figure 4-1 on the next page shows what SmartIcons look like on your screen.

OBJECTIVES

In this tutorial you will:

- Learn the definitions of SmartIcon, icon, and palette

- Load the SmartIcons add-in program

- Use a SmartIcon to retrieve a worksheet

- Use a SmartIcon to format a range

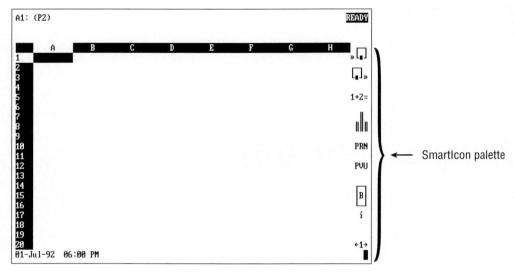

Figure 4-1a
SmartIcons
without WYSIWYG

Figure 4-1b
SmartIcons with
WYSIWYG

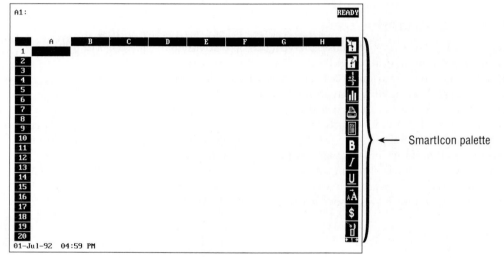

SmartIcons are grouped into columns called **palettes**. The icons in Figure 4-1 appear on palettes found to the right of the worksheets. In all, 1-2-3 Release 2.4 offers 77 icons grouped on several palettes. 65 of these icons are predefined Lotus commands or functions; 12 icons are user-defined and can be assigned to macros. The total number of palettes depends on the resolution of your screen and whether WYSIWYG is attached.

In this tutorial, you will learn how to load, access, and use SmartIcons.

Loading the SmartIcons Program

SmartIcons is an add-in program that is separate from the 1-2-3 program. You must attach the SmartIcons program before you can use SmartIcons. It is possible to run the SmartIcons and WYSIWYG programs at the same time; doing so will enhance the appearance of the icons, as in Figure 4-1b. However, since not all computers have enough memory to run both programs at once, we will assume in this tutorial that WYSIWYG is not attached. If WYSIWYG *is* attached on your system, the instructions in this tutorial will work, but the SmartIcons will look different on your screen.

If you do not see a SmartIcons palette on the right side of your screen, follow these steps to attach the SmartIcons add-in program. If SmartIcons appear on your screen the program is attached and you can go to "Using SmartIcons" on page L 358. Do not confuse SmartIcons with mouse icons. If your screen displays only a set of four triangles and a question mark along the right side, SmartIcons are not attached and you should follow the instructions for attaching them.

To attach the SmartIcons add-in program:

❶ Select */Add-in Attach* (**/AA**). A list of add-in programs appears. See Figure 4-2.

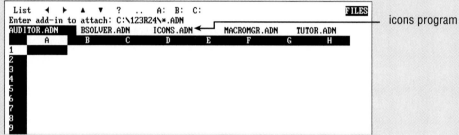

icons program

Figure 4-2
Add-in programs in
1-2-3 release 2.4

ICONS.ADN is the name of the SmartIcons program.

❷ Highlight ICONS.ADN and press **[Enter]**. The extension ADN stands for **AD**d-i**N**.

Once the SmartIcons program is loaded into memory, choose how you want to access the icon palettes using the keyboard. See Figure 4-3.

options →

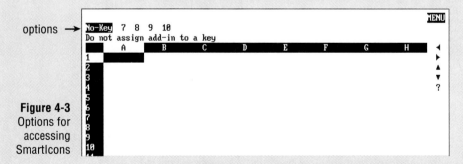

Figure 4-3
Options for
accessing
SmartIcons

If you choose *No-Key*, you cannot access the SmartIcons using the keyboard. You must use a mouse.

If you choose *7*, you press [Alt] [F7] to access the SmartIcons.

If you choose *8*, you press [Alt][F8] to access the SmartIcons.

If you choose *9*, you press [Alt][F9] to access the SmartIcons.

If you choose *10*, you press [Alt][F10] to access the SmartIcons.

❸ Highlight 7 and press **[Enter]**.

❹ Select *Quit* (**Q**) to leave the add-in menu and return to READY mode. The SmartIcons program is now attached to 1-2-3. Your screen should be similar to Figure 4-1a or 4-1b.

Using SmartIcons

Pauline wants to see how the worksheet will look if all of the values that represent currency are formatted as currency. We'll use SmartIcons first to retrieve a worksheet file, then to format a range as currency.

Using SmartIcons to Retrieve a File

First, let's use a SmartIcon to retrieve Pauline's final worksheet.

To retrieve Pauline's worksheet using the keyboard to access SmartIcons:

❶ Press **[Alt][F7]** to access SmartIcons. See Figure 4-4. Notice that the top icon is highlighted and that a brief description of its function appears in the control panel.

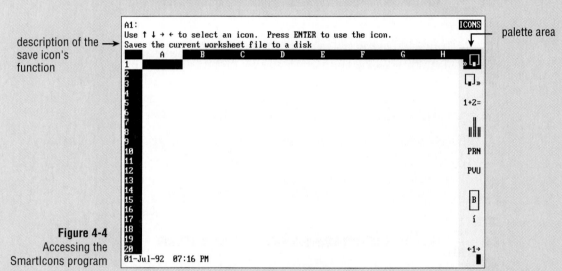

description of the save icon's function

palette area

Figure 4-4
Accessing the SmartIcons program

If you have a mouse, you can access SmartIcons by moving your mouse pointer anywhere into the palette area.

❷ Press **[↓]** once to highlight the next icon. A description of the highlighted icon is displayed on the control panel. See Figure 4-5.

If you have a mouse, you can see a description of a SmartIcon by holding down the right mouse button while you move the mouse pointer over that icon.

If the second icon on the current palette is not the retrieve file icon, continue pressing **[↓]** until the retrieve file icon is highlighted.

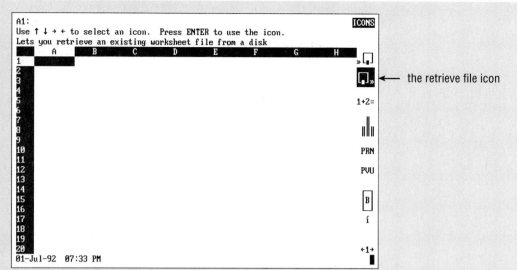

the retrieve file icon

Figure 4-5
Highlighting the
retrieve file icon

Now let's actually select the SmartIcon.

❸ Press **[Enter]**. A list of your worksheet files appears on the screen.

If you have a mouse, you can select SmartIcons by clicking the left mouse button while your mouse pointer is on that icon.

❹ Highlight the file M4BALBO1.WK1 and press **[Enter]**.

❺ Press **[PgDn]** to view the worksheet data. See Figure 4-6.

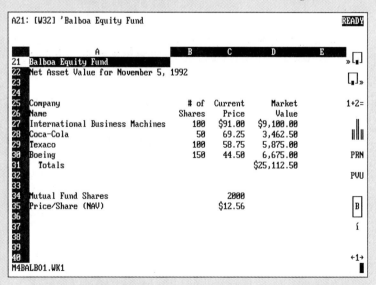

Figure 4-6

Formatting a Range as Currency

Before Pauline can change the format to currency, she needs to specify the range of cells that she wants to format.

To specify the range of data:

❶ Move the cell pointer to cell C28.

❷ Press **[F4]** to anchor the cell pointer.

❸ Highlight the range C28..D30 and press **[Enter]** to select them.

Because many SmartIcons perform their actions on a *range* of cells, learning how to prese-lect ranges is important. If the range you want to specify is a single cell, just move the cell pointer to the cell on which you wish to perform the action, then access SmartIcons.

Now that the range of data is specified it can be formatted. Pauline knows that the $ icon formats a selected range to currency with 2 decimals, but she can't remember on which palette she saw that icon.

To display another icon palette:

❶ Press **[Alt][F7]** to access SmartIcons.

❷ Move to the next palette by pressing **[→]**. See Figure 4-7.

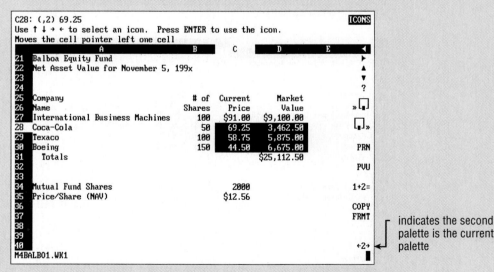

Figure 4-7
Second icon palette

The current palette is indicated by the number at the bottom of the palette area. To move to the previous palette, you would press [←].

If you have a mouse, you can move to the next palette by clicking the left mouse button on the arrow to the right of the palette number at the bottom of the palette

(See Figure 4-7). To move to the previous palette, click on the arrow to the left of the palette number.

In text mode, the currency format SmartIcon is not on the second palette. Let's look on the third palette.

❸ Press [→] to display the third palette. See Figure 4-8. The currency icon is on the third palette.

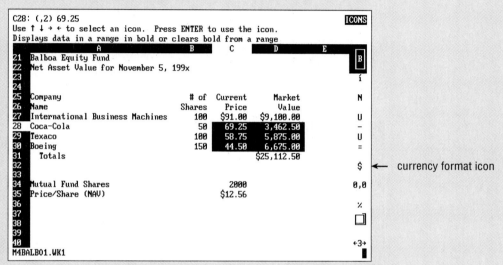

Figure 4-8
Third icon palette

← currency format icon

If the currency format icon is not on your third palette, use the [←] and [→] keys to search the other palettes until you find it.

Now format the range as currency format.

To select the currency format SmartIcon:

❶ Use [↓] to move the highlight to the currency format icon ($) and press **[Enter]**. The values within the specified range change to currency format. See Figure 4-9.

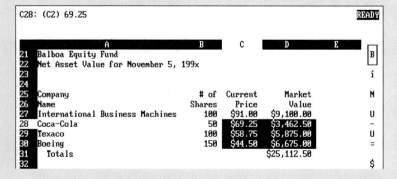

Figure 4-9
Currency format
applied to the range

Pauline decides the added dollar signs make the worksheet look cluttered. She decides to remove the currency format.

To turn off the currency format:

❶ Press **[Alt][F7]** to access SmartIcons.

Because the range C28..D30 remained highlighted after you selected currency format the first time, you do not have to preselect it again.

❷ Highlight the currency format icon and press **[Enter]**. The data changes back to general format. See Figure 4-10.

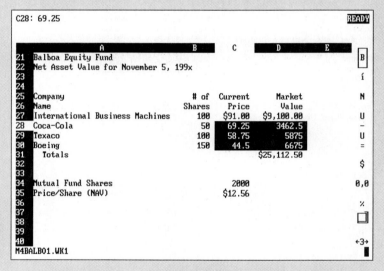

Figure 4-10
Range format changed back to general format

Reselecting the icon reverts the selected range to the Worksheet's global format. If you want the range to have two decimal places again, you would need to type /Range Format Fixed (/RF F), then press [Enter] to accept 2 as the number of decimal places.

Descriptions of the SmartIcons

Now that you know what SmartIcons are and how to use them, refer to Figure 4-11 to see a description of the SmartIcons. Some icons work only when WYSIWYG is attached. The icons in the first column are the icons that appear when WYSIWYG is attached. The icons in the second column are the icons that appear when WYSIWYG is not attached. Remember that by navigating through the palettes yourself, you can view descriptions of the icons and experiment with what they do.

Icons in WYSIWYG mode	Icons in text mode	Description
	»	Saves the current worksheet file to a disk.
	U _	This icon can only be used with WYSIWYG attached. Adds a single underline to data in a range or removes a single underline.
	U =	This icon can only be used with WYSIWYG attached. Adds a double underline to data in a range or removes a double underline.
	$	Formats values in a range with 2 decimal places, the default currency symbol, and the default thousands separator or restores the global format in the range.
	0,0	Formats values in a range with the default thousands separator and no decimal places or restores the global format in the range.
	%	Formats values in a range as % (percent) with 2 decimal places or restores the global format in the range.
	^{2}→2	This icon can only be used with WYSIWYG attached. Displays data in the highlighted range in the next available type style and/or point size.
	FGRD	This icon can only be used with WYSIWYG attached. Displays data in the highlighted range in the next available color.
	BGRD	This icon can only be used with WYSIWYG attached. Displays the background of the highlighted range in the next available color.
		This icon can only be used with WYSIWYG attached. Draws an outline around a range and draws a drop shadow below and to the right of the range or removes an existing drop shadow and outline.

	☐	This icon can only be used with WYSIWYG attached. Draws a single-line, double-line, or wide outline around a range or clears the outline, depending on the current type of outline.
	###	This icon can only be used with WYSIWYG attached. Adds light, dark, or solid shading to a range or removes the solid shading, depending on the current type of shading in the range.
	←L	Left-aligns labels in a range.
	←C→	Centers labels in a range.
	R→	Right-aligns labels in a range.
	ALGN TEXT	This icon can only be used with WYSIWYG attached. Centers text in a text range, aligns text evenly at both the left and right of a text range, right-aligns text, left-aligns text, or clears the alignment settings for a range, depending on the current alignment setting.
	+ROW	Inserts one or more rows above the highlighted range.
	+COL	Inserts one or more columns to the left of the highlighted range.
	−ROW	Deletes all rows in the highlighted range.
	−COL	Deletes all columns in the highlighted range.
	——— ---	Inserts a page break in the row that contains the cell pointer.
	┊┊	This icon can only be used with WYSIWYG attached. Inserts a page break in the column that contains the cell pointer.
	A→Z	Sorts a database in ascending order (A through Z and smallest to largest values), using the selected column as the sort key.
	Z→A	Sorts a database in descending order (Z through A and largest to smallest values), using the selected column as the sort key.

FILL   Fills the highlighted range with a sequence of values.

CALC   Recalculates all formulas in the worksheet.

DATE   Enters a number that corresponds to the current date and time in the current cell. If the cell is formatted with a date format, the date appears in the cell in that format. If the cell is not formatted with a date format, the date appears in the cell in the default date format. If the cell is formatted with a time format, the time appears in the cell in that format.

CRCL   This icon can only be used with WYSIWYG attached. Circles the data in the highlighted range. 1-2-3 creates the circle by adding a graphic to the highlighted range.

ZOOM   This icon can only be used with WYSIWYG attached. Enlarges the size of displayed cells and their contents to 125% or 150% of their normal size; reduces the size of displayed cells to 63% or 87% of their normal size; or displays cells at their normal size, depending on the current display size setting.

STEP   Turns on STEP mode, which executes macros one step at a time for debugging.

RUN   Lets you select and run a macro.

◀   Moves the cell pointer left one cell.

▶   Moves the cell pointer right one cell.

▲   Moves the cell pointer up one cell.

▼   Moves the cell pointer down one cell.

?   Starts the 1-2-3 Help system in READY mode.

⌐   Moves the cell pointer to cell A1. Equivalent to pressing HOME.

⌐   Moves the cell pointer to the lower right corner of the active area (the rectangular area between cell A1 and the lowest and rightmost nonblank cell in the worksheet).

	$\lVert \downarrow$ =	Moves the cell pointer down to the intersection of a blank and a nonblank cell. Equivalent to pressing END ↓.
	= $\lVert \uparrow$	Moves the cell pointer up to the intersection of a blank and a nonblank cell. Equivalent to pressing END ↑.
	→ == =	Moves the cell pointer right to the intersection of a blank and a nonblank cell. Equivalent to pressing END →.
	== == ←	Moves the cell pointer left to the intersection of a blank and a nonblank cell. Equivalent to press END ←.
	GOTO	Lets you move the cell pointer to a specified cell or range.
	FIND	Lets you find or replace specified characters in labels and formulas in a range.
	UNDO	Cancels your previous action or command if the undo feature is on.
	DEL	Erases the highlighted range.
	⌐•⌐ »	Lets you retrieve an existing worksheet file from a disk.
	1+2=	Sums values in the highlighted range, if you include empty cells below or to the right of the range; or, if the highlighted range is blank, sums values in the nearest area of data and places the results in the highlighted range.
	‖ ‖ ‖	Graphs the contents of the highlighted range or the data immediately adjacent to or surrounding the cell pointer. This icon displays the QuickGraph dialog box, which lets you change the settings for graph type, orientation, colors and 3-D effect and lets you graph data in columns or rows. If the cell pointer is not currently in an area that contains data, this icon lets you make changes to the current graph settings and displays the current graph.
	⌐‖ ‖ ‖	This icon can only be used with WYSIWYG attached. Adds the current graph to the highlighted range in the worksheet.

Icon	Label	Description
	VIEW GRPH	Displays the current graph. Equivalent to pressing F10 (GRAPH).
	EDIT TEXT	This icon can only be used with WYSIWYG attached. Lets you enter or edit text in a text range.
	PRN	Prints the range you specified with /Print Printer Range or :Print Range or, if no print range is specified, prints the highlighted range.
	PVU	This icon can only be used with WYSIWYG attached. Displays a preview of the range you specified with /Printer Printer Range or :Print Range or, if no print range is specified, displays a preview of the highlighted range.
	COPY	Lets you specify a range to copy the highlighted range to.
	MOVE	Lets you specify a range to move the highlighted range to.
	COPY FRMT	This icon can only be used with WYSIWYG attached. Applies the WYSIWYG formats of the highlighted range to a range you specify.
	REP DATA	Copies the contents of the current cell of the highlighted range in all other cells in the range.
	B	This icon can only be used with WYSIWYG attached. Displays data in a range in bold or clears bold from a previously formatted range.
	í	This icon can only be used with WYSIWYG attached. Displays data in a range in italic or clears italic from a previously formatted range.
	N	This icon can only be used with WYSIWYG attached. Clears all WYSIWYG formatting from a range and restores the default font.
		Adds an icon to your custom palette.
		Removes an icon from you custom palette.

Moves an icon to another location on your custom palette.

Displays descriptions of user icons U1 through U12, lets you assign one or more macros and descriptions to one or more user icons, and lets you copy the text of one or more macros to the worksheet so you can debug the macros.

Runs the macro you assigned to user icon U1. The SmartIcons add-in includes 12 user icons, labeled U1, U2, and so on through U12.

Lotus 1-2-3 Index

dBASE IV Tutorials

∎ ∎ ∎

Tutorial 1

An Introduction to Database Concepts and dBASE IV

OBJECTIVES

In this tutorial you will learn to:

- Define the terms *field, record, file,* and *database*

- Load dBASE

- Identify the components of the Control Center screen

- Use the menu system

- Get help while in the Control Center

- Switch from the Control Center to dot prompt mode

- Quit dBASE

Case: Wells & Martinez Advertising Agency — The Need for Computerization

Three years ago Nancy Wells and Martin Martinez founded the Wells & Martinez Advertising Agency (W&M) in Sante Fe, New Mexico. Their initial goal was to plan, prepare, and place advertising and other promotions for small to mid-sized local companies. Like many new, struggling businesses, W&M has experienced limited initial success providing advertising services to a few key clients. Their current client list includes a fashion boutique, a furniture designer, a caterer, a law firm, an automobile dealership, an insurance agency, and the town of Sante Fe's tourism board.

Recently, in an effort to attract more clients, Nancy and Martin launched an aggressive marketing campaign that focused on their agency's strengths — creativity, flexibility, and reasonable rates. The campaign generated increased interest among local companies, but, more important, it also attracted attention from several regional companies.

The prospect of increasing the size of their client list is both good news and bad news for Nancy and Martin. They have a limited budget and only six employees to help run the operations and creative activities of the agency. In addition the day-to-day administration of W&M is time-consuming. Nancy and Martin recognize that if they don't improve their own and their employees' efficiency, W&M might not be able to handle new business.

Martin directs the creative activities of W&M. He is responsible for generating advertising ideas and converting those ideas into print and broadcast messages. As the head of this part of W&M, Martin is primed and ready for the impending growth.

Nancy manages the administrative and production side of the agency. She has been struggling with the manual business systems that handle the billing, payroll, and general bookkeeping. Nancy knows that W&M has outgrown these basic systems, which she established three years ago; she expects to run into even more difficulty with possible new business.

Martin and Nancy have identified several problems with their current system. They are concerned about cash flow and that billings to clients are not always mailed promptly. Martin and Nancy have no way of knowing whether clients are being charged correctly or whether a specific job is profitable. In addition, their systems to track the various jobs and job-related expenses are inadequate. Finally, they know that the manual systems often supply erroneous information.

Nancy and Martin realize that computerization is the way to solve these administrative problems. But because of the cost of their recent marketing campaign, they cannot afford a computerized software package specifically designed for advertising agencies. They put their heads together and try to come up with a solution. If only they themselves knew about computers. Then Nancy remembers that Esther Wong, a recent business college graduate she hired 10 months ago, is familiar with accounting and microcomputer software. Nancy and Martin decide to talk to Esther and ask her to help them develop a computerized system in house.

Esther is flattered that Nancy and Martin have asked her to help, and she sets to the task immediately. She begins her analysis by first evaluating how work flows within W&M. She interviews Nancy, Martin, and the other employees to better understand how the advertising jobs are initiated, tracked, and billed.

After studying the work flow and discussing ways to improve the business systems, Esther outlines a possible solution. She presents her ideas to Nancy, Martin, and other staff members; they discuss her proposal, make several modifications, and then agree to create three files. First, a Clients file will store each client's identification code (ID), the names of the client companies, the names of the contacts at the client companies, and the clients' main telephone numbers. Second, a Jobs file will store information about each job that a client has authorized W&M to complete. The jobs file will include job numbers, client identification, brief descriptions of the jobs, due dates, and estimates of the costs to the clients. The third file, the Expenses file, will include for each expense the ID of the client to be charged; the job number; the billing category, which describes the expense, such as creative meeting, typesetting, copywriting, and so on; the date; the amount; and a brief explanation. Esther decides to use dBASE IV to create and maintain these files and thus computerize W&M.

Introduction to Database Concepts

Before you work along with Esther and begin the W&M database system, you need to understand a few important terms and concepts.

How Data Are Organized

Stored data, computerized or not, are commonly organized into a structure, or hierarchy, that starts at the bottom with fields and then builds to records, files, and then databases (Figure 1-1). This organization of data helps you to process and retrieve information.

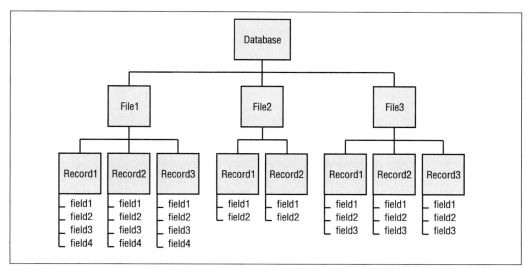

Figure 1-1
Data hierarchy

First let's look at a field. A **field,** also called a **data item** or a **data element**, is a characteristic of an object, person, place, or thing. For example, the client identification number, client name, client phone number, and name of contact person are fields that W&M wants to track for each client. Each field has a value. The *value of a field* is its specific contents. For example, the value of the field "phone number" might be (419)783-6210, and the value of the field "contact person" might be Gunther Williams.

If we group related fields together, they form what is known as a record. A **record** is a collection of data elements that describe an event, person, or object. For example, a complete client record at W&M consists of four related fields: client identification, client name, name of contact person, and phone number (Figure 1-2).

Figure 1-2
A client record

CLIENT ID	CLIENT NAME	CONTACT	PHONE
MOU	Mountain Top Ski	Gunther Williams	(419) 783-6210

value in CONTACT field

one record

A collection of related records is called a **file**. At W&M the nine client records collectively represent a file, in this case, the agency's clients file. Each record within the file contains the same four fields, but the data values in those fields vary from record to record. Figure 1-3 shows the complete W&M file CLIENT.

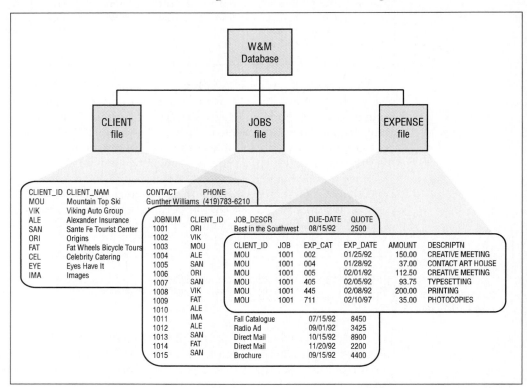

CLIENT ID	CLIENT NAME	CONTACT	PHONE	
MOU	Mountain Top Ski	Gunther Williams	(419) 783-6210	record 1
VIK	Viking Auto Group	Jeff Serito	(505) 984-9216	record 2
ALE	Alexander Insurance	Paul Alexander	(505) 883-9222	record 3
SAN	Santa Fe Tourist Center	Liddy Posada	(505) 986-5555	record 4
ORI	Origins	Gary Higgins	(505) 988-0733	record 5
FAT	Fat Wheels Bicycle Tours	Helen Carson	(505) 994-2432	record 6
CEL	Celebrity Catering	Linda Randall	(505) 883-9922	record 7
EYE	Eyes Have It	Sandy Alonso	(505) 780-2277	record 8
IMA	Images	Wendy Falchetti	(505) 898-1286	record 9

Figure 1-3
W&M's CLIENT file

Typically a company maintains several different files to store related data. A **database** is a collection of related files. For example, at W&M Esther's system will include a file to store basic data about clients, a second file to store data about each client's job on which W&M is working, and a third file to track the expenses incurred by W&M as they work on those jobs. These three related files can be thought of as W&M's database (Figure 1-4).

Figure 1-4
W&M's database

Database Management Systems

To create and manage its database, a company often purchases a database management system. A **database management system** (DBMS) is the software that lets you enter, maintain, manipulate, retrieve, and output data from a database.

A DBMS works as an "intermediary," that is, it serves as an interface between a database and the users who are seeking data from that database (Figure 1-5). A DBMS allows you to retrieve information from a database and to store data in a database conveniently and efficiently. Specifically a DBMS does the following:

- It creates the structure of the database files. In other words, it defines the fields in a record.
- It facilitates the initial loading of data into the database and enables you to update the database by adding, deleting, and modifying records.
- It allows you to ask questions by using query language and report generator software. A **query language** lets you obtain immediate responses to questions you ask about information in the database. You specify what you are looking for, and the DBMS searches the database and gives you the answers. The emphasis of a query is on quick response rather than well-designed output. A **report generator** allows you to develop professional-looking reports by including page numbers, report titles, column headings, and totals as part of the output.
- It provides a mechanism to protect the database from damage and unlawful use.

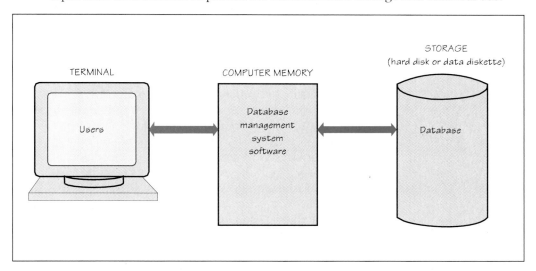

Figure 1-5
A database
management
system

How to Follow the Numbered Steps in the dBASE IV Tutorials

In the dBASE IV tutorials, you will follow step-by-step instructions. These are displayed as numbered lists on a blue-shaded background, for example:

❶ Press **[Esc]** to return to the Control Center.

Within the numbered lists are the following types of instructions:

- The letters, numbers, and special characters that you type are in boldface, for example: Type **browse**.
- Keys that you press are in brackets and in boldface, for example: Press **[Esc]**.
- Function keys are followed by the dBASE key name in parentheses, for example: Press **[F2]** (Data).

- Key combinations mean that you press and hold down the first key, and then while holding the first key, you press the second key. You then release both keys. An example of a key combination is **[Alt]T**.

- Menu options, which are in italics, are followed by a letter in parentheses and in boldface: you can select the option by pressing that key. An example would be *Modify catalog name* (**M**).

An Introduction to dBASE IV

dBASE IV, marketed by Borland International, is a DBMS package used to create, maintain, and manipulate database files. Currently it is one of the most widely used database software packages for IBM and compatible microcomputers. For the rest of this tutorial you will learn about different ways to use dBASE IV, and you will practice two of those methods. This practice will equip you for Tutorials 2 through 6, so you can work with Esther as she creates a database for W&M.

dBASE Modes

When you use dBASE IV (also referred to hereafter simply as dBASE), you can instruct the DBMS to do what you want in one of three ways. First you can use the **Control Center**, a graphic environment that provides an easy way to access your files. It is the gateway to accessing the dBASE menu system. With the Control Center you do not need an in-depth understanding of the dBASE commands. Second you can type in commands using dBASE's **Command mode**, or **dot prompt mode**. In this mode, you are presented with a blank screen except for a period (a dot) that appears near the bottom of the screen. The cursor is positioned after the period, which indicates that dBASE is ready for you to type your command. Third you can store commands in a program file and use dBASE's **Program mode**. You can then execute those commands by issuing a single command.

The Control Center is easy to understand because it includes the most frequently used dBASE commands. Some people, however, find the dot prompt mode to be faster and more flexible, so for each dBASE function introduced using the Control Center, the equivalent dot prompt command is also included.

Starting dBASE

Before you begin using the Control Center, you must first load dBASE into computer memory. If you are using your own computer and you have not already installed dBASE, see *Installing dBASE IV*, the instructions that accompanied your dBASE disks.

To start dBASE:

❶ Before you start dBASE, make sure you have the dBASE IV data diskette ready. If you haven't already created the dBASE IV data diskette, see the beginning of this book for instructions.

❷ Put your data diskette in drive A. If your data diskette matches drive B but not drive A, put your data diskette in drive B. Use drive B instead of drive A for all instructions that refer to your data diskette.

For the purposes in this text, we assume dBASE IV is stored on the C drive in the DBSAMPLE directory. If your system is different, check with your instructor. If you are using a network system, check with your technical support person for instructions on how to start dBASE and in which drive to put your data diskette.

❸ Make sure drive C is the current drive. Type **cd\dbsample** and press **[Enter]**. This makes the directory that contains the dBASE program files the current directory.

❹ At the DOS prompt, type **dbase** and press **[Enter]**.

dBASE is now loaded into computer memory. See Figure 1-6.

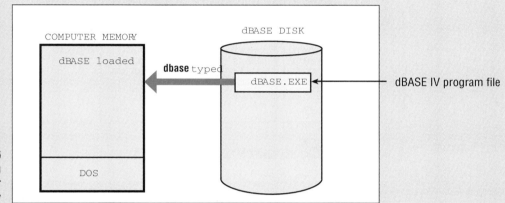

Figure 1-6
Process of loading dBASE into computer memory

dBASE IV program file

The dBASE copyright and license agreement appear briefly on the screen, then the dBASE IV Control Center screen appears. See Figure 1-7.

```
 Catalog   Tools   Exit                                        5:57:44 pm
                            dBASE IV CONTROL CENTER

                    CATALOG: C:\DBSAMPLE\SAMPLES\SAMPLES.CAT

      Data       Queries       Forms       Reports      Labels    Applications

   ┌─────────┐ ┌─────────┐ ┌─────────┐ ┌─────────┐ ┌─────────┐ ┌─────────┐
   │<create> │ │<create> │ │<create> │ │<create> │ │<create> │ │<create> │
   │         │ │         │ │         │ │         │ │         │ │         │
   │ CODES   │ │ GUESTS  │ │ ADDBOOK │ │ ALLNAMES│ │ CARDONLY│ │ AREACODE│
   │ CONTENTS│ │ LOCATOR │ │ CONTACTS│ │ CARDREC │ │ INVITES │ │ BUSINESS│
   │ EMPLOYEE│ │ NAMESQRY│ │ OBJECTS │ │ INVENTRY│ │ MAILALL │ │         │
   │ NAMES   │ │*ADDCODES│ │ PHONELOG│ │ REGIONAL│ │ NAMETAGS│ │         │
   │ PEOPLBAK│ │         │ │         │ │         │ │         │ │         │
   │ PEOPLE  │ │         │ │         │ │         │ │         │ │         │
   └─────────┘ └─────────┘ └─────────┘ └─────────┘ └─────────┘ └─────────┘

   File:        New file
   Description: Press ENTER on <create> to create a new file

   Help:F1  Use:◄┘  Data:F2  Design:Shift-F2  Quick Report:Shift-F9  Menus:F10
```

Figure 1-7
The Control Center

The dBASE IV Control Center

dBASE IV provides you with a comprehensive set of menus, screens, and prompts, collectively called the **menu system**. The menu system enables you to perform various tasks such as creating, modifying, organizing, and viewing your data.

You will access the dBASE IV menu system through the Control Center. The Control Center consists of six components, which are shown in Figure 1-8. Understanding these components will help you use dBASE more effectively.

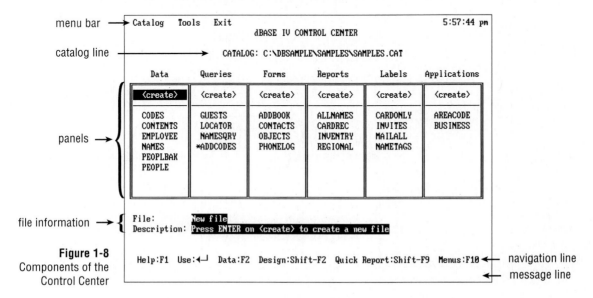

Figure 1-8
Components of the
Control Center

The components of the Control Center include the following:

- *Menu Bar.* The top line of the Control Center is called the **menu bar**. This line identifies the menus available to you from the Control Center. Each menu has a **pull-down menu** associated with it. For example, if you select the Tools menu, you can then copy a database file to another diskette.

- *Catalog line.* A **catalog** is a collection of related files. It is a tool for organizing related information in a database application. For example, you can store several database files and reports you create from those files in the same catalog. The catalog line indicates the default drive and directory and the name of the catalog currently in use.

- *Panels.* The center of the screen consists of six **panels**. Each panel is named by the type of file you can create or list from within that panel. The panels represent the operations you can perform through the Control Center. You create and maintain database files in the Data panel; you design searches to access data in the Queries panel; you create custom data-entry screens in the Forms panel; you design customized reports in the Reports panel; you create customized mailing labels in the Labels panel; and you write customized programs in the Applications panel. The files in the current catalog are listed in the panels under the appropriate file types. From these panels you select files and initiate database operations.

- *File information.* The section of the Control Center below the panels contains **file information**. This section lists the filename and a description of the file that is currently highlighted in the panel.
- *Navigation line.* The **navigation line** is at the bottom of the screen and lists the keys you can use to move the cursor. For example, Help:F1 tells you you can get help by pressing the function key [F1].
- *Message line.* The **message line** is below the navigation line. This line tells you what the current selection in the pull-down menu will do. This line is empty now because no menu option is selected.

Overview of the dBASE IV Menu System

Each set of menus in the dBASE IV menu system provides options that will help you build an effective database. The Control Center has three menus. The Catalog menu contains options to create and modify catalogs. The Tools menu contains options to aid in file management and to change the screen appearance. The Exit menu provides options to leave the Control Center or the dot prompt.

You will frequently use the menu system available in dBASE IV. You will have to be familiar with the methods of navigating through the menu system. Let's try one way now.

To view the menu options:

❶ Press **[Alt]C** to open the Catalog pull-down menu. See Figure 1-9. Pressing [Alt] and the first letter of a menu opens that menu.

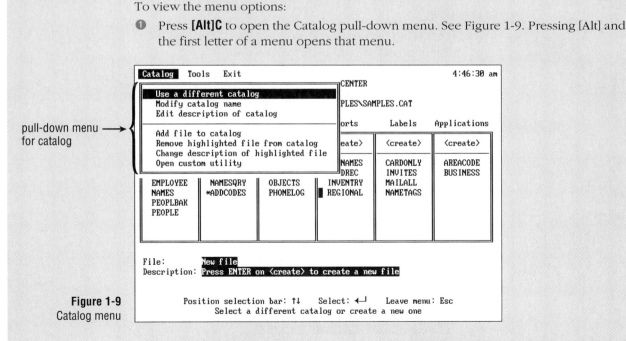

pull-down menu → for catalog

Figure 1-9
Catalog menu

There is a second method for accessing the menu bar. If you press [F10], the last menu used becomes highlighted.

Once the menu is open, press the first letter of one of the options listed to select that option. Or you can use [↓] to highlight the option you want to select, then press [Enter] to select it.

❷ Press **M** to select the *Modify catalog name* option. See Figure 1-10.

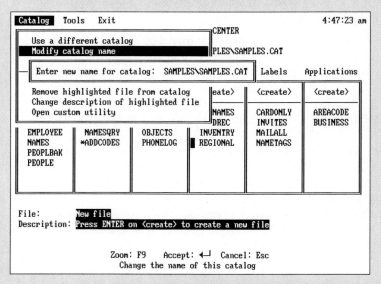

Figure 1-10
Prompt box for catalog name

You don't actually want to change the catalog name right now, so we'll cancel the last step by pressing [Esc].

❸ Press **[Esc]** to cancel the last step. You will see all the options in the Catalog menu displayed on top of the Control Center screen.

You can open a different menu from the menu bar by using [→] and [←].

❹ Press **[→]** to open the Tools menu. See Figure 1-11.

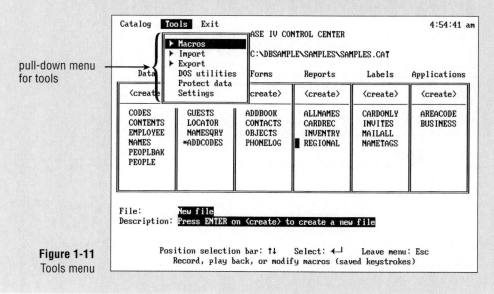

pull-down menu for tools

Figure 1-11
Tools menu

Notice that some options in the Tools menu have arrowheads in front of them. The arrowheads indicate that the option has another pull-down menu associated with it.

⑤ Press **[Esc]** again to close the Tools menu and return to the Control Center.

Changing the Default Drive

When the dBASE program is started, the default drive and directory are the same drive and directory where the dBASE software is stored. It's not a good practice to store your data files on the same directory as the dBASE software. Let's change the default drive and directory so that dBASE saves and retrieves your files to your data diskette.

To change the default drive and directory:

① Press **[Alt]T** to open the Tools menu.

② Press **[↓]** three times to highlight *DOS utilities.* See Figure 1-12.

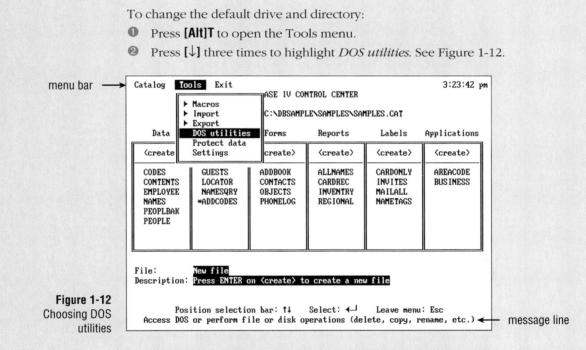

menu bar ⟶

Figure 1-12
Choosing DOS
utilities

⟵ message line

Notice the information in the message line. It now describes the *DOS utilities* option.

③ Press **[Enter]** or type **D** to select *DOS utilities.* See Figure 1-13 on the next page.

The Control Center screen is replaced with the DOS Utilities screen. This screen shows the list of files in the current DOS directory, C:\DBSAMPLE. Notice that this screen has a different set of menu names in the menu bar than the Control Center screen.

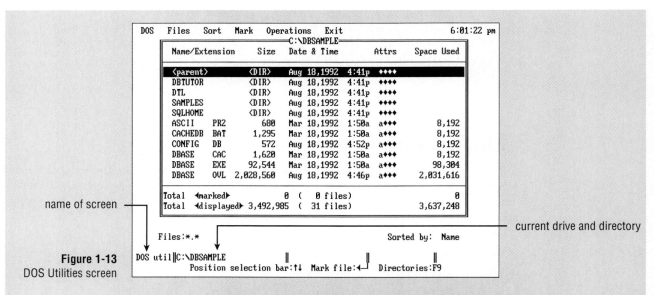

name of screen

current drive and directory

Figure 1-13
DOS Utilities screen

Now open the DOS option from the menu bar of the DOS Utilities screen.

③   Press **[Alt]D** to open the DOS menu. See Figure 1-14.

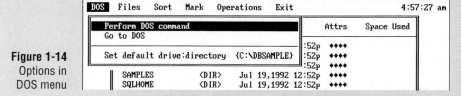

Figure 1-14
Options in
DOS menu

Now tell dBASE on what disk drive you have stored your database files.

④   Select *Set default drive:directory* (**S**). A prompt box appears that prompts you for the new default drive and directory. See Figure 1-15.

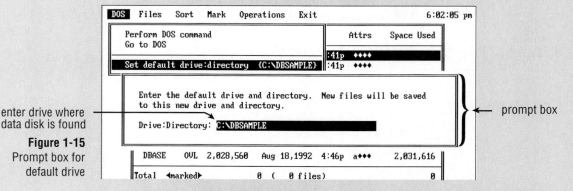

enter drive where
data disk is found

prompt box

Figure 1-15
Prompt box for
default drive

⑤   Type **a:**, press **[Spacebar]** to remove the remaining characters, and press **[Enter]**.

Now leave the DOS Utilities screen and return to the Control Center.

⑥ Press **[Alt]E** to open the Exit pull-down menu and press **[Enter]** to select the option *Exit to the Control Center*. The Control Center screen appears and now includes a list of all files associated with the catalog W&M found on the data diskette in drive A. See Figure 1-16.

current catalog →

database files →

```
Catalog  Tools  Exit                                        4:59:13 am
                        dBASE IV CONTROL CENTER
                        CATALOG: A:\W&M.CAT

     Data      Queries     Forms     Reports    Labels   Applications

  ┌─────────┬─────────┬─────────┬─────────┬─────────┬─────────┐
  │<create> │<create> │<create> │<create> │<create> │<create> │
  ├─────────┤         │         │         │         │         │
  │⌠CLIENT  │         │         │         │         │         │
  │⌡JOBS    │         │         │         │         │         │
  │         │         │         │         │         │         │
  │         │         │         │         │         │         │
  │         │         │         │         │         │         │
  │         │         │         │         │         │         │
  └─────────┴─────────┴─────────┴─────────┴─────────┴─────────┘

  File:        New file
  Description: Press ENTER on <create> to create a new file

  Help:F1  Use:◄┘  Data:F2  Design:Shift-F2  Quick Report:Shift-F9  Menus:F10
```

Figure 1-16
Control Center after
drive A made default

Selecting a Catalog

You will recall that a catalog is a file that groups information, including filenames, about associated files. You can identify catalog files on your data diskette because all catalog files have the extension .CAT. Your data diskette contains the nine catalogs listed in Figure 1-17. For example, the catalog named W&M groups the files associated with the Wells & Martinez application together, and the catalog named NBA groups the files that you will use if you are assigned the National Basketball Association case problem. Currently the W&M catalog and associated files appear in the Control Center. Only one catalog can be open at a time.

Catalog Name	Description
W&M	Files associated with Wells & Martinez case
NBA	Files associated with NBA case
BIG&HANG	Files associated with Biggs & Hang case
APPLTON	Files associated with Appleton & Drake case
MEDISRCE	Files associated with Medi-Source case
HOUSING	Files associated with Off-Campus Housing case
DEMO	Files associated with applications used in exercises
TUTOR2	Files associated with applications used in Tutorial 2
TUTOR6	Files associated with application in Tutorial 6

Figure 1-17
Catalogs on data
diskette

The information about the catalogs on your diskette and the catalog you used last is stored in a master catalog file called CATALOG.CAT. Each time you load dBASE and set the default drive and directory to the drive and directory containing the files for this text, the catalog last used will be restored to the Control Center.

Let's practice switching to the DEMO catalog.

To switch catalogs:

❶ Press **[Alt]C** to open the Catalog menu. See Figure 1-18.

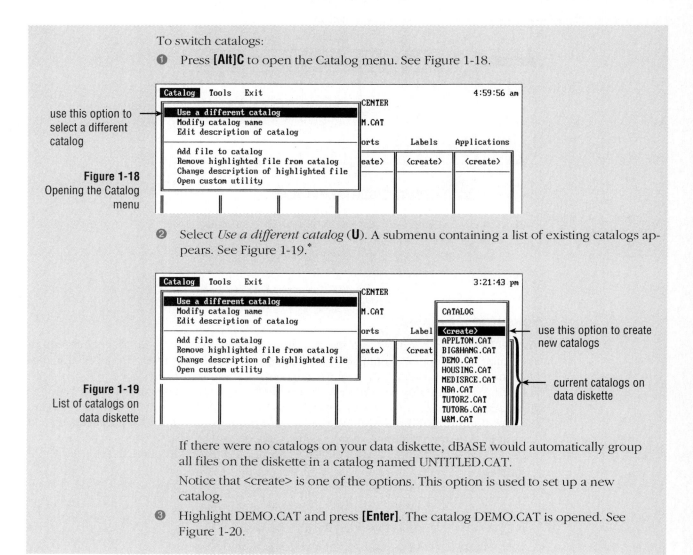

use this option to select a different catalog

Figure 1-18
Opening the Catalog menu

❷ Select *Use a different catalog* (**U**). A submenu containing a list of existing catalogs appears. See Figure 1-19.*

Figure 1-19
List of catalogs on data diskette

use this option to create new catalogs

current catalogs on data diskette

If there were no catalogs on your data diskette, dBASE would automatically group all files on the diskette in a catalog named UNTITLED.CAT.

Notice that <create> is one of the options. This option is used to set up a new catalog.

❸ Highlight DEMO.CAT and press **[Enter]**. The catalog DEMO.CAT is opened. See Figure 1-20.

---

* Your catalog listing may be slightly different.

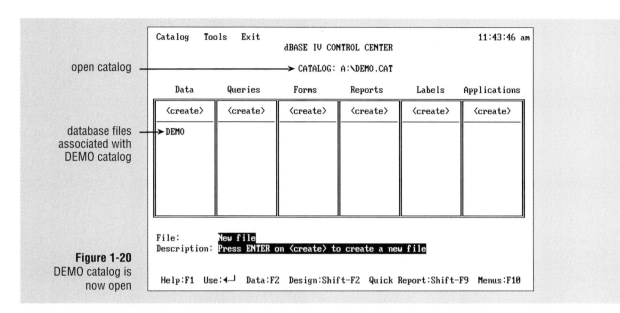

open catalog

database files associated with DEMO catalog

Figure 1-20
DEMO catalog is now open

Now let's switch back to the W&M catalog.

To switch catalogs:

❶ Press **[Alt]C** to open the Catalog menu.

❷ Select the *Use a different catalog* (**U**). A submenu containing a list of existing catalogs appears.

❸ Highlight the W&M catalog and press **[Enter]**. The W&M catalog is opened, and its associated files appear in the panels of the Control Center. See Figure 1-21.

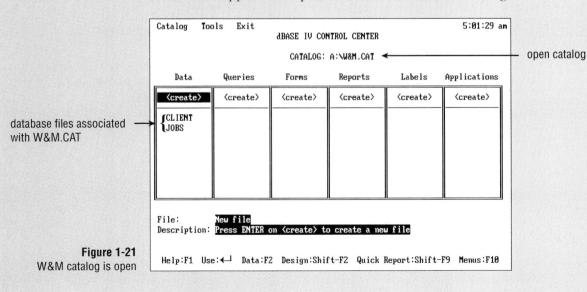

database files associated with W&M.CAT

open catalog

Figure 1-21
W&M catalog is open

Using the Control Center

Now that you have a basic understanding of database terms and concepts and are familiar with the dBASE IV Control Center, you are ready to work with Esther as she uses dBASE to build the Wells & Martinez database.

First let's look at some work Esther has already completed. She has created the database file CLIENT and entered the client data, which consist of each client's company name and ID, the name of the contact person at each client company, and each client's main telephone number. To familiarize you more with the Control Center, let's access W&M's CLIENT file.

Before you can view data from a database file, you must open the database file. Let's open the database file CLIENT.

To open a database file:

❶ Press [↓] to move the highlight to the CLIENT file in the Data panel and press **[Enter]**. You will see a prompt box that lists three things you can do with the database file. See Figure 1-22.

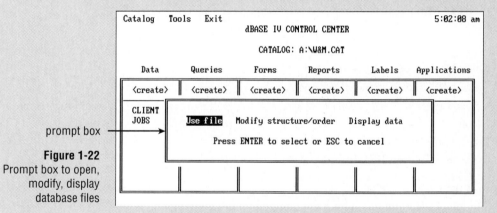

prompt box →

Figure 1-22
Prompt box to open, modify, display database files

❷ With the option *Use file* highlighted, press **[Enter]**. The *Use file* option opens the selected database file and places its name above the panel line. See Figure 1-23. When a filename appears above the panel line, the file is open.

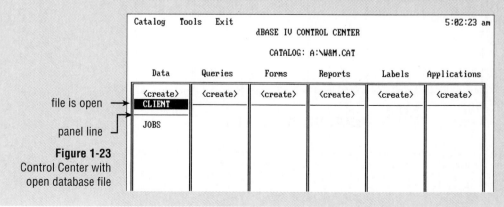

file is open →

panel line ⌐

Figure 1-23
Control Center with open database file

Now that you have opened the file, you can access the data in the file. Let's look at the data that Esther has entered in the W&M clients file.

To access the data in the database file CLIENT:

❶ Press **[F2]** (Data) to view the data in the file CLIENT. (Note that this key is listed on the navigation line.) Figure 1-24 shows the client data currently stored in the W&M file CLIENT.

```
 Records   Organize   Fields   Go To   Exit

 CLIENT_ID CLIENT_NAM                  CONTACT            PHONE

 MOU       Mountain Top Ski            Gunther Williams   (419)783-6210
 VIK       Viking Auto Group           Jeff Serito        (505)984-9216
 ALE       Alexander Insurance         Paul Alexander     (505)883-9222
 SAN       Sante Fe Tourist Center     Liddy Posada       (505)986-5555
 ORI       Origins                     Gary Higgins       (505)988-0733
 FAT       Fat Wheels Bicycle Tours    Helen Carson       (505)994-2432
 CEL       Celebrity Catering          Linda Randall      (505)883-9922
 EYE       Eyes Have It                Sandy Alonso       (505)780-2277
 IMA       Images                      Wendy Falchetti    (505)898-1286




 Browse  ‖A:\CLIENT            ‖Rec 1/9        ‖File ‖      ‖
```

Figure 1-24
Client data

❷ Press **[Esc]** when you are ready to return to the Control Center.

Getting Help in the Control Center

While in the Control Center you may need help understanding or using one of the options. To get additional information on any highlighted option, press the function key [F1]. When you request help, you will get help based on your current position in the menu system. This feature, known as *context sensitive help*, brings you information relevant to your current task. For example, let's get more information on using files in the Control Center.

To get help:

❶ With the cursor highlighting CLIENT in the Data panel, press **[F1]** (Help). See Figure 1-25 on the next page. A *Help box* appears containing either text about a particular topic or a table of contents for choosing other topics. In this case you get information on How to Use Files from the Control Center.

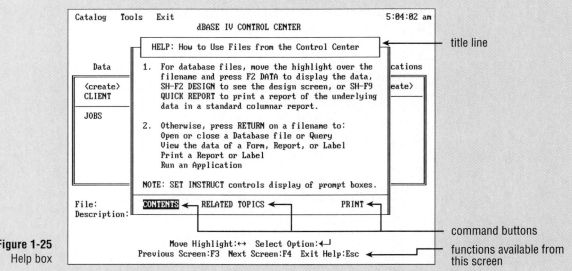

Figure 1-25
Help box

Each Help box contains a title line, which indicates the current topic. You can browse through the information on the help topic screen by pressing function keys [F4] and [F3]. Notice that these keys and the functions they perform are listed on the navigation line.

❷ Press **[F4]** to display the information on the next screen.

At the bottom of the Help box you will see several *command buttons*, which you use to choose different help functions. To move the highlight to a command button use [→], [←], [spacebar], and [Backspace]. When the desired button is highlighted, press [Enter] to select the button. The command buttons in Help perform the functions described in Figure 1-26.

Command Button	Function
CONTENTS	Displays a pop-up Table of Contents screen about the current information topic
RELATED TOPICS	Lists topics related to the current one, which pop up on the right section of the Help box
BACKUP	Returns to previously displayed Help screen
PRINT	Prints the current screen of Help information

Figure 1-26
Help screen
command buttons

For example, if How to Use Files is not the Help topic you're interested in, you can locate the appropriate help topic by searching the Help system's Table of Contents.

To get to the Help system's Table of Contents:

❶ With the CONTENTS button highlighted, press **[Enter]**. See Figure 1-27. The Table of Contents screen lists the topics about which you can get more detailed information. To select a topic from the current list, highlight the desired topic and press [Enter].

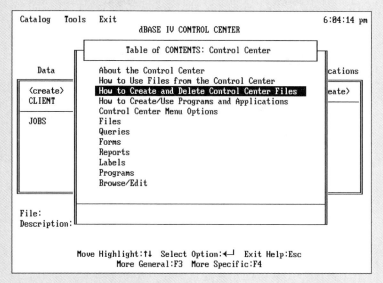

Figure 1-27
Help CONTENTS
screen

```
Catalog  Tools  Exit                                    6:04:14 pm
                        dBASE IV CONTROL CENTER
            ┌──────────── Table of CONTENTS: Control Center ──────────┐
   Data     │  About the Control Center                               │ cations
            │  How to Use Files from the Control Center               │
  <create>  │ ▓How to Create and Delete Control Center Files▓         │ eate>
  CLIENT    │  How to Create/Use Programs and Applications            │
            │  Control Center Menu Options                            │
  JOBS      │  Files                                                  │
            │  Queries                                                │
            │  Forms                                                  │
            │  Reports                                                │
            │  Labels                                                 │
            │  Programs                                               │
            │  Browse/Edit                                            │
            │                                                         │
  File:     └─────────────────────────────────────────────────────────┘
  Description:

            Move Highlight:↑↓  Select Option:◄┘  Exit Help:Esc
                      More General:F3  More Specific:F4
```

You can see more topics by using [↑] and [↓] to scroll through the list of topics. You can see a list of subtopics related to the highlighted topic by pressing [F4]. You can return to the Control Center from any screen in the Help system by pressing [Esc].

To exit Help and return to the Control Center:

➊ Press **[Esc]** to leave the Help box and return to the point from which you requested help.

Using Dot Prompt Mode

Now that you have had some experience with the Control Center, let's use dot prompt mode to list the clients in the Wells & Martinez database file CLIENT. As we discussed earlier in this tutorial, dot prompt mode requires you to enter commands.

First you need to learn how to switch dBASE from the Control Center to dot prompt mode.

To switch from the Control Center to dot prompt mode:

➊ Press **[Alt]E** to open the Exit menu.

➋ With the option *Exit to dot prompt* highlighted, press **[Enter]**.

The Control Center screen is erased, and a dot, called the *dot prompt*, appears near the lower left of your screen. See Figure 1-28. The dot prompt indicates that dBASE is waiting for you to type a dBASE command.

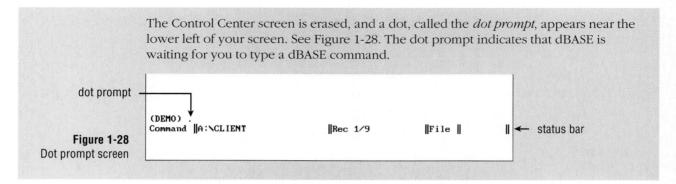

dot prompt

```
(DEMO) .
Command  ||A:\CLIENT              ||Rec  1/9        ||File ||         ||
```
← status bar

Figure 1-28
Dot prompt screen

The highlighted line near the bottom of the screen is called the **status bar**. It is divided into five sections, each displaying information about various aspects of dBASE's status. The first section describes the type of screen you are viewing, in this case, a Command screen; the second section indicates the default drive and directory and the database filename that is currently in use (if one is in use); the third section identifies the number of the current record and the total number of records in the current database; the fourth section indicates whether the source of the database data is a file or a view; and the fifth section indicates the keyboard mode (for example, [INS] appears if Insert mode is on and [CAP] appears if Caps Lock is on).

Since you opened the file CLIENT while you were in Control Center, you can now list all the clients in that database file.

To list all the clients in dot prompt mode:

❶ Type **browse** and press **[Enter]**. dBASE displays the clients currently stored in the W&M database file CLIENT on a Browse screen. See Figure 1-29.

```
 Records    Organize    Fields    Go To    Exit

 CLIENT_ID CLIENT_NAM              CONTACT          PHONE

 MOU       Mountain Top Ski        Gunther Williams (419)783-6210
 VIK       Viking Auto Group       Jeff Serito      (505)984-9216
 ALE       Alexander Insurance     Paul Alexander   (505)883-9222
 SAN       Sante Fe Tourist Center Liddy Posada     (505)986-5555
 ORI       Origins                 Gary Higgins     (505)988-0733
 FAT       Fat Wheels Bicycle Tours Helen Carson    (505)994-2432
 CEL       Celebrity Catering      Linda Randall    (505)883-9922
 EYE       Eyes Have It            Sandy Alonso     (505)780-2277
 IMA       Images                  Wendy Falchetti  (505)898-1286




 Browse  ||A:\CLIENT              ||Rec 1/9        ||File ||       ||
```

Figure 1-29
Browse screen

❷ Press **[Esc]** to return to the dot prompt command screen.

You may find changing the default drive from the Control Center cumbersome. As an alternative try using the dot prompt to change the default drive. Let's try it.

To change the default drive in dot prompt mode:
● Type **set default to a** and press **[Enter]**.

Tutorials 1 through 6 have you use the Control Center rather than the dot prompt. However, Dot Prompt boxes are included with each tutorial. The Dot Prompt boxes contain the syntax of the appropriate commands to perform the tasks that are being described in the tutorial. Optional parts of the command are shaded. Each Dot Prompt box has the following format: syntax, description, and example. For example, in Tutorial 3 you will learn how to access the Browse screen from the Control Center. At the end of that section, the Browse dot prompt command is shown in a Dot Prompt box.

Dot Prompt

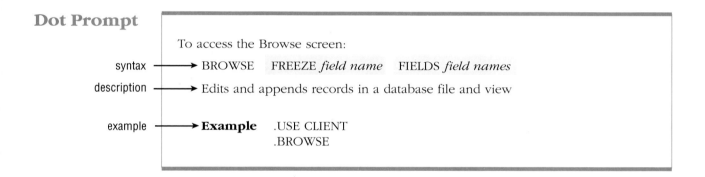

To access the Browse screen:

syntax ⟶ BROWSE   FREEZE *field name*   FIELDS *field names*

description ⟶ Edits and appends records in a database file and view

example ⟶ **Example**   .USE CLIENT
                              .BROWSE

That's all you will do in dot prompt mode for now. Let's leave dBASE.

Quitting dBASE

You have now completed Tutorial 1. Because you will be working primarily from the Control Center, you should know how to leave or quit dBASE from that screen.

You can switch from dot prompt mode to the Control Center at any time by using the Assist command. Let's do that now.

To switch to the Control Center:
● Press **[F2]** (Assist). The Control Center screen appears.

Alternatively, you can type assist and press [Enter] to return to Control Center from dot prompt mode.

To quit dBASE, you open the Exit menu from the menu bar.

To quit dBASE:

❶ Press **[Alt]E** to open the Exit menu. See Figure 1-30.

choose this option to
leave dBASE

Figure 1-30
Opening Exit Menu

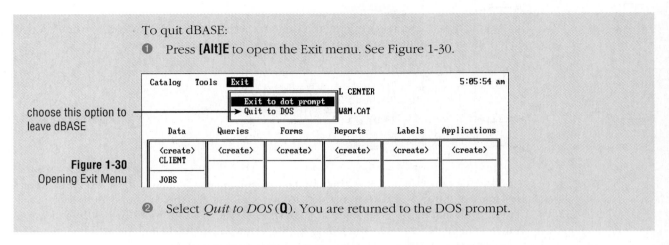

❷ Select *Quit to DOS* (**Q**). You are returned to the DOS prompt.

The *Quit to DOS* option closes all open files. *Be careful! If you turn your machine off before you issue the* Quit to DOS *option, you might lose any new data you typed this session.*

■   ■   ■

Exercises

1. Define the following terms:
   a. field
   b. record
   c. file
   d. database
   e. database management system

Use the data in Figure 1-31 to answer Exercises 2 through 6.

Library Card Holders

Card No.	Name	Street	City	State
2456	Ellery	17 Finch Rd.	Newport	RI
4687	Hemkin	1 Brook St.	Portsmith	RI
7991	Becker	323 High St.	Fall River	MA
9123	Drovsky	PO Box #12	Newport	RI

Books on Loan

Card No.	Book No.	Due Date
4687	12-32115	7/11/93
4687	18-23444	7/11/93
7991	17-23999	7/15/93
4687	22-95321	7/16/93
2456	14-11223	7/16/93

Figure 1-31

2. What are the fields in the library database?

3. How many fields are in the file BOOKS ON LOAN?

4. Identify the fields in the file LIBRARY CARD HOLDERS.

5. How many records are there in the file LIBRARY CARD HOLDERS?

6. The head librarian requests a list of all library cardholders. What steps in the Control Center would you take to provide this information?

7. At the DOS prompt what do you type to load dBASE IV?

8. In Control Center how do you do the following?
   a. quit dBASE
   b. get to dot prompt mode

9. In dot prompt mode what command do you use to get to the Control Center?

10. In Control Center what do you do to use the Help feature?

Tutorial Assignments

Load dBASE and set the default drive to the drive for your data disk. Do the following:

1. From the Control Center switch to the catalog DEMO.

2. Open the database file DEMO.DBF.

3. List on the screen the contents of this file.

4. Exit to the Control Center, then switch from Control Center to dot prompt mode.

5. While in dot prompt mode, list on the screen the contents of this file.

6. Return to the dot prompt, then switch from dot prompt mode to the Control Center screen.

7. Switch to the catalog W&M.CAT.

8. Quit dBASE.

Tutorial 2

Creating a Database File Structure

Case: Wells & Martinez — Creating the File Structure for WMJOBS

Early one morning Martin receives a phone call from Phyllis Higgins. Phyllis and her husband, Gary, are the owners of Origins, a Southwest fashion boutique, and have been W&M clients since Martin and Nancy started the agency. Phyllis tells Martin that she and Gary are very excited about their new line of Southwest fashion denim clothing for men and women and that they want W&M to develop an ad campaign to launch the new line. Later that day Martin tells Nancy about this new business from Origins. They decide that Martin and his creative team will put together a campaign plan. As soon as he has an outline of the plan, Martin will give the outline to Nancy, so she can estimate the costs of the job. They agree to have both the campaign plan and the cost estimate finalized and ready to present to Gary and Phyllis in two weeks.

Two weeks later Martin and Nancy meet with Phyllis and Gary Higgins and present the plan and the estimate. The Higginses are impressed and authorize W&M to begin work on the campaign — "Best in the Southwest" — immediately. They sign W&M's standard job authorization form, which authorizes Martin to begin working on the campaign and acknowledges the probable costs as Nancy has estimated them.

OBJECTIVES

In this tutorial you will learn to:

- Design the structure of a database file

- Create a dBASE database file

- Modify the structure of a dBASE database file

- Print the structure of a database file

When Nancy returns to the office, she meets with Esther and tells her that she wants to begin the new database system with the Origins campaign. She asks Esther what to do first. Esther tells Nancy that she needs a copy of the job authorization form, which summarizes key information about a new job and which must be filled out before any expenses can be charged to that particular job (Figure 2-1). Before the new database system this form would have been filed for future reference; now Esther will enter the data on the form into a file she will create and name WMJOBS.

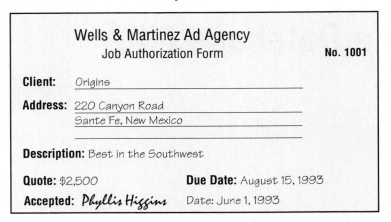

Figure 2-1
W&M job
authorization form

Esther has carefully studied the manual system that W&M had been using. She knows what type of information Martin and Nancy need about their clients, the individual jobs, and the costs of the jobs. She also has reviewed database design principles, which she learned in her courses at school, and the rules for designing a dBASE database.

Based on her study and review, Esther recognizes that the database system she is designing must track each job that W&M does for each client. For example, if next week Gary and Phyllis authorize W&M to begin an advertising campaign on Origins' new line of formal wear, someone at W&M would have to fill out another job authorization form. They could not use the same form that Nancy filled out for the "Best in the Southwest" campaign. Having a separate authorization form for each job will allow Martin and Nancy to track each job by its due date and to track costs *by job* rather than *by client*. They will be able to keep a closer watch over their costs for each job and to see how actual costs compare to Nancy's original estimates.

Esther decides to create a database file, which she names WMJOBS, in which she will store all the data on all the job authorization forms. Each record in the WMJOBS file will include an individual job's number, client ID, description, due date, and cost estimate.

Esther has already created the CLIENT file so that Nancy and Martin can track specific data about each client. In this tutorial you will create the WMJOBS database file.

Guidelines for Designing a Database File

Before you use any database software, you should plan and design the database you are going to build. If you plan first, your database is more likely to meet the goals for the new system.

When you design a database, you should follow these basic design principles:

- **Identify the type of information users will need from the database**. This will help you decide which data elements to track. For example, Martin and Nancy need information on their clients, the jobs their clients have authorized them to work on, and the costs for completing each job.
- **Group logically related fields in the same file**. For example, the fields that contain the client ID, the client's name, the contact's name, and the client's phone number are characteristics that describe clients and are included in the CLIENT file.
- **Include a common field in each related file (if your application has more than one file)**. Use this field to act as a connector when you need to combine data from related files. For example, the field CLIENT_ID is included in both the CLIENT and WMJOBS files and can be used to relate records in both files.
- **Avoid data redundancy**. Include data elements in a way that eliminates the need to enter the same information many times in many files. For example, Esther did not include company name, contact name, or phone number in the WMJOBS file. She already stores these data in the CLIENT file.

As you design a database file, for each field in a record you must:

- Assign a unique field name to identify the field
- Specify a maximum number of characters
- Assign a specific type of data — character, numeric, date, logical, or memo — to be stored in each field

Rules for Creating a dBASE Database File

As you design a database file, you must decide on the fields that are included in a record, the amount of space allotted to each field, and the type of data to be stored in each field. This information makes up the **file structure**. Later, when you are ready to develop the system, you must also consider the rules of the database software you will use. In our case dBASE has rules for naming files and fields and for handling data input to the files. Let's look at these rules.

Naming Files

It is always a good habit to choose descriptive names for your files that will help you identify their contents. For example, Esther's choices of CLIENT and WMJOBS are appropriate because the names help identify the data she plans to put into the files.

In dBASE a filename can contain up to eight letters, numbers, and/or special characters, such as _ - $ % &. Esther's choices follow these rules.

Naming Fields

You've already seen that each file is made up of records. For example, the WMJOBS file consists of a record for each job that W&M undertakes. Each of these records is made up of fields, and you must name each field. A **field name** describes the data stored in each field. Esther has named the fields in the CLIENT file CLIENT_ID, CLIENT_NAM, CONTACT, and PHONE. Field names help you work more easily with the data in a file.

Rules for naming fields in dBASE are as follows:

- A field name can be up to 10 characters long.
- A field name must start with a letter.
- A field name can consist of letters, numbers, and the underscore character but *not* spaces or hyphens. The underscore is used to connect words. For example, CLIENT_ID is permitted, but CLIENT-ID and CLIENT ID are not.

Data Types

For each field dBASE requires that you assign a **data type**, that is, the type of data a field can contain. Each field can store only one data type. You can choose from the following dBASE data types:

A **character data type** stores any sequence of letters, digits, blank spaces, and special characters, such as + - % $ &. The maximum width for a character field is 254 characters. In our W&M example the client's company name and the contact person's name would be stored in character data type fields. Fields that contain a sequence of digits that do not represent a quantity, such as zip codes or telephone numbers, are typically stored as character-type data.

A **numeric data type** stores values that are negative or positive, integer or decimal. The only characters permitted within a numeric field are the digits 0 to 9, a decimal point (.), and a sign (+ or -). No commas, parentheses, or dollar signs are permitted. You assign the numeric data type to fields that can be used in calculations. Numeric data are useful in business and financial applications. For example, the cost estimate for a job would be a numeric field.

A **float data type** also stores values that are negative or positive, integer or decimal. The characters permitted within a float numeric field are the same as those in a numeric field. The primary difference between numeric and float data types is how the number is stored internally in the database file. You assign the float data type to fields that are used in science and technical applications where very large or very small numbers are required or high levels of precision in calculations are necessary. For example, total world population in a population growth model would be a float field.

A **date data type** stores any valid date. Normally dates are entered and displayed in *mm/dd/yy* format, where *mm* represents a two-digit month, *dd* represents a two-digit day of the month, and *yy* represents the last two digits of the year. Dates stored using the date data type can be used in calculations. For example, say the due date is 30 days after the job was authorized. This due date can be computed by adding 30 to the date the job authorization form was signed. A date also can be stored as a character data type, but then that field cannot be used in calculations.

A **logical data type** represents values as either true or false. An entry of T or t (for true) or Y or y (for yes) represents a true value, while F or f (for false) or N or n (for no) represents a false value. For example, in an EMPLOYEE file the field US_CITIZEN would store the value true (T, t, Y, or y) if the employee were a U.S. citizen or false (F, f, N, or n) if the employee were not a citizen.

A **memo data type** stores large blocks of descriptive text. Though similar to the character data type, the memo data type is used when a field will contain a large amount of text. For example, an abstract of a book or a medical diagnosis would be stored as a memo data type.

Field Widths

When you use dBASE, you must indicate the number of characters, or the **width**, for each field. dBASE reserves a specified amount of space for each field. For some fields, deciding the width is a straightforward process. For example, Wells & Martinez uses the first three letters of a company's name as the client identification, so the width is 3. On the other hand, the job description field must be based on Esther's knowledge of the data. She knows that job titles vary in length but that most titles are shorter than Origins' "Best in the Southwest" description. Accordingly she has chosen a width of 25 characters, which allows each job description entry to be meaningful.

Numeric fields must be long enough to hold the largest possible number that will be stored in them, including a decimal point if the number has a fractional part and a sign if the number is negative. For example, W&M's cost estimate is always quoted to the nearest dollar. The largest estimate W&M has made so far is $32,500. Esther, however, has chosen a width of 6 to allow for estimates as large as $999,999. She has specified 0 for the number of decimal places because W&M cost estimates do not need decimal numbers.

The widths of logical, date, and memo fields are predefined by dBASE. For the logical data type the width is 1, for the date data type the width is 8, and for the memo data type the width is 5,000. Figure 2-2 summarizes the maximum widths of all dBASE data types.

Data Type	Maximum Width
Character	254
Date	8
Logical	1
Numeric	19
Memo	5,000

Figure 2-2
Widths of dBASE
data types

Preparing a File Layout Sheet

When you design a file for a computer system, you should document the structure of the records you will include in the file. For example, Esther sketched the structure of the WMJOBS file on a file layout sheet. A **file layout** is a document that describes the field name, the data type, and the length of every field in a record. The file layout sheet that Esther developed for the WMJOBS file is shown in Figure 2-3 on the next page.

WMJOBS File			
Field Name	**Data Type**	**Width**	**Decimal**
JOBNUM	Character	4	
CLIENT_ID	Character	3	
JOB_DESCR	Character	25	
DUE_DATE	Date	8	
QUOTE	Numeric	6	0

Figure 2-3
File layout for
WMJOBS file

How did Esther decide on this file layout? The first field, the job number, comes from the job authorization form, which is preprinted with a four-digit job number (Figure 2-1). Because these numbers will not be used for calculations, Esther did not need to use a numeric data type. Instead, she selected the character data type and assigned JOBNUM as the field name.

W&M uses the first three letters of the client's company name as the client identification. Esther named the client identification field CLIENT_ID. Because an ID always will be three letters, the data type is character and the length is 3.

Deciding the width of the job description field required Esther to make a judgment based on her knowledge of the data. The job descriptions vary in length, but none is longer than 25 characters. So Esther assigned the third field a width of 25, a field name of JOB_DESCR, and the data type character.

The fourth field is the date a project is due. In this field Esther stores dates in *mm/dd/yy* format. The field name is DUE_DATE, the data type is date, and the width is 8.

Esther chose numeric as the data type for the cost estimate because W&M personnel will use this field for calculations. As you've already seen, she knows that a numeric field must be long enough to hold the largest possible number that will be stored in it. W&M's cost estimates are always quoted to the nearest dollar, with the largest estimate so far being $32,500. Although no quote in the past has needed more than five digits, Esther chose a width of 6 in anticipation of larger projects. With a width of 6, dBASE can store quotes as large as $999,999. Esther specified 0 for the number of decimal places, because cost estimates are made to the nearest dollar. The field name is QUOTE, the data type is numeric, the width is 6, and the number of decimal places is 0.

Creating a Database File

Esther has documented the structure of the WMJOBS file in the file layout sheet. To define the structure of each database file in dBASE, Esther will use the Database Design screen. She will enter the information on the file layout sheet into dBASE. Let's try it.

To load dBASE and change the default drive:
● Load dBASE and be sure you're in the Control Center.

❷ Press **[Alt]T** to open the Tools menu.

❸ Select *DOS utilities* (**D**). The Control Center screen is replaced with the DOS Utilities screen.

❹ Press **[Alt]D** to open the DOS menu.

❺ Select *Set default drive:directory* (**S**) to tell dBASE on what disk drive you have stored your database files. A message window appears prompting you for the drive and directory where your data diskette is located.

❻ Make sure your diskette is in drive A. Type **a:**, press **[Spacebar]** as many times as necessary to remove the remaining characters, and press **[Enter]**.

Now leave the DOS Utilities screen and return to the Control Center.

❼ Press **[Alt]E** to open the Exit menu and press **[Enter]** to select *Exit to Control Center*. The Control Center screen appears and now includes a list of all files associated with the catalog W&M found on the data diskette in drive A. See Figure 2-4.

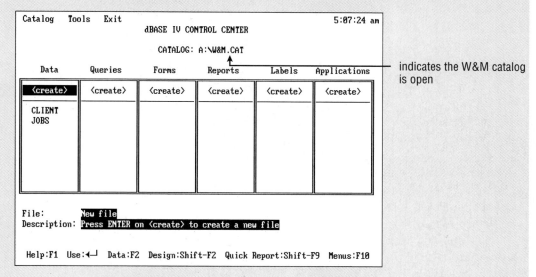

indicates the W&M catalog is open

Figure 2-4
Control Center screen with W&M catalog open

Dot Prompt

To set the default drive:

SET DEFAULT TO *drive*

Selects the drive where all operations take place and where all files are stored

Example   .SET DEFAULT TO a

Dot Prompt

To open a catalog file:

SET CATALOG TO *catalog filename*

Opens or creates a catalog file

Example   .SET CATALOG TO w&m

Now you can create the database file.

To create the database file named WMJOBS:
1. Make sure <create> in the Data panel is highlighted.
2. Press **[Enter]**. The Database Design screen appears. See Figure 2-5.

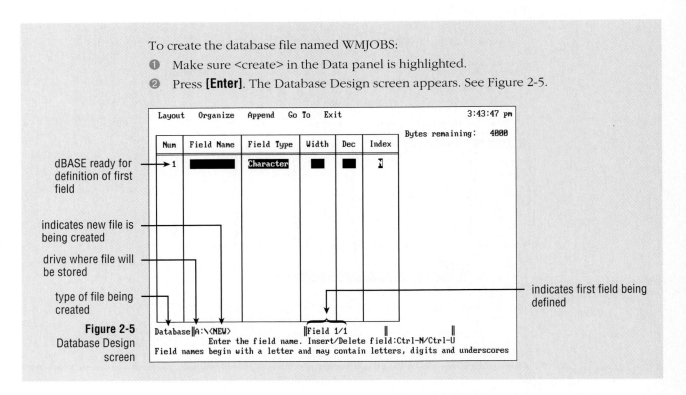

dBASE ready for definition of first field

indicates new file is being created

drive where file will be stored

type of file being created

indicates first field being defined

Figure 2-5
Database Design screen

For each field in the database file you enter its **definition**, which includes the field name, the data type, the width, the number of decimal places for numeric and float fields (Dec), and whether you want an index for this field. (You'll learn about indexes in Tutorial 5.) After completing this screen, you will have defined the structure of the WMJOBS file. Once you have defined the structure, all records in this file will have the same fields, and each field will have the same length and data type as defined in the Database Design screen.

You will recall that Esther plans to have five fields for each record in the WMJOBS file: job number, client identification, job description, due date, and quote. Esther uses the information from the file layout she created to help her define each field for the WMJOBS file.

The first field in the file layout sheet (Figure 2-3) is job number. Let's define this field.

To define the JOBNUM field:

❶ Type **jobnum** and press **[Enter]**. See Figure 2-6. You can type the field name in either uppercase or lowercase, but it will appear on screen in uppercase. The field name JOBNUM appears in uppercase, and the cursor moves to the Field Type column.

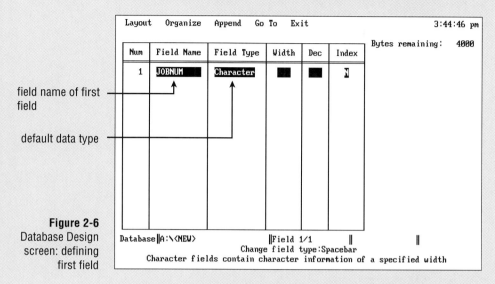

field name of first field

default data type

Figure 2-6
Database Design screen: defining first field

Esther's file layout shows that JOBNUM will be used to store character data. Because the job numbers will not be used for calculations, a numeric data type is not needed. Esther selects the character data type.

❷ Press **[Enter]** to select the character data type for the JOBNUM field. The cursor advances to the Width column.

If you do not select a specific data type, the default is the character data type. That is, unless you instruct it otherwise, dBASE assumes a field's data type is character.

Now enter the width, the maximum number of characters the field can store. You enter the field widths only for character and numeric fields. For fields defined as logical, date, and memo, the widths are predefined by dBASE. The JOBNUM field is character data type, and, as Figure 2-3 shows, its width is 4.

❸ Type **4** and press **[Enter]** to enter the width. See Figure 2-7.

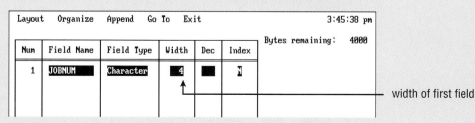

Figure 2-7
Database Design screen after width is defined for first field

width of first field

Notice that the cursor skipped the Dec (decimal) column. This is because we defined JOBNUM as a character field, and Dec is used only with numeric fields.

The cursor is now positioned in the Index column. For now accept the default N, for no index.

❹   Press **[Enter]**. See Figure 2-8.

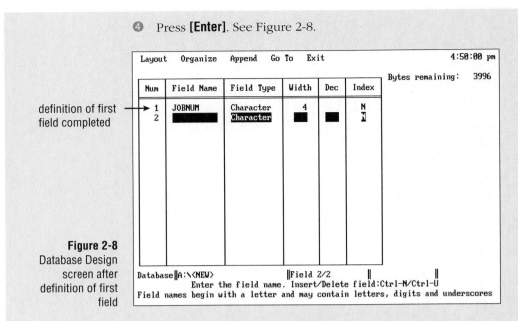

definition of first
field completed →

Figure 2-8
Database Design
screen after
definition of first
field

The definition of the first field is complete, and the cursor advances to the next row.
dBASE waits for you to enter the definition of the second field.

In Esther's file layout client identification is the second field in the WMJOBS record.
Esther has named this field CLIENT_ID, the data type is character, and the length is 3. Let's
define this second field.

To define the client identification field:

❶   Type **client_id** and press **[Enter]**. The cursor automatically moves to the Field Type
column.

Esther plans to use the first three letters of the company name as the client ID, so she
selects character as the data type for the CLIENT_ID field.

❷   Press **[Enter]** to select the character data type for the CLIENT_ID field.

Now enter the width, that is, the maximum number of characters the field can store. As
Figure 2-3 shows, the width of the CLIENT_ID field is 3.

❸   Type **3** and press **[Enter]**.

The cursor is now positioned at the Index column.

❹   Press **[Enter]**. See Figure 2-9.

You have now completed the definition of the second field. The cursor advances to the
next row, where you will enter the definition of the third field.

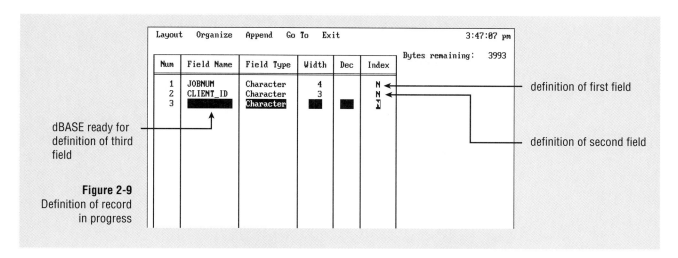

dBASE ready for definition of third field

definition of first field

definition of second field

Figure 2-9
Definition of record in progress

The third field is the job description. Again referring to the file layout in Figure 2-3, you can see that the field name is JOB_DESCR, the data type is character, and the width is 25. You will discover that the entries for this field are similar to the entries for the first two fields. Let's enter the information now.

To define the job description field:

❶ Enter the information for this field as it is shown in Figure 2-3. Don't worry if you make a mistake. You will learn how to fix it in the next section. Your screen should look like Figure 2-10.

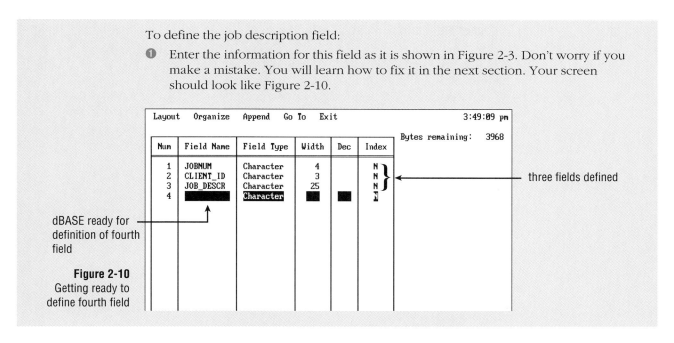

dBASE ready for definition of fourth field

three fields defined

Figure 2-10
Getting ready to define fourth field

The fourth field is the date the project is due. According to Esther's file layout, the field name is DUE_DATE, the data type is date, and the width is 8. Let's enter the due date field.

To define the due date field:

❶   Type **due_date** and press **[Enter]**. The cursor moves to the Field Type column.

Up until now you have selected only character data types, but this field requires a date data type. To change the data type, press the spacebar to move through the six available data types. When the data type you want is displayed, press [Enter] to select it. Alternatively you can select a data type by entering the first letter of the data type name: C, for character; N, for numeric; F, for float; D, for date; L, for logical; or M, for memo. For now select the date data type by pressing the spacebar.

❷   Press **[spacebar]** three times, then press **[Enter]** to select the date data type. The value of 8 is automatically entered as the width of the DUE_DATE field, and the cursor is now positioned at the Index column.

❸   Press **[Enter]** to accept the default of N for the Index column. The cursor advances to the next field. See Figure 2-11.

Figure 2-11
Definition of
DUE_DATE
complete

width automatically entered for date data type

The fifth field represents the W&M quote to the client. Figure 2-3 shows that the field name is QUOTE, the data type is numeric, the width is 6, and the number of decimal places is 0.

To define the QUOTE field:

❶   Type **quote** and press **[Enter]**. The cursor moves to the Field Type column.

Esther has chosen numeric as the data type because W&M personnel will use the QUOTE field for calculations. This time let's select the data type by typing the first letter.

❷   Type **n** to select numeric data type. The cursor moves to the Width column.

❸   Type **6** for width and press **[Enter]**. The cursor moves to the decimal place column.

The only time the cursor moves to the Dec column is when you have chosen either the numeric or the float data type. You must tell dBASE how many decimal places following the decimal point you want reserved for each number stored. Because W&M makes quotes only to the nearest whole dollar, Esther has chosen no decimal places for this field.

❹   Type the number **0** (zero) and press **[Enter]**. The cursor moves to the Index column.

❺   Press **[Enter]**. The cursor advances to the next field. See Figure 2-12.

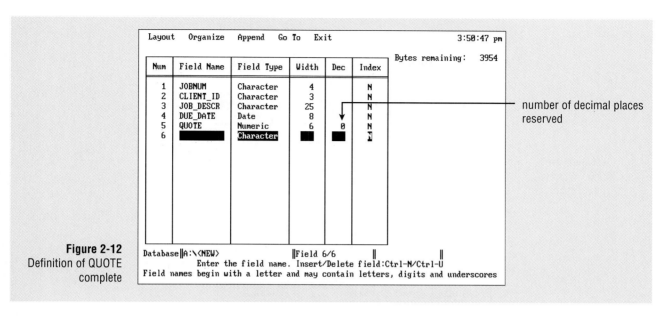

number of decimal places
reserved

Figure 2-12
Definition of QUOTE
complete

Now that you have defined each field, the structure of the WMJOBS file is complete. Look over your screen. It should be identical to Figure 2-12.

Correcting Errors

If you make an error while dBASE is displaying the Database Design screen, you can use the keys identified in Figure 2-13 to move the cursor so you can correct the field definitions.

Key	Action
[↑] [↓]	Moves highlight up or down one row
[→] [←]	Moves cursor one position to the right or left
[Tab]	Moves cursor one column to the right
[Shift][Tab]	Moves cursor one column to the left
[Ctrl]N	Inserts blank row above cursor position
[Ctrl]U	Deletes row where cursor is positioned

Figure 2-13
Keys used with the
Database Design
screen

If you made any errors when you defined the fields in this tutorial, make corrections now so that your screen matches Figure 2-12.

Saving the Database File Structure

When you have finished defining all the fields, you must save the database file structure. One way to save the file structure is to use the Exit menu.

To save the file structure:

❶ Press **[Alt]E** to open the Exit menu. See Figure 2-14.

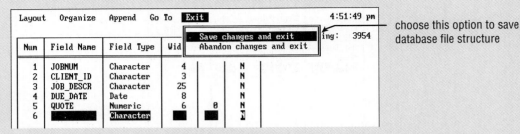

Figure 2-14
Saving the database
file structure

choose this option to save
database file structure

❷ Make sure the option *Save changes and exit* is highlighted and press **[Enter]**. dBASE prompts you for a name for the new database file. See Figure 2-15.

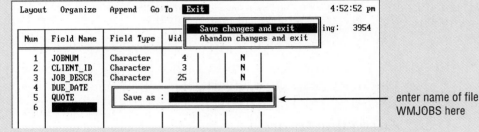

Figure 2-15
Enter name of
database file

enter name of file
WMJOBS here

❸ Type **wmjobs** and press **[Enter]**. You are automatically returned to the Control Center and WMJOBS appears in the Data panel. See Figure 2-16.

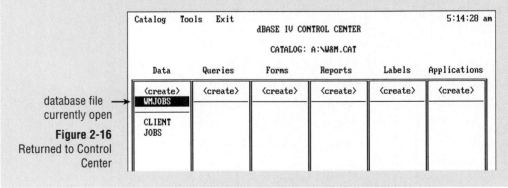

database file
currently open

Figure 2-16
Returned to Control
Center

dBASE saves the database file to the drive and directory you designated as the default. dBASE automatically adds a DBF extension to the filename. Thus, your database file is stored on your data diskette as WMJOBS.DBF. In addition to saving the database file to the disk, dBASE adds the filename WMJOBS.DBF to the open catalog, W&M.CAT.

As an alternative you could save the database structure and remain in the Database Design screen. Select the option *Save this database file structure* from the Layout menu, then enter the database filename and press [Enter] twice to accept the filename and return to the Database Design screen.

Figure 2-17 shows conceptually what takes place when you save a database file. Before you press [Enter] to save the database file, WMJOBS.DBF is not stored on your data diskette; it is stored only in computer memory (Figure 2-17a).

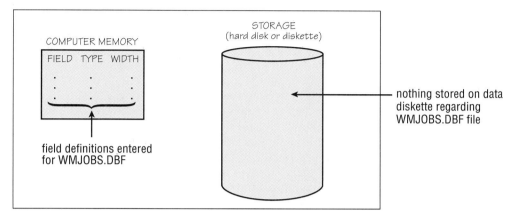

Figure 2-17a
Data definition in process

When you press [Enter] to save your file, WMJOBS.DBF is stored on your data diskette. At this point, no records are stored in the database file, only the database file structure (Figure 2-17b).

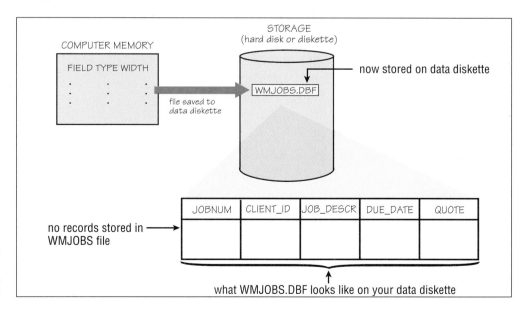

Figure 2-17b
After saving database file structure

Dot Prompt

To create a database file:

    CREATE *database filename*

    Builds a structure for a new database file

Example   .CREATE wmjobs

Modifying the Database File Structure

Now that Esther has created, saved, and viewed the WMJOBS database file, she is proud of herself and thinks her work is done. As she walks down the hall to get herself a cold drink, she passes Nancy and Martin in the hall; they are talking about how many jobs W&M has completed this month. Esther immediately thinks to herself, "What if Nancy or Martin want a list of completed jobs or jobs in process? I have no way to retrieve that information from the database." Esther realizes that her WMJOBS file has no field to enable her to distinguish between completed jobs and ongoing jobs. What can she do? She then remembers that dBASE has an option that allows her to change the file structure. Esther returns to her office to change the file structure of the WMJOBS file.

Referring to her file layout, she decides to add a field named STATUS after the QUOTE field (Figure 2-18). The STATUS field will use the code C to indicate if a job is complete or the code I if the job is in process, that is, incomplete.

WMJOBS File			
Field Name	**Data Type**	**Width**	**Decimal**
JOBNUM	Character	4	
CLIENT_ID	Character	3	
JOB_DESCR	Character	25	
DUE_DATE	Date	8	
QUOTE	Numeric	6	0
STATUS	Character	1	

Figure 2-18
Revised file layout
for WMJOBS file

Perhaps the data you originally planned for your database are not adequate to handle a particular business problem. Or perhaps a field is not long enough to store certain data values. You can use the *Modify structure/order* option in dBASE to change the structure of the file. This option allows you to add and delete fields and change a field's name, width, or data type. This is the option Esther will use to modify the structure of the WMJOBS file and add the field STATUS.

To modify the database file named WMJOBS:

❶ With WMJOBS highlighted in the Data panel, press **[Enter]**. The prompt box listing three things you can do with a database appears. See Figure 2-19.

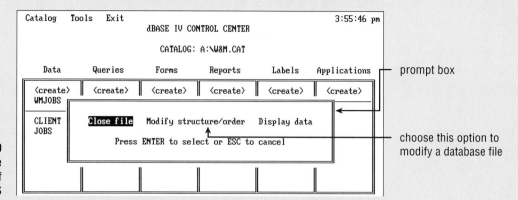

Figure 2-19
Modifying the structure of WMJOBS

❷ Highlight the option *Modify structure/order* in the prompt box, and press **[Enter]**. The Database Design screen appears with the Organize menu open. See Figure 2-20.

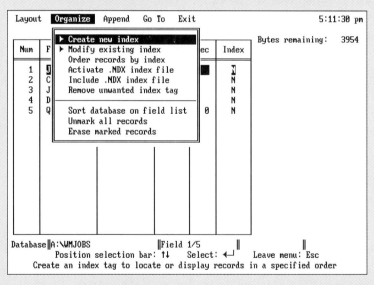

Figure 2-20
Organize menu appears over Database Design screen

❸ You don't need to use any of the options on this pull-down menu, so press **[Esc]** to close it. The current structure of the WMJOBS file appears on the Database Design screen. See Figure 2-21 on the next page.

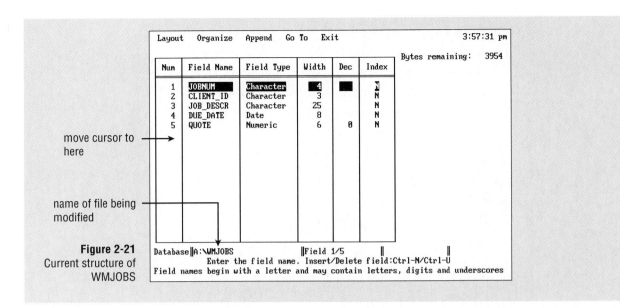

Figure 2-21
Current structure of
WMJOBS

move cursor to here →

name of file being modified

Now you can add the new field.

To add a new field:

❶ Move the cursor past field 5 to field 6, the first blank field.

Enter the name of the new field.

❷ Type **status** and press **[Enter]**. The cursor advances to the Field Type column. See Figure 2-22.

Figure 2-22
In process of modifying WMJOBS

new field being added →

Now enter the data type.

❸ Press **[Enter]** to accept the character data type for this field. The cursor advances to the Width column.

Next enter the width.

❹ Type **1** and press **[Enter]**. The cursor advances to the Index column.

⑤ Press **[Enter]**. The cursor advances to the next row.

You have just inserted a new field in the WMJOBS file. Look over your screen. It should be identical to Figure 2-23. If it is not, move to the STATUS field and make the appropriate corrections.

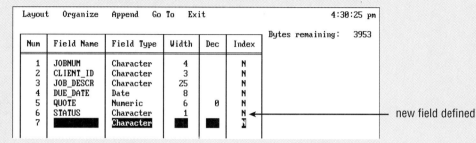

Figure 2-23
STATUS field added
to definition of
database file

Now let's save the modified database file structure.

To save the database file structure:

❶ Press **[Alt]E** to open the Exit menu.

❷ Select *Save changes and exit* (**S**). dBASE prompts if you're sure you want to make the changes.

❸ Select *Yes* (**Y**). You are automatically returned to the Control Center.

dBASE saves the database file to the drive and directory you designated as the default. dBASE automatically *writes over* the original database file and replaces it with the modified database file. dBASE stores the file as WMJOBS.DBF.

Figure 2-24 on the next page shows what has taken place on your data diskette. You stored WMJOBS.DBF on your data diskette, but you changed its structure from the original database file. Your new version includes the field STATUS.

Dot Prompt

To modify the database structure:

MODIFY STRUCTURE

Gives you access to the database Design screen

Example   .USE wmjobs
.MODIFY STRUCTURE

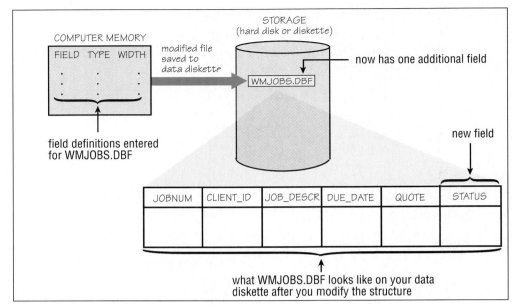

Figure 2-24
After modifying the
WMJOBS file structure

Printing the Database File Structure

Esther wants to verify that the database file structure has been modified as she specified in the file layout sheet. To do this, she can view the structure of the WMJOBS database file on the screen or print it. The Layout menu allows her to view or print the structure of a database file. You may also find this option helpful if you forget a field name or what data type you assigned to a particular field.

To print the file structure:

❶   With WMJOBS highlighted, press **[Enter]**. The prompt box appears.

❷   Move the highlight to the option *Modify structure/order* and press **[Enter]**. The Database Design screen appears with the Organize menu open.

❸   Press **[←]** to display the *Layout* option. See Figure 2-25.

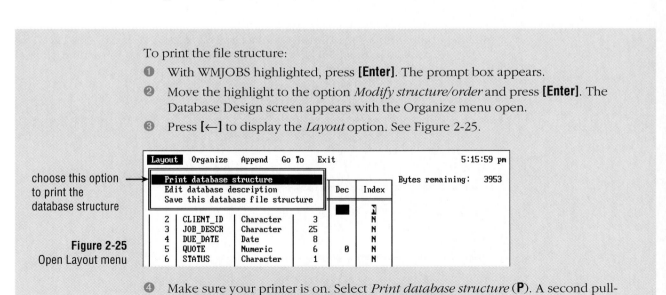

choose this option
to print the
database structure

Figure 2-25
Open Layout menu

❹   Make sure your printer is on. Select *Print database structure* (**P**). A second pull-down menu appears. See Figure 2-26.

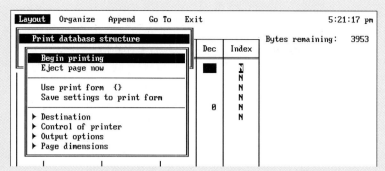

Figure 2-26
Choose Print option

⑤ Select *Begin printing* (**B**). You will receive a hard copy of the database file structure. Figure 2-27 displays the field name, the data type, and the width of each field in the record; the order in which the fields appear in the file structure; the number of records currently stored in the database; and the date the database file was last updated. When a database file structure is printed, if no number appears in the Dec column for numeric data, it means there are zero decimal places.

```
Page #    1

Structure for database: A:\WMJOBS.DBF
Number of data records:      0
Date of last update    : 06/01/92
Field  Field Name  Type        Width   Dec    Index
    1  JOBNUM      Character       4             N
    2  CLIENT_ID   Character       3             N
    3  JOB_DESCR   Character      25             N
    4  DUE_DATE    Date            8             N
    5  QUOTE       Numeric         6             N
```

Figure 2-27
Current structure of
WMJOBS database
file

If you add the numbers in the Width column, you will find that the total is one more than the sum of the individual field widths. dBASE automatically adds a one-character field at the beginning of each record to serve as an indicator (flag) as to whether the record is marked for deletion.

Dot Prompt

To print the database structure:

LIST STRUCTURE TO PRINTER

shaded portion of
the command is
optional

Displays field definitions of the specified file

Example   .USE wmjobs
                .LIST STRUCTURE TO PRINTER

Now return to the Control Center.

To return to the Control Center:

❶ Press **[Alt]E** to open the Exit menu.

There is no reason to save the file structure again since the field definitions have not changed.

❷ Highlight the option *Abandon changes and exit* and press **[Enter]**. You're now at the Control Center.

Esther is satisfied with the structure of the database file, and decides to quit dBASE for now.

Quitting dBASE

You have completed Tutorial 2. You will learn how to add data to a database file in the next tutorial. You may now quit dBASE.

To quit dBASE:

❶ Press **[Alt]E** to open the Exit menu.

❷ Select Quit to DOS (**Q**). You are returned to the DOS prompt.

Dot Prompt

To quit dBASE:

QUIT

Closes all open files, terminates the dBASE session, and returns control to the operating system

Example   .QUIT

Control Center Summary

To use a different catalog:

Press [Alt]C to open the Catalog menu.

Select *Use a different catalog* (U).

Highlight a catalog you want to use and press [Enter].

To create a database structure:

Highlight <create> in the Data panel and press [Enter].

Enter the specifications in the Database Design screen.

Press [Alt]E to open the Exit menu.

Select *Save changes and exit* (S).

Enter name of database structure and press [Enter].

To modify a database structure:

Highlight filename in the Data panel and press [Enter].

Select *Modify structure/order* (M).

Modify database structure.

Press [Alt]E to open the Exit menu.

Select *Save changes and exit* (S).

Answer Y to prompt.

To print database structure:

Highlight filename in the Data panel and press [Enter].

Select *Modify structure/order* (M).

Press [Alt]L to open the Layout menu.

Select *Print database structure* (P).

Select *Begin printing* (B).

To quit dBASE:

Press [Alt]E to open the Exit menu.

Select *Quit to DOS* (Q).

Exercises

1. Which of the following are valid dBASE filenames? For those names that are not valid, give the reason why.

    a. SALES HISTORY   d. SALESHISTORY

    b. SALES92   e. SALES

    c. 92SALES

2. Which of the following are valid dBASE field names? For those names that are not valid, give the reason why.

    a. CUST#   d. CUST:NUM   g. TR 1

    b. CUSTOMER_NUMBER   e. CUST92   h. CUST_NUM

    c. CUSTOMER   f. 1STQTR   i. CUSTNUM

3. Give an example of the values that can be entered for each of the following data types:

    a. logical   d. numeric

    b. date   e. memo

    c. character

4. What is the default data type?

5. Jim defines a phone number with a width of 7, using a numeric data type. Frank defines a phone number with a width of 14, using a character data type. How would each enter phone numbers? Give an example of a phone number that Jim would enter. Give an example of a phone number that Frank would enter.

6. If field names in dBASE are limited to 10 or fewer characters, how can you have a client named "Mountain Top Ski" stored in the database?

7. What file extension does dBASE use for database files?

8. Does the DOS command DIR help you determine if dBASE database files are stored on your data diskette? Explain.

9. Why would you want to print the structure of the database file?

10. Suggest a field name, a data type, and a width for each field in the invoice file shown in Figure 2-28.

Field Description

Invoice number (highest number is 4300)

Customer name (longest name is "Orlando Sand and Gravel Company")

Date of invoice

Amount of invoice (highest amount is $850.68)

Eligible for sales tax (y/n)

Figure 2-28

Activate the catalog TUTOR2 and use the record layout in Figure 2-29 to answer Exercises 11 through 16. The layout describes data on the faculty at a local college. The fields include a faculty identification number, faculty name, department, phone extension, and annual salary.

Field Name	Data Type	Width	Decimal
FID	Numeric	5	
FNAME	Character	15	
DEPT	Character	4	
EXTENSION	Character	4	
SALARY	Numeric	5	0

Figure 2-29

11. Use the <create> option in the Data panel of the Control Center to enter the definition of the faculty file using the file layout. Do *not* save the file.

12. Before saving the file you realize several changes need to be made. Make the following modifications to the field definitions:
    a. Change the first field, FID, to FACULTY_ID and the data type to character.
    b. Change FNAME to FACNAME.
    c. Delete the EXTENSION field from the record.
    d. Change the width of the SALARY field to 6.

13. Save the database file on your data diskette. Name the file FACULTY.

14. Print the file structure.

15. Modify the file structure to include a new field, the faculty member's hire date. The field name is HIRE_DATE, and the data type is date.

16. Save the file structure again, then print it.

Refer to Figure 2-30, which shows the structure of a database file, to answer Exercises 17 through 19.

```
Structure for database: A:student.dbf
Number of data records:    10
Date of last update   : 09/14/91
Field  Field Name  Type     Width   Dec
    1  SID         Character    3
    2  SNAME       Character   10
    3  SEX         Character    1
    4  MAJOR       Character    3
    5  GPA         Numeric      4    2
** Total **                    22
```

Figure 2-30

17. What is the name of the database file?

18. Identify each field.

19. How many records are currently stored in this file?

Tutorial Assignments

Esther decides to create an EXPENSES file for the third database file in the W&M database system. Each record in this file will represent an expense that W&M has incurred for a client, and each expense will be assigned to a specific expense category. Figure 2-31 shows the record layout for this file.

Field Description	Field Name	Data Type	Width	Decimal
Client ID	CLIENT_ID	Character	3	
Job number	JOBNUM	Character	4	
Billing category	CAT	Character	3	
Date of expense	DATE_EXP	Date	8	
Amount of expense	AMOUNT	Numeric	7	2

Figure 2-31

Activate the catalog TUTOR2 and do the following:

1. Create the database file and store it on your data diskette. Save the file as EXPENSES.

2. Print the structure of the EXPENSES database file.

3. Modify the EXPENSES file structure to include an additional field. Name this field DE-SCRIPTN and give it the data type character and a width of 30.

4. Save and print the modified structure of the EXPENSES database file.

Case Problems

> *Instructor's note: Students should create a separate data diskette for each of these case problems. To do this, see the section Creating Your Data Diskettes for the Tutorials at the front of this book.*

1. Biggs & Hang Investment Corporation

Biggs & Hang Investment Corporation (B&H Corp.) is an investment company located in San Francisco. Lavel Simpson, an executive assistant, notices that many of his manager's clients are asking for information on Japanese companies. Lavel suggests to his manager that B&H begin evaluating the investment potential of several companies listed on the Tokyo Stock Exchange. With his manager's approval, Lavel begins to compile a database of financial data about these companies.

    The design of his database is shown in the file layout in Figure 2-32.

Activate the catalog BIG&HANG and do the following:

1. Create a database file structure that matches the one shown in Figure 2-32 and save it to your data diskette as INVEST.

Field Description	Field Name	Data Type	Width	Decimal
Company ID	COMP_ID	Character	4	
Company name	COMP_NAME	Character	30	
Industry code	IND_CODE	Character	1	
Description	DESCRPT	Character	60	
Total assets	ASSETS	Numeric	10	0
Sales	SALES	Numeric	10	0
Profits	PROFIT	Numeric	10	0
Shares outstanding	OUT_SHRS	Numeric	10	0

Figure 2-32

2. Print the structure of the INVEST database file.

3. Add two new fields to the end of the database file. First add the company's highest price on the Tokyo Stock Exchange during the year. The field name is HIGH_PRICE, the data type is numeric, the length is 10, and the number of decimal places is 0. Second add the company's lowest price on the Tokyo Stock Exchange during the year. The field name is LOW_PRICE, the data type is numeric, the length is 10, and the number of decimal places is 0. Save the modified file.

4. Print the modified structure of the INVEST database file.

2. Medi-Source Inc.

Medi-Source Inc. distributes supplies to hospitals, medical laboratories, and pharmacies throughout the United States. Files of all Medi-Source customers and accounts receivable data are available to department managers on the company's mainframe computer.

Upon a recent review of the files Joan Glazer, the manager of the credit and collection department, notices that the outstanding balances of several Massachusetts and Rhode Island customers appear to be higher than that of the average Medi-Source customer, which is approximately $6,000. She decides to study the accounts in these two states more carefully.

Joan asks Bert Spivak, manager of the information systems department, to prepare several reports to help her analyze the data. Bert tells Joan that he and his programming staff are backed up on projects and will not be able to help her for four to six weeks. He suggests instead that he retrieve the Rhode Island and Massachusetts data from the mainframe database and provide her with a dBASE file, which she can analyze herself. Joan thinks this is a great idea. Bert says he'll have the data to her in two days.

Figure 2-33 on the next page shows the layout of the Medi-Source customer database file.

Field Name	Description	Data Type	Width	Decimal
CUSTID	A unique identification number assigned to each customer	Character	2	
CUSTNAME	Name of customer	Character	25	
TYPE	Code indicating type of business, e.g., P=Pharmacy, L=Laboratory, H=Hospital	Character	1	
STATE	Code of state: RI=Rhode Island, MA=Massachusetts	Character	2	
REP	ID of sales rep assigned to customer	Character	1	
CRD_LIMIT	Maximum amount of credit customer is allowed	Numeric	6	0
BAL_OWED	Amount customer currently owes Medi-Source	Numeric	9	2
YTD_SALES	Total sales to customer since beginning of year	Numeric	9	2

Figure 2-33

Activate the catalog MEDISRCE and do the following:

1. Create the database file structure and save it as a file named CUST.

2. Print the file structure of CUST.

3. Modify the structure of the CUST file to include a field for the date of the last sale. Insert the field after the YTD_SALES field and use the field name DATE_LSTSL and the date data type. Save the modified file.

4. Print the modified file structure of CUST.

3. Appleton & Drake Electrical Supply Company

Terry Rossati has worked at Appleton & Drake Electrical Supply Company for six months in the human resources (HR) department. He is amazed at the company's need for better and more up-to-date information about its employees. He knows he could be much more efficient and effective in his job if his department could be computerized.

Terry and his HR assistant have access to the company payroll database that was created and is maintained by the accounting office. But because this database was originally designed for accounting purposes, it is not helpful for HR needs. For example, Terry cannot get the payroll database to do something as simple as list the employees alphabetically by last name. The payroll system stores employees' first and last names in one field with first names entered first, as they would appear on payroll checks.

Terry needs to develop computerized Equal Employment Opportunity reports for the federal government; timely performance and salary review due date reports (each employee is reviewed on the anniversary of his/her date of hire); internal telephone directory reports; and marital status reports (to check eligibility for certain health benefits).

Currently Terry and his assistant must put together all these reports either manually or with partial information from the payroll system. When he does use the payroll system, Terry must still manipulate and recalculate the data before he can obtain the information he needs. Terry makes several requests to the data processing manager, Alice Austic, for help. But Alice tells him that her staff is too busy on other projects and will have no time this year to help the HR department.

Terry decides to assign Cheryl Muldoon, a recent business school graduate, to work with him to develop an HR information system. Cheryl studied database concepts and dBASE in school.

After studying the requirements of the HR department, Cheryl designs an employee file and creates the employee file layout shown in Figure 2-34.

Description	Field Name	Data Type	Width	Decimal
Employee number	EMP_NUM	Character	3	
Last name	LNAME	Character	15	
First name	FNAME	Character	10	
Sex (F/M)	SEX	Character	1	
Married (Y/N)	MAR	Character	1	
Number of dependents	DEP	Numeric	2	0
Annual salary	ANNSAL	Numeric	6	0
Department*	DEPT	Character	3	

* Codes are: SAL = Sales, COR = Corporate, ENG = Engineering

Figure 2-34

Activate the catalog APPLTON and do the following:

1. Create the database file structure using the employee file layout and save it as a file named EMP.

2. Print the structure of the EMP database file.

3. Modify the structure of the database file to include a field for the employee's hire date. Insert this field between the fields DEP and ANNSAL. Use HIRE_DATE as the field name and date as the data type. Save the modified file.

4. Print the modified file structure of the EMP database file.

4. National Basketball Association

Sharman Durfee is working as a summer intern at the National Basketball Association (NBA) headquarters in New York City. The NBA office receives numerous requests every day for information from sportswriters, TV announcers, team owners, agents, and other interested parties. Sharman's assignment is to set up a database of players' salaries to help NBA staff provide accurate information quickly and with little effort.

After studying the problem, she comes up with the file layout shown in Figure 2-35.

Field Description	Field Name	Data Type	Width	Decimal
Team ID	TEAM	Character	3	
Player's first name	FNAME	Character	12	
Player's last name	LNAME	Character	15	
Salary	SALARY	Numeric	10	0

Figure 2-35

Activate the catalog NBA and do the following:

1. Create the database file and name it PLAYER.

2. Print the structure of the database file.

3. A writer has expressed interest in seeing if there are salary differences by position. Modify the structure of the PLAYER database file to include a new field that represents the position an athlete plays. Use the codes shown in Figure 2-35 to represent the positions.

Code	Position
C	Center
F	Forward
G	Guard

Figure 2-36

Insert this field between the fields LNAME and SALARY. Name the new field POS and assign it a character data type and a width of 1. Save the modified file.

4. Print the modified file structure.

5. Off-Campus Housing at Ashland University

David Abelson is a sophomore at Ashland University. He works in the University's Housing Office, where he maintains a manual system for tracking the availability of off-campus housing. When landlords have vacancies, they call or come by the Housing Office to list their rental property with David. University students come in to seek off-campus housing. Using the current system, students look through the Housing Office's book of available off-campus housing units and try to find units that match their needs.

Although students do find available rentals, the system hasn't worked very smoothly. David has found that the system has several flaws. One problem is that too few copies of the housing book are available to meet student demands. In addition housing units that have been rented recently remain in the book after they are no longer available. Also students can't get a list of housing units that meet their specific criteria and they are forced to read *every* listing to find what they want. It would be helpful if students could specify their needs, such as maximum monthly rent, number of bedrooms, and distance from campus, and more quickly find the units that meet those needs.

David has recently completed a computer course, and he believes that this system is a perfect application for computerization. He suggests to his manager that the Housing Office create a database of available off-campus housing. Students would then be able to get lists of available units based on their specific needs.

Activate the catalog HOUSING and do the following:

1. Prepare a file layout based on the case description and sample off-campus-housing form (Figure 2-37).

AVAILABLE OFF-CAMPUS HOUSING FORM

1. Rental Address:

    _____
    Street Address

    _____
    City   State   Zip

2. Indicate name and phone numbers of owner of rental property

    _____
    Last Name   First Name

    _____
    Home Phone #   Work Phone #

3. Type of rental unit available (check one)
    ( ) House   ( ) Apartment

4. # of bedrooms: ___

5. How many miles is unit from campus? _____

6. Length of lease required (in months)?_____

7. Rent per month? _____

8. Date Available?   __/__/__

9. Please check all amenities that your rental unit features:
    ( ) Utilities included   ( ) Washer/dryer
    ( ) Furnished bedroom(s)   ( ) Dishwasher
    ( ) On bus line   ( ) Pets allowed
    ( ) Wheelchair accessible   ( ) Children allowed

Figure 2-37

2. Create the database file and name it HOUSING.

3. Print the structure of the HOUSING database file.

Tutorial 3

Keeping the Database Current

Case: Wells & Martinez — Updating the CLIENT and JOBS Files

Three weeks have passed since Esther created the JOBS file and added the first record. During this time she has entered all the data from W&M's job authorization forms into the database. Esther has also started to document the database by placing copies of the CLIENT and JOBS* file structures in a folder for easy reference (Figures 3-1a and 3-1b on the next page).

Today is the second Friday of the month, the day on which Nancy and Martin hold a staff meeting to let the employees know what's going on at W&M.

The meeting starts on time, and as usual Martin begins with any good news or success stories. He is happy to announce that W&M's marketing campaign for new clients has brought in two new clients: a local restaurant chain, Taco Heaven, and a retail shop that specializes in custom-made down comforters, Peaches & Ice. Esther jots a note to herself; after the meeting she must talk to Martin and get the information she needs to add these two clients to the database.

The next portion of the meeting is devoted to an update of the status of the various jobs in progress. The creative team discusses several of the larger jobs, sharing with everyone the nature of the various campaigns and their

OBJECTIVES

In this tutorial you will learn to:

- Open a database file

- Add records to a database file using both the Edit and Browse screens

- Edit records in a database file using both the Edit and Browse screens

- Mark records for deletion

- Permanently remove records from a database file

- Make a backup copy of a database file

---

* In Tutorial 2 you created the file structure WMJOBS. In the rest of this book you will use the file JOBS instead of WMJOBS. JOBS has the same file structure as WMJOBS, but it contains data on 20 W&M jobs.

progress. Martin announces with pride that the job for Images — a 20-page, full-color fall catalogue — was completed this week on schedule. He tells the group that two days ago Sledge Hill Printers delivered 2,000 catalogues to the mailing house. Esther pulls out her notes; she can change the JOBS file to show that the Images job has been completed.

```
Structure for database: A: CLIENT.dbf
Number of data records:  9
Date of last update: 07/01/92
Field   Field Name  Type         Width Dec
   1      CLIENT_ID   Character       3
   2      CLIENT_NAM  Character      25
   3      CONTACT     Character      20
   4      PHONE       Character      13
 **Total**                          62
```

Figure 3-1a
File structure for CLIENT file

```
Structure for database: A: JOBS.dbf
Number of data records: 20
Date of last update: 07/20/92
Field Field Name    Type         Width Dec
   1    JOBNUM        Character       4
   2    CLIENT_ID     Character       3
   3    JOB_DESCR     Character      25
   4    DUE_DATE      Date            8
   5    QUOTE         Numeric         6
   6    STATUS        Character       1
  **Total**                         48
```

Figure 3-1b
File structure for JOBS file

Martin then tells the group that despite their efforts, one of their clients, Eyes Have It, a specialty eyeglass store, has gone out of business. Esther makes another note — this time to delete Eyes Have It from the database.

Finally Martin asks if there are any other announcements. Nancy doesn't have any announcements, but she wonders if anyone has heard recently from Gunther Williams, W&M's contact person at Mountain Top Ski. Ann Lightfeather responds that the owner of Mountain Top Ski called yesterday and told her that Gunther had resigned and Victor Juarez is taking over his job. Nancy thanks Ann and asks Esther to update the database, but Esther is already adding this note to her list of things to do.

When the meeting is over, Esther asks Martin to write down the contacts and the phone numbers for Taco Heaven and Peaches & Ice and get that information to her as soon as he can. About 30 minutes later, Martin drops by her office and hands her a note (Figure 3-2).

Figure 3-2
Data on W&M's new clients

Esther, new client info:

Client name: Peaches & Ice
Contact: Alice Beaumont
Phone: (505) 728-5176

Client name: Taco Heaven
Contact: Bert Clinton
Phone: (505) 728-1295

Updating Database Files

What do all the tasks on Esther's list have in common? They affect the accuracy of the data in the W&M database. W&M, like any other business, must keep the contents of its database files up-to-date and accurate so the output from those files is meaningful and helpful in making business decisions. **File maintenance** — the adding, changing, and deleting of records — is a basic function you must perform when you have a DBMS. In this tutorial, you will learn how to use a variety of dBASE commands to update database files.

Opening a Database File

Esther is ready to add the two new clients to the CLIENT file. However, before she can update this or any other database file, she must first open the specific file she wants to update. The dBASE command USE tells dBASE to find a specific database file on your data diskette and to set aside a small portion of computer memory as a work area for that database file. This process is called *opening* the file.

When you open a file, dBASE does not display the data on the screen. You must first select other dBASE options before you can update, display, print, or manipulate records in a database file.

In Tutorial 1, Esther created the CLIENT database file and entered the client data. Let's open the CLIENT file and add the new clients to the file. To open the CLIENT database file, you use the Data panel of the Control Center.

To open the CLIENT database file:

❶ Load dBASE and change the default drive to the data diskette.

❷ Activate the W&M catalog.

❸ Highlight CLIENT in the Data panel and press **[Enter]**. The prompt box appears.

❹ With the option *Use file* highlighted, press **[Enter]**. CLIENT now appears above the panel line, indicating that the file is open.

Dot Prompt

To open a database file:

USE *database file*   ORDER *mdx tag*

Opens an existing database file and may open associated index files

Example   .USE client

Figure 3-3 on the next page will help you visualize what happens when you open a database file. Figure 3-3a illustrates the situation after you have loaded dBASE but have not opened a database file. No link exists between dBASE and any of the database files on your data diskette. Thus, you cannot update, list, or manipulate the records in any database file.

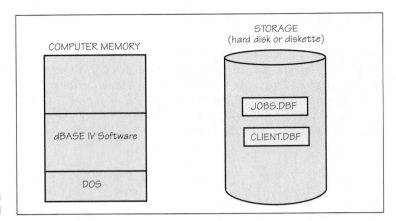

Figure 3-3a
No files opened

Figure 3-3b shows what happens after you open the CLIENT database file. dBASE has found your file on the data diskette and has set aside a portion of the computer's memory as a work area for the data in this file. The arrows between the work area in memory and the CLIENT file in storage indicate the CLIENT file is open. You can now update, list, and manipulate records in this file using dBASE.

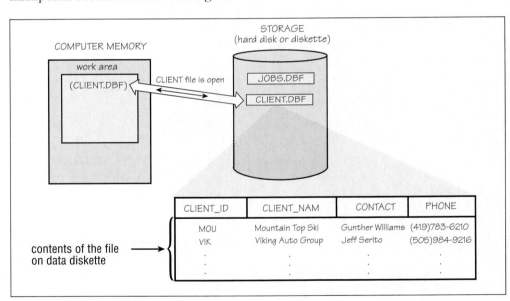

Figure 3-3b
CLIENT.DBF file
open

Adding Records to a Database File

Now that you have opened the CLIENT file, you can add the two new client records to it. You can use either the Edit or the Browse screen to add records. In some ways the choice of one screen over the other is simply a matter of preference. As you will soon see, each screen offers an advantage. With the Edit screen you focus on all the relevant information for one record. With the Browse screen, you see several records displayed at once. Let's try both so you can decide which you prefer.

Adding a Record Using the Edit Screen

You use the Edit screen when you want to view one record at a time. You can use the Edit screen to edit, delete, and add records to the currently open database file.

Let's add the new client records to the database file using the Edit screen.

To add a new record to the CLIENT database file using the Edit screen:

❶ With CLIENT highlighted in the Data panel press **[F2]** (Data). The Browse screen appears. See Figure 3-4. dBASE places the cursor at the first record in the database.

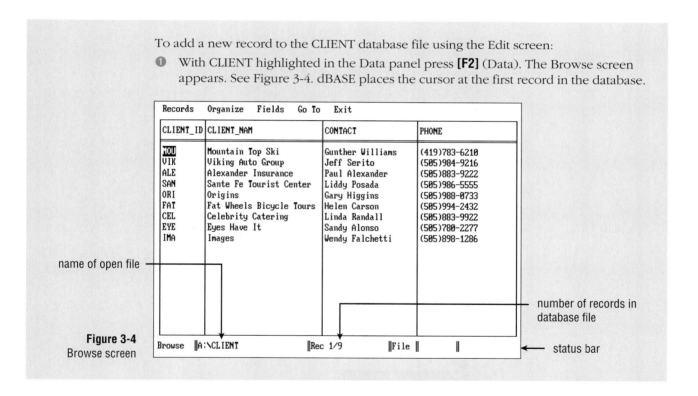

name of open file

number of records in database file

Figure 3-4
Browse screen

status bar

② Press **[F2]** (Data) to switch to the Edit screen. See Figure 3-5. dBASE shows the first record in the database file.

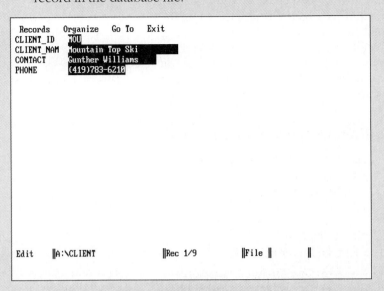

Figure 3-5
Edit screen

By pressing [F2] you can switch between the Edit and Browse screens. For now stay in the Edit screen.

Now indicate you want to add a record.

③ Press **[Alt]R** to open the Records menu. See Figure 3-6.

choose this option ⟶

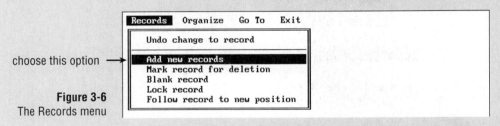

Figure 3-6
The Records menu

④ Select *Add new records* (**A**). dBASE displays a blank *data-entry form* on the Edit screen. See Figure 3-7.

Figure 3-7
Blank data-entry
form

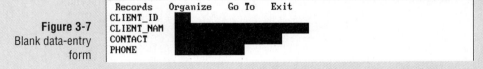

Notice that the form contains the field names Esther defined for the CLIENT file. An input area equal to the field's width follows each field name. You use this form to enter the data values for each client. Before you enter any data, the cursor is always in the first position of the first field.

Let's enter the data that Martin gave Esther for the new client, Peaches & Ice (Figure 3-2).

To enter data into the database file:

➊ With the cursor positioned in the CLIENT_ID field, type in uppercase **PEA**, the client ID that W&M will use for Peaches & Ice. The computer beeps and the cursor advances to the CLIENT_NAM field.

As you enter the data for this record, keep in mind the following guidelines:

• The entry of character data is *case-sensitive*, which means that uppercase and lowercase letters are stored exactly as you type them. For example, if you entered the CLIENT_ID for Peaches & Ice as "pea," it would be stored in lowercase; it would *not* be changed to uppercase and stored as "PEA."

• If the data you enter fill all the positions in the field, the computer will beep, and the cursor will automatically advance to the next field of the current record or to the first field of the next record (if the cursor is in the last field of the current record).

• If the data you enter do not fill the field, you must press [Enter] to move to the next field.

• If you enter an illegal character in a field, such as a letter in a numeric field, the computer will beep, and your entry will not appear. In that case just type a valid character.

• If you notice a typing error, you can move between fields within a given record by using [↑] or [↓]. You can then modify the contents of a field by typing over what you previously entered in the field.

Figure 3-8 summarizes the keystroke combinations you can use whenever you enter data in the Edit screen. You probably will not use them all right now, but they are listed here for your convenience and possible future use.

Keystroke	Function
[←] [→]	Moves the cursor one character to the left or the right
[↑] [↓]	Moves the cursor to the previous or next field in the record
[PgUp][PgDn]	Moves the cursor to the previous or next record in the database
[Ins]	Switches between insert and replacement modes
[Del]	Deletes the character the cursor is on
[Ctrl][End]	Saves all appended records, including the current record, and returns you to the Control Center or the dot prompt
[Esc]	Returns you to the Control Center or the dot prompt without saving the current record

Figure 3-8
Keystroke
combinations for
the Edit screen

Next let's enter the client's name.

To enter the client's name:

1 With the cursor in the CLIENT_NAM field, type **Peaches & Ice** and press **[Enter]**. Note that the cursor advances to the CONTACT field.

Next enter the name of the contact person.

2 Type **Alice Beaumont** and press **[Enter]**. See Figure 3-9. The cursor advances to the PHONE field.

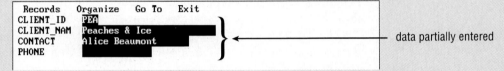

Figure 3-9
Adding data to data-entry form

data partially entered

3 Type **(505)728-5176**. The computer beeps, and a new blank data-entry form appears. See Figure 3-10.

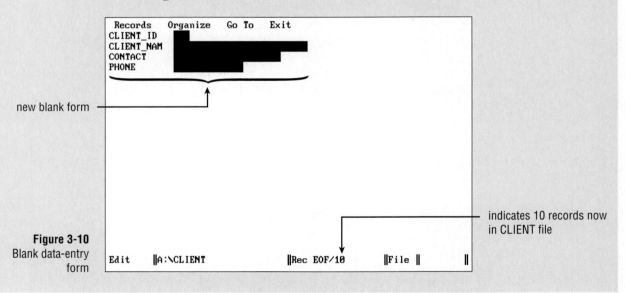

new blank form

indicates 10 records now in CLIENT file

Figure 3-10
Blank data-entry form

If you want to return to the record you just typed, press [PgUp] and the record will reappear. To correct any errors, move the cursor to the appropriate field and make your changes. When you are happy with what you see, press [PgDn]. You will be asked if you want to add a new record. Respond yes and you will be returned to the blank data-entry form.

Figure 3-11 illustrates the contents of the CLIENT file on your data diskette after you have entered the complete Peaches & Ice record. dBASE automatically saves the Peaches & Ice record, the tenth client, as record number 10 in the CLIENT file. Notice that the status bar indicates a total of 10 records (Figure 3-10). dBASE automatically assigns consecutive numbers, starting with 1, to the records you store in a database file. Thus, the first record you enter is assigned record number 1, the second record is assigned record number 2, and so on. You just added Peaches & Ice to the nine records already in the CLIENT file, so this record was assigned record number 10. dBASE IV refers to the assigning of record numbers in the order in which you entered the records as their *natural order*. When records are displayed, they are displayed in natural order, that is, in the order in which they were entered into the database.

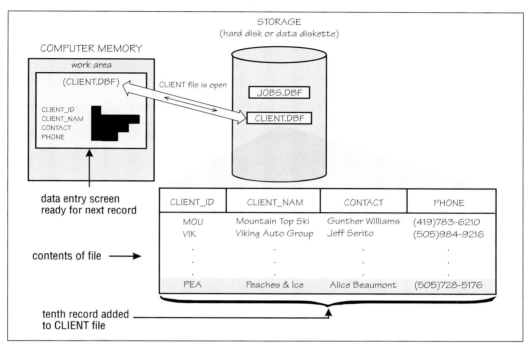

Figure 3-11

Dot Prompt

To add data to a database:

APPEND

Adds new records to the end of the active database file

Example   .USE client
                    .APPEND

The Record Pointer

dBASE keeps track of its place in the database file with a record pointer. The **record pointer** stores in the computer's memory the record number of the record that dBASE is currently "looking at." For example, 1/10 in the status bar means that dBASE is currently looking at the first of 10 records in a file. This record is called the **current record**. It is important for you to know about the concept of current records, because some dBASE commands process only the current record or begin processing at the current record.

Sometimes in the status bar you will see the letters EOF followed by a slash and a number. EOF is an abbreviation that means that the current record is the *end of the file*. EOF appears each time you add a record to a database file, because dBASE always adds a record to the end of a file.

Adding a Record Using the Browse Screen

Now that you have entered data into the last field of the Peaches & Ice record, a blank data-entry form appears. Recall, you can enter data using the Edit or the Browse screen. Let's use the Browse screen to add the Taco Heaven record. Unlike the Edit screen, which lets you view only one record at a time, the Browse screen lets you view several records at once. In the Browse screen you can see up to 17 records at one time, one record per line. (If a record is more than 80 characters wide — the screen's width — you have to scroll left and right to view the other fields.) Like the Edit screen, you can use the Browse screen to edit, delete, and add records to the currently open database file. Figure 3-12 summarizes the keystrokes you can use in the Browse screen.

Keystroke	Function
[←] [→]	Moves the cursor one character to the left or the right
[Home] [End]	Moves the cursor one field to the left or the right
[↓] [↑]	Moves the highlight to the previous or the next record
[PgUp] [PgDn]	Scrolls one screen up or down
[Ctrl][→]	Scrolls one field to the right
[Ctrl][←]	Scrolls one field to the left
[Ctrl] [U]	Marks or unmarks the current record for deletion
[Ctrl][End]	Saves all appended and edited records and returns you to the Control Center screen or the dot prompt
[Esc]	Saves all edited and appended records except the current one and returns you to the Control Center screen or the dot prompt

Figure 3-12
Keystroke combinations for the Browse screen

Let's enter the data for the second client using the Browse screen.

To add a new record to the CLIENT file using the Browse screen:

❶ Press **[F2]** (Data) to switch from the Edit screen to the Browse screen. The last record in the CLIENT file is highlighted.

❷ Press **[PgUp]** to view all the records in the CLIENT file from the Browse screen. See Figure 3-13. (If there were more records in the file than fit on the screen at one time, you could continue pressing [PgUp] until you saw the first record.)

```
 Records    Organize   Fields   Go To   Exit

 CLIENT_ID CLIENT_NAM               CONTACT          PHONE

 MOU       Mountain Top Ski         Gunther Williams  (419)783-6210
 VIK       Viking Auto Group        Jeff Serito       (505)984-9216
 ALE       Alexander Insurance      Paul Alexander    (505)883-9222
 SAN       Sante Fe Tourist Center  Liddy Posada      (505)986-5555
 ORI       Origins                  Gary Higgins      (505)988-0733
 FAT       Fat Wheels Bicycle Tours Helen Carson      (505)994-2432
 CEL       Celebrity Catering       Linda Randall     (505)883-9922
 EYE       Eyes Have It             Sandy Alonso      (505)780-2277
 IMA       Images                   Wendy Falchetti   (505)898-1286
 PEA       Peaches & Ice            Alice Beaumont    (505)728-5176 ◄──────── new record



 Browse   ||A:\CLIENT            ||Rec 1/10      ||File ||        ||
```

Figure 3-13
Browse screen after
Peaches & Ice
record added

Now tell dBASE your want to add a record.

❸ Press **[Alt]R** to open the Records menu.

❹ Select *Add new records* (**A**). The list of records scrolls up and the first blank row in the Browse screen is highlighted. See Figure 3-14.

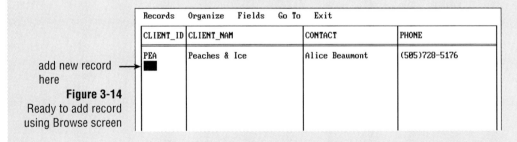

```
 Records    Organize   Fields   Go To   Exit

 CLIENT_ID CLIENT_NAM       CONTACT          PHONE

 PEA       Peaches & Ice    Alice Beaumont   (505)728-5176
 ■
```

add new record
here

Figure 3-14
Ready to add record
using Browse screen

You can now add a new client to the CLIENT file using the Browse screen.

To enter the data for the second new client:

❶ Type **TAC** in the CLIENT_ID column. The cursor moves into the CLIENT_NAM field.

❷ Type **Taco Heaven** and press **[Enter]**. The cursor moves into the CONTACT column.

❸ Type **Bert Clinton** and press **[Enter]**. The cursor moves into the PHONE column.

④   Type **(505)728-1295**. The cursor advances to the next row. See Figure 3-15.

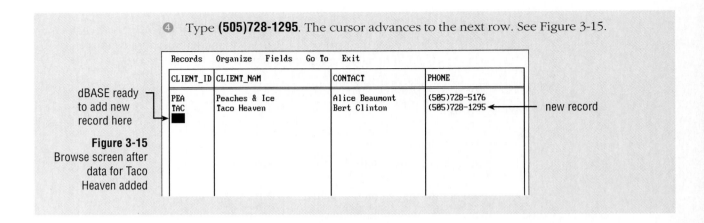

dBASE ready
to add new
record here

Figure 3-15
Browse screen after
data for Taco
Heaven added

Leaving the Browse Screen

After you have entered the data into the last field of the Taco Heaven client record, the status bar indicates that a total of 11 records are stored in the CLIENT file. The blank row that appears on the Browse screen is your indication that the record you just entered has been added to the CLIENT file. Now that you have entered the new records, how do you leave the Browse screen?

To leave the Browse screen:

①   Press **[Alt]E** to open the Exit menu.
②   Select *Exit* (**E**). The record is saved, and you return to the Control Center.

You would use the same method to return to the Control Center from the Edit screen.

Changing Records

Esther consults the list she made at the staff meeting. Since she already has the CLIENT database file open, she checks for any other changes she needs to make to this file. As she scans the list, she notices that she needs to delete Gunther Williams as the contact person for Mountain Top Ski and replace him with Victor Juarez.

   Esther can use either the Edit or the Browse screen to make a change like this. She decides to use the Edit screen.

Changing a Record Using the Edit Screen

You use the same data-entry form to enter changes to an existing record that you used when you originally entered the record. The only difference is that the values of the *current* record appear in the form. Let's use the Edit screen now to replace "Gunther Williams" with "Victor Juarez."

To change data in a record using the Edit screen:

❶ From the Control Center press **[F2]** (Data). The Browse screen appears rather than the Edit screen because it was the last screen used.

Now switch to the Edit screen.

❷ Press **[F2]** (Data). The Edit screen appears. See Figure 3-16.

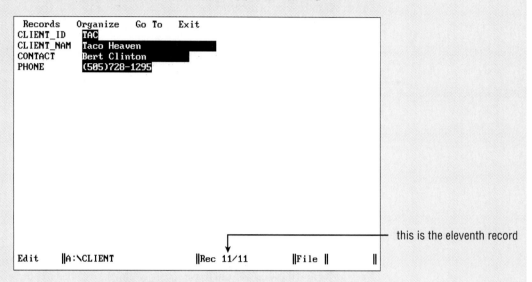

this is the eleventh record

Figure 3-16
Edit screen

The Edit screen displays the current record, Taco Heaven. But Taco Heaven is not the record you want to change. You can move to the next record by using [PgDn] or to the previous record by using [PgUp].

Now let's retrieve the Mountain Top Ski record, the record you want to edit.

❸ With the cursor positioned at the CLIENT_ID field, press **[PgUp]** until you see the Mountain Top Ski record displayed.

You can change the contents of any field by moving the cursor to the appropriate field and entering the changes. Let's try it.

❹ Press **[↓]** to move the cursor to the CONTACT field. Replace "Gunther Williams" by typing **Victor Juarez** over it. Then press **[Spacebar]** three times to erase the remaining letters. Press **[Enter]**. See Figure 3-17.

Figure 3-17
Edit screen after
change made

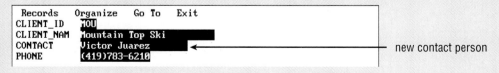

new contact person

If you mistakenly change data that you didn't intend to change, you can "undo" the change by accessing the Records menu ([Alt]R) and selecting the option *Undo change to record.* The contents of the original record will appear.

You can use the same keystrokes while editing a record that you used while adding a record to make changes to the data. Refer to Figure 3-8 for a summary of these keystrokes.

To exit the Edit screen, use the Exit menu. Now let's save the changes to the CLIENT file.

To save the changes to the CLIENT file and exit the Edit screen:

❶ Press **[Alt]E** to open the Exit menu.

❷ Select *Exit* (**E**). dBASE saves the changes and returns you to the Control Center.

If you do not want your changes saved to the database file, press [Esc] instead of opening the Exit menu.

Dot Prompt

To edit records in the Edit screen:

   EDIT *scope*   FIELDS *field list*

   Displays or changes the contents of a record in the active database file or view

   Example   .USE client
                  .EDIT 5

Now let's view the CLIENT database to verify the change has been made to the database file.

To view the clients in the CLIENT file:

❶ Press **[F2]** (Data). The Edit screen appears.

❷ Press **[F2]** (Data) to switch to the Browse screen. See Figure 3-18. Notice that Victor Juarez is listed as the contact person for Mountain Top Ski.

```
 Records    Organize   Fields   Go To   Exit

 CLIENT_ID CLIENT_NAM                CONTACT           PHONE

 MOU       Mountain Top Ski          Victor Juarez     (419)783-6210
 VIK       Viking Auto Group         Jeff Serito       (505)984-9216
 ALE       Alexander Insurance       Paul Alexander    (505)883-9222
 SAN       Sante Fe Tourist Center   Liddy Posada      (505)986-5555
 ORI       Origins                   Gary Higgins      (505)988-0733
 FAT       Fat Wheels Bicycle Tours  Helen Carson      (505)994-2432
 CEL       Celebrity Catering        Linda Randall     (505)883-9922
 EYE       Eyes Have It              Sandy Alonso      (505)780-2277
 IMA       Images                    Wendy Falchetti   (505)898-1286
 PEA       Peaches & Ice             Alice Beaumont    (505)728-5176
 TAC       Taco Heaven               Bert Clinton      (505)728-1295




 Browse  ||A:\CLIENT          ||Rec 1/11       ||File ||        ||
```

Figure 3-18
Client list in the
Browse screen

③ Press **[Esc]** when you are ready to return to the Control Center.

Changing a Record Using the Browse Screen

Esther consults her list again. She decides next to update the JOBS file to show that the Images fall catalogue job has been completed.

Let's use the Browse screen to change the status of Images' fall catalogue from in process (I) to completed (C). The CLIENT file is currently open, but you need to change a record in the JOBS file. Therefore, you must close the CLIENT file and open the JOBS file.

To open the JOBS database file:
① Highlight the JOBS file in the Data panel and press **[Enter]**. The prompt box appears.
② With the *Use file* option highlighted press **[Enter]**. See Figure 3-19. Notice JOBS appears above the panel line, indicating that the JOBS database file is now open. Also CLIENT appears below the panel line, indicating that it is now closed.

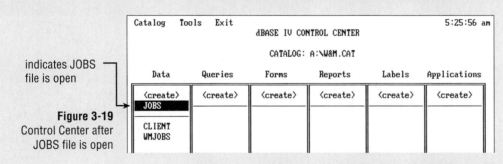

indicates JOBS file is open

Figure 3-19
Control Center after JOBS file is open

To help you visualize what has just occurred, look at Figure 3-20. Figure 3-20a illustrates the situation before you opened the JOBS database file, when the CLIENT database file was open. You were able to update, list, and manipulate the records in the CLIENT file.

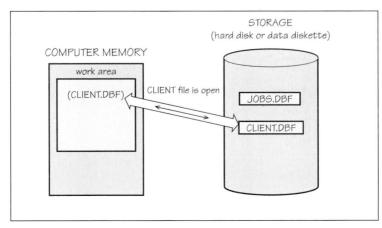

Figure 3-20a
CLIENT file open

Figure 3-20b shows what happened after you opened the JOBS database file. Now you have a link between the work area in the computer's memory and the JOBS file on your data diskette. You can update, list, and manipulate records in the JOBS file. However, you can no longer access any data in the CLIENT file.

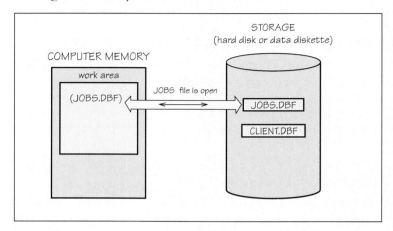

Figure 3-20b
JOBS file open

Let's select the Browse screen to change the job's status.

To use the Browse screen:

❶ Press **[F2]** (Data). The Browse screen appears. Remember, the last screen you used is the screen that is displayed.

❷ Press **[↓]** until you have highlighted job number 1011, Fall Catalogue.

❸ Press **[End]** to move the cursor to the STATUS field. Type uppercase **C** to change the job status to "completed." See Figure 3-21. The cursor advances to the next record.

```
  Records    Organize    Fields    Go To    Exit

  JOBNUM CLIENT_ID JOB_DESCR          DUE_DATE QUOTE  STATUS

  1001   ORI      Best in the Southwest  08/15/93   2500 C
  1002   VIK      Fall TV Ad             08/10/93  32500 C
  1003   MOU      Ski equipment sale     06/01/92   3000 C
  1004   ALE      B/W Magazine Ad        06/05/92   3500 C
  1005   SAN      Magazine Ad            06/10/92  22500 C
  1006   ORI      Fall Promotion         08/01/92   2200 C
  1007   SAN      Pamphlet               08/02/93   3000 C
  1008   VIK      Thanksgiving Promo     11/15/93  12000 I
  1009   FAT      Bicycle Magazine Ad    08/05/93   2500 C
  1010   ALE      Brochure               10/10/93   6000 I
  1011   IMA      Fall Catalogue         08/22/93   8450 C  ◄─── status field changed
  1012   ALE      Radio Ad               09/01/93   3425 I
  1013   SAN      Direct Mail            10/15/93   8900 I
  1014   FAT      Direct Mail            11/20/93   2200 I
  1015   SAN      Brochure               09/15/93   4400 I
  1016   IMA      Magazine Ad            10/15/93  10000 I
  1017   CEL      Flyer                  09/20/93    850 I

  Browse   ||A:\JOBS            ||Rec 12/24      ||File ||        ||
```

Figure 3-21
Browse screen after
record status
changed

Now exit the Browse screen.

To save the changes in the CLIENT file and exit the Browse screen:
1. Press **[Alt]E** to open the Exit menu.
2. Select *Exit* (**E**). dBASE saves the changes and returns you to the Control Center.

Dot Prompt

To edit records in the Browse screen:

> BROWSE   FREEZE *field name*   FIELDS *field names*

A full-screen menu-assisted command for editing and appending records in a database file and view

Example   .USE client
.BROWSE

Deleting Records

Esther has now completed three of the four items on her list. All that remains for her to do is to delete Eyes Have It from the CLIENT file. Because the company has gone out of business, this record is no longer needed.

To permanently delete a record from a database file, you take two steps: first you "mark" the record for deletion, then you "pack" the database file to permanently remove the record from the file. You delete in two steps so that you have the opportunity to reverse your decision. Until you "pack" the database, any records marked for deletion can be unmarked and thus not be permanently removed from the database. First let's discuss marking a record for deletion.

When you **mark** a record, dBASE places a code in the record indicating you want to delete the record. You have not yet physically removed the record from the database file during this step. You can still edit, list, and include in statistical calculations, among other dBASE actions, records marked for deletion.

Let's perform the first step in deleting Eyes Have It from the database file by marking this record for deletion. Currently you have the JOBS file open. However, the record you want to delete is in the CLIENT file. Thus, you must open the CLIENT file again.

To open the CLIENT database file:
1. Highlight CLIENT in the Data panel and press **[Enter]**. The prompt box appears.
2. With the *Use file* option highlighted, press **[Enter]**. CLIENT appears above the panel line, indicating that the file is open. The JOBS file has automatically been closed.

Marking Records for Deletion Using the Edit Screen

You can use the Edit or the Browse screen to mark a record for deletion. Esther decides to use the Edit screen to mark the Eyes Have It record for deletion, because it allows her to see the contents of only a single record at a time and verify that she has the correct record before she marks it for deletion.

To access the Edit screen:

❶ Press **[F2]** (Data). The Browse screen, the screen you used last, appears.

Switch to the Edit screen.

❷ Press **[F2]** (Data) to switch to the Edit screen. The current record is Mountain Top Ski.

Next you would scroll through the CLIENT file, using [PgDn], until you found the record you wanted to delete. But what would happen if you made a mistake and accidentally marked the wrong record for deletion? Let's *intentionally* mark a wrong record for deletion. You'll do this by marking Mountain Top Ski, the current record, for deletion using the keystroke combination [Ctrl]U.

To mark the client record Mountain Top Ski for deletion:

❶ Press **[Ctrl]U**. This action places a delete code in the current record. The status bar now shows "Del," which indicates that the current record is marked for deletion. See Figure 3-22.

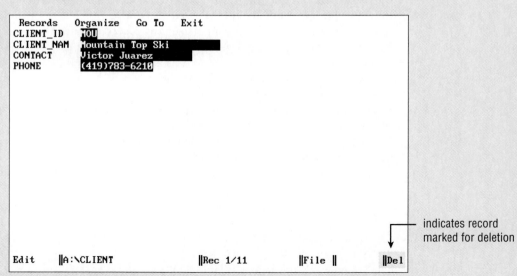

Figure 3-22
Record marked for
deletion

indicates record
marked for deletion

[Ctrl]U is a **toggle**, that is, it acts like an on/off switch. If you press [Ctrl]U one time, the record is marked for deletion. Press the keystroke combination a second time, and the record is no longer marked for deletion; press it again, and the record is marked for deletion; and so on.

Remember, the Mountain Top Ski record is marked for deletion in error. You need to "unmark" it.

To unmark the client record Mountain Top Ski for deletion:

❶ Press **[Ctrl]U** again. "Del" no longer appears on the status bar. See Figure 3-23. The current record is no longer marked for deletion.

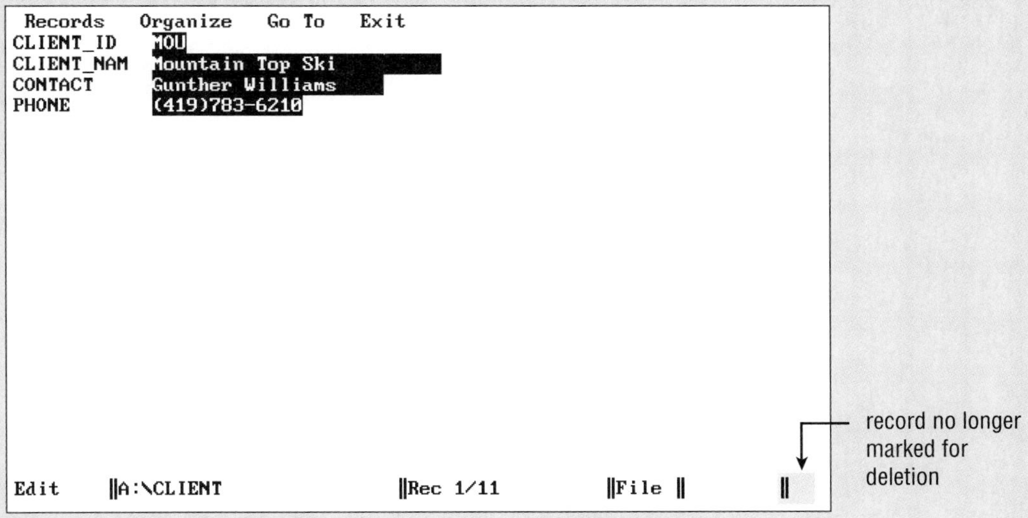

Figure 3-23
Mark for deletion removed

```
 Records    Organize   Go To   Exit
CLIENT_ID   MOU
CLIENT_NAM  Mountain Top Ski
CONTACT     Gunther Williams
PHONE       (419)783-6210




Edit    ||A:\CLIENT              ||Rec 1/11        ||File ||        ||
```

record no longer marked for deletion

This is a simple way to remove the "marked for deletion" status from the record. This is known as **recalling** the record. If you have marked several records for deletion and you want to unmark them, you can use the *Organize* option from the menu bar and select the option *Unmark all records.* This option is available in both the Browse and Edit screens.

Now let's mark the correct record for deletion.

To mark the client record Eyes Have It for deletion:

❶ Press **[PgDn]** until Eyes Have It is the current record.

❷ Press **[Ctrl]U**. Notice that "Del" appears on the status bar. See Figure 3-24 on the next page. The record is marked for deletion.

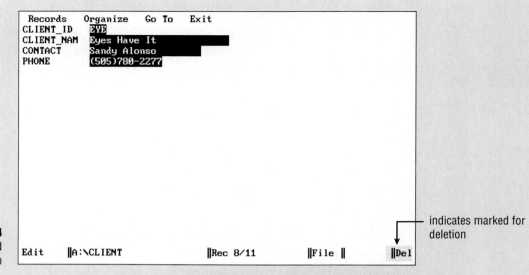

```
   Records   Organize   Go To   Exit
CLIENT_ID   EYE
CLIENT_NAM  Eyes Have It
CONTACT     Sandy Alonso
PHONE       (505)780-2277
```

— indicates marked for
   deletion

```
Edit    ||A:\CLIENT              ||Rec 8/11      ||File ||        ||Del
```

Figure 3-24
Eyes Have It record
marked for deletion

Now leave Edit mode with the Eyes Have It record marked for deletion.

❸ Select the *Exit* option from the Exit menu to return to the Control Center.

Dot Prompt

To mark records for deletion:

DELETE   *scope*   FOR *condition*

Marks a record in the active database file for deletion

Example   .USE client
                    .DELETE 5

Dot Prompt

To unmark records marked for deletion:

RECALL   *scope*   FOR *condition*

Reinstates records that are marked for deletion in the active database file

Example   .USE client
                    .RECALL 5

Packing the Database

When we first discussed removing records from a file, we said that removing a record is actually a two-step process: first you must mark the record to be deleted, then you must pack it. You have already learned that marking a record does not permanently delete the record. You can recall a record by using the keystroke combination [Ctrl]U to remove the "marked for deletion" code from a marked record. When you are ready to *permanently* remove a record, you use the *Erase all marked records* option in the Organize menu. This is called **packing** the database. *You cannot recover a marked record once the database file is packed.*

Before you use the *Erase all marked records* option, be certain that you have marked the correct records for deletion. Recall that when you use the Edit or Browse screen, you will know a record is marked for deletion if "Del" appears in the status bar when the record is the current record.

To verify that the correct record is marked for deletion:

❶ Press **[F2]** (Data). You are returned to the Edit screen. Notice that the "Del" indicator appears in the status bar for the record Eyes Have It.

Now pack the database. You must be in the Edit or Browse screen to pack the database.

To remove marked records permanently:

❶ Press **[Alt]O** to open the Organize menu. See Figure 3-25.

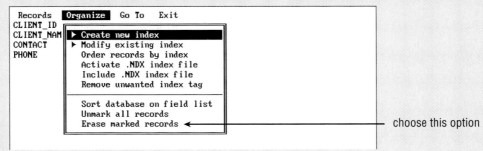

Figure 3-25
The Organize menu

choose this option

❷ Select *Erase marked records* (**E**).

You are asked if you are sure you want to erase all marked records. Answer yes to the prompt.

❸ Type **y**. You have now permanently removed the marked record from the database file. The message "10 records copied" appears briefly on your screen, which tells you that there are now 10 records in the CLIENT file. Before you executed the *Erase marked records* option, there were 11 records in the CLIENT file. Thus, one record has been removed from the CLIENT file.

To verify that the record is no longer in the CLIENT file, let's view the CLIENT file in the Browse screen.

To view the records in the CLIENT file:

❶ Press **[F2]** (Data) to move into the Browse screen. The data currently stored in the W&M CLIENT file appear. See Figure 3-26. Notice that the record for the company Eyes Have It does not appear in the Browse screen. That record has been permanently deleted.

```
Records   Organize   Fields   Go To   Exit

CLIENT_ID CLIENT_NAM              CONTACT           PHONE

MOU       Mountain Top Ski        Victor Juarez     (419)783-6210
VIK       Viking Auto Group       Jeff Serito       (505)984-9216
ALE       Alexander Insurance     Paul Alexander    (505)883-9222
SAN       Sante Fe Tourist Center Liddy Posada      (505)986-5555
ORI       Origins                 Gary Higgins      (505)988-0733
FAT       Fat Wheels Bicycle Tours Helen Carson     (505)994-2432
CEL       Celebrity Catering      Linda Randall     (505)883-9922
IMA       Images                  Wendy Falchetti   (505)898-1286
PEA       Peaches & Ice           Alice Beaumont    (505)728-5176
TAC       Taco Heaven             Bert Clinton      (505)728-1295
```

Figure 3-26
CLIENT file after
packing

❷ Press **[Esc]** to return to the Control Center.

Dot Prompt

To remove records permanently from a database file:

PACK

Removes records marked for deletion from the active database file

Example   .USE client
.PACK

Printing a Database File Using Quick Report

Two companies have been added and another deleted from the CLIENT file. Esther decides to give Nancy a printout of the revised client file. An easy way to print the contents of a database file is to use dBASE's Quick Report feature. Quick Report prints all the fields in the open database file.

To create a Quick Report:

❶ Make sure your printer is turned on.

❷ With CLIENT highlighted in the Data panel, press **[Shift][F9]** (Quick Report). The Print menu appears.

❸ From the Print menu select *Begin printing* (**B**). See Figure 3-27. Note that page numbers appear at the upper-left corner of the page, and the date appears immediately underneath the page number. The field names appear as column headings, and the data appear as single-spaced rows following the headings.

```
Page No.   1
07/16/92

CLIENT_ID  CLIENT_NAM             CONTACT          PHONE

MOU        Mountain Top Ski       Victor Juarez    (419)783-6210
VIK        Viking Auto Group      Jeff Serito      (505)984-9216
ALE        Alexander Insurance    Paul Alexander   (505)883-9222
SAN        Sante Fe Tourist Center Liddy Posada    (505)986-5555
ORI        Origins                Gary Higgins     (505)988-0733
FAT        Fat Wheels Bicycle Tours Helen Carson   (505)994-2432
CEL        Celebrity Catering     Linda Randall    (505)883-9922
IMA        Images                 Wendy Falchetti  (505)898-1286
PEA        Peaches & Ice          Alice Beaumont   (505)728-5176
TAC        Taco Heaven            Bert Clinton     (505)728-1295
```

Figure 3-27
Quick Report of
database contents

After the report has been printed, you are returned to the Control Center.

Backing Up a Database File

Esther has completed the updating tasks she planned for today, but before she quits dBASE, she knows she must make copies of the updated database files. The process of making a duplicate copy of each database file is called **backing up** the database file. Esther does this to protect her data in case the original database file is lost, stolen, damaged, or destroyed. The backup file can then be used in place of the original file.

In dBASE you use the *DOS utilities* option of the Tools menu to back up your database files.

To make a backup of the CLIENT database file:

❶ From the Control Center, press **[Alt]T** to open the Tools menu.

❷ Select *DOS utilities* (**D**) to open the DOS Utilities screen.

Now mark the files you want to back up by highlighting them and pressing [Enter].

❸ Highlight the file CLIENT.DBF and press **[Enter]** to mark the file. See Figure 3-28. Notice that an arrow appears in front of the filename to indicate the file is marked.

indicates file marked ⟶

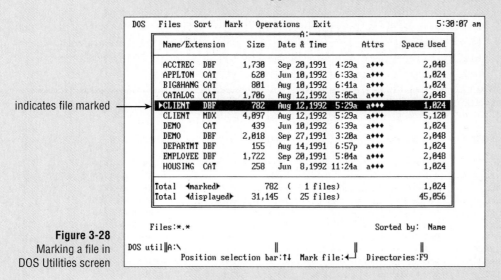

Figure 3-28
Marking a file in
DOS Utilities screen

❹ Press **[Alt]O** to open the Operations menu. See Figure 3-29.

Figure 3-29
The Operations
menu

❺ Select *Copy* (**C**). The Copy menu appears. See Figure 3-30. You can copy a single file, marked files, or displayed files. You want to copy a marked file.

Figure 3-30
Options available
for copying files

❻ Select *Marked files* (**M**). See Figure 3-31. The screen shows the message "All <marked> files in current directory." You are prompted to enter the destination information. The current drive and directory are the default choices. You want to save the backup file to your data diskette.

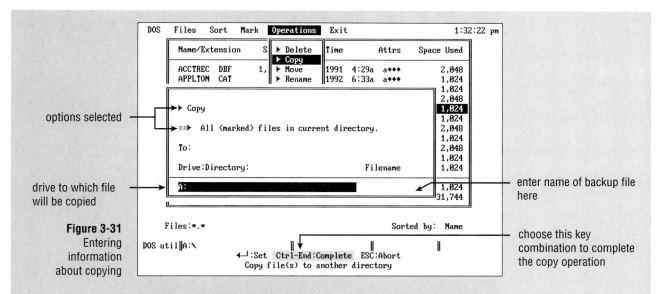

options selected

drive to which file will be copied

enter name of backup file here

choose this key combination to complete the copy operation

Figure 3-31
Entering
information
about copying

⑦ Press **[Enter]** to accept the current drive and directory and move the cursor to the filename.

You want to name the backup file CLIENTBK.DBF.

⑧ Type **clientbk.dbf** and press **[Enter]**.

If you store a backup file to the same diskette as the original file, the name of the backup file must be different from the original filename. Normally you will store the backup file on a separate diskette. Esther adds the letters BK, an abbreviation for backup, to the original filename to help her easily identify her backup files.

⑨ Press **[Ctrl][End]** to complete the copy operation. You are returned to the DOS Utilities screen. See Figure 3-32.

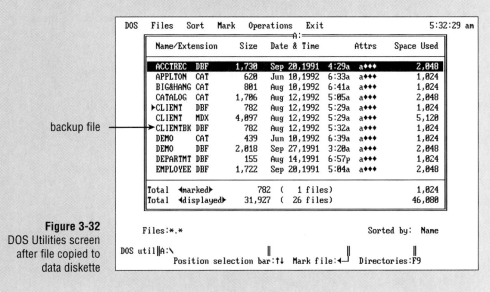

backup file

Figure 3-32
DOS Utilities screen
after file copied to
data diskette

Look at the files listed on the DOS Utilities screen (Figure 3-32). CLIENTBK.DBF is listed under the CLIENT.DBF file.

Now return to the Control Center.

⑩   Press **[Alt]E** to open the Exit menu and press **[Enter]**. You are returned to the Control Center.

As an alternative you can make a backup of your database file using the DOS COPY command after you quit dBASE. For example, to create a backup file named CLIENTBK.DBF on another diskette in the B drive, you would type COPY A:CLIENT.DBF B:CLIENTBK.DBF at the DOS prompt.

Dot Prompt

To back up a database file:

COPY TO *filename*

Makes a duplicate file of the active database file

Example   .USE client
.COPY TO clientbk

Quitting dBASE

Now that you have backed up the CLIENT file, you have finished this dBASE tutorial. You are ready to use the Exit menu to leave dBASE. When you leave dBASE using the *Quit to DOS* option, dBASE automatically closes all open files. If an open database file has not been properly closed, you may not be able to access all the data in that database file when you attempt to open the file again.

To quit dBASE:

❶   Press **[Alt]E** to open the Exit menu.

❷   Select *Quit to DOS* (**Q**). You are returned to the DOS prompt.

You have now completed Tutorial 3.

■   ■   ■

CONTROL CENTER SUMMARY

To open a database file:
>Highlight filename in the Data panel and press [Enter].
>Select *Use file* (U) from the prompt box.

To add records using the Browse screen:
>Highlight filename in the Data panel.
>Press [F2] until you access the Browse screen.
>Press [Alt]R to open the Records menu.
>Select *Add new records* (A).
>Enter data.
>Press [Alt]E to open the Exit menu.
>Select *Exit* (E).

To add records using the Edit screen:
>Highlight filename in the Data panel.
>Press [F2] until you access the Edit screen.
>Press [Alt]R to open the Records menu.
>Select *Add new records* (A).
>Enter data.
>Press [Alt]E to open the Exit menu.
>Select *Exit* (E).

To display data:
>Highlight filename in the Data panel.
>Press [F2] to access the Browse or Edit screen.

To print data:
>Highlight filename in the Data panel.
>Press [Shift][F9] (Quick Report).
>Select *Begin printing* (B).

To mark a record for deletion:
>Highlight filename in the Data panel.
>Press [F2] to display data in the Browse or Edit screen.
>Move cursor to the record you want to mark for deletion.
>Press [Ctrl]U.

CONTROL CENTER SUMMARY

To pack records:

Highlight filename in the Data panel.

Press [F2] to display data in the Browse or Edit screen.

In the Browse or Edit screen press [Alt]O to open the Organize menu.

Select *Erase marked records* (E).

Answer Y to prompt for confirmation.

To copy files:

Press [Alt]T to open the Tools menu.

Select *DOS utilities* (D).

Mark files.

Press [Alt]O to open the Operations menu.

Select *Copy* (C).

Select desired option.

Follow screen prompts for destination and filename.

Press [Ctrl][End].

Exercises

1. What information in the Control Center tells you which database file is open?

2. What line on the Edit screen tells you how many records are stored in the open database file?

3. How can you determine if any records are marked for deletion?

4. What is the difference between the Edit screen and the Browse screen?

5. After you mark a record for deletion, what option permanently removes a record from a database file?

6. What options from the Control Center would you select to make a backup database file?

Use the file layout in Figure 3-33 to answer Exercises 7 and 8. Assume employee 101 has skills in Lotus 1-2-3 (code = LOT123) and dBASE IV (code = DBASE4).

Field	Data Type	Width
EMPLOY_ID	Character	3
SKILL1_CD	Character	6
SKILL2_CD	Character	6
SKILL3_CD	Character	6

Figure 3-33

7. Sketch the blank data-entry form (in the Edit screen) that you would see if you selected *Yes* at "Add new records" from the Records menu.

8. Fill in the sketch from Exercise 7 using the data for employee 101.

Use the file layout in Figure 3-34 to answer Exercises 9 and 10. Assume employee 101 has skills in Lotus 1-2-3 (code = LOT123) and dBASE IV (code = DBASE4).

Field	Data Type	Width
EMPLOY_ID	Character	3
SKILL_CD	Character	6

Figure 3-34

9. Sketch the blank data entry form (in the Edit screen) that you would see if you selected *Yes* at "Add new records" from the Records menu.

10. How would you enter the data for employee 101? *Hint:* You need to add more than one record.

Tutorial Assignments

Instructor's note: The figures of the screens in Tutorial 4 reflect the updates to the CLIENT and JOBS files that students make in these assignments.

For the W&M CLIENT database file do the following file maintenance tasks:

1. Open the database file.

2. Print the file structure.

3. Add the record shown in Figure 3-35.

CLIENT_ID	MAM
CLIENT_NAM	Mama Lee's Pizza
CONTACT	Emma Lee
PHONE	(505)984-3245

Figure 3-35

4. Correct the phone number for Celebrity Catering from (505)883-9922 to (800)884-2321.

5. Print the CLIENT file.

For the JOBS database file do the following file maintenance tasks:

6. Open the JOBS database file.

7. Print the file structure.

8. Add the four records shown in Figure 3-36.

	Record 1	Record 2	Record 3	Record 4
JOBNUM	1021	1022	1023	1024
CLIENT_ID	ALE	MAM	TAC	PEA
JOB_DESCR	B/W magazine ad	Newspaper ad	TV ad	Brochure
DUE_DATE	11/10/93	12/01/93	12/15/93	11/30/93
QUOTE	6600	5300	14000	11000
STATUS	I	I	I	I

Figure 3-36

9. Print all the records in the JOBS file.

10. Make a backup copy of the JOBS file. Name the file JOBSBK.DBF.

Case Problems

To complete the Case Problems, you must change catalogs. Select *Use a different catalog* in the Catalog menu, then highlight the appropriate catalog name and press **[Enter]**.

1. Biggs & Hang Investment Corporation

Activate the BIG&HANG catalog and open the database file JAPAN.

1. Print the file structure.

2. Add the two records shown in Figure 3-37.

	Record 1	Record 2
COMP_ID	7272	7269
COMP_NAME	Yamaha Motor	Suzuki Motor
IND_CODE	A	A
DESCRPT	world's 2nd largest motorcycle manufacturer	world's 3rd largest motorcycle manufacturer
ASSETS	285833	551611
SALES	592559	982573
PROFITS	34933	27796
OUT_SHRS	230198	408612
HIGH_PRICE	1430	1040
LOW_PRICE	961	660

Figure 3-37

3. Change the PROFITS field from 210000 to 200585 for Honda Motor.

4. Print all the records in the file.

5. Make a backup copy of the database file JAPAN.DBF. Name the file JAPANBK.DBF.

2. Medi-Source Inc.

Activate the MEDISRCE catalog and open the database file ACCTREC.DBF.

1. Print the file structure.

2. Add the two records shown in Figure 3-38.

	Record 1	Record 2
CUST_ID	24	25
CUST_NAME	Rogers Hospital	Elmwood Pharmacy
TYPE	H	P
STATE	RI	MA
REP	4	4
CRD_LIMIT	15000	5000
BAL_OWED	0	0
YTD_SALES	0	0
DATE_LSTSL	no date	no date

Figure 3-38

3. Change the sales rep number for Bayshore Pharmacy from 3 to 1.

4. Print the ACCTREC file.

5. Make a backup copy of the database file ACCTREC.DBF. Name the file ACCTRBK.DBF.

3. Appleton & Drake Electrical Supply Company

Activate the APPLTON catalog and open the database file EMPLOYEE.DBF.

1. Print the file structure.

2. Add the two records shown in Figure 3-39.

3. Change Janet Krause's salary from 25800 to 27200.

	Record 1	**Record 2**
EMP_NUM	129	130
LNAME	Appleton	Lucas
FNAME	Kathy	Mark
SEX	F	M
MAR	Y	N
DEP	0	0
HIRE_DATE	6/2/92	8/15/92
ANNSAL	29000	27500
DEPT	ENG	SAL

Figure 3-39

4. Print the file.

5. Make a backup copy of the database file EMPLOYEE. Name the file EMPLOYBK.DBF.

4. National Basketball Association

Activate the NBA catalog and open the database file NBA.DBF.

1. Print the file structure.

2. Add the two records shown in Figure 3-40.

	Record 1	**Record 2**
TEAM	PHI	PHI
FNAME	CHARLES	JOHNNY
LNAME	BARKLEY	DAWKINS
POS	F	G
SALARY	2900000	1500000

Figure 3-40

3. KIKI VANDEWEGHE is the correct spelling of the player's name, not KIKI VANEWEGHE. Correct the name.

4. Print the file.

5. Make a backup copy of the database file NBA.DBF. Name the file NBABK.DBF.

5. Off-Campus Housing at Ashland University

Activate the HOUSING catalog and open the database file HOUSING.DBF.

1. Print the file structure.

2. Add the data in Figures 3-41 through 3-52 to the database.

AVAILABLE OFF-CAMPUS HOUSING FORM

1.   Rental Address:

39 Rippling Road
Street Address

Narragansett   RI   02894
City   State   Zip

2.   Indicate name and phone numbers of owner of rental property

Panza   Ronald
Last Name   First Name

(401) 555-9912
Home Phone #   Work Phone #

3.   Type of rental unit available (check one)
     (X) House   ( ) Apartment

4.   # of bedrooms: _3_

5.   How many miles is unit from campus? _8_

6.   Length of lease required (in months)? _9_

7.   Rent per month? _510_

8.   Date Available? _9/01/92_

9.   Please check all amenities that your rental unit features:
( ) Utilities included   ( ) Washer/dryer
(X) Furnished bedroom(s)   ( ) Dishwasher
( ) On bus line   (X) Pets allowed
( ) Wheelchair accessible   (x) Children allowed

Figure 3-41

AVAILABLE OFF-CAMPUS HOUSING FORM

1.   Rental Address:

28 Main Street
Street Address

Wakefield   RI   02893
City   State   Zip

2.   Indicate name and phone numbers of owner of rental property

Scalia   Vinnie
Last Name   First Name

(401) 555-8923   (401) 555-4444
Home Phone #   Work Phone #

3.   Type of rental unit available (check one)
     (X) House   ( ) Apartment

4.   # of bedrooms: _4_

5.   How many miles is unit from campus? _7_

6.   Length of lease required (in months)? _6_

7.   Rent per month? _500_

8.   Date Available? _9/03/92_

9.   Please check all amenities that your rental unit features:
( ) Utilities included   (X) Washer/dryer
(X) Furnished bedroom(s)   ( ) Dishwasher
(X) On bus line   ( ) Pets allowed
( ) Wheelchair accessible   (X) Children allowed

Figure 3-42

AVAILABLE OFF-CAMPUS HOUSING FORM

1.   Rental Address:

1 High Street
Street Address

Narragansett   RI   02893
City   State   Zip

2.   Indicate name and phone numbers of owner of rental property

Margolis   Jeanne
Last Name   First Name

(401) 555-2109
Home Phone #   Work Phone #

3.   Type of rental unit available (check one)
     ( ) House   (X) Apartment

4.   # of bedrooms: _1_

5.   How many miles is unit from campus? _7_

6.   Length of lease required (in months)? _3_

7.   Rent per month? _350_

8.   Date Available? _9/03/92_

9.   Please check all amenities that your rental unit features:
(X) Utilities included   ( ) Washer/dryer
(X) Furnished bedroom(s)   ( ) Dishwasher
( ) On bus line   ( ) Pets allowed
( ) Wheelchair accessible   ( ) Children allowed

Figure 3-43

AVAILABLE OFF-CAMPUS HOUSING FORM

1.   Rental Address:

61 Cheery Drive
Street Address

Narragansett   RI   02882
City   State   Zip

2.   Indicate name and phone numbers of owner of rental property

Ross   Maude
Last Name   First Name

(401) 555-9822   (401) 555-2291
Home Phone #   Work Phone #

3.   Type of rental unit available (check one)
     (X) House   ( ) Apartment

4.   # of bedrooms: _4_

5.   How many miles is unit from campus? _8_

6.   Length of lease required (in months)? _9_

7.   Rent per month? _600_

8.   Date Available? _9/05/92_

9.   Please check all amenities that your rental unit features:
( ) Utilities included   ( ) Washer/dryer
( ) Furnished bedroom(s)   (X) Dishwasher
(X) On bus line   ( ) Pets allowed
(X) Wheelchair accessible   (X) Children allowed

Figure 3-44

AVAILABLE OFF-CAMPUS HOUSING FORM

1. Rental Address:

915 Maple Street
Street Address

Wakefield   RI   _02894_
City   State   Zip

2. Indicate name and phone numbers of owner of rental property

Glass   _Fred_
Last Name   First Name

_(401) 555-9345_
Home Phone #   Work Phone #

3. Type of rental unit available (check one)
   ( ) House   (X) Apartment

4. # of bedrooms: _1_

5. How many miles is unit from campus? _7_

6. Length of lease required (in months)? _3_

7. Rent per month? _400_

8. Date Available? _9/03/92_

9. Please check all amenities that your rental unit features:
(X) Utilities included   (X) Washer/dryer
(X) Furnished bedroom(s)   (X) Dishwasher
(X) On bus line   ( ) Pets allowed
(X) Wheelchair accessible   ( ) Children allowed

Figure 3-45

AVAILABLE OFF-CAMPUS HOUSING FORM

1. Rental Address:

Crossways Apartments
Street Address

Wakefield   RI   _02879_
City   State   Zip

2. Indicate name and phone numbers of owner of rental property

Howard   _Frank_
Last Name   First Name

_(401) 555-9821_   _(401) 555-0982_
Home Phone #   Work Phone #

3. Type of rental unit available (check one)
   ( ) House   (X) Apartment

4. # of bedrooms: _1_

5. How many miles is unit from campus? _1_

6. Length of lease required (in months)? _9_

7. Rent per month? _350_

8. Date Available? _10/01/92_

9. Please check all amenities that your rental unit features:
(X) Utilities included   ( ) Washer/dryer
(X) Furnished bedroom(s)   ( ) Dishwasher
( ) On bus line   ( ) Pets allowed
( ) Wheelchair accessible   ( ) Children allowed

Figure 3-46

AVAILABLE OFF-CAMPUS HOUSING FORM

1. Rental Address:

50 Yankee Drive
Street Address

Narragansett   RI   _02882_
City   State   Zip

2. Indicate name and phone numbers of owner of rental property

Mason   _Jake_
Last Name   First Name

_(401) 555-1983_
Home Phone #   Work Phone #

3. Type of rental unit available (check one)
   (X) House   ( ) Apartment

4. # of bedrooms: _1_

5. How many miles is unit from campus? _7_

6. Length of lease required (in months)? _9_

7. Rent per month? _475_

8. Date Available? _9/01/92_

9. Please check all amenities that your rental unit features:
(X) Utilities included   ( ) Washer/dryer
( ) Furnished bedroom(s)   ( ) Dishwasher
( ) On bus line   ( ) Pets allowed
( ) Wheelchair accessible   ( ) Children allowed

Figure 3-47

AVAILABLE OFF-CAMPUS HOUSING FORM

1. Rental Address:

92 Worden Pond Road
Street Address

Kingston   RI   _02881_
City   State   Zip

2. Indicate name and phone numbers of owner of rental property

Kinyo   _Janine_
Last Name   First Name

_(401) 555-1195_   _(401) 555-5367_
Home Phone #   Work Phone #

3. Type of rental unit available (check one)
   ( ) House   (X) Apartment

4. # of bedrooms: _2_

5. How many miles is unit from campus? _2_

6. Length of lease required (in months)? _9_

7. Rent per month? _425_

8. Date Available? _9/01/92_

9. Please check all amenities that your rental unit features:
(X) Utilities included   (X) Washer/dryer
(X) Furnished bedroom(s)   ( ) Dishwasher
(X) On bus line   (X) Pets allowed
( ) Wheelchair accessible   ( ) Children allowed

Figure 3-48

AVAILABLE OFF-CAMPUS HOUSING FORM

1. Rental Address:

100 Point Judith Road
Street Address

Narragansett   RI   02882
City   State   Zip

2. Indicate name and phone numbers of owner of rental property

Franconi   Joe
Last Name   First Name

(401) 555-9921   (401) 555-1239
Home Phone #   Work Phone #

3. Type of rental unit available (check one)
   ( ) House   (X) Apartment

4. # of bedrooms: 2

5. How many miles is unit from campus? 8

6. Length of lease required (in months)? 9

7. Rent per month? 400

8. Date Available? 01/01/93

9. Please check all amenities that your rental unit features:
   ( ) Utilities included   ( ) Washer/dryer
   (X) Furnished bedroom(s)   ( ) Dishwasher
   (X) On bus line   ( ) Pets allowed
   ( ) Wheelchair accessible   ( ) Children allowed

Figure 3-49

AVAILABLE OFF-CAMPUS HOUSING FORM

1. Rental Address:

968 Ocean Drive
Street Address

Narragansett   RI   02882
City   State   Zip

2. Indicate name and phone numbers of owner of rental property

Marks   Heather
Last Name   First Name

(401) 555-9973
Home Phone #   Work Phone #

3. Type of rental unit available (check one)
   (X) House   ( ) Apartment

4. # of bedrooms: 3

5. How many miles is unit from campus? 10

6. Length of lease required (in months)? 9

7. Rent per month? 650

8. Date Available? 9/10/92

9. Please check all amenities that your rental unit features:
   ( ) Utilities included   (X) Washer/dryer
   ( ) Furnished bedroom(s)   ( ) Dishwasher
   (X) On bus line   ( ) Pets allowed
   ( ) Wheelchair accessible   (X) Children allowed

Figure 3-50

AVAILABLE OFF-CAMPUS HOUSING FORM

1. Rental Address:

1 Goat Island Circle
Street Address

Narragansett   RI   02882
City   State   Zip

2. Indicate name and phone numbers of owner of rental property

Razor   Charles
Last Name   First Name

(203) 555-9357   (203) 555-9111
Home Phone #   Work Phone #

3. Type of rental unit available (check one)
   (X) House   ( ) Apartment

4. # of bedrooms: 4

5. How many miles is unit from campus? 8

6. Length of lease required (in months)? 9

7. Rent per month? 700

8. Date Available? 09/01/92

9. Please check all amenities that your rental unit features:
   ( ) Utilities included   (X) Washer/dryer
   ( ) Furnished bedroom(s)   ( ) Dishwasher
   ( ) On bus line   ( ) Pets allowed
   ( ) Wheelchair accessible   (X) Children allowed

Figure 3-51

AVAILABLE OFF-CAMPUS HOUSING FORM

1. Rental Address:

12 Wooded Lane
Street Address

Kingston   RI   02881
City   State   Zip

2. Indicate name and phone numbers of owner of rental property

Johnston   Evan
Last Name   First Name

(401) 555-1357   (401) 555-4131
Home Phone #   Work Phone #

3. Type of rental unit available (check one)
   ( ) House   (X) Apartment

4. # of bedrooms: 1

5. How many miles is unit from campus? 1

6. Length of lease required (in months)? 12

7. Rent per month? 425

8. Date Available? 01/01/93

9. Please check all amenities that your rental unit features:
   (X) Utilities included   ( ) Washer/dryer
   (X) Furnished bedroom(s)   ( ) Dishwasher
   ( ) On bus line   ( ) Pets allowed
   (X) Wheelchair accessible   ( ) Children allowed

Figure 3-52

3. The rent per month for the property owned by Ronald Panza was entered incorrectly. Change it from $510 to $550.

4. Correct the work telephone number for Janine Kinyo, owner of the rental property at 92 Worden Pond Road, Kingston. The correct number is (401) 886-5637.

5. Fred Glass's rental property has been rented. Mark the record for deletion.

6. Fred Glass has just called to tell you his prospective tenant has backed out, so the property is still available. He asks you to continue listing the property.

Tutorial 4

Querying the Database

Case: Wells & Martinez — Retrieving Information from the W&M Database

One morning Esther finds two notes on her desk. One is a note from Nancy saying, "Need a printout of all W&M clients." Nancy explains in her note that she wants to give this list to potential clients who want to contact current clients for references on W&M's work. The second note is from Martin. He wants a list of all jobs currently in process that are due during this period. As Esther begins to work on Nancy's request, Martin pops in and asks for a list of all unfinished jobs and a list of unfinished jobs due after August 1, 1993. He needs the information so that Nancy and he can decide if they should hire more staff members. Then during coffee break Nancy finds Esther and makes another request — this time for completed jobs having a quote over $5,000.

As Esther walks back to her office, she bumps into Martin. Martin asks Esther for two more lists. He needs a list of all the jobs both completed and in process for Origins and for Alexander's Insurance. He also tells Esther that he's going on vacation from November 17 to December 6, 1993, and he wants a list of all jobs currently in progress that are due during that period.

Esther decides to use dBASE's querying capability to answer these requests for information.

OBJECTIVES

In this tutorial you will learn to:

- Use the different components of the Query Design screen

- Remove fields from output

- Rearrange fields in outputs

- Print the results of a query

- Build filter conditions using relational operators

- Save a query

- Build compound conditions

- Use condition boxes

- Use calculated fields

- Use aggregate operators to summarize data

- Use the Group By operator to group records

Introduction to Queries

Information systems are developed to provide information to help solve business problems. As computer professionals create these systems, they try to anticipate all the questions that managers may want answered from the data in a database and try to develop reports that can be produced on a regular basis. In spite of their efforts, however, computer professionals cannot anticipate all the questions that managers will ask.

When existing reports cannot answer their questions, dBASE users rely on the query facility of a DBMS. The query facility allows users to enter English-like commands to access the database and retrieve the records that will answer their questions. In this tutorial you will use dBASE's Query Design screen to develop the queries Esther needs to answer Nancy's and Martin's requests for information.

Understanding the Query Design Screen

The Query Design screen is a visual approach to querying known as **query by example** (QBE). In the Query Design screen, a picture of the database file in the form of a table with field names is presented to the user. The user forms a query by entering the criteria for selecting the records in the table. Like other screens, the Query Design screen includes a menu bar at the top of the screen and a status bar and a navigation line at the bottom. Figure 4-1 shows the elements that initially appear on the Query Design screen: the file skeleton and the view skeleton. Let's take a look at these two elements.

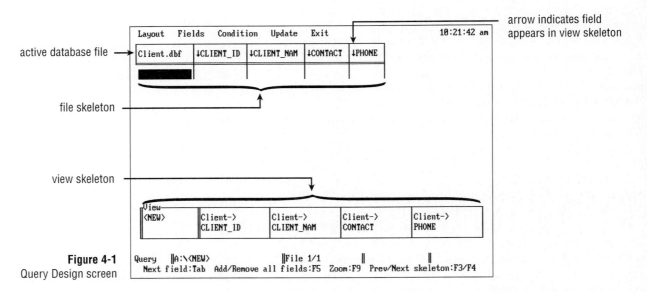

Figure 4-1
Query Design screen

The **file skeleton** appears near the top of the screen. It is a graphic representation of a database file. The name of the file appears in the first block. All the fields in the active database file appear in the rest of the blocks. The file skeleton is used to specify the conditions the data must satisfy in order for a record to be displayed.

The **view skeleton** is found near the bottom of the screen. The view skeleton contains only the fields that will be displayed when you see the results of the query that you created using the file skeleton. All the fields in the CLIENT database are now listed in the view skeleton because you have not yet created a query.

Using the Query Design Screen to View a Database File

Nancy has asked Esther for a list of all W&M's clients. Esther plans to use the Query Design screen to answer Nancy's request. But remember, a database file must be open before you can update, list, or perform calculations on any data in the file. So load dBASE, change the default drive, and activate the W&M catalog.

Now that dBASE is loaded, and the W&M.CAT catalog activated, open the CLIENT file, and then access the Query Design screen so you can prepare the list of clients for Nancy.

To open the CLIENT file and access the Query Design screen:

❶ Open the database file CLIENT.

A file must be open before you can create a query for it.

You use the Queries panel to create queries.

❷ Highlight <create> in the Queries panel. See Figure 4-2.

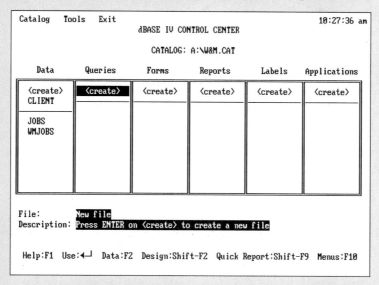

Figure 4-2
Accessing the
Query Design
screen

❸ Press **[Enter]**. The Query Design screen appears, as shown in Figure 4-1.

Notice that [↓] appears before each field name of the file skeleton. This indicates the field is included in the view skeleton. Initially all the fields are included in the view skeleton, so all fields in the file skeleton have [↓] in front of the field name.

Dot Prompt

To access the Query Design screen:

CREATE QUERY *query name*

Gives you access to the Query Design screen, which allows you to create query (QBE) files.

Example   .CREATE QUERY jobs

Let's try moving around the Query Design screen.

To move around the Query Design screen:

❶ Press **[Tab]** three times to move the highlight beneath the CONTACT field name.

To move the highlight to the left, use [Shift][Tab].

❷ Press **[Shift][Tab]** to move the highlight beneath the CLIENT_NAM field name.

Now move to the view skeleton. [F4] moves the highlight to the next skeleton on the screen.

❸ Press **[F4]** (Next). The highlight is now in the view skeleton. See Figure 4-3.

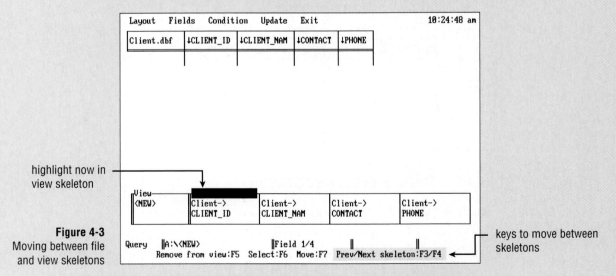

highlight now in view skeleton

Figure 4-3
Moving between file and view skeletons

keys to move between skeletons

[F3] moves the highlight back to the previous skeleton.

❹ To move the highlight back to the file skeleton, press **[F3]** (Previous). The highlight is again in the file skeleton.

Figure 4-4 lists the keys you can use to move around the Query Design screen.

Keystroke	Action
[Tab]	Moves highlight to next field (that is, one field to the right)
[Shift][Tab]	Moves highlight to previous field
[F3] or [F4]	Moves highlight between the file skeleton and the view skeleton
[↑] or [↓]	Moves highlight row by row up or down within a file skeleton
[→] or [←]	Moves cursor within highlighted field
[Home]	Moves to the first field in the file skeleton or the view skeleton
[End]	Moves to the last field in the file skeleton or the view skeleton

Figure 4-4
Keys used to navigate in the Query Design screen

To display all the records in the open database file, you don't enter any conditions in the Query Design screen; that is, the default query is to display the entire database. Just press [F2] to process the query. The results are displayed in the Browse screen.

To process the query:

❶ Press **[F2]** (Data). A list of all clients appears in the Browse screen. See Figure 4-5.*

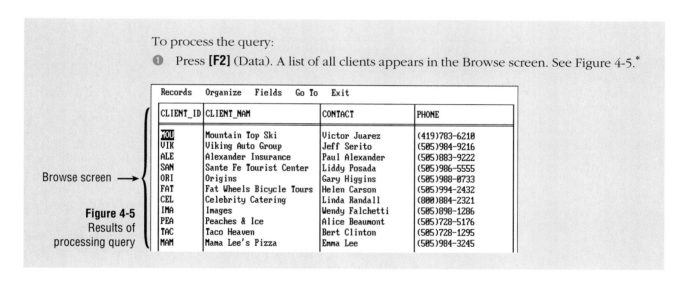

Browse screen ⟶

Figure 4-5
Results of processing query

Removing Fields from the View Skeleton

As Esther looks over the client list, she remembers that Nancy wants to use it as a reference list for prospective clients. She realizes that Nancy needs only the client name, the contact person, and the telephone number for each client. A prospective client doesn't need to know a reference's client ID. Esther can easily make this change. All she needs to do is to remove the CLIENT_ID field from the view skeleton. To remove a field name from the view skeleton, you can have the highlight on the field in either the file skeleton or the view skeleton. Let's remove the CLIENT_ID field now.

---

* The screen shots for the database file CLIENT include records that were added in the Tutorial Assignments in Tutorial 3.

To remove CLIENT_ID from the view skeleton:

❶ Press **[Shift][F2]** (Design) to return to the Query Design screen. The highlight is in the file skeleton.

❷ Move the highlight to the CLIENT_ID in the file skeleton and press **[F5]** (Field). The field CLIENT_ID disappears from the view skeleton, and [↓] no longer appears before CLIENT_ID in the file skeleton. See Figure 4-6.

down arrow does not appear

view skeleton does not include CLIENT_ID

Figure 4-6
Query Design screen after field removed from view skeletion

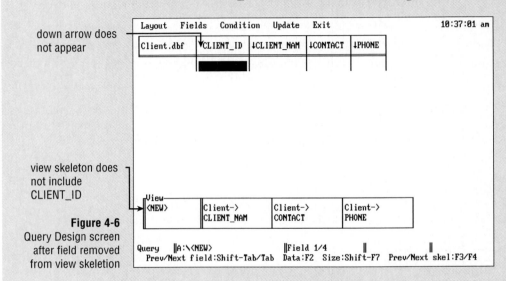

You can also remove a field from the view skeleton while the highlight is in the view skeleton. You would move the highlight to the file skeleton by pressing [F4] (Next), move the highlight to the field you want to delete, then delete that field by pressing [F5] (Field).

You can remove all the fields in the view skeleton at once by moving the highlight beneath the database filename in the file skeleton and then pressing [F5].

If you want to add a field back to the view skeleton once it has been removed, you would move the highlight to the field you want to add in the file skeleton then press [F5]. The field will appear as the last field in the view skeleton.

You are now ready to display the results of the query.

To process the query:

❶ Press **[F2]** (Data). The client data appear in the Browse screen. See Figure 4-7. Notice that the client ID is not displayed.

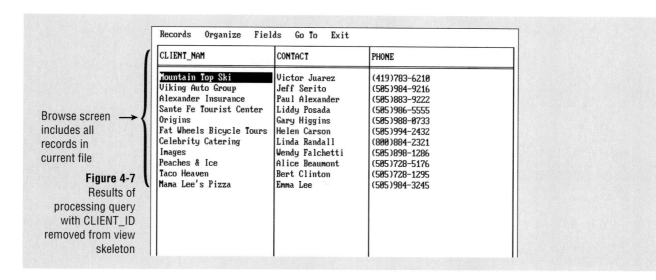

Browse screen includes all records in current file

Figure 4-7
Results of processing query with CLIENT_ID removed from view skeleton

Dot Prompt

To specify accessible fields:

SET FIELDS TO *field list*

Defines a list of fields that can be accessed in a file

Example   .USE jobs
.SET FIELDS TO client_id, jobnum, quote

Moving Fields in the View Skeleton

Esther looks at the results and decides she wants to display the phone number before the contact name. The order in which the fields appear in the view skeleton determines the order in which the fields appear when you see the results in the Browse screen. You can rearrange the order in which the fields appear in your output by changing their order in the view skeleton. Let's reverse the order of contact name and phone number.

To change the order of fields in the view skeleton:

❶   Press **[Shift][F2]**. You are returned to the Query Design screen.

Now switch the order of the contact name and the phone number.

❷ If you're not in the view skeleton, press **[F4]** (Next) to move to the view skeleton.

Highlight the field you want to move.

❸ Press **[Tab]** to move the highlight to the CONTACT field.

To identify a field you want moved, you select it.

❹ With the CONTACT field highlighted, press **[F6]** (Select). The entire box is highlighted. See Figure 4-8.

indicates field is selected

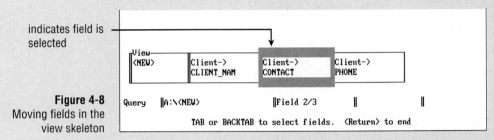

Figure 4-8
Moving fields in the view skeleton

If you change your mind and want to deselect the field, press [Esc].

Now complete the move by indicating where the selected field will be positioned.

❺ Press **[F7]** (Move), then press **[Tab]** once to move the field to the last position in the view skeleton.

❻ Press **[Enter]** to complete the move. The highlight on the box disappears and the standard highlight returns. See Figure 4-9.

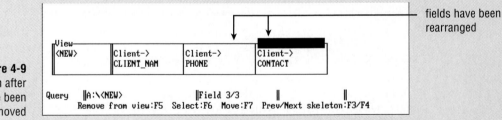

fields have been rearranged

Figure 4-9
View skeleton after fields have been moved

Now view the data.

To process the query:

❶ Press **[F2]** (Data). The phone number appears before the contact name. See Figure 4-10.

Records Organize Fields Go To Exit

CLIENT_NAM	PHONE	CONTACT
Mountain Top Ski	(419)783-6210	Victor Juarez
Viking Auto Group	(505)984-9216	Jeff Serito
Alexander Insurance	(505)883-9222	Paul Alexander
Sante Fe Tourist Center	(505)986-5555	Liddy Posada
Origins	(505)988-0733	Gary Higgins
Fat Wheels Bicycle Tours	(505)994-2432	Helen Carson
Celebrity Catering	(800)884-2321	Linda Randall
Images	(505)898-1286	Wendy Falchetti
Peaches & Ice	(505)728-5176	Alice Beaumont
Taco Heaven	(505)728-1295	Bert Clinton
Mama Lee's Pizza	(505)984-3245	Emma Lee

Figure 4-10 Browse screen shows fields rearranged

Printing a View Using a Quick Report

Nancy wants a printout of the client data. In Tutorial 3 you used a quick report to print the contents of a database file. You can also use a quick report to print the results of a query. A quick report prints all the fields in the view skeleton.

To create a quick report:

1. Make sure your printer is turned on.
2. The data you want to print appear in the Browse screen. Press **[Shift][F9]** (Quick Report). The Print menu appears.
3. From the Print menu select the option *Begin printing* (**B**). See Figure 4-11. Note that a page number appears at the upper left corner of the page, and the date appears immediately underneath the page number. The field names appear as column headings and the data appear as single-spaced rows below the heading.

Page No. 1
06/12/92

CLIENT_NAM	PHONE	CONTACT
Mountain Top Ski	(419)783-6210	Victor Juarez
Viking Auto Group	(505)984-9216	Jeff Serito
Alexander Insurance	(505)883-9222	Paul Alexander
Sante Fe Tourist Center	(505)986-5555	Liddy Posada
Origins	(505)988-0733	Gary Higgins
Fat Wheels Bicycle Tours	(505)994-2432	Helen Carson
Celebrity Catering	(505)883-9222	Linda Randall
Images	(505)898-1286	Wendy Falchetti
Peaches & Ice	(505)728-5176	Alice Beaumont
Taco Heaven	(505)728-1295	Bert Clinton
Mama Lee's Pizza	(505)984-3245	Emma Lee

Figure 4-11 Output from Browse screen using a quick report

After the report has been printed, you are returned to the Browse screen.

❹   Press **[Esc]** and select No (**N**) to the question about saving the query design. You are returned to the Control Center.

In this tutorial, Esther needs to print several reports for Martin and Nancy. Check with your instructor before printing the reports. If you do not want to print, simply skip the step that tells you to print a quick report.

Using Filter Conditions in a Query

Now that Esther has finished her first task for Nancy, she turns her attention to some of Martin's requests. She knows Martin wants to see a listing of jobs in process, not a listing of jobs that have been completed. How, Esther thinks, can I get this information from the database? To solve that problem, Esther must develop a query that contains a condition; that is, she must ask dBASE to search the entire database and display only those records that meet her criteria. Let's explore the concept of conditions.

A **condition** is the criterion that determines whether a record will be selected. For example, Esther wants records selected if they meet the condition that a job is still in process.

You express a condition in the Query Design screen by forming a **filter condition**, which has the following format:

relational operator   expression

A **relational operator** is a mathematical comparison of two expressions, such as less than, greater than, equal to, and so forth. Figure 4-12 lists the relational operators allowed in dBASE.

Operator	Description	Example
>	Greater than	> 5000
<	Less than	< 5000
=	Equal to	= 'ORI'
< > or #	Not equal to	< > 'ACC'
> = or = >	Greater than or equal to	>= 5000
< = or = <	Less than or equal to	<= 5000
$	Contains	$123
Like	Pattern match	LIKE '(505)*'

Figure 4-12
Relational operators
in dBASE

The expression in a filter condition is usually a numeric, character, or date constant. To form a filter condition, you combine the relational operator with the expression. In our example, jobs that are in process are assigned a code of I in the STATUS field, so the filter condition = *I* would select jobs in process.

Now that you know how to form a filter condition, how would you use it in dBASE? To select certain records based on a condition, as in Martin's example, you would include a filter condition in the file skeleton of the Query Design screen. The filter condition is entered in the space beneath the field names of the file skeleton.

Using Character Values in a Filter Condition

Now let's construct Martin's query. Let's create a filter condition to display the jobs in process. Your copy of the file CLIENT should still be open, so first you have to open the file JOBS and then access the Query Design screen.

To open the JOBS file and access the Query Design screen:

❶   Open the database file JOBS.

❷   Highlight <create> in the Queries panel and press **[Enter]**. The Query Design screen appears. See Figure 4-13.

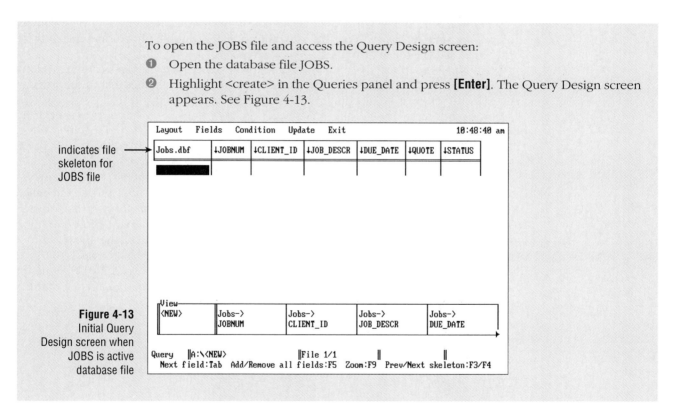

indicates file skeleton for JOBS file

Figure 4-13
Initial Query Design screen when JOBS is active database file

Now enter the filter condition. To enter a filter condition, you move the highlight to the field about which you are forming the condition, then you type the condition.

To enter a filter condition:

❶ Press **[End]** to move the highlight beneath the STATUS field name in the file skeleton.

You could also press [TAB] six times to move the highlight to the STATUS field name.

Now enter the condition.

❷ Type **='I'** and press **[Enter]**. See Figure 4-14.

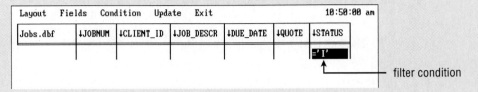

Figure 4-14
Enter filter condition
to select jobs "in
process"

Layout   Fields   Condition   Update   Exit   10:50:00 am

Jobs.dbf	↓JOBNUM	↓CLIENT_ID	↓JOB_DESCR	↓DUE_DATE	↓QUOTE	↓STATUS
						='I'

— filter condition

When the field being queried stores character data, you must enclose the character constant in quotation marks. You can use either single or double quotation marks, but be consistent. You will get an error message if you type ='I".

Recall that a relational operator is a comparison between *two* expressions. You don't need to include the first expression in a filter condition. dBASE assumes that the expression in the filter condition is being compared to the field being queried.

You do not have to enter the = symbol in front of the search value. However, if no operator appears in the condition, dBASE assumes you mean "equal to" the specified value. Thus the filter condition could have been entered as 'I' instead of ='I' and the same records would be retrieved.

Now that you have entered the filter condition for Esther's query, you can process the query. When you process a query, dBASE tests each record in the database file based on the filter condition to determine whether to select that record. In other words, for each record dBASE asks whether the filter condition is true or false. When the filter condition is true, the record is displayed; when the filter condition is false, the record is not displayed. For example, if the code in the STATUS field in the first record is I, then the filter condition ='I' is true (I is equal to I), and the record is displayed. If the status for the second record is C, then the filter condition = 'I' is false (C is not equal to I), and the record is not displayed. Figure 4-15 illustrates the logic of a query.

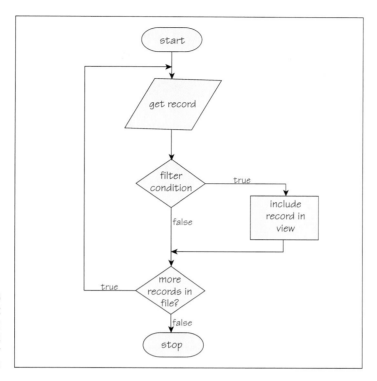

Let's process the query.

To process the query:

❶ Press **[F2]** (Data). dBASE searches all the database records and retrieves only the records with a status code equal to I. These are the only records displayed. See Figure 4-16.

JOBNUM	CLIENT_ID	JOB_DESCR	DUE_DATE	QUOTE	STATUS
1008	VIK	Thanksgiving Promo	11/15/93	12000	I
1010	ALE	Brochure	10/10/93	6000	I
1012	ALE	Radio Ad	09/01/93	3425	I
1013	SAN	Direct Mail	10/15/93	8900	I
1014	FAT	Direct Mail	11/20/93	2200	I
1015	SAN	Brochure	09/15/93	4400	I
1016	IMA	Magazine Ad	10/15/93	10000	I
1017	CEL	Flyer	09/20/93	850	I
1018	VIK	TV ads	01/15/94	35700	I
1019	SAN	Festival campaign	09/12/93	8900	I
1020	FAT	Mail order catalogue	10/10/93	9400	I
1021	ALE	B/W magazine ad	11/10/93	6600	I
1022	MAM	Newspaper ad	12/01/93	5300	I
1023	TAC	TV ad	12/15/93	14000	I
1024	PEA	Brochure	11/30/93	11000	I

Records   Organize   Fields   Go To   Exit

only jobs in process are retrieved

Next, Esther needs to print the report for Martin. Remember, check with your instructor before printing. If you do not want to print this report, skip to step 3.

❷ Print a quick report.

❸ Press **[Shift][F2]** (Design) to return to the Query Design screen.

Dot Prompt

To view records that meet specified conditions:

LIST *fields* OFF *scope* FOR *condition* TO PRINTER

or

DISPLAY *fields* OFF *scope* FOR *condition* TO PRINTER

Examples   .USE jobs
.LIST OFF client_id, jobnum, quote FOR status = 'C'

.USE jobs
.DISPLAY ALL OFF client_id, jobnum, quote FOR status = 'C'

Dot Prompt

To select records that meet a specified condition:

SET FILTER TO *condition*

Allows display of only those records in a database file that meet a specified condition

Example   .USE jobs
.SET FILTER TO quote > 5000

Using Dates in a Filter Condition

Martin also asked Esther for a list of all unfinished jobs due after August 1, 1993. This query requires a condition that compares a field that stores a Date data type with a date constant, that is, DUE_DATE greater than August 1, 1993. Let's construct a query to find all jobs due after August 1, 1993.

Before you enter the new filter condition, you need to remove the previous filter condition.

To remove a filter condition from the Query Design screen:

❶ Move the highlight so it is positioned on the filter condition you want to remove (in this case, beneath the STATUS field in the file skeleton).

Now remove the filter condition.

❷ Press **[Ctrl]Y**. The filter condition is removed from the file skeleton.

Now enter the new filter condition.

To enter a filter condition:

❶ Move the highlight beneath the DUE_DATE field.

To use a date in a filter condition, you must enclose the date you are searching for inside curly braces ({ }).

❷ Type **>{08/01/93}** and press **[Enter]**. See Figure 4-17. The date value must be entered in the format {mm/dd/yy}.

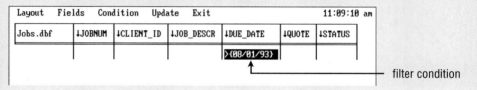

Figure 4-17
Enter filter condition
to retrieve jobs due
after 8/1/93

Layout	Fields	Condition	Update	Exit			11:09:10 am
Jobs.dbf	↓JOBNUM	↓CLIENT_ID	↓JOB_DESCR	↓DUE_DATE	↓QUOTE	↓STATUS	
				>{08/01/93}			

— filter condition

Now that the filter condition has been entered, you are ready to process the query.

To process the query:

❶ Press **[F2]** (Data). See Figure 4-18. Notice that only the records with a due date after August 1, 1993 are displayed.

— due dates after 8/1/93

Figure 4-18
Result of processing
query to select jobs
due after 8/1/93

Records	Organize	Fields	Go To	Exit		
JOBNUM	CLIENT_ID	JOB_DESCR		DUE_DATE	QUOTE	STATUS
1001	ORI	Best in the Southwest		08/15/93	2500	C
1002	VIK	Fall TV Ad		08/10/93	32500	C
1007	SAN	Pamphlet		08/02/93	3000	C
1008	VIK	Thanksgiving Promo		11/15/93	12000	I
1009	FAT	Bicycle Magazine Ad		08/05/93	2500	C
1010	ALE	Brochure		10/10/93	6000	I
1011	IMA	Fall Catalogue		08/22/93	8450	C
1012	ALE	Radio Ad		09/01/93	3425	I
1013	SAN	Direct Mail		10/15/93	8900	I
1014	FAT	Direct Mail		11/20/93	2200	I
1015	SAN	Brochure		09/15/93	4400	I
1016	IMA	Magazine Ad		10/15/93	10000	I
1017	CEL	Flyer		09/20/93	850	I
1018	VIK	TV ads		01/15/94	35700	I
1019	SAN	Festival campaign		09/12/93	8900	I
1020	FAT	Mail order catalogue		10/10/93	9400	I
1021	ALE	B/W magazine ad		11/10/93	6600	I

| Browse | ‖A:\<NEW> | ‖Rec 1/24 | ‖View ‖ | ‖ |

❷ Press **[PgDn]** to see the rest of the records.

❸ Esther needs to print the report for Martin. Print a quick report.

❹ Press **[Shift][F2]** (Design) to return to the Query Design screen.

Using Numeric Values in a Filter Condition

Next Esther turns her attention to Nancy's request for a list of all jobs that had quotes greater than $5,000. To specify which records have a quote greater than $5,000, you again enter a filter condition in the file skeleton. This time you place the filter condition beneath the field name QUOTE. Let's create a filter condition to display the jobs with quotes above $5,000. First you need to remove the previous filter condition from the Query Design screen.

To remove a filter condition from the Query Design screen:

❶ Make sure the highlight is beneath the DUE_DATE field in the file skeleton and press **[Ctrl]Y**. The filter condition is removed from the file skeleton.

Now enter the new filter condition.

To enter the filter condition:

❶ Move the highlight beneath the QUOTE field name.

❷ Type **>5000** and press **[Enter]**. See Figure 4-19. When the field being queried stores numeric data, you do not enclose the numeric constant in quotes or curly braces.

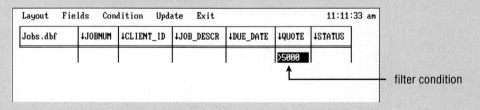

Figure 4-19
Enter filter condition for jobs having quotes above $5,000

Now that you have entered the filter condition for Esther's query, you can process the query.

To process the query:

❶ Press **[F2]** (Data). See Figure 4-20. Notice that only the records with a QUOTE above $5,000 are displayed.

Next, Esther prints the report for Nancy.

❷ Print a quick report.

③ After you've viewed the result of the query, press **[Shift][F2]** (Design) to return to the Query Design screen.

```
 Records   Organize   Fields   Go To   Exit
┌──────┬─────────┬──────────────────┬─────────┬──────┬───────┐
│JOBNUM│CLIENT_ID│JOB_DESCR         │DUE_DATE │QUOTE │STATUS │
├──────┼─────────┼──────────────────┼─────────┼──────┼───────┤
│1002  │VIK      │Fall TV Ad        │08/10/93 │32500 │C      │
│1005  │SAN      │Magazine Ad       │06/10/93 │22500 │C      │
│1008  │VIK      │Thanksgiving Promo│11/15/93 │12000 │I      │
│1010  │ALE      │Brochure          │10/10/93 │ 6000 │I      │
│1011  │IMA      │Fall Catalogue    │08/22/93 │ 8450 │C      │
│1013  │SAN      │Direct Mail       │10/15/93 │ 8900 │I      │
│1016  │IMA      │Magazine Ad       │10/15/93 │10000 │I      │
│1018  │VIK      │TV ads            │01/15/94 │35700 │I      │
│1019  │SAN      │Festival campaign │09/12/93 │ 8900 │I      │
│1020  │FAT      │Mail order catalogue│10/10/93│9400 │I      │
│1021  │ALE      │B/W magazine ad   │11/10/93 │ 6600 │I      │
│1022  │MAM      │Newspaper ad      │12/01/93 │ 5300 │I      │
│1023  │TAC      │TV ad             │12/15/93 │14000 │I      │
│1024  │PEA      │Brochure          │11/30/93 │11000 │I      │
```
quotes above 5000

Figure 4-20
Jobs with quotes above $5,000

Saving a Query to a File

If you think you will reuse a query, you can save it to a file. This enables you to reuse the query without reentering the filter condition. Esther believes that Nancy will want similar reports in the future, so she decides to save this query.

To save a query to your data diskette:
① Press **[Alt]E** to open the Exit menu.
② Select the option *Save changes and exit* **(S)**.

A prompt box appears asking you to enter a filename. You must enter a valid DOS filename (eight characters or less).

③ Type **job5000**, for jobs quoted above $5,000, and press **[Enter]**. You are returned to the Control Center. The name of the query file, JOB5000, appears in the Queries panel above the panel line. See Figure 4-21 on the next page.

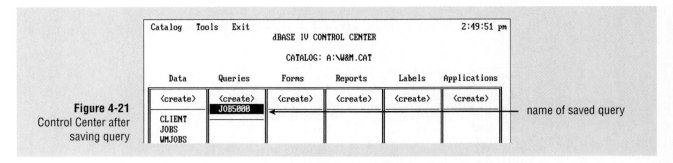

Figure 4-21
Control Center after
saving query

name of saved query

dBASE automatically adds a QBE extension to the filename and the file is stored on your data diskette, so the file is saved as JOB5000.QBE. The name of the saved query is also added to the current catalog, W&M.CAT. See Figure 4-22.

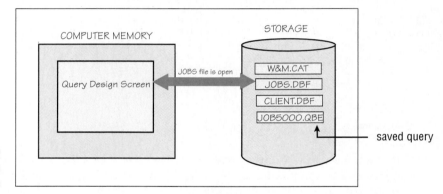

Figure 4-22
Storing a query to
your data diskette

saved query

In dBASE, a saved query is known as a **view**. It is called a view because the saved query does not contain data — it only stores the instructions that tell dBASE how you want to "view" the data in a database.

A saved query file appears in the Queries panel whenever you open the catalog with which it is associated. To reuse a saved query, you can select it just as you select a database file from the Data panel.

Dot Prompt

To change a saved query:

MODIFY QUERY *query name*

Gives you access to the Query Design screen, which allows you to modify query (QBE) files.

Example   .USE jobs
.MODIFY QUERY job5000

Using Compound Filter Conditions

As Esther looks over the results of the query, she realizes she hasn't followed Nancy's specifications. Nancy wants a list of *completed* jobs greater than $5,000. Esther's list includes all jobs that had quotes above $5,000. Esther decides to revise the query.

Esther's first query searched the database with only one condition. For many situations you need to enter only one condition to form the filter condition to select records from a database. There will be times, however, when you need to search a database based on two or more conditions. This is the case with Nancy's query about completed jobs quoted at more than $5,000. In these situations you use **logical operators**, which allow you to combine simple conditions.

If you place two or more conditions in the same row of the file skeleton, all the conditions must be met for a record to be displayed. This is called the **AND condition.** If you place two or more conditions in different rows of a file skeleton, only one of the conditions must be met for a record to be displayed. This is known as the **OR condition.**

Forming AND Conditions

Let's answer Nancy's query to list all the completed jobs with quotes over $5,000. To list these jobs, the filter condition consist of two conditions: the condition *status = 'C'* finds completed jobs, *and quote > 5000* finds jobs with quotes above $5,000. Both conditions must be met for the record to be retrieved.

Let's enter this query. Currently the Control Center indicates that the query file *JOB5000* is open (the filename appears above the panel line). To use the saved query file, highlight the name of the query file in the Queries panel. If you want to process the query, press [F2]. If you want to change the filter condition, press [Shift][F2] to access the Query Design screen. Let's return to the Query Design screen so you can modify the query.

To return to the Query Design screen:
1. Press **[Shift][F2]** (Design).

The Query Design screen appears with the the filter condition, *>5000,* already in the file skeleton. You do not have to enter the entire condition. Just modify the file skeleton so the filter condition = *'C'* is entered beneath the STATUS field.

Now enter the condition to search for completed jobs.

To enter an AND condition:
1. Press **[Tab]** to move the highlight beneath the STATUS field name in the file skeleton.
2. Type **='C'** and press **[Enter]**. See Figure 4-23 on the next page.

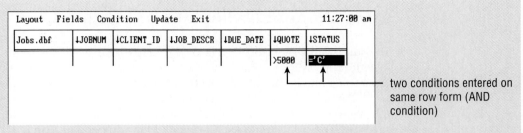

Figure 4-23
Entering filter conditions to find completed jobs with quotes above $5,000

two conditions entered on same row form (AND condition)

Remember to type an uppercase C for the status code. Otherwise no records will be retrieved. If you typed a lowercase c, just retype the entry.

There are now two conditions in the file skeleton. Since both conditions are in the same row, you have formed an AND condition.

Now process the query.

To process the query:

❶ Press **[F2]** (Data). See Figure 4-24. dBASE processes the query, and the records that meet both conditions, that is, with a status code equal to C and a quote greater than 5000, are displayed.

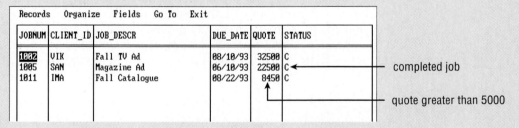

Figure 4-24
Result of processing query to select completed jobs with quotes above $5,000

completed job

quote greater than 5000

Esther writes a memo for Nancy listing the three completed jobs with quotes over $5,000.

❷ After you've viewed the result of the query, press **[Shift][F2]** (Design) to return to the Query Design screen.

When you search for data that fall within some range of values, you need to form an AND condition where both conditions apply to the same field. In this case you can use the >= operator before the low end of the range and the <= operator before the high end of the range. The two conditions must be separated by a comma. For example, suppose you wanted a list of jobs with quotes between $5,000 and $9,000. This condition would be entered under the QUOTE field as *>=5000,<=9000*.

Forming OR Conditions

Next, Esther works on Martin's request for a list of all the jobs for Origins (ORI) and Alexander's Insurance (ALE). This query requires a different type of logic from that of the previous query. Here you have a situation where either condition must be satisfied for a record to be retrieved, that is, CLIENT_ID = 'ORI' *or* CLIENT_ID = 'ALE'. This is an OR condition. To form such a query using the Query Design screen, you enter each condition on a separate row of the file skeleton. When you place the filter conditions on separate lines of the file skeleton, dBASE will retrieve records that match either condition.

Before you enter this new query, remember that you must remove the present filter conditions from the Query Design screen.

To enter the OR condition:

❶ First remove the filter conditions from the previous query.

❷ Move the highlight beneath the CLIENT_ID field.

❸ Type **='ORI'** and press **[↓]**. A new row is added to the file skeleton.

❹ Type **='ALE'** and press **[Enter]**. See Figure 4-25.

Figure 4-25
Entering filter conditions to select jobs for Origins or Alexander

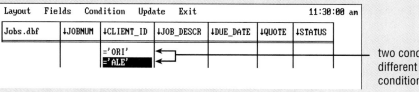

two conditions entered on different rows form (OR condition)

Since the conditions are entered on separate rows, you have formed an OR condition. Now process the query.

To process the query:

❶ Press **[F2]** (Data). Records with a client ID of either ORI or ALE are displayed. See Figure 4-26.

Figure 4-26
Result of processing query to select jobs for Origins or Alexander

Records	Organize	Fields	Go To	Exit			
JOBNUM	CLIENT_ID	JOB_DESCR			DUE_DATE	QUOTE	STATUS
1001	ORI	Best in the Southwest			08/15/93	2500	C
1004	ALE	B/W Magazine Ad			06/05/93	3500	C
1006	ORI	Fall Promotion			08/01/93	2200	C
1010	ALE	Brochure			10/10/93	6000	I
1012	ALE	Radio Ad			09/01/93	3425	I
1021	ALE	B/W magazine ad			11/10/93	6600	I

Esther writes a memo for Martin listing all the jobs for Origins and Alexander Insurance.

❷ Press **[Shift][F2]** (Design) to return to the Query Design screen.

Using a Condition Box to Form a Filter Condition

Esther now considers Martin's request for a list of the jobs currently in process that are due during his vacation, November 17 to December 6, 1993. Esther decides to use an optional feature in the Query Design screen known as the condition box . The **condition box** is a window that lets you enter the filter condition in a single visual area, rather than beneath specific fields in the file skeleton. If a condition is long, it may be easier to use a condition box (rather than a file skeleton) to express the logic of the query.

The syntax for a filter condition entered in a condition box differs from the condition entered in the file skeleton. You must specify the field name in the condition box so that dBASE knows the field to which the condition should be compared. In the condition box the filter condition is entered as

field name   relational operator   expression

The general form of a compound condition in the condition box is

conditional expression   logical operator   conditional expression

For example, to search for completed jobs, you would enter *STATUS = 'C'* in the condition box instead of *= 'C'* in the STATUS field of the file skeleton. Both approaches will retrieve only completed jobs.

Let's use the condition box to enter Martin's query. Remember to clear the previous filter condition before entering the new query.

To add a condition box to the Query Design screen:

❶ Clear the previous conditions.

❷ Press **[Alt]C** to open the Condition menu.

❸ Select *Add condition box* (**A**). The condition box appears on the lower right side of the screen. See Figure 4-27. You can now enter the new condition into the condition box.

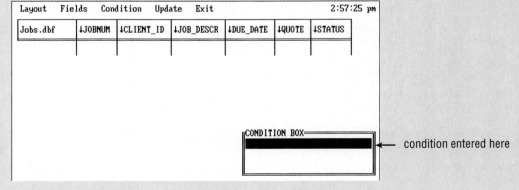

Figure 4-27
Query Design screen
with condition box

If your condition is long and you want to see the entire expression on the screen, you can press [F9] (Zoom) to enlarge the condition box. If you press [F9] again, the condition box is returned to its original size.

④   Press **[F9]** (Zoom). The condition box is enlarged.

Now enter the filter condition in the condition box.

⑤   Type **due_date >= {11/17/93} .and. due_date <= {12/06/93} .and. status = 'I'** and press **[Enter]**. See Figure 4-28.

Figure 4-28
Enlarged condition
box with filter
condition

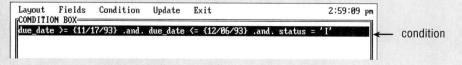

```
Layout   Fields   Condition   Update   Exit                    2:59:09 pm
┌CONDITION BOX
│due_date >= {11/17/93} .and. due_date <= {12/06/93} .and. status = 'I'
│
│
```

◄—— condition

You must put a period on each side of the logical operator. If you get a message telling you have a syntax error, check to make sure you typed it exactly as shown above.

Now process the query.

To process the query:

①   Press **[F2]** (Data). See Figure 4-29. Three jobs are due during Martin's vacation.

Figure 4-29
Jobs in process with
due dates between
11/17/93 and
12/06/93

```
Records   Organize   Fields   Go To   Exit

JOBNUM  CLIENT_ID  JOB_DESCR           DUE_DATE  QUOTE  STATUS
1014    FAT        Direct Mail         11/20/93   2200  I
1022    MAM        Newspaper ad        12/01/93   5300  I
1024    PEA        Brochure            11/30/93  11000  I
```

Esther notes the jobs due for Martin.

②   Press **[Shift][F2]** (Design) to return to the Query Design screen.

Before you can enter a different query, you need to remove the condition box.

To delete a condition box from the Query Design screen:

❶   Press **[Alt]C** to open the Condition menu.

❷   Select *Delete condition box* (**D**). The condition box disappears from the screen.

Case: Wells & Martinez — Using the Query Design Screen for Calculations

After lunch, Nancy asks Esther to stop by her office. She needs more information from the database. Nancy explains that she has received a request from Alexander Insurance. The client wants their radio ad, job number 1012, ready five days early, and is willing to pay a five percent premium over the quoted price. Nancy asks Esther to provide her with the proposed new due date and the amount of additional money W&M would earn.

Nancy also tells Esther that she believes that W&M's jobs have become more sophisticated and that quotations have become larger since W&M expanded. To find out if this is true, Nancy has asked Esther to calculate the number of completed jobs and the average quote for those jobs.

Using Calculated Fields in Queries

Esther decides to calculate the new due date for Alexander Insurance first. To do this, Esther will use a component of the Query Design screen called the calculated fields skeleton. The **calculated fields skeleton** enables you to create new fields, that is, fields not in the database but whose values can be determined from fields that are in the database. Once a calculated field is created, it can be used like any field in the file skeleton. Let's work on the two calculations in Nancy's request.

To include a calculated field for the new due date in a query:

❶   While the highlight is in the file skeleton, press **[Alt]F** to open the Fields menu.

---

❷ Select *Create calculated field* (**C**). The highlight appears in a new skeleton titled "Calc'd Flds." See Figure 4-30. dBASE is waiting for you to enter the calculations.

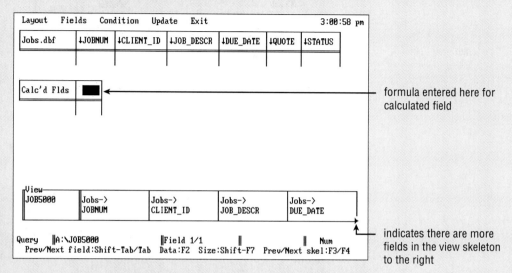

Figure 4-30
Query Design screen
with calculated fields
skeleton

formula entered here for
calculated field

indicates there are more
fields in the view skeleton
to the right

Now enter a formula to subtract 5 days from the DUE_DATE field. This is entered into the column heading of the calculated field skeleton.

❸ Type **due_date-5** and press **[Enter]**. See Figure 4-31.

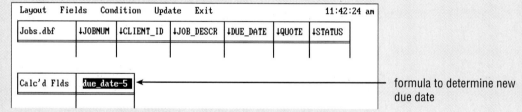

Figure 4-31
Calculating new
due date

formula to determine new
due date

Now you need to add the calculated field to the view skeleton.

❹ Press **[F5]** (Field). You are prompted for a field name to be assigned to the calculated field.

❺ Type **newdate** and press **[Enter]**.

Although you can't see the field NEWDATE on the view skeleton, it has been added. The arrow in lower right corner of the view skeleton indicates there are additional fields in the view skeleton.

❻ Press **[F4]** (Next) to move to the view skeleton.

❼ Press **[End]** to move the highlight to the last field in the view skeleton. The view skeleton scrolls to the left. See Figure 4-32 on the next page.

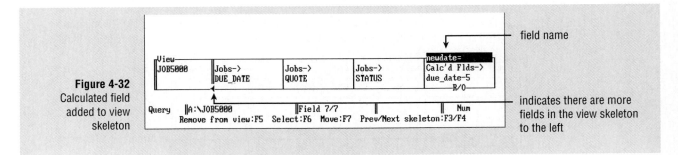

Figure 4-32
Calculated field added to view skeleton

dBASE allows up to 20 calculated fields in each query. The additional calculated fields are added to the calculated fields skeleton.

Let's add a second calculated field, to compute the additional money that W&M will receive.

To add a calculated field to the calculated fields skeleton:

❶ Press **[F3]** (Previous) to move the highlight back to the calculated fields skeleton.

❷ Press **[Alt]F** to open the Fields menu.

❸ Select *Create calculated field* (**C**). An additional column appears in the skeleton.

Now enter the formula to compute the five percent increase.

❹ Type **quote*.05** and press **[Enter]**.

Now add the calculated field to the view skeleton

❺ Press **[F5]** (Field). You are prompted for a field name.

❻ Type **premium** and press **[Enter]**. See Figure 4-33.

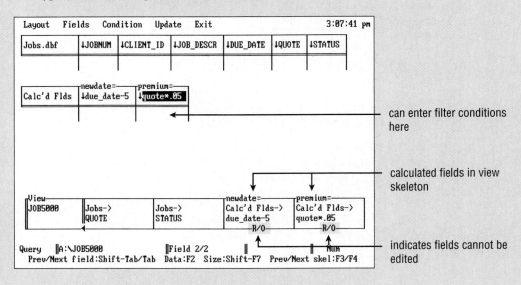

Figure 4-33
Query Design screen showing two calculated fields

The calculated fields, NewDate and Premium, cannot be edited. They derive their values through formulas, not through direct input. However, if any field that is included in the calculated field is updated, the calculated field also will be updated.

The query is not yet complete. You need to restrict the view to job number 1012, the job being reviewed. If you don't, you will calculate new due dates and premiums for all the records in the database.

To enter a filter condition:

❶ Press **[F3]** (Previous) to move to the file skeleton.

❷ Move the highlight to the JOBNUM field.

❸ Type **='1012'** and press **[Enter]**.

Esther doesn't need to see the job description and the status for this report, so she decides to remove JOB_DESCR and STATUS from the output.

To remove fields from the view skeleton:

❶ While in the file skeleton, move the highlight to JOB_DESCR and press **[F5]** (Field).

❷ Move the highlight to STATUS and press **[F5]** (Field).

Now you are ready to see the results.

Process the query:

❶ Press **[F2]** (Data). See Figure 4-34. The new due date for job 1012 is 8/27/93 and the client will pay a $171.25 premium.

Figure 4-34
Results of processing a query with calculated fields

Records	Organize	Fields	Go To	Exit	

JOBNUM	CLIENT_ID	DUE_DATE	QUOTE	NEWDATE	PREMIUM
1012	ALE	09/01/93	3425	08/27/93	171.25

Esther notes the new due date and the premium for Nancy.

❷ Press **[Shift][F2]** (Design) to return to the Query Design screen.

To remove all the calculated fields from the Query Design screen, use the Layout menu.

To remove the calculated fields skeleton:

❶ Move the highlight to any of the calculated fields in the calculated field skeleton.

❷ Press **[Alt]L** to open the Layout menu.

❸ Select *Remove file from query* (**R**). The calculated field skeleton disappears from the Query Design screen.

To delete a single calculated field, you would highlight the calculated field you want to remove, open the Fields menu, and select the option *Delete calculated field.*

Using Aggregate Operators in Queries

After calling Nancy to give her the information on Alexander's Insurance, Esther starts working on Nancy's second request. In this case, Esther doesn't want to display information about individual records; she wants summary information about the database.

Esther knows she can calculate statistical information such as totals, averages, and counts on all or selected records in a database file. To do this, she will use dBASE's aggregate operators, sometimes referred to as summary operators. **Aggregate operators** perform arithmetic operations on the records in a database. Figure 4-35 lists the aggregate operators used in dBASE.

Aggregate Operator	Calculation
AVG or AVERAGE	Divides the sum of all values in a column by the number of records, according to the records that meet the selection criteria.
CNT or COUNT	The number of records that meet selection criteria
MAX	The highest value in a field
MIN	The lowest value in a field
SUM	The total of all values in a field

Figure 4-35
Aggregate operators

In our example, one of the statistics Nancy wants to calculate is the average quote for completed jobs. To do this, Esther will use dBASE's AVG command. Let's calculate this statistic.

To calculate the average quote for completed jobs:

❶ Remove the filter condition from the previous query.

Now enter the new filter condition.

❷ Move the highlight to the STATUS field.

❸ Type **='C'** and press **[Enter]**.

Now include the aggregate operator in the query.

④ Move the highlight beneath the QUOTE field.

⑤ Type **avg** and press **[Enter]**.

Now process the query.

To process the query:

① Press **[F2]** (Data). See Figure 4-36. 8906 is the average quote for completed jobs.*

Figure 4-36
Results of
using AVG

Records	Organize	Fields	Go To	Exit

JOBNUM	CLIENT_ID	DUE_DATE	QUOTE
▉		/ /	8906

Notice that only the QUOTE field has a value in the Browse screen. When an aggregate operator is used in a Query Design screen, only fields that contain aggregate operators contain results. The rest of the fields are blank. Thus, the fields for JOBNUM, CLIENT_ID, and DUE_DATE are blank. For this reason you may want to remove the blank fields from the view skeleton so they do not appear when you process the query.

② After you've reviewed the result of the query, press **[Shift][F2]** (Design) to return to the Query Design screen.

Nancy also wants to know the total number of completed jobs as well as the average quote for those jobs. This requires two aggregate operators: CNT and AVG. Let's add the CNT operator to the Query Design screen.

To calculate the number of completed jobs:

① Move the highlight beneath the field JOBNUM in the file skeleton.

② Type **cnt** and press **[Enter]**. See Figure 4-37.

Figure 4-37
Query Design
screen using
aggregate operators

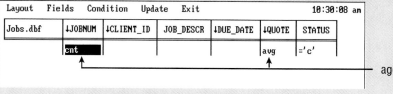

Layout	Fields	Condition	Update	Exit		10:30:08 am

Jobs.dbf	↓JOBNUM	↓CLIENT_ID	JOB_DESCR	↓DUE_DATE	↓QUOTE	STATUS
	cnt▉				avg	='c'

aggregate operators

Actually it doesn't matter whether you place CNT beneath JOBNUM, CLIENT_ID, or any other field in the file skeleton. The operator CNT counts the number of records that meet the filter condition. The placement of CNT determines only the column in the

---

* If you did not add the records in the Tutorial Assignments in Ttuorial 3, you will get 8963 for an average quote.

Browse screen where the count will be displayed. This is not the case for the other operators, where operator placement determines the fields to which calculations apply.

Before processing the query, let's improve the appearance of the output. Remove CLIENT_ID and DUE_DATE from the view skeleton.

To remove fields from the view skeleton:
1. Move the highlight to the CLIENT_ID field.
2. Press **[F5]** (Field). CLIENT_ID is removed from the view skeleton.
3. Repeat this step to remove the DUE_DATE field. When you have finished, only JOBNUM and QUOTE remain in the view skeleton.

Now process the query.

To process the query:
1. Press **[F2]** (Data). The screen shows that nine records were included in computing the average, $8,906. See Figure 4-38.

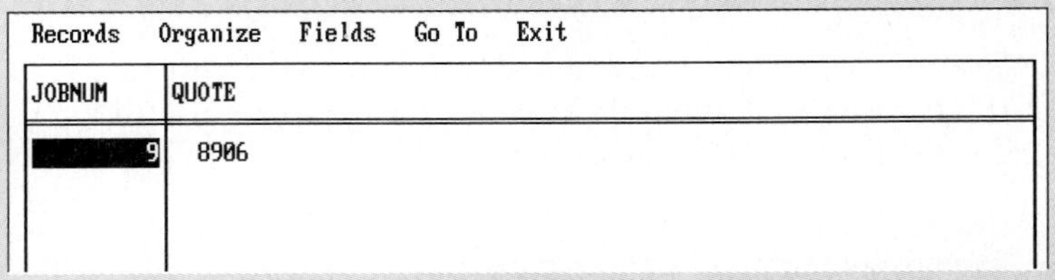

Figure 4-38
Results of query using two aggregate operators

```
Records   Organize   Fields   Go To   Exit

JOBNUM    QUOTE

       9  8906
```

Esther notes this information for Nancy.
2. Press **[Shift][F2]** to return to the Query Design screen.

Esther has now calculated the number of completed jobs, and the average quote for these jobs. She gives this information to Nancy.

Dot Prompt

To calculate an average:

AVERAGE *numeric fields* FOR *condition* TO *memory variable*

Calculates arithemetic mean of numeric expressions to memory variables

Example   .USE jobs
.AVERAGE FOR status = 'C'

Dot Prompt

To count the number of records:

COUNT FOR *condition* TO *memory variable*

Tallies the number of records in the database that match specified conditions

Example   .USE jobs
.COUNT FOR status = 'C'

Dot Prompt

To total numeric fields:

SUM *numeric fields* FOR *condition* TO *memory variable*

Totals numeric expressions to memory variables

Example   .USE jobs
.SUM FOR status = 'C'

Grouping Records in Queries

After reviewing Esther's data, Nancy decides it would also be helpful to compute the number of completed jobs and the average quote for completed jobs for each client. Esther knows that she can do this by using the Group By operator to obtain the results Nancy is looking for.

In the preceding query all completed jobs were summarized into statistics for all selected records. Often it's useful to group data by some characteristic of a group such as client ID, status code, or date so summary statistics about the group can be calculated. This process is known as **grouping**. In dBASE you use the Group By operator so all records with the same value on a designated field are summarized. When you process the query, dBASE applies the aggregate operators included in the query to each group of records that have matching values. Let's calculate the number and the average quote of completed jobs for each client.

To calculate summary statistics for each client:
❶ Make sure the highlight is beneath the CLIENT_ID field in the file skeleton.
❷ Type **group by** and press **[Enter]**. See Figure 4-39.

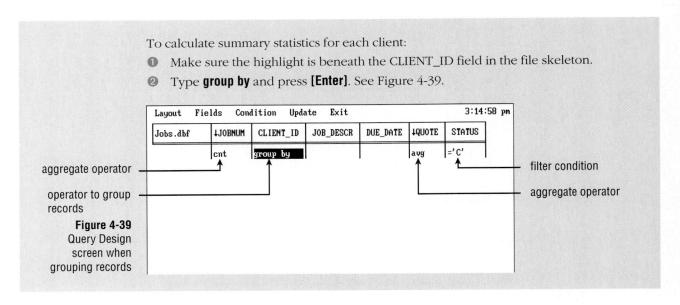

Figure 4-39
Query Design
screen when
grouping records

Now adjust the view skeleton to place CLIENT_ID before the other two fields.

To add a field to the view skeleton:
❶ With the highlight beneath the CLIENT_ID field, press **[F5]** (Field). The CLIENT_ID field is placed as the last field in the view skeleton.

Let's place the CLIENT_ID ahead of the other two fields. To do this, move to the view skeleton.

❷ Press **[F4]** (Next).
❸ Move the highlight to the CLIENT_ID field in the view skeleton.
❹ Press **[F6]** (Select) to select the CLIENT_ID field.
❺ Press **[F7]** (Move) and press **[Shift][Tab]** twice to move the field to the first position in the view skeleton.
❻ Press **[Enter]** to complete the move.

Now process the query.

To process the query:

❶ Press **[F2]** (Data). See Figure 4-40. Notice the statistics are summarized by client.

```
Records   Organize   Fields   Go To   Exit

CLIENT_ID JOBNUM        QUOTE

ALE                 1     3500
FAT                 1     2500
IMA                 1     8450
MOU                 1     3000
ORI                 2     2350
SAN                 2    12750
VIK                 1    32500
```

Figure 4-40
Results of query to
group records

Esther needs to print this information for Nancy.

❷ Print a quick report.

Esther collects the reports and memos she has produced and gives them to Nancy and Martin. You have now completed Tutorial 4. Remember to quit dBASE and return to DOS.

■   ■   ■

Control Center Summary

To access the Query Design screen:

Open database file.

Highlight <create> in the Queries panel and press [Enter].

To remove a field from the view skeleton:

While in the file or calculated fields skeleton:
Press [Tab] to move to the field you want to remove.
Press [F5] to delete field name.
Press [F2] to view data.

To add a field to the view skeleton:

While in the file or calculated fields skeleton:
Press [Tab] to move to the field you want to add.
Press [F5] to add field name.
Press [F2] to view data.

To move a field:

While in the view skeleton:
Highlight the field you want to move.
Press [F6] to select field.
Press [F7] AND move cursor to new position of field.
Press [Enter].

Control Center Summary

To enter a filter condition in the Query Design screen:

Highlight <create> in the Queries panel and press [Enter].

Tab to field name.

Enter filter condition:
    character value in quotes
    date value in curly braces
    AND operator in same row
    OR operator in different rows

Press [F2] to view data.

To add a condition box:

Press [Alt]C to open the Condition menu.

Select *Add a condition box* (A).

Enter condition.

Press [F2] to view data.

To create a calculated field:

Press [Alt]F to open the Fields menu.

Select *Create calculated field* (C).

Enter formula and press [Enter].

To save a query and remain in the Query Design screen:

Press [Alt]L to open the Layout menu.

Select *Save this query* (S).

Enter query name and press [Enter].

To save a query and return to the Control Center:

Press [Alt]E to open the Exit menu.

Select *Save changes and exit* (S).

Enter filename and press [Enter].

To print a Quick Report:

Highlight filename in Data panel.

Press [Shift][F9] (Quick Report).

Select *Begin printing* (B).

Exercises

1. Explain the purpose of each component of the Query Design screen:
   a. file skeleton
   b. view skeleton
   c. condition box
   d. calculated fields skeleton

2. Suppose you find a file on your data diskette named COMPLTED.QBE. What type of a file is this?

3. Use Figure 4-41 to answer the following questions:
   a. What is the filter condition, that is, which records will be retrieved?
   b. Which fields appear in the view?
   c. What does the calculated field compute?
   d. What is the name of the view?
   e. How would you add the field COST to the view?
   f. What does the triangle in the lower right corner of the view skeleton mean?

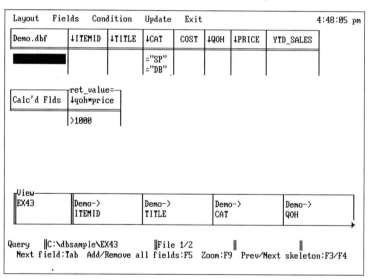

Figure 4-41

4. Explain the difference between the following filter conditions:

a.

QUOTE
>3000,<=4000

b.

QUOTE
<=3000
>4000

Use the file layouts shown in Figure 4-42 for an employee skills database to do Exercises 5 through 8.

File Layout 1		
Field	**Type**	**Width**
EMP_ID	Character	3
EMP_NAME	Character	30
SKILL1_CD	Character	6
SKILL2_CD	Character	6
SKILL3_CD	Character	6

File Layout 2		
Field	**Type**	**Width**
EMP_ID	Character	3
EMP_NAME	Character	30
SKILL_CODE	Character	6

Figure 4-42

5. For File Layout 1, what is the filter condition needed to find all employees who have experience using Lotus 1-2-3 (skill code LOT123)?

6. For the File Layout 2, what is the filter condition needed to find all employees who have experience using Lotus 1-2-3 (skill code LOT123)?

7. For the File Layout 1, what is the filter condition needed to find all employees who have experience using Lotus 1-2-3 (skill code LOT123) or dBASE IV (skill code DBASE4)?

8. For the File Layout 2, what is the filter condition needed to find all employees who have experience using Lotus 1-2-3 (skill code LOT123) or dBASE IV (skill code DBASE4)?

Tutorial Assignments

Activate the W&M catalog and open the database file CLIENT to complete Assignments 1 and 2. Use the Query Design screen to build each query and then use Quick Report to print the results.

1. For all clients list the fields CLIENT_NAM and PHONE.

2. For the client Origins list the CLIENT_NAM and PHONE.

Use the JOBS database to complete Assignments 3 through 5. Use the Query Design screen to build each query and then use Quick Report to print the results.

3. For all jobs still in process (status is I), print the fields CLIENT_ID, JOB_DESCR, and DUE_DATE.

4. For all Mountain Top Ski (MOU) jobs, print the fields CLIENT_ID, JOB_DESCR, QUOTE, and STATUS.

5. For all jobs with a status code of C or having a quote above $10,000, print the fields CLIENT_ID, STATUS, and QUOTE.

6. Use aggregate operators to determine the number of jobs in process (status is I) and the total quote.

7. Use aggregate operators to determine the average quote for jobs in process (status is I).

Case Problems

1. Biggs & Hang Investment Corporation

Activate the BIG&HANG catalog and open the database file JAPAN.DBF.

Use the Query Design screen to build each query and then use Quick Report to print the results.

1. For all companies, print the company name, the industry code, sales, and profit.

2. For all companies in the automobile industry (code = A), print the company ID, company name, industry code, sales, and profit.

3. For all companies with sales above 1,000,000 yen, print the company ID, company name, industry code, sales, assets, and profit.

4. For all companies with sales above 2,500,000 yen and profit above 300,000 yen, print the company name, industry code, sales, and profit.

5. For all companies with sales above 2,500,000 yen or profit above 300,000 yen, print the company name, industry code, sales, assets, and profit.

6. For all companies with a rate of return above 10 percent, print the company name, sales, profit, and rate of return. Rate of return is computed by dividing profit by assets.

7. Calculate the average profit for all companies in the database. Based on this calculation, print a list of all companies that had profits below the average. Include company names and profits in your listing.

8. Group the records in the JAPAN database by industry code and print a report similar to the one illustrated in Figure 4-43.

Industry Code	Average Sales	Average Profit
A		
E		

Figure 4-43

2. Medi-Source Inc.

Activate the MEDISRCE catalog and open the database file ACCTREC.DBF.

Use the Query Design screen to build each query and then use Quick Report to print the results.

1. For all customers, print the customer name, type of customer, and balance owed.

2. For all customers who are in the hospital (code = H) industry, print the customer name, type of customer, state, and balance owed.

3. For all customers whose balance owed is more than $6,000, print the customer ID, customer name, type of customer, and balance owed.

4. For all Rhode Island (RI) customers whose outstanding balance is greater than $6,000, print the customer name, type of customer, and balance owed.

5. For all Rhode Island (RI) customers or customers whose outstanding balance is greater than $6,000, print the customer name, type of customer, and balance owed.

6. Print the customer name, balance owed, ytd_sales, and ratio of balance owed to ytd_sales for any customer whose ratio of balance owed to ytd-sales is greater than .5. You compute the ratio by dividing balance owed by ytd_sales.

7. Calculate the average balance owed by all customers. Based on this calculation, print the customer name and balance owed for all customers who owe more than the average.

8. Group the records in the ACCTREC database by industry type and print a report similar to the one illustrated in Figure 4-44.

Type	Average Balance Owed	Total YTD Sales
H		
L		
P		

Figure 4-44

3. Appleton & Drake Electrical Supply Company

Activate the APPLTON catalog and open the database file EMPLOYEE.DBF.

Use the Query Design screen to build each query and then use Quick Report to print the results.

1. For all employees, print the last name, first name, sex, department, and salary.

2. For all female employees, print the last name, first name, sex, department, and salary.

3. For all female employees earning $35,000 or more, print the last name, first name, sex, and salary.

4. For all employees who are either in the SALES department (code = SAL) or married (code = Y), print the last name, first name, department, sex, marital status, and salary.

5. For all male employees earning less than $50,000 print the last name, first name, sex, and salary.

6. For all male employees or employees earning $50,000 or more, print the last name, first name, sex, and salary.

7. All the employees in the sales department will have their salaries increased by 7.5 percent. For all employees in the sales department, print the employee's last name, first name, department, and new salary.

8. Calculate the average salary paid to all employees. Based on this calculation, print the employee last name, salary, and date hired for all employees hired after December 31, 1989 and earning more than the average salary.

9. Group the records in the EMPLOYEE database by department and print a report similar to the one illustrated in Figure 4-45.

Dept	Average Salary	Number of Employees
COR		
ENG		
SAL		

Figure 4-45

4. National Basketball Association

Activate the NBA catalog and open the database file NBA.DBF.

Use the Query Design screen to build each query and then use Quick Report to print the results.

1. For all players, print the team ID, player's full name, position, and salary.

2. For all players playing center (code = C), print the team ID, player's full name, position, and salary.

3. For all players earning over $1 million, print the team ID, player's full name, position, and salary.

4. For all players who are members of the LA Lakers (code = LAK) or the Chicago Bulls (code = CHI), print the team ID, player's full name, position, and salary.

5. For all guards (code = G) earning under $500,000, print the team ID, player's full name, salary, and position.

6. For all guards (code = G) or any player earning under $500,000, print the team ID, player's full name, salary, and position.

7. Two percent of each player's salary is contributed to the NBA pension fund. Calculate each player's contribution. Output team, last name, salary, and pension fund contribution.

8. Calculate the average salaries paid to all players in the database. Print the average. How many earn more than the average salary?

9. Group the records in the NBA database by position and print a report similar to the one illustrated in Figure 4-46.

Position	Average Salary
C	
F	
G	

Figure 4-46

5. Off-Campus Housing at Ashland University

Activate the HOUSING catalog and open the database file HOUSING.DBF.

Use the Query Design screen to build each query and then use Quick Report to print the results. You decide on the appropriate fields to include in the output.

1. Include all housing units.

2. Include all housing units in Narragansett.

3. Include all housing units with a monthly rental below $600.

4. Include all housing units with a monthly rental below $500 in Narragansett.

5. Include all housing units with 3 or 4 bedrooms.

6. Include all housing units that are furnished apartments and cost under $550.

7. Use aggregate operators to output a report similar to the one in Figure 4-47.

House Type	Number of Units	Average Rent
A		
H		

Figure 4-47

Tutorial 5

More Querying the Database

Case: Wells & Martinez — Sorting the JOBS File

The next day Esther arrives at work to find another note from Nancy on her desk. Nancy wants to know the status of all the jobs in the database, in other words, which jobs are in process and which have been completed. Esther realizes that if she simply lists the JOBS file, she can easily provide this information to Nancy. She quickly lists the file to the printer and takes the printout to Nancy's office (Figure 5-1 on the next page).

As Nancy looks over the list, she shakes her head and apologizes for not making her needs clear. She explains to Esther that she wants the list to help her determine how many jobs W&M has completed for each client and how many jobs are in process for each client. Thus, Nancy says, this list would be more helpful if the jobs are arranged by client. Esther tells her not to worry — she can quickly and easily produce the list Nancy wants by sorting the data.

Nancy asks Esther if she would also be able to produce two more lists: one showing all jobs grouped by client and arranged by quote from highest to lowest, and one showing jobs arranged by status (completed or in process) and within status arranged by client.

OBJECTIVES:

In this tutorial you will learn to:

- Sort a database file

- Sort using primary and secondary sort keys

- Index a database file

- Create an index using multiple fields

- Search a database file using an index

- Link database files

Record#	JOBNUM	CLIENT_ID	JOB_DESCR	DUE_DATE	QUOTE	STATUS
1	1001	ORI	Best in the Southwest	08/15/93	2500	C
2	1002	VIK	Fall TV Ad	08/10/93	32500	C
3	1003	MOU	Ski equipment sale	06/01/93	3000	C
4	1004	ALE	B/W Magazine Ad	06/05/93	3500	C
5	1005	SAN	Magazine Ad	06/10/93	22500	C
6	1006	ORI	Fall Promotion	08/01/93	2200	C
7	1007	SAN	Pamphlet	08/02/93	3000	C
8	1008	VIK	Thanksgiving Promo	11/15/93	12000	I
9	1009	FAT	Bicycle Magazine Ad	08/05/93	2500	C
10	1010	ALE	Brochure	10/10/93	6000	I
11	1011	IMA	Fall Catalogue	08/22/93	8450	C
12	1012	ALE	Radio Ad	09/01/93	3425	I
13	1013	SAN	Direct Mail	10/15/93	8900	I
14	1014	FAT	Direct Mail	11/20/93	2200	I
15	1015	SAN	Brochure	09/15/93	4400	I
16	1016	IMA	Magazine Ad	10/15/93	10000	I
17	1017	CEL	Flyer	09/20/93	850	I
18	1018	VIK	TV ads	01/15/94	35700	I
19	1019	SAN	Festival campaign	09/12/93	8900	I
20	1020	FAT	Mail order catalogue	10/10/93	9400	I
21	1021	ALE	B/W magazine ad	11/10/93	6600	I
22	1022	MAM	Newspaper ad	12/01/93	5300	I
23	1023	TAC	TV ad	12/15/93	14000	I
24	1024	PEA	Brochure	11/30/93	11000	I

Figure 5-1
Esther's printout of
the JOBS file

Introduction to Sorting

You can rearrange data in a specific order through a process called **sorting**. As Nancy knows, records arranged in a particular order can make a report more meaningful.

To sort a file, you first must identify the **sort key**, which is the field that will be used to order the records in the file. For example, Esther wants to sort the JOBS file by client; thus, CLIENT_ID will be the sort key. If she wanted to sort the file by due date, then DUE_DATE would be the sort key. Sort keys can be numeric, character, or date fields.

You sort records in either ascending or descending order. Ascending means increasing order, and descending means decreasing order. For example, if you sort the JOBS database file in ascending order by job number, the record with the lowest job number will be the first record in the sorted file. The record with the highest job number will be the last record. When the sort key is a character field, ascending order means A through Z, and descending means Z through A. For example, if you sort the JOBS file in ascending order by client ID, the records in the sort file will be in alphabetical order, A to Z. When the sort key is a field that is defined with a date data type, ascending means earliest date to latest date, and descending means latest date to earliest date.

Sort keys can be unique or nonunique. Sort keys are **unique** if the value of the sort key field for each record is different. For example, the job numbers you use in the JOBS file are unique sort keys because each job has a different job number. Sort keys are **nonunique** if more than one record can have the same value in the sort key field. For example, the client ID in the JOBS file is nonunique because the same client can have more than one job.

When you use a nonunique sort key, dBASE groups together all records with the same value and lists the groups in either ascending or descending order. Within a group the records can be in any order. As Figure 5-2 shows, if you sorted the JOBS file by client ID, all records for Alexander's Insurance Company (ALE) would be listed before all job records for Celebrity Catering (CEL), which would be listed before all job records for Fat Wheels Bicycle Tours (FAT), and so on.

JOBNUM	CLIENT_ID	JOB_DESCR	DUE_DATE	QUOTE	STATUS
1004	ALE	B/W Magazine Ad	06/05/93	3500	C
1010	ALE	Brochure	10/10/93	6000	I
1012	ALE	Radio Ad	09/01/93	3425	I
1021	ALE	B/W magazine ad	11/10/93	6600	I
1017	CEL	Flyer	09/20/93	850	I
1009	FAT	Bicycle Magazine Ad	08/05/93	2500	C
1014	FAT	Direct Mail	11/20/93	2200	I
1020	FAT	Mail order catalogue	10/10/93	9400	I
1011	IMA	Fall Catalogue	08/22/93	8450	C
1016	IMA	Magazine Ad	10/15/93	10000	I
1022	MAM	Newspaper ad	12/01/93	5300	I
1003	MOU	Ski equipment sale	06/01/93	3000	C
1001	ORI	Best in the Southwest	08/15/93	2500	C
1006	ORI	Fall Promotion	08/01/93	2200	C
1024	PEA	Brochure	11/30/93	11000	I
1005	SAN	Magazine Ad	06/10/93	22500	C
1007	SAN	Pamphlet	08/02/93	3000	C
1013	SAN	Direct Mail	10/15/93	8900	I
1015	SAN	Brochure	09/15/93	4400	I
1019	SAN	Festival campaign	09/12/93	8900	I
1023	TAC	TV ad	12/15/93	14000	I
1002	VIK	Fall TV Ad	08/10/93	32500	C
1008	VIK	Thanksgiving Promo	11/15/93	12000	I
1018	VIK	TV ads	01/15/94	35700	I

Figure 5-2
JOBS file sorted by client ID

To arrange the records in each group in a certain sequence, you must specify a second sort key field. For example, you could arrange the jobs in alphabetical order by client ID and then for each client ID in descending order by quote. In that case, you would use two sort keys to sort the JOBS file: a primary sort key (CLIENT_ID) and a secondary sort key (QUOTE). The result of such a sort would look like Figure 5-3 on the next page.

JOBNUM	CLIENT_ID	JOB_DESCR	DUE_DATE	QUOTE	STATUS
1021	ALE	B/W magazine ad	11/10/93	6600	I
1010	ALE	Brochure	10/10/93	6000	I
1004	ALE	B/W Magazine Ad	06/05/93	3500	C
1012	ALE	Radio Ad	09/01/93	3425	I
1017	CEL	Flyer	09/20/93	850	I
1020	FAT	Mail order catalogue	10/10/93	9400	I
1009	FAT	Bicycle Magazine Ad	08/05/93	2500	C
1014	FAT	Direct Mail	11/20/93	2200	I
1016	IMA	Magazine Ad	10/15/93	10000	I
1011	IMA	Fall Catalogue	08/22/93	8450	C
1022	MAM	Newspaper ad	12/01/93	5300	I
1003	MOU	Ski equipment sale	06/01/93	3000	C
1001	ORI	Best in the Southwest	08/15/93	2500	C
1006	ORI	Fall Promotion	08/01/93	2200	C
1024	PEA	Brochure	11/30/93	11000	I
1005	SAN	Magazine Ad	06/10/93	22500	C
1013	SAN	Direct Mail	10/15/93	8900	I
1019	SAN	Festival campaign	09/12/93	8900	I
1015	SAN	Brochure	09/15/93	4400	I
1007	SAN	Pamphlet	08/02/93	3000	C
1023	TAC	TV ad	12/15/93	14000	I
1018	VIK	TV ads	01/15/94	35700	I
1002	VIK	Fall TV Ad	08/10/93	32500	C
1008	VIK	Thanksgiving Promo	11/15/93	12000	I

Figure 5-3
JOBS file sorted by
client ID and within
client ID by quote

Arranging the Database through Sorting

Esther needs to redo the job status listing for Nancy. This time she will sort the jobs by client ID before processing the listing.

Esther plans to reorder the database through a sorting operation available from the Organize menu. But first the file must be open. So load dBASE, change the default drive, and activate the W&M catalog.

When you sort a database field using the Organize menu while in the Edit or Browse screen, dBASE copies records from the currently open database file to a new database file. The records in the new file are physically rearranged according to the primary sort key field. The only difference between the two files is that the records are arranged in a different sequence.

To sort the database file:

❶ Highlight JOBS in the Data panel.

❷ Press **[F2]** (Data). The data are arranged in the order you entered the jobs.

❸ Press **[Alt]O** to open the Organize menu.

④ Select *Sort database on field list* (**S**).

⑤ Press **[Shift][F1]** (Pick) to access a list of possible field names. See Figure 5-4.

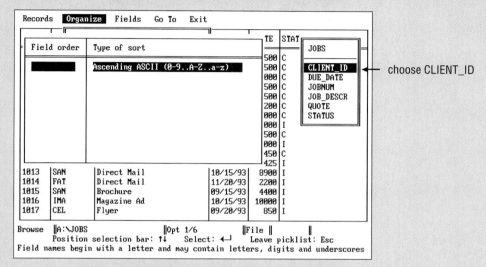

choose CLIENT_ID

Figure 5-4
Field name options
on which to sort

Highlight the name of the field you want to sort on.

⑥ Highlight CLIENT_ID and press **[Enter]**. CLIENT_ID appears in the first row of the *Field order* column.

⑦ Press **[Enter]** to move the cursor to the *Type of sort* column.

Choose the order of the sort.

⑧ Press **[Enter]** to accept the option *Ascending ASCII* as the sort order.

Now indicate you are ready to sort the database.

⑨ Press **[Ctrl][End]**. You are prompted for the name of the sorted file. Type **srt1jobs** and press **[Enter]**. A message appears briefly on the screen that says "Sort to a:\srt1jobs.dbf on client_id. 100% sorted 24 records sorted." When the sorting is complete, you are prompted "Edit the description of this .dbf file."

⑩ Press **[Enter]**. You are returned to the Browse screen.

Dot Prompt

To sort a database:

SORT ON *fieldname* /D TO *new filename*

Creates a new database file in which the records of the active database file are placed in alphabetical, chronological, or numerical order

Example .USE jobs
.SORT ON client_id TO srt1jobs

The sort operation does not automatically display the contents of the sorted file on the screen. The JOBS file is still open and its contents are displayed on the Browse screen in *natural* order, that is, the order in which they were entered into the database.

What has happened? dBASE has physically arranged each record by client ID and stored the results in a separate file. Figure 5-5a shows your data diskette after you opened the JOBS file, but before you issued the SORT command.

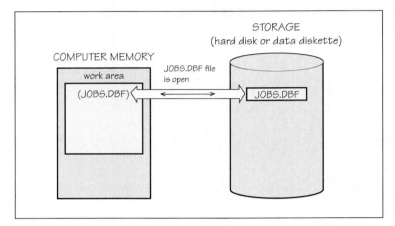

Figure 5-5a
Before sort on
CLIENT_ID

Figure 5-5b shows the contents of your data diskette after the sort. You now have a new database file on your data diskette named SRT1JOBS.DBF, which is the same as JOBS.DBF except that the records are sorted by client ID.

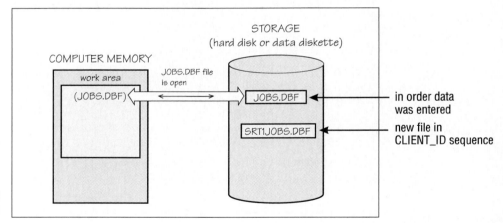

Figure 5-5b
After sort on CLIENT_ID

Let's view the sorted file. To view the sorted file, you must first open the SRT1JOBS file.

To view the jobs sorted by client ID:

❶ Press **[Esc]** to return to the Control Center.

❷ Highlight the SRT1JOBS database file and press **[F2]** (Data) to view the sorted results. The contents of the SRT1JOBS database file are displayed on the Browse screen in ascending order by CLIENT_ID. See Figure 5-6.

```
 Records   Organize   Fields   Go To   Exit

 JOBNUM CLIENT_ID JOB_DESCR              DUE_DATE QUOTE  STATUS

 1012   ALE       Radio Ad               09/01/93  3425  I
 1010   ALE       Brochure               10/10/93  6000  I
 1004   ALE       B/W Magazine Ad        06/05/93  3500  C
 1021   ALE       B/W magazine ad        11/10/93  6600  I
 1017   CEL       Flyer                  09/20/93   850  I
 1020   FAT       Mail order catalogue   10/10/93  9400  I
 1014   FAT       Direct Mail            11/20/93  2200  I
 1009   FAT       Bicycle Magazine Ad    08/05/93  2500  C
 1011   IMA       Fall Catalogue         08/22/93  8450  C
 1016   IMA       Magazine Ad            10/15/93 10000  I
 1022   MAM       Newspaper ad           12/01/93  5300  I
 1003   MOU       Ski equipment sale     06/01/93  3000  C
 1006   ORI       Fall Promotion         08/01/93  2200  C
 1001   ORI       Best in the Southwest  08/15/93  2500  C
 1024   PEA       Brochure               11/30/93 11000  I
 1015   SAN       Brochure               09/15/93  4400  I
 1007   SAN       Pamphlet               08/02/93  3000  C

 Browse   ||A:\SRT1JOBS         ||Rec 1/24      ||File ||        ||
```

Figure 5-6
SRT1JOBS file
sorted by
CLIENT_ID

Figure 5-7 shows a diagram of how the dBASE work area and data diskette now look. The arrow between the work area and the database file, SRT1JOBS, on the data diskette indicates SRT1JOBS is now open. You can also see that there is no arrow between the work area and the JOBS database file, which was automatically closed when SRT1JOBS.DBF was opened.

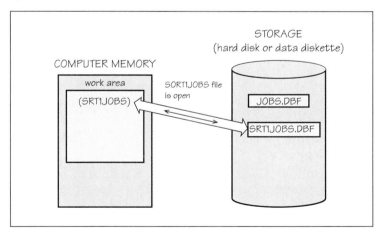

Figure 5-7
After SRT1JOBS
file is opened

Esther needs to print this report for Nancy. Remember, check with your instructor before printing.

To print a Quick Report and return to the Control Center:

❶ Print a Quick Report if requested to do so by your instructor.

❷ Press **[Esc]** to return to the Control Center.

Before continuing, let's close the file SRT1JOBS.

To close the database file:

❶ With the cursor on SRT1JOBS, press **[Enter]**. A prompt box appears.

❷ Select *Close file* (**C**). The file SRT1JOBS.DBF is closed, and SRT1JOBS appears below the panel line in the Control Center.

Sorting Using the Query Design Screen

Nancy's second request is for a list of all W&M's jobs grouped by client and sorted by quote from highest to lowest. As Esther prepares to sort the JOBS file again, she realizes that every time she uses the Organize menu to create and save a new sorted file, she uses more space on her disk. She remembers that she can also use the Query Design screen to accomplish the same results as using the Organize menu to create a new, sorted database file, opening the sorted file, and displaying the data. In other words, the results of queries can be sorted. Esther decides to sort the JOBS file again, this time using the Query Design screen.

Since you want all the records to be included in your output, you don't need to include a filter condition in the query. Before you process the query, you will tell dBASE you want the records arranged alphabetically by client ID. CLIENT_ID is the sort key, and the sort order is ascending.

Let's sort the job status listing using the Query Design screen.

To sort the database file using the Query Design screen:

❶ Open the database file JOBS.

❷ Highlight <create> in the Queries panel and press **[Enter]**. The Query Design screen appears.

❸ While in the file skeleton, move the highlight to the field you want to sort on, the CLIENT_ID field.

Select the Fields menu.

❹ Press **[Alt]F** to open the Fields menu. See Figure 5-8.

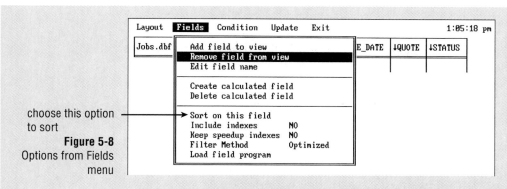

choose this option
to sort

Figure 5-8
Options from Fields
menu

⑤ Select the option *Sort on this field* (**S**). A submenu for defining the sort order appears. See Figure 5-9.

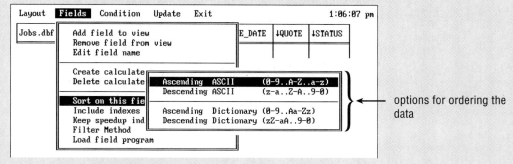

options for ordering the data

Figure 5-9
Different sort orders

Choose the sort order.

⑥ With the highlight on the option *Ascending ASCII*, press **[Enter]**. The entry Asc1 appears in the CLIENT_ID field of the file skeleton. See Figure 5-10.

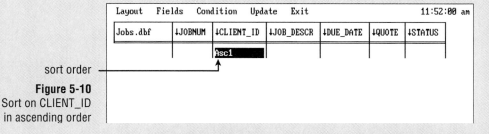

sort order

Figure 5-10
Sort on CLIENT_ID
in ascending order

Alternatively you can type the entry Asc1 directly in the file skeleton.

Now let's see the results.

To process the query:

❶ Press **[F2]** (Data). A list of all jobs ordered by CLIENT_ID appears in the Browse screen. See Figure 5-11 on the next page.

```
 Records   Organize   Fields   Go To   Exit

 JOBNUM CLIENT_ID JOB_DESCR            DUE_DATE QUOTE STATUS

 1004   ALE       B/W Magazine Ad      06/05/93  3500 C
 1010   ALE       Brochure             10/10/93  6000 I
 1012   ALE       Radio Ad             09/01/93  3425 I
 1021   ALE       B/W magazine ad      11/10/93  6600 I
 1017   CEL       Flyer                09/20/93   850 I
 1009   FAT       Bicycle Magazine Ad  08/05/93  2500 C
 1014   FAT       Direct Mail          11/20/93  2200 I
 1020   FAT       Mail order catalogue 10/10/93  9400 I
 1011   IMA       Fall Catalogue       08/22/93  8450 C
 1016   IMA       Magazine Ad          10/15/93 10000 I
 1022   MAM       Newspaper ad         12/01/93  5300 I
 1003   MOU       Ski equipment sale   06/01/93  3000 C
 1001   ORI       Best in the Southwest 08/15/93 2500 C
 1006   ORI       Fall Promotion       08/01/93  2200 C
 1024   PEA       Brochure             11/30/93 11000 I
 1005   SAN       Magazine Ad          06/10/93 22500 C
 1007   SAN       Pamphlet             08/02/93  3000 C

 Browse  ||A:\<NEW>            ||Rec 4/24      ||View ||        ||
```

Figure 5-11
JOBS file sorted
on CLIENT_ID in
ascending order

❷ When you have finished looking over the report, press **[Shift][F2]** (Design) to return to the Query Design screen.

When you view or print a query that contains the sort operator, dBASE sorts the records and saves them to a temporary database file. This temporary file is used by dBASE to output the results you see on the screen or in a hard copy. When the processing of the query is complete, dBASE automatically erases the temporary database file.

Why use the Query Design screen to sort? One major benefit is the ability to include filter conditions in the file skeleton along with the sort operator. Thus, you can obtain sorted output for any query.

Using Primary and Secondary Sort Keys

Nancy wants to see a list of all jobs grouped by client and for each client sorted by quote, with the highest quote first. Esther needs to rearrange the JOBS database file so that the jobs for each client are grouped together, then within each group the jobs are arranged by highest quote to lowest. This type of sort requires a primary and a secondary sort key. The primary key is arranged in ascending order, the secondary key in descending order.

The order in which you specify the sort key fields is important. The first field name specified is the **primary sort key**, and the second field is the **secondary sort key**.

Let's sort the database file again. Before you enter the new sort information, don't forget to remove the previous information in the Query Design screen.

Now sort the file. Because we want to sort by client and within client by quote, CLIENT_ID is the primary sort key and QUOTE is the secondary sort key.

To sort the database file using primary and secondary sort keys:

❶ Remove the existing information from the Query Design screen.

❷ With the highlight on the CLIENT_ID field, press **[Alt]F** to open the Fields menu.

❸ Select the option *Sort on this field* (**S**).

Choose the sort order.

❹ Move the highlight to the option *Ascending ASCII* and press **[Enter]**. The entry Asc2 appears in the CLIENT_ID field of the file skeleton.

Now select the secondary sort key.

❺ Move the highlight to the QUOTE field.

❻ Press **[Alt]F** to open the Fields menu.

❼ Select the option *Sort on this field* (**S**).

Choose the sort order.

❽ Move the highlight to the option *Descending ASCII*, press **[Enter]**. The entry Dsc3 appears in the QUOTE field of the file skeleton. See Figure 5-12.

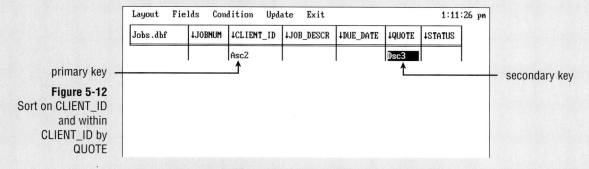

primary key

Figure 5-12
Sort on CLIENT_ID
and within
CLIENT_ID by
QUOTE

secondary key

As you define additional sort keys, dBASE assigns a number to each sort key in the file skeleton. The lowest number indicates the primary key, the next lowest is the secondary key, and so on.

Now process the query.

To process the query:

❶ Press **[F2]** (Data). See Figure 5-13 on the next page. A list of all jobs appears in the Browse screen. This time the data are arranged by CLIENT_ID and within CLIENT_ID by QUOTE, with the highest quote first.

Esther needs to print this report for Nancy.

❷ Print a Quick Report.

```
  Records   Organize   Fields   Go To   Exit

 ┌─────────┬──────────┬─────────────────────┬──────────┬───────┬────────┐
 │ JOBNUM  │ CLIENT_ID│ JOB_DESCR           │ DUE_DATE │ QUOTE │ STATUS │
 ├─────────┼──────────┼─────────────────────┼──────────┼───────┼────────┤
 │ 1021    │ ALE      │ B/W magazine ad     │ 11/10/93 │  6600 │ I      │
 │ 1010    │ ALE      │ Brochure            │ 10/10/93 │  6000 │ I      │
 │ 1004    │ ALE      │ B/W Magazine Ad     │ 06/05/93 │  3500 │ C      │
 │ 1012    │ ALE      │ Radio Ad            │ 09/01/93 │  3425 │ I      │
 │ 1017    │ CEL      │ Flyer               │ 09/20/93 │   850 │ I      │
 │ 1020    │ FAT      │ Mail order catalogue│ 10/10/93 │  9400 │ I      │
 │ 1009    │ FAT      │ Bicycle Magazine Ad │ 08/05/93 │  2500 │ C      │
 │ 1014    │ FAT      │ Direct Mail         │ 11/20/93 │  2200 │ I      │
 │ 1016    │ IMA      │ Magazine Ad         │ 10/15/93 │ 10000 │ I      │
 │ 1011    │ IMA      │ Fall Catalogue      │ 08/22/93 │  8450 │ C      │
 │ 1022    │ MAM      │ Newspaper ad        │ 12/01/93 │  5300 │ I      │
 │ 1003    │ MOU      │ Ski equipment sale  │ 06/01/93 │  3000 │ C      │
 │ 1001    │ ORI      │ Best in the Southwest│ 08/15/93 │  2500 │ C      │
 │ 1006    │ ORI      │ Fall Promotion      │ 08/01/93 │  2200 │ C      │
 │ 1024    │ PEA      │ Brochure            │ 11/30/93 │ 11000 │ I      │
 │ 1005    │ SAN      │ Magazine Ad         │ 06/10/93 │ 22500 │ C      │
 │ 1013    │ SAN      │ Direct Mail         │ 10/15/93 │  8900 │ I      │
 └─────────┴──────────┴─────────────────────┴──────────┴───────┴────────┘

  Browse  ‖A:\<NEW>‖              ‖Rec 1/24‖        ‖View ‖ReadOnly‖
```

Figure 5-13
JOBS file sorted
by CLIENT_ID
and within
CLIENT_ID by
QUOTE

Now return to the Control Center.

To return to the Control Center:

❶ Press **[Alt]E** to open the Exit menu.

❷ Select *Exit* (**E**) and select *no* (**N**) when prompted about saving the query.

Case: Wells & Martinez — Indexing the JOBS File

Martin calls Esther into his office. He is very excited about a new job he has landed, and he gives Esther a completed job authorization form. Mountain Top Ski, he announces, has decided to advertise their annual Christmas Weekend Getaway by having W&M launch a big ad campaign in the Sunday newspaper.

As Esther leaves his office, Martin asks her to enter the data from the job authorization form and then print a listing of all jobs by due date so he can include this new job in the work schedule.

Esther realizes that every time she adds a record to the JOBS file, such as for the new Mountain Top Ski job, the data in SRT1JOBS.DBF are no longer consistent with the data in the JOBS file. She would have to sort the JOBS file again before she could print the data; otherwise, the output would not be current. In addition, sorting requires a lot of disk space. A file equal to the size of the original file is created for each sort that uses a different sort key. Esther thinks about an alternative approach. She recalls that indexing saves disk space, requires less time to maintain, and is more flexible. She decides to use indexing with the JOBS file.

Introduction to Indexing

dBASE provides two methods for organizing data in your database file: sorting and indexing. Although both methods order the records in your database, the way dBASE goes about getting the end result for sorting is different than for indexing.

For example, when you used the Organize menu to sort the records in the JOBS file, the records were physically rearranged and stored in a second file. This second file was used to display your sorted results. When you use indexing to order the database, you do not physically rearrange the data in the database file. Instead, you create *another* file, called an **index file**, that controls the sequence in which the records in the database file are processed. Let's explore the concept of indexes.

In some ways an index file is similar to the index in a book. An index in a book is a list of items included in that book. It lists the items in alphabetical order and for each item includes the page number(s) where reference to that item can be found. In dBASE an index file contains a list of items found in another place, a database file. For each record in the database file, the index file stores a record with two fields: an indexing field and a location field. The **index key** or the **indexing field** stores the value of the field you want the database ordered by. The **location field** stores the record number of the record in the database file, thus serving as a "pointer" to the records in the database file.

When dBASE indexes a file, it arranges the records in the index file in a particular order based on the values in the indexing field. Thus, dBASE "sorts" the index file rather than the database file. To arrange the data in the sequence you want, dBASE scans the index file using the pointers in the index file to access records in the database file. Thus, when you look at the data in a file using an index, the records are displayed in the order of the index. You can index any field, and you can have several indexes related to one database file.

Figure 5-14 illustrates the relationship between a database file and an index file. This figure shows the JOBS database file and an index file that uses CLIENT_ID as the indexing field. Notice that the index file is a separate file, ordered alphabetically by client ID, that has one record for each database record. Each record in the index file "points" to one database record. When dBASE uses this index file to order the records in the database file JOBS, it scans the index file from top to bottom. In this case the first record in the index file, "ALE 4," results in record 4 from the database file JOBS being displayed first. The second record in the index file, "ALE 10," results in record 10 from JOBS being displayed second and so on. Thus, dBASE displays the jobs alphabetically by client ID without sorting the file.

Why use an index? Why not just sort? Indexing offers four advantages over sorting. First, indexing is more flexible, because a separate index is created for each field you want to sort. Thus, by maintaining several indexes at one time, you can process the database in a number of different ways without having to sort each time. Second, you can speed up database searches using indexes to look for data instead of searching through every record in the database. Third, when records are added to a database file that has been indexed, even new records will appear in the correct position when the database is displayed. If you add new records to a sorted file, these new records appear at the end of the listing when the database is displayed; the file is no longer in "sorted" order. In addition, the new records are not

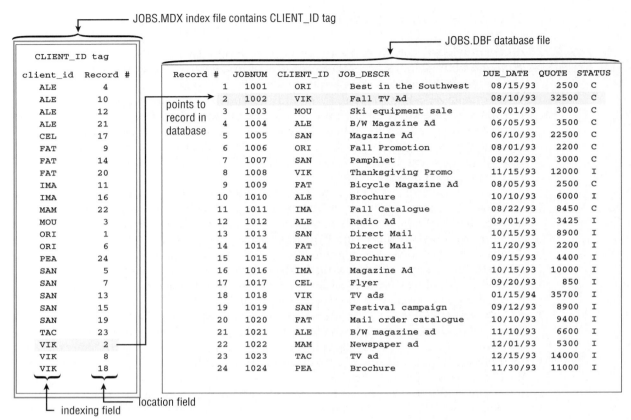

Figure 5-14
Relationship between an index file and a database file

automatically added to the original file, so the original file is not current. And fourth, sorting creates duplicate copies of the database file, which requires more disk space.

Now that you know some of the basic requirements and uses of indexing, let's learn how to create an index file.

Creating an Index on a Single Field

Esther decides to index the JOBS file on the client ID. Before you create the index, let's see how the data are displayed without an index.

To view the JOBS database without opening an index:

❶ Highlight JOBS in the Data panel.

Let's observe the order in which the database is currently displayed.

❷ Press **[F2]** (Data). Since there is no index controlling how the database is ordered, the data appear in the natural order. If you wanted to see the sorted data, you would have to open the sorted file, SRT1JOBS, or process a query.

❸ Press **[Esc]** to return to the Control Center.

Now create an index using CLIENT_ID as the index key. To create an index, you must give the index a name, sometimes referred to as an **index tag**. You also must specify **the index key**, that is, how you want the index ordered.

To create an index:

❶ Press **[Shift][F2]** (Design). The Database Design screen appears with the Organize menu open.

❷ Select *Create new index* (**C**). A prompt box appears. See Figure 5-15. You will use this box to enter the index name and the index key.

Figure 5-15
Defining an index

Now enter the index name.

❸ With the option *Name of index* highlighted, press **[Enter]** to open this area. The curly braces disappear.

Typically the field name is used as the name of the index.

❹ Type **client_id** and press **[Enter]**. The highlight moves to the *Index expression* option.

Now enter the index expression, that is, the index key. This entry determines the "sort" order.

❺ Press **[Enter]** to open this area. Type **client_id**. See Figure 5-16 on the next page.

❻ Press **[Enter]** to finish creating the index.

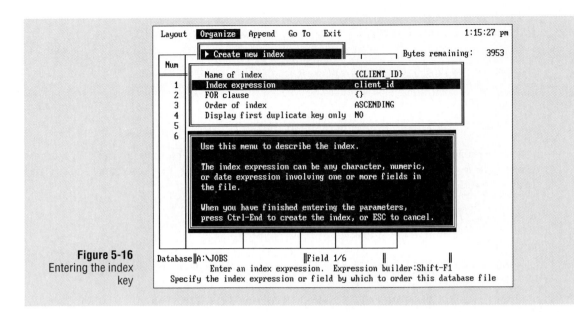

Figure 5-16
Entering the index
key

That's all the information required to create an index. The other choices are optional. Since the desired sort order is ascending and the default order is ascending, you have completed the definition of the index. To order the index in descending order, you press [spacebar] to switch between Ascending and Descending sort order.

Now save the index.

To save the index:

❶ Press **[Ctrl][End]**. A message appears briefly on the screen that says "INDEX ON client_id TAG CLIENT_ID 100% indexed 24 records indexed," then the Database Design screen appears.

dBASE saves the index in an index file called JOBS.MDX on your data diskette. dBASE uses the same name as the database file and automatically adds the extension MDX. MDX stands for *multiple index file*. Each index file can store up to 47 different indexes.

After the index file has been created, the Database Design screen appears. Notice that the option in the Index column for CLIENT_ID has changed from N (no) to Y (yes) because the CLIENT_ID field is now indexed. See Figure 5-17.

Figure 5-17
Database Design
screen after index
created

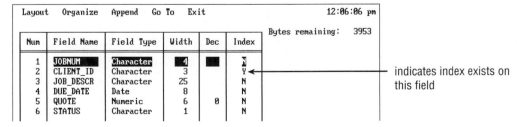

indicates index exists on
this field

Dot Prompt

To create an index:

INDEX ON *key expression* TAG *tag name*   DESCENDING

Creates an index in which records from a database file are ordered alphabetically, chronologically, or numerically

Example .USE client
.INDEX ON client_id TAG client_id

Figure 5-18 illustrates the files on your data diskette after the index file has been saved. The file JOBS.MDX contains only one index (CLIENT_ID) right now; if you created more indexes, they also would be saved in the JOBS.MDX file.

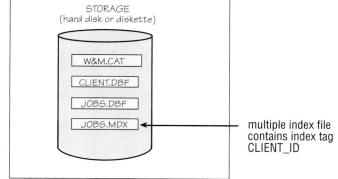

Figure 5-18
Index saved in
JOBS.MDX file

You can now use the index file to display or edit records in "sorted" order.

To view the data:

❶ Press **[F2]** (Data) to look at the data. See Figure 5-19 on the next page. Notice that the records are not displayed in natural order. The records are arranged alphabetically by client ID.

The index controls the order in which records are displayed. Remember, the index does not actually rearrange the records in the database file; it only controls the order in which they are displayed.

```
Records   Organize   Fields   Go To   Exit

JOBNUM  CLIENT_ID  JOB_DESCR              DUE_DATE  QUOTE  STATUS

1004    ALE        B/W Magazine Ad        06/05/93   3500  C
1010    ALE        Brochure               10/10/93   6000  I
1012    ALE        Radio Ad               09/01/93   3425  I
1021    ALE        B/W magazine ad        11/10/93   6600  I
1017    CEL        Flyer                  09/20/93    850  I
1009    FAT        Bicycle Magazine Ad    08/05/93   2500  I
1014    FAT        Direct Mail            11/20/93   2200  I
1020    FAT        Mail order catalogue   10/10/93   9400  I
1011    IMA        Fall Catalogue         08/22/93   8450  C
1016    IMA        Magazine Ad            10/15/93  10000  I
1022    MAM        Newspaper ad           12/01/93   5300  I
1003    MOU        Ski equipment sale     06/01/93   3000  C
1001    ORI        Best in the Southwest  08/15/93   2500  C
1006    ORI        Fall Promotion         08/01/93   2200  C
1024    PEA        Brochure               11/30/93  11000  I
1005    SAN        Magazine Ad            06/10/93  22500  C
1007    SAN        Pamphlet               08/02/93   3000  C

Browse   ||A:\JOBS              ||Rec 4/24        ||File ||         ||
```

Figure 5-19
Displaying the indexed file ordered by CLIENT_ID

❷ Press **[Esc]** to return to the Control Center.

Creating a Second Index

Martin wants a list of W&M's jobs ordered by due date. In a typical situation databases are indexed on several different fields. That's the case with W&M's database. Sometimes Esther processes the records in the JOBS database file by client ID, at other times by due date, and at other times by client ID and within client ID by due date. Esther needs to create a second index named DUE_DATE using the due date as the index key.

To create a second index:
❶ With the highlight on the open JOBS database file in the Control Center, press **[Shift][F2]** (Design). The Database Design screen appears with the Organize menu open.

②   Select *Create new index* (**C**). A prompt box appears.

③   With the option *Name of index* highlighted, press **[Enter]** to open this area.

Enter the name of the index, that is, the index tag.

④   Type **due_date** and press **[Enter]**. The highlight moves to the *Index expression* option.

Now enter the field the index is based on, that is, the index expression.

⑤   Press **[Enter]** to open this box. Type **due_date** and press **[Enter]**.

Now save the index.

To save the index:

①   Press **[Ctrl][End]**. A message appears briefly on the screen that says "INDEX ON due_date TAG DUE_DATE 100% indexed 24 records indexed."

After the due date index has been created, the Database Design screen appears. Notice that the option in the Index column for DUE_DATE has changed from N (no) to Y (yes) because the DUE_DATE field is now indexed.

dBASE adds the index, with the tag name DUE_DATE, to the multiple index file, JOBS.MDX, which is already on your data diskette. Figure 5-20a illustrates the updated file JOBS.MDX on your data diskette. Figure 5-20b illustrates the relationship between the multiple file index, JOBS.MDX, and the database file JOBS.DBF after the CLIENT_ID and DUE_DATE indexes have been created.

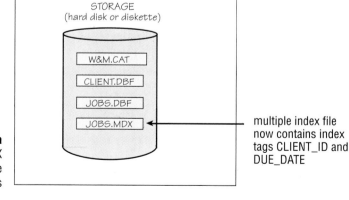

Figure 5-20a
JOBS.MDX
containing multiple
index files

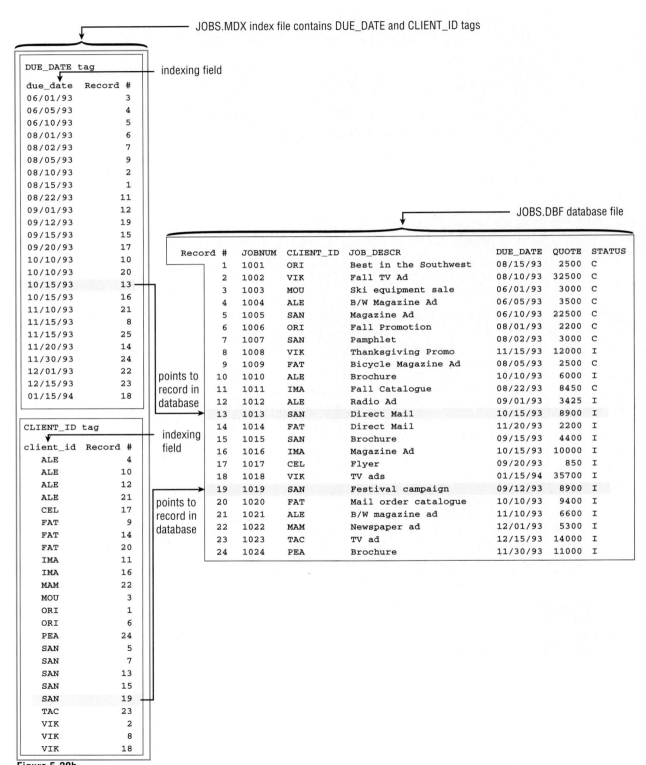

Figure 5-20b
Relationship between index files and database file

You can now use the index to display or edit records in sorted order by due date.

To view the data:

❶ Press [F2] (Data) to look at the data. See Figure 5-21. Because the DUE_DATE index is the active index, the records are now displayed in the order of their due dates.

JOBNUM	CLIENT_ID	JOB_DESCR	DUE_DATE	QUOTE	STATUS
1003	MOU	Ski equipment sale	06/01/93	3000	C
1004	ALE	B/W Magazine Ad	06/05/93	3500	C
1005	SAN	Magazine Ad	06/10/93	22500	C
1006	ORI	Fall Promotion	08/01/93	2200	C
1007	SAN	Pamphlet	08/02/93	3000	C
1009	FAT	Bicycle Magazine Ad	08/05/93	2500	C
1002	VIK	Fall TV Ad	08/10/93	32500	C
1001	ORI	Best in the Southwest	08/15/93	2500	C
1011	IMA	Fall Catalogue	08/22/93	8450	C
1012	ALE	Radio Ad	09/01/93	3425	I
1019	SAN	Festival campaign	09/12/93	8900	I
1015	SAN	Brochure	09/15/93	4400	I
1017	CEL	Flyer	09/20/93	850	I
1010	ALE	Brochure	10/10/93	6000	I
1020	FAT	Mail order catalogue	10/10/93	9400	I
1013	SAN	Direct Mail	10/15/93	8900	I
1016	IMA	Magazine Ad	10/15/93	10000	I

Records   Organize   Fields   Go To   Exit

Browse   ‖A:\JOBS   ‖Rec 3/24   ‖File ‖   ‖

Figure 5-21
Displaying an indexed file ordered by due date

❷ Press [Esc] to return to the Control Center.

Adding Records with Index Files

You will recall from Tutorial 3 that you use the Browse or Edit screen to add records to a database file. Esther now needs to enter the new Mountain Top Ski record to the JOBS file. She uses the job authorization form that Martin has filled out (Figure 5-22 on the next page).

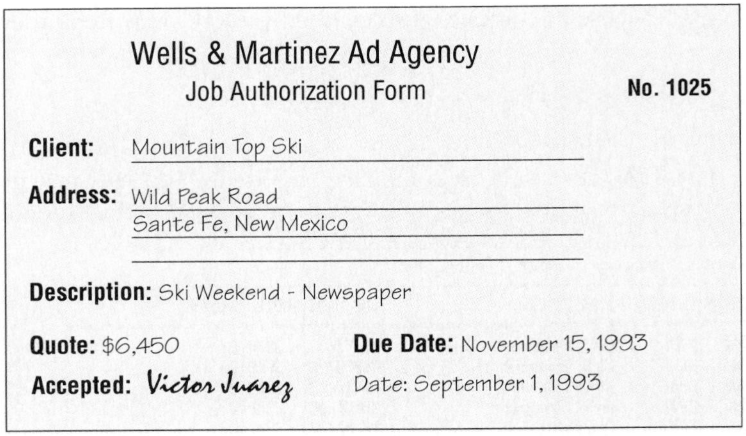

Wells & Martinez Ad Agency
Job Authorization Form   No. 1025

Client: Mountain Top Ski

Address: Wild Peak Road
Sante Fe, New Mexico

Description: Ski Weekend - Newspaper

Quote: $6,450   **Due Date:** November 15, 1993

Accepted: *Victor Juarez*   Date: September 1, 1993

Figure 5-22
Job authorization
for Mountain Top
Ski newspaper and
campaign

To add a new record to the JOBS database file:

❶ Press **[F2]**, open the Records menu, and select *Add new records* (**A**).

You can now enter data. As you have seen before, a blank row appears on the screen. Refer to Figure 5-22 to enter the data for the new Mountain Top Ski job. All index tags in the multiple index file are automatically updated whenever you add, change, or delete records.

After you have entered the data into the last field of the job record, a new blank row appears on your screen. You have no new records to enter, so you can leave the Browse or Edit screen by pressing [Esc] or by selecting the *Exit* option from the Exit menu. *Do not press [Ctrl][End] to leave the Browse screen after dBASE has moved to a blank row.* If you do, you will add a new blank record to the database file. dBASE saves the Mountain Top Ski record, the twenty-fifth record in the JOBS file. Notice that the status bar indicates a total of 25 records. Figure 5-23 shows the contents of the JOBS database file and the CLIENT_ID and DUE_DATE index tags after you have entered the new job record.

The last index activated stays in effect until you select another index or close the database file, so the file will be sorted by DUE_DATE. Esther needs to print a report listing jobs by due date. She can do this by using a Quick Report.

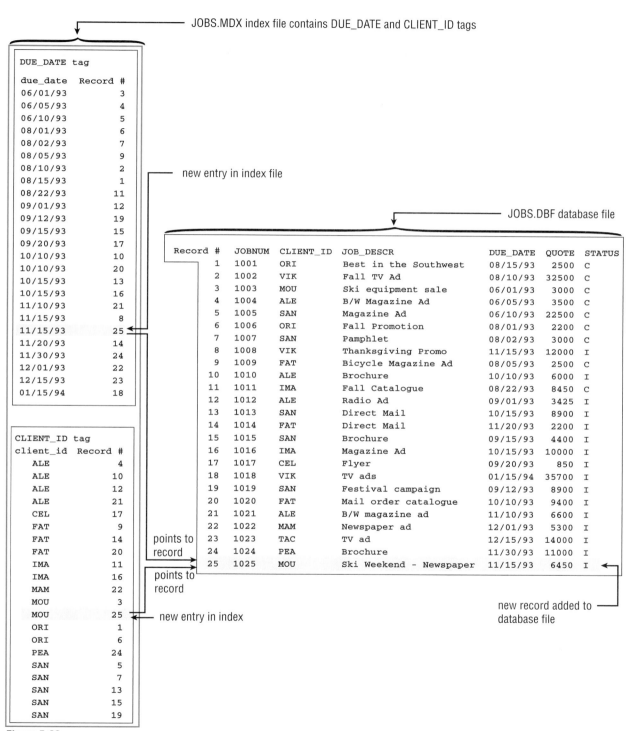

JOBS.MDX index file contains DUE_DATE and CLIENT_ID tags

DUE_DATE tag

due_date	Record #
06/01/93	3
06/05/93	4
06/10/93	5
08/01/93	6
08/02/93	7
08/05/93	9
08/10/93	2
08/15/93	1
08/22/93	11
09/01/93	12
09/12/93	19
09/15/93	15
09/20/93	17
10/10/93	10
10/10/93	20
10/15/93	13
10/15/93	16
11/10/93	21
11/15/93	8
11/15/93	25
11/20/93	14
11/30/93	24
12/01/93	22
12/15/93	23
01/15/94	18

new entry in index file

JOBS.DBF database file

Record #	JOBNUM	CLIENT_ID	JOB_DESCR	DUE_DATE	QUOTE	STATUS
1	1001	ORI	Best in the Southwest	08/15/93	2500	C
2	1002	VIK	Fall TV Ad	08/10/93	32500	C
3	1003	MOU	Ski equipment sale	06/01/93	3000	C
4	1004	ALE	B/W Magazine Ad	06/05/93	3500	C
5	1005	SAN	Magazine Ad	06/10/93	22500	C
6	1006	ORI	Fall Promotion	08/01/93	2200	C
7	1007	SAN	Pamphlet	08/02/93	3000	C
8	1008	VIK	Thanksgiving Promo	11/15/93	12000	I
9	1009	FAT	Bicycle Magazine Ad	08/05/93	2500	C
10	1010	ALE	Brochure	10/10/93	6000	I
11	1011	IMA	Fall Catalogue	08/22/93	8450	C
12	1012	ALE	Radio Ad	09/01/93	3425	I
13	1013	SAN	Direct Mail	10/15/93	8900	I
14	1014	FAT	Direct Mail	11/20/93	2200	I
15	1015	SAN	Brochure	09/15/93	4400	I
16	1016	IMA	Magazine Ad	10/15/93	10000	I
17	1017	CEL	Flyer	09/20/93	850	I
18	1018	VIK	TV ads	01/15/94	35700	I
19	1019	SAN	Festival campaign	09/12/93	8900	I
20	1020	FAT	Mail order catalogue	10/10/93	9400	I
21	1021	ALE	B/W magazine ad	11/10/93	6600	I
22	1022	MAM	Newspaper ad	12/01/93	5300	I
23	1023	TAC	TV ad	12/15/93	14000	I
24	1024	PEA	Brochure	11/30/93	11000	I
25	1025	MOU	Ski Weekend - Newspaper	11/15/93	6450	I

CLIENT_ID tag

client_id	Record #
ALE	4
ALE	10
ALE	12
ALE	21
CEL	17
FAT	9
FAT	14
FAT	20
IMA	11
IMA	16
MAM	22
MOU	3
MOU	25
ORI	1
ORI	6
PEA	24
SAN	5
SAN	7
SAN	13
SAN	15
SAN	19

points to record

points to record

new entry in index

new record added to database file

Figure 5-23
Contents of indexes and database file after new record is added to JOBS file

To print the contents of the JOBS file:

❶ Press **[Shift][F9]** (Quick Report). See Figure 5-24.

```
Page No.    1
06/30/92


JOBNUM   CLIENT_ID   JOB_DESCR                   DUE_DATE        QUOTE   STATUS

1003     MOU         Ski equipment sale          06/01/93         3000   C
1004     ALE         B/W Magazine Ad             06/05/93         3500   C
1005     SAN         Magazine Ad                 06/10/93        22500   C
1006     ORI         Fall Promotion              08/01/93         2200   C
1007     SAN         Pamphlet                    08/02/93         3000   C
1009     FAT         Bicycle Magazine Ad         08/05/93         2500   C
1002     VIK         Fall TV Ad                  08/10/93        32500   C
1001     ORI         Best in the Southwest       08/15/93         2500   C
1011     IMA         Fall Catalogue              08/22/93         8450   C
1012     ALE         Radio Ad                    09/01/93         3425   I
1019     SAN         Festival campaign           09/12/93         8900   I
1015     SAN         Brochure                    09/15/93         4400   I
1017     CEL         Flyer                       09/20/93          850   I
1010     ALE         Brochure                    10/10/93         6000   I
1020     FAT         Mail order catalogue        10/10/93         9400   I
1013     SAN         Direct Mail                 10/15/93         8900   I
1016     IMA         Magazine Ad                 10/15/93        10000   I
1021     ALE         B/W magazine ad             11/10/93         6600   I
1008     VIK         Thanksgiving Promo          11/15/93        12000   I
1025     MOU         Ski weekend - Newspaper     11/15/93         6450   I
1014     FAT         Direct Mail                 11/20/93         2200   I
1024     PEA         Brochure                    11/30/93        11000   I
1022     MAM         Newspaper ad                12/01/93         5300   I
1023     TAC         TV ad                       12/15/93        14000   I
1018     VIK         TV ads                      01/15/94        35700   I
                                                                225275
```

new record ⟶ 1025

Figure 5-24
Listing of JOBS file
by due date

The listing includes the new record you added to the file (Figure 5-20). Notice that although the new Mountain Top Ski record is the last record in the database file, the new record is in the twentieth position in the printed report. This is because DUE_DATE is the active index.

Creating an Index on Multiple Fields

Esther returns to her office after giving Martin the report listing jobs by due date. Looking over her notes, she realizes that she still needs to work on Nancy's request for a list showing jobs arranged by status and within status by client. She decides to create a third index that arranges the jobs by status and within status by client ID.

Usually the index key is a single field. However, you can create an index by combining two or more fields. An index that combines two or more fields is a **multiple field index**. For example, to arrange records by job status and within STATUS by CLIENT_ID, you can build a multiple field index on STATUS and CLIENT_ID.

The steps you follow to create a multiple field index are similar to the ones for creating a single field index.

To create a multiple field index:

❶ With the highlight on the open JOBS database file in the Control Center, press **[Shift][F2]** (Design). The Database Design screen appears with the Organize menu open.

❷ Select *Create new index* (**C**). A prompt box appears.

❸ With the option *Name of index* highlighted, press **[Enter]** to open this area.

Enter the index tag. Name the index STATCLNT.

❹ Type **statclnt** and press **[Enter]**. The highlight moves to the *Index expression* option.

❺ Press **[Enter]** to open this area.

Now enter the index expression that the index is based on. You enter multiple fields separated by a plus sign. The plus sign is used to combine two or more character strings. This is known as *concatenation*.

❻ Type **status+client_id** and press **[Enter]**. The client ID is added to the status code to create the index expression.

When you create a multiple field index, you can combine character fields with character fields, but you cannot combine character fields with numeric or date fields. Thus, you cannot directly index multiple fields that are not the same data type. You can get around this problem by using special operators known as functions. For example, the function DTOS (date to string) temporarily converts the contents of a field storing date data into a field storing character data; the function STR (string) temporarily converts the contents of a field containing numeric data into a field containing character data.

Now save the index.

To save the index:

❶ Press **[Ctrl][End]**. A message appears briefly on the screen that says "INDEX ON STATUS+CLIENT_ID TAG STATCLNT 100% indexed 25 records indexed."

dBASE adds the index STATCLNT to JOBS.MDX on your data diskette. The index file JOBS.MDX now contains three indexes.

Now use the index to display or edit records in "sorted" order by job status and within job status by client ID.

To view the data:

❶ Press **[F2]** (Data) to look at the data. See Figure 5-25 on the next page. Notice that the order of the data has changed again. The records are now displayed by STATUS and within STATUS by CLIENT_ID.

```
 Records   Organize   Fields   Go To   Exit

 JOBNUM CLIENT_ID JOB_DESCR              DUE_DATE QUOTE  STATUS

 1004   ALE       B/W Magazine Ad        06/05/93  3500  C
 1009   FAT       Bicycle Magazine Ad    08/05/93  2500  C
 1011   IMA       Fall Catalogue         08/22/93  8450  C
 1003   MOU       Ski equipment sale     06/01/93  3000  C
 1001   ORI       Best in the Southwest  08/15/93  2500  C
 1006   ORI       Fall Promotion         08/01/93  2200  C
 1005   SAN       Magazine Ad            06/10/93 22500  C
 1007   SAN       Pamphlet               08/02/93  3000  C
 1002   VIK       Fall TV Ad             08/10/93 32500  C
 1010   ALE       Brochure               10/10/93  6000  I
 1012   ALE       Radio Ad               09/01/93  3425  I
 1021   ALE       B/W magazine ad        11/10/93  6600  I
 1017   CEL       Flyer                  09/20/93   850  I
 1014   FAT       Direct Mail            11/20/93  2200  I
 1020   FAT       Mail order catalogue   10/10/93  9400  I
 1016   IMA       Magazine Ad            10/15/93 10000  I
 1022   MAM       Newspaper ad           12/01/93  5300  I

 Browse   ║A:\JOBS            ║Rec 4/25       ║File ║         ║          Ins
```

Figure 5-25
Displaying an
indexed file
ordered by job
status and client ID

Esther prints the report for Nancy.

❷   Print a Quick Report.

❸   Press **[Esc]** to return to the Control Center.

Activating an Index

You now have three indexes in the index file JOBS.MDX. Currently STATCLNT is the active index. What if you wanted to look at the data ordered by client ID again? You can tell dBASE from the Organize menu to activate a different index. Let's activate the CLIENT_ID index.

To activate the CLIENT_ID index:

❶   Press **[Shift][F2]** to open the Organize menu.

❷   Select *Order records by index* (**O**). A list of existing index names appears.

Choose the index you want to use to order your data.

❸   Highlight CLIENT_ID. Notice that when you highlight an index name, the index expression is displayed to the left of the index name as a reminder of the index order. Press **[Enter]**.

If you wanted to use the original order in which you entered data into the database, you would select *Natural order*, which appears at the top of the list of index names.

❹   To view the data, press **[F2]** (Data). The records are displayed in alphabetical order by client ID.

Once you activate an index, it stays in effect for any work you do with the database file until you select another index tag or close the database file.

Dot Prompt

To select an index tag as the controlling index:

SET ORDER TO TAG *tag name*

Opens index tag as the master or controlling index

Example   .SET ORDER TO TAG client_id

Using Indexes To Search For Records

Nancy sticks her head into Esther's office and asks if any jobs are due on December 15, 1993. Esther knows that you can use indexes to quickly find records in a database.

To efficiently search a database file for a specific record, the database should be ordered on that index key. First activate the DUE_DATE index.

To activate the DUE_DATE index:

① Press **[Shift][F2]** to open the Organize menu.

② Select *Order records by index* (**O**). A list of index names appears.

③ Highlight DUE_DATE and press **[Enter]**.

④ Press **[F2]** (Data) to view the data. The records are displayed in order by due date.

Now search for jobs due on 12/15/93.

To search for a specific record:

① Press **[Alt]G** to open the Go To menu.

② Select *Index key search* (**I**). See Figure 5-26. You are asked to enter a search string for the due date.

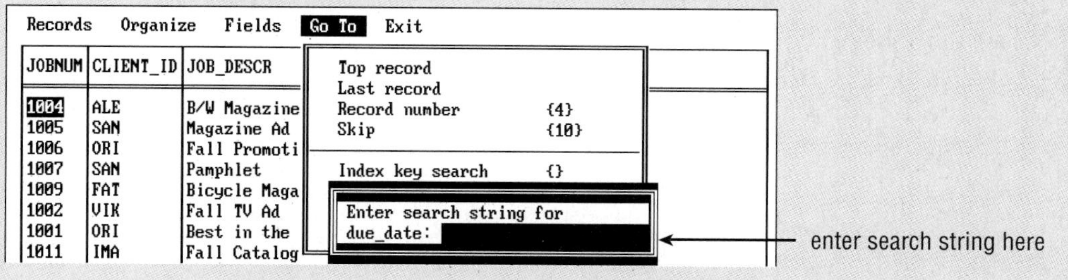

Figure 5-26
Entering search
information

```
 Records   Organize   Fields   Go To   Exit
┌────────┬─────────┬──────────┐  Top record
│JOBNUM  │CLIENT_ID│JOB_DESCR │  Last record
├────────┼─────────┼──────────┤  Record number    {4}
│1004    │ALE      │B/W Magazine  Skip              {10}
│1005    │SAN      │Magazine Ad │
│1006    │ORI      │Fall Promoti│  Index key search  {}
│1007    │SAN      │Pamphlet    │ ┌──────────────────────┐
│1009    │FAT      │Bicycle Maga│ │ Enter search string for│
│1002    │VIK      │Fall TV Ad  │ │ due_date: ████████     │ ←── enter search string here
│1001    │ORI      │Best in the │ └──────────────────────┘
│1011    │IMA      │Fall Catalog│
```

Enter the search value.

③ Type **12/15/93** and press **[Enter]**. The highlight goes immediately to the Taco Heaven record. See Figure 5-27 on the next page. You can now view or edit that record.

```
 Records   Organize   Fields   Go To   Exit
┌────────┬─────────┬──────────────────────┬─────────┬──────┬────────┐
│ JOBNUM │CLIENT_ID│ JOB_DESCR            │DUE_DATE │QUOTE │ STATUS │
├────────┼─────────┼──────────────────────┼─────────┼──────┼────────┤
│ 1023   │ TAC     │ TV ad                │12/15/93 │14000 │ I      │
│ 1018   │ VIK     │ TV ads               │01/15/94 │35700 │ I      │
│        │         │                      │         │      │        │
│        │         │                      │         │      │        │
└────────┴─────────┴──────────────────────┴─────────┴──────┴────────┘
 Browse   ║A:\JOBS           ║Rec 23/25    ║File ║      ║        Ins
```

Figure 5-27
Result of
DUE_DATE search

Esther calls Nancy to tell her that the Taco Heaven job is due December 15, 1993.

④ Press **[Esc]** to return to the Control Center.

When you use an index to search for a record dBASE searches the database using the index tag. If a value in the indexing field of the index matches the value you entered, dBASE moves to that record in the database. In this example, if there were more than one record with the same due date, dBASE would highlight the first record with that date. If there were no records with a 12/15/93 due date in the database, a message would be displayed indicating that no record was found.

Since W&M's database file JOBS is small, searching for a record using an index key does not appear to improve your search time. You just as easily could have pressed [PgDn] and found the record you were looking for. However, even if the database contained several thousand records, the indexed search would still take only a few seconds to look up the record. Without an indexed search, it might take several minutes to find the record.

Dot Prompt

To search for a record:

SEEK *expression*

Searches for the first record in an indexed database file with a key that matches a specified expression

Example   .USE jobs
.SET ORDER TO TAG client_id
.SEEK 'ORI'

Case: Wells & Martinez — Linking the JOBS File and the CLIENT File

Esther has just returned from the monthly staff meeting when Martin comes into her office and asks for help. Martin wants to modify the Jobs Due Listing Report for jobs in process. He now wants the report to provide all the information about a job and the client in one place. Specifically he wants to get a listing that includes the name of the client, job number, job description, due date, and quote for all the jobs in progress for each client and the name of the contact person for each client. He knows that all the information is in the database, but no one file contains all this information. He asks Esther what he should do.

Esther quickly examines the contents of the JOBS file; she points out to Martin that this file contains the jobs' due dates and quotes. She then lists the CLIENT file and notes that the remaining information he wants — client name and contact person — is in that file. Esther explains to Martin that he can get the information he wants in one listing by linking the two files.

Introduction to Linking Files

So far in this text you have queried the database and created reports by retrieving data from only one database file at a time. But what if answering a query or creating a report requires data from two or more files? For example, for Esther to display the listing that Martin needs, she must use data from both the CLIENT and JOBS database files.

A common way to retrieve data from two files is to link them. You can link two database files if the files have a common field. For example, because both the CLIENT and the JOBS files include the field CLIENT_ID, you can link them (Figure 5-28 on the next page).

Once these files are linked, you can perform tasks on the two files such as listing fields from both files as though they come from one file.

How can Esther link the two files? She can create a view that links the two database files by the common field, CLIENT_ID. This view is designed in the Query Design screen. The screen will contain two file skeletons, one for the CLIENT database and a second for JOBS. Identical values will be placed beneath the common field in both file skeletons to show dBASE that the files are to be linked. The identical values are referred to as **example variables**.

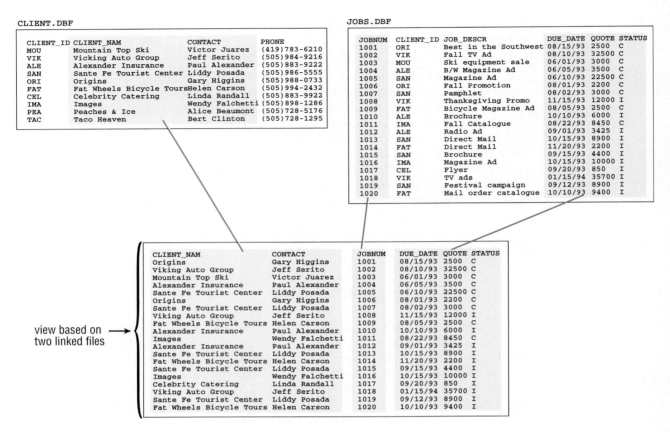

Figure 5-28
Linking database files

Let's build the view that links the CLIENT and JOBS database files. First the files must be added to the Query Design screen.

To open the CLIENT file and access the Query Design screen:

❶ From the Control Center open the database file CLIENT.

❷ Highlight <create> in the Queries panel and press **[Enter]**. The Query Design screen appears with a file skeleton of the CLIENT database.

Now make the indexes for the CLIENT file available to dBASE. This step is done to speed the time it takes to process the query. If you don't make the indexes available, dBASE will create temporary indexes to link the two database files. If dBASE creates these temporary indexes "on the fly," it takes longer for dBASE to link the files. So let's activate the indexes for the CLIENT file.

To open the indexes:

❶   Press **[Alt]F** to open the Fields menu.

❷   Select *Include indexes* (**I**). This sets the option to YES. You now see a triangle symbol in front of each field name in the file skeleton that is indexed.

Now add the related database file to the Query Design screen.

To add the JOBS file to the Query Design screen:

❶   Press **[Alt]L** to open the Layout menu.

❷   Select *Add file to query* (**A**). A list of database files appears.

❸   Highlight the JOBS file and press **[Enter]**. The file skeleton for the JOBS file is added to the Query Design screen. See Figure 5-29.

two file skeletons

symbol indicates index is activated

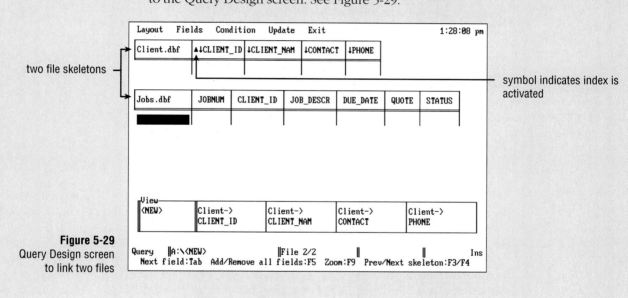

Figure 5-29
Query Design screen
to link two files

Now make the indexes for JOBS available to dBASE.

To open the indexes:

❶   Press **[Alt]F** to open the Fields menu.

❷   Select *Include indexes* (**I**). The option is changed to YES. You now see a triangle symbol in front of each field name of the JOBS file skeleton that is indexed.

Now you need to set up the link between the two database files. CLIENT_ID is the common field between JOBS and CLIENT and will be used to link the two files.

To set up a link between two files:

❶   Move the highlight to the CLIENT_ID field in the JOBS file skeleton.

❷   Type **link1** and press **[Enter]**.

Now move to the CLIENT file skeleton.

❸   Press **[F3]** (Previous) to move to the CLIENT file skeleton.

❹   Move the highlight to the CLIENT_ID field. Type **link1** and press **[Enter]**. See Figure 5-30.

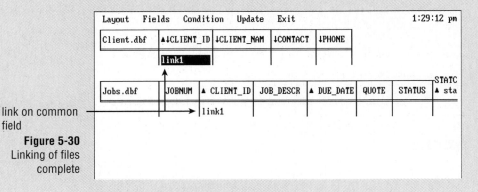

link on common field

Figure 5-30
Linking of files complete

You can also use the menus to link files. After both file skeletons have been added to the Query Design screen, you would open the Layout menu and use the option *Create link by pointing* to link the common fields. With this option you can "point" to the fields that establish the linkage between the files. Then you would place the highlight on the common field, CLIENT_ID, in the CLIENT file skeleton and select *Create link by pointing*. Then you would move the highlight to CLIENT_ID in the JOBS file skeleton and press [Enter]. After you created the link, the word LINK1 would appear below the CLIENT_ID field in both file skeletons.

Now that you have established the linkage between the two files, you can add a filter condition to the query so you retrieve only records of jobs that are in process, that is, jobs that have a status code of I.

To enter a filter condition:

❶   Press **[F4]** (Next) to move to the JOBS file skeleton.

❷   Move the highlight beneath the STATUS field name.

Enter the condition.

❸   Type **='I'** and press **[Enter]**.

Next modify the view skeleton to include the information that Martin wants to see. Currently all the fields from the CLIENT file are in the view skeleton. Martin is interested only in the client name and the contact name from the CLIENT file. Let's remove the other fields from the view.

To remove fields from the view skeleton:
❶ Press **[F3]** (Previous) to move to the CLIENT file skeleton.
❷ With the highlight beneath the CLIENT_ID field press **[F5]** (Fields) to remove the field from the view skeleton.
❸ Now remove the PHONE field from the view skeleton. Only CLIENT_NAM and CONTACT remain in the view skeleton.

Now you can add to the view skeleton the fields from the JOBS file that Martin wants to see: JOBNUM, JOB_DESCR, DUE_DATE, and QUOTE.

To add fields to the view skeleton:
❶ Press **[F4]** (Next) to move to the JOBS file skeleton.
❷ Highlight JOBNUM and press **[F5]** (Field). The field is added to the view skeleton
❸ Repeat this step for the other three fields: JOB_DESCR, DUE_DATE, and QUOTE. When you have finished, the view skeleton will look like Figure 5-31.

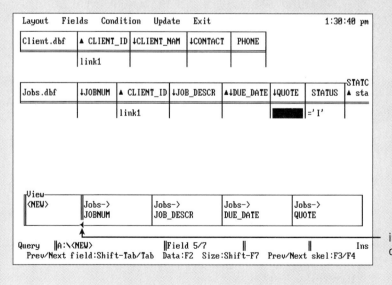

Figure 5-31
Query Design screen after modifying contents of view skeleton

indicates other fields to left of fields showing

Now you are ready to process the query.

To process the query:

❶ Press **[F2]** (Data). A list of all jobs in process appears in the Browse screen. See Figure 5-32.

fields from CLIENT database file

fields from JOBS database file

```
 Records   Organize  Fields  Go To   Exit

 CLIENT_NAM          CONTACT          JOBNUM JOB_DESCR

 Viking Auto Group   Jeff Serito      1008   Thanksgiving Promo
 Alexander Insurance Paul Alexander   1010   Brochure
 Alexander Insurance Paul Alexander   1012   Radio Ad
 Sante Fe Tourist Center Liddy Posada 1013   Direct Mail
 Fat Wheels Bicycle Tours Helen Carson 1014  Direct Mail
 Sante Fe Tourist Center Liddy Posada 1015   Brochure
 Images              Wendy Falchetti  1016   Magazine Ad
 Celebrity Catering  Linda Randall    1017   Flyer
 Viking Auto Group   Jeff Serito      1018   TV ads
 Sante Fe Tourist Center Liddy Posada 1019   Festival campaign
 Fat Wheels Bicycle Tours Helen Carson 1020  Mail order catalogue
 Alexander Insurance Paul Alexander   1021   B/W magazine ad
 Mama Lee's Pizza    Emma Lee         1022   Newspaper ad
 Taco Heaven         Bert Clinton     1023   TV ad
 Peaches & Ice       Alice Beaumont   1024   Brochure
 Mountain Top Ski    Victor Juarez    1025   Ski Weekend - Newspaper

 Browse  ‖A:\<NEW>        ‖Rec 8/25    ‖View ‖        ‖         Ins
```

Figure 5-32
Result of linking two database files

Notice that the Browse screen includes information from two database files: the CLIENT file (CLIENT_NAM and CONTACT) and the JOBS file (JOBNUM, JOB_DESCR, DUE_DATE, and QUOTE).

Esther prints the report for Martin.

❷ Print a Quick Report.

Now return to the Query Design screen.

❸ Press **[Shift][F2]** (Design).

Dot Prompt

To open a specified work area:
> SELECT *work area number*
> Specifies the active work area

> **Example**   .SELECT 1

Dot Prompt

To link files:

SET RELATION TO *common id field* INTO *open database file name*

Establishes a link between records in the active database and records in a second open database file

Example   .SELECT 1
.USE client ORDER client_id
.SELECT 2
.USE jobs
.SET RELATION TO client_id INTO client

Saving the Query

Esther decides to save this query before quitting for the day to avoid repeating these steps each time she wants information about jobs in process. Remember, when you save a query, it is added to your data diskette as a query file.

To save a query to your data diskette:

❶ Press **[Alt]E** to open the Exit menu.

❷ Select the option *Save changes and exit* (**S**).

A prompt box appears asking you to enter a filename. Enter a valid DOS filename (eight characters or fewer).

❸ Type **inproc** and press **[Enter]**. You are returned to the Control Center. The query file INPROC appears in the Queries panel.

dBASE automatically adds a QBE extension to the file, and the file is stored on your data diskette. The file is saved as INPROC.QBE. The saved query is also added to the current catalog, W&M.CAT (Figure 5-33).

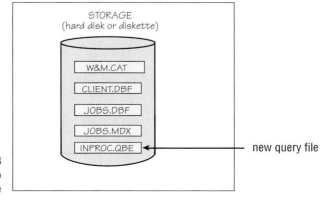

Figure 5-33
Query file added to
data diskette

You've now completed Tutorial 5. Remember to exit dBASE before turning off your computer.

■   ■   ■

Control Center Summary

To create a sorted file:

From the Data panel, highlight the database file you want to sort.

Press [F2] to view the data.

Press [Alt]O to open the Organize menu.

Select *Sort database on field list* (S).

Enter the field name you want to use to order the database.

Press [Enter] to move the cursor to the Type of sort column.

Choose the desired sort order.

Press [Ctrl][End].

Enter name of sorted file and press [Enter].

To sort a file using the Query Design screen:

With cursor in the file skeleton, move highlight to field you want to sort on.

Press [Alt]F to open Fields menu.

Select *Sort on this field* (S).

Choose the sort order and press [Enter].

To create an index:

Highlight filename in the Data panel.

Press [Shift][F2] to access Database Design screen.

From the Organize menu select *Create new index* (C).

Highlight *Name of index*, press [Enter], and enter index name.

Highlight *Index expression*, press [Enter], and enter index expression.

Press [Ctrl][End] to save the index.

To activate an index:

Press [Shift][F2] to open the Organize menu.

Select *Order records by index* (O).

Choose the index you want to use and press [Enter].

To search for specific records using an index:

Press [Shift][F2] to open the Organize menu.

Select *Order records by index* (O).

Control Center Summary

Choose the index you want to use and press [Enter].

Press [F2] to view the data.

Press [Alt]G to open the Go To menu.

Select *Index key search* (I).

Enter search string for <fieldname> and press [Enter].

To add a file to the Query Design screen:

Press [Alt]L to open the Layout menu.

Select *Add file to query* (A).

Highlight the database file you want to add and press [Enter].

To open indexes for use with a query:

Press [Alt]F to open the Fields menu.

Select *Include indexes* (I).

Exercises

1. Suppose you find a file on your data diskette named TITLE.MDX. What type of a file is this?

2. What file extension does a sorted file have?

3. Assume you have a database file named CONTACTS.DBF that contains three fields: NAME, CITY, and STATE. Figure 5-34 contains a sample of the contents of this file. Can you sort these data alphabetically by last name? Why or why not?

Name	City	State
Mike Franklin	Lincoln	NE
Heather Ennu	Tallahasee	FL
Ellen Jenks	Aberdeen	SD

Figure 5-34

Use Figures 5-35 and 5-36 to answer Exercises 4 and 5. These figures present information about customers (CUSTOMER.DBF) and their outstanding invoices (INVOICES.DBF).

Layout of CUSTOMER File — One Record per Customer

CUST_ID	Character	3
CUST_NAME	Character	25
ADDRESS	Character	20
CITY	Character	20
STATE	Character	2
ZIP	Character	5

Figure 5-35

Layout of INVOICE File — One Record for Each Invoice

INVOICE_NO	Character	5
CUST_ID	Character	3
INVCE_DTE	Date	8
INVCE_AMT	Numeric	8 2 (decimals)

Figure 5-36

4. Can these files be linked? Why or why not?

5. In the Query Design screen what files would make up the file skeleton if they were linked?

Tutorial Assignments

Open the W&M catalog, open CLIENT database file, and do the following:

1. Print the client data in the order in which the data were entered.

2. Print the CLIENT file sorted by client name in alphabetical order.

3. Create an index using client name as the index expression. Print the CLIENT file in alphabetical order using the client name index.

Open the JOBS file and do the following:

4. Sort by status and within status by quote. Arrange status in ascending order and quote in descending order. Print the JOBS file.

5. Using the Query Design file, link the JOBS database file and the CLIENT database file. For each of the following listings, include these fields: client name, job number, job description, due date, quote, and status. Save your query as TUT5.QBE.

6.   Print all jobs in the JOBS file.

7.   Print all completed jobs.

8.   Print all jobs with a quote over $5,000.

Case Problems

1.   Biggs & Hang Investment Corporation

Activate the BIG&HANG catalog and open the JAPAN database file.

1.   Use the Query Design screen to sort the companies in the file by sales with highest sales first. Include company name, industry code, and sales in your listing. Save your query as BIG5-1. Use Quick Report to print a ranking of the companies by sales.

2.   Use the Query Design screen to output companies in the automobile industry (industry code = A) in alphabetical order by company name. Include company name, sales, profits, and high price in your listing. Use Quick Report to print your results.

3.   Use the Query Design screen to sort the companies by industry and within industry by company name. Include industry code, company name, assets, sales, and profits. Use Quick Report to print a listing by industry.

4.   Create an index using PROFITS as the indexing field. Use this index to print company and profit.

5.   Open the database file INDUSTRY stored on your data diskette and print the contents of this file.

6.   Link the JAPAN and the INDUSTRY database files. Include the company name, industry name, sales, and profits in the view skeleton. Save this query as BIG5-6.

7.   Use the query developed in Problem 6 to print an alphabetical list of companies.

8.   Print a list of companies ordered by sales (highest to lowest). In your listing include the company name, industry name, sales, and profits.

2.   Medi-Source Inc.

Activate the MEDISRCE catalog and open the database file ACCTREC.

1.   Use the Query Design screen to sort the file by customer name. Include customer name, industry type, state, balance owed, and year-to-date sales in your output. Save this query as MEDI5-1. Use Quick Report to print a list of customers in alphabetical order.

2.   Use the Query Design screen to print a list of all companies in the hospital industry (industry code = H) in alphabetical order by customer name. Include customer name, credit limit, and balance owed.

3.   Use the Query Design screen to sort the customers by industry type and within industry type by balance owed with highest balance owed first. Include industry type, customer name, state, and balance owed in your output. Use Quick Report to print a listing by industry type.

4. Create an index using customer name as the indexing field.

5. Using the index you created in Problem 4, use the Query Design screen and Quick Report to print a list of all companies in the hospital industry (industry code = H) in alphabetical order by customer name. Include customer name, credit limit, and balance owed.

6. Create an index using YTD_SALES as the indexing field. Use Query Design and Quick Report to print a list of customers ordered by year-to-date sales. Include customer name, industry type, year-to-date sales, and balance owed.

7. Open the file named TYPENAME.DBF stored on your data diskette and print the contents of this file.

8. Link the ACCTREC and the TYPENAME database files. Include the company name, industry title, and balance owed in the view skeleton. Save this query as MEDI5-8.

9. Use the query developed in Problem 8 to print a list of companies.

3.   Appleton & Drake Electrical Supply Company

Activate the APPLTON catalog and open the file named EMPLOYEE.

1. Use the Query Design screen to sort the employees by their last names. Include employee first and last name, sex, department, and salary in the view skeleton. Save the query as APPL5-1. Use Quick Report to print a list of employees in alphabetical order.

2. Modify the query in Problem 1 to print all employees with salaries above $35,000.

3. Use the Query Design screen to sort the employees by department and within department by last name. Include department, employee first and last names, and salary in the view skeleton. Use Quick Report to print a listing by department.

4. Create an index using sex as the indexing field. Use the Query Design screen and Quick Report to print a list of all employees ordered by sex. Include each employee's first and last names, sex, department, and salary.

5. Create an index using salary as the indexing field. Use Quick Report to print a list of employees earning less than the company average. Include each employee's first and last names, department, sex, and salary. You will need to calculate the average salary first.

6. Open the file named DEPARTMT.DBF stored on your data diskette and print its contents.

7. Link the EMPLOYEE and the DEPARTMT database files. Include the employee's last name, full department name, and employee's annual salary in the view skeleton. Save the query as APPL5-7.

8. Use the query developed in Problem 7 to print a list of employees.

4. National Basketball Association

Activate the NBA catalog and open the NBA database file.

1. Use the Query Design screen to sort the records into alphabetical sequence using the player's last name as your sort key. Include the following fields: last name, first name, team, and salary in the view skeleton. Save the query as NBA5-1. Use Quick Report to print an alphabetical listing of all players.

2. Use the Query Design screen to sort the NBA file by team and within team by salary (highest salary first). Use Quick Report to print the team, last name, first name, and salary for players earning over $1,000,000.

3. Create an index using last name as the indexing field. Use the Query Design screen and Quick Report to print the NBA data in alphabetical order using your index file. Include each player's first and last names, team, and salary in your output.

4. Create an index file using position as the indexing field. Use the Query Design screen and Quick Report to print the NBA file ordered by position. Include all fields from the database in your printout.

5. Open the file named TEAMS.DBF stored on your data diskette and print its contents.

6. Link the NBA and the TEAMS database files. Include each player's last name, full team name, and each player's annual salary in the view skeleton. Save the query as NBA5-6.

7. Use the query developed in Problem 6 to print a list of players.

8. Print a second list of players, this time in alphabetical order using the query developed in Problem 6. In your listing include each player's last name, full team name, and each player's salary.

9. Use the Group By operator to calculate the total salary by team and output the table shown in Figure 5-37.

Team	Total Salary
Atlanta Hawks	
Boston Celtics	
Chicago Bulls	
Detroit Pistons	
LA Lakers	
NY Knicks	
Philadelphia 76ers	
Portland Trailblazers	

Figure 5-37

5. Off-Campus Housing at Ashland University

Activate the catalog HOUSING and open the database file HOUSING.

1. Use the Query Design screen to sort the records by city. Print the name of the owners and the addresses (street address, city, state, zip) of all rental properties.

2. Use the Query Design screen to sort the HOUSING file by type of rental unit and within rental units by city. Print the name of the owner, rental type, and the address (street address, city, state, zip) of each rental property.

3. Create an index file using the owner's last name as the indexing field. Print the HOUSING file in alphabetical order by owner's name and include the owner's home and work phone numbers.

4. Open the file named RENTTYPE.DBF stored on your data diskette and print the contents of this file.

5. Link the HOUSING and RENTTYPE database files. Include the description of each housing unit, the city where each rental unit is located, and the rent for each unit in the view skeleton. Save the query as HOUSE5-5.

6. Use the query developed in Problem 5 to print a list of rental units.

Tutorial 6

Using the Report Generator

OBJECTIVES

In this tutorial you will learn to:

- Use the Quick Layout feature to generate a report

- Use the Report Design screen to customize a report

- Use database files and views as a source of data for a report

- Save a report format file

- Print a report created using the report generator

- Include subtotals in a report

Case: Wells & Martinez — Generating the Completed Jobs Report

Nancy calls Esther into her office to discuss the W&M database. She thanks Esther for the work Esther has been doing and tells her how helpful the database has been.

Nancy then says that the listing of completed jobs has been so helpful that she wonders if Esther could update and print it regularly, perhaps once a month. Esther immediately recognizes that what Nancy is asking for is a report and that her request provides the perfect opportunity for Esther to use dBASE's report generator. Esther suggests that they discuss the design and format of the report to make it as useful as possible. Nancy agrees, and Esther begins to ask questions about the report and how it will be used. During their meeting they decide that the report will:

- Be issued monthly and be dated so Nancy will know when the printout was run

- Include a title that describes its contents, so Nancy can easily distinguish it from other reports

- Contain column headings that are more descriptive than the database field names dBASE automatically uses

- Omit the due date and status columns; Nancy wants only the completed jobs listed, so these fields are not needed

- Total the quote column, so Nancy can better track W&M's cash flow

- Order the job information by client ID

Esther takes this list and begins work.

Designing Reports

When Esther first developed the listing of completed jobs for Nancy, she paid little attention to the format. She wanted to answer Nancy's requests without delay, so she did what most people do when they query a database — she produced the printout quickly, without concern for its appearance. Thus, the headings were not as descriptive as they could have been, the printout was not titled, and other useful report features that make printed reports easy to read were also omitted.

Printed reports must provide information succinctly, clearly, and correctly. Before working at the computer, you should take the time to plan a report and its format. Ask yourself these general questions whenever you are planning a report:

- What information do I need?
- How much detail do I want to include? Do I need to display every record or only summary totals?
- How should I present the data? In columns? As a form? As a graph?
- How often will the report be prepared?

As part of your planning process you should prepare a report layout sheet. A **report layout** is a sketch of your report, which you can prepare on plain paper, graph paper, or special printer spacing charts. Figure 6-1 is the report layout sheet that Esther prepared after her meeting with Nancy.

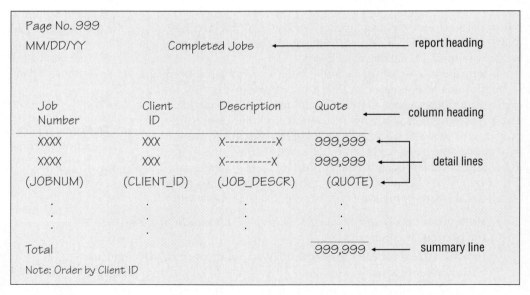

Figure 6-1
Esther's report
layout sheet

Your report layout should address the following questions:

- What items should be included in the report?
- Where on the report should each field be located?
- What report and column headings should be included?
- How should the records be ordered?
- Which groups of records should be subtotaled?

- Which fields should be totaled?

You can use a series of *X*s in the print positions to represent the character fields, a series of *9*s to represent numeric fields, and *mm/dd/yy* to represent date fields. If you have room, include the name of the field in parentheses under the symbols, as Esther did on her report layout sheet. For long fields you can do as Esther did for the field JOB_DESCR — put two *X*s connected by a line. You typically put only one or two lines on the report layout sheet to represent multiple lines that will contain the same type of information.

Esther's report contains several types of lines typical of many reports: heading lines, detail lines, and summary lines. **Heading lines** usually are printed at the top of each page to describe the nature of the data in your report. Column heading lines describe the columns of output. **Detail lines** are in the body of the report and provide detailed information about the results of processing. Typically you print one detail line for each record in the database. **Summary lines**, which are usually at the end of a report, give the totals of numbers from the detail lines.

You can use dBASE's report generator to build a report step by step. Using the report generator gives a report a professional appearance, including features such as the date on which you printed the report, page numbers, report titles, column headings, and totals.

Introduction to the Report Generator

After you have planned your report, you produce the report using dBASE's report generator. The report generator offers three general report layouts: column, form, and mailmerge, as shown in Figure 6-2.

- *Column layout:* The field information appears side by side in a columnar format. The records in the database are displayed in rows (Figure 6-2a).

- *Form layout:* The fields are laid out vertically. You do not have distinct columns in this report. Data is stacked or arranged in a free format (Figure 6-2b).

- *Mailmerge layout:* A large body of text from another application like a word processor is combined with information from a database (Figure 6-2c on the next page).

Figure 6-2a
Report using column layout

```
CLIENT_ID    CLIENT_NAM          CONTACT         PHONE
MOU          Mountain Top Ski    Victor Juarez   (419)783-6210
VIK          Viking Auto Group   Jeff Serito     (505)984-9216
ALE          Alexander Insurance Paul Alexander  (505)883-9222
.
.
.
```

Figure 6-2b
Report using form layout

```
Client ID: MOU     Client Name: Mountain Top Ski
Contact: Victor Juarez              Phone: (419)783-6210

Client ID: VIK     Client Name: Viking Auto Group
Contact: Jeff Serito                Phone: (505)984-9216

Client ID: ALE     Client Name: Alexander Insurance
Contact: Paul Alexander             Phone: (505)883-9222
.
.
.
```

from CLIENT
database file

Figure 6-2c
Report using
mailmerge layout

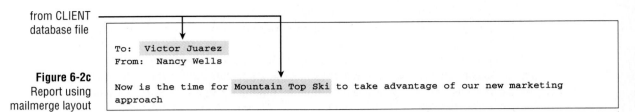

```
To:   Victor Juarez
From:  Nancy Wells

Now is the time for Mountain Top Ski to take advantage of our new marketing
approach
```

When you start designing a report, you can use dBASE's Quick Layout feature. The Quick Layout feature uses all the fields from the open database or view as the source of the data for the initial report. You can produce a report from this layout or modify the layout to resemble your report layout sheet.

Using the Report Design Screen

Let's work with Esther as she uses the report generator to create W&M's Completed Jobs report. You've already seen Esther's sketch of how she thought the report should look (Figure 6-1). The next step is to transfer the report layout to the Report Design screen. The Report Design screen contains a report's definition, that is, its titles, headings, columns, and fields.

Before you can create the report definition, you first must activate the W&M catalog and open the database file or view that will be used as the basis for defining the report. For the Completed Jobs report you will need the database file JOBS.

To open a database file:
1. Load dBASE, set the default drive and directory, and open the JOBS database file.

Since the report is to be ordered by client ID, you need to open the CLIENT_ID index tag you created in Tutorial 5.

To open an index tag:
1. Press **[F2]** (Data).
2. Press **[Alt]O** to open the Organize menu.
3. Select *Order records by index* (**O**).
4. Highlight CLIENT_ID and press **[Enter]**. The data on the Browse screen are rearranged by client ID.
5. Press **[Esc]** to return to the Control Center.

Now you are ready to design the report. Let's go to the Report Design screen.

To access the Reports Design screen:

❶ Move the highlight to <create> in the Reports panel and press **[Enter]**. The Layout menu appears.

Choose the *Quick layouts* option to build a report quickly.

❷ Select *Quick layouts* (**Q**). A submenu appears. See Figure 6-3.

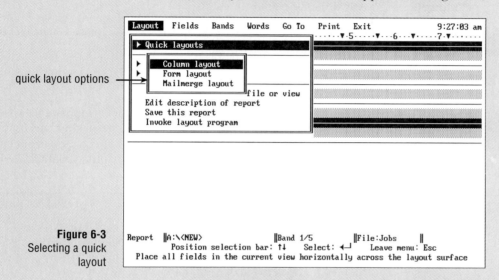

quick layout options →

Figure 6-3
Selecting a quick
layout

You can choose from three options: Column layout, Form layout, and Mailmerge layout.

❸ Select *Column layout* (**C**). See Figure 6-4. The Report Design screen showing the column layout appears.

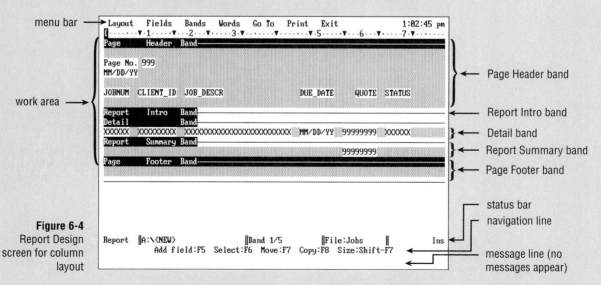

menu bar →
work area →

Page Header band
Report Intro band
Detail band
Report Summary band
Page Footer band

status bar
navigation line
message line (no
messages appear)

Figure 6-4
Report Design
screen for column
layout

Dot Prompt

To create a report:

CREATE REPORT   *report form filename*

Accesses the Report Design screen to create a new report

Example   .CREATE REPORT cmpltjb1

Understanding the Report Bands

Let's examine the Report Design screen shown in Figure 6-4. It includes a menu bar, work area, status bar, navigation line, and message line. The work area is the area where the report is defined. The work area is divided into **report bands**. Each report band is used to specify a different section of the report. Figure 6-5 describes the seven report bands available to help you design your report:

Report Band	Description
Page Header	Includes predefined fields for the date and page number, as well as the column headings for the report. Initially the field name of each database variable appears as a column heading. The items in this band are printed at the top of each page of the report.
Detail	Defines the body of the report. dBASE prints every record in the database or view according to the layout in the detail band. Initially this band consists of field templates for each field in the database or view. A **field template** is a set of symbols, one for each position in a field, that determines the width of the field and defines the appearance of each field when displayed or printed.
Report Summary	Includes summary totals such as totals and averages for all numeric fields printed in the Detail band. The items in this band are printed once at the end of the report.
Report Intro	Used for introductory text that appears near the top of the *first page* of the report. You include items such as title and author in this band. The items in this band appear only once in the report.
Page Footer	Used to place information at the bottom of each page of the report. Items such as page number or company name may be placed here.
Group Intro	Defines information you want to see before a group of records is printed. This band does not appear on the initial Report Design screen.
Group Summary	Defines summary statistics for a group of records. This band does not appear on the initial Report Design screen.

Figure 6-5
dBASE report bands

When you first open the Report Design screen, the Detail band contains field templates for each field in the database. A **field template** defines the width and the appearance of the field when it is displayed or printed. The format of the field template matches the format Esther used in her report layout sheet.

Viewing the Report

Let's view the report on the screen as it appears immediately after the *Quick layouts* option has been selected. You can compare the output from the quick layout with Nancy's specifications in the report layout to get an indication of the changes needed.

To view the report:

❶ Press **[Alt]P** to open the Print menu.

Now specify the destination of the report: the screen, the printer, or a file on your diskette.

❷ Select *View report on screen* (**V**). See Figure 6-6. All fields from the database file are included in the report. If the record is more than 80 characters wide, the line wraps around to the next line on the screen.

```
Page No.   1
09/04/92

JOBNUM  CLIENT_ID  JOB_DESCR                 DUE_DATE   QUOTE  STATUS

1004    ALE        B/W Magazine Ad           06/05/93    3500  C
1010    ALE        Brochure                  10/10/93    6000  I
1012    ALE        Radio Ad                  09/01/93    3425  I
1021    ALE        B/W magazine ad           11/10/93    6600  I
1017    CEL        Flyer                     09/20/93     850  I
1009    FAT        Bicycle Magazine Ad       08/05/93    2500  C
1014    FAT        Direct Mail               11/20/93    2200  I
1020    FAT        Mail order catalogue      10/10/93    9400  I
1011    IMA        Fall Catalogue            08/22/93    8450  C
1016    IMA        Magazine Ad               10/15/93   10000  I
1022    MAM        Newspaper ad              12/01/93    5300  I
1003    MOU        Ski equipment sale        06/01/93    3000  C
1025    MOU        Ski Weekend-Newspaper     11/15/93    6450  I
1001    ORI        Best in the Southwest     08/15/93    2500  C
1006    ORI        Fall Promotion            08/01/93    2200  C
1024    PEA        Brochure                  11/30/93   11000  I
1005    SAN        Magazine Ad               06/10/93   22500  C
1007    SAN        Pamphlet                  08/02/93    3000  C
          Cancel viewing: ESC,  Continue viewing: SPACEBAR
```

Figure 6-6
Output from Quick Layout

❸ Press **[Esc]** to return to the Report Design screen.

Dot Prompt

To print or view a report format file:

REPORT FORM *<report form filename>* <scope> FOR <condition> TO PRINTER

Prints information from active database or view using a report form file

Example .REPORT FORM cmpltjb2 FOR status = 'C'

Modifying the Detail Band

Based on Esther's sketch, the initial report needs to be modified in several ways. For example, the DUE_DATE and STATUS columns need to be removed from the report. In addition, the page title must be added and the column headings modified. To change the appearance of a report, you go to the specific band and make the appropriate modifications.

Removing Fields from the Detail Band

Let's begin by removing the DUE_DATE and STATUS columns. To do this, you remove the DUE_DATE and STATUS field templates from the Detail band.

To remove a field template from the Detail band:

❶ Use [↓] to move into the Detail band. Position the cursor at the DUE_DATE field template (MM/DD/YY). The field template is highlighted. See Figure 6-7.

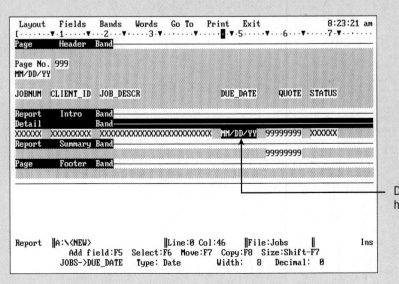

Figure 6-7
Preparing to remove the DUE_DATE field template from Detail band

DUE_DATE field template highlighted

❷ Press **[Del]**. The field template disappears from the screen.

Now remove the STATUS field template.

❸ Move the cursor to the STATUS field template and press **[Del]**. The field template for STATUS disappears.

If you accidentally delete a field, you cannot simply type the field template, such as 9999999 or xxxx, in the Detail line. To add a field template to a report, you would press [F5] and select the field you want to add from the field selection box that appears. dBASE would automatically place the field template in the Report Design screen.

Notice that the column headings for DUE_DATE and STATUS still appear in the Page Header band. We will remove these after we have finished making changes in the Detail band.

Moving Fields

When you remove a field template, the templates to the right do not automatically move over to replace the deleted items. To close up the space, you must move the remaining templates. Let's move the QUOTE template in the Detail band closer to the job description field.

To move a field template:

❶ Move the cursor to the field template for QUOTE. The template is highlighted. After positioning the cursor on the field template you want to move, you need to select it.

❷ Press **[F6]** (Extend Select), then press **[Enter]** to select the field.

If you wanted to move more than one template, you would press [F6], then use the arrow keys to highlight the field templates you wanted to move before pressing [Enter].

❸ Move the cursor to the position where you want the field template to begin. Look at the status bar and move the cursor to Line:0 Col:46 in the Detail band. This will position the QUOTE field two spaces after the end of the JOB_DESCR field template.

❹ Press **[F7]** (Move). A rectangle appears showing the new position of the field.

❺ Press **[Enter]** to complete the move. See Figure 6-8 on the next page.

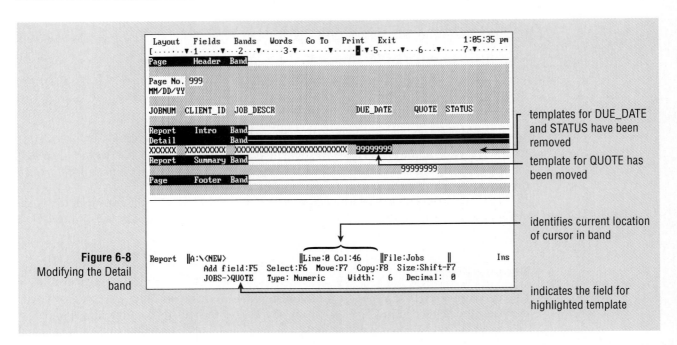

Figure 6-8
Modifying the Detail band

If you move a field template on top of another field template or on top of text, dBASE asks whether you want to delete the covered template or text. If you answer yes, the covered template or text is replaced by the moved field. If you answer no, the move does not take place.

Modifying Templates

When a field template initially appears on a Report Design screen, the symbols are based on the data as defined in the database. One way to make the data in your report more readable is to modify the template. For example, you can add commas to the field template so that commas will be displayed when a digit is present on both sides of the comma. Let's modify the QUOTE field so commas are included in the output for QUOTE.

To modify a field template:

❶ Position the cursor on the field template for QUOTE in the Detail band.

❷ Press **[F5]** (Field). The field definition prompt box appears. See Figure 6-9.

The top half of the field definition prompt box contains the field definition. This information cannot be changed. The information in the bottom half of the box can be modified.

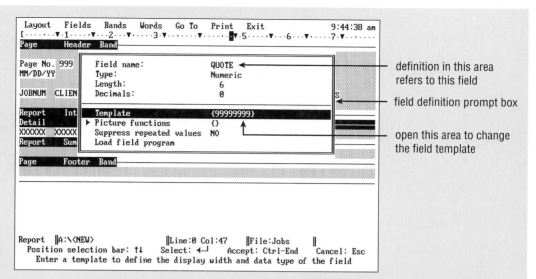

Figure 6-9
Modifying the
template for QUOTE

The *Template* option is highlighted. You will recall that the field template symbol controls what will be displayed in a particular position in the field. QUOTE is currently assigned a width of eight; thus, the template for this field is 99999999. Let's change the field template to 999,999.

③ Press **[Enter]** to open the template area.

④ Modify the entry in this area so the template appears as 999,999 and press **[Enter]**.

⑤ Press **[Ctrl][End]** to accept the new settings of the field definition prompt box. The revised field template appears in the Detail band. See Figure 6-10.

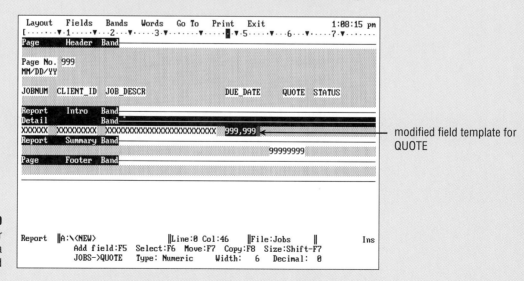

Figure 6-10
Field template for
QUOTE after comma
symbol inserted

Figure 6-11 lists the various template symbols that can be included in numeric fields.

Symbol	Description
9	Represents only digits and positive and negative signs
#	Represents only digits, spaces, and positive and negative signs
.	Specifies the decimal point
,	Displays a comma at this location if the number is large enough to require it
*	Displays leading zeros as asterisks; placed to left of most significant digit
$	Displays leading zeros as dollar sign; placed to left of most significant digit

Figure 6-11
Template
symbols for
numeric fields

If you accidentally press [Enter] while working on a detail line, you may find that the field templates following the cursor move to the next line. How do you move the field templates back to their original line? Try Select (F6) and Move (F7), which are described in the section "Moving Fields."

The changes to the Detail band are complete.

Modifying the Report Summary Band

The columnar report generated from the quick layout includes summary fields that total all numeric fields. These summary fields appear at the end of the report. QUOTE is the only numeric field in the JOBS database; therefore, there is only one summary field in the Report Summary band. After reviewing the output from the quick layout, Esther decides to make three changes to the Report Summary band. First, she wants to add the label "Total" to the summary line to describe the quote summary field; second, the quote summary field needs to be aligned under the quote field; and third, the quote summary field template should also include commas.

To add a label to the Report Summary band:

❶   Position the cursor at Line:0 Col:3 in the Report Summary band. Check the status line to locate the exact position of the cursor. See Figure 6-12 on the next page.

Enter the label.

❷   Type **Total**.

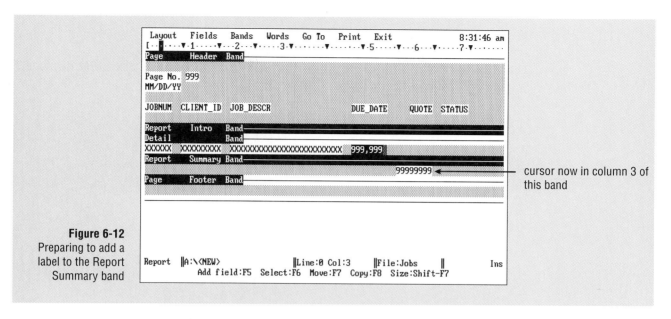

Figure 6-12
Preparing to add a
label to the Report
Summary band

Now move the quote summary field template so it is aligned under the quote template in the Detail band.

To move a field template:

❶ Move the cursor to the summary field template, Line:0 Col:56.

❷ Press **[F6]** (Extend Select) to begin the selection and press **[Enter]** to complete the selection.

❸ Move the cursor to Line:0 Col:46. This will align the quote summary field directly under the QUOTE field in the Detail band.

❹ Press **[F7]** (Move).

❺ Press **[Enter]** to complete the move.

Now change the summary field template to include a comma.

To include a comma when the summary field is displayed:

❶ Press **[F5]** (Field). A field definition prompt box appears.

❷ Select *Template* (**T**).

❸ Modify the template entry so it appears as 999,999 and press **[Enter]**.

❹ Press **[Ctrl][End]** to accept the new setting.

Adding Lines and Boxes

Lines and boxes can be added to a report to improve its appearance. Esther decides to add a single ruled line above the quote summary field.

To add a line to the report:

❶ Press **[Home]** to move the cursor to Line:0 Col:0 of the Report Summary band.

❷ Press **[Ctrl]N** to insert a blank line before the total line.

❸ Press **[Alt]L** to open the Layout menu.

Select the *Line* option.

❹ Select *Line* (**L**). A submenu appears.

Select a single or double line.

❺ Select *Single line* (**S**).

❻ Move the cursor to where you want the line to start, Line:0 Col:46.

❼ Press **[Enter]** to indicate the beginning of the line.

❽ Press **[→]** to draw the line over the field template. When you have finished drawing the line, the cursor should be positioned at Line:0 Col:53.

You can press [↓] to draw vertical lines.

❾ Press **[Enter]** to end the line. See Figure 6-13.

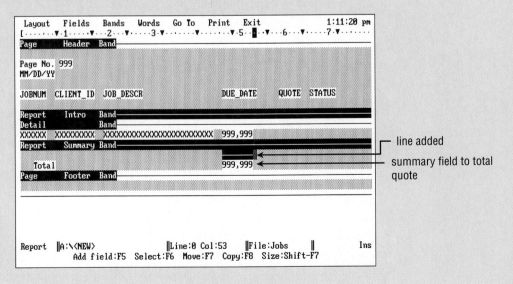

Figure 6-13
Modifying the
Report Summary
band

If you accidentally add a line to a band, how do you remove the line? Move the cursor to the line you want to remove. Press [Alt]W to open the Words menu and select *Remove line.*

The changes to the Report Summary band are complete.

Modifying the Page Header Band

According to her report layout sheet, Esther needs to add a page title and modify the column headings. Let's add the page title first. This is done in the Page Header band. According to her report layout sheet, Esther wants the title "Completed Jobs" to appear at the top of every page in her report.

To enter the page title:

❶ Move the cursor into the Page Header band. Move the cursor to Line:2 Col:17. The *Quick layouts* option automatically includes field templates for page number and today's date. Now enter the page title.

❷ Type **Completed Jobs**.

Now adjust the column headings.

To adjust the column headings:

❶ Move the cursor to line 4 of the Page Header band.

❷ Modify the column heading lines as illustrated in the report layout (Figure 6-1). Type the new heading over the current heading and delete the headings that are no longer needed. Remember to change the headings from all uppercase letters to uppercase and lowercase as shown in the report layout. This will be easier if Insert mode is off. (If you don't know what Insert mode is, check the status bar at the bottom of your screen. If the status bar shows Ins, press [Ins] to turn this mode off.)

As you enter column headings, you may not remember what field each template in the Detail band represents. If that's the case, highlight the template in the Detail band, and the message line will indicate the name of the field.

Esther decides that a line between the column heading and the first detail line will make the report easier to read. Let's add the line now.

To add a line to the report:

❶ Press **[End]** to move the cursor to the end of line 5 of the Page Header band.

❷ Press **[Ctrl]N**. A blank line is inserted in the Page Header band.

❸ Move the cursor to Line:6 Col:0 and follow the steps you used to add a ruled line in the Report Summary band. The line should begin at Col:0 and extend through Col:53. See Figure 6-14.

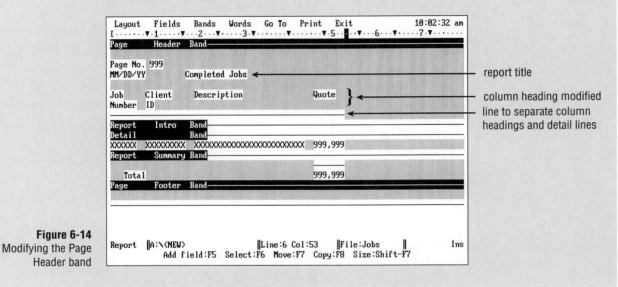

Figure 6-14
Modifying the Page
Header band

The modifications to the Page Header band are complete. Let's see what the report looks like.

Viewing the Modified Report

Now that you've made all the changes, look at the completed report to make sure it looks like your report layout sheet.

To view the report:

❶ Press **[Alt]P** to open the Print menu.

❷ Select *View report on screen* (**V**). See Figure 6-15.

❸ Press **[Esc]** to return to the Report Design screen.

```
Page No.   1
09/04/92        Completed Jobs

Job      Client   Description          Quote
Number   ID

1004     ALE      B/W Magazine Ad       3,500
1010     ALE      Brochure              6,000
1012     ALE      Radio Ad              3,425
1021     ALE      B/W magazine ad       6,600
1017     CEL      Flyer                   850
1009     FAT      Bicycle Magazine Ad   2,500
1014     FAT      Direct Mail           2,200
1020     FAT      Mail order catalogue  9,400
1011     IMA      Fall Catalogue        8,450
1016     IMA      Magazine Ad          10,000  ←
1022     MAM      Newspaper ad          5,300  ←
1003     MOU      Ski equipment sale    3,000
1025     MOU      Ski Weekend-Newspaper 6,450
1001     ORI      Best in the Southwest 2,500
1006     ORI      Fall Promotion        2,200
1024     PEA      Brochure             11,000  ←
1005     SAN      Magazine Ad          22,500
          Cancel viewing: ESC,  Continue viewing: SPACEBAR    ▮
```

report includes
jobs in process

Figure 6-15
Display of modified
report

Esther is pleased with the report format. The page title, column headings, and totals make the report easy to read. In addition, the records are ordered by client, making the report easier to use.

Now save the completed report format.

Saving the Report Format

Esther saves the report definition to a file so she can use this report format again without having to enter the specifications each time the report is run.

To save the report format file:

❶   Press **[Alt]E** to open the Exit menu.

❷   Select *Save changes and exit* (**S**).

Enter a report name

❸   Type **cmpltjb1** and press **[Enter]**. dBASE automatically returns to the Control Center, where the filename you entered is displayed in the Reports panel.

The report specifications are now saved on your data diskette. dBASE saved the report definition to a file named CMPLTJB1.FRM. dBASE automatically assigned the extension FRM to the file. In addition to DBF, MDX, and QBE files, your data diskette now contains FRM files, which are report format files.

Using Queries to Output a Report

The report is not yet complete. It includes all the records in the JOBS database, not just records of completed jobs. This is easily fixed. You can use a view as a source of data to generate your reports; that is, you can select the records to include in a report by creating a query to filter the records displayed in the report.

You can order the records and limit the records included in your report by designing a query in the Query Design screen. This query is used to control the records that are made available to the report generator.

Now prepare a query to select the completed jobs from the JOBS file.

To prepare a query:

❶ Highlight <create> in the Queries panel and press **[Enter]**. The Query Design screen appears.

Now enter the filter condition.

❷ Press **[End]** to move the highlight beneath the STATUS field name in the file skeleton.

❸ Type **='C'** and press **[Enter]**.

Now sort the database file.

❹ Move the highlight to the CLIENT_ID field.

❺ Type **Asc1** and press **[Enter]** to sort by client ID in ascending order. See Figure 6-16.

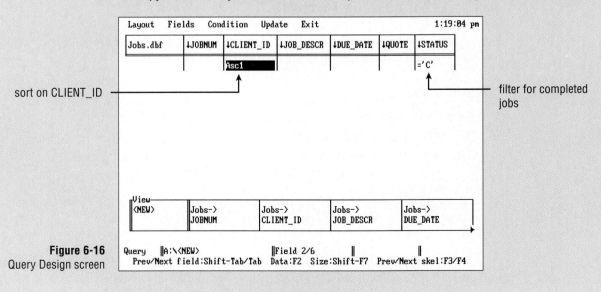

sort on CLIENT_ID

filter for completed jobs

Figure 6-16
Query Design screen

You must save this query in order to use it with the report format file.

To save a query to your data diskette:
1. Press **[Alt]E** to open the Exit menu.
2. Select *Save changes and exit* (**S**).

A prompt box appears, asking you to enter a filename.

3. Type **cmpltjob** and press **[Enter]**. You are returned to the Control Center. The query file CMPLTJOB appears on the Queries panel.

You may find it easier to use a view (a saved query) to design a report than to use the original database file. When you use a view you specify the fields and their order in the view skeleton. When you access the Report Design screen using the *Quick layout* option, only the fields specified in the view skeleton appear in the default report layout.

Esther is ready to output the report again. This time let's print the report.

To print the report:
1. Highlight **cmpltjb1** in the Reports panel and press **[Enter]**. A prompt box appears. See Figure 6-17.

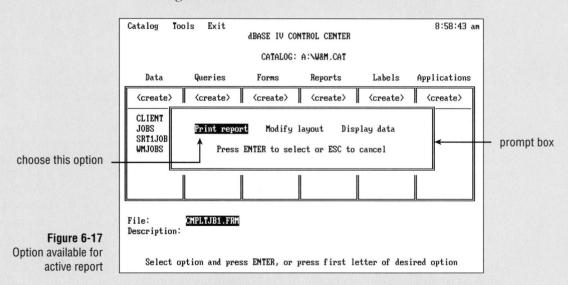

Figure 6-17
Option available for active report

2. Select *Print report* (**P**).

A prompt box appears asking you to choose either the current view or JOBS.DBF.
3. Select *Current view* (**C**). This is the view you just saved.
4. Select *Begin printing* (**B**). See Figure 6-18 on the next page. Now only completed jobs are output.

```
        Page No.  1
        06/22/93              Completed Jobs

        Job       Client    Description               Quote
        Number    ID
        ───────────────────────────────────────────────────
        1004      ALE       B/W Magazine Ad           3,500
        1009      FAT       Bicycle Magazine Ad       3,500
        1011      IMA       Fall Catalogue            8,450
        1003      MOU       Ski equipment sale        3,000
        1001      ORI       Best  in the Southwest    2,500
        1006      ORI       Fall Promotion            2,200
        1005      SAN       Magazine Ad              22,500
        1007      SAN       Pamphlet                  3,000
        1002      VIK       Fall TV Ad               32,500
                                                    ───────
           Total                                    80,150
```

Figure 6-18
Printout of
Completed Jobs
report

Although the ruled lines under the column heading and before the total quote appear as expected on the screen, some printers are not able to print lines and boxes. If your printer can't print graphic characters, remove this feature from the Report Design screen and output the report again.

Esther is pleased with the report, and she shows it to Nancy.

Including Subtotals in a Report

Later that day Esther finds the Completed Jobs report back on her desk with a brief note from Nancy saying she likes the report but she would like the report to include a subtotal of the quotes for each client.

To create a report with subtotals, you total one or more numeric fields for a group of records that have a common value in a specified field. For example, Nancy wants to total the quotes for all records that have the same client ID. To develop a report with subtotals, you need to process the records in sequence according to the field on which the records will be grouped. The field that determines how the records are grouped is called the **control field**. In this case, the client ID is the control field. This means that to subtotal by client, all the job records for ALE (Alexander's Insurance), for example, will be processed before any records for CEL (Celebrity Caterers).

To calculate a subtotal for the first group of records, those with the client ID ALE, dBASE adds together the quotes of all ALE records. The sum is the subtotal for the group ALE. A subtotal is displayed or printed when the value in the control field changes. In other words, when the client ID changes from ALE to CEL, dBASE displays or prints a subtotal for all previous records that have the client ID value ALE. The term **control break** is used to describe this change of value in the control field. When a control break occurs, a subtotal for the group of records just processed is displayed. This type of report, one that groups records by control field and includes subtotals, is called a **control break report**.

To prepare a control break report using the report generator, you add group bands. These bands organize records by collecting them into groups.

Modifying the Report

In response to Nancy's request, Esther prepares another report layout sheet to help her plan the revised report (Figure 6-19). In addition to including subtotals in the revised Completed Jobs report, she also decides to remove the client ID column from the report. Esther realizes that this column is no longer necessary since the client ID appears as a heading before each group of clients.

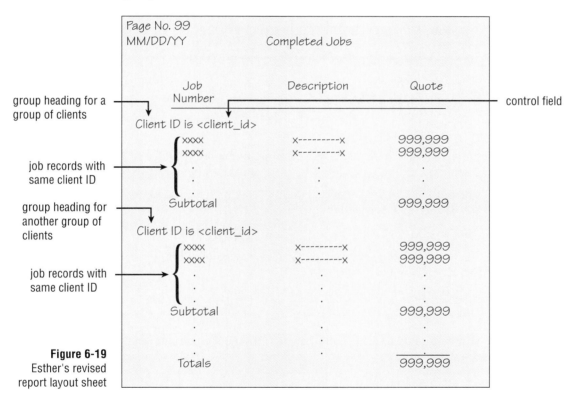

Figure 6-19
Esther's revised
report layout sheet

Esther is now ready to modify the Report Design screen. For a control break report to work properly, the database file must be sorted or indexed on the same field you used to group the records. For example, the revised Completed Jobs report must index (or sort) the records by CLIENT_ID to create a report where all clients are grouped together. Since the CLIENT_ID index was activated to prepare the previous report, there is no need to activate the index again. However, if this index were not activated, you would need to open this index before printing or viewing the report.

First you need to *access* the Report Design screen.

To return to the Report Design screen:

❶ Highlight CMPLTJB1 and press **[Enter]**.

❷ Select *Modify layout* (**M**).

A prompt box appears, to let you choose the current view or the JOBS database file.

❸ Select *Current view* (**C**). The Reports Design screen appears.

Dot Prompt

To modify a report:

MODIFY REPORT <*report form filename*>

Accesses Report Design screen to modify an existing report

Example   .MODIFY REPORT cmpltjb1

Now remove the CLIENT_ID column from the report.

To remove the field template and field name from the report:

❶ Move into the Detail band and position the cursor at the CLIENT_ID field template, Line:0 Col:8.

❷ Press **[Del]**. The template disappears.

Now remove the field name.

❸ Move into the Page Header band, Line:4 Col:8. Press **[F6]** (Extend Select) and press [→] and [↓] to highlight CLIENT_ID.

❹ Press **[Del]**. The heading disappears.

Now you need to add group bands to the Report Design screen. Group bands define subtotals for a group.

To insert a group band:

❶ Move the cursor to the Report Intro band border.

❷ Press **[Alt]B** to open the Bands menu.

❸ Select *Add a group band* (**A**). See Figure 6-20. A submenu appears.

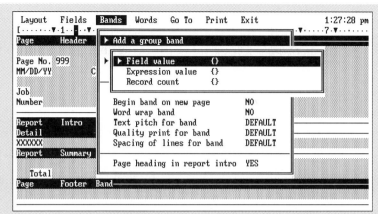

Figure 6-20
Adding a group
band

Indicate you want to group records on CLIENT_ID.

④ Select *Field value* (**F**) from the list of choices.

Select the field you want to group on.

⑤ Highlight CLIENT_ID and press **[Enter]**. See Figure 6-21. When you add a group band, two new bands appear in the Report Design screen. The *Group 1 Intro* band contains identifying text and data about a group and prints before the group of records. The *Group 1 Summary* band contains summary statistics for each group and prints after the group.

Group 1 Intro →
band

Group 1 →
Summary band

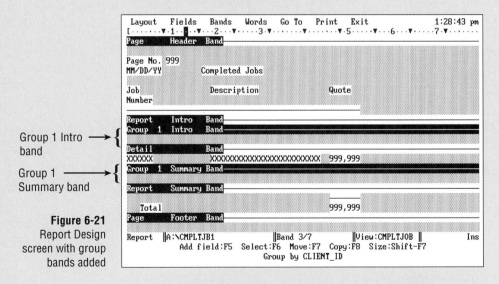

Figure 6-21
Report Design
screen with group
bands added

Now Esther is ready to add a group heading to the report format. Esther wants to add the heading "Client is ALE" on a separate line before the group of records for Alexander's

Insurance Company (ALE), and the heading "Client is CEL" on a separate line before the group of records for Celebrity Caterers (CEL), and so on.

To place a heading before each group to better describe the group of records that follows, you use the Group Intro band. Let's specify the group heading now.

To add a group heading:

➊ Move into the Group 1 Intro band. Position the cursor at Line:0 Col:3.

Enter the text for the heading.

➋ Type **Client ID is**.

Now add a database field to the group heading band.

➌ Move the cursor to Line:0 Col:17.

➍ Press **[F5]** (Field). The field selection box appears. See Figure 6-22.

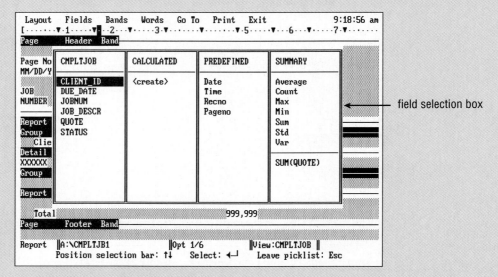

Figure 6-22
Adding a field to a
Group Header Band

Identify the field you want to add.

➎ From the CMPLTJOB panel highlight CLIENT_ID and press **[Enter]**. A field definition prompt box appears.

The field is defined as three characters. No changes are needed.

➏ Press **[Ctrl][End]** to accept the entries for the field definition. See Figure 6-23. The Report Design screen appears, showing the entry for the group heading. A field template representing the CLIENT_ID field also appears in the Group 1 Intro band.

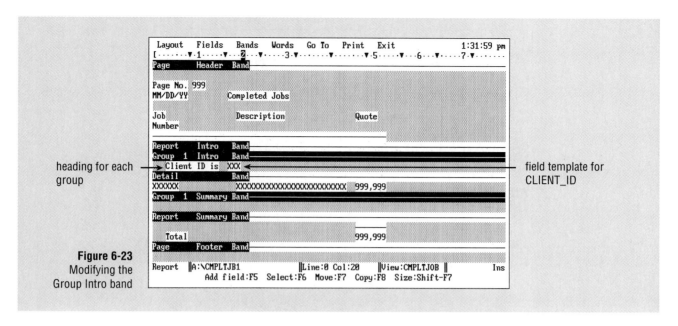

heading for each group →

field template for CLIENT_ID

Figure 6-23
Modifying the Group Intro band

Now add the specifications to sum the quotes for each client, that is, to define a summary field. This field is entered in the Group 1 Summary band.

To enter the specification for a group summary field:

❶ Move into the Group 1 Summary band and position the cursor at Line:0 Col:3.

Enter the description of the summary field.

❷ Type **Subtotal**.

❸ Move the cursor to the position where you want the summary field to begin, Line:0 Col:46.

Now define the summary field.

❹ Press **[F5]** (Field). A field selection box appears. Move the cursor to the SUMMARY panel. Seven types of summary fields are available: Average, Max, Min, Sum, Std, Var, and Count. See Figure 6-24 on the next page.

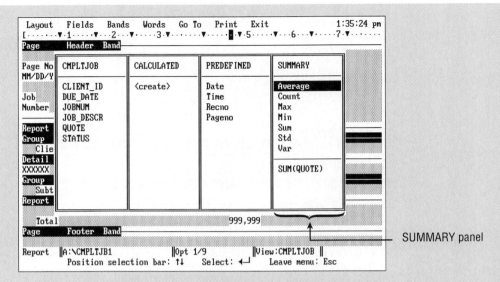

Figure 6-24
Field selection box
for summary field

⑤ Highlight Sum and press **[Enter]**. A field definition prompt box appears. See Figure 6-25.

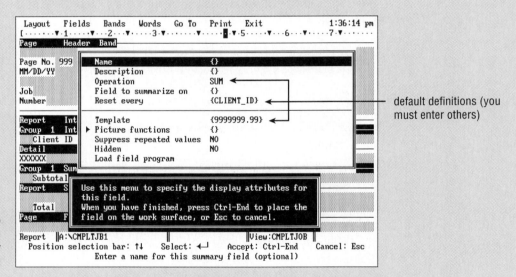

Figure 6-25
Field definition
prompt box for
summary field

Enter the name of the summary field.

⑥ Select Name (**N**), type **subquote**, and press **[Enter]**.

Indicate the field you want to summarize.

⑦ Select *Field to summarize on* (**F**). A list of field names appears.

⑧ Highlight QUOTE and press **[Enter]**.

Adjust the template for this field so it is consistent with the QUOTE field template in the Detail band.

⑨ Select *Template* (**T**), edit the template to read 999,999, and press **[Enter]**.

⑩ Press **[Ctrl][End]** to accept the current field definition. The Report Design screen appears, with the summary field added to the Group 1 Summary band. See Figure 6-26.

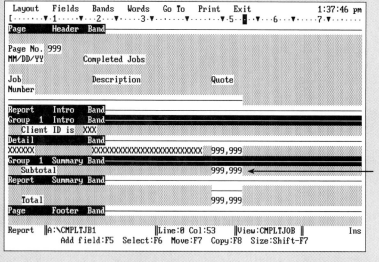

Figure 6-26
Defining the Group
Summary band

summary field template
subtotals for QUOTE

Esther decides a blank line between the subtotal for one group and the heading of a second group will improve the appearance of the report.

To insert a blank line:

❶ Move the cursor beyond the field template for SUBQUOTE in the Group 1 Summary band, Line:0 Col:53.

❷ Press **[Ctrl]N**. A blank line is inserted below the Subtotal line in the Group 1 Summary band.

Let's print the report.

To print the report:

❶ Press **[Alt]P** to open the Print menu.

❷ Select *Begin printing* (**B**). See Figure 6-27 on the next page.

```
Page No.    1
06/22/93              Completed Jobs

Job                       Description              Quote
Number
_____

   Client ID is   ALE
1004    ALE          B/W Magazine Ad            3,500
   Subtotal                                     3,500

   Client ID is   FAT
1009    FAT          Bicycle Magazine Ad        2,500
   Subtotal                                     2,500

   Client ID is   IMA
1011    IMA          Fall Catalogue             8,450
   Subtotal                                     8,450

   Client ID is   MOU
1003    MOU          Ski equipment sale         3,000
   Subtotal                                     3,000

   Client ID is   ORI
1001    ORI          Best in the Southwest      2,500
1006    ORI          Fall Promotion             2,200
   Subtotal                                     4,700

   Client ID is   SAN
1005    SAN          Magazine Ad               22,500
1007    SAN          Pamphlet                   3,000
   Subtotal                                    25,500

   Client ID is   VIK
1002    VIK          Fall TV Ad                32,500
   Subtotal                                    32,500

   Total                                       80,150
```

Figure 6-27
Printout with
subtotals

Esther looks over the report and sees that the records are printed in groups ordered by client ID. She has met Nancy's requirements, so she delivers the report. But first she saves this report. Rather than replacing the previous report definition with this revised definition, let's save this report to a different file.

To save a report and remain in the Report Design screen:

❶ Press **[Alt]L** to open the Layout menu.

❷ Select *Save this report* (**S**). A prompt appears, requesting a name.

❸ Edit the filename to read **cmpltjb2.frm** and press **[Enter]**. dBASE stores this file to your data diskette.

Now return to the Control Center.

To return to the Control Center:

❶ Press **[Alt]E** to open the Exit menu.

❷ Select *Abandon changes and exit* (**A**). Since you already saved the file, it's OK to make this choice.

Notice that the two reports you saved in this tutorial appear on the Reports panel. See Figure 6-28.

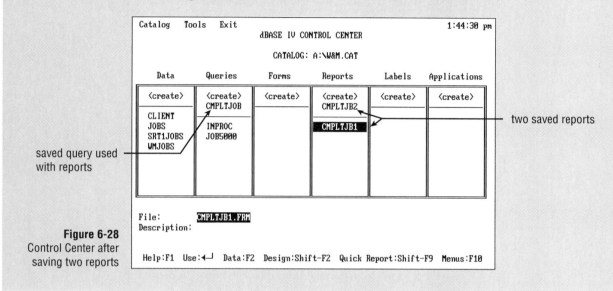

Figure 6-28
Control Center after saving two reports

You have now created, viewed, and modified a report. Remember to quit dBASE before shutting off your machine.

■   ■   ■

Control Center Summary

To create a quick layout report:

Open database file in the Data panel.

Highlight <create> in the Reports panel and press [Enter].

Select *Quick layouts* (Q). A submenu appears.

Select *Column layout* (C).

To select a field:

Move cursor to the field to be selected.

Press [F6] and press [Enter].

To delete a field:

Highlight the field template you want to remove and press [Del].

Control Center Summary

To move a field:

Move cursor to the field to be selected.

Press [F6] and press [Enter].

Press [F7] and move the cursor to new location.

Press [Enter].

To add a field:

Press [F5]. The field selection box appears.

Highlight the field that you want to use and press [Enter].

Fill in the field definition prompt box.

Press [Ctrl][End] when finished.

To add lines and boxes:

Press [Alt]L to open the Layout menu.

Select *Line* (L). A submenu appears.

Select *Single line* (S) or *Double line* (D).

Move the cursor to where you want to start.

Press [Enter] to indicate the beginning of the line.

Press [→] to draw a horizontal line or [↓] to draw a vertical line.

Press [Enter] to end the line.

To delete a blank line or a line of text:

Move cursor to the line you want to remove.

Press [Alt]W to open the Words menu.

Select *Remove line* (R).

To modify a field template:

Highlight the field template you want to modify.

Press [F5]. The field definition prompt box appears.

Make changes and press [Enter].

Press [Ctrl][End] to accept the new settings.

To add a group band:

Press [Alt]B to open the Bands menu.

Select *Add a group band* (A).

Select *Field value* (F) from the submenu.

Highlight the field you want to group on and press [Enter].

Control Center Summary

To save a report format:

Press [Alt]E to open the Exit menu.

Select *Save changes and exit* (S).

Enter a filename and press [Enter].

To print a report:

Press [Alt]P to open the Print menu.

Select *Begin printing* (B).

To view a report:

Press [Alt]P to open the Print menu.

Select *View report on screen* (V).

Exercises

1. If you see the file extension FRM on your data diskette, what do you know about this file?

2. What panel do you use to access the report format?

3. Your institution maintains a student transcript file named TRANSCPT, which contains records for all currently enrolled students. One of the fields in this file is each student's cumulative GPA. To develop a report of students on the dean's list (GPA above 3.25), what would be the source of data for the report?

4. In what band of the Report Design screen do you define report titles?

5. What is meant by the term *control break report*?

6. What section of the Report Design screen is used to define subtotals?

7. To include subtotals in a report, how must your data be organized?

8. Figure 6-29 on the next page is an inventory report created with the dBASE report generator.
   a. What band from the Report Design screen produced the item numbered 1?
   b. What band from the Report Design screen produced the item numbered 2?
   c. What band from the Report Design screen produced the item numbered 3?

```
Page No.      1
10/19/92
                              2  PC Mail Order Company
                                    Inventory Report

          1  Software           Type Quantity  Price/          Retail
             Package                 on Hand  Package          Value

             Lotus 123-2.0         SP        8   319.00        2552.00
             Lotus 123-3.0         SP        3   359.00        1077.00
             MS Excel              SP        4   284.99        1139.96
             MS Word 5.0           WP        3   199.99         599.97
             WordPerfect 5.1       WP        6   214.99        1289.94
             Quattro Pro           SP        3   257.00         771.00
             AMI Professional      WP        2   289.00         578.00
             PFS: Professional Write WP      4   127.00         508.00
          *** Total ***

                                                        3   8515.87
```

Figure 6-29

9. Figure 6-30 is a revised inventory report also created with the dBASE report generator.

```
Page No.      1
10/19/92
                                PC Mail Order Company
                                    Inventory Report

              Software             Quantity  Price/          Retail
              Package              on Hand  Package          Value

          1  ** Software Category: SP
             Lotus 123-2.0              8   319.00          2552.00
             Lotus 123-3.0              3   359.00          1077.00
             MS Excel                   4   284.99          1139.96
             Quattro Pro                3   257.00           771.00
             ** Subtotal **

                                                            5539.96


             ** Software Category: WP
             MS Word 5.0                3   199.99           599.97
             WordPerfect 5.1            6   214.99          1289.94
             AMI Professional           2   289.00           578.00
             PFS: Professional Write    4   127.00           508.00
             ** Subtotal **

                                                            2975.91

          *** Total ***

                                                            8515.87
```

Figure 6-30

a. What band from the Report Design screen produced the item numbered 1?

b. The column Retail Value has a subtotal, but the column Price/Package does not. What band from the Report Design screen was used to subtotal the retail value but not the price/package? How was it possible to get a subtotal for the retail value but not the Quantity on Hand field?

Tutorial Assignments

Activate the W&M catalog and use the CLIENT file to complete Assignments 1 and 2.

1. Use the report layout sheet shown in Figure 6-31 and the CLIENT database file to create a report format file. Name the report format file CLREPT.

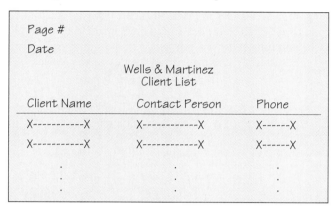

Figure 6-31

2. Use the report format file CLREPT and print W&M's clients in alphabetical order by CLIENT_ID.

Activate the TUTOR6 catalog and use the JOBS database file. Modify the layout of report format file STATUS1 to answer Assignments 3 through 6.

3. Print a report for each completed job having a quote under $10,000.

4. Modify STATUS1 to include a fifth column for the field STATUS. Also change the heading "Completed Jobs" to "Job Status." Save the report format as STATUS3.

5. Print the revised report in alphabetical order by client ID for all jobs. Use the index tag for CLIENT_ID.

6. Print the revised report in alphabetical order by client ID for all jobs having a quote between $5,000 and $15,000.

Open the report format file STATUS2 to answer Assignments 7 through 10.

7. Use STATUS2 from the Reports panel to print a report by client for all completed jobs having a quote greater than or equal to $2,000.

8. Modify STATUS2 to include a fourth column with the heading Due Date. Also change the heading "Completed Jobs" to "Job Status." Save the report format as STATUS4.

9. Print the revised report in alphabetical order by client ID for all jobs. Use the index tag for CLIENT_ID.

10. Print the revised report for all jobs having a quote between $5,000 and $15,000.

Case Problems

1. Biggs & Hang Investment Corporation

Activate the BIG&HANG catalog and open the JAPAN database file.

1. Use the report layout sheet in Figure 6-32 and the JAPAN database file to create the report format file JPRPT1. You may need to increase the width of the field templates in the number columns.

Figure 6-32

Page # Date				
		Japanese Companies Financial Data - 1990		
Company	Ind	Assets	Sales	Profits
X------X	X	99,999,999	99,999,999	99,999,999
X------X	X	99,999,999	99,999,999	99,999,999
		.	.	.
		.	.	.
		.	.	.
Total		999,999,999	999,999,999	999,999,999

Use the report format file JPRPT1 to complete Problems 2 through 4.

2. Print JPRPT1 in alphabetical order by company.

3. Print JPRPT1 with the companies ordered by industry.

4. Print JPRPT1 for companies with profits above 100,000 yen ordered by industry.

5. Use the report layout sheet shown in Figure 6-33 to modify JPRPT1. Save this revised report as JPRPT2.

```
Page #
Date
                          Japanese Companies
                         Financial Data - 1990
Company          Assets              Sales              Profits
Industry - <IND>
X------X         99,999,999          99,999,999         99,999,999
X------X         99,999,999          99,999,999         99,999,999
    .                .                   .                  .
    .                .                   .                  .
    .                .                   .                  .
Subtotal        999,999,999         999,999,999        999,999,999
Industry - <IND>
X------X         99,999,999          99,999,999         99,999,999
X------X         99,999,999          99,999,999         99,999,999
    .                .                   .                  .
    .                .                   .                  .
Subtotal        999,999,999         999,999,999        999,999,999
Total           999,999,999         999,999,999        999,999,999
```

Figure 6-33

6. Use JPRPT2 to print the companies with subtotals by industry.

2. Medi-Source Inc.

Activate the MEDISRCE catalog and open the ACCTREC database file.

1. Use the ACCTREC database file and the report layout in Figure 6-34 to prepare a report format file named MEDRPT1.

```
Page #
Date
                    Medi-Source Inc.
                    Outstanding Balance
Customer      Type      State     Balance
Name                              Owed
X--------X     X        XX        99,999.99
X--------X     X        XX        99,999.99
    .          .         .            .
    .          .         .            .
    .          .         .            .
Total                             999,999.99
```

Figure 6-34

Use the MEDRPT1 report format file to complete Problems 2 and 3.

2. Print the Outstanding Balance Report for all customers, with the customers in alphabetical order.

3. Print the Outstanding Balance Report for only those customers that have outstanding balances over $15,000. Arrange the customers in alphabetical order.

4. Use the report layout sheet in Figure 6-35 and the ACCTREC database file to create a report format file named MEDRPT2. The control field is TYPE (type of business).

5. Using TYPE as the indexing field, create the index tag named type.

Use the MEDRPT2 report format file to complete Problems 6, 7, and 8.

6. Print MEDRPT2 for all customers.

7. Print MEDRPT2 for customers who are not in the hospital industry (industry code = H).

8. Print MEDRPT2 for customers whose outstanding balance is over $5,000.

```
Page #
Date
                          Medi-Source Inc.
                        Outstanding Balance
                        By Type of Business
      Customer              State            Balance
      Name                                   Owed
      ─────────────────────────────────────────────
      Type of business <TYPE>

      X--------X            XX                99,999.99
      X--------X            XX                99,999.99

            .                 .                 .
            .                 .                 .
            .                 .                 .

      Subtotal                               999,999.99

      Type of business <TYPE>

      X--------X            XX                99,999.99
      X--------X            XX                99,999.99

            .                 .                 .
            .                 .                 .
            .                 .                 .

      Subtotal                               999,999.99
      Total                                  999,999.99
```

Figure 6-35

3. Appleton & Drake Electrical Supply Company

Activate the APPLTON catalog and open the EMPLOYEE database file.

1. Use the report layout sheet in Figure 6-36 and the EMPLOYEE database file to create the report format file EMPRPT1.

```
Page #
Date
                    Appleton & Drake
                    Employee Report
    Last Name       Dept      Sex        Salary
    X---------X     XXX       X          99,999
    X---------X     XXX       X          99,999
        .            .         .            .
        .            .         .            .
        .            .         .            .
    Total                                9,999,999
```

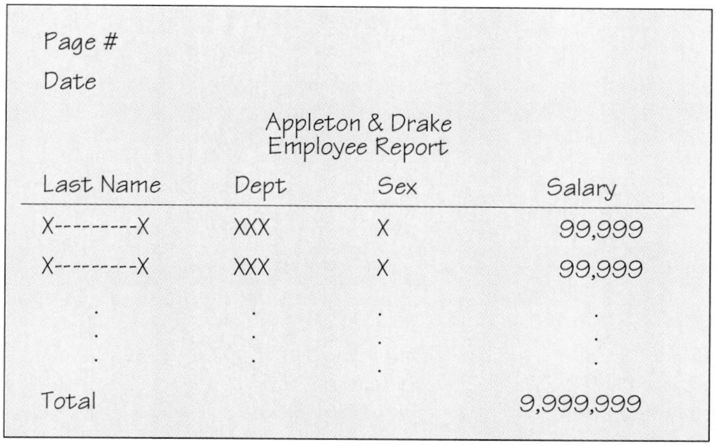

Figure 6-36

Use the report format file EMPRPT1 to complete Problems 2 through 4.

2. Print an alphabetized list of all employees.

3. Print a list of employees in alphabetical order for employees in the Corporate department (department code = COR).

4. Print the EMPRPT1 report for all employees earning under $30,000. Order the data by department; within each department, alphabetize by last name.

5. Use the report layout sheet in Figure 6-37 and the EMPLOYEE database file to create the report format file EMPRPT2. The control field is DEPT.

```
Page #
Date
                    Appleton & Drake
                    Employee Report
                    By Department
    Last Name          Sex        Salary
    ─────────────────────────────────────
    Department <DEPT>
    X---------X         X          99,999
    X---------X         X          99,999

           .           .            .
           .           .            .
           .           .            .

    Subtotal                      999,999
    Department <DEPT>
    X---------X         X          99,999
    X---------X         X          99,999

           .           .            .
           .           .            .
           .           .            .

    Subtotal                      999,999
    Total                       9,999,999
```

Figure 6-37

Use the report format file EMPRPT2 to complete Problems 6 and 7.

6.   Print EMPRPT2 for all employees.

7.   Print EMPRPT2 for all employees earning over $35,000.

4. National Basketball Association

Activate the NBA catalog and open the NBA database file.

1.   Use the report layout sheet in Figure 6-38 and the NBA database file to create the report format file NBARPT1.

```
Page #
Date
                              NBA Salary Report
    Last Name     First Name      Team      Pos       Salary
    ──────────────────────────────────────────────────────────
    X--------X    X---------X     XXX        X       9,999,999
    X--------X    X---------X     XXX        X       9,999,999

        .             .            .         .           .
        .             .            .         .           .
        .             .            .         .           .

    Total                                          99,999,999
```

Figure 6-38

Use the report format file NBARPT1 to complete Problems 2 and 3.

2. Print an alphabetized list of all players.

3. Print an alphabetized list of all players who play the position of forward (position code = F) or guard (position code = G).

4. Use the report layout sheet in Figure 6-39 and the NBA database file to create the report format file NBARPT2. The control field is TEAM. Create an index tag using TEAM as the indexing field.

```
Page #
Date
                      NBA Salary Report By Team
   Last Name        First Name        Pos              Salary
   Team <teamname>
   X--------X        X---------X        X            9,999,999
   X--------X        X---------X        X            9,999,999
       .                 .              .                .
       .                 .              .                .
       .                 .              .                .
   Subtotal                                         99,999,999
   Team <teamname>
   X--------X        X---------X        X            9,999,999
   X--------X        X---------X        X            9,999,999
       .                 .              .                .
       .                 .              .                .
       .                 .              .                .
   Subtotal                                         99,999,999
   Total                                            99,999,999
```

Figure 6-39

Use NBARPT2 to complete Problems 5 and 6.

5. Print a report by team.

6. Print a report by team for players earning over $1 million.

5. Off-Campus Housing at Ashland University

Activate the HOUSING Catalog and open the HOUSING database file.

1. Use the report layout sheet in Figure 6-40 to create a report format file. Name the report format file HSERPT1.

Page #
Date

Off-Campus Housing Report

Rental Street	Town/ City	Type	Rent	# of Bedrooms
X-------X	X-----X	X	9,999	X
X-------X	X-----X	X	9,999	X

Figure 6-40

2. Print a list of housing units ordered by town using your report format file.

3. Print a list of housing units ordered by type of housing unit.

dBASE IV Index

DOS QUICK REFERENCE

Set Up and Status

DATE *MM-DD-YY*	Set system date (e.g., 10-25-93)
TIME *HH:MM:SS*	Set system time (e.g., 13:00:00 for 1 PM)
VER	Show current DOS version
CLS	Clear screen
PROMPT PG	Change prompt to show drive and directory (e.g., C:\WP51)
d:	Change to drive *D*

Directories

DIR	Show file list of default directory
DIR *d:*	Show file list of files on drive *D*
DIR *dirname*	Show file list of indicated directory
DIR /P	Show file list, pausing when screen is full
DIR /W	Show filenames only (five columns of names)
CD *dirname* or CHDIR *dirname*	Change default directory to *dirname*
MD *dirname* or MKDIR *dirname*	Make directory *dirname*
RD *dirname* or RMDIR *dirname*	Remove directory *dirname* (must be empty)

File Management

COPY *file*	Copy file to current drive and directory
COPY *file file2*	Copy file to current drive and directory with name *file2*
COPY *file d:*	Copy file to drive *D*
COPY *file dirname*	Copy file to directory *dirname*
COPY *file path*	Copy file to indicated path (disk, directory, and filename)
DEL *file* or ERASE *file*	Delete file
REN *file file2* or RENAME *file file2*	Rename *file* to *file2*

Disk Management

FORMAT a:	Format diskette in drive A
FORMAT a:/s	Format diskette in drive A as system disk
DISKCOPY a: b:	Copy contents of diskette in drive A to diskette in drive B
DISKCOPY a: a:	Copy contents of diskette to another diskette by swapping them in drive A
CHKDSK a:	Check drive A and display report on screen

Paths and Files

When specifying file and directory names, use the conventions below. Wildcards can be used with COPY, DEL, REN, *and* DIR *to operate on multiple files at once.*

Example	Meaning
FILENAME.EXT	The file FILENAME.EXT in current drive and directory
\FILENAME.EXT	The file FILENAME.EXT in root directory of current drive
B:FILENAME.EXT	The file FILENAME.EXT in current directory of drive B
\DIRNAME\FILENAME.EXT	The file FILENAME.EXT in the DIRNAME directory of the current drive
C:\DIRNAME\FILENAME.EXT	The file FILENAME.EXT in the DIRNAME directory of drive C
\DIRNAME	The directory DIRNAME on the current drive (or all files in directory)
.	Wildcard: All files in current directory
*.EXT	Wildcard: All files with the extension EXT
FILENAME.*	Wildcard: All files with name FILENAME and any extension
FILENAME.?XT	Wildcard: Matches files where "?" is replaced by any legal character

WORDPERFECT 5.1 QUICK REFERENCE

COMMANDS

Block	[Alt][F4] or [F12]
Bold	[F6] or [Ctrl][F8],2,1
Cancel	[F1]
Case Conversion (block on)	[Shift][F3]
Center	[Shift][F6]
Center Page Top to Bottom	[Shift][F8],2,1
Conditional End of Page	[Shift][F8],4,2
Date Text	[Shift][F5],1
Delete Character Left	[Backspace]
Delete Character at Cursor	[Del]
Delete to End of Line	[Ctrl][End]
Delete to End of Page	[Ctrl][PgDn]
Delete Word	[Ctrl][Backspace]
End Field	[F9]
End of Record	[Shift][F9],2
Endnote	[Ctrl][F7],2
Exit	[F7]
Field	[Shift][F9],1
Flush Right	[Alt][F6]
Footers	[Shift][F8],2,4
Footnote	[Ctrl][F7],1
Format	[Shift][F8]
Hard Page Break	[Ctrl][Enter]
Headers	[Shift][F8],2,3
Help	[F3]
Hyphenation	[Shift][F8],1,1
♦ Indent	[F4]
♦ Indent ◀	[Shift][F4]
Justification	[Shift][F8],1,3
Line Format	[Shift][F8],1
Line Numbering	[Shift][F8],1,5
Line Spacing	[Shift][F8],1,6
List Files	[F5]
Macro Execute	[Alt][F10]
Macro Define	[Ctrl][F10]
◀ Margin Release	[Shift][Tab]
Margins Left/Right	[Shift][F8],1,7
Margins Top/Bottom	[Shift][F8],2,5
Merge	[Ctrl][F9],1
Merge Codes	[Shift][F9]
Move Block (block on)	[Ctrl][F4],1,1
Move Family (outline)	[Shift][F5],4,3
Move Paragraph	[Ctrl][F4],2
Move Sentence	[Ctrl][F4],1
New Page Number	[Shift][F8],2,6,1
Number of Copies	[Shift][F7],N
Outline	[Shift][F5],4
Page Numbering	[Shift][F8],2,6
Print	[Shift][F7]
Print Full Document	[Shift][F7],1
Retrieve Document	[Shift][F10]
Reveal Codes	[Alt][F3] or [F11]
Save Document	[F10]
Screen Rewrite	[Ctrl][F3],3
♦ Search	[F2]
◀ Search	[Shift][F2]
Search and Replace	[Alt][F2]
Setup	[Shift][F1]
Sort	[Ctrl][F9],2
Spell	[Ctrl][F2]
Split Screen	[Ctrl][F3],1
Style	[Alt][F8]
Suppress (Page Format)	[Shift][F8],2,8
Switch Document Screens	[Shift][F3]
Tab Set	[Shift][F8],1,8
Thesaurus	[Alt][F1]
Typeover/Insert Toggle	[Ins]
Undelete	[F1]
Underline	[F8] or [Ctrl][F8],2,2
View Document	[Shift][F7],6
Widow/Orphan Protection	[Shift][F8],1,9
Window	[Ctrl][F3],1

CURSOR CONTROL

Beginning of Document (before text)	[Home],[Home],[↑]
Begining of Document (before codes)	[Home],[Home],[Home],[↑]
Beginning of Line (before codes)	[Home],[Home],[Home],[←]
Beginning of Line (before text)	[Home],[Home],[←]
Character Left	[←]
Character Right	[→]
End of Document	[Home],[Home],[↓]
End of Line	[Home],[Home],[→] or [End]
Go To	[Ctrl][Home]
Line Down	[↓]
Line Up	[↑]
Next Paragraph Number (outline)	[Alt][→]
Next Paragraph Number, Same Level (outline)	[Alt][↓]
Previous Paragraph Number (outline)	[Alt][←]
Previous Paragraph Number, Same Level (outline)	[Alt][↑]
Screen Down	[Home],[↓] or + (Num Pad)
Screen Left	[Home],[←]
Screen Right	[Home],[→]
Screen Up	[Home],[↑] or – (Num Pad)
Word Left	[Ctrl][←]
Word Right	[Ctrl][→]

1-2-3 QUICK REFERENCE

Worksheet **R**ange **C**opy **M**ove **F**ile **P**rint **G**raph **D**ata **S**ystem **A**dd-In **Q**uit

PRESS /

Worksheet Commands

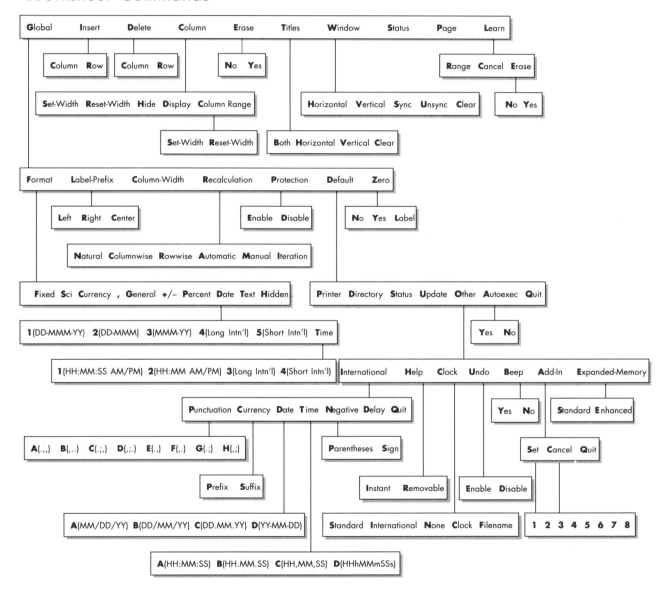

Range Commands

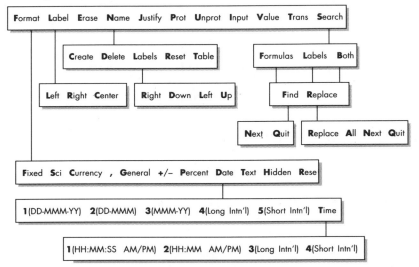

Format Label Erase Name Justify Prot Unprot Input Value Trans Search

Create Delete Labels Reset Table

Formulas Labels Both

Left Right Center

Right Down Left Up

Find Replace

Next Quit

Replace All Next Quit

Fixed Sci Currency , General +/− Percent Date Text Hidden Rese

1(DD-MMM-YY) 2(DD-MMM) 3(MMM-YY) 4(Long Intn'l) 5(Short Intn'l) Time

1(HH:MM:SS AM/PM) 2(HH:MM AM/PM) 3(Long Intn'l) 4(Short Intn'l)

File Commands

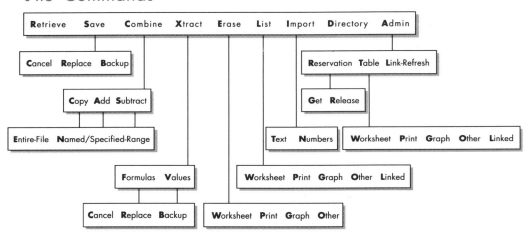

Retrieve Save Combine Xtract Erase List Import Directory Admin

Cancel Replace Backup

Reservation Table Link-Refresh

Copy Add Subtract

Get Release

Entire-File Named/Specified-Range

Text Numbers

Worksheet Print Graph Other Linked

Formulas Values

Worksheet Print Graph Other Linked

Cancel Replace Backup

Worksheet Print Graph Other

Print Commands

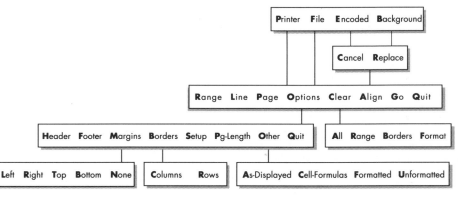

Printer File Encoded Background

Cancel Replace

Range Line Page Options Clear Align Go Quit

Header Footer Margins Borders Setup Pg-Length Other Quit

All Range Borders Format

Left Right Top Bottom None

Columns Rows

As-Displayed Cell-Formulas Formatted Unformatted

Graph Commands

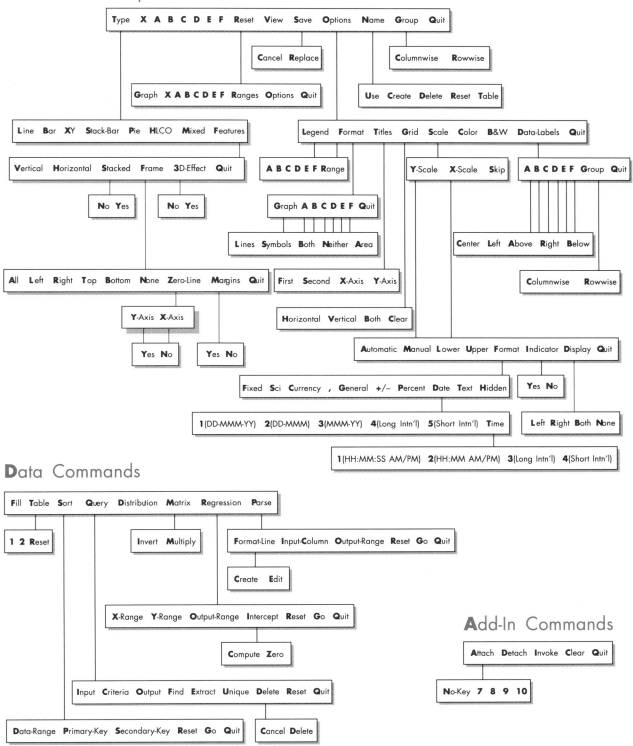

Data Commands

Add-In Commands

Course Technology, Inc.

1-2-3 WYSIWYG QUICK REFERENCE

Worksheet Format Graph Print Display Special Text Named-Style Quit

PRESS :

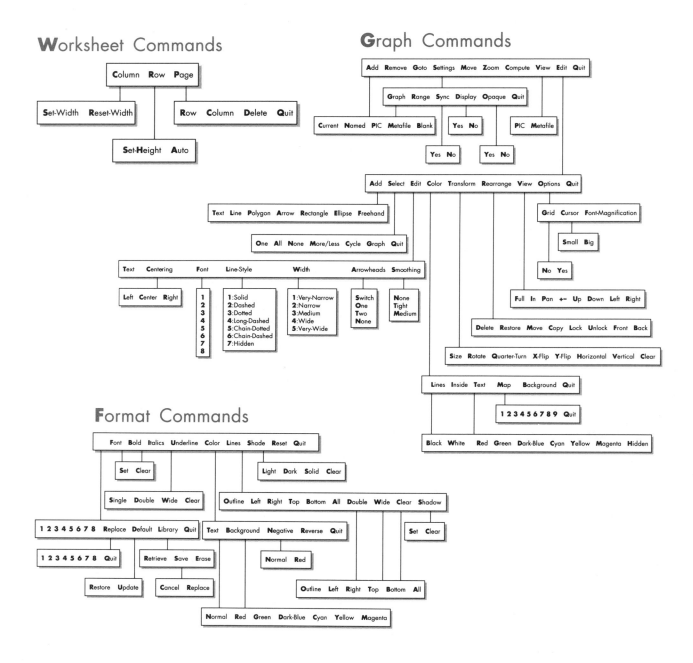

Print Commands

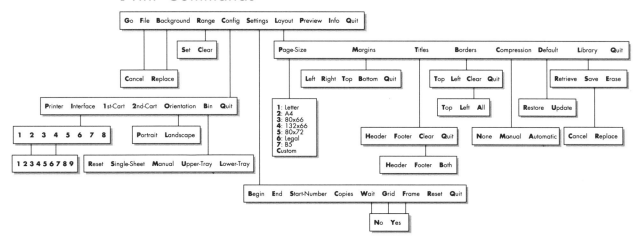

Display Commands

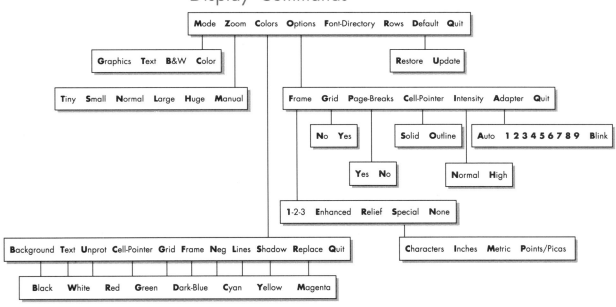

Special Commands

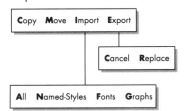

Text Commands

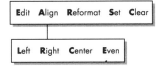

Named-Style Commands

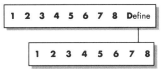

1-2-3 @FUNCTIONS

DATABASE @FUNCTIONS

@DAVG(*input,field,criteria*)	Average of values in database field.
@DCOUNT(*input,field,criteria*)	Number of nonblank cells in database field.
@DMAX(*input,field,criteria*)	Largest value in database field.
@DMIN(*input,field,criteria*)	Smallest value in database field.
@DSTD(*input,field,criteria*)	Standard deviation of values in database field.
@DSUM(*input,field,criteria*)	Sum of values in database field.
@DVAR(*input,field,criteria*)	Variance of values in database field.

DATE AND TIME @FUNCTIONS

@DATE(*year,month,day*)	Date-number for date specified.
@DATEVALUE(*string*)	Date-number for date-type string.
@DAY(*date-number*)	Day of month for given date-number.
@MONTH(*date-number*)	Month for given date-number.
@YEAR(*date-number*)	Year for given date-number.
@NOW	Date- and time-number of current date and time.
@HOUR(*time-number*)	Hour (1-23) of given time-number.
@MINUTE(*time-number*)	Minute (0-59) of given time-number.
@SECOND(*time-number*)	Second (0-59) of given time-number.
@TIME(*hour,minutes,seconds*)	Time-number for time specified.
@TIMEVALUE(*string*)	Time-number for time-like string.

FINANCIAL @FUNCTIONS

@IRR(*guess,range*)	Internal rate of return of cash flows.
@NPV(*interest,range*)	Net present value of cash flows.
@DDB(*cost,salvage,life,period*)	Double-declining balance depreciation (one period).
@SLN(*cost,salvage,life*)	Straight-line depreciation (one period).
@SYD(*cost,salvage,life,period*)	Sum-of-the-years'-digits depreciation (one period).
@FV(*payments,interest,term*)	Future value of series of equal payments.
@PMT(*principal,interest,term*)	Periodic payment for installment loan.
@PV(*payments,interest,term*)	Present value of series of equal payments.
@TERM(*payments,interest,fut-val*)	Number of payment periods to accrue future value.
@CTERM(*interest,fut-val,pres-val*)	Number of compounding periods to accrue future value.
@RATE(*fut-val,pres-val,term*)	Interest rate required to accrue future value.

STATISTICAL @FUNCTIONS

@AVG(*list*)	Average of values in list of ranges.
@COUNT(*list*)	Number of nonblank cells in list of ranges.
@MAX(*list*)	Largest value in list of ranges.
@MIN(*list*)	Smallest value in list of ranges.
@STD(*list*)	Standard deviation of values in list of ranges.
@SUM(*list*)	Sum of values in list of ranges.
@VAR(*list*)	Variance of values in list of ranges.

LOGICAL @FUNCTIONS

@FALSE	Logical value 0 (false).
@IF(*condition,x,y*)	*x* if *condition* is true, *y* if false.
@ISAFF(*name*)	1 for add-in function names, 0 otherwise.
@ISAPP(*name*)	1 for attached add-in names, 0 otherwise.
@ISERR(*x*)	1 if *x* is ERR, 0 otherwise.
@ISNA(*x*)	1 if *x* is NA, 0 otherwise.
@ISNUMBER(*x*)	1 for numeric value, 0 otherwise.
@ISSTRING(*x*)	1 for string, 0 otherwise.
@TRUE	Logical value 1 (true).

SPECIAL @FUNCTIONS

@@(*location*)	Contents of cell address.
@CELL(*attribute,range*)	Attribute information for first cell in *range*.
@CELLPOINTER(*attribute*)	Attribute information for current cell.
@COLS(*range*)	Number of columns in *range*.
@ROWS(*range*)	Number of rows in *range*.
@ERR	The value ERR.
@NA	The value NA.
@CHOOSE(*offset,list*)	Specified value in list of values.
@HLOOKUP(*x,range,row-offset*)	Horizontal lookup in range.
@INDEX(*range,col-offset,row-offset*)	Lookup value by row and column in range.
@VLOOKUP(*x,range,col-offset*)	Vertical lookup in range.

MATHEMATICAL @FUNCTIONS

@ABS(*x*)	Absolute (positive) value.
@EXP(*x*)	The value e^x.
@INT(*x*)	Integer portion of *x*.
@LN(*x*)	Natural logarithm (base *e*) of *x*.
@LOG(*x*)	Common logarithm (base 10) of *x*.
@MOD(*x,y*)	Remainder on dividing *x* by *y*.
@RAND	Random value from 0 to 1.
@ROUND(*x,n*)	Value of *x* rounded to *n* decimal places.
@SQRT(*x*)	Square root of *x*.
@ACOS(*x*)	Inverse cosine of *x*.
@ASIN(*x*)	Inverse sine of *x*.
@ATAN(*x*)	Inverse tangent of *x*.
@ATAN2(*x,y*)	Angle to point (*x,y*).
@COS(*x*)	Cosine of *x*.
@PI	Approximation to value of pi.
@SIN(*x*)	Sine of *x*.
@TAN(*x*)	Tangent of *x*.

STRING @FUNCTIONS

@CHAR(*x*)	Character in Lotus International Character Set (LICS).
@CLEAN(*string*)	*String* with certain control characters stripped.
@CODE(*string*)	LICS code for first character in *string*.
@EXACT(*string1,string2*)	1 if strings match exactly, 0 otherwise.
@FIND(*srch-string,string,start-num*)	Position of character search character in *string*.
@LEFT(*string,n*)	First *n* characters in *string*.
@LENGTH(*string*)	Number of characters in *string*.
@LOWER(*string*)	*String* converted to lowercase.
@MID(*string,start-num,n*)	*n* characters from middle of *string*.
@N(*range*)	Value in first cell of *range*.
@PROPER(*string*)	*String* with words capitalized.
@REPEAT(*string,n*)	*String* repeated *n* times.
@REPLACE(*orig-string, start-num,n,new-string*)	Replaces *n* characters in string with *new-string*.
@RIGHT(*string,n*)	Last *n* characters in *string*.
@S(*range*)	Label in first cell in *range*.
@STRING(*x,n*)	*x* converted to string with *n* decimal places.
@TRIM(*string*)	*String* with extra spaces stripped.
@UPPER(*string*)	*String* converted to uppercase.
@VALUE(*string*)	Number-type *string* converted to numeric value.

1-2-3 MODE AND STATUS INDICATORS

STATUS INDICATORS	MEANING
CALC	You need to recalculate: press [F9] (CALC).
CAPS	The Caps Lock key is on.
CIRC	A circular reference exists. Use /Worksheet Status to find it.
CMD	1-2-3 is pausing during a macro.
END	The End key is on.
LEARN	You pressed [Alt][F5] (LEARN). 1-2-3 is recording your keystrokes for a macro.
MEM	You are running out of memory.
NUM	The Num Lock key is on.
OVR	The [Insert] key is on.
RO	The worksheet has read-only status.
SCROLL	The Scroll Lock key is on.
SST	A macro running in single-step mode is waiting for user input.
STEP	You invoked STEP mode. A macro is running one step at a time.
UNDO	You can press [Alt][F4] (UNDO) to undo changes made.

MODE INDICATORS	MEANING
EDIT	You pressed [F2] (EDIT) to edit an entry.
ERROR	1-2-3 is displaying an error message.
FILES	1-2-3 is displaying a menu of file names in the control panel.
FIND	You selected /Data Query Find. 1-2-3 is highlighting a database record that matches your criteria.
FRMT	You selected /Data Parse Format-Line Edit to edit a format line.
HELP	You pressed [F1] (HELP). 1-2-3 is displaying a Help screen.
LABEL	You are entering a label.
MENU	You pressed [/] (Slash) and 1-2-3 is displaying a menu of commands.
NAMES	1-2-3 is displaying a menu of range names.
POINT	1-2-3 is prompting you to specify a range.
READY	1-2-3 is ready for you to enter data or specify a command.
STAT	You selected /Worksheet (Global Default) Status and 1-2-3 is displaying a status screen.
VALUE	You are entering a number or formula.
WAIT	1-2-3 is completing a process.
WYSIWYG	You pressed [:] (Colon). 1-2-3 is displaying a WYSIWYG menu.

—1-2-3 Task-Oriented Command Reference—

Retrieving a File

1. Select **/**F**ile** **R**etrieve (**/FR**).
2. Type or highlight the name of the file you want to work with. Press **[Enter]**.

Saving a File

1. Select **/**F**ile** **S**ave (**/FS**).
2. Press **[Enter]** to keep the existing filename, or type a new filename and press **[Enter]**.
3. When prompted, choose either **B**ackup (**B**) to save the file and create a backup copy of the old version, or **R**eplace (**R**) to save the file without creating a backup copy.

Copying and Moving Data

1. Select **/**C**opy** (**C**) or **/**M**ove** (**M**).
2. Enter the FROM range by highlighting the data you want to copy or move. Press **[Enter]**.
3. Enter the TO range by moving the cell pointer to the first cell in the range where you want the data to be copied or moved. Press **[Enter]**.

Changing the Width of Columns

To change the width of a single column:

1. Move the cell pointer to the column whose width you want to change.
2. Select **/**W**orksheet** **C**olumn **S**et-Width (**/WCS**).
3. Press [→] or [←] to widen or narrow the column, or type a number corresponding to the width you want (9 is the default). Press **[Enter]**.

To change the width of all the columns in a worksheet:

1. Select **/**W**orksheet** **G**lobal **C**olumn-Width (**/WGC**).
2. Press [→] or [←] to widen or narrow the columns, or type a number corresponding to the width you want (9 is the default). Press **[Enter]**.

Quitting 1-2-3

1. Select **/**Q**uit** **Y**es (**/QY**).

Inserting a Row or Column

1. Move the cell pointer where you want the new row or column.
2. Select **/**W**orksheet** **I**nsert **R**ow (**/WIR**) or **C**olumn (**/WIC**). Press **[Enter]**.

Erasing Data

To erase the data in a range:

1. Select **/**R**ange** **E**rase (**/RE**).
2. Highlight the data you want to erase. Press **[Enter]**.

To erase a worksheet from temporary memory and replace it with a blank one:

1. Select **/**W**orksheet** **E**rase **Y**es (**/WEY**).

To delete a file from disk:

1. Select **/**F**ile** **E**rase (**/FE**).
2. Choose the type of file you want to delete: **W**orksheet (**W**), **P**rint (**P**), **G**raph (**G**), or **O**ther (**O**).
3. Highlight the name of the file you want to delete. Press **[Enter]**, then choose **Y**es (**Y**).

Formatting Data

1. To format selected data, select **/**R**ange** **F**ormat (**/RF**). To format the entire worksheet, select **/**W**orksheet** **G**lobal **F**ormat (**/WGF**).
2. Choose the type of format you want; for example, **C**urrency (**C**).
3. If prompted, enter the number of decimal points you want; for example **2**. Press **[Enter]**.
4. If you are formatting a range, highlight the data you want to format.
5. Press **[Enter]**

Printing a Worksheet

1. Choose **/**P**rint** **P**rinter **R**ange (**/PPR**).
2. Highlight the data you want to print.
3. Press **[Enter]**.
4. Choose **A**lign **G**o **Q**uit (**AGQ**).

—dBASE IV Control Center Quick Reference—

General Commands

To use a different catalog:
Press [Alt]C to open the Catalog menu.
Select *Use a different catalog* (U).
Highlight a catalog you want to use and press [Enter].

To open a database file:
Highlight filename in the Data panel and press [Enter].
Select *Use file* (U) from the prompt box.

To quit dBASE:
Press [Alt]E to open the Exit menu.
Select *Quit to DOS* (Q).

Creating a Database Structure

To create a database structure:
Highlight <create> in the Data panel and press [Enter].
Enter the specifications in the Database Design screen.
Press [Alt]E to open the Exit menu.
Select *Save changes and exit* (S).
Enter name of database structure and press [Enter].

To modify a database structure:
Highlight filename in the Data panel and press [Enter].
Select *Modify structure/order* (M).
Modify database structure.
Press [Alt]E to open the Exit menu.
Select *Save changes and exit* (S).
Answer Y to prompt.

Maintaining Database Files

To add records using the Browse screen:
Highlight filename in the Data panel.
Press [F2] until you access the Browse screen.
Press [Alt]R to open the Records menu.
Select *Add new records* (A).

Enter data.
Press [Alt]E to open the Exit menu.
Select *Exit* (E).

To add records using the Edit screen:
Highlight filename in the Data panel.
Press [F2] until you access the Edit screen.
Press [Alt]R to open the Records menu.
Select *Add new records* (A).
Enter data.
Press [Alt]E to open the Exit menu.
Select *Exit* (E).

To display data:
Highlight filename in the Data panel.
Press [F2] to access the Browse or Edit screen.

To mark a record for deletion:
Highlight filename in the Data panel.
Press [F2] to display data in the Browse or Edit screen.
Move cursor to the record you want to mark for deletion.
Press [Ctrl]U.

To pack records:
Highlight filename in the Data panel.
Press [F2] to display data in the Browse or Edit screen.
In the Browse or Edit screen press [Alt]O to open the Organize menu.
Select *Erase marked records* (E).
Answer Y to prompt for confirmation.

To copy files:
Press [Alt]T to open the Tools menu.
Select *DOS utilities* (D).
Mark files.
Press [Alt]O to open the Operations menu.
Select *Copy* (C).
Select desired option.
Follow screen prompts for destination and filename.
Press [Ctrl] [End].

Designing Queries

To access the Query Design screen:

Open database file.

Highlight <create> in the Queries panel and press [Enter].

To remove a field from the view skeleton:

While in the file or calculated fields skeleton:
Press [Tab] to move to the field you want to remove.
Press [F5] to delete field name.
Press [F2] to view data.

To add a field to the view skeleton:

While in the file or calculated fields skeleton:
Press [Tab] to move to the field you want to add.
Press [F5] to add field name.
Press [F2] to view data.

To move a field:

While in the view skeleton:
Highlight the field you want to move.
Press [F6] to select field.
Press [F7] AND move cursor to new position of field.
Press [Enter].

To enter a filter condition in the Query Design screen:

Highlight <create> in the Queries panel and press [Enter].

Tab to field name.

Enter filter condition:
character value in quotes
date value in curly braces
AND operator in same row
OR operator in different rows

Press [F2] to view data.

To add a condition box:

Press [Alt]C to open the Condition menu.
Select *Add a condition box* (A).
Enter condition.
Press [F2] to view data.

To create a calculated field:

Press [Alt]F to open the Fields menu.
Select *Create calculated field* (C).
Enter formula and press [Enter].

To add a file to the Query Design screen:

Press [Alt]L to open the Layout menu.
Select *Add file to query* (A).
Highlight the database file you want to add and press [Enter].

To save a query and remain in the Query Design screen:

Press [Alt]L to open the Layout menu.
Select *Save this query* (S).
Enter query name and press [Enter].

To save a query and return to the Control Center:

Press [Alt]E to open the Exit menu.
Select *Save changes and exit* (S).
Enter filename and press [Enter].

Sorting Records

To create a sorted file:

From the Data panel, highlight the database file you want to sort.
Press [F2] to view the data.
Press [Alt]O to open the Organize menu.
Select *Sort database on field list* (S).
Enter the field name you want to use to order the database.
Press [Enter] to move the cursor to the Type of sort column.
Choose the desired sort order.
Press [Ctrl][End].
Enter name of sorted file and press [Enter].

To sort a file using the Query Design screen:

While in the file skeleton, move highlight to field you want to sort on.
Press [Alt]F to open Fields menu.
Select *Sort on this field* (S).
Choose the sort order and press [Enter].

Indexing Database Files

To create an index:
Highlight filename in the Data panel.

Press [Shift][F2] to access the Database Design screen.

From the Organize menu select *Create new index (C)*.

Highlight *Name of index*, press [Enter], and enter index name.

Highlight *Index expression*, press [Enter], and enter index expression.

Press [Ctrl][End] to save the index.

To activate an index:
Press [Shift][F2] to open the Organize menu.

Select *Order records by index* (O).

Choose the index you want to use and press [Enter].

To search for specific records using an index:
Press [Shift][F2] to open the Organize menu.

Select *Order records by index* (O).

Choose the index you want to use and press [Enter].

Press [F2] to view the data.

Press [Alt]G to open the Go To menu.

Select *Index key search* (I).

Enter search string for <fieldname> and press [Enter].

To open indexes for use with a query:
Press [Alt]F to open the Fields menu.

Select *Include indexes* (I).

Generating Reports

To create a quick layout report:
Open database file in the Data panel.

Highlight <create> in the Reports panel and press [Enter].

Select *Quick layouts* (Q). A submenu appears.

Select *Column layout* (C).

To select a field:
Move cursor to the field to be selected.

Press [F6] and press [Enter].

To delete a field:
Highlight the field template you want to remove and press [Del].

To move a field:
Move cursor to the field to be selected.

Press [F6] and press [Enter].

Press [F7] and move the cursor to new location.

Press [Enter].

To add a field:
Press [F5]. The field selection box appears.

Highlight the field that you want to use and press [Enter].

Fill in the field definition prompt box.

Press [Ctrl][End] when finished.

To add lines and boxes:
Press [Alt]L to open the Layout menu.

Select *Line* (L). A submenu appears.

Select *Single line* (S) or *Double line* (D).

Move the cursor to where you want to start.

Press [Enter] to indicate the beginning of the line.

Press [→] to draw a horizontal line or [↓] to draw a vertical line.

Press [Enter] to end the line.

To delete a blank line or a line of text:
Move cursor to the line you want to remove.

Press [Alt]W to open the Words menu.

Select *Remove line* (R).

To modify a field template:
Highlight the field template you want to modify.

Press [F5]. The field definition prompt box appears.

Make changes and press [Enter].

Press [Ctrl][End] to accept the new settings.

To add a group band:
Press [Alt]B to open the Bands menu.

Select *Add a group band* (A).

Select *Field value* (F) from the submenu.

Highlight the field you want to group on and press [Enter].

save a report format:

Press [Alt]E to open the Exit menu.

Select *Save changes and exit* (S).

Enter a filename and press [Enter].

To view a report:

Press [Alt]P to open the Print menu.

Select *View report on screen* (V).

Printing

To print a database structure:

Highlight filename in the Data panel and press [Enter].

Select *Modify structure/order* (M).

Press [Alt]L to open the Layout menu.

Select *Print database structure* (P).

Select *Begin printing* (B).

To print data:

Highlight filename in the Data panel.

Press [Shift][F9] (Quick Report).

Select *Begin printing* (B).

To print a Quick Report:

Highlight filename in Data panel.

Press [Shift][F9] (Quick Report).

Select *Begin printing* (B).

To print a report:

Press [Alt]P to open the Print menu.

Select *Begin printing* (B).

FOR STUDENTS ONLY
SPECIAL LOTUS SOFTWARE OFFER

If you didn't purchase this Course Technology textbook with software, you can purchase the Lotus 1-2-3 Release 2.4 software for just $34.95 plus shipping.

Now you can get your own copy of Lotus 1-2-3 Release 2.4, including WYSIWYG and SmartIcons, in a special version designed for students.

Important: Please read the information below before ordering

Hardware Requirements

- IBM personal computer or compatible
- Hard disk with 5MB free space
- One 3½-inch floppy drive (software *not* available on 5¼-inch disks)
- DOS 2.1 or higher
- Graphics adapter (VGA, EGA, high-resolution CGA, or Hercules) for WYSIWYG display
- At least 384K available RAM (conventional memory), 512K for WYSIWYG display

Also Supports

- L/I/M 3.2 expanded memory up to 8MB
- All the same printer drivers as the commercial version of 1-2-3
- Microsoft Mouse or compatible

Note

This version of Lotus 1-2-3 Release 2.4 does not include the Viewer, Auditor, Translate, and Backsolver utilities available with the commercial version. All printouts include your name and the words "Lotus 1-2-3 Spreadsheet Computing Series" at the top of each page. Technical support is not included.

See reverse side for details

Please send me Lotus 1-2-3 Release 2.4 student software

See reverse side for details

I have enclosed all of the following:

- This original coupon (no photocopies or reproductions please).
- A photocopy of my current student ID.
- A check or money order for $39.95 ($34.95 plus $5.00 shipping). Massachusetts residents must add $1.75 for sales tax. For rush handling (delivery in 5 to 10 days), add $7.50 (for a total of $47.45) and check here: ☐

You must include this original coupon, full payment, and a photocopy of your student ID. Incomplete orders will be returned. No credit card orders. Maximum one software order per person. For your own protection, do not send currency through the mail. Allow 4 to 6 weeks for normal delivery. All units are shipped on 3½-inch disks.

Make check payable to **Course Technology, Inc.**

Name_____

Address _____

_____

City _____

State_____**Zip**_____

Telephone _____

School _____

Send to:
Lotus 1-2-3 Student Upgrade Program
Course Technology, Inc.
One Main St.
Cambridge, MA 02142